P9-DBQ-049

LORE OF RUNNING

Third Edition

Tim Noakes, MD
University of Cape Town Medical School
South Africa

Leisure Press
Champaign, Illinois

Library of Congress Cataloging-in-Publication Data

Noakes, Timothy D., 1949-
   Lore of running / Timothy D. Noakes. -- 3rd ed.
     p.   cm.
   Includes bibliographical references and index.
   ISBN 0-88011-437-1. -- ISBN 0-88011-438-X (pbk.)
   1. Running. 2. Running--Training. 3. Running--Physiological
aspects.   I. Title
   GV1061.N6 1991
   796.42--dc20

90-29001
CIP

ISBN: 0-88011-438-X

Copyright © 1991 by Timothy D. Noakes

Copyright © 1986, 1985 by Oxford University Press

All rights reserved. Except for use in a review, the reproduction or utilization of this work in any form or by any electronic, mechanical, or other means, now known or hereafter invented, including xerography, photocopying, and recording, and in any information storage and retrieval system, is forbidden without the written permission of the publisher.

Acquisitions Editor: Brian Holding
Developmental Editors: Peggy Rupert and Christine M. Drews
Permissions Coordinator: Kari Nelson
Assistant Editors: Kari Nelson and Timothy Ryan
Copyeditor: Julie Anderson
Proofreader: Dawn Levy
Indexers: Alan M. Greenberg and Barbara J. DeGennaro
Production Director: Ernie Noa
Typesetters: Angela K. Snyder and Kathy Boudreau-Fouss
Text Design: Keith Blomberg
Text Layout: Denise Peters and Tara Welsch
Cover Photo: Kirk Schlea/Berg & Associates
Cover Design: Jack Davis
Printer: Versa

Leisure Press books are available at special discounts for bulk purchase for sales promotions, premiums, fund-raising, or educational use. Special editions or book excerpts can also be created to specification. For details, contact the Special Sales Manager at Leisure Press.

Printed in the United States of America

10 9 8 7 6 5 4 3 2

Leisure Press
A Division of Human Kinetics Publishers, Inc.
Box 5076, Champaign, IL 61825-5076
1-800-747-4457

Canada Office:
Human Kinetics Publishers, Inc.
P.O. Box 2503, Windsor, ON N8Y 4S2
1-800-465-7301 (in Canada only)

UK Office:
Human Kinetics Publishers (UK) Ltd.
P.O. Box 18
Rawdon, Leeds LS19 6TG
England
(0532) 504211

Contents

Foreword   vii

Preface   ix

Introduction: Some Reasons to Run   xiii

About the Author   xxviii

Part I   Physiology   1

Chapter 1   Muscle Structure and Function   2

Biochemical Events That Cause Muscle Contraction   6
Classification of Muscle Fiber Types   9
Classification of Exercise Based on Muscle Contractions Produced   12

Chapter 2   Physiology of Oxygen Transport   16

The Concept of $\dot{V}O_2$Max   18
$\dot{V}O_2$Max and the Concept of Running Economy   25
Other Factors Influencing the Oxygen Cost of Running   30
Implications of Research on Running Economy   36
Other Predictors of Running Performance   38
Summary of Performance Predictions From $\dot{V}O_2$Max Data   50
A Final Word on the $\dot{V}O_2$Max   53

Chapter 3   Energy Metabolism During Exercise   57

Digestion and Absorption   58
Body Fuel Stores   63
Preexercise Diet and Performance   80
Liver and Muscle Glycogen Replenishment After Exercise   84
Biochemical Changes During Supramaximal Exercise   84
Endurance Training and Skeletal Muscle Metabolism   96

Chapter 4   Control of Body Temperature During Exercise   104

Mechanisms for Heat Loss During Exercise   105
Dehydration   108
Clothing   109
Heat Acclimatization   110
Temperature Regulation When Running in the Cold   112
Fluid Intake During Exercise   115

Part II   Training   133

Chapter 5   Contribution of Arthur Newton   135

Newton's 9 Rules of Training   142
Applying Newton's Rules   152

Chapter 6   Theory and Practice of Training   166

Step 1: Analyze Your Levels of Motivation and Personal Discipline   167
Step 2: Decide Whether You Need Medical Clearance   169
Step 3: Choose Appropriate Running Shoes   171
Step 4: Choose Appropriate Running Clothes   182
Step 5: Commit the 15 Laws of Training to Memory   182
Step 6: Follow These Other Practical Tips   193
Step 7: In the Beginning Follow Some Kind of Training Program   199
Step 8: Enter Races of Progressively Longer Distances   205
Step 9: Learn From Personal Experience   205
Step 10: Beware of the Selfish Runner's Syndrome   215

Chapter 7   Training the Mind   217

Importance of the Mind in Sport   219
Psychological Preparation for Competition   220
Basic Concepts for Optimum Psychological Preparation for Sport   230
Psychological Preparation and Strategies for Competition   236
Psychological Benefits of Training   243
Potential Psychological Dangers of Training   247
Conclusion   259

Chapter 8   Training With the Expert Runners   261

Historical Overview   262
Marathon and Shorter Distances   263
Short Ultradistance Races: 50 to 100 Km   321
Long Ultradistance Races: 100 Km to 6 Days   343
Training Methods of the Elite   356

Chapter 9   Racing—10 Km, Marathon, and Longer   362

Physical and Practical Preparation   364
Race Day and Recovery   378
Racing With Arthur Newton   397

Chapter 10   Overtraining   408

Indicators of Overtraining   409
Preventing Overtraining   412
Whole-Body Damage and Recovery After Severe Exercise   423

Chapter 11   Limits to Running Performance   426

Scientific Predictions of World Records   427
The Effect of Age on Athletic Performance   438
Altitude and World Records   442
Biorhythms and World Records   442

The Effect of Lane Choice on Running Speed   445
The Effect of Track Compliance on Running Speed   445

Part III   Health and Medical Considerations   447

Chapter 12   Understanding Injuries   449

Running Injuries Are Not an Act of God   452
Each Running Injury Progresses Through Four Grades   456
Each Running Injury Indicates That the Athlete Has Reached the
    Breakdown Point   457
Virtually All Running Injuries Are Curable   459
X Rays and Other Sophisticated Investigations Are Seldom Necessary
    to Diagnose Running Injuries   459
Treat the Cause, Not the Effect   460
Rest Is Seldom the Most Appropriate Treatment   460
Never Accept as a Final Opinion the Advice of a Nonrunner   461
Avoid the Knife   462
There Is No Definitive Scientific Evidence That Running Causes
    Osteoarthritis in Runners Whose Knees Were Normal
    When They Started Running   462

Chapter 13   Avoiding Injuries   465

How Stretching Can Help You   466
Planning a Stretching Program   469

Chapter 14   Diagnosis and Treatment of Running Injuries   487

Step 1:   Decide Whether Your Injury Is Truly a Running Injury   488
Step 2:   Determine the Factors That May Have Caused the Injury
    488
Step 3:   Make an Accurate Diagnosis of the Injury and Institute
    the Most Appropriate Treatment   500
Psychology of Injury   549

Chapter 15   Nutrition and Weight Control   555

Basic Nutritional Principles   556
Dietary Practices of Athletes   577
Diet-Related Idiosyncrasies   580
Exercise and Weight Control   581
Anorexia Nervosa   586
Fad Diets   593
Vegetarianism   594

Chapter 16   Special Concerns for Women   598

Will Women Ever Run as Fast as Men?   601
Unique Considerations for Women Athletes   610

Chapter 17   Special Concerns for Children   630

Should Children Train Heavily or Compete Seriously?   631
Guidelines for Sports Participation of Young Children   639

Chapter 18   Medical Benefits and Hazards of Running   645

Environmental Hazards of Running   647
Running and the Prevention of Coronary Heart Disease   659
Exercise and Sudden Death in Athletes   669
Exercise and Longevity   676
The Respiratory System   680
The Gastrointestinal System   683
The Genitourinary System   687
The Hematological (Blood-Forming) System   691
The Immune System   699
The Central Nervous System   700
The Endocrine System   703

Postscript   706

References   711

Index   798

Foreword

One useful classification of our personality divides us into four categories: analytical, expressive, driver, amiable. Most of us have one primary characteristic. Many have two. A few have three. Timothy Noakes is one of the few people I have met that possess all four in almost equal degrees.

He is completely disarming in debate because he is so amiable. He is rarely without a smile on his face. He is a driver who pushes himself to the limit, both at work and in sports. He is a scientist devoted to exact proofs. An investigator who never allows emotion to get in the way of his judgment. At the same time he is an expressive who sees beyond all this logic and achievement to the nonrational areas of life. He allows himself to express the deepest and most fundamental human emotions. He is a rare combination and that makes this a rare book.

Noakes has a training, an intelligence, a sensitivity, and experience that few writers on the athletic life can equal. On every page we can see the work of the scientist. He has studied the physiology and pathology of athletic training in depth. No problem in running, whether it be an intractable orthopedic injury or sudden death on the road is foreign to him. He is not only familiar with the medical literature. In many instances he is the medical literature. His published material covers running in virtually every aspect. And he has explored the areas of living beyond the physical. He has integrated the science and art of living.

In this book we learn once again that the proper study of man is man. Each of us in some way follows that rule. Whatever we do for a living we must know something about the human animal. Whether our art is selling or parenting, nursing or teaching we are students of human nature and how it operates.

For the most part this specialization leads us to see only bits of man. Not, as D.H. Lawrence said, 'the whole hog.' We know man only in the scope of our own profession. The solution is to study ourselves. We must look inside and see all men. We must stretch our bodies and minds and spirits and thereby find our own limits.

Rarely do we do that. We may push ourselves to limits of what we consider our role in life. Nevertheless we remain specialists. Our avocations are diversions rather than a challenge to be our best. Our leisure is spent without attention to the peaks of human performance open to us. The possibility of a personal renaissance does not occur to us.

This book should change that. The subject of this book is man fully functioning . . . and, at the same time, man cognizant of the problems to be encountered in the pursuit of excellence. Timothy Noakes is a physician, intimate with the pathology of life. He has observed, diagnosed, and treated the disease that visit the best of us. He understands that disease is not always inevitable. There are ways to prevent unnecessary morbidity and mortality. But should disease come, especially those that plague the athlete, there are rational and effective ways to deal with it.

Noakes is also a physiologist and an expert in human performance. He tells us how to become and remain an athlete. This book instructs us on developing and maintaining our now buried capabilities for athletic endeavors. It teaches us how the body can be trained to function at its best.

Noakes is a runner who has gone through the varied experiences of running: The contemplation, the conversation, the competition. He is familiar with both the joy and the boredom of running. Its peaks and valleys, its elation and depression. If we are to study man we must study man in all aspects: body, mind, and spirit.

The result is a book that appears deceptively simple. Readers who have had the athletic experience may well say to themselves, "I could have written this book had I the time." This is the mark of writing that influences us. It puts into words our own thoughts as yet unexpressed and leads us to insights not yet discovered. We all have within us the drive toward excellence. Timothy Noakes writes of how he sought this excellence . . . and in so doing blazes a path for us all.

George Sheehan, MD
Red Bank,
New Jersey

Preface

"Running as an exercise can strengthen the limbs, develop the lungs, exercise the will and promote the circulation of the blood. The clothing should be light, the head bare and the neck uncovered. Care must be taken not to overdo. Running is well adapted to both young and middle-aged persons but not to those who are fat. Sedentary persons may find great benefit in it after the day's work is ended. If they live in cities, a quiet spot in the park may be selected and short trials adapted to the strength entered into. Girls can run as well as boys, and while they cannot go so fast, they can run much more gracefully."

Scientific American (1883)

"We must wake up to the fact that athletics is not, nor ever can be perfected; there will always be more to learn."

Arthur "Greatheart" Newton (1949)

"Athletics are an extension of the classroom."

Jumbo Elliot and Theodore Berry (1982)

"Winning the marathon in Munich made my running, in the eyes of others, legitimate. Suddenly it was okay to be a runner, to train for 2 and 3 hours a day. There was a purpose behind it, something to be gained. My running had been looked upon as a diversion, as a peculiar habit for a grown man. After all, it was not done on behalf of a university team. It was not earning me a decent living. It was not even making me look manly, skinny guy that I really was."

Frank Shorter (1984)

Before I became a scientist or a doctor, I was a runner. In fact, I became the scientist and doctor I am because of what I learned through running. This book is a product of that physical and intellectual quest.

In truth I initially wrote *Lore of Running* for myself. For when I started running, most of the running literature comprised mainly the anecdotal biographies of great athletes and their coaches; there was precious little scientific information about the sport. Exercise science, like running itself, was a neglected backwater, explored only by an eccentric group of tenacious dissidents.

So my running became both the instrument and the inspiration to scrutinize what was happening to me as I ran. I began with the belief that if I understood the science behind what I was doing, I would more likely be successful. So at the start I wished to discover how I should train to do my best and what physiological and other factors determined that best.

Fortunately, being (as George Sheehan described himself) a slow learner with poor protoplasm, I soon made every possible training error and incurred a series of debilitating injuries that landed me in the depths of despair. After fruitless months of searching for answers from my medical colleagues, I faced the stark realization that only I could help myself. And so my intellectual interest broadened to include running injuries and other medical aspects of running.

And as my involvement deepened, I became fascinated with the great running heroes and the proud history with which they had enriched the sport. Why, I wondered, had they achieved such excellence? What were their secrets? Analysis of their training and racing methods showed me that there truly were no secrets. Those who were most successful had independently adopted a similar approach that, if not previously described, was at least readily discernible.

Indeed, the experiences of these great runners suggested that the human body responds in a relatively fixed and uniform way to training. We now know that only the extent and rapidity of these adaptations differs between individuals: It turns out that the same principles discovered intuitively by these great runners apply, with minor modifications, to all runners regardless of their abilities. However, less skilled athletes should never try to reproduce exactly the training methods of the elite.

I was fortunate that my quest coincided with an unprecedented and universal explosion of interest in exercise, sport, and health. The turbulence generated by this revolution projected exercise science and sports medicine from their quiet backwaters into the mainstream as both attracted international attention and recognition. In the 1980s, these two Cinderella professions became among the most rapidly evolving, innovative, and exciting branches of science and medicine. My privilege was to have been there at the beginning and to have been a participant in the revolution.

So in the end what began as a private journal became a book for all athletes, regardless of their sport or level of ability. It is, I believe, as complete a book on this topic as any single person could write. While the book's bias is unashamedly factual and scientific, the emphasis is always on the specific information that is of the greatest practical value to the athlete. Like many, I have little interest in scientific information that has no practical application and certainly have no desire to inflict such information on any reader.

I begin this third edition of *Lore of Running* with some of my running experiences. In particular I have attempted to explain what I have learned about myself through running. I have tried to capture the essence and magic of those great moments that are achieved in competition when the mind and body are stretched beyond exhaustion.

How the body responds to exercise and training, plus the physiological and other factors that determine success, are then covered in detail. I have aimed to provide a text that is complete, current, and relevant. A reasonable grasp of this knowledge is essential if you are to understand the scientific methods for aiding performance.

In the past it has, of course, been possible to achieve greatness without this detailed scientific knowledge. This is proved by the success of those runners who preceded the present scientific era. It seems to me that these athletes owed their success to an intimate, almost mystical, understanding of their bodies and what was best for them.

One such runner was Arthur Newton, who in the 1920s formulated training principles whose merit has only recently been appreciated. Newton's ideas allowed me to formulate the 15 Rules of Training that apply to all athletes. This knowledge has been used to suggest training methods for both beginners and the elite. I am happy to know that more than one elite athlete has used the principles I describe in this book to reach the pinnacle of international sporting success.

Possibly the most important part of the training section emphasizes the dangers of doing too much—of overtraining. It is abundantly clear that more good athletes fail because they do too much training than too little. I have emphasized the dangers of overtraining almost to the point of boredom. Yet still the message seems not to penetrate everyone.

The remainder of the book addresses the medical aspects of running, including details on treating and preventing running injuries, the medical problems encountered by runners, and their psychological and nutritional needs. I also consider the special requirements of female and young runners. Again, my emphasis has been providing relevant, complete, and up-to-date information.

The first edition of this book took some 16 years from its conception to its publication in 1985. In 1986, a second edition was released. Naively, conceitedly, and possibly because of my mental exhaustion after finishing the book, I assumed that here, at last, was the final word on the topic.

But in my fatigue I forgot that science does not stand still. Within 3 years it was apparent that a revision was necessary. In particular, there was a need to catch up with recent scientific findings that made some of the ideas in the first 2 editions obsolete.

For example, the belief that oxygen transport definitely limits maximum exercise performance—the so-called $\dot{V}O_2$max concept—is now seriously in doubt.

So too is the idea that blood lactate concentrations show a true "threshold" phenomenon during exercise of increasing intensity. And there is new evidence showing the importance of drinking patterns during exercise in determining fluid and energy replacement.

There are also new data on the risks associated with drinking too much during prolonged exercise and, conversely, of the essential role of adequate carbohydrates in aiding performance. New information has also become available about the factors explaining fatigue during exercise of high intensity and of the importance of genetic factors in determining both athletic ability and the ability to adapt to training.

Another important change in this edition is the running and training histories of many more of the world's greatest runners. Sadly, too few runners record their training histories in any detail, and the records of others have passed into posterity. But since publication of the first edition, I have obtained almost all the biographies that were missing from that edition and have included those whose information is of value. This has broadened the international flavor of the book and has, I hope, added to its appeal.

On the advice of British running historian Andy Milroy, I have also added a separate section on the long ultradistance runners, athletes with expertise in races beyond 100 km. As Andy correctly pointed out, this is a special group of runners competing in racing distances that require different attributes than the shorter distances. This was not something I originally appreciated.

I have also updated and expanded the medical sections of the book, especially with new details about causes of running injuries. There is also exciting new information about the benefits of exercise, especially with respect to the prevention of heart disease and possibly even cancer.

The text has also been reorganized, and all these changes combine to considerably update, expand, and widen the international scope of *Lore of Running*.

Inasmuch as the first edition has been called the "bible" of running, so this edition is, I believe, only better.

Finally, I must reflect on the wisdom I have gained in rewriting this book, wisdom that is above and beyond the knowledge contained in these pages. I have been left in complete wonderment about the human body and its design. It is clear that the body was designed in anticipation of the demands that might be placed on it and with the capacity to adapt to those apparently unforeseen demands. Each new physiological discovery continues to reveal the harmony and the logic of the human design. One is left to wonder how this was brought about. Are there laws directing mammalian design, much like the physical laws that govern the universe? Who or what is it that determines these laws?

I hope this book will convey to you the joy of running, the wonder of science, and the marvel of the human body.

Introduction: Some Reasons to Run

"Even if the day ever dawns in which it will not be needed for fighting the old heavy battles against Nature, muscular vigor will still always be needed to furnish the background of sanity, serenity, and cheerfulness to life, to give moral elasticity to our disposition, to round off the wiry edge of our fretfulness, and make us good-humoured and easy of approach."

William James (1958)

"It is one of the strange ironies of this strange life that those who work the hardest, who subject themselves to the strictest discipline, who give up certain pleasurable things in order to achieve a goal, are the happiest men. When you see 20 or 30 men line up for a distance race in some meet, don't pity them, don't feel sorry for them. Better envy them instead."

Brutus Hamilton (Quoted by Doherty, 1964)

"From the outside, this runner's world looks unnatural. The body punished, the appetites denied, the satisfactions delayed, the motivations that drive most men ignored. The truth is that the runner is not made for the things and people and institutions that surround him."

George Sheehan (1978b)

> *"Running is the classical road to self-consciousness, self-awareness and self-reliance. Independence is the outstanding characteristic of the runner. He learns the harsh reality of his physical and mental limitations when he runs. He learns that personal commitment, sacrifice and determination are his only means to betterment. Runners only get promoted through self-conquest."*
>
> Noel Carroll (1981)

Like many, I discovered running quite by accident. In 1969, while training for rowing, I started running regularly and entered my first road races. But during those years, I seldom ran more than twice a week and never for more than 25 minutes until one day in 1971 when, for no logical reason, I decided to run for an hour. That run was absolutely decisive, because during it I finally discovered the sport for which I had been searching.

At school I had been taught that sport was cricket and rugby and that anything else was a trifle undignified for those of British ancestry. Of course, the pressure to conform to these sporting norms was extreme, and I was not then secure enough to question what was good for me. But personal doubts about the real attraction these games held for me first started at the age of 15 when I discovered surfing. For the first time, I discovered a sport that allowed me to be completely alone. I loved it—no rules, no guidelines, no teams, no coaches, no spectators, and (in those days) few other participants. Just me, my surfboard, my thoughts, and an almost empty ocean. In surfing I discovered a sport in which the external human factor was almost totally removed and nothing could detract from my enjoyment.

Surfing also brought me for the first time into direct physical contact with nature and its naked, frequently stark, and always awesome beauty. And sometimes when the water was cold and the offshore wind was strong, so that each passing wave left an icy, stinging spray that bit at my wet suit and scratched at my eyes, this starkness was intensified. And I knew that it was good to be alive, independent, vigorous, and so close to nature's embrace that with each wave I could hear nature's heartbeat. I found the attraction to surfing alarmingly powerful.

After school and the army I attended a university and for 4 years learned to row. In rowing I found a team sport that demanded total individual dedication, physical perfection, and an acceptance of physical pain and discomfort. Rowing first introduced me to my need for self-inflicted pain—the nauseating, deep-seated pain that accompanies repetitive interval training and racing. At first, I merely followed this need intuitively. Only later did I begin to suspect that continual exposure to and mastery of that discomfort are essential ingredients for personal growth. And in training for rowing, I was led to running. Now, 20 years down the road, this book provides the opportunity to reflect on what running has meant to me.

Running has taught me who I am and, equally important, who I am not. I learned through running that I love privacy and solitude. At best I mix rather poorly and then only with people who are equally as restrained and secretive as I am. At worst, I am a latent "sociophobe" with a tendency to become ill when forced to socialize too frequently.

I have come to accept that, in common with a good number of other runners, I share the emotional and personality traits that Sheldon and Stevens (1945) and Sheldon et al. (1954) ascribed to those they called *ectomorphs*, whose body builds resemble those of champion distance runners. I am not suggesting that you might mistake my generously endowed frame for that of a champion runner. Not so! Rather, I share the personality characteristics that Sheldon and colleagues attributed to that physical group: a love of privacy; an overwhelming desire for solitude and an inability to relax or talk freely in company; excessive concern with physical health; poor sleeping habits; chronic fatigue; and typical patterns of mental behavior that include daydreaming, absentmindedness, procrastination, and an inability to make decisions. According to Sheldon and colleagues, the ectomorph's eternal quest is to understand the riddles of life.

It's obvious why people with these characteristics are attracted to running. Running provides complete solitude. Even in the most crowded races, we reach points at which fatigue drives each of us back into ourselves, into those secluded parts of our spirits that we discover only under times of duress and from which we emerge with clearer perspectives of who we truly are. Running can also allay our excessive concerns with health by giving us evidence that we are still well and not aging or falling to disease. The emotional release and physical fatigue induced by running improve our sleep and blunt our natural flight responses when we are in company. Finally, running can provide a medium for us to look at the world and to explore those riddles of life, however insolvable they will always appear to us.

Running introduced me to my body, making me aware of my body and my responsibility to look after it. And as I perfected my body, I learned that without a perfect body, there can be neither mental nor spiritual perfection. I learned that the physically perfected body showed that I cared and that I had self-pride and, more important, self-discipline.

I am in illustrious company with this idea; Smuts (1951), Thoreau (1862), Emerson (1901), and Plato (428-238 B.C.) also expressed similar beliefs.

Running has also given me pride in what my body can do if I prepare it properly. Like the majority of today's runners, I am not really designed for running. I am too ungainly and far too tall, with too much fat, muscle, and bone. But these very disadvantages have heightened the rewards; the more effort that goes into skill acquisition and the more difficulties overcome, the more rewarding the result. I am in complete agreement with 2:11 marathoner Johnny Halberstadt, who said that once you have run an ultramarathon (any race longer than 26 miles) like the 56-mile Comrades Marathon, any failures you may have experienced are no longer that important.

Next I discovered that the successful completion of severe running challenges, like finishing an ultramarathon as fast as I could, gave me the self-confidence to believe that within my own limits I could achieve whatever physical or academic target I set, as long as I was prepared to make the necessary effort. I learned that rewards in running, as in life, come in direct proportion to the amount of effort I exert and the extent to which I can summon the required discipline and application.

Yet running also heightened my self-criticism and expectations. I realized that it is never possible to do one's absolute best or to reach the pinnacle of perfection. Beyond each academic or sporting peak there will always, indeed *must* always, be another peak waiting to be tackled. Mavis Hutchison realized this the very moment she completed her life's ambition—the run across North America. As she finished, she saw that she still had a lifetime ahead of her with other goals and other ambitions to achieve. Or as Percy Cerrutty (1964), coach to the invincible Australian miler Herb Elliot, once wrote, "If you do not have that almost constant feeling of dissatisfaction with everything, recognizing that no sooner is one pinnacle achieved, one goal realized, [there will be another], success may well elude you" (p. 38).

Running taught me that only I know whether I am a success or not. I now understand pianist Arthur Rubenstein's statement, made on his 90th birthday, that only he was close enough to his work to be aware of the tiny errors he made. The praise of others could not remove those errors or correct his failings.

Running in competition taught me the humility to realize my limitations and to accept them with pride, without envy of those who might have physical or intellectual gifts that I lack. Although I will never run like the elite runners described in chapter 8, I can still devote the same effort to my more mundane talents that they do to their talents, and so attempt to derive as much pleasure and reward as they do from running. I see these athletes as the glorification of all of us, the epitome of total human potential developed to its limit. These athletes provide examples for life that go far beyond running, examples that I have found in few other humans.

Personal success starts, I think, with modesty and self-criticism. Percy Cerrutty, who knew many great athletes, wrote that the really top athletes he had coached were never superior, insolent, or rude. Rather they were circumspect, modest, thoughtful, anxious to acquire new knowledge, and they hated flattery—attributes that I have found in virtually all the top runners I have had the privilege to know. Former Olympic gold medalist and world-record holder David Hemery (1986) drew the same conclusion from his study of 63 of the best-ever athletes. Indeed, I suspect that these characteristics are essential in sport, in which success and failure are so dreadfully visible and in which the duration of success is so ephemeral, lasting a bare handful of summers at most.

I suggest that to achieve real success in running, as in any worthwhile activity, we must always fear failure; we must have very real fears that the day will come when we will fail regardless of how hard we have prepared. It is that insecurity that keeps our carefully nurtured self-confidence from becoming blatant arrogance. And it is also in our inevitable failures that the seeds of real personal growth are sown and eventually blossom.

Running has taught me about real honesty; there is no luck in running. Results cannot be faked, and you can blame no one but yourself when things go wrong.

So running has shown me that life must be lived as self-competition and has made me appreciate what I now believe to be a very real weakness of many team and skill sports. In those sports you do not have to admit your imperfections; you can always blame someone or something else, if you so choose. Furthermore, the hereditary skill required for success in those sports can, like beauty, provide a shield to hide behind. If you are skilled or beautiful, life can be too easy. You may never need to display the humility, modesty, courage, and perseverance essential for success in individual sports like distance running.

In addition, pleasure and rewards in skill and team sports may depend on the failure and therefore unhappiness of one's opponents. Fortunately, in running this does not apply; in competition we are there to help one another. As George Sheehan (1978b, pp. 214-215; 1980, pp. 240-241) pointed out, *competition* means "to seek out in company" and *contest* means "to testify in company with others." So the real competitions are those in which we seek out and test ourselves in company with others, in which each of us is both the source and the recipient of this communal courage. A friend who achieved immortality in a skilled team sport had to run the Comrades Marathon before he could write, "You have not lived in the world of competitive sport until you have fought a battle that is not against an opponent, but against yourself" (Peter Pollock, personal communication, 1982).

The runner's prayer given by coach Fred Wilt to the second American ever to set a marathon world record, Buddy Edelen (Higdon, 1982), captures my friend's meaning.

> In every race there comes a critical point when victory hangs in the balance. At that instant, no matter how cleverly he has been coached, the issue of victory or defeat passes entirely to the athlete. Only then do the athlete's powers of physical and mental courage, will-power, tenacity and competitive desire stand naked and exposed in a moment of truth, which cannot be denied. (p. 78)

In recent years as I have progressed from the protection of my student days and been rudely exposed to an adult world, I have learned to use running for relaxation and creativity and as my form of play. I have found that running is one way to live with everyday mental hassles and to create, as Perry and Sacks (1981) described, "a magic world, while realizing at the same time that it is only make-believe" (p. 79). I have found that running provides time for the creativity that is important in my work. So I have written articles, prepared speeches, designed research experiments, and indeed refined this book during the hours that I have spent running. And I have found that my thinking during those hours is more precise and insightful than at any other time of my day.

Running taught me that creativity does not result solely from hard work. I feel that regular play, like running, provides the childlike activity necessary for the creative act to occur, for novel thoughts to appear apparently from nowhere, and for old established ideas to suddenly take on a new meaning. I am by no means the first to discover this. George Sheehan, whose writings are born during his 1-hour "river runs" (Sheehan, 1978b), has uncovered many examples of great writers and thinkers who used exercise to improve their creativity: U.S. President Thomas Jefferson, the poet Coleridge, the philosopher Nietzsche, the great statesman Jan Smuts, and the poet Wordsworth, who covered prodigious distances over the English countryside as he composed his poetry. According to Thoreau (1862), when a traveler asked Wordsworth's servant to show him the poet's study, she answered, "Here is his library, but his study is out of doors" (p. 596).

As the American mathematician Morris Kline has written, "The creative act owes little to logic or reason. Indeed it seems to occur most readily when the mind is relaxed and the imagination roaming freely." Or as the historian Gibbon wrote, "Solitude is the school of genius."

Finally, running can teach us about our spiritual component—the aspect that makes us uniquely human. I suspect this component involves the needs to discover, to perfect, and to keep moving forward. Running epitomizes that struggle by teaching us that we must not stop. "Standing water and a man that does not move are the same," wrote Paavo Nurmi. "You must move, otherwise you are bound for the grave." Arthur Newton (1949) felt similarly: "You never stay put at any stage; either you advance or slip back" (p. 41). So we inherit this desire to push ourselves to the limits to find out what makes us what we are and what is behind it all.

So it is, I believe, that our most remembered heroes and heroines are those who have willfully exposed themselves to the most extreme physical hardships to prove what the perfect human can do. The great mountaineers went to climb Everest, not because, as Mallory said, "it is there," but because the mountaineers were there and because they accepted the human responsibility to push constantly to their limits to discover and perfect humanity. An example is Robert Falcon Scott, who paid the supreme price in the wastes of Antarctica because his physical courage exceeded the bounds of common sense (Huntford, 1985). A memorial, erected where Scott's body and those of his companions Edward Wilson and Birdie Bowers were found, contains a line that possibly best describes our common need: "to strive, to seek, to find and not to yield."

I sensed this need when I watched the replays of Bruce Fordyce in the 1983 Comrades Marathon, Carlos Lopes in the 1984 Olympic Games Marathon, and world-record holder Belayneh Dinsamo in the 1988 Rotterdam Marathon. For the screen bore witness to something that was intangible, something that was beyond words: the great runners oblivious to the moment, entranced by their own most private thoughts, and showing that humans are indeed most marvelously made. Their running showed that action can make us immortal and that on occasion the bonds of gravity, fatigue, age, and that which ties us to our mortality can be tossed aside.

We recognize too that such moments come only rarely, when exceptional humans have searched for their peculiar brand of excellence. In the words of the college dean in the film *Chariots of Fire*, as he welcomed Harold Abrahams and his class to Cambridge, "Let each of you discover where your chance for greatness lies. Seize that chance and let no power on earth deter you."

And does this striving to the limit give us some deeper insights into our creation and into the meaning of life? In his book, *The Springs of Adventure*, Everest mountaineer Wilfred Noyce (1958) considers this to be the greater mystery. Edward Wilson, he relates, traveled to and died in the Antarctic, secure in the knowledge that he was following God's design.

> Surely God means us to find out all we can of His works, and to work for His salvation . . . and if it is right to search out His works in one corner of His Creation, it is right for some of us to go to the ends of the earth to search out others. (p. 206)

Noyce also relates stories of mountaineers and explorers who did not share Wilson's devout convictions yet experienced the feeling of another presence. An example is Frank Smythe, who climbed alone to 28,100 feet on Mount Everest certain that he was accompanied by a "strong, helpful and friendly presence" (p. 209) with whom he shared his food. Thomas Hornbein climbed Everest by the West Ridge and later wrote

> There was a hint of fear, not for our lives, but of a vast unknown which pressed upon us . . . the suspicion that maybe there was something more, something beyond the three-dimensional form of the moment. If only it could be perceived. (Hornbein, 1980)

I too have felt that presence.

And in training I have learned, as fellow ultramarathon runner Reverend Deric Derbyshire reminds us in his premarathon sermon, that in the fight with self the greatest battles of life are fought and won; I have learned of the Christian's need to dispense with excesses and of the discipline, determination, and proper training required to enter into what the Christian calls the glory of the Lord.

And the rewards of this striving are those that the runner experiences in the predawn excitement at the start of any marathon: "God made a home in the sky for the sun, it comes out in the morning . . . like an athlete eager to run a race" (Psalm 19, verses 5 and 6).

You may suspect that the 90-km Comrades Marathon is different, but at the start of the race you are certain of this. The atmosphere is like a carnival; we are an eccentric family doing for one day what we like best (Alexander, 1985). And no matter how humble the results, for 11 hours we will be loved and applauded for our efforts. From dawn until the sun sets in Durban, we are the children of the road, to be succored, encouraged, praised, and protected. On race day there can only be one outcome: each runner a winner, each a hero.

At the start, there is neither doubt nor fear. The outcome is predetermined. The Comrades family will ensure our safe passage to Durban. Even when we have spent our last ounce of energy, there will be an arm for support, a shoulder to steady our shaking legs, and someone to carry us over the finish line.

In faith then, at 6:00 a.m. on May 31 each year, the Comrades Marathon begins with each runner knowing that this is the year. This year he or she is at a peak and is older, wiser, and more experienced. This year at the moment of truth, when once more the pain and discomfort become intolerable and the desire to quit almost irresistible, the runner will fight back with more courage, greater energy, and supreme endurance. This year he will run the course on his own terms, or she will become the heroine she was always meant to be.

For the first 4 hours each year, I know all these things; I know that this is finally to be my year. The approach march has been easy. The first 40 km or more have passed effortlessly; the pace has been a pleasure. The friendship, the scenery, the weather— all have been perfect. But then, as always on the "down" run, the steep climb past the Alverston Tower up to Botha's Hill Village requires noticeable effort for the first time. (The race is run annually in opposite directions: one year "up" to Pietermaritzburg, the next year "down" to Durban, which sits 2,000 feet lower than Pietermaritzburg.) Quite suddenly I no longer have breath to spare for conversation. My horizon comes down to the few meters of road ahead, and I shorten my stride, looking for maximal efficiency. These kilometers must be run in earnest.

Soon enough, however, I crest the hill and feel the human warmth of the crowded village. It is time to take stock. The distance has by now removed just enough energy for my legs to become concerned. Sensing that today something extra is expected, they urge caution and argue for energy conservation—a shorter, less flamboyant stride. But even now I know that their warning has come too late, that I have again been carried away by the occasion. For however easy the first 4 hours may have felt, the cost has been too high. Within 1 hour I must pay for my early excesses; I must reenter the soul of the Comrades, that special confrontation between an exhausted body and mind and an ailing but unbeaten will.

Through Botha's Hill Village and Hillcrest, I must distract my mind from the oncoming holocaust. I wave, talk, and smile to every spectator, interested or otherwise. My mind, as if preparing for the coming onslaught, is sharpened and extrovert. These are magic miles; the best miles in reflection are always those immediately preceding the final collapse. Then too quickly I am past Hillcrest. Now alone and unaided, I must pass into the void beyond. It is here, in the sudden solitude of the quiet lane that meanders gracefully through Emberton and Gillitts, that for me the Comrades Marathon really begins. No longer do I progress on my own terms; the hopes and confidence stored in training now vanish before the reality. The course that I have held at bay for 57 km is now running me. I am approaching the line, isolated, uncertain, and caring only for survival.

My legs, detecting the first signs of an ailing will, begin their own mutiny, their tactics carefully prepared. They inform me that this is far enough. Geographically, they argue, the race is two thirds over. Why, they ask, must they continue to run, knowing that from here each step will become ever more painful, ever harder? After all there is always next year. Through the blanket of developing fatigue, I begin to appreciate the logic behind these questions; I begin to feel the attraction of that haven of rest at the side of the road, the bliss of not having to take even one more step toward Durban.

Around me, I know that each runner is engaged in this same battle. In common suffering, we are alone to find our individual solutions. A glance up the road shows a string of runners, each running alone, each separated by a constant distance from the runner in front and behind. A common thread holds us together, but only reluctantly do we defile the sanctity of the space that separates us; the space that is our universe—20 m of tarmac, our support team, and just enough room left over for our thoughts.

My willpower now comes from my assistant. Ever smiling, ever happy, he is pure encouragement, my sole precious link with a world that cares. In his hands he carries all our wealth: a bucket containing iced water, a sponge, and a choice of three different drinks. His presence confirms that it is all worthwhile, that to him and his world, I am the most important runner, and that together, whatever the cost, we must endure, we must both survive.

So despite the internal mutiny of an exhausted body, as I approach Kloof Station, my mind is still in control. But whatever mental reserves I retain, I know they are inadequate for the sight that now confronts me. From Kloof Station, at the top of Field's Hill, the Comrades plays its most evil trick. Experience tells me not to look, that should I for one second divert my eyes from the road, I will most likely not finish. But I have no discipline, and I see it laid before me: the final, infinite 25 km that separate me from Durban and the finish at the Kingsmead cricket ground.

In each race, I have learned, the desire to quit comes but once. It is a coward who once beaten does not return. But as I begin the descent of Field's Hill, even this knowledge is of no assistance. My second, who must wait anxiously 4 km away in Pinetown, is forbidden to help me on this major highway, and my mind hovers in the balance. I progress now only because it is automatic; it takes time to switch the engine off.

And here on this major descent I am joined by the final tormentor. The continual jarring of the sharp descents from Inchanga, Botha's Hill Village, and Hillcrest has taken its toll on my quadriceps, and every step now sends an ever-more-painful shock down each thigh. The muscles are in rebellion; depleted of energy, their connective tissues are now coming apart. I am a physical coward in the best of circumstances, and the added pain is too much; my tenuous willpower crumbles. I become Maurice Hertzog descending from his epic first ascent of Annapurna (Hertzog, 1952): "It's all over, Lionel, I am finished. Leave me alone and let me die" (Terray, 1975, p. 293).

You may think that even now I could still walk, that a few minutes of rest would restore the desire to live and would defeat the coward within. But you would be wrong, for the discomfort I feel exceeds my ability to recall or describe it. "After 18 miles," wrote David Costill (Sheehan, 1978b), the world's foremost running physiologist, "the sensations of exhaustion were unlike anything I had ever experienced. I could not run, walk or stand, and even found sitting a bit strenuous" (p. 204). Were the human brain able to recall the pain of Field's Hill, no one would ever run the "down" Comrades twice.

This, then, is the point that each runner must pass in order to arrive in Durban on two feet. It is here, stripped of any of society's false privileges, that we find no hiding place, no shelter of convenience. Face-to-face with ourselves we must look deep inside. "Those hills and the miles beyond," wrote George Sheehan (1978b, p. 215), "will challenge everything he holds dear, his value system, his life style. They will ask nothing less than his view of the universe."

For me, in 1978, that desire to live did not come from within, not from any universal insights. For coinciding with these darkest moments, 23 km away Alan Robb was just completing his greatest Comrades. I learned this from a lone spectator, perched on the embankment that skirts Field's Hill. Alan Robb, everyone's complete runner—quiet, undemonstrative, and humble in victory ("I owe everything to my seconds")—enshrines the Comrades ethic. He is a victory of purity, a victory for the human spirit, the affirmation of morality.

With renewed vigor and renewed faith that if the test is severe enough, goodness must always prevail, my gloom disappears and I enter Pinetown. Now I find sufficient energy to use the last trick of the ailing runner—a trick learned from Dave Levick, the man whose Comrades record is even then just being surpassed. "Run," he said, "from face to face. Look into the eyes of each spectator. Look at their joy. Imagine who they are, what they do, how much they want you to do well. Let them pull you through."

A thousand faces later, I have survived Pinetown and have climbed Cowie's Hill, to enter the last, dreadful 16 km.

Through Westville, the endless downhill reactivates the ice pick that hammers ever more painfully with each downhill stride. At 45th Cutting, I have but 41 minutes to cover the last 8 km to claim a silver medal. Down Black Hill I prepare for the last hill, the curving climb past the West Ridge tennis courts to Tollgate. Now I am reduced to running each step by itself. My eyes see only the road at my feet. I now must obey the Comrades runner's rule ("Don't look up"), because I have no choice. I no longer have the energy even to lift my eyes to the horizon.

Then, at first only gradually, I begin to perceive that the gradient has, at last, begun to relent. Soon I reach the summit ridge, a cruel 100 m from the top of the Tollgate ridge. My fatigue is extreme. No longer is there sufficient oxygen on the planet to keep me moving. My staggering gait and contorted face suggest imminent collapse. I wonder vaguely whether I will die, whether Harvard's former chief of psychiatry Gaylord P. Coon was right when he suggested that death may be the ultimate aim of marathoners. He likened us to the king's messengers, those who took pride in sacrificing themselves for their monarch (Guild, 1957).

> One always sees in these messengers a moment of exaltation, when they have finally won through and delivered the news; then it seems to be an almost inexorable destiny for them to drop dead—anything but death would be a dull, sodden anticlimax. (p. 1169)

But like Maurice Hertzog, I am to be spared. Slowly the gradient relents, and I spill over Tollgate encouraged by the spectators' assurances that from here it is all downhill.

Three minutes later the fire in my chest relents and the ache in my legs recedes. Now I know for sure that I will finish. But can I meet the 7-1/2-hour deadline? My second is adamant. There is to be no rest. The whip is now out; his attitude is quiet coercion, but I do not care to test the extent of his patience.

The minutes speed by, but the road seems to stand still. I am straining to deliver full power but sound as controlled as a steam engine at full throttle. I wobble and groan monstrously and begin to hope that something will burst.

Barely 8 minutes remain as I turn into Old Dutch Road and see my marker, the trees lining the road outside the Kingsmead cricket ground. Like the Chinese, who supposedly could run great distances in the mountains by fixing on a distant peak and entering a trancelike state, I see only these trees. I run oblivious to the noise and confusion around me of a Natal road under perennial reconstruction.

Finally the entrance to Kingsmead beckons. From inside, the noise of 2,000 voices is deafening. "Two-oo minutes, two-oo minutes." I comprehend the meaning but can no longer calculate distances and times. Halfway round the field, in unison, the crowd informs me that now only 1 minute remains. I rumble on, cursing that my victory lap has to be run in such an undignified race against the clock.

Then I see the finish line: on the left, a haggard group of runners, and on the right, pacing expectantly like Gary Cooper at high noon in Dodge City, the elegant figure of Mick Winn, the race organizer. In his right hand is the finishing pistol, the discharge of which will signal a bronze death.

I am still 10 m short of the line when he turns his back, and the pistol in his right hand arches agonizingly skyward. My last coherent thought is whether our happy friendship is about to end.

Later, from the warm comfort of the Kingsmead turf, when a measure of physiological normality has returned and I am secure in the knowledge that the last step has been taken, I know again why it is all necessary, what common bond unites all Comrades. Skill, you see, is not our requirement, nor has our race anything to do with winning and losing. These are the spoils of other, lesser games that are unable to transport us to the places we have been, we who have accompanied Hertzog to the summit of our own Annapurna.

For us the mountains had been a natural field of activity where, playing on the frontiers of life and death, we had found the freedom for which we were blindly groping. . . . The mountains had bestowed on us their beauties and we adored them with a child's simplicity. . . . Annapurna, to which we had gone empty-handed, was a treasure on which we should live the rest of our days. With this realization we turn the page: a new life begins. There are other Annapurnas in the lives of men. (Hertzog, 1952, p. 287)

Indeed, and the only requirement, the common bond that links all Comrades runners, is the need to look for the mountains in life. We need to take the paths least traveled, to go against the common stream, to search for the unattainable, and finally, as Menander said, to accept that we have no option. ''A man's nature and way of life are his fate, and that which he calls his fate is but his disposition'' (K. Moore, 1982, p. 68).

So because I have no choice but to follow my fate, on May 31, sometime between 6:00 a.m. and 5:00 p.m., you will find me in mind, if not in body, somewhere on the Old Main Road between Pietermaritzburg and Durban, secure in the knowledge that this is my year, that this year I shall finally defeat the coward within and so commence the hero's life.

Later, when I had reluctantly returned from the playground to the workbench, the inquisition began. Why, my colleagues wanted to know, had I been beaten by that woman? How was it that I, a 10-year veteran, could be beaten by a woman whose entire running career spanned less than 10 months? How could it possibly have happened that I, who postured as the running expert, had been beaten by a novice just barely out of her teens?

Of course I had no instant answers, at least none that could satisfy the ignorance of those who may never know that in distance running, as in life, the struggle is not man against woman or man against man. It is a personal battle; it is me against myself. And if I had not known it before, the race from which I had just returned had at least taught me that. It had, in those few, brief, lifelong hours, brought me face-to-face with Kierkegaard's truth: ''I myself am my only obstacle to perfection'' (Sheehan, 1978b, p. 55).

In the race, Isavel Roche-Kelly had come closest to her own perfection. At her first attempt she had run a world-class race. And the truth is that at her sport a world-class female athlete will always beat me and 99% of the other males on this planet. So, if you will, my best effort had been predictably surpassed by a champion with a fairy-tale athletic history.

Like most, Isavel's running began as a search for health, a desire to lose those few extra kilograms that had accumulated since she had become the desk-bound intellectual. Then, after only a month's jogging, she ran her first ''fun run,'' in which she was the third woman to finish. She saw that to become healthy was to go only halfway.

Her training miles increased, the excess weight melted off, and the races became longer until, after only 7 months, she was ready for a standard marathon, the race that many consider the ultimate challenge. But even that was not enough. For in only her second race over that distance, she had run the third fastest-ever time by a woman on the African continent. She needed something bigger, and for many nothing may be bigger than an ultramarathon.

So it was that on May 31, 1980, we stood together in the company of 4,207 others, below the Pietermaritzburg City Hall clock, awaiting the 6:00 a.m. chime that would send us on our 90-km journey through life to Durban.

My role that day was quite simple. After 10 years of running, my lack of talent had long since been ruthlessly exposed. And where there is lack of talent, survival must come through compensation. So my survival depends upon the metronome I carry in my head. This metronome beats at only one pace, a pace that if maintained will get me to Durban in 7:29, the time required to earn a Comrades silver medal, which before that 1980 race had not been won by a woman. This was a feat that tiny Isavel in her youthful innocence believed to be possible. So my appointed task for that day was to be the rabbit, to set that critically correct early pace that would give Isavel her best possible chance for a Comrades silver.

At last, after months of anxiety, the future was upon us. The town clock chimed, Max Trimborn crowed, the starting pistol fired, the crowd roared, and we shuffled forward in a jolting, disjointed, noisy mass. After 2 anxious stopwatch minutes—minutes that would have to be won back slowly during the next 7-1/2 hours—the shuffle became a fast walk and then a slow jog, and finally we were running down Commercial Street past the first spectators, the staff and patients who crowd the streetside balconies of Grey's Hospital.

In those early kilometers of each Comrades Marathon, we are children reborn. We are playful, carefree, and totally trusting. Our energy is limitless. The present and ourselves are our only concerns. The world we know is absolutely protective, totally supportive. Whatever may be, we know that the Comrades family will transport us safely through to Durban.

In just this attitude of total trust the greatest danger lies. During these early kilometers when we run at our most carefree, mindless of the future, the Comrades die is cast. For it is here that too fast an early pace will cause too rapid a breakdown of the runner's dearest commodity—muscle and liver glycogen stores. The body has no understanding of what lies ahead and only knows that after 3 days of carbohydrate gorging, it has a glycogen glut. So during this primary stage, the careless runner's body digs unrestrainedly into its glycogen stores, not realizing that it will come to regret any early excesses. Later, in a state of near-total carbohydrate depletion, the body will experience fatigue and discomfort never before imaginable. And because I have been there 3 times before, bitter experience has finally taught me to pay proper adult attention to these first few kilometers.

So as we set off past the market and into the countryside west of Polly Shorts, I set the metronome and checked the stopwatch as the kilometers clicked by steadily at the expected 5-minute intervals. I knew that in 6 hours the pace that now felt no more strenuous than a gentle jog would slowly, gradually, become ever more of an effort. I knew that by noon it would take everything I possess to maintain this now-gentle pace.

But it was not yet time to think of these matters. Our thoughts were absorbed in the present, with problems of water balance and heat exchange and with ensuring that we both received the correct quantities of fluid, glucose, and sponging from the endless rows of anxious, totally absorbed parental figures that lined the route.

Through Camperdown and Cato Ridge and on to the undulating hills known euphemistically as the Harrison Flats, we journeyed. By now there was little to say; the early morning childlike banter had been replaced by a restrained, adolescent concentration. And like those years, these miles were enjoyable. The body, now maturing to its chosen task, ran in harmony with the countryside, which bathed in an early-morning misty tranquility was exceptionally beautiful.

The mind was now content to be free with its own thoughts, meditating and quietly preparing for first the hills and later the endless downhill that lay ahead. In these kilometers as in no other, the runner truly becomes one with running. The movement is effortless and timeless so that, whatever his or her age, the Comrades runner approaching the Valley of a Thousand Hills recaptures for one brief hour that adolescent immortality.

But the harmony and tranquility cannot last. Ultimately even immortality must become boring. So shortly after 9:30 a.m. we were glad to descend into Drummond, the halfway mark, knowing that from here the race now began in earnest. Immediately ahead of us lay a foretaste of our predicament—a relentless climb out of the depths of the valley to Botha's Hill Village, a climb that showed us for the first time that our energy was not limitless. On this ascent, our breathing became harsher for the first time, our knee lifts became lower, our ankle drives became less decisive. On the road past the Alverston tower, we runners entered our middle years.

Appropriately, on this climb we met the first gentlemen of the road. When the work was in earnest, when each spoken word must be carefully chosen, the runners we passed had only praise and encouragement for Isavel's effort. On those long hills up to Botha's Hill Village, there was no room for chauvinism. Somewhere east of Drummond in the Comrades Marathon, the superficial differences that divide us no longer mattered. Here all that counted, all that would save us, was individual effort. The race asked only that we pile evermore effort on top of what we had already given until we had no more to give.

But that time was not yet. Soon enough the climb was over, and we entered the tree-lined road running through Botha's Hill Village to be met by the khakied Kearsney College boarders who, in their own private-school manner, cheered us on. At this point, still 40 km from Durban, we realized for the first time that Isavel could win this race. Over the toughest 6 km of the course she had closed by a minute on the lead woman. A new dimension entered the race. Until the finish in Durban, Isavel was now committed to a patient race for first place. And I knew that Isavel must win. For once you start slowing down in a race as long as the Comrades, you are in trouble. The lead woman had gone too fast over the first half, and somewhere before Durban she was passed.

I was not there to witness it. As we moved through Hillcrest and Winston Park and on to Kloof, I began to feel those first symptoms of the aged runner, a lightheadedness and difficulty in concentration that indicate a gradually developing hypoglycemia. They were the first symptoms announcing that the aged body has little more to give, that my race had been run. That from here on in, the strength of the aged body lies only in the spirit that it could command and in the knowledge that a liter of Coke drunk in the next 1-1/2 hours would still buy me 10 to 15 km of running. Enough at least, I calculated, to get me through Pinetown. I was not going to surrender easily this partnership before then.

But as my own condition gradually deteriorated, so Isavel became stronger. The doubt that she had entertained at Hillcrest had now vanished. At the top of Field's Hill from where she could see Durban for the first time, Isavel became suddenly transfixed. She could not believe that having covered 65 km, only 25 km remained. Her pace quickened and we parted: I bent on conservation, she, striking out down Field's Hill as if on a training run in the Newlands Forest.

About 2-1/2 hours later, when I had all but died and then recovered enough to suffer that endless 25-km downhill nightmare to Durban and Isavel had survived the incessant questioning of an incredulous press, we met again on the Kingsmead turf. In a field of exhausted runners she alone seemed to be without fatigue. Like the real champion, she showed no traces of the effort she had made. And she told me what she had achieved: She was the first woman in the race and the first-ever female Comrades silver medalist, and she set a new record time. It had been a peak experience.

Tragically, Isavel Roche-Kelly was killed while cycling in Ireland on January 8, 1985. She had turned to cycling in 1983 and wished to represent Ireland as a cyclist in the 1988 Olympic Games.

About the Author

Timothy Noakes was a runner "before running became popular" and has competed in more than 70 marathon and ultramarathon races. His experiences as a runner, a physician, and an exercise physiologist motivated him to write *Lore of Running*, the most complete book available on running.

Dr. Noakes is the Liberty Life Professor of Exercise and Sports Science and director of the Bioenergetics of Exercise Research Unit of the Medical Research Council of the University of Cape Town. He is an editorial board member for many international sport science journals and the 1991 president of the South African Sports Medicine Association. Noakes is also a Fellow of the American College of Sports Medicine.

Dedicated To My Best Friend
Marilyn Anne

Part I

Physiology

1

Muscle Structure and Function

"Muscle speed is inborne, varies with the individual and can be increased little—if at all—by training. To this extent, therefore, one might say an athlete and particularly a sprinter, is born and not made."

Franz Stampfl (1955)

"The complaint has been made to me—'why investigate athletics, why not study the processes of industry or of disease?' The answer is twofold. (1) The processes of athletics are simple and measurable and carried out to a constant degree, namely to the utmost of a man's powers: those of industry are not; and (2) athletes themselves, being in a state of health and dynamic equilibrium, can be experimented on without danger and can repeat their performances exactly again and again. I might perhaps state a third reason and say, as I said in Philadelphia, that the study of athletes and athletics is 'amusing': certainly to us and sometimes I hope to them. Which leads to a fourth reason, perhaps the most important of all: that being 'amusing' it may help to bring new and enthusiastic recruits to the study of physiology, which needs every one of them, especially if they be chemists."

A.V. Hill (1927b)

"We must wake up to the fact that athletics, like everything else, is not, nor ever can be perfected; there will always be more to learn."

Arthur Newton (1949)

"The human body is centuries in advance of the physiologist."

Roger Bannister (1955)

Muscle contraction is the essential physiological event that allows us to run. Thus, a description of how muscles are designed and how they contract is the logical departure point for an understanding of the physiology and biochemistry of running.

The body has three different types of muscle: heart, or cardiac, muscle; skeletal muscle, which is attached to the skeleton and contracts to produce locomotion; and smooth muscle, which forms the muscular linings of many organs, in particular, the digestive organs of the intestine. Although running does involve cardiac muscle, our attention will focus mainly on skeletal muscle structure and function (see Figure 1.1).

Each skeletal muscle is composed of a vast number of individual muscle cells or fibers lying parallel to each other and divided from one another by connective tissue that contains blood vessels and nerves. Humans have two different muscle cell or fiber types (slow twitch and fast twitch fibers), and these are mixed fairly randomly together in all the skeletal muscles in the body. Each muscle cell has its own nerve supply and is surrounded by a collection of tiny vessels, or capillaries, which supply blood to the muscle cell. In general, each muscle cell is surrounded by about five capillaries, a number that probably increases with training (Saltin & Gollnick, 1983).

As shown in Figure 1.1, every muscle cell is made up of a multitude of tiny rods called myofibrils, which are arranged parallel to each other. Each myofibril consists of many individual sarcomeres lying end to end. Each sarcomere, in turn, contains a vast number of even tinier rods, the myofilaments. A myofilament comprises two groups of individual muscle proteins—myosin molecules, which aggregate to make up the myosin (thick) filament, and actin molecules, which together with two other proteins, troponin and tropomyosin, form the thin filament. The complex interaction of the thick and thin filaments produces muscular contraction and therefore allows us to run.

An important feature of the sarcomeres is that they are striped or striated (see Figures 1.1 and 1.2); hence, the alternate term for skeletal muscle is striated

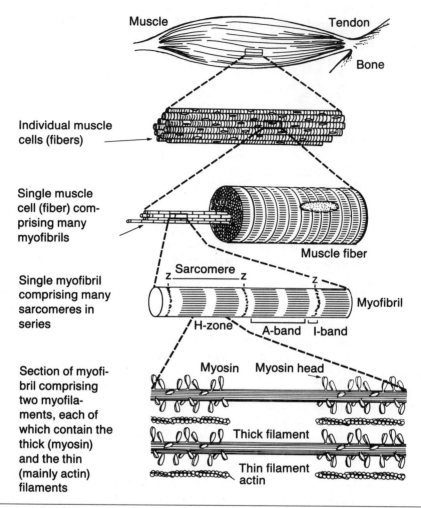

Figure 1.1   The structure of muscle showing the organization of thick and thin filaments into sarcomeres, myofibrils, and ultimately muscle cells.

muscle. These stripes are due to the regular arrangement of the thick filaments lying in the center of the sarcomere and the thin filaments extending from each end toward the center of the sarcomere.

The second important feature of the skeletal muscle cell, clearly shown on the electron microscopic picture in Figure 1.2, is the presence of semicircular structures called mitochondria. The principal function of these is to produce the energy needed to power muscular contraction. Mitochondria have been termed the "powerhouses" of the cell, and running ability and fitness are in part related to the total metabolic capacity of all the mitochondria that each runner has. Note

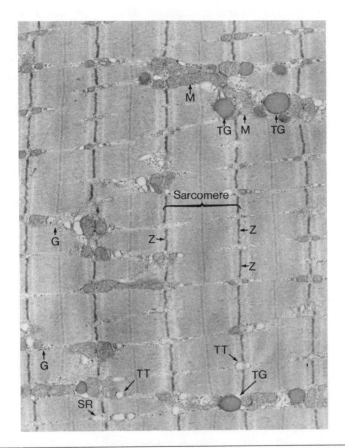

Figure 1.2 Electron microscopic view showing the detailed structure of muscle. Sample from Lindsay Weight, winner of the 1983 and 1984 Comrades Marathon. G = glycogen granules; M = mitochondria; SR = sarcoplasmic reticulum; TG = triglyceride droplets; TT = transverse tubules; Z = lines denoting end of sarcomeres.

that the mitochondria are strategically located next to the muscle filaments. In this way the energy produced in the mitochondria is readily transported to its site of use in the muscle filaments.

Our knowledge of the complex way in which mitochondria produce energy is incomplete. For our present purpose we should know that each mitochondrion consists of a bag of enzymes, or biological catalysts, that change the energy contained in the food we eat into the energy currency of the body—a molecule known as adenosine triphosphate (ATP).

A critical feature of mitochondria is that they function only in the presence of an adequate oxygen supply. Without sufficient oxygen, the mitochondria would be unable to produce ATP, and all cellular function would stop if an emergency system were not also available. Fortunately, there is such an emergency system made up of a group of enzymes or catalysts that exist in the sarcoplasm, an amorphous fluidlike substance bathing the myofilaments and the mitochondria. These enzymes constitute a metabolic pathway termed the *oxygen-independent glycolytic pathway*. This means that stored muscle glycogen (and blood glucose) can be utilized to produce energy independently of an oxygen supply. (Unfortunately, the incorrect term *anaerobic glycolysis* has persisted in the literature.)

A third important feature of muscle cells is the presence of circular fat droplets (see Figure 1.2). These consist of triglyceride molecules, a form in which fat is stored in the body. The triglyceride molecule comprises three fatty acid molecules linked to a single glycerol molecule. (*Cellulite* is a euphemistic term used to describe excessive accumulation of these molecules.)

For the triglyceride molecule to provide energy for muscular contraction, it must first be broken into its free-fatty-acid and glycerol components by the action of a specific biological catalyst, the enzyme triglyceride lipase. The free-fatty-acid molecules are then able to enter the bloodstream and travel to the muscle mitochondria where they are used as an important energy fuel. The liver uses the glycerol molecules to produce new glucose units in a metabolic process known as *gluconeogenesis*. Both these processes are important in providing energy during prolonged exercise, in particular during marathon and ultramarathon racing.

Also notable in the electron microscopic picture in Figure 1.2 are the clumps of fine granular material scattered throughout the cell. These granules are the second important form of intramuscular energy stores, comprising many individual glucose molecules bound together into long branching chains called glycogen. Glycogen is the only form in which both muscles and the liver store the carbohydrates eaten in the diet. As we shall see, these glycogen stores play a critical role in determining performance in marathon and ultramarathon races.

In vegetables and fruits, carbohydrates are stored as a different polymer—starch. Starch and its derivatives, in particular a short-chain polymer known as carbohydrate or glucose polymer, may have a special role in carbohydrate loading and fuel ingestion during exercise, a point that is discussed in greater detail in chapter 4.

With this background, we can now discuss the more detailed structure of the thick and thin filaments and how they interact to produce muscular contraction.

BIOCHEMICAL EVENTS THAT CAUSE MUSCLE CONTRACTION

In the early 1900s, researchers realized that when a muscle contracts the sarcomere shortens, so that whereas the A-band of the sarcomere (see Figure 1.1) remains the same width, the I-band becomes thinner. The British scientist A.F. Huxley proposed that the proteins of the I-band had "slid" or been pulled into the A-band by the action of the A-band proteins. For this sliding filament theory

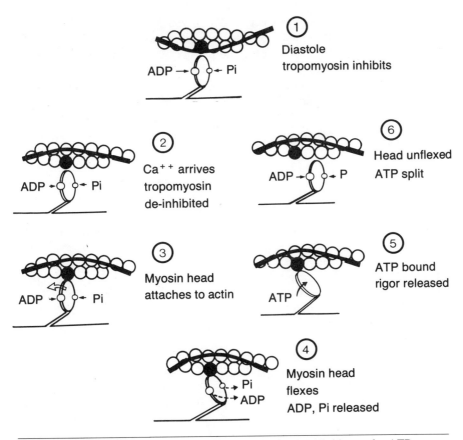

Figure 1.3 The molecular mechanisms involved in the cross-bridge cycle. ATP = adenosine triphosphate; ADP = adenosine diphosphate; Pi = phosphate.

of muscle contraction, Huxley won the Nobel prize for biology. Today there is general consensus that the Huxley hypothesis is essentially correct (Podolsky & Schoenberg, 1983).

In essence, the thick filaments that constitute the A-band comprise myosin molecules, each of which has a body and a "head" (see Figure 1.3). The individual myosin heads point toward the actin proteins of the thin filaments, and at each point where the myosin interacts with actin, the tropomyosin molecule is found. The presence of this molecule is necessary because the myosin head has a natural attraction for actin, and the absence of some blocking agent would mean that actin and myosin would be perpetually bound to each other, thereby causing persistent muscle contraction or, in running terms, muscle cramps. Before muscle contraction can occur, therefore, some mechanism must operate to move the tropomyosin molecule from its position between actin and myosin.

The trigger that does this is calcium. When you decide to move a particular muscle, the brain sends a message in the form of an electrical impulse down the spinal cord to the nerve that supplies the muscle. At the junction of the nerve and the particular muscle cell that it serves is a special site known as the motor-nerve end plate. Passage of the current through the motor-nerve end plate causes a special chemical messenger, acetylcholine, to be released into the gap between the motor-nerve end plate and the outer envelope or membrane of the muscle cell or its extensions that extend to the interior of the cell, the transverse tubules (see Figure 1.2).

Having traversed this tiny gap, the acetylcholine molecule binds to special acetylcholine receptors on the muscle cell. In a way that we still do not quite understand, this causes calcium that is stored deep inside the cell in another specialized structure in the cell gap, the sarcoplasmic reticulum, to be released very rapidly. The calcium then floods into the cell sarcoplasm surrounding the muscle filaments and binds to specific calcium-binding sites on the special calcium-binding protein, troponin-C, which is attached to both tropomyosin and actin. This binding of calcium causes the troponin-C molecule to undergo a complex twisting movement, the effect of which is to extricate the tropomyosin molecule from its blocking position between actin and myosin (see Figure 1.3). This allows the myosin head to attach itself to actin, the essential first step in muscular contraction.

The next ingredient required for muscular contraction is a source of energy, which is supplied by ATP molecules produced in the mitochondria that travel to specific ATP-binding sites on the myosin heads. Here the ATP is, in fact, stored as two ATP breakdown products, adenosine diphosphate (ADP) and phosphate (Pi).

When the energy-loaded myosin head attaches itself to actin, almost immediately the Pi and ADP are released in sequence by the myosin-binding site, which causes the myosin head to undergo a complex sequence of events in which its flexible "neck" is believed to "bend" 45° from its normal vertical angle (see Figure 1.3). This bending action causes the thin filaments to be pulled toward the center of each sarcomere. This movement, repeated in millions of thick and thin filaments in millions of sarcomeres in a single muscle, produces the visible muscle shortening that we recognize as movement.

The fully contracted position, in which the myosin head is bent to the 45° position and is bound to actin, is known as the *rigor complex*. To break the rigor complex, the mitochondria must supply fresh ATP to the ATP-binding site on the myosin head, and the calcium bound to the troponin-C must be removed so that tropomyosin can again move into its blocking position between the actin and myosin.

A muscle cramp is, of course, nothing more than the development of a rigor complex. Thus, we could speculate that a muscle cramp could occur either because no fresh ATP is available to the myosin head to allow relaxation or because a breakdown occurs in the mechanism whereby calcium is released from tropo-nin-C and pumped back into the sarcoplasmic reticulum.

CLASSIFICATION OF MUSCLE FIBER TYPES

Two principal types of muscle cells or fibers that are randomly mixed in all human muscles can be differentiated on the basis of their colors, the quantities of mitochondria that they contain, and the speeds with which they contract.

Using two of these three characteristics, Dubowitz and Pearse (1960) proposed a classification in which Type I fibers were colored red and were found to have high concentrations of mitochondria. The redness was due to a high content of the protein myoglobin, which transfers the oxygen carried in blood to the mitochondria and also acts as an oxygen store in the muscles. The Type II fiber was white, due to a low myoglobin content, and had a low mitochondrial content. An important weakness of this classification is that it takes no account of the different speeds at which the different muscle fibers can contract or, in more scientific terms, the rate at which the different fibers can complete the "cross-bridge cycle" of muscle contraction depicted in Figure 1.3.

Yet as early as 1873, the German physiologist Ranvier observed that "red" muscles contract and relax more slowly than "white" muscles. More recent work has confirmed this, so that the most modern classification of muscle fiber type is that fibers are either red, Type I, slow twitch (ST) fibers, or they are white, Type II, fast twitch (FT) fibers.

More recent evidence indicates that the speed of cross-bridge cycling in the different muscle fiber types is determined by the "strength" of the ATP-specific enzyme myosin adenosine triphosphatase (myosin ATPase), which sits in the myosin head and to which the ATP binds. Researchers have found that fast-contracting (FT) white muscle fibers have greater myosin ATPase activity than do slow-contracting (ST) red muscle fibers. However, it now seems that the situation is not quite this simple; the myosin ATPase activity is not simply either fast or slow, and grades of fastness or slowness among the FT and ST fibers may vary. Thus, the ST fibers of some athletes may have contraction speeds that approach those normally found in FT fibers.

In addition, the FT (Type II) fibers can be divided into three subtypes: FTa, FTb, and FTc. The FTa fiber is similar to the ST fiber in that it has a high concentration of mitochondria and therefore an increased capacity to produce ATP by oxygen-dependent metabolism in the mitochondria. This fiber type is found mainly in long-distance runners and other endurance athletes like cross-country skiers (Saltin et al., 1977). The FTa fiber is believed to be an FT fiber that is adapted for endurance exercise. The FTb fiber conforms to the classic description of the FT fiber in that it has low mitochondrial content, whereas the FTc fiber is of uncertain origin and may be an "uncommitted," primitive fiber, capable of developing into either an FTa or an ST fiber. Interestingly, the percentage of FTc fibers is highest in long-distance runners (Staron et al., 1984) and orienteers (Jansson & Kaijser, 1977).

Practical Implications of Different Muscle Fiber Types

Numerous studies show that the muscles of outstanding athletes exhibit specific and predictable patterns of muscle fiber content according to the sports in which the athletes excel. Thus, the muscles of sprinters, jumpers, and weight lifters contain high percentages of FT fibers whereas cyclists, swimmers, and middle-distance (400 m to 1 mile) runners tend to have equal proportions of both FT and ST fibers. In cross-country skiers and long-distance (10 km to 42 km) runners, on the other hand, the percentage of ST fibers is high (see Table 1.1).

These large differences between sprinters and distance runners are probably genetically determined; that is, the differences are inborn features of each athlete (Komi et al., 1977; Komi & Karlsson, 1979). If so, and if these different fiber patterns are essential for success in various sports, then an individual's ultimate potential for success in endurance sports may be determined, in part, by being born with a high percentage of ST fibers. Similarly, raw speed or weight-lifting strength may also be determined by the number of FT fibers with which one is born.

But three inconsistencies exist with these data. First, Alberto Salazar, who until recently held the world record for 8 km on the road, is hardly a slouch, yet he has a high percentage of ST fibers—92% (Costill, 1982). I suspect that he is

Table 1.1 Muscle Fiber Composition of Athletes

Sport	% Slow twitch fibers
Sprinters	26
Sprinters & jumpers	37-39
Weight lifters	44-49
Cyclists & swimmers	50
Middle-distance runners	45-52
Elite half-marathon runners	54
Canoeists	60
Elite oarsmen	60-90
Elite distance runners	79-88
Cross-country skiers	72-79

Note. Data compiled from numerous studies, including Saltin et al. (1977), Saltin and Gollnick (1983), and Noakes et al. (1990b).

a prime example of a person whose ST fibers are not really slow and may be able to contract almost as fast as the FT fibers of most other runners.

Second, we have a similar problem explaining the relatively low percentage of FT fibers in weight lifters. One would have suspected that, like sprinters, these athletes should have virtually all FT fibers. Possibly, like Salazar, these athletes' ST fibers are essentially fast twitching.

Third, I personally am not convinced that a high percentage of ST fibers is essential for success in prolonged endurance activities like marathon running. I suggest that the different muscle fiber compositions found between middle- and long-distance runners are artifactual and that within the next 20 to 50 years, the muscle fiber compositions of elite marathon runners will be found to approach those currently found in elite middle-distance runners (i.e., approximately 50% FT fibers). My reason for believing this is simply that those athletes who currently excel at the marathon distance probably do so because they are not quite fast enough (possibly because their muscles have too few FT fibers) for success in middle-distance running, in particular the 1-mile race. A good example is the former world marathon record holder Derek Clayton, who chose to specialize in the marathon when he realized he could not win middle-distance races or succeed in the mile (see chapter 8).

Thus, I suggest that selection pressures force these ''slow'' milers with low percentages of FT fibers to compete at the longer distances at which faster milers, who have faster muscles and higher percentages of FT fiber content, do not choose or indeed need to compete.

However, as the longer distance races, especially the standard marathon, become more lucrative and therefore more attractive than track running, these elite middle-distance runners with higher percentage FT fibers will begin to dominate these races. Thus, a repeat of the original study of David Costill and his colleagues on the elite American marathon runners of the 1970s (Fink et al., 1977) done in 10 or 20 years may show different results and could indicate that athletes with even mixes of ST and FT fibers are probably better able to succeed in marathon and ultramarathon races than are those with high percentages of ST fibers. Data on world-class black distance runners show this to be the case; these runners have 40 to 60% FT fibers (Noakes et al., 1989d).

Understanding the different muscle fiber types helps us to appreciate that during exercise the fibers in the active muscles have specific activation patterns. This is a function both of the type of exercise and of its intensity and duration. Thus, during low-intensity running, ST fibers are initially active, but as the exercise intensity increases, a greater number of FT fibers become active in the sequence of FTa → FTb (Saltin, 1981). Similarly, during prolonged exercise, a recruitment pattern occurs with the ST fibers being activated first. As the ST fibers become progressively energy depleted, the FTa fibers become active, followed finally by the FTb fibers. Thus the noncompetitive jogger who exercises at a low intensity for a short duration will train predominantly ST fibers, whereas the middle-distance runner who includes high-intensity training will train both ST and FT fibers.

Logically, we would think that optimal training should be at all running intensities so that all muscle fiber types are equally trained. Indeed, the success of the "peaking" training technique developed by Forbes Carlile (1963) and Arthur Lydiard (Lydiard & Gilmour, 1978) and described by Daws (1977), Osler (1978), and others (see chapter 5) may lie in the fact that the athletes achieve optimum training of FT fibers.

CLASSIFICATION OF EXERCISE
BASED ON MUSCLE CONTRACTIONS PRODUCED

Figure 1.3 shows that when an unloaded muscle contracts, it always shortens; this is called a *concentric* muscular contraction. In contrast, during an *eccentric* contraction, the muscle length increases. This occurs when a force applied to the muscle exceeds the force that the muscle can produce during contraction. In this type of contraction, the myosin heads are pulled out to angles of up to 90° or beyond during contraction, rather than flexing to 45° (see Figure 1.3). Eccentric muscle contractions use less oxygen and ATP and recruit fewer muscle fibers than do equivalent concentric contractions (Friden, 1984). Maximal power production is also greatest in eccentric contractions.

In running, eccentric muscle contractions occur, especially in the upper thigh muscles (quadriceps) during downhill running when the forces through these muscles become very large, particularly as the foot lands on the ground, and can equal 3 times the body weight. The initial contraction of the quadriceps is not quite strong enough to overcome this force; thus this muscle is stretched in an eccentric contraction for a brief instant every time either foot hits the ground. Muscles are not designed for repetitive eccentric contractions and are susceptible to damage when forced to contract this way (Friden, 1984). This explains why downhill running is especially painful and why it takes so much longer for the postrace muscle stiffness to disappear after downhill races than it does after uphill races. Chapters 10 and 14 discuss this concept of exercise-induced muscle damage in greater detail.

The final point about eccentric contractions is that during such contractions, the muscles act as brakes. During downhill running, muscles heat up just as brakes do when continually used. High-altitude mountaineers have always known this; they know that when descending a mountain they need to wear less clothing than they do when ascending, even though they are exercising at the same rate.

Static and Dynamic Muscle Contractions

When a muscle contracts concentrically, the contraction can either be sustained or it can be brief and followed by a relaxation period.

During *static muscle contractions* (static exercise) the active muscles remain contracted for the duration of the activity. An alternative term used to describe this type of contraction is *isometric* (*iso* means *same*; *metric* means *length*), meaning that the muscle maintains the same length during the contraction. In reality, few sporting activities involve muscle contractions that are exclusively static. Typical exercises in which static muscular contractions predominate are weight lifting, arm wrestling, pushing in the rugby scrum, and pulling at tug-of-war.

The important physiological effect of a sustained static muscular contraction is that the pressure inside the muscle rises dramatically. This exerts pressure on the (collapsible) arteries that traverse that muscle and provide oxygen and energy to it. If the pressure becomes sufficient to reduce or completely obstruct the muscle blood flow, the contracted muscle receives insufficient oxygen to sustain the mitochondrial production of ATP. Thus, the muscle cells have to rely on oxygen-independent mechanisms to produce the ATP necessary for contraction. Furthermore, the absence of an adequate blood supply prevents removal of certain toxic metabolic by-products, in particular hydrogen ions (protons) produced by oxygen-independent metabolism. Accumulation of these protons causes the acidity of the muscle to increase. This in turn ultimately inhibits further muscular contraction, in particular by preventing the binding of calcium to troponin-C, thereby preventing the interaction of myosin and actin. These two factors—an inadequate oxygen supply and an inability to remove metabolic by-products— explain why static muscle contractions are so painful and why they can be sustained for only relatively short periods of time.

The second important effect of a static muscle contraction is that it evokes powerful reflexes, probably in response to the reduced muscle blood flow (Mitchell et al., 1977), which cause the heart to pump more rapidly and more powerfully and the blood pressure to rise. This effect may be so marked that heart rates as high as 160 to 190 beats per minute and systolic blood pressures in excess of 300 mm Hg may occur.

However, these high heart rates and blood pressures do not mean that the athlete is achieving a training effect equivalent to that which he or she would achieve by running at an equivalent heart rate. For, as we shall see, training is absolutely specific. That is, the body adapts to the specific stress to which it is exposed, and because the physiological stresses of static exercise are exactly opposite of those of dynamic exercise (see Table 1.2), static exercise plays only a small role in improving running ability.

Training with static exercise causes the trained muscles to enlarge (hypertrophy) due to an increase in the number of myofilaments. This seems to occur without an increase in the total number of muscle cells (fibers). The important benefits of a static exercise like weight lifting are that when performed regularly, such exercise prevents the gradual loss of strength and bone mineral content that occurs naturally with age. Thus runners, who train only their lower limbs when

Table 1.2 Comparison Between Static and Dynamic Exercise

Static exercise	Dynamic exercise
Sustained muscular contraction	Repetitive muscle contraction/relaxation cycle
Reduced muscle blood flow	Increased muscle blood flow
No increase in muscle oxygen consumption	Increased muscle oxygen consumption
Oxygen-independent (anaerobic) energy production	Oxidative (aerobic) energy production
(Phosphagen stores; muscle glycogen → lactate; no increased uptake by muscle of blood-borne energy substrates)	(Muscle glycogen → CO_2 and H_2O; increased uptake by muscle of blood-borne energy substrates, in particular glucose and free fatty acids)

running, will benefit from using light weight training for their upper bodies. Many great runners, including Herb Elliott (Lenton, 1981), believe that training with static exercise improves running performance, although the scientific evidence is somewhat less optimistic.

Both Hickson (1980) and Dudley and Djamil (1985) found that the training-induced increase in maximum oxygen consumption ($\dot{V}O_2$max; see chapter 2) is not enhanced by combining static with dynamic exercise training. However, as we shall see, $\dot{V}O_2$max is not always a good measure of changes in running performance. Hickson et al. (1980) showed that a program of weight lifting did indeed improve running performance in short-duration, high-intensity exercise lasting up to 6 minutes. Furthermore, their subsequent study (Hickson et al., 1984) showed that heavy resistance training of the quadriceps increased endurance time during maximal cycling or running exercise by 47% and 12%, respectively, without causing an increase in $\dot{V}O_2$max. The physiological explanations for these findings are still a mystery. But the studies do show that many experimental circumstances exist in which changes in running performance are not matched by equivalent changes in $\dot{V}O_2$max, suggesting that the two are not causally related (Noakes, 1988b).

In contrast, the gains in strength that result from static exercise training appear to be impaired by concurrent dynamic exercise training (Dudley & Djamil, 1985; Hickson, 1980).

Training the quadriceps with eccentric contractions probably aids performance in marathon and ultramarathon racing by reducing muscle damage (see Bruce Fordyce's 9th point of ultramarathon training in chapter 8).

It seems that although strength training may indeed enhance running performance, running training impairs the muscles' abilities to adapt to strength training. Thus, those who wish only to develop strength would be unwise also to run.

The value of static exercise in terms of benefit to the heart and lungs is fairly limited. According to Mitchell and Wildenthal (1974), two leading U.S. cardiologists, "Whatever its aesthetic benefits for developing skeletal muscle size, from a cardiological viewpoint, isometric exercise is a relatively useless form of physical training and should not be recommended as a substitution for dynamic exercise" (p. 378-379).

During *dynamic muscle contraction* (dynamic exercise), the active muscle groups contract and relax repetitively, as in walking, running, skipping, cycling, swimming, and rowing. Therefore, during dynamic exercise (in contrast to static exercise) there is a period of muscular relaxation during which muscle blood flow can carry oxygen and energy substances to the muscle cells, where the mitochondria can utilize these substances to produce the energy required for prolonged muscular activity.

In summary, static exercise stresses power production by the muscle cells, whose performances are largely determined by the number and contractile qualities of the myofilaments they contain. In contrast, the performance of sustained dynamic exercise requires an adequate provision of oxygen and energy substances to the mitochondria for the uninterrupted production of energy. However, as we shall discuss, fatigue during sustained dynamic exercise can occur even when the supply of oxygen and energy substances to the muscles appears to be adequate.

2

Physiology of
Oxygen Transport

"There are two types of athletes . . . one type can run a terrific speed without training; he does 10.5s for 100 yds at school and he can continue this terrific speed up to the 1/4 mile—he probably manages 24s for the 220 and 51s for the 440.

"The other type—and I fall into this category . . . can't do the 100 in 12s, or the 220 in 30s or the 440 in 60s. We are able only through tortuous efforts to improve our speed, but with the slightest lay-off this hard-won ability vanishes.

"This first type of runner will always be the greatest . . . Herb Elliott is the first man of the speedy type to train and race the longer distances. I believe that, if he is interested, he will be able to make a clean sweep of all the records from 1,500 m to the marathon."

Gordon Pirie (1961)

"As far as I'm concerned, this sprint test is the best way to judge your potential. Your basic speed—not your build, leg length, or weight—should determine what distance you run. If you can't run the 200 faster than 26 seconds, for instance, forget all about half-miling. All the training in the world won't make you a champion at it. . . . If you can't run a 400 in 51 seconds, you can't run an 800 in 1:50. And if you can't do that, you don't have a chance in today's racing circles."

Arthur Lydiard and Garth Gilmour (1978)

*"If at first you don't succeed, you can always be-
come an ultramarathoner."*

Bruce Fordyce (1989)

Like those involved in other sporting pursuits, runners frequently assess what
their full potential may be. Most runners wonder, perhaps even daily, how fast
and how far they can run and why they can run only so fast and so far. The
answers to these questions may be found in the principles underlying the physiology of oxygen transport.

The pathway by which atmospheric oxygen, which constitutes 21% of the air
we breathe at sea level, is transported from the air to the mitochondria in the
muscle cells is shown diagrammatically in Figure 2.1.

When we inhale, oxygenated air is transported deep into the lungs into the
terminal air passages, which end in small sacklike projections called alveoli.
Each alveolus is really only a very thin semispherical membrane, on the surface

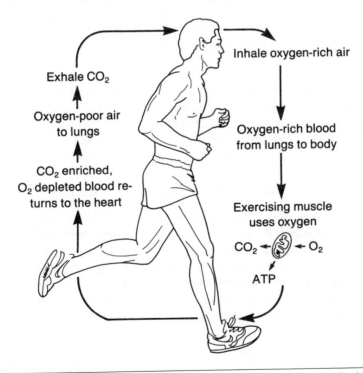

Figure 2.1 The pathways by which oxygen is transported from atmospheric air to the
active muscles.

of which run many small, equally thin-walled blood vessels, the capillaries of the pulmonary (lung) circulation. The alveolus is the meeting place of the oxygen in the air and the red blood cells contained in the blood. Red blood cells approaching the lung are oxygen depleted and carbon dioxide loaded (carbon dioxide is the major waste product of mitochondrial energy production).

As blood passes through the lungs, the carbon dioxide is released and a small fraction of the oxygen dissolves into the blood across the alveolar membrane, while a much larger fraction is taken up by the protein hemoglobin, which exists in the red blood cells and has a high attraction, or affinity, for oxygen. So combined, the oxygen is transported in the bloodstream to all the cells of the body, and the carbon dioxide is exhaled.

During exercise, the oxygen requirements of the active muscles can increase virtually instantaneously by as much as 20-fold, whereas the requirements of the inactive muscles remain unchanged. Clearly, some mechanism must exist to ensure that the increased blood flow during exercise goes to the right muscles. In brief, the increased activity of the skeletal muscles increases their demands for ATP to fuel the actin-myosin interactions. The metabolic breakdown products of ATP then act as a complex signal that causes both an increase in the rate at which fuels enter the mitochondria and an almost instantaneous dilation of the blood vessels supplying the active muscles. Simultaneously, these changes selectively increase both the energy and oxygen supplies to the active muscles.

Another mechanism for increasing blood supply to the active muscles has been termed the *splanchnic shunt*, with which blood is preferentially shunted away from the less active tissues, in particular those supplied by the splanchnic (''gut'') circulation (the intestine, kidneys, and liver), and redirected to the active tissues. All these tissues normally have an overabundant blood flow and can survive on a reduced blood supply for fairly prolonged periods, certainly for a few hours of exercise.

THE CONCEPT OF $\dot{V}O_2MAX$

As can be expected, an increase of oxygen consumption accompanies an increase in exercise intensity. The muscles recruit more myofibrils to produce more powerful muscular contractions. This demands increased amounts of energy, which in turn demand a greater oxygen supply. Two brilliant British physiologists, Nobel laureate A.V. Hill (see also chapter 11, Figure 11.1) and Hartley Lupton, were among the first to show that oxygen consumption increases as a linear function of increasing work output or running speed (A.V. Hill & Lupton, 1923; see Figure 2.2).

On the basis of certain assumptions that were probably incorrect (Noakes, 1988b), Hill and Lupton postulated that shortly before the individual reached maximum work capacity, or running speed, the rate of oxygen consumption

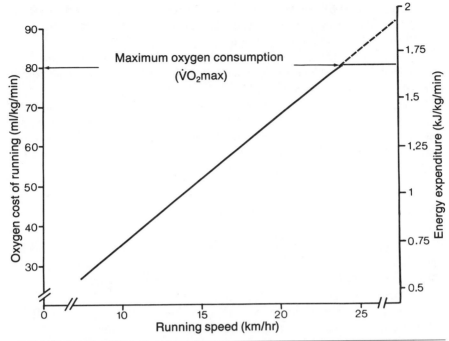

Figure 2.2 The linear relationship between oxygen consumption and running speed, showing the point at which maximum oxygen consumption ($\dot{V}O_2$max) is believed to occur.

reached a plateau and did not increase further. Although able to exercise a little harder, the athlete took up no more oxygen. At this point the athlete was said to have reached maximum oxygen consumption ($\dot{V}O_2$max; see Figure 2.2). The annotation V is simply scientific shorthand for a rate of volume flow. Thus $\dot{V}O_2$max is the maximum rate of oxygen flow and is usually expressed relative to body weight (i.e., ml/kg/min).

However, modern studies suggest that only approximately half of all tested subjects show true plateaus in oxygen consumption during maximal exercise; in the remainder no such plateaus are present, and the factors that determine these subjects' maximal exercise performances are presently unclear. I have suggested that factors related to muscle, not the cardiovascular system (and thus not oxygen transport), limit the maximal exercise performance of these persons (Noakes, 1988b). I suggest that whatever factors determine peak muscle-power production in short-duration, high-intensity exercise like running 800 to 1,500 m also determine performance in more prolonged exercise, including marathon and ultramarathon running. This would explain the observations by Lydiard and Gilmour

(1978) and Pirie (1961) that the distance runners who are fastest over the shortest distances will also be the fastest at all longer distances, including the ultramarathon. This is discussed further in chapter 8.

Obviously, these ideas are quite heretical, and it will be some time before they are either proven to be incorrect or are accepted by the international community of exercise physiologists (Noakes, 1988b).

Concerning those athletes who show true plateaus in oxygen consumption during maximal exercise, we assume but have not proven that a limitation in the rate of oxygen delivery to the muscles limits their maximal exercise performances (Noakes, 1988b). If this is indeed the case, in which section of the oxygen transport system does this limitation occur?

Factors Determining the $\dot{V}O_2$Max

We have good reasons to believe that the maximum rate at which oxygen can be transported to the alveoli does not limit maximum oxygen transport, at least in healthy individuals exercising at sea level. Even at rest, all healthy athletes can move more air into and out of their lungs than they ever require during exercise. This capacity is called the *maximum ventilation rate* (MVR). A typical MVR for a distance runner at rest would be in excess of 200 L/min, whereas elite athletes, even during maximum exercise, seldom require greater than 180 L/min (Pollock, 1977). Researchers have found that although the oxygen content of the blood sometimes falls during maximum exercise, this occurs only in some elite athletes with $\dot{V}O_2$max values greater than 70 ml/kg/min (Dempsey et al., 1982, 1984). It seems very unlikely that blood oxygen content falls during maximal exercise in the vast majority of nonelite athletes (Dempsey et al., 1984; S.K. Powers et al., 1988). If the lungs were the factor limiting maximum oxygen transport, even if the resting MVR were exceeded during maximum exercise, sufficient oxygen would still not be provided to the bloodstream, and the oxygen content (saturation) of blood would fall precipitously in all athletes, not just the very best.

The fact that blood oxygen saturation remains normal in the majority of subjects even during maximum exercise must also indicate that the rate of oxygen transport across the alveolar membrane into the blood, known as the maximum alveolar oxygen-diffusing capacity, also does not limit the $\dot{V}O_2$max of most athletes.

The amount of oxygen carried in the bloodstream is the next factor to consider. This is a function of the total hemoglobin content of the blood, which in turn is determined by the total number of red blood cells in the circulation and their hemoglobin concentration.

One of the experimental techniques used to determine whether the blood hemoglobin content limits the $\dot{V}O_2$max is called *blood doping*, in which red blood cells previously withdrawn from the athlete are reinfused 6 to 8 weeks later (see chapter 18).

The initial conclusion from these studies (Buick et al., 1980; Ekblom et al., 1976; Gledhill, 1982; Robertson et al., 1984) was that the blood hemoglobin content may well be a limiting factor for $\dot{V}O_2$max because blood doping increases running performance and $\dot{V}O_2$max at least for a few days (see chapter 18). The researchers presumed that the extra hemoglobin increases oxygen delivery to the muscles, and they further assumed that the increase in $\dot{V}O_2$max that occurs with blood doping indicates that when the working muscles are supplied with an increased oxygen supply, they have the capacity to increase their oxygen uptake by an equivalent amount. Thus, the researchers concluded that the rate of oxygen transport to the muscles, rather than the rate of oxygen utilization by the muscles, limits $\dot{V}O_2$max.

However, subsequent studies indicate that these conclusions may have been premature and were based on certain erroneous assumptions (Noakes, 1988b). In particular, the conclusions are based on the assumption that oxygen utilization limits performance during maximal exercise. This assumption has never been proven (Noakes, 1988b). Furthermore, the conclusions assume that blood doping affects only oxygen transport, whereas evidence now indicates that blood doping also favorably alters lactate metabolism (Celsing et al., 1987; Spriet et al., 1986). Thus, at present, we cannot determine the true implications of these findings.

Another factor potentially limiting the $\dot{V}O_2$max is the maximum rate at which that oxygen can be transported to the active tissues by the blood. This is measured as the maximum volume of blood that the heart can pump each minute (the cardiac output) and is calculated in liters per minute. Whether or not cardiac output limits the $\dot{V}O_2$max has not yet been determined.

Despite the close attention of some of the most eminent exercise physiologists in the world, the question of what limits the $\dot{V}O_2$max is still open and is unlikely to be answered definitively in the near future. My personal bias (Noakes, 1988b) is that the rate of oxygen transport is not the critical factor determining exercise performance. Rather, I suggest that the best athletes have muscles with superior contractility either on the basis of superior myosin ATPase activity or enhanced sensitivity to calcium (see chapter 1). Thus, they are able to achieve higher work loads and therefore higher rates of oxygen consumption during maximal exercise. The result is that their $\dot{V}O_2$max values will tend to be high, leading to the erroneous conclusions that $\dot{V}O_2$max is a good predictor of athletic potential and that oxygen availability must therefore be the most important factor limiting exercise performance.

However, studies show that the maximum achieved work load rather than the $\dot{V}O_2$max is the best predictor of running potential (Noakes et al., 1990a) and that skeletal muscle factors other than those regulating oxygen utilization determine the maximum achieved work load (Noakes, 1988b).

The Laboratory Measurement of $\dot{V}O_2$Max

Researchers have generally found that the highest $\dot{V}O_2$max values are reached during treadmill running to exhaustion, either uphill or on the flat. Highly trained competitive cyclists can achieve similar $\dot{V}O_2$max values on both the treadmill and the bicycle. On the other hand, trained runners and untrained subjects reach lower $\dot{V}O_2$max values on the bicycle than they do on the treadmill.

Quite why this happens is not clear, but it is apparent that researchers achieve optimum measurement of $\dot{V}O_2$max when the testing procedure faithfully recreates the activity for which the athlete is trained. Thus, the treadmill is the optimum testing apparatus for a runner, and the actual racing bicycle used by the cyclist in competition and pedaled at the correct cadence is optimum for a cyclist.

The Effects of Age, Gender, Training, and Altitude on $\dot{V}O_2$Max

Healthy but inactive subjects experience gradual declines in $\dot{V}O_2$max equivalent to about a 9% decrease per decade after the age of 25. Some evidence suggests that vigorous exercise maintained for life may reduce the age-related rate of decrease in $\dot{V}O_2$max, which has been estimated to be only 5% per decade in lifelong athletes (Heath et al., 1981; Pollock et al., 1987). The current belief is that the most important cause for the decrease in $\dot{V}O_2$max with age is an age-related decrease in maximum heart rate and therefore in maximum cardiac output. Alternatively, according to the theory that skeletal muscle contractility limits $\dot{V}O_2$max (Noakes, 1988b), the decrease in $\dot{V}O_2$max with age may reflect a progressive decrease in muscle contractility with age or, alternatively, a loss of muscle mass with age (Fleg & LaKatla, 1988).

Females have lower $\dot{V}O_2$max values than do males, in part because of a woman's higher body fat content, smaller muscle mass, and (probably most importantly) less "powerful" muscles (see chapter 16).

As far as training is concerned, healthy subjects who embark on a running program similar to that outlined in chapter 6 and Table 6.4 can expect an increase in $\dot{V}O_2$max of only about 5 to 15% (J. Daniels et al., 1978a). This indicates that $\dot{V}O_2$max is, per se, a poor measure of fitness. It also suggests that major differences (i.e., greater than 15%) in $\dot{V}O_2$max between subjects likely result from hereditary factors rather than from training. Age does not influence the degree to which $\dot{V}O_2$max increases with training; the increase is the same in the young and old (Hagberg et al., 1989; Meredith et al., 1989b).

Changes in altitude have the most marked effects on $\dot{V}O_2$max. With an increase in altitude, the barometric pressure and the oxygen content of the air decrease. This fall in the oxygen content of the air causes a predictable fall in $\dot{V}O_2$max equivalent to about 10% for every 1,000 m above 1,200 m (Squires & Buskirk, 1982). On the summit of Mount Everest (8,848 m), the $\dot{V}O_2$max of the average mountaineer is only 15 ml/kg/min, or about 27% of the sea-level value, and is barely greater than the lowest oxygen consumption required to sustain life—7 ml/kg/min (West et al., 1983a, 1983b). This explains why even when breathing supplemental oxygen, mountaineers struggle to climb near the summit of Everest and can take as long as 5 hours to climb the last 400 m to the summit.

Peter Habeler and Reinhold Messner, who successfully ascended Mount Everest without supplemental oxygen, described their ascent in the following way. "We can no longer keep on our feet to rest. . . . Every 10-15 steps we collapse into the snow to rest, then crawl on again" (Sutton et al., 1983, p. 435). Interestingly, the $\dot{V}O_2$max of Messner is only 48.8 ml/kg/min, essentially the same as that in Edmund Hilary (Pugh, 1958) and little better than values found in untrained, healthy subjects, whereas Habeler's is a far more respectable 65.9 ml/kg/min (Oelz et al., 1986). Thus, $\dot{V}O_2$max is certainly not a very good predictor of high-altitude mountain-climbing ability! Rather, performance ability at extreme altitude appears to be determined by the capacity to maintain very high rates of ventilation in response to the very low oxygen content of the inspired air (Schoene et al., 1984).

$\dot{V}O_2$Max Values of Elite Athletes

Given the linear relationship between oxygen consumption and running speed (see Figure 2.2), we might conclude that those elite athletes who have the abilities to maintain the fastest running speeds for prolonged periods of time must have much greater capacities for maximum oxygen consumption than do ordinary mortals. This is indeed so, and Table 2.1 shows the range of $\dot{V}O_2$max values recorded in some elite athletes.

The highest reported $\dot{V}O_2$max value for a male runner is that of Dave Bedford (85 ml/kg/min); the highest for a female runner is 77 ml/kg/min for a 2:36 marathoner (Gregor et al., 1981). The highest value ever recorded in any athlete is 93 ml/kg/min for a Scandinavian cross-country skier (Bergh, 1982). In contrast, $\dot{V}O_2$max values measured in otherwise healthy young men and women are much lower, usually between 45 and 55 ml/kg/min (Kruss et al., 1989; Wyndham et al., 1966), about 60% lower than in elite athletes. Because $\dot{V}O_2$max can be improved by only 5 to 15% even with intensive training, it is clear that the average healthy individual will never achieve a $\dot{V}O_2$max value anywhere near those of the elite athletes, no matter how much he or she trains. Therefore, because $\dot{V}O_2$max is an indirect measure of potential for success in endurance activities, it is clear that hereditary factors must play important roles in determining who will become champions.

Even among elite athletes with quite similar performances, $\dot{V}O_2$max values may vary quite dramatically. For example, consider the cases of Steve Prefontaine and Frank Shorter, two athletes whose $\dot{V}O_2$max values differed by 16% yet whose best mile times differed by less than 8 seconds (3.4%); their best 3-mile

Table 2.1   Maximum Oxygen Consumption ($\dot{V}O_2$max) Values in Elite Endurance Athletes

Athlete	$\dot{V}O_2$max value (ml/kg/min)	Major performance	Reference
Dave Bedford	85.0	10 km WR 1973	Berg (1982)
Steven Prefontaine	84.4	1 mile 3:54.6	Pollock (1977)
Gary Tuttle	82.7	2:17 marathon	Pollock (1977)
Kip Keino	82.0	2 km WR 1965	Saltin & Åstrand (1967)
Don Lash	81.5	2 mile WR 1937	Robinson et al. (1937)
Craig Virgin	81.1	2:10:26 marathon	Cureton et al. (1975)
Jim Ryun	81.0	1 mile WR 1967	Daniels (1974a)
Steve Scott	80.1	1 mile 3:37.69	Conley et al. (1984)
Bill Rodgers	78.5	2:09:27 marathon	Rodgers & Concannon (1982)
Matthews Temane	78.0	21.1 km WR 1987	Noakes et al. (1990b)
Don Kardong	77.4	2:11:15 marathon	Pollock (1977)
Tom O'Reilly	77.0	927 km in 6-day race	Davies & Tompson (1979)
John Landy	76.6	1 mile WR 1954	Åstrand (1955)
Alberto Salazar	76.0	Marathon WR 1981†	Costill (1982)
Johnny Halberstadt	74.4*	2:11:44 marathon	Wyndham et al. (1969)
Amby Burfoot	74.3	2:14:28 marathon	Costill & Winrow (1970a)
Cavin Woodward	74.2	48-160 km WR 1975	Davies & Thompson (1979)
Kenny Moore	74.2	2:11:36 marathon	Pollock (1977)
Bruce Fordyce	73.3*	80 km WR 1983	Jooste et al. (1980)
Grete Waitz	73.0	Marathon WR 1980	Costill & Higdon (1981)
Buddy Edelen	73.0	Marathon WR 1963	Dill et al (1967)
Peter Snell	72.3	1 mile WR 1964	Carter et al. (1967)
Zithulele Sinqe	72.0	2:08:05 marathon	Noakes et al. (1990b)
Frank Shorter	71.3	2:10:30 marathon	Pollock (1977)
Willie Mtolo	70.3	2:08:15 marathon	Noakes et al. (1990b)
Derek Clayton	69.7	Marathon WR 1969	Costill et al. (1971b)

Note. WR = world record.

*Predicted sea-level values from measurements recorded at medium altitude (5,784 feet) by adding 11%.

†Subsequently not ratified (short course).

times differed by even less (0.2 seconds). If $\dot{V}O_2$max is the sole explanation for differences in running performance, then Prefontaine should have been better by at least 16% in all distances. Similarly, why is Mark Plaatjies's marathon time not considerably faster than that of Zithulele Sinqe or that of Derek Clayton, who held the world marathon record despite such a relatively poor $\dot{V}O_2$max value of 69 ml/kg/min?

Why do some athletes with quite similar $\dot{V}O_2$max values have quite different running performances? For this we need to look no further than the examples provided by the American Alberto Salazar, the Norwegian Grete Waitz, and the Briton Cavin Woodward, whose best marathon times were greatly different despite similar $\dot{V}O_2$max values (see Table 2.2).

Table 2.2   Example of Three Athletes With Similar $\dot{V}O_2$max Values but With Greatly Different Standard-Marathon Times

Athlete (country)	$\dot{V}O_2$max value (ml/kg/min)	Standard-marathon time (hr:min:s)
Alberto Salazar (U.S.A.)	76.0	2:08:13
Grete Waitz (Norway)	73.0	2:25:29
Cavin Woodward (U.K.)	74.2	2:19:50

$\dot{V}O_2$MAX AND THE CONCEPT OF RUNNING ECONOMY

The idea that the $\dot{V}O_2$max test can predict how well any runner will ever perform on the road has been propagated in many scientific and lay publications (Costill, 1967; Costill et al., 1973; C.T.M. Davies & Thompson, 1979; C. Foster, 1983; C. Foster et al., 1978; Matsui et al., 1972; Miyashita et al., 1978; Wyndham et al., 1969). An important feature of all these studies is that they have looked at groups of athletes of quite different abilities, including the very good and the very bad. When this approach is used, the results are as expected. The slow athletes have low $\dot{V}O_2$max values, and the fast runners have much higher $\dot{V}O_2$max values.

However, when we study groups of athletes with very similar running performances, for example the athletes listed in Table 2.2, then we find that the $\dot{V}O_2$max becomes a far less sensitive predictor of performance (Conley & Krahenbuhl, 1980; Costill & Winrow, 1970a, 1970b; Noakes et al., 1990a; Pollock, 1977).

How, then, are we to explain these anomalies?

The most simple explanation for these discrepancies is that they are solely due to differences in motivation between the different athletes. Thus, runners with world-class $\dot{V}O_2$max values who run slowly must be underachievers. They must simply not be prepared to race or train hard enough to live up to their inborn potentials and therefore race at much lower intensities (i.e., at lower percentages of their $\dot{V}O_2$max values) than do runners with the same world-class $\dot{V}O_2$max values who achieve greatness.

On consideration, however, this explanation becomes somewhat less attractive. If correct, it would mean that compared to Frank Shorter, both Steve Prefontaine and Grete Waitz must be underachievers. This is a possibility that few would take very seriously. What is more, this line of reasoning cannot explain how runners with quite low $\dot{V}O_2$max values, such as Derek Clayton and Zithulele Sinqe, can still be among the most successful runners.

In fact, researchers have found that regardless of $\dot{V}O_2$max values, the top male and female runners run at very similar intensities (measured as a percentage of $\dot{V}O_2$max) during competition (Costill et al., 1971b; C.T.M. Davies & Thompson, 1979; Scrimgeour et al., 1986). Thus, this explanation for differences in running performance between athletes with equivalent $\dot{V}O_2$max values will not suffice.

David Dill and his colleagues (Dill et al., 1930), David Costill (Costill, 1979; Costill & Winrow, 1970b), and Jack Daniels (1974b) were probably the first scientists to suggest that there may be quite marked differences in the amount of oxygen different athletes actually require when running at the same racing speeds and that these differences in running "economy" or efficiency of oxygen utilization could be a major factor explaining differences in running performance in athletes with similar $\dot{V}O_2$max values (Noakes, 1988b).

In their study of Jim McDonagh and Ted Corbitt, top veteran ultramarathoners with similar $\dot{V}O_2$max values but with different running performances, Costill and Winrow (1970b) reported that the amount of oxygen each runner utilized when running at each of four submaximal (below 100% $\dot{V}O_2$max) running speeds of between 10.8 km/hr and 16 km/hr differed quite substantially. McDonagh required less oxygen to run at each running speed and was therefore labeled more economical or more efficient than Corbitt. The relative difference in their efficiencies was about 11%, which is about twice the difference (5%) in their best marathon times at the time they were studied. Dill et al. (1930) and more recently Sjödin and Schele (1982), J.T. Daniels et al. (1985), and Svedenhag and Sjödin (1985) reported that running economy can differ by as much as 30% even in trained athletes.

Other studies showed that marathon runners tend to be more efficient than other runners (Boileau et al., 1982; Costill & Fox, 1969; Costill et al., 1973; J. Daniels & Oldridge, 1970; Dill, 1965; Pollock, 1977; Pugh et al., 1967) and that world- class middle-distance runners tend to be more efficient than other lesser athletes (J. Daniels & Oldridge, 1970; Dill, 1965; Kollias et al., 1967). When tested on a bicycle, distance runners are more efficient than are sprinters (Stuart et al., 1981).

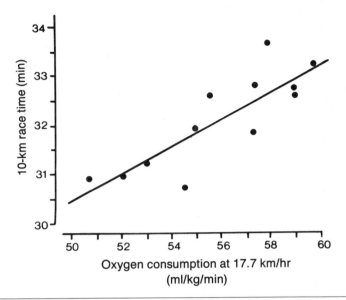

Figure 2.3 The relationship between running efficiently and 10-km race time.
Note. From D.L. Conley and G.S. Krahenbuhl, "Running Economy and Distance Running Performance of Highly Trained Athletes," *Medicine and Science in Sports and Exercise*, **12**(5), p. 359, 1980, © by American College of Sports Medicine. Adapted by permission.

In general, research has shown that the best athletes are usually the most efficient (Noakes, 1988b). This finding was most clearly shown by Conley and Krahenbuhl (1980), who studied a group of 12 runners whose best 10-km times were closely bunched between 30:31 and 33:33. The authors found that the runners' $\dot{V}O_2$max values, which ranged from 67 to 78 ml/kg/min, could not be used to predict their 10-km times. For example, the second fastest runner had the second lowest $\dot{V}O_2$max value. However, the researchers found excellent correlations between the amounts of oxygen that the runners used at each of three submaximal running speeds (14.5, 16.1, and 17.7 km/hr) and their best times for the 10-km race. Thus, the runners who used the least oxygen at each of these running speeds and were therefore the most efficient had the fastest 10-km running times (see Figure 2.3).

The authors suggested that they did not find $\dot{V}O_2$max to be a good predictor of running ability because they were dealing with a homogeneous group of runners with very similar 10-km race times. The authors concluded that a high $\dot{V}O_2$max (above 67 ml/kg/min) helped each athlete gain membership to this elite performance group, but within this selected group, running efficiency and not $\dot{V}O_2$max was the factor discriminating success in the 10-km race.

I will take their interpretation one step further. To gain entrance to the elite group of outstanding runners, the athlete needs muscles with superior contractility. These muscles then allow the athlete to achieve a high work load during the maximum test to exhaustion. The high work load demands a high rate of oxygen consumption, which is interpreted as a high $\dot{V}O_2$max (see Table 2.1). But the exact $\dot{V}O_2$max value that each athlete achieves will be determined by each person's running economy (Noakes, 1988b). Thus, among this select group of runners, $\dot{V}O_2$max values by themselves do not predict performance because they do not take into account differences in running economy or in peak achieved work load during the maximal test.

Thus, runners with very high $\dot{V}O_2$max values may have relatively less impressive running performances (e.g., Tuttle and Waitz in Table 2.1) because these runners are simply less efficient and require more oxygen than average to run at any speed. Similarly, the relatively low $\dot{V}O_2$max values of outstanding runners like Salazar, Clayton, Shorter, and Sinqe indicate that they are extremely efficient runners.

Some evidence of this hypothesis is provided by the data in Figure 2.4, which compares the running efficiencies of five great athletes—Derek Clayton (Costill et al., 1971b), Jim Ryun (J.T. Daniels, 1974a), Frank Shorter, Zithulele Sinqe, and Craig Virgin (Cureton et al., 1975)—with those of a group of children studied by C.T.M. Davies (1980a).

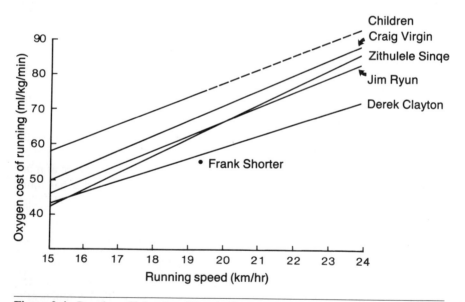

Figure 2.4 Running efficiencies of Derek Clayton, Jim Ryun, Frank Shorter, Zithulele Singe, and Craig Virgin.

It is clear that Clayton, Shorter, and Sinqe are the most efficient of the runners studied, that Ryun's efficiency is slightly better than the "average" runner shown in Figure 2.1, and that Virgin is the least efficient of these runners. The difference in efficiency between Clayton and Virgin ranges between 15 and 20% despite the fact that both these athletes were equally trained. This suggests that although training may improve running efficiency, inherent differences in running efficiency exist between different athletes, and these differences cannot be completely removed by training (J.T. Daniels et al., 1985). The nature of these differences is presently unclear.

Clayton (1980) described how he thinks he became an efficient runner.

When I started training for marathon distances, my style changed naturally. Running twenty miles a day cut down on my stride length. It also eliminated the tendency to lift my knees. Gradually, my power stride evolved into one of economy. Despite the energy-draining action of my upper body, I developed a very natural leg action I call the "Clayton shuffle." Through miles and miles of training, I honed my leg action to such a degree that I barely lifted my leg off the ground. The "Clayton shuffle" is probably the best thing that ever happened to my running. It was economical and easy on my body. (p. 62)

Figure 2.4 also shows that children are even less efficient than is Virgin and that at a running speed of 16 km/hr the difference in efficiency between Clayton and the children is 33%.

C.T.M. Davies (1980a) found that when these child runners ran with weights, their running efficiencies improved. He concluded that due to their light body weights, children were less able to transfer energy in the horizontal plane. When they were made artificially heavier by running with added weights, their vertical movement was reduced and they became more efficient.

Miyashita et al. (1978) recorded similar findings. In a group of runners of the same heights and weights and with similar $\dot{V}O_2$max values, the slower runners moved with a more upright stance, covered less ground, and used twice as much energy in the vertical axis as the faster runners. Dr. Ned Frederick has found that efficient runners glide along with very little vertical movement (Higdon, 1981).

This idea was beautifully illustrated in the television broadcast of the 1981 New York City Marathon, in which Alberto Salazar was filmed coming off the Queensborough Bridge. Only his head and shoulders were visible above the bridge wall, and it was clear that as he ran the top of his head remained absolutely parallel to the top of the wall. This indicates a negligible vertical component to the "Salazar shuffle."

Arthur Newton (see chapter 5) had similar advice about running style.

Learn to run in an easy and serene manner without an atom of wasted energy. Use short strides. *The longer your stride the more you bob up and down while enjoying it. You ought to almost slither your feet over the ground, going as near to touching it without actually doing it.* (Newton, 1935, pp. 21-22, 36; 1949, p. 87)

A possible explanation of these differences in running efficiency, which to my knowledge has not yet been resolved, is that with each running stride, the muscles of the landing leg store "impact energy" as they contract eccentrically to absorb the shock of landing (K.R. Williams, 1985). Some of the stored energy may then be used during the concentric muscle contraction that propels the body forward during the next stride. It is possible, although this is pure speculation, that the muscles of inefficient runners have less ability either to store or utilize this form of energy. Alternatively, other as-yet-unstudied biomechanical factors such as differences in limb lengths and body weight distributions could be equally, if not more, important in determining differences in running economy (K.R. Williams, 1985).

Finally, running economy may change for the same athlete during different types of exercise, for example, uphill or downhill running (Gregor, 1970), or during different activities such as cycling or step climbing (J.T. Daniels et al., 1985). Thus, it is possible that runners who are efficient on the flat may be inefficient while running either uphill or downhill. Alternatively, some efficient runners may be less efficient at cycling than are other runners who are less efficient runners.

The importance of running efficiency is that at any running speed an efficient runner will burn less fuel than will an inefficient runner. If depletion of body fuel stores explains fatigue during marathon racing, then the more efficient runner will be able to run farther on the same amount of fuel.

OTHER FACTORS INFLUENCING THE OXYGEN COST OF RUNNING

If running economy is so important, can it be altered? It seems that persons beginning exercise definitely become more efficient with training (Robinson & Harmon, 1941), as do persons who are already trained but who continue heavy training. Conley et al. (1981b) followed a single runner during 6 months of interval training and found that the subject's running efficiency improved by between 9 and 16% at three different speeds. However, his body weight also fell about 6%, which could have been the more important factor explaining the improved running efficiency. Subsequently these authors (Conley et al., 1984) showed that the running efficiency of Steve Scott, America's premier 1,500-m runner of the early 1980s, improved with interval training. Svedenhag and Sjödin (1985) showed that the running efficiencies of a group of elite Swedish distance runners improved between 1 and 4% during the course of 1 year, changes that were in the range (up to 4%) of those measured in the adolescent runners studied by J. Daniels and Oldridge (1971). Svedenhag and Sjödin (1985) speculated that the continual improvements in the running performances of these Swedish athletes were due to slowly progressive improvements in their running efficiencies rather than to increases in $\dot{V}O_2$max values, which were relatively fixed, increasing only during that phase of the season when the athletes were performing high-intensity interval-type training. This has indeed been shown in a group of elite Czechoslovakian runners (Bunc et al., 1989).

Athletes appear to choose stride lengths at which they are most efficient, that is, at which oxygen uptake is the least (Cavanagh & Williams, 1982). When forced to take either shorter or longer strides but to maintain the same running pace, athletes become less efficient and require an increased oxygen uptake. As Arthur Newton said, "Don't draw the line too fine about the length of your stride. . . . Just make a habit of acquiring a reasonable length and Nature will attend to the rest" (1935, p. 71). With training, runners increase the length of their strides and reduce their stride frequency (R.C. Nelson & Gregor, 1976). Some researchers believe that this optimizes running efficiency because increasing stride length is more economical than increasing stride frequency.

Children are less efficient runners than are adults (see Figure 2.4; Krahenbuhl & Pangrazi, 1983) but become more efficient as they age (J. Daniels & Oldridge, 1971), partly due to training (J. Daniels et al., 1978b) but also because of weight gain (MacDougall et al., 1983). Improvements in running performance in adolescents appear to be due to changes in running economy, not in $\dot{V}O_2$max (Krahenbuhl et al., 1989). Researchers found that instruction in running technique did not improve the running economies of 10-year-old boys (Petray & Krahenbuhl, 1985). Other researchers have suggested that children may be less able to store and utilize elastic energy during running (Thorstensson, 1986).

Although $\dot{V}O_2$max values do differ between the sexes, gender has no effect on running efficiency; trained men and women are equally efficient (J. Daniels et al., 1977; C.T.M. Davies & Thompson, 1979; P. Hopkins & Powers, 1982; Maughan & Leiper, 1983). Race may influence running efficiency; researchers have found that Asians and Africans utilize 17% less energy than Europeans when lying, sitting, or standing, but no studies have compared energy uses of these groups during exercise (Geissler & Aldouri, 1985). In a study of elite runners of different racial groups, researchers found no race-related differences in running economies (Noakes et al., 1990b).

Clothing weight is another factor that can influence an athlete's efficiency. Stevens (1983) calculated the effect of the weight of clothing on marathon racing performance. He found that the typical nylon vest and shorts worn by marathon runners weighed 150 g; 100% cotton shorts and vest weighed 234 g; and a heavy track suit weighed 985 g. Stevens calculated that changing from nylon to cotton clothing would increase a world-class runner's marathon time by about 13 seconds and an average 3:40 marathoner's time by about 23 seconds. Running in a full track suit would increase the average runner's marathon time by about 4 minutes.

However, laboratory experiments do not necessarily substantiate these calculations. Cureton et al. (1978) found that the addition of up to 5% of body weight (up to 4 kg in an 80-kg runner) to the torso increased the oxygen cost of running by only about 2.5%. Extrapolation of these data suggest that the addition of even 1 kg of extra weight to the torso in the form of clothing would increase the oxygen cost of running by less than 0.5%.

Extra weight added to the legs or feet appears to have a far greater effect on running economy. Martin (1985) found that the addition of 0.5 kg to each thigh or to each foot increased the oxygen cost of running by 3.5 and 7.2%, respectively, values considerably higher than those found by Cureton et al. (1978). A number of other studies (Catlin & Dressendorfer, 1979; Frederick et al., 1984; B.H. Jones et al., 1984, 1986; Martin, 1985; Stripe, 1982b) showed that the addition of 1 kg to the feet increases the oxygen cost of running by between 6 and 10%, or about 1% per 100 g increase in the weight of footwear. The increase is the same in men and women (B.H. Jones et al., 1986).

Clearly, a 1% savings in energy expenditure during a standard marathon race, for example, is not inconsiderable; if translated directly into a 1% improvement in performance it would mean a savings of 77 seconds at world-record marathon pace, equivalent to a sub-2:07 standard marathon. But we have yet to prove that this energy savings will cause an equivalent improvement in running performance.

In-shoe orthotics used in the treatment of a number of running injuries (see chapter 12, p. 449) will increase shoe weight and therefore might influence running economy adversely. In the study of Burkett et al. (1985), the addition of an 80-g orthotic device to each running shoe increased the oxygen cost of running by about 1.4%; smaller increases (0.4 to 1.1%) were reported by Berg and Sady (1985). These studies indicate that the added weight of the orthotic device decreases running economy in direct proportion to its weight.

Work at the Nike Sport Research Laboratory has shown that the air pocket used in the midsole of different Nike Air running shoes reduces the oxygen cost of running by 1.6 to 2.8% at a running speed of 16 km/hr (Frederick et al., 1983; Stripe, 1982a). If these savings directly translate into equivalent improvements in racing performance, then they are significant, at least for the top athletes. Further research is needed to study this possibility.

Obviously, prevailing conditions such as running surface, gradient, and wind speed and direction will have considerable effect on a runner's economy. The influence of the running surface on the oxygen cost of running was first noted by Passmore and Durnin (1955), who reported that the oxygen cost of walking across a plowed field was 35% greater than the cost of walking at the same speed on a smooth, firm surface. Running on sand has a similar effect (Wyngand et al., 1985). More recently McMahon and Greene (1979; see also chapter 11) suggested that optimizing the spring constant of a running track will likely improve running performance and running economy (and reduce injury risk).

One of the first scientists to study the influence of wind speed on running performance was the great British physiologist Dr. Griffiths Pugh, whose work on the effects of altitude on athletic performance is among the classic contributions on that topic (Pugh, 1958, 1967a). Pugh performed four different studies designed to measure how wind speed and the gradient of the running surface influence the oxygen cost of running (Pugh, 1970a, 1970b). His studies showed that the extra cost of running into a facing wind increased as the square of the wind speed. Thus the oxygen cost of running into a 66-km/hr head wind increases by 30 ml/kg/min. Similarly, running up an 8% incline increases the oxygen cost of running by about 20 ml/kg/min.

Figure 2.2 indicates that for each 1 km/hr increase in running speed, the oxygen cost increases about 4 ml/kg/min. Thus, the increased oxygen cost of 30 ml/kg/min caused by running into a 66-km/hr wind would cause a 7.5-km/hr reduction in running speed. Similarly, an 8% gradient would slow the runner by 5 km/hr.

Pugh also showed that at the speeds at which middle-distance track events are run (6 m/s or about 67 seconds per 400 m), about 8% of the runner's energy is used in overcoming air resistance. But by running directly behind a leading runner (or *drafting*) at a distance of about 1 m, the athlete can save 80% of that energy. In a middle-distance race this would be equivalent to a savings of about 4 seconds per lap. However, Pugh considers it unlikely that in practice the following athletes would ever be able to run as close to the lead runner to benefit to this extent. By running slightly to the side of the lead runner, the following runner would probably benefit by about 1 second per lap (Pugh, 1970a, 1970b).

Another researcher to study the benefits of drafting was Californian Chester R. Kyle (1979). His calculations suggest that at world-record mile pace, a runner running 2 m behind the lead runner would save about 1.66 seconds per lap, which generally confirms Pugh's estimations. Kyle calculated that the benefits of drafting in cycling are much greater than in running, some 30% or more. In addition, the larger the group and the farther from the front the cyclist rides, the more the cyclist benefits.

In contrast, the aerodynamic drag is *increased* when runners are positioned abreast because the larger frontal area results in a larger shared drag (L. Brownlie et al., 1987a).

These findings explain why track athletes find pacers to be such essential ingredients in aiming for world track records. In addition, these findings explain why world records in the sprints are set at altitude. During sprinting, the energy cost of overcoming air resistance rises to between 13 and 16% of the total cost of running. Thus, the sprinter benefits greatly by running at an altitude where air resistance is considerably reduced. It is interesting that when a runner is racing on a circular track, an optimum strategy is to accelerate into the wind and to decelerate when the wind is from behind, the opposite of what one would expect (Hatsell, 1974).

The Briton Dr. Mervyn Davies (C.T.M. Davies, 1980c, 1981) extended Pugh's findings. Davies used essentially the same techniques as Pugh but included observations on the effects of downhill running and of following winds of different speeds.

Davies found that when a runner was measured on the treadmill, facing winds of up to 18 km/hr had no effect on the oxygen cost of running. But the same conditions on the road will have a very marked effect. On the treadmill, the athlete does not move forward and thus does not expend energy overcoming air resistance. However, an athlete who runs on the road into a wind of 18 km/hr faces an actual wind speed equal to that of his or her running speed plus that of the prevailing wind.

The practical relevance of this is that on a calm day, anyone running slower than 18 km/hr (about a 2:21 marathon pace) will not benefit by drafting in the wake of other runners. However, runners stand to gain considerably by drafting when running at faster speeds or when running into winds that, when added to their running speeds, would make the actual wind speed greater than 18 km/hr.

Of course, the world marathon record is run at a faster pace than 18 km/hr. This means that athletes intent on setting world marathon records would be well advised to draft for as much of the race as possible. Front running in the marathon is almost as wasteful of energy as is front running on the track. One can only assume that as runners begin to realize this fact, we shall see pacers in marathon races just as we now have them in track races.

The only way besides drafting to reduce wind resistance is to run with a following wind, the speed of which is at least equal to that of the runner. Davies calculated that under these circumstances, the removal of the energy required to overcome wind resistance at world marathon pace (19.91 km/hr) would increase the runner's speed by about 0.82 km/hr, equivalent to a reduction in racing time of about 5 minutes. Similarly, drafting in a tightly knit bunch for the entire race would reduce air resistance by about 80%, allowing the runner to run about 4 minutes faster.

Davies found that the effect of a tail wind on the oxygen cost of running was about half that of a facing wind (although obviously this effect was to the runner's advantage). Thus, a following wind of 19.8 km/hr is of little assistance to runners running slower than 18 km/hr, but a following wind of 19.8 km/hr would assist a world marathon record attempt to the extent of a 0.5-km/hr increase in speed. Higher following wind speeds of 35 to 66 km/hr would improve running speeds by 1.5 to 4 km/hr.

At higher facing wind speeds, the oxygen cost of running increases enormously. Wind speeds of 35 km/hr would reduce running speeds by about 2.5 km/hr, speeds of 60 km/hr by about 8 km/hr (see Figure 2.5).

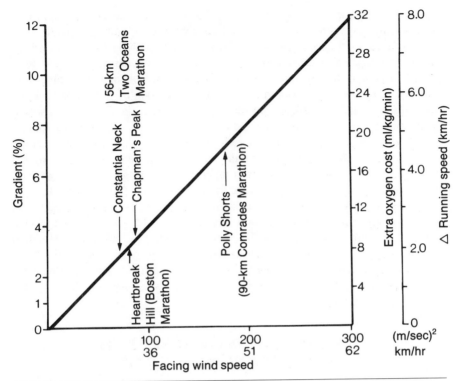

Figure 2.5 The additional oxygen costs of running up differing gradients or into facing wind speeds of different velocities.
Note. Based on data of C.T.M. Davies (1980c, 1981).

Finally, Davies calculated the additional oxygen cost of running uphill and the energy savings of running downhill. He found that the energy savings during downhill running equaled only half of the energy that would be lost when running on an equivalent uphill gradient. Thus, uphill running increased the energy cost by about 2.6 ml/kg/min for each 1% increase in gradient. This is roughly equivalent to a reduction in running speed of about 0.65 km/hr. Downhill running was associated with a reduction in the oxygen cost of running by about 1.5 ml/kg/min for each 1% gradient, equivalent to an increase in speed of about 0.35 km/hr.

The practical value of this information is twofold. First, it indicates that time lost going up a hill can never be fully regained by running an identical downhill gradient. Second, the data in Figure 2.5 can be used to estimate how much time you can expect to lose or gain on a particular section of a race (if you know the gradient of that section).

More recently, Chester Kyle and his colleagues (Kyle, 1986; Kyle & Caiozzo, 1986) studied the aerodynamic drag effects of athletic clothing and showed that the following factors increased the aerodynamic drag experienced by the runner (Kyle & Caiozzo, 1986): shoes with exposed laces (0.5%); hair on limbs (0.6%); long socks (0.9%); short hair (4%); loosely fitting clothing (4.2%), and long hair (6.3%). They also calculated that by reducing aerodynamic drag by as little as 2%, equivalent to a haircut, a runner would reduce his or her running time over 100 m by 0.01 seconds and in a standard marathon by 5.7 seconds. Even better results could be achieved by running in a custom-fitted speed suit with a tight-fitting hood to cover the hair and ears. Such a suit made of polyurethane-coated, stretchable nylon reduces aerodynamic drag by smoothing the airflow around the streamlined areas of the chin, ears, and hair, and by eliminating the flapping of loose clothing. Calculations suggest that wearing such clothing would reduce running time in the 100-m race by 0.284 seconds (3%) and by 1:34.50 (1%) in a standard marathon (L. Brownlie et al., 1987b). Unfortunately, this clothing is impractical for marathon runners because its streamlining prevents heat loss (L. Brownlie et al., 1987a). The first attempt to use the streamlined hood in Olympic relay competition also had a disastrous result—the 1988 United States Olympic Games 100-m relay team was disqualified when one runner received the baton outside the legal zone because he was unable to hear the approach of the other runner!

IMPLICATIONS OF RESEARCH ON RUNNING ECONOMY

Most of the early physiological research into the effects of running training focused almost exclusively on the effects of training on the athlete's $\dot{V}O_2max$. Yet we now know that the $\dot{V}O_2max$ of a healthy individual is relatively stable and changes relatively little, even with very intensive training (J. Daniels, 1974a; J. Daniels et al., 1978a; Svedenhag & Sjödin, 1985). Thus we may ask, Why does running performance continue to improve with training if the $\dot{V}O_2max$ does not increase in parallel?

One proven explanation is that training increases the running speed at the lactate turnpoint and that this change correlates closely with actual changes in running performance (Tanaka et al., 1984). Another important possibility is that an athlete who trains heavily shows a gradual and progressive increase in running efficiency, which continues to improve even for some years after the athlete's $\dot{V}O_2max$ has reached its highest possible value (Svedenhag & Sjödin, 1985).

Other findings are in accord with this interpretation. Scrimgeour et al. (1986) studied three groups of ultramarathon runners who trained at different weekly distances; the researchers found that the group of runners who trained the most (more than 100 km/week) differed only from the other groups in that they had superior running economy. The groups did not differ in their $\dot{V}O_2max$ values or in the percent $\dot{V}O_2max$ values that they sustained during races of 10 to 90 km.

In fact, the least-trained runners ran at significantly higher percent $\dot{V}O_2$max values during the 10-km race than did the runners who trained the most. Others have also noted that weekly training distance does not predict the percent $\dot{V}O_2$max that an athlete can sustain during competition, thus elite runners do not necessarily run at higher percent $\dot{V}O_2$max values during competition than do nonelite runners (C.T.M. Davies & Thompson, 1979; Maughan & Leiper, 1983; Sjödin & Svedenhag, 1985; Svedenhag & Sjödin, 1985; Wells et al., 1981; C. Williams & Nute, 1983). In the studies of Scrimgeour et al. (1986) and Sjödin and Svedenhag (1985), the runners who trained the most also ran the fastest but only because they were more efficient. Thus, at the same percent $\dot{V}O_2$max, the most-trained runners ran faster because they required less oxygen to run at any particular speed.

In summary, Scrimgeour et al. (1986) found that training more than 60 to 100 km/week did not increase the intensity of effort, measured as the percent $\dot{V}O_2$max, that athletes could sustain during marathon and ultramarathon races. However, the more heavily trained runners were more efficient. Thus, it seems that their extra training increased their running efficiencies so that for the same effort during competition, the more trained runners ran faster. Sjödin and Svedenhag (1985) reported essentially the same finding except that they concluded that the cutoff training distance was 120 km/week. Together these studies suggest that the sole benefit of a very high weekly training distance may be a progressive increase in running efficiency. In view of the risks associated with heavy weekly training distances (see chapter 10), we may ask, Are there better and less risky ways of improving running economy?

Unfortunately, at present our understanding of all the factors that determine running economy is incomplete; we do not know how these factors might be altered most effectively. The evidence presented so far does suggest that in order to optimize running economy, the runner needs to pay greater attention to the following: minimizing the weight of shoes and clothing worn during competition; developing a long stride length with a slow stride frequency; and minimizing the weight of the moving limbs, in particular the legs, in much the way that cyclists strive to keep the weight of their revolving wheels to a minimum. In addition, runners need to be more aware of their aerodynamic profiles. Thus Kyle (1986) suggested that runners who run with tightly fitting clothing, with short hair, and without socks can reduce aerodynamic drag 2 to 6%. This change would be the equivalent of running 4 inches less in the 100-m race and 30 m less in a standard marathon.

In the future we can expect major efforts by running shoe manufacturers to increase the contributions of their products to running efficiency; by the bioengineers to understand intrinsic anatomical factors that influence running efficiency; and by coaches to develop new training techniques to improve the running efficiencies of athletes. Even the psychologist may have a role, given the finding that hypnosis can influence running efficiency (Benson et al., 1978). One shoe manufacturer is already studying the possibility of "tuning" running shoes so that a maximum amount of energy is returned to the foot with each stride (Kyle, 1986), in much the same way that running tracks have been "tuned" in order to allow faster running times (see chapter 11).

OTHER PREDICTORS
OF RUNNING PERFORMANCE

A fascination with the belief that the $\dot{V}O_2$max is the alpha and omega of exercise physiology has blinded us to the possibility that other factors may be equal or better predictors of running performance (Noakes, 1988b).

My colleagues and I were first alerted to this possibility by finding that peak running velocity reached at exhaustion during the maximal treadmill test was a better predictor of running performance than was the $\dot{V}O_2$max (Scrimgeour et al., 1986). Krahenbuhl and Pangrazi (1983) reported a similar finding in children. We and others (D.W. Morgan et al., 1989) have since confirmed this in more detailed studies (Noakes, 1988b, 1990b). In all these studies, peak treadmill running velocity and the running speed at the "lactate turnpoint" were the best physiological predictors of running performance; $\dot{V}O_2$max was a less effective predictor, whereas running economy was without predictive value. The very best predictor of performance at any longer distance, even up to 90 km, was the 10-km run time.

To me, these results indicate the following.

1. A muscle factor determines running performance at any distance. This muscle factor involves the maximum power that the muscles can produce and is not likely related to factors determining oxygen transport to or oxygen utilization by the muscles (Noakes, 1988b).

2. Those runners with the best quality muscles for short-distance races (800 to 1500 m) also have the best muscles to race at any longer distance, even up to the extreme ultradistances (see chapter 8). Thus speed and endurance are not different physiological entities; they are intimately related.

This does not mean that the best sprinters will also be the best long-distance runners. Although they may have the best quality muscles for explosive exercise, factors such as temperament and body build prevent many top sprinters from achieving excellence at the longer running distances. Alternatively, muscles able to achieve very high rates of energy production for short duration may fatigue more rapidly than muscles that are not quite as powerful. Thus, at distances greater than 400 m, nonelite sprinters with the less powerful muscles may outperform the elite sprinters whose more powerful muscles fatigue too rapidly. However, I suspect that among trained distance runners, the best runners at any longer distance are those who are fastest over distances from 800 to 1500 m and possibly even shorter distances.

3. $\dot{V}O_2$max is an indirect measure of athletic potential, because it measures the oxygen consumption at the peak achieved work load or running velocity. Among runners who have equal running economies, the runners who reach the highest work loads will also have the highest $\dot{V}O_2$max values and will also be the best runners. But the true predictors of their potentials are the peak running velocities or work loads they achieve during the maximal test, not the actual $\dot{V}O_2$max values (Noakes, 1988b, 1989a).

4. The best predictor of running performance at any distance is a running test (time for races of 1500 m to 10 km). This is a most important finding, because it proves what the best athletes have always known—that one's state of preparedness for any long-distance race, including marathons and ultramarathons, can be predicted from one's recent 10-km times. Thus, it is not necessary to test your preparedness for a marathon, for example, by running the full distance. Timing a shorter run prevents the muscle damage and prolonged recovery that results from racing distances longer than 25 km.

5. Laboratory testing is not yet as effective as an actual running test for predicting performance. This indicates that we have yet to establish the exact physiological and biochemical factors that determine running performance. This finding also indicates that the tables predicting running performance on the basis of a hypothetical $\dot{V}O_2$max (Tables 2.3, 2.4, 2.6, 2.7) are accurate not because they are based on some unique physiological findings but because they predict performance at all distances on the basis of performance at shorter distances.

Practical Application of Research on $\dot{V}O_2$Max, Running Economy, and Peak Treadmill Running Velocity

Few athletes in the world have ready access to laboratories capable of measuring $\dot{V}O_2$max, running economy, or peak treadmill running velocity. Thus, the information that we have covered in some detail in the previous pages may be very interesting but may at first glance seem to be of little practical value to the average runner. However, because the best predictor of running performance at any distance is running performance at other shorter distances, you can predict with reasonable accuracy your potential running performances at all distances even without ever entering an exercise laboratory.

The C.T.M. Davies–Thompson Data (1979)

For reasons that are not absolutely clear, it is not possible to run at 100% $\dot{V}O_2$max for more than a few minutes. This concept has been most clearly researched by C.T.M. Davies and Thompson (1979), two eminent British physiologists who found that trained athletes could maintain an average of 94% (range: 89 to 100%) of their $\dot{V}O_2$max values for a 5-km race, 82% (range: 76 to 87%) for the standard marathon, and 67% (range: 53 to 76%) for the 85-km London-to-Brighton race.

These authors also collected data on a group of four elite British ultramarathoners, including former multidistance world-record holder Cavin Woodward. The authors were thus able to extend their data to include the percent $\dot{V}O_2max$ that could be sustained for races of up to 24 hours (see Figure 2.6).

These data generated Equation 2.1, which predicts the percent $\dot{V}O_2max$ that can be sustained for a given running time.

$$\%\dot{V}O_2max = 91.24 - \{[3.79 \times \text{time (hours)}] + [0.08 \times \text{time}^2 \text{ (hours)}]\}$$

Equation 2.1

Note that this equation relates percent $\dot{V}O_2max$ to running time, not to running distance. Thus, only those athletes who complete the marathon between 2:00 and 2:20 can sustain 87% of $\dot{V}O_2max$ for the distance. Athletes who run the distance in 4:00 can only expect to run the distance at 76% $\dot{V}O_2max$.

C.T.M. Davies (1980b) found that the percent $\dot{V}O_2max$ that can be sustained for various times in cycling is identical to the same value for running. However, because cycling is so much more efficient than running, the cyclist will cover about 2-1/2 times the distance covered by the runner in the same time.

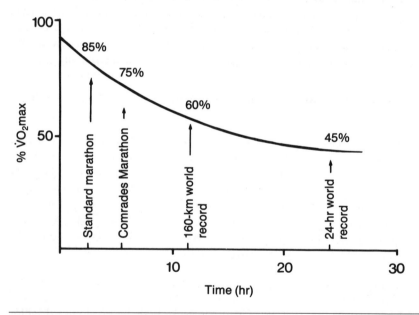

Figure 2.6 The sustainable exercise intensity (expressed as percent $\dot{V}O_2max$) falls progressively with increasing exercise duration.

Note. From "Aerobic Performance of Female Marathon and Male Ultramarathon Athletes" by C.T.M. Davies and M.W. Thompson, 1979, *European Journal of Applied Physiology*, **41**, p. 239. Copyright 1979 by Springer-Verlag Heidelberg. Adapted by permission.

Next C.T.M. Davies and Thompson (1979) showed that because the percent $\dot{V}O_2max$ that can be maintained for a certain time is predictable, we can predict an athlete's $\dot{V}O_2max$ from his or her 5-km racing time according to the formula contained in Equation 2.2.

$$\dot{V}O_2max \ (ml/kg/min) = 129.73 - [3.617 \times \text{5-km time (minutes)}]$$

Equation 2.2

C.T.M. Davies (1980b) also provided an equation (Equation 2.2a) for the prediction of $\dot{V}O_2max$ on the basis of best cycling performance over 16.1 km. This will interest athletes who both run and cycle:

$$\dot{V}O_2max \ (L/min) = -4.219 + (0.7727 \times V) \qquad \text{Equation 2.2a}$$

(V equals the speed in m/s that can be maintained for 16.1 km. To express $\dot{V}O_2max$ in ml/kg, simply divide the answer from this equation by body weight in kilograms.)

Now that we can predict an athlete's $\dot{V}O_2max$ and the percent $\dot{V}O_2max$ that he or she can sustain for a given period of time, we can calculate the rate of oxygen consumption that the athlete can sustain for a certain period of time.

For example, if the athlete has a $\dot{V}O_2max$ of 60 ml/kg/min and can sustain 50% of his or her $\dot{V}O_2max$ for 17 hours, then the athlete's average oxygen consumption during that period will be 30 ml/kg/min. To determine how fast the athlete will be running during that time, we need to know the running speed to which that rate of oxygen uptake corresponds. This is given in Equation 2.3.

$$\text{Running Speed (km/hr)} = [\text{Oxygen Uptake (ml/kg/min)} + 7.736] \div 3.966$$

Equation 2.3

Using an oxygen uptake of 30 ml/kg/min in this equation predicts that our athlete should be able to sustain a running speed of 9.5 km/hr for 17 hours. To know how far the athlete would run in 17 hours, we multiply calculated running speed in km/hr (9.5 km/hr) by running time to give a final distance of 161.8 km.

However, most athletes do not wish to know how far they will run in a certain time. Rather, they wish to know how fast they can run various distances. Mathematician J. Affleck-Graves, a marathon runner and former professor of business administration at the University of Cape Town, provided a formidable table (see Table 2.3), which gives all possible performances over virtually all possible distances that any runner would wish to race up to 24 hours. As running speeds will not be different for distances close to 90 km, reworking of the data will allow fairly accurate predictions of likely times for both the London-to-Brighton race (86.6 km) and the 100-km race. Distances below 5 km and beyond 24 hours cannot be accurately calculated, because the equation used by C.T.M. Davies and Thompson (1979) develops certain mathematical problems at very short and very long time periods (see Figure 2.7).

Table 2.3 Predicted Equivalent Running Times for Different Racing Distances Related to Predicted $\dot{V}O_2$max

Predicted $\dot{V}O_2$max (ml/kg/min)	Distance															24-hr distance (km)
	1,500 m	1 mile	5 km	8 km	10 km	16.1 km	21.1 km	30 km	32 km	42.2 km	50 km	56 km	90 km	100 km	160 km	
93.6	(3:50)	(4:07)	10:00	(20:43)	(25:59)	42:16	55:52	1:20:41	1:26:23	1:56:02	2:19:33	2:38:07	4:32:43	5:09:55	9:37:48	309.2
89.9	(3:59)	(4:16)	11:00	(21:29)	(26:57)	43:51	57:59	1:23:48	1:29:43	2:00:37	2:25:08	2:44:31	4:44:36	5:23:44	10:07:39	299.1
86.3	(4:08)	(4:26)	12:00	(22:19)	27:59	45:34	1:00:17	1:27:10	1:33:20	2:05:34	2:30:45	2:51:28	4:57:33	5:38:51	10:40:29	288.9
82.7	(4:18)	(4:36)	13:00	(23:12)	29:07	47:26	1:02:46	1:30:49	1:37:15	2:10:57	2:38:46	2:59:01	5:11:44	5:55:24	11:16:43	278.8
79.1	(4:28)	(4:48)	14:00	24:11	30:21	49:27	1:05:27	1:34:46	1:41:31	2:16:48	2:44:56	3:07:15	5:27:19	6:13:38	11:56:44	268.6
75.5	(4:40)	(5:00)	15:00	25:14	31:43	51:38	1:08:23	1:39:05	1:46:09	2:23:12	2:52:46	3:16:17	5:44:30	6:33:48	12:40:58	258.5
71.9	(4:43)	(5:14)	16:00	26:23	33:08	54:02	1:11:55	1:43:49	1:51:14	2:30:13	3:01:23	3:26:13	6:03:32	6:56:12	13:29:51	248.3
68.2	(5:06)	(5:29)	17:00	27:39	34:43	56:40	1:15:06	1:49:01	1:56:50	2:37:57	3:10:54	3:37:12	6:24:47	7:21:13	14:23:43	238.2
64.6	(5:22)	(5:45)	18:00	29:03	36:28	59:33	1:18:59	1:54:45	2:03:01	2:46:30	3:21:27	3:49:23	6:48:34	7:49:18	15:22:48	228.0
61.0	(5:38)	(6:03)	19:00	30:55	38:25	1:02:46	1:23:17	2:01:08	2:09:53	2:56:02	3:33:13	4:03:01	7:15:22	8:21:01	16:27:09	217.9
57.4	(5:57)	(6:23)	20:00	32:17	40:34	1:06:20	1:28:04	2:08:15	2:17:33	3:06:43	3:46:26	4:18:19	7:45:46	8:57:03	17:36:37	207.8
53.7	(6:18)	(6:46)	21:00	34:12	42:59	1:10:20	1:33:27	2:16:15	2:26:11	3:18:44	4:01:21	4:35:38	8:20:28	9:38:13	18:50:49	197.6
50.2	(6:41)	(7:11)	22:00	36:21	45:41	1:14:50	1:39:30	2:25:18	2:35:56	3:32:24	4:18:19	4:55:23	9:00:22	10:25:31	20:09:14	187.5
46.5	(7:08)	(7:39)	23:00	38:47	45:48	1:19:57	1:46:24	2:35:37	2:47:04	3:48:01	4:37:47	5:18:05	9:46:31	11:20:06	21:31:24	177.3
42.9	(7:38)	(8:12)	24:00	41:34	52:17	1:25:49	1:54:18	2:47:28	2:59:53	4:06:04	5:00:20	5:44:24	10:40:16	12:23:15	22:56:59	167.2
39.3	(8:13)	(8:44)	25:00	44:47	56:21	1:32:35	2:03:28	3:01:15	3:14:47	4:27:07	5:26:41	6:15:15	11:43:07	13:36:17	24:25:56	157.0
35.7	(8:54)	(9:33)	26:00	(48:32)	1:01:05	1:40:31	2:14:11	3:17:26	3:32:17	4:51:56	5:57:52	6:51:48	12:56:43	15:00:20	25:58:36	146.9
32.1	(9:41)	(10:24)	27:00	(52:57)	1:06:41	1:49:54	2:26:55	3:36:42	3:53:08	5:21:37	6:35:15	7:35:37	14:22:41	16:36:03	27:35:99	136.7
28.5	(10:39)	(11:25)	28:00	(58:16)	1:13:25	2:01:11	2:42:14	3:59:58	4:18:20	5:57:35	7:20:33	8:29:49	16:02:12	18:23:32	29:18:55	126.6
24.8	(11:48)	(12:40)	29:00	(1:04:44)	1:21:37	2:14:59	3:01:00	4:28:33	4:49:18	6:41:53	8:16:22	9:34:09	17:55:49	20:22:23	31:10:00	116.5
21.2	(13:15)	(14:13)	30:00	(1:12:48)	(1:31:51)	2:32:14	3:24:29	5:04:22	5:28:07	7:37:22	9:26:00	10:55:10	20:03:28	22:32:29	33:12:20	106.3

Note. Running times that appear in parentheses seem to be unrealistic. From "Aerobic Performance of Female Marathon and Male Ultramarathon Athletes" by C.T.M. Davies and M.W. Thompson, 1979, *European Journal of Applied Physiology,* **41**, p. 242. Copyright 1979 by Springer-Verlag Heidelberg. Adapted by permission. Calculations provided by J. Affleck-Graves.

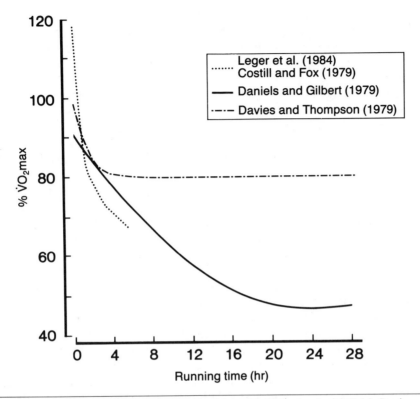

Figure 2.7 Comparison of graphs of J. Daniels and J. Gilbert and of C.T.M. Davies and M.W. Thompson to predict racing times at different distances. Also shown is the graph of L. Leger et al. (1984) and D.L. Costill and E.L. Fox (1967).

The practical relevance of this information lies mainly in demonstrating how hereditary factors can limit a runner and also in predicting the time a particular individual can expect to cover a certain distance on the basis of the time run for other distances.

As we have already established, $\dot{V}O_2$max (and by inference, performance in races of up to 10 km) is determined largely by hereditary factors; with even the most intensive training, $\dot{V}O_2$max can be increased by only 5 to 15%. Thus, if we take the typical healthy, untrained male who has a $\dot{V}O_2$max of about 50 ml/kg/min (Wyndham et al., 1966) and train him as we would a world champion, his $\dot{V}O_2$max might, with luck, increase to about 57 ml/kg/min, giving him a best 5-km time of about 20:00. Allowed to race the standard marathon, this highly trained runner would, according to the data in Table 2.3, run the race in a solid 3:06:43.

If we were now to enter this runner in a 90-km ultramarathon after he had trained every bit as hard as the top runners like Bruce Fordyce, Don Ritchie, and

Yiannis Kouros (see chapter 8) and if we were to ensure that he ran the race with the same degree of courage and intelligence as those great runners, his predicted race time would be 7:45:46. Even if he did everything right, the average male runner could only hope to finish an ultramarathon at least 2-1/4 hours behind the winner.

And now to add the final insult. According to Table 2.3, if the winner of that ultramarathon runs the distance in 5:27:19, he or she should have a predicted $\dot{V}O_2$max of 79 ml/kg/min, a value that is not very different from that recorded for Bruce Fordyce (see Table 2.1). If someone with this $\dot{V}O_2$max value were to run the race without any training whatsoever, so that he or she would be able to maintain about 50% $\dot{V}O_2$max for the race (equivalent to an oxygen cost of 39.5 ml/kg/min), this untrained runner would still complete the distance in 7:49:48, or just 4 minutes behind our highly trained, intensely motivated average runner.

Examples that confirm the general accuracy of this calculation do in fact exist. Bruce Fordyce's time in his first ultramarathon, for which he trained only moderately, was 6:45, equivalent to an effort of about 57% $\dot{V}O_2$max (see chapter 8).

So there it is. The famous Swedish physiologist Per-Olaf Åstrand said, "If you want to be a world beater then you must choose your parents carefully" (cited in Wyndham et al., 1969). Of course, most runners don't accept this; they assume that the rapid improvements they make when they start training will continue forever, that with training they too will become world champions. What happens instead is that after a year or so of running, they enter the area of diminishing returns. At first, performance and fitness improve dramatically, so that for a small input (e.g., 60 km training a week), our trained average runner with a $\dot{V}O_2$max of 57 ml/kg/min might be able to run the standard marathon at 50 to 60% of his or her $\dot{V}O_2$max for a finishing time of 3:58:48. But to improve his or her fitness by another 26% for a personal record of 3:06:43, this runner might have to increase training mileage up to 160 to 180 km a week. Although this training load might be acceptable for the potential champion looking to cut seconds off his time, for the average runner it is likely to result in injury, illness, overtraining, family disharmony, and poor racing form. Such a schedule will, of course, never allow the average runner to run faster than his or her 3:06:43 threshold.

Table 2.3 also allows runners to predict whether they will ever be able to complete longer distance races before the cutoff times for those races. Thus, to finish a standard marathon in under 4-1/2 hours, one must be able to run 5 km in about 25 minutes; to complete a 90-km ultramarathon in under 11 hours, one will need a slightly faster best 5-km time of about 24 minutes.

The J. Daniels–Gilbert Data (1979)

Working on the same principles as those of C.T.M. Davies and Thompson (1979), namely that the percentage $\dot{V}O_2$max that can be sustained falls predictably with the running time (see Figure 2.6) and that there is a predictable relationship between running speed and oxygen consumption, J. Daniels and Gilbert (1979) calculated predicted running times for virtually every possible racing distance on the track in metric or in yard/miles and for distances on the road from the half marathon to 50 km. Each performance time on each list was related to a reference $\dot{V}O_2$max value, as we have also done for the C.T.M. Davies–Thompson data (see Table 2.3). Table 2.4 lists all the distances also listed by C.T.M. Davies and Thompson up to 56 km. At those distances for which J. Daniels and Gilbert have not provided data, data have been calculated from the equations the authors provided.

Comparison of the J. Daniels–Gilbert data to those of C.T.M. Davies–Thompson will show agreement between their respective predicted marathon times based on 5-km times in the range 14 to 22 minutes, but outside these values the results are quite different, with the data of C.T.M. Davies and Thompson predicting marathon times that are considerably slower than those of J. Daniels and Gilbert.

The reason for this is that the equations derived by these two groups of workers relating the percent $\dot{V}O_2$max that can be sustained for running times shorter than 1 hour and for longer than 4 hours are quite different (see Figure 2.7).

The reason for this discrepancy is not clear, but it is probably explained by the fact that J. Daniels and Gilbert were more interested in races lasting less than 4 hours, whereas C.T.M. Davies and Thompson centered on races lasting from 4 to 24 hours. Note also that the C.T.M. Davies and Thompson graph, because it is based on a quadratic equation, predicts that the percent $\dot{V}O_2$max that can be maintained for races longer than 24 hours actually starts to increase as running time increases. This clearly is a mathematical, not a physiological, quirk. No runner is able to run faster in races lasting more than 24 hours than he or she can in shorter duration races!

We can use the data of J. Daniels and Gilbert to give reference $\dot{V}O_2$max values for all world records for males and females. Table 2.5 compares the relative quality of each world record and also compares the performances of males and females. The data in Table 2.5 show that the reference $\dot{V}O_2$max values for both male and female records fall with distance, which could indicate that athletes do not run as hard in the longer road races as they do in the shorter track races. It seems likely that environmental factors such as running gradients and wind could also be important factors explaining the relatively poorer performances at longer distances.

The $\dot{V}O_2$max reference values for the women's records are consistently at least 9 points lower at all distances than are those for the men. This suggests that until women can improve their performances over the shorter distances, they will not match men over the longer distances.

The Osler Data (1978)

Tom Osler, the veteran runner/mathematician/writer (see chapters 5 and 10), supplied a graph in his book *The Serious Runner's Handbook* (Osler, 1978)

Table 2.4 Predicted Equivalent Running Times for Different Racing Distances Related to a Reference V̇O₂max

Reference V̇O₂max value (ml/kg/min)	1,500 m	1 mile	5 km	8 km	10 km	16.1 km	21.1 km	30 km	32 km	42.2 km	50 km	56 km
112.1	2:40	2:53	10:00	16:29	20:52	34:25	45:46	1:06:31	1:11:15	1:35:44	1:54:44	2:09:24
100.2	2:56	3:10	11:00	18:07	22:55	37:47	50:17	1:13:08	1:18:21	1:45:17	2:06:08	2:22:14
90.5	3:12	3:27	12:00	19:44	24:57	41:10	54:50	1:19:49	1:25:31	1:54:53	2:17:35	2:35:05
82.4	3:28	3:45	13:00	21:22	27:01	44:35	59:25	1:26:32	1:32:42	2:04:31	2:29:02	2:47:55
75.5	3:44	4:02	14:00	23:00	29:04	48:01	1:04:02	1:33:16	1:39:56	2:14:09	2:40:29	3:00:44
69.7	4:01	4:20	15:00	24:38	31:08	51:28	1:08:40	1:40:02	1:47:10	2:23:47	2:51:55	3:13:31
64.6	4:17	4:38	16:00	26:16	33:12	54:56	1:13:19	1:46:48	1:54:25	2:33:25	3:03:19	3:26:16
60.2	4:34	4:56	17:00	27:54	35:17	58:25	1:17:58	1:53:35	2:01:39	2:43:01	3:14:40	3:38:57
56.3	4:51	5:14	18:00	29:33	37:21	1:01:54	1:22:38	2:00:21	2:08:54	2:52:34	3:25:58	3:51:34
52.8	5:08	5:33	19:00	31:11	39:26	1:05:23	1:27:19	2:07:06	2:16:07	3:02:06	3:37:13	4:04:08
49.7	5:25	5:51	20:00	32:49	41:31	1:08:53	1:31:59	2:13:51	2:23:19	3:11:35	3:48:24	4:16:37
47.0	5:42	6:09	21:00	34:28	43:36	1:12:22	1:36:36	2:20:34	2:30:29	3:21:00	3:59:32	4:29:01
44.5	5:59	6:28	22:00	36:06	45:41	1:15:52	1:41:18	2:27:15	2:37:37	3:30:23	4:10:35	4:41:21
42.2	6:16	6:46	23:00	37:44	47:46	1:19:21	1:45:57	2:33:54	2:44:43	3:39:42	4:21:34	4:53:36
40.1	6:33	7:05	24:00	39:22	49:51	1:22:50	1:50:34	2:40:32	2:51:47	3:48:57	4:32:28	5:05:47
38.3	6:51	7:24	25:00	41:00	51:56	1:26:18	1:55:11	2:47:07	2:58:48	3:58:08	4:43:18	5:17:52
36.5	7:08	7:42	26:00	42:38	54:00	1:29:46	1:59:46	2:53:39	3:05:46	4:07:16	4:54:03	5:29:52
35.0	7:25	8:01	27:00	44:16	56:04	1:33:12	2:04:20	3:00:09	3:12:42	4:16:19	5:04:44	5:41:47
33.5	7:42	8:19	28:00	45:53	58:08	1:36:38	2:08:53	3:06:37	3:19:34	4:25:19	5:15:09	5:53:37
32.2	7:59	8:37	29:00	47:30	1:00:12	1:40:04	2:13:24	3:13:01	3:26:24	4:34:14	5:25:51	6:05:22
30.9	8:16	8:56	30:00	49:07	1:02:15	1:43:28	2:17:53	3:19:23	3:33:10	4:43:06	5:36:17	6:17:01

Note. Based on equations derived from data in *Oxygen Power: Performance Tables for Distance Runners* by J. Daniels and J.R. Gilbert, 1979, Tempe, AZ: Oxygen Power. Copyright 1979 by J. Daniels and J.R. Gilbert. The exact data can be derived from *Oxygen Power.* The book can be purchased by writing to Jack Daniels, SUNY Cortland, Box 2000 Park Center, Cortland, NY 13045.

Table 2.5 Relative Performance Ratings of Male and Female World Records at Distances From 0.8 km to 42.2 km

Distance (km)	Time Male	Time Female	Reference $\dot{V}O_2$max (ml/kg/min) Male	Reference $\dot{V}O_2$max (ml/kg/min) Female
0.8	1:41.73 Coe, 1981	1:53.28 Kratochvilova, 1983	82.6	72.8
1.5	3:29.45 Aouita, 1985	3:52.47 Kazankina, 1980	82.1	72.7
1.6 (mile)	3:46.31 Cram, 1985	4:15.61 Ivan, 1989	82.1	71.0
2	4:50.81 Aouita, 1987	5:28.69 Puica, 1986	80.5	70.1
3	7:29.45 Aouita, 1989	8:22.62 Kazankina, 1984	81.1	71.9
5	12:58.34 Aouita, 1985	14:37.33 Kristiansen, 1986	82.1	70.6
10	27:08.23 Barrlos, 1989	30:13.74 Kristiansen, 1986	81.1	70.0
15	42:27 Musyoki, 1983	47:17 Kristiansen, 1987	79.9	70.6
20	57:24.2 Hermens, 1976	1:06:55.5 Mota, 1983	80.2	67.2
21.1	1:00:11 Temane, 1987	1:07:58 Kristiansen, 1983	81.1	70.5
25	1:13:55.8 Seko, 1981	1:31:04.3 Langlace, 1983	78.8	62.0
30	1:29:18.8 Seko, 1981	1:49:55.7 Langlace, 1986	79.4	62.5
42.2	2:06:50 Dinsamo, 1988	2:21:06 Kristiansen, 1985	80.6	71.2

Note. Data current to July 1989.

that showed equivalent effort performances in races ranging from 1 mile to the marathon. Osler does not mention how he arrived at these data; nevertheless, it is interesting to compare his data (see Table 2.6) with those of other researchers.

Osler's data compare quite accurately with both those of C.T.M. Davies and Thompson and those of J. Daniels and Gilbert, at least in the range of 5-km times between 12 and 22 minutes. Thereafter, Osler's data are remarkably close to those of J. Daniels and Gilbert.

The J.B. Gardner–Purdy Data (1970)

James Gardner and Jerry Purdy produced a series of tables in their book *Computerized Running Training Programmes* (1970). Table 2.7 contains the relevant data from their tables for the common racing distances from 100 m to 80 km.

The predicted times for races from 5 to 42 km based on 5-km times between 13 and 23 minutes are quite similar to those of all the other groups.

This table relates performance times at the sprint distances to those at the ultradistances. My hunch is that performance in distance races can indeed be predicted by time in the sprints, which echoes the opinions of Arthur Lydiard,

Table 2.6 Predicted Equivalent Running Times for Different Racing Distances Related to a Performance Rating

Performance rating[a]	Distance							
	1 mile	5 km	8 km	10 km	16 km	21.1 km	32 km	42.2 km
2000	3:34	12:00	20:53	26:43	44:25	59:53	1:33:28	2:05:52
1960	3:54	13:00	22:22	28:35	47:24	1:03:49	1:39:24	2:13:44
1910	4:18	14:00	24:02	30:39	50:42	1:08:11	1:46:03	2:22:29
1870	4:36	15:00	25:46	32:50	54:11	1:12:46	1:53:01	2:31:39
1830	4:54	16:00	27:26	34:54	57:30	1:17:08	1:59:38	2:40:24
1780	5:17	17:00	29:10	37:05	1:00:59	1:21:44	2:06:36	2:49:35
1740	5:34	18:00	30:44	39:03	1:04:08	1:25:53	2:12:54	2:57:53
1690	5:57	19:00	32:19	41:01	1:07:17	1:30:02	2:19:12	3:06:11
1650	6:15	20:00	34:08	43:18	1:10:55	1:34:50	2:26:29	3:15:48
1600	6:38	21:00	35:48	45:22	1:14:14	1:39:13	2:33:07	3:24:32
1560	6:55	22:00	37:27	47:26	1:17:33	1:43:35	2:39:45	3:33:17
1510	7:19	23:00	39:06	49:30	1:20:52	1:47:57	2:46:22	3:42:01
1470	7:37	24:00	40:46	51:35	1:24:11	1:52:19	2:53:00	3:50:46
1420	7:50	25:00	42:25	53:39	1:27:30	1:56:42	2:59:38	3:59:30
1380	8:07	26:00	44:05	55:43	1:30:48	2:01:04	3:06:15	4:08:15
1330	8:31	27:00	45:44	57:47	1:34:07	2:05:26	3:12:53	4:17:00
1290	8:49	28:00	47:24	59:52	1:37:26	2:09:48	3:19:31	4:25:44
1240	9:12	29:00	49:03	1:01:56	1:40:45	2:14:19	3:26:08	4:34:28
1200	9:29	30:00	50:42	1:04:00	1:44:04	2:18:33	3:32:46	4:43:13

Note. From *Serious Runner's Handbook* (p. 169) by T. Osler, 1978, Mountain View, CA: World Publications. Copyright 1978 by T. Osler. Adapted by permission.

[a]The performance rating is calculated as the year in which world records for the listed distances will equal the times given.

Table 2.7   Predicted Equivalent Running Times for Different Racing Distances Related to a Performance Rating

Performance rating[a]	Distance (m)					Distance (km)							
	100	200	400	800	1.6	5	8	10	16	32	42.2	50	80
1,080	9.85	19.8	44.1	1:41.3	3:45.1	13:00	21:31.7	27:14	45:07	1:34:24	2:06:18	2:33:04	4:16:47
950	10.42	21.0	47.0	1:48.5	4:01.7	14:00	23:11.4	29:21	48:39	1:41:53	2:16:22	2:45:19	4:37:34
840	10.95	22.1	49.8	1:55.3	4:17.8	15:00	24:48.6	31:25	52:06	1:49:12	2:26:13	2:57:19	4:57:59
740	11.47	23.2	52.6	2:02.4	4:34.3	16:00	26:29.6	33:34	55:41	1:56:50	2:36:30	3:09:50	5:19:19
650	11.99	24.4	55.4	2:09.5	4:51.2	17:00	28:13.0	35:45	59:22	2:04:41	2:47:05	3:22:45	5:41:20
570	12.50	25.4	58.1	2:16.6	5:08.0	18:00	29:56.8	37:57	1:03:04	2:12:36	2:57:46	3:35:46	6:03:36
500	12.97	26.5	1:00.8	2:23.5	5:24.3	19:00	31:38.7	40:06	1:06:43	2:20:24	3:08:17	3:48:38	6:25:38
440	13.41	27.4	1:03.3	2:29.9	5:39.8	20:00	33:15.7	42:10	1:10:11	2:27:51	3:18:21	4:00:56	6:46:44
380	13.88	28.4	1:05.9	2:37.0	5:56.9	21:00	35:22.2	44:28	1:14:03	2:36:08	3:29:34	4:14:38	7:10:18
330	14.30	29.3	1:08.3	2:43.4	6:12.4	22:00	36:42.0	46:34	1:17:36	2:43:47	3:39:55	4:27:19	7:32:07
280	14.75	30.3	1:10.9	2:50.3	6:29.4	23:00	38:30.6	48:53	1:21:31	2:52:13	3:51:21	4:41:19	7:56:17
240	15.13	31.1	1:13.2	2:56.3	6:44.2	24:00	40:05.5	50:53	1:24:56	2:59:37	4:01:23	4:53:36	8:17:32
200	15.52	32.0	1:15.5	3:02.8	7:00.1	25:00	41:48.4	53:04	1:28:40	3:07:41	4:12:20	5:07:02	8:40:48
170	15.83	32.7	1:17.4	3:07.9	7:12.8	26:00	43:11.7	54:50	1:31:41	3:14:14	4:21:13	5:17:56	8:59:43
130	16.26	33.7	1:20.1	3:15.3	7:31.1	27:00	45:11.6	57:25	1:36:03	3:23:42	4:34:05	5:33:44	9:27:11
100	16.60	34.4	1:22.2	3:21.2	7:45.9	28:00	46:49.2	59:29	1:39:36	3:31:25	4:44:36	5:46:40	9:49:42
70	16.96	35.2	1:24.2	3:27.4	8:01.7	29:00	48:33.9	61:43	1:43:25	3:39:46	4:55:57	6:00:37	10:14:04
40	17.34	36.0	1:26.7	3:34.1	8:18.5	30:00	50:26.9	64:08	1:47:33	3:48:47	5:08:15	6:15:45	10:40:32

Note. From *Computerized Running Training Programmes* by J.B. Gardner and J.G. Purdy, 1970, Los Altos, CA: Taftnews Press. Copyright 1970 by Taftnews Press. Selected data adapted by permission.
[a]Performance rating is an arbitrary scale indicating the relative quality of different performances; the higher the rating, the better the performance.

Garth Gilmour, and Gordon Pirie, which are quoted at the beginning of this chapter.

The Mercier/Leger/Desjardins Nomogram

Recently Daniel Mercier and his colleagues (Mercier et al., 1986) from the University of Montreal developed a nomogram (see Figure 2.8) to predict equivalent running performances at different distances. The nomogram is based on the authors' equations relating percent $\dot{V}O_2$max to duration of running (Leger et al., 1984). The predictions are not greatly different from those of Gardner and Purdy in Table 2.7, but the beauty of the nomogram is that it predicts performances from any best time for the common running distances, whereas Tables 2.3, 2.4, 2.6, and 2.7 predict performances for only a limited range of times at the different running distances.

The following technique is used to predict $\dot{V}O_2$max and performance at other distances on the basis of best running times at two other distances. Simply place a ruler connecting the two measured racing performances, and read along the edge of the ruler the times for equivalent performances at other racing distances. Estimated $\dot{V}O_2$max values are given on the scale that relates $\dot{V}O_2$max to 3-km running time (second column from the left).

You can also use the nomogram to predict the athlete's level of fitness. This is done by reading the values in Column A (extreme left side of the nomogram) and Column B (extreme right side of the nomogram) that correspond to the points at which the columns are crossed by the line that describes the athlete's performances at different distances. Subtracting the value in Column B from the value in Column A gives a fitness level on a scale of -100 to $+100$. A value of 100 corresponds to a horizontal line joining performances at 3 and 42.2 km and is equivalent to the performances of the world's best athletes.

SUMMARY OF PERFORMANCE PREDICTIONS FROM $\dot{V}O_2$MAX DATA

Much of the information in this chapter questions the credibility of the $\dot{V}O_2$max as a predictor of athletic performance, yet I have also used the data of C.T.M. Davies and Thompson; J. Daniels and Gilbert; and Mercier, Leger, and Desjardins to make the strongest possible case that $\dot{V}O_2$max can accurately predict performance. How can this anomaly be explained?

These tables actually show that performance at one distance can predict performance at another distance. Indeed, the nomogram of Mercier et al. (1986) is based entirely on tests of running performances at different distances (Leger et al., 1984). In addition, the tables provide a physiological explanation for this relationship, namely that a predictable relationship describes the percent $\dot{V}O_2$max (or, more accurately, the percentage of peak running speed) that can be sustained for a given running time.

However, the $\dot{V}O_2$max values contained in Tables 2.3 and 2.4 and Figure 2.8 are completely arbitrary and relate only to runners whose efficiencies fall within

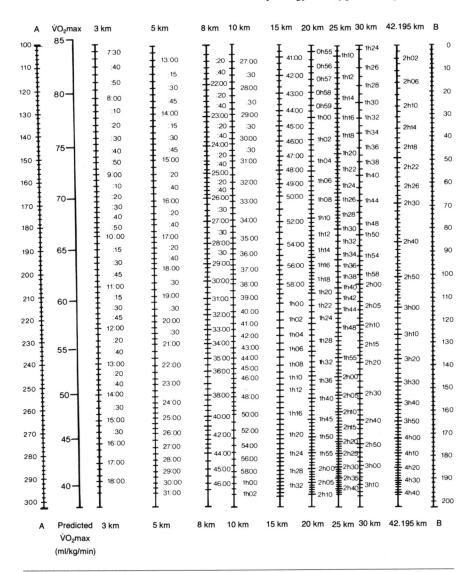

Figure 2.8 The Mercier/Leger/Desjardins (1986) Nomogram predicting running performance at distances of 3 to 42.2 km. For details of how to use the nomogram, refer to the text.

Note. From "Nomogram to Predict Performance Equivalence for Distance Runners" by D. Mercier, L. Leger, and M. Desjardins, 1986, *Track Technique*, **94**, p. 3009. Copyright 1986 by D. Mercier, L. Leger, and M. Desjardins. Adapted by permission.

the normal range of runners tested by the researchers. Problems arise when the efficiency of the runner differs dramatically from that of the prediction. Thus, using Table 2.1 we would predict that Derek Clayton's best marathon time would be only 2:23:47, based on his $\dot{V}O_2$max of 69.7 ml/kg/min (see Table 2.4). Craig

Virgin, with a $\dot{V}O_2$max of 81.1 ml/kg/min, would be expected to run the marathon in 2:04:31 (see Table 2.4). Both these predictions are wrong, because the two runners have different running efficiencies (see Figure 2.4). Thus Clayton's marathon time is underestimated, because he is more efficient than the average runner, whereas Virgin's time is overestimated, because he is less efficient than the average runner.

Thus, we cannot predict marathon performance on the basis of a $\dot{V}O_2$max value that takes no account of the runner's efficiency. The best predictor remains the performance in shorter distance races, particularly at 10 or 21.1 km (Noakes et al., 1990b). Noakes et al. (1990b) found that marathon time could be predicted from either 10-km or 21.1-km time according to the following equations.

Time for 42.2 km (minutes) = 5.48 × 10-km time (minutes) − 28.00

Equation 2.4

Time for 42.2 km (minutes) = 2.11 × 21.1-km time (minutes)

Equation 2.5

Equation 2.5 was found to be the more accurate predictor.

A final weakness of these predictions is that they take little account of the athlete's state of training. Jan Louw, Comrades Marathon runner and actuary working in the life insurance industry, has recently applied his mathematical genius to this problem (Louw, 1989).

He proposes that there are three laws governing training and performance. His first law is that a given amount of training time will produce equivalent training effects in all runners. Thus, provided they spend the same *total* number of hours training, a very fast and a very slow runner can expect the same training benefit even though the fast runner will have run much further in his training. (This assumption conflicts with the finding that the degree of adaptation to training is genetically determined, meaning not all persons adapt equally to the same training load. Nevertheless, when applied to a large group of runners rather than to individuals, this generalization is probably valid. Thus the time spent training rather than the distance covered should probably be the yardstick by which the training volumes of runners are compared.)

Louw also believes that there is an optimum training volume; for the Comrades Marathon, he considers the optimum volume to be about 156 hours training in the 5 months before the race.

Louw's second law is that performance in races of shorter distance predicts performance in longer distance races. The validity of this law has been discussed.

His third law is that there is a predictable deterioration in performance when the training volume is less than the predicted optimum.

On the basis of his three laws, Louw has produced Table 2.8 which predicts expected performance in a particular race, the "down" Comrades Marathon from Pietermaritzburg to Durban, on the basis of the athlete's most recent (index) performance at a shorter distance and the amount of training undertaken in the 5 months preceding the race.

Table 2.8 is used in the following way: The athlete first finds his or her most recent performance in a shorter distance race, the index run, in the columns under A (*Performance grid*). For example, let us assume that the athlete has recently completed a 5-km race in 19:12. This places the athlete in the ninth column over from the left. By now looking at B (*Training grid*), the athlete observes that his or her best possible Comrades time will be 7:30:00 if he or she trains a total of 1906 km during the 5 months leading up to the race. Training more will not improve the athlete's performance (notice the points in each column), because then the athlete would train for more than the optimum 156 hours and would therefore expect either no further improvement or a slight deterioration in performance.

Alternatively, if the same athlete runs only 800 km in training, he or she can expect to run no faster than 9:27:00 for the race.

Louw considers the accuracy of his predictions enhanced when allowance is made for the following factors:

- Women perform slightly better than do males with the same index performance. This difference is between 5 and 15 minutes with the greatest difference for the slower women runners.
- Runners who have run less than 15,000 km in their careers will run between 5 and 30 minutes slower than the prediction. The greatest difference will be for those who have done the least training and who run the slowest in the index race.
- The index run is for a recent sea-level performance.
- Runners who do neither hill nor speed training must add 10 and 15 minutes to their predicted times.
- Any increase or decrease in weight since the index run was performed are corrected by adding 3 minutes for each pound gained or subtracting 3 minutes for each pound lost.

This type of table allows each athlete to tailor his or her training according to the time he or she wishes to run in a particular race. It also indicates the range of performances the athlete can expect, most critically the performances that are beyond the genetically determined limits for the athlete. By providing a realistic time prediction for a particular race, the table will also ensure that the clever athlete does not overestimate his or her ability and therefore start running the race too fast, an error that always has dire consequences (see chapter 9).

A FINAL WORD ON THE $\dot{V}O_2$MAX

The $\dot{V}O_2$max measures the total oxygen-utilizing capacity of all the skeletal muscle mitochondria that are active during maximum exercise. Yet there are

Table 2.8   Performance Prediction for a 90-km Race Based on Current Performance and Recent Training in the 5 Months Before the Race

A (Performance grid)

Time (min.s or h.min)

Current performance: race distance (km)	14.05	14.43	15.22	16.00	16.39	17.17	17.55	18.34	19.12	19.51	20.29	21.07	21.46	22.24	23.03	23.41	24.19	24.58	25.36	26.15	26.53	27.32
5	14.05	14.43	15.22	16.00	16.39	17.17	17.55	18.34	19.12	19.51	20.29	21.07	21.46	22.24	23.03	23.41	24.19	24.58	25.36	26.15	26.53	27.32
8	23.16	24.20	25.23	26.26	27.30	28.33	29.37	30.40	31.44	32.47	33.51	34.54	35.58	37.01	38.04	39.08	40.11	41.15	42.18	43.22	44.25	45.29
10	29.32	30.52	32.13	33.33	34.54	36.15	37.35	38.56	40.16	41.37	42.57	44.18	45.38	46.59	48.19	49.40	51.01	52.21	53.42	55.02	56.23	57.43
15	0.46	0.48	0.50	0.52	0.54	0.56	0.58	1.00	1.02	1.04	1.06	1.08	1.10	1.12	1.15	1.17	1.19	1.21	1.23	1.25	1.27	1.29
21	1.06	1.09	1.12	1.15	1.17	1.20	1.23	1.26	1.29	1.32	1.35	1.38	1.41	1.44	1.47	1.50	1.53	1.56	1.59	2.02	2.05	2.08
32	1.42	1.47	1.52	1.56	2.01	2.06	2.10	2.15	2.20	2.24	2.29	2.33	2.38	2.43	2.47	2.52	2.57	3.01	3.06	3.11	3.15	3.20
42	2.18	2.24	2.30	2.36	2.43	2.49	2.55	3.01	3.08	3.14	3.20	3.26	3.33	3.39	3.45	3.51	3.58	4.04	4.10	4.16	4.23	4.29
50	2.48	2.55	3.03	3.10	3.18	3.26	3.33	3.41	3.48	3.56	4.04	4.11	4.19	4.27	4.34	4.42	4.49	4.57	5.05	5.12	5.20	5.27
56	3.13	3.21	3.30	3.39	3.48	3.56	4.05	4.14	4.23	4.31	4.40	4.49	4.58	5.06	5.15	5.24	5.33	5.42	5.50	5.59	6.08	6.17

Predicted 90-km race time (h.min):

	14.05	14.43	15.22	16.00	16.39	17.17	17.55	18.34	19.12	19.51	20.29	21.07	21.46	22.24	23.03	23.41	24.19	24.58	25.36	26.15	26.53	27.32
				5.30	•	•	•	•	•	•	•	•	•	•	•	•	•	•	•	•	•	•
			5.45	5.32	•	•	•	•	•	•	•	•	•	•	•	•	•	•	•	•	•	•
		6.00	5.47	5.34	•	•	•	•	•	•	•	•	•	•	•	•	•	•	•	•	•	•
	6.15	6.02	5.49	5.37	•	•	•	•	•	•	•	•	•	•	•	•	•	•	•	•	•	•

B (Training grid)

km/wk		Total
Jan & Feb	Mar & Apr	Jan to May
127	156	2600
121	149	2487
116	143	2383
112	137	2288

107	132	2200	5.39	5.52	6.04	6.17	6.30																
103	127	2118	5.42	5.54	6.07	6.19	6.32	6.45															
100	123	2042	5.45	5.57	6.10	6.22	6.34	6.47	7.00														
96	118	1972	5.48	6.00	6.12	6.25	6.37	6.49	7.02	7.15													
93	114	1906	5.51	6.03	6.15	6.28	6.40	6.52	7.04	7.17	7.30												
90	111	1845	5.54	6.06	6.18	6.31	6.43	6.55	7.07	7.19	7.32												
87	107	1787	5.57	6.09	6.21	6.34	6.46	6.58	7.10	7.22	7.34	7.45											
84	104	1733	6.00	6.12	6.25	6.37	6.49	7.01	7.13	7.25	7.37	7.47	8.00										
82	101	1682	6.02	6.15	6.28	6.40	6.52	7.04	7.16	7.28	7.40	7.49	8.02	8.15									
80	98	1634	6.05	6.18	6.31	6.43	6.55	7.07	7.19	7.31	7.43	7.52	8.05	8.17	8.30								
77	95	1589	6.08	6.21	6.34	6.46	6.59	7.11	7.23	7.35	7.47	7.55	8.07	8.20	8.32	8.45							
75	93	1546	6.10	6.24	6.37	6.49	7.02	7.14	7.26	7.38	7.50	7.58	8.10	8.22	8.35	8.47	9.00						
73	90	1505	6.13	6.26	6.39	6.52	7.05	7.17	7.30	7.42	7.54	8.02	8.13	8.26	8.38	8.50	9.02	9.15					
71	88	1466	6.16	6.29	6.42	6.55	7.08	7.21	7.33	7.45	7.57	8.05	8.16	8.29	8.41	8.53	9.05	9.17	9.30				
70	86	1430	6.18	6.32	6.45	6.58	7.11	7.24	7.36	7.49	8.01	8.09	8.20	8.32	8.44	8.56	9.08	9.20	9.32	9.45			
68	84	1395	6.20	6.34	6.48	7.01	7.14	7.27	7.40	7.52	8.04	8.13	8.24	8.36	8.48	9.00	9.11	9.23	9.35	9.47	10.00		
66	82	1362	6.23	6.37	6.50	7.04	7.17	7.30	7.43	7.55	8.08	8.16	8.28	8.40	8.51	9.03	9.15	9.26	9.38	9.50	10.02	10.15	
65	80	1330	6.25	6.39	6.53	7.07	7.20	7.33	7.46	7.59	8.11	8.20	8.32	8.44	8.55	9.07	9.18	9.30	9.41	9.53	10.05	10.17	10.30
63	78	1300	6.27	6.42	6.56	7.09	7.23	7.36	7.49	8.02	8.15	8.24	8.36	8.47	8.59	9.11	9.22	9.34	9.45	9.57	10.08	10.20	10.32
59	72	1200	6.35	6.50	7.04	7.19	7.33	7.47	8.01	8.14	8.27	8.40	8.53	9.05	9.18	9.30	9.42	9.53	10.05	10.16	10.28	10.39	10.48
54	66	1100	6.43	6.58	7.14	7.29	7.44	7.58	8.13	8.27	8.41	8.55	9.08	9.21	9.34	9.47	10.01	10.12	10.24	10.36	10.48	10.59	
49	60	1000	6.51	7.08	7.24	7.39	7.55	8.11	8.26	8.41	8.56	9.10	9.25	9.39	9.53	10.07	10.20	10.33	10.47	10.59			
44	54	900	6.59	7.17	7.34	7.51	8.07	8.23	8.40	8.55	9.11	9.27	9.42	9.57	10.12	10.27	10.42	10.56					
39	48	800	7.09	7.27	7.45	8.02	8.20	8.37	8.54	9.11	9.27	9.44	10.00	10.17	10.33	10.48							

Note. Times longer than 10.59 are not included because the Comrades Marathon, for which this table is constructed, has an 11.00 cut-off time. From "Predicting Your Comrades Performance" by J. Louw, 1989, *Comrades Marathon Update* (January). p. 12. Copyright 1989 by J. Louw. Adapted by permission.

additional sources of energy production for which oxygen is not needed, called *oxygen-independent ATP production*, which are not measured by $\dot{V}O_2$max testing.

Chapter 3 will discuss the nature of these biochemical pathways, which are very important during all short-term exercise lasting up to about 45 seconds. At present, the capacity of these oxygen-independent pathways for energy production are best measured in the field rather than in the laboratory. It makes little sense to devise a laboratory-based measure of sprinting ability when a time trial on a 100-m track will give the answers.

A final question that we need to ask is whether sprinting speed in running events lasting 2 to 4 minutes can predict running potential in endurance events. An affirmative answer is suggested by the observation, discussed in chapter 8, that the fastest middle-distance track runners are also the fastest marathon and ultramarathon runners, provided they have the appropriate body builds. Yet the fastest middle-distance runners are also the fastest over the sprint distances, as indicated by the quotes of Lydiard, Gilmour, and Pirie at the beginning of this chapter and by the findings of Krahenbuhl and Pangrazi (1983) in children. Noakes (1988b), Noakes et al. (1990b), and Scrimgeour et al. (1986) also found that the peak running speed that an athlete could achieve during a maximal treadmill test was the best predictor of performance in marathon and ultramarathon events, indicating a possible relationship between sprinting speed, which is a measure of the ability to produce energy by oxygen-independent pathways, and endurance capacity, which is believed to be a measure of the capacity for energy production by oxygen-dependent pathways. At present we have no easy scientific explanation for this apparent paradox.

3

Energy Metabolism During Exercise

"You will ask—I have often been asked, what happens to the body in training? I am sorry, I do not know. Perhaps the blood supply to the active muscles becomes better, the capillaries responding more rapidly to the needs of the muscles; perhaps more alkali is deposited in the fibres to neutralize the acid formed by exertion. More glycogen seems to be deposited in them as a store of energy, and certainly, . . . the nervous system which governs them learns in training to work more economically. Perhaps by training the recovery process is quickened. Maybe the actual mechanical strength of the muscle fibre and its surrounding membrane (sarcolemma) is increased by training so that it can stand, without injury, the strains and stresses of violent effort. All these factors may be at work, but at present we can only point to the importance and interest of the problem, and suggest that someone should investigate it properly."

A.V. Hill (1927a)

"Training is therefore, in some ways at any rate, just cleaning the channels through which energy flows."

Arthur Newton (1947)

We have discussed how muscles contract and how oxygen is transported from the atmospheric air to the mitochondria in the active muscle cells. This chapter will describe how the oxygen combines with various metabolic "fuels" in the mitochondria (in particular, breakdown products of carbohydrates and fats) to produce ATP, how those metabolic fuels are taken in from the diet, and how they are stored and then broken down to provide energy during exercise. We will pay particular attention to the effects of such factors as diet, exercise, and training on fuel storage and utilization during exercise and how depletion of one or more of these fuels might explain exhaustion during prolonged exercise.

DIGESTION AND ABSORPTION

Most of the food we eat is in the form of complex molecules that must be broken down until they are small enough to be absorbed through the linings of the intestines and enter the bloodstream. Once in the bloodstream, these molecules are transported to the appropriate organs, particularly liver, muscle, and fat (adipose tissue), for storage until required to provide energy (e.g., during exercise).

Food taken by mouth travels via the esophagus into the stomach (see Figure 3.1), where the food's presence stimulates the secretion of various digestive enzymes that begin to break down the complex carbohydrate and protein molecules into simpler constituents, in particular amino acids (proteins) and glucose, galactose, and fructose (carbohydrates).

When the composition of the food in the stomach fulfills certain criteria, shown in Table 3.1, the food is released into the upper reaches of the small intestine. Here digestive secretions from the liver, in the form of bile salts, and from the pancreas break the food down further. The bile secretions have a detergent effect, breaking the fats into an emulsion; the pancreatic and intestinal secretions contain the major portion of the enzymes that digest carbohydrates, fats, and proteins.

When the food enters the lower end of the small intestine, it has been broken down into its basic components and is ready for absorption. The carbohydrates, fats, and proteins are absorbed in the upper and middle portions of the small intestine; minerals, certain vitamins, and iron are absorbed at the lower end of the small intestine. The main function of the large intestine is to absorb the water that escapes absorption in the small intestine.

Blood Transport and Storage of Food Constituents

The fate of the various products of digestion is as follows.

Carbohydrates

The absorbed glucose, fructose, and galactose ultimately travel to the liver, where the fructose and galactose are converted to glucose. The studies of Katz and McGarry (1984) suggest that most of the ingested glucose must first be

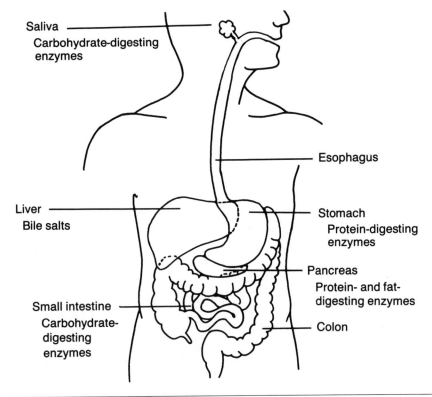

Saliva
Carbohydrate-digesting
enzymes

Esophagus

Liver
Bile salts

Stomach
Protein-digesting
enzymes

Pancreas
Protein- and fat-
digesting enzymes

Small intestine
Carbohydrate-
digesting
enzymes

Colon

Figure 3.1 Passage and digestion of food in the intestine.

metabolized to lactate by either skeletal muscle or possibly by the liver itself
(D.W. Foster, 1984). The lactate is then reconverted to glucose by the liver—the
so-called ''glucose paradox.'' Glucose may then be stored as glycogen in the
liver or may be exported to the skeletal muscles and heart, where the glucose is
stored as muscle glycogen if the glycogen stores in those muscles are reduced.
Alternatively, some of the glucose may be burned by certain tissues, such as the
brain and the kidney, and by the red blood cells, which all depend on blood
glucose for their normal function.

Once the liver and muscle glycogen stores are filled, any excess carbohydrate
is stored as fat (triglyceride) in the adipose tissue. It seems, however, that little
of the triglyceride stored in adipose tissue originates from carbohydrate; almost
all is derived from ingested fat.

Fats

The digested fats are transported to the major fat storage sites in adipose tissue
and in muscle, where they are stored as triglyceride molecules. Adipose tissue

Table 3.1 Factors Determining Gastric Emptying Rate

Accelerating factors	Decelerating factors	No effect
Large ingested volume	Small ingested volume	Training
Isotonic solutions	Hypertonic solutions	Rest
Fluids	Solids	Water or hypotonic solutions
Cold foods and beverages	Hot foods and beverages	
Low-fat/protein content	High-fat/protein content	
Carbohydrate content <0.30 kcal $\cdot$ ml^{-1}	Carbohydrate content >0.30 kcal $\cdot$ ml^{-1}	
Running at $<75\%$ $\dot{V}O_2$max	Any exercise at $>75\%$ $\dot{V}O_2$max	
Calm mental attitude	Anxiety	
	Dehydration	
	Severe environmental conditions	

is distributed widely throughout the body, forming the subcutaneous fat layer (which conserves heat) and surrounding major organs such as the heart, kidney, and intestines. In women, fat is concentrated in the breasts, upper thighs, and buttocks, whereas in men, fat tends to settle around the abdomen.

Proteins

The absorbed protein digestion products—the amino acids—go to the liver, where they may serve as precursors for glucose and glycogen production. More importantly, all body tissues, in particular muscle, use amino acids to replace proteins that are continually being broken down.

Mobilization and Utilization of Stored Fuels

Once exercise begins, the fuels that have been stored during the resting period must be mobilized to provide the ATP necessary for muscular contraction.

Carbohydrates

Glycogen stored with water in the liver and muscle is hydrolyzed in a reaction controlled by the enzyme phosphorylase to form glucose 1-phosphate and then glucose 6-phosphate. In the liver another enzyme, glucose 6-phosphatase, acts on the glucose 6-phosphate to produce glucose. This glucose then enters the bloodstream, from which it is later extracted by the muscles, brain, kidney,

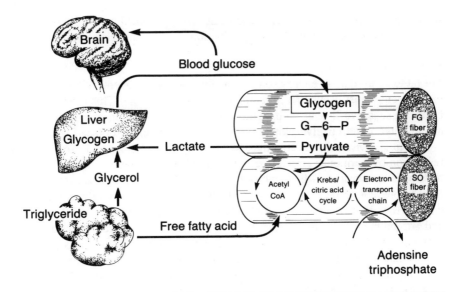

Figure 3.2 The pathways for carbohydrate and fat metabolism by liver, muscle, and brain. FG = fast glycolytic; SO = slow oxidative.

and red blood cells. During exercise the main site of blood glucose uptake and utilization is skeletal muscle (Figure 3.2).

Blood glucose levels represent a balance between the rate of glucose production by the liver and the rate of glucose utilization by muscle and other tissues. When the rate of blood glucose utilization exceeds the rate of production by the liver, blood glucose levels fall, causing impaired function, particularly of the brain, which depends on carbohydrate for its energy. The relevance of this to fatigue in ultramarathon running is discussed subsequently.

Muscle lacks glucose 6-phosphatase and is therefore unable to produce glucose from glycogen. Instead, the glucose 6-phosphate enters another metabolic pathway known as glycolysis, the end product of which is pyruvate.

An important feature of the glycolytic pathway is that it can proceed without the provision of an adequate oxygen supply. This is called "oxygen-independent" glycolysis. This term supercedes the old term "anaerobic glycolysis," which suggests that glycolysis occurs only when there is anaerobiosis (i.e., an inadequate oxygen supply). This is quite incorrect. We know that glycolysis becomes very active during high-intensity exercise such as sprinting, even though there is an adequate oxygen supply to the muscles.

Most of the pyruvate produced by glycolysis will cross the mitochondrial membrane, in which the enzyme pyruvate dehydrogenase is embedded. This enzyme converts pyruvate into acetyl-CoA, which then enters the final common metabolic pathway called the *citric acid* or *Krebs cycle*. At various points in the

Krebs cycle, hydrogen is released and transferred to a third metabolic pathway, the electron transport chain, for the production of mitochondrial ATP.

Fats

For fat to be used as an energy source, the fatty acid components of the triglyceride molecule must first be freed from the glycerol molecule. This is achieved by hormone-sensitive lipase, an enzyme that exists in the adipose cell membrane and that hydrolyzes triglyceride to free fatty acids and glycerol (see Figure 3.2).

Hormone sensitive indicates that the activity of the enzyme is sensitive to regulation by hormones circulating in the bloodstream. The two most important hormones are insulin, which inhibits or reduces the hormone-sensitive lipase thereby preventing fat mobilization, and adrenaline, which strongly activates the enzyme thereby accelerating fat mobilization. During exercise, insulin levels fall and adrenaline levels rise so that fat mobilization is stimulated. In contrast, a high-carbohydrate meal, especially of simple carbohydrates such as glucose, causes insulin levels to rise and impairs fat oxidation. Physical training, on the other hand, increases the sensitivity of hormone-sensitive lipase to the stimulatory effects of adrenaline (Wahrenberg et al., 1987).

Following their release from triglyceride molecules in adipose tissue, free fatty acids and glycerol easily cross the fat cell membrane to enter the bloodstream. In order to be soluble in the blood, the free-fatty-acid molecules must be bound to a carrier protein, in this case albumin. Although this binding is very tight, some free-fatty-acid molecules do exist in solution, and these unattached free-fatty-acid molecules are metabolized by muscle. Newsholme and Leech (1983) contend that the low concentration of unbound free fatty acids in the bloodstream limits the rate at which they can be transported into the cell and may therefore limit the rate at which energy can be produced from fat oxidation in the Krebs cycle. Although this contention remains unproven, the body certainly appears unable to extract energy at a high rate from fat metabolism during exercise of high intensity. As we shall see, the limited rate at which fats can produce energy has certain serious consequences for metabolism during very prolonged exercise.

When free-fatty-acid molecules reach the capillaries supplying the muscle cell, the unbound-fatty-acid molecules are taken up by the cell and either metabolized in the Krebs cycle to produce ATP or re-formed and stored as muscle triglyceride.

Evidence now shows that these muscle triglyceride stores provide important fuel during prolonged exercise; evidence also shows that an important effect of training is to increase the amount of muscle triglyceride utilized for energy while sparing muscle glycogen (Hurley et al., 1986).

Proteins

The major function of the protein stores in the body is to produce movement (see Figure 1.3). The body uses protein as an energy source during exercise, but only under extreme conditions such as complete starvation or prolonged exercise (especially under conditions of carbohydrate depletion) does protein's contribution reach even 10% of the total energy production (Lemon & Mullin, 1980). Under such conditions, protein's major role is to provide the liver with substrates from which the liver can produce glucose when the liver glycogen stores are low.

BODY FUEL STORES

In medical science it is traditional to consider that the average or normal person is a 70-kg (154-lb) healthy male. The following discussion will use this average subject as a reference point.

Table 3.2 lists the weights of the different organs of the body in a 70-kg (154-lb) man. The largest organ is muscle, which comprises about 26 kg (about 57 lb) of total body weight, followed by fat tissue (10.5 kg or 23 lb) and bone (10 kg or 22 lb). The amount of fat tissue in different individuals varies greatly; for our average healthy male we will assume that the value is about 15% of total body weight.

Table 3.2 shows that water is the major constituent of the human body, comprising as much as 64% of body weight. But the most important point shown in the table is that fat is the largest energy store in the body. By comparison, the carbohydrate stores are quite trivial. To emphasize the importance of this difference, let us consider how long our sample subject could run at world-class marathon pace if burning exclusively carbohydrates or exclusively fats.

The oxygen cost of running at world-record marathon pace (19.8 km/hr) for an athlete of average efficiency is 66.5 ml/kg/min. The total oxygen consumption by a 70-kg runner running at 19.8 km/hr would therefore be 70×66.5 ml/min, that is, 4.66 L/min. We know that each liter of oxygen utilized produces approximately 20 kJ; thus our runner will burn 93.1 kJ/min (1 calorie = 4.2 kJ). Table 3.2 shows that at this rate of energy consumption, the total-body carbohydrate store in this particular athlete would last only 126 minutes (2:06:00), whereas the body fat stores would last about 59:49:00.

But our empirical observation is that no world-class marathon runner could ever hope to run at 19.8 km/hr for close to 60 hours. Clearly, fats cannot provide all the energy required at world-class marathon pace. We will consider this topic in greater detail subsequently.

Factors Controlling the Size of Fat Stores

Table 3.2 assumes that fat constitutes 15% of the body weight of our average subject. In reality, individuals vary widely in percent body fat.

Figure 3.3 shows the distribution of body fat of male and female medical students at the University of Cape Town (Koeslag, 1980). Body fat percentages of the subjects are described by symmetrical, convex curves. As shown by these

Table 3.2 Weights of Different Organs of the Body and Their Composition

Tissue	Wet weight of tissue (kg)	Water content (kg)	Protein content (kg)	Carbohydrate content (kg)	Fat content (kg)
Skeletal muscle	26.0	20.0	5.0	0.6	0.5
Fat tissue	10.5	1.9	0.2	—	8.4
Bone	10.0	8.0	2.0	—	—
Skin	6.0	5.0	1.0	—	—
Blood	5.5	5.0	0.5	0.005	0.001
Liver	1.8	1.5	0.3	0.1	?
Brain	1.5	1.4	0.2	—	—
Heart	0.4	0.3	0.1	—	—
Other	8.3	1.7	1.7	—	—
Totals (kg)	70.0	44.8	11.0	0.705	8.901
Kilojoule (kJ) equivalents of energy stores	—	—	—	11.681	333.788
Running time in minutes at an energy cost of 93 kJ/min	—	—	—	126	3589

Note. 1 g carbohydrate provides 16.6 kJ; 1 g fat provides 37.5 kJ (Newsholme & Leech, 1983). To convert kg to lb, multiply kg by 2.2. To convert kJ to calories, divide kJ by 4.2. From *The Biochemistry of the Tissues* (p. 89) by P. Banks, W. Bartley, and L.M. Birt, 1976, London: John Wiley & Sons. Copyright 1976 by John Wiley & Sons. Reprinted by permission of John Wiley & Sons.

curves, small numbers of people are at the extremes of very low and very high percent body fat (the left and right ends of the curves), but the average or middle readings in the curves are about 15% for males and 25% for females. These figures are probably very similar to statistics for other, similar groups of young Caucasian adults around the world.

Elite marathon runners are represented at the extreme left corner of the curves. Studies by Costill et al. (1970) and Pollock et al. (1977) show that male marathon runners have 2 to 7% body fat, or about half that found in untrained persons. The lowest percent body fat that has been measured in the University of Cape Town's laboratory is that of "Mosquito" Madibeng (3.5%), the ninth fastest half-marathon runner of all time. A study of the top American female distance runners of the early 1970s found that the average percent body fat was 15%, with the lowest value being 6% (Wilmore et al., 1977); a more recent study reported essentially identical findings (Graves et al., 1987). Grete Waitz, former world-record holder for the marathon, reportedly has 8% body fat (Costill & Higdon, 1981).

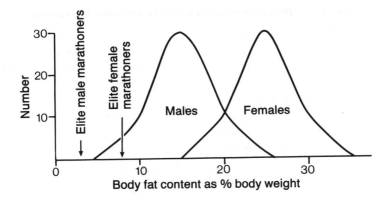

Figure 3.3   Percent body fat in males and females.
Note. From "Obesity" in *Basic Medical Sciences* (Third series, p. 147) by J.H. Koeslag, 1980, Cape Town, South Africa: University of Cape Town Postgraduate Medical Centre. Copyright 1980 by J.H. Koeslag. Adapted by permission.

It therefore seems fair to conclude that female distance runners have greater fat stores than do male distance runners but that both have considerably less fat stores than the average healthy untrained person.

Factors Controlling the Size of Carbohydrate Stores

Although Table 3.2 might suggest that the body can only store a fixed amount of carbohydrate, this amount can in fact be quite different between individuals and may vary greatly in the same person at different times. Let us consider the factors that explain this observation.

One factor is the level of training. The concentration of glycogen in the leg muscles of untrained subjects who eat normal diets is about 14 g/kg of wet muscle (Blom et al., 1987a; Hultman, 1967), whereas values of up to 36 g/kg are usually found in trained athletes who have not exercised for 24 to 48 hours (Costill et al., 1981; Noakes et al., 1988b; W.M. Sherman et al., 1983; see Table 3.3). Average muscle glycogen levels in athletes during training are lower, about 21 g/kg.

A small part of this difference is a result of a dietary change, because as people become more fit they naturally tend to eat diets higher in carbohydrate, which will increase muscle glycogen stores. However, untrained subjects eating high-carbohydrate diets increase their muscle glycogen stores to about 18 g/kg (Hultman, 1967; Jardine et al., 1988) or about half the values measured in trained athletes. Similarly, muscle glycogen levels in trained subjects eating low-carbohydrate diets are about twice the values measured in untrained subjects eating the same diet.

Table 3.3 Effects of Different Interventions on Muscle and Liver Glycogen Stores (g/kg wet tissue)

Subjects	Type and time of diet	In muscle	In liver
Untrained	Average (45%) CHO diet	14	54
	High (70%) CHO diet	18	70
Trained	When training daily (low-CHO diet)	14	30
	When training daily (high-CHO diet)	21	70
	24-hr fast	21	10
	"Glycogen stripping" (3 days low-CHO diet with exercise)	7	10
	Immediate premarathon (3 days CHO loading)	36	90
	Immediate postmarathon	4.5	23[a]
	24 hr postrace (high-CHO diet)	15	90
	48 hr postrace (high-CHO diet)	27	90
	1 week postrace (high-CHO diet)	30	90

Note. To convert from g/kg to mmol/kg wet muscle, multiply by 5.56. Notice that although liver glycogen stores are intact after a 42-km race, muscle glycogen levels are very low. CHO = carbohydrate. [a]Calculated at a liver glycogen utilization rate of 40 g/hr during exercise at 75 to 85% $\dot{V}O_2$max (Ahlborg & Felig, 1982) for an athlete running 42.2 km in 2.5 hours and not ingesting carbohydrate.

Additional evidence that training increases the muscle's capacity to store glycogen is provided by the finding that the muscle glycogen content of the legs is greater than that of the arms, almost certainly because the legs are used more and are therefore "fitter" (Hultman, 1967).

Liver glycogen levels are about 54 g/kg (Hultman & Nilsson, 1971; Nilsson & Hultman, 1973) and increase to about 90 g/kg when the subject eats a high-carbohydrate diet.

Another factor influencing the size of body carbohydrate stores is the effect of different diets, including fasting. Table 3.3 shows that a high-carbohydrate (greater than 70%) diet causes a small increase in muscle glycogen levels, from 14 g/kg to about 18 g/kg in untrained subjects and from 14 g/kg to about 21 g/kg in trained subjects. A 24-hour fast causes a very rapid depletion of liver glycogen stores but has little effect on muscle glycogen stores.

The rapid fall in liver glycogen levels results from the use of liver glycogen in maintaining the blood glucose level. At rest, liver glycogen is used principally by the brain, which (at least in the short term) can really only utilize glucose for its energy. The brain's daily glucose requirement is about 125 g. If we assume that the liver weighs about 1.8 kg (see Table 3.2), its total store when the subject eats a high-carbohydrate diet is only about 162 g. Thus the brain's daily glucose requirement alone is almost sufficient to deplete the liver glycogen stores within

24 hours. Note that liver glycogen stores fall about 9 g/hr, so liver glycogen depletion can occur after a fast of only 18 hours.

In contrast, either eating a low-carbohydrate, high-protein, high-fat diet or fasting for up to 5 days causes muscle glycogen levels to fall by only about 30 to 40% if the subject performs only normal daily activities (Hultman, 1971). This indicates that muscle glycogen levels fall only if the subject performs vigorous exercise. Furthermore, glycogen levels fall only in the exercised muscles (Hultman, 1971).

How Intensity and Duration of Exercise Affect Glycogen Use

During exercise, muscle glycogen levels fall progressively as a semilogarithmic function of time (Hultman, 1971), as shown in Figure 3.4. The rate of glycogen breakdown is greatest during the first 15 to 20 minutes of exercise, after which, for reasons that will become clear later, the rate falls. The rate of glycogen breakdown is critically dependent on the intensity of exercise, so that the higher the exercise intensity (expressed as percent $\dot{V}O_2$max), the more rapid the rate of glycogen utilization (Saltin & Karlsson, 1971).

Figure 3.4 also shows that severe muscle glycogen depletion does not occur during continuous exercise at very high intensities (greater than 90% $\dot{V}O_2$max). This is because at such high exercise intensities, hydrogen (protons) rapidly accumulates within the muscle cell, which causes a marked fall in muscle pH, which ultimately prevents muscle contraction.

However, if exercise of high intensity is performed intermittently (dotted lines in Figure 3.4), which would allow for the metabolism of the excess protons during recovery, then a very marked degree of muscle glycogen depletion can occur within a very short period of time.

Continuous exercise at 70 to 85% $\dot{V}O_2$max that is sustained for prolonged periods of time (longer than 2 hours) causes the greatest degree of muscle glycogen depletion. Therefore, at least theoretically, only performance in exercises such as long-distance running, cycling, or swimming events that last more than 2 hours is likely to be aided by manipulations aimed at increasing initial pre-event muscle-glycogen stores or at slowing the rate of glycogen utilization during exercise.

Researchers generally agree that during prolonged exercise at 70 to 90% $\dot{V}O_2$max, glycogen depletion occurs to the greatest extent in the ST muscle fibers (Thomson et al., 1979), somewhat less in the FTa fibers, and least in the FTb fibers (Andersen & Sjogaard, 1976; Gollnick et al., 1973, 1974; Vollestad & Blom, 1985). After a subject runs a standard marathon race, his or her ST and FTa fibers are completely glycogen depleted, with only the FTb fibers retaining some glycogen (W.M. Sherman et al., 1983). During supramaximal (>100% $\dot{V}O_2$max) exercise, all three fiber types become glycogen depleted, although

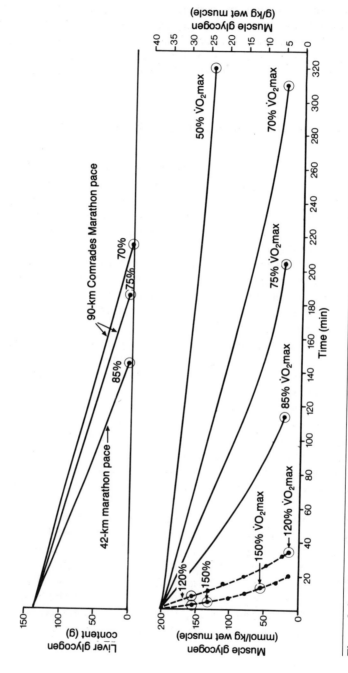

Figure 3.4 Rates of liver and muscle glycogen utilization as a function of exercise intensity.

depletion is greatest in the FTb fibers, least in the ST fibers, and intermediate in the FTa fibers (Essén, 1978; Thomson et al., 1979). At lower exercise intensities (40 to 60% $\dot{V}O_2$max), the greatest glycogen breakdown occurs in the ST fibers (Vollestad & Blom, 1985).

Vollestad and Blom (1985) also found that the rate of glycogen breakdown is the same in all ST fibers for the duration of exercise; the authors found that the rate of breakdown in FTa fibers increases after the first few minutes of exercise and thereafter stays the same in all fibers, whereas the rate of glycogen break-down in FTb fibers is quite variable.

Liver glycogen levels also fall during exercise, but this rate of decrease has not been studied in the same depth as has that of muscle glycogen. This is because the biopsy technique used to collect samples of liver for glycogen analysis is far more painful and potentially more dangerous than is the technique for muscle biopsy; thus both researcher and subject are much more reluctant to undertake this procedure!

However, indirect evidence suggests that the rate of liver glycogen utilization increases linearly with increasing exercise intensity and averages 0.9 to 1.1 g/ min at exercise intensities of 70 to 85% $\dot{V}O_2$max. Figure 3.4 shows that if the total liver glycogen stores are 135 g before a marathon race (see Table 3.3), these stores will be completely depleted within 140 to 215 minutes of exercise at 70 to 85% $\dot{V}O_2$max if the subject takes no carbohydrate by mouth during that period. This means that during prolonged exercise at 70 to 75% $\dot{V}O_2$max, liver glycogen depletion is likely to occur before muscle glycogen depletion in the athlete who takes no carbohydrate by mouth during exercise.

In summary, the extent of muscle and liver glycogen depletion during exercise depends on the intensity and duration of the exercise and will be greatest after prolonged exercise at standard marathon (85% $\dot{V}O_2$max) or ultramarathon (70 to 75% $\dot{V}O_2$max) pace. However, at exercise intensities of 70 to 75% $\dot{V}O_2$max, depletion of liver glycogen stores is likely to precede depletion of muscle glyco-gen stores. The importance of this is discussed next.

Effect of Time and Diet Since Last Exercise Bout on Glycogen Stores

Immediately after the exercise bout is completed, the glucose produced by the liver is used to ensure that the blood glucose level is returned to normal, and then it is used to restock the glycogen stores first of the heart and then of the skeletal muscles (Gaesser & Brooks, 1980). Only when all these stores are replete do the liver glycogen stores begin to be filled.

This resynthesis is aided by a high-carbohydrate diet. Trained athletes who eat high-carbohydrate diets can probably restock their entire carbohydrate stores within 24 hours of moderate exercise (Brouns, 1988; Costill & Miller, 1980). The rate of muscle glycogen resynthesis after a standard marathon race (see

Table 3.3) is somewhat slower (W.M. Sherman et al., 1983), probably because racing-induced muscle damage slows the normally high rate of glycogen resynthesis in trained subjects.

The classic studies of the effects of exercise and dietary manipulation on muscle glycogen levels were performed in 1967 by Scandinavian groups led by Jonas Bergström (Bergström et al., 1967a; Bergström & Hultman, 1967a, 1967b) and Bjorn Ahlborg (B. Ahlborg et al., 1967a, 1967b). These studies led directly to the widespread use by marathon runners in the 1970s of the prerace "carbohydrate-depletion/carbohydrate-loading" diet. Figure 3.5 is a synthesis of the findings of B. Ahlborg et al. (1967a).

B. Ahlborg and his colleagues took three groups of Scandinavian army conscripts (Groups A, B, and C) and exposed them to the following experimental regime.

Group A subjects performed exercise to exhaustion on Day −3 and then ate high-fat, high-protein, low-carbohydrate diets for the next 3 days. On Day 0 they again exercised to exhaustion, and for the next 7 days (Days 1 through 7) they ate high-carbohydrate (90%) diets.

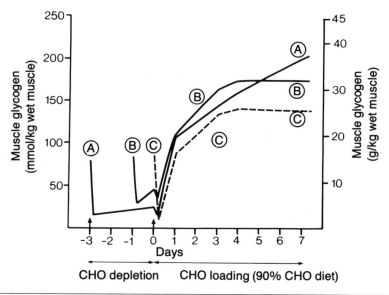

Figure 3.5 The effects of the carbohydrate-depletion/carbohydrate-loading exercise diet regime on muscle glycogen levels. A, B, and C represent three groups of exercisers. CHO = carbohydrate.

Note. Adapted from data in "Human Muscle Glycogen Content and Capacity for Prolonged Exercise After Different Diets" by B. Ahlborg, J. Bergström, J. Brohult, L.G. Ekelund, E. Hultman, and G. Maschio, 1967a, *Förvarsmedicin*, **3**, p. 91.

Group B exercised to exhaustion on Day −1. Then, after 24 hours on high-fat, high-protein diets, they again exercised to exhaustion (Day 0) before eating high-carbohydrate diets for the next 7 days. Group C performed only one exercise bout on Day 0 and then ate high-carbohydrate diets for the next 7 days.

This experiment showed the following.

- The exhaustive exercise caused muscle glycogen levels to fall to very low levels.
- Researchers observed minimal glycogen resynthesis when a high-fat, high-protein diet (carbohydrate depletion) was eaten by Group A between Day −3 and Day 0 and by Group B between Day −1 and Day 0.
- A high-carbohydrate (90%) diet (carbohydrate loading) caused muscle glycogen levels to be resynthesized rapidly, so that preexercise levels were exceeded within 24 hours (see lines for all groups between Day 0 and Day 1).
- The muscle glycogen levels in Groups B and C peaked after 4 days of carbohydrate loading and rose no further. The final values in Group B were about twice the normal resting values.
- Muscle glycogen levels in Group A continued to increase for the entire duration of the experiment and reached final values close to 3 times the normal resting values.
- The subjects tested were relatively unfit. This is shown by their low starting muscle glycogen levels of about 14.4 g/kg wet muscle, a value that corresponds to those found in untrained subjects (see Table 3.3).

On the basis of these studies, the carbohydrate-depletion/carbohydrate-loading (carbo-loading) diet was popularized, with which athletes followed the same exercise/diet regime undertaken by Group A in Figure 3.5 and ate high-carbohydrate diets for the last 3 days before a race. Yet Figure 3.5 shows that optimum carbohydrate loading would have been expected to occur only if the carbohydrate-loading phase had lasted for 7 days.

The next research group to add to these original studies was that of David Costill at Ball State University in Muncie, Indiana. Costill and his colleagues first showed that progressive muscle glycogen depletion occurs when vigorous and prolonged exercise is undertaken on consecutive days (Costill et al., 1971a) but that athletes can reduce the extent of this progressive depletion of muscle glycogen stores by eating high-carbohydrate (>70%) diets (Costill & Miller, 1980; Kirwan et al., 1988; see Figure 3.6). This confirmed the finding of B. Ahlborg et al. (1967a; see Figure 3.5) that muscle glycogen resynthesis is very rapid when the subject eats a high-carbohydrate diet. However, even an intake of 560 g of carbohydrate per day could not prevent some reduction in muscle glycogen stores in runners training hard daily for 5 consecutive days (Kirwan et al., 1988).

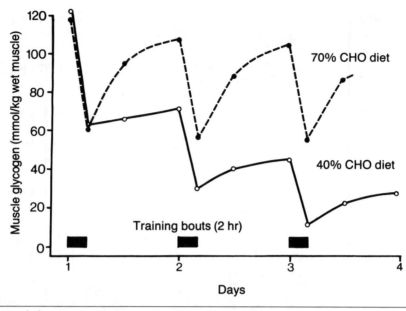

Figure 3.6 The effects of successive days of heavy training on muscle glycogen levels when low- (40%—solid line) and high- (70%—broken line) carbohydrate (CHO) diets are followed.
Note. From "Nutrition for Endurance Sport: Carbohydrate and Fluid Balance" by D.L. Costill and J.M. Miller, 1980, *International Journal of Sports Medicine*, **1**, p. 5. Copyright 1980 by Georg Thieme Verlag. Adapted by permission.

Next, Costill et al. (1981) showed that the rate of muscle glycogen resynthesis after exercise increases linearly with increasing daily-carbohydrate intake and was greatest when the daily-carbohydrate intake was 525 g or more. The authors also found that the rate of glycogen resynthesis was greatest when complex (unrefined) carbohydrates such as starch were eaten. A more recent study (K.M. Roberts et al., 1988), however, showed the opposite; the rate of muscle glycogen resynthesis in this study was fastest in those who ate simple carbohydrates. The authors suggest that the optimum strategy is to eat simple carbohydrates for the first part of the carbohydrate-loading phase and to then switch to a diet rich in complex carbohydrates.

Two more recent studies confirmed most of the findings of Costill's group. Blom et al (1987b) showed that the rate of muscle glycogen repletion for the first 6 hours after exhaustive exercise was maximal when subjects ingested approximately 25 g of glucose or sucrose each hour, equivalent to a 24-hour carbohydrate intake of 600 g. Doubling the rate of carbohydrate intake did not increase the rate of glycogen resynthesis. Interestingly, the rate of muscle glycogen resynthesis after fructose ingestion was approximately half the rate that followed an

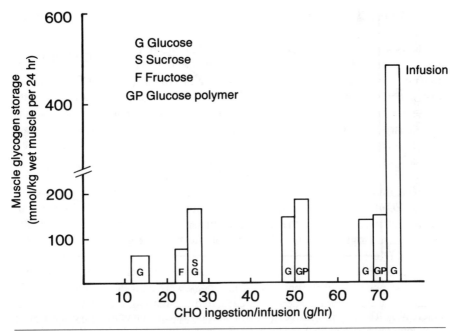

Figure 3.7 Relationship between the rate of muscle glycogen storage and the rate of carbohydrate ingestion or infusion.

Note. Based on data of Bergström and Hultman (1967b), Keizer et al. (1987), Blom et al. (1987b), Reed et al. (1989), and Ivy et al. (1988).

equivalent glucose intake (see Figure 3.7), as also noted by others (Bergström & Hultman, 1967b; Nilsson & Hultman, 1974).

Keizer et al. (1987) also showed that a very high carbohydrate intake (70 g/hr) for the first 4-1/2 hours after exhaustive exercise did not produce a higher rate of glycogen resynthesis than that measured by Blom et al. (1987b) at an intake rate of 25 g/hr. Two other studies (Ivy et al., 1988; Reed et al., 1989) also found that higher hourly carbohydrate intakes (50 to 70 g/hr) did not result in higher rates of muscle glycogen resynthesis. The Ivy study also established that muscle glycogen resynthesis was most rapid if the carbohydrate was ingested immediately after exercise; the Reed study found that, provided the same amount of carbohydrate was given, the rate of muscle glycogen resynthesis was the same for liquid carbohydrate (glucose polymer solution), solid carbohydrate (rice/banana mixture), and glucose infusion into the bloodstream.

Thus, it seems that a carbohydrate intake of 25 g/hr produces the optimum rate of muscle glycogen resynthesis. If a subject maintained this rate of carbohydrate intake for 24 hours and if the rate of glycogen resynthesis remained the same for that period (which seems unlikely—the rate would be expected to slow with time), total muscle glycogen repletion would occur within 18 to 24 hours, as found in professional European cyclists (Brouns, 1988; Brouns et al., 1989a, 1989b).

Also shown in Figure 3.7 is the rate of muscle glycogen resynthesis when glucose is infused directly into the bloodstream at a rate of 70 g/hr. The very high rates of muscle glycogen resynthesis result from the very high blood glucose levels achieved during this procedure. When a subject takes glucose by mouth, the secretion of insulin from the pancreas regulates blood glucose levels, and they do not fluctuate dramatically. This control is less effective when glucose is infused directly into the bloodstream; blood glucose levels are much higher during such an infusion.

The practical relevance of this information is that a subject could achieve complete muscle glycogen resynthesis within about 7 hours after exhaustive exercise if the glucose were infused rather than ingested by mouth. However, this would not necessarily ensure complete normalization of endurance capacity; postexercise fatigue persists even when complete muscle glycogen repletion has occurred (Keizer et al., 1987).

W.M. Sherman et al. (1981) studied the extent of muscle glycogen storage at various stages using different diets. The stages were as follows: after the traditional 7-day carbohydrate-depletion/carbohydrate-loading diet and exercise regime used by B. Ahlborg et al. (1967a; see Figure 3.5); after eating a 50% carbohydrate diet for the entire 7 days of the study; and after eating a 50% carbohydrate diet for the first 3 days of the study followed by a high-carbohydrate (75%) diet for the last 3 days (see Figure 3.8).

The results showed that the traditional carbohydrate-depletion/carbohydrate-loading diet (Group A in Figure 3.8) did not raise muscle glycogen levels any higher than did the high-carbohydrate diet eaten for only the last 3 days before competition (Group C). As expected, muscle glycogen levels were lowest in subjects who ate the 50% carbohydrate diet for the entire duration of the experiment (Group B). The extent of muscle glycogen depletion during a 21-km time trial on Day 7 was the same in all groups regardless of the initial prerace muscle glycogen levels.

Finally, Blom et al. (1987a) showed that the amount the subject runs on the last 3 days before the start of the carbohydrate-loading phase does not influence the extent to which muscle glycogen levels rise when the subject practices carbohydrate loading. In fact, the authors were unable to detect the so-called "supercompensation effect," in which prior exercise and carbohydrate loading supposedly lead to higher muscle glycogen levels than were present at the start of the experiments, as shown in Figures 3.5 and 3.6 in both trained and untrained subjects. We cannot ascribe this failure to an inadequate carbohydrate intake, because the subjects ingested 600 g of carbohydrate daily when carbohydrate loading. Roberts et al. (1988) also showed that optimum glycogen storage can be achieved without a carbohydrate-depletion phase.

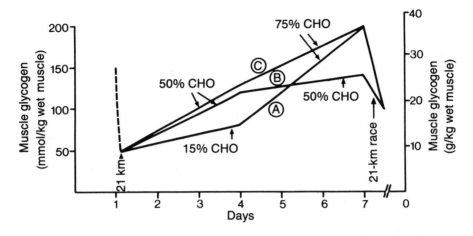

Figure 3.8 Muscle glycogen changes in trained athletes undergoing the modified carbohydrate (CHO)-loading regime. A: traditional carbohydrate-depletion/carbohydrate-loading diet; B: 50% carbohydrate diet; C: high-carbohydrate diet for 3 days before competition.

Note. From ''Effect of Exercise-Diet Manipulation on Muscle Glycogen and Its Subsequent Utilization During Performance'' by W.M. Sherman, D.L. Costill, W.J. Fink, and J.M. Miller, 1981, *International Journal of Sports Medicine*, **2**, p. 116. Copyright 1981 by Georg Thieme Verlag. Adapted by permission.

Studies in rats (Conlee et al., 1987) and humans (Bergström & Hultman, 1967b; Blom et al., 1987b; Nilsson & Hultman, 1974) show that fructose ingested or infused during the recovery period after exercise is a poor precursor for muscle glycogen resynthesis but is as effective as glucose for rapid liver glycogen resynthesis.

In summary, these studies confirm that the athlete's level of training and the amount of carbohydrate ingested daily are the principal determinants of muscle glycogen levels during carbohydrate loading.

Now that we have an idea of the body's energy fuel stores and how they are mobilized, we can look at factors that determine in what proportions the body uses these fuels during exercise.

Factors Influencing the Choice of Fuel Used During Exercise

A number of factors determine whether the body will choose to burn fats, carbohydrates, or protein during exercise.

Intensity of Exercise

As the intensity of exercise increases, the contribution of carbohydrates to energy production increases. The increased rate of carbohydrate oxidation is due to an increased rate of both muscle glycogen and blood glucose utilization. The increased rate of muscle glycogen utilization becomes progressively more marked at exercise intensities above 75% $\dot{V}O_2$max. At exercise intensities greater than 95% $\dot{V}O_2$max, only carbohydrate is burned (Saltin, 1973). The reason for this is not established, but Newsholme and Leech (1983) suggested that the slow rate of transport of free fatty acids into the cell limits the rate at which fats can be converted into usable energy (see Figure 3.2). Researchers believe that the oxidation of fat alone can sustain exercise only up to levels of about 50% $\dot{V}O_2$max.

Duration of Exercise

As the duration of exercise increases at any exercise intensity, fat becomes an increasingly important energy source (G. Ahlborg & Felig, 1982; G. Ahlborg et al., 1974).

For example, in the study of G. Ahlborg et al. (1974), in which athletes exercised at 30% $\dot{V}O_2$max for 4 hours, fat oxidation accounted for only 37% of the energy production after 40 minutes of exercise but increased to 62% after 4 hours of exercise (see Figure 3.9). Costill (1970) found similar changes during 120 minutes of treadmill exercise at 65% $\dot{V}O_2$max. At the start of exercise, 39% of the energy came from fat oxidation, whereas at the finish, 67% of the energy came from that source.

The change from predominantly carbohydrate oxidation to predominantly fat oxidation as the exercise duration increases is due more to a slowing of the rate of muscle glycogen breakdown than to a reduced rate of blood glucose uptake by the muscles. In fact, the rate of glucose uptake by muscle actually increases with increasing duration of exercise (compare 60-minute and 90-minute values with those at 30 minutes in Figure 3.9). Ultimately, however, liver glycogen depletion occurs, causing the relative contribution of blood glucose to total muscle carbohydrate utilization to fall (see values at 180 minutes and 210 minutes in Figure 3.9).

State of Athletic Training (Fitness)

The physiological and biochemical adaptations that occur with dynamic exercise training are reviewed in some detail later in this chapter. The major effect of these adaptations is that during exercise of any intensity or duration, more energy comes from fat oxidation rather than from carbohydrate oxidation (Henriksson, 1977; Hurley et al., 1986). The result is that increased fitness reduces the amount of carbohydrate burned during exercise. Researchers believe that this adaptation

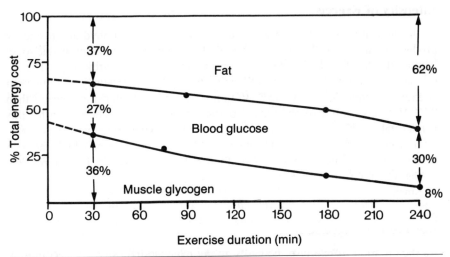

Figure 3.9 Changes in the relative contributions of fat, blood glucose, and muscle glycogen to total energy expenditure during prolonged exercise.
Note. From "Substrate Turnover During Prolonged Exercise in Man. Splanchnic and Leg Metabolism of Glucose, Free Fatty Acids, and Amino Acids" by G. Ahlborg, P. Felig, L. Hagenfeldt, R. Hendler, and J. Wahren. Reproduced from the *Journal of Clinical Investigation*, 1974, 53, p. 1086, by copyright permission of the American Society for Clinical Investigation.

allows the trained person to run farther before becoming exhausted due to carbohydrate depletion.

Carbohydrate Levels at the Start of Exercise

As early as the 1930s, researchers knew that the preexercise diet influenced fuel utilization during subsequent exercise (E.H. Christensen & Hansen, 1939). These researchers noted increased fat oxidation during exercise that followed a few days of a carbohydrate-free diet. They also noted that the length of time that a subject could sustain exercise was influenced by the preexercise diet and was greatest after a high-carbohydrate diet and least after a high-fat, high-protein diet. Subsequently, Bergström et al. (1967) showed that this difference could be explained on the basis of dietary-induced differences in preexercise muscle glycogen levels.

W.M. Sherman et al. (1981), however, suggested that additional glycogen stored as a result of a high-carbohydrate diet is burned more rapidly than glycogen stored following a lower carbohydrate diet (see Figure 3.8).

These studies could throw serious scientific doubt on the actual benefits of carbohydrate loading, but such an argument may be fallacious for reasons discussed subsequently.

The Time Since the Last Meal and the Nature of That Meal

As a general rule, the amount of energy that the exercising muscles can produce from fat metabolism is determined by the rate at which free fatty acids are supplied to the muscles via the bloodstream (Newsholme & Leech, 1983). This rate, in turn, is a function of the blood free-fatty-acid concentrations and the rate of blood flow to the active muscles. For a given muscle's blood flow, a greater percentage of the total exercise energy bill can be paid from fats when blood free-fatty-acid concentrations are high. Conversely, when blood free-fatty-acid levels are low, the muscles must burn alternative energy fuels, in particular muscle glycogen and blood glucose.

Therefore, the amount of fat the muscles can burn during exercise (thereby preserving the body's limited carbohydrate stores) can be increased two ways. Either the blood flow to the exercising muscles must be increased, or blood free-fatty-acid levels must be raised.

As yet, we know of no procedure by which blood flow can be artificially increased during exercise. Thus, fat metabolism during exercise can only be enhanced if blood free-fatty-acid concentrations are elevated either before or during exercise.

Three components of the last meal can influence blood free-fatty-acid levels and therefore influence the pattern of fuel utilization during exercise: caffeine, fat:carbohydrate ratio, and nicotinic acid.

Caffeine ingestion (250 to 350 mg or 5 mg/kg body weight) causes blood free-fatty-acid concentrations to rise, reaching peak values after about 1 hour but remaining 3 to 4 times normal values for up to 4 hours (Bellet et al., 1968; Weir et al., 1987). This effect is delayed for the first 2 hours if sugar is taken with the caffeine (e.g., in coffee), but after 4 hours, sugar intake does not affect blood free-fatty-acid concentrations.

Essig et al. (1980) noted that during subsequent exercise, the elevated blood free-fatty-acid concentrations may contribute to a reduced rate of muscle glycogen utilization, although Ravussin et al. (1986) found this claim unlikely. Berglund and Hemmingson (1982) noted that these elevated levels may enhance endurance performance. Thus, during exercise after caffeine ingestion, the body may utilize 40% less carbohydrate (Costill et al., 1978). However, more recent studies (Casal & Leon, 1985; Erickson et al., 1987; Weir et al., 1987) have been unable to confirm all these benefits.

Weir et al. (1987) found that carbohydrate loading combined with a high-carbohydrate meal prevented the normal effect of caffeine on blood free-fatty-acid concentrations. Thus, caffeine ingestion prior to exercise did not cause blood free-fatty-acid concentrations to rise, and it did not stimulate fat metabolism in runners who had undergone the normal prerace dietary modifications of carbohydrate loading and ingesting a high-carbohydrate meal 3 hours before exercise.

Caffeine does, however, have a direct stimulatory effect on skeletal muscle contractility (Lopes et al., 1983), and any ergogenic effects of caffeine may result from this direct effect on muscle. Thus, the question of whether or not caffeine ingestion really helps performance is unresolved.

A drug that has a similar effect to caffeine is *heparin*. The main action of heparin, a substance first isolated from snake venom, is to prevent blood clotting. However, like caffeine, heparin also stimulates the release of free fatty acids from adipose tissue (see Figure 3.2), causing blood free-fatty-acid levels to rise rapidly, reaching peak values within 60 minutes (Costill et al., 1977). Like caffeine, heparin may reduce the rate of muscle glycogen utilization during subsequent exercise (Costill et al., 1977).

Blood free-fatty-acid levels rise after a fatty meal. A high-carbohydrate meal causes blood insulin levels to rise and to be elevated for up to 60 to 90 minutes thereafter.

Insulin is the "antiexercise hormone," because it inhibits fatty acid mobilization from fat cells and also inhibits the breakdown of glycogen in the liver. The result is that during exercise after a high-carbohydrate meal, there will be increased carbohydrate oxidation (G. Ahlborg & Bjorkman, 1987; Coyle et al., 1985a). If exercise starts when blood insulin levels are high, the rate of muscle glycogen utilization may increase; there is also a risk that blood glucose levels will fall precipitously, causing hypoglycemia, although this is not always found (Devlin et al., 1986).

Nicotinic acid is a vitamin that when present in the blood in high concentration has an insulinlike effect and inhibits fat mobilization (Bergström et al., 1969; Carlson et al., 1963). Nicotinic acid will therefore have the same effect as insulin on metabolism during exercise.

Fasting increases blood free-fatty-acid levels so that fat metabolism is increased during exercise after fasting. However, performance in both submaximal (Loy et al., 1986) and maximal (Gleeson et al., 1987) exercise is impaired by fasting; the former because of the premature onset of hypoglycemia, and the latter because of changes in acid-base status, with the buffering capacities of muscle and blood being reduced during fasting. Interestingly, dogs show no such impairment of running performance after fasting.

Fuel Ingested During Exercise

Studies show that glucose either taken by mouth or infused into the bloodstream during exercise does not reduce the rate of muscle glycogen utilization (B. Ahlborg et al., 1967b; Bergström & Hultman, 1967b; Coyle et al., 1986a; Noakes et al., 1988b). Rather, this glucose is burned by the muscles in place of blood glucose derived from the liver. Thus, glucose or other forms of carbohydrate ingested during exercise will reduce the rate of liver glycogen depletion.

Environmental Temperature

The rate of muscle glycogen utilization appears to increase during exercise in the heat (Fink et al., 1975; Kozlowski et al., 1985; Kruk et al., 1985). This may be one factor explaining impaired running performance in hot conditions.

Practical Implications

The practical implications of all this information are many. The evidence provided so far indicates that when the body's carbohydrate stores are depleted, the exercise intensity must fall because the alternate fuel, fat (see Figure 3.2), cannot be metabolized quickly enough to provide the required energy.

Exercise performance during prolonged exercise can potentially be enhanced by increasing the amount of carbohydrate stored before exercise, by reducing the rate at which those stores are burned during the initial stages of subsequent exercise, and by maintaining a high rate of carbohydrate utilization, particularly when fatigued, via ingestion of carbohydrates in the appropriate amounts.

PREEXERCISE DIET AND PERFORMANCE

Figures 3.5 and 3.8 show that a high-carbohydrate (75 to 90%) diet eaten for the last 3 days before exercise causes maximum filling of muscle and liver glycogen stores. Figure 3.7 also shows that the carbohydrate content of the diet needs to approach 500 g a day for optimum filling of these stores. (Chapter 15 provides practical dietary advice for achieving these goals.)

The length of time for which prolonged submaximal exercise can be sustained is closely linked to the size of the preexercise muscle glycogen stores. Karlsson and Saltin (1971) found that time in a 30-km race was best when the prerace muscle glycogen levels were 21.9 g/kg wet muscle (high-carbohydrate diet) but that the time was 12 minutes slower when prerace muscle glycogen levels were only 11.2 g/kg (high-fat, high-protein diet). Extrapolated to the marathon distance, these data suggest that an athlete who eats a low-carbohydrate diet will run about 30 to 40 minutes slower than one who eats a high-carbohydrate diet.

In a more recent laboratory study, Bebb et al. (1984) showed that subjects who carbohydrate loaded before exercise were able to run 12% longer at 70% $\dot{V}O_2$max than those who ate only their normal diets for the 3 days before the exercise.

If a high-carbohydrate diet is so beneficial for prolonged submaximal exercise, does it have any role in exercise at 100% or more of $\dot{V}O_2$max? At present, the answer seems to be affirmative.

Maughan and Poole (1981) and Greenhaff et al. (1987a, 1987b) showed that athletes could exercise longer at higher intensities after ingesting high-carbohydrate diets, and I. Jacobs (1987) found that the work performed during 50 maximal muscle contractions improved 10 to 20% with carbohydrate loading. Greenhaff et al. (1987a, 1987b, 1988a, 1988b) found that blood pH, blood bicarbonate levels, and blood-base excess before, during, and after maximal exercise were all higher after carbohydrate loading, indicating that this diet favorably affects blood and muscle acid-base status by reducing the decrease in pH during exercise. The authors suggested that the improved exercise performance during maximal exercise after carbohydrate loading may be due to an enhanced buffering capacity in muscle and blood. They also noted that those subjects who ate low-carbohydrate diets had increased dietary acid intakes.

Muscle Glycogen Use During Exercise

Figure 3.8 shows that the rate of muscle glycogen utilization during exercise is greatest when prerace muscle glycogen levels are highest. Thus it follows that if one has taken the trouble to carbohydrate load before exercise, that athlete must also try to prevent those stores from depleting too rapidly.

A technique that might prevent this rapid depletion is to elevate preexercise blood free-fatty-acid levels by ingesting caffeine, a high-fat meal, or both, 3 to 5 hours before exercise. The use of heparin injections to elevate blood free-fatty-acid levels should be considered purely experimental because of the risks involved. The experimental evidence supporting these practices is, as described, quite slim (Ravussin et al., 1986; Weir et al., 1987).

Liver Glycogen Use During Exercise

Failure to maintain liver glycogen levels during exercise will cause blood glucose levels to fall. Because the brain depends on an adequate glucose supply, falling blood glucose levels (hypoglycemia) ultimately lead to exhaustion due to impaired brain functioning.

The typical symptoms of hypoglycemia are incoordination, inability to concentrate or to think clearly, and extreme physical weakness leading to collapse.

Probably the first report of hypoglycemia in marathon runners was that provided by a group of doctors from the Peter Bent Brigham Hospital in Boston (Levine et al., 1924). These doctors studied six runners competing in the 1924 Boston Marathon and found that postrace blood glucose levels were decreased in all runners. The doctors also noted a strong correlation between the conditions of the athletes at the end of the race and their blood glucose levels; athletes with low blood glucose levels showed asthenia, pallor, and prostration. For the next race, these researchers encouraged those runners who had developed hypoglycemia in the 1924 race to eat high-carbohydrate diets for the last 24 hours before the race and to start eating candies after they had run about 24 km (Gordon et al., 1925).

These techniques were very effective. The runners on the ''carbohydrate trial'' completed the race in excellent physical condition; their postrace blood glucose levels were elevated, and their performances were improved. This study had such an effect that for the next 56 years, most authorities virtually dismissed the possibility that hypoglycemia could be a factor in fatigue during marathon running (Felig et al., 1982).

My personal interest in this problem arose during the 1980 Comrades Marathon, a race for which I had not prepared properly. After 60 km I started to have difficulty concentrating. My mind would clear for 5 to 10 minutes every time I drank 100 ml of cola. By 65 km my pace began to fall, and by 80 km I was forced to sit on the side of the road lest I fall over. After about 5 minutes I recovered sufficiently to return to the road to walk the remaining 10 km to the finish. On the road I met two other runners who had suffered the same fate. Like me, they had started to feel faint and giddy and could simply not continue running. We all had intense hunger and cravings for sweets.

Subsequently, two famous incidences of what was almost certainly hypoglycemia in elite Comrades Marathon runners came to my attention. In the 1979 race, his first attempt at a race longer than 56 km, Johnny Halberstadt led the race convincingly from the start and established a record time at the halfway mark. On the morning of the race he did not eat breakfast and during the race he drank an electrolyte-containing ''athletic drink'' that had a very low carbohydrate content. He dominated most of the race, but 14 km from the finish he became disoriented, was unable to concentrate, and had to lie down to prevent himself from falling over. He also had an intense craving for something sweet. Shortly after drinking 1 L of Coke, which contains about 100 g of carbohydrate, Halberstadt took off with renewed vigor, just failing to win the race.

This remarkable recovery is identical to those reported by pioneering Scandinavian exercise physiologists who showed that exhausted, hypoglycemic subjects were able to exercise without distress after consuming drinks with a high-carbohydrate content (Boje, 1936; E.H. Christensen & Hansen, 1939).

In the same 1979 Comrades Marathon, a young and unknown runner, Bruce Fordyce (see chapter 8), also went through a ''bad patch'' at about the same point as Halberstadt—20 km from the finish. Fordyce recalls that quite suddenly he was unable to maintain his running pace. His father forced him to drink a high-carbohydrate solution (cola with added sugar). The results were quite dramatic—Bruce finished strongly in third place, and the career of one of the greatest ultradistance racers had begun.

Why should hypoglycemia occur specifically in elite ultramarathon runners but be apparently uncommon in standard marathon runners (Noakes et al., 1988b)? The answer would appear to lie in Figure 3.4. If we assume that total muscle glycogen stores are about 460 g and liver glycogen stores are about 135 g, an athlete running at standard marathon pace (85% $\dot{V}O_2max$) will use up muscle glycogen stores at a rate of 3.8 g/min (with total stores lasting about 120 minutes) and will use up liver glycogen stores at 1.1 g/min (with stores lasting 122 minutes). In addition, the liver has the ability to produce new glucose (glycogen) at a rate of about 10 g/hr. Thus, after 122 minutes of exercise, the liver will still have sufficient glycogen for another 25 minutes of exercise.

However, an athlete running at ultramarathon pace (70 to 75% $\dot{V}O_2$max) will use muscle glycogen at a rate of only 1.5 g/min (with stores lasting 310 minutes). The study of C.T.M. Davies and Thompson (1986) supported this finding; they showed that complete muscle glycogen depletion did not occur in a group of ultramarathon runners who ran for 4 hours at 67 to 73% of $\dot{V}O_2$max. The authors' data therefore fit the prediction of Figure 3.4 quite accurately.

The rate at which liver glycogen is used at this pace drops to 0.8 g/min, and stores will last 220 minutes. So liver glycogen stores will be depleted long before muscle glycogen stores during an ultramarathon race, and hypoglycemia will develop unless something is done to boost liver glycogen levels.

An athlete who drank 250 ml of Coke (which has a carbohydrate content of 100 g/L) for every hour of running would extend the time to hypoglycemia, so that he or she would become hypoglycemic after about 5 hours and 10 minutes. This is remarkably close to the time it took both Johnny Halberstadt and Bruce Fordyce to become hypoglycemic during the 1979 Comrades Marathon.

Arthur Newton (see chapter 5) made a striking observation:

When you have gone some thirty-five miles . . . something in connection with digestion or assimilation of food is apt to make you think that you are getting badly tired. I haven't yet solved this to my complete satisfaction though I seem to be getting near a likely cause. It may be that you have utilized all the immediately available energy from your last meal and on top of that used all your extra and ordinary reserves. (1935, pp. 191-192)

Newton seems to be describing the inevitable hypoglycemia that occurs after 4 or so hours of running if the athlete has ingested inadequate carbohydrate during the race. Because Newton never really learned to take in sufficient carbohydrate during his races lasting less than 24 hours, it is possible that he never completely found the answer to this problem, which almost certainly was a detriment to his performance. This is particularly surprising, because Newton clearly appreciated the critical importance of a high-sugar intake during multiday events, in particular the Transcontinental Races of 1928 and 1929, about which he wrote: "It was sugar that sustained practically every one of us: sugar and a liquid to dissolve it in—lemonade or tea or, in a few cases, wine" (1940, p. 118).

As discussed subsequently, present evidence suggests that the optimum carbohydrate source to prevent hypoglycemia during ultramarathon running is a glucose or glucose polymer solution.

LIVER AND MUSCLE GLYCOGEN REPLENISHMENT AFTER EXERCISE

Athletes whose training involves prolonged high-intensity daily exercise must eat high-carbohydrate diets in order to maintain their liver and muscle glycogen levels (see Figure 3.6). As shown in Figure 3.7, the greater the carbohydrate content of the diet, the more rapid the rate of glycogen resynthesis. At present we do not know which carbohydrate source (glucose, sucrose, maltose, or glucose polymer) is preferable when taken orally; fructose does not appear to be an effective source for muscle glycogen resynthesis. As discussed, the continuous intravenous infusion of glucose causes the most rapid muscle glycogen resynthesis.

Thus in practice, the athlete wishing to restock liver and muscle glycogen stores as rapidly as possible should eat the same high-carbohydrate diet as is recommended before competition. An athlete competing on consecutive days for more than 4 hours daily can ensure optimum muscle glycogen resynthesis each day only if he or she also ingests high-carbohydrate solutions during competition (Brouns, 1988).

A DISCLAIMER: CARBOHYDRATE INTAKE IS NOT THE COMPLETE ANSWER!

Having read this far, you might conclude that fatigue during prolonged exercise could be due only to either hypoglycemia or muscle glycogen depletion.

The truth is that hypoglycemia or muscle glycogen depletion may cause premature fatigue in runners who fail to follow all the guidelines we have discussed. However, athletes who follow the advice exactly will eventually become fatigued even though they are neither hypoglycemic nor muscle glycogen depleted and even when their rates of carbohydrate oxidation remain relatively high (Coyle et al., 1986a; C.T.M. Davies & Thompson, 1986). Thus, other factors must be operative.

Current evidence suggests that the contractile ability of the muscle falls progressively during prolonged exercise (C.T.M. Davies & Thompson, 1986), possibly on the basis of thermal damage to muscle. Alternatively, muscle fiber recruitment may progressively fail due to damage to the sarcoplasmic reticulum (Byrd et al., 1989) or to inhibition of nerve impulses traveling from the brain (central fatigue) or in the peripheral nerves (peripheral fatigue).

BIOCHEMICAL CHANGES DURING SUPRAMAXIMAL EXERCISE

Up to this point we have confined our discussion to metabolism during prolonged exercise at intensities that are less than 100% $\dot{V}O_2$max and for which virtually all the energy comes from oxygen-dependent mitochondrial metabolism (see Figure 3.2).

Yet it is clear that some distances, such as the 100-m and 200-m sprints, are run at speeds that require energy production well beyond anything that could be sustained by purely oxidative metabolism, that is, greater than 100% $\dot{V}O_2$max. Thus a 100-m sprint run in 10 seconds, a speed of 36 km/hr, would require an oxygen consumption of 140 ml/kg/min, far greater than the highest value ever measured in a human (see Table 2.1). Clearly, the body must be able to produce energy from other oxygen-dependent pathways in each cell; such pathways are described next.

ATP Stores

The muscle cell stores about 6 mmol of ATP per kilogram of muscle. This ATP is used during explosive, single muscular contractions and can sustain about 1 second of sprinting.

Creatine Phosphate Stores

The size of intramuscular creatine phosphate (PCr) stores can provide energy for about 6 seconds of sprinting. Creatine phosphate is used to resynthesize the ATP broken down by muscular contraction according to the following reaction.

$$\text{Creatine Phosphate} + \text{ADP} + \text{Pi} \xrightarrow{\text{Creatine Kinase}} \text{ATP} + \text{Creatine}$$

Equation 2.4

Thus creatine phosphate does not participate directly in energy transfer in cross-bridge cycling (see Figure 1.3) but is used to resynthesize the ATP broken down to ADP and phosphate (Pi) during muscular contraction.

Oxygen-Independent Glycolysis

If intense activity like sprinting lasts more than a few seconds, the metabolic pathway known as glycolysis (see Figures 3.2 and 3.10) becomes the only pathway that can generate ATP rapidly enough to sustain very high intensity exercise.

Theoretically, muscle has sufficient glycogen to maintain a maximum sprint for at least 80 seconds (Newsholme & Leech, 1983). Yet we all know from watching sports events that even the world's best sprinters cannot maintain peak sprinting speed for more than about 20 seconds. Why should this be?

Important by-products of glycolysis and of ATP and PCr hydrolysis are lactate, protons (H^+), Pi, and magnesium (Mg^{++}). The accumulation of H^+ causes the muscle pH to fall. Researchers have calculated that if all the muscle glycogen stores were converted to lactate at the maximum rates measured in humans, the muscle pH would fall to below 5.0 within 3 minutes. Levels of pH below 6.2

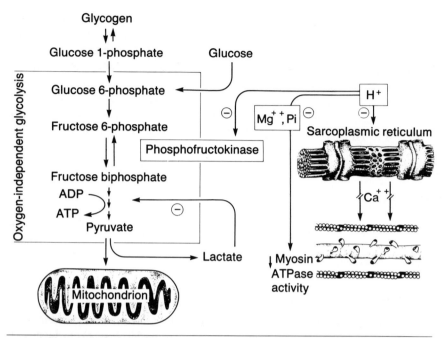

Figure 3.10 The metabolic pathways for glycogen breakdown. ADP = adenosine diphosphate; ATP = adenosine triphosphate; Pi = phosphate; Mg^{++} = magnesium; H^+ = hydrogen; ATPase = adenosine triphosphatase; Ca^{++} = calcium.

are incompatible with life; thus, the muscle cells must have protective controls that will prevent this from happening.

The body prevents a catastrophic fall in muscle pH by using the products of rapid energy utilization (H^+, Pi, Mg^{++}, and lactate) to reduce the rate at which energy can be utilized. Thus, as the muscle pH falls, the maximum rate at which the contractile machinery of the muscle can use the abundant available energy is rigorously reduced. Because the body is unable to utilize energy rapidly, the rate of production of H^+ falls; thus, catastrophically low muscle pH levels can never be reached. This control mechanism is evident as the reduction in running speed that runners can sustain in sprints of increasing distance.

Increased muscle concentrations of H^+, Pi, Mg^{++}, and lactate impair muscle contraction in the following ways (Parkhouse & McKenzie, 1984). First, the activity of the key glycolytic enzyme, phosphofructokinase (see Figure 3.10), is reduced by increased acidity; thus, glycolysis is inhibited. Second, the accumulated H^+, Pi, and Mg^{++} interfere with calcium regulation of the cross-bridge cycle by interfering with calcium binding to troponin-C, by impairing calcium release from the sarcoplasmic reticulum, and by reducing the activity of the myosin ATPase (Blanchard et al., 1984; Cooke & Pate, 1985; Donaldson, 1983;

Donaldson & Hermansen, 1978; Donaldson et al., 1978; Fabiato & Fabiato, 1978; Nakamura & Schwartz, 1972). In addition, these changes may ultimately prevent the normal depolarization of the cell necessary to produce muscle contraction (Donaldson, 1986; Lindinger & Heigenhauser, 1988; Sjogaard et al., 1985).

The result of these control mechanisms is that during exercise, the normal human muscle can never deplete its ATP content or reduce its pH to such low levels that muscle rigor develops and causes irreversible muscle damage and muscle cell death.

We will now examine the exercise durations for which each of these intracellular fuels is especially important during high-intensity exercise such as sprinting (see Figure 3.11).

A single maximal muscle contraction utilizes only ATP. Thereafter, creatine phosphate splitting and glycolysis are maximally activated, peaking within about 3 to 6 seconds (Boobis, 1987; Hultman et al., 1987; Spriet, 1987). Next, the control mechanisms come into play so that the rates of creatine phosphate splitting and glycolysis become progressively inhibited and so that oxidative (mitochondrial) metabolism becomes increasingly important.

After 90 to 120 seconds, oxidative metabolism becomes the predominant energy source. Note that the rate of energy production from the breakdown of the phosphagens (ATP and creatine phosphate) and from glycolysis exceeds, by far,

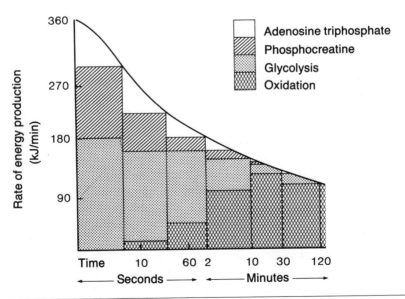

Figure 3.11 Maximum exercise for different durations stresses different metabolic pathways.

that from purely oxidative pathways. This explains why it is possible to do very intense exercise only for brief periods of time.

This information helps explain the different metabolic pathways that are activated by high-intensity interval training of different durations and the nature of the fatigue experienced during very high–intensity exercise of different durations.

Interval training is a form of supramaximal exercise in which the athlete alternates periods of high-intensity exercise with periods of either rest or mild exercise. During these rest periods the energy systems depleted during exercise have a chance to completely or partially replenish themselves.

Åstrand and Rodahl (1977) conducted an interesting experiment in which three groups of subjects performed the same total amount of exercise using three different combinations of intervals. Each group followed an exercise:rest ratio of 1:2, but the durations of exercise periods were 10, 30, or 60 seconds, and corresponding rest periods were 20, 60, or 120 seconds, respectively (see Figure 3.12, a and b).

The striking result was the blood lactate levels in the subjects exercising for the shortest time did not rise, whereas blood lactate levels in the subjects exercising for 60 seconds each interval rose progressively.

The explanation for this difference would be that the group exercising for only 10 seconds each interval utilized mainly their intracellular ATP and creatine phosphate stores. During recovery, these stores were rapidly replenished by ATP produced in the mitochondria. Because glycolysis was only marginally activated during this exercise, muscle glycogen levels fell only very gradually (see Figure 3.12a).

In contrast, the group exercising for 60 seconds per interval activated glycolysis maximally (Figure 3.11) and produced more lactate and protons during exercise than they could metabolize during the recovery period. Had the researchers also measured muscle glycogen levels, they would likely have found these levels to have fallen precipitously (Figure 3.12a); thus, both very high muscle proton levels (and therefore low muscle pH) and low muscle glycogen levels would have terminated the interval session.

Subjects in the middle group showed little change in blood lactate levels after the first 3 exercise bouts. This indicates that glycolysis was initially stimulated but that the rate of lactate removal from muscle during the rest period equaled the rate of lactate production during the preceding interval. Thus a steady state was reached in which muscle and blood pH levels did not change further. Glycogen depletion in the muscle, rather than pH changes, would ultimately limit this type of exercise.

The practical implication of this study is that you should alter the length or intensity of the training interval according to which metabolic pathways you wish to train. Exercise to exhaustion in less than 6 to 10 seconds stresses creatine phosphate and glycolytic metabolism maximally and is probably limited by the accumulation of Pi, H^+, and Mg^{++}; blood lactate levels remain relatively low.

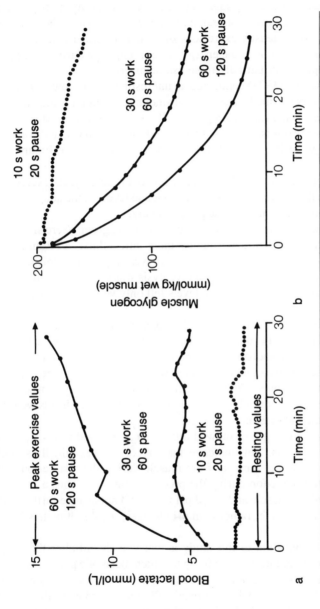

Figure 3.12 Blood lactate (a) and muscle glycogen (b) concentrations during interval training. Total work output and the ratio of exercise to rest were the same, but the duration of exercise was 10, 30, or 60 seconds.
Note. From *Textbook of Work Physiology* (p. 309) by P.O. Åstrand and K. Rodahl, 1977, New York: McGraw-Hill. Copyright 1977 by McGraw-Hill. Adapted by permission.

During intervals lasting 6 to 30 seconds glycolysis is the predominant energy source, but the recovery period allows sufficient time for removal of all the lactate and protons produced during the exercise period. Thus, steady-state blood lactate levels are reached after two or three intervals. The benefit of this form of interval training may be to speed up the rate of lactate removal from muscle during the recovery period.

Finally, interval sessions of longer than 30 seconds cause a maximum contribution of glycolysis to energy production resulting in a progressive accumulation of lactate and protons, because recovery metabolism is too slow to prevent their accumulation. This type of interval training stresses the buffering systems of muscle maximally and will adapt the muscle for continued performance at low pH levels (Sahlin & Henrikksson, 1984).

Lactate Metabolism

Blood lactate levels can also rise during submaximal exercise at intensities less than 100% $\dot{V}O_2$max. Figure 3.13 shows that blood lactate levels measured during the same progressive treadmill test used to determine the $\dot{V}O_2$max remain low at low running speeds. Ultimately, a running speed is reached above which blood lactate levels appear to rise more precipitously. This point has by convention

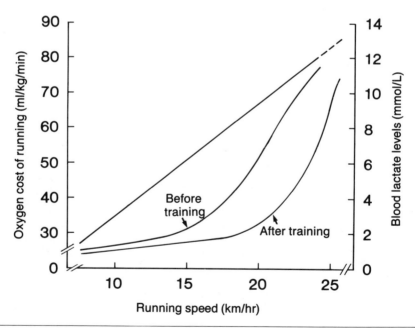

Figure 3.13 The lactate turnpoint. Training shifts the lactate turnpoint to a higher running speed or percent $\dot{V}O_2$max.

become known as the *lactate turnpoint* or the *anaerobic threshold*. It seems that both terms are incorrect.

The original explanation for the rise in blood lactate concentrations at the lactate turnpoint was that at the turnpoint, the oxygen supply to the muscles was inadequate to cover their oxygen demands. The muscles therefore became "anaerobic" and, as a result, released lactate in increasing amounts. The origin of this belief can probably be traced to the influence of A.V. Hill who proposed that lactate was the signal that initiated muscle contraction and that the "function of oxygen is to remove the (lactic) acid, once it has been formed" (1927, p. 66). It is now clear that lactate is a product of, not the cause of, muscle contraction. More importantly, there is little evidence that lactate is released only by muscles that are anaerobic or that muscles become anaerobic during exercise.

First, muscles can release lactate even when their oxygen supply is more than adequate (Connett et al., 1984, 1986). Thus muscle lactate production is not synonymous with anaerobic conditions in the muscles.

Second, there is no conclusive evidence that muscles become anaerobic during exercise at intensities approximating the lactate threshold (Connett et al., 1985; Gayeski et al., 1985) or even during maximal exercise (Graham & Saltin, 1989). For these reasons the term *anaerobic threshold* is clearly inappropriate.

Third, it now seems that the blood lactate concentrations do not show a clearly defined, abrupt threshold effect during exercise of progressively increasing intensity. Rather, blood lactate concentrations begin to rise as soon as progressive exercise commences. However at low exercise intensities, the rate of rise is slow and is therefore barely noticeable. Only when the exercise becomes more intense does the rise become more noticeable; hence the concept of an abrupt increase in blood lactate concentrations at the lactate threshold.

When mathematical techniques are used to quantify these changes, they show that blood lactate concentrations rise as a continuous function of the exercise intensity without showing an abrupt threshold effect (M.E. Campbell et al., 1989; Dennis et al., 1991; Hughson et al., 1987).

For all these reasons, the terms *anaerobic threshold, lactate threshold,* and *lactate turnpoint* are no longer acceptable. But no term has yet been proposed as a replacement. Accordingly, the term *lactate turnpoint* will continue to be used in this text. This term refers to the exercise intensity at which blood lactate concentrations begin to rise visibly (Figure 3.13). The term suffers from the twin limitations that it identifies a point which is determined visually, not mathematically, and that it suggests some sort of abrupt threshold, when no such threshold exists.

More accurate techniques to define this same point mathematically rather than visually are available (Campbell et al., 1989; Dennis et al., 1991; Hughson et al., 1987). They measure the gradient of the slope of increasing blood lactate concentrations (Figure 3.13). Thus the lactate turnpoint can be defined as a point on the curve at which the gradient for increasing blood lactate concentrations is, for example, 10°.

What are the biochemical explanations for the continuous rise in blood lactate concentrations with progressive exercise?

As the exercise intensity increases, so does the rate of carbohydrate utilization until at high exercise intensities (greater than 85 to 95% $\dot{V}O_2max$), only carbohydrate is burned. This means that the rate of flux through the glycolytic pathway (see Figure 3.10) increases steeply with increasing exercise intensity. The result is that the rates of both pyruvate and proton production increase, and when these rates exceed the rate at which both can be transported into the mitochondria, protons combine with pyruvate to produce lactate. Thus, during submaximal exercise, lactate production occurs as a result of a "glycolytic overflow" of pyruvate and protons that exceeds the rate at which these glycolytic products can be metabolized further in the mitochondria of the skeletal muscle or heart (see Figure 3.2).

An important aspect of endurance training is that it shifts the lactate turnpoint to a higher percent of $\dot{V}O_2max$, and changes in the lactate turnpoint appear as an early response to training. In one 36-week study, as a group of subjects increased their weekly training distances from 20 km/week to 73 km/week in preparation for a marathon race, their lactate turnpoints increased from 63 to 71% $\dot{V}O_2max$ within the first 12 weeks of training and did not change thereafter. Their maximum oxygen consumption levels continued to increase for 24 weeks before stabilizing (D.A. Smith & O'Donnell, 1984). Gaesser and Poole (1986) showed that the rate of change in the lactate turnpoint was fastest in the first 2 to 3 weeks of training. Subsequently, Gaesser and Poole (1988) have shown that the half-time for this adaptation is 10.5 days; that is, half of the total adaption (to the constant workload) will be achieved within 10.5 days of training. This study also showed that the time schedule of adaptations in $\dot{V}O_2max$ and in the lactate turnpoint are different.

Following is clarification of six final points regarding lactate metabolism.

1. *Muscles may "shuttle" lactate*. Professor George Brooks (1986a, 1986b) of the University of California at Berkeley has pioneered the concept of the *lactate shuttle*. He suggests that lactate is not a useless by-product of glycolysis but is possibly the most important metabolic fuel used by muscle, especially during exercise.

Brooks proposes that both at rest and during exercise, the skeletal muscles actively produce and consume lactate. He suggests that the lactate produced in one part of the muscle, possibly by FT glycolytic fibers, is transported to and consumed by other fibers, possibly ST oxidative fibers. As the exercise intensity increases, the rate of lactate production in both ST and FT fibers rises (Ivy et al., 1987) so that at the lactate turnpoint, lactate production exceeds the local rate of lactate consumption in the skeletal muscles. Lactate then appears in increasing amounts in the arterial and venous blood. In this way, lactate is "shuttled" to other tissues, in particular the liver, the heart, and the inactive skeletal muscle. The liver may use lactate as a gluconeogenic substrate for the production of glucose and glycogen; in the heart, the lactate becomes the preferred fuel for oxidative (mitochondrial) metabolism. The inactive muscles "store" the lactate, thereby lowering the lactate concentrations in the blood and active muscles.

An important feature of the lactate shuttle is that it allows carbohydrate to be transferred from one muscle group to another while the muscles are at rest or during exercise. Because muscles, unlike the liver, lack the enzyme glucose-6-phosphatase, they are unable to export glucose derived from glycogen into the bloodstream for use by other glycogen-depleted muscles. The lactate shuttle, therefore, provides a convenient method by which body carbohydrate stores can be redistributed from glycogen-replete areas to glycogen-depleted areas during and especially after exercise (G. Ahlborg et al., 1986). Thus during and after leg exercise, for example, glycogen reserves in the inactive arms are mobilized to lactate, which is transported via the blood to serve as an additional carbohydrate energy source for the active leg muscles and to assist in the replenishment of the leg-muscle glycogen stores after exercise.

2. *Lactate, per se, is not the cause of fatigue in any form of exercise.* Lactate is a totally innocuous substance that, if infused into the bloodstream, has no noticeable effects. Rather, it is the excess protons released during rapid glycolysis that cause fatigue during high-intensity exercise. In addition, the low lactate levels found after prolonged exercise cannot explain fatigue in marathon and longer distance races.

3. *Lactate is rapidly removed from muscle and blood after exercise.* A frequent question is whether the stiffness that athletes feel after a hard training session or, in particular, after a marathon race is caused by the presence of lactate in these stiff muscles.

Within an hour after an intensive interval training session during which blood lactate levels reach the highest achievable values (15 mmol/L), muscle lactate levels will return to normal (Peters-Futre et al., 1987). Furthermore, the worst muscle soreness is always evident after very long races that are run at speeds below the lactate turnpoint and that do not, therefore, elevate either blood or muscle lactate levels. For both these reasons, lactate cannot be a cause of the muscle soreness or stiffness felt after exercise (Schwane et al., 1983). In chapter 10 we see that this stiffness is almost certainly due to racing-induced muscle cell damage.

4. *The lactate visually determined turnpoint is an accurate predictor of marathon performance.* A number of recent studies suggest that the visually determined lactate turnpoint may be the best predictor of marathon running performance. This was first shown by Farrell et al. (1979), who found that the paces runners were able to maintain for the standard marathon were 0.45 km/hr faster than the treadmill speeds at which their lactate turnpoints occurred.

Other studies confirmed these findings in race walkers (Hagberg & Coyle, 1983), in road racers competing at distances from 5 to 21 km (Kumagai et al., 1982; LaFontaine et al., 1981; S.R. Powers et al., 1983; Tanaka et al., 1983;

C. Williams & Nute, 1983), and in marathoners (Lehman et al., 1983; Noakes et al., 1990a; Sjödin & Jacobs, 1981; Sjödin & Svedenhag, 1985; Tanaka & Matsuura, 1984). In addition, Sjödin and colleagues (1981) showed that a runner's lactate turnpoint was related to the percentage ST fibers and the capillary density in the runner's leg muscles and to the runner's training volume. Thus, the greater the percentage of ST fibers, the greater the training volume; also, the more muscle capillaries the athlete had, the greater the speed at which the runner's lactate turnpoint occurred and therefore the faster the runner's marathon pace. Training-induced changes in road racing performance at distances from 5 to 10 km also correlate best with changes in the lactate turnpoint (Tanaka et al., 1984).

Recently, researchers have proposed a practical method to predict the lactate turnpoint on the basis of heart rate changes during exercise. Italian researchers (Conconi et al., 1982) recorded the heart rates of a group of athletes during track running. During the experiment, the runners ran on a 400-m track; they started running at 12 to 14 km/hr and increased their running paces each lap by about 0.5 km/hr until they were exhausted. Exhaustion usually occurred within 8 to 12 laps, with the runners having reached speeds that ranged from 18 to 25 km/hr. Their heart rates were measured electronically at the end of each lap. A few days later the athletes underwent a conventional treadmill test to determine their lactate turnpoints. The results of the experiment showed that at low to moderate running speeds, there was a linear increase in heart rate measured on the track, and this increase corresponded to a gradual rise in blood lactate levels measured during the treadmill test. However, at and above the running speeds that corresponded to the lactate turnpoint in the treadmill test, heart rates measured on the track no longer rose linearly but reached plateaus, giving a heart rate inflection or breakpoint (see Figure 3.14).

The authors suggested that determination of the speed at which the heart rate breakpoint occurred would allow prediction of the lactate turnpoint. The authors also showed that this test could be used to measure training improvement, signal established illness, and predict overtraining and imminent illness. The authors found that correct training caused the heart rate breakpoint to occur at a higher running speed, whereas overtraining or illness caused the heart rate breakpoint to occur at a lower running speed (see Figure 10.3). The method has also been used in cyclists, cross-country skiers, rowers, and walkers (Droghetti et al., 1985) and appears to be particularly reliable in children (Gaisl & Wiesspeiner, 1988).

A more recent study (Ribeiro et al., 1985) suggested, however, that only about 50% of subjects show true heart rate breakpoints; the authors also found that in those in whom a breakpoint does develop, this point occurs at work loads well beyond the true lactate turnpoint, shown diagrammatically in Figure 3.14. If this is indeed the case, it means that Conconi's method overestimates the true lactate turnpoint. It also means that runners who use Conconi's method to determine

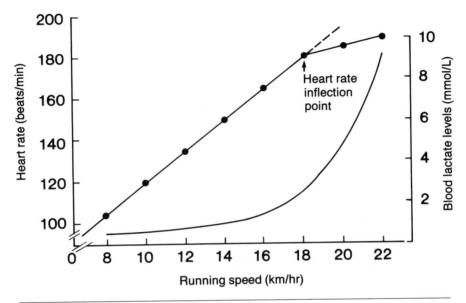

Figure 3.14 Postulated relationship between the lactate turnpoint and the heart rate inflection point.

exercise intensities that boost them to or beyond their lactate turnpoints would exercise at intensities that are too high and would thereby increase the risk of overtraining (see chapter 10). This issue is currently unresolved. Some studies have failed to confirm the existence of a heart rate breakpoint (Dennis et al., 1991). Similarly, Kuipers et al. (1988) found that the heart rate breakpoint, when present in cyclists, did not coincide with the lactate turnpoint, and in runners they could not identify a heart rate breakpoint; thus they also question the validity of the heart rate breakpoint.

5. *High-intensity (peaking) training influences lactate metabolism without increasing* $\dot{V}O_2max$. As we shall discuss in chapter 5, probably the most important technique for rapidly improving one's running performance is to include high-intensity training (so-called peaking training) for a short period of time. The effects of peaking training are usually dramatic, but the physiological explanation for these effects has until recently not been determined.

Edmund Acevedo and Allan Goldfarb (1989) have shown that high-intensity training improves running performance and lowers blood lactate concentrations at the high exercise intensities used in training, without altering the $\dot{V}O_2max$. This indicates that the addition of peaking training will further improve the changes in lactate metabolism produced by more gentle endurance (base) training (see chapter 5). These changes in lactate metabolism are likely either directly or indirectly responsible for the enhanced performance resulting from peaking training.

6. *Performance in high-intensity, short-duration exercise is improved by alkali ingestion—"soda loading."* If high-intensity exercise is limited by proton accumulation, which causes a fall in muscle pH that ultimately prevents muscle contraction, it follows that performance might be enhanced if the buffering capacity of the muscle were increased. In part, this is one result of high-intensity interval training; the resistance of the muscle cells to a fall in pH is increased so that the muscle can continue working at lower muscle pH than before training (Parkhouse & McKenzie, 1984). Recent work (Gledhill, 1984; Lavender & Bird, 1989; R.J. Robertson et al., 1987; Wilkes et al., 1983) suggests that an added effect can be gained if the athlete ingests alkali by mouth before exercise, presumably because the alkali is able to buffer some of the protons produced during exercise.

The alkali sodium bicarbonate, taken at a dose of 300 mg/kg body weight, increased the performances of a group of athletes by an average of 2.9 seconds in an 800-m race (Wilkes et al., 1983). Performance in interval-type exercise was also enhanced with the effect increasing as the number of intervals increased (Lavender & Bird, 1989; D.C. McKenzie et al., 1986). A disadvantage was that the high dose of alkali caused quite marked diarrhea within about 1 hour in 50% of subjects.

Soda loading clearly contravenes the doping regulations controlling athletics, and the alkali is likely to soon be listed as a banned agent. In addition, soda loading is relatively easily detected; within a short time of soda loading, the urine contains a vast excess of bicarbonate. I mention the procedure not to condone it but merely because it allows further practical insights into the factors that limit running performance.

As we might expect, the ingestion of acidic substances before exercise impairs performance (Hultman et al., 1985).

ENDURANCE TRAINING AND SKELETAL MUSCLE METABOLISM

Previous sections have briefly mentioned four metabolic adaptations that occur with training: (a) an increased $\dot{V}O_2max$ indicating an increased capacity for oxygen consumption by the mitochondria, (b) an increased capacity to store muscle and liver glycogen (see Table 3.3), (c) an increased rate of fat oxidation with decreased glycogen utilization during exercise at all work loads, and (d) a shift in the lactate turnpoint to a higher running speed or percent $\dot{V}O_2max$ (see Figure 3.13).

The biochemical adaptations in the skeletal muscles that explain these metabolic adaptations are as follows.

Increased Number of Blood Capillaries

Evidence shows that the number of blood capillaries surrounding muscle fibers increases with training (Andersen & Henriksson, 1977; Leinonen, 1980), which facilitates transport of both oxygen and fuel to the muscle mitochondria.

This adaptation may be especially important for facilitating free-fatty-acid uptake by the muscle mitochondria, which is the step that seems to limit the rate of fat oxidation during exercise at intensities greater than about 50% $\dot{V}O_2$max (Newsholme & Leech, 1983).

Adaptations in Metabolic Pathways

The major adaptations to training occur in the glycolytic pathway with sprint training and in the mitochondria with endurance training.

Supramaximal (Sprint) Training

Sprint training increases not only the activities of certain glycolytic enzymes (A.D. Roberts et al., 1982; see Figure 3.10) but also the abilities of the muscle fibers to continue exercising despite a low intracellular pH. Muscle buffer capacity is also increased (R.L. Sharp et al., 1986). Mitochondrial enzyme activities remain unchanged (K.J.A. Davies et al., 1982a; Gillespie et al., 1982; A.D. Roberts et al., 1982).

Submaximal (Endurance) Training

An important adaptation to submaximal (dynamic) exercise training occurs in the mitochondria: They increase in number and size (Kirkwood et al., 1987) and alter in composition. The mitochondrial enzyme content, particularly of those enzymes in the Krebs cycle and in the respiratory chain (see Figure 3.2), increases during submaximal training. Another increase occurs in the concentration of enzymes associated with fatty-acid metabolism and with the shuttle systems that transfer protons (that are generated by glycolysis and ATP breakdown) into the mitochondria for utilization in the respiratory chain (K.J.A. Davies et al., 1981; Holloszy & Coyle, 1984). An additional adaptation is the increase of resting muscle glycogen, triglyceride, and myoglobin stores; the increase in the capacity for muscle glycogen storage can be identified as early as the fourth day of training (H.J. Green et al., 1989).

The way in which the increased mitochondrial enzyme content might lead to the increased rate of fat oxidation and the shift in the lactate turnpoint after training could be explained as follows (Gollnick & Saltin, 1982; Saltin & Gollnick, 1983).

An important signal that controls cellular metabolism is the ratio of ATP to its breakdown products, ADP and Pi, represented scientifically as the (ATP)/

(ADP)(Pi) ratio. During exercise, the ratio falls progressively as the exercise intensity increases. A fall in this ratio increases the rate of carbohydrate metabolism by activating glycogenolysis and glycolysis. In this way carbohydrate becomes the preferred energy fuel during high-intensity exercise, when the intracellular (ATP)/(ADP)(Pi) ratio falls.

The pretraining Line A in Figure 3.15 shows that the rate at which ATP can be produced by oxidative metabolism in the mitochondria from untrained muscle increases with increasing provision of substrate, for example the free fatty acids carried in blood. However, the rate of ATP production approaches its maximum value at relatively low substrate concentrations and can be increased relatively little even with further large increases in substrate supply. The practical implication is that the capacity of untrained mitochondria to produce ATP rapidly from a substrate like blood-borne free fatty acids is relatively limited. Thus, even at quite low work loads, mitochondria initially utilizing mainly fats would experience a fall in the (ATP)/(ADP)(Pi) ratio, which would be the signal to increase energy provision from alternate substrates, especially carbohydrates.

However when the number and volume of mitochondria increase as a result of training (posttraining Line B in Figure 3.15), the immediate effect is that the

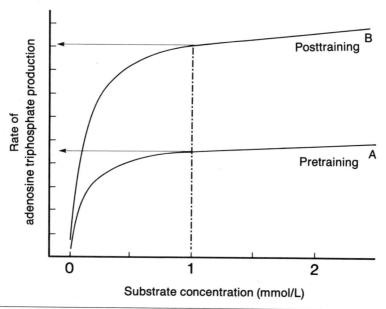

Figure 3.15 Training increases the rate of energy production from the oxidation of substrates, especially free fatty acids.

Note. From ''Hypothesis: Significance of Skeletal Muscle Oxidative Enzyme Enhancement With Endurance Training'' by P.D. Gollnick and B. Saltin, 1982, *Clinical Physiologist*, **2**, p. 4. Copyright 1982 by Blackwell Scientific Publications. Adapted by permission.

capacity of each mitochondrion to produce ATP at any substrate concentration is greatly enhanced. Thus at any rate of energy production (exercise intensity) each mitochondrion will be able to work at a higher (ATP)/(ADP)(Pi) ratio and will therefore be less dependent on carbohydrate metabolism for energy.

This means that after training, fat can provide more energy at higher exercise intensities than it can before training, with less need to activate carbohydrate metabolism. So the rate of lactate production is reduced after training; this explains, in part, the shift in the lactate turnpoint with training (Figure 3.13). Dudley et al. (1987) have shown that the muscle (ATP)/(ADP)(Pi) ratio is indeed higher during exercise in trained than in untrained muscle.

Finally, because the capacities of the shuttles that transfer protons from cytoplasm to mitochondria are increased through submaximal training, there will be a lesser accumulation of protons during exercise. Thus, the escape mechanism for proton transfer onto pyruvate to produce lactate (see Figure 3.2) is reduced, causing a further shift of the lactate turnpoint to a higher running speed or percent $\dot{V}O_2$max.

In addition, evidence now indicates that the abilities of tissues such as the heart, kidney, liver, and inactive and active skeletal muscles to utilize any lactate produced by the active muscles during exercise are also increased through submaximal training (Donovan & Brooks, 1983). These authors consider this adaptation the most important explanation for the reduced rate of blood lactate accumulation during exercise—a proposal that is in line with more recent findings (MacRae et al., 1991).

Adaptations in Muscle Contractility

The fascination that modern exercise physiologists have had for the theory that oxygen alone determines exercise performance may have blinded us to other possibilities (Noakes, 1988b). One possibility is that muscle power or contractility may determine performance (see chapter 2, p. 21) and that training may effect important changes in muscle contractility (Noakes, 1988b). These changes would likely result from increased skeletal muscle myosin ATPase activity and enhanced calcium handling by the sarcoplasmic reticulum.

The Time Course of the Mitochondrial Adaptations: The Effects of Detraining

The adaptations of $\dot{V}O_2$max to training occur very quickly, so that it is possible, for example, to show an increase in $\dot{V}O_2$max within a week of beginning an intensive training program (Hickson et al., 1977). Changes in heart rate, blood pressure, the lactate turnpoint, and glycogen storage can be detected even earlier (H.J. Green et al., 1989; M.A. Rogers et al., 1988). Unless the intensity of the training program is increased progressively, the total increase in $\dot{V}O_2$max will be achieved within 3 weeks (Hickson et al., 1981). Detraining brings about a rapid fall in $\dot{V}O_2$max in the first 2 to 3 weeks with a more gradual decrease thereafter (Coyle et al., 1984).

The time course of muscle enzyme changes with training has been less clearly defined, but in studies lasting up to 12 weeks, enzyme levels appear to show a gradual and progressive increase. At present, it seems that the rate and magnitude of these changes are functions, within limits, of the total amount of muscle contractile activity. The rate can be increased either by performing more contractions in a given time period (i.e., increasing exercise intensity) or by maintaining the same frequency of contraction for a longer period (i.e., increasing exercise duration; Holloszy & Coyle, 1984).

In a study of rats, Dudley et al. (1982) found that at any exercise intensity, 60 minutes of training 5 days a week produced maximum adaptation in mitochondrial enzyme content. Longer daily training periods produced no further increase in mitochondrial oxidative enzyme changes. The authors found that high-intensity interval training at approximately 116% $\dot{V}O_2$max for relatively short periods (15 min/day) produced as great an increase in mitochondrial enzyme content as did exercise for 90 min/day at 83 to 94% $\dot{V}O_2$max.

A number of researchers have used the decrease in mitochondrial enzyme content that occurs when training stops as a measure of the rate at which fitness is lost when one stops training. In addition, they have studied the amount of exercise required to maintain these adaptations.

In rats and humans trained for 8 to 15 weeks, elevated mitochondrial enzyme contents are lost within about 8 weeks in rats and about 4 to 8 weeks in humans (Coyle et al., 1985b; Holloszy & Coyle, 1984; R.L. Moore et al., 1987) with no further loss thereafter (Coyle et al., 1985b). However, humans who have trained for much longer (6 to 20 years) show much more gradual declines in mitochondrial enzyme content; even after 12 weeks of inactivity these people have mitochondrial enzyme contents at least 40 to 50% above untrained levels (Chi et al., 1983; Coyle et al., 1984, 1985b). This is compatible with the empirical observation that once an athlete has trained for a few years, even 1 or 2 months of complete inactivity do not cause that athlete to go back to total unfitness. In these studies, $\dot{V}O_2$max declined by 7% over the first 12 days of detraining and by 16% after 8 weeks, at which level it stabilized (Coyle et al., 1984). The work load or oxygen consumption at the lactate turnpoint declined by 20% after 8 weeks before stabilizing at that level (Coyle et al., 1985b).

On the other hand, tapering by reducing training from 110 km/week to 40 km/week for 10 days neither decreased nor increased $\dot{V}O_2$max and exercise time to exhaustion in trained distance runners (Houmard et al., 1989).

Hickson and his colleagues (Hickson & Rosenkoetter, 1981; Hickson et al., 1982) exercised groups of subjects 40 minutes a day, 6 days a week, for 10 weeks, after which the subjects exercised either less frequently (2 or 4 days a week) or for shorter times (13 min/day or 26 min/day) but at the same intensities and frequencies. The authors found that the fitness levels of the subjects were maintained even though the times that some subjects spent exercising had been reduced by almost two thirds. However, similar one-third or two-third reductions in exercise intensities failed to maintain the elevated $\dot{V}O_2max$ values resulting from training (Hickson et al., 1985).

Interestingly, these researchers found that with detraining, performance time to exhaustion during short-duration (5 minutes) and prolonged (200 minutes) exercise did not decrease to the same extent as did the $\dot{V}O_2max$, which again suggests that other factors, possibly muscle contractility, are important in determining performance during short-duration and prolonged exercise.

Researchers have also shown through studies of rats a dissociation of changes in running performance, in $\dot{V}O_2max$, and in muscle mitochondrial adaptations, which also suggests that an unmeasured factor, probably muscle contractility (Noakes, 1988b), also changes with training and is an important, albeit unrecognized, component of those training adaptations that increase running performance (Lambert & Noakes, 1989).

Another interesting finding is that the decrease in $\dot{V}O_2max$ that results with detraining can be reversed simply by increasing the blood volume with a dextran/saline infusion (Coyle et al., 1986b). We would not expect such an infusion to alter the muscle mitochondrial enzyme activities, thus this finding again shows a dissociation between changes in $\dot{V}O_2max$, running performance, and mitochondrial enzyme activities.

Nevertheless, these studies have important implications for those who wish to become "fit" in a short period of time but who are then unwilling to continue exercise for the same amount of time after achieving this goal. Continuing to exercise at high intensity will maintain fitness most effectively.

Practical Implications of Training

Of what practical value is this knowledge of the muscle adaptations to training? First, the fact that the mitochondrial adaptations to training occur only in the trained muscles and only in the muscle fibers that are active during that exercise indicate that training for a particular event or sport must use the correct muscle groups and more specifically the appropriate muscle fibers and the appropriate metabolic pathways in those fibers. For example, the runner who trains exclusively on the flat is untrained for uphill running because different muscle groups are involved in these two activities (Costill et al., 1974). Similarly, the noncompetitive jogger will train a different fiber type than will the middle-distance runner who exercises at a higher intensity and therefore activates both ST and FT muscle fibers.

Second, studies of detraining show that it is not necessary to maintain the same high intensity of training year-round; a reduction in training by as much as two thirds may maintain a decent level of fitness. This becomes important when we consider the concept of peaking.

Third, the concept of different training intensities producing different training effects allows the tailoring of individual training goals. Sprinters must aim to increase muscle contractility and the rates of glycolysis and creatine kinase reactions, whereas middle-distance runners must adapt the muscles so that they become progressively more resistant to low pH levels. Marathon runners, on the other hand, must shift their lactate turnpoints to higher running speeds; these runners must increase their capacities for fat oxidation so that they can "spare" carbohydrate stores during racing. They must also maximize their abilities to store liver and muscle glycogen before exercise and must increase their capacities to absorb carbohydrate during competition. Ultramarathon runners must, in addition, adapt their muscles so that they are resistant to racing-induced muscle damage.

The Heritability of the Capacity to Adapt to Endurance Training

The concept that the $\dot{V}O_2max$ is determined largely by hereditary factors has been described. We now also know that endurance performance during a prolonged exercise test is even more strongly determined by genetic factors (Bouchard et al., 1986), as is the degree to which any individual can adapt to an endurance training program (Bouchard & Lortie, 1984; Hamel et al., 1986; Prud'homme et al., 1984; Simoneau et al., 1986). Thus, 70 to 80% of both endurance performance and the adaptability to training is determined by genetic factors.

Researchers have identified high and low responders to training, with low responders (Lortie et al., 1984; Prud'homme et al., 1984) showing none of the adaptations to training that this chapter has described. These individuals simply do not and cannot improve with training regardless of their efforts. Attempts to identify genetic markers for high and low adaptors are currently in progress (Bouchard et al., 1989). Interestingly, the extent to which other beneficial changes develop with training, including the reduction in serum cholesterol concentrations, may also be genetically controlled (Després et al., 1988).

Thus, elite athletes are not only superiorly endowed with those attributes necessary for success—such as high $\dot{V}O_2max$ values, lactate turnpoints that occur at fast running speeds, fast peak treadmill running speeds (Noakes et al., 1990b), and muscles with a higher capacity to generate ATP from oxidative metabolism even when untrained (Park et al., 1988)—but they also have genetic gifts that enable all these variables to adapt to the greatest possible extent with training.

The Role of Arm Training and Cross-Training for Activities That Involve Mainly the Legs

Part of the accepted dogma of training is that all training is absolutely specific. Thus it is believed that the greatest benefit is achieved if one trains only in the specific activity in which one wishes to compete (Clausen, 1977).

While this is essentially true, some evidence suggests that arm training added to normal leg training may enhance performance during leg exercise more than leg training alone (Loftin et al., 1988). Both the mechanism and the practical value of this finding are presently unclear. The trained arm muscle may be better able to remove lactate during high-intensity exercise and conversely store more glycogen prior to endurance exercise. By releasing lactate from those glycogen stores during prolonged exercise, the arms could make an important contribution to overall carbohydrate balance during prolonged exercise.

A related consideration is the value of cross-training for runners. The growth of the triathlon in the mid-1980s was sustained largely by an influx of runners keen to tackle a new sport. Subsequently, elite triathletes have shown themselves to be not only exceptional swimmers and cyclists but also runners of very high class. For example, in 1989, American Mark Allen had to complete the final 26-mile marathon of the 139-mile Hawaiian Ironman Triathlon in 02:40:04 in order to win by 58 seconds. To what extent does cycling hinder or enhance running performance? At present, cycling's effects are not entirely clear, but certain possibilities are apparent.

Young competitive runners probably should run only; cycling will be detrimental to their running performance. However for marathon and ultramarathon runners, cycling allows the metabolic demands of prolonged exercise to be simulated without the same risk of muscle damage or injury. Dave Scott, the athlete beaten by Mark Allen, believes that a heavy cycling program aids distance-running performance and that this explains why elite triathletes seldom run more than 60 to 80 miles a week.

My experience is that cross-training with cycling offers the greatest benefits for those whose running training is limited by frequent or resistant injuries. Supplementing a less demanding running program with cycling may well produce the same benefits as a more strenuous running program but with a lesser risk of injury.

4

Control of Body Temperature During Exercise

"Oh, everybody was affected by the heat [in the 1956 Olympic Marathon in Melbourne]. I think that 13 boys were carried from the route on stretchers. We all knew that the heat would not agree with us; in fact, the great Zatopec, just before the race, looked up at the sun in the sky and said, 'Today, we all die.' "

Dean A. Thackwray (Guild, 1957)

"Yet, I repeat, these symptoms, however unpleasant and alarming have no baleful significance as of danger. One recalls the historic Marathon race in London in 1908 when the Italian, Dorando, staggered blindly disorientated into the Stadium and fell, lying, according to picturesque journalistic phraseology, for a time between life and death. Yet by the following morning he had completely recovered and subsequently ran a considerable number of Marathon races.

"At that time biochemistry was in its infancy; modern researchers have made us familiar with the true significance of these symptoms and have taught us to transfer the lesion from the heart, about which solicitude is mistakenly expressed, to less vital structures."

Sir Adolphe Abrahams (1961)

The runner faces a major problem: the excess heat produced by muscle contraction. Humans are homeotherms, and to live they must keep their body temperatures within a narrow range (35 to 42 °C) despite wide variations in environmental temperatures and differences in levels of physical activity.

During exercise, however, the conversion of chemical energy stored in ATP into mechanical energy is extremely inefficient, so that as much as 70% of the total chemical energy used during muscular contraction is released as heat rather than as athletic endeavor.

Thus, when Bruce Fordyce or Don Ritchie (see chapter 8) wins an ultramarathon at an average pace of 16.3 km/hr, he utilizes about 56 kJ of energy every minute (see Figure 4.1, a and b) or about 18,480 kJ in the 5-1/2 hours that he runs. Of this, only 5,940 kJ help transport the athlete from the start to the finish of the race; the remaining 12,540 kJ are nothing more than a hindrance, as they serve only to heat the athlete. Were the athlete unable to lose less than one tenth (1,115 kJ) of that heat, his body temperature would rise above 43 °C, causing heatstroke.

To prevent disastrous overheating and heatstroke and to control the increased heat associated with exercise, the body must be able to call upon a number of very effective heat-losing mechanisms.

MECHANISMS FOR HEAT LOSS DURING EXERCISE

As exercise begins, the blood flow to the muscles increases. Not only does the heart pump more blood, but blood is preferentially diverted away from nonessential organs and toward the working muscles and skin. As blood passes through the muscles, it is heated, and it distributes the added heat throughout the body, particularly to the skin. In this manner, as well as by direct transfer from muscles lying close to the skin, heat is conducted to the skin surface. Here, circulating air currents convect this heat away, and any nearby objects whose surface temperatures are lower than the skin temperature attract this heat, which travels by electromagnetic waves in a form of energy transfer known as radiation.

In another method of heat loss, surface heat evaporates the sweat produced by the sweat glands in the skin. Sweating itself does not lose heat; heat is lost only when that sweat actually evaporates. The efficiencies of all these mechanisms depend on a variety of factors, most of which are open to modification by the athlete.

The Exercise Intensity

As the intensity of exercise increases, the body must decide whether to pump more blood to the muscles to maintain their increased energy requirements or to assist heat dissipation by increasing the skin blood flow. Faced with conflicting demands, the body always favors an increased blood flow to the muscles. The result is that while body heat production is increased, the ability to lose that heat is decreased.

It appears that athletes running at world-record speeds, at least in races up to 16 km, develop marked limitations to skin blood flow and therefore have limited abilities to lose heat. They thus run in microenvironments in which their abilities to maintain heat equilibrium depend entirely on the prevailing environmental conditions (Pugh, 1972). If these conditions are unfavorable, the athletes will continually accumulate heat until their body temperatures reach the critical level at which heatstroke occurs.

Two famous athletes running at world-record pace who developed heatstroke when forced to race in unfavorable environmental conditions were Jim Peters in the 1954 Empire Games Marathon (see chapter 8) and Alberto Salazar in the 1980 Falmouth 12-km Road Race.

Environmental Factors Affecting Heat Loss

The air temperature and wind speed determine the amount of heat that can be lost from the skin by convection, which is the heating of the surrounding air by the skin.

High facing-wind speeds cause a large volume of unwarmed air to cross the skin in unit time and therefore allow for greater heat loss by convection. Running itself produces an effective wind speed that aids convective heat loss but may not be sufficient to increase heat loss adequately in severe environmental conditions. Obviously, a wind coming from behind the runner at the same speed that the runner is moving forward will cause him or her to run in a totally windless environment, which will prevent convective heat loss. In contrast, the wind speed developed by cyclists appears to be sufficient to compensate even for severe conditions, which explains why heat is not as great a problem for endurance cyclists as it is for runners.

At rest, the body skin temperature is about 33 °C. If you exercise in environmental temperatures greater than 33 °C, heat cannot be lost by convection, because the air temperature is higher than that of the body surface. In this case the direction of heat transfer is reversed, and the superficial tissues gain heat from the environment. In these conditions, the only avenue for heat loss is by sweating. Sweating removes 1,092 to 2,520 kJ of heat per liter of sweat evaporated (see Figure 4.1), depending on whether all the sweat evaporates or, as usually happens, a large percentage drips from the body without evaporating. As the air humidity increases, the body's ability to lose heat by this mechanism decreases.

The body can absorb additional heat from the environment, in particular from the sun. The body temperature is cooler than that of the sun, thus, the body will absorb radiant energy from the sun. Obviously, the amount of radiant energy to

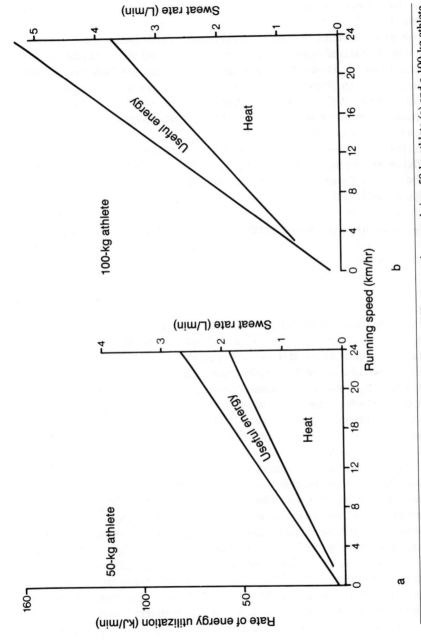

Figure 4.1 The rates of energy expenditure and sweating at different running speeds in a 50-kg athlete (a) and a 100-kg athlete (b).

Note. From ''Sweating: Its Composition and Effects on Body Fluids'' by D.L. Costill, 1977, *Annals of the New York Academy of Sciences*, **301**, p. 162. Copyright 1977 by the New York Academy of Sciences. Adapted by permission.

which the athlete is exposed is greatest when there is no cloud cover and is least when cloud cover is absolute.

These three environmental factors that determine the athlete's ability to lose heat—wind speed, the humidity and temperature of the air, and the radiant energy load—are measured in the wet bulb globe temperature (WBGT) index.

The WBGT index integrates the measurement of radiant energy (as the temperature of a black globe—the globe temperature) with the wet bulb temperature (measured by a thermometer covered by a wick permeated with water). The difference between the wet bulb temperature and the prevailing air (dry bulb) temperature is a measure of the humidity of the air and therefore is also a measure of the ease with which sweat will evaporate from the athlete. Furthermore, wind blowing over the wet wick of the wet bulb thermometer will increase the rate of evaporative cooling and will therefore lower the wet bulb temperature. In this way, the prevailing wind speed also influences the WBGT index.

Chapter 9 and Table 9.4 describe the use of the WBGT index to determine precautions that should be taken to prevent heat injury during marathon races. Recently, the corrected environmental temperature (CET) has been proposed as an even better predictor of heat stress during running. This is discussed in greater detail in chapter 9.

DEHYDRATION

With sweating, fluid is removed from the body causing dehydration, which may be compounded by vomiting and diarrhea. Whyndham and Strydom (1969) drew attention to what they believed to be the dangers of dehydration in predisposing the athlete to heatstroke. They studied runners in a 32-km road race and showed that the body temperatures of athletes who became dehydrated by more than 3% of their body weights approached values previously recorded only in victims of heatstroke. In addition, the researchers found that athletes weighing 70 kg or more who had not drunk during the race incurred 5% water deficits and had markedly elevated body temperatures after the race.

The conclusions that these authors drew are now believed to be incorrect (Noakes, 1990a, 1990b; Noakes et al., 1988a, 1991a). In particular, it seems that dehydration is not the most important factor determining the body temperature during exercise. Nevertheless, the findings of Wyndham and Strydom (1969) drew attention to the potential dangers of the International Amateur Athletic Federation Rule Number 165:5, which stipulated that marathon runners could drink no fluids before the 11-km mark of the standard marathon and thereafter could drink only every 5 km. This ruling discouraged marathon runners from drinking during races and promoted the idea that drinking during running was unnecessary and a sign of weakness. This rule was eventually repealed.

That early marathon runners were not used to drinking fluids regularly during races is shown by the trivial amounts drunk by Arthur Newton during his races (see chapter 9). Indeed, Jim Peters described the conventional wisdom of the day in the following statement about marathon racing (J.H. Peters et al., 1957):

> There is no need to take any solid food at all and every effort should also be made to do without liquid, as the moment food or drink is taken, the body has to start dealing with its digestion and in so doing some discomfort will almost invariably be felt. (p. 114)

Although dehydration is not the critical factor predisposing athletes to heatstroke during exercise, marked dehydration does have detrimental effects. Skin blood flow is reduced (Nadel et al., 1980), and body heat storage (and therefore body temperature) is increased by dehydration (Gisolfi & Topping, 1974). However, the effects are somewhat less dramatic than generally believed (Noakes, 1990b; Noakes et al., 1988a, 1991a).

CLOTHING

Apart from aesthetic reasons, the rationale for wearing clothing is to trap a thin layer of air next to the body. Because air is a poor conductor of heat, this thin layer rapidly heats to body temperature and acts as an insulator preventing heat loss. Clearly, any clothing that is worn during exercise in the heat must be designed for the opposite effect—to promote heat loss.

Marathon runners have learned that light, porous clothing such as "fish net" vests best achieve this heat loss. In contrast, T-shirts or heavy rugby jerseys, particularly when soggy with sweat, become very good insulators, preventing adequate heat loss.

Novice runners, particularly those who might consider themselves overweight, often train in full track suits in the heat. Many neophyte athletes probably believe that the more they sweat, the harder they must be exercising and therefore the greater the weight they stand to lose. The unfortunate truth is that in running, the energy cost is related only to the distance run. Thus, to lose more weight, one needs to run a greater distance.

Excessive sweating will effect a sudden loss of weight by dehydrating the body; this is the procedure used by boxers, jockeys, and wrestlers in "making the weight." By exercising in the heat for as little as half an hour, one can "lose" as much as 1 kg, but this is a fluid loss that will be rapidly replaced if the athlete rehydrates by drinking. In contrast, to lose a real kilogram of body weight one must expend about 37,500 kJ of energy, equivalent to running about 160 km!

The insulating qualities of different clothing is expressed as CLO units. One CLO unit is equivalent to the amount of insulation provided by ordinary business apparel that provides comfort at temperatures of 21 °C when both wind speed and humidity are low. The clothing of the Eskimo provides 10 to 12 CLO units and is essential for life in arctic conditions. However, because of the considerable heat production during exercise, clothing that will provide 1 CLO unit of insulation is all that is required when running in temperatures as low as −22 °C, provided there is little or no wind.

Thus, a runner who lives in a moderate climate seldom (if ever) needs to train for any period in a track suit. By doing so, the runner merely increases discomfort and promotes conditions favorable for heatstroke.

HEAT ACCLIMATIZATION

When athletes who have trained exclusively in cool weather are suddenly confronted with hot, humid conditions, they suffer immediate and dramatic impairments in performance. However, with perseverance and continued training in the heat, performance soon improves, returning to normal within a short period.

The process underlying this adaptation is termed *heat acclimatization*. It begins after the first exposure to exercise in the heat, progresses rapidly, and is fully developed after 7 to 10 days. Only by exercising in the heat can one become heat acclimatized. The optimum method for achieving this is to train daily in the heat for periods of 2 to 4 hours for 10 days. Once established, heat acclimatization is fully retained for about 2 weeks. Thereafter, it is lost at rates that vary among individuals. It is best retained by those who stay in good physical condition and who reexpose themselves to exercise in the heat at least every 2 weeks.

Important changes occur with heat acclimatization: Heart rate, body temperature, and sweat salt (sodium chloride) content during exercise decrease, whereas sweating rate increases due to increased secretory capacity of the sweat glands (Buono & Sjoholm, 1988). In addition, metabolic rate and the rate of muscle and blood lactate accumulation are decreased by heat acclimatization (A.J. Young et al., 1985), as is the rate of muscle glycogen utilization (King et al., 1985; Kirwan et al., 1987).

Heat acclimatization confers considerable protection from heat injury; equally important, in competition in the heat, the heat-acclimatized athlete will always have the "edge" over an equally fit, but unacclimatized opponent.

Chapter 9 describes the way in which Ron Daws (1977) used heat acclimatization to qualify for the 1968 Olympic Games.

Sponging

As the skin temperature rises, it causes blood to pool in the veins of the arms and legs. This is because the elevated skin temperature "paralyzes" the veins, which dilate and soon fill with a large volume of blood.

This blood is effectively lost from the circulation and can only be returned to the circulation if the skin temperature is again lowered. This can be achieved by *sponging* (literally wetting the skin with a sponge).

A recent study confirmed that wetting the skin did indeed lower the skin temperature during exercise but did not aid heat loss (Bassett et al., 1987). Thus the benefits of sponging during exercise probably relate to its effect on the central circulation.

Factors Explaining Impaired Running Performance in the Heat

Anyone who has run a marathon or longer race in the heat knows that such races are much more difficult than are races of the same distance run in cool conditions. The most likely explanation for this comes from recent studies showing that precooling of the body or of the active muscles either prior to or during exercise prolongs endurance time to exhaustion in both dogs and humans (Kozlowski et al., 1985; Kruk et al., 1985; Olschewski & Brück, 1988; Schmidt & Brück, 1981). This cooling keeps the muscle temperature lower during subsequent exercise and alters the metabolic response by decreasing the rates of muscle glycogen utilization, muscle lactate accumulation, and the fall in muscle high-energy phosphate content (Kozlowski et al., 1985), thereby allowing the cooler muscles to exercise for longer. By inference we may conclude that the sustained elevation of muscle temperature that occurs during prolonged exercise may be one of the most important factors limiting endurance performance.

Calculating Sweat Rate During Exercise

To calculate your sweat rate or to figure how much your current drinking pattern during races falls short of replacing your sweat losses, you could try the following experiment.

Weigh yourself (naked) on a scale reading in kilograms, immediately before (WB) and immediately after (WA) a run in conditions and at a pace to which you are accustomed. Measure carefully the total amount of fluid (F) in liters that you ingest while running. You can then calculate your sweat rate fairly accurately.

$$\text{Sweat Rate (L/hr)} = \frac{(\text{WB} - \text{WA}) + \text{F}}{\text{Running Time (hours)}}$$

Your fluid replacement will have been adequate if, after races longer than 30 km, you have lost less than 2 to 3 kg and are not dehydrated by more than 3%, calculated by this equation:

$$\text{Dehydration (\%)} = \frac{\text{WB} - \text{WA}}{\text{WB}} \times 100$$

TEMPERATURE REGULATION WHEN RUNNING IN THE COLD

The essential problem encountered during hot-weather running is the dissipation of sufficient heat to prevent heat storage and a dangerous rise in body temperature. When running in extreme cold, the critical danger is that the rate of heat loss from the body may exceed the rate of body heat production, causing the body temperature to fall. Once the temperature falls below 35 °C, mental functioning is impaired and the blood pressure falls. Below 33 °C, mental confusion develops and the limb muscles become rigid and immobile. Unconsciousness develops shortly thereafter, which leads to death from hypothermia if the body is not rapidly rewarmed.

As Roald Amundsen, the first man to reach the South Pole, noted, the exercising body is a furnace (Huntford, 1985) so that with appropriate clothing, the human can survive even under the most unfavorable environmental conditions. Only under certain well-defined conditions does the rate of heat loss from the body exceed its rate of production during exercise, thereby leading to hypothermia.

Survival in severe environmental conditions is, however, critically dependent on the choice of appropriate clothing, because despite its ability to produce an enormous amount of heat during exercise, the body has a relatively limited ability to reduce its rate of energy transfer to the environment. Thus avoiding hypothermia when exposed to the cold depends on two important factors: the choice of appropriate clothing and the maintenance of a high rate of heat production, as occurs during exercise. As described earlier, the insulating qualities of different clothes are rated in CLO units. At an environmental temperature of −50 °C, a resting human would need to wear 12 CLO units of clothing to maintain body temperature (see Figure 4.2a), whereas a person running at 16 km/hr in the same conditions would be adequately protected by only 1.25 CLO units of clothing. Allowance must also be made for clothing that becomes wet; the insulating properties of clothing are greatly reduced when they become wet, because unlike air, water is a very poor insulator (i.e., a good conductor of heat). This explains why exposure to cold water (less than 10 °C) can induce hypothermia in lean swimmers within less than 30 minutes.

We can predict that hypothermia is likely to occur during exercise in those who either start exercising in clothing that is inappropriate for the environmental conditions or who dress in clothing that is appropriate for high rates of energy expenditure but which becomes inappropriate as the subjects become tired and slow down, thereby reducing their rates of energy expenditure. Hypothermia is also likely to affect those whose clothing becomes wet.

Hypothermia usually develops as a consequence of all these mechanisms acting in fatal concert (Pugh, 1966, 1967b). Maintenance of body temperature during exercise in the cold, therefore, depends on choosing clothing that is appropriate

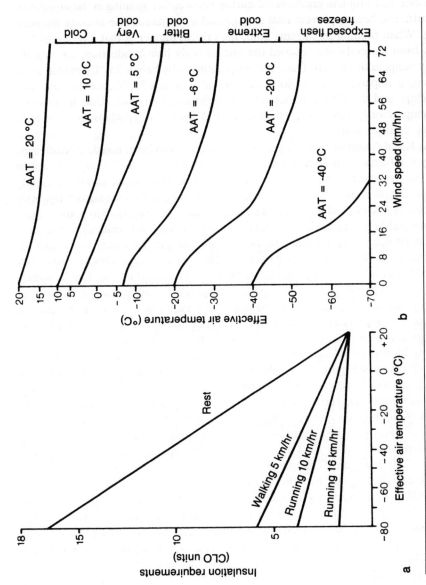

Figure 4.2 Insulation requirements during exercise at different effective air temperatures (a) and the effects of different wind speeds on the effective air temperatures at different ambient air temperatures (AAT) (b).

for the predicted rate of energy expenditure in the expected environmental conditions and keeping the clothing dry, especially if a strong wind is blowing.

To calculate the coldness of the environment in which you exercise, you must know both the dry bulb temperature and the expected wind speed and direction. Wind dramatically increases the "coldness" of any given dry bulb temperature, in effect reducing the effective temperature to which the body is exposed, thereby increasing the rate of energy loss from the body. This is known as the *wind chill factor*. Figure 4.2b is a plot of the effective temperature for different actual still-air dry bulb temperatures and wind speeds. To calculate the effective temperature, remember that your running speed into the wind increases the effective wind speed by a speed equal to your running speed, whereas running with the wind behind you reduces the effective wind speed by an equivalent amount. Notice also that it is not safe to run at effective temperatures below about −56 °C. At lower temperatures, exposed flesh freezes within 30 seconds, leading to "frostnip" or frostbite (see chapter 18).

Figure 4.2 can help you decide how much clothing to wear depending on the speed at which you will be running and the effective air temperature. Note that even when you are running at quite slow speeds (10 km/hr) in effective air temperatures as low as −50 °C, as little as 3 CLO units will provide adequate protection. Appropriate clothing under these most extreme conditions would include the following: cotton T-shirt; two nylon sweat shirts; underpants (one or two pairs); cotton, polypropylene, or Lycra long johns; shorts; sweat pants; hood; mittens; ski mask or face protector including a sweatband to protect the tip of the nose; shoes; and socks. If there is precipitation, you must also wear a rainproof jacket with hood. At higher temperatures, you can discard the outer layers of clothing as you warm up.

You should try to wear sufficient clothing to keep warm but not so much that you start to sweat profusely, because sweat reduces the insulating properties of your clothing. Always start your run facing into the wind and finish with the wind behind you. In this way the cooling effect of the environment is greatest when you are freshest, running the fastest, and therefore generating the most body heat; cooling is least when you are tired, running the slowest, and producing the least heat. Always plan to run in well-populated areas so that help is always close at hand should hypothermia develop; never run so far that you might become tired and have to walk. As shown in Figure 4.2, compared to running, walking dramatically increases the amount of clothing you need to wear to keep warm at low effective air temperatures. Finally, wear clothing that is easily adaptable, like a lightweight rain jacket with a zip-up front and a hood, which can be worn either zipped or unzipped or with or without the hood or that can be carried with equal ease. Also choose running routes that provide as much shelter from the wind as possible.

FLUID INTAKE DURING EXERCISE

If dehydration is a factor in the cause of heatstroke during prolonged exercise, it follows that adequate fluid ingestion should be an important factor preventing heat injury during exercise. However, the major factors causing heatstroke during races are the environmental conditions, the speed at which the athletes run, and individual susceptibility (Noakes et al., 1988a, 1991a). If longer distance races are held when either the WBGT index or the dry bulb temperature is greater than 23 °C, heat injury will occur in a significant number of competitors regardless of how much they drink and sponge during the race or how they are dressed. Adequate fluid replacement during racing is only one of many factors that reduce the risk of heat injury; it is certainly not the only factor and may not be even a very important factor (Noakes, 1991b; Noakes et al., 1988a, 1991a).

How Much Should You Drink?

From the results of their original study, Wyndham and Strydom (1969) concluded that marathon runners should aim to drink 250 ml of fluid every 15 minutes during exercise; this advice has been perpetuated in the Position Statement of the American College of Sports Medicine (1987). It is now clear that this advice applies only to a small number of runners. Wyndham and Strydom's own data show that the marathoners in their study actually drank only about 100 ml/hr, and more recent studies confirm that the voluntary fluid intakes by runners during races are closer to 500 than to 1,000 ml every hour (Maughan, 1985; Noakes et al., 1988a; Shephard & Kavanagh, 1978).

Furthermore, Shephard and Kavanagh (1978) pointed out that during marathon running, the metabolism of glycogen releases the water stored in the glycogen. This makes an additional important source of water available to offset the dehydration caused by sweating; the volume of this fluid can be as much as 2 L.

Thus, a runner who sweats at a rate of 1 L/hr during a 4-hour marathon race and who therefore suffers a 4-kg weight loss (1 L sweat = 1 kg) during the race would incur an actual dehydration of only 2 kg, because 2 L of water would be released by glycogen metabolism. Therefore, during the race, that runner only needs to drink 500 ml/hr to maintain fluid balance.

Only recently have researchers noted the dangers of drinking too much fluid, especially during an ultramarathon race (e.g., drinking 1,000 ml or more instead of 500 ml each hour). Noakes et al. (1985a) reported four cases, two of which were serious, of runners who developed *hyponatremia* (water intoxication) during ultramarathons or ultratriathlons when they drank fluid in excess of their requirements. Of 17 runners who were hospitalized after the 1985 Comrades Marathon, 9 had hyponatremia; after the 1987 race 24 such cases were reported (Noakes et al., 1990c). Among these were runners who were critically ill, three of whom nearly died. All these runners were uniquely predisposed to developing the condition because they were unable to prevent increases in blood volume that followed dilution of their blood sodium contents when they ingested too much fluid during prolonged exercise (Irving et al., 1991). Similar cases have also been described in American ultramarathon (Frizzell et al., 1986) and marathon (M. Young et al., 1987) runners.

Typically, runners who are affected by hyponatremia are not elite, competitive runners but are completing these ultramarathons in 9 to 11 hours. Their slow running speeds allow them ample time to drink fluid from the vast number of feeding stations available during these races. But, more importantly, the slow running speeds and therefore the low metabolic rates of these athletes cause them to sweat at much slower rates than the rates calculated previously by researchers who studied only elite marathoners (Pugh et al., 1967; Wyndham & Strydom, 1969). It is clear that sweat rate calculations based on elite runners cannot be applied to the average runner of the same body mass who runs much slower.

For example, researchers originally believed that if a 50-kg runner loses 5.5 L of sweat during a 5:30:00 ultramarathon, then that runner should obviously drink 1 L every hour to maintain a water balance. (This calculation ignores the water lost from glycogen, which does not have to be replaced.) Thus, the general (but incorrect) rule was devised (American College of Sports Medicine, 1975) that a 50-kg person should drink 1 L of fluid for every hour of running, and those who are heavier should drink a little more.

But we now know that this advice is safe only if the runner is able to finish the race in 5:30:00. A less competitive 50-kg runner who religiously followed that advice but took 10:00:00 to complete the race would finish the race with a fluid credit of 4 L, enough to cause water intoxication (Noakes et al., 1985a) if the runner is predisposed to the condition (Irving et al., 1991). The finding that the incidence of hyponatremia is on the increase among slower ultramarathon runners (Noakes et al., 1990c, 1991c) suggests that this is happening more frequently.

What factors, then, determine sweat rate? Probably the most important factor is metabolic rate, which is affected by the speed of running and by body weight (Costill, 1977). Figure 2.2 shows that the rate of oxygen consumption and therefore the rate of metabolic heat production increases linearly with increasing running speed. Because sweating is the most important avenue of heat loss during running, it is likely that the sweat rate also increases linearly with the increasing rate of heat production, that is, with increased running speed (see Figure 4.1).

Increased body mass increases metabolic heat production at any given running speed in proportion to the increased body mass (see Figure 4.1). Thus, a 100-kg runner will produce twice as much heat as a 50-kg runner when they both run at the same speed. The 100-kg runner's sweat rate will also likely be twice as high (see Figure 4.1).

What happens, of course, is that during competition, the smaller runners run faster for a shorter time and the heavier runners run slower for a longer time. If their finishing times are in the same ratio as their body weights, their total sweat losses should be very similar.

It follows that if we assume that a 50-kg runner sweats at a rate of about 1 L/ hr during competition and needs to replace only half that loss each hour during exercise lasting up to 5 hours, then a fluid intake of 500 ml each hour is probably adequate for runners of all weights, provided they run proportionately slower than the 50-kg runner.

Surprisingly, mild environmental temperature seems to have little influence on sweat rate during competition; even in cold running conditions (dry bulb temperature 11 to 12 °C), sweat rates of 1.2 L/hr are recorded in the fastest runners (Maughan, 1985), and these values are not different from values measured at dry bulb temperatures of 14 to 17 °C (Wyndham & Strydom, 1969) and 22 to 23 °C (Noakes et al., 1988a; Pugh et al., 1967).

Thus, we may conclude that running speed and body weight are the most important determinants of sweat rates during running, and that on average, an hourly fluid intake of 500 ml should cover the requirements of most runners under most conditions (Noakes et al., 1988a, 1991a).

These ideas are formalized in Figure 4.3, which shows postrace rectal temperatures, rates of water loss, and weight losses of 70- to 80-kg runners completing standard marathons at different speeds. Note that the postrace rectal temperatures are not greatly elevated; that the rates of water loss rise with increasing running speeds, as would be expected, and are quite low in the slowest runners; and that only the very fastest runners finish the race mildly dehydrated. As most of the other runners do not lose more than 2 kg, equivalent to the masses of water and glycogen stored before the race, they finish the race moderately overhydrated.

What Should the Ingested Fluid Contain?

The fluid taken should contain certain substances to restore the body's supplies. One possible aim of fluid ingestion during exercise might be to match the electrolytes that are lost in sweat. *Electrolytes* are chemical substances that, when dissolved or melted, dissociate into electrically charged particles (or *ions*, such as sodium, potassium, etc.). Electrolytes are essential to the normal functioning of all cells. Table 4.1 compares the electrolyte content of sweat (Costill, 1977; Verde et al., 1982) with that of blood.

It is clear from Table 4.1 that both fitness and heat acclimatization reduce the sodium content of sweat. Thus, the amount of sodium lost in the sweat of the heat-acclimatized, fit athlete is really quite trivial, amounting to little more than

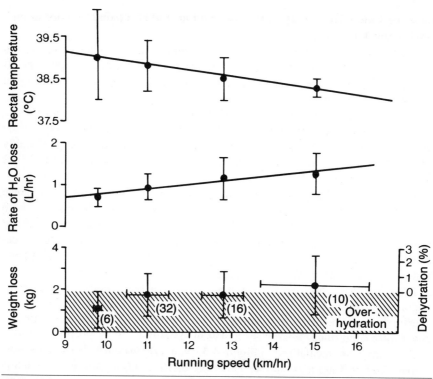

Figure 4.3 Postrace rectal temperatures, rates of water loss, and weight losses in 70- to 80-kg runners completing standard marathon races at different running speeds.
Note. From "Fluid and Mineral Needs of Athletes" by T.D. Noakes in *Current Therapy in Sports Medicine* (p. 146) edited by J.S. Torg, R.P. Welsh, and R.J. Shephard, 1990, Philadelphia: B.C. Decker. Copyright 1990 by B.C. Decker. Adapted by permission.

2 g/hr (assuming a sweat rate of about 1 L/hr), or about 6 to 8 g in a standard marathon and 10 to 16 g in an ultramarathon.

As we will discuss in chapter 15, the average daily salt intake of the common runner exceeds his or her requirement by about 8 g and is therefore more than enough to cover the salt requirements of running as much as a marathon per day. Even after an ultramarathon, the runner's normal daily salt intake would replace sodium losses within 24 hours. For this reason, one might argue that extra salt is not required when one exercises. However, we now know that the issue is somewhat more complex.

Calculations (Noakes et al., 1990c) suggest that during prolonged exercise, the body is forced to deplete its fluid stores as a consequence of the sodium chloride losses in sweat. If this did not occur and if the body fluid stores were allowed to remain normal, then a dilutional hyponatremia with potentially catastrophic effects would develop in all runners competing in races lasting more than 4 hours.

Table 4.1 Electrolyte Contents of Sweat and Blood and the Effects of Fitness and Heat Acclimatization

Electrolyte	Blood	Sweat of unacclimatized, unfit subject	Sweat of fit but unacclimatized subject	Sweat of fit, acclimatized subject
Sodium (Na$^+$)	140 (6.1)	80 (3.5)	60 (2.6)	40 (1.8)
Potassium (K$^+$)	4.0 (0.1)	8.0 (0.2)	6.0 (0.15)	4.0 (0.1)
Magnesium (Mg$^+$)	1.5 (0.1)	1.5 (0.1)	1.5 (0.1)	1.5 (0.1)
Chloride (Cl$^-$)	101 (2.9)	50 (1.4)	40 (1.1)	30 (0.9)

Note. All values in mmol/L (g/L). Based on data from "Sweat Composition in Exercise and in Heat" by T. Verde, R.J. Shephard, P. Corey, and R. Moore, 1982, *Journal of Applied Physiology*, **53**(6), pp. 1541, 1543, and "Sweating: Its Composition and Effects on Body Fluids" by D.L. Costill, 1977, *Annals of the New York Acadamy of Sciences*, **301**, p. 162. Copyright 1982 and 1977 by the American Physiological Society and the New York Academy of Sciences, respectively. Adapted by permission.

It follows that the only way in which dehydration can be prevented during exercise is to replace both the sodium and the water lost through sweat as these losses develop (Carter & Gisolfi, 1989; Ryan et al., 1989). Runners are not at risk of developing deficiencies of either magnesium or potassium during exercise, thus neither need to be replaced.

More important is the fuel content of the fluid. Chapter 3 explained that athletes must ingest carbohydrate during prolonged exercise at up to 75% $\dot{V}O_2$max lasting more than 4 hours. To choose the most appropriate type of carbohydrate, we need to look more closely at factors that determine the rate at which fluid leaves the stomach (gastric emptying) and can be absorbed into blood from the intestine (gastrointestinal absorption).

Table 3.1 lists some of the factors that influence the rate of gastric emptying. Costill and Saltin (1974) first studied these factors in detail, and the results of their experiments are depicted in Figure 4.4, a to d.

These authors found that up to an exercise intensity of 60% $\dot{V}O_2$max (Figure 4.4a), the rate of gastric emptying is about 750 ml/hr with a 2.5% glucose solution, but thereafter the rate falls steeply and is only about 320 ml/hr at an exercise intensity of 90% $\dot{V}O_2$max.

Gastric emptying falls with increasing temperature (Figure 4.4b) of the ingested fluid and is only 350 ml/hr at a temperature of 40 °C, whereas emptying is almost 900 ml/hr at 5 °C.

The rate of gastric emptying falls with increasing glucose content (Figure 4.4c) of the ingested fluid and is about 100 ml/hr at a glucose concentration of 10 g per 100 ml (10%). Also shown on this graph are the gastric emptying rates of

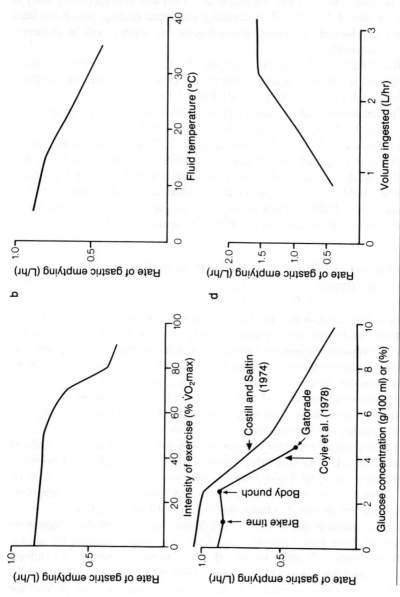

Figure 4.4 The effects of exercise intensity (a), fluid temperature (b), glucose concentration (c), and ingested volume (d) on the rate of gastric emptying.

Note. From "Factors Limiting Gastric Emptying During Rest and Exercise" by D.L. Costill and B. Saltin, 1974, *Journal of Applied Physiology*, **37**, p. 681. Copyright 1982 by American Physiological Society. Adapted by permission.

three drinks—Brake Time, Body Punch, and Gatorade—studied by Coyle et al. (1978).

The amount of liquid emptied by the stomach increases with increasing volume ingested (Figure 4.4d) and was maximum in Costill and Saltin's (1974) study at an ingestion rate of 2.4 L/hr. This critically important finding, which has been completely overlooked by exercise physiologists and athletes, will be discussed in detail subsequently.

Costill and Saltin (1974) did not study the effects of increasing the osmolality of the ingested solution by adding electrolytes. However, hypertonic solutions are known to delay gastric emptying (see Table 3.1).

More recent studies indicate that many additional factors influence the rate of gastric emptying. Both dehydration (Neufer et al., 1989a) and severe environmental conditions (>35 °C dry bulb temperature, 20% relative humidity; Neufer et al., 1989a) impair gastric emptying, but running at exercise intensities less than 75% $\dot{V}O_2$max is associated with increased rates of gastric emptying (Neufer et al., 1986, 1989b). Training appears not to influence the rate of gastric emptying (Rehrer et al., 1989a), which is also the same during cycling and running at the same exercise intensities (Neufer, 1989b; Rehrer et al., 1990).

Intestinal Absorption and Muscle Uptake of Carbohydrate

Most researchers assume that the rate at which the energy contained in the ingested drink reaches the muscle where it will be utilized is determined by the rate at which the solution empties from the stomach. But this ignores the obvious anatomical consideration that once past the stomach, the solution must still be absorbed from the intestines into the bloodstream, where its glucose content is taken up by the muscles and used as a fuel for oxidative metabolism.

Thus any of these four processes—gastric emptying, intestinal absorption, muscle glucose uptake, or oxidation—could be the real factors limiting the rate at which carbohydrate provided exogenously by mouth can actually be utilized by the active muscles. Accordingly, solutions that empty rapidly from the stomach might not produce the highest rates of fuel provision to, and fuel utilization by, the active muscles if the factors controlling the rates of gastric emptying (intestinal absorption, muscle glucose uptake, and utilization) differ.

At present, exercise physiologists have fastidiously ignored this problem so that we do not know for certain which of these processes determines the rates at which the muscles can oxidize exogenously supplied fuels. Studies in the University of Cape Town laboratory (Hawley et al., 1991; Moodley et al., 1991) suggest that the limiting factors do indeed lie distal to the stomach so that, at least for ingested carbohydrate, the rate at which the exercising muscles oxidize the ingested carbohydrate is *less* than the rate at which the ingested carbohydrate leaves the stomach. This suggests that the optimum solution for ingestion during prolonged exercise cannot be chosen purely from knowledge of the gastric emptying characteristics of different solutions, as these same characteristics will also influence rates of intestinal absorption and muscle carbohydrate uptake and utilization.

The factors that influence the rate at which water, electrolytes, and energy fuels are absorbed in the intestine—the rate of intestinal absorption—are relatively well understood. In brief, when a solution enters the intestine it is rendered isotonic by the addition of either body water or electrolytes, which move from the cells or surrounding extracellular space into the intestine. Thus an ingested hypotonic solution is rendered isotonic in the intestine by the addition of body electrolytes; an ingested hypertonic solution is made isotonic by the addition of body water (Leiper & Maughan, 1988). The result is that water absorption is fastest from an ingested solution that is hypotonic, whereas electrolytes are absorbed most rapidly from ingested hypertonic solutions.

The picture is rather complicated because glucose, sodium, and chloride are absorbed from the intestine in equal amounts, and each interacts to accelerate the absorption of the others (Schedl & Clifton, 1963). Thus an increased sodium chloride content will expedite the rate at which the carbohydrate is absorbed from that solution and vice versa; the sodium concentration that optimizes carbohydrate absorption is about 90 to 120 mmol/L, while the optimum osmolality to achieve the same effect is believed to be in the range of 200 to 250 mmol/kg (Leiper & Maughan, 1986).

The rate of intestinal absorption of carbohydrate is more rapid from glucose polymer than from glucose solutions (B.J.M. Jones et al., 1983, 1987), but the influence of glucose polymers on the rates of electrolyte and water absorption are not known (Leiper & Maughan, 1988). Presumably glucose polymers would expedite both.

Finally, those factors in the ingested solution that influence the rate at which the active muscles take up and oxidize the ingested carbohydrate during exercise are not particularly well known.

The fate of the ingested carbohydrate is the same whether it is taken 3 hours before (Jandrain et al., 1984) or 15 or 120 minutes after the start of exercise (Krzentowski et al., 1984; see Figure 4.5). The ingested carbohydrate is burned by the muscles in place of blood glucose derived from the liver. The rate of combustion of the ingested carbohydrate increases with increasing exercise intensity (Pirnay et al., 1982) and the amount ingested (Pallikarakis et al., 1986). When ingested as a 25% solution at a rate of 100 g/hr during 4-3/4 hours of exercise at 45% $\dot{V}O_2max$, ingested glucose was combusted at a rate of 70 g/hr, thereby providing between 85 and 90% of the total carbohydrate expenditure during the latter phase of exercise (Pallikarakais et al., 1986).

Massicotte et al. (1986) have shown that ingested glucose is oxidized more rapidly than ingested fructose. They found that 75% of a glucose load ingested during 3 hours of exercise was metabolized, but only 56% of an equivalent

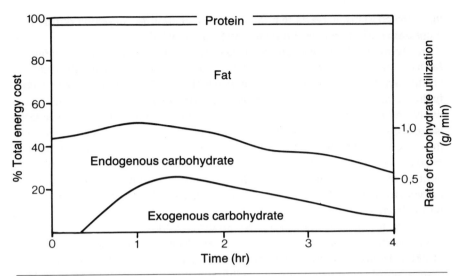

Figure 4.5 Carbohydrate ingested during or prior to exercise (exogenous carbohydrate) is utilized by the muscles as an energy fuel in place of (blood) glucose derived from the liver (endogenous carbohydrate).

Note. From "Effect of Glucose Ingestion on Energy Substrate Utilization During Prolonged Muscular Exercise" by F. Pirnay, M. Lacroix, F. Mosora, A. Luyckx, and P. Lefebvre, 1977, *European Journal of Applied Physiology*, **36**, p. 250. Copyright 1977 by Springer-Verlag Heidelberg. Adapted by permission.

fructose load was utilized as fuel during the same period of exercise. Furthermore, whereas glucose was being used as a fuel within 20 minutes of ingestion, ingested fructose first contributed to energy metabolism 40 minutes after ingestion. The authors concluded that ingested fructose is less available for muscle metabolism than is glucose, because the fructose must first be converted to glucose in the liver before it can be oxidized by muscle, and the activity of this metabolic pathway in the liver is low. The intestinal absorption of fructose is also slower than that of glucose. Thus fructose ingestion is not more beneficial than glucose ingestion during prolonged exercise. Two additional studies (Guezennec et al., 1989; Massicotte et al., 1989) have confirmed these results. Fructose solutions also are more likely to cause gastrointestinal distress during exercise than are equivalent glucose or sucrose solutions (R. Murray et al., 1989).

Studies have also found that the more carbohydrate delivered to the intestine, the faster the rate at which the active muscles can utilize that carbohydrate. Moodley et al. (1991) found that glucose polymer solutions were more rapidly oxidized than were equivalent glucose or sucrose solutions, whereas Hawley et al., (1991) showed that starch was the most rapidly oxidized of all the carbohydrates. Others have not found this effect, possibly because they studied glucose polymers at low concentrations (Massicotte et al., 1989) or only when solutions were ingested before exercise (Guezennec et al., 1989).

In summary, the problem in determining the optimum carbohydrate solution for ingestion during exercise is that the very factors which expedite the intestinal absorption of the carbohydrate present in a solution, especially increased electrolyte and carbohydrate content, are also the factors which may *retard* the rate at which the solution empties from the stomach (Table 3.1). The only exceptions are glucose polymer and starch solutions, which empty either at the same rate or more rapidly from the stomach than do equivalent glucose solutions (Sole & Noakes, 1989) and are also more rapidly absorbed from the intestine. Either or both of these facts could explain why the rate of muscle glucose oxidation is greatest from glucose polymer and starch solutions (Hawley et al., 1991; Moodley et al., 1991).

Before deciding how all these factors influence the choice of the drink for ingestion during exercise, we will first consider the evidence that shows that the drinking pattern adopted during exercise, rather than the electrolyte and carbohydrate content of the ingested fluid, is the primary factor determining the rate of carbohydrate utilization by muscle.

Drinking Patterns and Rates of Carbohydrate and Fluid Delivery

Figure 4.4c suggests that increasing the carbohydrate content of the ingested solution beyond about 6% begins to have a rather marked effect on the rate of gastric emptying.

Costill and Saltin's (1974) studies were performed in subjects who ingested the solutions only once, and the rate of gastric emptying was averaged over the sampling period, which was usually about 20 minutes. However, more recent studies show that this is an inaccurate method for determining the rate of gastric emptying. Furthermore, during competition athletes ingest fluid repeatedly, and the effect of repeated bouts of fluid ingestion needs to be considered.

These more recent studies have found that if the solutions are ingested *repeatedly* during exercise, so that the stomach is kept in a more distended state during exercise, then higher rates of gastric emptying can be achieved, as predicted by Costill and Saltin (1974; Figure 4.4d). Thus, differences in the rates of gastric emptying between water and solutions with quite high carbohydrate and electrolyte content are minimized when both solutions are ingested repeatedly during prolonged exercise (Davis et al., 1987; J.B. Mitchell et al., 1988, 1989, 1991; Owen et al., 1986; Ryan et al., 1989).

Indeed, for practical purposes, the rates of gastric emptying for water and for carbohydrate solutions at concentrations up to 10% are essentially the same at rest and even during exercise at up to 70% $\dot{V}O_2$max (J.B. Mitchell et al., 1989,

1991; Rehrer et al., 1989a; Sole & Noakes, 1989). However, higher carbohydrate concentrations (>15%) empty significantly slower than does water both at rest (Rehrer et al., 1989a; Sole & Noakes, 1989) and during exercise (Davidson et al., 1988; Davis et al., 1987; Moodley et al., 1991; Rehrer et al., 1989a). However, the rate of carbohydrate delivery to the intestine from these more concentrated drinks *increases* with increasing carbohydrate content even up to 18% carbohydrate solutions (Davidson et al., 1988; J.B. Mitchell et al., 1989, 1991; Moodley et al., 1991; Rehrer et al., 1989a; Sole & Noakes, 1989). Higher concentrations have not been studied, but there is no reason to believe that the rate of carbohydrate delivery would not continue to rise with further increases in the carbohydrate concentration of the ingested solution.

The reason that frequent drinking effects the rate of gastric emptying can be inferred from the detailed studies of Rehrer et al. (1989a). The critical finding in these studies was that the rate of gastric emptying for any solution is a logarithmic function of the amount of fluid present in the stomach at that time; in essence this means that during any equivalent time period, a constant percentage of the drink that was present in the stomach at the start of that period would have been emptied. They found that approximately 65% of a water solution, 50% of an isotonic 7% carbohydrate solution, and 25% of a 15% glucose or 18% glucose polymer solution would be emptied during successive 10-minute time periods when exercising at approximately 70% $\dot{V}O_2$max.

This information has been used to construct Figure 4.6, which shows the volume of fluid remaining in the stomach at successive 10-minute intervals after the initial ingestion (at Time 0) of 400 ml of water and a 7% or 18% glucose polymer solution. Figure 4.6 shows that the most important factor determining the rate of gastric emptying is the volume of the solution in the stomach and not its carbohydrate content.

For example, the rate of gastric emptying of the 18% carbohydrate solution between 0 and 10 minutes is 100 ml per 10 minutes, which exceeds the rate of emptying of water at all times after 10 minutes (<92 ml per 10 minutes) and of the 7% glucose polymer solution at all times after 20 minutes (<50 ml per 10 minutes).

Figure 4.7 uses this information to show the hypothetical effects of two different drinking patterns on carbohydrate and water delivery during exercise. Figure 4.7a shows a practical drinking pattern for an athlete who is able to run with a stomach containing 800 ml of fluid; Figure 4.7b depicts the drinking pattern of an athlete who can tolerate a stomach volume of only 400 ml. This drinking pattern is actually not the optimum but is one that can be applied practically at least while running races. The optimum method, which could be used by cyclists and canoeists who carry their fluids with them, would be to drink fluid continuously at a rate exactly equaling the rate of gastric emptying, thereby maintaining a constant gastric volume and maximizing the rate of gastric emptying.

Using the more practical approach of drinking at regular intervals, both runners would fill their stomachs to capacity immediately prior to exercise. Every

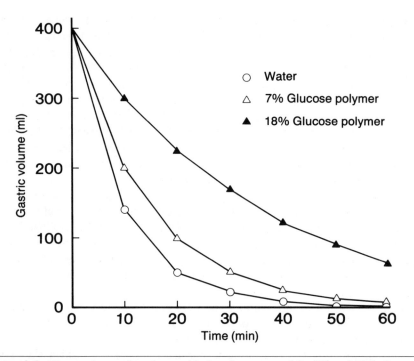

Figure 4.6 Changes in gastric volume with time for water and for 7% and 18% glucose polymer solutions.
Note. From T.D. Noakes, N.J. Rehrer, and R.J. Maughan, "The Importance of Volume in Regulating Gastric Emptying," *Medicine and Science in Sports and Exercise*, **23**(3), 1991, © by American College of Sports Medicine. Adapted by permission.

10 minutes thereafter, each would again drink sufficiently to replace the volume of the solution that had emptied during that 10-minute period, thereby refilling the stomach to the individual maximum tolerable gastric volume. The volumes of fluid that each could ingest every subsequent 10 minutes would obviously depend on the carbohydrate content of the ingested solution and would be 65% of the initial volume of water ingested (520 or 260 ml), 50% of the 7% isotonic carbohydrate solution (400 or 200 ml), or 25% of the 18% glucose polymer solution (200 or 100 ml). At the completion of exercise, total fluid delivery from the three solutions during 1 hour would have been 3120, 2400, and 1200 ml respectively for the athlete able to maintain a gastric volume of 800 ml (Figure 4.7a) and half that (1560, 1200, and 600 ml) for the athlete able to maintain a gastric volume of only 400 ml during exercise (Figure 4.7b). The respective rates of carbohydrate delivery for these drinking patterns would be 0, 108, and 216 g/hr (Figure 4.7a) and 0, 54, and 108 g/hr (Figure 4.7b).

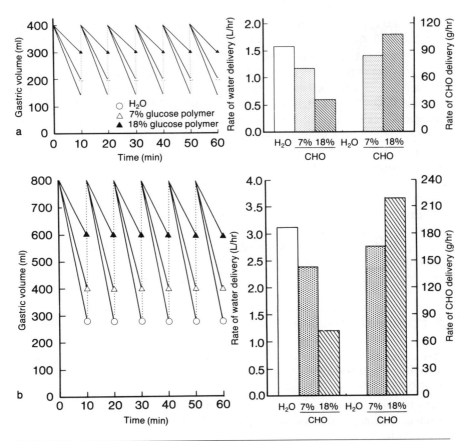

Figure 4.7 Changes in gastric volume with time and rates of water and carbohydrate delivery from two different drinking patterns for water and for 7% and 18% glucose polymer solutions. In the top graphs, the athlete maintains a gastric volume of 400 ml every 10 minutes; in the lower graphs, a volume of 800 ml every 10 minutes. The figure shows that it is possible to provide high rates of water and carbohydrate delivery even from solutions with high carbohydrate contents.

Note. From T.D. Noakes, N.J. Rehrer, and R.J. Maughan, "The Importance of Volume in Regulating Gastric Emptying," *Medicine and Science in Sports and Exercise,* **23**(3), 1991, © by American College of Sports Medicine. Adapted by permission.

The general accuracy of these predictions is indeed confirmed by the results of two recent studies. Ryan et al. (1989) reported a rate of gastric emptying in excess of 1 L/hr in subjects who drank 5% glucose, glucose polymer, or glucose polymer/fructose solutions at rates of 350 ml every 20 minutes, similar to the drinking pattern proposed in Figure 4.7b. In contrast, a rate of gastric emptying of only 460 ml/hr for a similar (6%) carbohydrate solution was reported by J.B. Mitchell et al. (1989) in subjects who ingested only 150 ml every 15 minutes.

These calculations demonstrate two very important points. First, it is theoretically possible to ingest very large volumes of fluid during exercise if one drinks frequently and maintains a large gastric volume. This would explain why it is possible to develop water intoxication (hyponatremia) during exercise. Second, different drinking patterns can produce the same rates of carbohydrate delivery during exercise from solutions with quite different carbohydrate concentrations (compare total carbohydrate delivery from the 7% carbohydrate solution in Figure 4.7a with the 18% carbohydrate solution in Figure 4.7b).

In summary, the critical practical relevance of this finding is that the maximum rate at which the carbohydrate and water content of an ingested solution can be delivered to the intestine is determined solely by the average volume of fluid the athlete will allow to have in his or her stomach during exercise. The greater the degree of gastric distension the athlete maintains during exercise, the more carbohydrate and water that will be delivered to the intestine regardless of the carbohydrate content of the ingested solution (Noakes et al., 1991b).

A Proposed Solution

This argument has shown that the fluid requirement for most runners during exercise is about 500 ml/hr. Thus the key in developing the optimum replacement fluid for ingestion during exercise is to develop a drinking pattern that will provide optimum carbohydrate replacement at a gastric emptying rate of 500 ml/hr without causing gastric distress by forcing the athlete to maintain a very large gastric volume.

The proposal outlined in Figure 4.7 shows that even an 18% carbohydrate solution ingested at a rate of 100 ml every 10 minutes in an athlete prepared to maintain a gastric volume of 400 ml would provide a gastric emptying rate in excess of 600 ml/hr. The same athlete could achieve the same results from a 7% carbohydrate solution if he or she also ingested 100 ml every 10 minutes and maintained a gastric volume of only 200 ml. The latter is probably the more usual drinking pattern chosen by most athletes during competition.

Thus, it is clear that many different carbohydrate concentrations ingested in different ways could provide the required fluid replacement of 500 ml/hr but would provide quite different rates of carbohydrate delivery.

The rate of carbohydrate delivery, rather than the rate of water delivery, may really be the more important factor to consider (Noakes et al., 1990b).

The ingestion of carbohydrate during prolonged exercise delays fatigue and enhances performance (Coggan & Coyle, 1987, 1988, 1989; Coyle et al., 1983, 1986a; Ivy et al., 1983; W.M. Sherman et al., 1989) probably by delaying the onset of liver glycogen depletion and therefore hypoglycemia. This has been most clearly shown in the recent studies of Coyle et al. (1986a) and Coggan and Coyle (1987, 1988, 1989).

In their first significant study, these authors (Coyle et al., 1986a) compared the blood glucose concentrations and the rates of carbohydrate oxidation and muscle glycogen utilization in cyclists who ingested either a placebo (no carbohydrate) or a glucose polymer solution (approximately 400 g in 4 hours) during prolonged exercise.

They found that glucose polymer ingestion improved endurance performance by preventing hypoglycemia and maintaining a high rate of carbohydrate oxidation (Figure 4.8). Interestingly, carbohydrate ingestion did not reduce the rate of muscle glycogen utilization, as also found in runners during marathon and short ultramarathon races (Noakes et al., 1988b). Their subsequent work (Coggan & Coyle, 1988) has shown that glucose infused at a rate in excess of 1 g/min, beginning at the point of exhaustion, can prolong performance. Carbohydrate ingestion at the point of exhaustion was less effective probably because the rate of delivery from the intestine was unable to match the high rate of oxidation (Coggan & Coyle, 1987). Exercise performance was even enhanced if the carbohydrate was ingested late in exercise but prior to the onset of exhaustion (Coggan & Coyle, 1989). The authors suggested there might be no benefit of ingesting carbohydrate throughout prolonged exercise. Ingesting a high carbohydrate load 30 or more minutes before the time at which exhaustion is expected to occur might have the same effect. It is still too early, however, to accept this possibility unconditionally.

These studies suggest that the rate of carbohydrate oxidation of about 1 gm/min is required to support prolonged exercise at the point of exhaustion. Researchers have found (Moodley et al., 1991) that at an exercise intensity of 70% of $\dot{V}O_2$max, about 50% of the carbohydrate delivered to the intestine from glucose polymer solutions is oxidized by the muscle; therefore, the rate of carbohydrate delivery to the intestine from the stomach would need to be about 120 g/hr. As shown in Figure 4.7, the only realistic way to achieve this would be to ingest 600 ml/hr of an 18% carbohydrate solution and to maintain a gastric volume of 400 ml.

Whether such a concentrated carbohydrate drink should be ingested for the entire duration of exercise is not known. Perhaps a less concentrated drink could be ingested initially and the more concentrated solution saved for the final third or final quarter of an endurance race when the rate of exogenous carbohydrate oxidation becomes the vital factor determining performance.

The ingested solution should probably be hypotonic (200 to 250 mmol/kg) with a sodium chloride content of up to 100 mmol/L in order to optimize intestinal absorption of carbohydrate and water. However, these proposals are based on the results of studies performed at rest. They need to be confirmed by studies performed during exercise, because intestinal water and electrolyte absorption may be altered during exercise (Barclay & Turnberg, 1988).

The hypotonic solution will, however, ensure high rates of gastric emptying (Rehrer et al., 1989a). The carbohydrate should be a glucose polymer, but the optimum chain length of the polymer has still to be determined (Moodley et al., 1991). Recent evidence suggests that, in theory at least, soluble starch may be

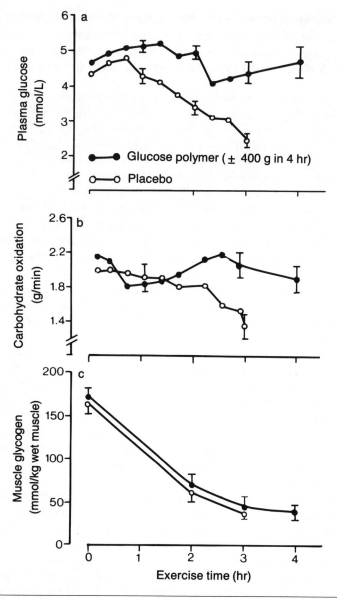

Figure 4.8 Effects of carbohydrate ingestion on plasma glucose levels (a) and on the rates of carbohydrate oxidation (b) and muscle glycogen utilization (c) during prolonged exercise at 70% V̇O₂max.

Note. From "Muscle Glycogen Utilization During Prolonged Strenuous Exercise When Fed Carbohydrate" by E.F. Coyle, A.R. Coggan, M.K. Hemmert, and J.L. Ivy, 1986, *Journal of Applied Physiology,* **61,** p. 167. Copyright 1986 by the American Physiological Society. Adapted by permission.

the best because it produces the fastest rates of muscle carbohydrate oxidation (Hawley et al., 1991).

Other Energy Sources

Other studies have shown that the ingestion of glycerol (Gleeson et al., 1986; J.M. Miller et al., 1983) or medium- or long-chain fatty acids (Ivy et al., 1980) during exercise is of no benefit, whereas the ingestion of alcohol is contraindicated because it impairs liver glucose production thereby increasing the risk that hypolgycemia will develop during prolonged exercise. Furthermore, alcohol per se cannot be utilized directly by muscle as a fuel; it must first be changed to acetaldehyde in the liver. Even then, acetaldehyde is a very inferior fuel, not nearly as effective as glucose, lactate, or free fatty acids. One study suggests that the ingestion of high-fat foods (e.g., almonds) delays the onset of the subjective feelings of fatigue during prolonged, low-intensity exercise (Arieli et al., 1985). Medium-chain triglycerides are oxidized during exercise but to a lesser extent than glucose (Satabin et al., 1987).

Part II

Training

Training

5

Contribution of Arthur Newton

"If any psychologist will take the trouble to trace out the history of each of our prominent pedestrians he will discover that a very large proportion of them have been subject to some form of madness."

Quoted by Sir Adolphe Abrahams (1961)

"Perhaps the greatest debt of all is owed to the late Arthur Newton, who, more than any other man, showed the way to success by daily and hard training, in season and out."

Percy Wells Cerutty (1964)

"Arthur Newton was at the same time a very strange and remarkable man, and perhaps no one has ever or will ever really understand him—but he may just have been, in his own way, the greatest runner ever seen.

"He was a strange man because he remained aloof even from his closest associates, and yet, if one thing stands out above all others, it must be the honesty and trust of the man, the sheer goodness—it shows out in any photograph."

Ron Clarke and Norman Harris (1967)

"Arthur Newton was the finest gentleman I have ever met in athletics. Although one of the greatest distance runners of all time he was totally modest and portrayed everything that is good in human nature. He was a totally honest man, and he was so

> *uncomplicated that he made everything he dis-*
> *cussed on life appear so simple. A more honest man*
> *never donned a pair of running shoes."*
>
> John Tarrant (1979)

> *"Hitherto we have been taught to believe that present-*
> *day methods were all that could be desired, but the*
> *sooner we question this and discover something in*
> *advance, the better for all of us."*
>
> Arthur Newton (1949)

After 15 years as a self-coached runner I have learned this truth: To be coach/ manager/runner on your own one-person running team is to invite disaster. Sadly I suspect that most of us runners have no option but to go it alone—to perpetuate an annual cycle of disaster and to repeat the same idiotic training and coaching errors each new running year.

Our problem is that running is not a sport for coaches. Sanity prevents even the most community-minded enthusiast from monitoring our training schedules during the strange hours and in the distant places we perfect our ritual.

And those potential coaches whose outlooks are less philanthropic provide even less cause for enthusiasm. For it takes neither a trained eye nor even a glance at last year's racing form to know that from among my friends and especially in me, no coach will ever uncover a potential world champion.

So we runners are left to our own devices. But we soon discover that those very characteristics that attract us to this unsophisticated, uncomplicated, intellectual sport are the very factors that hamper our success as complete, one-person running teams.

For those distracted runners who, like me, suffer perpetually from chronic indecision and malignant forgetfulness, each day's training poses mental challenges far beyond their limited cerebral resources. So we can seldom reach final decisions on exactly how we should train each day, what we should wear, when and where we should run, what we should eat, and how often we should race each year.

But occasionally there are self-coached runners who can identify, interpret, and correct their own errors. Among the first was the remarkable Arthur "Greatheart" Newton, whose competitive career spanned 13 years, from May 1922 to June 1935. During that time he won five of the six 90-km Comrades Marathons that he entered and also set the "up" and "down" records. (The

Comrades Marathon is run annually in opposite directions. The "up" from Durban climbs 2000 ft to Pietermaritzburg; the "down" run to Durban falls the same amount. The record for the "down" run is usually 5 to 10 minutes quicker than the "up" run.) He held the 86-km London-to-Brighton record; the world 30-, 35-, 40-, 45-, 50-, 60-, and 100-mile records; and the world 24-hour running record, covering 102,735 miles in training (Newton, 1935; see Table 5.1). In an era when it was usual for top athletes to train 30 miles a week (with the possible exception of the American marathoner Clarence de Mar; see chapter 8), Newton ran as much as 30 miles a day, 7 days a week.

In his day, Newton was described variously as "the most phenomenal distance runner the world has ever known" (Newton, 1935, p. 5); "one of the marvels of all time" by *London Observer*; and "the greatest runner ever seen" (Clarke & Harris, 1967, p. 76).

Probably the greatest tribute paid to Newton was the retrospective award of the Helms Trophy for "outstanding sportsman on the African Continent in 1925." This is the only occasion on which the Helms trophy, first awarded in 1936, was awarded retrospectively.

Although Newton had belonged to an athletic club in England, where he was born, and had run races of up to 25 miles (40 km), it was only after he moved to South Africa that he became seriously committed to long-distance running. Andy Milroy (1987) found evidence to show that Newton finished fourth with a time of 1:31:00 in a 20-km race in Howick, Natal, on February 1, 1908, and ran 16 km with a time of 1:01:30.4 in December 1910 on the Scottsville race course in Pietermaritzburg.

But his return to competitive running 12 years later was instigated by various governmental actions and omissions that caused Newton to suffer serious financial losses and ultimately led to his bankruptcy. To draw national attention to his predicament, Newton decided that "genuine amateur athletics were about as wholesome as anything on earth; any man who made a really notable name at such would always be given a hearing by the public" (Newton, 1940, p. 20).

On January 1, 1922, the 38-year-old Newton restarted his running career with a run of 2 miles including a "longish" stop halfway. For the next 2 days he was so "abominably stiff" that he was unable to run but walked instead. After 5 days of recovery he was able to run 4 miles. But Newton was not satisfied by this improvement. "Instead of using what common-sense I possessed, I did what the text-books recommended: make the stop-watch your master and try to improve your times slightly every day" (Newton, 1940, p. 29). Newton eventually decided to stick to common sense; he started training more slowly and ran the first 10-mile race of his new career 5 weeks later.

On May 24, 1922, just 20 weeks after starting his second running career, Newton lined up at the start of the second-ever Comrades Marathon, which was run from Durban to Pietermaritzburg. Newton started that race slowly, moving into second place at the top of the Inchanga Bank (see Figure 5.1). Just before

Table 5.1 Arthur Newton's Comrades Training and Racing Record

Year	Age	Comrades direction	Comrades time (hr:min:s)	Position	Total training distance (January–May) (km)	Monthly distances (January–May) (km)	Total distances from June–January previous year (km)
1925	42	down	6:24:54	1	3,592	(752; 815; 791; 902; 322)	3,988
1927	44	down	6:40:56	1	4,288	(890; 811; 1,043; 886; 658)	5,830
1923	40	down	6:56:07	1	4,760	(847; 968; 1,269; 1,035; 641)	3,446
1924	41	up	6:58:22	1	4,321	(763; 1,074; 1,006; 766; 712)	7,283
1926	43	up	7:02:00	2	3,962	(832; 678; 816; 850; 786)	2,766
1922	39	up	8:40:00	1	1,535	(143; 145; 306; 386; 506)	0

Note. Notice that Newton ran his best race in 1925 on his second-lowest total training distance leading into the race. The Comrades Marathon is run annually in opposite directions: one year "up" to Pietermaritzburg, the next year "down" to Durban, which sits 2,000 feet lower than Pietermaritzburg. From Newton (1925).

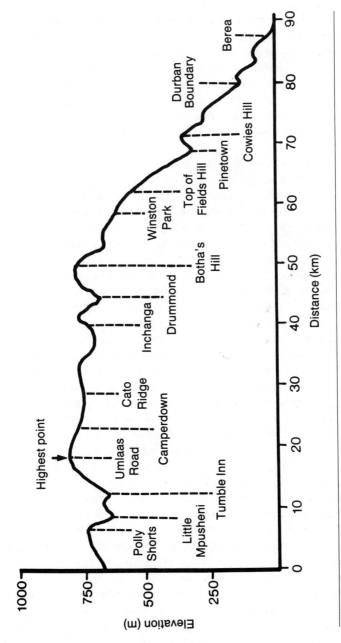

Figure 5.1 Outline of the Comrades Marathon course.

Camperdown, Newton wrested the lead from Purcell of Greytown and continued on to win the race in 8:40:00.

The following year (1923) Newton lined up for his second Comrades Marathon. This time he was more properly prepared; in the 12 months since his last race he had covered a staggering 6,610 miles in training—5,096 miles of running and 1,524 miles of walking. His training methods began to evolve: He aimed to run 100 miles in 6 days of training per week (see Table 5.1).

On this second attempt Newton won by 52 minutes, finishing in 6:56:07 and beating the old record by 2 hours and 3 minutes. His achievement was so unexpected that it was only by chance that two race officials reached the finish in time to record his finishing time on the nearest clock—the post office clock about 600 m away.

That single performance heralded the beginning of the modern training approach to distance running, which advocated year-round training of 2 or more hours per day for peak performance. Although by the 1940s Newton had described the essence of his training methods, it was really only the arrival of athletes like Zatopek and Peters (see chapter 8) in the 1950s and the training schools of Cerutty and Lydiard in the 1950s and 1960s that began to propagate widely the ideas Newton had discovered in the 1920s in Natal.

After his decisive victory in the 1923 Comrades Marathon, Newton decided to attempt the world 50-mile running record of 6:13:58, set by the Englishman Lloyd in 1913. A 50-mile out-and-back course on the Comrades route, beginning in Pietermaritzburg and therefore including Polly Shorts (see Figure 5.1) on the return journey, was measured out. Despite the uneven, dusty, and untarred road, Newton ran the distance in 5:53:05, thereby lowering the record by 20 minutes, a feat described as "impossible" by incredulous English road running officials.

In 1924, Newton again won the Comrades Marathon, this time by the large margin of 75 minutes, finishing in 6:58:22. To prove the credibility of his "impossible" 50-mile time, he traveled to England where he set a new London-to-Brighton record of 5:53:43, an improvement of 65 minutes on the old record (see Figure 5.2). En route, he set world records at 30, 35, 40, 45, and 50 miles. He also passed the 42-km standard marathon mark with a time that was 9 minutes faster than that of the first English finisher in the 1924 Olympic Games. The performance ensured that when the London-to-Brighton race was revived in 1951, the magnificent winner's trophy would bear Newton's name.

Newton's success continued with wins in the 1925 and 1927 Comrades Marathons and world records at 30, 40, 50, 60, and 100 miles. His 60-mile time of 7:33:55 and his 100-mile time of 14:43:00 represented improvements of 50 and 105 minutes on the respective former records.

In January 1928, Newton traveled to England where, on the Bath Road in snow and floods, he lowered his 100-mile record by another 21 minutes, to 14:22. In March 1928 he started in the professional Transcontinental Race, which was run in about 80 daily stages of between 30 and 75 miles each, from Los

Figure 5.2 Arthur Newton finishing his London-to-Brighton run in 1924.
Note. Photo courtesy of Vernon Jones.

Angeles to New York, for a prize of $25,000. A fictional story, *Flanagan's Run* (McNab, 1982), is based on that race, but those who wish to read a faithful record of what actually happened in the race should read *Running in Three Continents* (Newton, 1940). Newton also competed in the 1929 Transcontinental Race but retired after being struck by a car and fracturing his arm.

In 1930 and 1931, Newton teamed up with the Englishman Peter Gavuzzi for the two-person, 500-mile Distillers' Corporation Montreal-Quebec-Montreal International Snow Shoe Race in Canada, and on both occasions they won handsomely. Toward the end of 1931 Newton ran what was probably his greatest race—the 24-hour world record. This race, which cost Newton $1,000 to enter, was run on a tiny, indoor, square (to avoid giddiness) track that measured 13 laps to the mile and was located at the Arena in Hamilton, Ontario. Newton's final distance of 152 miles and 540 yards remained the world's best for 22 years until it was surpassed by another South African and Comrades Marathon legend, Wally Hayward (see chapter 8), who ran 159 miles 562 yards in 1953.

In 1933, Newton returned to the Bath Road in England where, despite Achilles tendinitis and the fact that he did not complete the full distance, his time of 7:15:30 at 60 miles was good enough for another world record.

In 1934 Newton chose to make a final attempt at the 100-mile record, again on the Bath Road. On July 20 of that year, the 51-year-old Newton completed his last race and successfully lowered his time to 14:06:00. Regrettably, it seems that Newton was disappointed with that run, because he wrote the following:

There was no good fighting shy of the fact as far as the ''hundred'' was concerned, I had completely failed to put up a reasonable time on the course, and I was too old to think of continuing for another year or two. (Newton, 1949, p. 45)

After his last 100-mile world record, Newton continued to run although no longer competitively. He lived in Middlesex, England, and busied himself by writing the four books that are his legacy (Newton, 1935, 1940, 1947, 1949).

As a person, and as a runner, Newton was entirely exceptional: His four books exemplify this. They carefully chronicle a training approach that I believe is the forerunner of the modern training approach to distance running, which came into use in the 1960s and 1970s. In particular, his ideas of year-round training, long-slow-distance training up to 160 km per week, specialization, racing infrequently, and mental preparation were innovative.

NEWTON'S 9 RULES OF TRAINING

Newton's books, written over a period of 12 years, cover the same topics in slightly different detail. There were nine aspects of training about which he frequently wrote: I call these *Newton's 9 Rules of Training* and have drawn them up in this section as a synthesis of material taken from the text of his four books (1935, 1940, 1947, 1949). With each rule, I provide an extract that paraphrases portions of these works.

Rule #1: Train Frequently Year-Round

First practice your event as often as possible, paying less attention to other activities. If you want to be a good athlete you must train all the year round, no matter what. What is really required is a little exercise constantly; this will benefit you permanently to a far greater degree than single heavy doses at long intervals.

This advice no longer sounds particularly remarkable, yet it certainly was for the amateur runners of Newton's era. When Newton started running in 1922, the great amateur distance runners of the day or of the immediate past were Walter George, Alf Shrubb, Hannes Kolehmainen, Paavo Nurmi, and Clarence de Mar (see chapter 8). Of these, only Clarence de Mar trained consistently all year round. Shrubb and probably Kolehmainen trained only 64 km (40 miles) a week and George no more than 2 miles a day (Krise & Squires, 1982; Lovesey, 1968).

Even Nurmi trained for only 5 months of the year (between April and September) and before 1924 seldom ran more than 10 km a day (see chapter 8).

The books about marathon training that Newton might have read were those by Thom (1813), Downer (1900), George (1902, 1908), Shrubb (1908, 1909), Andrews (1903), Hardwick (1912), Mussabini and Ransom (1913), and A. Nelson (1924). Shrubb's advice was the following:

> The principal item [for marathon training] is walking. Get out for a sixteen-mile walk three or four times a week, and walk at a four-and-a-half-miles-an-hour pace. On the other days, go eight miles only at about five miles an hour, saving one day for a sixteen-mile steady road run. (Shrubb, 1910, p. 64)

Shrubb suggested that this training program should be followed for 4 to 6 weeks. He recommended that for the last month before the race, the long run should be increased to 20 or even 25 miles and that this distance should be run either twice a week or 3 times every 2 weeks. Andrew's advice (1903) was similar, although he emphasized the need to run more distance:

> To train for long distances a great amount of walking must be done. . . . It is necessary to negotiate many miles both of walking and running at a stretch, the distance to be regulated according to the number of miles a man is training for. . . . At first long road-walks, fifteen, twenty or thirty miles a day, alternate with runs of a like distance on the track, but at the easiest of speeds. (pp. 72-73)

The advice of Alec Nelson (1924), who set the professional half-mile record in 1905 and who was coach to Cambridge University and the British Olympic Team, was very similar: "First of all, then, to build up the body and stamina it is necessary to specialize in long strong walks" (p. 75). He suggested that the athlete train in two sessions per week—one long walk and a run of gradually increasing distance. He added that "if the athlete feels that he is quite capable of turning out more frequently, additional runs of from 6 to 8 miles may be included" (p. 75). Nelson also provided a 16-week marathon training program that is reproduced in Table 5.2.

Only Thom (1813) and Downer (1900) refer to the more exacting training methods of the professional pedestrians (see chapter 8), whose approaches were more similar to Newton's.

Thus, Newton really broke new ground for amateur runners when he stated that training must continue year-round, that it must occur as frequently as possible, and that runs of 20 miles should be undertaken daily, not weekly. His subsequent contact with Walter George, who was a friend of the great pedestrian Charles Rowell (see chapter 8), likely exposed Newton to the training methods

Table 5.2   Alec Nelson's 16-Week Marathon Training Program

Week	Walking distance (km) (one session)	Running distance (km) (one session)	
1	24	8	
2	24	8	
3	24	8	
4	16	16	
5	16	24	
6	16	16	Training speed 4:04/km to 4:23/km
7	24	24	
8	16	41	
9	24	20	
10	16	48	
11	24	16	
12	16	16	
13	16	32[a]	
14	24	16	Training speed 3:45/km
15	16	24	
16	24	16	

Note. From Nelson (1924, pp. 75-76).

[a]Final trial

of the pedestrians. It is likely that Newton ultimately revised his ideas on the basis of that additional information (Milroy, 1987).

Rule #2: Start Gradually and Train Gently

Second, never practice anywhere near 'all out'. You ought never to get really breathless or to pant uncomfortably. So in running as in most athletics, it is essential to 'take to it kindly'.

My advice is this—train gently and gradually. Nearly all of us dash into it hoping for and expecting results which are quite unwarranted. Nature is unable to make a really first class job of anything if she is hustled. To enhance our best, we need only, and should only, enhance our average. That is the basis we ought to work on, for it succeeds every time when the other fails.

In this rule Newton proposed that the most effective training method was to run long distances at a comfortable pace (much slower than race pace) and not to race in training. In the 1960s this type of training was rediscovered and termed *long slow distance* (LSD) by the American Joe Henderson (1969, 1974, 1976, 1977).

The wisdom in Newton's idea that one should train at 20 to 25% below racing speed is borne out by the training methods of the modern distance exponents, who do most of their running at slower than race pace (see chapters 6 and 8) and who in practice sessions are never able to reproduce their racing performances over distances longer than about 21 km.

How the body is able to produce competitive performances that greatly exceed what is achieved in training is not known, but it must relate to the higher levels of mental stimulation achieved during racing. It is clear that this is a very real phenomenon that must be appreciated if the athlete is ever to achieve lasting success. A runner who repeatedly attempts to reproduce racing performances in training simply becomes overtrained (see chapter 10).

Rule #3: Train First for Distance (Only Later for Speed)

If you are going to contest a 26-mile event, you must at least be used to one hundred miles a week . . . As it is always the pace, never the distance, that kills, so is it the distance, not the speed, that has to be acquired. In the early days of training you must endeavour only to manage as great a distance on each practice outing as you can cover without becoming abnormally tired. Your business therefore is to develop your ordinary standard by continuous practice.

Your aim throughout, should be to avoid all maximum effort while you work with one purpose only; a definite and sustained rise in the average speed at which you practice, for that is the whole secret of ultimate achievement. This enables you to build up considerable reserves and to add continually to them. You must never, except for short temporary bursts, practice at racing speed; the most useful pace should be nine miles an hour up and down hills. The more hills you practise on the better for your ultimate form.

This is really a corollary to Newton's Rule #2, in which he warned against the dangers of excessive speed training. In Rule #3 he elaborated on his principal belief that the goal of training is to gradually increase the speed that can be maintained for long distances. And this, he believed, could only be achieved by training that emphasized distance, not speed. Interestingly, Alf Shrubb (1910) drew the same conclusion: "It is the distance and not the pace that is going to kill in the long-distance race" (p. 64).

Newton was the first to describe two components that are central to the training beliefs of the New Zealand running coach Arthur Lydiard: the 100-mile training week and the belief that humans already have sufficient speed and what they lack is endurance.

However, as we shall discuss later, Newton's advice that one should never undertake speed training applies only to beginning runners and to athletes who run for enjoyment and who are not concerned with improving their speeds. There is no doubt that the standard of competitive running has progressed enormously since Newton's day, and it would be unthinkable for a modern elite distance athlete to try to succeed in competition without attention to speed training. As we shall see when we discuss the training methods of Don Ritchie, Bruce Fordyce, and Eleanor Adams (see chapter 8), it is now clear that even ultradistance runners need speed training. Thus I have modified what Newton actually believed ("train only for distance") into this: Train first for distance, only later for speed.

Rule #4: Don't Set a Daily Schedule

Don't set yourself a daily schedule; it is far more sensible to run to a weekly one, because you can't tell what the temperature, the weather or your own condition will be on any day.

With this rule, Newton introduces the concept of "listening to your body," an idea subsequently popularized by George Sheehan (1972, 1975). Using this technique, runners monitor how they feel before and during runs and then adjust training on any day according to how they feel during each run. The practical application of this rule is described in more detail in chapters 6 and 10.

Rule #5: Don't Race When You Are in Training, and Run Time Trials and Races Longer Than 16 km Only Infrequently

I decry such things as time-trials. . . . I am convinced that they are nothing but a senseless waste of time and energy. They can't tell you any more than the race itself could.

I am convinced that it doesn't help in any way at any time to practice sheer speed. Actual racing and running or all-out exertion in any other form of sport should be confined solely to the competition for which you are training. Your business is to build up, not to break down. You will find the speed is there and doesn't need practice.

But by all means enter for a race now and then, but beyond making a good shot of it, leave time-trials and anything of that sort very much alone.

Racing, then, should be the only time-trials, and should be run only every two weeks—preferably three—apart . . . six weeks between events would be more suitable for a marathon man, once in two months is probably better.

Remember to "bank" your racing powers until you seriously require them, and you will then find that the interest is there as well as the capital when you start to draw on the account; there is no safer, saner or surer method of training.

Newton was strongly opposed to time trials and races other than the major event for which he was training. One must presume he was referring to time trials over marathon distances rather than over distances of 8 to 12 km, which seem essential for elite marathon and ultramarathon runners and probably for any experienced athletes wanting to improve their performances. However, I believe that all beginning runners should initially avoid time trials and should follow Newton's ideas about building endurance and not speed.

The accuracy of Newton's observation that a period of 6 to 8 weeks must separate longer distance races has only been proven in recent years. We now know that races longer than about 25 km produce quite marked muscle damage, which takes a considerable time to repair (see chapter 10), probably longer than Newton estimated.

Rule #6: Specialize

Specialization nowadays is a necessity. Modern exponents have raised the standards to such a height that nothing but intensive specialization can put a fellow anywhere near the top.

Before the 1914-1918 war, the marathon was considered an event for only the favoured few who had unusual toughness and stamina.

It takes anything from 18 months to 3 years to turn a novice into a first class athlete. You will have to drop the bulk of your present recreations and spend the time in training; anything from 2 to 3 hours a day will have to be set aside. Athletics must be your major engagement for at least two years on end, your business or means of making a livelihood being at all times of secondary importance.

To drop anything at any time during that period whether for a holiday or anything else is to throw overboard part of your hard-earned ability: the longer the holiday, the more serious your relapse.

The idea that only a special breed of person could run the marathon probably stems from Andrews (1903), who wrote the following:

It requires strength and a dogged determination to become a successful long-distance runner. . . . Every man will improve with training, but only those possessed of the above qualifications, and are also blessed with a strong stomach and sound digestive organs, should go in for long-distance work, as it is particularly trying to these parts of the constitution. (p. 71)

In this rule then, Newton suggested nothing less than making running a profession, a choice he personally made when he entered the 1928 Transcontinental Race.

Until recently, Newton's idea was quite contrary to prevailing thought, which was epitomized by Sir Roger Bannister (1955), who viewed sport as a diversion rather than a profession.

I believe . . . that running has proved to be a truly amateur activity after all, on which it is neither necessary nor desirable to spend unlimited time and energy. Fitting running into the rest of life until one's work becomes too demanding—this is the burden and joy of the true amateur. (p. 221)

Times have changed since Bannister wrote this, and what Newton foresaw more than half a century ago has materialized. (Today, of course, the top runners are professional in everything but name.)

For those of us whose talents are not in running and who will never break into the professional ranks, I like to think that this rule stresses the importance of specific training. For we now appreciate that training is absolutely specific and that we are fit only for what we train.

Most runners will have already experienced this. They will know that although they can run effortlessly for hours, they are quite unable to swim comfortably for even a few minutes. The reason for this is that running and swimming train different muscle groups. When the runner exercises his or her untrained upper body in swimming, for example, the body responds as if it were essentially untrained.

This distinction may be even more subtle within an activity. Beginning runners frequently find hill running difficult. This is because uphill running stresses, in particular, the quadriceps (Costill et al., 1974)—a muscle that is much less important during running on the flat and is therefore undertrained in persons who run exclusively on the flat.

Training specificity also involves training speed, hot-weather training, and altitude acclimatization. As discussed in chapter 1, the speed or intensity of training determines which muscle fibers will be active in the particular muscle groups that are being exercised. So, if you train only at slow speeds and then race at a faster pace, you may utilize muscle fibers during the race that are relatively untrained. Similarly, to race effectively in the heat or at altitude, you need to train under those specific conditions (see chapters 4 and 18).

In this context, it is interesting to note Newton's comment on the role of walking and cycling as additional training methods for long-distance running. Walking was much in vogue in the 1920s, and many popular walking races were held, including the London-to-Brighton Stock Exchange race, the predecessor of the London-to-Brighton running race. Shrubb (1910) and Andrews (1903) believed that walking should be the major component for long-distance training and that runners in training should run only once a week. Even Nurmi walked long distances. Yet Newton's attitude was clear: Walking is a waste of time. Long walks, even quick walks, do not help a person to run.

Given Newton's attitude, it is difficult to understand why he walked more than 47,000 km during his running career (see Table 5.2). His explanation was this:

> There was a definite purpose in this walking, viz., to make me used to being on my feet nearly all the time . . . though at a much later date I decided it might have been better to run, for running was my job not walking. (Newton, 1947, p. 64)

Ultimately he concluded, "The average young man would be better off if he left long walks until later on in life when strenuous exercise won't have so great an appeal" (Newton, 1949, p. 56).

In keeping with his ability to foresee trends in physical activity 50 years ahead of time, Newton also expressed some ideas about training for the triathlon (i.e., about the effects of cycling and swimming on running performance). He commented that walking, cycling, and swimming did not affect his running ability, but did serve to keep him thoroughly fit.

> I came to the conclusion that practically all sport should be taken on in moderation without any fear of spoiling you for your pet event, the only important point being that your specialized training must continue without serious interruption, all other exercise being treated as temporary "asides". (Newton, 1947, p. 65)

Rule #7: Don't Overtrain

> Perhaps one of the chief points is to regulate your training so as to be sure of always being on the safe side: the least trifle of overdose if persisted in, will surely lead to trouble of one sort or another. . . .
>
> Go so far every day that the last mile or two become almost a desperate effort. So long as you're fit for another dose the following day, you're not overdoing it. But you must never permit yourself to approach real exhaustion, you must never become badly tired.
>
> A good way to judge whether you are overdoing it is by your appetite. A really fearsome thirst is a definite sign that either the pace or the distance has been too much. Not only are you unbearably thirsty, but your appetite has entirely disappeared even for many hours after the event. Curiously enough, it is almost always the pace that is to blame.

Newton mentions only a few symptoms that the overtrained athlete will experience. Probably this is because Newton seldom, if ever, wore himself down by training too much and was thus unaware of the myriad of other symptoms that appear when the athlete trains too hard. Of course, Newton lived in an era when there were few races in which to run and few financial incentives to entice him to race too frequently.

Once again, Newton was 50 years ahead of scientists in his observation that increased thirst is an early indicator of overtraining. Richard Brown, exercise physiologist and former coach of the Athletics West Club in Eugene, Oregon, reported that one of the earliest indicators of overtraining is an increased fluid intake in the evening (R.L. Brown, 1983).

Chapter 10 contains a complete description of overtraining and offers guidelines for avoiding this syndrome.

Rule #8: Train the Mind

The longest and most strenuous mental and physical exertions all come at the start; get on with it at once and you will soon be through the worst. If you can stick it out for a few months, things will become altogether easier, because by that time, . . . your active mind will have handed over to the subconscious a whole series of almost interminable details in the form of habits; and what formerly necessitated a continual effort will then become more or less automatic. Stamina seems to me to be just as much a mental attribute as a physical one.

Make your mind healthy and it will do the rest. If it is not normally healthy, you will never make a decent job of anything. Success depends far more on what use you make of your head than on anything else.

The idea that the mind plays an important role in a sport such as running is not always appreciated, even today. Indeed, until very recently the entire running literature contained few contributions about the mental aspects of training; even reviews of how training methods have evolved over the years pay scant attention to mental preparation for running (Burfoot, 1981a). Chapter 7 is my attempt to correct this omission.

Rule #9: Rest Before the Race

You should cut out all racing of every description during the last month of your training; . . . you will need certainly three weeks to put the finishing touches to your stamina and reserve of energy. . . . When you consider what a vast amount of work you have already gone through you will admit that a fortnight or so longer is a relatively trifling matter.

Endeavour to keep all your spare time fully occupied with reading, writing, or anything that will keep you still—anything to divert your mind from harping on the forthcoming event.

It seems that no writer before Newton discussed the importance of resting before a major race (also called *tapering*). Certainly Alf Shrubb trained hard right up to the day of competition; 4 days before he set his 16-km and 1-hour world records, he ran a 16-km time trial in 50:55, just 15 seconds slower than his subsequent world record! Shrubb was successful even though he did not taper, probably because he was remarkably gifted, because he was not a heavy trainer, or because he did not race distances longer than 18 km. I believe that the harder the athlete trains and the longer the distances he or she races, the more vital the tapering process.

Other distance runners of the day were unaware of the importance of tapering. The day before the 1912 Stockholm Olympic Marathon, the South African who finished second in that race, Christian Gitsham, set out to run the complete marathon distance. Fortunately, his coach caught up with Gitsham after he had run 20 km and angrily returned him to his hotel. Eleven days before the 1920 Antwerp Olympic Marathon, the team of four United States runners ran the course in 2:46:55, a time they could barely repeat on race day (Temple, 1981).

One of the first authors to discuss the importance of resting before competition was Stampfl (1955), who insisted that his distance athletes rest for 4 full days before competition. But it was really Carlile (1963) who first emphasized the importance of tapering before competition. Incidentally, the term *tapering* was first coined by Carlile and Professor Frank Cotton in 1947.

Carlile and Cotton found that after 2 or 3 months of hard training, swimmers performed best if they eased their training for the last 3 weeks before major competition. At the end of the first week of tapering, the swimmers would complete a time trial. "A poor time generally indicates that the swimmer needs more rest" (Carlile, 1963, p. 33).

The 1962 European Swimming Championships proved the correctness of this approach. Before the championships, Carlile was appointed national coach to the Dutch swimming team, which had previously performed very poorly. Carlile's approach was to send each swimmer a document that warned of the dangers of hard training during the last 3 weeks before competition.

The swimmer who feels that he *must* be training very hard close to an important contest, as far as swimming knowledge is concerned, is still a child. . . . On occasions a week or more of complete rest, out of the water, should be taken even during the final preparation for a big event. . . .

. . . I give notice here to members of the Dutch National Team, that within a week or so of International contests, I shall be using the "rest principle" very much more than the "train hard" principle. My experience as coach has convinced me of the great importance of the "rest principle" in making peak performances. (Carlile, 1963, pp. 43-44)

At the championships, all members of the team swam their best times of the year, and all but two achieved personal bests as they "swept all before them," winning the Braedius Cup for European Swimming Supremacy (Carlile, 1963, p. 44). The studies of Costill and his colleagues (Costill, 1985; Costill et al., 1985), which confirm that swimmers perform best when they taper for at least a week before competition, are described in chapter 10.

Today runners are beginning to realize the importance of an adequate taper. Frederick (1983b) used the term "Zatopek phenomenon" to emphasize the importance of resting before competition. The author relates that Emil Zatopek (see chapter 8) was training very intensively for the 1950 European Games in Brussels when he became so ill that he required hospitalization for 2 weeks. He was released only 2 days before the 10,000-m race, which he won by a full lap, thanks to the enforced rest. A few days later, he won the 5,000-m race by 23 seconds.

Other famous examples exist. Dave Bedford (see Chapter 8) set the 10,000-m world track record in 1973 after injury kept his training to a minimum for some months. Toward the end of 1973, Derek Clayton (see chapter 8) ran a 2:12 marathon after one of his "easiest preparations" (Clayton, 1980). Four months later he failed to complete the 1974 Commonwealth Games Marathon due to injury. "I think," he later wrote, "there is a message here as I often thought I trained harder than necessary" (Clayton, 1980, p. 130). British marathoner Ron Hill reported essentially the same experience (see chapter 8).

APPLYING NEWTON'S RULES

Newton's rules accurately describe most of the major errors that runners make when they first start training or racing or when they become proficient racers and are tempted to race too frequently.

Let us summarize these errors. Beginning runners start too rapidly and train too hard; they emphasize speed rather than distance, religiously following rigid training schedules without listening to their bodies. Then, when they become racers they overtrain; they race in training and run time trials and races too frequently; they fail to train specifically; they do not rest sufficiently before races; and they ignore the importance of mental preparation for competition. Newton's ideas about these points laid the groundwork on which all subsequent training theories have evolved.

North American Pat Dengis, ignoring Newton's caution on burnout, was hospitalized and was seen as a "has-been." With initial reluctance, he followed Newton's training ideas and later credited them for his return to supremacy, which included running the world's fastest marathon in 1938 (2:30:28).

Ultradistance runners Wally Hayward and Jackie Mekler (see chapter 8) followed Newton's ideas and became world-record holders. In Australia, Percy Wells Cerutty embraced Newton's genius but argued that his training methods did not lead "to a full and proper development of the whole musculature" (Cerutty, 1964, p. 59). New Zealander Arthur Lydiard performed essentially the same training experiments on himself as had Newton 30 years previously and introduced Newtonian principles of overdistance training to his most famous protégé, Peter Snell; it seems likely that Lydiard knew of Newton's ideas and may well have read Newton's first book. The similarity of Lydiard's and Newton's beliefs regarding the 160-km training week, the need to emphasize endurance rather than speed training, and the dangers of racing too frequently suggest a common source.

Finally, the writings of Joe Henderson (1969, 1974, 1976, 1977), who discovered that repetitive time trials and interval training left him sore and disinterested, popularized the pattern of long-slow-distance training first described by Newton.

To claim that no progress in training methods has been made since Newton would be patently incorrect. It is now clear that Newton's training methods were suboptimum in four important areas.

First, Newton did not believe in specific speed training; he believed that the speed was always there and did not need to be developed. He thought that the runner who felt "extra good" at the end of a training run should give it a "full go" for a few miles. This approach is no longer effective in competitive running, at least for elite athletes at distances up to 90 km and longer.

Second, Newton appears to have trained very similarly each day. Today we believe that the intensity and duration of each day's training must be varied in order to achieve an optimum training effect.

Third, Newton did not alter his training prior to a race. Besides tapering, he did not specifically alter his training in the last 6 to 10 weeks before the race. Thus, it seems that he was unaware of the method of "peaking" for a race.

Fourth, Newton did not train with a coach. In this he really had no choice, because he certainly knew more about running than did anyone else. Today, to my knowledge, the majority of elite runners train under coaches, which suggests that they find this practice beneficial.

In the following section I have added four additional training rules to correct these four omissions in Newton's rules of training. I have also added two additional rules that Newton almost certainly followed, although he did not specifically mention them. Finally, I have revised Rule #3 to bring it into line with modern thinking, as explained next.

Since Newton's era, training has evolved considerably, with more emphasis placed on the need for speed training, or *speed work*. The first reference I have found to an athlete who regularly performed speed training was made by Shrubb (1910). At least twice a week, Shrubb ran at close to race pace for distances from 2 to 10 miles. Hannes Kolehmainen probably also performed speed training and has been credited as one of the first runners to practice speed play (also called *fartlek*), in which the athlete runs fast for varying distances, usually on the road or across country (Doherty, 1964). Kolehmainen also probably influenced the next great Finnish runner, Paavo Nurmi, to include speed work in his training. As described in chapter 8, Nurmi considered his early years of training less than optimum because he had not included sufficient speed training. He considered this to be the explanation why he remained a "slow trudger" until 1924, when he first included regular speed-training sessions.

Nurmi's principal method of speed training was interval repeats, first of 80 to 120 m and later of 400 to 600 m. This type of training was subsequently refined independently by the German team of physiologist Dr. Hans Reindell and coach and professor Woldemar Gerschler (Burfoot, 1981a; Doherty, 1964; Pirie, 1961) and by Franz Stampfl, British coach of Roger Bannister (Lenton, 1983a; Stampfl, 1955). Bannister used solely interval training to break the 4-minute mile barrier, and Zatopek also used this technique to achieve his unique greatness.

The wide acceptance of speed work indicates that it is effective and is essential for elite runners. But this should not detract from Newton's observation that the greatest performance improvements occur, at least initially, after the athlete has developed a strong endurance base through long-slow-distance training. I feel that speed work should be approached with extreme caution, preferably with the help of a knowledgeable coach.

With this evidence, I have (as mentioned previously) altered Rule #3 as follows: Train first for distance and only later for speed.

The First Additional Rule of Training: Alternate Hard and Easy Training Days

It is generally believed that Bill Bowerman and Bill Dellinger, the coaches behind the dynasty of great runners who have emerged from the University of Oregon at Eugene, were the first to teach that training should not always be of the same intensity and duration each day (Burfoot, 1981b). Bowerman and Dellinger observed that their runners progressed best only when they were allowed a suitable recovery period after each hard training session. For some runners, this period was only 24 hours; for others it was as long as 48 hours. This has been called the *hard-day/easy-day* training program. Kenny Moore, who trained under Bowerman and Dellinger (K. Moore, 1982) and who was one of the runners needing 48 hours of recovery, called his personal variation the *hard/easy/easier* training method (Galloway, 1983).

Dellinger claims that the hard-day/easy-day description of the Oregon training approach is incorrect.

> Strictly speaking, it's misleading to say that we follow a hard-day/easy-day pattern. Our kids run two workouts that I consider fairly hard, on Tuesday

and Saturday. On Thursday they might do a little quality work, but it's short and not very intense. (Burfoot, 1981b, p. 57)

Researchers have not established why the body is unable to train hard every day, but it is probably due to muscle damage of the same type (but less severe) as that caused by marathon racing (see chapter 10). Muscles damaged to this lesser degree require about 24 to 48 hours to recover fully, rather than the 6 to 8 weeks needed after a 42-km marathon.

Training is certainly not simply a matter of stoking up with fuel and repeating the previous day's training. You must learn that if the previous training session was hard, you must allow your body a period of recovery to restock its energy stores and to repair the microdamage caused by the previous day's heavy training, regardless of what your mind tells you or what you imagine your competitors are doing in training. Hard training when the body is not fully recovered simply compounds damage already done.

You must establish for yourself how frequently you can train hard; your success will, in large measure, depend on whether or not you achieve this balance. When training hard, I have found that three moderately hard sessions a week were optimum, but only for 6 to 8 weeks at a time.

The Second Additional Rule of Training: Incorporate Base Training and Peaking

This rule implies that peak racing performance occurs only when a period of high-intensity, low-volume training (*peaking*) follows a prolonged buildup period consisting of low-intensity, high-volume training (*base training*).

Franz Stampfl, the coach who had more to do with the first sub-4-minute mile than is generally acknowledged, was one of the first coaches to introduce the idea of base and peaking training (Stampfl, 1955). But unquestionably, the coaches who refined this concept and first described it in detail were the Australian swimming coach Forbes Carlile (Carlile, 1963) and New Zealand running coach Arthur Lydiard (Lydiard & Gilmour, 1978).

In his book, Carlile (1963) provided the first detailed description of peaking I have found. Figure 5.3 summarizes his training plan for swimming.

Carlile divides the year into four quarters (Periods 1 through 4) and designates it either a "one-peak" or "two-peak" year. For a one-peak year, Period 1 comprises a complete rest from hard training, with emphasis on forms of exercise other than swimming. During Period 2, swimming training is increased with the emphasis on technique, and Period 3 is reserved for very heavy swimming training. Period 4 is the competitive period, during which the athlete tapers while competing regularly. In a two-peak year, all four periods are shortened, and less heavy training is done during Period 3. Lydiard similarly combined different

Time	Southern hemisphere	Northern hemisphere	Relative amounts of training	
			One-peak year	Two-peak year
Period 1 Recuperation	April-June	November-January		
Period 2 Gentle training	July-September	February-April		
Period 3 Hard training	October-December	May-July		
Period 4 Hard competition	January-March	August-October		

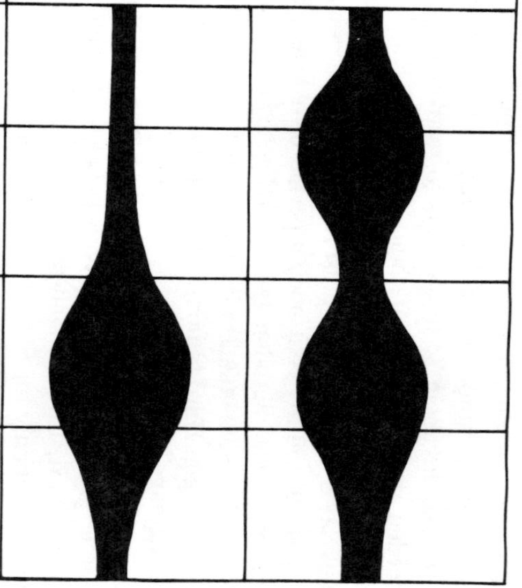

Figure 5.3 The Forbes Carlile yearly training plan.

Note. From *Forbes Carlile on Swimming* (p. 17) by F. Carlile, 1963, London. Published by Pelham Books, © 1963 by Forbes Carlile. Adapted by permission.

training phases—base training, hill training, and sharpening—in the methods he devised for runners (Daws, 1977; Lydiard & Gilmour, 1978).

Two runners who achieved their greatest success using this Carlile/Lydiard method of peaking were the New Zealander Peter Snell and the "Flying Finn" Lasse Viren. Their stories illustrate the value of peaking.

Snell, the 1960 800-m Olympic gold medalist, had been "written off" by the press 4 weeks before the 1964 Olympic Games because he was unable to run the mile in under 4 minutes in competition. When the finals arrived Snell was unbeatable. Whereas his competitors had already peaked by the time they arrived at the Olympics, Snell had used the heats as the speed work he needed to bring him to his peak. In January 1962, Snell completed what Doherty (1964) considered the greatest middle-distance running the world had ever seen. In early December 1961, Snell completed a standard marathon as part of Lydiard's base training program and began sharpening training in mid-December. With only 2-1/2 weeks of speed training, Snell ran a mile in 4:01.3. During the following 5 weeks of competition, he ran 880 yd in 1:48.3 and 1:47.3; 800 m in 1:46.2; a mile in the world-record time of 3:54.4; a world-record 800 m in 1:44.3; and 880 yd in 1:45.1. Snell fulfilled Lydiard's belief that his system would bring "[you] to your peak slower than many other runners and you will be running last when they are running first. But when it is really important to run first, you will be passing them" (Lydiard & Gilmour, 1962, p. 33).

Viren, a winner of very little besides four gold medals, two each at 5,000 m and 10,000 m in the 1972 and 1976 Olympic Games, appears to be an ordinary athlete who beat the world by following Lydiard's ideas and choosing to peak only once every 4 years. I vividly recall watching a replay of the 1976 Olympic Games 10,000-m final. With Viren leading the British hopeful, Brendan Foster, by half a lap, English broadcaster Ron Pickering remarked in dismay, "but Brendan Foster has beaten Lasse Viren four times this year." Viren spent 4 years of background training preparing for a single peak at the Olympic Games. And when he peaked, no one was near him. Of this ability, Viren commented, "Some do well in other races, some run fast times, but they cannot do well in the ultimate, the Olympics . . . The question is not why I run this way, but why so many cannot" (Daws, 1978, p. 73).

This method is worth studying in more detail. The sources I have referred to are the books by Carlile (1963), Osler (1967, 1978), Daws (1977), and Lydiard and Gilmour (1978), to which readers are referred for more detailed explanations of the ideas and programs followed by these runners. I personally found the books of Daws and Osler the most readable and easiest to follow.

Base Training

Base training consists mainly of long-slow-distance (LSD) running. The aim is to run as high a mileage as possible without overtraining and to increase gradually the average speed and distance of the training sessions.

Tom Osler (1978; see Figure 5.4) suggested that base training should continue for at least 6 months and preferably 1 year before any sharpening training begins. He also wrote that the guiding principle during base training is that after any training session, the runner should feel able to complete the same workout again if demanded.

According to Osler (1967, 1978), base training

- develops "robust health,"
- conditions the cardiovascular system,
- helps, via the slow pace, to keep injuries to a minimum,
- effects a continuous, slow improvement in the runner's base performance level,
- has a desharpening effect, and
- conserves what Osler calls "adaptation energy."

No one knows precisely what Osler meant by "adaptation energy." Osler also referred to this energy form as "competitive juices." He suggested that we all

Figure 5.4 Tom Osler in the 1975 New York City 50-mile (80-km) race.
Note. Photo courtesy of Ed Dodd.

have limited reserves of these "juices," which we must expend with care. This concept is similar to that proposed by Hans Selye in his general adaptation theory and was also alluded to by Moran (1945) when he described the battle-weary troops he doctored in the trenches during World War I (see chapter 10, p. 419).

Osler contends that stressful conditions use up these competitive juices, and when they are exhausted, the athlete is no longer able to perform to his or her potential. This idea has been confirmed by Barron et al. (1985), who showed that overtrained runners are unable to respond normally to stress because they cannot release the appropriate stress hormones or "juices."

Osler warns that although base training is a very safe training method, it fails to prepare either body or mind for the stresses of racing. In particular, base training fails to develop the coordination and the relaxation at speed that are necessary for peak performance. Also, it fails to produce those biochemical adaptations that are specific to speed training (see chapter 3).

Thus the athlete who practices only base training may be able to run forever at a slow pace and will recover very quickly from even the most demanding performance but will never run to his or her potential. All these authors agree that to achieve that potential, each athlete must undergo a period of *sharpening*, which is described next.

Typical of Osler's homespun but incisive and individualistic advice is this analogy:

A runner who conditions himself with slow running first is like a builder laying a strong and deep foundation for a skyscraper. The runner who begins with speedwork (sharpening) is like a builder who lays a weak foundation so as to get the first few stories of his structure up quickly. So it is that the runner who begins with speedwork shows the fastest initial improvement. However, just as the builder who laid a weak foundation, is severely limited in the height to which he can raise his structure, so it is that the future performances of our hasty runner will be limited. Whereas our runner who started slow, will eventually surpass the other for his foundation will provide the base from which higher and higher performances will be launched. (Osler, 1967, p. 12)

Peaking (Sharpening)

Peaking consists of any of a number of different training methods, which are all performed at race pace or faster for varying lengths of time. The most common sharpening techniques are hill work, short races or time trials of up to 8 to 10 km, and speed play (or fartlek) and interval running (Daws, 1977; Doherty, 1964; Galloway, 1983; Glover & Schuder, 1983; Lydiard & Gilmour, 1978; Osler, 1967, 1978; see also chapter 8). These sessions become the focal point of training and may be practiced 1 to 3 times weekly, depending on the experience and physical strength of the athlete.

According to Osler, an important advantage of peaking is that it teaches one to run relaxed even at race pace. More importantly, it produces specific physiological adaptations that produce quite dramatic improvements in racing performances, as shown by the experience of Peter Snell. Osler reports that after 8 weeks of sharpening, he runs 10 to 20 s/mile faster than previously and gains an 11-minute improvement in his marathon time.

But sharpening training has serious disadvantages, even more than base training. In particular, sharpening is very taxing and uses up what Osler called adaptation energy; sharpening increases the risk of injury and reduces resistance to infection. When sharpening, the athlete is on the knife's edge that divides a peak performance from a disastrous race. For this reason, sharpening can be maintained for only relatively short periods of time, with a probable maximum of between 8 and 12 weeks. I believe that this rule applies to all human activities, mental or physical. How then, to achieve a peak?

Osler (1967) formulated the diagram in Figure 5.5, which owes nothing to science and everything to the anecdotal experiences of great runners like Viren and Snell and great runner/thinkers like Osler and Fordyce (see chapter 8). The diagram compares the performance improvements that would be experienced by a runner following two different training methods for 36 weeks each.

If you chose to do only base training in the 36-week period, you could expect to improve your racing performance along Points A to I. Osler calls this the improvement in base performance level.

If, however, you chose to start sharpening at the 6-week point on the graph (Point B), so that instead of training only with LSD running you would also include speed training, your racing performance would immediately improve quite dramatically, along Points B, C, and D of the graph. Six weeks after starting sharpening training, your potential racing performance would probably start to plateau (Point D). Note that the time intervals shown on the graph are somewhat arbitrary and have been derived from empirical observation of rather small numbers of runners rather than by careful scientific study. Some runners will take either longer or shorter periods to arrive at the various points on the diagram.

To my knowledge, the first author to point this out was Prokop (1963-1964), who noted that there are two types of athletes: the ''short-swing'' and the ''long-swing'' types. Short-swing athletes are able to improve their conditions very quickly but can maintain their performances for only short periods of time before they must return to base training. These athletes are able to peak several times during the season. The long-swing types need considerably more training to reach their peaks, which they can sustain for much longer.

Prokop reported that his athletes usually required 7 to 8 weeks of sharpening training to reach a peak that would last 3 to 6 weeks before their performances would start to fall.

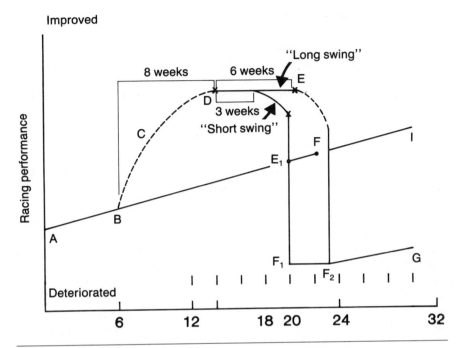

Figure 5.5 The theory behind peaking.
Note. Based on data from *The Conditioning of Distance Runners* (p. 8) by T. Osler, 1967, Mountain View, CA: Runner's World Publications, and *Serious Runner's Handbook* (p. 31) by T. Osler, 1978, Mountain View, CA: World Publications. Copyright 1967, 1978 by T. Osler. Used by permission.

Two great athletes who observed this in their own performances were Derek Clayton (1980) and Ron Hill (R. Hill, 1981, 1982; see also chapter 8), who found that their running performances improved steadily for approximately 10 weeks. Beyond this period they were easily tired, slept badly, were often injured, and raced poorly.

Once you reach your peaking plateau (Points D to E in Figure 5.5), you are ready for your best race, and all you need do is maintain your sharpening training. As coach Jumbo Elliott said, "After you start hard racing, hard training will get you nowhere" (Liquori & Parker, 1980, p. 150).

A frequent problem is that once runners realize they are peaking, they are seldom happy with just one good race, unless that race happens to be in the Olympics. Inevitably, the now-greedy runners try to pack in too many races, the last of which they run when their performance levels are already on the precipitous downward slide of the performance curve (Points E to F in Figure 5.5). The result is that such runners end up injured, ill, and thoroughly overtrained, depicted as Points F_1 and F_2 on the diagram and described in detail in chapter 6.

An important feature of Points E to F_2 is the steepness of the line they create. I suspect that it takes only 3 weeks to go from a best-ever performance to the point where one is physically incapacitated.

Two final points shown in Figure 5.5 are the slow rate of recovery from overtraining (Points F to G) and the way in which a sharpening runner can perform either much better (Point E) or much worse (Point F_2) than the runner who performs only base training (Points E_1 and F).

Monitoring the Success of Peaking

Just as you will develop specific warning symptoms (see chapter 10) if you overtrain, so will your body tell you when you are sharpening correctly. Osler (1967, 1978) was the first to record these symptoms.

During speed-training sessions, you no longer need to force your body through the session. Rather, your body "surges forward at its own will" and "thirsts to accelerate" (Osler, 1967, p. 23). In the hour following training, you feel supreme vigor, quite unlike the normal postexercise feelings of mild fatigue. Everyday physical activities, like climbing stairs, become easier. You become increasingly sensitive to everyday situations. You are mildly irritable as your body is "prepared for action and is ready for the fight" (Osler, 1967, p. 24). As your body becomes flooded with previously latent energy, a heightened sexual awareness is often evident (Osler, 1967, p. 24).

The Third Additional Rule of Training: Train Under a Coach

When I began running, I was totally unaware of the potential value of a coach. Now that I have read more widely and have met many excellent coaches in different sports, I see that the successful coach is a very skilled artist whose work is infinitely more difficult than is that of scientists like myself. Performing experiments in the laboratory in which virtually all factors are rigorously controlled is a thousand times easier than trying to do the same with athletes who live in the real world and must therefore cope with the problems that life brings and that inevitably threaten their running performances.

The more I have read, the more I have realized that the coach is not needed for the physical preparation of the athlete as much as for inspiration and support and to provide an objective analysis of the athlete's training. Stampfl (1955) said as much:

> The coach's job is twenty per cent technical and eighty per cent inspirational. He may know all there is to know about tactics, technique and training, but if he cannot win the confidence and comradeship of his pupils he will never be a good coach. (p. 146)

In *Testament of a Runner*, Loader (1960) said much the same, and James Counsilman (see also chapter 10), the brilliant swimming coach of Indiana University, added another important role of the coach: "The most practical judgment of the point at which the swimmer has had exactly enough training is exercised by the coach. Perhaps the ability to do this effectively marks the difference between a good and a poor coach" (Counsilman, 1968, p. 235). Counsilman (1986) also wrote that the coach must contribute enthusiasm, create team unity, and provide guidance:

> I prefer to visualize our experience as that of a well-informed coach talking to an intelligent group of athletes in a situation in which everyone has a common goal, that of achieving the full potential of each person and of involving each intellect in the process. (Counsilman, 1986, p. 4)

I now believe that athletes are not made by training—chapter 8 shows that there really are no training secrets known only to the great athletes. Many runners train just as hard as the great athletes, if not harder in some cases, yet they never achieve the same degrees of success.

Marti Liquori, the American miler who trained with Villanova's Jumbo Elliott, the coach generally considered to be the greatest ever produced in the United States (J.F. Elliott & Berry, 1982), wrote, "Much of running is mental, and the guru coaches . . . probably have been successful more because they knew how to harness a runner's heart and mind than because of any mysterious secret training formula" (Liquori & Parker, 1980, p. 35). Of Jumbo Elliott himself, this was written: "His 'method'—the mystical basis for his success in turning out champions—was a 'non-method'. . . . He insisted on their attention to studies. . . . His 'method' was in the application of his knowledge of the athletes, knowing which psychological approach would be most effective and when his man was ready" (J.F. Elliott & Berry, 1982, pp. 186-187).

This, I think, is the crux of good coaching—treating each athlete as an individual and knowing which psychological approach will work best for each athlete. For the athlete, the challenge remains to find the coach with whom the athlete feels most comfortable and to whom the athlete best relates. That coach should be sufficiently knowledgable to prevent the athlete from overtraining and should be able to extract the most out of the athlete. In Arthur Lydiard's words (Lenton, 1981), "Two brains are better than one" (p. 69).

The Fourth Additional Rule of Training: Keep a Detailed Logbook

A well-kept logbook is a runner's best friend, for it records the path that has been traveled in the search for fitness. It also provides a continuing source of motivation and, most importantly for the competitive athlete, it can provide important clues as to which training methods have been successful or not so successful.

One athlete who believes implicitly in the importance of keeping a detailed logbook is ultramarathoner Bruce Fordyce (see chapter 8), who calls his logbooks his "textbooks" (Fordyce, 1983). By comparing his performances in the same types of training sessions over the years, he is able to judge his fitness at any time of the year with pinpoint accuracy. The result is that he is always "right" on race day and has thus established a degree of consistency never before seen in ultradistance running and equaled by only very few athletes.

The Fifth Additional Rule of Training:
At First, Try to Achieve as Much as Possible on a Minimum of Training

As we shall see in chapter 8, many outstanding athletic performances are achieved on very little training. Exceptional runners like Walter George and Alf Shrubb achieved quite remarkable performances on very little training; Walter George ran a 4:10.6 mile and a 49:29 16-km time on 2 miles of training a day! Even Paavo Nurmi, the most medaled Olympic runner of all times, trained pathetically little but performed exceptionally even by today's standards. The exceptional performances of African runners from Kip Keino to Matthews Temane (see chapter 8) have also been achieved on relatively light training.

The genius of Bruce Fordyce (see chapter 8) has been his realization that if he could run well in ultramarathons without doing heavy mileage, then possibly mileage was not the answer. His unique ultramarathon record and the experiences of the other experts discussed in chapter 8 prove this to be correct.

My own experience has also backed this up. If I could start my running career over again, I would seldom run more than 120 km a week, the maximum training distance suggested by Oregon's Bowerman and Dellinger. I would first see what I could achieve by running that training load for a few years. If I still wished to improve I would then increase the amount of my speed training and perfect the peaking technique. Only when these methods failed to improve my running would I consider increasing my training distances further.

Sixth Additional Rule of Training:
Understand the Holism of Training

The term *holistic running* was first coined by Kenneth Doherty (1964), who made the very simple but profound observation that most training methods "limit their attention to what happens during the few training hours each day and ignore the remaining 20 or more hours, which are often just as effective in determining success in running" (p. 121).

Thus, athletes need to be aware that they are in training 24 hours a day, and everything they do can affect their running.

But runners should also be aware that there is a holism to training itself. Thus, in his analysis of the different methods of training, Doherty (1964) suggested that the success of Lydiard's training was due to the balance Lydiard achieved between many factors: training and competition; races that are important and those that are merely training; mileage and enjoyment; different kinds of terrain; endless year-round training and maintaining motivation through six different types of training; and steady-state and uneven speed running. Clearly, you should try to achieve this balance in your own training.

In this chapter we have looked at the training methods that were first described by Newton and have discussed how these have been refined by other incisive thinkers such as Stampfl, Gerschler, Reindell, Bowerman, Dellinger, Lydiard, and Osler. Chapter 6 consolidates their combined teachings into the 15 Laws of Training and discusses their practical applications. Chapter 8 also considers the training methods of some of the best runners the world has ever known.

6

Theory and Practice of Training

"Training is principally an act of faith."

Franz Stampfl (1955)

"Most people, including coaches, thought I was mad, but . . . I became the fastest miler by using the ideas of a distance runner. There is no universal formula which suits everyone. That is the fascination about running."

Derek Ibbotson (T. O'Connor, 1960)

"I am never happy about setting out a training programme, mainly because we can never stick to the details of one ourselves."

Forbes Carlile (1963)

"The runner must learn early in his career to observe keenly the symptoms his body reveals when responding favourably and unfavourably to a training programme."

Tom Osler (1967)

"There is a time to run and there is a time to rest. It is the true test of the runner to get them both right."

Noel Carroll (1981)

This chapter aims to provide some practical training advice while incorporating the theoretical wisdom of the previous chapter. It is written particularly for

166

the neophyte runner. More experienced runners or those who want more exact details of training programs are referred to the books of J. Gardner and Purdy (1970), Henderson (1977), Daws (1977), Osler (1978), Lydiard and Gilmour (1978), Galloway (1983), and Glover and Schuder (1983). I have steered clear of giving any detailed training programs because my personal inclination has always been to train according to a general plan and to run each day as I feel. But I am equally aware that some runners will benefit by a more regimented approach.

STEP 1: ANALYZE YOUR LEVELS OF MOTIVATION AND PERSONAL DISCIPLINE

At least in the beginning, running is neither easy nor enjoyable. You need great motivation and personal discipline to survive the first 3 months before, as Newton said in his eighth rule of training, running becomes a habit controlled by the subconscious. The result is that many beginners, who possibly see only the glamour of marathon running and are unaware of the demands of the sport, soon fall by the wayside.

I suspect that those who stick with a running program have previously exhibited perseverance, are mentally healthy, and usually have succeeded in whatever they have done. In contrast, those who drop out are more likely to have failed previously and may have low levels of self-esteem (Lobstein et al., 1983). Indeed, studies of cardiac patients who drop out of exercise programs to which they have been referred after suffering heart attacks showed that these patients were more depressed, hypochondriacal, anxious, and introverted and had lower ego strength than those who remained in such programs (Blumenthal et al., 1982a).

At present, our knowledge of how best to help those likely to drop out of a regular running program is limited, so adherence essentially becomes an individual problem for each runner. Realize your weaknesses, and get others to help and support you. In particular, you should plan to run in a group of people who meet regularly and who will assist in motivating you. Unfortunately, the running clubs in most countries have not yet evolved a system whereby they guide beginning runners through these first difficult steps; hopefully this will change in the future. John Martin and Patricia Dubbert from the University of Mississippi at Jackson (J.E. Martin & Dubbert, 1984) suggest the following strategies to assist the beginner.

Shaping

This is a process in which a target behavior (e.g., becoming fit enough to run a marathon) is broken up into a series of gradual steps that eventually lead to the desired goal. J.E. Martin and Dubbert (1984) suggest starting with a simple, easily performed task. In running, the initial shaping goal during the first 8 to 12 weeks should therefore not be to become fit, but rather to develop the habit of regular exercise.

Reinforcement Control

Any encouragement that reinforces the exercise habit will be beneficial (e.g., social support gained from running in a group or increased physical fitness gained from exercise).

Stimulus Control

This involves the use of stimuli or prompts that encourage exercise. Examples of such stimuli are laying out running clothing the night before a planned run, wearing exercise clothes around the house, and always having exercise attire in the car. Associating with regular exercisers, discussing personal training and performances, and reading about running also increase the desire to exercise.

Goal Setting

Always set achievable short-term goals in training (either distance or time run each day or week), but also have long-term goals like running in a fun run or marathon.

If you are a highly dedicated person, rather than doing too little, you are likely to aim too high too soon. It is important to set realistic goals and then start gradually. Please be aware that in the beginning, your mind, heart, and lungs are infinitely stronger than are the bones, tendons, and ligaments of your lower limbs and that a serious running injury is virtually guaranteed to anyone who starts training too intensively too soon.

Associative/Dissociative Strategies

This concept is discussed in greater detail in chapter 7. In short, when running you should either think about everything but what you are doing (dissociation) or concentrate purely on the activity and how your body feels as you run (association). In general, it is believed that competitive runners do best if they associate during races. However, it also appears that novice runners do best if they dissociate. If you associate and think about your running and how your body is hurting, you are less likely to continue exercising. Running in pleasant and varied surroundings rather than on monotonous roads and tracks helps the dissociation process.

Coping Thoughts

The novice runner must learn positive self-talk (see chapter 7): "I'm doing well to exercise at all today since I wasn't looking forward to it . . . I'm nearly halfway finished . . . Let me notice what's going on around me—that sunset is beautiful."

At first, it is better for the novice to be excessively self-congratulatory about personal efforts. Stricter self-evaluation can be instituted once the exercise habit is ingrained.

STEP 2: DECIDE WHETHER YOU NEED MEDICAL CLEARANCE

A question that inevitably arises is whether persons taking up exercise in middle age should have exhaustive medical evaluations before they start. Ideally the answer should be an unqualified *yes*, because anyone with a medical problem that could be aggravated by running should be identified early and advised appropriately.

This type of logic led the American College of Sports Medicine (1976) to advise that anyone over 35 years of age who planned to start an exercise program should have a full medical examination, including an electrocardiogram recorded before, during, and after maximal exercise (a maximal exercise or stress test). In addition, the College felt that persons under 35 who have certain risk factors for heart disease (e.g., a family history of heart disease or a personal history of heavy smoking, high blood pressure, or high blood fat levels—cholesterol or triglycerides or both) should also undergo this test. The maximal exercise test would identify all those who have heart disease and who are therefore at high risk of dying suddenly and unexpectedly during exercise.

Subsequent research has shown this method to be inconclusive and prohibitively expensive. When formulating these guidelines, the American College of Sports Medicine was unaware that maximal exercise testing is a relatively insensitive method for identifying those persons who have the type of heart disease likely to cause sudden death during exercise. Worse, some people who do *not* have heart disease may have electrocardiographic responses to exercise that are identical to those of persons with the disease; thus, the maximal exercise test cannot conclusively diagnose heart disease.

At present the best method to determine without doubt whether a person has serious heart disease is to perform a *coronary angiography*, a specialized procedure performed only in the cardiac unit of a major hospital. In this procedure a small plastic tube (or catheter) is introduced into a large leg or arm artery and carefully guided until it enters, in sequence, each of the arteries supplying the heart muscle—the coronary arteries. A dye is injected into each coronary artery, and X rays are taken as the dye travels down the arteries. Any irregularities in the arteries are shown as narrowings, which indicate the presence of coronary atherosclerosis (hardening of the arteries), the disease most likely to cause sudden death in older (over 40 years) athletes during exercise.

However, coronary angiography is not without important limitations. It is a specialized procedure requiring admission to a hospital, and it is not without risk. For every 1,000 coronary angiographies performed, there is likely to be one death attributable to the procedure. In addition, coronary angiography identifies only those persons who have coronary atherosclerosis. If we were to perform coronary angiographies on all runners we would expect that 20 to 30% (the national average for most Western countries) would have coronary atherosclerosis of varying grades of severity. Yet data show that very few, possibly 1 per 6,000 to 7,000 runners, develop cardiac problems during any single year (Noakes et al., 1984a; P.D. Thompson et al., 1982). At present we are unable to separate those few runners with severe coronary atherosclerosis who are at risk of sudden death during exercise from that much larger group of other runners with equally severe coronary atherosclerosis but for whom, for reasons unknown, exercise does not pose such an inordinate risk of sudden death.

Bearing in mind the risks involved in these medical tests and their present costs, the U.S. National Heart, Lung and Blood Institute (1981) formulated the following guidelines. Anyone who conforms to one or more of the following eight criteria should consult a doctor before beginning an exercise program.

1. You are over age 60 and not accustomed to vigorous exercise.
2. You have a family history of premature coronary artery disease (under 55 years of age).
3. You frequently have pains or pressure in the left- or midchest area, left neck, shoulder, or arm (as distinct from the "stitch") during or immediately after exercise.
4. You often feel faint or have spells of severe dizziness, or you experience extreme breathlessness after mild exertion.
5. Your doctor has said your blood pressure is too high and is not under control. Or, you do not know if your blood pressure is normal.
6. Your doctor has said that you have heart trouble, that you have a heart murmur, or that you have had a heart attack.
7. Your doctor has said you have bone or joint problems, such as arthritis.
8. You have a medical condition not mentioned here that might need special attention in an exercise program (e.g., insulin-dependent diabetes).

I certainly agree with this advice and would submit to an exercise test only if I had symptoms suggestive of heart disease.

There are ways, however, in which you can protect yourself without recourse to medicine. First, start your exercise program gradually and train gently. If heart disease is present, it will show itself when your heart is forced to work harder than it is able.

Second, be aware of those specific symptoms that might develop during exercise and that indicate heart disease. In the largest such studies of sudden deaths and heart attacks in marathon runners, Noakes (1987b) and Noakes et al. (1984a) found that the majority (81%) had warning symptoms that they chose to ignore. These symptoms included severe chest pain and shortness of breath sufficiently severe to prevent normal running. Despite this, a number continued to train and even to race; three even completed the Comrades Marathon despite marked chest pain and shortness of breath.

In two of the runners we studied, the symptoms of heart disease were misinterpreted by their doctors, who may have concluded that because the runners were so "fit" they could not possibly have heart disease. This error could also possibly be traced to those medical zealots who popularized the incorrect theory that marathon running absolutely prevents heart disease (Bassler, 1977).

The message is simple: Before starting an exercise program, check the eight starting criteria provided by the National Heart, Lung and Blood Institute. If your responses to these statements indicate that an exam is necessary, visit your general practitioner, who will decide what else needs to be done. Regardless of whether or not you initially consult your doctor, you should consult him or her immediately if you develop any of the suspicious symptoms described earlier, either during or after exercise. If your doctor considers it likely that the symptoms come from your heart, he or she will advise you to be evaluated exhaustively in a hospital, and it is likely that you will undergo at least a maximal exercise test and possibly a coronary angiography as well.

Unfortunately, even if everyone religiously followed the guidelines described here, there would still be runners who die during exercise. Part of the reason for this is that some such deaths are caused by a form of heart disease known as *hypertrophic cardiomyopathy*, which is extremely difficult to detect medically. It frequently causes no symptoms, and worse, the enlarged heart of the athlete with hypertrophic cardiomyopathy may, with current methods of detection, be indistinguishable from the normally enlarged heart of the athlete.

Also, some persons with coronary atherosclerosis have no symptoms and will die suddenly during exercise without prior warning.

STEP 3: CHOOSE APPROPRIATE RUNNING SHOES

Once you have the go-ahead to start running, the next step is to choose an appropriate pair of running shoes.

This is easier said than done. The choice of running shoes has become enormously complex, and there are probably over 100 different models of running shoes on the market.

This problem is compounded further by our inabilities to define those minor individual differences in body structure that determine which shoes are best for us (Cavanagh, 1980). I feel that the choice of the appropriate running shoe is determined by two principal factors:

1. Whether or not you are a novice.
2. If you are not a novice, whether or not you are injured.
   - If you are uninjured, (a) whether you run enough to warrant expensive shoes and (b) for what activities you want to use the shoes.
   - If you are injured, what type of injury you have.

Shoe Advice for the Novice

It is always best to start running in a relatively modestly priced pair of shoes, bought from a reputable running shoe dealer. If after some months of running you have an injury, the nature of the injury will indicate what type of shoe is likely to help cure that injury and prevent further similar injuries. This is discussed further in chapter 14.

If you enter that running shoe shop prepared to buy a modestly priced running shoe, you should know something about the different features of running shoes and how these features affect the performance of any particular model.

Anatomy of the Running Shoe

Any running shoe has six major anatomical features: the outer sole, the midsole, the presence or absence of slip or board lasting, the heel counter, the shoelast (straight or curved), and the medial and lateral midsole heel flares (see Figure 6.1).

The Outer Sole

The outer sole is that part of the shoe that comes into direct contact with the ground. Today, outer soles are made from a variety of different materials and are of different designs. The main design variation is whether or not the sole has "waffles." Bill Bowerman (see chapter 5) filled a waffle-toasting iron with urethane, producing the first outer sole with this characteristic pattern—hence the name.

Waffles were originally designed for cross-country, not road, running because they give better traction on uneven ground (Cavanagh, 1980); they also increase shock absorption. However, waffles do not wear as well as flat-surfaced outer soles.

The most important feature of the outer sole is that it should not wear down too quickly. It should have the greatest durability in the areas of greatest wear, particularly at the outer heel edge. This type of outer sole has been called the nonuniform outer sole. Very durable material is not used throughout the entire outer sole, because the more durable the material, the heavier it is. Thus, the

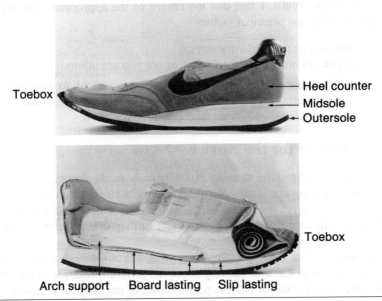

Toebox

Heel counter
Midsole
Outersole

Toebox

Arch support   Board lasting   Slip lasting

Figure 6.1 Important anatomical features of the running shoe (the inner sole has been rolled back in the bottom photograph).

nonuniform outer sole saves weight. The only benefit of a soft and therefore nondurable outer sole is that it provides additional cushioning, which may be useful to those runners for whom exceptional shock absorption is essential.

I do not believe that the outer-sole wear at the heel should necessarily be repaired even if it threatens to wear through to the midsole; the heel wears in order to accommodate the natural heel strike of the athlete. The athlete whose foot lands with the heel in marked supination will tend to show heavy wear at the heel. To patch such a heel prevents proper adaptations of the shoe to your particular heel strike pattern. You would probably be better off allowing the outer sole to wear out completely, even exposing the midsole.

The important features of the outer sole are durability and traction.

The Midsole

The midsole is the real heart of the shoe and is the feature of the shoe that I always notice first. The most important feature of the midsole is the degree of softness or hardness.

The midsole has three different functions: It must absorb the shock of the heel strike and the forefoot strike; it must be strong enough to resist excessive inward rotation of the ankle (pronation) as the foot progresses from heel strike to toe-off (see Figure 12.3); and it must be able to flex at a point about two thirds from the heel as the heel starts to come off the ground leading to toe-off (see Figure 12.2).

Prior to the mid-1970s, midsole material was made only from rubber, which has dual disadvantages of being heavy and a relatively poor absorber of shock. In 1974, Jerry Turner, then of the Brooks Shoe Company, contracted a chemical engineer, David Schwaber, to produce a lighter material with better shock-absorbing properties (Cavanagh, 1980). The result was a compound called *ethylene vinyl acetate* (EVA). Tiny gas bubbles are trapped in the EVA when it is cooled at high pressure; these bubbles make the material light and able to absorb shock. The major disadvantage is that with wear, the tiny gas bubbles are expelled from the EVA, which flattens out, becomes harder, and absorbs shock less well. When the EVA becomes unevenly compacted either in the heel or the midsole, the shoe distorts badly, which may be an important cause of injury (see Figure 14.1).

Another problem arises from the manufacturing process; it is difficult to produce EVA of consistent hardness. As a result, the quality of the midsole can vary from shoe to shoe.

For these reasons, it is essential to compare the midsole hardness of all the shoes you look at and to learn to use the "thumb compression test" (see Figure 6.2) to determine the type of midsole that best suits you.

In this test, you squeeze the midsole at both the heel and forefoot to determine the relative hardness of the midsole. The greater the degree of midsole indentation produced by this method, the softer the shoe and therefore the more shock the shoe can absorb. However, the added shock absorption is bought at a price; the softer the shoe, the quicker it will tend to compress. Conversely, the less indentation that is caused by the thumb compression test the harder the shoe is and the less shock it will absorb, but also the less likely it is to compress rapidly.

The midsole must combine a capacity for shock absorption with capacities to control ankle pronation and provide adequate flexibility. Yet to some extent, two of these characteristics are mutually exclusive; an EVA that has good shock absorption will be soft and therefore have good flexibility but very poor pronation control, whereas EVA that provides good control of pronation will be hard and inflexible and have poor shock-absorbing characteristics.

In an attempt to compensate for these mutually exclusive characteristics, shoe manufacturers have used midsoles of different hardness in different areas: a soft, shock-absorbing material along the outer heel border and under the ball of the foot to increase shock absorption and flexibility plus a firmer material along the inner border of the shoe, extending from heel to midfoot, to control pronation.

These techniques have largely been successful. The only problem that has not been effectively solved concerns the midsole underneath the ball of the foot. This area does not absorb the highest forces during landing—the heel does this—but this area is exposed to moderately high pressure for a much longer time; thus, it will tend to compress even more than the heel. Yet it must be soft enough to allow flexibility.

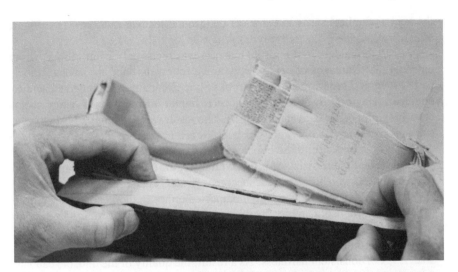

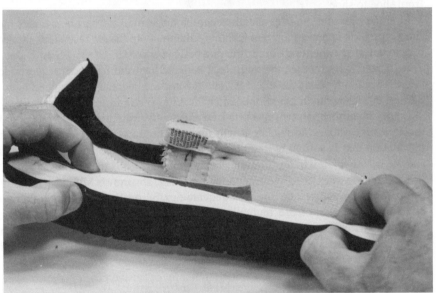

Figure 6.2 The thumb compression test. A hard or firm midsole compresses very little (top); a softer midsole compresses more, providing greater shock absorption.

One attempt to solve this problem resulted in the Nike Tailwind, first released in 1979. The midsole of this shoe contained a series of five polyurethane tubes extending from heel to forefoot into which Freon gas was injected at a pressure of about three atmospheres (Cavanagh, 1980). Although this shoe ultimately proved unsatisfactory because it had poor rearfoot control, its offspring have clearly shown that the air sole does not become compressed in the same way as does conventional EVA. However, in not all of these shoes does the air sole extend to the forefoot. If the air sole is present only in the heel, the EVA under the forefoot will still be prone to compression for those runners who land heavily on the forefoot (see Figures 14.3 and 14.4). In 1987, Asics running shoes introduced a gel-containing midsole, which, like the air midsole, resists compression yet likely has equivalent if not superior shock-absorbing capacity than EVA. More recently, other major shoe manufacturers including Reebock, Converse, Hi Tec, Saucony, and Turntec have introduced so-called "energy return systems" to their midsoles. These are discussed in chapter 14.

In summary, the features of the midsole that require consideration are its hardness and whether or not it is made of mixed material. Those who require shock absorption in their running shoes because they have "rigid" lower-limb structure must look for shoes with soft midsoles; those with "mobile" feet need firmer shoes (see chapter 14).

The Presence of Slip or Board Lasting

During the construction of running shoes, the nylon material that constitutes the shoe upper—the part that covers the top of the foot—is stitched together, and its lower part is glued onto the top of the midsole. If this part of the upper is stuck directly to the midsole and no additional material overlies it, the shoe is said to be *slip lasted*. If a brown-colored board overlies and hides the tucked-under portion of the upper, the shoe is said to be *board lasted* (see Figure 6.1).

Board lasting increases the ability of the shoe to resist pronation. The board may extend from heel to toe, in which case the board lasting is *conventional*, or the board may end just behind the ball of the foot, in which case it is called *partial* or *combination lasting*. The benefit of partial board lasting is that it does not reduce flexibility in the forefoot yet retains some ability to resist ankle pronation. Figure 6.3 demonstrates a technique for testing a shoe's pronation-resisting qualities.

In general, board-lasted shoes will benefit those runners who require shoes that control excessive ankle pronation, whereas slip-lasted shoes are best for those with rigid feet that require as much movement as possible.

Heel Counter With or Without Heel Stabilization

The heel counter is made from a firm thermoplastic material that is molded into the correct shape during a special heating process (Cavanagh, 1980). Some heel counters extend further on the inner than on the outer side of the shoe, and today most are associated with special stabilizing structures that tend to bind the heel counter more firmly to the midsole (see Figure 6.4).

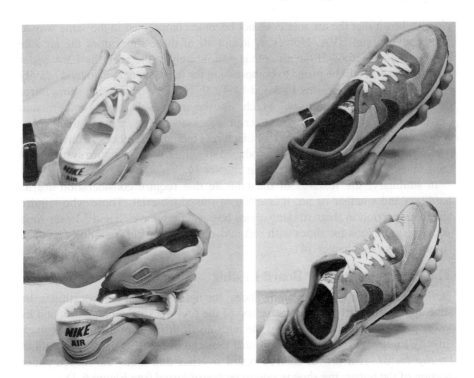

Figure 6.3 The Noakes Running Shoe Pronation-Testing Technique. The shoe on the left is easily rotated in the vertical plane, whereas the shoe on the right is designed to resist ankle pronation.

The aim of the heel counter is to reduce ankle pronation. The athlete who requires a shoe that will limit ankle pronation should obviously choose a shoe with a strong heel counter.

There are two ways to test the strength of the heel counter. First, pinch the middle of the heel counter on its inner and outer edges between the thumb and the index and second fingers of your dominant hand (see Figure 6.4, a and b). Determine how much pressure is required to distort the heel counter toward the center of the shoe. Second, holding the heel counter as before, grasp the midsole of the shoe in the palm of the other hand and determine how much torque is required to distort the heel counter to the inside or to the outside of the shoe (see Figure 6.4, c and d).

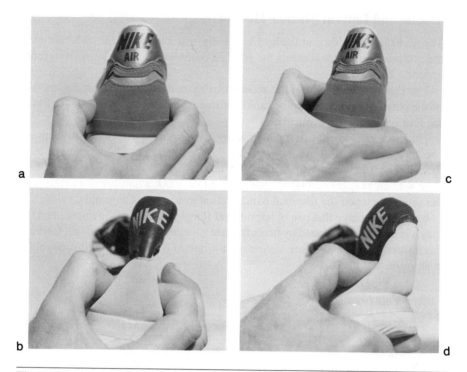

Figure 6.4 Testing the strength of the heel counter of the running shoe. The heel counter of the shoe at the top resists deformation better than does that of the shoe on the bottom and would likely control ankle pronation more effectively.

The less distortion produced by these maneuvers, the stronger the heel counter.

Straight or Curved (Banana) Lasting

A straight-lasted shoe is one that, when viewed from the bottom, is symmetrical in relation to a line drawn from the middle of the heel to the middle of the toe. In contrast, the front of a curved (banana) or inflared-lasted shoe bends inside a line drawn from the middle of the heel to the middle of the midfoot.

In general, a straight-lasted shoe, because it contains considerable additional midsole material under the midfoot, will help resist ankle pronation and should therefore be used by runners who require such control. In contrast, the curve-lasted shoe is of benefit to those athletes looking for increased foot movement and shock absorption. Such athletes usually have high-arched feet, tend to wear the outer edges of their shoe soles (see Figure 14.6c), and usually run with their toes pointing inward (toeing in).

Medial and Lateral Midsole Heel Flares

The midsole of the shoe at the heel is usually wider on both sides where it meets the ground than where it meets the foot; in other words, it is flared from foot to ground.

The flare on the inside of the shoe probably resists ankle pronation; the flare on the outside probably increases ankle pronation because it acts as a lever forcing the foot inward at the heel strike.

Thus, it seems likely that the medial heel flare may be of value to runners who need control of ankle pronation, but the lateral flare is probably more of a hindrance than a help to these runners. In the mid-1970s, when Nike introduced a shoe with an exaggerated lateral flare, the LDV 1000, a number of runners using the shoe developed the iliotibial band friction syndrome (Cavanagh, 1980).

It seems probable that use of lateral heel flares will stop in the future, and they may eventually be replaced by heels that are rounded at the lateral edge. Certainly the injured runner who uses a shoe with a lateral heel flare would probably do best to file that flare off.

Other Features

A number of other, less important features are worthy of note. All modern shoe uppers are made of nylon. Leather tends to stretch when wet, and it needs to be dried slowly.

Additional arch support systems are provided in some running shoes, as shown in Figure 6.1. These systems offer little to help runners who pronate excessively but may assist those with only minor degrees of abnormal ankle pronation.

The *Achilles tendon "protector"* is the extension of the material at the top of the heel counter. Although some suggest that this protector may be the cause of inflammation in the Achilles tendon, I have not found this. Should the protector cause you discomfort, simply remove it; it does not affect the function of the shoe in any way.

The way in which a shoe is laced may affect its comfort. The two most common lacing methods are variable-width lacing and speed lacing. Variable-width lacing uses two rows of nonaligned eyelet holes, which allow the athlete to choose either a narrower or a wider lacing system. In speed lacing, plastic D-rings are substituted for the conventional leather eyelets. The friction between the plastic and the lace is considerably less than between lace and leather; thus, lacing is quicker and pressure distribution is said to be more even with the D-rings. However, plastic D-rings are hard and can cause considerable pressure on the top of the foot.

A recent innovation in lacing has been the use of Velcro strips in place of laces. Some shoes also have supplementary lacing systems in which tabs at either the midfoot or the heel allow the laces to be attached to the midfoot, the rearfoot, or both.

Final Considerations

Having decided what model shoe you are going to buy, make sure that the shoe fits. Here four rules apply.

1. The shoe should be fitted in the afternoon and should be slightly larger than your conventional shoes. This is because your foot swells about one half size during the day and during running. The width of your index finger should be able to fit between the end of the longest toe (not always the big toe!) and the front end of the shoe upper.

2. The width of the shoe must be right, and there must be sufficient height in the toe box to allow free up-and-down movement of the toes (see Figure 6.1). Athletes with very wide or very narrow feet will need to look for manufacturers whose normal width ranges tend to be either broader or narrower than the average running shoe. The most important width fitting is over the middle (bridge) of the foot.

3. The shoe must feel good when you buy it. A shoe that feels uncomfortable in the shop will only become even more so once on the road.

4. The heel must not slip out of the heel counter at toe-off.

Shoe Choice for Uninjured Runners

After you have been running for some time and have not experienced an injury, you become an uninjured nonnovice runner, and the choice of your second pair of shoes requires several new considerations. If you suffer an injury that may be related to your choice of running shoe, then you become an injured runner and your choice of shoe is determined by a different set of factors. These are detailed in chapter 14.

Uninjured runners fall into two categories: those who are at risk of injury but who are not yet running enough to become injured and those fortunate few who can do whatever they like without ever becoming injured. This latter group are experienced runners; their choices of shoes can be made entirely without recourse to any of the information contained either here or in chapter 14. They could probably run barefoot if they trained for it.

One way to check whether you may be injury prone is to try the "pinch test." The pinch test is effective because damaged tissues become tender to the touch long before they actually cause pain during or after running. A feeling of tenderness or discomfort when the Achilles tendon is pinched between the thumb and forefinger or when firm pressure is applied along the borders of the shinbone (the tibia) or the kneecap indicates trouble. If allowed to go unchecked, this symptom may lead to a debilitating injury.

Tenderness in any of these areas indicates, among other things, that the foot is being allowed to pronate excessively and that a shoe that restricts ankle pronation should be worn.

Do not race in shoes that are either too light or too worn out. The muscles normally provide a good measure of overall shock absorption during running, but near the end of a long race they become too exhausted to help, so the shoe is left to absorb the shock unaided. A shoe that feels adequate at the start of the race may not be optimum when it must cope without the help of the muscles.

All running shoes with EVA midsoles have limited life expectancies—a probable maximum of 6 months of daily wear— before their abilities to absorb shock or control the foot are lost (see chapter 14). So you should change such shoes about every 6 months if you run daily.

Runners frequently ask whether they should train in shoes that are heavier than the ones in which they normally race. I don't really think that the weight of the training shoe makes any real difference to the overall training effect. Distance and speed are the factors that count in training, and shoes should be chosen that are comfortable and protective. Shoes for cross-country racing can sacrifice some cushioning and should have a thin midsole, especially at the heel, to increase stability on uneven ground. Shoes for ultramarathon races need more cushioning, as do shoes used if you are training at high mileages. Joggers who train less than 3 times a week or who run less than 20 km a week probably do not need the additional protection built into the very expensive running shoes, although such joggers may need such protection if they become injured.

As far as different brands or models of shoe are concerned, if you are comfortable in a particular brand of shoe, you should stay with that shoe. I have found that I am comfortable in only a small number of models. Any number of other shoes that seem to have the identical characteristics as these shoes are (for no apparent reason) simply not comfortable.

In summary, my advice for uninjured runners is to stay with the shoes you find comfortable and to choose shoes that are appropriate for racing and training and for different distances.

Many uninjured runners who are unable to justify the high price of modern running shoes ask how the great runners of the past were able to do so much running in cheaper, more basic shoes. I believe that in those days, runners underwent a vigorous process of self-selection. Only those with perfect biomechanical functions were able to survive training; those with less-than-perfect functions were soon injured and dropped the sport.

Today, many runners who have very bad biomechanics are able to run prodigious distances only because of the very real improvements in the design of running shoes. In the past, these runners would simply have had to stop running due to recurring injuries.

I had the opportunity to advise Wally Hayward (see chapter 8) about what running shoes he should choose. In his first 50 years of running in plimsolls he had few injuries besides recurrent calf-muscle tears, which probably bear little relationship to shoe choice. But since he had been running in modern shoes he had suffered a series of knee injuries. Following the reasoning outlined above, I advised him to go back to plimsolls, but with an elevated heel. He seemed perfectly happy with that advice!

STEP 4: CHOOSE APPROPRIATE RUNNING CLOTHES

The key to choosing appropriate running clothes is to dress lightly when running. In most countries during the summer, a pair of shorts and a T shirt are all that you need. When it is hot, you should wear only the lightest, most porous clothing. This is because when running, your body produces an enormous amount of heat and experiences great difficulty losing that heat. The tendency when exercising in mild to warm conditions is to overheat, and wearing a track suit during exercise will only exacerbate this. You should wear a track suit only when the temperature is near 0 °C, when a strong, cold wind is blowing, or when you are trying to acclimatize to hot-weather running (see chapter 4).

Beginning runners often exercise in track suits in the mistaken belief that they will lose more weight that way. This is not true; exercising in a track suit simply causes you to sweat more. The only way to lose real body weight with exercise is to burn more calories of energy, and this is achieved only by doing more exercise. Even then the amount of weight lost may be quite disappointing if you don't follow a fairly strict diet in addition to exercising.

STEP 5: COMMIT THE 15 LAWS OF TRAINING TO MEMORY

The last step before actually starting to run is to memorize the 15 laws of training (see Table 6.1) that are based on the rules listed in chapter 5. We will now review these laws and include some additional practical points.

The 1st Law of Training: Train Frequently Year-Round

This is known as the "consistency ethic" (Liquori & Parker, 1980). When you start a running program, the key is to train regularly. For the jogger interested only in improving health, 30 minutes of exercise 3 or 4 times a week is probably all that is required (American College of Sports Medicine, 1978). The competitive runner will obviously need to train at least 6 days a week.

Although elite runners probably need to train 11 months of the year, I suggest that others should probably train no more than 10 months a year and take a full 2 months of rest each year.

Table 6.1   The 15 Laws of Training

1. Train frequently year-round (Newton's 1st Rule).
2. Start gradually and train gently (Newton's 2nd Rule).
3. Train first for distance, only later for speed (Newton's 3rd Rule).
4. Don't set yourself a daily schedule (Newton's 4th Rule).
5. Alternate hard and easy training (Bowerman/Dellinger's Rule).
6. At first try to achieve as much as possible on a minimum of training.
7. Don't race when you are in training, and run time trials and races only infrequently (Newton's 5th Rule).
8. Specialize (Newton's 6th Rule).
9. Incorporate Base Training and Peaking (sharpening) (The Carlile/Lydiard Rule).
10. Don't overtrain (Newton's 7th Rule).
11. Train with a coach.
12. Train the mind (Newton's 8th Rule).
13. Rest before a big race (Newton's 9th Rule).
14. Keep a detailed logbook.
15. Understand the holism of training.

The 2nd Law of Training: Start Gradually and Train Gently

We now know that the bones, tendons, and muscles, even of young healthy humans, are simply not able to adapt overnight to the cumulative stress of regular training. For this reason it is best to begin training with a period of walking and to start jogging slowly at first and for only short periods of time. The training program included under Step 7 of this chapter incorporates such an initial walking period.

It is only necessary and possible to train at race pace for 5 to 10% of your total training distance. Most of the world's best runners do most of their training at speeds between 30 and 50 s/km slower than their race paces. Two excellent examples are Alberto Salazar and Rob De Castella (see chapter 8), both of whom do most of their training at 3:45/km, yet race standard marathons at close to 3:00/km. Wally Hayward seldom trained faster than 5:00/km, yet set world records in ultramarathon races by averaging 4:05/km for up to 90 km.

This means that the novice runner who ultimately plans to run a standard marathon in 4:30 will need to run the marathon at about 6 min/km, so his or her training speed should be between 6 and 7 min/km.

The best way to achieve the correct intensity of training is to monitor how your body responds to the effort. While running, you should feel that the effort is comfortable. You should be able to carry on a conversation with your running companions (the talk test). Should the effort of the run become noticeable and cause you to be unable to talk, you are "straining, not training" and should slow down.

Never be ashamed to walk during a training run if you find yourself becoming overtired. At the start, at least, always finish each run feeling only pleasantly tired, knowing that if you had to, you could comfortably run the same distance again.

The first scientist to observe that athletes could accurately predict how hard they were exercising on the basis of how they felt was Dr. Gunnar Borg from Sweden. Borg (1973, 1978) noticed a close relationship between exercising heart rate (which is directly related to the intensity of the exercise) and how the athlete actually perceives his or her effort. Borg produced a scale that provides a scoring system from 6 to 20 according to how the athlete feels when running (see Table 6.2a). The figures Borg chose relate quite closely to the heart rate (divided by 10) that the athlete would achieve while exercising at those different ratings.

More recently, the original Borg scale has been modified to come into line with the observation that the perception of effort does not increase linearly with increasing exercise intensity. Rather, as the runner approaches lactate turnpoint, the perception of effort increases very steeply. The new Borg scale (B.J. Noble

Table 6.2a   Ratings of Perceived Exertion (RPE) Scale: The Original Borg Scale

Rating	Perception of effort
6	
7	Very, very light
8	
9	Very light
10	
11	Fairly light
12	
13	Somewhat hard
14	
15	Hard
16	
17	Very hard
18	
19	Very, very hard
20	

Note. From G. Borg, "Perceived Exertion: A Note on History and Methods," *Medicine and Science in Sports and Exercise*, **5**(2), p. 92, 1973. Copyright © by American College of Sports Medicine. Adapted by permission.

et al., 1983; see Table 6.2b) takes account of this by reducing the range of ratings that describe mild to moderate exercise (0 to 3) and increasing the range of ratings for heavy exercise (4 to 10). Using the scale, the athlete is able to accurately describe the exact intensity of any exercise, particularly that of more vigorous exercise. One of the best uses to which you can put the new Borg scale is to record in your logbook the intensity of your training sessions.

Another method for determining effort during running is to monitor heart rate during exercise. We know that maximum heart rate falls with age. A simple equation to remember is that the maximum heart rate (in beats/min) can be calculated as 220 minus age in years. Thus the maximum heart rate at age 40 is 220 minus 40, which equals 180 beats/min. Two other factors that reduce the maximum heart rate are endurance training and heart disease. All young highly trained athletes and most patients with heart disease have maximum heart rates that are lower than expected for age.

Maximum benefit from training is achieved by training at between 60 and 90% of maximum heart rate. Ideally, heart rates should fall between these values for most of the training time. Values higher than these should be achieved only during short-duration speed training, lower values only when you are jogging

Table 6.2b   Ratings of Perceived Exertion (RPE) Scale: The Category-Ratio Scale of Perceived Exertion—the New Borg Scale

Rating	Perception of effort	
0	Nothing at all	
0.5	Very, very weak	(just noticeable)
1	Very weak	
2	Weak	
3	Moderate	
4	Somewhat strong	
5	Strong	(heavy)
6		
7	Very strong	
8		
9		
10	Very, very strong	(almost maximal)
>10 (any number)		(maximal)

Note. From B.J. Noble, G. Borg, I. Jacobs, R. Ceci, and P. Kaiser, "A Category-Ratio Perceived Exertion Scale: Relationship to Blood and Muscle Lactates and Heart Rates," *Medicine and Science in Sports and Exercise*, **15**(2), p. 523, 1983. Copyright © by American College of Sports Medicine. Adapted by permission.

during the days of recovery from hard training or racing. Table 6.3 can help you control your exercise intensity on the basis of your exercising heart rate.

The heart rate ranges in Table 6.3 are for persons with normal hearts. Anyone with known heart disease should first get a specialist's advice before embarking on an exercise program.

To use this method to control exercise intensity, you must measure your pulse rate accurately. This can be done by counting your pulse rate at any convenient spot where you feel a pulse. The most common spot is the artery on the thumb side of your wrist. Touch this spot lightly with three fingers until you feel a pulse. Start counting immediately after exercise and count for 10 seconds only, because the pulse rate returns to slower resting levels very rapidly. Then multiply the 10-second count by 6 to get a heart rate in beats per minute. Check either of these two counts against the values in Table 6.3, which lists training heart-rate ranges for normal people.

Exercising heart rates between 60 and 90% of the maximum heart rate correspond to a rating of perceived exertion of 10 to 12 on the Borg scale, an effort perception best described as comfortable.

Table 6.3   Maximum Heart Rates and Target Heart Range for Different Ages

Age	Maximum heart rate (Beats/60s)	Target heart rate range (Beats/60s)	Target heart rate range (Beats/10s)
20-29	200	120 to 180	20-30
30-39	190	114 to 168	19-28
40-49	180	108 to 162	18-27
50-59	170	102 to 150	17-25
60-69	160	96 to 144	16-24
70+	150	90 to 132	15-22

The 3rd Law of Training:
Train First for Distance, Only Later for Speed

The initial key to successful training is the amount of time you spend running each week and the distance you cover rather than the speed at which you run.

Therefore, at first you should aim to run for a certain time each session. You will run farther when fresh and rested than when you are tired. Remember, the initial goal in distance training is to gradually increase the speed or effort that you can maintain for prolonged distances.

If you train only for distance, your performance will reach a definite plateau after a few years of training. To improve further, you must either increase the distance you run in training or run the same distance but run some of that distance at a faster pace (i.e., train for speed).

The evidence clearly indicates that increasing the distance run in training is frequently counterproductive, particularly when the weekly training distance goes beyond about 190 km a week. Rather, the judicious use of a limited amount of speed training at the correct time can produce quite dramatic improvements in performance (see Figure 5.5).

If you wish to try speed training, my advice is to first read all you can about the different methods of speed training (see chapter 8; Daws, 1977; Galloway, 1983; J.B. Gardner & Purdy, 1970; Glover & Schuder, 1983; Henderson, 1977; Lydiard & Gilmour, 1978; Osler, 1978). Then speak to the experts—the speed-trained athletes and their coaches—and find a group of experienced runners whose running performances are similar to yours but who perform regular speed training as part of their peaking programs.

The reasons for speed work relate to both physical and mental needs. Faster running trains the quadriceps and the fast twitch muscle fibers in all the leg muscles. These are the muscle groups and the muscle fibers that you need during the marathon but that remain untrained if you run only slowly during training. Another benefit of speed training is learning to relax at speed. Furthermore, fast running likely adapts the ventilatory muscles for high work rates and may help in prevention of the "stitch."

Speed work is also a psychological necessity, because a target is set and a time is laid down. Like the race, speed work is a test of the will. The choice is simply between doing and not doing the chosen task, and there is no place for explanations, excuses, and rationalizations. Only when you have successfully faced that reality in the unforgiving solitude of the track are you ready for that best race.

But speed work is not without risk; the twin dangers are running the sessions too often and running too fast. The athlete who is as idle as myself is not likely to fall into these traps. My ideas about this type of training are described in greater detail at the end of this chapter, and the ideas of some of the world's greatest runners are in chapter 8.

The 4th Law of Training: Don't Set Yourself a Daily Schedule

Novice runners often choose to run each day according to a prearranged schedule. This approach is less than ideal because, as Newton pointed out, the weather may not always be appropriate and the body may not always be ready to undertake the training scheduled for that day. In particular, factors either within the body (e.g., minor illness or muscle soreness indicating lingering fatigue from the last workout) or external to it (e.g., work and family commitments, lack of sleep, and travel) may reduce the body's ability to perform on that day and, more important, its ability to benefit from that particular training session. Inappropriate training performed with sore and damaged muscles will not only be ineffectual, because the damaged muscles are unable to perform properly, but will also delay muscle recovery.

A daily schedule should act only as a guideline. Knowing how much to train on any given day comes from learning to "listen to your body." This, of course, is much more difficult than religiously following a detailed training schedule, because it demands insight and flexibility, attributes not everyone possesses. Yet the ability to know how much training to do on any particular day ultimately determines running success. There is immense wisdom in Liquori's statement: "What is pain or discomfort to a relatively inexperienced runner is merely information to the elite runner" (Liquori & Parker, 1980, p. 78).

Other methods of regulating training are described in chapter 10 in the section on preventing overtraining.

Probably the most effective technique I can suggest is to monitor how your legs feel at the start of and during each run. When you are training hard, it is usual for your legs to feel slightly tired and lethargic at the start of a run. This feeling should lift rapidly as the run progresses. Muscle stiffness and soreness that either persist or get worse during the training run indicate that you should abandon the run and observe a period of rest to allow muscle recovery before you undertake another hard or long training session. When 24 to 48 hours of rest do not return a feeling of strength to your legs, then you are well on the road to overtraining.

The 5th Law of Training: Alternate Hard and Easy Training

This law was discussed in detail in chapter 5. The law does not really mean you should train hard every second day with only one rest day in between; rather, train hard only twice a week.

The 6th Law of Training: At First Try to Achieve as Much as Possible on a Minimum of Training

For some reason, part of the "macho" image of running is the belief that the top runners achieve greatness by enduring training programs quite beyond the levels of the rest of us. The best runners, some believe, are those who train the hardest. Seldom do you ever read about the many great athletic performances that have been achieved on very little training or about how very well these top runners perform even when they train very little, as described in chapter 8.

It is clear that genetic abilities have more effect on the performances of great athletes than do their "harder" training programs; there is no earthly way by which training can reduce the gap that separates these runners from the rest of us.

Unfortunately, too many runners believe that they must train very hard to run very well, and so they end up doing too much to try to compensate for their genetic deficits. But by starting with a modest training program and then gradually increasing and modifying the balance between increasing training distance and training speed (see Bruce Fordyce, chapter 8), you can avoid the crossover point where increased training leads to worse, not better, performance and to increased risk of injury.

The 7th Law of Training:
Don't Race When You Are in Training, and Run Time Trials and Races Longer Than 16 km Only Infrequently

This law was reviewed in detail in chapter 5 and is discussed further in chapter 8. The essential point to remember is that fast running exhausts not only the body but also, equally important, the mind. Thus, the amount of fast training and racing that you do must be very carefully controlled.

The rule of thumb is that the shorter the race, the more frequently it can be run; approach runs beyond 25 km with caution, because it appears that racing-induced muscle damage starts to occur in races longer than 25 km.

As a general rule, only two to three races longer than 32 km should be raced each year. By *racing* I mean running to total exhaustion. You can certainly enter shorter races more frequently, but again you must exercise extreme caution and restraint, as discussed in more detail in chapter 9.

Lydiard (Lydiard & Gilmour, 1978) advocated running regular time trials during the peaking phase. Yet he shared Newton's concerns about the dangers of racing in training:

> The words "time trials" often give a wrong impression of their use. Basically they are used to develop coordination in running races over certain distances, and to find weaknesses and use the appropriate training to strengthen them. Time trials should not be run at full effort, but with strong, even efforts, leaving you with some reserves. (Lydiard & Gilmour, 1978, p. 76)

Lydiard spoke out strongly against racing in training and placing too much reliance on the stopwatch. He noted that too much concern with time can cause the athlete to lose confidence, a feeling that would be exacerbated by fatigue from heavy training: "Remember that when you are doing time-trials, you are still training hard, so good times cannot always be expected. You cannot train hard and perform well simultaneously" (Lydiard & Gilmour, 1978, p. 77).

In running regular time trials, many runners err by thinking that each trial must be faster than the last. This is neither desirable nor possible. The surest indication that you are improving is if you are able to run the same or better times in successive time trials but at a lower heart rate, with less effort, and with a more rapid recovery.

The 8th Law of Training:
Specialize

All training is specific to the exercise type, and there is little crossover of the training effects. Running trains only the legs, leaving the upper body relatively untrained, whereas canoeing and swimming train mainly the upper body, leaving the legs untrained. Thus, swimming and canoeing do not improve running ability, or vice versa. Other examples of training specificity, in particular adaptation to uphill versus flat running, to high-altitude running, and to hot-weather running, have been described in previous chapters.

The closer you tailor your training to the specific demands of the sport for which you are training and to the environment in which you will compete, the better you will perform.

The 9th Law of Training:
Incorporate Base Training and Peaking (Sharpening)

This law was fully covered in chapter 5. The important practical point is that you must perform your most intensive training only during the last 6 to 8 weeks before any competition. Furthermore, once you have peaked you can maintain that peak for only 4 to 8 weeks. During that period you should only race and should do no hard training (see Figure 5.5).

The 10th Law of Training:
Don't Overtrain

Overtraining can lead to such symptoms as poor racing performance, extreme fatigue, and illness. This law is so important that chapter 10 is dedicated entirely to a detailed review of this very major problem.

The 11th Law of Training:
Train With a Coach

Many runners fail because they do not have someone to motivate or guide them. The successful coach is the person who can provide these vital functions. The coach can immediately assess when the athlete is doing too much and can provide the vital inspiration, guidance, and mental comfort necessary.

The 12th Law of Training: Train the Mind

Success in running is ultimately determined not so much by training your body but by training your mind. This helps explain why consistently successful runners always perform well, why equally trained runners seldom perform equally, and why some runners who perform superbly in training never succeed in racing.

Percy Wells Cerutty was one of the first coaches to identify the importance of mental preparation for running. Certainly Cerutty recognized that his greatest protégé, Herb Elliott, was mentally different:

> Elliott . . . had the ''gift'' of being able to exhaust himself. That is shared by very few. It is a type of personality, individuality, not of training. You have it—or you do not have it. . . . Elliott had it 100 percent. His greatness as a runner rested in this. (Cerutty, 1964, p. 29)

Later, Elliott wrote:

> If you emphasize the physical side of training you may become superbly conditioned but mentally not advanced at all. On the other hand, if you concentrate on the mental aspect, it is inevitable that the physical side will follow. My golden rule is to train for the mental toughness and don't train for the physical development. (Lenton, 1981, p. 32)

Another great miler, Marti Liquori (Liquori & Parker, 1980) wrote in a similar vein: ''The athletes who truly make it . . . are mentally some of the toughest people in the world. No one is born with that kind of toughness, and it doesn't come overnight. You must develop it, cultivate it, cherish it'' (p. 149).

Chapter 7 examines in greater detail the mental side of running.

The 13th Law of Training: Rest Before a Big Race

Tapering is the reduction in training load that occurs in the period leading up to the race. No one knows precisely how long one should taper before a big race, but I believe that it may take at least 10 to 14 days and possibly even longer for the body to recover fully from months of heavy training and racing. Chapter 5 contained examples of athletes who performed exceptionally and who set world records when they were forced to do little or no training because of serious injuries that occurred shortly before those events. This is called the Zatopek phenomenon.

Specific guidelines for tapering are provided in chapter 9.

The 14th Law of Training:
Keep a Detailed Logbook

Chapter 5 emphasized the importance of a well-kept logbook. The essential information that should be included in the logbook are the date, the training route, the details of the training session, the shoes worn, the running time and distance, running partners, and the weather. This provides the basic descriptive data to which you will return over the years to see, for example, how much and how fast you are running in comparison to what you did in the past or to see with whom you have run over the years.

Nine additional pieces of information must be included in the logbook, not because they have any value initially but because they will eventually tell you whether you are overtraining.

1. *Note how each run feels.* Pay particular attention to muscle soreness, the level of fatigue, and the intensity of your effort. The way you can use this information is described in greater detail in chapter 10.

2. *Record the effort rating of each run.* For this, use the new Borg scale (see Table 6.2). This information tells you when you are reaching your peak, because you will run at a higher perceived intensity but will feel less fatigued. In contrast, high ratings of perceived exertion during exercise of low intensity indicate that you are tired and need to rest.

3. *Rate the enjoyment rating of each run* (J.E. Martin & Dubbert, 1984). On this scale, a score of 1 indicates a very unenjoyable run; a score of 3, a neutral run; and a score of 5, a very enjoyable run. If your running sessions score consistently low on the enjoyment rating scale, then you need to analyze the cause. You may be running too much and may therefore be overtired, or you may be running at too high an intensity. If the running continues to be unenjoyable, the chances are that you will drop out and stop exercising. Urgent action needs to be taken if your running continues to be unenjoyable.

4. *Record your waking pulse rate,* that is, the pulse rate measured within a few minutes of waking in the morning. If your waking pulse rate suddenly increases more than five beats a minute above the normal value, you have done too much the previous day and should either train very little that day or rest completely (see chapter 10).

A refinement of this technique is to remeasure your heart rate exactly 20 seconds after first getting out of bed in the morning. Your heart rate increases when you stand up, and the degree of this increase is also used as an early indicator of overtraining (see Figure 10.2).

5. *Record morning body weight.*

6. *Record postworkout body weight.* As described in chapter 10 (p. 416), Richard Brown, an exercise physiologist from Eugene, Oregon, showed that these measurements (Numbers 5 and 6) also indicate when an athlete is overtraining.

7. *Record the time you go to bed and the number of hours you sleep.* Again, changes in sleeping patterns provide another easily measured indicator of overtraining.

8. *Record heart rate after each interval.* This is important if you regularly perform speed work sessions.

9. *Women should record their menstrual cycles.* This helps a woman determine whether her performance is influenced by her menstrual cycle and, if so, whether she wishes to alter the timing of menstruation, particularly before competition.

The 15th Law of Training: Understand the Holism of Training

The holism of training encompasses two ideas. First, training itself must be balanced and varied; second, what happens in the hours that we are not running also has a major influence on how we run.

It is vital to realize that everything affects how you run and train. Unfortunately, only the professional athletes are ever able to manipulate their lives so completely that running becomes their central focus. For the rest of us, running must compete with various other activities. To do our best, we must first recognize these enemies and try to keep their interference with our running to a minimum.

The four factors that need careful attention when you are training hard are diet, sleep, other physical effort during the day, and work stress.

When training heavily I like to reduce my total caloric intake and avoid fatty foods and red meat. I have no idea why this is necessary. However, I was glad to read that Galloway (1983) has also found that fatty foods seem to impair running performance and that this effect becomes more marked with age.

When training hard, I generally sleep an additional hour per night on those days that I train hard or long, and I also try to nap for an hour on both Saturday and Sunday afternoons.

As my work is totally cerebral, I have no need to avoid physical effort during the day. But those who are required to do some physical work during the day should, if possible, try to limit the amount of that work, especially when training hard or when preparing for a major race.

Finally, avoiding excessive work stress, such as overtime, excessive travel, and endless meetings, is another essential training trick. This is discussed further in Step 6—*don't let running become just another stress.*

STEP 6: FOLLOW THESE OTHER PRACTICAL TIPS

Learn How to Breath Properly

Runners should learn yoga breathing, or "belly breathing," which involves breathing predominantly with the diaphragm rather than with the chest muscles.

With belly breathing, the chest hardly moves at all. Rather, it appears that the abdomen (stomach) is doing all the work; as you breathe in, your stomach goes out, and when you exhale, your stomach retracts (see Figure 6.5). Note that the term belly breathing is incorrect, albeit descriptive. The diaphragm, not the belly, does the work.

Proper breathing prevents the development of the "stitch," a condition that occurs only during exercises that are undertaken in the erect posture and that involve running, jolting, or both (A. Abrahams, 1961; Rost, 1986; Sinclair, 1951). The pain of the stitch is usually felt on the right side of the abdomen, immediately below the rib margin. Frequently the pain is also perceived in the right shoulder joint, where it feels as if an ice pick were being driven into the joint. The pain is exacerbated by downhill running and by fast, sustained running

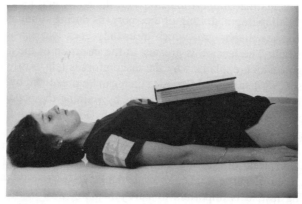

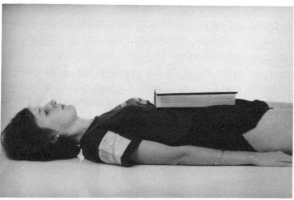

Figure 6.5 Learning how to belly breathe. A book placed on the abdomen will rise on the intake of breath (inspiration) and fall when the breath is expelled (expiration).

as in short road races or time trials. Other factors that predispose you to the development of the stitch are lack of training, weakness of the abdominal muscles, cool weather, nervousness, starting a race too fast, and eating and drinking before exercise (Rost, 1986). In addition, constitutional factors seem to be involved, because only certain people are susceptible to the condition.

You can immediately stop an attack of the stitch by lying down with your hips elevated; this also helps differentiate the stitch from other conditions, including chest pain due to heart disease. About 20% of athletes have residual discomfort on deep inspiration for 2 to 3 days after an attack of the stitch (A. Abrahams, 1961).

For various complex anatomical reasons, the fact that the stitch causes discomfort in the shoulder joint suggests that the diaphragm is the cause of the pain. The historical (A. Abrahams, 1961; Sinclair, 1951) explanation which is still favored (Rost, 1986) for this condition is based on the anatomical finding that a group of ligaments that support the stomach, the liver, and the spleen are also attached to the diaphragm. Jolting of these organs during running is believed to cause strain on the diaphragm, which ultimately goes into spasm, causing the pain of the stitch. The tension is greatest at the insertion of the diaphragm into the rib margin, which explains why the discomfort is felt mostly under the rib margin. Rost (1986) suggested that the stitch can be prevented by avoiding food and water for 2 to 4 hours before exercise, by training the abdominal muscles with appropriate sit-ups (see chapter 13), and by learning how to breathe with the diaphragm—to belly breathe.

To belly breathe, lie on the floor and place one or more large books on your stomach. Concentrate on making the books rise when you breathe in and fall when you exhale. Because it takes about 2 months to learn to do that movement while running fast, it is important to start practicing well before an important race.

A change in breathing pattern may help relieve the stitch. Within a short period of starting a running session, breathing becomes synchronized with footfall. Thus, one automatically breathes in when landing on one leg and out when landing either on the same leg or on the opposite leg. This phenomenon was first reported by Bramble and Carrier (1983). Of particular interest was their finding that most runners are "footed," that is, the beginning and end of their respiratory cycle occurs on the same foot, usually in a stride:breathing ratio of either 4:1 while jogging or 2:1 while running faster. Runners, then, become habituated to breathing out on the same leg. This produces asymmetrical stresses on the body and could be a factor in both the stitch and in certain running injuries.

Train With Company

When starting training you should train with others, because this helps to maintain interest and motivation. Train with experienced runners only if they will run at a slow pace. Generally, they will run faster than the novice and are uncomfortable when running at the much slower pace of the beginner. Do not try to impress experienced runners by trying to stay with them in training. The end result will be that you run too far, too fast, too soon and develop the inevitable running injury, in particular shinsplints or a stress fracture.

At First, Train Only on the Flat

Hill running stresses the quadriceps, which are usually untrained, particularly in people who previously have walked only on the flat, an activity that stresses mainly the calf muscles.

For this reason, it is better to initially walk and jog on the flat, using muscles that are not totally untrained. Only when able to run comfortably on the flat for about 30 minutes should you attempt hills.

Run in Scenic Areas

Before I started running, I did not appreciate the scenic beauty that surrounds me. I feel that one of the beauties of running is that it can bring us back into contact with our environment and thus enhance our awareness of nature.

When on the Road, Run Defensively

Once fitness improves, it becomes necessary, sooner or later, to run on the roads. Once that happens, you become exposed to the runner's greatest enemy—the car. I have lost two friends who were knocked down and killed while running; another three were lucky to live after cars hit them. As the number of runners on the roads continues to escalate, the potential for these tragedies only increases.

Many of these tragedies can be avoided, as shown by A.F. Williams (1981), whose study of American runners revealed that collisions between joggers and automobiles typically occurred after dark when the jogger was running on the road in the same direction as the traffic. Most often, the runner who was struck was running abreast of another runner and was closest to the road (A.F. Williams, 1981). In only 27% of the cases were the drivers primarily responsible for the collisions, and in most such cases, the drivers were under the influence of alcohol or drugs. Thus, in the vast majority of cases, the jogger was either totally or partially responsible for the collision. Adherence to the following simple rules will greatly reduce the risk of these tragedies (Osler, 1978; A.F. Williams, 1981).

- Adopt a defensive attitude when running on the road.
- Constantly watch every oncoming car, and listen for cars coming from behind. Be ready to jump to safety at the first indication of potential trouble.

- Always select roads with little traffic and very wide shoulders.
- Run facing the oncoming traffic.
- Run on the edge or shoulder, not on the road itself.
- Run in single file or not more than two abreast. Large running groups are particularly dangerous, especially when runners are on both sides of the road. When this happens, the drivers of oncoming cars are unable to drive onto the edge in the case of an emergency.
- If you must run at dusk or at night, choose a safe, well-lit route and wear clothing of bright, visible colors with reflective material attached. Osler (1978) wrote, "Yellow, orange and red might not be the colours you prefer from the standpoint of fashion, but you must make yourself as visible as possible to motorists. Never wear blue, brown or dark gray" (p. 59).
- Be especially careful when you are tired. Fatigue impairs the concentration, slows the reflexes, and seems to make runners feel they are indestructible, a combination of factors not unlike the effects of alcohol intoxication.
- The most worrysome situation is, as Osler (1978) pointed out, the overtaking car that comes up from behind runners on their side of the road. The nearest I have ever been to being hit by a car has always occurred in this situation.

I was not always as careful as I now am when running on the roads. But I have learned my lessons and have (I hope) grown up. Nevertheless, I remain gravely concerned by the needlessly cavalier attitudes that many runners have toward road safety. These runners seem to act as if they own the roads, and they exhibit extreme arrogance toward other road users. This attitude is not only unnecessary but is extremely stupid. For in an accident with a car, the only loser is the runner, regardless of whether or not that runner is at fault.

Do Regular Stretching and Strengthening Exercises

Running causes the muscles that are active to become strong and less flexible, whereas the opposing muscles that are relatively underused become weaker. To maintain flexibility and the correct balance between opposing muscle groups, you need to perform special exercises on a regular basis. Chapter 13 gives examples of the appropriate stretching exercises that runners, particularly those who are injured, should consider doing regularly.

Eat as You Feel

The special nutritional requirements of endurance athletes are described in detail in chapter 15. All beginners need know is that the body will dictate its requirements. Thus there is no need to follow a special diet.

As an individual becomes more active, the major alterations that occur in dietary preference are the desires to eat more carbohydrates (starches), in particular sweets and fruits, and to increase fluid intake. These are natural responses. The carbohydrate content of the diet determines how rapidly the muscle and liver glycogen stores will be replenished after exercise, and a high-carbohydrate diet best ensures that these stores will be rapidly replaced (see chapter 3). Fluid intake increases spontaneously to replace that which is lost in sweat and from the lungs with breathing. Drink fluid during exercise only if the exercise bout lasts more than an hour. About 500 ml of fluid—cold water or a favorite refreshment—should be drunk for every hour that you run (see chapter 4).

Salt losses during short-duration exercises are relatively trivial, so it is not necessary to increase salt intake when training. There is also no need to increase protein intake, and we have no convincing evidence that the intake of vitamins and minerals should be increased above the extra intake that will result from the increased intake of food.

Sleeping Time

Although the amounts of time that individuals sleep can vary quite remarkably, with some sleeping as little as 4 hours a night, the average person sleeps between 7 and 8 hours a night. With harder training, the amount of time you need to sleep will likely increase.

Arthur Newton described the changes in sleeping patterns that occur with an increase in physical activity:

> Physical exercise . . . needs more time for recuperation than mental work. While indulging in a heavy dose of this latter only, I used to find five hours' sleep quite sufficient; but no sooner did I sheer off into rigorous training that I noticed a seven to eight hour stretch, or even more, was desirable. . . . When it is a matter of super-intensive training, you may require as much as nine hours abed each night. (Newton, 1935, pp. 172-173)

Many runners don't get enough sleep because they don't budget for that time taken out of the day. If you are running 2 hours a day and sleeping an extra hour every night, then you need to budget 3 hours a day for training.

Weather Conditions

You need to take special precautions if you wish to exercise in severe environmental conditions (see chapter 4). For more mild conditions, I advise runners not to exercise vigorously in the very early morning if the temperature is very cold (below freezing). The likelihood of developing upper respiratory tract infections seems to increase if one consistently trains very hard in very cold air. Also, wear rainproof clothing if it is raining heavily and a strong wind is blowing. Wind increases the windchill factor, and if your clothes are wet you could develop a critical reduction in body temperature (hypothermia) if you run for too long under such conditions (see chapter 4).

This advice differs slightly from that of Newton, who, as a competitive runner, was less inclined to let the weather affect his training. He also observed correctly, despite incorrect reasoning, that running in the cold weather is altogether less taxing than is running in the heat.

Don't Let Running Become Just Another Stress

I frequently see runners who can't understand why they are unable to work and run hard at the same time. They are unaware that running is an additional stress that, when added to their already highly stressful lifestyles, may prove too much.

Runners are usually people involved in many demanding activities, each of which we try to do with the same perfection we desire of our running. But once the total stress from all our various activities exceeds our stress-coping capacities, then we will in time break down, the most obvious indication of which is the overtraining syndrome. A typical example of this phenomenon is that of a runner who wrote to me.

This runner tried to combine training for the standard marathon with a very heavy work load. This meant he had to run early in the morning under very cold conditions and often had to work very late. Added to this were the stresses of a high-powered business environment, all of which led to recurring bouts of flu. Although he aimed to run a 3:30 marathon, he was forced to walk from 23 km to the finish and completed the distance in a shade under 5 hours. The athlete stayed in bed for the next 3 days.

This neophyte runner thought he could add the stress of running to his already overstuffed life without taking something else away to make room. By getting up early he was reducing his sleep; worse, he was running in very cold air temperatures, which increase the likelihood of respiratory infection. A vicious cycle developed in which he was simply becoming progressively more fatigued and therefore less able to cope not only with running but also with all the other aspects of his life.

STEP 7: IN THE BEGINNING FOLLOW SOME KIND OF TRAINING PROGRAM

Although following a rigid daily training program violates the fourth law of training, I have found that most beginning runners require some kind of training program to assist them in the initial year of running. In particular, the program allows them to run without constantly worrying about what they should be doing.

Many different training programs have been drawn up for those wishing to start running, and these are available in a variety of publications (Bloom, 1981;

Galloway, 1983; Glover & Schuder, 1983; Henderson & Maxwell, 1978; Squires, 1982; Temple, 1980). I am sure that they are all very similar and will be equally effective. However, to my knowledge, none of them has been scientifically tested in a sufficiently large group of subjects to determine real effectiveness in practice. The training program included in this chapter has undergone at least some field testing.

From August 1982 to March 1983, our research group trained a group at the University of Cape Town of 32 previously sedentary subjects to run a standard marathon. In the end, 26 finished the standard marathon in times ranging from 2:59 to 6:05. The program these runners followed was modeled on the Henderson and Maxwell (1978) marathon training program, to which an initial 8-week walking program was added. The original program was adjusted slightly in light of the results achieved:

• Even reasonably healthy, young, and otherwise athletic individuals will most certainly develop injuries between the 8th and 12th weeks of training if they do not first start with a solid base of walking.

• The original program of 7 months was too short a training period for the average beginner to train for a standard marathon; certainly, very athletic individuals can do it in this time, but the average person requires 8 to 9 months.

• Performances suddenly improved dramatically after 20 weeks of training.

The 36-Week Training Program for 10- to 42-km Races

The 36-week training program (see Table 6.4) was designed to allow a novice to complete a 10-km race after 25 weeks and a marathon after 36 weeks. The table lists the time (in minutes) you should exercise each day. Thus the code *W 20* for Day 1 of Week 1 means that you should walk for 20 minutes on that day.

Although most people think that to become runners they must begin by running, it is essential to only walk for at least the first 3 weeks and then to introduce running very slowly. It is in fact, far better to walk for the first 6 weeks of the program rather than risk an injury, which might force you to stop running for 6 weeks. The initial walking period allows the bones time to strengthen (second law of training) so that they can resist the more demanding stresses to which they will be exposed subsequently. This period also provides the opportunity of ensuring that your heart is sound and not causing symptoms that require medical evaluation (see Step 2). The main aim is to acquire the exercise habit rather than to become fit—the concept of shaping described earlier in this chapter.

On the 1st day of the 4th week, running finally begins. The designation *W15.R5* for that day indicates that you should walk for 15 minutes and jog/run for 5 minutes. Over the next 14 weeks the amount of time spent jogging will gradually increase, until after 17 weeks each training session includes only running, which is shown by the *R30* designation.

Table 6.4   10- to 42-km Races: 36-Week Training Schedule

Day	Week 1	Week 2	Week 3	Week 4	Week 5	Week 6
1	W20	—	W20	W15, R5	—	W10
2	—	W20	W20	W20	W20	W20, R5
3	W20	—	—	—	—	—
4	—	W20	W20	W20	W20	W15, R5
5	W20	—	W10	—	—	—
6	—	W20	W20	W20	W15, R15	W15, R5
7	W20	—	—	W10	—	—

Day	Week 7	Week 8	Week 9	Week 10	Week 11	Week 12
1	W5, R5	W5, R5	W5, R5	R10	W15, R5	W10, R10
2	W15, R5	W20, R5	W20, R5	W20, R10	W20, R10	W15, R15
3	—	—	W10, R10	—	—	—
4	W15, R5	W15, R5	—	W20, R10	W20, R10	W20, R10
5	—	—	W10, R10	—	—	—
6	W15, R5	W20, R5	—	W20, R10	W20, R10	W15, R15
7	—	—	W15, R10	—	—	—

Day	Week 13	Week 14	Week 15	Week 16	Week 17	Week 18
1	W10, R10	W10, R10	W5, R15	W5, R25	R30	R30
2	W10, R20	W10, R20	W5, R25	—	—	—
3	—	—	—	R30	R30	R30
4	W15, R15	W10, R20	W10, R20	W5, R15	R20	R20
5	—	R10, W10	W5, R25	R30	R30	—
6	W10, R20	W10, R20	—	—	—	R30
7	—	—	W10, R10	W5, R15	R20	R20

Day	Week 19	Week 20	Week 21	Week 22	Week 23	Week 24
1	R30	—	—	—	—	—
2	—	R30	R30	R25	R35	R20
3	R30	R20	R30	R40	R30	—
4	R30	—	—	—	—	R20
5	—	R30	R35	R30	R25	R45
6	R20	R30	R25	R25	R35	—
7	R20	R15	R20	R20	R20	R20

Day	Week 25	Week 26	Week 27	Week 28	Week 29	Week 30
1	R40	R45	R30	R30	R35	R35
2	R20	R30	R45	R55	R60	R70
3	—	—	R30	R30	R35	R35
4	R20	R30	R50	R55	R60	R70
5	R50	R50	—	—	R35	R35
6	—	R45	R60	R80	R90	R100
7	R30 (or 10-km race)	—	—	—	—	—

Day	Week 31	Week 32	Week 33	Week 34	Week 35	Week 36
1	R40	R40	R40	R40	R40	R40

(Cont.)

Table 6.4 **(Continued)**

Day	Week 31	Week 32	Week 33	Week 34	Week 35	Week 36
2	R80	R90	R90	R90	R90	R20
3	R40	R40	R40	R40	R40	R30
4	R40	R90	R90	R90	R30	—
5	R35	R40	R40	R40	R40	—
6	R110	R120	R150	R100	R80	—
7	—	—	—	—	R20	Marathon

Note. All measurements are in minutes. W = walk; R = run.

During the period from the 4th, to 17th weeks, certain symptoms may appear for the first time. These include persistent calf-muscle soreness and discomfort along the border of the shinbone—the tibia. This condition is known as shin-splints, which tends to disappear with time without recourse to the more involved treatment regime described in chapter 14.

These symptoms indicate that training, however light it might seem, is too intensive and that at least for a few weeks until the symptoms abate, more rest days are required and less distance should be run. If these simple measures do not alleviate the symptoms, you should consider changing running shoes and possibly seeking professional advice (see chapter 14).

All running must be done at a comfortable pace, without concern for speed (second law of training). The essential feature during this period of running is not to become breathless or overly tired. The average training pace will probably be 5 to 7 min/km; if you are able to train at that pace, you will be able to run the marathon.

If after some months you are still unable to run comfortably at 7 min/km or better, this indicates that your $\dot{V}O_2$max is too low to allow you to complete a marathon in under 4:30:00 (see chapter 2). Runners in this predicament might as well accept their genetic limitations and restrict their interests to shorter races.

Resist any desire to start running earlier than is indicated on the schedule, bearing in mind the risk of injury occurring after 10 to 12 weeks. Why the risk of injury is so high during this stage is unknown; this phenomenon has also been noted in army recruits who become most prone to injury after about 2 months of training.

Evidence indicates that the bones in the lower limbs undergo some demineralization during the first 3 to 5 months of training before becoming stronger after about 10 months (Kuusela et al., 1984; see chapter 14). Unfortunately, fitness starts to improve dramatically after about 10 weeks of training, and the novice will want to start training more intensively at the very time when the bones are weakest. For this reason, it is best to start slowly so that both the extent of bone demineralization and the rate of fitness enhancement are reduced.

Interestingly, there are few studies of the real distances people run in training for a marathon. Researchers from Glasgow University (S.J.Y. Grant et al., 1984) studied 88 runners in the 1982 Glasgow Marathon and found that the average distance run was 60 km/week for the 12 weeks prior to the race and that distances ranged from 24 to 103 km. The authors concluded that no relationship exists between weekly training distance and marathon time (as also shown by Franklin et al., 1978) and that despite apparently inadequate training, runners did not slow down dramatically after hitting their predicted "collapse points" at about 27 km. Thus, the authors could find no evidence for the "collapse-point theory" proposed by K. Young (1978), which holds that runners who do not train more than 101 km/week collapse during the race and are reduced to a shuffle when they race distances that are more than 3 times their average daily training distances for the last 8 weeks before the marathon. Finally, as in the study of Franklin et al. (1978), these novice marathoners were unable to predict their marathon times accurately. However, the accuracy of their predictions did improve the nearer those predictions were made to race day.

Beginning Runner's Ultramarathon Training Program

Surprisingly, there are some runners for whom the marathon is not enough. Those who have completed a marathon and who wish to tackle an ultramarathon of up to 90 km can do so by following the 22-week training schedule listed in Table 6.5. For example, the coding of this table on Day 1 of Week 1—*48 (8 km)*—means that you should run for either 48 minutes or for 8 km, whichever is shorter.

It should be apparent that these distances and times are calculated for an athlete whose normal speed is about 6 min/km, the training speed of the bulk of recreational ultramarathon runners. If your training speed is faster than 6 min/km, pay attention to the distances given on the training schedule. If your training speed is slower than 6 min/km, pay attention to the times given in the training schedule. The slow runner who tries to run the distances listed will be doing too much.

The major difference between training for 10 to 42 km and for over 42 km is the length of the long weekend runs, which gradually increase from 16 km to the longest of 60 km. I believe that the long weekend training run is the most important feature of any training program for marathon and longer races. If you were to drop some of your training, the only thing you should not drop is the long training run on weekends. Anyone able to complete two 32-km training runs in the final 6 weeks before a marathon can be confident of finishing that race regardless of how well the rest of the training has gone. More advice about training, including training for distances up to 1,000 km, is provided in chapter 9.

Table 6.5   Ultramarathon: 22-Week Training Schedule

Day	Week 1	Week 2	Week 3	Week 4	Week 5	Week 6
1	48 (8)	—	—	—	—	—
2	60 (10)	48 (8)	96 (16)	96 (16)	96 (16)	96 (16)
3	60 (10)	60 (10)	96 (16)	96 (16)	66 (11)	66 (11)
4	78 (13)	96 (16)	78 (13)	78 (13)	96 (16)	96 (16)
5	—	78 (13)	96 (16)	96 (16)	96 (16)	114 (19)
6	96 (16)	—	—	—	—	—
7	—	114 (19)	114 (19)	144 (24)	156 (26)	192 (32)

Day	Week 7	Week 8	Week 9	Week 10	Week 11	Week 12
1	—	—	—	—	—	—
2	114 (19)	114 (19)	114 (19)	114 (19)	96 (16)	96 (16)
3	72 (12)	72 (12)	96 (16)	96 (16)	132 (32)	132 (22)
4	96 (16)	96 (16)	96 (16)	96 (16)	96 (16)	96 (16)
5	132 (22)	132 (22)	114 (19)	96 (16)	114 (19)	114 (19)
6	—	—	—	—	—	—
7	240 (40)	120 (20)	240 (40)	120 (20)	288 (48)	120 (20)

Day	Week 13	Week 14	Week 15	Week 16	Week 17	Week 18
1	—	—	—	—	—	—
2	96 (16)	96 (16)	96 (16)	96 (16)	114 (19)	78 (13)
3	132 (22)	132 (22)	132 (22)	132 (22)	114 (19)	96 (16)
4	96 (16)	96 (16)	96 (16)	96 (16)	96 (16)	114 (19)
5	114 (19)	114 (19)	114 (19)	132 (22)	96 (16)	132 (22)
6	—	—	—	—	—	—
7	288 (48)	240 (40)	120 (20)	288 (48)	360 (60)	120 (20)

Day	Week 19	Week 20	Week 21	Week 22
1	—	—	48 (8)	48 (8)
2	96 (16)	96 (16)	96 (16)	48 (8)
3	132 (22)	114 (19)	96 (16)	30 (5)
4	96 (16)	96 (16)	114 (19)	—
5	132 (22)	96 (16)	96 (16)	—
6	—	—	—	—
7	240 (40)	120 (20)	60 (10)	Ultramarathon

Note. All measurements are in minutes (kilometers).

A Final Word

The training programs listed in Tables 6.4 and 6.5 have been designed solely for neophyte runners who wish to complete races of 10 to 90 km in relative comfort. Almost anyone can follow the first 25 weeks of training on Table 6.4, and for many this will be sufficient. Those who continue training at that level for the rest of their lives will expend between 6,000 and 7,000 kJ of energy per week and can expect reductions in heart attack risk of about 25% (see Figure 16.4) and increases in life expectancy of 1 to 2 years, depending on the age at which they first started running (Paffenbarger et al., 1986).

Before advancing to the ultramarathon program listed in Table 6.5 you should either have run your first marathon in under 3:45 or have been running for 1 to 2 years. However, if you wish ultimately to be a very good marathon or ultramarathon runner, you should not follow these programs. Rather, you should first race at short distances on the track, on the road, and cross-country. Only when you are running your fastest possible over 10 km should you consider entering marathon and ultramarathon races. In chapter 8 we discuss further this concept that the training that is best for 10-km races is, with some minor modifications, also best for races of up to 100 km. As Grete Waitz (Waitz & Averbuch, 1986) wrote, "The roots of every great runner, and all great running, are on the track" (p. 102).

These programs should be followed in spirit rather than to the letter. Daily training sessions should be modified according to your feelings on the day. Take particular care to avoid the symptoms of overtraining described in chapter 10. Set aside 2 days a week for rest, more when you are fatigued.

STEP 8: ENTER RACES OF PROGRESSIVELY LONGER DISTANCES

Running races is totally different from training, because racing produces its own peculiar stresses: the presence of a large number of experienced runners, learning to pace oneself, fighting to grab sponges, and the confusion caused by trying to drink at tables.

So it is best to run a number of short-distance races before you tackle a standard marathon. Thus, by the time you run your first marathon you can concentrate on what it takes to go the distance rather than be confused by all the distractions that surround racing. I suggest that you run races of 4, 8, 10, 12, 16, 21, 24, and 32 km before trying the marathon. You should run a 56- to 60-km race before tackling an ultramarathon of 90 to 100 km.

These races will also provide opportunities to practice the advice for racing given in chapter 9 and to establish a pace you will likely run in a marathon.

STEP 9: LEARN FROM PERSONAL EXPERIENCE

Every athlete is different. Although the training approach described in this chapter has general application to all athletes, the specific details will vary from individual to individual. In particular, the relative emphasis that different athletes will place on different aspects of their training will vary.

The only way to determine what is most appropriate for you is to observe carefully how you personally respond to different training methods. Continue experimenting until you finally discover the training methods that produce the best results for you, regardless of how unusual such methods may be.

Virtually all that I have written and quoted from great runners in this book has had to be selective and will necessarily be biased. Thus, I consider it important to describe in some detail what I have learned from my personal experiences and how the knowledge I gained writing this book has altered my training beliefs.

In general my training approach has always been like that of Newton—lots of long slow distance to the exclusion of speed work. For the first 6 to 8 years of my running career I trained exclusively by running long slow distances. However, I now firmly believe that this training approach, which emphasizes distance training to the virtual exclusion of speed work, although very safe, is really not the best way to train for any distance, including ultramarathons. I agree with Bannister, who said that high-mileage distance training increased the athlete's speed of recovery from effort but that it had not been shown to increase racing speed. To increase racing speed, the athlete must do just enough and not too much speed training.

The evidence shows, without doubt, that the fastest middle-distance and cross-country runners are the best runners at all distances, even up to the very long ultramarathons (see chapter 8).

With this background, I will detail my training practices.

The 20-Week Hard-Training Program

The initial goal of my hard-training program is to condition myself to be able to run 112 km/week, a distance that I have also found to be optimal for the majority of recreational runners who have major time constraints. Recent studies have been unable to show that training more than 120 km/week produces any additional physiological benefits to competitive racers (Sjödin & Svedenhag, 1985). This weekly distance is also used by the middle-distance athletes trained under Bill Bowerman (see chapter 5) and was also advocated by Herb Elliott (Lenton, 1981). This distance is about twice that I normally run when not training hard. An important reason I do not run further in training is that when I start running further (e.g., up to 160 km/week) I begin to feel that I am doing nothing but running. I feel rather like Ron Daws, who trained for the 1968 Olympic Marathon in the dark mornings and evenings of a Minnesota winter (Daws, 1977). He wrote that at times he returned from his runs not knowing whether he should be going to bed or getting ready for a day's work. Once I reach that state, I am no longer able to maintain my interest in running.

Worse, though, heavy training unquestionably affects one's creativity; such training interferes with other commitments and may introduce other adverse stresses such as inadequate sleep, excessive fatigue, family disharmony, and missed deadlines. Having written previously that running enhances one's productivity and creativity, I must now admit that too much training has the opposite effect. As always, Arthur Newton recognized this:

> Aggressively serious physical effort left me with a positive disinclination to study anything that needed real brain work . . . so much of my available energy was used for training that only a mere trickle was left over for recreational purposes, not nearly enough to permit me to delve into metaphysics or similar intricate matters which always beckoned me. I regretted it all the time, for I felt I was losing a great deal in the way of education, yet to neglect even a small part of my training might make all the difference between reasonable certainty and chance, and I distrusted and dislike the latter. (Newton, 1947, p. 66)

I suspect that the biochemical explanation for this is that heavy training causes depletion of certain brain chemicals, the reduction of which also explains the relaxing and tranquilizing effects of running and, in the long term, leads to the overtraining syndrome (see chapter 10). This effect is also the reason serious runners cannot work at jobs that demand excessive mental effort, particularly in the afternoons; this is especially true during periods of intensive training.

For approximately the first 10 weeks of my hard-training program I gradually increase my training from 90 to 110 km/week. At first, my average training speed will be slower than 5 min/km; I will struggle up each hill, and the longer runs will be particularly tiring. I judge the stressfulness of these runs not only by how I feel during the run but also by how quickly I recover after the run. A run that has been too long or too hard will make me want to sleep for an hour or two, I will be unable to do any mental work that day, and the following day I will run tiredly. A run that is just the right length will leave me a little tired; I will need to sleep for only a short time, after which I will be able to do an hour or two of mental work if I so choose. By the following day's run my body will have recovered so that my gentle recovery run of 6 to 14 km is effortless. During this phase, I will run three to five short races of up to 16 km. Any longer races that I might enter will constitute long training runs.

This break-in phase, the details of which are contained in Table 6.6, lasts for 10 to 12 weeks, during which time my long weekend runs will be no less than 24 km and no longer than 32 km. The major indications that this phase has had its desired effect is that I start to finish the long runs so fresh that I want to run farther on the following long run; simultaneously my average training speed starts to increase, and the hills that I run become easier. When this happens I am ready to move onto the second (peaking) phase of my program.

I do most of this training to and from work, and all is over hilly terrain. Tuesday and Thursday afternoon runs will occasionally include slightly faster runs, either track or hill repetitions.

Table 6.6   Tim Noakes's Typical Base Training Week

Day	Morning	Evening
Monday	5 km	7 km
Tuesday	7 km	7 km
Wednesday	7 km	7 km
Thursday	7 km	7 km
Friday	5 km	5 km
Saturday	24-32 km	—
Sunday	—	8-14 km
Total	96-110 km	

The Peaking Program for a 10-km Race or for the Standard Marathon

The First 6 Weeks

The next phase of my 20-week hard-training cycle differs depending on whether I am preparing for a 10-km race, a standard marathon, or an ultramarathon. The essential difference is that for the 10-km race and the standard marathon, I mostly emphasize speed training and maintain a weekly training distance of about 120 km/week; for the ultramarathon, I emphasize distance training and long weekend runs and add speed training only when I have completed the heavy distance training.

My training for the 10-km race and the standard marathon differs from that in Table 6.6 only in that I will emphasize speed-training sessions either on a Tuesday or a Thursday each week and will run 2 or 3 races of 10 to 16 km but no further under any circumstances. I have found that these are, for me, the optimum racing distances to prepare for both the 10-km race and for the marathon. Longer races tend to cause more severe damage to my muscles, which slows my recovery. Also, from a psychological viewpoint, the marathon breaks up neatly into two 16-km and one 10-km race, so that during the marathon race, I concentrate on running as close to my best times for each of these distances as is possible. When properly prepared, one can come remarkably close to this goal.

Speed Work

As far as speed work goes, I have observed the following:

1. *Proper speed work probably requires the presence of a coach (11th law of*

training). Speed work requires more finesse and understanding than does long-slow-distance running because speed work is more likely to cause injury or physical breakdown. For these reasons, it is essential to work with someone who can objectively analyze whether the speed work is having the desired effect.

The following statement by Lydiard may at first seem to contradict this advice.

> There is no coach in the world who can say exactly what an athlete should do as far as the number of repetitions, distances, and intervals are concerned. Not even physiologists can tell an athlete that. The important point is that the athlete knows what he is trying to achieve and goes out and works at it until he does. (Lydiard & Gilmour, 1978, p. 12)

I believe Lydiard is saying that the coaching of athletes doing interval training is just as empirical as are all forms of coaching, which is all the more reason to have two heads working on the problem rather than just one.

2. *Fast running is best done when the body and mind demand it.* Fast running should be an enjoyable change from the occasional monotony of long training runs. When fast running is not enjoyable, this indicates that the body is too tired, and the session must be postponed until the speed session again becomes pleasurable. Remember the different approaches of John Walker and Derek Clayton. If Walker struggles in an interval training session he packs up and goes home; when Clayton struggled he carried on until he had completed what his mind said that his body should do. Such obsession is inevitably destructive and explains why Clayton was so frequently injured (see chapter 8).

3. *Speed training cannot be done indefinitely.* Carlile and Lydiard taught us that 6 to 8 weeks of intensive training, when added to a solid training background, are all that is needed for a peak performance; many researchers seem to agree (Daws, 1977; Dellinger & Freeman, 1984; Galloway, 1983; Glover & Schuder, 1983; Osler, 1967, 1978). Even Clayton (1980) wrote that he could sustain heavy training for only 10 weeks before his performances began to deteriorate. Significantly, Hill came to precisely the same conclusion (R. Hill, 1982): "My ideal build-up to a peak occupies a period of 10 weeks" (p. 160). When two of the world's best marathoners come to the same conclusion independently, then there is likely to be some truth in it. Yet often I have known not only runners but other endurance athletes who have tried to maintain heavy training for longer than this period and who have all come badly unstuck either because of injury or overtraining. This is always a tragedy: They have invested much effort, which, for the want of just a little knowledge, has been wasted.

4. *The most beneficial forms of speed training for marathon and ultramarathon runners seem to be hill running and fast, long intervals on the track.* The

principles of hill training have been best described by Daws (1977). Although Lydiard includes the use of short intervals (100 and 200 m) in his marathon training methods, I think that longer intervals (800 m to 1 mile) are probably better for 10-km and marathon training.

5. *One of the joys of speed training is the rapid improvement that is felt.* Very little effort produces remarkable rewards. I have found that when I start my interval training sessions, I may be able to run only two or possibly three 1-mile repetitions, each of which are very tiring. But after four or five such sessions, I am able to do twice as many repetitions, and I can run them much faster and without the distress I experienced in the first session.

As long as I am running as fast as or faster than before with the same or less effort, I know that the speed training is beneficial. However, if the sessions become increasingly difficult and if my interval times start to slow, I know that I am in trouble and that my body is telling me it has done too much and requires rest, not more training.

Many runners make a critical error in believing that decreases in performance during these sessions indicate they are not sufficiently motivated and are not trying hard enough. So, instead of resting, they try harder and simply compound their errors and the risks of overtraining. There is a danger that by training under these conditions, not only do the runners damage themselves physically, but they use up the motivation they should conserve for their one all-out racing effort.

6. *Short races of 5 to 16 km are excellent forms of speed training.* These races should be run as hard efforts controlled by the sensation of effort rather than by the stopwatch (seventh law of training).

When I am peaking, I use such a race as the equivalent of a hard interval session. I do this by starting the race at a comfortable pace, which I increase gradually with each kilometer. By the end of the race I will have run 4 to 8 km at a hard pace (equivalent to an interval session of three to five 1-mile repetitions). But because I start slowly without concern for my total time and do not race the entire distance, the overall stress is reduced and I recover more quickly.

Another reason for running short-distance races is that they usually fall on weekends, when I need a long training run. Galloway (1983) and Glover and Schuder (1983) emphasized that speed work or a race should never be combined with a long training run on the same weekend: "Never put two stress days together under any circumstances" (Galloway, 1983, p. 134). Indeed Galloway suggested that even after a race of only 10 km, you should have about 1 week of easy running before tackling speed work or another long run. He also stressed that 2 easy days should follow each hard session or long training run (fifth law of training).

By racing half or less of the total goal-race distance in these "training" races, I can run them more frequently.

7. *The total number of speed sessions during the peaking phase should be between 7 and 10.* This conforms closely to Galloway's suggestion that one should perform only one speed session a week when training for 10 km and one every 2 weeks when training for the marathon.

8. *Always keep your goal race pace in mind.* My best marathon pace is about 4:00/km. Therefore, any session in which I run under 3:45/km becomes a speed session, and running any faster really makes no sense.

Galloway (1983) provided additional useful guidelines for interval training: Run 400-m repetitions at approximately 5 to 7 seconds faster than your goal race pace; run 800 m at 10 seconds faster than your goal pace; and run 1 mile at 15 to 20 seconds faster than your goal pace. If you are unable to achieve these goals during interval training, you are almost certainly training at too high a mileage and will need to cut back if you are to benefit optimally from this type of training.

9. *Rest for as long as desired between each interval repeat.* You should never complete an interval session feeling totally fatigued. The key in the interval sessions is to complete the required number of repetitions at the required speed; the total time required to achieve that is unimportant.

You can use the nomogram in Figure 2.8 as a guide to the training speeds you should attempt during training. Burfoot and Billing (1985) suggested that optimum training is achieved by including regular runs at three different intensities in one's weekly training. They suggest that most of your training needs to be done at intensities of between 65 and 75% $\dot{V}O_2$max, which are lower than the pace at which you run the marathon. The purpose of these runs, the authors suggest, is to improve running efficiency. Once a week, you should schedule a run of 5 to 10 km at 85% $\dot{V}O_2$max. The purpose of this run is to shift the lactate turnpoint to a higher percent $\dot{V}O_2$max. This exercise intensity corresponds to the speed one can maintain during races of 10 to 21 km. It is not necessary to run the 5 to 10 km of this session continuously. Rather, the authors suggest, this workout can be run on the track or road as a series of repeat runs of 2 to 3 km each.

Finally, you should run one session a week at a running pace eliciting a $\dot{V}O_2$ value that corresponds to the speed at which you can run 3 km (see Figure 2.8). Run this as an interval session on the track, and follow the guidelines already described. Burfoot and Billing suggest that this session should comprise three to six 800-m intervals or eight to twelve 400-m intervals. I think that these distances are too short for less competitive marathon runners.

Notice that as you become fitter and your performances on the Mercier/Leger/Desjardins nomogram improve, so the speed at which these workouts should be run will also increase.

Costill (1986) also provided a list of what he considers appropriate times for different intervals based on best 10-km time (see Table 6.7). He divides the interval sessions into *anaerobic, aerobic*, and *aerobic-anaerobic*. He suggests that the *anaerobic* sessions should comprise ten 200-m intervals with 2 minutes of rest between intervals; the *aerobic* sessions twenty 400-m intervals with 10 to 15 seconds of rest; and the *aerobic-anaerobic* sessions ten 400-m intervals with 60 to 90 seconds of rest between intervals.

Competitive runners who wish to read a review of the methods of speed training are referred to Dellinger and Freeman (1984), a book based on the Oregon system of training distance runners.

The Last 2 Weeks

During the second to the last week before the 10 km or the marathon, I reduce my training to 50 to 80 km of easy running, and I rest and carbohydrate load for the last 3 days before the race. The intervening 4 days incorporate 3 days of mild carbohydrate restriction and runs of 12 to 18 km, depending on how I feel.

The Peaking Program for the Short Ultramarathon (56 Miles)

The First 6 Weeks

Having completed a 10-week break-in period similar to the one described under training for the 10-km race or standard marathon, I am ready to start increasing the weekly distances I run in training with the aim of peaking with 2 weeks of 160 km (see Table 6.8).

Notice that the major difference between the training program described in Table 6.8 and that in Table 6.6 is that the total running distance on Tuesdays and Thursdays is greatly increased in Table 6.8, as is the distance of the long weekend-training runs. The relative rest days of Monday, Wednesday, Friday, and Sunday remain the same.

The key during this phase is to increase gradually the total distance run each week by increasing the amount run on the 3 hard-training days. I pay exquisitely careful attention to the symptoms of overtraining, and if any of these develop, I don't run on the relative rest day and I approach the next hard-training day with utmost caution. Should these symptoms remain even after a full day's rest, then

Table 6.7   Optimum Running Times for 10 km

| | Intervals | | |
Best 10-km time (min:s)	200 m (anaerobic)	400 m (aerobic)	400 m (aerobic-anaerobic)
46:00	00:46	2:00	1:51
43:00	00:43	1:52	1:44
40:00	00:40	1:45	1:37
37:00	00:38	1:37	1:29
34:00	00:36	1:30	1:16

Note. Adapted from *Inside Running: Basics of Sports Physiology* (pp. 98, 101, 103) by D.L. Costill, PhD, 1986, Benchmark Press, Canmet, IN. Copyright 1986 by Benchmark Press, Inc.

Table 6.8   Tim Noakes's 6-Week Peak Training Program for the Short Ultramarathon (90 km)

Day	Morning	Evening	Effort rating
Monday	5 km	7 km	Jog
Tuesday	16-21 km	8-15 km	Moderate
Wednesday	7 km	7 km	Jog
Thursday	16-21 km	8-15 km	Hard
Friday	5 km	5 km	Jog
Saturday	42-60 km	—	Moderate
Sunday	—	12-16 km	Jog
Total	138-182 km		

the next hard-training day becomes a light-training day, and this continues until all symptoms have disappeared. What is really remarkable is how quickly the body recovers when given a chance. With just 24 hours of rest I am usually fully recovered, and the next training session is inevitably a delight.

Two other important indicators of whether the training load is optimal are the times run over a regular training course and performance in interval sessions or time trials. I frequently run the same course between my work and home. By regularly checking my running times over that course, I can immediately spot when I am doing too much, because the run will take longer and will require more effort. Conversely, fast, effortless runs indicate that I am approaching my peak.

A question that is yet to be resolved is whether, when one is training hard, each training week should be of the same distance or whether there should be a varied pattern in which, for example, the normal mileage of 140 km is run the 1st week, reduced by 20% (to 112 km) for the 2nd week, increased by 15% (to 160 km) for the 3rd week, and reduced by 50% (to 70 km) for the 4th week. The need for variation is argued by both Galloway (1983) and Costill (1979). Galloway feels that we all need one week of reduced training each month to allow our bodies to repair themselves. My own feeling is that Galloway is probably correct and that altering weekly training distances probably also reduces the risk of overtraining. But the 6-week hard-training program is probably just short enough to reduce the risk of overtraining, particularly because the program leads directly into the tapering and sharpening period. The athlete who plans a longer buildup should consider varying the training distances.

The Last 4 Weeks

During the last 4 weeks before the ultramarathon, I reduce training distance according to the formula that Fordyce developed (see Table 8.27): from 100% in the 5th to the last week before the race to 26% during the last week before the race.

During this period, the emphasis shifts to speed work sessions. I try to run four or five such sessions during the 4-week period. These should especially emphasize hill running if the ultramarathon is to be run on a hilly course.

The Effects of Age

When I first penned these pages I was enjoying the peak physical age of the early 30s. I could not conceive that with the passage of just a few short years, much of what I took for granted would need to be modified.

Now that I am over 40, I know there are concessions one has to make to aging. One simply can no longer train with the same intensity. One of the first great runners to consider this possibility was Jeff Galloway, who represented the United States in the 10,000 m in the 1972 Olympic Games and held the American 10-mile record.

As he prepared to turn 40, Galloway (1984) realized that the runner's dream of racing and training immortality is a myth. He accepted that his future enjoyment of running would require a more measured approach than he had previously practiced. Based on his observations of the successful adaptations made by other older runners, Galloway has concluded that the older runner requires a day of rest after each day of running. He believes that recovery from a hard workout does not occur as quickly in the older runner.

Does this mean that the older runner can no longer expect to run well? Apparently not. Galloway refers to the experience of former 2:11 marathoner Jack Foster, who celebrated his 50th birthday by running a 2:20 marathon. His weekly training at the time comprised 3 days of running, with a long cycle of 3 to 4 hours on the weekends. George Sheehan also ran his fastest-ever marathon at age 62 on three 10-mile runs a week.

When I visited Galloway in Atlanta, I learned firsthand that he now practices this approach; he runs only every 2nd day and limits his running to 30 miles a week. Despite this, he still runs 10 km in under 32:00.

My own approach has been influenced by Galloway. I now run less and include swimming and especially cycling in my training schedule. On many days my muscles are either too stiff or too fatigued to run; cycling provides a gentle alternative, especially after hard races or training. Recovery from long cycling rides, which seem to be of equivalent health and possibly training benefit, is much more rapid than from long runs.

STEP 10: BEWARE OF THE SELFISH RUNNER'S SYNDROME

Noel Carroll, the Irish double Olympian who began running at the age of 15 and has been running for more than 25 years, was the first runner to dare suggest that everything might not be absolutely rosy on the runner's home front. He wrote, "Runners make better lovers but sometimes lousy spouses: that is the problem" (Carroll, 1981, p. 65).

But his message does not end at that. "Runners are an introverted lot. They like to keep their thoughts to themselves. Their behaviour is at best anti-social, at worst utterly selfish. . . . It can create an atmosphere that does nobody any good and certainly not the runner" (p. 13).

Running can indeed become an extremely selfish activity. I once asked one of the world's most lauded ultradistance runners what running had taught him. His answer was that it had taught him how incredibly selfish he is. And to compete at his level, running must come first. But in his case, such selfishness can be justified by his lack of family commitments, by the level of excellence he has achieved, and by the fact that without such selfishness he would not have reached the same heights. He warns, however, that one must not be too antisocial: "So don't run in a world of your own: it's everybody else's world as well. You must consider your family, friends and workmates. You must consider those who you expect to tolerate you. You must be prepared to compromise" (Carroll, 1981, p. 68).

The problem of the Selfish Runner's Syndrome is most acute for those of us who have family commitments and who lack the champion's talent. I have found that to balance everything, paying appropriate attention to work and family, requires almost as much effort as does running. To put all our reason for living into racing is inappropriate and ultimately may be harmful. The joy of running should be that it adds to, rather than detracts from, our lives.

7

Training the Mind

"That the mental is destined to play an even more important part in sport than ever before is, however, my firm conviction. Physical attributes are essential to success in sport but their full use in exercise can be obtained only by the correct mental and physical control."

Jack Lovelock (Tobin, 1984)

"Mind is everything: muscles—pieces of rubber. All that I am, I am because of my mind."

Paavo Nurmi (Lovesey, 1968)

"Running or any natural exercise is physical as well as mental development, and makes the whole machine more capable. . . . When your physique is about as near perfection as Nature can make it, all your abilities become greatly enhanced; you can work better, think more clearly and play more actively and intensely than before. . . . A welcome result is that you get a lot more enjoyment out of life, which is what we look for: we only do things because we consider the result will bring us pleasure on one way or another, even if it is only indirectly."

Arthur Newton (1949)

"Together Cerruty and Elliot have brought athletics to the threshold of a new era. They have proved conclusively that not only the body but also the mind must be conquered."

Derek Ibbotson (T. O'Connor, 1960)

"A man runs with his mind and emotions, just as much as with his legs and circulatory system. . . . The mental-emotional aspects of training should be just as carefully planned as the physical aspects."

Kenneth Doherty (1964)

"If you want to be a champion, you will have to win every race in your mind 100 times before you win it in real life that last time."

Marti Liquori and John Parker (1980)

"There's probably going to be a quantum leap forward when we understand our minds better. I believe that we just barely understand our physical capabilities at this stage of the game. There will come a time when knowledge of ourselves will enable us to tap that physical resource. At this time, we'll see a quantum leap in all sports."

Herb Elliot (K. Peters, 1981)

"The difference between my world record and many world class runners is mental fortitude. I ran believing in mind over matter."

Derek Clayton (1980)

"Running is not like a team sport. You have to be egocentric. But you also have to separate the race from the rest of your life; you shouldn't become an egocentric personality."

Grete Waitz and Gloria Averbuch (1986)

Despite all I have written about preparing the body for running, I suspect that the preparation of the mind is the more important factor determining running success.

In the first portion of this chapter I will try to shed some light on how the mind should be prepared for competition and how the mind should be occupied during competition. Next we will look at the psychological changes that occur with training, and finally we will examine the issue of "running addiction."

IMPORTANCE OF THE MIND IN SPORT

We shared a place where no man had yet ventured—secure for all time, however fast men might run miles in the future. We had done it where we wanted, when we wanted, how we wanted. . . . In the wonderful joy, my pain was forgotten. (p. 193)

The words are, of course, those of Roger Bannister (1955), the man who as a medical student, training as little as 1 hour a day during his lunch hour, was the first to run the mile in under 4 minutes.

Latterly, it has become popular to conclude that Bannister's knowledge of medicine and of exercise physiology (Bannister et al., 1954a, 1954b) explained why he and not other, possibly more gifted, runners like Arne Anderson, Gunder Haegg, Wes Santee, or John Landy had been the first to break that mystical 4-minute barrier. This is an assumption that we have, to our detriment, been making far too long.

Bannister himself would never have considered that his scientific knowledge gave him any sort of advantage. He saw that his medical training really taught him to observe and understand himself better: "A medical training aims at increasing the power of careful observation and logical deduction. Because understanding other people starts from understanding ourselves, the self-analysis which sport entails can be very helpful to the medical student" (Bannister, 1955, p. 121).

What, then, was Bannister's secret? I think success came first to him because he, better than anyone, perceived that the battle for the 4-minute mile was fought in the mind, not in the body. Gunder Haegg, the man who in 1945 came within 1.3 seconds of breaking the 4-minute mile, wrote this about 1 month before Bannister's great race: "I think Bannister is the man to beat four minutes. He uses his brains as much as his legs. I've always thought the four-minute mile more of a psychological problem than a test of physical endurance" (Doherty, 1964, p. 216).

Bannister's genius told him what was most important—the conditioning of the mind until it would "release in four short minutes the energy I usually spend in half an hour's training" (Bannister, 1955, p. 184).

In his preparation Bannister reduced the race to its simplest common denominator—400 m in 60 seconds or multiples thereof. He trained until running 60 seconds a lap, 24 km/hr, became automatic. "In this way a singleness of drive could be achieved, leaving my mind free from the task of directing operations so that it could fix itself on the great objective ahead" (Bannister, 1955, p. 184).

And when he achieved that great objective at Oxford's Iffley Road track on May 6, 1954, Bannister's unique experience allowed him to write one of the most significant paragraphs in the running literature:

> Though physiology may indicate respiratory and cardiovascular limits to muscular effort, psychological and other factors beyond the ken of physiology set the razor's edge of defeat or victory and determine how closely the athlete approaches the absolute limits of performance. (Bannister, 1956, p. 224)

That few runners or their coaches have ever grasped the implications of what Roger Bannister said is shown by an almost total dearth of material about the mental side of training and competition. To correct this, we will compare Roger Bannister's intuitive approach to mental preparation for racing with the approaches suggested in other modern books that I found to be useful (Garfield & Bennett, 1984; Kauss, 1980; Liebetrau, 1982; Nideffer, 1976, 1985; Orlick, 1980; K. Porter & Foster, 1986; Rushall, 1979).

PSYCHOLOGICAL PREPARATION FOR COMPETITION

Brent Rushall (1979), professor of physical education at Lakehead University, Ontario, Canada, studied the mental practices of a large number of Canadian elite sportspersons from a variety of sports. He found the majority of these athletes used quite similar psychological strategies for mental preparation before and during competition. This suggests that regardless of their sports, successful competitors employ similar mental approaches to competition, and these approaches are different, presumably, than those used by unsuccessful athletes. Table 7.1 provides a synthesis of Rushall's findings.

We will now review the evidence that reveals Roger Bannister's intuitive approaches along these same lines.

Bannister's Mental Preparation

Concentration on a single goal during training. More so than most athletes, Bannister needed a supreme goal to justify the sacrifices he made. In particular, he had to justify the time spent away from his medical studies. Beaten into fourth place in the 1952 Olympic Games 1,500-m final because he was "not nearly tough enough" to run two heats and a final in 3 days, Bannister found his goal.

> My running had become something of a crusade. It was as if I were preaching about a special attitude towards running that I felt was right. . . . I could accept being beaten in the Olympics—that had happened to many stronger

Table 7.1   Mental Attributes and Approaches to Competition of Elite Canadian Athletes

1. The successful athlete has the ability to concentrate totally on the upcoming competition throughout the training period.
2. The successful athlete has the ability to put more into competition than into training.
3. The successful athlete has absolute confidence in his/her ability to perform up to expectation.
4. The successful athlete has the ability to judge very accurately how he/she will perform in competition.
5. The successful athlete has a detailed competitive strategy; the more detailed the strategy, the greater the athlete's confidence.
6. The successful athlete's competitive strategy includes what to do if things go wrong.
7. Before competition, the successful athlete performs as many mental rehearsals of the competition as is possible.
8. The successful athlete is not upset by any small distractions or problems that may arise before competition.
9. If troubled before competition, the successful athlete knows what to do to regain composure.
10. If the successful athlete becomes too excited before competition, he/she knows what to do to calm down.
11. If the successful athlete loses confidence before competition, he/she knows what to do to calm down.
12. The successful athlete is not affected by unfamiliar competitive arenas.
13. The successful athlete is able to handle any unusual circumstances or distractions that may occur at the site of competition.
14. The successful athlete does not worry about other competitors before a competition.
15. The successful athlete prefers to be alone immediately before competition and prefers to warm up alone.
16. The successful athlete does not need a coach to be present at the warm-up.
17. The warm-up of the successful athlete contains practices of things to be done during competition.
18. The successful athlete exhibits controlled levels of nervousness and tension at the start of the competition.

Note. From *Psyching in Sport. The Psychological Preparation for Serious Competition in Sport* (pp. 20-26) by B.S. Rushall, 1979, London. Published by Pelham Books, © 1979 by Professor Brent S. Rushall. Adapted by permission.

favourites than me. What I objected to was that my defeat was taken by so many as proof that my way of training was wrong. (Bannister, 1955, p. 164)

And so, with the significant help of his coach, Franz Stampfl (Lenton, 1983a, 1983b; K. Moore, 1982), and his running companions, Chris Brasher and Chris

Chataway, Bannister set out to prove that it was still possible to be a champion on as little as 1 hour of training a day. Then, in December 1952, the Australian John Landy ran a mile in 4:02.1, and the race for the 4-minute mile began in earnest.

The ability to put more effort into racing than training. This is shown by Bannister's comment that he needed to "release in four short minutes the energy I usually spend in half an hour's training."

The ability to perform up to expectation. In June 1953 Bannister and Chris Brasher ran a 4:02 mile during an invitational race at a school's athletic meeting. Having come so close under such artificial conditions, Bannister realized that he was capable of running a 4-minute mile.

In contrast, Landy, who had by April 1954 run the mile under 4:03 on six occasions, said: "It is a brick wall. I shall not attempt it again" (Bannister, 1955, p. 181).

The ability to judge competitive ability. Bannister trained principally by running repetitive intervals of 400 m. In April 1954, when he was able to run ten 400-m intervals in 59 seconds each, with a 2-minute rest between intervals, he considered that he was ready. Then, 8 days before his greatest day, he ran a three-quarter mile in a high wind. The watch recorded a time of 2:59.9. "I felt that 2 min. 59.9 sec. for the 3/4-mile in a solo training run meant 3 min. 59.9 sec. in a mile race" (Bannister, 1955, p. 185).

Having a detailed competitive training plan. Bannister realized that there were four essential requirements for a sub-4-minute mile: a good track, the absence of wind, warm weather, and even-paced running. He knew that only Landy could ever beat him to a 4-minute mile, but that if he waited until they happened to race each other, it might be too late. Thus, the famous Iffley Road race was conceived, and the details of how Chris Brasher and Chris Chataway would pace Bannister during the epic race were planned by their coach, Franz Stampfl (Lenton, 1983a, 1983b).

Concerning the tactics he used in his famous race with Landy, Bannister wrote the following:

> Tactical plans for big races have to be thought out in advance. The runner must be prepared both to meet possible moves by an opponent and to retain the flexibility to modify his scheme if something happens unexpectedly. The simpler such plans can be, the better, because the mind can be free during the race. . . . This makes it easier to relax and run "more economically."
>
> My plans were extremely simple. I had to force John Landy to set the pace of a four minute mile for me. . . . I must reserve my effort of will power for the moment when I would fling myself past him at the finish. Until then I would be entirely passive, thinking of nothing else throughout the whole race. (Bannister, 1955, p. 203)

To ensure that Landy did not choose to run from behind in the race, Bannister, in his last mile race before the Empire Games, ran easily for the first 3 laps and finished with a final lap in 53.8 seconds. He hoped that this would convince Landy, who lacked finishing speed, that he would have to lead from the start.

Having a plan that allows for the unexpected. In his race with Landy, Bannister exhibited his ability to change plans during the race. When Landy had built up a commanding lead by the end of the second lap and showed no signs of tiring, Bannister realized that he would have to forego his prerace plan.

To have any "finish" left I must be able to follow at his shoulder throughout the early part of the last lap. How could I close the gap before the bell? If I were to stand any chance of winning I must reach his shoulder before then. I must abandon my own time schedule and run to his. This was the turning point of the race. (Bannister, 1955, p. 214)

Mental preparation. For the last 5 days before the Iffley Road race, Bannister rested as he began to store "nervous energy." Then he began to run the race in his mind.

Each night in the week before the race there came a moment when I saw myself at the starting line. My whole body would grow nervous and tremble. I ran the race over in my mind. Then I would calm myself and sometimes go off to sleep. (Bannister, 1955, p. 186)

Not being upset by problems before competition. This was one area in which Banister's approach was less than ideal, and in which he required guidance from others.

For on the day Bannister set the 4-minute mile, the wind only abated almost the moment Bannister stepped onto the track. Stampfl (Lenton, 1983a, 1983b) recalls that this upset Bannister, who was "in a blue mood." Only constant persuasion from Chataway and Brasher finally enticed Bannister to the start. Stampfl was convinced that Bannister must run and that if he missed that opportunity, there would not be another.

I knew a bit of rain or wind would make no bloody difference because he was capable of a 3:56 or 3:57 mile. So maybe he'll run a little slower but he would still break four minutes. If he doesn't do it today he'll never do it because . . . how is he going to build up again? When will there be another occasion? What about coping with this kind of mental pressure? How do you know the weather will be better at some future date? For all these reasons Bannister, in my opinion, would never have done it again. (Lenton, 1983a, p. 30)

But Bannister did, in the end, make the right decision. He overcame a potential inability to cope with an unexpected problem.

The ability to regain composure before competition. Bannister appears to have been well composed before most of his races, although his confidence threatened to desert him on occasion, especially before the Iffley Road mile. Yet in the end, he also overcame these barriers.

The ability to calm down before competition. In the hours before setting the 4-minute mile, Bannister "forgot some of my apprehensions" by staying with his friends, the Wendens, at their house, which had "become a second home" for him during his studies at Oxford. "The calm efficiency of Eileen had often helped to still my own restless worries. Never was this factor so important as on this day" (Bannister, 1955, p. 189).

Before his victories at the Empire and European Games, Bannister went for long walks "seeking the mental calm I needed" (Bannister, 1955, p. 17).

The ability to regain confidence before competition. In the hours before both the Iffley Road race and his race with Landy, Bannister suffered a loss of confidence, as previously described. Yet he recovered his composure on both occasions.

Adaptability to unfamiliar surroundings. Bannister makes no mention of his concern about competing in unfamiliar surroundings. Perhaps this was not Bannister's strongest characteristic: His choice of the Iffley track and the familiar surroundings of Oxford for his first attempt at the 4-minute mile indicate that, like everyone, he appreciated the importance of the "home ground" advantage.

Ability to handle unusual circumstances at competition. Although Rushall (1979) found this characteristic in many Canadian elite athletes, I could find no illustrative examples of this in Bannister's running history.

Not worrying about other competitors. By carefully planning his racing tactics in great detail and correctly predicting how his opponents would run, Bannister was able to concentrate on his own running rather than on that of his opponents.

Not requiring a coach at the warm-up. Bannister believed in individual experience: "The things a man learns for himself he never forgets. . . . The things a man does by himself, he does best" (Bannister, 1955, p. 204). Thus, he was reluctant to have a coach.

But in Franz Stampfl, Bannister found a coach who complemented him exactly: "Franz Stampfl's greatness as a coach rests on his adaptability and patience. He watches and waits for the moment when the athlete needs him. . . . Franz is an artist who can see beauty in human struggle and achievement" (Bannister, 1955, pp. 187, 204).

For the historical record, we should note that Stampfl's crucial contributions to Bannister's success in the Iffley Road race were understated by Bannister in his autobiography (Bannister, 1955). Stampfl (Lenton, 1983a, 1983b) claims that the major achievement in the Iffley Road mile was not having Bannister run 3:59 but was getting Chataway and Brasher to the point where they were able to pace Bannister for the first three and a quarter laps. When Stampfl first arrived at Oxford, Brasher was unable to run two laps in 2 minutes, yet in the Iffley Road race he ran two and a half laps at that pace. Similarly, Chataway had a best mile time of only 4:08, yet in the Iffley road race he ran three and a quarter laps at sub-4-minute mile pace. In addition, Stampfl subsequently trained Chris Chataway and Brian Hewson to become the world's fourth and fifth sub-4-minute milers after Bannister, Landy, and the Hungarian Laszlo Tabori.

Chris Brasher confirmed that Stampfl was the major planner of the race but that his omission from Bannister's book would not have been a falsehood in Bannister's eyes: "He had laboured through eight years of preparation, all of it inspired by a dream of self-reliance, of doing it alone. When the time came, he wrote the dream instead of the reality" (K. Moore, 1982, p. 92). Thus, it seems that Bannister's success did not prove that a coach is unnecessary.

The need to be alone at the warm-up. Bannister makes no mention that this was his preference. Certainly, he preferred his own company in the days before competition.

The warm-up contains practice of things to come in the race. Bannister makes no mention of this.

Being nervous at the start. Bannister's nervousness at the start is shown by his anger at a false start in the first sub-4-minute mile race: "I felt angry that precious moments during the lull in the wind might be slipping by. The gun fired a second time" (Bannister, 1955, p. 191). The rest is now history. Bannister went on to run the world's first sub-4-minute mile.

Psychological Strategies During Competition

Before we consider Bannister's mental strategies during competition, let us return briefly to Rushall and detail the competitive behaviors that he found to be exhibited by successful, elite Canadian athletes (see Table 7.2).

Several quotes from Bannister's book indicate that he exhibited most of the behavioral characteristics identified by Rushall.

1. *Not saving himself for a good finishing effort.* According to Rushall, this attribute indicates that in competition elite athletes prefer to stamp their authority on the event from the beginning. Clearly this is not always appropriate in track running, particularly for an athlete like Bannister whose major competitive attribute was his fast finish. Thus, Bannister's major racing tactic was indeed to save himself for the finish, but when this approach was clearly inappropriate, as it threatened to be in his race with Landy in the 1954 Empire Games, Bannister was prepared to risk everything by running himself out.

2. *The ability to concentrate on a strategy throughout the entire contest, to concentrate on technique when tired, and to handle the pressures in the final*

Table 7.2   Competitive Behaviors of Successful, Elite Athletes

1. Elite athletes do not save themselves in order to make a good finishing effort.
2. These athletes are not deterred by the punishing aspects of competition, and they have abilities to concentrate on strategy throughout each contest. When tired, these athletes try harder and concentrate on technique; they are able to handle pressure in the final stages of a close competition.
3. These athletes exert maximum efforts even if they know that they cannot improve their situations. When beaten, they still try to produce best-ever performances.
4. Elite athletes use information and experiences gained in a contest to modify strategies for the next competition.

Note. From *Psyching in Sport. The Psychological Preparation for Serious Competition in Sport* (pp. 26-30) by B.S. Rushall, 1979, London. Published by Pelham Books, © 1979 by Professor Brent S. Rushall. Adapted by permission.

stages of a close competition. Bannister wrote the following about his race with Landy in which he had been forced to change his tactics halfway through the race (see Figure 7.1):

> If I were to stand any chance of winning . . . I must abandon my own time schedule and run to his. This was the turning point of the race. . . . I won back the first yard, then each succeeding yard, until his lead was halved by the time we reached the back straight on the third lap. . . . I had now "connected" myself to Landy again, though he was still five yards ahead. I was almost hypnotized by his easy shuffling stride. . . . I tried to imagine myself attached to him by some invisible cord. With each stride I drew the cord tighter and reduced his lead. . . . As we entered the last bend I tried to convince myself that he was tiring. With each stride now I attempted to husband a little strength for the moment at the end of the bend when I had decided to pounce. . . . When the moment came my mind would galvanize my body to the greatest effort it had ever known. I knew I was tired. There might be no response, but it was my only chance. This moment had occurred dozens of times before. This time the only difference was that the whole race was being run to my absolute limit. . . . Just before the end of the last bend I flung myself past Landy. . . . In two strides I was past him, with seventy yards to go, but I could not accelerate further. (Bannister, 1955, pp. 215-216)

He also described this ability to extend himself when exhausted when he wrote about the closing stages of the 4-minute mile race:

Figure 7.1 Roger Bannister chases John Landy in the "Mile of the Century" at the Vancouver Empire Games, 1954.

Note. Photo courtesy of Die Burger (Photopress, Cape Town).

My body had long since exhausted all its energy, but it went on running just the same. The physical overdraft came only from greater willpower. . . . With five yards to go the tape seemed almost to recede. . . . I leapt at the tape like a man taking his last spring to save himself from the chasm that threatens to engulf him. (Bannister, 1955, p. 192)

Bannister's ability to handle the pressures in the final stages of a close race was obviously well shown in both the 4-minute mile and his race with Landy, but it was also shown in the 1,500-m final of the European Games:

Never did my finishing burst serve me so well. There was no longer any need to call on emotion to produce this ability to take an overdraft on my energy. There had been times in other races when I felt real fear as I tore down the finishing straight as if my life depended on it. . . . This time it was different—I was calm. . . . My mind remained quite cool and detached. It merely switched over the lever, and well-worn channels carried to my body the extra energy that my mind unleashed. (Bannister, 1955, p. 24)

3. *The ability to produce a maximum effort even when beaten.* Reading between the lines, I believe that one of Bannister's learning experiences was the 1952 Olympic Games. Shortly before the Games it was announced that for the first time there would be semifinal heats in the 1,500-m race. This immediately put Bannister at a disadvantage that he knew was fatal, because he was not trained to run three hard races in 3 days. Then, at the Games, Bannister and Chataway saw the awesome running of Zatopek: "Zatopek isn't human in his achievement. . . . While he goes for a 20-mile training run on his only free day, we lie here panting and moaning that the Gods are unkind to us" (Bannister, 1955, p. 154). At the same Games Bannister experienced the special pressures of the Olympic Games: "Now with the whole athletic world concentrated in a few square miles all sense of perspective was lost. Around me every man was giving his best—fighting to the last gasp" (Bannister, 1955, p. 156). And in the emotional stresses that this produced, Bannister and the other British athletes "tied in knots with anxiety . . . realized more about our weakness and strength as we wound up our minds for the trial" (Bannister, 1955, p. 157).

Bannister also realized that he had much to learn about his own self-control, a realization that almost certainly helped him in his later races.

Finally, after days of mental torture, Bannister went out to contest the 1,500-m final:

I hardly had the strength to warm up. As I walked out in front of those 70,000 spectators, my step had no spring, my face no colour. The ruthless fighting of the semi-final, the worry and lack of sleep, had exhausted me. (Bannister, 1955, p. 158)

Despite this Bannister ran the best he could. Lying second at the last bend, he reached down for his finishing kick, but it was not there. "My legs were aching, and I had no strength left to force them faster. I had a sickening feeling of exhaustion and powerlessness as Barthel came past me, chased by McMillen" (Bannister, 1955, p. 159). Despite this, Bannister would finish in fourth place, only 0.8 seconds behind the winner.

4. *The ability to learn from each race and to modify racing strategies accordingly.* Bannister clearly stated his feelings on this topic:

Improvement in running depends on continuous self-discipline by the athlete himself, on acute observation of his reactions to races and training and above all on judgment, which he must learn for himself. The runner has to make his own decisions on the track—he has no coach there to help him. If a man coaches himself then he has only himself to blame when he is beaten. (Bannister, 1955, p. 63)

Each race is an experiment. There are too many factors that cannot be completely controlled for two races to be the same, just as two similar scientific experiments seldom give exactly the same results. By learning, often unconsciously, from mistakes, I discovered my reaction—both desirable and undesirable—to many of the situations I was likely to meet in big races. . . . It was my aim to minimize the effect of the undesirable factors in my running which I could not entirely eliminate, so that my running in a big race would have the spontaneous joy I felt as a boy running wildly along the shore. I wanted to remove all uncertainty and worry except the great uncertainty of victory which is the main driving force. Only in this way could my whole being become absorbed in the struggle. (Bannister, 1955, p. 121)

Summary of Bannister's Legacy

It is clear that a great deal of Bannister's success must have come from his intuition, which convinced him of the importance of his mind in determining his racing performances. It is also clear that he came upon these conclusions quite by himself and had little help from coaches or, more importantly, professional psychologists.

We will now consider how the mind works and how it can be controlled to produce optimum competitive performance. You can find more detailed discussions of this topic in any of the psychological texts to which I have already referred. I think that every athlete at whatever level would benefit by reading at least one of these books.

BASIC CONCEPTS FOR OPTIMUM PSYCHOLOGICAL PREPARATION FOR SPORT

Our psychological makeup comprises our thoughts, emotions, and behaviors and how we interact with others. Each of these factors exerts major influences on how we ultimately behave (perform) in sports. It follows that control of these psychological variables is essential if we wish to ensure that we can always produce a particular behavior (winning).

As a first step to understanding how this control is achieved, consider the following diagram:

STIMULUS $\longrightarrow$ RESPONSE (Behavior)

This simple diagram indicates that observable behavior occurs in response to various stimuli. However, the behavior of different humans to the same stimulus is not always predictable, and, alternatively, different stimuli can produce the same response in different people. This is because behavior is not a simple reflex response to each and every stimulus. A stimulus is processed in the brain and is interpreted in terms of what psychologists call each individual's "belief system" according to the diagram below.

STIMULUS $\longrightarrow$ BELIEF SYSTEM $\longrightarrow$ RESPONSE (Behavior)

Your belief system is an inbuilt system that interprets all incoming stimuli and then activates the response that is appropriate for you, depending on what you believe about yourself and the situation in which you find yourself.

Another important concept is that your belief system, although strongly ingrained, is not fixed and is subject to modification. Thus, many athletes perform less well than they should because they have belief systems that are programmed for failure; such athletes will perform up to their potentials only if their belief systems can be successfully reprogrammed.

To make these concepts more understandable, let us consider a hypothetical situation. Imagine that you are leading the Olympic Games Marathon, with 10 km to go. It has been your life's ambition to win the Olympic marathon. You have paced yourself well, you are running as well as you possibly can, and you are beginning to think that this might just be your year. Quite suddenly and somewhat unexpectedly, another athlete appears at your shoulder.

In this situation you are likely to respond in one of three ways: You will surge immediately and try to break your challenger; you will run with your challenger and try to break away at a later stage of the race; or you will throw in the towel and immediately drop behind. Can you predict what you would do in this situation?

Your response to the challenge will be determined by how you process the stimulus of being passed, how you relate this stimulus to the beliefs you have about yourself (your self-concept), and which thoughts and emotions (in particular those in response to the possibility of defeat) the stimulus arouses.

These in turn are modified by your attitude toward the specific event in which you are competing (i.e., how important it is to you) and, most importantly, by your attitude to the person who is passing you. If, for example, you know that the athlete passing you has won his or her last five marathons and is known for strong finishes, your response to the runner is likely to be very different than your response to another runner who is known to fade badly in the last 10 km of the race.

The kinds of thoughts and emotions that may cross your mind in this imaginary race might lead you to make a verbal comment indicating your distaste for this particular runner. What actually happens in your mind in this type of situation is shown in Figure 7.2.

The stimulus activates emotions and thoughts, termed *self-talk*, which will be either positive or negative, having either a beneficial or a detrimental effect on your performance. The behavior that results, whether positive or negative, will

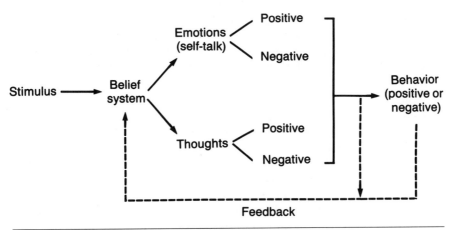

Figure 7.2 The stimulus-belief system behavior diagram.

feed back into your belief system so that the next time you are in the same situation, you will likely respond in the same way.

If you go on to win the race, you will have a greater belief in your self and will consider yourself a winner. But if you fade out of contention, chances are that your belief system will be imprinted with the loser's image and the next time around you will again act as a loser.

This example should be enough to convince you that the control of emotions and thoughts is essential to produce optimum performance. As Liebetrau (1982) said, "Emotions put the fuel in the tank and thoughts provide the steering and other skills of driving" (p. 7). We will now consider emotions and thoughts in more detail and discuss how these might be controlled.

Emotions and Their Control

There are seven basic emotions: joy, sadness, anger, love, fear, shame, and surprise. Other emotions are considered to be combinations of these basic seven.

The emotions you feel in any situation and how you respond to them will depend on four factors: your basic personality, how much control you have over your emotions, your emotional reactivity, and your flexibility. Control of these emotions is achieved by controlling the thoughts that cause them.

Thoughts and Their Control

The thoughts that we experience are influenced by the concepts or attitudes we have toward ourselves and our opponents. Attitudes are the collections of thoughts and emotions that we have about ourselves and others, and these attitudes help to determine which emotions we will feel at any time.

For example, let us return to our previous analogy. The arrival of another athlete at your shoulder 10 km from the end of the Olympic Marathon could engender several lines of thought that would result in quite different outcomes in the race. You will probably drop off the pace and fall back if you have these thoughts: "This year I really thought I had it. I have worked so hard and now I have blown it. I really am a loser." Whereas you will have a far greater chance of success if your thoughts run as follows: "Well, here is the person they call the best marathon runner ever, who has only been able to catch me after 32 km. What I will do is just tuck in behind the about-to-become-ex-Number-One, who can do the work for a change and who I'll try to break later. After all, my 10-km time is as good as this runner's and in close finish I have the crowds behind me, because they always back the upstart."

The difference between a strong or weak belief system is determined by your self-concept (what you believe about yourself), which is in turn established by your record of past performances, your body image (what you honestly believe you can achieve in sport), and the attitudes that the significant people in your life, such as your parents, spouse, friends, and coaches, have toward you and your participation in sport. The self-concept can be further divided into what you really think about yourself (your real self) and what you would like to be (your ideal self).

How the significant others in your life influence your performance can be shown by extending the imaginary example a little further. Had you fallen off the pace in the last 10 km of the Olympic Marathon, your coach or other important person in your life might have said the following to you: "You really were awful. We were sure you had it sewn up and then you let that fool beat you. How could you?"

This type of verbal abuse is likely to stimulate a response. You may think, "That's true. I really am a loser. I will never win a major marathon." Or you may think, "No, that is wrong. I ran my heart out, which my coach couldn't know. Now I am more determined than ever to show them what I can do." (A third response may be to rid yourself of anyone who could be stupid enough to say such a thing!)

Our next step is to analyze the self-concept and discuss how we can improve those areas in which we may have specific weaknesses.

Analysis of the Self-Concept

In his excellent book, Liebetrau (1982) proposed the following approach to the analysis of self-concept.

To begin with, he suggested dividing a few pages in a notebook or training logbook into the following three columns:

STIMULUS	SELF-TALK/BELIEF SYSTEM (Thoughts)	RESPONSE (Emotions and Behaviors)

The idea is to complete this form by first describing your responses (in terms of emotions and behaviors) to a variety of sporting situations. For example, in the situation we have already imagined in the Olympic Marathon, the emotions that might have been aroused could have been fear, anger, and frustration at being passed, or you could have felt joy that another runner was going to make you earn your victory.

The next step is to record the stimulus that caused your particular response; in this case the stimulus was being passed at 32 km in the Olympic Marathon. Finally, list the thoughts that were evoked by that sporting situation. In the Olympic Marathon example, these thoughts could indicate the belief system of a winner (''I can stay with this runner—I am just as good'') or that of an also-ran (''I have blown it—I really am a loser'').

Liebetrau believes that the analysis of detailed records of about 20 such sporting situations in both racing and training will immediately point to a strong relationship between a positive belief system and a favorable (i.e., winning) response. Conversely, negative thoughts usually result in an unfavorable result.

The second reason for writing down these responses is to show the importance of being able to analyze all sporting situations in terms of the three components listed previously (stimulus, belief system, and response). Liebetrau suggested that with the help of a coach, the athlete must learn to dispute bad or negative thoughts as they occur. In addition, the athlete should practice applying positive self-statements as often as possible in all sporting situations. The more frequently you make these statements, the more likely they are to become fixed beliefs.

One important point made by Liebetrau is that the word *must* should never be used unless you are 100% sure of achieving an easy goal, because if this statement is followed by failure, you will not be able to trust in your future beliefs. Liebetrau indicated that the catastrophic consequences of a *must* statement are best shown by completing the second half of such statements, for example, ''I must win the Olympic Marathon, or else I am a failure.'' Failure to win at the Olympics will then have very serious consequences on your belief system; failure will undermine whatever confidence you might have had in yourself and so will make it even less likely that you will succeed in your next attempt at that goal.

Training to Improve the Self-Concept

Central to this notion of the importance of psychological factors in determining racing performance is the idea that a positive self-concept is associated with a strong belief system. But self-concept is not static; each day brings new challenges to the self-concept that will either enhance or detract from it. In a sense there is a vicious cycle; success breeds success and failure breeds failure. The only way to break this cycle, therefore, is to strengthen the self-concept.

Liebetrau's approach to strengthening the self-concept is as follows. Write down the person you aspire to be, your ideal self. Next, describe the person you consider yourself to be, your real person. Include in these descriptions lists, real versus ideal in each case, of the following: personal attributes; sporting achievements and motivations; dedication and training habits; relationship with coach and team members (if applicable); overall and specific fitness levels; sporting skills or talents; and sporting achievements.

Liebetrau suggested that training the self-concept should be approached in the following way. First, imagine your real and ideal selves as two separate identities following each other around in your daily life. Pay special attention to the attributes in the ideal and real self that differ the most. The next step is to imagine the two selves in various sporting situations that you experience. At first the ideal self goes through the same motions as the real self; ultimately the abilities of the ideal self surpass those of the real self and so produce the performance you desire.

Next, begin to visualize yourself as the ideal self in everyday situations. And finally, imagine how your ideal self would have coped with previous competitive failures. In a similar way, rehearse forthcoming competitive events by imagining how your ideal self will successfully complete such events.

Clearly these are difficult techniques that are not mastered overnight, nor are they probably ever developed to maximum benefit without the assistance and advice of a qualified professional such as a sport psychologist.

The Failing Athlete

We all know of athletes who perform exceptionally in training only to fail miserably in competition. Although some such individuals simply overtrain (see chapter 10), probably a large number suffer from various psychological syndromes.

One such syndrome has been termed the "fear-of-success/competitive-inhibition" syndrome (Ogilvie, 1980). Ogilvie listed the following five stresses, which can be bred by success and which are believed to contribute to this syndrome:

1. *Social and emotional isolation.* Success may isolate athletes from their friends and families (in particular their spouses) and may invoke jealousy among others with whom athletes come into contact. Paradoxically, increased acceptance by fans only intensifies this loneliness, because the fans expect athletes to be superhuman.

2. *Guilt about displaying the aggression necessary for athletic success.* The athletes who have been taught since childhood that aggression is bad may have difficulty expressing the necessary aggression during competition.

3. *Fear of discovering physical limits.* Athletes who as children were rewarded only for winning or for extreme excellence may be unwilling to test themselves to the limits lest they fail. They therefore rationalize their needs not to compete by falsely denying the importance of competition, success, or failure and therefore assiduously avoiding such competition.

Another way such athletes can avoid competition is being perpetually injured during training—so-called "training-room athletes" (Ogilvie & Tutko, 1971). Such athletes have strong feelings of inferiority but cannot simply opt out of the sport because of fear of isolation or rejection. Injuries allow training-room athletes to avoid competition that they fear might expose physical limits but to remain members of the team, thereby preserving their egos. In addition, injuries allow such athletes to believe that but for the injuries, they would be exceptional athletes.

4. *Fear of displacing idols.* Athletes who have used idolization of former champions to motivate performances may become anxious when in positions to challenge these idols' records.

5. *The responsibility of being first or the champion.* Once an athlete sets a record, fans expect him or her to set records at each competition. Thus, only perfection becomes acceptable to the fans, who may resent any performance below a record.

The fear-of-success syndrome is only one of many psychological causes of competitive failure. I have used it only as one example to show that you must consider psychological factors when analyzing competitive failures and that you should seek the help of the appropriate specialist when you suspect that perpetually poor performances are due to psychological factors.

Summary

My aim in this section, as indeed in this entire chapter, is not to provide final answers on all aspects of the psychology of running. Rather, I have aimed to outline how the mind affects sport performance and to show that it is possible to improve mental attitudes to competition, thereby improving running performance. Runners who agree with these ideas and who feel they could benefit from the application of some of the training techniques outlined should read more about sport psychology and seek the help of appropriately trained professionals.

The 1970s became the decade in which great strides were made in the management of running injuries; the 1980s saw similar great advances in the understanding of exercise physiology and biochemistry. I have a feeling that the 1990s will be the decade in which we finally come to understand the importance of the mind.

PSYCHOLOGICAL PREPARATION AND STRATEGIES FOR COMPETITION

Anxiety and Arousal

As competition approaches, athletes tend to become more anxious and begin to experience precompetition arousal. Anxiety that leads to controlled arousal is necessary, but anxiety that leads to inappropriate thinking can be detrimental.

Rushall (1979) suggested that the nature of the thoughts aroused by anxiety indicate whether the anxiety is likely to be harmful or detrimental. He classified these thoughts as being either irrelevant, self-oriented, or task-oriented. Of these, self-oriented thoughts are the most dangerous and take the form of worry about minor aches and pains and possible equipment failure. These thoughts obstruct

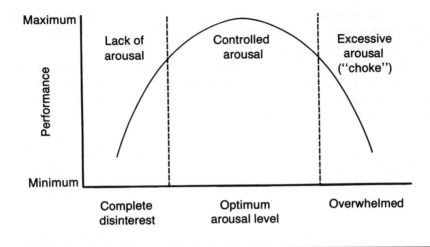

Figure 7.3 The simplified arousal diagram.
Note. From *Psyching in Sport. The Psychological Preparation for Serious Competition in Sport* (p. 54) by B.S. Rushall, 1979, London. Published by Pelham Books, © 1979 by Professor Brent S. Rushall. Adapted by permission.

the athlete's mental preparation. Thus, the athlete who is worried by such thoughts before competition clearly needs professional help.

The concept of arousal is shown in Figure 7.3. Researchers have found that athletes perform best when their levels of arousal immediately prior to competition are in the midrange (optimum arousal level). Inadequate or excessive arousal levels lead to reduced performance.

This concept was refined by Cratty (1983), who proposed that the optimum arousal level differs for different activities. Optimum performance in a simple, well-rehearsed activity like running can occur over a wide range of arousal levels. But as the activity becomes more complex and less well rehearsed, the range of arousal levels that will allow optimum performance becomes very narrow (see Figure 7.4).

Runners are generally left to their own devices to control anxiety and arousal levels. Clearly, both levels are vital to superior performance, and athletes who recognize their weaknesses in these areas will best be helped by professionals. Nevertheless, some guidelines can be given.

Relaxation for Controlling Arousal

There are two important techniques for controlling arousal. Both require your active involvement and teach you to regulate your physiological and mental arousal state.

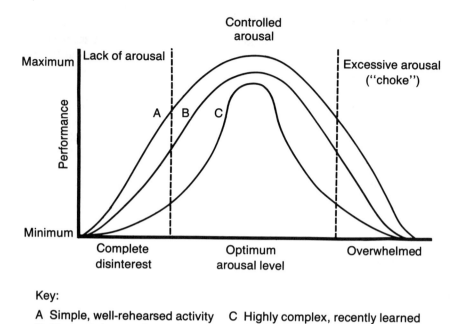

Figure 7.4 The influence of task complexity on optimum arousal patterns.

Autogenic phase training concentrates on your muscular and autonomic functions (e.g., heart and breathing rate) and on your mental state. You lie in a relatively relaxed body position (preferably outstretched on your back) and imagine that your limbs and abdominal area are growing warmer. Once these areas have become warm, you imagine that they have become heavier, and once this has been achieved, you begin to repeat a personal autogenic phase (like "I feel strong, relaxed, and confident") that reflects your desired mental and physical arousal state.

Frequent repetition of this procedure establishes a conscious association between the desired arousal state and the autogenic phrases, so that when you repeat your personal autogenic phrases, the conditioned controlled arousal response is elicited. This technique can induce changes in muscle temperature, in heart and respiratory rates, and in the brain's electrical wave patterns (Duffy, 1976).

The second technique for controlling arousal is the thought-stopping strategy (Ziegler, 1978). Negative thoughts and speculations invariably increase feelings of apprehension and tension, so that once you start imagining your "inevitable" failure, doubt, fear, and panic set in. These negative thoughts must be stopped and replaced by positive thoughts and self-statements and by task-oriented association. In this way, you shift your focus of attention to the positive aspects of your performance.

The Progressive Relaxation Technique

Progressive relaxation, the technique used to induce muscular relaxation, was developed by Jacobson (1929). It is particularly effective for persons who have trouble falling asleep (Berkovec & Fowles, 1973).

With this technique, you contract and then relax your muscle groups, progressing from one muscle group to another until the major muscle groups have exercised. The reason for first contracting each muscle group is to teach you to appreciate what muscle tension feels like. Without conscious recognition of the two extreme sensations of muscle tension and muscle relaxation, you will not be able to voluntarily induce the appropriate degree of muscle relaxation. Like all psychological techniques, progressive relaxation should be practiced regularly some months before a major competition so that you acquire the appropriate proficiency with the technique by the time you need to use it.

Progressive relaxation is best practiced in a quiet, comfortable room that is free from distractions. The best place is usually a heated and carpeted room with the lights dimmed. You follow the following five-step sequence:

1. Lie on your back on the floor with your hands resting on or next to your abdomen, with your legs extended and feet rotated outward. Ensure that you are comfortable, and then relax as much as you can.

2. Next, clench your right fist and feel the tension in your right fist, hand, and forearm.

3. Then relax and feel the fingers of your right hand become "loose." As you do so, contrast the feelings of contraction and relaxation.

4. Repeat this procedure first with the right hand again, then with the left hand twice, and then with both hands at the same time.

5. Now repeat the same sequence for all the major muscle groups in your body, particularly the muscles of the face, neck, shoulders, upper back, chest, stomach, lower back, hips, thighs, and calves. Exercise all muscle groups, taking care not to rush the sequence. At all times, carefully note the extent of the difference in the sensations of relaxation and contraction.

Practice the complete sequence of progressive relaxation exercises 3 times a day for 15 minutes, with the last session scheduled immediately before going to sleep. The beneficial effects of the procedure should become apparent within a few weeks.

Mental Imagery/Mental Rehearsal

Mental imagery means running the race in your mind beforehand. The importance of this is shown by Marty Liquori's statement that the race must be won in the mind 100 times before it is finally won in reality.

There are two important features of mental imagery: (a) "segmenting," or breaking up the event into manageable segments and (b) setting individual goals for each segment and an overall goal for the event. Rushall (1979) provided the following guidelines for this approach.

Establish an overall goal that is realistic. Novice runners are usually quite unable to set realistic racing goals; some realistic race times are listed in Tables 9.1 and 9.2.

After you have set a realistic overall goal, segment the event and set realistic intermediate goals for each of these segments. For example, if you wish to run the standard marathon in 3:30, a pace of 5 min/km, you would set 1-, 8-, 10-, 16-, and 32-km intermediate goals of 5, 40, 50, 80, and 160 minutes, respectively. Note that the early goals are much easier to achieve than are the latter, because you tire and find it more difficult to maintain pace as the race progresses. However, the achievement of intermediate goals stimulates you to keep trying. Setting goals that are initially too high will only undermine your motivation.

Another important reason the initial goals should be realistic is so that the "stopping wish" can be more easily overcome. Rushall (1979) stated that in each race there is a stage, usually after 80 to 85% of the activity has been completed, when athletes ask whether they should continue. Athletes who still have realistic chances of achieving overall goals when they first experience the stopping wish will probably continue.

In addition, the more detailed and precise the preplanned goals, the more pain and discomfort you will endure to achieve your goal.

Rushall pointed out that the performance is likely to be better if the final evaluation allows for the attainment of a number of different goals rather than a single goal. He also stressed that initial competitive goals should not be set too high and should allow for a gradual improvement in performance over the years so that the athlete's motivation is not decreased by continued failure. Bruce Fordyce's running record (see Table 8.26) is an excellent example of this approach.

Mental imagery allows you to practice the activity an unlimited number of times and to review past successes and failures. You can also imagine yourself exceeding performances achieved in practice.

Finally, a number of additional pointers can aid performance and should therefore be remembered during the practice of mental imagery (Liebetrau, 1982; Rushall, 1979):

- Make a public commitment to your goal.
- Play your game and not your opponent's game.
- Enjoy the challenge and the event; participate as if you were a child.
- Play as well as you can, and don't play against your opponent. The issue of whether or not you are a better athlete than your opponents is one you can do nothing about; you have your equipment and they have theirs. What

you can do something about is how much of your physical and mental equipment you will be able to put into use.
- Concentrate on yourself and not on your opponent or on your previous success; build on your confidence with self-congratulation.
- Keep a narrow focus of attention.
- Think about the significance of the event.

Mental Strategies During Competition

In order to cultivate a positive and constructive mental dialogue during racing, we each need to discover the specific thoughts and ideas that can spur us on. I think in time we will learn that we run our best when we concentrate very intensely and purposefully on what we are doing, thereby excluding all extraneous thoughts, including those relating to pain.

Experimental evidence for this has been provided by Dr. William Morgan, an exercise psychologist from the University of Wisconsin (W.P. Morgan, 1978; W.P. Morgan & Pollock, 1977; Sachs, 1984a). He reported a study that contrasted the mental strategies used during competition by a group of elite, world-class American marathon runners (including Frank Shorter, Kenny Moore, Don Kardong, and Jeff Galloway) with the strategies used by a group of nonelite, average runners.

Morgan found that during competition, the elite runners exhibited "associative characteristics," that is, their thoughts were totally absorbed in the race itself. They concentrated on strategy, on staying "loose," and on running as efficiently as possible by closely monitoring subtle physiological cues from their feet, calves, thighs, and respiration patterns. These athletes' marathon paces were governed not by the clock, but by "reading their bodies."

Surprisingly, these elite runners did not accept the concept of the marathon "wall," and all seemed able to choose exact racing speeds that avoided sudden and precipitous falloffs in performance. One said, "The wall is a myth. The key is to read your body, adjust your pace, and avoid getting into trouble" (W.P. Morgan, 1978, p. 43).

The wall, these athletes suggested, befalls only those who ignore the subtle physiological cues that differentiate between the correct racing pace and one that is too ambitious.

Another essential strategy used by these runners was segmenting, also called "framing." With this technique the athletes concentrated on running the race in sections without being influenced by what was still to come in the race. Thus, as they ran, they concentrated only on holding the correct pace for the kilometer they were actually running, rather than concerning themselves with the fact that they had many more kilometers to run after that.

In contrast, Morgan found that the average marathon runners tended toward dissociation during competition. That is, they transfixed their minds on subjects totally unrelated to running. Morgan also reported that the need for the average runner to dissociate became overwhelming as the race progressed and the runner was overcome by discomfort.

In more recent research, my colleague at the University of Cape Town, Dr. Helgo Schomer (1984, 1986, 1987) studied the relationship between marathon runners' perceptions of effort and the mental strategies these runners employed during exercise of different intensities. Using lightweight microcassette recorders, he recorded the thought patterns during training of three distinct groups of marathon runners: a group of beginner runners who were training for their first marathon, a group of average marathon runners, and a group of elite runners with best marathon times in the region of 2:20. These runners were encouraged to speak into the tape whatever went through their minds.

The surprising finding, which contrasts with that of W.P. Morgan (1978), was that all runners, regardless of their levels of proficiency, spent progressively more time in associative thought as the intensities of their perceived efforts, measured on the Borg scale (see Table 6.2), increased. Thus, regardless of whether they were elite or beginner runners, as they perceived their exercise becoming harder, they altered their thinking from being mainly dissociative to mostly associative. The findings of Sachs (1984a) are in line with this interpretation.

Schomer (1987) also found that associative thoughts could be classified as

- body monitoring,
- personal commands or instructions,
- reflection on the athlete's emotional state, or
- pace monitoring.

Schomer concluded that athletes who wish to use associative thoughts optimally must discipline their minds to focus on the task at hand, with careful monitoring of energy reserves and emotional states. Athletes should also encourage and praise themselves for their efforts and should calmly consider the correctness of their paces in relation to those of their opponents.

Similarly, Schomer found that dissociative thoughts during running typically comprised

- reflections on the runner's life,
- personal problem solving,
- work and career planning,
- considerations of the environment and the course, and
- conversational chatter.

Although these thought patterns are probably beneficial for the novice runner in that they maintain motivation by distracting the runner's thoughts from the discomfort he or she may be feeling, for the more serious runner, dissociative thinking patterns, particularly during races, probably indicate that the athlete is not really running as hard as would be possible if he or she trained more seriously.

PSYCHOLOGICAL BENEFITS OF TRAINING

When I began running, I perceived the benefits as being purely physical. I have since discovered that the real benefits of exercise are in the mind. The most persuasive evidence for this is provided in the classic running books of Sheehan (1975, 1978b, 1980, 1983) and Fixx (1977).

A criticism that can be leveled at some of these writings is that we runners are too neurotically involved in the activity to be totally objective. For this reason, we will next review some of the more scientific studies that provide evidence for psychological gains from exercise. But equally important is a consideration of the possibility that if running has so much psychological benefit to offer, it can be too much of a good thing for some people. The most detailed scientific review of this topic can be found in the monograph by Sachs and Buffone (1984).

Exercise and Happiness

In one random survey (R. Carter, 1977), it was found that 72% of those who exercised sufficiently to maintain moderate levels of fitness—equivalent to 30 Cooper points per week (K.H. Cooper, 1968), which in turn is equivalent to running 10 km/week—claimed that they were "very happy." In groups of subjects who answered that they were either "pretty happy" or "not so happy," only slightly more than one third were physically fit.

Therefore, a significant association was found between happiness and optimum physical fitness. This does not necessarily prove that exercise increases happiness. Happiness should be a factor that determines whether people will choose to exercise or not.

(Cooper points are a measure of the energy expended during different activities of different durations. They provided the first method by which the amount of energy expended in different sports [tennis, running, etc.] and recreations [walking] could be compared. Cooper was the first to propose that you had to expend so much energy to be healthy. He was correct, but his point system is inaccurate and not scientifically based.)

Reduction of Tension and Anxiety

Anxiety levels in both normal and anxious people are reduced after vigorous exercise in both the laboratory and out of doors (Bahrke & Morgan, 1981). Chronic exercise (training) also decreases anxiety levels (Topp, 1989), and trained persons have lower levels of anxiety than nonexercisers (Nuori & Beer, 1989; Stephens, 1988). Running has been used in the management of those with severe anxieties (Berger, 1984). Other diversional activities such as biofeedback, meditation, or just quiet rest are apparently equally effective (Bahrke & Morgan, 1981), but I have found that exercise has a specific effect on my anxiety that is not achieved in any other way. In addition, the anxiolytic effect of exercise may last longer than that produced by other methods (Raglin & Morgan, 1987).

When compared to a single dose of tranquilizer, a single exercise bout (15 minutes walking at a heart rate of 100 beats/min) has a significantly greater effect on resting muscle tension. De Vries (1981) concluded that exercise has a substantial acute and long-term tranquilizing effect. Runners also exhibit less anxiety about death than do nonrunners (Guyot et al., 1984).

Depression

Jogging has proved to be an effective adjunct in the treatment of depression and may be at least as effective as, and considerably cheaper than, conventional drug therapy in cases of mild depression (Berger, 1984; Buffone, 1984; Griest et al., 1981; Kostrubala, 1984; Martinsen et al., 1985; McCann & Holmes, 1984). Cross-sectional studies show that depressive symptoms decrease with increasing levels of physical activity (Farmer et al., 1988; Ross & Hayes, 1988; Stephens, 1988). Farmer et al., (1988) suggest that physical inactivity may be a risk factor for depressive symptoms.

Quality of Life

University students who participated in a 15-week jogging program showed significant increases in their reported quality of life, whereas a control group showed no such change (A.E. Morris & Husman, 1978). Female long-distance runners also scored higher on this scale than did college students and nonrunners (A.F. Morris et al., 1982).

Personality

A number of studies have focused on the effects of exercise training on personality (Dienstbier, 1984). Canadian researcher McPherson and his colleagues (1967) reported that healthy adults who had exercised regularly for 4 or more years exhibited greater energy, patience, humor, ambition, and optimism and were more amiable, graceful, good-tempered, elated, and easygoing than were a group of persons just commencing an exercise-training program. Similarly, Ismail and Trachtman (1973) from Purdue University, Indiana, reported that high-fitness adults had greater emotional stability, imaginativeness, and self-sufficiency than did adults with low levels of fitness. Membership in the high-fitness group was associated with self-assurance, imagination, emotional stability, and self-sufficiency.

Subsequent studies showed that exercise training increases self-confidence, emotional stability, self-sufficiency, conscientiousness, and persistence (Buccola & Stone, 1975; M.W. Sharp & Reilley, 1975; R.J. Young & Ismail, 1976a, 1976b, 1977); reduces anxiety, tension, depression, and fatigue; and increases vigor (Blumenthal et al., 1982b).

Runners in particular were found to be more introverted, stable, self-sufficient, and imaginative than inactive controls, and the runners were also low on anxiety and high on self-esteem (Hartung & Farge, 1977). It also appears that these benefits increase with increasing amounts of exercise. Thus, marathon runners score higher on these variables than do joggers who, in turn, score higher than do those who are inactive (Wilson et al., 1980). Body image and self-esteem are also increased in persons who exercise regularly (Eide, 1982). Exercise training also increased self-concept and mood in incarcerated delinquent adolescents (MacMahon & Gross, 1988).

These studies led the eminent sport psychologist Bruce Ogilvie, coauthor of the classic text *Problem Athletes and How to Handle Them* (Ogilvie & Tutko, 1971), to state the following:

> Distance running has character strengthening effects as well as physical effects. Running can generate certain qualities that have tremendous payoffs in our society; qualities such as dependability, organization, the willingness to take risks and push to the limit, and tenacity; qualities we need to survive in our world today. The nature of distance running demands and nurtures these qualities. (Ogilvie, 1981, p. 52)

Stress Resistance

I have no doubt that exercise greatly increases the ability to cope with minor irritations and stresses that we experience each day, especially at work. I have noticed this particularly since I began running to work some 9 years ago. On those days that I do not run to work, I am unquestionably less relaxed and I experience more stress and discomfort when coping with daily problems. It is as if running allows us to see the triviality of the problems that we must cope with daily. Also, prior exercise may alter the concentrations of certain chemical transmitters in the brain, including endorphins, which may then dampen our responses to subsequent stressful events.

Suzanne Kobasa and her colleagues (1982) postulated that there might be a special, "hardy" personality that would enable a person to cope with stress better than others. Kobasa and her colleagues found that "hardiness" protected against illness, particulary under severely stressful conditions, and that the hardiness of these "hardy personalities" was increased by regular exercise. Thus, stress resistance was greatest in those hardy personalities who also exercised. Dienstbier et al. (1981) studied a group of runners at different times: when they had not run or after they had run either 10 km or a standard marathon. The subjects' physiological responses to various stimuli including noise and cold exposure were less after they had run than when they had not run. Furthermore, when tested after running, the runners perceived these factors to be less stressful. An important observation was that in this experiment, the subjects were tested up to 5 hours after they had run; thus, the stress-reducing effect of running lasted for at least that long, something I have also observed with my own running.

Howard and his colleagues (1984) found that persons who exercise regularly are more resistant to the detrimental physiological and psychological effects of "stressful life events." The stressful life events include divorce, financial hardship, or loss of a spouse. Thus, for example, physically active persons were better able to cope with the loss of a spouse than were their inactive peers. The same conclusions were drawn from a study of adolescents who had experienced stressful life events. Those who were physically active were less debilitated by these events (J.D. Brown & Lawton, 1986; J.D. Brown & Siegel, 1988).

In addition, Roth and Holmes (1987) showed that exercise training was the most effective method for reducing the depression that resulted from a stressful life event. In their review of all the published studies relevant to this topic, Crews and Landers (1987) concluded that the endurance-trained subjects show reduced physiological responses to psychosocial stress.

Minor Medical Complaints

Although not strictly a psychological benefit of exercise, it has been shown that physically fit women complain less of minor medical conditions such as colds, allergies, fatigue, menstrual discomfort, backaches, and digestive disorders than do less fit women (Gendel, 1978). The author concluded that many of these complaints may be due simply to a lack of physical fitness.

Mental Functioning

Two preliminary studies (Ismail & El-Naggar, 1981; Lichtman & Poser, 1983) suggested that exercise training increases mental functioning, as shown by scores in a variety of tests of mathematical and other reasoning abilities; scores increased when subjects took the tests after exercising. Rats that exercise for life also show improved memory retention as they age (Samorajski et al., 1985).

Health Awareness

I have found that of all sports persons, runners and other endurance athletes are by far the most conscious of their physical and mental health. This results, I suspect, from the process whereby endurance athletes learn to "listen to their bodies." Early in their athletic careers, endurance athletes learn that the physical demands of running and other endurance activities are such that these activities can only be performed with pleasure and satisfaction if the body is well cared for.

The result is that endurance athletes become aware of their health and follow good health practices (Heinzelman & Bagley, 1970), not because they are primarily health conscious but because they are performance conscious. The potential long-term health benefits of this attitude should not be dismissed lightly. For example, Breslow (1979) showed that longevity and physical health are very strongly influenced by seven health practices: avoiding smoking; exercising regularly; eating moderately and controlling body weight; eating regularly; eating breakfast; drinking alcohol moderately or not at all; and sleeping 7 to 8 hours per night. It was found that a 45-year-old person who followed all seven health practices had a life expectancy of some 11 years over a similarly aged person who followed three or less of these rules (Belloc, 1973). By comparison, the greatest medical advances we have known, which have taken place since the turn of this century, have increased the longevity of men and women aged 45 by a mere 4 years (Breslow, 1979). Thus, Breslow has concluded that "the patterns of daily living, including eating, physical activity, use of alcohol and cigarettes, largely determines both health and how long one lives" (p. 2093).

On this basis we can say that running, because it positively influences all these behaviors, is one of the most powerful health tools we have ever known.

How Runners Perceive These Psychological Benefits

Now that we have reviewed what the scientists think running does for our minds, we should consider what runners themselves think of these benefits.

Callen (1983) used a questionnaire to survey 424 runners of both sexes in the small college town of Columbia, Missouri, and his results are contained in Table 7.3.

This table shows that the surveyed runners believe they derive important mental and emotional benefits from exercise, in particular relief from tension and enhanced self-image, mood, and self-confidence. Sixty-nine percent of the runners experienced a "high" during running. This occurred more commonly in those who ran more than 35 km/week and had been running for more than 15 months. The high—which was described as a feeling of euphoria with a lifting of spirits, increased creativity and insight, and a sense of well-being—usually occurred in the second half of the run; it occurred roughly every second run and became more likely to occur the longer the run. Callen suggested that the high may be a form of autohypnosis, with the first half of the run being used to induce the hypnotic state.

POTENTIAL PSYCHOLOGICAL DANGERS OF TRAINING

As the running revolution of the 1970s took hold and the literature describing its benefits grew, it was only natural that a counterliterature should develop. The

Table 7.3   Summary of Survey of 424 Runners

Responses	% of total[a]
1. Reasons for starting running	
To improve health	70
For fun	55
Weight control	54
Competition	32
2. Mental and emotional benefits from running	
Relieves tension	86
Better self-image	75
More relaxed	75
Better mood	66
More self-confident	64
Others (happier, more alert, relieves depression, more content, think more clearly)	53-58
3. Experienced the "runner's high"	69
4. Experienced a trance or altered state of consciousness during running	56

Note. Modified from "Mental and Emotional Aspects of Long-Distance Running" by K.E. Callen, 1983, *Psychosomatics*, **24**(2), pp. 139, 145. Copyright 1983 by American Psychiatric Press. Adapted by permission.

[a]Respondents could list as many benefits as they wished.

major contention of this countermovement was that running is detrimental because it is "addictive" (Sachs & Pargman, 1984). For the remainder of this chapter we will consider the arguments surrounding "running addiction."

Researchers have described the criteria that should be fulfilled for a diagnosis of "exercise dependence" (de Coverley Veale, 1987). One definition states that addiction occurs when involvement in an activity eliminates choice in all areas of life. On this basis, an addiction must be distinguished from a habit, commitment, or compulsion, none of which exclude all other activities. My experience is that a great majority of runners are not addicted to the extent that running completely dominates all other aspects of their lives. Rather, I believe that running fits the description of a compulsion and that the term *addiction* is inappropriate.

We should also note that society is selective in its judgment of compulsion. As James Fixx (1980) noted, "Practically no one, after all, uses the word addiction when referring to people who spend inordinate amounts of time making money, playing at politics, or pursuing the opposite sex" (p. 41). Fixx suggested that these activities may be even more hazardous than "spending a quiet hour or two in a park or on a country road'' (p. 41). But we should not allow Fixx's masterful English to disguise the possibility that running in a park for up to 2 hours a day could in fact be as much a behavior disorder as working 12 or more hours a day.

A feature of an addictive state is that withdrawal symptoms develop when the addict cannot partake of the addiction. Two authors have described the withdrawal symptoms that they consider indicative of running's addictive nature. W.P. Morgan (1979) listed the following array of withdrawal symptoms:

> Depression and anxiety are usually accompanied by restlessness, insomnia and generalized fatigue. Tics, muscle tension and soreness, decreased appetite and constipation or irregularity often develop. In general, the benefits of vigorous exercise are reversed. . . . Exercise addicts give their daily run(s) higher priority than job, family, or friends. They run first, and then if time permits, they work, love, and socialize. And, they often exercise to the point where overuse injuries have near crippling effects, the pain becomes intolerable, and they search for the perfect shoe, orthotic, injection, or psychological strategy that will enable them to run ('shoot up') again. (p. 59)

Sacks (1981) noted that running addiction usually starts during a period of increased emotional stress. In this regard, running is especially attractive because it is an easy skill to acquire and therefore provides a simple and rapid solution to emotional distress.

So powerful is this addiction that Willoughby (1977) has suggested that the United States Congress should enact legislation requiring the following warning to be displayed on all running shoes, shorts, or books:

WARNING: The Psychiatrist General has determined that jogging and running are hazardous to mental health and present a grave risk of contracting contagious quasirandomous wanderitis (QW) or "jogging about." (p. 17)

Sacks (1981) emphasized particularly the psychological component of these withdrawal symptoms:

> The running addict is characterized by a compulsive need to run at least once and sometimes twice a day. . . . If prevented from running, such runners become irritable, restless, sleepless and preoccupied with guilty thoughts that the body will decondition or deteriorate in some way. The running addict recognizes the irrationality of those feelings and thoughts, but they are inescapable and can be relieved only by running. (p. 128)

With this background, let us consider in more detail the arguments for and against the addictiveness of running.

The Arguments for a Running Addiction

The Biochemical Argument

This argument contends that running is addictive because it stimulates the release of certain hormones inside the brain, the endorphins or enkephalins, which give runners pleasurable feelings when they are jogging—the so-called runner's high (Callen, 1983). The brain then becomes dependent on these pleasure-producing substances just as it does with other potentially addictive substances like heroin, cocaine, or morphine. But, as with all addictions, the euphoric feelings can only be maintained if the dosage (i.e., running distance) is continually increased.

The Psychological Argument

Other writers have noted that the withdrawal symptoms described by runners who are forced to stop running for a period of time are mainly of a psychological, rather than a physical, nature. The psychological withdrawal symptoms that they describe include guilt, irritability, anxiety, tension, restlessness, and depression. These writers also note that runners, possibly like myself, tend to lay too much emphasis on the mental benefits of running; the writers suggest that this may indicate that such addicted runners use their running to cope with major underlying psychological problems. Altshul (1981b) suggested that if jogging is indeed able to mask anxiety and depression, as these runners testify, albeit for relatively short periods, then it follows that many people with these psychological abnormalities will use running as an effective and cheap home remedy.

Like Sacks, Altshul (1981b) also noted that compulsive running frequently starts in response to a major emotional upheaval.

> My impression . . . is that if . . . a lean, athletic man is consciously or unconsciously contemplating divorce, there is at least a 75% chance that he is or will be a compulsive runner. Thus, I would claim not that running causes divorce, but rather that divorce, among other forms of human misery, causes running. (p. 52)

A number of abnormal psychological states possibly present in addicted runners are described next.

Primary Affective Disorder. Apparent evidence for the postulate that running might attract persons more likely to suffer from anxiety or depression comes from a study by New York physician Dr. Edward Colt and his colleagues (1981). In a group of 61 runners who were participating primarily in a study of physiology, not psychology, the researchers found a high incidence of *primary affective disorder*. Persons with this condition suffer from more anxiety and depression than is normal and frequently require psychiatric assistance, including psychotherapy. Among the group were some elite athletes who showed this disorder.

Colt et al. (1981) concluded that these data indeed suggest that running may be particularly rewarding to those runners with affective disorders. The authors also noted that some runners said that they became "revved up" after very intensive training sessions and that these workouts were frequently followed by insomnia. These symptoms, which I have certainly experienced, are said to indicate *hypomania*. One question that Colt suggested needs to be answered is this: What happens to competitive athletes when they retire from competition? Do they become depressed? If so, he asks, could this explain those suicides that occur among retired athletes?

The Athletic Neurotic. Psychological dependence on running may occur not only because running helps control primary affective disorders but also because it may provide an essential coping mechanism for those who have neurotic fears of illness. Some indication for this was first provided by Leeds psychiatrist Dr. Crawford Little (1969) in a paper that went largely unnoticed prior to the current interest in running addiction.

Little noted that among patients referred to him for the treatment of neuroses, 42% were completely unathletic; they showed not the slightest interest in any form of physical activity. However, 39% were the precise opposite. These "athletic neurotics" seemed to overvalue the importance of health and fitness and revealed "inordinate pride" in their previous sickness-free progress through life and their excess physical stamina, strength, or skills.

Subsequently, Little (1981) concluded that athletic neurosis is not a trivial, short-lived illness. He suggested that although excessive athleticism is not in itself neurotic, because it does not cause any suffering in either the subject or his or her family, it can place the subject in a vulnerable preneurotic state, leading to a manifest neurosis in the event of an appropriate threat. Despite this, Little concluded that the overall benefits of the exercise movement of the 1980s far outweigh the small danger that this movement will produce some athletic neurotics.

Since rereading Little's article, I have become more aware of athletic neurotics. One recent example was the 45-year-old man who wanted to know whether he should take anabolic steroids to improve muscle bulk and strength. My suggestion that at his age he shouldn't be so vain was clearly quite inappropriate, because his athletic neurosis demanded that he should go to inordinate lengths to insure that he did not become weak.

The Obsessive-Compulsive Athlete. In its extreme form, obsessive-compulsive behavior is characterized by a rigid, intensely focused attitude; preoccupation with technical detail; excessive reliance on intellectuality with a loss of emotional responsiveness; worry and marked self-criticism; overconcern for moral and professional responsibility, with emphasis on what *should* be done; and a constant routine activity performed with the use of a schedule and checklists.

Running is attractive to the obsessive-compulsive person because it provides a rigidly defined goal (such as running an ultramarathon) that justifies a constant, routine activity (i.e., training) and preoccupation with detail (e.g., training methods, diet, shoes, and reading this book). Signs that suggest an obsessive-compulsive attitude to running include a need to run every day (the "training streak") and a need to run every race on the calendar.

Narcissism/Masochism. An interesting observation made by Arnold Cooper (1981), professor of psychiatry at Cornell University, New York, is that you "scratch marathoners once, and they tell you how wonderful they feel. Scratch them twice and they tell you about their latest injuries" (p. 267). This made Cooper consider the masochistic needs of runners.

Cooper stated that narcissism refers to behaviors derived from interest, concern, and satisfaction with oneself. Healthy narcissism is reflected by the self-confidence that enables one to pursue goals with pleasure and by the high self-esteem that follows achievement of those goals. Pathological narcissism, on the other hand, involves an endless series of maneuvers designed to disguise a shaky self-esteem and feelings of lack of self-worth.

Cooper contended that the body is central to narcissism, so that the more narcissistic an individual is because of low feelings of self-worth, the more likely he or she is to demonstrate a bodily preoccupation expressed either as a need for maintaining strength and beauty or by endless hypochondriacal complaints.

Masochism, the ability to extract pleasure from pain is, according to Cooper, linked to narcissistic needs developed early in the child's development. Cooper stated that growing children are faced with two tasks: developing healthy narcissism about their self-images, their bodies, and their needs and developing autonomy from their mothers. By their nature, these two processes cannot fail to produce a conflict that is typically expressed with childhood tears. Forced to realize that they are not omnipotent and that painful realities cannot be avoided, children engage in certain mental maneuvers to protect their fantasies. They begin by constructing a black-and-white world in which everything good that happens to them is their own doing; everything bad is the fault of someone else, usually their mothers. Gradually, however, they realize that their mothers are not all bad; thus the children must find other ways to explain their failures at omnipotence. Cooper suggested that children do this by using the following logic (or illogic): They conclude that if they are experiencing frustration, this is neither because they lack the power to control it nor because their mothers are unremittingly bad, but because they (the children) actually enjoy this frustration. It is, as Cooper noted, a classic example of "If you can't beat them, then join them!"

Thus, children take credit for actively pursuing and enjoying those pains that they cannot avoid.

Pain, then, is a part of the process of separation from one's mother, and the mastery of this pain is linked to the self-definition of learning that one is separate from another. Persons who exhibit masochistic tendencies may be unable to successfully achieve this self-identity and therefore a healthy narcissism.

The inescapable feature of running is the masochistic need to inflict pain by running great distances. This, A.M. Cooper (1981) concluded, "seems to be a repetition of the infant's desperate need to create everything—even their own pain" (p. 271). By completing a marathon, the runner demonstrates omnipotence by triumphing over his or her frailty while secretly enjoying the self-inflicted pain, which would normally be forbidden by the runner's and society's consciences. Together these victories provide illusions of immortality. "The result is a hypomanic state experienced as the runner's high" (p. 272).

Cooper concluded that we all share pathological narcissistic and masochistic tendencies but that most find ways to divert these tendencies toward useful activities. The marathon runner is likely to be quite far along the narcissistic-masochistic spectrum and

> almost uniquely, carries on a useless activity that symbolizes society's need for a special hero who will enact the infantile triumphs requisite for healthy functioning, and who also enables the audience to share vicariously in some of his or her forbidden pleasures. (A.M. Cooper, 1981, p. 272)

Thus, runners with more than their fair shares of narcissistic and masochistic pathologies are likely to use running as pseudosolutions for avoiding problems in life, and Cooper suggested that the running addiction, in particular the need to inflict the pain suffered during a marathon, is "best understood in terms of its contribution to the masochistic psychic balance, with overtones of perverse satisfaction rather than in terms of addiction, which denies the psychological issues" (p. 273).

The Anorexic Personality. That some obsessive male runners show personality characteristics similar to those of females with anorexia nervosa will be discussed in more detail in chapter 15. Once again, the suggestion is that running provides a socially sanctioned diversion for those persons to cope with their disturbed psychological states.

The Addictive Personality. I suspect that for various reasons, some people are especially prone to becoming addicted to alcohol, cigarettes, or other drugs. Furthermore, my experience with some such individuals suggests that they find that running is a counteraddiction that allows them to live without recourse to these drugs.

The Arguments Against a Running Addiction

Withdrawal Symptoms in Runners

The published evidence of the withdrawal symptoms experienced by runners who are forced to stop running shows that these symptoms are somewhat less dramatic than W.P. Morgan (1979) and Sacks (1981) would have us believe.

In one of the few scientific studies of these symptoms, Baekeland (1970) found that daily exercisers refused to participate in a study for which they would be paid to stop exercising for a month. Many asserted that no amount of money would stop them from exercising. Baekeland was therefore forced to study less addicted people who exercised only 3 times a week. He found that a month-long period without exercise impaired sleep, increased sexual tension, and increased the need to be with others. Thaxton (1982) found that runners who trained 5 days a week were more depressed if they did not run on a scheduled running day.

It is also enlightening to look at the scientific evidence that W.P. Morgan (1979) provided to support his description of the runner's addiction and the withdrawal symptoms that result. He provided eight brief case reports involving the following: two runners who developed withdrawal symptoms when they were forced to stop running because of injury; three joggers who continued to exercise with chronic injuries; one person who missed a staff meeting and went running instead; a counseling psychologist who expressed guilt because his midday run cut into 30 minutes of his counseling time, for which he was being paid; and an Olympic wrestler who in addition to training for wrestling would awaken in the middle of the night and run 8 to 10 km.

It certainly seems that the documented evidence for the withdrawal symptoms in runners is distinctly sparse. My personal experience is that such symptoms are usually of a psychological, not a physical, nature and only occur when I stop running while I am still working. I have never developed these symptoms when I have stopped running even for as long as 4 weeks while on holiday. This indicates that these withdrawal symptoms are not solely due to stopping running. Clearly, we require more than eight brief case reports from one scientist to confirm the existence of a withdrawal condition.

The Biochemical Argument

Evidence now shows that endorphin levels in the blood rise during exercise (Francis, 1983; Harber & Sutton, 1984), that the degree to which they rise correlates with the increase in the feelings of pleasantness engendered by the exercise (Wildmann et al., 1986), and that blocking the action of these endorphins prevents some of the euphoric feelings experienced after running (M.E. Allen &

Coen, 1987; Janal et al., 1984) and may impair performance during submaximal exercise (Surbey et al., 1984). These findings therefore support, at least superficially, the premise that elevated endorphin levels caused by exercise could explain the addictive nature of running. However, there are two weaknesses in this argument.

First we now know that endorphins play an integral part in the normal stress response of the body. Thus, any stress to which the body is exposed will cause endorphin levels to rise; we know not all stresses, for example being chased by a lion, are likely to be addictive!

Second, because the proposed mechanism for the running addition is neurochemical (i.e., addiction to endorphins), the implication is that anyone who ever runs will become addicted in the same way as someone who takes an addictive drug. Thus, a runner who makes a rational decision to begin running would ultimately become dependent on a neurochemically based addiction, which would override the runner's rational thinking process, making it impossible for him or her to stop.

But the evidence shows that not all joggers experience the runner's high (Callen, 1983; Sachs, 1984b), and not all are addicted to the extent of developing the symptoms described by W.P. Morgan (1979) and Sacks (1981). The fact that the runner's withdrawal symptoms are mainly a psychological rather than physical nature further suggests that the addiction is not neurochemically based. Thus, an entirely different explanation must be sought.

The Psychological Explanation

I find it difficult to dispute the contention that certain categories of runners are attracted to running because it provides a psychological support system that allows them to cope with their particular psychological disorders. In this group we would include those who suffer from anxiety and depression, the athletic neurotics, the obsessive-compulsives, the anorexics, and those with addictive-dependent personalities. Probably there are many more such categories. An important point is that running, far from being an addiction, may in fact be a very beneficial method of treatment for persons with these conditions (Thaxton, 1982).

But this explanation can hardly hold for the vast majority of runners who both outwardly and when tested scientifically seem to enjoy excellent psychological health. We have already described a number of studies that have shown that runners exhibit increased emotional stability and score low on neuroticism and anxiety (W.P. Morgan & Costill, 1972). Indeed, even obligatory runners enjoy excellent psychological health (Blumenthal et al., 1984). Runners are also cleverer than average, are of higher socioeconomic status, and are more imaginative and self-sufficient than average, although they tend to be more introverted. In addition, runners have been shown to score higher on psychological scales that measure needs for "thrill and adventure," and one study suggested that running may be an important method for thrill and adventure seekers to acquire sufficient sensory input to keep their needs satisfied (Pargman, 1980).

Thus, it seems that an explanation for attraction or addiction to running must take into account all these psychological attributes of runners. One suggestion (Pargman, 1980; Sachs & Pargman, 1984) is that adherence to running is either a *commitment/dedication* on an intellectual basis or an *addiction/dependence* on a psychochemical basis. Thus, the committed runner may run regularly for health or social reasons (e.g., the desire to forestall a heart attack), for financial reasons, or for prestige, power, or narcissism. In this view, a professional runner is not addicted to running but committed to earning a living. Sachs and Pargman (1984) suggested that involvement of the committed runners in their sports should be termed "healthy habits," not addictions. The addicted runner, on the other hand, runs not for any intellectual reasons but because running offers opportunities for mind-bending experiences, for euphoria, or for escape from depression or anxiety (Sacks, 1981).

Two psychologists from the University of Illinois, Mary Ann Carmack and Rainer Martens (1979), were the first to attempt a more complete explanation of the way in which social, psychological, and physiological factors interact to determine the extent of an individual's involvement in running. They quantified the extent of this involvement on the basis of assessing the following aspects of the runner's lifestyle: the time spent thinking and reading about running; the distances involved in traveling to races and the frequency of competition; the number of marathons run; the number of friends who are runners; the percentage of new friends met since starting running who are also runners; the amount of money spent on books and magazines about running and on running equipment and accessories; the extent to which changes in eating, drinking, and other lifestyle patterns are made to accommodate the daily run; and the duration and intensity of running itself.

Two North American sociologists, Paul Joseph and James Robbins (1981), used this information in a novel study of the sociological factors that influence running addiction. The authors noted that Western society is quite unusual in its view of work as the activity contributing most to a sense of self-esteem and sense of accomplishment, but they also concluded that this is in the process of changing. Currently only 20% of North Americans consider their work to be a more important source of personal identity than their leisure activities; over the past 20 years, the number of men in Sweden who consider leisure to be more important than work has doubled. The authors wondered if the extent to which runners were committed to running might also reflect a shift in their sources of self-identity from work to leisure.

Using this Carmack/Martens Commitment to Running Scale, Joseph and Robbins (1981) studied four groups of runners whose commitments to running were classified according to the following criteria; the authors related the subjects' levels of commitment to various indexes of work satisfaction and commitment.

Group 1 *Running as the most important commitment.* Subjects in this group ran at least 64 km/week and raced often; most of their friends were runners, and they read about running at least weekly.

Group 2 *Running as a crucial commitment.* Subjects in this group ran between 18 and 64 km/week and raced frequently. They were less involved in the running subculture than were Group 1 runners.

Group 3 *Running as a hobby.* Subjects in this group also ran between 18 and 64 km/week but had no interest in the running subculture.

Group 4 *The occasional runner.* Runners in this group ran just when they felt the urge. They usually stopped running in winter or during bad weather.

The authors made three important findings. First, they found that all runners, regardless of their levels of commitment, valued self-involvement at work, but this self-involvement had to be active, one in which the employees were able to focus on themselves and the contributions they could make.

Second, the authors found that the more committed these runners were to their running, the greater the tendency to rank running as a more important source of self-identity than work. Thus, the more committed the person to running, the more that person feels he or she can be best understood through running.

Finally, the greater the dissatisfaction with certain aspects of work, in particular the potential it gave for self-development, self-involvement, or competition, the greater the tendency to rank running over work as the more important source of self-identity. This was particularly marked in those who were dissatisfied with the capacity for self-development offered by their work and who hence shifted their identities from that of worker to runner.

Joseph and Robbins concluded that those associating with the leisure role, in this case the runners, are affected by one of two things: (a) They are attracted to a particular set of work needs, really a philosophy of work that stresses the *cultivation of self* (i.e., a chance to relax, to be alone with one's problems, to counter the seriousness of life, and to forget about personal problems), or (b) they are frustrated by their job experiences because these experiences fail to provide opportunities for self-development in terms of, for example, control over outcome of their efforts; the ability to see the unambiguous results of those efforts; the chance to be totally involved and to make a contribution to society; and the chance to find challenge, adventure, and friendship.

These authors suggested that in sociological terms, their findings indicate that society is gradually rejecting the previous social norm that individuals should identify themselves exclusively through their work. Running, the authors suggested, "represents a quiet but legitimate rebellion against the unwarranted hegemony of work as the primary focus of self-identity" (Joseph & Robbins, 1981, p. 142).

They also pointed out that this shift in identity would not have been possible if there had not also been an expansion of leisure time. However, they noted that this is selective and does not involve all social classes. Thus, runners come from a social class that enjoys the privilege of an expanded leisure time and therefore the possibility for this shift in self-identity.

The authors concluded that the very existence of this need to search for alternative or supplemented areas of self-understanding indicates that ambiguity exists. If running is then to take on compulsive and irresponsible features of its own, the authors maintained, running itself contains elements of pathos, uncertainty, and insecurity. The unsettling element of the search for self-identity through running is the implication that all is not as it should be in other aspects of the runner's life. By pouring ourselves into running, Joseph and Robbins suggested we unconsciously adopt a form of social amnesia and therefore escape from activities that continue to be important.

Yet another explanation for the attraction to running has been advanced by Blumenthal et al. (1985), who proposed that habitual or obsessive running is best understood as a coping strategy for the regulation of a person's emotional state or affect. They point out that our emotional states comprise positive affects such as excitement and enjoyment and negative affects such as distress, tension, anger, fear, and shame; the authors suggested that running enhances positive affects and reduces negative affects. Thus, they postulated running represents one method by which individuals learn to regulate their emotional states.

In addition, the authors suggested that different runners may learn to use running either as a stimulant to improve feelings of self-esteem and self-worth or as a reward for some actions of which they are proud; these runners may actually run only when they are happy (positive-affect runners) or they may run only as an antidote to control their distress (negative-affect runners). In this scheme, the negative-affect runners are at risk if they begin to believe that running is their sole method of reducing distress. As running replaces other effective methods of stress management and affect control, the runners begin to believe that the only way to reduce distress is to "engage in running behavior." This belief heightens dependence on running, thus the development of an addiction.

Two other explanations have been offered for commitment to running that do not evoke an abnormal psychological state. Fred Graham (1981), professor of religious studies at Michigan State University, pointed out that four major anxieties color our lives: death, guilt, meaninglessness, and loneliness. He suggested that a recent addition is the anxiety of terminal helplessness or living death. This, he suggested, has arisen through the introduction of hospital intensive-care units that raise the specter of a living death in which the terminally ill patient, too ill to function, loses control of his or her life and is at the mercy of machines and the unfortunate medical ethos of preserving life at all costs. Graham noticed that a statement frequently made by runners is typified by the following:

I am going to run until I'm 90. If the weather is bad on my last day, I'll collapse and die on an indoor track. Don't let anyone try to keep me alive, Fred. Just take a pushbroom and shove me off the running surface. Then, when you have finished your run, call the coroner.

Graham also suggested that part of the explanation for the withdrawal symptoms that occur when one misses a few days of training is that this causes anxiety because it induces thoughts about the body aging and the time of terminal helplessness drawing closer.

These feelings engendered by the anxiety of terminal illness are well described by Noel Carroll's (1981) book:

His controlled fear is that all his precious training will go down the drain if he eases up for a single day. I have lived all my running life with this anxiety and I know I share it with other runners: an inability to sleep if a day's training is missed; the guilty feeling that overwhelms with gloom and despondency; the remorse for reneging on your commitment; the realization that you have let yourself down. (p. 41)

But finally, many of us may run simply because it provides us with a simple way to "play." Another pair of American psychiatrists, Samuel Perry and Michael Sacks (1981), pointed out that the word *sports* comes from the word *disport*, which means "to carry away" (i.e., from work). They pointed out that three features of sport also make it play: Sport produces nothing in the real world, and once sport has purpose, it is no longer play but becomes work; play is separate from the real world (the opposite of play is not work, but reality); and although play is a purposeless activity in a make-believe world, the feelings expressed through play can be very real and very intense.

Thus, for many of us running provides the make-believe world of our childhood in which we can do anything, including win the Olympic Marathon in our dreams. "Like children, we pretend because we can never completely accept reality for what it is. Pretending is make-believe, an illusion" (Perry & Sacks, 1981, p. 74).

So running is our personal, private playground in which we develop our personal, private creations. In running, we are able to control how, when, where, how far, and how fast we run; we can call "time out" when we have had enough and can set our own goals, all the ingredients essential to a play activity.

And the success of this make-believe is shown by the answer to this question: Who really but a runner could be proud of finishing 10,000th in a marathon?

CONCLUSION

The most important lesson I have learned in researching this section on running addiction is that psychology provides few definitive answers. In part this is because of the extreme complexity of human nature and the fact that psychology is a relatively young science and therefore is in a state of continuing flux. There seem to be many possible explanations for any particular observation but few firm data to identify which theory is correct.

In providing a broad range of possible psychological explanations for this attraction to running, I have not tried to conclude which theories are more likely. Rather, I have provided readers with a core of ideas that will allow them to make some commonsense deductions about their own motives for running.

By understanding our addictions, we may be better able to manage them and so avoid the most dangerous of pitfalls in running—the selfish runner's syndrome (see chapter 6).

8

Training With the Expert Runners

"Train little, hard, and often."

Jim Peters (personal communication, 1955)

"The more I speak to athletes, the more convinced I become that the method of training is relatively unimportant. There are many ways to the top, and the training method you choose is just the one that suits you best. No, the important thing is the attitude of the athlete, the desire to get to the top."

Herb Elliott (1964)

"Develop a base of several months of long aerobic runs, then begin interspersing several interval workouts per week while attempting to maintain the same mileage level. These interval workouts should be of varying distances, from 220s through 880s, should start at gentle paces but culminate with much sharper sessions as the runner approaches a targeted race. The recovery interval will for the most part be the same distance as the effort run, and will generally (but not always) be in the form of jogging. That's it. That's the only training you need to win a gold medal in the Olympics."

Marti Liquori and John Parker (1980)

"No one can dogmatically say that this is the best way for an athlete to reach the top because it isn't necessarily. Most of all he has to experience and evolve his own system . . . I trained every day for

eight years irrespective of illness or injury. I was wrong."

Ron Clarke (Lenton, 1981)

"*Again choose quality rather than quantity when training. Train for speed not distance. Speed is the killer. It is infectious. It has spread. To win mile races you have to be fast. To win marathons you have to be fast. The top ultramarathoners are now showing that to win ultras you have to be fast as well.*"

Bruce Fordyce (1989)

In this chapter, we look at the training methods of those runners who have reached the pinnacle of excellence in the past century. The chosen athletes have been included not only because of their levels of excellence but also because we know at least something of their training methods. Regrettably, the majority of great athletes record the barest details of their training methods for posterity.

The athletes described in this chapter represent middle- and long-distance running up to the marathon, short ultramarathon running at distances up to 100 km, and long ultramarathon running at distances from 100 to 700 km.

HISTORICAL OVERVIEW

Milroy (1981), who has traced the roots of modern distance running, relates that foot messengers used by the Greeks and Romans to carry letters and messages ran up to 100 km at a time and that a 237-km race was held in the Circus Maximus in Rome at the height of the Roman Empire.

The first reference to British foot messengers dates to A.D. 1040; the first reference to European and Turkish messengers dates to the 15th century. By the end of the 18th century, improvements in the conditions of roads, particularly in Britain, made the continued use of messengers unnecessary. Messengers were retained only for racing, but they were soon supplanted by the growth of professional pedestrianism in Britain in the first half of the 18th century.

According to Milroy (1981), it is difficult to explain why professional pedestrianism first developed in Britain. Three essential components—good roads, accurately measured courses, and accurate and cheap pocket watches—were also available in other parts of Europe, including France. He suggested that the fascination of the British upper class for gambling was the pivotal factor. However, it is also clear that organized running events had evolved in Britain and were well established by the 17th century; thus the groundwork for professionalism was well established (F.J.G. van der Merwe, 1987).

From the outset, a clear distinction was made between professional and amateur running. Professional running was the domain of the lower, working classes, and the earliest races were usually sponsored by traditional pubs that built their own running tracks (Lovesey, 1968). The aim was to make money, not to enjoy sport, and any working class youth who showed promise in athletics soon became a professional runner.

The more conventional (amateur) running probably arose in the English public schools and soon spread to Oxford and Cambridge (Krise & Squires, 1982). Eton was probably the first British school to introduce formal athletics for students in 1837; less formal cross-country running for schoolboys in the form of games like "hares and hounds" and "paper chases" became popular at about the same time. The 20-m Crick Run, held annually since 1837 at Rugby School, is the oldest long-distance run in the world.

Road running, especially marathon and ultramarathon running, seems to have evolved from the professional sport. Professional road records antedate those of the amateurs by more than 70 years (Milroy, personal communication, 1987). Track running also evolved from the professionals—the amateurs wished to have similar events but "without the air of disreputability that surrounded the professional scene" (Milroy, personal communication, 1987)—but continued as the domain of the amateurs. The 1896 Olympic Games formalized the marathon as an amateur event (at least until the upheaval in the early 1980s); the modern interest in ultramarathon running can be traced, at least in part, to the influence of Newton and the Comrades Marathon (see chapter 5).

MARATHON AND SHORTER DISTANCES

Deerfoot

Probably the first great runner of modern times was Deerfoot, the North American Indian from Cattaraugus.

Deerfoot first became an international celebrity in September 1861, when at the age of 36 he visited "a secure and insular" Britain (Lovesey, 1968) to test his running skills against the leading British professionals of the day. Deerfoot's exceptional talent had first come to the attention of a British promoter and former runner, George Martin. Earlier that year, Martin had taken three leading British pedestrians to North America to compete in a series of races against the leading American runners. It was in those races that Deerfoot's potential had become apparent.

Deerfoot's tour of Britain lasted until May 1883, during which time he visited all the major cities in the United Kingdom. In one 4-month period alone, he ran

400 miles in competition (Lovesey, 1968); in the first 14 weeks of his tour he ran 16 races of distances from 1 to 11 miles against the best British runners and lost only twice, both times under unusual conditions.

Only near the end of his tour was Deerfoot's invincibility challenged, in part because he had overraced and had become "rather too fond" of the British way of life and apparently of British beer.

Among his greatest performances was, in 1861, a 10-mile race run in 53:35; 1 week later he became only the fourth man in history to cover 11 miles in less than 1 hour. In 1862 he established the world record for distance run in 1 hour, and in the first 4 months of 1863, he improved on that distance 3 times. His last race in Britain was one of his greatest. Passing 10 miles in 51:26, he completed 11 miles 970 yards in 1 hour and 12 miles in 1:02:02.05. It was not until 1953, 90 years later, that another British amateur, Jim Peters, exceeded that distance by running 16 yards farther in 1 hour. As we shall see, Peters may have been the greatest marathoner of all time.

When asked how he trained, Deerfoot replied, "I have never trained" (Lovesey, 1968, p. 39). Lovesey (1968) wrote that Deerfoot's "invasion" of England had three major effects on distance running. First, Deerfoot exposed the "cautious, strength-preserving" tactics of the British runners as unprogressive and unnerved his opponents with his frequent switches of pace during the race. Second, he brought social respectability and wide public appeal to running, and third, he inspired an exceptional group of British runners who established running records that would last for 16 to 60 years.

Walter George

The next great distance runner after Deerfoot was Walter George (see Figure 8.1), who in the 1880s earned the title "champion of champions" for a series of remarkable running performances. Together with Deerfoot, Shrubb, Nurmi, and Zatopek, George is considered one of the "kings of distance" by Peter Lovesey (Lovesey, 1968).

In 1882, at age 23, George set world marks at every running distance from the 3/4 mile to 10 miles (Krise & Squires, 1982; Lovesey, 1968) and failed by just 37 yards to beat Deerfoot's 1-hour record; George won a string of British track and cross-country titles and lowered the world amateur mile record from 4:25.5 to 4:18.4. In 1885 he ran a mile in training in 4:10.2 on a course that was too long by 6 yards. Later he ran an unofficial 10 miles in 49:29.

Probably his most famous races were those that he ran in 1885 against the Scotsman William Cummings, who was the professional counterpart of George, holding all the professional records at the same distances at which George competed (Lovesey, 1968). In the first 3 races that they contested, George won the first, a mile in 4:20.2, and Cummings won the second and third at 4 and 6 miles,

Figure 8.1 An elderly Walter George poses with Arthur Newton.
Note. Photo courtesy of Vernon Jones.

respectively. George's disappointment led to the scheduling of the "Mile of the Century" run between the two great rivals on August 23, 1886. The contestants completed the first lap in 58.25, completed the half mile in 2:01.75, and were still locked together at the end of the third lap, run in 3:07.75. Then Cummings suddenly sprinted to a 10-yard lead.

But he had gone too soon. George caught Cummings in the back straight, winning in the world-record time of 4:12.75. Cummings collapsed 60 yards from the finish. George's performance nearly matched a prediction he made at age 19, only 3 months after he had started running, that he would one day run the mile in 4:12 (Lovesey, 1968), a 12-second improvement on the then–world record.

By modern standards, George trained only very lightly. For the first 6 years of his running career he trained only with his "100-up" exercise (George, 1908; Lovesey, 1968). This exercise basically involved running in place so his knees were alternatively flexed to hip level. The goal was to repeat the exercise 100 times at the maximal possible speed. By 1882, George ran every morning and afternoon, alternating slow runs of 1 to 2 miles with faster runs of 400 to 1,200 yards and some sprinting. He finished all his long runs with a sustained burst of fast running, and he included one 100-up exercise each day plus occasional walks (Lovesey, 1968).

Cummings, on the other hand, seems to have trained mainly with walking up to 10 miles a day. He included a slow daily run of 1 mile with faster runs once or twice a week (Lovesey, 1968).

Lovesey (1968) suggested that George's contribution to running was that he brought a sense of purpose to the sport with his daily training and with his intellectual approach.

In his later life, George, who had been born in the village of Calne, Wilshire, on the Box-to-London 100-mile course, was chief timekeeper in most of Arthur Newton's record attempts in Britain (R. Clarke & Harris, 1967).

Len Hurst

The next great British distance runner, Len Hurst, left more complete details of his training methods (Downer, 1900; Milroy, 1983).

Hurst was born in Kent on December 28, 1871 and ran his first professional race at age 15, winning a 6-km race worth "sterling" 10 (Milroy, 1983). In the early years of his athletic career, Hurst ran only short distance races, but in 1893 he switched to longer distances and covered 294.6 km in a 4-day, 30-hour event (7-1/2 hours of running each day).

In 1896 he won the inaugural 40-km Paris-to-Conflans marathon in 2:31:00, a time that was 27 minutes faster than Spiridon Louis's winning time in the inaugural Olympic Games Marathon, also run over 40 km that year. Hurst won the Paris-to-Conflans marathon twice more with a best performance of 2:26:48 in the 1900 race. A month later he ran 50 km in 3:36:45, a time that Milroy (1983) considered to have been a likely world record. The following year Hurst easily defeated the American Bob Hallen in the "40-km championship of the world."

In 1903 Hurst won the first professional London-to-Brighton race by 40 minutes in a time of 6:32:34, a 26-minute improvement on the previous record. In the next unofficial running of this event in 1929, Newton lowered the record a further 38 minutes. In his last major running success, two months later at the Preston Park cricket ground in Brighton, Hurst set a new world amateur and professional 40-km track record of 2:33:42.

Hurst retired in 1908 and became the licensee of a public house. A quiet man, he refused to write his life story and reportedly died of cirrhosis of the liver, an occupational hazard, in 1937 at age 66. His achievements are commemorated each year with the award of the Len Hurst Belt to the winning team in the London-to-Brighton race; this award is believed to have been won by Hurst in that race in 1903.

Of his training methods, Hurst wrote the following (Downer, 1900):

For a youth to attain anything like 'class' honours in events from ten miles and upwards, he . . . will have two or three year's steady work ahead of him, and must be satisfied to plod along at what, to his ambitious mind, must appear a very slow pace. . . . Experience teaches us that it is impossible for a man to possess both speed and endurance for long distance running without a thorough training.

I should, therefore, advise . . . any amount of walking exercise, right from the time they start running. . . . Remember never overdo yourself or pump yourself quite out. (pp. 117-118)

He summarized his daily training as follows:

Rise at six o'clock in summer and seven o'clock in winter; . . . steady walk; 8.30 breakfast; easy till 9.45; walk till 11 o'clock; run about three miles; dinner, 12.45; bed, 1.45; out for walk at three o'clock; track at four; three mile spin with sharp finish, shower and rub down; tea, 5.30; walk, 6.30 to 8.30 . . . bed at ten o'clock. Never forget grooming on rising from bed at anytime, and take sponge and shower baths cold. (Downer, 1900, p. 119)

Thus, it seems that Hurst's training included between 5-3/4 and 6-3/4 hours of walking each day and between 10 and 30 km per day of running (when training for a marathon).

His nutritional preference was for roast beef, roast and boiled mutton or chicken, a limited amount of vegetables, and bread washed down with half of a pint of good bitter ale. During races he reportedly drank a mixture of egg and sherry (Milroy, 1981).

Joe Binks

In 1902 Joe Binks surpassed George's amateur world mile record by running the distance in 4:16.8. Binks's training was even more farcical than was George's. Binks trained one evening a week for about 30 minutes, during which he ran five or six 110-yard intervals at top speed, finishing with a "fast 200 or 300 yards" (Burfoot, 1981a).

Later Binks became a journalist, a close friend of Arthur Newton, and organizer of the 1937 London-to-Brighton race, in which Hardy Ballington beat Newton's course record by 1 second.

Alfred Shrubb

Born in Sussex on December 12, 1878, 4-1/2 years before Newton, Alfred Shrubb set amateur and professional world records at distances from 2 to 5 miles and from 8 to 11 miles, including the record for the greatest distance run in 1 hour.

He also won 20 British Championships between 1900 and 1904. His amateur world records, all set in 1904, included 2 miles in 9:9.6, 10 miles in 50:40.6, and the 1-hour run of 11 miles, 1,137 yards. In the 10-mile race he surpassed George's 22-year-old record of 51:20. In the next 50 years, only one Englishman would run faster.

Shrubb was "discovered" by Harry Andrews, who saw him win a number of races and immediately appreciated his talent. The following spring, Andrews traveled to Horsham to train Shrubb for 3 weeks. He began with a "good dose of medicine. First, a little salt and senna leaves, and then a little ginger and Spanish liquorice. It is the finest medicine I have ever struck, and does not purge a man too much" (Andrews, 1910, p. 2).

For the first week of training, Shrubb and Andrews walked 15 to 20 miles every day. In the second week, Andrews prescribed "running exercises round the local football field" (Andrews, 1910, p. 2). In the third week, Shrubb ran a 4-mile time trial on a loose, heavy, and potholed track in 8 seconds over the record time. Apparently, Andrews's methods were paying off!

Compared to George and Binks, Shrubb trained heavily. He was one of the first runners to record his training ideas and methods in book form (Shrubb, 1910). His training program for the 12 days before he set the 10-mile record on November 5, 1904, is set out in Table 8.1. Shrubb's training for the week of October 24 to 30 totaled 42 miles, of which 14 miles were run at race pace on consecutive days. Note also that just 5 days before his official race, Shrubb even beat George's 10-mile record in a training run.

In his book, Shrubb (1910) expressed his views on a wide range of topics, including the American runner, who "takes his sport more seriously . . . is more highly-strung . . . and seems to set his mind more determinedly on winning than does his British rival" (p. x); child athletes, "The less serious running of any description which an athlete indulges in before eighteen, the better for his future prospects" (p. 17); and alcohol, "Never touch spirits of any kind. They are the worst thing an athlete can go for" (p. 71).

Shrubb entered two marathon races in 1909, but it is not clear whether he finished either (D.E. Martin & Gynn, 1979). On February 5 of that year he collapsed when in the lead after 39 km of a marathon run in the Madison Square Gardens on a track measuring 160 m per lap. On April 3, he led for the first 40 km of a Marathon Derby run on an outdoor track at the New York Polo Grounds (320 m per lap) but failed to place even third in that race. His book includes training advice for the marathon race; this training consisted mainly of walking.

Hannes Kolehmainen

Hannes Kolehmainen was the first in the dynasty of outstanding Finnish long-distance runners that included Paavo Nurmi and Lasse Viren and that completely

Table 8.1   Training of Alf Shrubb (October 24 to November 4, 1904)

Day	Morning	Afternoon
Monday 24	4 miles (steady)	2 miles in 9:17.8
Tuesday 25	—	10-mile time trial in 51:02
Wednesday 26	4 miles (steady)	2 miles in 9:18.6
Thursday 27	8 miles (steady)	—
Friday 28	—	—
Saturday 29	4 miles (steady)	8 miles (slow)
Sunday 30	—	—
Monday 31	—	—
Tuesday 1	3 miles (steady)	10 miles in 50:55
Wednesday 2	2 miles (fast)	5 miles (steady)
Thursday 3	8 miles (steady)	4 miles (fairly fast)
Friday 4	Rest	Rest

Note. From Shrubb (1910).

dominated all the Olympic 5,000- and 10,000-m races and the world records at those distances from 1896 to 1948.

In 1910, aged 20, Kolehmainen started training in earnest for the 1912 Stockholm Olympic Games. At those Games, in the space of 8 days, he won gold medals in the 5,000 m (in a world-record time of 14:36.6), in the 10,000 m (also in a world-record time—31:20.8), and in the 8,000-m cross-country race. He also set the fastest time in the 3,000-m team event, in another world record time of 8:36.6. At the next Olympic Games in Antwerp in 1920, Kolehmainen won the marathon in 2:32:35.8.

Unfortunately, no record of his training methods exists, although it is thought that he included speed play (fartlek) in his training and did little if any training on the track (Doherty, 1964). Almost certainly his training must have been based on the Finnish training methods later described by Mikkola (1929). It is also certain that Kolehmainen influenced Nurmi to include speed work in his training. In letters written to Nurmi in 1918, Kolehmainen urged Nurmi to vary the speed of his training runs and to include frequent sprints, balanced by slower "shacking" (Lovesey, 1968, pp. 94-95). Kolehmainen's other great contribution was that he introduced meticulous pacing to the longer track races. The world record he established in the 5,000-m Olympic Games Final was the first such race run with almost even splits (7:17.0; 7:19.6) and resulted in an improvement of 25 seconds on the previous record.

Clarence DeMar

Clarence DeMar (see Figure 8.2) is to the Boston Marathon what Arthur Newton is to the Comrades Marathon; both achieved legendary performances that helped popularize those races.

DeMar won the Boston Marathon an unequaled 7 times; his last victory in 1930 came when he was 41 years old. He ran in the 1912 and 1924 Olympic Games Marathons, finishing third in the 1924 race (DeMar, 1937).

His achievements were the more remarkable by the fact that between the ages of 22 and 33, he ran the Boston Marathon only once (in 1917). DeMar gave three reasons for this. First, he had been told that he had a heart condition and had been advised not to run. An autopsy performed after his death from bowel cancer in 1958 showed that he had no serious cardiac abnormalities and that his coronary arteries had only mild atherosclerosis (Currens & White, 1961). These findings indicate that the heart murmurs that had been heard so many years before were

Figure 8.2 The legendary Clarence DeMar, "Mr. de Marathon," in the Boston Marathon.
Note. From The Bettmann Archive.

probably due to his high level of training and were a feature of what is now called the "athlete's heart."

Second, DeMar's deep religious beliefs as a Baptist led him to question whether running for "selfish victory" was actually the most appropriate activity for him. He noted that some church leaders later denounced the 1928 Olympic Games as a "carnival of flesh," a denouncement that, he wryly observed, insured that those Games had the greatest attendance yet.

Finally, his work as a printer combined with his studies at the University of Vermont prevented DeMar from training properly.

DeMar was the subject of many scientific studies performed by the legendary physiologist David Dill and his colleagues at the Harvard Fatigue Laboratory (Bock, 1963; Bock et al., 1928; Dill, 1965; Dill et al., 1930). DeMar was found to have good running efficiency, low blood lactate concentrations during exercise, a 'lactate turnpoint' that occurred at a fast running speed, a powerful heart, and a very high $\dot{V}O_2$max, estimated to be 76 ml/kg/min at age 36 and measured at 60 ml/kg/min at age 49. Dill (1965) also estimated that DeMar ran his best marathons at about 77% $\dot{V}O_2$max.

In his autobiography first published in 1937 and subsequently reprinted in 1981 (DeMar, 1937), DeMar provided few details of his training methods. He wrote that for his first Boston Marathon in 1910, he "trained by running leisurely (to work) with my clothes on, my only speed work being 10 mile races. Several times I had been out fifteen or twenty miles instead of the usual seven to or from work" (p. 19). Before the 1911 Boston Marathon he ran approximately 100 miles a week for 2 months before the race and included "several 20 mile jaunts." Most of his running was done at 8 mi/hr (5 min/km), and his speed work was again confined to an occasional 10-mile race. These training methods were almost identical to those of Newton with the exception that time constraints prevented DeMar from training as much. Like Newton, DeMar continued to run exceptionally well even when well into middle age.

Paavo Nurmi

Paavo Nurmi (see Figure 8.3), the "Flying Finn," was born in 1897 and began running in 1908 at age 11. By the time his competitive career ended prematurely in 1932, he had competed in three Olympic Games, had won a total of six Olympic races, was second in three other Olympic races, and was first in a team event. He had also set 20 official world records (Lovesey, 1968).

Nurmi began more serious training in 1912 at age 15. Of this period in his running career he later wrote (Doherty, 1964; Wilt, 1973), "My training was very one-sided. I practiced only in summer. Actual winter training was hardly known in those days . . . I had no idea of speedwork, so it was no wonder I remained a slow trudger for so many years!" (Wilt, 1973, p. 77). It was only

Figure 8.3 Paavo Nurmi, the ''Flying Finn,'' whose athletic performances included 10 Olympic and 19 world records.
Note. From *The Kings of Distance* (p. 112) by P. Lovesey, 1968, Norfolk, England: Eyre and Spottiswoode. Copyright 1968 by The Press Association.

after his correspondence with Kolehmainen that Nurmi altered his training methods to include more speed work.

In 1918, Nurmi entered military service and had more time to train. He also began to experiment with different training speeds. The results were, at least outwardly, impressive. At his first Olympic Games in 1920, Nurmi finished second in the 5,000 m and first in the 10,000 m. He also won individual and team gold medals in the 10,000-m cross-country race, an event no longer contested at the Olympics. The domination of the Finns in the 1920 Olympic long-distance running events was completed by Kolehmainen's victory in the marathon. Yet, in retrospect, Nurmi felt that his training had been less than optimum: insufficient and with too much emphasis on long distances.

From 1920 to May 1924, Nurmi trained 6 months of the year, between April and September, according to the following schedule (Doherty, 1964; Wilt, 1973).

Morning: Walk 10 to 12 km with some sprints in order to "supple up" for the afternoon run.

Afternoon: Run 4 to 7 km with fast speed over the last 1 to 2 km, finished off by four to five 80- to 100-m sprints.

For the remaining 6 months of the year, Nurmi did not train. In addition to his Olympic achievements, using this quite meager training Nurmi set a new world mile record of 4:10.4 in August 1923. In the same year he also set world records for the 1,500-m race and the 3-mile race.

In May 1924, as Nurmi prepared for the Paris Olympic Games, he changed his training to include a late-morning run during which he ran four to five 80- to 120-m sprints, followed by a timed 400- to 1,000-m run, followed by 3,000 to 4,000 m at even speed with "the last lap always very fast" (Wilt, 1973, p. 78). It seems likely that Nurmi must also have begun running longer intervals of up to 600 m during this period.

Nurmi's Olympic performances were again impressive; he won the 1,500 m and 5,000 m within 1 hour of each other, the 3,000-m team race, and the 10,000-m cross-country race. In the 1,500-m race he passed the first 500 m in a time that was faster than that of either Herb Elliott or Jim Ryun in their world 1,500-m records set in 1960 and 1967 (Lovesey, 1968). At the 1928 Olympics in Amsterdam, Nurmi won the 10,000 m and was second in both the 5,000-m race and the 3,000-m steeplechase.

Regrettably, that was to be his last Olympic Games, for in 1932 Nurmi was declared a professional, apparently on the evidence of a check paid to him by an American race organizer (Krise & Squires, 1982). Nurmi had planned to run the marathon at the 1932 Games and in training had run a 40.2-km road race in 2:22:04, equivalent to a 2:29:04 marathon.

Nurmi continued to run competitively in America for a further few years. His death from heart disease at age 75 was most likely a result of a hereditary predisposition, because his father had died of the same disease. In his will Nurmi left a large bequest for heart disease research, which has been used to fund a series of "Paavo Nurmi Symposia" on heart disease research.

According to Webster (1948), the successes of the Finnish long-distance runners of the 1920s were due largely to their systems of winter training.

The details of their winter training methods were contained in a booklet written by Mikkola (1929), an English translation of which was discovered by Newton's great friend, Vernon Jones, in Newton's correspondence.

Mikkola records that the Finnish runners began their walking training at a time that depended on the distances they raced; marathon runners started in January, and 1,500-m and 5,000- to 10,000-m runners started in February or March. The distances walked also depended on the distances the runners would race; marathon runners walked longer distances (15 to 35 km) than did the 5,000- to 10,000-m runners (10 to 20 km) and the 1,500-m runners (8 to 15 km). Basically, each group would walk these distances 2 to 4 times a week until the end of March. After about 6 weeks' training, they would run the last 3 to 10 km of the workout. By April, the athletes would train 4 to 5 days a week, usually twice a day; cross-country runs of 6 to 8 km would be added as would track sessions involving sprints of 150 to 300 m and continuous runs of 1,000 to 2,000 m at a relatively easy pace. Walking would be gradually discontinued. By the end of March, the 5,000- to 10,000-m runners were walking 60 km and running 18 km a week; the marathon runners were walking 120 km and running 24 km a week. The peak sharpening precompetition training programs that were reached in May by the 1,500-m, 5,000 to 10,000-m, and marathon runners are listed in Tables 8.2, 8.3, and 8.4.

Mikkola wrote that only "an experienced and hardened man" could stand the training program of the 5,000- to 10,000-m runners and that to avoid going stale,

Table 8.2   Precompetition Training Program for a Finnish 1,500-m Olympic Competitor (Circa 1920)

Date	Morning	Afternoon
May 2	8-km walk	800 m (75%)
4		2,000 m (easy)
		2 x 150 m (100%)
6	3-km run	1,000 m (100%)
		4 x 60 m (100%)
7	8-km walk	500 m (75%)
		2,000 m (85%)
8		2 x 150 m (100%)
		800 m (75%)
11		1,500 m (90%)
13		600 m (90%)
		1,000 m (easy)
14		3 x 150 m (100%)
		2,000 m (easy)
16		300 m (75%)
		1,800 m (easy)
17		3 x 60 m (100%)
		1,000 m (75%)
19		200 m (100%)
		1,500 m (easy)
20		300 m (85%)
		1,000 m (easy)
21		800 m (jog)
24		Race

Note. Information courtesy of Arthur Newton and Vernon Jones.

Table 8.3   Precompetition Training Program for a Finnish 5,000 to 10,000-m Olympic Competitor (Circa 1920)

Date (in May)	Morning distance	Afternoon distance (effort)
2	10-km walk	2 x 150 m (100%) 3,000 m (75%)
4		5,000 m (85%)
6	15-km walk	3 x 150 m (100%) 2,000 m (75%)
7	6-km run	600 m (75%) 1,500 m (easy)
8		5 x 50 m (100%) 1,000 m (easy)
9	8-km walk	4,000 m (easy)
11		10,000 m (67-75%)
13	8-km walk	300 m (75%) 2,000 m (easy)
14		8-km run
16		3 x 150 m (100%) 3,000 m (easy)
18		1000 m (90%) 3-km run
20	4-km run	3 x 50 m (100%) 600 m (75%)

Note. Information courtesy of Arthur Newton and Vernon Jones.

the younger runners should confine themselves only to the running workouts. Only experienced 5,000- to 10,000-m runners were advised to attempt the marathon. Runners at all distances were advised to taper for races, with the last 2 to 3 days being for complete rest.

During competition, marathon runners were advised to race to win and not to set records because it was considered useless to make schedules for such an unpredictable race. "The only 'schedule' which a marathoner can make, and which is dependent on good fortune, is 'if nothing extra-ordinary happens during two hours and thirty minutes, then I shall succeed'" (Mikkola, 1929). Although the best tactic was considered to be even-paced running, Mikkola noted that this was seldom possible in "big" competition, because the leaders tended to start fast. Runners were advised to run with their competitors for the first 21 to 28 km of the race and then to "try the ice" by sprinting to break contact, if they had the energy. Otherwise, they were to reserve enough strength for the last kilometers, "in case someone should surprise." Mikkola also recognized that good marathon runners required both speed and the ability to change pace during competition.

Table 8.4   Precompetition Training Program for a Finnish Olympic Marathon Competitor (Circa 1920)

Date	Morning	Afternoon
April 1	18-km walk	10-km run
2		15-km run
4	45-km walk	
6	25-km walk	
7	20-km walk	15-km run
9	15-km walk	15-km run
11		20-km run[a]
13	15-km walk	10-km run
14	15-km run	

Note. Information courtesy of Arthur Newton and Vernon Jones.

[a]Two to three 30-km runs were included in April, including one at race pace 4 weeks before the competition.

Emil Zatopek

The Czech Emil Zatopek (see Figure 8.4) is the last of Lovesey's "kings of distance." Like Nurmi, Zatopek completely dominated distance running in his era. In the 1948 London Olympics Zatopek won the 10,000 m, and at the Helsinki Games in 1952 he became the only man in Olympic history ever to win the three long-distance events—the 5,000 m, 10,000 m, and the marathon—the latter in his first race over the distance. In all these races he set Olympic records. By the end of 1948 Zatopek held every world record from 10,000 m to the marathon, and in 1954 he added the world record for the 5,000 m as well.

Zatopek's basic training was interval work (Doherty, 1964; Wilt, 1973). His rationale for this type of training was simple:

> When I was young, I was too slow . . . I thought, "I must learn to run fast by practising to run fast." So I ran one hundred metres very fast. . . . People said, "Emil, you are crazy. You are practising to be a sprinter. You have no chance." I said, "Yes, but if I run one hundred metres twenty times, that is two kilometers and that is no longer a sprint" (Benyo, 1983, p. 80).

Up to 1947, Zatopek reportedly had two basic training programs, which he alternated daily (Doherty, 1964; Wilt, 1973):

> **Day 1:**   Five 150-m intervals with 150-m jogs between, twenty 400-m intervals with 150-m jogs between, and five 100- to 150-m intervals. The 400-m intervals were run in times varying between 67 and 77 seconds, and the shorter sprints were run slightly faster.

Day 2: Five 150-m intervals, twenty 400-m intervals, and five 200-m intervals.

By 1948, Zatopek had refined his daily training to become essentially five 200-m intervals, twenty 400-m intervals, and five 200-m intervals with a 200-m (about 1-minute) jog between intervals. The 200-m intervals were run in 34 seconds, and the 400-m intervals were run between 56 and 75 seconds or slower, starting at the faster speed and gradually slowing down. The total distance covered each day was about 18 km (11 miles). In October 1949 Zatopek increased his training to equal 28 km (17.5 miles) a day.

From the beginning of 1954, age and increasing foreign competition forced Zatopek to train twice a day. In April of that year he increased the intervals to a total of ten 200-m intervals and fifty 400-m intervals, thereby covering more than 30 km a day.

We don't know how fast Zatopek ran these intervals. Certainly they were nowhere near the 60 seconds per lap that has entered the running folklore. It seems that "the times of the intervals were mostly slow and quite irregular. Many were practically 'walks,' but others were sprightly—around 65 seconds.

Figure 8.4 Emil Zatopek nears the finish of the 1952 Olympic marathon in Helsinki.
Note. Photo courtesy of Die Burger (Photopress, Cape Town).

The plan was to cover the distance first, then to try to run the intervals faster, but always a week before the race he severely reduced the distance and speeded up the intervals" (Doherty, 1964, p. 233).

An interesting observation by Zatopek relates to the importance of setting realistic goals:

"You can't climb up to the second floor without a ladder . . . When you set your aim too high and don't fulfill it, then your enthusiasm turns to bitterness. Try for a goal that's reasonable, and then gradually raise it. That's the only way to get to the top." (Doherty, 1964, p. 6)

Jim Peters

Jim Peters (see Figure 8.5) is the next in our parade of running greats. Between 1952 and 1954, Peters became the first man to break the 2:20 barrier for the marathon, reducing the world marathon record from the old mark of 2:26:07 to a new 2:17:39. When he retired prematurely after the Vancouver Marathon in 1954, Peters held four of the six fastest-ever marathon times. No marathoner before or since has equaled these performances, and for this reason I consider Peters the greatest marathoner ever.

Regrettably, Peters is best remembered for two events over which he really had little control. First, as the world-record holder and clear favorite for the 1952 Olympic Marathon, Peters was badly beaten by Zatopek in that race. History records that at about the 18-km mark in that race, Zatopek asked Peters

Figure 8.5 Jim Peters, arguably the greatest marathoner of all time.
Note. Photo courtesy of Die Burger (United Press Photos).

whether the pace they were running was "good enough." When Peters replied that the pace was too slow, Zatopek speeded up, and Peters was unable to respond. Within a few kilometers Zatopek had a 10-second lead over Peters, passing the 30-km mark only 12 seconds shy of Peters's world record. Peters retired from the race shortly after 30 km (Benyo, 1983; Krise & Squires, 1982; J. Peters, 1955).

Many assume that Zatopek psyched out Peters, which I feel is an extremely unfair assumption. Two less well-known factors may explain Peters's poor performance in that race. Six weeks prior to the race, Peters had won the British AAA Marathon in an astounding 2:20:42, an astonishing improvement of more than 4-1/2 minutes on the world record. British athletic officials, including Harold Abrahams, expressed doubts that Peters would be able to recover sufficiently for the Olympic Marathon (J. Peters, 1955). Their doubts were justified.

The second factor was Peters's mode of travel to the Games. Unable to afford seats on a scheduled airline, the British athletic officials were forced to charter a four-engined York transport plane to take their team to Helsinki. The flight lasted 9 hours, during which time the plane was struck by lightning and Peters, exposed to a very cold draft, became violently ill. He arrived in Helsinki feeling sick and stiff and with a headache.

Peters is also remembered for his collapse from severe heatstroke in the 1954 Vancouver Empire Games Marathon (see Figure 18.1). Unlike Peters, who believed that extreme heat was no deterrent to a very fast marathon time, two South Africans in the race, Jackie Mekler and Jan Barnard, were accustomed to the dangers of hot-weather running and ran very conservatively, finishing second and third. Both entered the stadium more than 20 minutes behind Peters, but Peters did not finish the race.

Peters is another of the few runners to have left details of his training methods (J. Peters, 1955; J. Peters et al., 1957). The keys to his training seem to have been a gradual increase in his weekly training distance and its intensity, a slow introduction to marathon racing, and sustained, hard effort in all his training runs. For the first 4 years of his running career, between 1946 and 1949, Peters ran track, cross-country, and road races of up to 16 km (J. Peters, 1955) and was the British champion at 6 and 10 miles. He also ran in the 1948 Olympic Games 10,000-m final, in which he was lapped by Zatopek. Deeply embarrassed by his loss, Peters decided to retire and in 1949 ran only one race. But his coach, Johnny Johnston, eventually persuaded him to continue running, and in November 1949 he again began regular training with the idea of becoming a specialist marathon runner. A year later, in October 1950, his training program read as shown in Table 8.5 (J. Peters et al., 1957).

Although Peters's total training distance at this stage was very low, his average speed was good (3:57/km).

By the following February, Peters had increased his regular 4-mile run to 6 miles and by April to 9 miles. Once a week he ran a faster 4-mile time trial in about 23 minutes. By the first week of April 1951, Peters's training was as shown in Table 8.6 (J. Peters et al., 1957).

Table 8.5   Jim Peters's Training Program for October 1950

Date	Distance Km	Miles	Time (hr:min:s)	Comment	Speed (min:s/km)
2	6.4	4	25:30	Fast trot	3:59
3	6.4	4	24:00	Fast trot	3:45
4	—	—			
5	4.8	3	18:00	Fast (shorts)	3:45
6	—	—			
7	9.6	6	40:00	Cross-country run	4:10
8	—	—			
Total	27.2	17	1:47:30		3:57

Note. From *Modern Middle and Long-Distance Running* (p. 135) by J.H. Peters, J. Johnston, and J. Edmunson, 1957, London: Nicholas Kaye. Copyright 1957 by Nicholas Kaye.

By this stage, his average speed was below 3:45/km (6:00/mile) but was not near the 3:08/km (5:00/mile) pace for which he strove.

In April and May that year, Peters ran two 32-km (20-mile) races, and in June he ran his first full marathon in a course- and British-record time of 2:29:28, just 4 minutes off the then–world record. His training leading into that race was as shown in Table 8.7 (J. Peters et al., 1957).

We can make four observations about Peters's training at this stage of his career. First, although he was running longer distances in training, his average speed had improved from 3:57/km (see Table 8.5) to 3:37/km (see Table 8.7). Second, his weekly training distance was only about 105 km (65 miles) a week, and this training distance had brought him within 4 minutes of the then–world standard-marathon record. Third, he did not reduce his training during the last week before the race. Fourth, all his training was done in single runs.

In 1952 Peters started training twice a day. At midday he would run 9.6 km (6 miles) on the track in about 30 minutes (3:08/km). In the evening he would run either 8 or 16 km at between 3:08/km and 3:17/km. He began running cross-country and shorter road races, setting personal bests at 6 miles and 20 miles and breaking Walter George's 69-year-old record for the 1-hour track run. Peters also finished 11th in the 1953 World Cross Country Championships. The record that we have of his training during this period was for June 1953, leading up to his third world marathon record (see Table 8.8; J. Peters et al., 1957).

Peters's training for the rest of his career remained essentially the same. His last great race was on June 26, 1954, when he ran 2:17:39.4 for the AAA Marathon. Shortly after that race, he ran his best ever 6-mile race on the track—28:57.8. In the 10 months leading up to that race, he had covered 7,158 km (4,474 miles). Ironically, Peters's hard training and his subsequent collapse

Table 8.6 Jim Peters's Training Program for April 1951

Date	Distance Km	Miles	Time (hr:min:s)	Comment	Speed (min:s/km)
2	14.4	9	50:30	Terribly stiff, but made it	3:31
3	9.6	6	35:00	Still stiff and tired	3:38
4	14.4	9	51:00	Still stiff	3:32
5	14.4	9	51:00	Bit better, very tired	3:32
6	—	—	—		
7	24	15	1:36:00	Nasty day	4:00
Total	76.8	48	4:43:30		3:41

Note. From *Modern Middle and Long-Distance Running* (p. 136) by J.H. Peters, J. Johnston, and J. Edmunson, 1957, London: Nicholas Kaye. Copyright 1957 by Nicholas Kaye.

in the Vancouver Marathon were contrasted to the performance of Roger Bannister, who trained lightly and who did not collapse after his "mile of the century" race against Landy at the same Games (see Figure 11.1). Thus, the illogical conclusion was drawn that hard training explained Peters's collapse in the Vancouver Marathon (Ward, 1964). Six weeks after the Vancouver Marathon, Peters retired, largely because he was scared that he might kill himself if he ran another marathon in the heat. He believed it likely that the one race he still longed to win, the 1956 Olympic Marathon in Melbourne, would be run in the heat, and he was not prepared to risk his life again (Benyo, 1983).

Few marathon runners before or since have equaled the ferocious and unremitting intensity with which Peters (and indeed Zatopek) trained. Peters expressed his belief in the importance of intensive training in the following manner:

> The body has got to be conditioned to stand up to the stresses and strains which it is going to meet in an actual race and therefore it is useless training at 6-min-per-mile pace if you hope to race at 5-1/2 min per mile. (J. Peters et al., 1957, p. 110)

And later he said, "I rarely ran more than sixteen miles a day in training. But I did good, fast quality miles. You see, speed and stamina are yoked together. And if you do a lot of speed work, the more you do, you build up the stamina to do a marathon" (Benyo, 1983, p. 64). Peters's training advice inscribed on the inside of a copy of his autobiography given to ultramarathoner Jackie Mekler sometime after the Vancouver Marathon was this: "Train little, hard and often."

Peters warned against overtraining and suggested there should be a gap of at least 3 weeks between 32-km races and 4 to 5 weeks before a race of any kind

Table 8.7 Jim Peters's Training Program for June 1951

Date	Distance Km	Miles	Time (hr:min:s)	Comment	Speed (min:s/km)
2	25.6	16	1:35:00		3:43
3	—	—	—		
4	20.6	13	1:15:00		3:38
5	—	—	—		
6	23.2	14.5	1:27:00		3:45
7	16	10	58:00	Fast. Legs stiff.	3:38
8	19.2	12	1:10:30	Fast. OK.	3:40
9	20.8+	13+	1:18:00	Tired.	3:45
10	—	—	—		
11	19.2+	12+	1:11:00	Fast run. OK.	3:42
12	16+	10+	56:00	Fast. Hot. OK.	3:30
13	16+	10+	56:30	Fast. Hot. Terrific wind.	3:32
14	16+	10+	1:00:00	Fast. Hot. OK.	3:45
15	—	—	—		
16	42.2	26.2	2:29:28	1st. Hot, tired but happy.	3:32
Total	234.7+	146.7+	14:06:28		3:37

Note. From *Modern Middle and Long-Distance Running* (p. 137) by J.H. Peters, J. Johnston, and J. Edmunson, 1957, London: Nicholas Kaye. Copyright 1957 by Nicholas Kaye.

should be attempted following a marathon. "Your body and *mind* must be given ample time to recover from the effort" (J. Peters et al., 1957, p. 111). Like Zatopek, Peters did not alternate hard and easy training days and did not taper for his races. One wonders whether these modifications might have made him even faster.

Gordon Pirie

The next great British runner after Peters was Gordon Pirie, who was born in Yorkshire in 1931. He was the son of Alick Pirie, a Scottish international runner who introduced his son to competitive running. After leaving school in 1948, Pirie continued to run regularly but without competitive ambition. His desire for greatness was aroused when he witnessed Zatopek winning the 10,000 m at the 1948 Olympic Games in Wembley. Pirie resolved to one day beat Zatopek.

Pirie soon became disenchanted with the training methods of the other top British runners of the day, Roger Bannister and Chris Chataway. Pirie thought

Table 8.8   Jim Peters's Training Program for June 1953

Date	Distance Km	Miles	Time (hr:min:s)	Comment	Speed (min:s/km)
7	25.6	16	1:31:15		3:34
8	12.8	8	42:47	Fast. OK.	3:20
9	9.6	6	31:40	OK.	3:20
	19.2	12	1:07:06	OK.	3:29
10	9.6	6	31:35	OK.	3:20
	16	10	56:03	OK. Easing down.	3:20
11	9.6	6	32:10	OK.	3:21
12	10.4	6.5	33:23	OK.	3:13
13	42.2	26.2	2:18:40	World record.	3:17
Total	154.7	96.7	8:44:39		3:23

Note. From *Modern Middle and Long-Distance Running* (p. 139) by J.H. Peters, J. Johnston, and J. Edmunson, 1957, London: Nicholas Kaye. Copyright 1957 by Nicholas Kaye.

these British runners too "amateur," too talented, and therefore too ready to undervalue the importance of heavy training. He wondered whether they found their training somewhat boring and decided that Zatopek's superiority over the British runners was due to his attitude and his training methods. Pirie found in Zatopek an openness, a willingness to share secrets, and an enthusiasm that he admired. Zatopek never became bored and approached life with an infectious sense of fun; he was as enthusiastic helping his competitors as he was in running them off their feet. Nor did Zatopek appear to feel the stress of competition; running and racing were simply joys. Zatopek embodied the ideal for which Pirie would strive.

In June of 1949, Pirie started his 2 years of national service in the Royal Air Force. During this period he adopted the training methods of Zatopek and progressed to become one of the leading British track runners. In July 1951, Pirie set the British record for 6 miles (29:32) and in the following year for 3 miles (13:44.8). In July 1952, he traveled to the Helsinki Olympic Games in the same plane as Jim Peters and finished seventh in the 10,000 m (in a personal best time of 30:04.2) and fourth in the 5,000-m (also in a personal best time—14:18).

Two months later he set his third British record at 2,000 m (5:21.2), and in 1953 he established new British records for 6 miles (once), 3 miles (thrice), 3 km (thrice), 5 km (once), 10 km (once), and 2 miles (twice). In addition, he set world records at 6 miles (28:19.4) and 4 miles (18:35.4) and was a member of the British relay team that established the world record for 4 × 1,500 m.

Additional highlights in his career that would last until 1961 were world records in the following: the 1-mile race on grass (4:05.2 in 1954); 1-1/2 miles (6:26 in 1955); 2 miles (8:39 in 1958); 3000 m (twice—best time 7:52.8 in 1956); and 5000 m (best time 13:51.6 in 1958). In the 1956 Olympic Games at Melbourne, he was involved in an enthralling battle with Vladimir Kuts in the 10,000-m final before slipping exhausted into eighth place. In the 5,000-m final, Pirie finished second to Kuts. Even in the twilight of his career, at the 1960 Olympic Games, Pirie ran a personal best in the 10,000 m, finishing 10th in 29:15.6.

Pirie's average heavy-training day is described in his book (Pirie, 1961; see Table 8.9). It seems that by 1956 he followed this routine 4 or 5 days a week. On the remaining 2 to 3 days of the week he would complete only one training session.

Table 8.9   Gordon Pirie's Heavy-Training Day

Morning session (10 a.m.)	Afternoon session (6 p.m.)
30-min warm-up	30-min warm-up
800 m in 1:56	10 x 400 m in 1:01 with 300 m recovery
10-min jog	15-min cool-down
3.2 km in 8:46.6	
4 x 800 m in 2:08 with 400 m recovery	
15-min cool-down	

Note. From *Running Wild* (pp. 24-26) by G. Pirie, 1961, London: W.H. Allen. Copyright 1961 by W.H. Allen.

One of the most interesting quotes to be found in Pirie's book (Pirie, 1961) is the following:

There are two types of athletes. They don't differ in size or muscular development. There is no apparent difference at all. But one type can run a terrific speed without training; he does 10.5s for 100 yds at school and he continues this terrific speed up to the 1/4 mile—he probably manages 24s for the 220 and 51s for the 440. These fellows can't run slowly when they try. . . .

. . . The other type—and I fall into this category . . . can't do the 100 in 12s, or the 220 in 30s or the 440 in 60s. We are able only through torturous efforts to improve our speed, but with the slightest lay-off this hard-won ability vanishes.

This first type of runner will always be the greatest. . . . Herb Elliott is the first man of the speedy type to train and race the longer distances. I believe that, if he is interested, he will be able to make a clean sweep of all the records from 1,500 m to the marathon.

The second type of runner is the fellow who flogs and flogs himself to great heights and is liable to fall quickly. But he can't possibly compete with the speed man. Trainers tell us that if you only do "so-and-so" you can run much faster. But I've tried every "so-and-so" methods, and I can assure anyone that it is not so. (pp. 72-73)

Herb Elliott

Many consider the Australian Herb Elliott (see Figure 8.6) the greatest distance runner ever. In part this is because of his unequaled record; during his career as a senior athlete he was never beaten in the mile or 1,500 m.

Elliott was born in Perth, Australia, on February 25, 1938. Like Alick Pirie, Elliott's father was a competitive athlete who encouraged his son to run at a young age. At primary school, Elliott excelled in the sprints. He ran his first mile at age 14, finishing in 5:35. Later he ran the mile in 5 minutes and concluded that any 14-year-old able to run a mile in 5 minutes could ultimately run the mile in under 4 minutes. Two years later he won the State 16, 800 m in 2:10:40. In 1954 he set the world junior mile record of 4:25:60 and the Australian national junior 800-m record of 1:55.7. In his final year at school, besides continuing his running achievements, he was head prefect, he rowed in the school's first eight, and he was on the school's first hockey team. He was also an accomplished swimmer.

In October 1956, like Pirie 8 years earlier, he attended the Olympic Games at Perth in the company of his father. Just as Pirie had been inspired by the performances of Zatopek, so Elliott was fascinated by the running of Vladimir Kuts in his races with Pirie. Elliott decided to commit himself seriously to running, so he left home to train at Portsea with Percy Cerutty, so becoming Cerutty's most famous protégé.

The following year Elliott set the world junior mile record twice, lowering it to 4:04.4, more than 2 seconds faster than Ron Clarke's previous best. Elliott also set the world junior 800-m record (1:50.8), the world senior 3,000-m record (8:45.6), and the world senior 3-mile record (14:02.4). In March he won the Australian Senior Mile Championships in 4:00.4, the 11th fastest time ever, and set the Australian record for 800 m (1:49.3).

On January 25, 1958, the 19-year-old Elliott became the youngest runner to break 4 minutes for the mile, finishing in 3:59.9. At the Empire Games in Cardiff, Wales, in July that year he won the 800 m and the mile, and on August 6th he set the world mile record in Dublin (3:54.5), an improvement of 2.7 on

Figure 8.6 Herb Elliott leads the field in the 1,500 m at the 1960 Rome Olympic Games, in which he set a new world record.
Note. From *The Golden Mile* (p. 146) by H.J. Elliott, 1961, London: Cassell and Co. Copyright 1961 by Keystone Press Agency.

the previous record. Three weeks later in Gothenberg, Sweden, he set the world record in the 1,500 m (3:36.0).

By 1959, Elliott's enthusiasm for running was on the wane as he studied for a scholarship to enter Cambridge University after the 1960 Olympic Games. He raced very little, and on Boxing Day, with no little lack of enthusiasm, he began training for the 1960 Rome Olympics. Despite less-than-optimum training and little racing, he won the 1,500 m at those Games in a new world record time of 3:35.6. In the 3 weeks following the Games he ran four sub-4-minute miles and then retired.

During his career, Elliott was unbeaten over 1,500 m and the mile, running 17 sub-4-minute miles in 2 years. He seldom ran more than 120 km per week in training, and his average training week was as shown in Table 8.10 (H.J. Elliott, 1961).

He also found it was unnecessary to train hard during the competitive season, providing he raced twice a week and ran an occasional 16 km at peak speed.

Table 8.10   Herb Elliott's Training Week in 1956

Monday:	6-10 x 400 m or 800 m followed by 3 to 5 km of free running
Tuesday:	8 km at peak speed
Wednesday:	Training with sprinters
Thursday:	30 minutes of sprint-jogging on a track; he sprinted for 30 s, then jogged 190 s before repeating the sprint
Friday:	Rest
Saturday:	4 to 10 km at peak speed on the track
Sunday:	16 km hard

Note. Data compiled from *The Golden Mile* (p. 148) by H.J. Elliott, 1961, London: Cassell and Co. Copyright 1961 by Cassell and Co. Ltd.

That Elliott was remarkably talented is shown by his performances in 1956, when he trained sporadically after a foot injury and spent most of his evenings in a coffee bar with another "half-hearted" athlete inventing excuses for why they should not train. Despite this lack of training, he wrote, "strangely my athletic form never deserted me" (H.J. Elliott, 1961, p. 29).

Although he "caroused about the country" for a month in July 1958 following the Empire Games, abusing his body by consuming too much rich food and champagne, he ran the 800 m, his weakest event, in 1:47.3, the fastest-ever half mile in Europe and only 5 seconds outside the world record. "To this day," he wrote, "that performance remains a mystery to me" (H.J. Elliott, 1961, p. 89).

Ron Clarke

Another Australian, Ron Clarke (see Figure 8.7), followed Herb Elliott as the preeminent distance runner of the early 1960s. The high-altitude conditions of the 1968 Olympic Games in Mexico City robbed him of the Olympic gold medal that would have crowned his extraordinary athletic career.

Clarke started racing in 1953 at age 16 and first came to public notice during 1955 and 1956, when he set Australian junior records at distances from 800 yards to 3,000 m. In 1956, he also set the Australian senior 2,000-m record and was rewarded by being invited to carry the torch that lit the flame opening the 1956 Melbourne Olympic Games. Shortly thereafter Clarke married, fathered three children in quick succession, and began to concentrate on his career. By the time of the 1960 Rome Olympics, Clarke was a 23-year-old former athlete. The following year he started running again, and at the 1962 Commonwealth Games in Perth, Australia, he ran second to New Zealand's Murray Halberg in the 3-mile race. In July that year he set Australian records for both the 10-mile race (50:02) and for the greatest distance run in 1 hour (19.36 km).

Figure 8.7 Ron Clarke leads Michael Jaxy in the 5,000 m final in the 1965 World Games in Helsinki.
Note. From "A Matter of Priority" in *The Unforgiving Minute* (p. 65) by R. Clarke, 1966, London: Pelham Books. Copyright 1966 by Ron Clarke.

The following year at Olympic Park in Melbourne, he set his first world records at 6 miles (27:17.8) and 10,000 m (28:15.6). The following year at the same venue he added the 3-mile world record (13:07.6), and at the Olympic Games held in Tokyo that year, he finished third in the 10,000 m after being passed by the first 2 runners in the last 60 m. He also finished ninth in both the 5,000 m and the marathon, the latter in an Australian record time.

In 1965, Clarke set 9 world records including the 5,000 m (twice; best time 13:25.8), 3 miles (twice; best time 12:52.4), 6 miles (26:47.0), 10,000 m (27:39.4, an improvement of 35 seconds on the old world record), 16 km (47:12), 20,000 m (59:22.8), and distance covered in 1 hour (20.24 km). In 1966, Clarke set the Australian 30-km record (1:34:35), set world records for 3 miles (12:40.4) and 5,000 m (13:16.6), and won silver medals in the 5,000 m and 10,000 m at the Commonwealth Games in Jamaica. In December he ran the second fastest 6 mile ever (26:52), and in June 1967 he set a world 2-mile record of 8:19.8.

By 1968 he was ready to change his image as a world-record holder who could not win major international competitions. He quit his job, mortgaged his house, and took his family with him to the French Olympic training camp at Fontromeu, which lies at an altitude of 2,200 m in the French Pyrenees, the same altitude as Mexico City. For 3 months the Clarke family lived rent-free in the flat that belonged to the mayor of Bolquere, a tiny village just below Fontromeu. The mayor bestowed this privilege because he liked the amateur Clarke.

Twice during this period Clarke returned to sea level to race at Crystal Palace in London. In the first trip he broke the world 2-mile record; in the second he finished 6 seconds outside his 10,000-m world record despite racing in gale-force conditions. During the latter race he lapped Dave Bedford (who finished second) an extraordinary 3 times. He believed then, as did most others, that he would have beaten his world record by 20 seconds had he raced in good weather conditions. Had he broken his record, the new record would have stood for close to 20 years.

The 10,000-m race at the Mexico City Olympics was run in the evening of the first day of the Games. With two laps to go, a group of six runners was in the lead. With 600 m to go, Clarke made his move and for 200 m led the race. With 400 m to go, the Ethiopian Malmo Waldi and the Kenyan Naftali Temu passed Clarke, who began to struggle. He remembers little of the last lap, which he completed in 85 seconds, collapsing at the finish line. The Australian team doctor, Dr. Corrigan, who attended the collapsed Clarke feared for his life. After 20 minutes Clarke had recovered sufficiently to stand, but he could not speak. It was an hour before he managed to speak, asking simply, "Where am I?"

That was to be Clarke's last great race. He retired in 1970 after a career in which he won 202 of the 313 races he had entered and set 17 world records. A measure of the esteem in which he was held was shown by Emil Zatopek when Clarke visited him in Prague in July 1966. As they parted at the airport, Zatopek gave Clarke a small gift with the words "not out of friendship but because you deserve it" (K. Moore, 1982). It was the gold medal Zatopek had won in the 10,000 m at the 1952 Helsinki Olympic Games.

Clarke's training methods have been described by Wilt (1972), who reports that Clarke trained almost daily year-round with little variation from one season to another. Any variation was unintentional. Each day's workout was remarkably similar, and he did not attempt to peak. Rather he remained racing fit year-round, gradually increasing the quality of his training over his athletic lifetime. He seldom trained on the track, did not keep a training diary, and never used a stopwatch during training. Most of his training was done on grass and roads, and much of it was done over extremely hilly courses.

Clarke trained 3 times a day but regarded the evening workout as the truly important part of each day's training. On weekday mornings between 6:30 a.m. and 7:15 a.m. he ran 5 km continuously at a fast pace and thereafter did some gym work. From 1:00 p.m. to 1:45 p.m. he ran 10 to 12 km continuously at a fast pace, and in the evening from 5:15 p.m. to 7:30 p.m. he ran 16 to 25 km, also at a fast pace. He usually did this workout while wearing a full track suit unless the weather was extremely hot. On Tuesdays and Thursdays he included gym training. On Saturdays he trained only once, usually running 16 to 25 km, and on Sundays he also trained only once, covering 28 to 34 km at a continuous fast pace over a remarkably hilly course.

Occasionally, but not more than once or twice a week, he would run ten 200-m or ten 400-m intervals with equivalent recovery jogs between repetitions. The remainder of his training was mainly long, fast, continuous running at under 3:08/km for distances up to 16 km and close to 3:08/km for distances up to 24 km. He ran hard and forced the pace almost without exception on most of his training runs.

Clarke seldom missed an opportunity to enter track, road, or cross-country races, and he usually raced more than once a week. He enjoyed running races of 800 to 1600 m as preparation for longer distance races. During competition on the track, his main racing tactic was to share the early pace with another runner, to increase his pace in the middle third of the race to break the rest of the field, to start surging with four laps to go, and to sprint the last two laps (Lenton, 1981).

Leonard "Buddy" Edelen

Edelen's career started in high school in Sioux Falls, South Dakota, where in 1955 he won the South Dakota state mile championship in 4:28. While attending the University of Minnesota, he became the 1958 Big Ten cross-country champion and set a conference record for 2 miles. During the 1960 indoor track season, Edelen won two mile races at two major meets and set an American record of 29:58.9 for the 10,000 m. The following year he moved to Europe, and between 1962 and 1966 he ran 13 marathons, winning seven and never finishing lower than ninth (Higdon, 1982). Edelen set eight American track records and won the 1962 British AAA 10-mile (16-km) title. On June 15, 1963, he ran his greatest race, winning the Polytechnic Marathon from Windsor Castle to Chiswick in a world's-best time of 2:14:28, becoming the first American ever to set the world marathon record (see Figure 8.8).

Edelen (1964) considered that natural speed was not a prerequisite for marathon success—his best 400- and 800-m times were 00:55 and 1:58, respectively. Like Peters, Edelen believed in a gradual introduction to racing the full marathon distance and suggested starting by racing 6 to 10 miles and progressing to a few 15- to 20-mile races before tackling the full marathon. His weekly training for the marathon included one long run of 32 to 37 km (20 to 23 miles) at a steady pace, a midweek run of 19 to 24 km (12 to 15 miles) at a faster pace, a high-volume workout of repeated 400- to 800-m intervals at medium pace, and some repetition sprint work. Like DeMar, Edelen did much of his training on the way to and from his work. His typical training week was as shown in Table 8.11 (Edelen, 1964).

Figure 8.8 Leonard "Buddy" Edelen sets a new world standard marathon record on June 15, 1963.
Note. Photo courtesy of Buddy Edelen.

Table 8.11 "Buddy" Edelen's Training Week

Day	Morning distance km	miles	Evening distance km	miles	Comment
Sunday	35-37	22-23	8-9	5-6	
Monday	—	—	7	4.5	
Tuesday	7	4.5	7	4.5	Followed by 20-25 x 400 m in 68-70 s with 60-s recovery.
Wednesday	7	4.5	24	15	
Thursday	7	4.5	7	4.5	Followed by 2-3 sets of (10-15 x 100 m) in 14-15 s with 110 m jog recovery.
Friday	7	4.5	8	5	
Saturday	8	5	Race		

Note. From "Marathon Running" by L.G. Edelen in *Run Run Run* (p. 154) edited by F. Wilt, 1964, Los Altos, CA: Taftnews Press. Copyright 1964 by Track and Field News. Adapted by permission.

Edelen trained about 160 km (100 miles) per week. Other advice that he offered was to train twice daily, to rest for 2 days before competition, and to not start too fast in the marathon: "Attempting a pace, which is too ambitious usually results in disaster the last few miles!" (Edelen, 1964, p. 155). He felt it was best to run a bit slower for the first half to three quarters of the race and then to speed up. He emphasized the importance of the mental tenacity required not only in racing the marathon but also in training for it: "The miler knows that in just over 4 minutes the pain of severe effort will subside . . . But the marathoner must be able to tolerate pain and fatigue for over two hours" (Edelen, 1964, p. 155).

Hezekia Kipchoage (Kip) Keino

The first glimpse of the distance-running potentials of runners from the African continent was provided at the 1960 Olympic Games by the Ethiopian Abebe Bikila, who, running barefoot, won the marathon in a new Games-record time of 2:15:16.2. In 1964 Bikila became the first runner to win the marathon in consecutive Olympics, winning in 2:12:11.2.

Yet it was the next Olympic Games held in Mexico City in 1968 at which the true magnitude of the potentials of the African runners first became apparent. In those Games, African runners won every race longer than 1,500 m, including the 3,000-m steeplechase. Nineteen years later, at the 1987 IAAF World Athletics Championships, African runners would repeat that performance, winning the 800 m but losing the 3,000 m steeplechase. With African Americans winning all the shorter sprints, the domination by runners of African descent was complete.

The athlete who best epitomized the African running revolution in the 1960s was unquestionably Hezekiah Kipchoage (Kip) Keino.

Born in Kipsamo, Kenya, on January 17, 1940, Keino began his competitive running career in 1960. His first major championship, the 1962 Commonwealth Games in Perth, Australia, was less than auspicious; Keino finished last in the 3-mile race and was beaten in the mile heats but set a national 1-mile record of 4:07. In the 1964 Olympics, he finished fifth in the 5,000 m.

In 1965, Keino beat Ron Clarke in two of three races over 5,000 m and set world records at 3,000 m (7:39.35) and 5,000 m (13:24.2), the latter eclipsing Ron Clarke's record. Keino also came close to the world mile record with a time of 3:54.2 and won the 1,500 m and the 5,000 m at the first African Games.

In 1966 he won gold medals in the 3-mile race (12:57.4) and 1-mile race (3:55.3) at the Commonwealth Games and ran what was then the second-fastest mile in history (3:53.4). At the 1968 Mexico City Olympic Games, he won the 1,500 m in 3:34.9, beating the favorite Jim Ryun in a remarkable performance; Keino repeated this performance at the 1970 Commonwealth Games, winning in 3:36.6. In 1972, he earned his second Olympic Gold medal by winning the steeplechase in 8:23.6, and he also finished second in the 1,500 m that year. He won bronze medals in the 1968 Olympic Games 5,000 m and the 1970 Commonwealth Games 5,000 m.

At the time of the 1968 Olympics, Keino was self-coached, and his training (Wilt, 1972) was 10-km cross-country runs in the early mornings on Mondays, Wednesdays, and Fridays. On Monday and Wednesday afternoons he ran four to eight 400-m intervals in 55 to 58 seconds each, with 400-m recoveries between intervals. On Fridays he ran four 800-m intervals in 1:53 to 1:56 with 5 minutes of recovery between sessions. He did no formal training on the 4 other days of the week, nor did he train in the rainy season. All his training was at medium altitude (2000 m).

Wilt (1972) remarked that Keino's training was "unusually light by modern standards" and suggested that his daily work as a physical education instructor must have successfully supplemented his formal training. Alternatively, Keino may have been, like Herb Elliott, extraordinarily gifted and may not have needed to train even as little as did Elliott. The abilities of the top African runners to achieve exceptional performances on quite modest training are shown also by the world-class South African runners, Matthews Temane and Xolile Yawa.

Derek Clayton

The Australian Derek Clayton was the first runner to break the 2:10 and the 2:09 time barriers for the standard marathon. His world record of 2:08:34, set in Antwerp on May 30, 1969, lasted 12 years until officially broken by Robert de Castella in the 1981 Fukuoka Marathon.

Clayton is another example of a frustrated miler who found his niche in the marathon. Possessed of only "mediocre" 400-m speed (52.8), Clayton realized that he would never emulate the achievements in the mile of that greatest of all Australian runners, Herb Elliott (Clayton, 1981). Clayton gradually lengthened the distances he raced on the track to 5,000 m and then in his first serious marathon in October 1965 became the Australian record holder with a time of 2:22:12. "Suddenly," he later wrote, "I was number one in something I never planned to excel in—the marathon. Suddenly I had proof that I wasn't wasting my time. After years of searching, I had found my distance. I was on my way to the top" (Clayton, 1980, pp. 42-43).

Clayton's training was very hard. He regularly ran between 192 and 256 km (120 to 160 miles) a week and on two occasions ran over 320 km (200 miles) in a week. Clayton's training week is detailed in Table 8.12 (Wilt, 1973).

His total mileage for this average week was approximately 240 km (150 miles). He also wrote that his interval training consisted of four 1-mile intervals, and he recognized overtiredness, lethargy, and quick temper as features of overtraining (Clayton, 1980).

Two features of Clayton's running career suggest he trained too hard. He suffered a string of injuries, many of which required surgery. These included

Table 8.12 Derek Clayton's Training Week

Day	Morning	Afternoon
Monday	8-11 km (easy)	27 km (fast)
Tuesday	8-11 km (easy)	19 km (medium)
Wednesday	8-11 km (easy)	22 km (fast, hills)
Thursday	8-11 km (easy)	22 km (fast, hills)
Friday	8-11 km (easy)	16 km (easy)
Saturday	7 km (easy)	40 km in ± 2:20
Sunday	27-32 km (hills)	16 km (medium)

Note. From *How They Train: Vol. Two: Long Distances* (2nd ed., p. 34) by F. Wilt, 1973, Los Altos, CA: Tafnews Press. Copyright 1973 by Track and Field News. Adapted by permission.

four operations on his Achilles tendons, two on his knees, and one for a heel spur (Clayton, 1980). Looking back, he wrote:

> Unfortunately, I didn't heed my injuries, I challenged them . . . Now, I would show an injury the respect it deserves. I would rest it, exercise it, and if need be, stop running until it healed. Such an attitude during my competitive years might have kept me off the operating table a few times. (Clayton, 1980, p. 120)

Also, most of his world records came in the wake of protracted layoffs from serious injuries (the Zatopek phenomenon; see chapter 6), indicating that had he rested more he would probably have been even better (Benyo, 1983). Thus, Frank Shorter has suggested that Clayton's marathon world record came after Clayton had been injured and resting for as long as 5 weeks (O'Brien, 1982).

Ron Hill

The British runner Ron Hill (see Figure 8.9) ran his best marathon races in 1969 and 1970, including the world's second-fastest-ever marathon (2:09:28) and was favored by many to win the 1972 Olympic Games Marathon. His PhD in chemistry from Manchester University makes Hill the most academically qualified of all elite marathon runners. Hill is further unique among these runners in that he wrote two autobiographical books (R. Hill, 1981, 1982) that detail his running career in what some critics have considered to be rather self-indulgent detail. His courage in detailing both his successes and his failures will ensure that his books fulfill one of the goals Hill had in writing them, namely to teach runners where he went wrong in the hope that they would not repeat his errors.

Figure 8.9 Ron Hill wins his greatest race, the 1970 Commonwealth Games Marathon in Edinburgh. His winning time of 2:09.28 was the then second fastest marathon performance of all time and may have been the fastest-ever on an accurately measured course. *Note.* From *The Long Hard Road. Part One. Nearly to the Top* (p. 118) by R. Hill, 1981, Cheshire, England: Ron Hill Sports. Copyright 1981 by Ron Hill. Reprinted with permission.

I was particularly interested to see whether Hill's books contained any clues to explain why he had not won the 1972 Olympic Marathon. It was an analysis that, surprisingly, Hill had not made himself.

Hill was born in 1938 and finished ninth in the first race that he ran, his school's cross-country championships in 1951; in 1954 he joined the local running club, and for the next 2 years his training was "infrequent, unplanned and unscientific" (R. Hill, 1981, p. 18). He was coached by a man who trained only in winter and who "speeded up whenever he came near passers-by and then slowed down when there was no one around" (p. 18). When he enrolled at Manchester University in 1957, Hill started to train and race cross-country and short road races regularly, and he ran his first marathon in 1961, finishing first with a time of 2:24:22. For the 7 weeks before that race, Hill had averaged about 120 km per week. He entered a further five marathons (best time 2:14:12 on June 30, 1964) before finishing 19th with a time of 2:25:34 in the October 1964

Olympic Games Marathon in Tokyo. This characteristic of running extremely well in training but failing in major Olympic competition was to become a depressing feature of Hill's running career.

Hill's book (1981) details that he ran that race on "dead legs," a usual sign of overtraining (see chapter 10), but the other features of the overtraining syndrome, in particular a series of poor running performances preceding the really bad race, are not mentioned in his book. In his last two races at distances up to 11 km, run in the last 2 weeks before the 1964 Olympic Marathon, Hill had set two personal records. Thus, the explanation for his poor performance in those Olympic Games is not clear. Possibly, his performance was affected by his traveling to and competing in a foreign country.

During the next 4 years leading up to the 1968 Olympic Games in Mexico City, Hill continued to specialize mainly in short-distance racing on the track, on the roads, and cross-country. During this period he ran a total of six marathons, five in a range of times between 2:20:55 and 2:27:21; his best marathon (the only one he ran in 1968) produced the second-best time of his career at that point—2:17:11. At this stage of his career, Hill's weekly training routine was as shown in Table 8.13.

Using this training schedule, Hill set a world record for 16 km on the track and ran an exceptional 10,000 m at medium altitude in the 1968 Olympic Games, finishing seventh with a time of 29:53. He was the first athlete who had not trained at altitude for any meaningful period to finish the race, and he was only one place behind Ron Clarke, who almost certainly would have won the race had it been run at sea level. On the strength of this performance, Hill decided to attempt the 10,000-m/marathon double in the 1969 European Games, and so he began to race marathons more frequently and at higher intensities.

In the next 2 years, Hill ran eight marathons including the 1st (2:09:28), 2nd (2:10:30), 3rd (2:11:13), 5th (2:12:39), 9th (2:13.42), 11th (2:14:35), 12th (2:15:27), and 15th (2:16:48) fastest times in his serious marathon racing career, which was still to last a further 7-1/2 years. Interestingly, Hill's three best marathon races were run in ascending sequence between December 7, 1969, (the Fukuoka Marathon) and the Commonwealth Games marathon in July 1970 (see Figure 8.10). This was to be the premature peak of Hill's career, and he would never again be the same force in world marathon running.

During this period, Hill also began to experiment with the carbohydrate-depletion/carbohydrate-loading diet (see chapter 3) and used it successfully in all his best marathons.

The first inkling of future disaster came at the Fukuoka Marathon in December 1970, when Hill finished a disappointing ninth in 2:15:27. He commented after the race that he never believed he would ever run so slowly again. However, he later raced a slower marathon in the race he most wanted to win—the 1972 Olympic Games Marathon.

The explanation for Hill's poor race in 1970 is not difficult to find; he commented that in training for that race he altered his training methods:

Table 8.13 Ron Hill's Training Week for October 1968

Day	Morning	Afternoon
Monday	11 km	16 km including fartlek
Tuesday	11 km	14. 5 km including 12 x 70 second bursts with 50 second intervals in sets of 2, 4, and 6
Wednesday	11km	19 km including two sets of number stride fartlek, usually up to 55 strides then down[a]
Thursday	11km	13 km
Friday	11km	11 km
Saturday	Race	
Sunday	33 km with one monthly run of 45 km	

Note. Hill alternated two different cycles of training on Monday, Tuesday, and Wednesday afternoons. On the 1st and 3rd week of any month he would perform the training described above; on the 2nd and 4th week of the month he would do the following:

   Monday—Two 2-min bursts with 90-s rest interval; up to twenty 30-s bursts with 30-s rest interval; two 2-min bursts.
   Tuesday—3 x 1.6-km fast with 0.8 km rest interval.
   Wednesday—Hard bursts on all the hills.

From *The Long Hard Road. Part One: Nearly to the Top* (pp. 386-387) by R. Hill, 1981, Cheshire, UK: Ron Hill Sports Ltd. Copyright 1981 by Ron Hill Sports Ltd. Adapted by permission.

[a]Hill does not define exactly what "number stride fartlek" entails.

I wondered what would happen if I went beyond my 120-130 miles per week. Would I reach another plane of fitness and capability? I had to find out. . . . But I was never really happy. A lot of the time I felt slightly fatigued and towards the end of this increased training stint I seemed to be doing nothing but changing in and out of running gear. (R. Hill, 1982, pp. 130-131)

The week before the race, Hill ran his highest-ever mileage, a massive 264 km (see Figure 8.11), which left him with a sore throat and no competitive desire during the race.

   For the next 3 months Hill was troubled by a succession of throat and chest infections, six in all. He continued to train despite very severe symptoms, shown in his diary as the following typical entry: "Chest so tender I could hardly

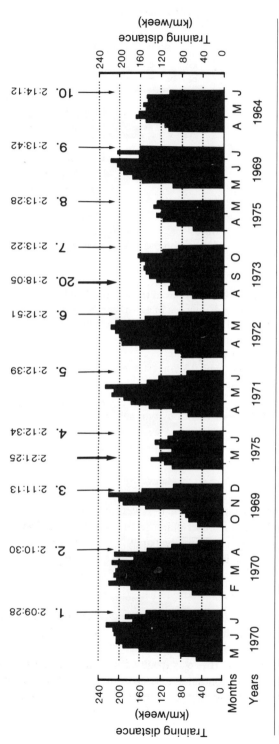

Figure 8.10 Ron Hill's weekly training distances for his 10 fastest marathons.

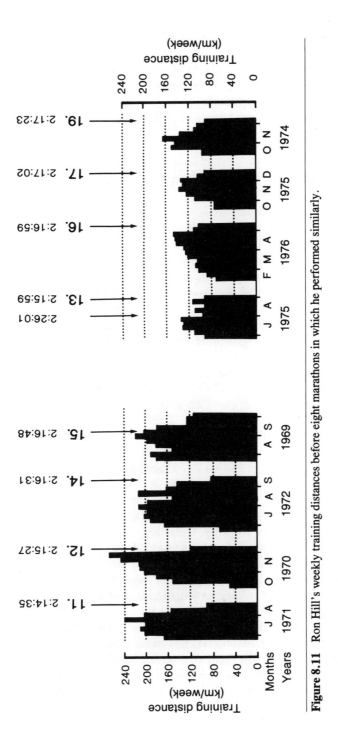

Figure 8.11 Ron Hill's weekly training distances before eight marathons in which he performed similarly.

bear to cough—chest aching too—felt weak physically—thought I was going to collapse a couple of times—couldn't eat anything when I got back'' (R. Hill, 1982, p. 137). Hill continued to train up to 190 km per week and raced frequently with atrocious results. Finally in April, he reduced his average weekly training distance to 105 km and was well enough to run a 2:12:39 marathon in July and a 2:14:35 marathon in August in the European Marathon Championships in Helsinki. These races would prove to be the 5th and 11th fastest of his career.

After the Helsinki marathon, Hill wrote the following:

> The successful pattern of training I have evolved over the years I feel is unique amongst marathon runners. This involves a series of peaks, averaging about three per year, followed by "rests". My usual "rest" is about four weeks averaging 40 miles per week and my ideal build-up to a peak occupies a period of 10 weeks. (R. Hill, 1982, p. 160)

Hill was also critical of the need to prequalify for selection to the Olympic and other teams by running marathon races within approximately 3 months of the competition, and he wrote that ''once the trial race is over, a large measure of inspiration has gone, and the feeling is 'I've made it' when this is not the case at all. Usually there is not enough left for the really big race'' (R. Hill, 1982, pp. 160-161). He also wrote something that would ultimately apply to his own career:

> You may have noticed that most top marathon runners do not last long. Bikila was an exception and he raced infrequently. The others have been more or less specialist marathon men and I am convinced that you can become marathon "punch drunk". These people usually retire or deteriorate rapidly. (R. Hill, 1982, p. 161)

In March 1972, Hill began his 8-week buildup for the British Olympic Marathon trial, in which he finished second in 2:12:51, the sixth-best time of his career. After a month of reduced training, he commenced his buildup for the Olympics with two important changes in his usual routine. First, he planned to continue his peaking for 10, not 8, weeks because he ''hoped that this extra work would lead to an extra special performance'' (R. Hill, 1982, p. 198). This despite the fact that on the last occasion when he had done ''extra work''—before the Fukuoka Marathon—the results had been disastrous.

Second, he planned to train at altitude for 3 of the last 4 weeks before the marathon, despite the fact that he had previously only ever trained at altitude for a few days in his life. By contrast, the athlete who would ultimately win the 1972 Olympic Marathon, Frank Shorter, had found through personal experience that after training at altitude, he required at least 2 weeks at sea level before his speed returned. At altitude Hill was faced with the unexpected problem of cold; he did not reduce the amount he trained, with the result that most of the time he felt "knackered," and his speed sessions were poor, which he said was "disappointing" but not surprising considering the state of my legs" (R. Hill, 1982, p. 204). Going to the start of the marathon, he noted that he did not "feel as bouncy or springy as I have felt before some marathons" (p. 214). During the first 800 m of the race he noted that the pace seemed much faster than he was actually running, this almost certainly because at altitude he had not been able to train at his peak speed and had not left himself sufficient time to reacclimatize once he returned to sea level.

During the race Hill was never a contender, feeling "rough" after only 5 km at which point he fell off the pace, ultimately finishing a tired sixth in 2:16:31. For the man who had predicted on national television that the Olympic Marathon gold medal was his, this must have been a humiliating experience.

The remainder of Hill's running career is notable for two reasons. First, he continued to train twice a day and once on Sundays as he had since 1964—the world's longest running streak. This is a compulsion that tells much about Hill's personality and may explain some of the errors he made in his career. Second, after 1972 he ran some very good marathons on considerably less training than he had done prior to the 1972 Olympic Marathon. For example, he ran the fourth (2:12:34) and eighth (2:13:28) fastest marathons of his career in April and June 1975 during a period when his average weekly training distance was "only" 112 km (see Figure 8.10). After a similar experience in 1973 he wrote this:

Well, well, well. Winning the Enschede at the end of a rest period, on an average of only 56 miles a week. And in 2:18:06, on a hot day, and with very little effort. It made me think. Yes! It made me think that 120 to 130 miles per week perhaps weren't absolutely necessary for good marathon performances. (R. Hill, 1982, p. 253)

We can learn a number of important lessons from Hill's career. First, he shows that each marathon runner has only a certain number of outstanding races before becoming "punch drunk" and starting to race less effectively. Hill ran three world-class marathons in a 9-month period and never again reached the same heights despite intense motivation and heavy training. Recent international examples of the same phenomenon include Alberto Salazar, Dick Beardsley, Rob de Castella, Carlos Lopes, Geoff Smith, and Steve Jones.

Second, Hill's racing record again confirms that heavier training is as likely to produce worse racing performances as it is better performances. This is clearly shown in Figure 8.10, which depicts Hill's weekly training distances during his buildup periods for his 10 best marathon races. As mentioned earlier, Hill ran his fourth and eighth best marathons on his lightest training. Similarly, Figure 8.11, a and b, compares Hill's training for other races in which his performances were quite similar but his training was quite different. Figure 8.11a shows races for which he trained heavily; Figure 8.11b shows races for which he trained relatively lightly yet performed no worse than when he ran almost twice as far in training.

If we were to apply statistical techniques to analyze the relationship between Hill's training load and his marathon performances, we would be forced to conclude that no statistical relationship exists between the amount of training he did for his various races and his subsequent performances in those races. In other words, the amount of training Hill did was not the most important factor determining his marathon performances. That he was able to run a 2:12:34 marathon on a training load of about 120 km per week clearly reaffirms the critical importance of genetic ability, not training, in determining racing ability. Remember also that when Hill trained an average of 190 km per week for 10 weeks leading up to the 1972 Olympic Marathon, he could only manage a time of 2:16:31.

Third, Hill's marathon performances started to deteriorate when he started racing marathons regularly in place of competing in regular cross-country and short road races. Alberto Salazar suffered the same fate in the early '80s and blamed his failures specifically on an overemphasis of training distance at the expense of quality training.

Fourth, Hill suffered a prolonged 3-month period of ill health that started immediately after he had run six marathons (including his three best-ever marathons) in one 18-month period. Clearly he was marathon "punch drunk." One wonders whether irreparable damage was done to his body or his mind during this period, damage that might explain why he never again reached the same athletic heights.

Fifth, Hill continued to train enormous weekly mileages even when he was quite ill. As he wrote, "Illness—colds, chest infections, bugs, sore throats— didn't stop me, just occasionally lowering the weekly mileage when I was really bad" (R. Hill, 1982, p. 137). He apparently was unaware that illness is an important sign of overtraining (see chapter 10) and indicates the absolute and urgent need for more rest, not more training.

Sixth, Hill did not taper adequately for his major races, and this must surely have affected his performances adversely.

Seventh, Hill made the fundamental error of introducing change for change's sake at the most critical times in his career. This was most apparent before the 1972 Olympic Games Marathon when, despite never having trained at altitude for more than a few days, he committed himself to 3 weeks of altitude training just 4 weeks before the most important race of his life. There was no evidence then, as there is no evidence now, to suggest that a period of training at altitude inevitably improves sea-level racing performance (see chapter 9).

Immediately prior to the 1972 Olympic Marathon, he changed his proven formula for success by increasing his peak training period from 9 to 10 weeks (see Figure 8.11). This may seem a small change, but it might have been critical if, as I suspect, he really only needed to peak for 6 weeks and was, in reality, already going downhill physically when he ran his best races after the 9-week peaking period. Under those circumstances, the extra week of heavy training would make an enormous difference.

The evidence contained in his books that suggests that Hill probably needed to peak for only 6 weeks is his statement that he usually felt a training breakthrough after about 5 weeks of heavy training, after which his relatively poorer racing performances (due to his heavy training) suddenly improved dramatically so that despite the continued heavy training, he was running near-personal-best times. If only he had begun his taper then, rather than killing himself by continued excessive training, the outcome may have been different.

That Hill was unable to stick to the winning formula he discovered in 1969 and 1970—but chose rather to train harder, hoping that this would improve his performance—is such a common response among runners that it must be considered almost natural. His experience brings to mind the wisdom in coach Bill Bowerman's famous dictum: "If it works, don't fix it."

Eighth, Hill was unquestionably hindered in his running career by having to hold down a full-time job. The fact that he had to work probably contributed to his poor performance at the 1972 Olympic Games, when he was forced to compete against athletes like Frank Shorter who had no such commitments.

But in the final analysis, I have a feeling that Hill's fanaticism was the real cause of his downfall; he simply wanted too much to win. This certainly was the belief of the winner of the 1972 Olympic Games Marathon, Frank Shorter, who thought Hill to be "too precise, too compulsive and . . . seems possessed with the scientific method" (Shorter & Bloom, 1984, p. 77). Shorter preferred his own more intuitive approach (Shorter & Bloom, 1984).

Frank Shorter

American Frank Shorter (see Figure 8.12) has been labeled "the man who invented the marathon," a title he vigorously denies. His victory in the 1972 Munich Olympic Marathon and his second place in the 1976 Montreal Olympic Marathon, both of which were screened live on American television, are often cited as important factors behind the subsequent running explosion in the United States (Benyo, 1983).

I include Shorter in this chapter not because he used any spectacular training methods but rather to make three important points.

First, Shorter was not a champion athlete at school or even for most of his university career. This fact becomes important when we consider whether young athletes should be encouraged to strive for international success at young ages (see chapter 17).

Shorter studied law at Yale, a university with no athletic scholarship program and with only a volunteer track team. Conflicting interests in skiing, studying, and singing in the choir kept Shorter from any intensive training during his first 3

Figure 8.12 Frank Shorter during the 1972 Olympic Games Marathon. *Note.* From The Bettmann Archive.

years at Yale. Only in his senior year, when his coach Bob Giegengack suggested Shorter could become the world's best marathoner, did he start to train seriously, winning the American Collegiate 6-mile title and achieving second place in the 3-mile event (Shorter & Bloom, 1984).

After graduation, Shorter's performances on the track improved progressively and his interest in the marathon was kindled. Besides his Olympic victories, Shorter's outstanding marathon performances included his string of four consecutive victories between 1971 and 1974 in the Fukuoka Marathon, including the third-fastest-ever marathon in the 1972 race.

The second important feature of Shorter's running career was that he trained initially as a track and cross-country athlete. He specialized in the 10,000 m but was also very competitive at distances as short as 2 miles.

Shorter was by no means the first athlete with a track background to run the marathon, although some authors have suggested this. Of the runners already mentioned in this chapter, Kolehmainen, Nurmi, Zatopek, Peters, Edelen, Clayton, and Hill were all fast track or cross-country runners who moved up to the marathon.

The third point is that from the time Shorter ran his first serious marathon in June 1971, in which he finished second in 2:17:45, until his last competitive marathon race on October 24, 1976, he completed a total of 13 "serious" marathons, winning the first 11 and finishing second in his last 2 major marathons including the 1976 Olympic Games Marathon. He made his career-best time of 2:10:30 in only his sixth marathon; his second to last serious race, the 1976 Olympic Games Marathon run in wet conditions that did not suit him, produced the second-best time of his career (2:10:46). In all, Shorter ran 5 races faster than 2:12 and 10 faster than 2:16.

The explanation for Shorter's exceptional winning record, made over what for a marathon runner was a very long career, must be found in his belief in the importance of peaking and of running only a few serious races each year. He wrote that it was "almost impossible to be in peak form *twice* in the same season, especially in the distance events" (Shorter & Bloom, 1984, p. 66), and for this reason the only races for which he ever peaked were the Fukuoka and Olympic marathons. His inspiration for this approach seems to have come from other great "peakers," for he wrote this:

Historically, the peakers—the real peakers, who pick their spots—win at the Olympics. Look at Lasse Viren or Waldemar Cierpinski or Kip Keino or Miruts Yifter or even me. . . . It's almost impossible for a distance runner to do both—to race frequently in top form in major competitions year in and year out and also fare well in the Olympics. . . . Viren, at his best, was always in control. He had the peaking process down pat. (Shorter & Bloom, 1984, pp. 149-150)

Unfortunately little is recorded of how Shorter actually trained. Two quite different sample training weeks are found in an article by Wilt (1973) and in Shorter's autobiography (Shorter & Bloom, 1984). The latter is included in Table 8.14.

Table 8.14   Frank Shorter's Training Week

Day	Morning	Afternoon
Monday	11 km at 4:00-4:23/km	16 km at 4:00/km
Tuesday	As for Monday	4 x 1,200 m (3:06-3:12/km)
Wednesday	As for Monday	As for Monday
Thursday	As for Monday	12 x 400 m (60-61 s)
Friday	As for Monday	As for Monday
Saturday	As for Monday	Race or 16 km
Sunday	32 km (first 16 km at 4:00/km; last 16 km at close to 3:07/km)	

Note. From *Olympic Gold. A Runner's Life and Times* (pp. 146-149) by F. Shorter and M. Bloom, 1984, Boston: Houghton Mifflin. Copyright 1984 by Houghton Mifflin. Adapted by permission.

Shorter, in his autobiography, also said that after a period of training at altitude he required a period of 10 to 14 days at sea level before he was again at his best. It is likely that the muscles require this time to readapt to the faster running speed possible at sea level. As discussed, Ron Hill failed to allow for this recovery period at sea level immediately before the 1972 Olympics and paid the price for this error.

Shorter also wrote that he did not run well in the rain because "I dissipate heat very well and get cold easily. Rain stiffens me up, tightens my muscles, so I'm not as loose as I might be. My stride changes; therefore my form changes" (Shorter & Bloom, 1984, p. 104). All these symptoms suggest that Shorter's body, particularly his muscles, were exquisitely sensitive to the cold; even under what might normally be considered quite mild conditions, his muscle temperature was likely to fall, causing the muscle stiffness that he described. As discussed in chapter 4, evidence now shows that body temperatures can indeed fall during marathons run in cold conditions, and athletes like Shorter are particularly prone to this hypothermia because of their low body fat and muscle contents.

Shorter also noted that he could run a hard 10,000-m race a week before a marathon—as he did at the 1972 Olympics, in which he finished fifth in the 10,000-m final just 5 days before his marathon victory—but that he could not run a hard marathon even 10 weeks before another marathon. He also found that he could tell "in the first quarter-mile of a race whether or not I'll have a good day" (Shorter & Bloom, 1984, p. 78). This feeling he described as "either being there or it isn't. I've learned I can't talk myself into this feeling" (p. 78).

Shorter is also one of the few Olympic Marathon champions about whose physiology we have some information. As reported in chapter 2, his V̇O₂max value in 1976 was 71.3 ml/kg/min (Pollock, 1977), and his gastrocnemius muscle comprised 80% slow twitch fibers (Fink et al., 1977); his height was 1.78 m, his weight 61 kg, and his body-fat content 2.2% (Pollock et al., 1977). We also know that Shorter was an extremely efficient runner (Pollock, 1977) whose running economy was equivalent to that of Derek Clayton (see Figure 2.4). Calculations show that Shorter sustained an exercise intensity of at least 80% when he won his Olympic gold medal (Pollock, 1977), an intensity equivalent to that sustained by other world-class runners (see Figure 2.6).

Grete Waitz

Of all the athletes both male and female who have achieved excellence in the past decade, the Norwegian Grete Waitz (see Figure 8.13) has probably been the most charismatic. Certainly no other runner has done so much to promote women's running. Her influence on the progress of the women's world marathon record between 1978 and 1980 was similar to that of Jim Peters between 1952 and 1954.

Waitz started running at 12 years of age and won her first race, a 400-m cross-country event, when she was 14. By 16 she was the Norwegian Junior Champion at 400 m and 800 m. The following year (1971) at age 17, she set Norwegian records in the 800 m and 1,500 m and competed in her first European Championships. In 1972 she recorded her personal best 1,500-m time of 4:16 at the Munich Olympic Games. In 1974 she finished third in the same event at the European Championships in Rome and was named Norwegian Athlete of the Year for 1974.

The next year she married, was ranked Number 1 in the world in the 1,500 m and 3,000 m, and set a world record in the 3,000 m (8:46.6). In 1976, she reached the 1,500-m semifinals at the Montreal Olympics and set another world record in the 3,000 m (8:45.4). In 1977 and 1978 she was again ranked Number 1 in the world in the 3,000 m after winning that race at the 1977 World Cup and finishing third in the same race in the 1978 European Championships. However it was only when she turned to road running that Waitz became an international running celebrity.

In her first major road race, the 1978 New York City Marathon, she set a world best time of 2:32:30. In the 1979 race she became the first woman to run 42.2 km in less than 2:30, finishing in 2:27:33, and in 1980 she lowered the world record further to 2:25:42. To date she has won the New York City Marathon eight times. In addition, between 1978 and 1983 she won the IAAF World Cross-Country Championships five times; in 1983 she set another world marathon best of 2:25:29 in the London Marathon and won the inaugural IAAF World

Figure 8.13 Grete Waitz wins the 1986 London Marathon.
Note. From Sporting Pictures U.K. Ltd.

Championships Marathon in 2:28:09. The following year she was second in the inaugural Los Angeles Olympic Games Marathon in 2:26:18. Five times between 1978 and 1983 she was ranked first in the world in the woman's marathon by *Track and Field News*.

Her consistency in marathon running is matched by her success in cross-country and road racing, in which events she was unbeaten until 1982 and 1983, respectively. In Norway she was unbeaten in competition between 1972 and 1984.

In her book, Waitz provides a beginners' training program, which she proposes will allow former "armchair athletes" to run 5 km continuously within 10 weeks (Waitz & Averbuch, 1986).

During the first 4 weeks—the break-in period—novices are warned to pay close attention to their bodies and to learn to read signals of fatigue or stress (see chapter 10). Each session should be comfortable, and a warm-up and cool-down are advocated. There should be no hesitation to walk during training. Exercise sessions are scheduled 3 days a week and take approximately 45 to 60 minutes, including 5 to 10 minutes warming up and cooling down followed by stretching and strengthening exercises. There should be 1 day of rest between training sessions. The program is as shown in Table 8.15.

Waitz advises that in the beginning, the main objective of the running program is simply to go out and move. She suggests that beginners should not worry about how they look. Running should be done joyfully, and if runners feel self-conscious, that is the first incorrect attitude that needs to be corrected.

Waitz suggests that running should be a group experience, and the beginning runner should find a group of running partners. Consistency is vital, but interest should be maintained by varying the course, the terrain, and the location of one's runs.

She also writes that it is natural to feel discouraged, bored, or apathetic at times. These mood swings in running are natural, but negative feelings should be translated into positive ones. Thus, the experience should be seen not as a struggle to get into shape but as a new way of feeling and a new and better way of life. Finally, she suggests that the beginner should run at least 1 to 2 years before considering training for a marathon or other long race.

Table 8.15 Grete Waitz's Beginner's Training Program

Week 1:	Alternately jog and walk 100 m for a total of 1.6 km. Repeat three times during the week.
Week 2:	Alternately jog and walk 200 m for a total of 2 km. Repeat twice during the week for a total of three exercise sessions during the week.
Week 3:	Alternately jog and walk between 200 and 400 m for a total of 2-1/2 km. Repeat twice during the week.
Week 4:	Alternately jog and walk, but walk only half the distance of each jog. Vary the distances between 400 to 800 m for a total of 3 km.
Week 5:	Session 1—Alternate 800 m jogging with 400 m walking for a total of 3.2 km.
	Session 2—Alternate 1.2 km jogging with 800 m walking for a total of 3.2 km.
	Session 3—Jog 3.2 km without walking.
Week 6:	Session 1—800-m jog followed by 400-m walk, followed by 1,200-m jog, followed by 400-m walk, followed by 800-m jog; for a total of 3.6 km.
	Session 2—1.6-km jog followed by 400-m walk, followed by 1.6 km-jog, for a total of 3.6 km.
	Session 3—3.6-km jog with no walking.
Week 7:	3.8-km jog on 3 days of the week.
Week 8:	4.4-km jog on 3 days of the week.
Week 9:	4.8-km jog on 3 days of the week.
Week 10:	5-km jog on 3 days of the week.

Note. Reprinted by permission of Warner Books/New York. From *Grete Waitz—World Class* (pp. 57-59) by G. Waitz and G. Averbuch, 1986, New York: Warner Books. Copyright © 1986 by Grete Waitz and Gloria Averbuch.

In common with the elite male runners quoted in this chapter, Waitz stresses that training for competitive racing is very individual and that the elements of her personal training program should be seen as the building blocks from which anyone can fashion an adequate training program. She believes that the experiences of other runners constitute one of the greatest resources available for any runner and that all should learn and profit from each other.

She lists five training guidelines.

1. Have a definite goal.
2. Set realistic goals and be flexible.
3. Don't add to or change your running program too quickly; the body needs time to adapt.
4. When something works for you, don't change it.
5. Follow the hard-easy principle.

She states that hard-easy is a relative principle and its application to the individual runner depends on experience and ability. For some, one hard training session a week is sufficient; others can handle three or even four, whereas still others incorporate moderately difficult training sessions between their hard and easy days. Table 8.16 lists Grete Waitz's sample training week.

The crux of her training program is the inclusion of at least two or often three quality sessions (one of long intervals, one of short intervals, and one of fartlek)

Table 8.16 Grete Waitz's Training Week

Day	Morning 5 a.m. to 6 a.m.		Afternoon 4 p.m. to 5 p.m.	
	Distance	Time	Distance	Time
Monday	10-15 km	40-60 min	10-15 km	40-60 min
Tuesday	10-15 km	40-60 min	6-8 x 1,000-m intervals, 1- to 2-min rest breaks (pulse 180)	
Wednesday	10-15 km	40-60 min		Rest
Thursday	10-15 km	40-60 min	Fartlek, 13 km: several 500-m sprints	
Friday	10-15 km	40-60 min	10-15 km	40-60 min
Saturday	10-15 km	40-60 min	15-20 x 300-sprints (pulse 180)	
Sunday	20-33 km fast-paced distance run			Rest

Note. Reprinted by permission of Warner Books/New York. From *Grete Waitz—World Class* (p. 106) by G. Waitz and G. Averbuch, 1986, New York: Warner Books. Copyright © 1986 by Grete Waitz and Gloria Averbuch.

per week and one longer run. All speed sessions are done in the afternoon in racing shoes.

On the day of a quality workout session, she begins her preparation by mentally rehearsing the workout. She takes these hard workouts very seriously and avoids a busy schedule on the days she runs these sessions. She will usually nap beforehand in order to ensure that she feels rested and prepared to run hard.

A typical long-interval workout on the track is six 800-m intervals run at faster than 10-km race pace with 400-m recoveries between intervals. If she does not have access to a track or other measured distance, she substitutes this workout with six 2-1/2-minute intervals of hard running with 2-minute recoveries between intervals. During these sessions she concentrates on doing more repetitions at a fast pace rather than fewer repetitions at maximal effort. To progress she does not try to run each interval faster; rather she shortens the recovery period between each interval.

Waitz's short-interval session consists of twelve 200-m intervals run at close to 800-m race pace. In contrast to her approach with the longer intervals, as she progresses she does not shorten the recovery period but runs each interval faster. The purpose of these short intervals is to maintain her leg speed and efficiency. This is the only session during which she times herself on the track. She considers it to be mentally the most difficult workout for her and one that helps toughen her mind. The final type of speed work that Waitz employs is a time trial in which she races up to two thirds of the distance of an upcoming race at 5 to 10 seconds per kilometer slower than her race pace. She uses this session to assess her likely race pace. If she is able to run at or near her goal 10-km pace for 5 or 6 km in training and feels under control, then she knows she will be able to repeat that speed in a race. Because she races frequently, she uses these time trials only occasionally, particularly when there are gaps in either her racing schedule or in her confidence.

Waitz also considers attitude an important factor in running; she suggests that you should reduce the expectations you and those around you have of yourself. She believes in having a winning attitude but suggests that this should be kept to oneself and not broadcasted: "It's great to be confident, but let your achievements speak louder than your words. . . . I have never made a bold public statement. I think the need to proclaim invincibility is often a sign of insecurity. Some runners do it just to convince themselves" (pp. 158-159).

In contrast to other successful runners, Waitz has not practiced peaking except for the two major races of her career, the 1983 World Championships Marathon and the 1984 Los Angeles Olympic Games Marathon. She "focused" on both these races for a full year.

In general she follows the approach of Pat Clohessy and Rob de Castella, both of whom consider it too risky to sacrifice everything for a single distant goal. She also finds that the mental pressure of this approach takes the enjoyment out of her training.

Waitz believes that quality speed training is important for all runners, even for those who just want to complete the distance regardless of time.

She emphasizes that her training for the marathon is fundamentally the same as her training for 3,000-, 5,000-, and 10,000-m races except that her total mileage is higher. The major difference is the addition of a weekly long run of approximately 24 to 30 km leading up to the race. This approach is the same as that of the elite male marathon and ultramarathon runners.

Waitz believes that getting to the start line healthy and running conservatively are vitally important, and she suggests that one should always start slowly, run conservatively, and aim to run a negative split.

Waitz states that she has never started a marathon race with the intent of running a particular time and that during the race she does not pay close attention to her time because this is too stressful. The few occasions on which she ran races specifically to break records taught her that the pressure of this approach was just too great and she was unable to relax. The result was that she did not pay sufficient attention to her body cues.

She therefore suggests that the marathon is too unpredictable a race to allow even the top runners to predict their probable finishing times with certainty. She suggests that "the marathon is the kind of race you must take one mile at a time, being flexible enough to adapt to the unknown and the unexpected" (p. 134).

For the first 2 weeks after a marathon, Waitz runs as she feels and does no speed training. She feels that regardless of the competitive ability of the athlete, there should be a minimum of 6 months between marathon races. In her entire career up to 1986, she has run only 10 marathons. She feels she is physically able to run three marathons a year, but mentally she finds it difficult to run more than one a year.

Dave Bedford

Dave Bedford, the British runner of the 1970s, set a world record of 27:30.8 for 10,000 m on the track in 1973 but achieved little other international success. I have included his training methods in Table 8.17 not because Bedford was a great marathon runner but to warn future runners of the dangers of trying to do too much.

Temple (1980) stated that 10 or 20 years will pass before we can say whether Bedford trained too much. I have no doubt that Bedford, like Clayton, tried too hard and trained too much. The proof lies in the fact that Bedford ran his best when his training had been curtailed by injury; another example of the Zatopek phenomenon. Bedford's relatively poor competitive record in major international races might indicate that he lacked the winner's mind and so tried to run his doubts away by training hard, but this I find difficult to believe. More likely, he was always overtrained and was therefore able to run to his potential only occasionally.

Table 8.17 Dave Bedford's Training Week

Day	Morning	Noon	Afternoon
Monday	16 km	10 km	19 km
Tuesday	16 km	10 km	8 km plus 8 x 800 m in 2:12/interval
Wednesday	16 km	10 km	16 km
Thursday	16 km	10 km	15 km plus 30 x 200 m
Friday	8 km	10 km	24 km
Saturday	8 km	24 km	16 km (fartlek)
Sunday	8 km	32 km	8 km
Total	300 km		

Note. Data compiled from *Cross-Country and Road Running* (p. 95) by C. Temple, 1980, London: Stanley Paul. Copyright 1980 by Stanley Paul.

Bedford once stated that only five times in his career did he ever run more than 320 km in a week and that his average weekly training distance was between 260 and 280 km (Aitken, 1984). I conclude, then, that 260 km/week of training is too much.

Robert (Deek) de Castella

Robert (Deek) de Castella began running at the age of 12; at age 14 he was coached seriously, for the first time, by the Australian national distance coach Pat Clohessy (de Castella & Jenkinson, 1984; Lenton, 1982, 1983b).

Clohessy started the young Deek on a training program of 60 to 80 km/week, including a long run of up to 21 km, shorter recovery runs, and hill and track work typically consisting of six to eight repetitions of 200 to 400 m. By the age of 18, he had set Australian under-19 records from 3,000 to 10,000 m, and his junior time of 8:44 for 2 miles eclipsed the previous Australian record held by Herb Elliott.

De Castella's performance improved little from 1976 to 1979, but his eighth-place finish in the 1979 Cinque Mulini International Cross Country made him realize that he had the potential to rise to the top. Determined to succeed, he started the training program that he still follows today (see Table 8.18; de Castella & Jenkinson, 1984; Lenton, 1982).

On this training scheme, de Castella ran the world's fastest marathon (2:08:18 at Fukuoka in 1981; the fastest time ever on an out-and-out back course) and convincingly won the 1982 Brisbane Commonwealth and 1983 Helsinki World

Table 8.18   Rob de Castella's Training Week

Day	Morning	Afternoon
Monday	10 km (38:00)	16 km (60:00)
Tuesday	10 km (38:00)	10 km (38:00) 12 x 200 m
Wednesday	10 km (38:00)	29 km (hilly; 1:50:00)
Thursday	10 km (38:00)	10 km (38:00) 8 x 400 in 63-64 s with a 45-s recovery
Friday	10 km (38:00)	18 km (64:45)
Saturday	19-21 km (3:36/km); 6 x 100 m	Race or 10 km (38:00)
Sunday	33-36 km (2:15:00-2:40:00)	8 km (31:00)
Total	208 km	

Note. From *Deek—The Making of Australia's World Marathon Champion* (pp. 33-34) by R. de Castella with M. Jenkinson, 1984, Australia: William Collins (PTY) Ltd. Copyright 1984 by R. de Castella and M. Jenkinson. Adapted by permission.

Games marathons. His 1981 Fukuoka Marathon time was an improvement of 2:26 on his previous best, and his time of 2:09:18 in the Brisbane Commonwealth Games Marathon on a hilly course is considered by some, including Ron Clarke, to be the best marathon time ever run before 1982.

The years 1984 and 1985 proved to be relative low points in de Castella's career; he failed badly in the 1984 Olympic Games Marathon, finishing fifth, and was well beaten by Steve Jones in both the 1984 and 1985 Chicago marathons. De Castella ascribes his failures in part to being overmotivated and to training a little too hard, particularly when he was tired (Mehaffey, 1986). However, his relocation to the medium altitude of Boulder, Colorado and his move to a more relaxed approach, including less training, particularly when tired, apparently rejuvenated de Castella, and his 2:07:55 in the 1986 Boston Marathon made him the then–world's third fastest marathoner behind Lopes and Jones.

De Castella does not believe in Lydiard-type peaking but rather mixes all his training, including hill running, intervals, and long runs, into each week. He stresses the importance of the long runs, which he runs at between 3:54 to 4:03/km (6:15 to 6:30/mile): He believes that if athletes are forced to reduce their training leads, they should avoid reducing their long runs because these are a vital source of "strength."

He considers that 210 to 230 km/week is adequate training and that further improvements in the world marathon record will come with improvements in diet and shoes and in pacing during the race. He is concerned not with expectations of the general public but only with his own expectations and those of the people who are close to him.

Steve Jones

Steve Jones was born in Tredegar, South Wales, on August 4, 1955, and it was only in his late teens that, almost by chance, he began running. As a cadet in the Air Training Corps stationed in his town, Jones was enticed to run an intersquadron cross-country race. His fifth-place finish qualified him for the British National Championships, in which he finished 29th. He realized then that he had found something he could do "reasonably well."

In 1974, Jones joined the Royal Air Force and for the first time in his life began training regularly, this under the influence of his first and only coach, Bob Wallis. Jones's break into international running came in 1977 when he won the Welsh National Cross-Country Championships, earning a place in the World Cross-Country Championships, in which he finished 103rd. Up to 1986, he won the Welsh Cross-Country Championships every subsequent year except 1982. By July 1984, his only major international successes were third place in the 1984 World Cross-Country Championships and eighth place in the Olympic 10,000-m final.

It therefore came as something of a surprise when on October 21, 1984, in his first complete marathon, Jones lowered the world record to 2:08:05, beating Olympic Marathon champion Carlos Lopes by 61 seconds. In the 8 weeks leading up to that race Jones ran the following weekly distances: 160, 134, 114, 114, 160, 152, 154, and 92 km, respectively. His typical training week during that period is shown in Table 8.19.

Table 8.19 Steve Jones's Training Week

Day	Morning	Afternoon
Sunday	24-32 km at 3:45/km	19 km at 3:07/km
Monday	12-16 km at 3:07/km	10-16 km
Tuesday	11 km including 4 x 5 min hard	Cross-country or track race
Wednesday	11 km	10-16 km
Thursday	Hills (10 repetitions)	8-20 km
Friday	10-12 km	Race or track session (16 x 1 min
Saturday		or 10 x 2 min or 16-24 x 45 s)
Total	135-180 km	

Although Jones later lost his world marathon record to Carlos Lopes, he set a world-record time of 1:01:14 in the half marathon (21.1 km) at Birmingham,

England, in August 1985. His 2:07:13 performance 2 months later in the 1985 Chicago Marathon made him the then–second fastest marathoner of all time.

The principal aim of Jones's training is to improve his performances on the track, in particular at 10,000 m. This he believes, and has indeed shown, is the key to fast marathon performances. Thus, his overall weekly training distance is quite low but includes four sessions of speed training (either in the form of track or cross-country races), intervals on the track or road, and hill repetitions.

Carlos Lopes

Carlos Lopes began running in his native Lisbon, Portugal, in his late teens and first tasted international success when he won the 1975 World Cross-Country Championships. At the 1976 Montreal Olympics, he finished second to Lasse Viren in the 10,000 m. Thereafter his international career wavered, and his performances gave no indication of what was to follow. But in the short period from March 1983 to April 1985, the then–38-year-old moved from the status of superstar to running legend and became the supreme inspiration for all those who thought they might be through with racing after the age of 35.

Lopes's comeback began in March 1983, when he completed his first standard marathon at Rotterdam in 2:08:39 and was outsprinted in the last few hundred meters by Robert de Castella. In the same year Lopes won the World Cross-Country Championships for the second time, and in the 1984 Rotterdam Marathon he ran with the leaders before dropping out after 29 km. Later he told Frank Shorter that he had run the race for one reason only—to see how fit he was. When Lopes found that running with the leaders required only "modest effort," he knew he was in excellent shape. He dropped out so that he would not show his opponents how fit he was and so he would not risk wasting his fitness on an all-out marathon only a few months before the Olympic Games.

Three months later, on July 2, he ran the world's second fastest 10,000 m ever (27:17:48), and 5 weeks later, in only his second-ever completed marathon, he won the Olympic Marathon gold medal with a time of 2:09:21. Interestingly, Lopes was hit by a car 10 days before that race and was unable to train again before the race. He finished the race in exceptional condition; another example of the Zatopek phenomenon.

Ten weeks after that, with a period of relaxed training behind him, he was still able to run 2:09:06, finishing second to Steve Jones's world-record performance of 2:08:05. In 1985, Lopes won the World Cross-Country Championships for the third time, and on April 29 at the Rotterdam Marathon, running alone for most of the race, he finished in 2:07:11, thereby beating Steve Jones's record by 54 seconds. Lopes commented that with more competition he could have run 2 minutes faster, a view that few would challenge lightly.

Published details of Lopes's training methods are scanty. In an interview with Frank Shorter, Lopes stated that he trains hard all the time and even when training at medium altitude seldom runs slower than 3:30/km. He did not change his training substantially before the Olympic Games Marathon except that he increased his long runs from 90 to 120 minutes, covering about 35 km.

Shorter considers that there are three secrets to Lopes's success. First is his innate ability to read his body signals in both training and racing so that he is always in control (as shown at the 1984 Rotterdam Marathon). Second is his ability to peak, as proven by his victories in the World Cross-Country Championships, and third is his ability to focus on his primary goals. He defeated more favored runners in the 1984 Olympic Marathon because he focused specifically on that event and was not sidetracked, as were many others, by the financial lure of other less important races in the 12 months before the Olympic Games.

In addition, Lopes confirms that the fastest runners at the shorter distances are the best marathon runners.

Matthews Selepe Temane

One of the few runners to surpass Steven Jones's half-marathon world record is the South African runner Matthews Selepe Temane (see Figure 8.14), who set a new world 21.1-km best of 1:00:11 in East London on July 25, 1987.

Temane was born of Tswana parents in Hammanskraal, South Africa, on December 14, 1960. His first ambition, expressed from an early age, was to become a famous soccer player. Although he won the majority of the middle-distance races that he entered at school, his sporting ambitions focused exclusively on soccer. The only specific running that he did was jogging to school and back, a total of 15 km a day.

Eventually his mother, sensing that her son's real athletic talent lay in running, encouraged him to pursue running as a career. Accordingly he joined the Vaal Reefs Gold Mining Company in Johannesburg in 1981 as a sports officer and came under the care of Richard Turnbull, the coach who was to guide Temane in his formative years as a runner.

His first major race was the 1981 national under-21 track championships, in which he placed third in the 5,000 m despite stopping to attend to his feet during the race. Since then he has won national track, cross-country, and road titles at distances from 1.5 to 21.1 km; in 1987 he won every major national road and cross-country title. His best performances include the following: 1.6 km in 3:55.4, the world's fastest time for the mile at medium altitude; a national record at 5,000 m on the track (13:25.2); a national record at 10 km on the road (28:29 on a certified course, 28:03 on an uncertified course); and the world's fastest 21.1 km (1:00:11).

Turnbull believes that Temane's greatest running assets are his natural speed; his disciplined training approach stressing rest and the avoidance of overtraining; and his meticulous peaking technique, with which he can reach a peak performance with only 4 weeks of intensive training. He drinks no alcohol, tea, or coffee and eats few sweets or chocolates.

Figure 8.14 Matthews Temane, holder of the world's fastest time for the half-marathon.
Note. Photo courtesy of The Argus Mease.

The principles of Temane's training program have been described in detail (Turnbull, 1985). The program aims to produce a versatile athlete able to compete effectively from 1,500 m to 5,000 m during the track season and from 10 km to 21.1 km during the winter cross-country and road season.

Turnbull divides the training program into a preparatory period, which may last up to 6 weeks; a basic period, which may last up to 10 weeks; and a specific period, which may last for 2 to 5 weeks and which is always followed by a period of 1 to 4 weeks of active rest (see Figure 8.15). During the preparatory period, Temane does no speed training but combines slow- and medium-paced runs with hill running, stretching exercises, and weight training. Intervals, fast continuous runs, and fartlek are added during the basic period, which serves as an introduction to the more intensive specific period, during which the intensities of the interval and fartlek sessions are increased and the recovery periods between intervals are lengthened. Tables 8.20, 8.21, and 8.22 provide details of Temane's training in the basic and specific training periods (Turnbull, 1985).

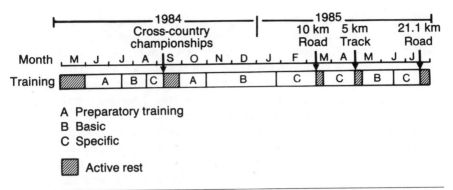

Figure 8.15 The 15-month training periodization program devised by Richard Turnbull for Matthews Temane.

Note. From "Turnbull and Temane—The Team Triumphant" by R. Turnbull, 1985, *South African Runner* (November, p. 26). Copyright 1985 by South African Runner. Adapted by permission.

Table 8.20   Matthews Temane's Late Basic/Early Specific Training Program for Road and Cross-Country Running

Day	Time of day	Distance (pace)
Monday	a.m.	16 km (medium)
	p.m.	Weight training
Tuesday	a.m.	15 km (fast)
	p.m.	10 km (easy)
Wednesday	a.m.	16 km (easy)
	p.m.	8 x 400-m hill runs (90% effort)
Thursday	a.m.	10 km (easy)
	p.m.	10 km (medium)
Friday	a.m.	10 km (easy)
	p.m.	Fartlek
Saturday		20-25 km (easy)
Sunday		Rest

Easy pace = 3:50/km
Medium pace = 3:20/km
Fast pace = 3:00-3:10/km

Note. From "Turnbull and Temane—The Team Triumphant" by R. Turnbull, 1985, *South African Runner* (November, p. 27). Copyright 1985 by South African Runner. Adapted by permission.

When tested in a laboratory (Noakes et al., 1990b), Temane's $\dot{V}O_2$max was 78 ml/kg/min; his running economy was the same as that reported for Frank Shorter and Derek Clayton (51.1 ml/kg/min at 17 km/hr); and his lactate turn-point occurred at 21 km/hr. His body-fat content was 7.4% and his mass 53 kg. Most importantly, he was able to run 1 minute longer during the maximal tread-mill test than any previous athlete tested in the same laboratory, including the runner who was ranked fourth fastest miler in the world in 1987.

Temane's success at distances up to 21.1 km seems to stem from the fact that like the other world-class black South African distance runners, he is a very fast miler who chooses also to run on the roads. He exemplifies what former world mile record holder John Walker (1988) said: "If the best milers came off the track, they'd clean up on the roads" (p. 29).

Table 8.21   Matthews Temane's Late Basic/Early Specific Training Program for Track Running

Day	Time of day	Distance (pace)
Monday	a.m.	16 km (medium)
	p.m.	Weight training
Tuesday	a.m.	10 km (easy)
	p.m.	1 set (2 x 600 m) each in 1:27 with 30 s rest between intervals
		1 set (2 x 400 m) each in 57 s with 30 s rest between intervals
		1 set (4 x 300 m) each in 38 s with 1 min rest between intervals
		6 min rest between the sets
Wednesday	a.m.	10 km (easy)
	p.m.	8 x 300-m hill runs (fast)
Thursday	a.m.	16 km (easy)
	p.m.	4 sets (2 x 400 m) each in 56 s with 30 s rest between intervals and 4 min rest between sets
Friday		10 km (easy)
Saturday		18-20 km (medium)
Sunday		Rest

Note. From "Turnbull and Temane—The Team Triumphant" by R. Turnbull, 1985, *South African Runner* (November, p. 27). Copyright 1985 by South African Runner. Adapted by permission.

Table 8.22 Matthews Temane's Training Program 2 Weeks Before His World 21.1 km Record

Day	Morning	Afternoon
Monday	40 to 50 min jog	16 km (48-50 min)
Tuesday	40 to 50 min jog	Track:
		2 x 800 m (2:07, 2:10)
		2 x 600 m (94 s, 95 s)
		2 x 400 m (57 s, 58 s)
Wednesday	40 to 50 min jog	Cross-country 12 km
Thursday	40 to 50 min jog	8 x 400 m hills (60 s)
Friday	40 to 50 min jog	8 km time trial (23 min)
Saturday	40 to 50 min jog	Fartlek; 3 sets
		3 min fast; 5 min jog
		2 min fast; 5 min jog
		1 min fast; 5 min jog
Sunday	Rest	

Note. From "Fast and Furious for Matthews" by South African Runner, 1987, *South African Runner* (September, p. 33). Copyright 1987 by South African Runner. Adapted by permission.

Xolile Yawa

Another South African runner of whose training methods something is known and whose performances are almost on a par with Matthews Temane is Xolile Yawa. At age 23, Yawa ran a world-class medium-altitude half marathon in 1:02:37 in 1986; in 1987 he finished third behind world half-marathon record beaters Matthews Temane and Zithulele Sinqe with a time of 1:00:56. His training methods, listed in Table 8.23, show a low overall mileage but high intensity.

SHORT ULTRADISTANCE RACES: 50 TO 100 KM

Besides Arthur Newton (see chapter 5), the achievements of four modern runners set them apart in the short ultradistance races of 50 to 100 km: These runners are Wally Hayward and Jackie Mekler of South Africa and Don Ritchie and Bruce Fordyce of Great Britain. Three of these runners achieved greatness in the 90-km Comrades Marathon, which Arthur Newton popularized and which, with more than 10,000 entrants annually, is the most competitive short ultradistance race in the world.

Table 8.23 Xolile Yawa's Training Week

Day	Time	Regimen
Monday	a.m.	30-min fartlek
	p.m.	Hard 10 km (29:15-29:40)
Tuesday	a.m.	10-min fartlek
	p.m.	Intervals: 2,000 m—5:21; 1 mile—4:12; one-lap jog; 1,200 m—2:56;
Wednesday	a.m.	800 m—1:55; 400 m—55-58 s
	p.m.	8 km—medium (25-26 min)
Thursday	a.m.	30-min fartlek
	p.m.	Fast 5 km (less than 15 min)
Friday		Intervals: 6 x 1,000 m in 2:33-2:35; 4-min rest between intervals
Saturday		Easy 1-hour run on golf course, track, or road
Sunday		12 km—medium to fast (37-39 min)
		20 min—200-m sprints

Note. From "Xolile Yawa" by South African Runner, 1987, *South African Runner* (June, p. 45). Copyright 1987 by South African Runner. Adapted by permission.

Wally Hayward

Wally Hayward was born on July 10, 1908, and ran his first competitive "race" as a teenage diamond staker during the 1920 South African diamond rush.

Hayward started running seriously in 1925 at age 17. During the first 5 years of his career, Hayward concentrated on races of up to 16 km until in 1930, aged 21, he entered the 88-km Comrades Marathon for the first time. His longest previous run had been 50 km, and his inexperience in ultramarathon tactics was soon apparent as he ran very fast from the start and was leading by 16 minutes at halfway. After 65 km, Hayward was clearly in trouble; he was forced to walk all the hills, and his lead over the last 30 km was cut by a minute per kilometer. Yet he persisted, winning by 37 seconds.

In training for the 1931 Comrades, Hayward fractured his ankle and as a result turned his attention again to shorter distance races. Between 1930 and 1937, he won national titles at 3 and 10 miles, including the national record. In 1936 he finished third in the national marathon championships, and in 1938 he competed at the Empire Games in Sydney, finishing third in the 6 miles.

After World War II, Hayward decided to switch to longer distance races, winning the 1946 national marathon title. Between 1950 and 1954 he won the 52-km Pieter Korkie Marathon five times, and in 1950, after a gap of 20 years, he again won the up-Comrades, this time by 13 minutes, an improvement of more than 40 minutes on his 1930 time.

In 1951 Hayward won the down-Comrades in 6:14:08, a new official record by 8 minutes and an improvement of 22 seconds on Arthur Newton's unofficial record set in 1925. In 1951 Hayward was awarded the Helms trophy for the outstanding sportsman on the African continent. The following year he finished 10th in the Olympic Marathon, 7 minutes behind Zatopek, and in 1953 he became the first man to break 6 hours for the Comrades, winning in 5:52:30. His time for the second half of the race, 2:59:28, was not surpassed until 1969. It was to be the start of his greatest running year.

In August 1953 Hayward, accompanied by the 20-year-old Jackie Mekler, who had finished fifth in that year's Comrades in 6:52:59, traveled to England to renew the challenge on the London-to-Brighton and Bath 100-mile races. During this time they stayed with Arthur Newton at his home in Middlesex.

On September 26 Hayward duly shattered the existing London-to-Brighton record by 22:42, finishing in 5:29:40 and in the process establishing his first world record for 50 miles on the road (5:14:22). Jackie Mekler finished fourth in 5:48:03.

Less than a month later, on October 24, both were on the road again to tackle Hardy Ballington's 100-mile record on the Bath Road. Again Hayward won, running the distance in 12:20:28, more than an hour faster than the old record of South African Hardy Ballington—13:19:00. Mekler also beat Ballington's old record and finished in 13:08:36. On the strength of these performances, Newton suggested that Hayward, together with Mekler, should attempt the 24-hour track record. Interestingly, Mekler was only 1 month older than 21 years and thus became one of the world's youngest ultramarathoners.

On November 20 at Motspur Park, Hayward again set out after Newton's 24-hour record (see Figure 8.16). Running at a steady 12.8 km/hr (8 mi/hr), Hayward passed 100 km in a new world-record time of 7:41:36 and 100 miles in a new world (track) record time of 12:46:34.

Hayward was running comfortably until, against his better judgment, he let Newton persuade him to come off after 160 km for a shower and a rubdown, something Newton found to have an "almost magical" effect. Unfortunately, the shower proved disastrous. Hayward's muscles tightened up; he struggled to run and though he had run 150 km (94 miles) in the first 12 hours of the race, he could manage only a further 106 km (66 miles) in the last 12 hours, giving him a finishing distance of 256.4 km, an improvement of 11.3 km on Newton's old track record.

Hayward later described the unremitting boredom of that race:

You run purely mechanically; all you can see is the track. . . . You run like a pig . . . who puts his nose to the ground and just runs. Later you think of just one thing, that the 24-hours must finally end. And then when it was finally over, I said: "Thank the Lord that I've finished" and "never again." (Hauman, 1979, pp. 41-42)

Figure 8.16 Wally Hayward receives a drink from Arthur Newton during his 24-hour world-record run in November 1953.
Note. Photo courtesy of Die Burger (Photopress, Cape Town).

The magnitude of Hayward's achievement on that day is shown by the length of time it took for his records to be broken. The 100-km and 160-km records were broken only in 1969 and 1968, respectively, by South African Dave Box; by 1979 Hayward's 24-hour record had been broken by only one man, Briton Ron Bentley.

Hayward was clearly at the peak of his powers in 1953 and continued in the same vein the following year, winning the 1954 Comrades Marathon for a fifth time, in 6:12:55. Then, on August 12, 1954, he was declared a professional for having accepted money to cover part of the cost of going to England. Only in the mid-1970s was Hayward's amateur status renewed, and he celebrated this in 1978 by setting a world marathon age record of 3:06:24 for 70-year-olds. In 1988, at age 79, he ran his sixth Comrades Marathon, the first he ever lost, finishing in 9:44:15, equivalent to a time of 4:48 for a 30-year-old (see Table 9.4).

When measured in 1978, Hayward's $\dot{V}O_2$max was 56.8 ml/kg/min (Maud et al., 1981), and it was estimated that he had run at 86% $\dot{V}O_2$max when setting the world marathon age record for a 70-year-old. No heart or other abnormalities were noted during those examinations; in particular, his back, hip, and knee joints showed no evidence of osteoarthritis, and he was considered to be in excellent health.

Like all the runners of his era, Hayward knew little of science. His training methods were very simple. At the start of his career all his training had been short and fast, but after World War II he slowed down and ran farther distances. From 1946 to 1954 the basis of his training was 100 miles a week mostly at 5:00/km. On Sunday he ran 48 to 80 km with a recovery 8-km run on Monday. From Tuesday to Friday he ran 16 to 24 km a day, and on Saturday he rested or ran a cross-country race. He included some speed training (fartlek) and ran cross-country races in winter. His pre-Comrades long runs were of 48 to 112 km (30 to 70 miles), and he ran four to six runs longer than 70 km in the 5 months leading up to the Comrades. These long runs gave him the confidence he needed for the Comrades, and his last long run would be 3 to 4 weeks before that race.

Jackie Mekler

When Hayward traveled to England in 1953 he was accompanied by Jackie Mekler (see Figure 8.17), a 20-year-old protégé whose running success would ultimately rival his own.

Figure 8.17 Jackie Mekler winning the Comrades Marathon.
Note. Photo courtesy of *Natal Daily News*.

Jackie Mekler's competitive running career started on December 27, 1945, at the tender age of 13. Mekler won the Comrades Marathon five times, setting the up-Comrades record of 5:56:32 in 1960, beating Hayward's record by 16 minutes and becoming the first runner to beat 6 hours on the "up" run. At the time, this was considered the greatest-ever feat in the Comrades. He set the down-Comrades record of 5:51:20 in 1963 only 10 days after running a 2:36 marathon in Greece, from which he had returned only the night before the Comrades. He also finished second and third twice each in the Comrades, winning in all 10 Comrades gold medals (for finishing in the top six). Further, he won the 50 to 60 km Pieter Korkie Marathon six times, three of which he won in record time, and he won the 1960 London-to-Brighton race, also in the record time of 5:25:26. In 1954 he set world track records at 30, 40, and 50 miles and finished second in the 1954 Empire Games Marathon in Vancouver, the race in which Jim Peters so tragically collapsed (see chapter 18).

Mekler's early running started as an expression of his aloneness. He found in running an escape from the restrictions of the orphanage in which he grew up. He learned that he enjoyed his own company, and throughout his career he seldom trained with others.

Table 8.24 lists all the distances that Mekler ran in training. It shows that he started training more intensively in 1952. In that year he saw an advertisement for Newton's books in a running magazine; he wrote to the listed address and was surprised to find that the letter was answered by Newton himself. Mekler read and absorbed all Newton's ideas but did not follow them unreservedly, because he did not believe that any single approach could suit everyone. Nor did he feel that he could commit himself to one line of thinking. During his first trip to England in 1953 with Hayward, Mekler stayed with Newton, and their mutual respect soon developed into a lasting friendship.

The result was that Newton insisted that Mekler should return to England and stay with him for as long as he liked. In 1955 Mekler took this opportunity and stayed with Newton for 1 year. From this experience, he concluded that Newton taught an outlook on life rather than a training method. Central to that philosophy was the belief that the individual had to overcome problems alone; if unable to do this, the individual could not be a champion.

All of Mekler's training was done outside of working hours. Up until 1955 he ran mostly to and from work, sometimes covering as much as 50 km before work. Later he ran 8 to 15 km before or after work or both, always ending with a fast finish. Like Hayward, but unlike Newton, Mekler raced on the track at distances up to 6 miles and regularly competed in cross-country races. He did not specialize for the Comrades and ran all his training on the hardest courses he could find.

Table 8.24 shows that his heaviest training years (1953, 1958, 1959, and 1969) did not produce his best ultramarathon performances. It also seems that the distances he ran between June and December each year had little effect on his

Table 8.24 Jackie Mekler's Training and Comrades Marathon Record and Training Distances (km) (1952-1969)

Year	Age	Comrades direction	Comrades time	Position	Total Jan.-May	Monthly distances Jan.-May	Total June-Jan. previous year
1969	37	down	6:01:30	3	3,255	(499, 506, 633, 704, 913)	2,050
1968	36	up	6:01:11	1	3,513	(525, 472, 1,032, 784, 783)	1,610
1965	33	down	5:56:19	2	2,130	(177, 185, 448, 663, 657)	1,134
1964	32	up	6:09:54	1	2,368	(530, 454, 501, 390, 493)	2,536
1963	31	down	5:51:20	1	2,536	(488, 497, 470, 469, 612)	2,759
1962	30	up	6:04:04	2	2,174	(486, 204, 385, 554, 543)	1,670
1960	28	up	5:56:32	1	2,857	(673, 493, 564, 549, 578)	3,494
1959	27	down	6:35:52	3	3,494	(557, 644, 541, 892, 860)	2,692
1958	26	up	6:26:26	1	4,038	(834, 831, 857, 741, 775)	4,561
1953	21	down	6:52:59	5	3,688	(630, 736, 681, 853, 788)	3,779
1952	20	up	7:45:08	7	2,219	(227, 235, 592, 610, 555)	1,286

Note. Information courtesy of J. Mekler.

subsequent performances. Thus his victory in the 1968 Comrades Marathon came after he had trained only 200 km/month from June to December the previous year.

Table 8.25 lists the number of training runs longer than 32 km that he ran in the 5 months between January and May 31 each year leading up to the Comrades Marathon. These long runs (greater than 56 km) were run at 4:24/km. Before his 1960 race, arguably his best, Mekler ran two runs longer than 70 km (one in January and one in April), six longer than 56 km, nine longer than 42 km, and one longer than 32 km. Conversely, in 1963, 1968, and 1969, he ran more runs longer than 70 km, fewer at distances between 42 and 56 km, and many more at 32 km. Thus, as his total training distance came down in his later years, Mekler increased the number of both very long (greater than 70 km) and shorter (32 km) training runs.

Mekler, who ran to win or to beat a record in every race he entered, said that he instinctively knew what pace was right. When asked to list those factors that he would change if he had his running career over again, he replied that he would choose his parents carefully, live near his work, pay more attention to the mental aspects of training and racing, and choose a career in the army or police or in the mines. ''Professionalism,'' he told me, ''is being paid to rest.'' He felt that if one is employed in a full-time occupation, one can forget about winning. In particular, one cannot do the appropriate speed training after a hard day at work.

Table 8.25   Record of Jackie Mekler's Pre-Comrades (January to May 31) Long Training Runs

Year	1958	1960	1963	1965	1968	1969
Comrades result (time) position	(6:26:26) 1	(5:56:32) 1	(5:51:20) 1	(5:56:19) 2	(6:01:11) 1	(6:01:30) 3
Runs: ≥ 70 km	1	2	4	3	6	6
≥ 56 km	5	6	1	5	2	4
≥ 42 km	17	9	4	2	3	2
≥ 32 km	7	1	7	7	10	13
Total:	30	18	16	17	21	25

Note. Information courtesy of J. Mekler

Don Ritchie

In his remarkable and still unfinished career, the Scotsman Don Ritchie (see Figure 8.18), who was born on July 7, 1944, has set nine world best times on the track at 50 km (twice), 64 km (40 miles), 80 km (50 miles; twice), 100 km, 150 km, 160 km, and 200 km and three world records on the roads at 100 km on a certified course, 100 km on an uncertified course, and 160 km. He also has a formidable road racing record and has won eight major European 100-km races at least once each.

Ritchie first began running competitively as a track runner when he joined the Aberdeen Athletic Club in September 1963 and began competing at distances from 400 to 1600 m in the following year at age 19. By 1966 he was training 120 km per week, and he ran his first marathon in that year, finishing in 2:42. In 1967 he trained harder, finishing second in the Scottish Marathon Championships in 2:27:48. The following year he improved his marathon time further to 2:24:48.

His first ultramarathon race was the 1970 58-km Two Bridges race in Scotland, in which he finished seventh in 3:50:50. During the next 4 years he continued to race cross-country, on the track, and on the road at distances up to the marathon and achieved his fastest-ever time for 16 km (49:54) and greatest distance run in 1 hour (19.241 km). In his first London-to-Brighton race in 1974 he finished third in 5:25:00. His first major international successes came in April 1977 with a world 50-km record of 2:51:38 followed by victory in September 1977 in the London-to-Brighton race in 5:16:05, at that time the fourth fastest–ever time. Later that year he ran a world 15-km/100-mile best of 11:30:51. The following year he won the London-to-Brighton in 5:13:02 at the fastest average pace until then, and he won the Hartola 100 km in 6:18:00, also the then–fastest time. Also

Figure 8.18   Don Ritchie after 48 km in the 1978 London-to-Brighton race, which he won in 5:13.02.
Note. Photo courtesy of Don Ritchie.

in 1978 he set world track records at 80 km (4:53:28), 100 km (6:10:20), and 160 km (11:30:51) and world road records at 80 km (4:51:48) and 100 km. In June 1979, he added the world 160-km road best (11:51:12) and improved his own world 50-km best to 2:50:30.

A period of injuries followed, but in October 1982 he returned with a world 100-km road best of 6:28:11 in the Santander race in Spain. A month later in the Barnet Copthall track 100-km race in North London, he set a new world 64-km (40-mile) best of 3:48:35, and the following year he broke his own 50-mile record with 4:50:11. In October 1983 on the Coatbridge track, at age 39, he set the world 200-km track record of 16:32:30 despite having to contend with gale force winds and lashing rain for most of the race, and in the same year ran his best marathon of 2:19:34 in the London Marathon.

Despite the advance of the years, Ritchie has slowed hardly at all. In 1984 he ran 5:28:27 in the London-to-Brighton race with a world Veteran's record of 5:07:08 for 50 miles. In February 1985 he ran 2:56:51 for 50 km, and in April of that year he completed the London Marathon in 2:21:26. His most recent excellent performance was the Veteran's record of 6:36:02 for the 100-km Turin-to-St. Vincent race in Italy in May 1986.

During his entire running career, Ritchie (Ritchie, personal communication, 1987) has been self-coached and writes that he has gleaned his ideas from many sources. He has used this empirical approach to discover what best suits his style.

As a beginner he was inspired by *Run to the Top* (1962) written by Arthur Lydiard and Garth Gilmore. Later he introduced interval training based on the principles espoused by Gerschler and Reindell and began to include the ideas of another British runner, Bruce Tulloh.

After graduating from college in August 1972, Ritchie began work in the aerospace industry until 1975, when he retired from running and went to work on an oil rig in the North Sea. An accident in which he was thrown into the sea convinced him to return to dry land in August 1976, when he started teaching high school physics and resumed his athletic career. His training at that time comprised mainly long runs of medium pace with two hard runs with his running club each week. He increased the tempo of his runs and included long rambling runs through forests and cross-country. The result was that between 1977 and 1980 he ran his best races. In June 1980 he was injured, and when he could again resume heavy training in early 1982, he began to include a hard 30-km midweek training run with a friend. In July 1983 he married and decreased his training. The result is that he now runs less but at a higher intensity.

He now stresses consistency, usually running about 160 km/week but he has run as little as 32 km/week and as much as 258 km/week. Included in his training program are sessions of fartlek on grass and forest roads and hard efforts of from 1 to 5 minutes on the road. Because he puts on weight easily, he feels that he needs to run high weekly mileages. He is nevertheless particularly aware of the dangers of overtraining, which he notices as painful muscles.

Ritchie varies his training throughout the year. He runs twice a day Monday to Friday with single longer runs on Saturday and Sunday. His usual training pace is 16 km/hr or quicker, and all his training is done alone. He includes three effort sessions per week: a 16-km run broken up by 1- and 2-minute hard runs alternating with equal recovery intervals; a 25-km run doing 1, 2, 3, 4, 5, 4, 3, 2, and 1 minutes hard with equal recovery intervals, then repeating; and a third session on the hills. He believes that the key to his training is the weekly long runs. He runs a 50-km course on roads and forestry tracks 2 or 3 times a month. He finds longer training runs to be too time consuming, and he does not think that they contribute any additional benefits to his condition.

Prior to an important race he embarks on a 10-week buildup, increasing his mileage from 160 to perhaps 260 km/week. In the spring he starts training for a marathon in mid-May and a 100-km race in June or July before easing back in the summer holidays, when he races every week at 16 to 21 km. In August he again starts training for a 100-km race. This variety keeps his enjoyment alive.

He writes that he loves running and especially loves racing well. His racing strategy when he is fully fit is to run as hard as possible from the start of each race without becoming overtly short of breath. He naturally slows as the race progresses. When not fully fit he runs more cautiously and lets others dictate the pace while he awaits developments. During ultradistance races he drinks approximately 200 ml of a glucose polymer/electrolyte solution every 20 minutes. Once an hour he also ingests 200 ml of a 10% glucose polymer solution. He started this practice as early as 1977, well before other runners (see chapter 4), and considers that this gives him a physiological and psychological advantage.

Ritchie is a close friend of Aberdeen's exceptional exercise physiologist Dr. Ron Maughan, who besides being a former Scottish 1,500 m champion, has contributed so much to our understanding of the physiology of long-distance running (Maughan, 1985, 1986, 1990; Maughan & Leiper, 1983; Maughan & Poole, 1981). Maughan was also instrumental in having Downer's historic book (Downer, 1900) republished and is one of the most approachable and helpful scientists I have ever met.

Bruce Fordyce

According to his mother, Bruce Fordyce (see Figure 8.19) won his first race at the age of 3 and then did little serious running until after he had left school (Aitken, 1983). Then at age 20, during an Old Boy's rugby match, he became aware that his fitness had fallen precipitously, and he resolved to start running. In June 1976 he heard about the Comrades Marathon and started training with the idea of running the race the following year.

In his first run in 1977, Fordyce finished 43rd in 6:45. Only the following year, when he finished in 14th place in 6:11, did his potential become apparent. Since then his running has improved greatly (see Table 8.26). He has won the Comrades Marathon eight times in succession and the London-to-Brighton Marathon three times, a feat never before achieved. He has thrice lowered the up-Comrades record, has set the down-Comrades record, and ran 4:50:21 for 50 miles during the 1983 London-to-Brighton race.

His racing performances have improved gradually and progressively virtually every year, with one of his best runs being in 1988. This indicates that each year he has learned something that has allowed him to get inexorably closer to his genetic limits.

But most remarkable has been the manner in which he has achieved his most recent victories. A friend who watched the television broadcast of the 1983 Comrades told me that watching Bruce run was an ethereal experience. Later when I saw a recording of the race, I too was transfixed by what I saw. For the screen bore witness to something that was intangible, something beyond words.

Figure 8.19 Bruce Fordyce with his sister Oonagh during the 1982 London-to-Brighton race.

Note. Photo courtesy of Red Daniels.

Never before had the Comrades seen such poetic running, such effortless mastery, and such athletic perfection—indeed, such complete excellence.

What he has perfected is consistency. He has never yet had a bad race. This must be because he has controlled all the variables that determine ultramarathon success. And in doing so, he has made the most important observations about training for the short ultramarathons since Arthur Newton. Let us see how he came to his ideas (Fordyce, 1985).

Table 8.27 details all the training distances Bruce has run up to May 1988. As can be seen, he ran his first Comrades in 1977 on little training (1,575 km between January 1 and May 31). Then, in training for the 1978 race, the single event that probably fashioned Bruce's thinking more than any other occurred. In January that year, he became injured and was able to run a total of only 285 km in January and February (compared to 472 km the year before). The injury resolved, Bruce increased his training and subsequently finished 14th in that

Table 8.26 Bruce Fordyce's Ultramarathon Progress

Year	Race	Position	Time
1977	Comrades Marathon (up)	43	6:45:00
1978	Comrades Marathon (down)	14	6:11:00
1979	Comrades Marathon (up)	3	5:51:15
1980	Comrades Marathon (down)	2	5:40:31
1981	Comrades Marathon (up)	1	5:37:28 (Record)
	London-to-Brighton	1	5:21:15
1982	Comrades Marathon (down)	1	5:34:22
	London-to-Brighton	1	5:18:36
1983	Two Oceans Marathon	4	3:14:02[a]
	Comrades Marathon (up)	1	5:30:12 (Record)
	London-to-Brighton	1	5:12:32[b]
1984	Comrades Marathon (down)	1	5:27:18 (Record)
	A.M.J.A. 80-km Marathon	1	4:50:50 (Current American record)
1985	Pieter Korkie Marathon	1	3:21:48
	Comrades Marathon (up)	1	5:37:01
1986	Comrades Marathon (down)	1	5:24:07 (Current record)
1987	Comrades Marathon (up)	1	5:37:01
	Nanisivik Midnight Sun 80-km Marathon	1	6:33:00 (Current record)
1988	Comrades Marathon (up)	1	5:27:42 (Current record)
1989	Standard Bank 100-km Challenge	1	6:25:07 (Current record)
1990	Comrades Marathon (up)	1	5:40:25

[a]Run as a training run. [b]Including 4:50:21 for 50 miles.

year's Comrades Marathon. He is convinced that with a little more racing experience he might have done even better.

Bruce subsequently told me that this performance made him suspect that runners like Newton (see Table 5.1) and Mekler (see Table 8.24) had possibly trained too much for the race. Bruce was particularly impressed by Dave Levick's Comrades performance in 1971, when on a grand total of only 130 km training in January and February, he ran one of the great Comrades, finishing second in 5:48:53 and going on to win the 1971 London-to-Brighton race in record time. Thus Fordyce concluded that high training mileage in January and February was probably not necessary.

With the insight of the athletic genius that he is, Fordyce resolved not to follow the usual pattern exhibited by most runners who, tasting success for the first time in a marathon or ultramarathon, conclude that they would do even better next time by training a much higher mileage. (For example, compare Jackie Mekler's

Table 8.27   Bruce Fordyce's Training and Comrades Marathon Record and Training Distances (km) (1977-1990)

Year	Age	Comrades direction	Comrades time	Position	Total Jan.-May	Monthly distances Jan.-May	Total June-Jan. previous year
1990	34	up	5:40:25	1	2,884	(525, 488, 520, 767, 584)	3,132
1988	32	up	5:27:42	1	2,901	(534, 440, 577, 734, 616)	2,901
1987	31	up	5:37:01	1	2,872	(513, 483, 563, 792, 521)	3,389
1986	30	down	5:24:07	1	2,960	(508, 518, 564, 750, 620)	2,779
1985	29	up	5:37:01	1	2,844	(568, 429, 500, 747, 600)	3,168
1984	28	down	5:27:18	1	2,713	(498, 404, 488, 760, 563)	2,993
1983	27	up	5:30:12	1	2,904	(498, 488, 552, 752, 614)	3,055
1982	26	down	5:34:22	1	2,960	(544, 283, 665, 786, 682)	3,495
1981	25	up	5:37:28	1	3,047	(619, 561, 561, 768, 538)	3,139
1980	24	down	5:40:31	2	2,925	(570, 410, 645, 610, 690)	3,226
1979	23	up	5:51:15	3	2,698	(503, 400, 423, 738, 634)	2,472
1978	22	down	6:11:00	14	1,887	(204, 81, 400, 670, 532)	1,890
1977	21	up	6:45:00	43	1,575	(216, 250, 359, 345, 405)	1,146

Note. Information courtesy of B. Fordyce.

Comrades training in 1958 and 1959 versus 1963 and 1965 (see Table 8.24).) Rather, Fordyce decided to keep his total training distance down, and following the lead of another Comrades multiwinner, Alan Robb, Fordyce introduced more speed work and hill training.

So for the 1979 race, he increased his training distance for January to May by only 800 km and has since kept this distance at about 2,900 km for the last 5 months each year before the race. Since then, his major training refinements have been to define exactly what type of speed training he requires and when. He has also discovered that it is not possible to race ultramarathons too frequently, particularly leading up to the Comrades.

Running the Comrades and London-to-Brighton ultramarathons within 14 weeks of each other has led Fordyce to conclude that many long runs are not essential for successful distance running. Because he takes 4 to 6 weeks to recover from the Comrades and tapers for the last 2 weeks before the London-to-Brighton race, he has only 6 to 8 weeks to prepare for the latter. During the period between these two races in 1983, he was able to run only two runs of 50 km or longer. Despite that, he ran one of the world's fastest times for 50 miles in the 1983 London-to-Brighton race.

The only hiccups in his progress have been injuries that occurred in March of 1979 and 1980 and in February 1982. He believes that these resulted from starting specific Comrades training too soon, and this has further convinced him of the need to be careful in January and February and to introduce intensive speed training only later. Of particular interest is that despite the low mileage he ran in February 1982 (282 km) due to injury, he still won the Comrades that year.

Bruce's training ideas are frighteningly simple. When asked to list the reasons for his success, he offered the following:

- Rarely doing too much
- Leg strength
- Extreme caution—never losing his head
- His natural speed, which has been improved by racing on the track at 1,500 to 10,000 m in the summer off-season*
- Minute attention to all possible details, to the point of paranoia
- Altitude training

Recently he has found that with age he has had to reduce slightly the intensities of his interval and hill sessions.Despite this, or possibly because of it, his racing performances have improved further.

I will consolidate these ideas into *Fordyce's 9-Point Approach to Training* for the short ultramarathons, which in this case would be run at the end of May or beginning of June.

Point 1: Start Gently in January and February Regardless of How Fit You Are

Train hard over distances of 6 to 10 km, and do not run more than 110 km/week with long weekend runs of up to 25 km. Bruce includes one speed session a week on the track during January and February.

Point 2: Start Specific Ultramarathon Training Only in the Middle of March

In March, Bruce begins to move towards his peak by increasing his training distance to 130 km/week; in April, which he considers to be the most important month, this rises to 176 to 192 km/week. This heavy training (beyond 130 km/week) is sustained for a maximum of *only* 8 weeks.

---

*This has had the effect of increasing his peak "cruising speed," particularly in the second half of ultramarathon races. This was best exemplified in the 1987 Comrades Marathon in which he was 4-1/2 minutes behind the leader with 20 km to go, but won by 6-1/2 minutes, the latter all made up in the last 8 km. During that race he was timed at 3:20/km between 60 and 70 km, equivalent to a standard marathon in 2:20, or only 3 minutes slower than his best.

Further support for this 6- to 8-week training rule is provided by a study that showed a dramatic fall in both performances and $\dot{V}O_2$max values during the 6th week in athletes who underwent an intensive laboratory-based 6-week peaking training program (Mikesell & Dudley, 1984).

Point 3: Do Specific Speed Training

Bruce's speed sessions include hill training (which he hates but believes to be absolutely vital), time trials of 8 to 10 km, cross-country races of up to 12 km, and track intervals. For hill training he runs a 400-m hill in 90 seconds and repeats it 5 to 8 times for the last 4 to 5 weeks before the race. Done any more frequently, this hill training causes fatigue the next day, which Bruce considers to be a bad sign. For the first session he will run six to eight hills at a slow pace; in the last two sessions he will run fewer hills but at a faster pace.

Interval sessions on the track are six 800-m intervals run at 2:15 to 2:00/800 m, four 1-mile intervals run at 4:45 to 4:50/mile, or a combination of intervals from 800 to 1,200 m. Combined with track sessions and time trials, his typical training week during the 6 to 8 weeks of heavy training is as shown in Table 8.28.

In the 8-week period he averages between 11 and 14 hard training sessions on Tuesdays and Thursdays and runs two cross-country races of 12 km. Bruce summarizes his ideas in these words:

> Choose quality rather than quantity when training. Train for speed not distance. Speed is the killer. . . . The idea is not to be able to sprint fast, after all most ultramarathons are decided long before the final meters are run, but to be able to raise cruising speed. I know that if I can race 10 kilometers in under 30 minutes, I am going to find 3-1/2 minute kilometers fairly easy. (Fordyce, 1989, p. 32).

Table 8.28   Bruce Fordyce's Training Week During His 6- to 8-Week Peak Training Period

Day	Morning	Afternoon
Monday	8 km	16 km
Tuesday	8 km	8 km (time trial/interval session/hills)
Wednesday	24 km (easy)	—
Thursday	8 km	10 km (hills in April; interval sessions in May)
Friday	16 km	8 km
Saturday	8-16 km	(cross-country race)
Sunday	Long run (42-64 km)	

Note. Information courtesy of B. Fordyce.

He considers that his training is not very different from that of the standard-marathon runners, such as Rob de Castella (see Table 8.18), with the exception that Fordyce believes the ultramarathoner needs to run more very long runs than do those who concentrate purely on the standard marathon (Aitken, 1983).

After his fifth Comrades victory in 1985, Bruce went through a period in which his running enthusiasm waned. His answer was to start racing on the track between November and March. His specific track training resulted in his achieving the following personal-best times: 1,500 m, 3:59 (altitude); 1 mile (road), 4:10; 3,000 m, 8:36 (altitude); 5,000 m, 14:28; and 10,000 m, 30:28. The result has been that his "cruising speed" in the latter stages of the ultramarathon has increased.

Point 4: Don't Do Too Many Very Long Runs

Bruce does very few long runs during the ultramarathon buildup (one 56- to 70-km run, eight 42- to 56-km runs, three 32- to 42-km runs, and six 32-km runs) and has never yet finished his club's 70-km pre-Comrades training run. He told me that after 5-1/2 hours on his feet he has had enough and just "gets into the nearest car."

Point 5: When in Doubt, Rest

My training advice is going to be different from a lot of advice you will be given. This is because I place my emphasis on rest and recovery. I do believe in hard training, but there is only so much hard training that the body can take, and the timing and duration of any hard training phase is very important.

During the hard training phase never be afraid to take a day off. If your legs are feeling unduly stiff and sore, rest; if you are at all sluggish, rest; in fact, if in doubt, rest. (Fordyce, 1981, pp. 4-5)

Point 6: Do Not Run an All-Out Marathon or Longer Race in the Last 10 to 12 Weeks Before the Ultramarathon

Another vital lesson that Bruce has taught us is the need to select races very carefully:

If you want to do well on the day that really matters, don't try to do well on the days that aren't as important. . . . Enter as many marathons as you like, but treat them as training runs—don't race! I enter a lot of local marathons as I find them an extremely pleasant way to run a weekend 26-mile training run. I probably only race hard once (over the full marathon distance in the five months) before Comrades. (Fordyce, 1981, p. 5)

As discussed in chapter 10, it seems that this specialization is necessary because of the muscle damage caused by ultramarathon racing and because of the muscles' slow recovery. So the runner who races too often and trains too much will be running on muscles that are continually damaged and cannot perform optimally. Thus a hard ultramarathon race in April destroys April's training, the very month that is the most important for the Comrades.

Bruce and I discussed his slightly poorer run in the 1985 Comrades Marathon. We considered the possibility that his more hectic lifestyle, his many commitments, his increasing age, and the years of heavy training and competition could explain why he performed less well than he had in 1983 on an identical training program and racing buildup (see Tables 8.26 and 8.27). Our tentative conclusion was that he should race only one ultramarathon every year and should be more circumspect about any races he enters during his Comrades Marathon buildup.

Point 7: Undergo a Decent Taper Before the Race

Prior to Bruce's Comrades ascendancy, it was generally held that the last month before the race was the time to train the hardest. Thus the training mileages of previous Comrades greats including Newton (see Table 5.1) and Mekler (see Table 8.24) show that they all trained their greatest distances in May.

Yet Bruce has modified this by resting more in May and training hardest in April (see Table 8.27). He achieves this by following a definite taper, not dissimilar to that advocated by Newton (see Table 8.29).

For the final 10 days before the race, he reduces his training precipitously and rests frequently. Before the 1980 race, his training for the last 10 days before the race was as shown in Table 8.30 (Fordyce, 1981).

Table 8.29   Bruce Fordyce's Training Taper Before the Comrades Marathon

Week	Training distance	% of maximum
Last week April	180 km	100
First week May	160 km	88
Second week May	128 km	71
Third week May	112 km	62
Last week May	48 km	26

Note. Information courtesy of B. Fordyce.

Table 8.30   Distance Run (in km) by Bruce Fordyce Before the 1980 Comrades Marathon

Date	Morning	Afternoon
May 20	5	5
May 21	—	6
May 22	—	—
May 23	—	8.5
May 24	10	—
May 25	20	—
May 26	5	—
May 27	6	—
May 28	5	—
May 29	—	—
May 30	—	—
May 31	Race	

Note. From *The Distance Runner's Log: To the Lonely Breed* (9th ed., p. 5) by Collegian Harriers, 1981, Pietermaritzburg: Collegian Harriers. Copyright 1981 by Collegian Harriers. Adapted by permission.

Point 8: Gauge Your Fitness by Performance in Short-Distance Races and Speed Sessions

The need to gauge fitness at any point in training was discussed in chapter 4. Two refinements that Fordyce has developed are the abilities to gauge his fitness on the basis of performance in short-distance races and speed sessions.

Bruce wrote that when he can run 8 km in close to 25:00 (at altitude), he is ready for the Comrades (Fordyce, 1984). American marathoners Frank Shorter and Alberto Salazar have said essentially the same for the standard marathon. Both judge their preparedness for the standard marathon on the basis of their times over 10 km. Not that this is anything new! At the turn of the century, the pedestrian Barclay wrote the following:

> In the progress of his training, his condition may as well be ascertained . . .
> by the manner in which he performs one mile at the top of his speed, as to
> walk a hundred; . . . if he performs this short distance well, it may be
> concluded that his condition is perfect. (Downer, 1900, p. 143)

The short races that Bruce runs before the Comrades include six to seven 8-km time trials, one 10-km race, two 12-km cross-country races, one 21.1-km half marathon, and one 32-km race. Note that he races nothing longer than 32 km before the Comrades. As suggested in chapter 10, it seems that muscle damage becomes progressively worse in races longer than about 28 km. Thus Bruce races frequently at safe distances that are unlikely to cause muscle damage.

Bruce has learned to gauge his fitness by his performance during his training sessions, as described in chapter 5 in the fourth additional rule of training keeping a detailed logbook.

Point 9: Do Specific Strength Training for Downhill Ultramarathons

After his first down-Comrades victory in 1982, Bruce remarked that the down-Comrades was not a race but a "survival trip." He referred to the more severe muscle damage caused by the downhill nature of the course. Before the 1984 race, he decided that he would have to do something to reduce that damage.

The evidence suggests that strength training of the quadriceps group may reduce the degree of muscle damage during downhill running. So for the 1984 race, Bruce underwent a weekly program of strength training for his quadriceps and included more regular downhill running sessions.

Frith van der Merwe

The South African Frith van der Merwe (Figure 8.20) was born in Johannesburg on May 26, 1964. In junior school she participated in tennis and netball, and she gained state colors for tennis at age 16 while still in high school.

Her interest in running began in 1979 when she won her school's 4-km cross-country race despite never having trained specifically for running. In 1981, her final year of high school, she trained more consistently, and won the local inter-schools 1,500 m in 4:48.

For the following 4 years, van der Merwe attended the University of the Witwatersrand where she trained more regularly but with no greater ambition than representing her university at the annual Inter-University Championships. Despite this relatively low-key approach, she received state colors for 15-km road racing and cross-country.

In 1986, her final year at the university, van der Merwe entered her first marathon, finishing in 3:24. In the following year she ran two marathons, breaking 3 hours for the first time in October; she also finished seventh in the 56-km Two Oceans Marathon (4:20) and sixth in the 90-km Comrades Marathon (7:22) of that year. She recalls that breaking 3 hours in the marathon was the turning point that inspired her to aim for greater running achievements.

Her performances in 1988 proved that her ambitions were not misplaced. In January and again in February, she won standard marathons at medium altitude in 2:47; in March she won the 56-km Milo Korkie Marathon at medium altitude in 3:54; in May she won the 90-km up-Comrades Marathon in 6:32; and in July she won the 50-km City-to-City Marathon, also at medium altitude, in 3:16. In

Figure 8.20 Frith van der Merwe finishing 15th overall in the 1989 Comrades Marathon.
Note. Photo courtesy of Die Beeld—Jan Hamman.

all five races, she set new course records. She completed 1988 with a personal best of 2:43 in the Egoli Marathon run at medium altitude.

In January 1989 she again won the Benoni standard marathon in a new personal and course record time of 2:40:45; the following month she lowered her best marathon time to 2:30:25 when she won the South African Marathon Championship in a new national record time. This is the fastest marathon ever run by a woman in February, and it was the eigth fastest time in the world in 1989. In March, she won the 56-km Two Oceans Marathon in a new record time of 3:30:36, finishing in 22nd position overall. During the race she established new world best times for 30 miles (3:01:16) and 50 km (3:08:39). Six weeks later, she set the South African and All-African records for 32 km (1:53:40).

As remarkable as these performances were, they pailed somewhat when, on May 31, 1989, van der Merwe finished 15th overall in the 90-km "down"-Comrades Marathon in a time of 5:54:43. That performance may have been the greatest-ever Comrades Marathon run by any athlete. The overall downhill gradient of the course prevented her time from being considered a world record.

Her calculated time at 50 miles (5:24:37) is 52:53 faster than the recognized world record held by West German, Monika Kuno.

During the remainder of 1989, van der Merwe won a further marathon (2:38) run on a hilly course; she lowered her record time for the 50-km City-to-City Marathon to 3:04:34; and in November she ran 49:48 for 15 km at sea level. By the end of the year she had been awarded national colors for 15 km, the marathon, and the ultramarathon in the same year. On February 24, 1990, she improved her national record to 2:27:36 in the national marathon championships, and on March 18, 1990, she finished in 10th place overall in the 56-km Milo Korkie Marathon, lowering her previous record by 22 minutes to 3:32:42.

Some of the features van der Merwe believes are important for her success are the devoted support and love she receives from her family, especially her mother who takes care of all the small but essential comforts necessary for the competitive athlete; her personal dedication and discipline; her enjoyment of running; and the fact that she was never pushed to train hard at school. She is entirely self-coached because, as she writes, she has "always been an independent, headstrong person" who "prefers doing things my own way" (F. van der Merwe, 1990, p. 38). In less public moments, she admits that she does not like being told what to do. She also writes, "I'm the best person to know how my body feels and will train accordingly" (F. van der Merwe, 1990, p. 38). She believes that by training herself, she has been able to avoid serious injuries.

Van der Merwe's approach to ultramarathon training and racing has been strongly influenced by Bruce Fordyce, whose advice she has sought and followed since she began serious training. Her average training week is listed in Table 8.31. Her typical weekly training distance varies from 120 to 130 km depending on the length of the long weekend run. Prior to the Comrades Marathon she increases this to about 140 km/week in February and to 160 to 170 km/week in March, April, and the first 2 weeks of May. Her training during the last 2-1/2 weeks before the Comrades is very similar to the taper used by Bruce Fordyce for that race.

In this chapter, we have discussed the value of the long-distance training runs that are a feature of the training programs of most ultradistance runners. It would seem that, like Bruce Fordyce but unlike many other great ultradistance runners, van der Merwe does not believe that such runs are of great value. Prior to her record-breaking run in the 1989 Comrades Marathon, she completed only the following long training runs: January—one 42-km race; February—two 42-km races; March—one 56-km race; April—one 45-km training run; May—one 59-km training run.

Like many of the great male distance runners, van der Merwe is an excellent example of an athlete who developed her true potential only after leaving school and indeed after leaving the university. She began intensive training when she was 23, yet set world records by age 25. She again shows that the best ultramarathon runners will come from those who are fastest over 10 to 42 km.

Table 8.31 Frith van der Merwe's Training Week

Day	Time	Regimen
Monday	a.m.	10 km—easy
	p.m.	Gym (upper body)—40 min; 45-min fartlek—hard
Tuesday	a.m.	10 km—easy
	p.m.	Gym (legs)—45 min; 10 km (occasional time trial)—hard
Wednesday	a.m.	12 km—very easy
	p.m.	20 km—easy
Thursday	a.m.	10 km—easy
	p.m.	Gym (upper body)—45 min; hill sprints (10 x 150 m hills); 8 km—easy
Friday	a.m.	8 km—easy
Saturday	a.m.	25-30 km—long, hilly, fairly hard
Sunday		20-30 km—long, slow; the distance of this run increases from January to May in preparation for the Comrades Marathon

LONG ULTRADISTANCE RACES: 100 KM TO 6 DAYS

The true history of the origins of long ultradistance running is still being compiled (Milroy, 1981).

Captain Barclay

One of the first modern references to an unusual ultradistance performance named a Captain Barclay, who in 1806 walked 160 km in 19 hours. Three years later he ran 1 mile every hour for 1,000 consecutive hours (41 days and 16 hours) thereby earning sterling 16,000 (Van der Merwe, 1987).

Barclay was clearly an unusual man. A wealthy landowner, the sixth Laird of Vry, he had at age 21 submitted to the training of a tenant farmer, Jackey Smith, then the most celebrated British trainer of pedestrians. This involved a major role reversal, which was not common in a society in which a gentleman never accepted orders from those who were his social inferiors.

Smith's training program lasted 4 to 6 weeks and included running, walking, and hard physical labor (Radford, 1985). Smith was a hard taskmaster, once forcing Barclay to complete a 110-mile "time trial." The training that Barclay received from Jackey Smith provided the basis for Barclay's training methods when, after 1807, he himself became an athletic trainer.

Barclay first achieved notoriety as a trainer of the pugilist Tom Crib, whose victory over Tom Moulineux for the "Championship of the Pugilistic Prize Ring" in Vry, Scotland, in 1811 was ascribed largely to Barclay's training methods (Radford, 1985).

In *Walkers Manly Exercises* (cited in Doherty, 1964), *Running Recollections and How to Train* (Downer, 1900), and Thom's *Pedestrianism* (1813), Barclay gave the following advice for the beginning runner who had already undergone a 12-day period during which the runner took a course of "physic," comprising a dose of "Glauber's salts," and was therefore ready to start training.

> When the object in view is the accomplishment of a pedestrian match, his regular exercise may be from 20 to 24 miles a day. He must rise at five in the morning, run half a mile at the top of his speed uphill, and then walk six miles at a moderate speed, coming in about seven to breakfast, which should consist of beefsteaks or mutton chops underdone, with stale bread and beer. After breakfast, he must again walk six miles at a moderate pace, and at twelve lie down in bed without his clothes, for half an hour. On getting up, he must walk four miles, and return by four to dinner which should also be beefsteaks or mutton chops, with bread and beer, as at breakfast. Immediately after dinner, he must resume his exercise, by running half a mile at the top of his speed, and walking six miles at a moderate pace. He takes no more exercise for that day, but retires to bed about eight; and the next morning he proceeds in the same manner. (Doherty, 1964, pp. 224-225)

After 3 or 4 weeks on this regime the athlete was advised to "take a four mile sweat." This involved the athlete running 4 miles in flannel clothing, drinking a hot beverage on return, and then going to bed for 25 to 30 minutes, covered by six to eight blankets. After a gentle 2-mile walk, "well wrapped in his great coat," the trainee returned to breakfast before beginning the normal exercise routine. Three or four of these sweats were recommended leading up to the race. Another component of the Barclay method was time trials. This was a feature of the training of Walter George and Alfred Shrubb.

The origin of these training ideas is unknown. Radford (1985) suggests that they were linked inseparably with the training of animals, especially fighting cocks and racing horses. He notes that details of the training methods for fighting cocks were available long before those for humans and that these included the same four central components—purging, sweating, watching one's diet, and exercising. In addition, cockfighting was the oldest sport and possibly the first "national" sport in Britain, reaching back at least to the time of the Romans. Furthermore, trainers like Jackey Smith knew as much about the training of horses as they did of humans. Radford (1985) suggests that the training of humans evolved from that of animals on the basis of a "continuous verbal tradition stretching down the centuries" (p. 82).

Barclay also paid great attention to diet (Downer, 1900; Thom, 1813). He preferred foods of animal origin, in particular lean beef, mutton (occasionally), and the legs of fowl. All veal, lamb, pork, fish, eggs; fatty or greasy substances, in particular milk, butter, and cheese; and salts, spices, and seasonings were prohibited. Vegetables were also avoided, and biscuits and stale bread were the only preparations of vegetable origin that were allowed. The only liquor allowed was old home-brewed beer (not exceeding 3 pints a day) and half a pint of red wine after dinner.

Hereditary factors seem to have been important in Barclay's success. His father was said to be so powerful that "finding a stray horse in one of his fields, he lifted it on to his shoulders and threw it over the hedge" (Downer, 1900, p. 131); when a member of Parliament, his grandfather would walk to Westminster from his home in Urie at the start of each Parliamentary session and "would pick up many a prize hat for cudgel play, and wrestling on the road" (p. 131). Barclay was also very strong; he once lifted a 100-kg man with one hand and placed him on a table (Milroy, personal communication, 1987)!

Edward Payson Weston

The next great ultramarathon walker was the American Edward Payson Weston, the man who was to inspire one of the most heroic and interesting eras in the history of running.

Weston, who became known as the "father of pedestrianism," was born in Providence, Rhode Island, on March 15, 1839 (Osler & Dodd, 1977, 1979). He first gained fame in 1861 by walking 713 km from Boston to Washington DC in order to attend the inauguration of President Lincoln. In 1867 he walked 2,135 km from Portland, Maine, to Chicago in 26 days. Thereafter his goal became that of covering 800 km in 6 days or 144 hours. He finally succeeded at his third attempt in December 1874, thereby winning a gold watch plus the title "Pedestrian Champion of the World."

The following year Daniel O'Leary, an Irish immigrant to North America, walked 800 km in Chicago and challenged Weston to a match to decide the "world champion." The race, held from November 15 to 20, 1875, was won by O'Leary, who covered 800.4 km to Weston's 720 km.

The following winter Weston traveled to England, where he was unbeaten in a series of races. His best performance (801.6 km) was achieved at the Agricultural Hall in London, where he met Sir John Drysdale Astley, a Baron and member of Parliament, who agreed to back Weston against anyone else in the world.

Meanwhile O'Leary, learning of Weston's great successes in England, traveled to London and challenged Weston to a showdown in London in April 1877. Again O'Leary triumphed with a new world record of 837 km to Weston's 816 km. Despite losing £20,000 on Weston, Sir John Astley decided to sponsor the

official world pedestrian championship. He donated the Astley Belt, valued at
£100, and £2,000 in other prizes for the "Long-Distance Challenge Championship of the World."

The Astley Belt Races
and the Rise of Charles Rowell and Daniel O'Leary

The first Astley Belt race was held at the Agricultural Hall in London in March
1878 and the second at Madison Square Gardens in October 1878. Both were
convincingly won by O'Leary with a best distance of 837.7 km, a new world
record. Weston entered neither.

Despondent at the American domination of this event, Astley began the search
for a British pedestrian who could tackle foreigners. He chose Charles Rowell,
a 24-year-old boat boy from Maidenhead, Kent, with little athletic experience
besides a modest best–15-km time of 60 minutes. Rowell, who was 5 feet 6
inches tall, and weighed 63 kg, was given support and time to train. In the winter
of 1879 he set sail for America to vindicate British pedestrianism.

The third Astley Belt contest was held in March 1879 at Madison Square
Gardens. O'Leary, worn out from too much racing, was no match for Rowell,
who won with a distance of 800.2 km, a quite remarkable performance for a
novice. O'Leary retired on the third day of the race.

Three months later, the fourth Astley Belt was contested in London. Rowell
was unable to compete because of injury. Weston, who had watched Rowell's
progress, had by this time realized that a good runner like Rowell would always
beat a good walker. Before the race Weston had started running training. Utilizing his new technique, Weston took the lead on the fourth day of the race,
finishing with a new world record of 880 km.

Three months later, the fifth Astley Belt was contested at Madison Square
Gardens. Rowell regained the championship belt with a distance of 843.8 km
and returned to Britain.

One week after the finish of the fifth Astley Belt race, the first O'Leary Belt
race, sponsored by Daniel O'Leary, was held in Madison Square Gardens.
O'Leary's stated purpose in sponsoring the race was to develop a pedestrian
capable of bringing the Astley Belt back to the United States, but financial motives may also have played a role—O'Leary and his supporters reportedly made
close to $60,000 profit from the race.

The O'Leary Belt was won by the novice Nicholas Murphy, who finished with
a total of 808 km. One of the athletes initiated to the sport by the race was Patrick
Fitzgerald of Long Island, who had earlier run 17.6 km in 59:50. Fitzgerald then
competed in a number of 6-day, 14-hr/day contests and within 2 months finished
his first full 6-day event with 838.5 km.

The second O'Leary Belt race was held in Madison Square Gardens in April 1880. This was a far more competitive race and was won by Frank Hart, who covered 909.7 km, a new world record. En route he set an American 24-hour record of 210.9 km. Three of the top American finishers in that race, William Pegram, John Dobler, and H. Howard, then challenged Rowell for the Astley Belt. Hart and O'Leary could see no reason for traveling to Britain. Instead they invited Rowell to a return race in America.

The sixth Astley Belt race began at the Agricultural Hall in London on November 1, 1880. Included in the field were the Britons "Blower" Brown, who had previously set a world record of 890.5 km, and George Littlewood from Sheffield, the latter competing in only his second 6-day event.

Rowell took off quickly, going through 160 km in a record 13:57:13 en route to a world 24-hour record of 235.2 km covered in 22:27. By the end of 3 days he had covered 547.4 and he finished with a new world record of 911.4 km. Littlewood was second with 756.7 km. The first American to finish was Dobler, who completed 724.5 km. The failure of the Americans was put down to the poor condition of the Agricultural Hall, which was described in the following terms: "Madison Square Gardens bears about the same relationship to it as a lady's boudoir in Fifth Avenue does to a log hut in the Western wilds" (Osler & Dodd, 1979, p. 117).

With three Astley Belt victories, Rowell needed only one more victory to obtain absolute possession of the coveted Astley Belt. He was challenged by Weston in the seventh and last Astley Belt race, which was held in June 1881 at the Marble Rink in London. With Weston came Daniel O'Leary, Frank Hart, Charles Harriman, and John Ennis, the latter two who had also competed in the third Astley Belt race. Regrettably, Weston fell ill the night before the race and withdrew on the third day after completing 323.6 km to Rowell's 450.8 km.

The world 6-day record was improved three times by Americans in 1881; the last by Patrick Fitzgerald, who covered 937 km at the American Institute Building in Manhattan in December. Rowell, who was in attendance, vowed to start training the next day for a race to take place the following February. In this race, which Rowell stated was to be his last, he wished to set a record that would last forever—1127 km (700 miles) in 6 days.

The race was held from February 27 to March 4, 1882, in Madison Square Gardens. Included in the race were the American current and former world-record holders Patrick Fitzgerald and John Hughes. In training for the race, Rowell ran and walked 64 km/day at the American Institute Building in Manhattan.

During the race, Rowell passed 160 km in 13:26:30 and after 22-1/2 hours had completed 241.8 km, both new world records. He passed 320 km (200 miles) in 35:09:28, setting his third world record, and after 48 hours had completed 416 km for his fourth world record. On the 3rd day he passed 480 km (300 miles) in 58:17:06, finishing the day with 568.5 km, his fifth and sixth world records, respectively.

On the morning of the 4th day Rowell accidentally ingested a cupful of vinegar and retired from the race shortly thereafter. The race was won by the Englishman George Hazael with a new world-record distance of 967.8 km with Fitzgerald second with 929.2 km.

Rowell was clearly not prepared to retire after such a disappointment. He entered another 6-day race in September 1882 but retired after the 3rd day because of an illness that was diagnosed as malaria. He went home to Britain and rested on his farm for 1 year. In October 1883 Rowell returned to New York and started training for a return match with Fitzgerald to be held in the Madison Square Gardens from April 28 to May 3, 1884.

This proved to be a remarkable race. On the afternoon of the 6th day, Rowell closed the gap on the exhausted Fitzgerald to less than 3 km, at which point Fitzgerald's medical adviser, a Dr. Taylor, lacerated Fitzgerald's legs with a mechanical scarifier. The treatment was apparently effective; the exhausted Fitzgerald was sufficiently revived to hold off Rowell's final challenge and to complete a new world-record distance of 982 km to Rowell's 969.2 km.

During 1888, the last three important 6-day events were held in Madison Square Gardens. In the first, James Albert from Philadelphia increased the world record to 1001 km; in May, George Littlewood returned from Britain and completed 984.1 km, the second-best performance ever. Then in November, Littlewood completed 1004.2 km in 4 hours less than 6 days. It was the final great race. Despite attempts at a renaissance in 1901, 6-day racing would be dead for more than 90 years.

Of the great pedestrians, Weston and O'Leary continued to walk for the rest of their lives. O'Leary made a custom of walking 160 km within 24 hours on each of his birthdays and was able to keep this up to his 75th birthday, when he completed the 160 km in 23:54. O'Leary died at the age of 87; Weston, who at age 70 walked from New York City to San Francisco (6,279 km) in 105 days, died at 90. Osler and Dodd (1979) noted that the other pedestrians were not as fortunate—Rowell died at 55, Fitzgerald at 53, and Brown at 41. The authors wonder whether Weston's self-control, in particular his ability to quit rather than to force himself when he was overextended, might not have been a factor in his greater longevity.

Training and Racing Methods of Pedestrians

Andy Milroy (1983) made the most detailed analysis of the techniques employed by the top pedestrians. He found that professional pedestrians usually came from working-class families and were lured to this most grueling activity by the remarkable financial incentives—one victory in a 6-day race could provide financial security for life. Only the very best athletes became pedestrians, and many were world-record holders at shorter distance races; Patrick Fitzgerald held the United States 1-hour record with 17.76 km; George Hazael held the world 32-km 20-mile) record; and George Mason and James Bailey held world records at 40 km (25 miles) and 64 km (40 miles), respectively. Prospective pedestrians graduated to the full-blown 6-day events by way of nursery events in which they ran continuously for 12 to 14 hours a day for 6 days.

Milroy's (1983) analysis shows that the pedestrians aimed to maintain speeds of between 8.4 and 9.6 km/hr, usually averaging about 8.8 km/hr. Rowell, in particular, could run tirelessly at 9.6 km/hr for hours on end. Together with Walter George, Rowell perfected a most economical running style that produced hardly any knee bend or leg lift; the "trailing leg swung through naturally, like a pendulum, bringing the heel in contact with the ground" (Dillon & Milroy, 1984, p. 48). The benefit of this technique may have been that the absence of any knee bend reduced the amount of eccentric contraction in the quadriceps, thereby protecting the muscle from injury (see chapter 10). Littlewood, too, is thought to have perfected a flat-footed, shuffling gait.

Milroy (1983) concluded that the pedestrians did not alternate walking and running but continued to run for as long as possible each day before starting to walk. At the end of each day they would sleep as little as 3 hours a night; in a fiercely competitive race they would sleep as little as 2 to 2-1/2 hours, an athlete with a good lead might sleep for 4 hours a night. Sleep usually followed a hot bath and massage.

We have little documented evidence of the training methods of the pedestrians. Milroy (1983) suggested that this was because they did not wish their opponents to discover their secrets. It seems that most adhered to the training methods proposed by Barclay and Hurst, in which they alternated walking and running for 6 to 8 hours a day. According to Burfoot (1981a), Rowell "walked and ran up to 50 miles a day" (p. 35). According to Dillon and Milroy (1984), Rowell "would run eight hours a day and put in a sixty mile run twice a week. On his hard day he would go out for a second session" (p. 48). He apparently thought nothing of running to London from his home in Chesterton near Cambridge (about 96 km) in under 8 hours and returning the next day. Similarly, Littlewood trained three times a day, alternating walking and running, including trips from his home to Doncaster and back (116 km).

The pedestrians followed diets similar to those described by Len Hurst (Milroy, 1983) and Captain Barclay (Thom, 1813): roast beef, roast and boiled mutton or chicken, and limited vegetables and stale crusty bread, all washed down with bitter ale. The meat, often in the form of chops, was usually taken before the longest unbroken period of each day's training. While on the move, the pedestrians ate meat protein in semiliquid form (e.g., mutton stew, calf's-foot jelly, or eel broth) using an invalid feeding cup like a small gravy boat with a long, thin spout. The favorite liquid intake was beef tea or beef broth. Other fluids taken were tea, coffee, ginger ale, and milk as well as more potent beverages. When the pedestrians became exhausted, they successfully used alcoholic drinks like champagne and brandy. Often more drastic measures were needed, including morphine, strychnine, and belladonna intake; electric shocks; and even the mechanical scarification to which Fitzgerald was subjected during his final race with Rowell in 1884.

Milroy (1983) concluded that the pedestrians' successes were probably due to their willingness to cut their sleep to 3 hours or less a night; their running to preplanned schedules of rest (at least at the start); and their abilities to walk at 6.4 km/hr for long periods even when utterly exhausted. But the most important factor, Milroy believes, was the prospect of overnight wealth for poor men.

The Modern Pedestrians

The demise of public interest in extreme ultradistance races occurred at the exact time that interest in marathon running was rekindled by the inclusion of that race in the first modern Olympic Games in Greece in 1896.

The next ultradistance events of importance were the second running of the London-to-Brighton race in 1899; the first professional London-to-Brighton race, won by Len Hurst in 1903; and the first running of the Comrades Marathon in 1921. Out of interest in the Comrades Marathon, Arthur Newton traveled to Britain to set a new London-to-Brighton record in 1924 and a new 160 km road record in 1928 before traveling to Canada in 1931 for the first "modern" indoor 24-hour run (see chapter 5), in which he eased past Rowell's 1-day best with 152 miles 540 yards. Another 20 years passed before another 24-hour race was staged, in which Wally Hayward eclipsed Newton's record; only in 1973 were 24-hour track races again held on a regular basis in South Africa, Italy, and Great Britain. In the first such British race, Ron Bently eclipsed Hayward's 24-hour mark by running 259.7 km, a 1-day record that stood until 1979. In May 1981 Jean-Gilles Boussiquet of France extended the record to 272.7 km; he had previously set world records of 260.8 and 264 km. The following year the British runner Dave Dowdle increased this to 274.6 km, a distance that has since been surpassed by the modern Greek phenomenon Yiannis Kouros.

Events longer than 24 hours have an even briefer modern history. In May 1979, the American Don Choi organized a race that was the first 48-hour race in well over 80 years. A year later he organized the first 6-day race, which he won with a distance of 645.6 km. The remaining history of the modern 6-day events revolves around one runner—Yiannis Kouros—who has now set more than 56 world records at distances from 160 to 1,000 km.

Yiannis Kouros

Yiannis Kouros began running as a child because, being from a poor family, he could not afford the entertainment luxuries available to other youngsters. By age

16 he was ranked among the top three schoolboys in Greece at 1,500 and 3,000 m with best times of 4:09 and 9:03, respectively, for those distances.

He sprang to international prominence when he won the inaugural 240-km Spartathlon from Sparta to Athens in September 1983. His winning time of 21:53:42 was greeted with some skepticism, particularly because he won the race by 2 hr 45 min and because other competitors were known to have accepted car rides during the race.

Any doubts about his abilities and integrity were dispelled in April 1984 when he won each stage of the 3-day, three-stage, 320-km Danube race and finished with a total time of 23:16:15, 3 hours ahead of the second runner. Less than 10 weeks later, between July 2 and 8, 1984, he competed in his first 6-day race on Randall's Island, New York (see Figure 8.21). After 48 hours he had completed 428.8 km, an improvement of 8.8 km on Ramon Zabalo's record set earlier that year; after 6 days Kouros surpassed George Littlewood's 1888 mark of 1004.2 km with a final distance of 1022.5 km. Four months later in November, running on a 1-mile circuit in Queens, New York, he set world road bests of 11:46:37 for 160 km and 15:11:48 for 200 km and a new 24-hour world best of 285 km.

Figure 8.21 Yiannis Kouros setting the world 6-day record in New York in 1984.
Note. Photo courtesy of Stan Wagon/*UltraRunning Magazine.*

Three weeks later, in his second 6-day race, from Melbourne to Colac, Australia, he increased his world 6-day record by just over a kilometer to 1023.6 km.

In March the following year, in a 2-day race in Montauban, France, he improved his world 200-km best to 15:11:09 and his world 48-hour best to 452.8 km. One month later he won the Sydney-to-Melbourne 966-km race in 125:07, and at the end of the year in Queens, he again improved his world 24-hour best to 286.6 km. In February 1986, competing in a 24-hour indoor race on a track measuring 11 laps to the mile, he set indoor world records at distances up to 100 km and beyond 200 km and ended with 251 km, a new world indoor best (albeit only 6 km better than Newton's 1931 indoor performance in Hamilton, Ontario).

Another best performance came in March 1987, when Kouros again won the 1,060 km Sydney-to-Melbourne race in 134:47, equivalent to 1,127 km (700 miles) in 6 days, the distance for which Rowell had first aimed 105 years earlier.

An important factor that helps to explain Kouros's remarkable success is that for an ultramarathon runner he has, like Fordyce and Ritchie, a relatively fast best marathon time (2:24:01). He also has a quite remarkable ability to go without sleep for prolonged periods of time. In the Colac race, in which he set the current 6-day world record, he was off the track for only 4 hours during the entire 144 hours of the race. Like the famous pedestrians, he has taught himself to race walk at 6.4 km/hr for prolonged periods, and his approach in these races, like Rowell's, is to run hard from the start and then to walk a great deal. Of his training we know little except that he runs 20 to 25 km per day. He is also a vegetarian and enjoys races of 100 to 300 km the most.

Physiological information on Kouros has recently been published (Rontoyannis et al., 1989). At the time of testing, Kouros was 1.71 m tall, weighed 64 kg with 8% body fat and had a $\dot{V}O_2max$ of 63 ml/kg/min. Data for his energy balance during the 1985 960-km Sydney-Melbourne race, which he won by more than 24 hours finishing in 125:07, were also provided.

During the 5 days of that race, Kouros averaged 11.7, 8.3, 8.1, 8.9, and 6.2 km/hr which corresponded to 57, 41, 40, 44, and 30% of his $\dot{V}O_2max$; he slept for a total of 4 hours 40 minutes and rested for an additional 9 hours 40 minutes. His daily energy expenditure ranged from 15,367 Kcal on the first day to 7,736 Kcal on the fifth day, and his daily energy intake varied from 13,770 Kcal on the first day to 7,800 Kcal on the fifth day. Overall, his total estimated energy intake (55,970 Kcal) exceeded his energy expenditure (55,079 Kcal).

To maintain this high rate of energy consumption, Kouros ate every 15 minutes; his intake included Greek sweets, dried fruits and nuts, biscuits soaked in honey or jam, and fresh fruit such as pears, melon, watermelon, grapes, apples, bananas, plums, pineapples, dates, and raisins. His only meat intake was a small amount of roast chicken on the morning of the fourth day. Carbohydrates provided 96% of his total energy intake.

Kouros drank small amounts of either water, fruit juice, or Gatorade every 10 to 15 minutes. His daily fluid intake varied from 22 litres on the first day to 14.3 liters on the fourth day and averaged 800 ml per hour that he ran. He finished the race 1 lb lighter than he started.

His only medical complaints were severe constipation and frequency of urination, the latter possibly due to what may have been an excessively high fluid intake for his rate of energy expenditure (see Chapter 4). Bladder trauma resulting from the continuous running (see chapter 18) may also have contributed.

Clearly, two factors contribute most significantly to Kouros's success. First, he has a remarkable ability to go without sleep for prolonged periods. Second, he has a capacity to maintain a high rate of energy consumption during these races. This parallels findings in cyclists competing in the formidable Tour de France. Only those cyclists whose rates of daily energy consumption equal their rates of energy utilization are able to finish the race (Brouns et al., 1989a, 1989b; Saris et al., 1989). Interestingly, the daily rates of energy expenditure of cyclists in the Tour de France (24,000 kJ; 5,700 Kcal) are considerably lower than the 7,736 to 15,367 Kcal achieved by Kouros during his ultradistance races.

Eleanor Adams

Englishwoman Eleanor Adams (see Figure 8.22) is considered by many to be the greatest woman ultradistance runner ever; in fact, her competitive abilities over a range of running distances have never been matched by any other male or female. She has set world track and road records at distances from 40 to 1,600 km and holds the women's course records for the 240-km Sparta-to-Athens Spartathlon, the 1,060-km Sydney-to-Melbourne race, and the 234-km Death-Valley-to-Mount-Whitney race in Death Valley in California, in which race she has recorded the second fastest ever time by any competitor of either gender. This is particulary remarkable for a native of Britain who trains in very moderate environmental conditions. In addition, she won the 86-km London-to-Brighton race in 1986.

Adams first began competitive running at school and represented Yorkshire on the track and in cross-country events at distances from 800 m to 4 km. She was also the county school champion at 800 m.

After leaving school she went to a university to study physical education and continued to compete in cross-country events. But after graduation, she taught, married, and soon had three active children and insufficient time to do much more than regular jogging. Her competitive instincts were reawakened in 1979, when she finished second in her age group in a 4-km fun run in Hyde Park. The next week she joined a local running club and entered an 8-km race. For the next year she raced regularly in road and cross-country races and in 1980 ran her first standard marathon, finishing second in the women's division in 3:24.

Figure 8.22 Eleanor Adams during a 6-day race in New York.
Note. Photo courtesy of Stan Wagon/*UltraRunning Magazine*.

In 1982 she won the same marathon in 2:54 and in the same year achieved her then-best standard marathon time of 2:49:52. Inspired by the first modern British 6-day race held in Nottingham in 1981, she entered her first 12-hour ultradistance race at Barnet in 1982 and set an unratified world track record at 50 miles (6:41:02). In October 1982 she set new world records at 20 miles (2:13:19) and at 25 miles (2:53:54) in a 100-km track race. In November she entered her first 24-hour race in Nottingham, completing 175 km and winning the mixed race. En route she set world records at 30 miles (3:35:42), 50 km (3:44:08), and 40 miles (4:55:17). The following year at the same site she set the then–world best of 653 km in the 6-day race. In the same year she set the women's record of 32:20 in the 240-km Spartathlon.

Her record-breaking zeal did not slow down in 1984. In February at Milton Keynes, she set the world 24-hour indoor record of 121-3/4 miles and set seven additional indoor records at 30 miles, 50 km, 40 miles, 50 miles, 100 km, 150 km, and 100 miles. In March in the 48-hour Mountauben race, she set new world records for 300 km (42:28:48), 200 miles (47:24:51), and 48 hours (202 miles and 77 yards). In July in a 6-day race in New York, she completed 734 km and in November in the Colac 6-Day Race she set a new world record with 806 km.

In the 1985 Montauben 48-hour race she set a new world record (207 miles 988 yards), and at the Nottingham 24-hour race in August she set world records at 200 km (20:48:35.3) and at 24 hours (138 miles 777 yards). In October she completed the Chicago 80-km race in 6:04:28, the second fastest ever time by a woman. In 1985 and 1986 she won the 1,060-km Sydney-to-Melbourne race, and in February 1986 she set a new 6-day race record of 808 km. In July of that year in Honefoss, Norway, she set track records at 160 km (15:25:46) and at 200 km (20:09:28). In September she won the London-to-Brighton race in 6:42:40.46.

In February 1987 in the Milton Keynes indoor race she set an absolute world 24-hour best of 227.26 km and also set world indoor records for every distance from 30 miles upward. In May she completed a 1,600-km round-Britain race in 16 days, 22 hours, and 51 minutes. In July, she completed the 234-km Death-Valley-to-Mount-Whitney run from the lowest to highest points in the United States in 53:03, the second fastest time ever by a runner of either gender.

In describing her training approach (E. Adams, 1987), Adams considers that good organization is the key to success for a woman ultradistance runner. She points out that after running, many women (unlike many men) return home to cook meals and attend to her children's needs. As a single parent, Adams has the added responsibility of providing for the financial needs of her children. She therefore has to fit her training around her family and her career.

She presently works as a substitute teacher and aims to work 3 days a week with 2 free weekdays, on each of which she runs 32 to 36 km in a single run. On workdays, she completes two to three sessions for a total of 32 km a day, giving an average weekly total of 160 km. Prior to the 1,600-km race around Britain, she increased her weekly average to 200 to 220 km/week. All her training is done alone at about 11 km/hr. On weekends she races any distance but chooses the longest available race. In summer she will also often race in midweek. These races form part of her speed training for the long ultradistance races, and she does not rest for these races. Nor does she train specifically for marathons; thus, she feels that her best marathon time of 2:48:23 run 6 weeks after the Death Valley run could be considerably improved.

Adams prefers to compete in a long race about every 6 weeks for a total of six to seven ultramarathons a year. She does not feel it necessary also to do very long runs in training.

Her racing advice for the very long ultradistance races is to first work on a support crew so that you get an impression of what happens in these races. She warns the prospective competitor always to expect the worst and to take everything that you expect to need and extras besides. This includes food, hot drinks, clothing for all weather, and several pairs of shoes. She notices that one's feet swell during a 6-day race so that it is necessary to take larger shoes as well. She also includes plans for when the race is done: Must she cook a meal for her family?

Adams's best times for different distances are the following: 10km— 36:04; 16 km—57:36; 21.1 km—1:18:21; 42.2 km—2:48:23, and 100 km—8:04:48.

Modern Training and Racing Methods for the Long Ultramarathons

The fact that Don Ritchie, whose training methods are not dissimilar to those of Bruce Fordyce, has achieved success in races of up to 200 km suggests that these methods would likely be optimum for races lasting up to 24 hours. Whether that approach is also optimum for distances up to 1,000 km or more is not known largely because few of the athletes competing at those distances have yet recorded how they train. One who has is Dave Cooper (1986), who has completed fifteen 24-hour races and is recognized as one of the world's most consistent performers in that event.

Cooper suggests that the preparation for a long ultramarathon should take about 16 weeks; the athlete increases training distance successively every second week from a base of 96 km/week to 112, 132, 148, and finally 160 km after 8 weeks. The athlete then runs 160 km/week for 6 weeks before tapering for the last 2 weeks before the competition. Cooper feels it is not necessary to train more than 160 km/week for these races, which suggests that the Fordyce/Ritchie approach for the short ultramarathon races is also appropriate for the long ultramarathons.

The racing strategy Cooper follows is the following:

Break the 24-hour race into three 8-hour periods and plan to run hardest in the last 8 hours. Break the 8-hour periods into hourly segments and walk for 100 to 200 m every 20 minutes. Drink and eat during these walking breaks. After 2 hours, start taking some solid food. (Cooper's favorite foods are chocolate bars, biscuits, sausage rolls, pork pies, and bananas, eaten frequently in small amounts.)

During a 48-hour race, eat a large meal after every 8-hour stretch, then sleep for about an hour.

During a 6-day race, run for the first 16 hours with the usual 20-minute walking breaks; then eat a large meal and sleep for about 2 hours. Break every day at noon and midnight for a short break and a light meal; break at 4:00 p.m. and 4:00 a.m. for a larger meal and a 2-hour sleep.

TRAINING METHODS OF THE ELITE

The overriding conclusion I have drawn from this survey of the training methods of some of the elite runners of the past 100 years is that available records are very inadequate. Thus, I suspect that at least some of what is written in this chapter may yet prove to be inaccurate. Nevertheless, the six points I have learned from these runners are as follows:

1. *Many of the athletes achieved remarkable performances on little training.* Examples of this are Walter George, who ran 16 km in under 50 minutes after training 2 miles/day; Deerfoot, who ran only marginally faster than George without ever training outside of actual racing; Alf Shrubb, who ran similar times on 67 km/week training; Paavo Nurmi, who trained only 6 months of the year and then only about 16 km/day, and Jim Peters, who in his marathon debut came within 4 minutes of the world marathon record despite training only 77 km/week. Similarly, Ron Hill ran some phenomenal marathons on relatively little training. Attention has also been drawn to the low training mileages but high training intensities of African runners like Kip Keino, Matthews Temane, and Xolile Yawa. It would be of great interest to know whether the same applies to the East African runners who now dominate world distance running.

This emphasizes the importance of genetic ability—not everyone can achieve such performances on so little training—and the law of diminishing returns. To improve their performances further, these athletes had to increase their training quite markedly. For example, Jim Peters had to double his training distance and maintain the same intensity in order to lower his marathon time by a further 12 minutes.

2. *The majority of these outstanding athletes were not outstanding athletes as children.* Neither Arthur Newton, Emil Zatopek, Jim Peters, Gordon Pirie, Kip Keino, Ron Hill, Frank Shorter, Steve Jones, Carlos Lopes, Matthews Temane, Wally Hayward, Jackie Mekler, Don Ritchie, Bruce Fordyce, Frith van der Merwe, or Charles Rowell gave notice of their subsequent talent while schoolchildren. On the other hand, Herb Elliott, Ron Clarke, Buddy Edelen, "Deek" de Castella, Yiannis Kouros, Grete Waitz, and Eleanor Adams all performed exceptionally while still young. This point is discussed further in chapter 17.

3. *Most of these athletes trained quite similarly.* Jim Peters ran 160 km/week at high intensity, averaging approximately 3:20/km. Grete Waitz also trains about 160 km/week. Edelen, Clarke, Hill, Shorter, de Castella, and Jones all ran up to 180 to 200 km/week, probably at similar intensities to that of Jim Peters but without apparent detriment to their performances. But Clayton, Pirie, and Bedford, who tried on occasion to run up to 256 km/week, probably proved that such weekly training distances are too great.

On the other hand, Herb Elliott, Kip Keino, and Matthews Temane all trained considerably less (up to 110 km/week), yet all set world records at distances from 1.5 to 21.1 km.

The best modern short- and long-ultramarathon runners, including Wally Hayward, Jackie Mekler, Don Ritchie, Bruce Fordyce, Yiannis Kouros, Frith van der Merwe, and Eleanor Adams, seldom ran much more than 160 to 180 km/week, considerably less than the training distances of Arthur Newton and the pedestrians like Charles Rowell, who ran up to 300 km/week!

Thus it seems that elite runners perform best when they train between 120 and 200 km/week, with an increasing likelihood that they will perform less well when they train more than 200 km/week, as vividly shown by the experiences of Ron Hill (see Figure 8.11). This is confirmed by the more recent experiences of Alberto Salazar, who set the since-disallowed world marathon record in 1981. Following his early marathon successes, which directly followed impressive performances, particulary at 10,000 m on the track, Salazar increased his weekly training distance from 176 to 208 km. He reasoned that more distance would allow him to run faster marathons. The result was that his training intensity fell, he was running "tired" most of the time, and his performances in both the 10,000 m and the marathon fell off alarmingly, culminating in a disappointing run in the 1984 Olympic Marathon. Salazar subsequently stated he would return to those training methods that originally worked for him (lower mileage, more speed work), he would again train as a 10,000-m runner, and he would only run another marathon when he was again able to run 10,000 m in a world-class time (Higdon, 1985). His retirement, announced in 1988, indicated that he had been unable to recapture the physical condition that had made him the world's most exciting marathoner of the early 1980s.

4. *Virtually all great runners achieved success at shorter distance races before gravitating to marathon and ultramarathon races.* Kolehmainen, Nurmi, Zatopek, Peters, Edelen, Clayton, Hill, Shorter, de Castella, Salazar, Jones, Lopes, Temane, and Waitz were all excellent track or cross-country exponents before they achieved success at longer distances on the road, especially in the marathon.

Similarly the great ultramarathon runners, Hayward, Mekler, Ritchie, Fordyce, Rowell, Kouros, and van der Merwe have all run fast over distances from 10 to 42.2 km.

This evidence proves beyond doubt that the faster the athlete at short distances, the greater that athlete's potential in the marathon and ultimately in the ultramarathon, as also shown in scientific studies (see chapter 2).

This truth was again confirmed in the 1984 Olympic Marathon, won by 1984 World Cross-Country champion Carlos Lopes, who 2 months before the Games ran the second fastest 10,000 m ever (27:17:41). Second place in the Olympic Marathon went to John Tracy, also a former World Cross-Country champion, who was running his first-ever marathon. Alberto Salazar ran his best marathons when he was training for 10,000 m on the track, and Steve Jones set his 1984 world marathon record in his first marathon, which he ran after training specifically for track and cross-country racing.

Thus it comes as no surprise that Matthews Temane, who has run the fastest mile at altitude, holds the world 21.1 km best; that Bruce Fordyce has the fastest mile, 5,000-m, and 10,000-m times of anyone running the Comrades Marathon; that Frith van der Merwe and Eleanor Adams are the fastest female marathon runners currently competing in the short and long ultramarathons; and that Yiannis Kouros is the fastest marathon runner competing in the long ultramarathons.

The truth is that if you are unable to beat these runners at 1 mile or 10,000 m, you will also never beat them at any other distance, even up to 700 km!

5. *All runners included regular speed work in their training.* Rowell, Hurst, Newton, De Mar, Hayward, and Mekler achieved greatness without paying much attention to speed training. Yet they were the last of that breed, and subsequent runners have shown that regular speed training is absolutely essential for success in marathon and ultramarathon races. Nurmi, Zatopek, Pirie, Keino, Edelen, and Shorter stressed interval training on the track; Peters, Elliott, Clarke, and Clayton ran at high intensity most of the time; and Hill, de Castella, Jones, Temane, Ritchie, Fordyce, Waitz, and Lucre combine hill training and interval sessions on the track. Clearly, no single method of speed training works for everyone.

The universal importance of speed training has been proven most convincingly by the ultramarathon runners, in particular by Bruce Fordyce and Don Ritchie, who have completed the training circle that began with the pedestrians like Charles Rowell and Arthur Newton.

Fordyce and Ritchie have shown that the Newtonian approach of running high mileage remains as a basic training principle but that subsequent improvements in running performance will not come simply by running more miles at the same relatively slow pace. Newtonian training is probably not even appropriate for the very long ultramarathon races of up to 700 km, as shown by the performances of Yiannis Kouros and Eleanor Adams, both of whom have achieved exceptional performances in races of up to 1,100 km on about one half the training of Rowell and Newton.

Runners such as Kouros and Adams have shown that improvement in the ultramarathon comes with better speed training, and they have proved that the statement of Krise and Squires (1982)—''There's nowhere to hide from speed; it will inevitably inhabit every distance'' (p. 102)—applies to the ultramarathon just as it does to all other distances.

Similarly, the low-mileage, high-intensity approaches of Matthews Temane and Xolile Yawa are reminiscent of the approaches of Jim Peters and Herb Elliott and suggest that the great distance runners of the future will be those who are genetically endowed to cope with short periods of very-high-intensity peaking training.

6. *The majority of these runners ran their best marathon races when they were still relatively inexperienced, and they did not improve much thereafter.* This was most clearly shown by Ron Hill, who ran his best marathon race in 1970 after he had been racing marathons seriously for only 1 year. During the

remaining 7-1/2 years of his serious athletic career, he would never again run as fast.

Similarly, despite his peaking approach to marathon racing, Frank Shorter ran his best-ever marathon in only his sixth attempt at the distance and did not improve further his last eight serious marathons. Rob de Castella set the world marathon record at his sixth attempt at the distance in 1981 and failed to improve further during the next 4 years despite heavy training and high expectations, especially for the 1984 Olympic Games Marathon (de Castella & Jenkinson, 1984). A similar fate has struck Steve Jones (whose average time for the first three marathons of his career was sub-2:08) and Carlos Lopes, both of whom have run poorly in recent years and shown relatively large decreases in performances.

It seems that each runner can run only a limited number of very fast marathons and that the runner's career will be foreshortened if those races are run in rapid succession, as in the cases of Hill, Lopes, and Jones. Sub-2:09 marathoner Mark Plaatjies, a former South African who now lives in the United States, has suggested that elite marathoners should race a maximum of one or two marathons a year for 2 years before taking a complete break from marathoning for a full 2 years. He notes that the cofavorites for the 1984 Olympic Marathon, de Castella

Table 8.32   Prior Marathon Racing Experience of the Olympic Games Marathon Winners (1932-1988)

Olympic year	Athlete	Number of marathons run before Olympics
1932	Juan Carlos Zabala	1
1936	Kitei Son	"A few"
1948	Delfo Cabrera	1
1952	Emil Zatopek	0
1956	Alain Mimoun	0
1960	Abebe Bikila	1
1964	Abebe Bikila	4
1968	Mamo Wolde	Unknown—converted track runner
1972	Frank Shorter	4 (in 13 months)
1976	Waldemar Cierpinski	4
1980	Waldemar Cierpinski	13
1984	Carlos Lopes	1
1988	Joan Benoit	11
	Gelindo Bordin	~6

Note. From "Olympic Marathon: Experience Not Required" by H. Beinart, 1986, *Track and Field News* (May), p. 45. Copyright 1986 by Track and Field News. Adapted by permission.

and Japan's Toshihiko Seiko, took 2 years to recover from their disappointing performances in that race (Plaatjies, 1986).

Another finding that adds credence to this general belief is that with only one exception, the winners of the Olympic Games Marathon up to 1984 have been relatively inexperienced marathoners (Beinart, 1986; see Table 8.32). If you were going to pick future winners of the Olympic Marathon, it seems that you should back the very fast 10,000-m runners who have run either no marathons or only one previous marathon.

9

Racing— 10 Km, Marathon, and Longer

"In every race there is a crucial moment when the body wants to quit. Then it needs imagination and mental tenacity to survive the crisis. Otherwise the penalty is defeat."

Derek Ibbotson (T. O'Connor, 1960)

"The music of the marathon is a powerful martial strain, one of those tunes of glory. It asks us to forsake pleasures, to discipline the body, to find courage, to renew faith and to become one's own person, utterly and completely."

George Sheehan (1980)

"If people were possessed by reason, running marathons would not work. . . . but we are not creatures of reason. We are creatures of passion. We do need reason, of course, to steer the ship. But if the winds of passion are not in our sails, all the steering in the world would get us nowhere."

Noel Carroll (1981)

"I like the marathon because it's one race where you can find out who's really the toughest. On the track, sometimes a guy can just pull away, and you want to stay with him but you don't have the leg speed. The marathon is slow enough that anyone

362

can stay with you if he wants, if he has the will. The marathon is ultimately a test of will.''

Alberto Salazar (1981)

"Rumour has it that there is life after running. There is even life after—or without—marathoning.''

Bob Glover and Pete Schuder (1983)

"The ability to run a race is an art unto itself.''

Liquori and Parker (1980)

"Every athlete has a certain number of races in him. There just isn't an infinite supply. When you get fit and good you can't just keep churning them out week after week.''

Brendan Foster (Lenton, 1983b)

"There's a little bit of the actor in all of us. We like being watched. We may run the race for ourselves, but it's significant that we do it in front of specta- tors. Without being on that stage, it just isn't the same—not for me, anyway.''

Grete Waitz and Gloria Averbuch (1986)

"Like many runners, I have a love/hate relation- ship with the race.''

Grete Waitz and Gloria Averbuch (1986)

The marathon is less a physical event than a spiritual encounter.

In infinite wisdom, God built into us a 32-km racing limit, a limit imposed by inadequate sources of the marathoner's prime racing fuel—carbohydrates. But, in human wisdom, we have decreed that the standard marathon must be 42.2 km long.

So it is in that physical "no-man's-land" that begins after the 30-km mark that the irrepressible appeal of the marathon lies. In those miles, as we approach the limits of human endurance, the marathon ceases to be a physical event. At this point runners learn something about themselves and their own views of life. Marathon runners have termed this point "the wall."

In this chapter we look at the techniques necessary to give the body its best chance over 10-km, marathon, and longer races, and we review how Arthur Newton prepared for his own races. We will see that each race is a carefully controlled experiment in which the results are essentially predictable; these results are predictable in direct relation to the care with which the athlete controls variables that determine racing performance. Only those athletes who see racing in this light are ever likely to do well on a regular, rather than a haphazard, basis.

We have looked at the variables that determine how well the body is physically prepared for the marathon, and we have discussed the variables determining mental preparation. The three most important physical variables, encompassed in the 9th and 13th laws of training and in Bruce Fordyce's points for ultramarathon training, are as follows: whether the athlete peaked for the race, whether the athlete underwent an adequate taper, and how recently the athlete ran a major race. The important mental variables are as follows: whether the athlete has analyzed his or her self-concept and trained to improve that concept, whether the athlete has practiced mental imagery and visualized the race beforehand, and whether the athlete has controlled arousal levels immediately before the race.

In this chapter we refine these concepts and consider other important variables that need equally careful control.

PHYSICAL AND PRACTICAL PREPARATION

Months 9 to 3 Before the Race

**RUN A SERIES OF PROGRESSIVELY LONGER RACES
BEFORE ATTEMPTING RACES OF 10 KM, 42 KM, OR LONGER**

This provides you with the opportunity to become accustomed to the many distractions that accompany races, and offers a chance to practice any strategies you might have evolved.

Weeks 12 to 4 Before a Marathon or Longer Race

**DO NOT COMPETE IN A RACE LONGER THAN 28 KM IN THE LAST
12 TO 16 WEEKS BEFORE A MARATHON OR ULTRAMARATHON**

Part of the tapering process is deciding how many races to run in the weeks and months leading up to the race (Newton's 5th rule of training; Fordyce's 6th point of ultramarathon training). Other experienced runners who have expressed themselves on this topic include Osler (1978), Galloway (1983), Squires (1982), and Glover and Schuder (1983).

All these writers agree that you need at least an 8-week recovery period after an all-out standard marathon race. I feel that this advice is too liberal and that full recovery of both muscles and mind takes a minimum of 12 to 14 weeks after a standard marathon.

Thus my advice is this: Don't race marathons competitively more than once every 4 to 6 months. Recovery from races shorter than 25 km is probably much quicker because these races do not appear to cause significant muscle damage. For these races, Osler's rule of 1 day of recovery per mile (or 2 kilometers) raced is probably adequate for the experienced runner; I suggest that the novice allow 2 days of recovery for each mile or 2 kilometers raced.

I believe that recovery from ultramarathon races probably takes disproportionately longer. I have found that I need a minimum of 12 weeks to even begin to start training properly after a short ultramarathon race of 90 km; I need a further 4 to 8 weeks before I can consider racing again. Furthermore, I have noticed that runners who compete in 160-km or 24-hour races may take 9 to 12 months of rest before they are able to race effectively. I suggest that although one may be able to race two marathons a year, anyone who wishes to race ultramarathons regularly for more than a few years should definitely limit these to one per year, possibly running one other long race either 3 to 4 months before or 4 to 5 months after that ultramarathon.

Bruce Fordyce has used this knowledge to his best advantage by not running any marathon or longer races at 100% effort in the months before the Comrades Marathon. Athletes who have tried to do otherwise have inevitably paid the price for their indiscretions (Fordyce's 6th point of ultramarathon training; Fordyce, 1985).

Fordyce has been able to win the London-to-Brighton race (which is held barely 3 months after the Comrades) 3 years in succession (1981 to 1983), and he established one of the world's fastest 80-km times in the 1983 London-to-Brighton race. He also won the 1984 American Medical Joggers Association (AMJA) 50-miler in Chicago and the 1987 80-km Nanisivik Midnight Sun Marathon, two races held soon after the Comrades Marathon. This I ascribe to the fact that he starts the Comrades Marathon slightly undertrained and, with the exception of 1982 and 1985, has not run himself out in any long-distance race.

I believe it is much better to race short distances more regularly during the buildup for a marathon or ultramarathon and to save the pain and the muscle damage for one all-out effort. I believe that the athlete is capable of only so many really good races and must use this capability with the utmost discretion. Furthermore, I have learned that performance in your own chosen race cannot be predicted from how you performed in any marathon you might have run during the 12 weeks before that race. Rather, I suspect that the best measure of condition for both marathon and ultramarathon distances is your most recent time over a short distance event of 8 to 16 km (Fordyce's 8th point of ultramarathon training) provided, of course, that you have been training for a distance event.

Weeks 4 to 1 Before the Event

ACCLIMATIZE YOURSELF TO HEAT
IF THE RACE IS TO BE RUN IN THE HEAT

An important problem faced by many runners is that most of their training is done in the cooler times of the day, either in the early mornings or late evenings. The result is that most of us are not adequately acclimatized for exercise in the heat. Thus we run less well in the heat than we might otherwise. Fortunately, most races are now held in the early morning, when environmental conditions are usually mild. However, for races that either start at midday or last most of the day, chances are that on occasion the environmental conditions will be unfavorable. Faced with this possibility, the wise athlete will undergo a period of heat acclimatization (see chapter 4).

Some degree of heat acclimatization can be achieved quite rapidly. Five to eight exercise sessions, each up to 2 hours, on consecutive days in the heat produce acclimatization that lasts for several weeks. However, it seems that there are quite large differences in the length of time different marathon runners believe they require for full acclimatization (Browne, 1986). Some feel that acclimatization can be achieved in days; others believe that even 6 months is too little (Browne, 1986). Heat acclimatization likely is only ever optimum in those who are born in the hotter parts of the world and who train regularly in the heat.

Thus, sometime in the weeks leading up to a hot-weather race, you should undergo heat acclimatization either by running in the midday heat or by training in a track suit. How Ron Daws used the track suit technique to earn a place in the 1968 Olympic Marathon is detailed in his book (Daws, 1977) and should be read by those who are forced to compete in the heat but who live and train in cool climates.

In brief, Daws collapsed with heat exhaustion at the 40-km mark of the 1964 United States Olympic Marathon trials, run at midday in New York City with dry bulb temperatures of 96 °F. The race was won by Buddy Edelen (see chapter 8), who had been training in England in temperatures of approximately 50 °F. Edelen's secret was that he trained each day wearing five layers of clothing. Daws subsequently used the same method for heat acclimatization; his technique was to train with five layers of clothing 4 days a week for 3 weeks, a total of 12 training days. He found that it was not possible to train each day with full clothing, so he trained in normal running attire on alternate days.

As a result of his attention to detail, Daws comfortably won positions on United States marathon teams, the selection races for which were run in extreme heat on each occasion.

If your race is to be run at a time of day at which you do not normally train, then doing at least some training at that time of day will probably be helpful.

ACCLIMATIZE YOURSELF TO ALTITUDE
IF THE RACE IS RUN AT ALTITUDE

If you reside at sea level and are forced to compete at altitude, you should undergo at least some short-term altitude acclimatization. However, certain absolutes exist about competing at altitude, and these should be understood by all sea-level athletes who, by choice or necessity, must compete at altitude.

Performance at altitudes greater than 1,000 m (3,281 feet) is always inferior to sea-level performance in all races lasting more than 2 minutes. In contrast, performance in shorter races is enhanced by altitude, and the majority of the men's world records in running events of 400 m or shorter have been set at altitude (see Figure 11.8).

We don't know why performance is impaired in races lasting longer than 2 minutes. One theory is that the major portion of energy utilized during such races comes from oxygen-dependent pathways (see Figure 2.1). As the oxygen content of the air decreases with increasing altitude, so the maximum oxygen-transport capacity ($\dot{V}O_2$max) falls, resulting in a reduced ability for energy production by oxygen-dependent pathways. I believe that the oxygen deficit either acts directly to impair muscle contractility or causes the athlete's blood lactate levels to rise more rapidly and to reach limiting steady-state levels at a lower running speed than occurs at sea level. Runners who try to run at the same speeds at altitude as

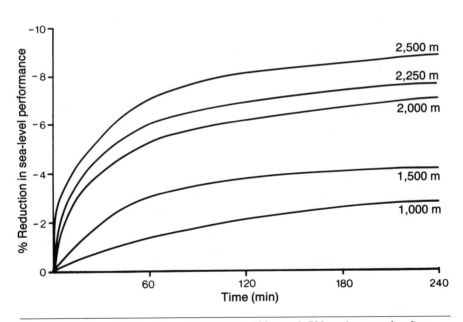

Figure 9.1 The effect of different altitudes (1,000 m to 2,500 m above sea level) on running performance.

at sea level may become excessively short of breath because their blood lactate levels, which indirectly stimulate breathing, are higher than usual. Interestingly, residence and training at medium altitude do not alter the detrimental effect of increasing altitude on $\dot{V}O_2$max; neither do they increase $\dot{V}O_2$max at sea level (Tucker et al., 1984). The extent to which performance is reduced in races of different durations at different altitudes is shown in Figure 9.1.

Performance in the sprint events from 100 to 400 m is improved because air resistance is reduced at altitude (see Figure 11.8). In addition, these events are not affected by the body's reduced capacity for oxygen transport, because they rely on energy produced mainly by oxygen-independent pathways (see Figure 3.11). The 800-m race appears to be the race in which the benefits of the reduced air resistance exactly match the detrimental effects of the reduced oxygen-transport capacity. Thus, at the 1968 Olympics the time in the 800-m race equaled the world record, whereas times in all the shorter sprints were improvements on the existing world records (see Figure 11.8).

The second absolute of altitude competition is that sea-level athletes are always at a disadvantage when competing at altitude against altitude residents in events lasting longer than 2 minutes. This is because the sea-level athlete suffers a dramatic fall in work performance and in $\dot{V}O_2$max immediately upon arriving at altitude, and this reduction corrects only slowly. Thus, $\dot{V}O_2$max may fall as much as 15% on the second day after the athlete arrives at altitude of 2,200 m above sea level. Over the next few weeks, $\dot{V}O_2$max gradually improves to return to a value, at altitude, 10% below the sea-level $\dot{V}O_2$max (Dill, 1968). The practical implications of this are that the sea-level athlete who must compete at altitude should compete either immediately upon arriving at altitude or not until 3 or more weeks after arriving at altitude. The worst time to compete at altitude is within 3 to 6 days after first arriving at that altitude.

In reality, however, the best way to acclimatize to altitude is to live at altitude 22 hours a day and to travel to sea level for training sessions. The benefits are that the body acclimatizes to altitude by living there, not by exercising there. Indeed the problem with training at altitude is that because of the reduced oxygen content in the air, the athlete is never able to train quite as fast as he or she would at sea level. Thus, when training at altitude, the athlete's racing fitness for sea-level competition falls slightly, despite an enhanced ability to perform at altitude. By training at sea level and living at altitude, the athlete adapts to altitude without losing sea-level racing edge, thus enjoying the best of both worlds.

Incidentally, the same argument explains why training at altitude does not improve sea-level performance, at least in the shorter track and distance races in which "leg speed" is essential: It is not possible to train sufficiently fast at altitude. On the other hand, altitude training could conceivably enhance performance in ultramarathon races, which are run at much slower speeds (approximately 16 km/hr). The good athlete who trains at altitude will have no difficulty running faster than 16 km/hr in training and therefore will retain sufficient leg speed for ultramarathon races. Yet that athlete will always be running at a higher percentage of $\dot{V}O_2$max, at higher blood lactate levels, and therefore harder than he or she would if training at the same speed at sea-level.

UNDERGO A DECENT TAPER

The critical importance of a decent taper was described in chapter 5 (Newton's 9th rule of training).

Indeed, if athletes do the same amount of training, they will benefit more by performing that training at altitude, as their performance at both sea level and altitude will increase more than if they did *the same volume of training* at sea level (Terrados et al., 1988). Altitude training reduces blood lactate levels more during submaximal exercise than does sea level training and increases muscle capillarization more (Terrados et al., 1988).

Bruce Fordyce tapers for the last 3 weeks before his ultramarathons and runs very little in the last 10 days before a race (see Tables 8.27 and 8.28). This tapering procedure has worked for him and I suggest that his is a basic approach that could be followed by all.

Arthur Newton's rule was to reduce training by 15% 3 weeks before the race and by a further 10% 2 weeks before the race. He continued to train quite hard until 4 days before competition. Thus, he tapered much less than does Fordyce.

Few other authors have discussed the importance of tapering. Galloway (1983) advised that training should be reduced by 30% 2 weeks before a marathon race and that one should only run 30% of the usual weekly total distance in the first 4 days of the last week before the race. For the last 3 days he suggested running only 2 to 5 km daily.

The Last Week Before the Race

DECIDE ON THE EFFORT OR PACE THAT YOU WILL EXPEND DURING THE RACE

There are essentially two ways to run a race: according to your body or according to your watch. When running according to your body, you monitor effort; when running according to your watch, you monitor pace.

For the first few races, run according to your body and start every race very slowly at an effort you are certain you can maintain for the entire distance. It is disastrous to start too fast in any race but starting too fast is especially bad in your first long race. Bitter experience has shown me that any time gained in the first half of any race is paid for in double during the second half.

The first-time racer certainly can follow no better advice than the motto of a popular North American running club: "Start slowly, then taper off."

The golden rule is that the effort for both halves of the race must be as equal as possible. Never listen to those who advocate running the first half of any race faster so that you will have spare time to cushion your reduced pace in the second half. In fact, the fast early pace is the very reason for the fade in the second half. The great runners have exquisite abilities to judge not only pace but effort. My personal preference, gained from many unhappy experiences, is to aim to run the second half of each race slightly faster than the first. I have found that it is always preferable to speed up in the second half when others are slowing down. This gives the impression that you are running much faster than you really are, and the mental lift of passing others is great.

Even when you are running a race according to effort rather than pace, you need to have some idea of how fast you are likely to run. This is another important reason you need to have run previous races of 10, 16, 21.1, and 32 km before attempting a marathon; the times you run in those races will allow you to predict the time you can expect to run in the marathon. The tables devised by C.T.M. Davies and Thompson (1979; Table 2.3), J. Daniels and Gilbert (1979; Table 2.4), Tom Osler (1978; Table 2.6), Gardner and Purdy (1970; Table 2.7) and Mercier et al. (1985; Figure 2.8) give predicted marathon and ultramarathon times on the basis of performances in shorter races.

For example, let us assume that your times in races of those four distances were 37:21, 1:01:54, 1:22:38, and 2:08:54. Table 9.1 shows that according to the data of J. Daniels and Gilbert (1979), each of these performances equates to a $\dot{V}O_2$max of 56.3 ml/kg/min and a final marathon time of 2:52:34. This indicates that you are well trained, because your performances do not deteriorate with distance.

In contrast, if your times for those races are as shown in Table 9.2, your performance clearly deteriorates with increasing distance. You are obviously inadequately trained for the longer distances and cannot expect to run the standard marathon even in the time predicted from your 32-km time. You should probably aim to run the marathon as if your predicted $\dot{V}O_2$max were only 40.1 ml/kg/min, which would give you a predicted marathon time of 3:48:57.

Table 9.1 Predicting Likely Standard Marathon Times on the Basis of Performance in Shorter Distance Races

Distance (km)	Your time	Predicted $\dot{V}O_2$max (ml/kg/min)	Predicted time
10	37:21	56.3	2:52:34
16	1:01:54	56.3	2:52:34
21.1	1:22:38	56.3	2:52:34
32	2:08:54	56.3	2:52:34

Table 9.2   Predicting Likely Standard Marathon Times on the Basis of Performance in Shorter Distance Races

Distance (km)	Your time	Predicted $\dot{V}O_2max$ (ml/kg/min)	Predicted time
10	37:21	56.3	2:52:34
16	1:05:23	52.8	3:02:06
21.1	1:31:59	49.7	3:11:35
32	2:37:37	44.5	3:30:23

Predicting the time you are likely to run in the standard marathon on the basis of your times at shorter distances is important because very few novices have the slightest idea of the times they are likely to run in their first marathons. One North American study (Franklin et al., 1978) revealed that 65% of first- and second-time marathoners predicted they would run faster than they actually did. Worse, 15% of the first-time and 8% of the second-time marathoners predicted they would run 1 hour faster than they subsequently did! In contrast, the authors found that experienced marathoners could predict their marathon times to within a few minutes.

If you are running the marathon "cold," never having competed in any of these distances and having no idea of what you can do, only one tactic remains. Line up 5 m behind the last row of runners at the marathon start and start the race in the slowest pace that will get you to the finish in under 4:30 (i.e., 6:23/km), if that is the final cut-off time. If after the 34-km mark you are sure that this pace is too slow, then, and only then, is it safe to speed up.

Having decided on the pace at which you will run the marathon, you can then calculate the split times you will run at 1, 8, 10, 16, 21.1, and 32 km (see Table 9.3). How this information is incorporated in the prerace mental strategy is described later.

CARBOHYDRATE LOAD WITH OR WITHOUT THE CARBOHYDRATE-DEPLETION REGIME

The scientific rationale for the carbohydrate-depletion/carbohydrate-loading regime was detailed in chapter 3 (see Figure 3.5), and sample diets for the carbohydrate-depletion and carbohydrate-loading phases are included in chapter 15.

To recap, the basic theory holds that the body's carbohydrate stores are filled more completely if a very-high-carbohydrate diet is eaten for the last 3 to 7 days before competition. In this carbohydrate-loaded state the athlete can expect to

Table 9.3 Pacing Schedules for the Standard Marathon

Distance (km)	1	8	10	16	21.1	32	42.2
Time	3:00	24:00	30:00	48:00	1:03:18	1:36:00	2:06:36
	3:10	25:22	31:42	50:43	1:06:53	1:41:26	2:13:46
	3:20	26:38	33:18	53:17	1:10:16	1:46:34	2:20:32
	3:30	28:00	35:00	56:00	1:13:51	1:52:00	2:27:42
	3:40	29:22	36:42	58:43	1:17:26	1:57:26	2:34:52
	3:50	30:38	38:18	1:01:17	1:20:49	2:02:34	2:41:38
	4:00	32:00	40:00	1:04:00	1:24:24	2:08:00	2:48:48
	4:10	33:22	41:42	1:06:43	1:27:59	2:13:26	2:55:58
	4:20	34:38	43:18	1:09:17	1:31:22	2:18:34	3:02:44
	4:30	36:00	45:00	1:12:00	1:34:27	2:24:00	3:09:54
	4:40	37:22	46:42	1:14:43	1:38:32	2:29:26	3:17:04
	4:50	38:38	48:18	1:17:17	1:41:25	2:34:34	3:23:50
	5:00	40:00	50:00	1:20:00	1:45:30	2:40:00	3:31:00
	5:10	41:22	51:42	1:22:43	1:49:05	2:45:26	3:38:10
	5:20	42:38	53:18	1:25:17	1:52:28	2:50:34	3:44:56
	5:30	44:00	50:00	1:28:00	1:56:03	2:56:00	3:52:06
	5:40	45:22	56:42	1:30:43	1:59:08	3:01:26	3:59:16
	5:50	46:38	58:18	1:33:17	2:03:01	3:06:34	4:06:02
	6:00	48:00	1:00:00	1:36:00	2:06:36	3:12:00	4:13:12
	6:10	49:22	1:01:42	1:38:43	2:10:11	3:17:26	4:20:22
	6:20	50:38	1:03:18	1:41:17	2:13:34	3:22:34	4:27:08
	6:30	52:00	1:05:00	1:44:00	2:17:09	3:28:00	4:34:18
	6:40	53:22	1:06:42	1:46:43	2:20:44	3:33:26	4:41:28
	6:50	54:38	1:08:18	1:49:17	2:24:07	3:38:34	4:48:14
	7:00	56:00	1:10:00	1:52:00	2:27:42	3:44:00	4:55:24
	7:10	57:22	1:11:42	1:54:43	2:31:17	3:47:26	5:02:34
	7:20	58:38	1:13:18	1:57:17	2:34:10	3:54:34	5:09:20
	7:30	1:00:00	1:15:00	2:00:00	2:38:15	4:00:00	5:16:30
	7:40	1:01:22	1:16:42	2:02:43	2:41:20	4:05:26	5:23:40
	7:50	1:02:38	1:18:18	2:05:17	2:45:13	4:10:34	5:30:26
	8:00	1:04:00	1:20:00	2:08:00	2:48:48	4:16:00	5:37:36
	8:10	1:05:22	1:21:42	2:10:43	2:52:23	4:21:26	5:44:46
	8:20	1:06:38	1:23:18	2:13:17	2:55:16	4:26:34	5:51:32
	8:30	1:08:00	1:25:00	2:16:00	2:59:21	4:32:00	5:58:42
	8:40	1:09:22	1:26:42	2:18:43	3:02:56	4:37:26	6:05:52
	8:50	1:10:38	1:28:18	2:21:17	3:06:19	4:42:34	6:12:38
	9:00	1:12:00	1:30:00	2:24:00	3:09:54	4:48:00	6:19:48
	9:10	1:13:22	1:31:42	2:26:43	3:13:59	4:53:26	6:26:58
	9:20	1:14:38	1:33:18	2:29:17	3:16:22	4:58:34	6:33:44
	9:30	1:16:00	1:35:00	2:32:00	3:20:27	5:04:00	6:40:54
	9:40	1:17:22	1:36:42	2:34:43	3:24:02	5:09:26	6:48:04
	9:50	1:18:38	1:38:18	2:37:17	3:27:25	5:14:34	6:54:50
	10:00	1:20:00	1:40:00	2:40:00	3:31:00	5:20:00	7:02:00

perform better, especially in events lasting longer than 90 minutes but also probably in events as short as 4 minutes. The issues that remain unresolved are

- whether the 3-day carbohydrate-depletion phase that precedes the carbohydrate-loading phase is necessary,
- whether any dangers are associated with the depletion phase of the diet,
- for how long one should load carbohydrates (see Figure 3.5),
- what type of carbohydrate (simple or complex) one should eat,
- the exact amount of carbohydrate (in grams) one should eat each day during the loading phase, and
- whether one needs to supplement the carbohydrate intake by drinking commercially available "carbohydrate-loading drinks" during the loading phase.

All these questions are answered in greater detail in chapter 15. I feel that it is probably unnecessary and unwise to follow an absolutely rigid 3-day depletion phase and that a modified depletion phase in which carbohydrate is restricted and one runs only short distances in training is probably better. However, I am not convinced that the depletion phase is necessarily as dangerous as some have suggested.

The loading phase need last only 3 days, during which you should mainly eat complex carbohydrates. The amount of carbohydrate eaten each day during the loading phase should be 500 g. Thus, you need to take some form of carbohydrate-loading drink during this period, because it is essentially impossible to eat 500 g of carbohydrate on a normal diet (see Table 15.2).

BEGIN THE MENTAL PREPARATION FOR THE RACE

Most of the details of the psychological aspects of running are discussed in chapter 7. The essential features are to understand yourself, your mental weaknesses and strengths, and your self-concept. When you are competing, it is important to control your anxiety and arousal levels before the race and to "run the race in your mind" (i.e., visualize the race) as often as possible. Another feature not mentioned by psychologists is to store "creative energy" by avoiding all creative activities in the last few days before the race.

Storing Creative Energy.   During this period of mental preparation, runners are frequently at their most eccentric.

A colleague who missed one ultramarathon because of influenza now refuses to work for the last 7 days before the race. When not running during this period, he dons a surgical mask, takes leave of his family, and cloisters himself in a sterile environment, accompanied only by a library of Eastern philosophy. At such times, only those who are known to be free of marathon-destroying germs have access to him.

This reaction should not be regarded as unusual. The correctly trained runner is on the knife's edge and is mildly irritable and at an increased risk for infection.

The runner has worked hard for what will be a once-only chance and is physically ready. Now this runner must seek out the correct environment so that the final arbiter of marathon performance—the mind—can be equally well prepared.

Like my colleague who finds his answers in Eastern philosophy, the runner aiming for a best marathon must devote time during the last week to mental preparation for the race. For the lonely long-distance runner about to face a most taxing ordeal, this mental preparation, I suspect, is best done in solitude.

The first priority is to store creative energy. As discussed in chapter 5, running requires mental energy; if this energy has been exhausted in other pursuits, there will be insufficient energy remaining to compete the race successfully. I discovered this as a surgical intern when working over 100 hours a week. In a standard marathon after 30 km, for the first and only time I lacked the mental energy to pull me through the wall. Now I do not race marathons when I am working too hard. Should I wish to race during such times, the race must be run at a gentle, sociable pace with absolutely no concern for my finishing time.

There are at least three ways by which runners harness their creative energies prior to a race. First, they reduce their training loads. This not only allows the body time to recover but stores the mental energy normally used during training. Second, they begin to sleep more, to relax, and to avoid any extraneous stresses, particularly at work. Acute sleep deprivation impairs performance during prolonged exercise (B.J. Martin, 1981) and is therefore to be avoided. Interestingly, resistance to this effect differs markedly between individuals (B.J. Martin, 1981). Third, runners preparing for a race avoid any new creative activities at work.

Run the Race in Your Mind (Mentally Rehearse).   The next important mental strategy is to run the race in your mind beforehand. The importance of setting realistic goals and then "segmenting" the distance into manageable proportions is described in chapter 7. Clearly these skills are not developed overnight; you will need many years of practice and many races to properly develop this ability.

After you have established realistic goals along the lines set forth earlier in this chapter, your task is to mentally break up the race into small segments and to imagine yourself running each of these sections in turn, finishing the sections in the times (see Table 9.3) that you have set for yourself.

I have found that the 10-km race must be segmented into single kilometers; this race is really too short to require additional tactics. The standard marathon breaks up into two 16-km races with a final 10-km stretch tacked on the end. Thus, when preparing to race the standard marathon I set myself time goals for the 16- and 32-km markers. In this way I never concentrate on a goal more than 16 km away. To ensure that everything is going according to plan during the race, I might check my pace over various individual kilometers along the route. The positive reinforcement engendered by knowing that you have run another kilometer in the correct time has a remarkable psychological effect.

In mental practice for the marathon I visualize the times I have set for myself. Then, for the last 10 km of the actual race I run from each kilometer marker to the next, timing myself for each marker. If I am on time at 32 km the motivation to maintain my pace through each of those last 10 individual markers is very high. On the other hand, if these intermediate goals are not achieved, it means that I am having a bad day, and my subsequent goals in this race must be modified accordingly.

Of course, today's runner has it very easy. When I ran my first marathons in the early 1970s, the only marker board we were likely to see was at 32 km. Thus, it was impossible to segment to the same degree as is now possible with marker boards placed every kilometer or mile, even in the ultramarathons. The mental agonies we endured because we had no such marker boards were enormous.

The final essential mental rehearsal is to visualize the last section of the race and to visualize how to deal with what runners call "bad patches" (which Rushall, 1979, refers to as "dead spots") and the very real fatigue that develops during races.

Dead spots occur when you lose mental control either because you have grown tired of concentrating on the same mental track or because a powerful distraction has suddenly appeared.

When you hit a dead spot, try to avoid panic and try to regain mental control as rapidly as possible. The best way to do this is to introduce positive self-statements. My approach is to concentrate on the goals in the race I have already achieved; I remind myself how well I am doing and how proud I will be of my performance. If this fails, I think about some aspect of my work that is going well and is giving me pleasure.

The second problem is how to cope with the very real fatigue that occurs after 32 km in the standard marathon and, to a far worse degree, after 70 km in a short ultramarathon or after 120 km in a long ultramarathon.

The key is to prepare mentally for when the pain will begin. In the marathon, the pain begins to become a problem after about 28 km and in the ultramarathon after either 60 or 100 km. Thus, in your mental preparation you must imagine the feelings of increasing fatigue that you will experience and how these will affect you.

Another important mental tactic is to know that when the discomfort comes, it is at first worse on the uphills. I comfort myself by saying that the next downhill will allow me to recover. Because I already know the course, I know precisely when the next downhill section is due and so can more easily motivate myself to hang on just a little bit longer until the next downhill.

However, when the fatigue becomes all-embracing and running downhill is just as tiresome as running uphill, then you must confront the pain, accept it, and concentrate all your effort on not allowing the pain to slow you down. This is done by concentrating on your time through each successive kilometer. A technique I have found useful is to think only of getting to the next marker in a particular time. However tired I am, I can usually imagine getting to the next marker. With time, the individual kilometers add up, and finally I arrive within striking distance of the finish. Usually I know I am home when I get to within 4 km of the finish. Once again, positive self-statements during this phase of the race are very helpful.

Having decided on a clear running strategy, you only have to convince yourself that it is possible.

Arriving at the Site of Competition

If the competition is to be held at altitude and you reside at sea level, the best time to arrive is either immediately before or 3 or more weeks before competition.

If the competition is to be held away from your home but at low altitude, the following rules apply:

- Arrive at least 2 days before the race and allow 1 day of recovery for each day spent driving there.
- Allow 1 day of recovery for each 3 hours spent flying there.
- If the competition is very far away so that traveling involves crossing one or more time zones, allow 1 day of recovery for each time zone crossed.

When possible you should check the following points about travel and accommodation arrangements so that the effects of all unfamiliar events and sights are reduced to a minimum and as many minor frustrations as possible are avoided (Liebetrau, 1982).

If you are flying to the site of competition, you should ensure that travel to the hotel has been organized. Check that the hotel rooms are comfortable, free from noise, and close to those of your friends. Noisy rooms in hotels are those near the street fronts, the kitchen, the lounge, the dining room, and the bar; all these must be avoided. Arrange this well in advance by asking the hotel manager for details about the allocated room. At the same time, inquire about the availability of any special foods that you require and other facilities such as saunas and swimming pools that you may need. Finalize travel plans to the site of competition.

On arrival 2 days before the race, familiarize yourself with the room. Liebetrau (1982) suggested that you reduce the unfamiliarity of the room by taking along some personal possessions such as photographs, the pillows on which you normally sleep, and the bedding and pajamas in which you have recently slept. This ensures that unfamiliar smells and skin contact do not interfere with your ability to fall asleep and to stay asleep.

The Day Before Competition

DRIVE OVER THE COURSE FOR A FINAL TIME, PAYING SPECIAL ATTENTION TO THE LAST SECTION OF THE RACE

Even if you know the course very well and have visualized yourself running it, you should still drive the course one last time, paying special attention to the last section. As you drive the course, again imagine how you will feel on race day as you run the various sections, and remind yourself of the positive self-statements that you will use as you become progressively more tired.

EAT WISELY

A disconcerting experience for any runner is to have the race interrupted by an unscheduled "pit stop." The emotion of the moment combined with a few hours of hard running will shake loose even the most resolute bowels.

One way to avoid a pit stop is to ensure that your intestine is empty before the race. This is achieved by eating only highly refined, low-bulk carbohydrate foods that leave little residue (e.g., white bread, cookies, sweets, rice, and potatoes) for the last 16 to 24 hours before the race.

Recently, I have begun to suspect that another reason many runners have to visit the toilet during marathon races is because they have very mild forms of milk or other food intolerances. Sheehan (1975) was the first to observe that the stress of competitive running caused some athletes to have gastrointestinal disturbances, which were prevented if the athlete avoided milk or other dairy products either completely or for the last 24 hours before competition. I have cured my own racing pit-stop problems in this way and have helped others with this simple advice. It is also possible that intolerance to other foods, such as gluten, may be the problem.

ASSEMBLE YOUR RUNNING GEAR THE NIGHT BEFORE AND ENSURE THAT YOU HAVE EVERYTHING

Pin your race numbers to your vest and drape the vest on a chair near your bed. Seeing your racing numbers on awakening will help motivate you. Pack a gym bag with petroleum jelly, toilet paper, extra safety pins, any food supplements you require during the race, and a snack for after the race. Also include alternate clothing, in case of weather changes before or during the race, a change of shoes, and clothing for after the race. If you are unsure whether or not water will be provided at the start of the race, also pack a bottle of water.

GET ADEQUATE REST

Go to bed at your normal time. This is necessary because you are conditioned to awakening at a certain time each morning, and this time is not influenced by how late you go to bed. Going to bed late at night thinking that you will simply awake later the next morning will not work. You will wake at the same time and therefore will sleep fewer hours. It is especially important to go to bed very early the second to the last night before the race and sleep as many hours as possible that night.

But despite having gone to bed at the correct time, you may experience any of three types of sleeping disorders, especially the night before competition. You may not be able to go to sleep, you may awaken frequently throughout the night, or you may awaken early and be unable to go back to sleep.

To enable yourself to fall asleep quickly, use the relaxation procedure described in chapter 7. Another technique suggested by Liebatrau (1982) is the "calm scene" visual imagery. With this technique, you imagine that you are in a tranquil place that you have previously visited. Imagine in the greatest possible detail every feature of the place, including all the sensations that you can see, hear, smell, or feel. As you practice this technique, the scene becomes more vivid and more detailed. After many trials, you can identify which scene works most effectively.

Even when using these techniques, you probably will not sleep very deeply the night before a major race. This is something that many novice runners fear because they are concerned that this may make them run less well. In fact, the opposite is probably true. The night before the race the mind is restless because it is preparing for what lies ahead. My impression is that a good night's sleep before the race probably indicates that the runner is not properly psyched up for the race. The time to sleep well is the last week before and especially the second to the last night before the race.

What about sex the night before the race? Old ideas, it seems, die hard. Tom Osler (1978) wrote that in ancient Greece "sexual intercourse (for athletes) was strictly prohibited" (p. 125) because it was believed to sap the athlete's strength. The earliest reference I could find to this topic was mentioned "as delicately as possible" by Andrews (1903), because it had not "been treated in any previous text-book on training." He wrote the following:

> I have come to the conclusion, based upon long experience, that the married state is not the best for an athlete, and that in all cases continence is essential to success.

> When, under my system, every organ of the body is being brought by strict training to the fullest state of health and vigour, there may very probably be a tendency to involuntary losses during sleep. These losses are so weakening, and so certain to defeat all the trainer's best endeavours, that they must be effectually prevented. (p. 57)

Current feeling is that sexual activity, in moderation, has no effect whatsoever on physical performance. In the words of the famous American baseball coach Casey Stengel: "It's not the sex but the staying up all night looking for it, that fatigues the athlete" (Mirkin & Hoffman, 1978, p. 169).

RACE DAY AND RECOVERY

The Day of Competition

WAKE UP CORRECTLY

Both Liebetrau (1982) and Rushall (1979) stressed the importance of correct waking procedures for determining how you will feel and perform during the rest of the day. These authors give the following guidelines:

- Avoid the use of an alarm clock with a loud and jarring ring, because this will awaken you with a shock. You should be "nudged" awake by a gentle alarm or by a quiet knock on the door. My approach is to use the same (gentle) alarm that I use each morning and to which I am therefore accustomed.

- The drink of your choice should be available so that you can awake gradually while enjoying the sensory pleasure of drinking.

- Repeat some positive self-statements about how well you feel, what a beautiful day it is, and how excited you are about the race.

- Smile and generally get yourself into a happy, humorous frame of mind. Then do some stretching and deep-breathing exercises. As soon as you are in a good, positive mood, get dressed but continue repeating positive self-statements.

- Avoid thinking about the competition, because this will produce anxiety and high levels of arousal too early before competition. If you begin to feel anxious or excited, practice the mental-relaxation techniques described in chapter 7.

DRESS APPROPRIATELY FOR THE RACE CONDITIONS

Heat is a major problem in many summer marathons, so it is essential to dress as lightly as possible. Running pants and vests should be lightweight and porous. The best racing vests are of the nylon "fish net" variety. However, when conditions are likely to be cold, especially if it's also wet and windy, runners are at risk for hypothermia (see chapter 18), especially thin runners with little muscle bulk. Under these conditions, wear more than one layer of clothing, cover your arms, and make every attempt to stay as dry as possible. Wind when combined with wet conditions is the greatest enemy, and the only sure protection under such conditions is to wear rainproof clothing at least over your upper body. Goretex running jackets appear to be the most effective such clothing.

The shoes you race in should be sufficiently broken in, to be comfortable, but not so old they are worn out. To prevent having a pair of shoes wear out a few days before a major race, leaving no time for breaking in a new pair, I keep aside a pair of broken-in shoes, and use them only for racing. One absolute rule is never to run a long race in a pair of shoes you have not previously used in one or more long training runs.

I wear socks during ultramarathon races. If I am concerned about the possibility of blistering, I apply petroleum jelly to my feet before putting on the socks.

A question that always arises is whether the weight of racing shoes influences the time taken to complete the course. In fact, some evidence shows that very light racing shoes can reduce the energy cost of running up to 3%, and over 42 km that is quite a saving (Cavanagh, 1980).

But the reason that racing shoes (racing flats) are able to save this energy is because they sacrifice on certain other important characteristics. For example, Cavanagh (1980) found that when comparing the best training shoe with the worst racing flat, there were differences of 100% and 400% in rearfoot and forefoot cushioning in favor of the training shoe. He concluded that it is unwise for all but the best runners to race in racing shoes, because the risks are likely to outweigh the benefits. And the risks are sore feet, added stress on the musculo-skeletal system, and a greater chance of injury.

So especially for the novice unused to the stress of marathon running, it is safest to run in a comfortable, sturdy training shoe. Fancy racing shoes should be avoided until you are an expert or have been running and racing for 2 or more years without injury.

A final essential piece of "clothing" is sufficient sheets of toilet paper for one pit stop in a marathon, two in an ultramarathon. Enclose these in a plastic bag with a watertight seal of the type used by banks as money containers. Then store the bag in a pocket in your running shorts. The pocket should also be large enough to accommodate any food that you may wish to take with you, especially if you are running an ultramarathon. If your shorts do not have such a pocket, sew one into them.

The final prerace preparations are to apply petroleum jelly to those areas of the body that are liable to chafe (in particular the groin), to cut the toenails, and to apply sticking plaster to the nipples to prevent "jogger's nipples" or "jogger's breasts."

MAKE YOUR PRERACE MEAL A WINNER

This is another topic that causes great anguish among novice runners. In fact, what you eat for breakfast before an early-morning marathon probably does not greatly influence running performance. This is because virtually all of the energy required for the marathon has been stored before the race. Figure 3.8 shows that muscle glycogen stores are near maximum after 3 days of carbohydrate loading and will certainly not be increased in any meaningful way by the small amount of additional carbohydrate eaten at breakfast.

Why bother eating breakfast at all? The reason for this is to restock the glycogen stores in the liver. After an overnight fast, the liver carbohydrate stores will be depleted by about 50 g, and optimum liver carbohydrate stores are essential if blood glucose levels are to be maintained near the end of marathon or longer races. However, even after an all-night fast, liver glycogen stores will be adequate to prevent hypoglycemia from developing during a 10-km race. Thus, there is no need to eat breakfast before a 10-km race.

The prerace breakfast should contain easily digestible carbohydrates (e.g., bread, cornflakes, sugar, or honey) and must be eaten at least 2 or 3 hours before the race starts. Food that is eaten within 1 hour of the race stimulates the release of the hormone insulin, which, for the reasons discussed in chapter 3, leaves the runner a "metabolic cripple" who will burn carbohydrates more rapidly than normal and so have an earlier encounter with "the wall."

The final breakfast supplement that you may choose is two cups of coffee. Previously it was thought that the 200 mg of caffeine contained in that coffee prime the body for prolonged exercise by stimulating the release of those body hormones that mobilize free fatty acids from fat tissue. More recent evidence suggests that caffeine offers no such metabolic advantage, at least in runners who have carbohydrate loaded and eaten breakfast (Weir et al., 1987), and that if caffeine has any beneficial effects on performance, these probably result from its action as a mental stimulant.

Because caffeine is a drug that also acts as a mental stimulant, its use "to excess" constitutes doping and is in contravention of the rules governing competition under the International Amateur Athletics Federation. There is no evidence that taking more than about 300 mg of caffeine, equivalent to about two and a half to three cups of coffee, has any additional benefits for the runner, so there is no need to take caffeine in large amounts.

One possible complication of caffeine is that it promotes urine formation (diuresis). Thus, the 1 or 2 minutes of benefit that the caffeine-loaded runner might gain from the stimulatory effects of caffeine may be lost if the runner has to urinate during the race.

A fatty meal (steak, eggs, bacon, or dairy product) with some carbohydrate (breakfast cereal or bread and honey) eaten 4 to 5 hours before the race may be of greater benefit than eating carbohydrates alone. This is because the fatty meal causes blood free-fatty-acid levels to rise and could therefore have a carbohydrate-sparing effect. Indeed, many legendary ultramarathon runners including Arthur Newton and Wally Hayward ate fatty meals before their ultramarathon races.

ALLOW YOURSELF AMPLE WARM-UP TIME

Having prepared both mentally and physically, you are finally ready to take to the road. Check in early at the race start, and leave yourself at least 30 minutes for adequate stretching and warm-up and a final mental tuning.

Stretching is necessary to overcome the overnight tightness and inflexibility that will have developed in your most-trained muscles—calves, hamstrings, and back muscles. You should set aside 15 minutes for this. Some runners have told me that a hot bath before the race is also helpful in overcoming this early-morning stiffness.

A warm-up is necessary only if the race is short and you are competitive; this time also allows the solitude necessary for the final mental planning. My approach is that if I am racing to do my best, I will warm up with jogging for 15 to 20 minutes and a few bursts at a race pace. I feel that when I'm unfit and noncompetitive, this warm-up is an unnecessary drain on my limited energy reserves. Under such conditions, I will warm up during the first 5 km of a 10-km race and the first 41 km of the marathon and be happy to race only thereafter.

Having stretched and warmed up, with 5 minutes to go before the race start, drink 200 to 300 ml of cold fluid, either water or the carbohydrate-containing solution that you prefer to drink during the race. This fluid will help reduce the extent of dehydration during the race by ensuring that even as the race starts, fluid is being absorbed from the intestine.

Then, as you amble nervously over to the horde of gathered runners, you need to take the "starting-line test." This test, first described by Osler (1978), states that if while standing at the start in your skimpy running clothes you do not feel cold, then the weather for that day is too hot for you to run your best marathon. That being the case, remember the running axiom—"in the cold you run for time, in the heat you run for a place"—and set your pace accordingly.

The novice runner might beat the distance but will never beat the heat. The novice who is too ambitious in the heat will suffer the ultimate indignity of turning to pulp and being passed by experienced runners like myself who know that the heat is the great equalizer. In the heat, youth and those with much speed are the runners we "elders" most like to pass.

Since Osler (1978) described the starting-line test, a more scientifically accurate measure of the environmental heat load, the wet bulb globe temperature (WBGT) index, has become available (see chapter 4). Guidelines for how athletes should conduct themselves in races run at different WBGT indexes have been proposed by Hughson et al. (1983; see Table 9.4) and adopted by the American College of Sports Medicine (1975, 1987).

In races in which the WBGT index is not routinely measured, the following guidelines should be followed (see Table 9.5). Note that these guidelines are based on the dry bulb temperature, that is, the temperature measured with an ordinary thermometer. The dry bulb temperature is also the temperature that is reported in the news media.

Unlike the WBGT index, the dry bulb temperature takes no account of the relative humidity of the air or the amount of solar radiation. On humid days when there is no cloud cover (and therefore no protection from solar radiation), the dry bulb temperature seriously underreads the heat load to which the runner is exposed (Browne, 1986). Table 9.5 makes provision for this.

Based on their decade-long experience in treating large numbers of heat-related casualties in one of the world's largest fun runs (Sydney's annual 14-km City-to-Surf run, which attracts in excess of 25,000 runners), Richards et al. (1984) suggested that the WBGT index is in fact not the best predictor of heat injury risk during distance running and proposed an alternate index, the corrected effective temperature (CET). The authors point out that the WBGT taken at the start of the race may not reflect conditions later in the day as the race progresses and that the WBGT value may not necessarily apply for all sections of the course. In addition, they suggest that the WBGT takes too little account of the two factors that make a very large difference to the runner's ability to stay in thermal balance during distance races—the amount of radiation from the sun (global radiation) and the wind velocity. The CET gives adequate weighing for both these factors (see Figure 9.2, a-c).

Figure 9.2 shows how the CET is derived from the dry bulb temperature and humidity (Figure 9.2a) and from the global radiation and the wind velocity (Figure 9.2b). Figure 9.2a shows that at any given dry bulb temperature, the effective temperature falls with decreasing humidity. Thus, for example, when the humidity

Table 9.4 Heat Stress Warnings for Runners Based on Wet Bulb Globe Temperature (WBGT) Index[a]

WBGT color warning code	Risk	Warnings
White	Risk of hypothermia	Hypothermia may develop in slow runners in long races and in wet, windy conditions.
Green Below 18 °C	Low	Heat injury can occur, so caution is still needed.
Yellow 18-22 °C	Moderate	Runners should closely monitor for signs of impending heat injury and slow pace as necessary. Environmental conditions may deteriorate as race progresses.
Red 23-28 °C	High	Runners must slow their running pace and be very aware of warning signs of heat injury. Do not run if unfit or ill or if sensitive to heat or humidity.
Black Above 28 °C	Extremely high	Even with considerable slowing of pace great discomfort will be experienced. Races should not start under these conditions.

Note. From "Monitoring Road Racing in the Heat" by R.L. Hughson, L.A. Staudt, and J.M. Mackie, 1983, *The Physician and Sportsmedicine*, **11**(5), p. 102. Copyright 1983 by McGraw-Hill. Adapted by permission.

[a]Runners who are not accustomed to running in the heat must exercise greater care at any temperature.

is only 20%, a dry bulb temperature of 30 °C corresponds to a CET 6-1/2 ° lower—23-1/2 °C. Similarly, increasing wind velocity decreases the rise in CET for any given amount of global radiation. Thus, whereas full sun conditions in late winter in Sydney (latitude 34° South) cause an elevation of CET by 5 °C; at a wind velocity of 20 m/s full sun conditions increase the CET by only 0.75 °C.

Figure 9.2c shows the value of the CET in predicting the likely number of heat-related casualties in the Sydney City-to-Surf race. The number of casualties rises from less than 0.02% of starters at CET values of 10 °C or less to more than 0.25% (a 15-fold rise) at CET values of 22 °C or greater. Richards et al. (1984) found that the CET was better able to predict the number of heat casualties occurring in their race than was the WBGT. They warned, however, that in order to provide an adequate margin of safety, race officials should be prepared to care for 50% more heat casualties than predicted by their data.

Browne (1986) has provided a simple diagram from which runners can assess heat stress associated with running in different environmental conditions of humidity and air temperature (Figure 9.3). This figure shows that running at air

Table 9.5 Heat Stress Warnings for Runners Based on Dry Bulb Temperature

| | Color warning code | | |
Season[a]	Green[b]	Yellow[c]	Red[d]
Spring	Less than 12 °C	12-23 °C	Greater than 23 °C
		Or less than 12 °C but humidity greater than 50% and a cloudless day	Or temperature between 12-23 °C but humidity greater than 50% and a cloudless day
Summer	Less than 18 °C	18-27 °C	Greater than 27 °C
		Or less than 18 °C but humidity greater than 50% and a cloudless sky	Or temperature between 18-27 °C but humidity greater than 50% and a cloudless sky
Winter	Less than 10 °C	10-20 °C	Greater than 20 °C
		Or less than 10 °C but humidity greater than 50% and a cloudless sky	Or temperature between 10-20 °C but humidity greater than 50% and a cloudless sky

Note. From "Primary Prevention of Heat Stroke in Canadian Long-Distance Runs" by R.L. Hughson, 1980, *Canadian Medical Association Journal*, **122**, p. 1119. Copyright 1980 by Canadian Medical Association. Adapted by permission.
[a]The season influences the runner's resistance to heat by altering the level of heat acclimatization which is best in summer, less in spring, and least in winter. [b]Green indicates go. [c]Yellow indicates run with caution and be aware of the risk of heat injury. Runners should monitor themselves carefully for the early warning symptoms of heat injury and must be prepared to slow their paces should these occur. [d]Red indicates extreme caution. Athletes uncertain of their abilities to complete the distance should not run. The only way to finish is by running much slower than normal.

temperatures of up to 25 °C is relatively safe even at relative humidities up to 100%. However, once the air temperature exceeds about 27 °C, increasing humidity is associated with progressively greater stress and increasing likelihood that the danger limit will be approached.

Although we do not yet know the extent to which racing performance is affected at higher environmental temperatures, C. Foster and Daniels (1975) calculated that for each 1 °C the dry bulb temperature is above 7 °C, the final running time will be increased by 40 seconds. E.C. Frederick (1983a) reported that the average marathon winning time is least in races run at dry bulb temperatures of 12 to 13 °C (see Figure 9.4). This is in line with the world male and female marathon records, both of which were set at dry bulb temperatures between 10 and 12 °C. On the basis of questionnaire data, Browne (1986) has concluded that

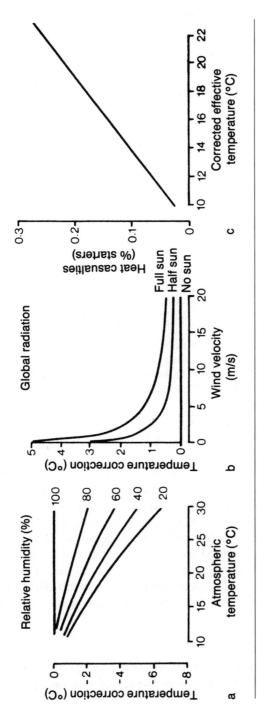

Figure 9.2 The corrected effective air temperature (CET).

Note. From "Method of Predicting the Number of Casualties in the Sydney City-to-Surf Fun Runs" by R. Richards, D. Richards, and R. Whittaker, 1984, *Medical Journal of Australia,* **141**, p. 806. Copyright © Medical Journal of Australia. Adapted by permission.

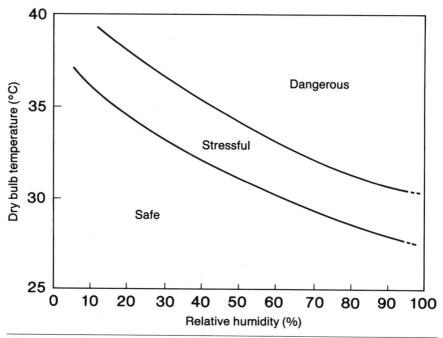

Figure 9.3 Assessment of heat stress associated with running in different environmental conditions of humidity and air temperature.
Note. From "What Do We Mean by Heat" in *A Complete Guide to Running in the Heat* (p. 23) by S. Browne, 1986, Hong Kong: Travel Publishing Asia Ltd. Copyright 1986 by S. Browne.

at temperatures greater than 77 °F, marathon finishing times will be 7 to 10% slower. Thus a 2:16 marathon in the heat is equivalent to a 2:10 marathon in cold conditions.

Thus, the runner who takes the starting line test and who knows the likely dry bulb temperature that will be reached during the race should adjust the racing time accordingly. The final problem that you will face before you actually start the race is to decide where you will stand in this heaving, jovial horde. My advice to the novice runner is to start as close to the back as possible. In all races, there is such a wealth of racing talent that the frontrunners will always start very fast. And a fast start always has a ripple effect—it tends to make everyone start too fast. The further back you are in the pack, the less is this effect. If your aim is just to finish a marathon or ultramarathon race, then you must be in the back row from the start.

At the Gun

The first action to take when the gun goes off is to start the stopwatch on your digital wristwatch. You will soon learn that next to your running shoes, a digital

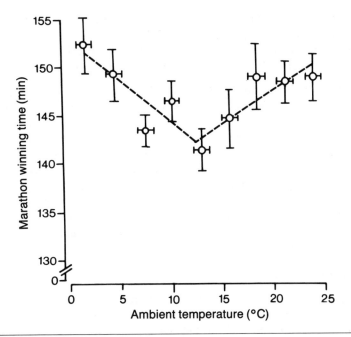

Figure 9.4 The influence of the ambient dry bulb temperature on the average winning times in standard marathons.
Note. From "Hot Times" by E.C. Frederick, 1983, *Running*, **9**, p. 52. Copyright 1983 by E.C. Frederick. Adapted by permission.

stopwatch is your most critical companion in any race, the more so the longer the race.

After you start the stopwatch and the race, hopefully at the same time, your immediate priority is to achieve the correct running pace as quickly as possible. For novice runners, this is the single most difficult achievement; it is the one thing they do very badly and the one that causes them the most grief. The only way to correct this is to calculate the running pace over each of the first 2 km by checking the time as you cross the start line and at the 1- and 2-km marks.

The 1st Kilometer

Pacing. At the 1-km mark, you must check your stopwatch time. By subtracting the time when you crossed the start from your time at the 1-km mark, you can calculate your running pace for the 1st kilometer. If your pace is far too fast, as it usually is, the only way to get into the correct pace is to walk for a short distance. This breaks the running rhythm and will allow a fresh start at a slower pace. Without this walking break you will find it absolutely impossible to slow down adequately. This process should be repeated at each kilometer mark until you finally slot into the correct pace.

Although this approach may sound very artificial, it is the only way novices will definitely protect themselves from running too fast early in the race.

Running in a Group. Chapter 2 discussed the importance of "drafting" during cycling and racing on the track and suggested that drafting may be of value even during marathon racing.

Yamaji and Shephard (1987) found that competitors in the two leading Japanese distance races—the Fukuoka and Tokyo marathons—form clusters, the densities of which increase linearly with increasing running speed. Clustering was therefore most apparent among the best runners. Runners probably cluster because this reduces wind resistance, increases the competitive spirit, allows each runner to survey the other runners, and reduces uncertainty about the correct racing pace (Yamagi & Shephard, 1987). These are the benefits that result from running in a group.

The 3rd Kilometer

Drinking and Sponging. By about the 3-km mark, you will need to take a first drink and, if it is a warm day, you will need to sponge for the first time. It is important to start drinking early, as the rate of fluid absorption from the intestine continues at a constant rate and cannot make up for time lost if the intestine is empty at the start of the race.

Chapter 4 discussed which fluid is the best to drink during racing. To recap, I believe that at least some of the discomfort experienced by the less trained but nevertheless competitive runners during the last 10 km of the standard marathon and, more especially, by the highly competitive runners in the last 30 km of the short ultramarathon, results because they do not ingest sufficient carbohydrate to maintain blood glucose levels during the latter sections of these races. I believe that some form of high-carbohydrate drink or food should be taken regularly by competitive runners after 50 km of ultramarathons, particulary if symptoms of hypoglycemia such as depression, light-headedness, and difficulty in concentrating develop. If you experience the same symptoms in the standard marathon, you should follow the same advice.

The amount of fluid that you should drink is about 500 ml/hr; this fluid should be cold.

These considerations do not apply in races of 10 km, in which fluid ingestion is probably of little importance.

Mental Imagery. Once you have settled into the race after a few kilometers and are running at the appropriate pace, it becomes essential to start "associating."

The key to associating is to concentrate all your attention on precisely what you are doing each step of the way. I have only ever achieved this degree of involvement in one marathon race, which, not surprisingly, was my best. In this race I felt that my involvement with the present was so intense that time stood still. I experienced something in that race that I later heard marathoner Johnny Halberstadt describe: an intense concentration on only what I was doing—on breathing, on efficiency of movement, on running as fast as possible. There was no room for extraneous thoughts or for considering how well I was running. As Halberstadt said, "Once you think you are running well, you have already lost it" (Halberstadt, personal communication, 1983).

When I finished I remembered little of the last 10 km of the race, only the incredible rapidity with which (in contrast to all other races) those kilometers had seemed to pass. I am not sure how one learns to associate, but I do not think it just happens. I suspect that it needs considerable practice.

For further advice on this topic I refer you to the real experts—the top runners—and the relevant psychological texts referred to in chapter 7. Learn from these sources how to associate. Learn from them the implications of concentrating for the entire race.

Kilometers 10 to 32 in the Standard Marathon

These kilometers usually pass quite uneventfully. The best running in the standard marathon occurs between 14 and 28 km. I have found that without any increased effort I usually run at a slightly faster pace during this section of the race. Thus, I have learned to save my effort for the second 16 km of the marathon, during which I will actually pick up 1 or 2 minutes. Nevertheless, a number of problems may occur during these kilometers.

In every good race I have run, I have had the desire to quit. I am not sure whether this is a personal idiosyncrasy or whether it is common to all runners. However, I have only ever "bailed" in one race, so this desire cannot be very strong and is usually quite easily overcome.

It is essential not to bail from any long race unless you are an elite athlete or have a medical condition. Failure will stay with you for a very long time and will increase the likelihood that you will fail again in the next race. Extreme fatigue is, by itself, certainly not a reason to quit any race. Much of the marathon battle is mental anyway, and often fatigue becomes more bearable as you approach the finish. Elite runners who race poorly almost always do so because they are overtrained. It makes no sense for them to try to finish races in which they are running poorly, because the races will only compound their overtraining, prolong their recovery periods, and seriously affect their future chances of again running well.

So however fatigued you might feel when the desire to quit arises, remember that if you bail, that is it for the year—you have no second chance. Don't get into the nearest car; just start walking and keep walking until the race is officially over. Don't worry that you progress at only a very slow pace. Take heed of ultramarathoner Jackie Mekler's (see chapter 8) advice: "At all costs, keep moving *forward* [italics added]" (Mekler, personal communication, 1979). You have to be extremely well disciplined to restart any race once you sit or lie down. Worse, particularly in a long race, you have trouble restarting because the exhausted muscles may seize up and prevent further running.

There are, however, some occasions when it is essential to stop running. The following indicate that you should quit the race:

• Severe diarrhea or persistent vomiting. Both of these indicate that something is seriously wrong. Furthermore, they compound the normal fluid losses incurred by sweating. In addition, they may cause marked loss of sodium chloride, which must be replaced by drinking salt-containing drinks, which are usually not available at drinking tables during the race. Replacing fluid losses from diarrhea without also replacing the salt losses could possibly lead to water intoxication.

• Light-headedness, drowsiness, or aggressiveness. These symptoms indicate that you may be hypoglycemic or may be suffering from hyperthermia or hypothermia. If these symptoms do not respond within 15 minutes to adequate carbohydrate ingestion, then you are probably either hyperthermic or hypothermic and should follow the advice described in chapter 4.

• Chest or stomach pain that is obviously not due to a stitch, that is severe enough to cause you to walk, and that does not disappear very rapidly particularly if you lie down. These symptoms may indicate something rather more ominous than a stitch and must therefore be taken very seriously. On occasion, they may indicate an impending heart attack, which although very uncommon has occurred in marathon runners during races (Noakes, 1987b).

If you experience any of these symptoms, don't try to be heroic. Look for medical advice. Strange things do happen in marathons, just as they happen in every other sport, and these are best treated immediately. The medical literature is replete with examples of athletes who continued to run when they should have stopped.

Provided all is going well and you are not forced to stop for any of the reasons above, you may find you have a desire to walk. As I have said, walking during a marathon is certainly not a crime. But what is a crime is to start walking when you are already exhausted. If prior to the race you are unsure whether you can cover the entire distance without walking, plan when and for how long you will walk during the race; don't wait until you are too exhausted to continue running.

If you are unsure of your ability to run the entire marathon or ultramarathon distance, alternate regular running and walking, for example, 20 to 25 minutes of running followed by 5 to 10 minutes of walking. By spreading your walking distance over the entire course instead of walking just at the end, you have a chance to recover every 20 minutes or so, and the result is that you cover the same distance with much less discomfort and probably also in a shorter time.

Osler (1978) was one of the first modern proponents of regular walking in racing and training, an idea he borrowed from the 19th-century pedestrians like Rowell (see chapter 8). Osler concluded that anyone capable of running 42 km can easily run 80 km by alternating regular walking and running in the ratio described previously.

One other approach is to walk only on the uphills; this is good advice for hilly ultramarathons but does not allow much walking time on a flat marathon course.

Often encountered is the problem of the stitch. The nature and postulated cause of the stitch were described in chapter 6. The most likely explanation is that the stitch is due to spasm of the diaphragm caused by breathing with the chest rather than with the diaphragm. Shallow, rapid breathing, as occurs when one runs fast and which allows the diaphragm to be in a shortened position, may also predispose one to the stitch.

The best form of treatment is prevention—learn to breathe with the diaphragm and strengthen your abdominal muscles with regular sit-ups. Should the stitch develop during a race, two measures frequently help: (a) Alter your breathing pattern so that you breathe *out* when you land on the foot opposite to the side on which you feel the pain, and (b) exhale forcefully (grunt) with each breath. I suspect that these techniques help because the grunting breaks the diaphragmatic spasm and breathing out on the foot opposite to the pain reduces cecal slap.

Cecal slap is a descriptive term first used by a British physician, who noted that he developed diarrhea and pain in the right side of his abdomen after running his first marathon (A.M.W. Porter, 1982). He suggested that this was due to contact of the first part of the large bowel, the cecum (which sits immediately above and to the right of the pelvis), with the anterior abdominal wall, and this caused bruising of the cecum.

I suggest that the stitch may also be exacerbated by contact of part of the large bowel with the diaphragm. If the cecum can slap against the anterior abdominal wall, other parts of the bowel probably can also hit the diaphragm. If you get a stitch on your right side it may be that landing on your right foot drives the right side of the large bowel into your diaphragm. By breathing out when you land on your left foot, you may reduce the amount of contact between the bowel and the right side of the diaphragm, thereby alleviating the stitch.

The stitch frequently occurs on a long downhill that follows a tough uphill section in a race. This may be due to sudden contact of the cecum with the anterior abdominal wall and to contact between the large bowel and the diaphragm as you run downhill. The bowel then becomes irritable, as does the diaphragm, causing the stitch.

Another source of discomfort on a downhill stretch may be the road surface or its camber. Many downhill sections of races, especially ultramarathons, are characterized by severely cambered roads, which add additional stress to one side of the body and can be very tiresome, particularly when the runner is fatigued.

My solution to this is to run in the gutter or ditch, which is usually relatively flat. The only drawback is that you are forced to share the gutter with stones, bottles, and assorted litter. As marathons become more popular, perhaps more attention will be paid to keeping the gutters clean.

A slippery road is another cause of considerable distress during a race; the gutter is usually less slippery and may be preferable.

A final problem is the need to visit the toilet. The key here is to find an appropriate spot as soon as possible. If you are well prepared, you will have your own toilet paper with you and will thus be spared the agony of having to look for some. In an urban marathon, service station rest rooms provide the most convenient pit stops; in country races, the nearest bush is the best.

In a race in which time is of the essence, you should be prepared to urinate on the run. For those who like myself are somewhat modest, this is best done when you have just passed a refreshment station so that the water or sponge can be used to disguise your actions. The attention of the other runners is usually diverted at those moments in the race, and they are less likely to notice!

Kilometers 32 to 42.2 in the Standard Marathon

It is in these kilometers that the marathon really begins. From 32 km to the finish, your body speaks of logic and therefore appeals to your mind. Your body will argue that there is no justifiable reason to continue. Your only recourse is to call on your spirit, which fortunately functions independently of logic. Your spirit accepts that marathon running goes beyond logic, that we were not designed to race marathons any more than we were designed to scale Everest. And the human spirit soon learns that the marathon is one way for ordinary people to define irrevocably their own physical, mental, and spiritual limits. By the 32-km marker, you must be ready to define your limits.

The only advice I have is ignore all logic, take solace in the realization that every other runner feels as bad as you, and view your own efforts as being every bit as important as anything else you have ever done.

Special Considerations for Ultramarathon Races

There are really only three additional considerations for ultramarathon racing.

First, pacing must be far more precise. For example, bad pacing in a standard marathon may leave you with, at worst, 12 to 14 km that are very difficult. The same mistake in the short ultramarathon can leave you with 30 km or more to struggle through.

The answer is to start the ultradistance race conservatively, aiming to run the first half easily, according to your body, and using what energy you have left in the second half. I have observed that all the experienced runners do this. As I discussed earlier, it is usually best to get that section of the race that is the most difficult—the last quarter—over as quickly as possible, and this is best done by starting very conservatively.

The second important consideration in ultramarathons is the question of food and fluids during the race. I now believe that the evidence is incontestable that any athlete running hard in any race lasting more than 4 hours must take in an additional source of carbohydrate during the race. Many of the conventional drinks provided during races do not contain sufficient carbohydrate; thus, you may need additional carbohydrate.

On a cold day you should worry less about the total volume that you drink and more about the amount of carbohydrate you are ingesting. On a hot day, you should run slower and take more care about the volume of fluid you ingest; because you are running more slowly, your glucose requirements will be less, but near the end of the race, when you are still reasonably hydrated, you should switch to high-carbohydrate drinks.

The third extra point for ultramarathon running is to take additional clothing to the race. The athlete who may be on the road up to 24 hours must be prepared for every eventuality and should take four sets of clothes—one each for hot, cold, and intermediate temperature and a separate kit for a race run in the rain. In a rainy ultramarathon you must stay as dry as possible. This is especially important if it is also cold and windy, when you need some form of protection from the rain to prevent the development of hypothermia.

Table 9.6 provides a prerace checklist that you should copy and place in a prominent place. By checking the list regularly, you will ensure that you do not overlook anything and that your racing preparation is optimum.

After the Race

After the race, the fast runner's immediate priority is to drink sufficient liquid to correct any dehydration and sodium chloride loss that may have occurred during the race. This ensures that the kidneys start working again. The best drinks to correct this dehydration are those that have a diuretic (urine-forming) effect: tea, coffee, and alcoholic beverages. Slower runners who have drunk adequately during the race and who may be slightly overhydrated (see chapter 4) need to be sure that they do not drink too much after the race, thereby becoming water intoxicated (hyponatremic).

It now seems that the body can correct water losses after exercise only if the sodium chloride losses are replaced at the same time (Nose et al., 1988a, 1988b). The body concerns itself with correcting the sodium chloride losses first and allows the water deficit to be restored only when the sodium chloride deficit has been corrected.

Thus, it is important to ingest some salt, probably in the form of salty food like potato chips, after prolonged exercise.

Table 9.6   Prerace Checklist for Marathons

Weeks 36 to 13 before race day

Run a series of progressively longer races to get used to the atmosphere of races, to practice pacing, and to learn how to drink while running. Make sure that you have a digital watch with a stopwatch function to time yourself during these races.

Send in your race entry form in good time (i.e., 3 months before the race).

Weeks 12 to 5 before race day

During the last 12 weeks before the race, *no* races longer than 28 km should be run. The period from the ninth to the fourth last week must be reserved for heavy (peaking) training.

Ensure that the shoes you plan to race in are broken in.

If racing out of town, check that you have comfortable and quiet accommodation at the site of the race and that the food choice and other amenities are satisfactory. If travelling by air, check that you have organized a lift from the airport to your hotel.

Weeks 4 to 1 before race day

Start your taper by reducing training to 70%, 50%, and 40% of maximum for the fourth, third, and second last training weeks. Save the shoes you are planning to race in by running in them only once or twice a week.

Consider the need for heat acclimatization.

Decide on the pace you plan to run in the marathon.

Study the course, especially the last 10 km of the standard marathon and the last 25 km of an ultramarathon.

Begin mental preparation by visualizing yourself running on the course and passing the 1, 10, 16, 21, and 32 km marks at the times appropriate for your pacing schedule. Memorize the exact details for the last 10 km, in particular the number and length of all the uphills and downhills and when they come and for how long they last. Imagine yourself running that section and think about how you will cope with the inevitable fatigue you will feel.

Check that all your racing gear fits and is in perfect condition. Attach your race numbers to your racing shirt and pack all your racing gear in a special bag.

Days 7, 6, and 5 before the race

If on the carbohydrate-depletion diet, run a longish run (up to 21 km) on Day 7, and thereafter begin the low-carbohydrate diet for 2-1/2 to 3 days. Run up to 12 km on Days 6 and 5. Sleep as much as possible at night, and try to nap in the afternoons. Be less fastidious than usual at work.

Days 4 and 3 before the race

Run very little (up to 5 km) or not at all. Eat a high-carbohydrate diet as outlined in chapter 3. Rest and sleep as much as possible. Don't think too much about the race.

Day 2 before the race

Do not run. Continue eating a high-carbohydrate diet and resting as much as possible. Travel to the site of competition if the race is out of town. Remember to take your own bed linen and other personal possessions from your room. Drive over the course, particularly the final section. Go to bed early.

The day before the race

Do not run. Continue eating a high-carbohydrate diet but switch to low-residue carbohydrates. Avoid all dairy produce and other foods to which you may be allergic. Spend the day relaxing and keep your mind occupied with things other than the race. Lay out all the clothing you will need for the next day.

Get into bed well before 10:00 p.m. Before going to sleep set at least two alarm clocks to wake you.

If unable to fall asleep, practice relaxation procedures or calm-scene visual imagery.

Race day

Wake up slowly. Drink your favorite early morning beverage. Repeat positive statements.

Dress for the race, applying vaseline where necessary and taping the nipples.

Check that you have toilet paper for the race. Check the weather to see whether you will need to wear or take additional clothing with you to the start.

Eat a light breakfast 2 to 2-1/2 hours before the start of the race. Use the toilet.

Arrive at the race start no later than 30 minutes before the scheduled start. Take the starting-line test and if it is clearly going to be a hot day, adjust your race schedule accordingly.

Line up in the appropriate position and think about the race; visualize your race one more time.

Start the race slowly.

RELAX!

Usually, you should urinate within 6 hours of completing a marathon. Inability to do so could indicate acute kidney failure. Certainly, if you have not passed urine within 12 hours of completing a race you must contact a doctor, preferably a kidney specialist. If you are developing acute kidney failure, the earlier you get to a doctor the more likely the severity of the failure can be lessened and the need for blood dialysis prevented.

A runner's appetite is usually reduced for many hours after a marathon; when your appetite returns you will usually have a mild craving for high-fat/high-protein foods like steak. Fordyce says that the only time he eats steak is for the first 3 days after the Comrades and London-to-Brighton ultramarathons. It is probable that the protein in the steak is needed to repair the racing-induced muscle damage.

The day after the race is usually characterized by mild to marked depression and a very washed-out feeling. Typically, your legs are stiff due to muscle damage of varying degrees, and anything except sleeping will seem to require more energy than you have. This usually lasts for 48 hours after a standard marathon and for 7 to 10 days after a short ultramarathon.

You can do little about these feelings besides accept them as normal, sleep a lot, and avoid excessive physical and mental activity. I suspect that the depression is due to depletion of brain neurotransmitters, an exaggerated response of the same type that in a milder form explains the ability of running to reduce anxiety.

From the 2nd day after the race the likelihood of infection increases. In a study of the incidence of upper-respiratory-tract infections (sore throats, nasal symptoms, cough, fever) after the 56-km Two Oceans Marathon, Edith Peters and Professor Eric Bateman (1983) found that 47% of runners who ran the race in less than 4 hours developed such infections in the first 14 days after the race, whereas only 19% of those finishing the race in between 5-1/2 and 6 hours developed infections. The infection rate in the slow runners was the same as that of members of their households during the same period, whereas the infection rate of the fast runners was much higher. These infections were not trivial, and in 47% of runners they lasted for more than 7 days.

A general rule that I have found, which is contrary to all medical teachings, is that when one is training or racing hard, it is essential to take a powerful antibiotic at the first sign of an upper-respiratory infection. I have found if I do not take effective antibiotics early, I soon develop sinusitis and am then quite ill. However, taking antibiotics early has never failed to abort the attack for me. Like the runners studied by Peters and Bateman, my resistance to infection falls when I have done too much and results in an infection that spreads rapidly. Of course, once I have developed such an infection I know that I have again over-trained and need to rest. I also know that it is unlikely that I will run a good race within 4 to 6 weeks of that infection.

About a week after the race, when your enthusiasm for running starts to return, you need to start analyzing the race in detail to determine the errors you made in both the race and in training. If you ran well, clearly your training was correct and you paced the race well; if you ran badly, training was probably at fault or you ran too fast too early in the race.

The most common error is overtraining; training too hard and too close to the race without a decent taper or racing too frequently and too recently. Also pay attention to the question of balance between speed and distance training. Was the balance correct in your training? Did you carbohydrate load effectively or did you become hypoglycemic during the race? If you quit mentally during the race, analyze your responses. Did you start having negative thoughts at some point in the race?

Race Recovery—When to Race Again

When I started running seriously, no one seemed to bother about how long to rest between races. My coach, Dave Levick, raced a marathon and an ultramara-thon within 6 days of each other, only weeks before his record victory in the 1973 Comrades Marathon.

I think people are now far more cautious. Fordyce (see chapter 8; Fordyce, 1985), more than anyone, has forced us to realize the damaging effects of mara-thon races and the slow recovery from them. The studies of muscle damage due to marathon running seem to confirm his ideas (see chapter 10).

To reiterate the point made earlier in this chapter, I suggest that you *race* only two marathons a year, or one marathon and one ultramarathon. Ideally, you should wait at least 4, but preferably 6, months between these races.

Remember also that if you develop an infection after any race, regardless of its length, then you should definitely not race again for another 4 to 6 weeks, because the result will only be a disaster.

Finally, remember that the temptation to experiment with something new increases as the race approaches: Never try something new for the first time in any important race. The time to experiment with alterations to the guidelines provided here is in minor races, the results of which are not critical to your running career.

RACING WITH ARTHUR NEWTON

In writing this chapter I have relied heavily on my own experiences. This has been necessary because, with the exception of Bruce Fordyce's book (1985), very few of the running books I have studied mention the finer details of actually racing the marathon. Possibly this is because athletes, at least the better ones, do not wish to share their secrets.

But one who did share secrets was Arthur Newton, who covered this topic in his usually precise and insightful way. The remainder of this chapter will be devoted to my comments on some of Newton's more relevant ideas, which, as we have come to expect, are uncannily accurate.

Predicting Racing Performance

There are times when you line up feeling completely ready and thoroughly prepared to achieve your best ever, yet while you are at it you discover that something, too nebulous perhaps to be clearly recognized, is steadily applying the brakes and you can't do as well, anything like as well, as you know you ought to. (Newton, 1949, p. 65)

Comment:

Ideally, you should be able to predict exactly when you are ready to run well. Newton's statement suggests that he was less well able to do this. Possibly because he was unaware of the technique of peaking (9th law of running), he probably ran more training miles than he needed, and he probably tapered too little, too late.

Optimum Environmental Conditions for Racing

I know a distinctly moist day, cloudy, the thermometer about 55 degrees and with little or no wind is what suited me for racing purposes. (Newton, 1935, p. 81)

Comment:

This seems to be about correct. Optimum marathon times are run in dry bulb temperatures of about 10 °C (50 °F) with cloud cover reducing the radiant energy load (see Figure 9.4). These conditions have produced the current world male and female standard-marathon records.

The Influence of Altitude on Racing Performance

Judging from personal experience I should say that anything up to 2,000 feet above sea level makes so little difference as to be practically negligible but from that height upwards the effect becomes quite marked. . . . My best marathon times at each level give a good illustration of the difference: 2 h. 55 min. at Bulawayo and 2 h. 42 min. 43 s. for the same distance during a fifty mile race at sea level.

At 6,000 ft (1,829 m), Johannesburg, I was all but incapable as a runner: my marathon time there was in the region of three and a half hours, and the effort left me considerably distressed—for hours afterwards I was seized with fits of gulping like a fish out of water. (Newton, 1947, p. 39)

Comment:

The effects of altitude on running performance were reviewed earlier in this chapter (see Figure 9.1). Again, Newton's observations are remarkably accurate: Distance-running performance begins to be affected noticeably at altitudes greater than 1,000 m. Newton seems to have overestimated the effect of altitude on standard-marathon performance. The world's best time for a standard marathon at medium altitude was set in Johannesburg by Mark Plaatjies (2:14:45) and is 6 minutes (4.7%) slower than his best time at sea level. This is in line with the prediction in Figure 9.1.

The Effects of Body Weight on Racing Performance

Each of us has a minimum weight below which we are not at our best. . . . I found also that my chances were altogether healthier when I was a trifle overweight rather than the least bit on the light side: I suppose it meant extra reserves to draw on. Trying to reduce your weight by dieting seems to me almost as great a mistake. . . . You should rely on the training to effect the reduction. (Newton, 1947, pp. 28, 31)

Comment:

Many runners believe they can never be thin enough. Like Newton, I have observed that each runner has an optimum weight at which he or she performs best. Going below that weight will lead to worse, not better, performances.

Tapering

Newton's tapering approach was to reduce his training distance by 15% the 3rd week before the race and by a further 10% in the 2nd week before the race, so that he was still running 75% of his usual mileage only 7 days before the race. He maintained this for the first 3 days of the last week, then ran 16 km, 8 km, and 3 km, respectively, on the last 3 days before the race.

By comparison, Bruce Fordyce rests much more during the last 10 days before competition (see Table 8.30) than did Newton, despite the fact that Fordyce runs less total training mileage. This suggests that Newton probably did not rest sufficiently before races and might explain why his racing performances didn't always please him.

The Course

You can put up a better time and with much less effort on a road you know well than you are ever likely to make on an untried route. . . . It will greatly benefit your ultimate performance if you can manage to practice over the actual route beforehand until you get to know it thoroughly. (Newton, 1935, pp. 179-180)

Comment:

I agree absolutely with Newton and have found that knowledge of the course, in particular the last 10 km of a standard marathon and the last 25 km of a short ultramarathon, is essential for best performances.

With the advent of home video productions, today's runners can film most or all of the course should we so wish. My advice to the elite runner competing on an unfamiliar course is to film the course beforehand on video and to use that film not only to learn the course but also to help with mental preparation for the race.

The Night Before the Race

The evening before your race you turn in about the usual time—a trifle later if you wish . . . get hold of a book and go on reading until you fancy there really is a chance of dropping off. As soon as you put the book down your mind incontinently bolts in the forbidden direction; pull it up sharp and turn it any other way. Be very careful not to fidget; just lie there enjoying a downright royal slack for once in a way. (Newton, 1935, p. 180)

Comment:

Newton describes the typical mental response of dwelling on the next day's race and being unable to sleep. To overcome this problem, do the mental relaxation procedure described in chapter 7 and use the "calm scene" imagery described earlier in this chapter.

The Prerace Breakfast

Newton wrote the following before his 100-mile world record on the Bulawayo Road:

> I put away a real good breakfast at the last possible moment . . . and was driven out to the starting point. . . . I ambled along at a serenely easy seven miles per hour knowing I had to save every atom of energy lest I should fail from exhaustion. For the first score or so of miles I had to carry on like this while the breakfast settled down. (Newton, 1949, p. 19).

Comment:

By eating "at the last possible moment," Newton prevented the development of the reactive hypoglycemia described in chapter 3. We now know that running at a relatively low intensity (less than 75% $\dot{V}O_2$max) allows the digestive processes to continue unaffected (Cammack et al., 1982). Thus, by running relatively slowly, Newton allowed his food to be gradually digested, thereby providing an excellent source of energy during very long races.

Note that Newton was used to running immediately after eating, and he always ate a breakfast with a fairly high fat content before he ran each morning.

At the Starting Gun

> At the signal for "Go", take an easy walking step forward, another a bit quicker, a third which is half a trot and in the first twenty yards work up to the pace you have decided. . . . So keep your wits about you and don't go streaking off after the majority of the field: they can carry on like this if it pleases them but you're not having any. As far as you can manage it, take no notice at all of any other competitor at any time; you have enough work of your own to keep you busy, and so has the other man if only he knew it.

> . . . it is a mistake in these races to start off with the pace you intend to rely on; you should always begin a trifle below and work up quite gradually to your reasonable maximum. What really spoils any hope of winning is running a bit wild at the start. If you travel moderately for the first six to eight miles of the marathon, you will not weaken so badly and will be able to extend yourself later on.

> In a race you ought to go off at a pace that you know you can keep up quite easily for more than half the distance; no! it's not as fast as you can run; but if you let out any more you won't stand a reasonable chance at the finish whereas the other man, who has acted on this, will.

As soon as ever your wind has settled down use it as your guide. Take mighty good care that you never get completely "blown" during the course of a race; . . . your wind, being a product of your condition, will let you know at any time where you stand.

It is always the output that should remain a constant factor, not the speed.

Once a fellow is absolutely "beat," anyone with a trifle in reserve can overtake him with ease; recovery on the spot is hopeless, and he is compelled either to drop out or to drag himself along knowing that neither excitement nor will power can add anything worthwhile to his speed.

Make a note of that point next time you race, for it's one of the most valuable and least practised by marathon men. (Newton, 1935, pp. 185-186; 1949, pp. 28, 25; 1935, pp. 46-47; 1935, p. 155; 1949, p. 34)

Comment:

Earlier in this chapter I placed much emphasis on correct pacing at the start of the race. The longer the race, the more important this becomes.

Note in particular Newton's statements about keeping "output . . . not the speed" constant during the race and the use of "his wind" to determine the correct effort level during the race. These two statements indicate that Newton listened to his body and used the subtle clues mentioned earlier in the chapter to ensure that his pace was appropriate for each race.

Mental Association During the Race (Segmenting)

While you were out practising you kept your mind largely off running, but when the genuine trial at record comes along all that will have to be altered and every ounce must be focused, if it is only once in a lifetime, on the immediate concern. . . . Never forget for a moment that it is your mind that can make or mar your prospects if you let it.

When you get really desperately tired, you can't keep your mind off your condition; it won't answer to the helm as it does when you are fighting fit, and I remember thinking that never again would I dream of risking such punishing discomfort though, having already undergone so much, I'd have to battle through the remaining hours.

But I had only one job just then, and that was to travel along with the most perfect rhythm I was capable of. . . . Every mile seemed a weary long way—ten miles was too tiring even to be thought about. Yet I knew that if I went on, the ten would turn up, and another ten after that, and still another, till the actual 150 was in sight. . . . So I'd just got to hang on no matter how tired I felt. (Newton, 1935, pp. 186-187; 1949, pp. 40-41)

Comment:

Newton is talking about the importance of associating during racing, which was discussed in detail in chapter 7.

Tactics

I never believed, as many apparently do, in running only to win an outstanding event; it always seemed to me to be only proper, in fact only sensible, to do your actual best, no matter whether you happen to be miles ahead or miles behind. Remember, you want to measure YOUR abilities—not the other fellow's failings.

If I wanted to pass a man, I used to keep behind him for a minute or so—he would be going just too slow for me and therefore I'd be saving up a trifle of energy during this period to make up for extra expenditure. This would be required when I started to pass him. As soon as I was ready I would go slightly faster, . . . and if he still stuck to me would keep it up and listen to his breathing. I nearly always learnt what I wanted in this way. If a couple of hundred yards made much difference to his respiration I knew I was safe and kept going till he dropped back; if however he still managed to get along quite comfortably I might try even half a mile an hour faster and again "listen in." All this time I would be going somewhat faster than I wanted to and if my rival still appeared to be quite perky I should deliberately drop behind him until, a mile or two later, I'd start the business all over again. Rarely indeed did it fail to work: when it did I had either to "kill" my man or accept defeat.

The reverse of this is simple. When another tries to pass let him get on with it. If you're in better condition he's bound to make the discovery later on. (Newton, 1940, p. 65; 1947, pp. 56, 59-60)

Comment:

The idea that you perform better if you race yourself and not your opposition is supported by most sport psychologists (Kauss, 1980; Liebetrau, 1982; Rushall, 1979).

To my knowledge, very few competitive runners ever discuss how they determine when to pass another runner as Newton does in this series of quotations. Bruce Fordyce's simple explanation is the following:

In ultra-marathoning it is quite important, if you start to establish a lead, to relax, do it gradually. If you have taken the lead, then that's because the other runners can no longer take that pace, so if you can just hold that pace you will continue to pull away. I tended to think "Oh God, I am in the lead now"; you have got to get a gap, and you push yourself. I pushed myself a bit hard for no reason and then I suffered a little towards the end. (Aitken, 1983, p. 6)

Sugar-Containing Drinks

Water? You would say it is the most natural, wouldn't you? Yet I am not so sure that it is . . . almost every drink you take while racing, or even practising, would be better were salt and sugar added . . . and they should be cold, next to, but not quite icy. . . . When it came to open competition it was tea every time . . . with rather more than the usual amount of sugar in it. For a long journey I like about three piled-up teaspoonfuls to a half pint of liquid.

By the way, don't be afraid of the sugar. . . . It's as well to remember that without sugar they are not really effective—it's their sugar content that makes them worthwhile. . . . The harder the physical work the more sugar I find I can do with. If you find your ability to get along weakening considerably, . . . get a sweetened drink as soon as possible and set your mind to work at once to reason the position out.

You should not suck sweets or keep anything in your mouth, as that would put an end to anything approaching regularity in your breathing. So there is only one course left; dissolve the sugar and drink it. This absorbs less time than any other method, yet apparently acts just as well.

On October 3rd, 1924, I was racing from London to Brighton. At twenty odd miles the heat was having a very noticeable effect on my pace, but I soon worked out what was wrong and asked for a really cold lemonade containing salt and extra sugar. . . . Ten minutes after it was despatched I had added a mile an hour to my pace and was feeling very much better. Thereafter, with a similar drink every six to eight miles and an occasional douche of cold water, there was no further trouble. . . . When you take a drink while on the run make sure it is available at the foot of a long incline if possible . . . don't put it away just before descending a hill, as that would almost certainly spell stitch or other discomforts. (Newton, 1935, pp. 103, 91, 95, 93; 1949, p. 70; 1935, pp. 94, 105)

Comment:

The drink to which Newton refers was probably the "corpse reviver," a drink developed by Newton that contained 1 tablespoon sugar, 1/2 teaspoon salt, 3/4 teaspoon bicarbonate of soda, and water and lemonade mixed in a ratio of 1:3 to make up a large glass. This was drunk every 16 km or 2 hours.

Newton clearly believed in the importance of sucrose intake during ultramarathon running, but the surprising aspect is how infrequently he drank. In addition, the concentration of his sucrose drinks was low, approximately 4 to 5%—3 teaspoonfuls ($\pm$ 12 g) in 1/2 pint (300 ml). Thus, his carbohydrate intake during many races could not have been optimum and certainly was less than the required amount of 25 to 40 g/hr (see chapters 3 and 4). For some reason he found sugar more effective than glucose: "Don't try and substitute glucose for sugar; no matter what the text-books tell you it's not in the same street so far as merit is concerned" (Newton, 1949, p. 70).

Salt-Containing Drinks

The man who does anything more than a little in the running line should take extra salt as a regular item of his diet if he feels inclined to.

Most drinks during a very long race should have a little salt in them to partly balance the loss that is going on through perspiration.

If you drink quantities of liquid without any salt you will be apt to suffer from what might be called water poisoning. . . . In addition to the above, if you add a little extra salt to your regular diet you will be far less liable to attacks of cramp. . . . I can only find two causes of cramp—over-exertion (practically synonomous with undertraining, of course), and a lack of the necessary amount of salt in your system. . . . undertrained I got cramp, in reasonable form I did not.

If you get an attack while you are on the road, . . . the only remedy I can think of is to shorten your stride and take a drink with salt in it. (Newton, 1935, pp. 89-90, 134-135)

Comment:

Runners probably need to ingest some salt but only during very prolonged exercise when the sodium chloride losses become important (Noakes et al., 1988c; see chapter 4). Without ingesting salt, the body cannot completely correct its fluid losses. However, the fact that millions of athletes have run countless races without ingesting salt and without too many problems, suggests that salt ingestion during exercise is a refinement rather than an absolute requirement.

We do not know if salt deficiency causes cramps or can help alleviate them.

Alcohol

At times I got most desperately exhausted with exercise and this brought up the question of stimulants. . . . If alcohol . . . would be of distinct benefit, . . . I meant to find out. . . . Presently I went out for a forty miler . . . and called in for the brandy with only five miles of downhill remaining to be covered. . . . So I put about six tablespoons of water to the spirit, gulped it down, and started at once on the last lap.

This is what happened—I felt less tired and my pace increased. But it did not last very long; by the time I had covered some four miles I could distinctly notice that the effects were beginning to wear off. Nevertheless, the experiment was certainly valuable.

Now was that first experiment a fluke, or could it be relied on to produce the same effects at any time? I decided I had better put it to the test once more. . . . So once more I set out to make myself excessively tired, once more I swallowed a teaspoonful of brandy in six or seven of water, and again I found the conditions were eased. Good enough; I knew that when it came to the fifty-four mile [Comrades Marathon] race I was training for, . . . I would arrange for precisely the amount of dope that experiences had taught me was beneficial. The race came off; at fifty miles I downed the noisome stuff, and I was a winner by nearly half an hour.

I am convinced that there are times such as these when spirits in strict moderation are of real benefit. (Newton, 1935, pp. 99-102)

Comment:

Scientifically, I see no reason why alcohol should be of any value during races. Indeed, studies show that alcohol affects performance adversely (McNaughton & Preece, 1986).

Alcohol is a poor energy source; it is clearly inferior to carbohydrate. Worse, alcohol inhibits liver glucose production, thereby increasing the likelihood of hypoglycemia developing if alcohol is ingested during very prolonged exercise. But if Newton found it to be of some benefit, then it may well be. Certainly, I am aware of runners who regularly ingest alcohol in ultramarathon races without apparent detrimental results. But the winners are not among them!

Food Intake During Races

For distances up to sixty miles, I have found it unnecessary to take any solid food along the road, but a hundred is a different matter on account of the time involved. When it comes to this latter distance, you will probably require a light but nourishing meal anywhere between forty and fifty miles.

[During] a trial at the 100 miles world record, . . . I had two or three drinks from a thermos between twenty-five and forty-five miles and was beginning to feel decidedly hungry . . . and welcomed the meal which had been ordered and was ready. My fodder was soup, chicken and vegetables, and fruit pie (pastry!). . . . Twelve minutes later, I was out on the road again. . . . That meal certainly helped me along wonderfully and I felt the benefit of it for the next twenty miles.

You must work out for yourself what the food is to be, though no doubt soup and some kind of sandwich is about as good as anything. The soup should be a trifle more salty than usual, and as hot that you can only just drink it straight off. Be careful not to overdo the salt. . . . Personally I rely on thin bread, preferably brown, with quite a lot of butter and solidified honey (or minced roast chicken in place of the latter). The honey should be of the solid kind or it won't stick there, and unless you have plenty of butter to lubricate it you will find it a tiresome job to despatch the fodder. (Newton, 1935, pp. 193-195; 1949, p. 19)

Comment:

I suspect that time will prove that food intake is probably essential during very long races and that Newton ate too little, especially during the 24-hour race.

Pacing

Any alteration during the progress of the race ought to be tackled almost infinitesimally; just a fraction more speed for a hundred yards and the results carefully noted; if there is a suspicion of it being too fast drop back to the as-you-were stage which was evidently correct. So long as you watch your wind carefully and treat it kindly you can average a better pace than any other method will give you. (Newton, 1935, pp. 46-47)

Comment:

As described in chapter 7, elite runners monitor many body signals to determine their levels of effort; here Newton again discusses the use of one of these, breathing, to determine his effort level.

Hill Running in Competition

When you start climbing a hill the first thing to make sure of is that your "wind" doesn't suffer too greatly. . . . Keep on moving with exactly the same number of strides to the minute as you would employ on the level, but shorten them in accordance with the gradient. . . . Your wind will tell you precisely what length is best . . . never under any circumstances permit yourself to be absolutely blown by the climb. . . . Do NOT purposely lean forward . . . when you go uphill. Nothing but your wind can tell you whether your pace is correct for conditions at the time, for your breathing is entirely dependent on the amount of energy you are bringing into use.

When you come to a downhill stretch you may employ a distinctly longer stride than the one you take on the level. (Newton, 1935, p. 32; 1949, pp. 79-80)

Stopping During Very Long Races

Before the start he and I had agreed to retire for a quick hot bath after we had completed a hundred miles. . . . A short and really hot shower is more refreshing and re-invigorating than any food or drink. (Newton, 1949, p. 39).

Comment:

Although this advice clearly aided Newton, when Wally Hayward tried it during his own 24-hour race, disaster occurred (see chapter 8). The response of two individuals to the same procedure can be quite different; you must discover for yourself what works for you.

Recovery From Racing

You don't recover from racing a 150-miler in a day or two or even in a week; to be quite at my best I needed rather more than a month. You might feel perfectly fit a few days later but another trial, if you were foolish enough to risk such a thing, would prove at once that you were still far from top form. (Newton, 1949, p. 35)

Comment:

Bruce Fordyce essentially echoed these words (Fordyce, 1985). He wrote that his main opponents in the 1981 Comrades Marathon and the London-to-Brighton race of the same year had chosen to run hard immediately before those races; this he felt had adversely affected their performances in both races.

The length of time that should be allowed for recovery after distance races was discussed in detail earlier in this chapter.

10

Overtraining

*"There were two holders of world swimming re-
cords. Both were in the final period of their training
for the Helsinki Games in 1952. Both had been
training consistently and hard, up to six miles a day
and recording close to their best times. Then their
times started to fall off. One swimmer believed he
should train harder for as he said 'did not slower
speed show the need for more training', the other
swimmer eased off and swam slowly when he
trained. . . . He spent most of his time in bed . . .
The wrongly advised, energetic one by a long way
failed to come up to his previous standard but the
'lazy' one, who had developed a sound basic philosophy on the subject of training, won his Olympic
race in record time."*

Forbes Carlile (1964)

*"I remember talking to John Walker, former world
record holder in the mile, about his training. He let
his body dictate his schedule. For instance, if he
planned to run ten hard quarters for an evening
workout and felt terrible after running one, he
would pack up and go home. I thought that was
great. I could never do that. If I planned fifteen, I
ran fifteen."*

Derek Clayton (1981)

*"Overtraining is to my way of thinking, the biggest
medical problem incurred by talented runners who
lack the experience or discipline to cope with their
own enthusiasm."*

Marti Liquori and John Parker (1980)

> *"The last couple of years I thought that if 110 [miles a week] got me a 2:08 [marathon], if I went to 130 I could run 2:07. That didn't happen. Sooner or later, you cross that borderline between proper training and overtraining."*
>
> Alberto Salazar (Higdon, 1985)

> *"Overtraining is wasted training."*
>
> Grete Waitz and Gloria Averbuch (1986)

From the moment you file that first race entry form, you become a racer and enter a new world. You will become aware of the threshold you have crossed—the threshold that divides jogging for health from training for peak racing performance. And in that first race, the former jogger in you suddenly discovers that singular endeavor that demands nothing less than total harmony between the perfect spirit and your newly perfected body. With that first race, you catch the first glimpse of your true potential.

Of course, the danger of all this is that as a neophyte racer you will inevitably try to achieve too much. The mind, reaching for perfection, will soon demand more than the body can deliver. And when the mind really gets going, the impetuous and greedy racer is on the verge of the athlete's most common and least understood illness—overtraining.

Despite my decade of experience in the sport, each year my avaricious mind ensures that I spend a few weeks rediscovering this overtraining illness in myself. I am not alone in this, and I am frequently visited by runners whose training greed has reduced them to the walking wounded. Some suffer generalized fatigue, recurrent headaches, diarrhea, weight loss, sexual disinterest, and little appetite for food or work. Others are no longer able to sleep properly and complain they are troubled by early morning wakening, inabilities to relax, and generally listless attitudes toward life. Generalized swelling of lymph glands may suddenly appear, allergies may worsen, and colds, influenza, or respiratory infections may resist all conventional therapy.

All these symptoms are diagnostic. These runners have stretched their bodies beyond their individual breaking points. They are told that rest, not more training, is required and that all they can do is get some rest and wait for nature to heal what medicine does not yet comprehend.

INDICATORS OF OVERTRAINING

Probably the earliest scientific reference to overtraining was made by R.T. McKenzie (1923), who noted that exhaustion after exercise was of three kinds: acute exhaustion accompanied by marked breathlessness, from which recovery was rapid; fatigue of the whole muscular system, which required 1 or 2 days of rest; and chronic fatigue, caused by "slow poisoning of the nervous system" (p. 66), which he called "staleness," and from which recovery was very prolonged and could last weeks or even months. McKenzie described staleness in the following way:

> The vitality declines as the day progresses. He [the athlete] is unable to concentrate on study or work and takes but little interest in the world about him. He awakens tired after sleeping and his sleep is frequently broken. He finds it difficult to hold his attention on any subject. The physician notes that the eye is sunk deep in its socket, the face is pinched, the appearance dejected, the temper peevish and distrustful, aggravated by little things. Wounds and scratches heal slowly. Sudden rise to the standing position shows an increase in the pulse-rate of 20 beats or more. . . . There is gradual loss of weight from day to day, and the weight lost during exercise is not replaced within twenty-four hours as it should be. (p. 67)

The next important observation was made by Heiss (1971), who described an increased susceptibility to infection as an important component of the overtraining syndrome. He noted that the incidence of upper respiratory tract infections among competitors at the 1928 winter Olympics increased sharply both immediately before and during the competition. At subsequent Olympics, this trend was again apparent, and Heiss considered these infections to be a late sign of overtraining.

Subsequent descriptions of the overtraining syndrome (Bresnahan & Tuttle, 1950; Carlile, 1963, 1964; Counsilman, 1968; Karpovich & Sinning, 1971; Keretzty, 1971; Mellerowicz & Barron, 1971; Reidman, 1950; Ryan, 1983; Webster, 1948; Wolf, 1971) did not add materially to these observations; Tom Osler was the first runner to synthesize these ideas in readily understandable terms.

In his 30-page classic entitled *The Conditioning of Distance Runners*, Osler (1967) described the symptoms he observed in himself when he had trained too much. Table 10.1 contains a fairly comprehensive listing of indicators of overtraining, drawn from a large number of sources.

Of course, the runner's natural response to these indicators, most particularly to the combination of a poor racing performance followed by illness, is to think that more training is in order. What other possible explanation can there be for a bad performance? And the urgency to train hard is only exacerbated by the time lost as a result of illness. But because these assumptions are wholly incorrect, the athlete's bout of intensive training only compounds an already grave situation. The truth is that once you are even mildly overtrained, you are already past your best. And the only way to help the situation is to stop training immediately until the desire to run and compete again returns.

Table 10.1   Indicators of Overtraining/Staleness Syndrome (References in Parentheses; See Key)

Emotional and behavioral changes

Loss of enthusiasm and drive; generalized apathy; an "I don't care" attitude; loss of joy of life (1, 5, 6, 8-10).

Loss of joy of and thirst for competition. Desire to quit during competition (2, 4-9, 11).

Lethargy; listlessness; tiredness (1, 2, 4-6, 10, 11).

Peevish; complaining; easily irritated; miserable; anxious; depressed; ill-humored; unable to relax; bored (1, 2, 4-8, 10, 11).

Inability to concentrate at work; impaired academic performance (1).

Changes in sleeping patterns, in particular, insomnia (1, 2, 4-7, 11). Sleep does not refresh (1, 5, 10).

Loss of appetite (1, 2, 4-8, 10).

Loss of libido.

Poor coordination; general clumsiness (9).

Increased fluid intake at night; feeling thirsty (1, 12).

Physical changes

Impaired physical performance, in particular, inability to complete routine training sessions (1-7).

Gradual loss of weight (1, 2, 4, 6-8, 11).

Athlete looks drawn, sallow, and dejected with sunken eyeballs (1, 2, 8).

Increase in early morning heart rate of more than five beats per minute (12, 17). Abnormal rise in heart rate on standing (1, 2, 15) and during (4, 14) and after a standard workout (7). Slower recovery in heart rate after exertion (8, 11). Postural hypotension (2, 11).

Heavy leggedness. Sluggishness that persists for more than 24 hours after a workout (9).

Muscle and joint pains (4, 7). Persistent muscle soreness increases from session to session (9, 11).

Swelling of lymph glands (4, 8).

Gastrointestinal disturbances, in particular, diarrhea (4).

Increased susceptibility to infections, allergies, headache, and injury (3, 4, 7-9, 11, 16).

Minor scratches heal slowly (1, 2).

Loss of menstruation (amenorrhea) in women.

Increased blood eosinophil count. Serial T wave changes on the electrocardiogram (4).

Key to references

1. McKenzie (1923).
2. Webster (1948).
3. Heiss (1971).
4. Carlile (1963, 1964).
5. Karpovich and Sinning (1971).
6. Bresnahan and Tuttle (1950).
7. Mellerowicz and Barron (1971).
8. Counsilman (1968).
9. Osler (1967).

10. Wolf (1971).
11. Ryan (1983).
12. Brown (1983).
13. Czajkowski (1982).
14. Conconi et al. (1982).
15. Reidman (1950).
16. Peters and Bateman (1983).
17. Dressendorfer et al. (1985).

The single most important reason we are all prone to overtraining is, I believe, that we lack objective assessments of our ultimate performance capabilities. We simply will not accept that we are mortal and that we have built-in performance ranges beyond which training cannot take us. We believe that the harder we train, the better we will perform, and we ignore the evidence that indicates that this is blatantly untrue (see chapter 2). So we train harder and then run worse. And then, in the act of ultimate stupidity, we interpret our poor races as indications that we have undertrained. And so we go out and train even harder.

Personal experience gained from my own running and from treating overtrained runners forces me to conclude that the overtraining syndrome develops in one of two ways: It occurs either in athletes who have been training very intensively for protracted periods or else in those who run series of races in short succession, also following periods of intensive training.

PREVENTING OVERTRAINING

The essential element in avoiding overtraining is to understand the different stages of the overtraining syndrome. Especially important is the ability to distinguish between the generalized fatigue that appears to be an essential ingredient of proper training and the slightly increased degree of fatigue that indicates too much training. In my opinion, the person who has best distinguished between these very subtle grades of fatigue is James Counsilman, swimming coach at Indiana University and author of the classic swimming book *The Science of Swimming* (Counsilman, 1968). My regard for Counsilman is heightened by the knowledge that he is one of the oldest men ever to have swum the English Channel.

The Three Stages of the Overtraining Syndrome

Counsilman stresses that feeling tired does not, by itself, mean that the athlete has done too much, especially if the athlete's training performance is stable or improving.

> As long as the swimmers keep swimming fast in practice, doing good repeats and good efforts, work them hard or harder. Even after they begin having the feeling of general fatigue, they will continue to swim well in practice, so keep them working hard up to the point at which their performances in practice begin to suffer. At this point they should be watched carefully and the coach should be ready to reduce the workload. (Counsilman, 1968, pp. 237-238)

Counsilman believes that his swimmers should never be allowed to recover fully before the next training session. He feels that allowing swimmers to recover fully before the next training session was never as effective as keeping them in the "valley of fatigue."

To give visual expression to this ideas, Counsilman produced a figure on which Figure 10.1 is based. The three lines (A, B, and C) indicate changes in fatigue levels in three different athletes who train hard for 5 consecutive days, with rest or recuperative training days on Saturday and Sunday. As the athletes become progressively more tired from Monday to Friday, their levels of fatigue increase and encroach upon the fatigue zone or the "valley of fatigue."

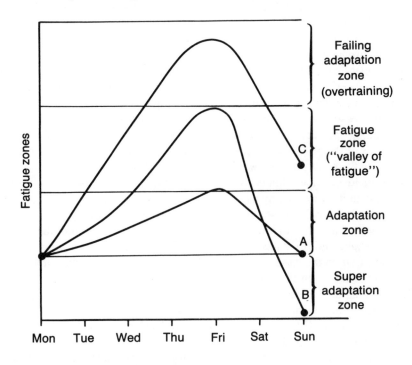

Figure 10.1 The fatigue zones of Counsilman.
Note. From J.E. Counsilman, *The Science of Swimming,* © 1968, p. 236. Adapted by permission of Prentice Hall, Englewood Cliffs, New Jersey.

Line A represents changes in fatigue levels in an athlete who trains only moderately hard and becomes only mildly fatigued after 5 days of training, barely reaching the fatigue zone. During the recovery period on Saturday and Sunday, this athlete's fatigue level decreases to a level slightly lower than it was the previous Monday. Line B represents the same changes in an athlete who is pushed to the upper limit of the "fatigue zone." Upon recovery, this athlete's body superadapts to a fatigue level very much lower than that at which it started.

Counsilman's inference is that this athlete's fitness and ability to resist training fatigue would increase correspondingly. The athlete depicted in Line C trains the hardest of the three. So this athlete's fatigue level goes through the fatigue zone and deep into the failing adaptation (overtraining) zone. Even after resting on Saturday and Sunday, this athlete does not recover before the start of the following week. If this athlete recommences hard training before fully recovering, the level of fatigue will increase further and the athlete will be on the road to overtraining.

Counsilman suggested that the first and, unfortunately, the most subtle indicator that the athlete has dropped too far into the fatigue zone and is therefore overtraining is that performance in training falls off. Arthur Newton noted this also, because he wrote, "Inability to produce your best when you are apparently in good form is the first sign of incipient staleness" (Newton, 1947, p. 22). Of course, athletes who do not carefully monitor their training performances will never spot this very subtle indicator, and I suggest that this is the single most important reason why all athletes should record and analyze the results of all their training and racing in great detail. Certainly one of the essential factors in the success of Bruce Fordyce (see chapter 8) has been his method of meticulously monitoring the results of each workout he has ever run. By comparing his performances in identical workouts over many years, he knows precisely what his physical condition was at any day of any year.

Indeed, I believe the reason for the time trials suggested by Lydiard (see Rule #5 in chapter 5 and the 7th law of training in chapter 6) is to monitor the athlete's level of fatigue and resistance to the stress of fast running, *not* against the stopwatch but first on the basis of the level of effort required to produce that performance and second on the basis of the athlete's rate of recovery after the time trial. As long as the athlete's performance is improving, as shown by a faster running time for the same effort and by a more rapid recovery, then the athlete is not overtraining. Once the athlete has to run harder to achieve the same time, overtraining has occurred.

If the athlete fails to identify this indicator of overtraining and continues to train hard or, more commonly, believes that a fall in performance indicates the need for more intensive training, that athlete is likely to develop what Bruce Fordyce calls the "plods." The most common symptoms of the plods are sore muscles, a heavy-legged and sluggish feeling, generalized fatigue, malaise, and diarrhea. The plods always disappear completely within 24 to 48 hours if the athlete is sensible enough to rest completely or to jog only a few kilometers; this rapid response to rest is what differentiates the plods from a more serious state of overtraining. The first run after the rest should be an absolute pleasure; there should not be the slightest trace of muscle soreness, and the athlete should run an effortless 30 s/km (or more) faster than normal. Grete Waitz calls the plods a "miniburnout" (Waitz & Averbuch, 1986).

Of course, the problem is that when you are training hard, it is usual for your legs to feel slightly stiff and lethargic at the start of a run, but this feeling should lift as the run progresses. One method of deciding when the level of muscle soreness is inappropriate is to score all training runs on the basis of how your legs felt during each run. Muscle soreness that either persists or gets worse during the training run indicates that you should abandon that particular run and rest for 24 to 48 hours to allow full muscle recovery before undertaking another hard or long training session. If in the next run following the rest period your legs do not feel "strong," then you have the "superplods" and must rest for a further period until your legs fully recover.

The athlete who continues to race or to train hard despite having the superplods can only crash into what we recognize as the full-blown overtraining state, with some or all of the symptoms listed in Table 10.1. Of these symptoms, the most common found in a group of overtrained runners (Barron et al., 1985) were persistent muscle soreness, loss of interest in training and competition, increases in resting heart rate, and changes in sleeping patterns. Once these symptoms were present, recovery took between 5 and 8 weeks, during which time there was absolutely no possibility that the athlete could train properly, let alone race. Grete Waitz labels this a "maxiburnout" (Waitz & Averbuch, 1986).

Other Factors Predisposing the Athlete to Overtraining

Although training and racing too much are the usual ingredients essential for overtraining, various authors have listed other factors that predispose athletes to overtraining. These factors include poor nutrition, drug use, lack of sleep and inadequate rest, adverse climatic conditions, "irregular living," work pressures, emotional conflicts, emotional unrest, monotonous training, and miscellaneous stress—the "everyday wear and tear of living" (Carlile, 1963).

Always remember that training is a "holism" (15th law of training) and that certain aspects of your lifestyle will contribute to overtraining.

Monitoring the Early Signs of Overtraining

Obviously, very few runners develop the full-blown overtraining syndrome, yet many run races less well than they should because they fail to observe these early symptoms of the plods and the superplods. The only practical way to prevent overtraining is to recognize the early symptoms, and this is probably best done by an independent and therefore objective observer such as a coach.

Certainly, the runner will seldom be sufficiently objective about his or her overtraining symptoms. My own ability to recognize overtraining in others but not in myself is a typical example.

The signs that provide the earliest clues that the athlete is overtraining have been detailed by Richard Brown through his studies of athletes running for the Athletics West Track Club in Eugene, Oregon (R.L. Brown, 1983). The pointers, which were also discussed in chapter 10, include the athlete's afternoon weight and fluid intake, time of going to bed, total number of hours slept, and early morning pulse rate.

Brown found that the first indicator of overtraining was a fall in the athlete's afternoon postworkout weight. The next indicator was an increased fluid intake in the evening, and the third was the time the athlete went to bed. Athletes who were overtraining went to bed later than normal but woke either at the same time or earlier than normal. Thus they slept fewer hours than normal, the fourth indicator of overtraining. The fifth indication was a rise in the early morning (waking) pulse rate.

Czajkowski (1982) reported the results of a simple test he used to monitor the training status of Polish cross-country skiers. Each morning the skiers measured their heart rates on awakening and again exactly 20 seconds after they had stood up. Czajkowski found that as the skiers became overtrained, their waking pulse rates rose, but more importantly, the differences between their lying and standing heart rates increased (see Figure 10.2).

The final technique that has been described to identify overtraining is the same as that described by Conconi and his colleagues (1982) to determine the anaerobic threshold. They showed that as athletes became overtrained, their heart rates

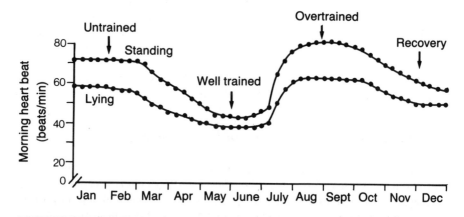

Figure 10.2 The effects of training and overtraining on early morning lying and standing heart rates.

Note. From "A Simple Method to Control Fatigue in Endurance Training" by W. Czajkowski in *Exercise and Sport Biology*, International Series on Sports Sciences (Vol. 12, p. 210) edited by P.V. Komi, 1982, Champaign, IL: Human Kinetics. Copyright 1982 by Human Kinetics. Adapted by permission.

were higher at any given running speed (see Figure 10.3). This, of course, is exactly opposite to the training response to correct training, in which the heart rate at any running speed is reduced. Interestingly, Carlile recorded essentially the same observation in his swimmers some 20 years earlier (Carlile, 1963).

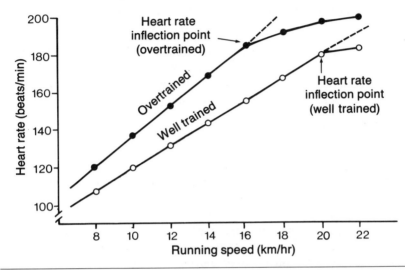

Figure 10.3 The heart rate inflection points in a well trained and an overtrained athlete.
Note. From ''Determination of the Anaerobic Threshold by a Non-Invasive Field Test in Runners'' by F. Conconi, M. Ferrare, P.G. Ziglio, P. Droghetti, and L. Codeca, 1982, *Journal of Applied Physiology*, **52**(4), p. 871. Copyright 1982 by the American Physiological Society. Adapted by permission.

The reason the resting heart rate rises with overtraining is unknown. Dressendorfer et al. (1985) studied 12 runners running 500 km in 20 days and found that the early morning heart rates fell for the first 8 days of the race (as the athletes became fitter) but thereafter rose progressively, presumably as the athletes became overstressed and overtrained. The authors hypothesized that the rising heart rates might indicate progressive fatigue of the heart muscle.

The heart rate is an easy factor to measure during training, so it is surprising that few athletes and their coaches have used this measurement. One who has reported using exercising heart rate to indicate his physical condition during training is Lasse Viren. In July 1972, prior to the Munich Olympic Games, Viren set a world record for 2 miles (8:14), raising the possibility that he had peaked too soon for the Games, which were to be held in September. To check for this, his coach instructed Viren to run a standard workout of twenty 200-m intervals; Viren's time for each repeat and his heart rate were measured immediately after he finished (Daws, 1978). In June, Viren averaged 30 seconds and 192 heart beats per minute; in July, before the 2-mile record, he averaged 29.3 seconds and 186 beats per minute; and in August, he averaged 28.2 seconds and 172 heart beats per minute. Clearly, he was continuing to improve.

One of the modern runners who has written the most about overtraining is Grete Waitz (Waitz & Averbuch, 1986). Her remarkable consistency must be due in part to her ability to detect the early signs of overtraining:

> I judge my fatigue more by my moods. . . . If it's hard to sleep or I'm cranky, impatient or annoyed, I'm probably overtraining. In my case, family and friends often know when I'm overtraining even before I do. When I begin to snap at Jack [her husband], he knows it's time to analyze my training and probably cut back. (Waitz & Averbuch, 1986, p. 74)

She suggests that answers in the affirmative to three or more of the following questions probably indicate that it is time to reduce one's training:

1. Does your normally comfortable pace leave you breathless?
2. Do your legs feel "heavy" for far longer than usual after a hard workout or a race?
3. Do you find it especially hard to climb steps?
4. Do you dread the thought of training?
5. Do you find it exceptionally hard to get out of bed in the morning?
6. Do you have a persistent loss of appetite?
7. Are you more susceptible to colds, flu, headaches, or infections?
8. Is your heart rate 5 to 10 beats higher than usual?
9. Is your heart rate during exercise higher than usual?

Grete writes that the feelings in her legs and the way she breathes during exercise indicate when she can no longer push herself in training. Usually, heaviness in her legs goes away after a few minutes of running. When the feeling persists, she knows she should rest rather than train.

Her advice to avoid overtraining is never to try overcoming fatigue by force. Like Bruce Fordyce, she stresses that when in doubt, one should rest rather than train hard; one should not be overambitious and one should not overrace.

Treatment of the Overtraining Syndrome

Once the athlete has developed the full-blown overtraining syndrome, he or she must rest completely for anything between 6 and 12 weeks. Continued training or racing when seriously overtrained is totally counterproductive because the athlete's racing performance will be abysmal and because continued training will probably result only in injury or a major infection. My observation is that even early overtraining (the superplods), shown by a cold or other infection 7 to 14 days before a standard marathon or an ultramarathon, will slow the runner between 5 to 20 minutes and 45 to 60 minutes in those respective races.

In addition, continued training when one is overtrained will only prolong the period for which the athlete will finally have to rest. The sooner an athlete accepts the inevitable, the better.

The advice I give to overtrained runners is that they start running again only when they have the desire, and then only slowly. But for many of us, overtraining is usually a chronic, relapsing condition, so that we need some intellectual insight for its prevention.

Marathon running is deviant behavior; the human body was not designed principally for running 42 km or more at maximum possible speed. The fact that some athletes run marathons with distinction does not prove that the human body is a marathon machine any more than the conquest of Everest indicates that humans are high-altitude animals. Both simply indicate the remarkable flexibility of adaptation we have inherited. But although we can adapt well to a wide variety of opposing stresses, we are generalists, and we lack abilities to adapt specifically to any single severe stress for any length of time.

Bodily Changes With Overtraining

No one as yet knows the exact bodily changes that cause the overtraining syndrome.

There are, of course, those armchair experts who will tell you that overtraining is all in the mind, that it is purely due to a mental failure—the sporting equivalent of a "lack of character." All that such statements show, I believe, is that these experts have yet to learn firsthand that when physically stretched, the body—not the mind—is always the first to quit. The overtrained runner finds that although the mind is ready to run, the body would much rather be asleep in bed. And the more the mind forces one to train, the more the body resists until, in the race, the body has the final say.

I formerly believed that the superplods experienced after either a single long training run or after an unbroken period of heavy training were probably due to complete depletion of body carbohydrate stores. But that explains neither why the superplods last for much longer than the 24- to 48-hour period required to restock body carbohydrate stores nor why it is not possible to run good marathons within about 8 to 12 weeks of each other. It seems that this prolonged period of recuperation after races and long training runs must indicate the presence of other recovery processes, either in the muscles or in other parts of the body or in both. The prolonged recovery from overtraining supports this idea. Let us consider both these processes.

Evidence for Muscle Damage and Its Recovery After Severe Exercise

A number of studies show that muscles are damaged by severe, prolonged exercise like marathon running or heavy daily training, and that recovery from this damage takes a long time (see chapter 14).

Hikida et al. (1983) performed muscle biopsies on a group of marathon runners the day before, immediately after, and at 3, 5, and 7 days after a competitive marathon. The authors found strong evidence for muscle cell damage, which was the worst at 1 and 3 days after the race but was still present in the sample taken 7 days later. Worse, some runners' muscles showed damage even in the prerace samples. The authors concluded that both the intensive training and the marathon itself induce muscle cell damage, which explains the muscle cell soreness that accompanies heavy training and, in particular, marathon racing. The authors' data show that recovery from this damage is prolonged.

In a related study, P. Matin et al. (1983) injected a radioactive substance (technetium 99 m pyrophosphate) into the blood of ultramarathon runners after races of 80 and 160 km. By scanning the athletes with special cameras, the researchers were able to identify where the radioactive material, which is taken up by damaged cells including heart, muscle, and bone, was concentrated. There were abnormally high concentrations of radioactivity localized exclusively to the muscles of the lower limbs of all athletes. After uphill running, the increased radioactivity was found in the abductors (inner thigh muscles), whereas after downhill running the hamstrings, quadriceps, and buttock muscles were the most affected. The authors also noted that the runners who complained of the worst postrace muscle soreness had the greatest abnormalities on scanning.

The authors suggested that the greater the muscle pain after a race, the longer the recovery time required. Table 10.2 is a simple classification of muscle soreness and the length of time that hard training and racing should be avoided if the different grades of muscle damage develop.

Warhol et al. (1985) performed serial muscle biopsies on a group of 40 runners for up to 12 weeks after a standard marathon. Biopsies taken 48 hours after the race showed varying degrees of damage to the myofibrils, mitochondria, and sarcoplasmic reticulum. The damage was patchy and, at worst, affected 25% of the fibers in individual runners; in other runners little damage was apparent.

Table 10.2 Classification of Muscle Soreness

Grading	Symptoms	Indication
0	No discomfort.	Continue training.
1	Some discomfort on feeling muscle.	Reduce training for 7 days. No racing for 2 weeks.
2	Discomfort on walking. Unable to squat without discomfort.	Reduce training for 14 days. No racing for 1 month.
3	Severe pain. Walking with difficulty.	Reduce training for at least 1 month. No racing for 2 months.

Biopsies taken 7 days after the marathon showed beginning resolution of the acute injuries. The contents of the damaged myofibrils had been removed, leaving only empty or "ghost" muscle tubes. There was also evidence for an ingrowth of satellite cells, which would ultimately replace the damaged muscle cells.

One month after competition, there was little evidence of residual damage but clear evidence for muscle cell regeneration and repair. Evidence of regeneration was more marked in biopsies taken 8 to 10 weeks after the race.

The authors concluded that damage occurred to myofibrils that were depleted of their glycogen and lipid stores; that the injuries were focal and seldom exceeded more than 10% of the myofibrils examined; that the degrees of injury varied among runners; that the injuries did not induce necrosis (death) of muscles or activate inflammatory responses, rather the injuries were characterized by muscle fiber degeneration and "dropout"; and that the injuries were completely reversible within 10 to 12 weeks. The authors did notice, however, that veteran runners did have some areas of fibrosis in muscle, suggesting incomplete repair.

More recent studies have confirmed all these findings. Kuipers et al. (1989) followed a group of novice runners training for a 42-km marathon and showed that as the length of the athletes' training runs increased, so did the incidence of pathological changes in their muscles. They considered that these findings reflected a continuous degeneration and regeneration of muscle.

Sjostrom et al. (1987) performed muscle biopsies on a single athlete who ran an average of 44 miles (72 km) a day for 7 weeks. The biopsy taken before the run was normal. However, marked abnormalities were present in the biopsy taken 7 weeks later, after completion of the run. The muscle-fiber sizes varied considerably and regenerating and necrotic muscle fibers were observed. Average muscle-fiber size was reduced. The researchers found evidence of increased connective tissue and an infiltration of inflammatory cells. Similar changes were subsequently found in the muscles of a group of sub–2:40 marathon runners (Sjostrom et al., 1988).

These findings indicate that heavy training is associated with muscle damage. It seems reasonable, therefore, to suggest that the persistent muscle weakness and soreness so characteristic of the plods, the superplods, and the full-blown overtraining syndrome indicates severe and persistent muscle damage. Indeed, Sjostrom et al. (1987) reported that the "running speed" of the subject who ran 42 miles a day for 7 weeks "has continuously decreased since the experiment" (p. 519). As described elsewhere, we have also observed that athletes who race marathon and ultramarathon races frequently in any single year usually perform poorly for some considerable time thereafter.

More recent studies suggest that postexercise muscle soreness is probably a separate condition and is due not to the muscle damage described previously, but to damage to the connective tissue elements within the exercising muscles (D.A. Jones et al., 1987; see chapter 14).

The question that remains is, How far can we race before inducing this muscle damage? One obvious way to discover this is to monitor muscle soreness after races of different distances. Distances that do not cause muscle soreness do not, presumably, cause muscle damage. My experience is that races of up to 21 km usually do not result in marked postrace muscle soreness.

To study this, Strachan et al. (1984) monitored a blood protein (C-reactive protein), the levels of which rise when there is tissue death anywhere in the body. These researchers found the C-reactive protein levels rose markedly after marathon and ultramarathon races; after the 90-km Comrades Marathon, these levels equaled those normally found in patients with minor heart attacks. In races shorter than 21 km, essentially no rise occurred. This suggests that muscle cell damage starts to occur only in races longer than 21 km and becomes progressively worse the longer the race. Kuipers et al. (1989) have drawn the same conclusion.

Evidence for the Development of Chronic Muscle Fatigue With Daily Training

Research in swimmers has shown that even daily training produces chronic muscle fatigue from which muscles recover only with a quite prolonged period of reduced training or rest.

Costill (1985) and his colleagues (Costill et al., 1985) showed that the peak muscle power of a swimmer is least when the swimmer is training the most, and power increases progressively during a 7-day taper immediately prior to competition. This finding confirms the importance of a relatively long taper prior to competition, as first proposed by Forbes Carlile (1964) and now advocated by many elite athletes including ultramarathon runner Bruce Fordyce (see chapter 8). The subtle biochemical changes that explain this phenomenon are not clear, and the optimum duration of the taper has not been established.

Psychological Changes With Overtraining

W.P. Morgan and his colleagues (1987) reported the first detailed study of psychological changes with overtraining. They studied groups of swimmers and showed that mood disturbances characterized by reduced vigor and increased feelings of fatigue, depression, and anger developed during the periods of most intensive training. These changes, which are similar to those found in persons with marked depression, reversed spontaneously with rest or tapering for 3 to 6 weeks. The authors suggested that monitoring mood states with the appropriate psychological questionnaires may prevent the development of staleness and overtraining (W.P. Morgan et al., 1988).

WHOLE-BODY DAMAGE AND RECOVERY AFTER SEVERE EXERCISE

The best lead we have toward understanding the nature of the whole-body damage that occurs with overtraining comes from the landmark studies of the legendary Canadian biochemist Hans Selye, the man who developed an animal model that closely resembled overtraining. Selye (1957) exposed laboratory animals to a variety of stressful situations and observed their behaviors. His observations are summarized in Figure 10.4. He hypothesized that an organism exposed to a specific stress initially undergoes an "alarm reaction," during which resistance to that stress is reduced. If the organism survives this alarm reaction, it passes into the "stage of resistance" in which the organism has increased resistance to the specific stress to which it has now become adapted but reduced resistance to other stresses. But because all organisms have limited "adaptation energy" (Selye, 1950), when exposed to an unremitting stress, each organism must ultimately reach the "stage of exhaustion."

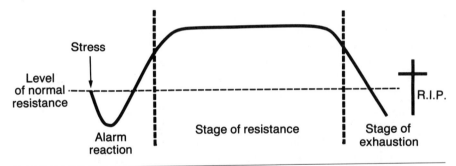

Figure 10.4 The general adaptation syndrome of Hans Selye.

Could it be that the overtrained runner is behaving like Selye's experimental animals, entering this exhaustion phase with impaired resistance to the specific stress of running and to less specific stresses such as allergy and infection? This would help explain the overtrained runner's increased susceptibility to infection (see Table 10.1).

In studying the biochemical basis of the overtraining syndrome, Barron et al. (1985) used heresay evidence that suggested that an even more severe form of the overtraining syndrome had been observed in athletes from East European countries who continued to overtrain for months, possibly years, and finally developed an illness known as Addison's disease. This condition is marked by depression, progressive weight loss, an inability to maintain blood pressure when standing (postural hypotension), and severe physical incapacitation. Similar but less severe symptoms have been described in overtrained runners (see Table

10.1). The cause of Addison's disease is a failure of the adrenal gland to secrete adequate amounts of certain hormones essential for life, in particular the hormone cortisol.

Following this lead, my colleague Dr. Geoff Barron (Barron et al., 1985) set out to determine whether overtrained runners were able to secrete cortisol normally in response to an appropriate biochemical challenge. A strong yet safe stimulus for cortisol secretion is a fall in the blood glucose level, which can be induced experimentally by injecting an appropriate dose of insulin into an obliging subject.

The researchers tested a group of overtrained runners to see how they responded to the stress of having their blood glucose levels dropped precipitously by an insulin injection. As predicted, these runners exhibited an abnormal cortisol response; they were unable to increase their blood cortisol levels appropriately in response to the massive challenge of severe hypoglycemia. This abnormality was not due to a failure of the adrenal gland itself, as originally suggested by Webster (1948) and Selye (1950), but rather to "exhaustion" of the hypothalamus, the gland that orchestrates the entire hormonal response of the body (see chapter 18). This fits well with the other overtraining symptoms of depression, loss of appetite, and loss of libido, all of which are also influenced by the functioning of the hypothalamus.

After a 6-week period, during which the overtrained runners rested and jogged only occasionally, their hormonal responses to insulin-induced hypoglycemia returned to normal, but this occurred some time before they had fully recovered. This suggests that some other recovery processes may also be required before the overtrained athlete can again run normally. A. Luger et al. (1988) recently reported that heavy training alone produces changes in the hypothalamic-pituitary-adrenal axis similar to those reported by Barron et al. (1985). A. Luger et al. (1988) noted that these changes are "reminiscent of those seen in patients with anorexia nervosa and depression" (279).

Another study (MacConnie et al., 1986) confirmed that intensively training athletes running 125 to 200 km/week also show hypothalamic dysfunction but to lesser degrees than Barron et al. (1985) found in overtrained runners. Specifically, the subjects studied by MacConnie et al. (1986) showed reduced spontaneous luteinizing-hormone (LH) release from the pituitary, the same abnormality found in female runners with menstrual abnormalities (see chapter 16). It is possible that these changes may be related to the negative changes in mood state reported by W.P. Morgan et al. (1987).

Different research groups have attempted to use this information to predict which athletes are overtraining. O'Connor et al. (1989) have shown that in response to large increases in training, salivary cortisol concentrations increase. Heavy training also causes serum testosterone levels to fall (see chapter 18); thus the ratio of serum testosterone to cortisol concentrations also falls with heavy training (Urhausen et al., 1987). However, no one has been able to use this information specifically to differentiate athletes who are overtraining from those who are training intensely but adapting effectively to that training.

So, until we have further, more definitive studies, I am happy to conclude that the overtraining syndrome is caused by a very major disruption of the body's ability to respond to normal stresses such as infection or running. It is possible that this quite gross abnormality represents the protective response of a totally exhausted body. Rather than suffer additional damage that would result if the body were allowed to continue training in this depleted state, the body responds by making training impossible. We must learn to respect the messages that our bodies give us when they are trying to tell us they have done too much.

11

Limits to Running Performance

"The man who has made the mile record is W.G. George . . . His time was 4 minutes 12.75 seconds and the probability is that this record will never be beaten."

Harry Andrews (1903)

"It is evident, then, that a man's best time for protracted competition must be assessed from a combination of physical and mental maxima, and this leaves us with a range of from about twenty-five to forty-five years."

Arthur Newton (1949)

"It's amazing that the record breaking in distance running has come from very small areas in the world. The Germans haven't produced anybody in 100 years . . . The Americans haven't really produced anybody . . . But take New Zealand; Australia; England; a small part of the African continent in Ethiopia, Tanzania and Kenya and maybe Finland. These countries have produced the record breakers."

Ron Clarke (Lenton, 1981)

"People talk about the possibility of a 2-hour marathon, but I think 2 hours 5 minutes would be a more realistic limit. . . . When it is reached, it will be done by a 10,000 metres runner who is motivated towards the marathon."

Ron Hill (Temple, 1981)

Just how fast can men and women run? Most theories on this topic are unsatisfactory because they are instinctive answers based largely on personal beliefs rather than on any scientific information. But do we in fact have any scientific basis for projecting how running records will improve in our lifetimes?

SCIENTIFIC PREDICTIONS OF WORLD RECORDS

The first scientist to consider this question was Professor A.V. Hill (1925). To determine how long a given effort can be maintained, Hill plotted the average speeds for all male and female world records in running against the times for which those speeds had been maintained (see Figure 11.1). From the graphs that were generated, he made the following conclusions.

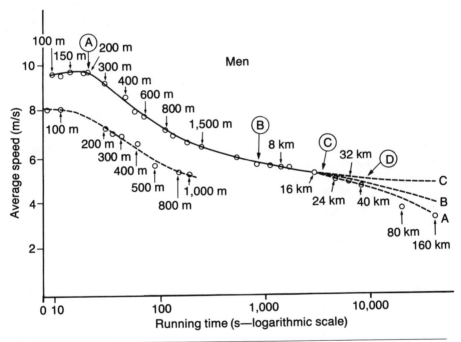

Figure 11.1 Professor A.V. Hill's plot of average running speeds for male and female world record holders up to 1925.
Note. From "The Physiological Basis of Athletic Records" by A.V. Hill, 1925, *Lancet,* **2,** p. 484. Copyright 1925 by The Lancet Ltd. Adapted by permission.

First, very high running speeds could be maintained for only relatively short times, the fastest running speeds being recorded in the 200-m race (Point A). Second, running speeds fell rapidly in events lasting more than 20 seconds and leveled off only in events lasting for more than 10 to 15 minutes (Point B). Third, in running events lasting more than 60 minutes, a further reduction in performance occurred, and this became exaggerated the longer the performance (Point C). This reduction was particularly marked in races longer than 40 km (25 miles; Point D). Fourth, the women's world running records achieved levels of only 79% of the corresponding male records. Fifth, Hill noted that some records were less good than others and would therefore be easier to break. He advised any "enterprising and scientific [male] athlete" to concentrate on the 120- and 500-yard and the 3/4- and 3-mile races and to avoid the 200- and 440-yard and 1- and 6-mile races. Female athletes were advised to try the 500-m race and to avoid the 300-m race.

Hill then considered the physiological basis of these observations. He estimated that the oxygen debt mechanism would support exercise for at least 50 seconds and concluded that the decrease in performance after 20 seconds of exercise must occur because the body was unable to release all its available energy stores in such a short time. He proposed that mechanical and nervous factors rather than depletion of energy reserves must be the critical factors limiting performance in explosive short-term activities.

To explain why there was only a gradual decline in the speed that could be maintained in events lasting between 10 and 60 minutes, Hill concluded that these activities were limited only by the athlete's maximum ability to consume oxygen, the $\dot{V}O_2$max value. As this was preset before the athlete began the race, the distance of the race would not influence performance greatly.

Next, Hill offered two suggestions to explain why a further, more rapid deterioration occurred in the speed that could be maintained in races between 10 and 100 miles (Line A in Figure 11.1).

First, he postulated that fatigue in these events might be due to "exhaustion of the material of the muscle or to incidental disturbances which may make a man stop before his muscular system has reached its limit" (A.V. Hill, 1925, p. 485). He suggested that a runner's glycogen supply would need to be bolstered by carbohydrate to sustain the effort required to maintain speed.

Second, Hill felt that the greatest athletes had confined themselves to distances of up to 10 miles and that had athletes of the caliber of Alf Shrubb and Paavo Nurmi regularly run marathon and longer races, they would have broken the records "very effectively" by producing performances that lay along either Line B or, better still, Line C.

To explain the inferior performances of the women, Hill concluded that this could be a result only of females' lower capacities for power production. As he described in his autobiography (A.V. Hill, 1965), this statement subsequently caused him considerable embarrassment: "The now defunct *Westminster Gazette* said that I had insulted the whole female sex; other papers took it up; and angry strong women came to my laboratory demanding to be 'tested'. . . . I have often wondered what it is about me that attracts lunatics" (p. 89).

The next scientist to consider the physiological implications of world sporting records was Ernst Jokl, who is emeritus professor of physical education at Kentucky University. Professor Jokl and his colleagues (1976) undertook a mathematical analysis of world records at different sporting events by plotting the measured variable (time, height, or distance) against the year in which the world record was established. They reasoned that in each event there must be a speed, height, weight, or distance that would prove to be the ultimate limit for human performance. This limit could be mathematically predicted because as any particular record approached this limit, each improvement on the previous record would be even smaller and the time period between each new record would grow ever longer. Thus, the curve of any graph plotting these records would start to flatten out; in mathematical terms the curve would become asymptotic. Records that were not approaching their limits would continue to improve linearly, or in cases in which rapid improvement was occurring, the graph might even ascend.

Professor Jokl concentrated on nonrunning events and noted that, with two exceptions, all these world records showed linear improvements, indicating that the ultimate performance limits in these events were not yet in sight and were therefore not currently predictable.

The exceptions to this pattern were the record curves for the women's 400-m freestyle swimming event and for the men's long jump. At the time of Jokl's study, the women's swimming record had taken a recent and dramatic upward curve. Furthermore, when Jokl wrote the article, the gap between the men's and women's records for this event was closing, and this raised the statistical possibility that in the late 1980s or early 1990s, women would swim the 400 m as fast as men.

The women's standard-marathon record has shown a similarly dramatic improvement in the last 20 years, and were this improvement to be maintained, the women's record would equal the men's record in the early 1990s (see Figure 11.2). This rapid improvement represents a sociological, not a physiological, phenomenon. As the number of women marathoners has increased, better female athletes have been attracted to the marathon and the marathon record has improved phenomenally.

However, in the past few years, the women's marathon curve has flattened predictably (Line D in Figure 11.2) as the record has become more representative of women's physiological limits. Now one can safely predict that until women can run short distances as fast as can men (Figures 11.1 and 16.4), the curve showing women's future improvements in marathon times will remain lower than that of the men, in proportion to how much slower women are than men at the shorter running distances.

The second exception to the rule of linear improvement in world records that Professor Jokl noted occurred in the men's long jump, in which the record curve started to become asymptotic in 1935 when Jesse Owens jumped 8.13 m. In the following 33 years, the record improved a scanty 0.22 m. Then the impossible

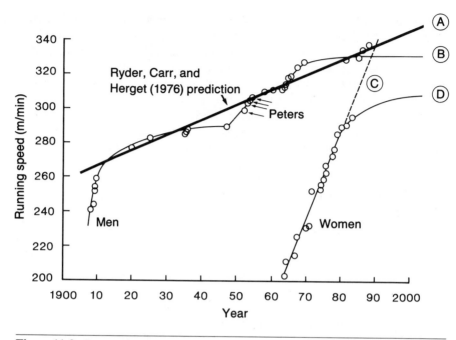

Figure 11.2 Progression of men and women's world standard marathon records.

occurred. At the 1968 Mexico Olympics, Bob Beamon added 0.55 m to the record, an estimated record progression of 84 years and roughly equivalent to a 6-second improvement in the 400-m world record or a 24-second improvement in the mile running record. It was, according to Jokl, the greatest single feat in the recorded history of athletics and a record that, as shown in Figure 11.3, should be safe for another 84 years. The factors contributing to Beamon's remarkable performance were the altitude and the following wind speed, which at 2.0 m/s was the maximum allowable (Brearly, 1977). Both these contributed to his reaching a higher sprinting speed than had previously been achieved by a long jumper (Ward-Smith, 1986).

But as I write this just 20 years later, the American Carl Lewis seems destined to break Beamon's record. If this occurs, it will suggest that the previous men's long-jump record was, in reality, not limited by human physiology. Rather, the long-jump training techniques of the past might have been inadequate and stagnant or the athletes best suited to long jump might simply not have been attracted to that event.

Three Chicago physicians, Ryder, Carr, and Herget (1976), have analyzed men's running records in detail. By plotting the speed (in m/min) of every world record ever set at both metric and nonmetric running distances against the year

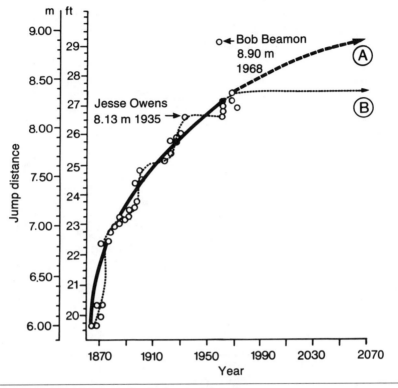

Figure 11.3   Record progression in the men's long jump.
Note. From "Advances in Exercise Physiology" by E. Jokl, R.L. Anand, and H. Stobody, 1976, *Medicine and Sport*, **9**, p. 7. Copyright 1976 by S. Karger AG, Basel. Reprinted by permission.

in which the record was established, the authors found that in the speed of every record in each event, there was a linear improvement equivalent to about 0.6 m/min/year for the 100 m and 0.9 m/min/year for the standard marathon (see Figure 11.4).

Ryder and his colleagues did not study records for races longer than the standard marathon. To see whether the same rules applied to longer races, I applied the same mathematical techniques used by Ryder and his colleagues to the records in races from 48 km to 24 hours. Unfortunately, in most of these races there are too few results to allow any reasonable inferences to be drawn. However, two ultramarathon races, the 83- to 87-km London-to-Brighton race and the 90-km Comrades Marathon, produce sufficient records to allow reasonable graphs to be drawn.

The records of both these races show the same pattern as that found by Ryder and his colleagues in the shorter distances; there is a linear improvement in running speeds ranging from 0.88 to 1.11 m/s/year.

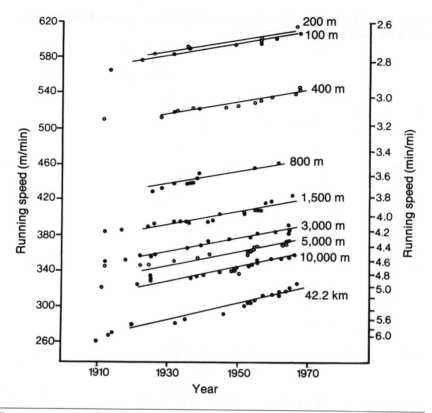

Figure 11.4 World-record progression for running distances from 100 m to 42.2 km appears to be linear.

Note. Adapted from "Future Performance in Footracing" by H.W. Ryder, H.J. Carr, and P. Herget, 1976, *Scientific American*, **234**, p. 112. Copyright © 1976 by Scientific American, Inc. All rights reserved.

Two interesting points follow from these observations. First, on the assumption that the improvement in world records is indeed linear, we can predict future world records. The men's 10,000-m record should be below 26 minutes by the turn of the century, the men's marathon world record below 2 hours by 2004, the men's 5,000-m record below 12 hours by 2020, and the men's mile below 3:30 by 2028 (see Table 11.1).

Second is the authors' explanation for the linear progression in records. Ryder and his colleagues explained this phenomenon in the following way:

The champions stop not at a given speed but when they set a record. Succeeding champions do the same. They telescope in their relatively short racing lives all the achievements of the great runners of the past and then stop with a gold medal, just as their predecessors did. Since it is the medal

Table 11.1   World-Record Predictions for Male Running Races From 100 m to 42 km for the Years 2004 and 2028

| | Time (hr:min:s.hundredth) | |
| | Year | |
Distance (m)	2004	2028
100	9.56	9.34
200	18.97	18.52
400	42.49	41.32
800	1:38.30	1:35.10
1,000	2:08.80	2:04.30
1,500	3:22.20	3:14.70
1,609 (1 mile)	3:38.30	3:30.00
2,000	4:40.00	4:28.90
3,000	7:12.10	6:54.10
5,000	12:24.80	11:51.90
10,000	25:44.00	24:31.00
16,000	42:48.00	40:39.00
20,000	53:57.00	51:09.00
24,000	1:06:50.00	1:03:17.00
30,000	1:24:42.00	1.20:01.00
42,200	2:00:00.00	1:53:13.00

Note. Adapted from "Future Performance in Footracing" by H.W. Ryder, H.J. Carr, and P. Herget, 1976, *Scientific American*, **234**, p. 112. Copyright © 1976 by Scientific American, Inc. All rights reserved.

and not the speed that stops them, the speeds they reach cannot be considered in any way the ultimate physiological limit. (Ryder et al., 1976, p. 114)

This explanation seems eminently reasonable. Almost certainly, throughout their careers the elite athletes condition themselves to run just fast enough to win gold medals or to set world records. It makes no sense to run 30 seconds faster than the opposition if one thousandth of a second will do. Furthermore, this explanation is compatible with a belief that many elite athletes hold, including former world record holders Roger Bannister, Herb Elliott, and Derek Clayton, that psychological rather than physiological factors ultimately separate the elite from the less good runners.

A possibility not mentioned by these authors and to which we must not be blind is that the linear improvements in these athletic records may be artifacts of the relatively short period during which these records have been recorded. Although humans have been running for millions of years, for only the past 100 or so years have we recorded accurate running records, and the data used by Ryder and his colleagues cover only the past 60 years.

What seems more likely is that the current world records are already on the asymptotic part of the record curve and that the linear part of the curve is hidden in our prehistory before the advent of the stopwatch, the measuring rod, and the human desire to measure oneself in athletic competition.

That this explanation is probably valid becomes more apparent if we consider the world records for the extreme ultradistance races. In those races few records have been set, but more importantly, some of the best records were set 100 years ago and have since improved little, if at all. Thus, in February 1882, Charles Rowell (see chapter 8) set world records for 160 km and 24 hours that were to last 71 and 49 years, respectively, before they were broken by Wally Hayward and Arthur Newton, both of whom were competing in single-day events. Yet, when Rowell established these records, he still faced 5 days of competition. During the next 2 days he set records that were finally broken only in 1984 by Yiannis Kouros (see chapter 8).

Another scientist who considers that world running records may already show evidence of becoming asymptotic is Hugh Morton, a statistician at Massey University, Palmerston North, New Zealand (Morton, 1983, 1984). Morton has paid particular attention to the progress of the men's 1,500-m world record since that record was first recorded in the late 19th century. Using sophisticated mathematical techniques, he has provided strong evidence, both mathematically and visually (see Figure 11.5), that the record progression in the men's 1,500-m race is best described by a curve, not by the straight line of Ryder et al. (see Figure 11.4). Certainly a straight line can be fitted to these data, but the curve fits better, suggesting very strongly that a true asymptote is being approached in this event. When he applied the same mathematical techniques to other races, Morton found essentially the same results: All track records were best considered to be asymptotic.

Using his equations, Morton predicted the ultimate male records for certain distances and the times that we can expect to see run each decade for the next 120 years (see Table 11.2).

The striking feature of Morton's predictions when compared to those of Ryder and his colleagues (see Table 11.1) is how very much more conservative they are. Ryder at el. (1976) predicted that by 2028 the mile will be run in 3:30, whereas Morton offered us only a 3:41.9 mile by 2030. Similarly, the prediction of Ryder et al. for the 10,000 m in 2028 is some 95 seconds faster than that predicted by Morton.

My personal inclination is to believe that Morton's ideas are probably closer to the truth. For example, a close look at the men's world standard-marathon record (see Figure 11.2) shows that the straight line of Ryder et al. (Line A) does not actually intersect all the points that represent record times, whereas a line that does intersect these points (Line B) seems to be made up of two asymptotic

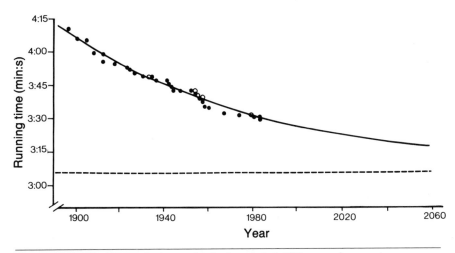

Figure 11.5 World-record progression in the men's 1,500-m running event.
Note. Reprinted from R.H. Morton, "You Can't Catch Me: I'm the Gingerbread Man" in *The Fascination of Statistics* edited by R.J. Brook, G.C. Arnold, T.H. Hassard, and R.M. Pringle, Marcel Dekker Inc., NY, 1984, p. 272, by courtesy of Marcel Dekker Inc.

lines. The first asymptote ends in 1952 with the appearance of Jim Peters and his dramatic 7-minute improvement in the men's world record in just 2 years. The second asymptote has only just ended with the recent spate of improvements in the men's world marathon record. Whether these improvements will continue or whether the record will fall progressively further behind the prediction line of Ryder and his colleagues remains to be seen.

Someone who agrees with Morton and me is British Olympian Ron Hill, who in 1970 ran the marathon in 2:09:28, then the world's fastest marathon time (chapter 8). Hill (Temple, 1981) has since stated the following:

> Unless doctors find a method, or evolution results in bigger people with longer legs, we'll never get down to 2 hours. I think it's impossible simply because I don't believe the human body is capable of carrying that much energy store in available glycogen or fat. (p. 68)

Before concluding this section, we must include Osler's (1978) running predictions (see Table 11.3). You will recall from chapter 2 that Osler used this graph to predict performances at different distances on the basis of performance at other distances (see Table 2.6). Each performance was given a value that equaled the year in which that particular performance would have been a world record.

Like Ryder and his colleagues, Osler predicts a linear improvement in world records, which, as Morton has shown, is probably unrealistic.

Table 11.2 Hugh Morton's Predicted Male World Running Records (min:s.hundredths) From 1980 to 2100

Distance (m)	1980	1984	1990	2000	2010	2020	2030	2040	2050	2060	2070	2080	2090	2100	Ultimate
100	9.87	9.95	9.80	9.74	9.68	9.63	9.58	9.54	9.50	9.47	9.44	9.41	9.39	9.37	9.15
200	19.98	19.72	19.81	19.66	19.52	19.40	19.29	19.19	19.09	19.00	18.92	18.85	18.79	18.73	18.15
400	44.08	43.86	43.70	43.34	43.01	42.71	42.44	42.18	41.95	41.74	41.54	41.36	41.20	41.04	39.33
800	1:42.6	1:41.7	1:41.7	1:40.9	1:40.1	1:39.4	1:38.7	1:38.1	1:37.6	1:37.1	1:36.7	1:36.3	1:36.0	1:35.7	1:33.0
1,500	3:32.5	3:30.8	3:29.9	3:27.5	3:25.4	3:23.5	3:21.8	3:20.2	3:18.8	3:17.6	3:16.4	3:15.3	3:14.4	3:13.6	3:05.7
1,609[a]	3:50.7	3:47.3	3:48.6	3:46.7	3:44.9	3:43.3	3:41.9	3:40.6	3:39.5	3:38.4	3:37.5	3:36.6	3:35.8	3:35.1	3:28.4
3,000	7:31.5	7:32.1	7:24.6	7:18.0	7:12.1	7:06.9	7:02.1	6:57.8	6:53.9	6:50.4	6:47.2	6:44.3	6:41.7	6:39.4	6:16.9
5,000	13:10.5	13:00.4	13:00.3	12:51.0	12:42.6	12:35.0	12:28.5	12:23.0	12:16.3	12:11.2	12:06.6	12:02.5	11:58.7	11:55.3	11:22.9
10,000	27:42.5	27:22.4	27:21.8	27:03.0	26:46.0	26:30.1	26:16.8	26:04.2	25:52.8	25:42.5	25:33.2	25:24.8	25:17.1	25:10.2	24:04.6

Note. From H. Morton, personal communication, March 1984.

[a] 1,609 m = 1 mile.

Table 11.3 Tom Osler's Predicted Male World Running Records (hr:min:s.hundredths) From 1980 to 2050

Distance (m)	1980	1990	2000	2010	2020	2030	2040	2050
1,609[a]	3:45	3:40	3:35	3:30	3:25	3:20	3:15	3:10
10,000	27:37.5	27:11.3	26:41.3	26:15	25:48.8	25:18.8	24:48.8	24:15
16,000	46:09.9	45:20	44:30	43:49	43:00	42:09.9	41:20	40:49.9
24,000	1:11:15	1:10:12	1:09:00	1:07:59	1:07:03	1:05:42	1:04:30	1:03:27
42,200	2:09:41	2:07:52	2:05:46	2:04:27	2:02:21	1:59:59	1:57:54	1:56:35

Note. From *Serious Runner's Handbook* (p. 171) by T. Osler, 1978, Mountain View, CA: World Publications. Copyright 1978 by T. Osler. Adapted by permission.

[a]1,609 m = 1 mile.

THE EFFECT OF AGE ON ATHLETIC PERFORMANCE

Another interesting insight that a study of world records allows concerns the effects of age on human performance capacity. The first scientist to suggest this use of athletic records was L.E. Böttiger of Stockholm's Karolinska Hospital (Böttiger, 1971, 1973).

By studying the average finishing times of competitors of different ages in a 30-km cross-country running race and in the 90-km Vasa cross-country ski race, Böttiger showed that the fastest runners in the shorter race were aged 26 to 30 years, whereas the best performers in the longer race were aged 31 to 36 years. After these ages, performances fell uniformly 5 to 10% per decade.

A similar study was carried out by Dan Moore (1975) of the Lawrence Livermore Laboratory in California. He plotted the 1974 world age records for the 200 m and the standard marathon and noted that performances in these races reached a peak in the age range of 20 to 30 years. Thereafter, performances in both races fell quite steeply, but the decrease in speed was greater in sprint than in distance running. This suggests that speed deteriorates faster with increasing age than does endurance. The reduction in speed with age was 6.9 and 10% per successive decade after age 30 in sprinting and 4.8 and 8% per successive decade in marathon running.

However, a recent study using more modern data refutes this finding. In a study of the running and swimming records of Masters athletes, Stones and Kozma (1986) found that endurance falls more rapidly with age than does speed. In my experience this is certainly true in swimming. Masters sprint swimmers are able to equal or better performances they established 20 or more years previously.

Another interesting observation is that the age at which peak performances have been achieved in Olympic track, field, and swimming events has remained remarkably constant for the past 100 years (Schulz & Curnow, 1988). This study confirms that the age of peak performance increases with the length of the foot-race but that women generally achieve peak performances at younger ages. The average age of peak performance in male long-distance runners is about 28 years of age; I am not aware of similar data yet available for women. I have subsequently plotted 1983 world standard age records and compared these with the current age records for the up-Comrades Marathon (see Figure 11.6).

Figure 11.6 shows that peak performances in both races occur in the range of 23 to 30 years and that after the age of about 40 years there is an almost linear and parallel decline in performances in both races. The slope of the fall in performance with age is quite similar to the curve describing the reduction in $\dot{V}O_2max$ with age. The phenomenal performance of 79-year-old Wally Hayward (see chapter 8) in the 1988 Comrades Marathon is also indicated on the figure.

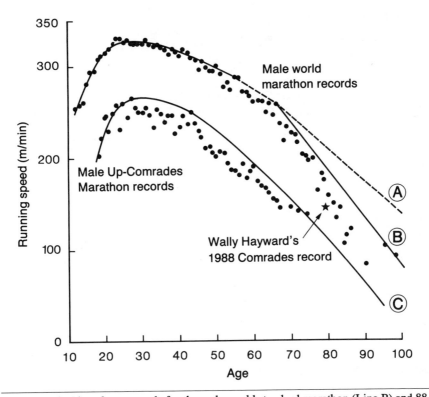

Figure 11.6 Plot of age records for the male world standard marathon (Line B) and 88- to 90-km Comrades Marathon (Line C) records. ''Up'' Comrades = the uphill run from Durban to Pietermaintzburg. Line A = optimum projection/prediction of performances, that is, what the results should be if more older people ran marathons and if there were no sudden aging effect at 65.

When runner Willie Loedolff noted this regular predictable decline in running performance with age, he suggested that this could be used as a system for age handicapping in long-distance races.

The curves for the world age records for the standard marathon and the Comrades Marathon show that the peak performances in each race are achieved at ages 25 and 26, respectively. This performance then becomes the standard for the race. Equivalent relative performances at different ages are calculated by dividing the time (in seconds) of the standard performance into the time (in seconds) of the records at all other ages. Thus, the world marathon record at age 25 is 2:08:13 (7,963 seconds) and that at age 95 is 6:42:10 (24,130 seconds). Thus, the relative performance of the 95-year-old record is 7,963 ÷ 24,130, which equals 0.33. Using this idea to calculate the relative performances at all ages allows us to draw Figure 11.7.

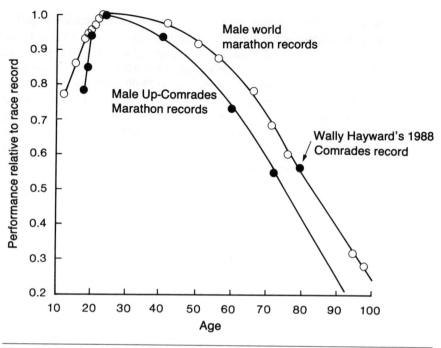

Figure 11.7 Plot of relative performances at different ages in the standard marathon and the 88- to 90-km Comrades Marathon.

Note that Figure 11.7 includes only the best age records at both these distances. This can be justified on the assumption that the best records are set by the athletes who come closest to the physiological limits set by their ages and that the weaker records are not representative of the true physiological limits at that age. For example, the fastest runners at those ages may be less gifted (i.e., they might have disproportionately lower $\dot{V}O_2$max values than runners at other ages) or they may not train as hard.

The curves in Figure 11.7 show that relative performances in the standard marathon are better than they are in the Comrades, particularly between ages 40 and 66. Thereafter the lines are almost parallel. Either performance falls off more precipitously in ultradistance races than it does in the standard marathon, or, more likely, the Comrades Marathon age records are "soft" (easier to break) compared to world marathon records. The athletes competing in the Comrades Marathon are relatively few in number, whereas many thousandfold more compete in standard marathons. That the performance of Wally Hayward in the 1988 Comrades Marathon falls closer to the line for the standard marathon than for the Comrades suggests that Comrades runners, in general, underachieve compared to the world's marathon runners.

From these figures we can draw up a table of relative performances for different ages at the standard marathon and ultramarathon distances (see Table 11.4). These figures can then be used as an age-handicapping system in marathon and ultramarathon races. For example, if the winner in a particular standard marathon race is 26 to 30 years old and runs a time of 2:20:00 then that time (8,400 seconds) becomes the reference standard. A 100-year-old runner who competed in the same race should have a performance relative to that of the winner by 0.25; that is, the 100-year-old should take 1 ÷ 0.25, or 4 times as long (33,600 seconds = 9:20), to run the race. Thus, a centenarian who completed the race quicker than 9:20 would have performed statistically better than the winner.

Table 11.4 Equivalent Relative Performances for 5-Year Age Groups in the Standard Marathon and 90-km Ultramarathon

Age	Reference values for standard marathon	Reference values for 90-km Ultramarathon
15-20	0.82-0.96	0.78-0.95
21-25	0.97-1.00	0.97-1.00
26-30	1.00-0.99	1.00-0.98
31-35	0.99-0.99	0.98-0.96
36-40	0.99-0.98	0.96-0.94
41-45	0.98-0.95	0.93-0.90
46-50	0.94-0.92	0.89-0.85
51-55	0.91-0.88	0.84-0.80
56-60	0.87-0.84	0.79-0.74
61-65	0.83-0.79	0.72-0.66
66-70	0.78-0.71	0.64-0.58
71-75	0.69-0.62	0.56-0.50
76-80	0.60-0.54	0.49-0.42
81-85	0.53-0.47	0.41-0.33
86-90	0.45-0.39	0.32-0.26
91-95	0.37-0.31	—
96-100	0.30-0.25	—

Note. Find the reference value for your age group. Divide 1 by your reference value, then multiply this quotient by the winner's time (in seconds). This determines your equivalent relative performance, which indicates the time that is statistically equal to the winner's time for your age.

Unfortunately, I could not find world age records for distances shorter than the standard marathon. Such records, were they to be kept, would obviously be of considerable value because they would allow an appropriate handicapping system to be developed for races of distances shorter than the marathon.

An important advantage of this type of handicapping system is that it is independent of the difficulty of the course or the prevailing environmental conditions, because these will be the same for all the competitors. The first competitor to finish the race will be either helped or hindered by the environmental conditions of the course, and the index will be automatically corrected for that. I hope that at some time in the future, this handicapping index will become a feature of all running races.

Interestingly, sprinting speed in both running and swimming falls less rapidly with age than does speed in longer distance races (Stones & Kozma, 1986). Furthermore, freely chosen walking speed falls relatively little up to age 62. Thereafter, the rate of decline increases 10-fold, suggesting that a major biological change occurs at that age (Himann et al., 1988).

ALTITUDE AND WORLD RECORDS

The 1968 Olympic Games, held in Mexico City at an altitude of 2,500 m, provided an opportunity to study the effects of this altitude on human performance. By comparing the winning times at various running distances with the world records for those distances, researchers found that performances at distances below 800 m were improved, whereas performances at greater distances were impaired, progressively more with increasing distance.

Figure 11.8 provides a composite picture of these results and shows that performances in races of 100 to 400 m were enhanced by 1 to 2%, whereas performances in races from the 3,000-m steeplechase to the standard marathon were impaired by 5 to 7%.

The reasons for these opposing effects of altitude on running performance at short and long distances were discussed in chapter 9, and Figure 9.1 compares the effects of different altitudes on running performance.

BIORHYTHMS AND WORLD RECORDS

Recently much interest has focused on the concept that biorhythms can predict when any athlete will perform either well or badly on a particular day.

This concept holds that from the moment of birth, each human acquires three biorhythm cycles of fixed, but different, periods that continue unaltered for life (see Figure 11.9). The physical cycle is said to affect the person's energy, aggressiveness, strength, endurance, resistance, and physical condition; this cycle lasts 23 days. The emotional or sensitivity cycle influences optimism, judgment, temper, mood, and teamwork and lasts 28 days. The intellectual cycle, which supposedly regulates mental alertness, intelligence, logic, memory, concentration,

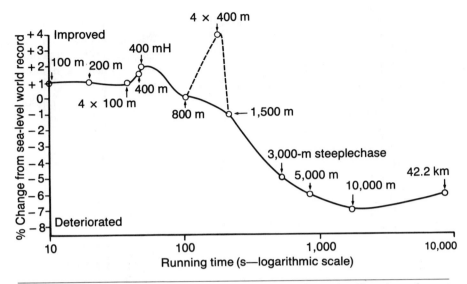

Figure 11.8 The effect of medium altitude on athletic performance. Experience from the 1968 Olympic Games.

responsiveness, presence of mind, and speed of comprehension lasts 33 days. The first half of each of these cycles is positive, and the second half is negative. Critical days occur at the beginning of each cycle as the cycle turns from negative to positive and again at the middle as the cycle turns from positive to negative.

Thus, when applied to sport, the biorhythm theory holds that athletes will perform best during the positive phases of their cycles, particularly the physical cycles, and less well during the negative phases of these cycles. Performances on critical days are likely to be particularly unfavorable. To ensure that this theory can be turned to commercial advantage, various enterprising individuals have developed computer programs for either hand-held calculators or microcomputers that will help the athletes decide when their biorhythms are either favorable or unfavorable.

Little, if any, scientific information has emerged to support this biorhythm theory in sports or in other areas.

In an attempt to find out whether biorhythms do in fact influence athletic performance, Brian Quigley (1982) of the University of Queensland, Australia, performed an ingenious study. He calculated the frequencies at which 700 world (metric) athletic records, set in track and field events between 1913 and 1977, had occurred in the positive, negative, or critical phases of the record setters' biorhythm cycles. If the biorhythm theory is correct, virtually all such records must have been set during the positive phase of each athlete's cycle, with none during the negative or critical phases.

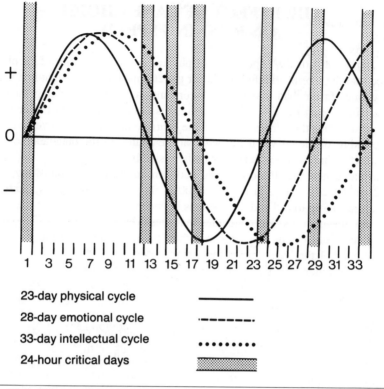

23-day physical cycle   ————

28-day emotional cycle   ·———·

33-day intellectual cycle   • • • • • • • •

24-hour critical days

Figure 11.9 The biorhythm cycles.

Quigley found that the number of records set during each of these phases fitted an entirely random distribution. This led Quigley to conclude that world athletic records occur randomly and are not influenced by biorhythms.

Variables other than biorhythms explain good and bad performances in competition, as discussed in detail in chapter 9.

However, we should note that the body does have a well-established 24-hour (circadian) rhythm and that those parameters determining athletic performance reach a maximum between noon and 9:00 p.m. and then decline to a minimum between 3:00 a.m. and 6:00 a.m. (Winget et al., 1985). Thus, performance is always better in the afternoon than in the morning, and races held in the early morning are less likely to produce records than are races held in the afternoon under identical environmental conditions.

This might be an important consideration for runners intent on setting world records for any distance but especially for the marathon, which is usually raced in the early morning.

THE EFFECT OF LANE CHOICE ON RUNNING SPEED

P.C. Jain (1980) of the department of physics at the University of Zambia observed that the world running record for the 200 m run in a straight line is about 0.4 seconds faster than that run on a conventional, curved running track. The slower time when running on a track results from overcoming the centripetal force as one runs the curves. Because the centripetal force is an inverse function of the radius of the curve, it follows that the runner in the outside lane will be less affected than will be the runner in the inside lane.

Jain calculated that the difference between adjacent lanes constitutes about 0.012 and 0.024 seconds in 200- and 400-m races, respectively, accounting for a difference of up to 0.8 and 1.6 seconds between the inside and outside lanes in 200- and 400-m races. He concludes that these differences are sufficiently important to be corrected. He suggests either that the distance of the inside lanes be shortened or that these races start *before* rather than *on* the curve. Thus, the start for the outer lane should be moved from *on* the curve (as is the present practice) to the point where the straight part of the track meets the curved section. In this way, the athlete in the outside lane would run the entire curve and would therefore run a longer distance on the curve (because of the greater radius of the curve), whereas the runner in the inside lane would run a shorter distance on the curve. In this way, the advantage gained by running in the outside lane would be neutralized, because runners in that lane would be exposed to the same centripetal force as before but for a longer time.

THE EFFECT OF TRACK COMPLIANCE ON RUNNING SPEED

In 1976, two Harvard University engineers, Thomas McMahon and Peter Greene (T.A. McMahon & Greene, 1978; 1979), were approached by the athletics department of that university to design an indoor running track that would both reduce the risk of injury and optimize the athlete's running speeds during competition.

The engineers' intuition told them that the softer or more compliant the track surface, the lower the risk of injury. But a soft surface would not optimize running speeds, because when running on an absorbing surface, the athletes would spend so much time sinking into and rebounding from the surface that their speeds would be considerably reduced.

To establish a surface compliance that would optimize both running speed and low injury risk, McMahon and Greene performed a series of experiments to determine the effects that surfaces of differing hardness had on the two important components of running speed—ground-contact time and stride length. Contrary to expectations that an unyielding, hard surface would be fastest, the researchers discovered that due to an inbuilt shock-absorbing or "damping" component in muscle, ground-contact time was least and stride length greatest when the running surface was of intermediate hardness, specifically when the track compliance was in the range of 2 to 4 times the compliance of human muscle. The stiffness of the track and that of the athletes' muscles had to be "tuned" for each other. When this was achieved, the authors predicted that the runner's track times would be reduced by between 2 and 3%, a predicted improvement on the world mile record of up to 7 seconds.

Their prediction has yet to be validated, because few if any outdoor tracks have yet been built to the specifications determined by these innovative workers.

Part III

Health
and Medical
Considerations

12

Understanding Injuries

"It is not unusual for an athlete to tear a tendon, or to strain a muscle, and not unknown even for him to pull off a piece of a bone by an exceedingly violent effort. We are obviously not far from our limit of safety. If we doubled our speed of movement, the number of breakages would increase very many times, and athletics would become a highly dangerous pastime."

Archibald Hill (1927)

"First of all find the cause."

Arthur Newton (1935)

"Treat the reason, not the result. Treat the cause, not the effect."

George Sheehan (1978a)

"If athletes were given less care and more thought, the doctors might come up with some original ideas on why illness persists, why injury doesn't clear up. If more non-physicians—podiatrists and physio-therapists, for instance—could be induced to lend their ideas and talents, we might see a completely new approach to sports medicine. And if the athlete had to wait longer for surgery, he might have time to recover from his ailments."

George Sheehan (1975)

Runners often hear dire warnings about the dangers of running to their physical well-being if not to their very lives. For example, American cardiologists Friedman et al. (1973) and Burch (1979) described jogging as a form of mass suicide, and they see runners as deserving prey for the automobile or our own coronary arteries. Some orthopedic surgeons dismiss running as an outrageous threat (Apley, 1978), especially to the integrity of the human knee. Such activity, they predict, will leave us with ''knees so badly deteriorated as to be crippling'' (Sonstegard et al., 1978, p. 44).

Because health is not our aim, these dire threats of imminent cardiological demise or chronic orthopedic disability quite miss the point. They are just so much hot air and are not even true. Studies by disinterested scientists, rather than antijogging activists, found that ''daily physical activities or sports cannot be incriminated as an important contributory factor in sudden death in the general population'' (Vuori et al., 1978, p. 287; see also chapter 18) and that long-distance running cannot be considered a factor in the development of osteoarthritis, at least of the hip (Puranen et al., 1975).

The dire medical warnings fail to impress us runners because they come from those who have learned everything from the outside without ever bothering to undertake that most fundamental learning process—personal experience.

The single running danger that really does concern us is the epidemic of running injuries—the modern-day athletic pandemic. What makes running injuries so dangerous is that doctors often fail to think about the root cause, and so treatment fails. Running injuries have a unique feature; an identifiable and treatable cause. And until that cause is rectified, the conventional approach—the rest, drugs, injections, and surgery—is just an expensive waste of time.

The first to conclude this was Dr. George Sheehan (1972, 1975, 1978a). Suffering perpetually from injuries, Sheehan was the first to admit that his colleagues could not help him. The medical elite were powerless to cure, much less to prevent, his myriad running injuries.

At the same time, Sheehan wrote the world's only medical column in a running magazine (*Runner's World*). In his writings Sheehan espoused the traditional orthopedic advice: The runner's injury must be initially treated with rest, physiotherapy, and drugs. When these measures failed there would have to be cortisone injections and ultimately surgery. Even then the outlook was grave. In the early 1970s, most injured runners soon became ex-runners.

But through his special pipeline to the running world, Sheehan learned of those runners' experiences that suggested that this traditional approach was off target. Sheehan learned of a high school runner whose knees hurt only when he trained in a particular pair of shoes. Another suffered pain only when he ran continuously in one direction on a banked track. Someone else found that running on the outside of his foot helped alleviate a painful knee. Sheehan himself observed that the slant of the road seemed to be a factor, because he experienced discomfort only when running continually on one side of the road but was pain free when running on the opposite side.

The ultimate revelation came from the experience of the ex-marine who refused to stop running despite severe knee pain, which resisted every possible therapeutic intervention that Sheehan or anyone else prescribed. The marine was finally saved when he developed foot pain in addition to his knee injury and was referred to a foot specialist (podiatrist). The in-shoe foot support (orthotic) that was prescribed to relieve the foot pain cured not only the runner's foot injury but also his knee pain. From this fortuitous event, Sheehan drew the empirical conclusion that the foot might have something to do with running injuries in other parts of the leg.

Later, there were Dave Merrick's famous knees (Sheehan, 1978a). Merrick, a champion high school runner, was sidelined at college with severe knee pain for which he received the textbook treatment: 14 months of rest, corrective exercises, drugs, cortisone injections, and finally surgery. When surgery proved unsuccessful, the whole process was started again and continued a further 18 months, until surgery was again suggested. But that time Merrick demurred. Instead he sought out Sheehan to find out whether the runners might know something not yet in the medical textbooks.

As Merrick later told the press, the meeting nearly started badly: "I thought Dr. Sheehan was nuts at first. I thought he was some kind of quack. Here, my knees are all swollen and he looks at my feet" (Sheehan, 1978a, p. 117). By that time Sheehan had sufficient experience to believe that when Merrick's feet were corrected, the injured knees would take care of themselves. And so they did. Within a week of fitting a pair of custom-made in-shoe supports, Merrick was back on the road. Within 6 weeks, he had won his college 2-mile indoor championship, and within a further 3 months he was the university cross-country champion. Inexpensive in-shoe supports had succeeded where expensive conventional therapy had failed.

In the years since these first therapeutic miracles Sheehan and others have taught us that the key to the successful treatment of running injuries is to be on the lookout for that mysterious ''X factor,'' that hidden factor that is responsible for the runner's injury. We have learned that those very factors that make the athlete great—genetic endowment, training methods, and training environment—are the same factors responsible for injuries. A myriad of inbuilt afflictions exist, each a potential destroyer—the internal twist of the femur or tibia, the squinting patellae, the bow legs or knock-knees, the short leg, and the flat or high-arched feet.

When these genetic factors are exposed to the hostile environment of shoes and surfaces and are expected to withstand impossible training loads, injury becomes not only possible but inevitable. Treatment of that injury must take into account every possible contributory factor—the genetics, the environment, and the training.

Experience with my own running injuries is not dissimilar from that of Sheehan. A few months after my first Comrades Marathon in 1973, I developed a persistent injury that resisted all the conventional medical advice. Only when I attended the 1976 New York Academy of Science Conference on the Marathon (Milvy, 1977) and heard the presentations by doctors George Sheehan, Richard Schuster, and Steven Subotnick did I begin to appreciate that attention to my running shoes and the use of an orthotic might cure my injury. These measures worked, and since then I have not suffered any further major running injuries.

This experience, together with knowledge gained from treating those injured runners kind enough to risk my advice, led me to formulate 10 laws of running injuries (see Table 12.1), which need to be appreciated especially by injured runners.

Table 12.1   The 10 Laws of Running Injuries

1. Running injuries are not an act of God.
2. Each running injury progresses through four grades.
3. Each running injury indicates that the athlete has reached the breakdown point.
4. Virtually all running injuries are curable.
5. X rays and other sophisticated investigations are seldom necessary to diagnose running injuries.
6. Treat the cause, not the effect.
7. Rest is seldom the most appropriate treatment.
8. Never accept as a final opinion the advice of a nonrunner.
9. Avoid the knife.
10. There is no difinitive scientific evidence that running causes osteoarthritis in runners whose knees were normal when they started running.

THE 1ST LAW OF RUNNING INJURIES:
Running Injuries Are Not an Act of God

Injuries that occur in sport fall into two groups: *extrinsic* and *intrinsic*.

Extrinsic injuries result when an external force acts on the body, for example in contact sports like rugby, American football, and boxing. The first sports medicine specialists were probably those doctors who looked after the Roman gladiators. In modern times, the first orthopedic surgeons who cared for athletes in major contact sports were indeed the first modern sports medicine doctors. The result of this has been that textbooks of orthopedics and sports medicine have until very recently been restricted to extrinsic injuries and have essentially ignored injuries occurring in noncontact sports.

Intrinsic injuries, on the other hand, result from factors inherent in the body itself and have nothing to do with external trauma. These injuries result from the interaction of at least three identifiable factors: the athlete's genetic build, training environment, and training methods. Only the genetic factor remains constant; environment and training methods are forever changing.

The critical genetic factor that predisposes one to running injuries is lower limb structure, because this largely determines how our hips, knees, and ankles and their supporting structures—muscles, tendons, and ligaments—function during running. Because of differences in genetic structure, virtually no two runners function identically. More importantly, perfect mechanical function is exceedingly rare and is restricted to a handful of top runners. The rest of us run despite varying grades of biomechanical imperfection. Back in the pack where I run you will discover the "Bad Genes Bunch." Take any 10 of us and you will have every possible biomechanical running abnormality ever described (and a few that defy description).

In short, it seems that we have not yet adapted to an upright posture; our feet and lower limbs are better adapted to climbing trees than they are to running on a flat surface (see Figure 12.1). As Amberson (1943) wrote, "When man's subhuman ancestors dared to rise and walk upon their hind legs, they essayed a physiological experiment of no mean difficulty" (p. 143).

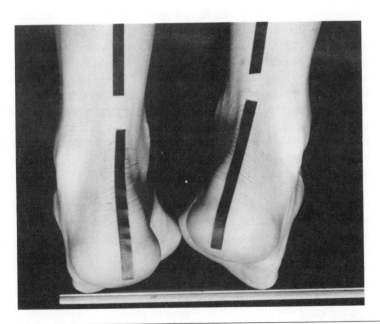

Figure 12.1 Feet assume the neutral position when not bearing weight. The deviation from the vertical at the heel in this picture is known as rearfoot varus; the deviation from the horizontal on the forefoot is known as the forefoot varus.

The list of genetic afflictions that can predispose us to running injuries includes the following: leg-length asymmetry (short-leg syndrome); genu varum (bow legs); genu valgum (knock-knees); forefoot or rearfoot malalignment; and, in their worst form, the "malicious or miserable malalignment syndrome," comprising twisting (internal rotation) of the femur, squinting or "kissing" patellae, knock-knees, externally rotated tibia, and flat feet (excessive foot pronation).

The description in the early 1970s of the manner in which these structural abnormalities interfere with the normal functioning of the foot and lower limb during running and how they interact with running surfaces, shoes, and training methods was the single most important advance in sports medicine in the past 20 years. Although not yet fully understood, a common pathway seems to exist by which these abnormalities cause running injuries.

The running stride is divided into two major phases: the short support or stance phase and the longer swing or recovery phase. One running cycle is from heel strike to the next heel strike of the same foot. During each running stride, the leg rotates in the following sequence (see Figure 12.2). During the swing or recovery phase of the cycle (Positions 5 to 11, right leg), the leg rotates inward (internal rotation), and this continues during the first part of the support or stance phase (Position 1). By midsupport (Position 2), the direction of rotation reverses to one of outward (external) rotation, which continues at toe-off (Positions 3 and 4).

As soon as the foot is planted on the ground (Position 1), the frictional forces between the sole and the surface prevent the foot from passively following the internal/external rotation sequence occurring in the lower limb. Therefore a mechanism has to be present to allow the rotation sequence of the upper limb to continue without involving actual movement of the foot in relation to the ground. To achieve this, the subtalar component of the ankle joint acts as a universal joint, transmitting the internal rotation of the lower limb (in the transverse plane) into an inward rolling or pronatory movement at the ankle (in the frontal or horizontal plane; see Figure 12.3). As the ankle joint pronates, it unlocks the joints of the midfoot, allowing these also to roll inward. The importance of this movement is that it absorbs and distributes the shock of landing and allows the foot to adapt to an uneven running surface.

In the athlete with normal running mechanics, after 55 to 60% of the stance phase as been completed, the upper limb begins to rotate externally, and the ankle rotation reverses itself and rotates outward (supination) until, just before toe-off, the ankle and midfoot joints lock in a fully supinated position. This results in the lower limb becoming a rigid lever allowing for a powerful toe-off.

In the ideal running gait there is an early, limited degree of pronation followed sometime near the middle of the stance phase of the running stride by supination of the subtalar joint.

Unfortunately, only a very small percentage of runners have sufficiently normal biomechanical structures to allow this normal sequence of events. Most of

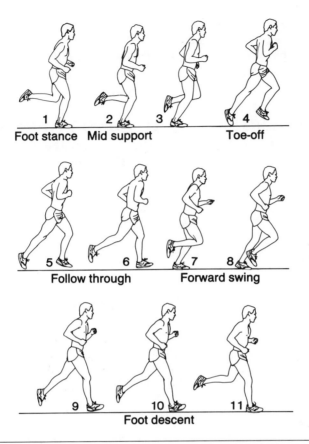

Figure 12.2 The running stride. Stance phase 1-3; swing phase 4-11.

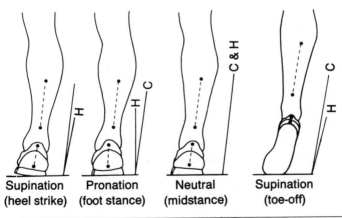

Supination	Pronation	Neutral	Supination
(heel strike)	(foot stance)	(midstance)	(toe-off)

Figure 12.3 Ankle joint pronation during the foot contact phase. C = calf alignment; H = heel alignment.

us are saddled with feet that either do too much rolling (the hypermobile foot) or too little rolling (the so-called rigid or "clunk" foot). And when these feet are attached to minor malalignments in the lower limbs, it becomes remarkable that any runner can escape injury.

THE 2ND LAW OF RUNNING INJURIES:
Each Running Injury Progresses Through Four Grades

Unlike extrinsic injuries, in which the onset is almost always sudden and dramatic (e.g., the football player caught in a ferocious tackle), the onset of intrinsic running-related injuries is almost always gradual. Running injuries become gradually and progressively more debilitating, typically passing through four stages or grades.

- *Grade I*. Causes pain only after exercise and is often felt only some hours after exercise has ceased.
- *Grade II*. Causes discomfort, not pain, during exercise but is insufficiently severe to reduce the athlete's training or racing performance.
- *Grade III*. Causes more severe discomfort, recognized as pain, that limits the athlete's training and interferes with racing performance.
- *Grade IV*. So severe that it prevents any attempts at running.

Appreciating these distinctions in the severity of running injuries allows a more rational approach to treatment. An athlete with a *Grade I* injury requires less active treatment than does the athlete with a *Grade IV* injury. Similarly, the athlete with a *Grade I* injury does not have to be excessively concerned about the injury as long as it does not progress to a *Grade II* injury. Should this happen, more serious attention should be paid to the injury.

The runner certainly need not fear that a chronic *Grade I* injury will suddenly deteriorate overnight to a *Grade IV* injury; the only exceptions to this rule are stress fractures and the iliotibial band friction syndrome, both of which can become incapacitatingly severe very rapidly.

The grade of the injury helps the doctor define each athlete's pain or anxiety threshold. The athlete who seeks attention for an injury only when it reaches *Grade IV* clearly has a different anxiety threshold than does the athlete who seeks urgent attention for a *Grade I* injury. Obviously, the advice given for each type will also differ greatly; the former requires little psychological support, the latter much more.

THE 3RD LAW OF RUNNING INJURIES:
Each Running Injury Indicates That the Athlete Has Reached the Breakdown Point

This law is really a corollary to the 1st law, which holds that running injuries occur for a reason. The 3rd law simply emphasizes that once an injury has occurred, it is time to analyze why the injury has happened at all. This will frequently be because the athlete has reached the breakdown point, usually because of some change in training routine. He or she may be training harder or running farther or may be running on a different terrain or in different or worn-out running shoes.

My belief is that every athlete has a potential breakdown point, a training intensity and a racing frequency at which the athlete breaks down. This point could be a weekly total of 30 km or 300 km in training and a racing frequency of 1 or 50 races a year.

The key in the prevention and treatment of injuries is to understand that just as most of us will never win a big race, because of certain genetic limitations, so our genes limit our choice of shoes, influence what surfaces we can safely train on, and ultimately determine what training methods we can survive. Only when we learn this will we have sufficient wisdom to be injury resistant. The corollary, of course, is that athletes who are frequently injured aren't yet wise enough to appreciate these points. When a running injury occurs, the factors that the wise runner needs to consider are the following: training surfaces, training shoes, and training methods.

Training Surfaces

Running surfaces are often too hard or too cambered. The ideal running surface is a soft, level surface such as a dirt road. Unfortunately, we are usually forced to run on tar roads or concrete sidewalks. Furthermore, roads are usually cambered, which forces the foot on the higher part of the slope to rotate inward (pronate) excessively and reduces the range of movement of the foot on the lower part of the slope. In addition, the leg on the lower side of the camber is artificially shortened and therefore acts as a "short leg."

Grass surfaces, although soft, are uneven, and the sand on beaches is either too soft (above the high-water mark) or too cambered (below the high-water mark). Athletic tracks are of varying hardnesses and introduce the problem of running continuously in one direction. This causes specific stresses on the outer leg, which must overstride to bring the athlete around each corner.

Similarly, uphill running stretches the Achilles tendon and calf muscles and tilts the pelvis forward, whereas downhill running accentuates the impact shock of landing and pulls the pelvis backward, thereby extending the back. Downhill running also causes the muscles to contract eccentrically, thereby increasing muscle damage (Schwane et al., 1983). Overstriding, which is more common when running downhill, also increases the loading on the anterior calf muscles.

A running injury may first occur shortly after the athlete has changed to uphill or downhill running, to running on the beach or on a "Tartan" or cinder track, or to running continuously on an unfavorable road camber.

Training Shoes

Injury may follow a recent change in shoes, either a switch from training shoes to racing flats or spikes or a switch from one pair of shoes to another or, more commonly, from one model to another. Running in worn-out shoes with worn-off heels or with heel cup and midsole molding to the genetic foot faults, usually collapsing inward (see Figure 14.1), or running in shoes in which the midsole has become compacted or hard (see Figures 14.3 and 14.5), can also cause injury.

Training Methods

Injury frequently follows a sudden increase in training distance or speed (training too much, too fast, too soon, too frequently), or it occurs when too many races or long runs have been undertaken or when insufficient stretching has been done before or after running.

Novice runners, women in particular, are especially prone to injury if they run too much and are too ambitious during their first 3 months of running. It seems that beginning runners who increase their training according to the rapid improvement in the fitness of their hearts, lungs, and leg muscles may exceed the capacities of their bones (which adapt more slowly) to cope with the extra load caused by running and may develop shinsplints or stress fractures.

Training also promotes muscle strength/flexibility imbalances. Every mile that we run increases the strength and inflexibility of the muscles most active in endurance running—the posterior calf, hamstring, and back muscles—and correspondingly reduces strength in their opposing muscles—the front calf, front thigh, and stomach muscles. This strength/flexibility imbalance may ultimately become an important factor in injury, and many authorities (B. Anderson, 1975; Beaulieu, 1981; Uram, 1980) but not all (Osler, 1978) believe that it is important to maintain flexibility. For this reason, flexibility (stretching) exercises are usually prescribed to both prevent and cure injuries. How well these work I am not sure. However, full description of the commonly prescribed stretching exercises is provided in chapter 13.

THE 4TH LAW OF RUNNING INJURIES:
Virtually All Running Injuries Are Curable

Only a minute fraction of true running injuries are not entirely curable by quite simple techniques, and surgery is required in only very exceptional cases. For example, in a study of 200 consecutive running injuries seen at a sports injury clinic, Pinshaw et al. (1983) found that within 8 weeks of following the simple advice described in this book, nearly three-fourths of the injured runners were pain free and running almost the same training distance as before injury. In addition, most of the runners who were not helped had not adhered to the treatment protocol.

Armed with this knowledge, my first priority is to reassure injured runners that they can almost certainly be completely cured. The only possible exceptions to this rule are the following types of injuries:

- Injuries that occur in runners with very severe biomechanical abnormalities for which conventional measures are unable to compensate adequately. Such runners are likely to become injured whenever they train sufficiently hard. However, I have found that only a small number of runners have such severe mechanical abnormalities that they are unable to run without injury.

- Injuries that result in severe degeneration of the internal structure of important tissues, in particular the Achilles tendon.

- Injuries that occur in those who start running on abnormal joints, in particular hips, knees, and ankles. Typical patients with this problem are former football players who damaged one of these major joints and required major surgery. The joint is never again quite the same after major surgery, and by the time such players start to run, usually in their late 30s, their joints have often degenerated to the point where they cause pain during running.

An important corollary to this law is that if you are not completely cured of your running injury by the experts you initially consult, you should look for help elsewhere. But treat even the advice of runners with some caution, and do not accept such advice unconditionally.

THE 5TH LAW OF RUNNING INJURIES:
X Rays and Other Sophisticated Investigations Are Seldom Necessary to Diagnose Running Injuries

Most running injuries affect the soft tissue structures (tendons, ligaments, and muscles), particularly those near the major joints. These structures do not show up on X rays; thus, you should be wary of the practitioner whose first reaction to your injury is to order an X ray. Unless that X ray can be justified, you are probably better off putting the money that you would have spent on the radiological examination into a good pair of running shoes.

The diagnosis of most running injuries is made with the hands, so practitioners who do not carefully feel the injured site with their hands must always be suspect.

THE 6TH LAW OF RUNNING INJURIES:
Treat the Cause, Not the Effect

Because each running injury has a cause, it follows that the injury can never be cured until the causative factors are eliminated.

Therefore, surgery, physiotherapy, cortisone injections, drug therapy, chiropractic manipulations, and homeopathic remedies are likely to fail if they do not correct all the genetic, environmental, and training factors causing the runner's injury. It is wise to remember the following axiom: The runner is an innocent victim of a biomechanical abnormality arising in the lower limb. First treat the biomechanical abnormality, and *then* treat the injury.

Unfortunately, some runners' injuries exist more in their heads than in their legs. This group is characterized by failure to respond to those forms of treatment that would normally be expected to succeed.

THE 7TH LAW OF RUNNING INJURIES:
Rest is Seldom the Most Appropriate Treatment

If an injury is caused solely by running, then the logical answer for those who know no better is to advise rest as the obvious cure. Rest does indeed cure the acute symptoms, but like any therapy that does not aim to correct the cause of the injury, rest must ultimately fail in the long term, because as soon as the athlete stops resting and again starts running, the lower limbs are exposed to the same stresses as before, and the injury must inevitably recur. Furthermore, there is no doubt that rest is "the most unacceptable form of treatment for the serious runner" (S.L. James et al., 1978, p. 45).

Rest is unacceptable, because running involves a type of physical and emotional dependence. Athletes who are forced to stop running for any length of time usually develop overt withdrawal symptoms, and either they (or their spouses) will immediately start searching for anything that will allow the distraught runners to return to their former "running" tranquility.

The only injuries that require complete rest are usually those injuries that make running impossible. For example, athletes with stress fractures simply cannot run, however much they may wish to.

I advise runners to continue running but only to the point where they experience discomfort. They are not allowed to run so far that their injuries become frankly painful.

If the treatment is effective, then discomfort should lessen during runs, allowing the athlete to run progressively farther. If the pain does not improve with treatment, then either the treatment is ineffective (occasionally because the runner has a psychological basis for the injury, in which case an alternate method of treatment must be tried) or else the diagnosis is wrong.

Furthermore, if the injury does not respond to adequate treatment within 3 to 5 weeks, then the alarm bells must ring very, very loudly. The failure of an injury to respond can indicate two things: an obscure injury, such as effort thrombosis of the deep veins in the calf, or an injury unrelated to running, such as bone cancer, for which another form of treatment may be urgently required.

THE 8TH LAW OF RUNNING INJURIES:
Never Accept as a Final Opinion the Advice of a Nonrunner

Over the years I have come to the conclusion that everyone considers himself or herself an expert on sport. People who are otherwise extremely wary about expressing opinions on subjects about which they may even know something feel no such restraint when the topic of sport arises. This applies as much to medical practitioners as it does to anyone else.

How, then, do you know whose advice you can trust? I suggest four simple criteria.

1. Your adviser must be a runner. Without the firsthand experience of running, he or she won't have sufficient insight to help you. Of course, this doesn't mean that all the advice you get from runners will be sound, only that there is a greater probability that the advice will be correct.

2. Your adviser must be able to discuss the details. This person must understand the genetic, environmental, and training factors likely to have caused your injury. If not, together you will go nowhere.

3. If your adviser can't cure your injury, this failure should hurt him or her as much as it does you. Your adviser must understand the importance of your running to you. It is patently ridiculous to accept advice from someone who is antagonistic to your running.

4. Your adviser shouldn't be expensive.

Other advice given by Osler (1978) is that injured runners should consider the possibility of treatment only after all choices are clear and the runners have had time to reflect on these choices. After hearing what treatment the practitioners suggest, runners should go home and discuss it with other runners. At all times, runners should be conservative in the advice they accept. Finally, Osler reminds runners that "God heals and the doctor sends the bills."

THE 9TH LAW OF RUNNING INJURIES:
Avoid the Knife

The only running injuries for which surgery is the first line of treatment are muscle compartment syndromes and interdigital neuromas. Surgery may also have a role in the treatment of chronic Achilles tendinitis of 6 or more months' duration (Smart et al., 1980), low back pain due to a prolapsed disc (Guten, 1981), and the iliotibial band friction syndrome (C.A. Noble, 1979, 1980), but only when all other forms of nonoperative treatment have been allowed a thorough trial.

The obvious danger of surgery is that it is irreversible; what is removed during surgery cannot be put back. It is a tragedy (one I have seen on more than one occasion) to undergo major knee, ankle, or back surgery for the wrong diagnosis. Not only will that surgery fail to cure the injury but it may seriously affect the unfortunate athlete's future running career.

Remember that surgery should only be considered for a few certain injuries and only when such injuries are *Grade III* or *IV*.

THE 10TH LAW OF RUNNING INJURIES:
There Is No Definitive Scientific Evidence That Running Causes Osteoarthritis in Runners Whose Knees Were Normal When They Started Running

Osteoarthritis is a degenerative disease in which the articular cartilage lining the bony surfaces inside the knee joint becomes progressively thinner until the bone beneath the cartilage on both sides of the joint ultimately becomes exposed. In the advanced stages of osteoarthritis, the exposed bones rub against each other causing pain and severely limited joint movement. Some orthopedic surgeons believe that this degenerative process can be initiated and exacerbated by long-distance running (Sonstegard et al., 1978). However, the balance of evidence at present does not support this extreme position.

Puranen and his colleagues (1975) obtained the hip X rays of 74 former champion Finnish athletes who had run for a mean duration of 21 years. Advanced degenerative osteoarthritic changes were found in a total of three runners (4%) but were present in more than twice as many (9%) in a control group of persons who were treated at that hospital for conditions other than hip diseases. In two runners with advanced radiological changes, their symptoms were insufficiently severe to restrict their running, even at the ages of 75 and 81! The authors reported that despite what the 75-year-old runner's radiograph showed, he would not even consider interrupting his lifelong obsession with marathon running.

In other studies of highly active sports persons, including professional soccer players (I.D. Adams, 1976), physical education teachers (Bird et al., 1980; Eastmond et al., 1980), and even sport parachutists (Murray-Leslie et al., 1977), the incidence of osteoarthritis was found to be no higher than that found in the nonathletic population. Neither Wally Hayward (Maud et al., 1981) nor Jackie Mekler (see chapter 8) show any evidence of osteoarthritis despite the prodigious distances they have run in their lives. In no large series of persons with osteoarthritis is there a preponderance of athletes (Jorring, 1980), which would be expected if sport were a significant cause of osteoarthritis.

Sohn and Micheli (1984) reported that the incidence of osteoarthritis in a group of runners who competed between 1930 and 1960 at seven universities in the eastern United States was *lower* than that of a matched group of swimmers who competed at the same universities at the same time and whose joints had not been exposed to the same poundings as had the runners' joints.

Finally, in the most extensive study yet undertaken, Lane et al. (1986) reported that the incidence of osteoarthritis was not higher in a group of 41 runners aged 70 to 72 than it was in a matched control group. A similar finding was reported by Panush et al. (1986). Lane and his colleagues (1986), who plan to follow these runners indefinitely, also found that the bone mineral contents of the runners, both male and female, were approximately 40% greater than those of the controls.

In a related study, Lane et al. (1987) showed that with age, runners develop fewer musculoskeletal disabilities and develop them at slower rates than do nonrunners. Thus, far from making runners more infirm and disabled, running preserved the functional integrity of their subjects' joints and muscles. Female former college athletes were found not to be at increased risk of developing osteoporotic fractures in later life than were nonathletes (Wyshak et al., 1987).

Other evidence supports this belief: Osteoarthritis in rabbits is not made worse by running (Videman, 1982); the absence rather than the presence of normal weight bearing across a joint leads to degenerative changes similar to those found in early osteoarthritis (Palmoski et al., 1980); and even in patients with the more serious form of arthritis (rheumatoid arthritis), regular exercise seems to delay rather than to expedite the progression of the disease (Nordemar et al., 1981).

Sports participants who develop osteoarthritis usually have had previous joint surgery. In the study of Murray-Leslie et al. (1977), 75% of sports parachutists who developed osteoarthritis had undergone previous surgery for removal of a torn cartilage (meniscectomy). It was those athletes who exercised on abnormal joints who ultimately developed osteoarthritis.

The sports injuries that require surgery are the extrinsic injuries that typically occur in contact sports. Thus, persons who blame running as the sole cause of osteoarthritis are barking up the wrong tree. They should rather blame contact sports. Of course, that is an unpopular stance in many countries and could explain why those who should know better have not yet singled out the real issues surrounding osteoarthritis in athletes.

Two studies linked physical activity with an increased risk of osteoarthritis. In the Framingham study, the most physically active were at increased risk of osteoarthritis as were those who were the most obese (Felson et al., 1988). In a 15-year study of 27 long-distance runners, researchers found that those who were running the fastest in 1973, when the study began, had the most marked radiological changes of degenerative hip disease at follow-up. The authors concluded that past long-term, high-intensity, and high-mileage running cannot be dismissed as a potential risk factor for premature osteoarthritis of the hip (Marti et al., 1989). If this is indeed so, it is not entirely clear why other studies of former runners did not come to a similar conclusion. Clearly, more studies of this important question are needed.

In summarizing these 10 laws, it seems that in many ways the medical approach to running injuries is the medicine of a bygone era. A correct diagnosis requires a careful, unhurried approach in which the patient is given sufficient time to detail symptoms, theories, and training methods. The doctor must have time and the patience to listen carefully and sympathetically. Seldom is it necessary to utilize expensive tests to establish the diagnosis, and the correct treatment is usually very simple. Indeed, I believe that 60% of a doctor's success is due to an ability to understand what the injury means to the patient, the fears that the injury engenders, and how best to allay those fears. For this the doctor needs to understand the patient's psyche as well as the patient's motivations in having the injury examined.

13

Avoiding Injuries

"So there I was at the end of 1979: atrophy in the left leg, 'hot spots' up and down the body, a possible stress fracture in the back, and more. And not willing to let some very fine physicians help me. Of course, that didn't stop me from running the Honolulu Marathon.

"The same personality—independent, introverted, single-minded, self-reliant, self-confident, distrusting—that enabled me to excel as an athlete in full health hindered me when I became an athlete in pain."

Frank Shorter (Shorter & Bloom, 1984)

"It is impossible to overemphasize the importance of injury prevention and treatment to the career of a successful athlete. It has been noted that the champion athlete is very often one who has attained a high level of lay expertise and downright craftiness with regard to injuries, whereas novices seem to keep getting hurt.

"Very often the difference between the perennial champion and the perennial bridesmaid is just that edge: an ability to avoid and/or recover quickly from physical trauma."

Marty Liquori (Liquori & Parker, 1980)

"The money and the fame are irrelevant really. I'm just a hamstring away from oblivion; you've got to look at it like that."

Steve Jones (Holmes, 1986)

465

Avoiding injury revolves around three important steps: Start training gently, choose appropriate running shoes, and make stretching exercises part of your daily routine.

HOW STRETCHING CAN HELP YOU

Stretching is not something that most runners do willingly. Runners who will somehow squeeze in 1 or 2 hours of running a day never seem quite able to find the additional 5 to 10 minutes needed for adequate stretching. I think there are a variety of reasons for this. We inflexible runners are unconvinced that stretching is beneficial, and we are ignorant of what stretching involves. Experience has taught us that stretching hurts, and we are haunted by suspicions that we may be doing it wrong anyway. There are now four excellent references to the question of stretching (B. Anderson, 1975; Beaulieu, 1981; Shellock & Prentice, 1985; Uram, 1980), and the following is a synthesis of their ideas.

The Benefits of Stretching

Beaulieau (1981) presented evidence that there are three main benefits of stretching: a reduced risk of injury, less muscle soreness after exercise, and improved athletic performance.

I have personal experience of these last two benefits. I have observed that after a race or long training run I am most stiff in the muscles that were the least supple before the run. I also suspect that my exceptional inability to run fast downhill is because I am too tight in both the hamstring and quadriceps muscle groups. Tightness in either of these muscle groups must limit stride length and therefore speed when running downhill, particularly near the end of a race when fatigue has caused the muscles to become even tighter. However, evidence appears to show that runners who stretch are not less prone to injury (S.J. Jacobs & Berson, 1986).

The Dangers of Stretching

Beaulieu (1981) acknowledged that runners may become sore and even injured after stretching. But this, he argued, is because these runners do not stretch properly; if runners better understood the physiology of stretching, they would be less likely to injure themselves while stretching.

The Physiology of Stretching

Muscles have a complicated mechanism that prevents their ever being damaged by overstretching. Muscles contain tiny *stretch receptors*, which are attached to the working part of the muscle—the muscle fibers. When a muscle is stretched, the degree of stretch is sensed by the stretch receptors. They send messages back, via the spinal cord, to the nerves that control the contraction of the muscles in which the receptors lie (i.e., the stretched muscle). As the intensity of the stretch increases, so the stretch receptors begin to fire more rapidly and more strongly. Ultimately, these impulses exceed a certain threshold, and the stretched muscle contracts and shortens, thereby preventing overstretching.

A general rule is that the intensity of the muscle contraction induced by a stretch reflex varies with the rapidity with which the stretch is applied. The faster the stretch is applied, the more powerful the contraction it evokes. This is an important consideration in ballistic stretching.

Another important stretch reflex, the *inverse stretch reflex*, performs a function exactly opposite of that of the conventional stretch reflex. The receptors for this reflex are centered not among the muscle fibers but in the muscle tendons. These receptors are sensitive to the tension present in the muscle tendon.

As a muscle contracts, the tension in the tendon rises and the tension receptors are activated. As in the conventional stretch reflex, these receptors send messages to the nerves controlling the contraction of the muscles in which these receptors lie. But in contrast to the conventional reflex, when these tension receptors in the inverse stretch reflex are activated, they inhibit the contraction of that muscle. Therefore, the inverse stretch reflex provides a protective mechanism that prevents a muscle from contracting so strongly that it can rupture its own tendons. If the tendons sense that the muscle is contracting too powerfully, the tendon receptors cause the contraction to be switched off.

Applied Physiology of Stretching

How does this information help us arrive at the most effective stretching techniques?

This information indicates that the stretch must always be applied gradually. A slow buildup of stretch has the least stimulatory effect on the stretch receptors. Thus, these receptors remain quiescent, and the tension in the stretched muscle is kept to a minimum. This is important, because some experts feel that the best stretches are achieved when the tension inside the stretched muscles is low.

The inverse stretch reflex explains why a muscle that has been gradually stretched for 60 to 90 seconds will suddenly ''give'' as the inverse stretch reflex relaxes any remaining tension in the stretched muscle.

Stretching Techniques

There are four basic stretching techniques: *ballistic*, *passive*, *contract-relax*, and *static*.

Ballistic Stretching

This is the technique beloved of school coaches and football players, the flamboyant bobbing up and down that looks impressive. Unfortunately, ballistic stretching is probably worse than useless. All that ballistic stretching achieves is activation of the stretch reflex, causing the stretched muscle to contract rapidly and the athlete to bob up with remarkable speed.

The tension inside the muscle during ballistic stretching is about twice that in a static stretch. Thus, the risk of injury is increased during this type of stretching.

Passive Stretching

In this method of stretching, a partner applies additional external pressure to increase the extent of the stretch. This method is particularly popular among gymnasts. Beaulieu's (1981) opinion is that this stretching method is valuable for expert stretchers but potentially risky for inexperienced stretchers.

Contract-Relax Stretching

The muscle to be stretched is first actively contracted and then stretched immediately after it relaxes. The theory behind this technique is that the active muscle contraction activates the inverse stretch reflex; thus, the muscle tension during the subsequent contraction should be reduced. In fact, it has been found that this does not occur. Rather, the contracted muscle continues to be slightly active during the subsequent stretch. So the tension in the stretched muscle is actually higher, not lower, than during a static stretch.

A variant of this stretching technique is the contract-relax-antagonist-contract method, in which the muscle that is the antagonist of the muscle being stretched is contracted immediately following relaxation of the stretched muscle.

Static Stretching

The stretch position is assumed slowly and held for at least 30 to 60 seconds. There is a slow buildup of tension in the muscle; thus, the stretch reflex is not activated. As the tendons are gradually stretched, the inverse stretch reflex is activated and muscle tension falls so that the muscle can be stretched further. As static stretching causes the least muscle tension buildup, it is believed to be the most effective stretching technique.

Comparing the Techniques

The scientific evidence that is currently available indicates that the contract-relax-antagonist-contract technique is superior to the contract-relax technique for increasing flexibility (Etnyre & Abraham, 1986). The ballistic stretch technique is the least effective (Wallin et al., 1985).

Furthermore, holding the stretch for 10 seconds at a time produces the same benefits as does stretching for 30 seconds at a time, provided the total duration of the stretching sessions are the same (Borms et al., 1987).

Once the desired degree of flexibility has been achieved, a single stretching session per week will maintain that flexibility. Continuing to stretch three to five times a week will produce further improvements in flexibility (Wallin et al., 1985).

PLANNING A STRETCHING PROGRAM

Most of the following guidelines for a successful stretching program were provided by Beaulieu (1981).

- Expect results after weeks or months. Thus, you should follow a stretching program year-round, or, for a seasonal sport, you should commence a stretching program at least 6 weeks before the beginning of a season.

- Don't jog first before starting to stretch; this is not necessary. Beaulieu's contention that stretching should follow a gentle warm-up (e.g., a 5-minute jog) because warm muscles stretch better and are less likely to be injured is now known not to be true (Williford et al., 1986).

- Stretch both before and after exercise. If this is not possible, at least stretch before exercise. The increased muscle flexibility that results after a period of stretching lasts for up to 3 hours.

- Select stretching exercises carefully. Start with the easiest and build up to the more advanced.

- Alternate the muscles that are stretched.

- Assume the stretching position slowly and hold for 30 to 60 seconds. Stretch the muscle to the point where you feel tightness in the muscle. At no time should the stretch cause discomfort or pain.

- Use stretches that have been chosen by Beaulieu for runners, shown in Figure 13.1. Beaulieu suggests that Exercises 1, 2, 3, 5, 9, 10, 15, and 16 can be used if insufficient time is available for the total program. Beaulieu considers that some exercises commonly used by runners (Exercises 18 to 20) are too risky for inexperienced stretchers and should be replaced by appropriate choices from Exercises 1 to 16.

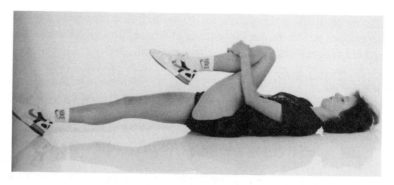

Exercise 1 Hamstrings: Pull the knee to the chest and raise the head to the knee.

Exercise 2 Quadriceps: Grab the left foot with the right hand. Pull the left foot toward the buttock. Repeat with the right foot. Note that this exercise and Exercise 1 should be avoided by athletes who have injured knees. Flexion of the knee joint in these positions may be painful. A healthy athlete should have no difficulty with these exercises if they are performed correctly.

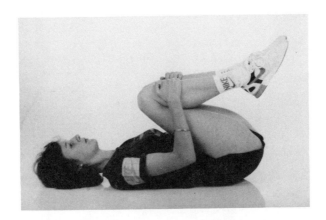

Exercise 3 Back: Rock gently back and forth 8 to 10 times.

Exercise 4 Back: Bring the legs over the head. Use your arms to keep balance.

Exercise 5 Abdomen and chest: Push the upper torso back with your arms. Push head as far back as it will go.

Exercise 6 Groin: With back straight and feet together, push down on knees.

Exercise 7 Hip and sartorius: With legs together, move your legs to one side. Repeat with the other side.

Exercise 8 Shoulders: Put one elbow behind your head. Gently pull elbow toward the center of the back. Repeat with the other arm.

Exercise 9 Lower leg: Leaning on wall, keep your back foot flat and your head up. Slowly bend arms and lower body toward wall.

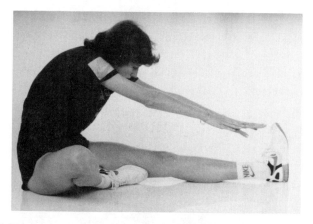

Exercise 10 Hamstrings: From position shown, grab ankle and pull body forward. Repeat with other leg.

474

Exercise 11 Quadriceps: Lie on back with knee up and foot pulled toward buttocks. Slowly lower knee. For persons with knee injuries, the same rule applies as for Exercise 2.

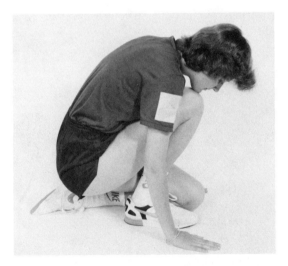

Exercise 12 Lower leg: From position shown, push right knee forward by pressing the chest against the knee. Keep toes of right foot even with knee of left leg.

Exercise 13 Hamstrings: While lying on your back, grab leg below the calf and pull toward head.

Exercise 14 Abdomen and chest: While lying on your stomach, grab both feet above the ankles. Arch the back and pull the feet toward the head.

Exercise 15 Groin: Put bottoms of feet together, pull heels toward groin, and pull body forward.

Exercise 16 Hip and sartorius: Cross right leg over left and bring left arm to right side of right knee as shown. Push on right leg with left arm and twist body. Turn head to the side. Repeat with other side.

Exercise 17 Iliotibial band: Put weight on right leg and cross left leg in front. Bend toward the left, pushing hips toward right as shown. This stretches the right iliotibial band. To stretch the left side, reverse all positions.

Exercise 18 This exercise, called the plow, places excessive strain on the lower back and should be excluded from most conditioning programs. However, Exercises 3 and 4 provide excellent alternatives for stretching the upper and lower back and hamstrings. Exercise 3 should always precede Exercise 4 because it gently prestretches the back muscles. In Exercise 4 the legs should be brought slowly into position, not thrust over the head quickly. Exercise 4 is safer because the hands support the trunk throughout the exercise and the ankles are flexed, which prevents you from stretching further than your flexibility will safely allow. Athletes with lower back problems should avoid the plow and its variations.

Exercise 19 Many athletes use this exercise to stretch the hamstrings. The force of gravity pulling on the trunk places an excessive load on the spine and lower back muscles, and an athlete with lower back problems may find that this exercise may aggravate and prolong those problems. It can even injure a healthy athlete if done with improper warm-up or with bouncing.

Exercise 20 This is a popular exercise among many runners who find it convenient to walk up to a wall and throw their legs up against it. In this position they begin with an attempt to extend the leg to 90 degrees or greater and then apply force. Unfortunately, most runners do not have sufficient flexibility, and the chance of injury is very high. This very advanced exercise should be excluded from almost all athletic conditioning programs

Note. Exercises 1-20 from ''Developing a Stretching Programme'' by J.E. Beaulieu, 1981, *The Physician and Sportsmedicine*, **9**, pp. 62-64. Copyright 1981 by McGraw-Hill. Adapted by permission.

Exercises 21 to 29 are specifically designed to prevent and treat low back pain. Each can be repeated up to 10 times, as frequently as required.

Exercise 21 Pelvic tilt: Lie on your back with knees bent, feet flat on the floor, and arms at your sides. Tighten your stomach muscles and flatten the small of your back against the floor, without pushing down with the legs. Hold for 5 seconds, then slowly relax.

Exercise 22 Knee to shoulder: Starting in the same position as for the pelvic tilt, grasp your left knee, and gently pull it toward your left shoulder. Return to the starting position and repeat with the right leg.

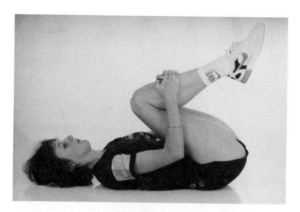

Exercise 23 Double knee to chest: Starting in the same position as for the pelvic tilt, use your hands to pull your right leg close to your chest, and then pull the left leg even with the right. Grasp both knees and pull toward your shoulders. Let the knees return to arm's length and repeat.

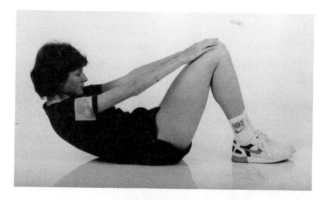

Exercise 24 Partial sit-up: Do the pelvic tilt, and while holding this position, curl your head and shoulders up and forward. Hold briefly. Return slowly to the starting position.

Exercise 25 Hamstring stretch: From the same starting position as for the pelvic tilt, bring one knee to your chest and then straighten the leg vertically, stretching the heel toward the ceiling. You should feel the stretch behind your knee. Bend the knee and return the leg to the starting position. Repeat with the other leg.

Exercise 26 Rotational sit-up: Do the pelvic tilt, and while keeping your hips flat, rotate your upper body so that the weight rests on the left shoulder. Then, curl your head and shoulders upward, raising your right shoulder higher than the left. Hold briefly before returning to the starting position. Rotate your upper body to the right and repeat the movement, this time raising the left shoulder higher than the right.

Exercise 27 Cat and camel: On your hands and knees, relax your abdomen and let your back sag downward. Then tighten your stomach muscles and arch your back. Repeat.

Exercise 28 Trunk flexion, prone: Starting on your hands and knees, tuck in your chin and arch your back upward, and then slowly sit back on your heels while letting your shoulders drop to the floor. Relax. Return to the starting position, keeping stomach tight and back arched. Repeat.

Exercise 29 Trunk flexion, seated: Sitting near the edge of a chair, spread legs apart and cross arms over your chest. Be sure the chair will not slip backward or tip. Tuck your chin and slowly curl your trunk downward. Relax. Uncurl slowly into an upright position, raising your head last.

Note. Exercises 21-29 from "Low Back Pain in Athletes" by G.D. Rovere, 1987, *The Physician and Sportsmedicine*, **15**, pp. 105-117. Copyright 1987 by McGraw-Hill. Adapted by permission.

14

Diagnosis and Treatment of Running Injuries

"If I had my competitive career to run over again, I would change some of my attitudes to injuries. I would show them more respect. Because after all, injuries weren't some unknown barrier that I was trying to crash through. Injuries were simply my body telling me that something wrong was happening."

Derek Clayton (1980)

"Finally, remember that God heals and the doctor sends the bills. Give nature every chance to do her own good work."

Tom Osler (1978)

"One of the basic rules of health is 'Listen to your body.' I am responsible for my health, and to respond to my body I must listen to it, learn from it."

George Sheehan (1978a)

Boston podiatrist Dr. Rob McGregor tells his injured running patients that they must not contact him until they have tried everything they can think of to cure their own injuries. Only when they have run out of ideas are they allowed to consult him.

The kind of self-help approach prescribed by Dr. McGregor is the correct one. Because running injuries have identifiable causes, it follows that the runner, the person closest to these causes, should be in the best position to analyze and correct them. Furthermore, the development of virtually all running injuries

487

(with the possible exception of stress fractures) is a gradual process. So, with very few exceptions, the runner will have a fairly long warning period. During this time the clever runner will begin to analyze why the injury developed; the following guidelines can aid this analysis.

STEP 1: DECIDE WHETHER YOUR INJURY IS TRULY A RUNNING INJURY

Although virtually all running injuries are intrinsic injuries, occasionally a runner has an injury that causes discomfort during running yet was actually caused by a non-running-related incident that was so mild it was disregarded. Thus a very trivial knee or ankle injury, suffered in a long-forgotten football or basketball game, may cause symptoms only when the person takes up running many years later. The importance of identifying these injuries lies in the fact that they will not respond to the treatment approach prescribed in these pages and may ultimately require surgical correction.

So the first priority is to ensure that the injury is truly running related and is not due to external trauma. If there is doubt, remember the following:

• Intrinsic injuries come on gradually and never involve the joints. One of the most common injuries, runner's knee, causes pain around the joint but is not a joint injury.

• With the possible exceptions of chronic muscle injuries, some types of stress fractures, and occasionally the iliotibial band friction syndrome, all running injuries will be cured, albeit temporarily, after 4 to 12 weeks of complete rest. Injuries then recur only when the athlete again reaches that weekly training distance equivalent to the breakdown point (the 3rd law of running injuries). In contrast, extrinsic injuries do not improve no matter how long they are rested, and they cause discomfort virtually immediately after running is resumed.

If you are certain that your injury is a true running injury, proceed to Step 2. You can, of course, consult a doctor at this stage, but the cure may be as simple as changing to a better pair of running shoes, in which case the visit to the doctor will waste both your time and the doctor's time.

STEP 2: DETERMINE THE FACTORS THAT MAY HAVE CAUSED THE INJURY

This step involves establishing whether the injury has occurred simultaneously with a change in one or more factors in your milieu. Although a correct diagnosis is always helpful, empirical treatment based on recent changes in your routine may be sufficient to cure the injury, and an accurate diagnosis may not be necessary. So we will start on that tack.

Shoe Choice

HAVE YOU RECENTLY CHANGED TO A DIFFERENT TYPE OF RUNNING SHOE?

If you train in your normal way but become injured within 2 to 4 weeks after changing to different running shoes, you must consider that the new shoes are causing the injury. In this case the treatment is obvious. Either go back to the old pair of running shoes or, if these are in bad repair, start running in a new pair of the same model.

IF THE SHOES ARE NOT NEW, ARE THEY WORN OUT?

The major areas of failure in the running shoe are the heel counter, the midsole, and the outer sole. The heel counter can lose its rigidity and drag inward as shown in Figure 14.1. This is the typical pattern in athletes whose feet rotate inward (pronate) excessively. Athletes who run in shoes similar to these are said to be running "next to" their shoes.

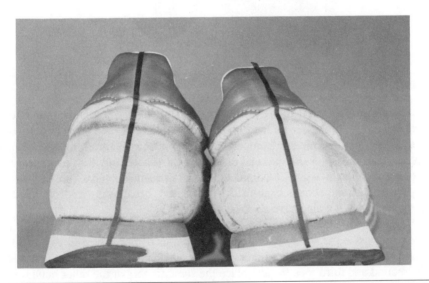

Figure 14.1 Running shoes showing collapsed heel counters, the typical effect of excessive ankle pronation.

The midsole material in the heel is particularly prone to compaction, especially in running shoes in which the midsole material is very soft. In the shoes depicted in Figure 14.2, the height of the midsole at the heel is 2.5 cm on the outside and 1.5 cm on the inside. This means that the midsole underneath the inside heel is compacted by 40%. This degree of imbalance (1 cm) in the heel is more than sufficient to produce a running injury. These considerations indicate the importance of checking the heels of your shoes regularly; be sure to view them from the perspective shown in Figure 14.2.

Collapsed midsole

Figure 14.2   Running shoes showing collapsed midsole material at the heel.

The midsole material in the forefoot can also compact, particularly in "forefoot strikers," runners who land mainly on the balls of their feet. Figure 14.3 shows this marked midsole compaction. The midsole material under the small and big toes measures 0.8 cm, and that under the second and third toes measures 0.6 cm, again showing 25% compaction. Note that this compaction may not be apparent when the shoe is examined from behind, because the midsole material at the heel may not also have compacted.

The only way to detect this midsole compaction under the forefoot is to put one hand inside the shoe and the other outside, as demonstrated in Figure 14.4. Place your index and middle fingers of the inside hand into the indentation where the second and third toes fit, and place the same fingers of the other hand on the outer sole overlying this area. Then assess the thickness of the midsole by squeezing it between your fingers and comparing the midsole thickness at that site with the thickness of the rest of the forefoot. Frequently, the midsole under the forefoot is completely compacted so that the fingers of the inner and outer hands are separated only by the thickness of the outer sole.

Runners whose shoes reach this state will usually know about it, because when they land on a stone underneath their big toes, they feel immediate pain.

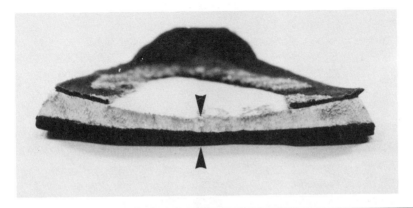

Figure 14.3 Running shoe in cross section showing compaction of the midsole material under the forefoot.

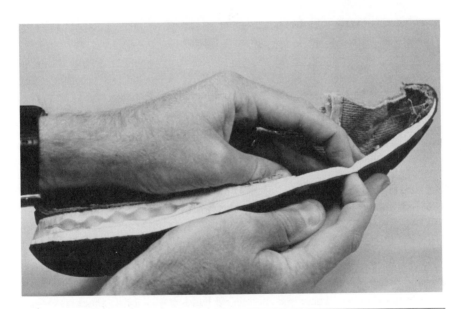

Figure 14.4 Testing for midsole compaction under the forefoot.

The final way in which the midsole may wear out is that it may harden or "bottom out." Figure 6.2 shows the thumb compression test, which is used to compare the relative hardness of the midsoles of different running shoes and also the degree to which a particular shoe has bottomed out. With experience you will

Figure 14.5 The thumb compression test fails to make any impression on the "fossilized" midsole of this running shoe.

learn how much indentation is appropriate for your own shoe. The test is also essential to check loss of shock-absorbing capacity, which happens over time. For example, Figure 14.5 shows the indentation test being performed on a 5-year-old running shoe. This shoe allows no indentation; the midsole has essentially fossilized, and the owner of these shoes might just as well run barefoot on the tarmac. The tarmac would probably be softer.

Shoes differ in the rapidity with which the midsole compacts or turns to "stone." Cavanagh (1980) tested 28 randomly chosen pairs of running shoes, of which each pair had been used for between 640 and 3,200 km of training. He found that the average loss of shock absorption was 11% in the heels and nearly 40% in the forefoot. The worst shoe tested had lost 40% of its shock-absorbing capacity in the heel and 70% in the forefoot. As Cavanagh noted, these shoes had clearly changed since the day they were bought; he also noted that if shock absorption is important to a particular athlete, then this degree of loss may be more than enough to produce an injury.

Cook et al. (1985a, 1985b) reported even more alarming results. These workers found that after between 400 and 800 km of use, running shoes had lost 45% of their original cushioning. The authors also noted that the greater the original cushioning of the shoe, the more rapid the deterioration in cushioning. Thus, a shoe initially selected for its ability to absorb shock might prove to be inappropriate in the long term. Finally, the authors noted that wetness reduced the cushioning properties of the shoes. However, once the shoes dried, they returned to the level of cushioning consistent with the mileage they had "run."

Thus, injured athletes must remember to check that the midsoles of their running shoes have not compacted completely.

The final important area of shoe wear is the outer sole. Figure 14.6 shows the different wear patterns found in three different running styles. In the normal wear pattern (see Figure 14.6a), the outer sole wears first at the outer edge of the heel, then under the ball of the foot between the first and second toes, and then at the front of the sole underneath the second and third toes. In contrast, the extreme pronator (see Figure 14.6b) strikes on the inside of the heel and wears all along the inside border of the sole and, in particular, underneath the big toe. The third type of sole wear is found in the runner whose foot supinates excessively during running. The supinator's sole wear pattern is the exact opposite of that found in the pronator; the supinator's main wear is concentrated on the outer border of the sole, from heel to toe (Fig. 14.6c).

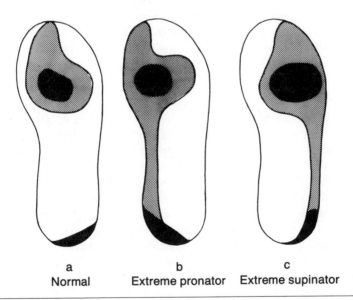

| a | b | c |
| Normal | Extreme pronator | Extreme supinator |

Figure 14.6 Outer sole wear patterns of the shoes of three different runners.

I am not sure to what extent excessive outer sole wear, particularly at the heel, influences injury risk. There is indeed some merit in the argument that wear, particularly at the heel, is an adaptation to that athlete's particular mechanical makeup. Thus, the athlete who wears rapidly at the heel has a reason for doing so. Indeed, one shoe company produced shoes with heels that were rounded in the direction of the heel wear. This type of heel reduces the extent and rate of pronation (Nigg, 1985) and may therefore be of value in the treatment of pronation-related injuries like runner's knee. This type of heel does, however, increase peak landing forces at heel strike.

This argument suggests that applying excessive repair patching on the heel is probably not beneficial and may be a factor in injury.

Biomechanical Structure

In fairly broad terms, the lower limb mechanics of injured runners usually exhibit one of two characteristic patterns: Either the foot rotates inward (pronates) too much or it does not pronate enough. The foot that rotates too little is frequently referred to as the clunk foot, whereas the foot that pronates too much is referred to as hypermobile, flexible, or simply flat.

A popular method that has been advocated to determine the presence of a hypermobile or clunk foot is called the "bathroom test." In this test, you place your wet foot on the bath mat first when you are sitting and then when you are standing. The imprint that most runners make when they are sitting looks like Figure 14.7a. If your standing foot imprint is like Figure 14.7b, you have a rigid (or clunk) foot, whereas an imprint like Figure 14.7c indicates a flat (hypermobile) foot. Identifying your foot type is important, because these two foot types cause injuries for different reasons.

The Clunk Foot

The clunk foot is a rigid, stable, immobile, high-arched structure that is unable to perform the most basic function of the running foot, that is, provide adequate shock absorption through controlled, appropriate pronation. Because of its stability, the clunk foot provides a powerful lever at push-off and so is the ideal foot for the sprinter. But in long-distance running, in which adequate shock absorption is essential (particularly during days of heavy training or during a long race when fatigued muscles lose their ability to absorb shock), the clunker is a major source of disaster. In fact, possibly 30 to 40% of injured runners have this type of foot. Because the high-arched foot is unable to absorb sufficient shock, it places additional stresses on other shock-absorbing structures, particularly the knee, which may break down.

The Hypermobile Foot

The hypermobile foot is an excellent shock absorber because of its ability to pronate, but it is very unstable during the push-off phase of running. Instead of having a firm lever with which to push off, the runner with the hypermobile foot is all but attached to the ground by a bag of delinquent bones, each going its own

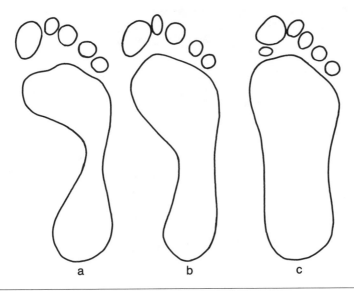

Figure 14.7 The bathroom test to detect rigid or flat feet: (a) normal imprint, (b) rigid imprint, (c) flat imprint.

way and causing the lower libs to rotate too far inward during the stance phase of running. This excessive inward rotation causes the most common running injuries.

The common injuries that accompany these two foot types are listed in Table 14.1 (McKenzie et al., 1985).

The Intermediate Foot

In between these two types of running feet is an intermediate foot, which combines the weaknesses of both; this foot is high arched and also malaligned. It combines rigidity with instability so that the treatment that works for either of the other foot types may be useless for this type. Another danger inherent in this foot type is that if its pronation is too well controlled with appropriate shoes and orthotics, the original injury may be cured but another injury may be caused because the foot can no longer absorb shock adequately.

Shoe Design

Until very recently, manufacturers who developed running shoes paid little attention to the possibility that they could cause running injuries. But science and public demand have since forced the running shoe manufacturers to produce shoes that will not only reduce the risk of injury but will cure injuries that are already present.

Table 14.1   Injuries That May Be Associated With Specific Foot Types

Clunk foot	Hypermobile foot
Stress fractures	Plantar fasciitis
Iliotibial band friction syndrome	Achilles tendinitis
Gastrocnemius/soleus muscle strain	Runner's knee
Trachanteric bursitis	Shinsplints
Plantar fasciitis	
Achilles tendinitis	
Ill-defined muscle and joint pain, particularly after long races	
Metatarsalgia	

Note. From "Running Shoes, Orthotics, and Injuries" by D.C. McKenzie, D.B. Clement, and J.E. Taunton, 1985, *Sports Medicine*, **2**, p. 337. Copyright 1985 by Adis International Limited. Adapted by permission.

Choosing running shoes that are appropriate for the different injuries and foot types is important. In particular, the two different foot types and injury categories require quite opposite shoe characteristics to compensate for inherent weaknesses in the foot.

Running shoes must therefore be designed either for adequate shock absorption or for motion control. These are two quite different characteristics that can be built into the same shoe only with great difficulty. In general, the more motion-controlling ability a shoe has, the more rigid it must be and consequently the less shock it can absorb. Conversely, the better the shock-absorbing capacity of the shoe, the less able it is to control motion.

The principle characteristic that makes a shoe soft enough for a rigid foot is a very soft midsole. Thus, the thumb compression test will show that the EVA, air, or gel component of the midsole compresses easily (see Figure 6.2). In addition, the heel counter must be ineffective and should be made of a flexible, nonrigid material (see Figure 6.4). This shoe should also be slip lasted and should fail the Noakes Running Shoe Pronation-Testing Technique (see Figure 6.3).

The features that increase a shoe's ability to resist pronation are the exact opposite of these. Thus, the antipronation shoe requires a firm midsole. Some manufacturers have selectively increased the firmness of the midsole material on the inner side of the shoe and added softer material laterally. In addition, the shoe should be straight lasted (see chapter 6) and must have a firm board last; the heel counter must be rigid and durable. Another innovation introduced by some shoe manufacturers involves incorporating additional material that attaches the heel counter more firmly to the midsole. This helps prevent separation of the heel counter from the midsole, a not-uncommon problem for runners who pronate excessively.

Few researchers have studied the effects of shoe design on ankle movement during running. A study by T.E. Clarke et al. (1983a) showed the following:

- Shoes with soft midsoles (25 durometer, Shore A scale) allowed significantly more pronation than did shoes with either medium (35 durometer) or hard (45 durometer) midsoles. This finding has since been confirmed (Stacoff et al., 1988).
- Heel height had no effect on the extent of pronation. Others have found different results (Frederick, 1986).
- Shoes with O° heel flare allowed significantly more pronation that did shoes with 15° or 30° heel flares. However, other studies show that the lateral heel flare increases initial pronation (Nigg et al. 1987; Nigg & Bahlsen, 1988; Nigg & Morelock, 1987; Stacoff et al., 1988), whereas the medial flare reduces pronation (T.E. Clarke et al., 1983a). As discussed, the "negative flare" or rounded heel reduces pronation (Nigg & Morlock, 1987).

More recently, Clarke et al. (Stripe, 1983) showed that a straight-lasted shoe controls pronation more effectively than does a curve-lasted shoe even if the midsole is of the same hardness. To my knowledge, the effects of board lasting have not yet been studied. The dual density midsole (chapter 6) increases rearfoot control (Nigg et al., 1988).

The softness of the midsole has no marked effect on landing forces during running (T.E. Clarke et al., 1983b; Frederick, 1986; Nigg et al., 1987). It seems that runners alter their gaits and muscle activation patterns (Komi et al., 1987) when running in harder shoes or when running barefoot. Thus, the degree of pronation is reduced when one runs barefoot (Frederick, 1986; L.S. Smith et al., 1986), a reduction due to changes in running patterns. In particular the maximum rate at which the knee bends at landing *increases* with barefoot running and with the hardness of the shoe (Frederick, 1986). This is thought to be an energy-inefficient mechanism that could make barefoot running less efficient than running in soft shoes (Frederick, 1986).

One problem with the cushioning properties of the shoe is that the tendons and ligaments of the foot are designed to absorb shock when one runs barefoot (R.M. Alexander, 1987). Furthermore, these structures in the foot act as highly efficient springs, converting as much as 93% of the energy they absorb on landing into elastic recoil at toe-off. Compared to these structures, the midsoles and outer soles of running shoes are relatively inefficient, because they convert only 40 to 50% of this energy back into elastic recoil (Alexander, 1987; Alexander & Bennett, 1989); the remainder of that energy heats up the midsole. Shoe manufacturers, who have considered only the shock-absorbing function of the midsole, have only recently turned their attention to this property (Alexander & Bennett, 1989; A. Turnbull, 1989). Those companies that have made claims for the value of their "energy return systems" would seem to have overstated their cases; few differences in "energy return" capacity have been found between different running shoes (Alexander & Bennett, 1989). Even a shoe that was 100% effective in energy return would save the runner only about 10% of the energy lost from his body with each step (Alexander & Bennett, 1989).

Specific Running Shoes for Specific Problems: The *Runner's World* Shoe Survey

When the sports world began to realize that running shoes should be designed for either shock absorption or motion control, the need arose to grade the different models of running shoes according to their relative capacities for shock absorption or motion control.

Since 1975, *Runner's World* magazine has devoted each October issue to evaluating a large number of running shoes and grading them according to how well they fulfill the functions of shock absorption and motion control. This annual survey provides essential, up-to-date information about the popular running shoes and should be consulted by any runner preparing to buy new running shoes, particularly if injury necessitates buying a particular type of shoe. Another important resource with detailed information regarding shoe choice is Cavanagh's book (Cavanagh, 1980).

The Effects of Orthotics

There is a general consensus that orthotics reduce both the total amount of rearfoot pronation and the maximum rate of pronation (Bates et al., 1979; Frederick, 1986; L.S. Smith et al., 1986; Taunton et al., 1985). This is compatible with the belief that orthotics can cure running injuries that are caused by excessive subtalar-joint pronation.

The Effects of Viscoelastic Shoe Insoles

Viscoelastic shoe insoles are frequently used by runners who believe that these insoles will reduce landing forces. It appears, however, that these insoles are without significant effect (Nigg et al., 1988).

Training Methods

HAVE YOU RECENTLY CHANGED YOUR TRAINING METHODS OR RACING PATTERNS?

Recent changes in training methods or racing patterns might be factors explaining an injury.

The common changes that occur in training methods are an increase in the amount of speed work done, either in the form of harder or more frequent interval sessions, speed-play sessions, or time trials; an increase in the total distance run in training, in particular the introduction of single long training runs; or the introduction of uphill or downhill running. Running too many races too close together is another important precipitating factor (S.J. Jacobs & Berson, 1986). Injury risk seems to increase linearly with increasing running speed, daily and weekly running distance, and number of days run per week (Blair et al., 1987; S.R. Jacobs & Berson, 1986; Koplan et al., 1982; Marti, 1988; Powell et al., 1986; Samet et al., 1982).

If the injury occurred after a change in any of these, then it is logical to go back to the training schedule you were following before the injury occurred and to reintroduce the causative factor very gradually.

Training Surfaces

HAVE TRAINING SURFACES RECENTLY CHANGED?

The most important features of training surfaces are hardness and degree of camber. Hard running surfaces include roads, pavements, and some running tracks; softer surfaces include dirt roads, grass, and beach sand.

Most road surfaces are cambered to ensure adequate drainage of rain water into the gutters at the roadside. When you run on a cambered road, the foot nearest the center of the road will be forced to pronate excessively, whereas the foot nearest to the edge will have restricted pronation. This apparently trivial difference can be sufficient to cause injury on one side of the body. For example, the athlete with flexible feet, which have increased tendencies to pronate, may develop an injury such as runner's knee on the leg that is positioned closest to the center of the road. This is because the foot on that side will be forced to pronate even more to compensate for the road camber, and this may be just sufficient to cause the injury.

Although grass surfaces are soft and not usually cambered, they are uneven. This unevenness detracts from the overall attractiveness of grass as a running surface, because unevenness will tend to favor excessive ankle pronation. Similarly, beaches are highly cambered below the high-water mark and are very soft above it.

If you have changed shoes and corrected any possible errors in training or in your choice of running surfaces, it is entirely possible that the injury will be cured. Studies (Lindenberg et al., 1984; Pinshaw et al., 1983; Pretorius et al., 1986) show that these simple procedures are effective enough to cure more than 60% of injured runners within 3 to 6 weeks. This indicates that some running injuries can be cured without an accurate diagnosis ever being made. However, if injury persists despite these simple measures, then an accurate diagnosis must be made.

STEP 3: MAKE AN ACCURATE DIAGNOSIS OF THE INJURY AND INSTITUTE THE MOST APPROPRIATE TREATMENT

Running injuries typically affect the following structures, in roughly the order of frequency listed.

- Ligament-to-bone and tendon-to-bone attachments
- Bones
- Muscles
- Tendons
- Bursas (fluid-filled sacs that lie between tendons and bones and allow free movement of the tendons over the bones)
- Blood vessels (arteries and veins)
- Nerves

Each injury has certain characteristics that help in the diagnosis, and each will be discussed in appropriate detail with comments about its correct treatment. But first we will discuss the relative frequencies of these injuries and note how that frequency has changed over the past decade as the quality of running shoes has altered.

Four different surveys (Cavanagh, 1980; Clement et al., 1981; James et al., 1978; Pinshaw et al., 1983) found that knee injuries are by far the most common running injuries (comprising 19 to 44% of all such injuries) followed by shin-splints (15 to 18%). Less common injuries are Achilles tendinitis (5 to 11%), plantar fasciitis (5 to 14%), stress fractures (5 to 6%), and muscle injuries (5 to 6%). Studies show that the most common knee injury is runner's knee, with the iliotibial band friction syndrome accounting for only about one fifth to one third of the total running injuries to the knee.

The major changes that have occurred in the patterns of running injuries since 1970 have been a decrease in the incidence of Achilles tendinitis (from about 20 to 5% of all injuries) and increases in the incidence of shinsplints (from 10 to 18%) and the incidence of runner's knee (from 23 to 44%). This fall in the incidence of Achilles tendinitis may be a result of the increased heel height in modern running shoes and increased time spent stretching by modern runners (McKenzie et al., 1985). The reason incidences of the other injuries have risen may be due, as Cavanagh (1980) suggested, to the introduction of softer running shoes, which control pronation rather poorly.

Ligament-to-Bone and Bone-to-Tendon Attachment Injuries

The four common injuries that I include in this group are runner's knee, the iliotibial band friction syndrome, plantar fasciitis, and the Osgood-Schlatter syndrome.

Runner's Knee (Peripatellar Pain Syndrome; Medial Patellar Retinaculitis)

The term *runner's knee* was first coined by Dr. George Sheehan in the early 1970s to describe a running injury that produces a set of very specific and characteristic symptoms.

- The pain is localized around the kneecap.
- The pain first occurs during running and does not result from external trauma.
- The pain usually comes on after a predictable distance.
- The pain becomes gradually worse but is exacerbated by very long races.
- Walking up or down steps causes discomfort, as does squatting on the haunches.
- Sitting with the knee bent for any length of time causes discomfort. (Insall et al., 1976, called this the ''movie sign,'' because patients with this injury soon learn to choose aisle seats at the movies so that they can periodically stretch their knees into the aisle, thereby relieving the pain.)
- The conventional medical approach to sporting injuries—cortisone injections into the painful area—never provides a permanent cure for runner's knee, as in most running injuries.

In the original description of runner's knee, it was thought that the damaged tissues in this injury lay behind the kneecap in the cartilaginous lining of the knee joint between the kneecap and the tibia and femur (the two other bones that constitute the knee joint). Thus, runner's knee was considered to be chondromalacia patella—a condition well recognized by orthopedic surgeons that is marked by degeneration of the joint cartilage on the undersurface of the kneecap.

If this were indeed the case it would mean that running had caused degeneration of the joint cartilage, which, in time, would almost certainly lead to arthritis. Following this logic, it is a small step to conclude that runners who have a high incidence of the prearthritic condition, chondromalacia patella, must ultimately develop arthritis. The 10th law of running injuries counters this untruth.

Fortunately, we now know that runner's knee is not chondromalacia patella and has nothing to do with the cartilage lining the undersurface of the kneecap (Pretorius et al., 1986). Dr. Stan James (an orthopedic surgeon, a runner, and the man whose medical expertise helped Joan Benoit win the first women's Olympic Marathon) and his colleagues (1978) were the first to notice that the area of most severe knee pain in runners with this condition was actually on the inner or outer border of the kneecap, at the site where the patella tendon and the medial and lateral retinacula (see Figure 14.8) attach. Clearly, these sites are not those affected by chondromalacia patella. James and his colleagues (1978) therefore coined the term *peripatellar pain syndrome* to describe this condition; others use the terms *medial patellar retinaculitis* (Clancy, 1980) or *patellofemoral pain syndrome* (Clement et al., 1981).

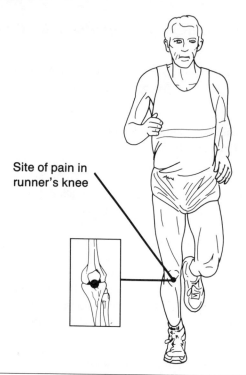

Site of pain in
runner's knee

Figure 14.8 The kneecap and related anatomy showing sites where the pain may be felt in the runner's knee syndrome.

Stan James's hunch has since been confirmed by sophisticated studies showing that the tendons and indeed the bone in this condition are abnormal (Devereaux et al., 1986); studies also show degenerative changes that almost certainly explain the marked pain caused by this injury (Merkel et al., 1982).

If the history of injury is suggestive, the diagnosis of runner's knee can be confirmed by a simple test shown in Figure 14.9. In this test the runner lies supine on the examining couch and relaxes the quadriceps. The examiner's left hand pushes the top end of the patella so that the bottom tip comes away from the knee joint. Firm pressure applied by the second and third fingers along the lower border of the patella reproduces the pain the athlete feels when running.

Runner's knee is the injury that, par exemplar, is caused by excessive ankle pronation. This occurs because the runner has hypermobile feet that pronate excessively either because the foot itself is at fault or because it is compensating for other abnormalities in the lower limb (Pretorius et al., 1986). This hyper-mobile foot then fails to resupinate after the midstance of the running cycle. Rather, it acts like a bag of delinquent bones, each going its own way and failing to produce the firm lever required for a strong toe-off. The excessive pronation

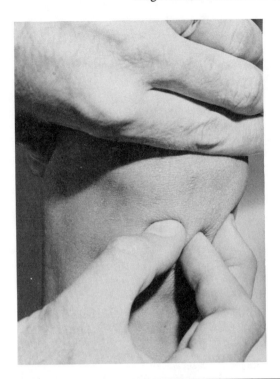

Figure 14.9 Palpating the kneecap to make a diagnosis of runner's knee.

causes a twisting force to develop at the knee (see Figure 14.10). This pulls the kneecap out of its correct alignment, causing increased stress on the kneecap-anchoring ligaments shown in Figure 14.8. With time, this abnormal movement, repeated sufficiently frequently, causes the bone to which the ligaments are attached to develop a stress response, ultimately causing pain.

Other factors may be associated with this injury.

1. *Shoes.* The most important additional factor associated with runner's knee is inappropriately soft running shoes that fail to control pronation adequately and that may have collapsed to the inside, as have the pairs shown in Figures 14.2 and 14.3.

2. *Training errors and training surfaces.* Other likely factors include training too far, too hard, and too soon; always running on the same side of a cambered road; interval training; and racing too often (Pretorius et al., 1986). Note that this injury is more likely to occur in the leg nearest to the middle of the road, because this foot has to pronate more to compensate for the road camber.

3. *Hereditary factors.* The most important hereditary factor causing the ankle to pronate excessively in runners with this injury is hypermobile feet. In addition,

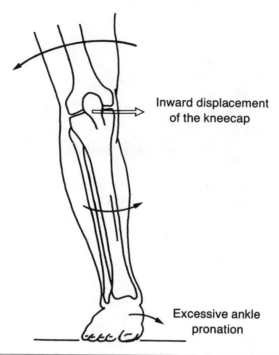

Inward displacement
of the kneecap

Excessive ankle
pronation

Figure 14.10   The biomechanical basis of knee pain in runner's knee.
Note. From *Cures for Common Running Injuries* (p. 12) by S.I. Subotnick, 1979, New York: Macmillan. Copyright 1979 by S.I. Subotnick. Adapted by permission.

other abnormalities may cause the kneecap to drift inward during the stance phase of running (e.g., an abnormal inward twist in the large thigh bone, the femur).

The treatment of runner's knee must be aimed at correcting the biomechanical factors causing the injury. If the biomechanical cause is not corrected, the kneecap will continue to be pulled out of alignment with each running stride, and this will successfully defeat all medical efforts that aim simply to treat the painful area on the kneecap. The principal aim of treatment of this injury must be to reduce excessive ankle pronation during running. This is achieved by running in shoes that limit ankle pronation and, if this fails, to have a custom-built orthotic (arch support) made. That orthotics do indeed control ankle pronation has been shown (Bates et al., 1979).

Using this simple approach to treating runner's knee, Pretorius et al. (1986) were able to cure 68% of runners in their sample within 4 weeks of only one 20-minute consultation.

Other less essential methods of treatment include calf-muscle stretching and correcting any possible muscle strength/flexibility imbalances between the quadriceps and hamstring muscles. The role of muscle imbalance in this injury has not yet been established.

Appropriate Shoes for People With Runner's Knee. All the major running shoe manufacturers have developed shoes that specifically limit ankle pronation during running, so-called antipronation shoes. The clinical effectiveness of these shoes improves each year.

As described earlier, antipronation shoes have firm midsoles when tested with the thumb compression test (see Figure 6.2), they have rigid heel counters (see Figure 6.4), and they are straight lasted with combination or board lasting (see Figure 6.1). Most importantly, when tested with the Noakes Pronation-Testing Technique, these shoes are extremely resistant to vertical torque, as is the shoe shown in Figure 6.3.

Additional shoe advice for the runner who needs an antipronation shoe can be found in the most recent Shoe Survey issue of *Runner's World* magazine, in which a group of shoes that have good antipronation features are listed. The runner should also discuss these shoes with other runners and particularly with the shoe salesclerk at a specialty running shoe shop to determine which of these shoes have proven to be successful on the road.

Orthotics (Arch Supports). If the choice of more appropriate running shoes does not cure the injury, then the only hope for long-term pain-free running is to have a custom-built orthotic made.

Unfortunately, in all countries except in some parts of the United States, people who are sufficiently qualified to make such supports are difficult to find. And unless the orthotic is correctly made, the injury will not improve. The best advice I can offer is to find runners who are wearing orthotics with which they are pleased and find out where they had the orthotics made. At present, orthotics that can be bought over-the-counter at pharmacies and running shoe shops are usually not sufficient for persons who pronate excessively, although these devices may help runners with only very mild degrees of abnormal pronation.

First Aid Treatment. The first aid treatment of runner's knee is to apply ice to the sore area for about 20 minutes twice daily. Two aspirins (or equivalent) taken 30 minutes before exercise are also said to be quite helpful. Cortisone injections into the knee joint, although suggested by some writers, must be avoided at all costs because these injections do not reach the site of the injury, which, as was shown in Figures 14.8 and 14.9, is around the kneecap, not in the knee joint itself.

Runners with this injury who fail to improve within about a month must realize that the shoes and orthotics that they are using have failed to control their ankle pronation sufficiently and that further correction is necessary.

The Iliotibial Band Friction Syndrome

The iliotibial band is a thickened strip of fascia (tendon) that extends from the hip across the outside of the knee and inserts into the large shinbone (the tibia), immediately below the line of the knee joint (see Figure 14.11). When the knee is straight, the fascia lies in front of a bony prominence at the outside of the knee, the femoral epicondyle, but as the knee bends the fascia begins to move toward that bony point. When the knee has bent through about 30°, the fascia may contact the femoral epicondyle, and it is this contact that is believed to cause pain in this condition.

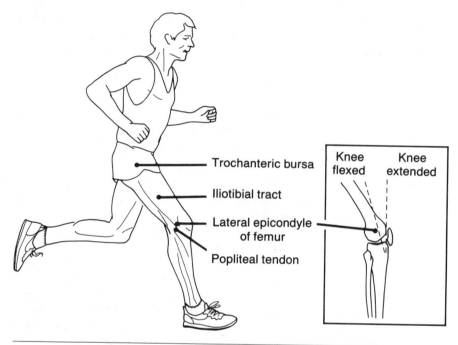

Figure 14.11 The anatomy of the iliotibial band showing the area of localized pain experienced in the iliotibial band friction syndrome.

The classic feature of this injury is severe pain, well localized over the outside of the knee, directly over the lateral femoral epicondyle. The pain is absent when the runner is at rest and only comes on during exercise. Even though the athlete may be quite unable to run, he or she is usually able to walk long distances or play other sports (e.g., squash, football, or tennis) without discomfort, although walking downstairs may be painful.

During running, the pain usually becomes so severe that it limits the runner to a specific running distance that may be as little as 100 m in some cases and as much as 16 km in others. The pain usually comes on rapidly and once present stops further running. Downhill running, in particular, aggravates the symptoms in all runners. Sometimes, but rarely, symptoms are only present during downhill running; in such cases, the runner may be able to continue running on the flat or uphill but must avoid the downhills.

Another important feature of this injury is that the pain subsides almost immediately after the athlete stops running. For this reason, athletes are frequently reluctant to see their doctors lest they be considered hypochondriacal. However, should the athletes again try to run, the pain returns rapidly. (My colleagues and I use this feature to help in the diagnosis. If an athlete describes an injury that sounds like the iliotibial band syndrome, but we can find no sign of injury, we simply ask the athlete to go for a run and to return when pain develops. After the athlete has a short run, the site of the pain and therefore the diagnosis of the injury usually becomes obvious.)

The most important finding during an examination of the knee is an area that is exquisitely tender to pressure. This area is well localized to the outside of the knee joint, immediately overlying the femoral epicondyle (see Figure 14.11). Downhill running aggravates the pain. The diagnosis is confirmed by a test first described by a South African orthopedic surgeon (Noble, 1979, 1980). In the Noble test, pressure is applied to the lateral side of the knee directly over the femoral epicondyle. The knee is slowly straightened from about 90° of flexion. At about 30° of flexion, as the band slips over the femoral epicondyle directly underneath the examiner's finger, the pain that the athlete feels during activity is reproduced.

At present there is no consensus of how this injury occurs. But some of the factors that Lindenberg et al. (1984) and others have isolated include the following.

1. *Training errors*. It seems that heavy training mileages, sudden increases in training, and too much racing are important training errors that explain why this injury occurs most commonly in the peak racing season.

2. *Training surfaces*. Excessive downhill running and running on hard surfaces seem to be factors in this injury. Another important factor identified by Lindenberg et al. (1984) was that injury occurred on the side of the body corresponding to the side of the road on which the runner most often ran. Runners who ran on the right-hand side of the road normally developed the injury on their right-hand sides.

3. *Shoes*. Of the sample of Lindenberg et al. (1984), 66% of injured runners were running in "hard" running shoes with poor shock-absorbing properties at the time of injury.

Hard shoes are those designed to limit ankle pronation, which are therefore normally prescribed for the treatment of runner's knee and shinsplints. Indeed, it is not uncommon for an athlete treated too enthusiastically for either runner's knee or shinsplints to return some weeks or months later with the initial injury cured but with an iliotibial band friction syndrome that has been caused by shoes and orthotics that restricted ankle pronation too effectively.

4. *Hereditary factors.* The most important hereditary structural factors associated with this injury are bowlegs and high-arched, rigid feet (Sutker et al., 1981). Rigid feet are unable to adequately absorb the shock of landing, which is then transferred in some way to the iliotibial band, ultimately leading to the injury.

In my experience, about 70% of cases of the iliotibial band friction syndrome occur in runners whose lower limbs fail to absorb shock adequately, mainly because their ankles do not pronate sufficiently. Thus, treatment must aim to increase the limb's ability to absorb shock, which can be achieved in a number of ways.

Shoes. Initially, all injured runners should be advised to buy "soft" running shoes that do not resist pronation. Typically, these are shoes that have very soft midsoles when tested with the thumb compression test (see Figure 6.2), they have weak heel counters (see Figure 6.4), and they are curved and slip lasted (see Figure 6.1). When tested with the Noakes Pronation-Testing Technique (see Figure 6.3), these shoes have very little resistance to vertical torque and bend easily. In addition, the shoe must not have an outside heel flare, because this has been specifically implicated as an important factor causing injury. The shoe can be modified by filing down the heel flare on the outer side of the shoe that is worn on the injured leg.

Finally, in runners with severe bowlegs or very high-arched, rigid feet, it may be necessary for an orthopedic technician to build a lateral (outside) wedge into the midsole of the shoe. This wedge forces the foot to pronate inward, thereby improving its shock-absorbing capacity. In addition, if the athlete has a short leg, the sole of the shoe on the short-leg side should be built up to compensate for the imbalance.

Training. Athletes are encouraged to reduce their training. They are allowed to run with discomfort, but once the injury becomes frankly painful, they must stop.

Training Surfaces. Training should be done on flat, soft surfaces, and all downhill running should be avoided until the injury has healed.

Stretching. Two special lateral stretches are prescribed. For the first, place all your weight on the injured leg and bend your upper body in the direction of the uninjured leg, without twisting your trunk. This stretches the iliotibial band and should be performed for 10 minutes daily (see Figure 13.1, Exercise 17). Perform the second stretch while sitting. Place both hands on the injured knee and pull the knee across your body toward the opposite armpit.

Roadside. Because we and others (Firer, 1989; Lindenberg et al., 1984) found that the majority of injuries occurred on the leg farthest away from the center of the road (i.e., the left leg of a runner running on the left-hand side of the road), all runners were encouraged to switch the side of the road on which they ran. (Please note that this advice is potentially dangerous, because it is not safe to run with your back to the traffic. Thus, this advice must be followed only with the greatest caution.)

Other Forms of Treatment. Other treatment options for the iliotibial band friction syndrome include icing the tender area of the knee or injecting hydrocortisone into the tender area. Occasionally, in very resistant cases, a small surgical procedure is performed in which the section of the tendon that comes to ride over the femoral epicondyle is excised (Noble, 1979, 1980). Although the results of surgery are most encouraging (Firer, 1989; Martens et al., 1989), I feel that surgery and hydrocortisone injection should only be tried after all the other treatment options previously described have been tried, or if the athlete simply cannot afford the time necessary for conservative treatment to succeed.

Using simple methods of treatment outlined in this section, 83% of the injured runners in the sample studied by Lindenberg et al. (1984) were cured completely of their injuries; 58% of all injured runners were cured within 3 weeks and the remaining runners, who were completely cured, became symptom-free within 6 weeks to 6 months.

However, of all running injuries, the success rate in this injury is the most disappointing. So if you have to be injured, please choose any injury other than the iliotibial band friction syndrome! Lindenberg et al. (1984) were unable to fully cure 17% of the injured runners, and of these one half stopped running. Interestingly, the ones who continued were ultimately helped when they were placed in hard running shoes and prescribed arch supports (orthotics) to limit ankle pronation, the reverse of what had been suggested initially.

The iliotibial band friction syndrome remains one of the most difficult running injuries to treat. Unlike runner's knee and shinsplints, both of which respond very quickly to simple measures, the iliotibial band friction syndrome can drag on endlessly in some runners. This may well indicate that we do not fully understand the mechanics causing the injury.

Plantar Fasciitis

This is one of the less common injuries, accounting for only about 5 to 14% of running injuries.

The symptom is pain directly in front of the heel that is usually first noticed during running and then becomes noticeable when the patient gets up in the morning. For the first few steps the patient hobbles by putting all weight on the heel and will not extend the ankle or push off with the big toe. (The same features are present in Achilles tendinitis.) Someone suffering from a heel bruise, on the other hand, will hobble on the toes in order to prevent the bruised heel from coming into contact with the ground.

On examination, the diagnostic feature is extreme point tenderness at the origin of the plantar fascia from the calcaneus (see Figure 14.12).

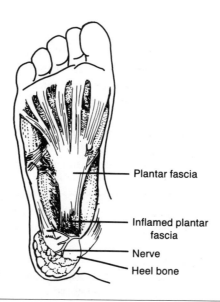

Plantar fascia

Inflamed plantar fascia

Nerve

Heel bone

Figure 14.12 The anatomy of the plantar fascia, showing the area that may become inflamed after injury.

The mechanism of injury in this condition is believed to be excessive subtalar joint pronation (as for runner's knee), which causes a bowstring stretching of the plantar fascia, especially if toe-off occurs with the ankle fully pronated. Confirmation of this concept, however, is still lacking (B.L. Warren, 1984), and it is easier to identify those unlikely to develop the injury than those who either have or have had the injury (B.L. Warren & Jones, 1987). Others suggest that the injury is more common in those with cavus feet that fail to pronate sufficiently (McKenzie et al., 1985).

Until the exact mechanism of this injury has been determined, efforts to treat this injury should initially include measures to stop excessive ankle pronation. Thus, the injured runner should try all the measures described for the treatment of runner's knee and Achilles tendinitis. It may be necessary to adjust the orthotic slightly to ensure that it does not contact the painful area under the heel bone. Calf-muscle stretching (see Figure 13.1, Exercise 9) seems to be especially important (B.L. Warren, 1984). Uphill running and speed work should be avoided until the injury has resolved. If this approach fails to be effective, the possibility that the injury is due to inadequate pronation should be considered. For runners in whom symptoms persist for more than 12 months despite all these measures, surgery may prove very effective (Snider et al., 1983). In these runners, there is evidence of major histological changes in the fascia at the site of pain.

The Osgood-Schlatter Syndrome

This is a condition specific to growing children who develop discomfort that is well localized over the tibial tubercle into which the patella ligament inserts.

In growing children the tibial tubercle is an epiphysis, and repetitive contractions by the powerful quadriceps muscle, which inserts via the patella tendon into the tibial tubercle, can cause minor separation of the epiphyseal cartilage from the underlying bone. The condition is resolved when the cartilage in the epiphysis is replaced by bone, usually at the age of about 15 years.

In the past, immobilization of the knee was a popular method of treating this condition. But we have since learned that this is unnecessary and that time alone will cure the injury. Until the tibial epiphysis fuses, the athlete with this condition can continue exercising with discomfort but not with pain. Activities that cause pain sufficiently severe to limit exercise must be avoided.

Bone Injuries

The two common bone injuries in runners are shinsplints and stress fractures.

Shinsplints (Medial Tibial Stress Syndrome)

Before the running revolution of the 1970s, there was really only one running injury. If you were a runner and you hurt somewhere between your big toes and your hip, then you had shinsplints. Actually, this lack of diagnostic precision was probably not really much of a handicap, because our understanding of running injuries was so rudimentary that whatever therapy was suggested invariably failed.

Today, however, shinsplints is a diagnosis reserved for one specific and curable injury—a bone injury localized to one or both of the calf bones (the tibia and the fibula) in one or more of three positions (see Figure 14.13). Most experts feel that the term *shinsplints* should be replaced by one of the anatomically more correct terms: *posterior tibial syndrome* (S.L. James et al., 1978), *tibial stress syndrome* (Clement, 1974; Clement et al., 1981), or *medial tibial stress syndrome* (Mubarak et al., 1982).

Shinsplints typically develops through four stages of injury (2nd law of running injuries). In the first stage, vague discomfort, poorly localized somewhere in the calf, is noted after exercise. As training continues, the discomfort comes on during exercise. At first it is possible to "run through" this pain, but if training continues without treatment, the pain soon becomes so severe that proper training

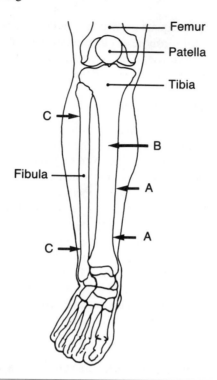

Figure 14.13   The anatomy of shinsplints. Posterior shinsplints (A), anterior shinsplints (B), and lateral shinsplints (C).

is neither enjoyable nor possible. This is a Grade III injury. Ultimately, the injury may be so bad that anything more strenuous than walking is impossible. At this point the Grade IV shinsplints injury has, in fact, become a stress fracture.

In diagnosing shinsplints, the examiner must differentiate the injury from a chronic tear in the tibialis anterior or tibialis posterior muscles. This is done by feeling for the site at which maximal tenderness is felt. In shinsplints, this site is always along either the front (anterior shinsplints) or back (posterior shinsplints) borders of the tibia or along the outside edge (lateral shinsplints) of the fibula (see Figure 14.13). Usually, the bone in the affected area has a rough, corrugated feeling due to the buildup of a new bony (periosteal) layer at the site of the irritation. When the examiner applies firm finger pressure to these areas, the patient feels exquisite, well-localized, nauseating tenderness. The discomfort so produced is usually severe enough to cause the injured runner to screech involuntarily and pull the leg away. Frequently there is also mild swelling over the injured bone so that when the finger pressure is released, a small indentation is left in the tissues overlying the injured bone.

There are several elaborate explanations for what causes shinsplints, but I am not sure that all are entirely satisfactory. In the mid-1970s, the most popular explanation was that the buildup of pressure in one or more of the tight muscular compartments of the leg during exercise caused shinsplints (see Figure 14.14). Thus, the logical treatment was to prevent the effects of this pressure buildup by performing a surgical procedure in which the tight lining of the muscular compartment was cut. Certainly, this type of treatment is very effective for the compartment syndromes, in which there is just such an increase in pressure, but it is without effect in true shinsplints (M.J. Allen & Barnes, 1986).

We now know that in true shinsplints there is no such pressure buildup (Detmer, 1986; Mubarak et al., 1982; Wallensten & Eriksson, 1984). It appears that shinsplints is a bone injury that is caused either by excessive ankle pronation (Viitasalo & Kvist, 1983) or by exposure to excessive shock to which the bone is initially unable to adapt. Interestingly, as early as 1938, Webster (1948) suggested that "shin-soreness" was often, but not always, caused by the "lowering of the arches of the foot" (p. 80).

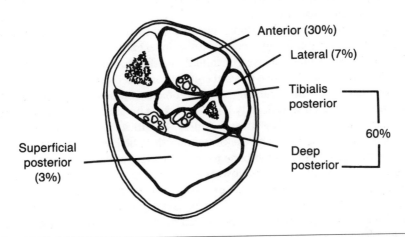

Figure 14.14 The muscle compartments of the calf. The relative frequency of involvement of the different compartments is shown.
Note. Based on data of Martens et al. (1984).

Michael and Holder (1985) suggested that the area of abnormality in some cases of shinsplints is restricted to a narrow band of bone along the inner border of the tibia, into which the thick covering (fascia) of the soleus muscle inserts. These authors postulated that excessive ankle pronation causes increased tension in this fascia, the so-called soleus syndrome, ultimately leading to the bone injury of shinsplints. They therefore suggested that if control of excessive ankle pronation does not cure the injury, then surgical dissection of the fascia is likely to be successful. Detmer (1986) called this injury the *Type II medial tibial stress syndrome* and also suggested that surgical resection of the fascia of the posterior compartment and attention to the damaged periosteal lining is usually required.

But the most likely explanation for the majority of cases of shinsplints is that the injury occurs in bones that are undergoing remodeling in response to an increased loading stress.

It is now clear that the initial response in bones subjected to increased loading is the activation of specialized cells, *osteoclasts*, whose function is to cause bone resorption (Johnson et al., 1963; Li et al., 1985). The resorbing bone also becomes highly vascular and, possibly because of this increased vascularity, may be identified by bone scanning (Matheson et al., 1987) or by magnetic resonance imaging (Lodwick et al., 1987). This phase has been termed "osteoclonal excavation" (Lodwick et al., 1987). During this phase the bone strength is likely reduced, placing the bone at increased risk of fracture (Scully & Besterman, 1982). Movement at the site of bone weakness induced by exercise could explain the deep-seated pain of shinsplints.

The phase of osteoclonal excavation passes gradually into another phase in which new bone is laid down at the site of bone resorption by other specialized bone cells, the *osteoblasts*.

My interpretation is that shinsplints and stress fractures develop in athletes either whose bones undergo excessive osteoclonal excavation or whose osteoblastic responses are either delayed or initially ineffectual. Indeed, Margulies et al. (1986) showed that the bone mineral contents of Israeli army recruits who failed to complete their basic training, most commonly because they suffered stress fractures, increased significantly less than did the bone mineral contents of those recruits who did not suffer stress fractures. Significantly, 85% of the fractures occurred within the first 8 weeks of training. It is believed that at least 90 days are required for the resorbed bone to be completely replaced by mature, strong bone; the rate of this response slows with increasing age (Johnson, 1964). Thus, I suggest that shinsplints indicates excessive osteoclonal excavation with the development of focal or diffuse areas of bone weakness. These weaker areas are sensitive to touch and to the increased loading stress of exercise. Myburgh et al. (1990) have indeed shown that athletes with stress fractures have reduced bone density due to a low calcium diet, menstrual disturbances, or both.

It has also been suggested that overstriding is a factor in the development of anterior shinsplints. Overstriding is especially common during fast downhill running. When overstriding, the athlete uses a stride that is too long and causes the shoe to strike the ground forcibly at the extreme back of the heel, causing the forefoot to slap onto the ground. It is believed that in trying to prevent this slapping movement, the muscles in the front of the calf are forced to overwork, and ultimately pain develops at the point where they attach to the tibia.

Posterior shinsplints, by far the most common form of shinsplints, is almost certainly caused by either excessive ankle pronation (Messier & Pittala, 1988;

Viitasalo & Kvist, 1983) or by the inadequate shock-absorbing abilities of bones unused to the stresses of running. In my experience, most novice runners who develop shinsplints within their first 3 months of running usually get better without any specific treatment other than possibly changing to more appropriate running shoes. This suggests that the bones get "stronger" and therefore become better able to absorb the shock of running. On the other hand, we do know that when excessive ankle pronation is controlled in experienced runners with shinsplints, they are usually cured within a short time.

Exactly how these two mechanisms cause the bone pain of shinsplints is not known. My guess is that abnormal ankle pronation causes a torque or twisting force to develop in the tibia and the fibula and that this eventually leads to minute bone cracks (Grade I to III injuries) at the sites of greatest bone resorption. Ultimately, these may progress to stress fractures (Grade IV injury). How inadequate shock absorption causes the identical injury is not presently known.

Shinsplints is most common among three groups of athletes: middle-distance high school track athletes; beginning joggers and army recruits, particularly during their first few months of training; and more experienced runners, particularly when they start training intensively for competition. Factors associated with the injury are as follows.

1. *Training errors, training surfaces, and running shoes.* I suspect, although there is no published evidence to support this, that high school track athletes are particularly likely to develop shinsplints. These athletes train very little in the off-season so that when the new school year begins, they usually have about a month in which to prepare for the first track meet. So each day the athletes are exposed to impossible training loads (too much speed work, too often, too soon with no hard-day/easy-day routine) under the worst possible environmental conditions (running continually in one direction on a hard, unforgiving running surface in hard, uncompromising shoes). Unless the athletes have perfect lower limbs, the results are predictable: By the time the first major track meet arrives, the athletes either have such bad shinsplints that they are unable to do their best or else they are watching from the sidelines, nursing stress fractures.

Joggers and long-distance runners who develop shinsplints may exhibit some of the same behavior patterns as the high school students but may be affected by some additional factors as well. Typically, joggers with shinsplints have been running for 5 to 12 weeks; frequently they are running to lose weight so may be a shade heavy; they have trained in sneakers on hard surfaces; and they have progressed too rapidly (Devas, 1958; Myburgh et al., 1988; Richie et al., 1985). For whatever reason, female joggers seem to be at greater risk than are men. This high risk of shinsplints in beginning joggers is the reason why I advocate a period of walking in the first weeks of the beginner's training program (see Table 6.4).

Trained distance runners who have recently developed shinsplints have usually altered their training methods in one or more ways described previously. The runners may have suddenly increased training distances or introduced speed work or hill-running sessions. Alternatively, they may have recently resumed training after a rest and pushed it too hard, too soon. Their training shoes may be inappropriate, or their shoes may be worn out in one or more of the ways described earlier in this chapter; usually, either the shoes will have collapsed to the inside or else the midsoles may have hardened to the consistency of stone.

2. *Hereditary factors.* These are essentially the same as those causing runner's knee—in particular, hypermobile feet (Devas, 1958; Michael & Holder, 1985; Myburgh et al., 1988; Viitassalo & Kvist, 1983) and a leg-length discrepancy (Friberg, 1982). In addition, there may be inadequate flexibility of the ankle caused by tight calf muscles. A squatting test has been designed to identify those with the greatest degrees of lower limb malalignment, who are at greatest risk of injury (M. Allen et al., 1986).

3. *Muscle imbalance and inflexibility.* Although tight calf muscles may be inborn, they may also develop in athletes who train hard without stretching adequately.

Hard training also develops muscle imbalances; it is believed that running increases the strength of the posterior calf muscles more than it increases the strength of the anterior (front) calf muscles. This strength imbalance may then play a role in injury.

4. *Menstrual abnormalities, a low-calcium diet, or both.* There is growing evidence (see chapter 16) that the majority of female sports enthusiasts who have abnormal menstrual patterns also restrict their dietary energy intakes (Cann et al., 1984; Cook et al., 1987; Drinkwater et al., 1984; E.C. Fisher et al., 1986; Lindberg et al., 1984; Marcus et al., 1985; M.E. Nelson et al., 1986). The result is that their trabecular bones (in particular the vertebrae) but not their cortical bones, or limbs (Gonzàlez, 1982; K.P. Jones et al., 1985; Linnell et al., 1984; Lutter, 1983), are likely to become weaker for two reasons: (a) The blood levels of the female hormone estrogen that are required for normal bone mineralization are depressed, and (b) these women's dietary calcium intakes may be too low to maintain normal bone mineral content. Their weaker bones are more prone to the development of shinsplints, stress fractures, and curvature of the spine (scoliosis) in early adult life (Barrow & Saha, 1988; Lindberg et al., 1984; Lloyd et al., 1986; Marcus et al., 1985; M.P. Warren et al., 1986); these bones are certainly prone to more serious problems like pathological hip fractures complicating severe osteoporosis in older age. The extent of this bone weakness is very serious; the young amenorrheic 25-year-old women in these studies had bone mineral contents comparable to postmenopausal women of 50 to 60 years of age. Fortunately, resumption of menstruation is associated with an increase of bone mineral content, whereas continuing amenorrhea causes a further loss of bone (Drinkwater et al., 1986).

In addition, Myburgh (1989) and Myburgh et al. (1988, 1990) showed that the dietary calcium intakes of sports participants with shin soreness (shinsplints and stress fractures) is abnormally low and is a predisposing factor for the injury.

The treatment of shinsplints depends upon the severity of the injury and its location. Grade I injuries, which cause pain only after exercise, do not require heroic measures. The first priority, as in all injuries, is to determine whether anything has changed recently in the runner's training methods. A return to previous training methods (if possible) may be all that is required to cure the injury. For example, track athletes who develop injuries shortly after the introduction of regular speed sessions on the track should simply run fewer intervals, run them less often, and run them more slowly until the injuries clear up. Alternatively, the athletes should run their intervals on softer surfaces in running shoes that absorb shock better than do spikes.

Novice runners who have been running for less than 3 months can be assured that their injuries will likely disappear in 4 to 10 weeks without any specific treatment and even without reductions in training. This group of runners must especially pay attention to their running gaits; in particular they must run with a shuffle and avoid overstriding. Another trick is to avoid pushing off with the toes; the toes should be allowed to float inside the shoe. Some podiatrists suggest that padding should be placed under the toes to help achieve this.

The next option is to consider a change in running shoes. If examination of an old pair of shoes shows that the runner pronates excessively, then the runner must buy a shoe that will resist pronation.

If the old shoes do not reveal patterns of excessive pronation, the problem becomes one of deciding whether the shoe is too hard or not quite hard enough to control ankle pronation. Under these circumstances, I usually advise the runner to buy a slightly softer shoe than the one in which he or she has been running. Should that prove ineffective, I still have the option of prescribing an arch support to control ankle pronation.

A third treatment option is to do specific calf-muscle stretching and strengthening exercises. Appropriate calf-muscle stretching exercises are shown in Figure 13.1, Exercise 9.

A specific form of treatment is to apply ice massages to the sore areas for 20 to 30 minutes a session, 2 to 3 times a day. The ice should be placed in a plastic container and then massaged gently up and down the leg over the sore areas. I do not know whether physiotherapy, drugs, or injections really make any difference at this stage of the injury. Certainly, they do not substitute for a thorough evaluation and correction of the factors causing the injury.

A woman who is not menstruating regularly should consider that a lack of circulating estrogen may be contributing to her injury. If she is knowingly restricting her food intake, she should consider increasing her food intake until a normal menstrual pattern returns. Alternatively, she should consult a gynecologist for an opinion about the advisability of taking replacement estrogen and progesterone therapy.

Those women who are menstruating normally but who are restricting their dietary calcium intakes, usually by avoiding dairy produce, which provides most of the calcium in the diet, should consider taking supplementary calcium in the form of calcium tablets (500 to 1000 mg/day; see also chapter 16).

Other risk factors for the development of osteoporosis in women include alcohol or tobacco use, a sedentary lifestyle, and the use of certain drugs, in particular anticonvulsant drugs and thyroid hormone. White and Oriental women who are slenderly built, who undergo early menopause, and who have family histories of osteoporosis are particularly at risk (Johnston & Slemenda, 1987).

It is important to stress that exercise, particularly when combined with a high dietary calcium intake, increases bone mineral content and reduces the risk of osteoporosis and its complications in all persons at all ages with the sole exception of young, amenorrheic women whose blood estrogen levels are low (Chow et al., 1987; Dalsky et al., 1988; Johnston & Slemenda, 1987; E.L. Smith & Raab, 1986).

When, despite trying everything listed previously, the athlete always feels pain during running (Grade II and III injuries), the only real hope for a cure is to acquire an adequate custom-built arch support (orthotic) to wear when running. When the injury advances to this stage, it indicates that the runner's genetic structure will never, by itself, cope with the amount of training the mind wants the body to do. And the only way to compensate for those genetic limitations is by wearing an orthotic. But remember that only when the orthotic is correctly adjusted will it cure the injury. If the orthotic fails to cure the injury, it likely has not been made sufficiently well to provide the precise degree of control required to cure the injury. Usually all that is required is further minor corrections to the orthotic. If the injury fails to respond to conventional treatment, the athlete may have the "soleus syndrome" of Michael and Holder (1985) and should seek a surgeon's opinion.

If the level of a Grade IV injury is reached—the stage of stress fracture—the treatment is physical rest and mental exercise (i.e., deciding what caused the injury). Whether a first stress fracture is an indication to buy an orthotic depends largely on the major factor causing the injury. If a major error has been made in the training methods, then this error should be corrected first. If, in spite of careful attention to all the factors previously listed, the injury returns, then an orthotic is likely to be the only long-term solution to the injury. The most frustrating aspect of a stress fracture is the enforced layoff from exercise that it entails. Exercise that the athlete is allowed to do while recovering from a stress fracture is described subsequently.

Stress Fractures

Unlike the common bone fractures occurring in contact sports like football, in which a single external blow causes the bone to fracture, the runner's bone may fracture as a result of repetitive minor trauma accumulating over weeks or months. This is a concept that runners usually find difficult to accept. How can something as strong as bone fracture so easily? We do not know, but it happens quite frequently.

Probably the first doctor to recognize this injury was Breihaupt (1855), a German military doctor. Because such fractures occurred most commonly in new army recruits recently introduced to marching, the fractures became known as "march fractures," a name that persists today. Only three animals, all athletes, develop these injuries: humans, racehorses, and greyhounds.

The symptom produced by a stress fracture is simple and unmistakable: a quite rapid onset of pain that is well localized to any of a number of the bones, usually of the lower limbs. (Stress fractures of the vertebrae, ribs, and upper arms have been described, but these are uncommon in runners.) In a Scandinavian study of 142 stress fractures in athletes, Orava et al. (1978) found that 54% of the fractures occurred in the tibia, 18% in the metatarsal (toe bone), 14% in the fibula (small calf bone), 7% in the femur (thigh bone), 1% in the navicular (ankle bone), and 1% in the groin (pubic bone; see Figure 14.15).

The pain is usually bearable when the patient is at rest or is walking, but as soon as any running is attempted, the pain becomes quite unbearable and running is impossible.

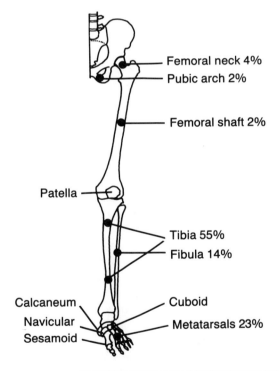

Femoral neck 4%
Pubic arch 2%
Femoral shaft 2%
Patella
Tibia 55%
Fibula 14%
Calcaneum
Cuboid
Navicular
Metatarsals 23%
Sesamoid

Figure 14.15 The anatomical distribution of stress fractures in runners.
Note. From "Stress Fractures Caused by Physical Exercise" by S. Orava, J. Puranen, and L. Ala-Ketola, 1978, *Acta Orthopaedica Scandinavica*, **49**, p. 22. Copyright 1978 by Munksgaard International Publishers, Ltd., Copenhagen, Denmark. Adapted by permission.

The diagnosis of stress fracture is quite simple. First, the injury is usually of quite sudden onset, and there is no incident of external violence. Warning symptoms are usually mild; runners get little notice of the tragedy about to befall them, but suddenly they are no longer able to run. Second, the runners will find that hopping on the injured leg (the "hop test") is painful (Matheson et al., 1987); in those with fractures of the pelvis, standing on one leg (the "standing test") is very painful and may be impossible (Noakes et al., 1985b). Third, the diagnosis may be confirmed if tenderness is felt localized to the bone. Even quite gentle pressure on the injured bone will elicit exquisite, nauseating pain. For absolute diagnostic certainty, however, a fourth feature is required: The injury heals itself completely within 2 months of complete rest.

Unfortunately, few runners will accept a 2-month rest period without some visible evidence that the diagnosis is correct. So doctors usually have to resort to X rays and bone scans, both of which have their own drawbacks. In quite a high percentage of cases, up to 57% (Matheson et al., 1987), X rays will fail to reveal the presence of a stress fracture if they are taken earlier than 3 weeks after the initial injury. In effect, the fracture is so small that it cannot be seen. Only when new bone is being formed, which is more dense than the old bone it replaces, does the fracture show as a line on the X ray (see Figure 14.16).

Convention dictates that the runner with a stress fracture that fails to show up on the first X ray is asked to come back 3 weeks later for a second X ray. In fact, the runner need not bother, because that first X ray has already revealed the most important information—that the pain is not due to a bone infection or other bone abnormality like a bone cancer, which is quite unrelated to running and which requires rather more energetic medical attention than do stress fractures. If the X ray shows nothing but the runner is unable to run, the injury is certainly a stress fracture.

A new technique that can be used to detect stress fractures is *bone scanning*. This involves injecting a radioactive material into the bloodstream; at least in theory, this radioactive material is taken up by bone cells that are extremely active. These active cells then show up as an area of increased radioactivity, a "hot spot," when photographed through a special camera (see Figure 14.17), and they indicate areas of active bone resorption and bone remodeling. Virtually all runners who have the clinical features of a stress fracture but who have normal X rays usually have these hot spots, indicating that the runners do indeed have stress fractures that for some reason (probably because they are too small) could not be identified on X ray. However, even this technique may not reveal every stress fracture. Furthermore, for each symptomatic fracture that the bone scan identifies in any individual, another two sites of increased uptake of radioactivity are present somewhere else in the athlete's skeleton (Matheson et al., 1987). These sites are asymptomatic; they do not cause the athlete noticeable discomfort. Matheson et al., (1987) coined the term "bone strain" to identify areas of active bone remodeling that can be identified by bone scanning. When the area of

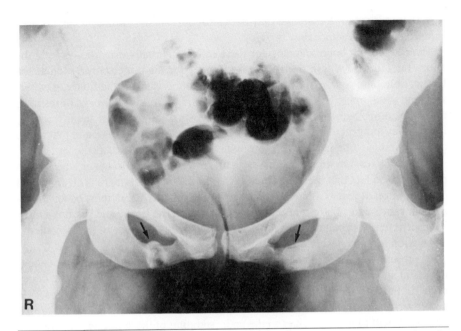

Figure 14.16 Pelvic X ray showing a healing stress fracture on the left (arrowed) and a bone traction injury on the right.

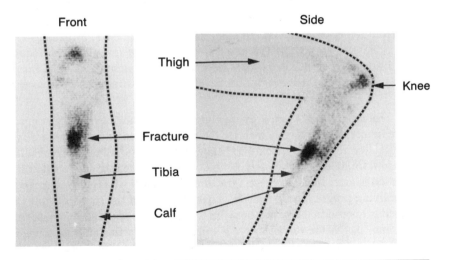

Figure 14.17 Bone scan showing a stress fracture with a well-localized increased radioactive material in the left tibia.

Note. From A. Fatar, MD, Department of Radionuclear Medicine, Groote Schuur Hospital, Cape Town, South Africa.

remodeling is small, the athlete may complain only of shinsplints; when the area is large, a stress fracture may develop.

My view is that bone scanning for these injuries is really only necessary if the injury fails to heal within 6 to 12 weeks (longer for the larger bones such as the femur, tibia, and pelvis; shorter for the smaller bones such as the fibula, metatarsals, and small ankle bones) or if the injury recurs within a few weeks of resumption of training. Neither of these features suggests a conventional stress fracture. Rather they suggest that something unrelated to running is going on in that bone, and they indicate the need for a thorough evaluation by an orthopedic surgeon.

The exact reason stress fractures occur is not known. However, the reason must lie in the fact that the bone fractures at the site at which there is an abnormal concentration of forces. Thus, two factors are involved: There must be an abnormal concentration of stress at one particular site in the bone, and the bone must be insufficiently strong to resist those forces, probably because of the osteoclonal excavation already described.

At present we do not know the exact biomechanical reasons these forces accumulate at specific sites in the different fractures, nor do we know why the bones of some but not all runners are insufficiently strong to resist those forces. We do, however, know that there are a number of risk factors for this injury, which ultimately will give us the clues to the understanding of these injuries. Six factors associated with stress fractures are as follows.

1. *Female sex.* Women are more prone to stress fractures than are men (Hulkko & Orava, 1987; Kannus et al., 1987). This became especially apparent after women were accepted to the American military academies and began to perform the same training programs as did men (Brudvig et al., 1983; Protzman, 1979; Scully & Besterman, 1982). The frequency of stress fractures in these women is up to 12 times higher than in the men. Recently it has been suggested that amenorrheic women are especially at risk for developing stress fractures (Marcus et al., 1985).

2. *Training errors.* Most stress fractures occur in novice runners or in competitive runners who suddenly increase their training loads, run one or more very long races, or return too quickly to heavy training after a rest. It seems likely that hard training during the early period of bone weakening due to osteoclonal excavation is more likely to cause a fracture. In runners who followed the beginner's training program described in chapter 6, most of the stress fractures that occurred happened in the period between 8 to 12 weeks after the commencement of training, just as the runners were getting sufficiently fit to run more than 10 km regularly. Their increased levels of muscle and heart fitness occurred at just the wrong time, when their bones were not yet sufficiently strong to cope with the added stress of suddenly running much longer distances.

Another adverse result of a sudden increase in training distance is that it causes accumulated muscular fatigue, which may then reduce the muscles' abilities to absorb shock. When the muscles are tired and unable to absorb shock, that function is passed over to the bones, which therefore become more likely to fracture.

3. *Shoes.* Excessively hard running shoes, in particular training spikes, may be a factor explaining this injury, especially in track athletes. However, my impression is that shoes play less of a role in this injury than do major errors in training methods.

4. *Genetic factors.* Three principal genetic factors are associated with stress fractures: (a) the high-arched foot, which fails to absorb shock adequately and is associated with fractures of the femur and metatarsals (Matheson et al., 1987); (b) the pronating low-arched foot, which causes abnormal biomechanical function in the lower limb, part of which may actually be a shearing motion in the tarsal bones, the tibia, and the fibula, predisposing those bones to fracture (Matheson et al., 1987); and (c) leg length inequalities. The importance of leg length inequalities in this injury was shown by Friberg (1982), who found that 87% of army recruits with stress fractures had leg length inequalities. The author found that 73% of fractures of the femur, tibia, and metatarsals occurred on the side of the long leg, whereas 60% of fibular stress fractures occurred on the side of the short leg.

Thus, runners with stress fractures must check their old shoes to determine whether they are too hard or whether they indicate excessive pronation (see Figures 14.1, 14.2, and 14.6). To determine whether a runner has a leg length inequality, he or she will usually have to be examined by a doctor or physiotherapist, but the side and site of the stress fracture may suggest which leg is short.

5. *Menstrual abnormalities, a low-calcium diet, or both.* This was detailed in the previous section. Recent studies (Myburgh, 1989; Myburgh et al., 1990) found that stress fractures were 12 times more frequent in persons with low dietary calcium intakes. In these studies, a low calcium intake was by far the best predictor of risk of stress fracture.

6. *Low bone density.* Myburgh et al. (1990) found that stress fractures occur in athletes who have reduced bone density as a result of an inadequate calcium intake (in men) or of menstrual dysfunction (in women).

7. *Race.* People of African descent are apparently less prone to stress fractures than are people of European descent (Blickenstaff & Morris, 1966; Brudvig et al., 1983).

The only treatment required for most stress fractures is 6 to 12 weeks of rest. Because these fractures seldom become unstable and therefore liable to go out of alignment, they do not require placement in plaster. In fact, complete immobilization of a stress fracture in plaster of paris may reduce the speed with which the injury heals. Immobilized muscles weaken considerably, and the bone may become demineralized. The latter two effects will, of course, be corrected once the athlete starts exercising again, but they are unnecessary complications. Instead of using plaster of paris, the athlete can try some form of bandaging, which may reduce discomfort in the early weeks following injury. Recently, interest has been shown in the possibility that exposing the fracture to an electrical field may speed recovery, but this possibility requires further research.

Runners who simply will not rest can possibly continue exercising in water in a specially designed pool using a flotation device. I first saw such a pool in Eugene, Oregon, in the practice of Dick Brown, former coach of Alberto Salazar and Mary Decker-Slaney. Brown was enthusiastic that this activity appeared to increase the rate of healing of fractures of the lower limb. Alternatively, runners with fractures of the tibia or fibula may achieve complete relief from their symptoms and may be able to continue their activities simply by wearing a pneumatic leg brace (T.D. Dickson & Kichline, 1987).

There is one exception to the general rule that stress fractures do not need to be immobilized. A stress fracture of the neck of the femur (see Figure 14.15) is an extremely serious injury and requires the urgent attention of an orthopedic surgeon, because the injury can have very serious sequelae.

The real challenges for the runner recovering from a stress fracture are to keep physically active and thus avoid the runner's withdrawal symptoms and to find out why the injury happened in the first place and how to prevent its recurrence.

Muscle Injuries

Muscle injuries in runners fall into four categories:

- delayed muscle soreness,
- acute (sudden) muscle tears,
- chronic (insidious) muscle tears, and
- muscle cramps.

Delayed Muscle Soreness

This is the feeling of muscle discomfort that comes on hours or days after unaccustomed or particularly severe exercise (Armstrong, 1984; Friden, 1984). It is not due, as many consider, to an accumulation of lactate (lactic acid) in the stiff muscles, because the lactate concentration in muscles exhibiting delayed muscle soreness is not elevated. The likely cause of this delayed muscle soreness is damage of the muscle cells, in particular the connective (supporting) tissue as well as the contractile proteins.

Recent evidence suggests that there are at least three types of muscle damage that occur with exercise. The first type occurs 24 to 48 hours after unaccustomed exercise in *trained* persons and is associated with the leakage of moderate amounts of muscle enzymes into the bloodstream; peak enzyme leakage occurs at the time of peak muscle soreness, that is, 24 to 48 hours after exercise (Noakes 1987a; Noakes et al., 1983a).

The current belief is that this soreness, better termed *stiffness*, is due to damage to the connective tissue in the muscle (D.A. Jones et al., 1987). The characteristic feature is that pain develops when the muscle is forcefully stretched.

The second type of muscle damage occurs approximately 4 to 6 days after unaccustomed eccentric exercise in *untrained* persons (D.A. Jones et al., 1986; Newham et al., 1986). It is associated with much higher rates of enzyme leakage into the blood, infiltration of the muscle by inflammatory cells (Round et al., 1987), and degeneration of muscle cells, with the latter peaking 10 to 12 days after exercise (D.A. Jones et al., 1986; O'Reilly et al., 1987). Muscle glycogen content is also reduced in the damaged muscle (O'Reilly et al., 1987). Replacement of damaged muscle cells is already well advanced 20 days after exercise.

The third type of muscle damage was described in detail in chapter 10. It is the chronic damage that occurs in trained runners who run long distances in training and is the probable cause of the impaired muscle performance found in overtrained athletes.

M.W. Abraham (1979) was the first to study the biochemical basis for this phenomenon. He showed that the excretion in the urine of connective tissue breakdown products is increased in persons with delayed muscle soreness and that peak urinary excretion coincides with the time when the subjects report the greatest muscle soreness.

Armstrong (1984) postulated that repetitive powerful muscle contractions, especially those occurring during eccentric contractions (see chapter 1), cause muscle cell damage, allowing calcium to flood into the cells and leading to cell death that peaks 48 hours after exercise (see chapter 10). Initiation of an inflammatory response stimulates nerve endings in the damaged tissue, causing the typical pain of delayed muscle soreness. The site of maximal damage appears to be the Z-band of the sarcomere (see Figure 1.2), the point at which the thick filaments (see chapter 1) are anchored and which is therefore the intrasarcomeric structure that is subjected to the greatest strain during eccentric muscle contractions, particularly during downhill running (Friden, 1984; Friden et al., 1983b, 1984) and possibly sprinting (Friden et al., 1988a). This suggests that the initial damage results from mechanical trauma; damage may be more pronounced in ST, Type II fibers (Snyder et al., 1984).

Z-band disruption with release of protein breakdown products may then lead to fluid accumulation and swelling of the muscles (Bobbert et al., 1986), which may in turn cause the delayed muscle soreness. Protein degradation may also be due to the activation of special intracellular enzymes, the lysozymes (Friden, 1984; Salminen et al., 1985). Friden et al. (1986, 1988b) showed that intramuscular pressure is greater during and after eccentric exercise than after concentric exercise, whereas Bobbert et al. (1986) found that legs with muscle soreness had increased volumes. These studies suggest that an elevated intramuscular pressure resulting from muscle fiber swelling may be an important factor in delayed-onset muscle soreness (Friden et al., 1988b).

An alternate postulate is that oxygen-centered free radicals that are released into tissues that are actively utilizing oxygen, as do muscle during exercise, may explain this damage (K.J.A. Davies et al., 1982b). These free radicals are believed to attack lipids, particularly in cell membranes, damaging them in a peroxidation reaction. It is postulated that vitamin E deficiency exacerbates this process, but there is no evidence that this damage can be prevented by an excessive vitamin E intake (Jackson, 1987). Donnelly et al. (1987) showed that the blood level of serum lipid peroxides rises after eccentric exercise and follows the same time course as do changes in serum enzyme activities.

Finally, Aldridge et al. (1986) showed that there is an increase in the concentration of inorganic phosphate in muscles with delayed soreness, due possibly to accumulation of phosphate at the sites of damage.

There are some important practical points to remember about delayed muscle soreness: This soreness indicates that the muscle has been overstressed; persistent muscle soreness is a very strong indicator of overtraining; and the muscle requires considerable time to recover fully from this injury (see Table 10.1). (Refer also to material about race recovery in chapter 9.)

We know of only three ways to reduce the degree of muscle soreness and therefore of muscle damage during prolonged exercise.

- Distance training.
- Training downhill or with eccentric exercise (Byrnes et al., 1985; Friden et al., 1983a; Schwane & Armstrong, 1983; Schwane et al., 1987), because the eccentric contractions that occur during downhill running cause the most muscle damage. The study of Byrnes et al. (1985) showed that a single bout of downhill running offered protection from muscle damage during a similar bout of downhill running for up to 6 weeks. This effect may be due either to an increase in the number of sarcomeres or, more likely, to an increase in Z-band strength (Friden, 1984; see chapter 10) or reduced lysosomal activation (Salminen et al., 1985).
- Weight training to increase the strength of the quadriceps muscle (see Fordyce's 9th Point of Ultramarathon Training). Interestingly, antiinflammatory agents appear to have no effect on delayed muscle soreness (Donnelley et al., 1988; Editorial, 1987).

Acute (Sudden) Muscle Tear

This is the classic muscle injury of the explosive sports like sprinting, football, squash, soccer, and tennis. The athlete is suddenly overcome by agonizingly severe pain in the affected muscle; there is immediate loss of function. The muscle is in spasm, is extremely tender, and over the next few hours swells, and the skin overlying the injury may show bruising.

Acute muscle tears are believed to result from a combination of muscle strength imbalance between opposing muscle groups (Burkett, 1970), inflexibility of the affected muscles, and inadequate warm-up (Sutton, 1984). The theory is that the sprinter's hamstring tear is caused by an activity (very fast running) that overdevelops the front thigh muscles (quadriceps) at the expense of the hamstrings, which become correspondingly weaker. When this strength imbalance reaches a critical value, the quadriceps literally overpowers the hamstring, causing a severe muscle tear.

The immediate treatment of the acute muscle tear is to apply ice to the tender area without delay, to rest and elevate the injured limb, and to apply a firm compression bandage over the site of the tear as soon as the initial ice application is completed. Athletes below 18 years of age should be examined by an orthopedic surgeon to check that they have not pulled off the pelvic epiphysis, to which the hamstring muscles are attached. Next, and most importantly, comes specific treatment and early rehabilitation.

Until relatively recently a serious acute muscle tear was considered to be such a severe injury that rest for 6 to 8 weeks was the only treatment prescribed. In the early 1970s a group of Sydney doctors under the leadership of Dr. Anthony Millar, head of the Institute of Sports Medicine, developed a treatment regime that clearly showed that such a conservative approach was not necessary. They found that an intensive regime involving vigorous treatment of the injured muscle together with muscle stretching and strengthening for as many as six half-hour sessions a day, beginning 48 hours after injury, could return most athletes with serious acute muscle injuries to competitive sport within 10 to 14 days (Millar, 1975, 1976).

Unfortunately, few centers provide such expert therapy, which clearly is vital for all top-class athletes. I am always saddened when I read (quite frequently) in the local or international press that an international athlete will be out of competition for 6 weeks because of an acute muscle tear.

The critical issue in acute muscle injuries, particularly those of the hamstring, is to prevent their recurrence. This can only be achieved if the muscle balance is corrected by strengthening the hamstrings. One of the most effective ways to achieve this is to run long distances, because unlike sprinting, distance running develops principally the hamstrings, not the quadriceps. Preferably, though, specific muscle-strengthening exercises should be performed on an isokinetic exercise machine, under expert supervision. Hamstring stretching (see Figure 13.1, Exercises 1, 10, and 13) should also be performed religiously, also under supervision, and no fast running must be undertaken unless there has been an adequate warm-up and the hamstring-to-quadriceps strength ratio is correct. When these procedures are followed, the incidence of hamstring injuries in persons participating in explosive sports is reduced (Heiser et al., 1984).

More recently it has been suggested that acute hamstring muscle tears occur when the muscle is contracting eccentrically, that is, when it is contracting but lengthening during the swing phase of the running cycle, as the foot is decelerated immediately prior to heel strike (Positions 8 to 11 in Figure 12.2). The tear is more likely to occur during the eccentric phase of the muscle contraction because the intramuscular forces are greatest during eccentric contractions.

To increase eccentric hamstring muscle strength, do the following exercise either standing or lying prone on a couch. Kick your leg into rapid knee extension and stop the movement suddenly 20° to 30° before full knee extension, allowing the hamstring to contract concentrically thereafter. Perform three sets of 15 repetitions every second day, starting without weights and gradually introducing weights, increasing in increments of 1/2 kg. Powerful sprinters may reach a maximum weight of 5 kg after about 8 weeks of training.

The effects of this training method can be measured only with isokinetic dynamometers, which analyze both eccentric and concentric muscle function.

The site of the muscle tear can now be identified with computed tomography (Garrett et al., 1989), which shows that inflammation and edema rather than bleeding are the major components of the injury.

Chronic (Insidious) Muscle Tears (Muscle Knots)

These are probably the most common injuries seen in elite long-distance runners.

The chronic muscle tear is probably the third most common injury among all groups of runners (Pinshaw et al., 1983) and is especially common among the elite runners. Chronic muscle tears are usually misdiagnosed, can be very debilitating, and will respond only to one specific form of treatment. Remarkably, this group of injuries has been described adequately in only one German textbook (Krejci & Koch, 1979).

The injury is usually reasonably easy to recognize. The characteristic feature is gradual onset of pain, in contrast to the acute muscle tear's dramatically sudden onset of pain. At first the pain of the chronic muscle tear comes on after exercise. When the pain starts to occur during exercise, the athlete can at first run through the pain. But the pain gets progressively worse until it interferes with training, so that speed work in particular becomes impossible. The pain is almost always localized to a large muscle group, either the buttock, groin, hamstring, or calf muscle; the pain is deep seated and can be very severe but passes off rapidly with rest. Typically there are other features suggesting that the damaged muscle has gone into protective spasm (e.g., the inability to push off properly with the toes).

In contrast to bone or tendon injuries, both of which improve with sufficient rest, chronic muscle tears will never improve unless the correct treatment is prescribed. So the patient can rest for months or even years without any improvement. Indeed, I have seen one runner who struggled for 5 years with a chronic muscle injury, having given up all hope that he could ever be cured.

To confirm that the injury is indeed a chronic muscle tear, the runner (or preferably a physiotherapist) needs only to press firmly with two fingers into the affected muscle in the area in which the pain is felt. If it is possible to find a very tender, hard "knot" in the muscle, then the injury is definitely a chronic muscle tear. I cannot emphasize sufficiently just how sore are these knots are—they are excruciating! Finally, because the injury occurs in muscle, it will not show on an X ray; attempting to diagnose this injury with X rays is futile.

The mechanism of injury in chronic muscle tears is unknown. I am impressed by the fact that the individual who has recurrent chronic muscle tears will tend to tear the same muscles at the same site every time, usually when he or she starts doing either more speed work or more distance training. I have five specific muscle sites (right groin, left calf, outside calf, both hamstrings, right buttock) at which I develop chronic tears, and they affect me only when I am training more than 130 km/week, including regular speed-work sessions. Similarly, Bruce Fordyce suffers from chronic tears of his calf muscles virtually every March, as he begins his intensive Comrades Marathon preparation.

I conclude that chronic muscle tears occur in the various muscles at specific sites that, for reasons unknown, are exposed to very high loading. This loading is especially high during faster running. Because the loading is so concentrated over a small section of the muscle, an initial small tear develops at that site as the muscle gives way. The tear is initially too small to cause discomfort. However, once the initial tear has occurred, a cycle of repair and retear develops that leads ultimately to the large tender knot, which probably comprises muscle fibers surrounded by scar tissue, as found in experimental muscle injuries (Nikolaou et al., 1987).

Conventional treatment, including drugs and cortisone injections, is a waste of time in this injury; the only treatment that works is a physiotherapeutic maneuver known as *cross frictions*, first popularized by Cyriax (1978). A better term would be "crucifixions," because nothing, not even the runner's toughest-ever race, is as painful as cross frictions applied (however gently) to a chronic muscle tear.

And therein lies the key to the treatment of these injuries. A chronic muscle tear will only get better if (a) the cross frictions are applied to the injury site, in this case the tender knot in the muscle, and (b) they are applied sufficiently vigorously. If the cross friction treatment does not reduce the athlete to tears, either the diagnosis is wrong and should be reconsidered or the physiotherapist is being too kind. This is the one treatment for which you must have a physiotherapist who has big hands, the forearms of a gorilla, and unbridled sadism!

Most chronic muscle tears respond rapidly to a few sessions of cross frictions. The treatment is correct if the pain during running becomes gradually less so that progressively greater distances can be covered. Most injuries will require between 5 and 10 sessions of therapy, each lasting 5 to 10 minutes, after which most runners should be able to run entirely free of pain. Injuries that have lasted for 6 months or more may require longer periods of treatment.

I have mentioned that these injuries tend to recur. To prevent recurrence, you should be especially fastidious about stretching the muscles that tend to be injured, especially before any fast running and in particular before early morning races. Furthermore, it is essential that at the first sign of reinjury, you immediately have more "crucifixions." A little treatment early on in these injuries saves a great deal of agony later.

Muscle Cramps

These are spasmodic, painful, involuntary contractions of muscles. Although muscle cramping is an important feature of some very serious muscle disorders, the cramps experienced by runners are usually of little medical consequence (despite the inconvenience and discomfort they cause) and tend to occur either at night (usually in elderly people—nocturnal cramps) or during unusually prolonged exercise (exertional cramps).

The propensity for cramping differs among individuals; some are almost never affected, whereas others will always develop muscle cramps provided they run far enough. One unfortunate ultramarathon runner informed me that in 10 attempts, he had never been able to run more than the first 50 km of a 90-km race because of severe cramping that developed as soon as he went farther than 50 km. His propensity to cramping was not influenced by how much he trained or what he ate or drank before or during the race. I conclude that he has a minor muscle or nerve abnormality that becomes apparent only during very prolonged exercise.

Exertional cramps tend to occur in persons who run farther or faster than they are accustomed. Thus, the athlete whose longest regular training run is 30 km is likely to develop muscle cramps during the last few kilometers of a standard marathon. A possible cause of these cramps is that a portion of exercised muscle is simply exhausted, possibly glycogen depleted (see chapter 3), or may be damaged as described in the previous section. There is no evidence for a gross disturbance in blood electrolyte levels in runners with cramps (Maughan, 1986), and no evidence shows that ingesting electrolytes like sodium chloride, magnesium, or zinc will prevent cramps. Dehydration also seems an unlikely candidate; thus, an excessive fluid intake is not likely to be of value. Indeed, hyponatremia induced by an excessive fluid intake can lead to cramping (see chapter 4).

Therefore, the only factor that appears to reduce the risk of cramping is simply more training, especially long-distance runs for those who run marathons and longer races. Attention to adequate fluid and carbohydrate replacement before and during exercise and avoiding running too fast too early in the race may also be of value.

The cause of nocturnal cramps is unknown but is likely different from that producing exertional cramps. Stretching the affected muscles before retiring each night has been found to completely prevent this form of cramp.

Tendon Injuries

Unlike muscle injuries, which are usually poorly recognized by runners and their advisers, tendon injuries do not usually present a diagnostic problem to anyone, particularly when they occur (as they invariably do) in the Achilles tendon.

The first inkling of disaster usually comes with what one shoe manufacturing company advertised as the most difficult step in the runner's day—that first step out of bed in the morning. As soon as the afflicted foot touches the ground, there is a feeling of discomfort or stiffness behind the ankle. This discomfort is usually enough to cause some initial limping and tends to wear off after a few minutes of walking. These symptoms constitute a Grade I injury. If the condition is allowed to progress unchecked, discomfort may also be noted after exercise, particularly after long runs or fast intervals (Grade II), and the condition may deteriorate gradually through Grades III and IV of injury (2nd law of running injuries).

Most runners will realize that the injury is Achilles tendinitis, because the pain will be well localized to the tendon, which will be tender to touch at one or more sites. However, two serious conditions involving the Achilles tendon that need to be differentiated from Achilles tendinitis are partial or complete tendon ruptures. In these conditions, either a large portion of the tendon or the complete tendon ruptures causing sudden, dramatic pain and weakness in the affected ankle. Although complete Achilles tendon rupture is an uncommon injury in distance runners, it tends to occur in middle-aged undertrained athletes involved in sports in which the Achilles tendon is exposed to sudden violent eccentric stretching (as occurs in squash, tennis, or sprinting). The incomplete tear is, however, not infrequently seen in distance runners.

It is important to recognize complete or partial Achilles tendon ruptures, because they are conditions for which early surgery is essential (Ljungqvist, 1968).

Thus, if the onset of Achilles tendon pain is sudden and debilitating, unlike the gradual onset described for typical Achilles tendinitis, then it is essential that you present yourself without delay to a surgeon experienced in the care of running injuries so that the appropriate surgery can be performed immediately. The area of torn tendon begins to degenerate shortly after injury, making surgery extremely difficult after any delay.

The diagnosis of Achilles tendinitis is usually very easy. The discomfort is localized to the tendon, and on pinching the tendon between the thumb and index finger, you can locate one or more exquisitely tender areas. A partial tendon rupture will feel exactly the same, whereas in a completely ruptured tendon you should be able to feel a complete gap in the tendon. An important feature of a complete tendon rupture is that it prevents normal walking on the affected side, the runner with a completely ruptured Achilles tendon is unable to push off with that ankle, because the calf muscles that provide the power for push-off are no longer attached to the ankle by the Achilles tendon.

The most plausible explanation for how Achilles tendinitis occurs has been offered by Clement et al. (1984). They hypothesized that excessive ankle pronation causes a whipping action or bowstring effect in the Achilles tendon. They also noted that the Achilles tendon has a relatively poor blood supply in the area in which the injury typically develops, that is, 2 to 6 cm above the site of insertion of the tendon into the heel bone. The authors suggested that this whipping action interferes with the already tenuous blood supply to the area, leading ultimately to death (necrosis) of small areas of the tendon in that region.

A number of factors may be associated with this injury.

1. *Training factors.* These include any sudden increases in training distances, in particular single, very long runs; too many speed sessions, including track or fast hill running, particularly if these are done by running mainly on the toes (as opposed to the heel-toe pattern of long-distance running); a sudden return to heavy training after a layoff; and increased inflexibility of the calf muscles caused by too much training and too little stretching (Clement et al., 1984; Smart et al., 1980).

2. *Shoe problems.* These include running in heelless spikes or low-heeled shoes (racing flats) or in running shoes that either are worn out or are inappropriate to that runner's specific biomechanical needs, in particular, shoes that do not control pronation adequately or that have heel height less than 12 to 15 mm and very stiff soles that fail to bend easily at the forefoot. Wearing high heels at work during the day promotes calf-muscle shortening so that when the runner changes to lower heeled running shoes, the Achilles tendon is suddenly stretched. The only time it is a good idea to wear high-heeled shoes is during the early treatment phase of this injury.

3. *Genetic factors.* These include tight, inflexible calf muscles; hypermobile feet; and in a small percentage of runners, the high-arched cavus or clunk foot (Clement et al., 1984). Loss of the shock absorbing capacity of the heelpad has also been implicated (Jorgensen, 1985).

The initial treatment for the injured Achilles tendon is to apply an ice pack to the sore area for as long as is possible each day. An orthopedic colleague maintains that his Achilles tendinitis was cured by keeping the injured foot in an ice bath for up to 8 hours a day, which is fine if you don't trade your Achilles tendinitis for severe frostbite!

A less demanding schedule would be to apply an ice pack for at least 30 minutes 3 times a day, especially immediately before and after running.

Appropriate calf-muscle stretching exercises must be done for between 10 and 20 minutes each day. The most effective stretching exercises for this injury are those shown in Figure 13.1.

In addition, eccentric loading of the Achilles tendon may be very helpful. Stanish et al. (1985, 1986) noted that Achilles tendon ruptures occurred most frequently when the Achilles tendon was being stretched eccentrically and that those with Achilles tendinitis complained of the greatest pain when the tendon was stretched eccentrically during downhill running or when it was stretched experimentally in the laboratory. Accordingly, the authors developed an eccentric stretching program to increase the strength of the Achilles tendon during eccentric loading.

This program of eccentric exercise is performed with the patient standing with the ball of the foot on the edge of a step and the heel extending over the edge. Under the influence of the body's weight, the heel is gradually lowered until the Achilles tendon is fully stretched. Contraction of the calf muscle returns the heel to its horizontal position, whereafter the sequence is repeated. Three sets of 10 repetitions each should be repeated daily. For the first 2 days the sets are performed slowly, for the next 3 days at a moderate pace, and thereafter at the fastest speed that does not induce pain. After seven sessions, the subject starts adding weights in the form of sandbags over the shoulders. The strength-training activity is continued until the condition resolves.

Antiinflammatory drugs and cortisone injections can be used, but my personal approach is to avoid both drugs and injections if at all possible in this injury, for the following reasons.

This type of treatment can suggest to the runner that a cure can be bought or swallowed, whereas what is really essential is that the runner learns why the injury occurred. Only that way will the runner ever learn how to avoid repeated injury.

This treatment has a cost, and I question whether that money could not be better spent elsewhere (e.g., buying a new pair of shoes).

With regard to cortisone injections, there is a general feeling that cortisone should never be allowed near an Achilles tendon unless the injector is extremely knowledgeable. The risk is that cortisone injected in to the tendon may make it more liable to rupture completely (Ryan, 1978).

Others justify the use of drugs in this injury because they feel that Achilles tendinitis is a serious injury that requires whatever treatment is possible. I think that this is a reasonable assumption, although I am not aware of a single scientific study showing that drug therapy improves the outcome in this injury. My approach is, as always, to treat any factors that might cause or exacerbate the injury.

Shoes

My general rule is that an injury is an absolute indication to buy a new pair of shoes, probably a different model. When choosing a shoe to treat Achilles tendinitis, look for those "antipronation" models with rigid heel counters and firm midsole materials that best reduce excessive ankle pronation. The rigid heel counter may also increase the capacity of the heelpad to absorb shock (Jorgensen & Ekstrand, 1988).

Most authorities agree that a 7- to 15-mm heel raise should be added to the running shoe, either as an addition to the heel or as firm felt material inside the running shoe (Clement et al., 1984). This is especially important for persons who have tight calf muscles, cavus feet, or leg length inequalities.

If the Achilles tendinitis resists all the previously described treatments, then an in-shoe device (orthotic) is indicated. Ideally, these should be professionally made, because they usually require expert readjustment before they are completely effective. Another factor that helps you decide whether an orthotic should be prescribed is the degree to which the foot overpronates during running. The athlete who pronates so badly that his or her shoes look like those in Figures 14.1 and 14.2 will almost certainly require an orthotic.

Rest or Modification of the Training Schedule

Many authorities feel that an attack of Achilles tendinitis is an absolute indication for total rest until the injury has healed. Their rationale is that the injury can cause adhesions to develop between the Achilles tendon and its sheath; growth of these adhesions may be stimulated by continued running. But few runners will even consider this advice.

A more acceptable approach is one of modified rest tailored to the grade of injury. In general, as long as the injury remains in the first injury grade, it is probably not necessary to alter one's training program dramatically. But for a Grade II injury (pain coming on during exercise), a reduction in all speed running (particularly hill running), racing, long runs, and weekly training distance is advisable. When the injury reaches Grade III (pain coming on during exercise and impairing performance), only short-distance jogging, cycling, and swimming are allowed; in Grade IV (pain prevents running), there should be no running whatsoever, only swimming and possibly cycling.

One way of tailoring training to the injury is to use the pinch test after each run. If the pinch test indicates that the tendon is becoming progressively more tender after each run or after a particular training session, then either the total training should be reduced or that particular training session should be avoided. Alternatively, if the tendon becomes progressively less tender, then the treatment is succeeding and training distance and intensity may be gradually increased.

Physiotherapy

This is advised for all tendon injuries and should be mandatory for all injuries worse than Grade I. The most effective type of physiotherapy is vigorous cross frictions applied to the tender areas of the tendon.

Surgery

The ultimate danger in recurrent Achilles tendinitis is that the scarring process, which initially starts inside the tendon, progresses to involve the sheath surrounding the tendon. When this happens, adhesions (connections) are formed between the tendon and its sheath. As this happens, the free movement of the tendon inside its sheath becomes progressively more impaired, and the tendon becomes susceptible to repetitive attacks of tendinitis, each of which leave the runner progressively more debilitated until ultimately he or she can run very little.

Fortunately, this injury can now be very effectively treated by a delicate surgical procedure that removes the tendon sheath together with any areas of tendon scarring. When performed by an experienced surgeon, this procedure has a very high success rate (Smart et al., 1980). However, surgery should only be considered when all other techniques, including repeated sessions of vigorous cross frictions, have been without effect.

Table 14.2 summarizes one approach to the treatment of Achilles tendinitis. The critical points to remember are (a) that the injury must be differentiated from partial or complete Achilles tendon ruptures, both of which require urgent surgery and (b) that during the acute injury episodes, anything that will provoke further damage should be avoided, because the greater the amount of damage the more likely it becomes that surgery will ultimately become necessary.

The results of this type of treatment approach are usually very encouraging. Of a total of 86 runners treated in this way, 73 (85%) reported an excellent result and only one (less than 1%) graded his result as "fair" (Clement et al., 1984).

Table 14.2   An Approach to the Treatment of Achilles Tendinitis

---

Grade I injury (morning discomfort in the tendon)
  Ice injury before, during, and after running.
  Stretch calf muscles (total stretching time at least 20 minutes a day).
  Try new running shoes (models that prevent excessive pronation).
  Add 7- to 15-mm heel raise to running and day shoes.
  Continue training as before.
  Monitor injury progress with the "pinch test."
  Physiotherapy and drug therapy are optional and determined by the cost factor.
Grade II injury (pain during running but not affecting performance)
  Repeat everything as above.
  Modify training (reduce speed work, hill running, long runs, and weekly distance).
  Try an orthotic.
  Try physiotherapy; in particular, cross frictions.
Grade III injury (pain during running and affecting performance)
  Repeat everything as above.
  Try regular cross frictions.
  Undertake absolutely no serious running; only jogging, cycling, or swimming, until
    injury reverts to Grade II; then try serious running only when injury goes back to
    Grade I.
  If attacks occur repetitively (every 3 months or so), consider visiting an orthopedic
    surgeon who has experience with the surgical demands of this injury.
Grade IV injury (running impossible)
  Try everything above. If this fails, visit an experienced orthopedic surgeon. However,
    surgery should be considered only when all other techniques, including repeated
    sessions of vigorous cross frictions, have been without effect.

Other Tendon Injuries

Achilles tendinitis is by far the most common form of tendinitis. The only other form that is frequently seen involves the popliteus tendon, which runs around the outside of the knee. This injury causes pain on the outside of the knee just below the site at which the iliotibial band syndrome causes pain (see Figure 14.11). The injury is said to occur with downhill running, although no one has yet studied a large enough number of runners with this injury to confirm this observation.

The treatment that I prescribe for this injury is the same as that used in the treatment of Achilles tendinitis, in particular, the control of ankle pronation during exercise with the use of the appropriate shoes and orthotics.

Other forms of tendinitis should also be treated according to the regime described for Achilles tendinitis.

Injuries Due to Interference With Blood Circulation

Acute and Chronic Compartment Syndromes

This group of injuries occurs infrequently and in the past has been confused in the literature with shinsplints.

In the compartment syndromes, exercise causes an abnormal rise in pressure in one or more of the muscular compartments of the lower leg (Davey et al., 1984; Detmer et al., 1985; Martens et al., 1984; Rorabeck, 1986; Rorabeck et al., 1988; Wallensten, 1983; Wiley et al., 1987; see Figure 14.14). It is likely that the pressure rise occurs because fluid accumulates in the muscles during exercise. Normally these compartments have sufficient space for the muscles to swell without causing any increase in pressure. However, in persons who develop this injury, the muscle compartments do not allow sufficient room for such swelling. Thus, the pressure rises abnormally in those compartments during exercise, and the resulting pressure increase may be so great that it obstructs the blood flow to the muscles, causing them to become painful (Styf et al., 1987).

At present, the only factors known to be associated with this injury are hereditary—muscle compartments that are too small to accommodate the normal swelling of their contained muscles during exercise or muscles that are simply too big for their compartments.

The most common symptom in the chronic form of this injury is the onset of pain during or after exercise. At first, the pain is mild and disappears rapidly as soon as the runner stops running. However, with time, the pain becomes progressively more severe and begins to interfere with running. Ultimately, the pain is so severe that it forces the patient to stop running.

The runner usually has no difficulty localizing the site of pain, which occurs in one or more large muscle groups, usually the deep posterior calf muscles or less commonly the anterior and lateral calf muscles (see Figure 14.14). If observant, the runner may also notice that as the affected muscles become painful, they lose their normal suppleness and become very hard to the touch. But as the pain disappears, so the hardness gradually dissipates.

Although most cases of compartment syndrome are marked by gradual (chronic) development of symptoms, there is another extremely dangerous presentation. In this acute form, the athlete's muscles become suddenly painful after a single exercise session, with no previous warning. Rather than abate with rest, the pain intensifies and soon becomes so bad that the runner is quite unable to do anything but think of the painful leg. The runner may also notice loss of sensation in the skin overlying the muscles, and ultimately there may be paralysis of those muscles, which become "board hard." In addition, the arterial pulses in the foot disappear.

This injury is an emergency. The pressure inside the muscles has built up to such an extent that it has caused complete obstruction of blood flow to the involved muscles. Because these muscles have an inadequate blood supply, they begin to die.

The treatment is to relieve the pressure without delay. This is achieved by the same surgical procedure used in the management of the more insidious (chronic) form of compartment syndrome (Rorabeck et al., 1983). The only difference is that with this acute form, the surgery must be performed as an absolute emergency, as soon as it becomes clear that the pain will not subside.

Differentiation of Compartment Syndromes From Shinsplints. I estimate that the ratio of runners suffering from true shinsplints to those with the compartment syndrome is between 100:1 and 200:1. This indicates just how uncommon this injury is.

A true compartment syndrome can be differentiated from shinsplints with relative ease.

- A compartment syndrome causes pain localized to the muscles, not to the bones, of the lower limb.
- The pain usually gets worse after running (acute compartment syndrome).
- The injury never gets better even after months of rest (whereas after a few months of rest, the runner with shinsplints will usually be pain free until again reaching the breakdown training level; see the 3rd law of running injuries).
- After running, the involved muscles become absolutely rock hard and the foot may be pulled into a strange position (because of transient muscle paralysis).
- There may also be changes in skin sensation, and occasionally there will be severe muscle cramping.

The only type of treatment for this injury is a surgical procedure in which the lining of the tight compartment is split, allowing the muscle to expand freely inside its compartment (Detmer, 1986; Detmer et al., 1985; Rorabeck et al.,

1983). Rest and other forms of conservative treatment are almost always unsuccessful (Rorabeck et al., 1988; Wiley et al., 1987). It is important that all the involved compartments are identified and surgically treated (Martens et al., 1984; Rorabeck, 1986; Rorabeck et al., 1988).

The response to treatment will be excellent if the initial diagnosis was correct; the athlete will again be able to run pain free as soon as the surgical wound has healed. If, on the other hand, the initial diagnosis was in error and the athlete was suffering from true shinsplints, then the surgery will obviously not result in any improvement (M.J. Allen & Barnes, 1986).

Popliteal Artery Entrapment Syndrome

This is an extremely uncommon injury that causes pain in the leg during exercise. It is caused by the contraction of an anomalous portion of the gastrocnemius muscle that surrounds the popliteal artery, the main artery in the calf. Contraction of that muscle during exercise causes obstruction of the artery, preventing blood flow to the calf. This absence of blood flow causes the pain during exercise.

This is a diagnosis only for the experts, and the only effective treatment is surgery.

Effort Thrombosis of the Deep Calf Veins

Clotting of blood (thrombosis) in the deep veins of the calf is an extremely dangerous condition that can be precipitated by exercise. Ultramarathoner Len Keating described his own experiences with this injury (Keating, 1982).

Keating related that he continued training and racing through pain that started in his calf and then spread to the back of the knee. He initially ascribed his problems to Achilles tendinitis, then to hamstring troubles. The day after racing a half-marathon

> I couldn't walk or even sit without pain. About six days later the pain subsided and I continued running. I decided to run a 50 km race and for the first time in my entire running career, I pulled out of a road race—at the 40 km mark—limping badly and in some distress. (p. 18)

After continuing to train lightly, Keating found that he could not walk the day after "a hard 16 km" and that his leg, in particular his calf, had begun to swell. A visit to his doctor confirmed a deep vein thrombosis with clotting stretching from Keating's ankle through to his abdomen.

Effort thrombosis of the deep calf veins is another very uncommon injury; I probably see and hear of less than 10 such cases each year. The factors precipitating the clotting are unknown. Once the clot has formed it blocks the main route for blood to return from the legs to the heart. The blood then accumulates in the legs, causing at first the pain that Keating described; later, as the extent of the clot increases, the leg will begin to swell.

The main danger of this condition is that a part of the blood clot can dislodge and travel through the heart to lodge in the arteries of the lungs. If sufficiently large, the dislodged clot can cause death within minutes; if smaller, it causes death of small areas of the lung. When this occurs the patient will experience marked chest pain and may cough up blood.

The only treatment is immediate hospitalization to allow for the safe administration of drugs that reduce blood clotting; supportive bandaging of the leg; and a complete avoidance of all exercise for a period of up to 6 to 12 months. During this period, blood clotting is controlled with appropriate medication. Fortunately, recovery is usually complete. (In 1984, Keating returned to racing to win a 161-km road race in 13:32.)

Nerve Injuries

Recently it has become apparent that a group of nerve entrapment syndromes can cause pain, especially in the foot. These injuries are resistant to all forms of conventional therapy (Henricson & Westlin, 1984; Murphy & Baxter, 1985). The nerves involved in these conditions are the following:

1. The nerve to the abductor digiti quinti. This nerve runs deep to the plantar fascia in the foot and, when entrapped, causes pain that is indistinguishable from plantar fasciitis.

2. The deep peroneal nerve at the point where it crosses either the talus or the tarso-metatarsal joint. Entrapment of this nerve can cause pain at the site of the entrapment on the top of the foot, often with radiation of the pain to the toes.

3. The posterior tibial nerve by an accessory navicular bone (os trigonum). Entrapment of this nerve causes pain to be felt on the bottom (plantar surface) of the foot as well as on the inside of the heel.

4. The medial plantar nerve below the calcaneonavicular joint. This entrapment causes pain to be felt on the inside of the foot just above and in front of the site at which the plantar fascia is tender in persons with plantar fasciitis.

5. The peroneal nerve as it crosses the head of the fibula. Entrapment of this nerve causes pain and tingling to be felt on the lateral aspect of the lower leg (Leach et al., 1989). Surgical decompression of these nerves at the site of entrapment is the only effective form of treatment.

The Heel Bruise

An injury that is less understood is the heel bruise.

In this condition, pain is felt in the heelpad directly under the calcaneus. On examination, a small exquisitely tender area can be palpated. The site of maximum tenderness is usually in the middle of the heel; this distinguishes the injury from plantar fasciitis in which the pain is located nearer to the arch of the foot (Figure 14.12), or from a calcaneal stress fracture, in which the pain is best reproduced by compressing the calcaneus between the thumb and forefinger on both sides.

The heelpad comprises specialized tissue designed both for shock absorption and energy return (Jorgensen, 1985). With age, the thickness and therefore presumably the functional capacity of the heelpad decreases, and this may predispose the runner to injury.

The most effective treatment for this condition is the use of a special heelcup designed to maintain the mobile tissues of the heelpad underneath the heel at heelstrike. This prevents the heelpad from compression and dispersion on both sides of the heel. When this is achieved, the shock-absorbing capacity of the heelpad is enhanced (Jorgensen & Ekstrand, 1988).

Injuries That Occur at Specific Sites in the Body

We have now described the most common running injuries. To complete the picture we will look at the anatomical sites at which running injuries occur (see Figure 14.18, a-c).

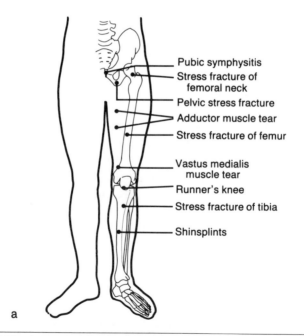

a

(Cont.)

Figure 14.18 Anatomical distribution of the common running injuries viewed from the front (a), the back (b), and the inside (c).

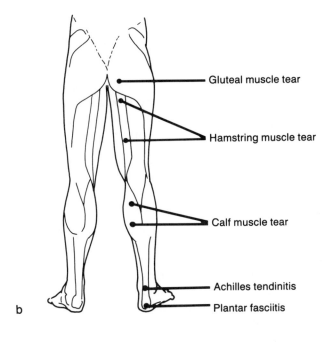

Gluteal muscle tear

Hamstring muscle tear

Calf muscle tear

Achilles tendinitis

Plantar fasciitis

b

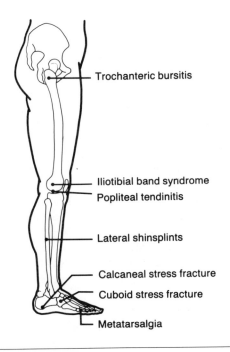

Trochanteric bursitis

Iliotibial band syndrome
Popliteal tendinitis

Lateral shinsplints

Calcaneal stress fracture

Cuboid stress fracture

Metatarsalgia

c

Figure 14.18 (Continued)

Back

About 70% of all adults complain of moderate or severe low back pain (Frymoyer et al., 1983); the management of this condition in anyone, runners included, is a very specialized area of medicine. Runners with this complaint are advised to consult only those specialists who have expert knowledge in this field.

I classify low back pain in runners into two groups: pain that is a result of degeneration of the disc between the vertebrae in the lower back and pain that arises from other tissues, for example, ligaments, muscles, and the small joints of the back. Of these two groups, the former is far more serious and is likely to require some modification of training; the second is somewhat less serious and may be adequately controlled by appropriate low back stretching and strengthening exercises (see Figure 13.1).

I am beginning to think that the low back is the area of the body that is least well designed to cope with the stresses of running. Some evidence shows that a disproportionate number of joggers and cross-country skiers are among those who complain of moderate low back pain (Frymoyer et al., 1983). In part this is probably due to the loading on the back during running, but it could also stem from the fact that running promotes strength imbalances between the abdominal and back muscles and inflexibility of the hamstring muscles, all of which aggravate the back pain. Pain may also be aggravated by an associated short-leg syndrome or prolonged ankle pronation during running. Thus, effective treatment of low back pain in a runner requires careful evaluation of the injury and, when appropriate, prescription of appropriate low back exercises. The value of manipulation would not seem to have been scientifically evaluated.

Other factors outside of work that are related specifically to severe low back pain due to a prolapsed lumbar disc are the male gender, cigarette smoking, and driving a German or American car (Kelsey et al., 1984). Drivers of Japanese or Swedish cars were found to be at much lower risk of acute disc prolapse!

Interestingly, Kelsey et al. (1984) as well as Frymoyer et al. (1983) found that jogging and other sporting activities were not associated with severe low back pain. Thus, it seems that the worst physical activities for the back are those encountered at work, in particular those that combine weight lifting with twisting of the spine. Jogging and other leisure activities may increase the symptoms of moderate but not severe low back pain. Paradoxically, lack of fitness is strongly associated with an increased incidence of low back pain. A reduced capacity to absorb shock in the trunk and upper body has also been implicated (Voloshin & Wosk, 1982).

Should the runner who has severe lumbar disc degeneration undergo surgery? Here again the general advice is that surgery should always be delayed for as long as possible. However, should surgery be necessary, the good news is that in runners, at least, the results are usually successful (Guten, 1981).

Some low back pain in runners is actually buttock pain due to chronic muscle tears either in the glutei or pyriformis muscles. Also, stress fractures of the sacroiliac region, causing low back pain, have been described (Marymont et al., 1986).

Buttock Pain

Pain caused by chronic tears of the pyriformis or glutei muscles is usually quite easily diagnosed, because the runner will complain of discomfort in the buttock and will usually be able to localize the site of discomfort to the affected muscle.

The diagnosis is confirmed by finding the tender knot, described earlier under chronic muscle injuries. The only effective treatment is vigorous cross frictions and appropriate stretching exercises.

Groin Pain

Groin pain may be due to chronic muscle tears of the adductor muscles, to a stress fracture of the pelvis or sacrum (Volpin et al., 1989), or to an ill-defined injury known as osteitis pubis, literally inflammation of the pubic bone.

Chronic muscle tears of the adductor muscles in the groin (see Figure 14.18a) are diagnosed in the same way as are all such injuries. On palpation of the painful area, the examiner feels a tender knot. Vigorous cross frictions are the only effective treatment.

A stress fracture of the pelvis (see Figure 14.16) may initially be confused with a chronic adductor muscle tear, an error I have frequently made. At first, there is ill-defined discomfort in the groin, but (in contrast to a muscle tear) if the athlete continues to run, the discomfort soon becomes so severe that running is impossible. When that occurs, the diagnosis of a stress fracture is no longer in doubt.

An important diagnostic feature found in a series of 12 pelvic stress fractures (Noakes et al., 1985b) is what is called the "standing test." The researchers found that each athlete with a pelvis stress fracture experienced pain or discomfort in the groin when asked to put all of his or her weight on the leg that was on the same side as the fracture. To my knowledge, this symptom is not present in any other injury.

The mechanism of injury in this fracture is unknown but almost certainly involves abnormal shearing stresses across the pelvis, of the same kind that cause osteitis pubis. The injury is far more common among women than among men and seems to affect those women who train hardest, are the most competitive, and may have amenorrhea (see Figure 14.17; Noakes et al., 1985b).

As with all stress fractures, the only treatment is rest. This particular fracture usually takes 8 to 12 weeks to heal properly.

Pubic symphysitis or *osteitis pubis* is an ill-defined injury in which the athlete complains of pain over the symphysis pubis (see Figure 14.18a), often at the point of attachment of the large muscles that form the anterior abdominal wall.

Typically, the pain comes on after the runner has run a set distance, and it persists until running stops. Usually the pain is of a nagging, annoying quality but seldom becomes severe enough to prevent running. Sit-ups reproduce the pain.

On palpation the symphysis pubis is usually very tender, and on X ray specific radiological features are apparent that suggest the diagnosis. The cause of the injury is unknown but probably involves the same shearing forces across the joint that cause pelvic stress fractures and adductor muscle tears.

I have not yet worked out an appropriate and effective way to treat this injury, nor am I aware of anyone who has. The approach should be to correct any overt biomechanical lower limb abnormalities, but in some cases, surgery may be the ultimate resort. Cortisone injections into the tender area have also been used, but their effectiveness is unproven.

Another technique that some physiotherapists practice for the treatment of this injury involves mobilizing the symphysis pubis, and this is achieved in the following way: The athlete lies supine on the examining couch with knees and hips flexed, the knees to 90°. The physiotherapist, with hands clasped together, places his or her arms around the patient's knees so that the knee farthest from the physiotherapist contacts the physiotherapist's hands and the closest knee presses against the physiotherapist's chest.

The patient then presses the knees outward with maximal force against the resistance applied by the physiotherapist. The patient repeats this contraction 3 times, each lasting 5 seconds, the first with the knees together, then 5 cm apart, and finally about 15 cm apart. After the third contraction, the physiotherapist places one hand on the inside of each of the patient's knees, which remain 15 cm apart, and asks the patient to push inward maximally against the pressure. At this time the mobilization of the symphysis pubis occurs and is usually clearly audible as a grinding sound or a loud click.

Whether or not this technique will prove to be any more effective than others for the treatment of this injury is unknown. However, given that this is an injury that stubbornly resists most forms of treatment, the technique is probably worth a try.

Back of Thigh and Calf

The three injuries that affect this anatomical region are chronic hamstring tears, chronic calf muscle tears, and Achilles tendinitis (see Figure 14.18c), the treatments of which have already been covered adequately.

Front Thigh

Chronic muscle tears of the psoas, quadriceps, and vastus medialis muscles and stress fractures of the femur are the four common injuries at the front of the thigh (see Figure 14.18a). The diagnoses and treatments of the three muscle injuries are the same as that already described for chronic muscle tears at other sites.

Femoral stress fractures can occur in the femoral neck or in the midshaft of that bone (see Figure 14.15). Fractures in both places are uncommon, and the diagnoses, particularly of femoral neck fractures, are frequently missed or delayed.

Femoral neck stress fractures cause pain in the front of the hip, and, as with most fractures, the pain is always so severe that running is impossible. This is a serious fracture because the fracture line crosses the blood vessels that keep the head of the femur, the part that fits into the hip joint, alive. If the blood vessels are severely damaged, the head of the femur may die because its blood supply has been interrupted. Death of the head of the femur will ultimately lead to osteoarthritis of the hip.

Alternatively, the fracture may move out of its normal anatomical alignment (displace) and lead to a fracture that either does not heal (nonunion) or heals in the incorrect alignment (malunion).

For this reason, pain in the front of the hip that prevents running must be taken very seriously and must be evaluated immediately by an orthopedic surgeon. The fracture frequently fails to show up on X ray, so a bone scan (see Figure 14.17) may be required. Even then, the fracture may not show, thus, the diagnosis must often be made solely on clinical grounds.

There is no absolute consensus of how this injury should be treated (Blickenstaff & Morris, 1966; Fullerton & Snowdy, 1988; Kaltsas, 1981). Based on their experience with 54 such fractures occurring in military recruits during the first 14 weeks of basic training, Fullerton and Snowdy (1988) suggested that the injury should be treated on the basis of the radiological changes.

Those in whom there was clinical and bone scan evidence but no radiological evidence of fractures were treated with crutches so that they walked without bearing weight. Provided no evidence of fracture developed, they were allowed to gradually return to full activity.

Those in whom there was clear radiological evidence of healing fractures (bone sclerosis) were prescribed bed rest until their pain resolved. They were then allowed out of bed to walk in a non-weight-bearing manner with crutches.

Those who showed radiological evidence of cracks in the bone but who did not experience displacement were hospitalized (with strict bed rest), and the fractures were carefully monitored. Any evidence that the fracture sites were widening was taken as an indicator for surgical pinning of the fracture.

Finally, those who showed evidence of crack fractures that had widened or who had frankly displaced fractures were hospitalized for emergency pinning of the fractures.

My experience has been that most runners with this injury show no radiological evidence of fracture and only seek medical advice when their symptoms are already subsiding. Most can therefore be safely treated with the use of crutches or bed rest. However, the sudden onset of symptoms suggests a displaced fracture that may require surgical treatment.

Outside Leg

Bursas are fluid-filled sacs that prevent tendons from rubbing directly on bone. The trochanteric bursa lies between the trochanter of the femur and the iliotibial band. When inflamed, the bursas cause pain to be felt over the bony trochanter at the side of the leg. This condition is known as *trochanteric bursitis*.

The causes of trochanteric bursitis are probably the same as those of the iliotibial band friction syndrome, and the treatment is essentially the same: prescription of soft running shoes from which the lateral heel flare has been removed; lateral stretching exercises (see Figure 13.1); and, most importantly, shoe modifications to correct for any leg length inequalities. Frequently, a single cortisone injection into the bursa, given by an experienced orthopedic surgeon, may be particularly effective.

The iliotibial band friction syndrome and popliteus tendinitis, which affect the outside leg, were described earlier.

Fibular shinsplints and fibular stress fractures cause pain localized to the fibula (see Figure 14.15) and are probably brought about by presently unknown biomechanical factors that cause a concentration of stress in the fibula, as occurs in the conventional forms of tibial shinsplints.

The treatment is the same as that for posterior (tibial) shinsplints and involves the correction of any biomechanical factors that may be present.

Knee and Front of Lower Leg

Runner's knee, jumper's knee, and anterior shinsplints have all been described.

The only injury affecting the front of the calf is a stress fracture of the anterior border of the tibia (see Figure 14.15), which is uncommon and is treated in the same way as are all stress fractures.

Inside Leg, Lower Calf

Posterior shinsplints has been described in detail. Other injuries from which this injury must be distinguished are tibial stress fractures and chronic muscle tears of the overlying tibialis posterior muscle.

The chronic muscle tear causes pain to be felt maximally in the muscle, as distinct from shinsplints and stress fractures, which cause symptoms to be felt only in the bone. The distinction between shinsplints and a stress fracture is made on the basis of whether the pain is so severe that it prevents running, in which case it is a stress fracture.

The most common sites at which tibial stress fractures occur are immediately below the tibial plateau, 5 cm below the knee, or at the junction of the lower third and upper two thirds of the tibia (see Figure 14.15). The reason for the different locations of these fractures is unknown. My experience is that the fracture below the medial tibial plateau is especially common in novice runners.

Top of Foot

Pain felt on the top of the foot is usually due either to pressure on the nerves (*digital neuritis*) or to stress fractures of one or more of the metatarsal bones (see Figure 13.15).

Digital neuritis is caused by pressure from the shoe upper, in particular from the shoe laces, on the small digital nerves that run over the bony prominences on the back of the foot. The treatment is to isolate the site at which the nerve is tender and alter the shoe-lacing pattern so that no laces cause pressure on that site. A lacing system that achieves this is shown in Figure 14.19. Shoes with the D-ring lacing system may be particularly liable to cause this injury. If altering the lacing pattern does not cure the injury, some form of additional padding (e.g., Spenco material) should be glued to the back of the shoe tongue to protect the site of pain.

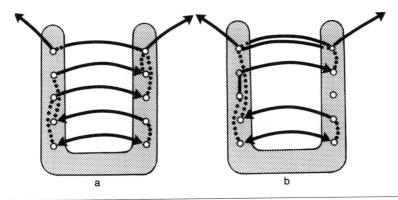

Figure 14.19   The different lacing patterns to prevent digital neuritis: the Arthur Lydiard method (the laces run only in front of the lace hole border) (a) and the modified method (the laces do not cross the tender area of the foot) (b).
Note. Excerpted from *Galloway's Book of Running* © 1983 by Jeff Galloway. $8.95 Shelter Publications, Inc., P.O.B. 279, Bolinas, CA 94924, USA. Distributed in bookstores by Random House. Reprinted by permission.

Stress fractures of the metatarsals cause severe pain that prevents running. The pain can be reproduced by pressing the top of the injured metatarsal. The treatment is 6 weeks of rest from running, during which time the athlete should analyze why the injury developed. The athlete may swim and cycle during this period.

The two groups of runners who are particularly prone to this injury are female runners who start training too hard and too soon and more experienced runners who have rigid feet and who run in hard running shoes.

Medial Side of Ankle

We have already considered plantar fasciitis. Another cause of pain in the ankle may be stress fractures of the talus or navicular bones (see Figure 14.15). These are uncommon stress fractures that cause pain well localized to those bones. The fractures do not usually show on conventional X rays, and special techniques including bone scans must be used (Pavlov et al., 1983). The only effective treatment is 6 weeks of rest.

Tendinitis of the tibialis posterior tendon and *subtalar pronation syndrome* both cause pain immediately below the lower tip (medial malleolus) of the tibia. The distinction between the two conditions is of little practical importance, because both are due to excessive ankle pronation and respond only to adequate control of this tendency.

Thus, the treatment of these injuries is the same as that for runner's knee, Achilles tendinitis, and plantar fasciitis.

Lateral Side of Ankle

Inflammation of the peroneus tendon, *peroneus tendinitis*, is an uncommon injury of unknown biomechanical etiology. Frequently, stress fracture of the cuboid bone (see Figure 14.18b), over which the peroneal tendon runs, is confused with peroneus tendinitis. Unlike other stress fractures, a feature of the cuboid fracture is that it does not usually cause pain that is sufficiently severe to prevent all running. Thus, the important diagnostic feature is persistent discomfort over the cuboid bone that does not resolve within 3 to 5 weeks. The injury is usually only apparent on bone scan, not on X rays. In my experience the injury usually resolves after 5 to 8 weeks of rest.

Bottom of Foot

Two distinct injuries occur on the bottom of the foot—*digital neuroma* and *metatarsal trauma*.

In digital neuroma, one of the small nerves on the bottom of the foot, immediately beneath the metatarsal bones, becomes inflamed, hard, and tender. This causes marked, well localized pain under the affected metatarsal. The pain becomes progressively worse the farther the athlete runs. The most important diagnostic feature is a tender knot of nerve and scar tissue, about the size of half a peanut, that causes a distinct, painful click as it is rolled from side to side over the head of the nearest metatarsal. The only effective treatment is surgical removal of the neuroma.

Metatarsal trauma causes more diffuse pain, which spreads across two or more of the metatarsal bones. It is due to excessive landing pressure on the bones of a foot that is biomechanically imbalanced so that landing force is localized to these bones, rather than distributed across all the bones of the forefoot.

The treatment is to use softer running shoes with a sorbothane or Spenco insole to absorb additional shock. Should that fail, an orthopedic technician should be consulted to apply a "metatarsal bar" to the outside of the shoe immediately behind the ball of the foot. Alternatively, an orthotic should be used in an attempt to distribute landing forces more evenly across the foot. Usually these measures cure the injury, but they may require some months of adjustment before they are totally effective.

A *heel bruise* is treated with a heelcup and the use of softer running shoes.

The possibility of a nerve entrapment syndrome should be considered when chronic foot pain persists despite appropriate treatment that would be expected to cure the common foot injuries.

PSYCHOLOGY OF INJURY

Now that we have the knowledge, the tools, the shoes, and the orthotics to theoretically cure all runners, we are discovering that other factors limit our effectiveness in treating some runners. We are beginning to learn that these now-conventional remedies cure the majority of runners but are quite useless for some. The remedies are useless because, like a good percentage of ordinary medical patients, some runners can never get better. Their problems are more mental than physical—perhaps this problem could be termed "excessive pronation of the brain."

Over the years I have had my fair share of failures with these runners. I am gradually becoming aware of some of the psychological factors that determine how each individual will respond to injury and, more importantly, how we will respond to each other should the runner consult me.

Personal Factors in Reacting to Injuries

Certain factors in athletes influence how they will interact with their injuries and with the persons they consult about the injuries (Nideffer, 1983).

The Athlete's Need to Be in Control

There are essentially two groups of injured runners: those who wish to be in control of their treatment and those who wish to be controlled.

Obviously, their needs are quite different. The former requires little more than simple advice of the type provided in this book. The latter requires very precise and detailed instructions and is likely to recover only if he or she can find an adviser capable of giving advice in that manner.

I like to be in control, and I expect athletes to do the same. For this reason I am relatively ineffective with injured runners who need to be controlled.

The Athlete's Level of Self-Confidence and Self-Esteem

Athletes whose self-confidence levels are low usually require their doctors to take charge of their treatment. If left to do things by themselves, these athletes become excessively stressed and anxious.

The opposite extreme is the athlete whose level of self-confidence is too high, frequently unjustifiably so. Such athletes find it difficult to trust and listen to the opinions of others. They have unshakable confidence in their own ways of doing things and know better than their doctors how to do things. Under pressure, this tendency often becomes more extreme. All doctors will have difficulty with this type of athlete.

The Speed of Decision Making

Persons differ in the speeds at which they make decisions. I tend to make quick decisions and therefore become frustrated with persons who take a long time to consider all the possible consequences of their decisions.

The Athlete's Degree of Extroversion/Introversion

Quiet, introverted athletes become even more so when injured, and it is often extremely difficult to extract all the necessary information about their injuries from them. In contrast, the extroverted athlete may use denial and joking to avoid facing the reality of the injury. This approach will pose a problem if it prevents the athlete from facing up to the seriousness of the injury.

Interpersonal Expressiveness

The ways we express ourselves have intellectual and emotional components, and the amount we attach to either will differ. The expressiveness of some of us, academics particularly, is dominated by intellectual ideas. These people tend to be logical and rational, operate via so-called "left-brain dominant" behavior, and usually do not express much emotion. When such a person is injured, a structured treatment protocol, rather than understanding and commiseration, is required.

Others who are "right-brain dominant" may express themselves more through emotions, which might be positive and supportive, negative and critical, or confrontational. Patients who become negative and critical when injured are unlikely to elicit sympathy from those they consult.

The Normal Psychological Patterns of Response to Injury

Regardless of personality types, athletes will go through typical patterns of response to injury.

Denial

At first, the athletes refuse to accept that they are injured. They simply deny the possibility of injury. Examples of runners who ran to their deaths, denying that they could possibly have heart disease, are detailed in chapters 6 and 18.

Anger (Rage)

When the injuries can no longer be denied, the athletes become enraged and blame either their doctors, their spouses, or some third party. Occasionally, athletes will blame their bodies for betraying them and may even subject their bodies to further abuse.

Depression

When denial and rage no longer work, the stage of depression sets in.

Acceptance

Finally, after some months, the athletes learn to accept their injuries and to modify their ambitions to accommodate the inadequacies of the mortal body. When this occurs, the athletes are likely to be over the injuries.

However, sooner or later, ambitions will again rise, desires to do more will again increase, and the athletes will enter what Altshul (1981a) labeled the "stage of renewed neurotic disequilibrium." In this stage, neurosis is caused by the athlete's rational realization that he or she must stay within the limits of personal talent (and injury risk) and the neurotic need to train more to achieve ever-greater running ambitions. "In running, as in all human endeavours," Altshul concluded, "the battle for mature self-acceptance must be perpetually fought" (p. 12).

Some Psychological Injury Patterns

The Munchausen Syndrome

Baron von Munchausen lived in Hanover in the mid-18th century and achieved notoriety as a teller of extraordinary tales about his life as a soldier in the Russian army and as a hunter and sportsman. The connection of Munchausen's name to a medical condition was made by Asher (1951), who described a group of patients who were so addicted to surgery that they learned to tell detailed, very appropriate, but totally untrue stories about their imagined illnesses. In this way, they fooled the surgeons into believing that the patients desperately needed whichever surgical operation they desired.

Asher recognized three types of Munchausen syndrome patients: the neurological type, who complains of paroxysmal headache, fits, or loss of consciousness; the hemorrhagic type, who specializes in bleeding from the lungs, stomach, or other sites; and the acute abdominal type (laparotomophilia migrans), who describes severe abdominal pain that mimics a surgical emergency.

The Munchausens are probably excessively rare among runners. Yet I have met one or two runners whose love of running was, I suspect, exceeded only by their love of surgery.

The Runner Who Does Not Want to Get Better

A variant of the Munchausen syndrome is the runner who has a simulated injury that is incurable, even through surgery. Conventional medical practice views such patients as having dependent personalities and using their simulated illnesses to avoid work or family responsibilities. To be successful, such a patient requires a sympathetic, long-suffering audience, such as an overattentive, soft-hearted spouse or sympathetic hospital doctors and nurses.

I view runners with simulated injuries as being totally harmless. They benefit from the attention and care they receive, benefits that might not be forthcoming in other areas of their lives. I have learned to view all running injuries as potential attention-seeking behaviors. Some runners need to be treated as if they are special, even for only a few minutes each month. The doctor's duty is to identify these patients and respond appropriately.

Iatrogenic Injury Syndrome

Iatrogenic is Greek for "doctor induced." There are a number of ways doctors, either alone or in combination, can ensure that certain running injuries never heal.

First is the situation in which the runner with a real injury suffers the misfortune of being shunted from one disinterested doctor to another without ever getting better. The runner soon concludes or is told openly that the injury is incurable, that he or she will never run again, or that arthritis will eventually develop (a particular favorite; see the 10th law of running injuries). It is understandable that after such provocation any subsequent minor twinge or ache confirms the runner's sorry plight and produces the "arthritic cripple."

A related injury is induced by society, not by doctors. Formerly a condition of men, it is now becoming common among women, particularly among those who live in communities in which women's running is still unacceptable. Such people usually seek help for injuries that soon prove to be trivial or imagined.

Again the approach must be direct. I point out the patent superiority of runners. I remind these patients of the scientific studies that show that runners are brighter, more intelligent, more self-confident, and more emotionally stable than nonrunners. I suggest that they ignore the opinions of those nonrunners who are too dull to appreciate the special beauty of runners.

The "Psyche-Out" Injury Syndrome (Injury as an Escape)

This is one of the most common psychological running injuries. In this case, the runner uses injury either to explain a poor performance or to prevent a good performance in a race. This idea was presented in chapter 7, in which the concept of the "training-room athlete" was discussed.

Another variant is the runner who becomes psychologically injured shortly before an extreme event such as an ultramarathon. These runners lack the psychological mechanisms to cope with these longer races and are best encouraged to stick to the shorter distances. There is no disgrace in being scared of overextending oneself.

The "Overeager Parent" Syndrome (Injury as a Weapon)

This injury syndrome is forever linked in my mind with the case of the schoolboy athlete whose father asked me to help his son, who was going to captain his country's schoolboy rugby team 3 months later. Apparently the boy had been unable to play for some months because of a back injury that had resisted the attention of the best physicians, orthopedic surgeons, chiropractors, physiotherapists, acupuncturists, homeopaths, and naturopaths in the entire country.

The boy did not have a serious back injury, nor did he ever play for his country. Rather, he was an extremely talented but reluctant athlete who was forced to play by an athletically frustrated father. As Ogilvie and Tutko (1971) pointed out, by being "injured" the reluctant athlete achieves several objectives: He or she can make the parent feel guilty for applying pressure, can frustrate the parent's misplaced aspirations, and can avoid the undesired competition.

Two clues make the diagnosis very likely: the overbearing presence of a parent whose desire for the child's success is clearly abnormal and the extreme reluctance of the "injured" athlete even to try participating in the sport. Thus, all encouragement for the athlete to return to the sport is vigorously rejected. This contrasts absolutely with the usual situation of the athlete with a real injury who must be restrained from returning too quickly to the sport.

The "My-Injury-Is-Unique" Syndrome

This category is a wastebasket for a group of conditions that I, as yet, cannot accurately subdivide.

Runners with this syndrome are usually outwardly intelligent and successful people. They usually contend that their injuries are unique, that I will most certainly know nothing about the injuries, and that I definitely will not be able to help them. These runners usually exude a certain degree of hostility. Indeed, one such runner even introduced himself by asking whether I had a good medical protection in case he had to sue me. Another variant of this syndrome is the runner who vehemently accuses me of causing the injury, either because of something I wrote or failed to write or because of something someone said I had said or written.

I suspect that these runners are simply venting their own psychological insecurities on me.

Understanding the psychology of injury helps us understand why we respond to injuries in our own peculiar ways. By understanding why we respond as we do, we gain better insights into our psychological makeup and the types of medical approach that will be most likely to get our minds over the injuries.

15

Nutrition and Weight Control

"The only definite dietary rule that can be laid down for all and sundry would be 'eat what you like'. Nature generally knows what is needed, and what is needed is right. Satisfy your digestion with anything that you seem to fancy and you need have no qualms."

Arthur Newton (1949)

"If you see an adolescent girl in our culture and she is dieting, that is probably normal. If you see one who is dieting successfully, she has an eating disorder until proved otherwise."

Dr. Preston Zucker (1985)

"The very fat this culture so obsessively attempts to deny and eliminate is depositing itself over our bodies according to laws which no one understands."

Hilary Bichovsky-Little (1987)

Some years ago a medical friend and I ran a marathon on pangamic acid—purely in the interests of science. Reports in the medical literature had claimed that pangamic acid (that imposter "vitamin B_{15}") worked better than training (Pipes, 1980). A group of 12 male college athletes who had used the substance for just 1 week had reportedly increased their $\dot{V}O_2$max values by 28% and their times to exhaustion while running on the treadmill by 24%—increases that you or I would be lucky to achieve in a lifetime of training. When my friend and I lined up for that marathon all those years ago, we were looking not so much for personal bests but for world records.

In the end, I am glad to report, vitamin B_{15} was a total, unmitigated failure. The runner/doctors had come back with a pair of career worsts; we had learned that vitamin B_{15} was no replacement for training.

Do not believe, however, that these failures will convince me or should convince you to give up the search for those missing nutritional elements that will finally allow us to run faster on the same amount of training.

BASIC NUTRITIONAL PRINCIPLES

There are three basic rules of nutrition. First, the body requires essential nutrients: carbohydrates, proteins, and fats (the energy-supplying nutrients) and the vitamins, minerals, trace elements, and water that are necessary for the utilization of that energy. Second, these nutrients are contained in four basic food groups: the meat, fish, and meat-substitute group; the fruit and vegetable group; the milk and dairy produce group; and the bread and cereal group. Third, items from these four basic food groups should be eaten in the following portions each day: meat and fish, two portions; milk and dairy produce, two portions; bread and cereal, four portions; and fruits and vegetables, four portions.

Let us consider these three principles in greater detail.

The Six Basic Nutrients

Carbohydrate

Previous chapters have emphasized the important role of dietary carbohydrate in exercise performance.

- The body has limited carbohydrate stores (see Tables 3.2 and 3.3).
- These carbohydrate stores are utilized at rates proportional to the intensity of exercise (see Figure 3.4).
- The larger the carbohydrate stores before exercise, the better the performance (see chapter 3).
- The extent to which the body carbohydrate stores are filled depends on the carbohydrate content of the diet and can be increased by the carbohydrate-loading diet (see Figures 3.5, 3.6, 3.7, and 3.8).

These are the theoretical considerations. The practical questions that arise are these: What foods comprise mainly carbohydrates? How much carbohydrate should be eaten when training? How does one carbohydrate load? Are there any dangers involved in this practice?

Carbohydrate-Containing Foods. Some high-carbohydrate foods, all of which comprise at least 90% carbohydrate with less than 5% protein and 5% fat, are listed in Table 15.1. These are the types of carbohydrate-containing foods that should be eaten during heavy training and when you are carbohydrate-loading.

Thus, a high-carbohydrate diet consists almost exclusively of fruits, vegetables, and cereals (bread, pasta, rice, potatoes, and breakfast cereals). Sweets, chocolates, and other confectioneries may have relatively lower carbohydrate contents because of high fat contents. It is best to eat more natural high-carbohydrate foods, in particular potatoes, during carbohydrate loading.

Table 15.1 High-Carbohydrate Foods (Less Than 5% Fat and 5% Protein)

Potatoes	Sugar	Grapes	Carrots
Rice	Honey	Raisins	Parsnips
Macaroni	Marmalade	Oranges	Artichokes
Beetroot	Jams	Bananas	Turnips
Porridge	Stewed fruit	Prunes	Fruit juices
Crispbread	White bread	Molasses	

The Carbohydrate Content of the Diet During Heavy Training. The work of Costill and Miller (1980) showed that muscle glycogen levels in athletes eating normal mixed diets (40% carbohydrate) fell progressively when these athletes exercised for up to 2 hours a day. This fall was prevented when the athletes ate a high-carbohydrate diet in which 70% of the dietary energy was provided by carbohydrate (70% carbohydrate diet; see Figure 3.6).

In practice, few athletes eat diets that contain as much carbohydrate, largely because such diets are extremely bland and unappetizing. Unfortunately, it is the protein and fat content of food that increases its palatability.

Table 15.2 provides a simple base for a high-carbohydrate diet that could be followed during both heavy training and carbohydrate loading.

The Carbohydrate-Loading/Carbohydrate-Depletion Diet. For reasons discussed in detail in chapter 3, highly trained athletes should not undergo the carbohydrate-depletion phase and should rather ingest adequate amounts of carbohydrate during prolonged exercise, especially exercise that lasts more than 4 hours. By avoiding the carbohydrate-depletion phase, they also avoid some potential dangers that will be described subsequently.

Less well trained runners may benefit from the carbohydrate-depletion phase. Using this technique, they may store more muscle and liver glycogen than they would by only eating a high-carbohydrate diet for the last 3 days before competition (see Figure 3.5). For this reason, I have always followed a modified carbohydrate-depletion/carbohydrate-loading diet before my major races. I also think that the less well trained runners, because they are not as finely tuned, are less

Table 15.2   Suggested Base for a Simple High-Carbohydrate Diet

Food/fluid	Quantity
Orange juice	1 L
Skim milk	0.2 L
Whole corn bread	10 slices
Cereals or muesli	50 g
Bananas	3
Apples	2
Potatoes or pasta	200 g

Note. This diet provides approximately 400 g carbohydrate, 45 g protein, 10 g fat, and more than 100% of the RDA for thiamin, riboflavin, niacin, vitamin C, calcium, magnesium, and iron. From "High-Carbohydrate Diet for Long-Distance Runners—A Practical View Point" by M. Fogelholm, H. Tikkanen, H. Naveri, and M. Harkonen, 1989, *British Journal of Sports Medicine,* **23**, p. 95. Copyright 1989 by British Journal of Sports Medicine. Adapted by permission.

likely to be adversely affected by the carbohydrate-depletion phase than are the elite runners.

Two final points made in chapter 3 require reemphasis. First, it was originally thought that complex (unrefined) carbohydrates such as potatoes and bread induce more complete carbohydrate storage during carbohydrate loading than do simple carbohydrates (Costill et al., 1981). This is no longer believed to be the case (Roberts et al., 1988). The optimum strategy is to eat simple carbohydrates for the first 24 to 48 hours of the carbohydrate-loading diet and thereafter to eat mainly complex carbohydrates. Second, the rate of muscle glycogen storage is determined by the carbohydrate content (in grams) of the diet and is maximum on a diet providing 500 to 600 g of carbohydrate per day (see Figure 3.7). Athletes eating 25 g of carbohydrate per hour resynthesize glycogen at a rate of 170 mmol (31 g) per kilogram of wet muscle every 24 hours and are therefore able to completely restock their muscle glycogen stores within 24 hours of being totally carbohydrate depleted. Athletes involved in prolonged (4 to 6 hours) daily exercise, like cyclists in the Tour de France, can restock their muscle glycogen stores each day only if they ingest high-carbohydrate solutions both during and after exercise.

How do you know that you are eating sufficient carbohydrates when carbohydrate loading?

Probably the safest way to carbohydrate load before a race is simply to modify your diet in the following ways.

- Eat cereals, bread (with honey), fruit, and fruit juices for breakfast. Use skim milk in place of whole milk, because skim milk has a lower fat content.
- Substitute pasta (e.g., macaroni and spaghetti) for meat, and eat more potatoes.
- If you are still hungry, eat sweets, but not to the point of gluttony.
- Supplement the diet with 200 g of high-carbohydrate "carbo-loading" athletic drink.

Table 15.2 provides an outline of the composition of the optimum carbohydrate-loading and carbohydrate-depletion diets, and Table 15.3 lists the carbohydrate content in grams of various commonly eaten foods.

Table 15.3   Carbohydrate Content of Various Common Foods

Food	Carbohydrate content (g)
Biscuit (100 g)	65
Chocolate milk shake (large)	60
Cake with chocolate icing (150 g)	58
Chocolate bar (100 g)	57
Brown bread (100 g)	50
Breakfast cereal (100 g)	43
(Fruit) mince pie (100 g)	25
Macaroni (100 g)	23
Spaghetti (100 g)	23
Banana (100 g)	19
Baked potato (100 g)	19
Apple (100 g)	13
Orange juice (unsweetened, 100 ml)	11
Cola drink (glass = 200 ml)	11
Grapefruit (half)	10
Peach (100 g)	9

Note that the carbohydrate-depletion diet is no longer considered to be an essential method for optimum carbohydrate loading, at least for well-trained athletes (see Figure 3.8).

The best sign that sufficient carbohydrate has been stored during the loading phase is an increase in body weight. For every 1 g of carbohydrate that is stored, approximately 2 to 3 g of water are also stored. If the body carbohydrate stores were completely empty before carbohydrate loading commenced, body weight should increase 2.0 to 2.5 kg (equivalent to a total carbohydrate store of 600 g) during the loading phase.

Are any other food supplements necessary during carbohydrate loading?

Clearly, fluid intake needs to be increased during the loading phase so that sufficient water can be stored with glycogen. The best guide to the adequacy of fluid supplementation is urine color. A light-colored urine indicates an adequate fluid intake.

Potassium is also stored with glycogen. Thus, potassium requirements must also increase, and you can best meet these by eating oranges, tomatoes, and bananas, which are good sources of both potassium and carbohydrate. There is tentative evidence to suggest that the requirements of the B-group vitamins thiamine and niacin may be slightly increased during the loading phase (Jetté et al., 1978).

I usually take a vitamin supplement while carbohydrate loading. But one should never take vitamin-B-complex tablets immediately before exercise, particularly those containing nicotinic acid. When present in high concentrations in the blood, nicotinic acid prevents the mobilization of free fatty acids. Thus, if taken in high doses shortly before exercise, nicotinic acid will impair endurance performance by increasing the rate of muscle glycogen utilization during exercise.

Are there any dangers in the carbohydrate-depletion/carbohydrate-loading diet?

Carbohydrate loading does not suit everyone. Although most will probably run better after loading, a few runners may be adversely affected (Slovic, 1977) and will curse the day they ever heard about this diet.

The main risk is that the high content of carbohydrate in the loading diet may cause intestinal distress, in particular diarrhea, that may persist until the race. For this reason, you should experiment with the diet by initially deviating as little from your normal diet as possible. With time you will learn which carbohydrates to avoid and how much you need to eat to achieve maximum benefit.

The second major problem of the diet is that during the carbohydrate-depletion phase, physical performance capacity falls steeply. After about 24 hours without carbohydrates, any physical effort much greater than a walk becomes very tiresome. Worse, after 36 hours of carbohydrate depletion, even the most docile, congenial runner becomes an irritable, aggressive, short-tempered monster of impossible proportions.

In addition, it seems that the long depletion run originally advocated by Scandinavian researchers (see Figure 3.5), coming as it does only 7 days before a major race, must be detrimental. For this reason, it is probably better to run relatively short distances on the 3 days of carbohydrate depletion rather than a single long run. In addition, there is no evidence that the depletion run by itself increases muscle glycogen storage (see chapter 3).

Other medical risks that have been described include acute kidney failure (Bank, 1977), induced by the depletion phase in two athletes who almost certainly suffered from obscure muscle cell metabolic abnormalities. Although the high-carbohydrate diet would be expected to affect blood fat levels adversely, causing blood cholesterol and triglyceride levels to rise, this has not been found (Blair et al., 1980). In general, even the carbohydrate-depletion phase of this diet appears to be very safe (Forgac, 1979).

It is generally held that carbohydrate loading should be undertaken two to three times a year and only before major races. However, you certainly should not try it for the first time before a major race. In addition, the diet should be gradually adapted to the individual's needs and should certainly not be followed blindly without modification. Elite athletes should probably avoid the depletion phase altogether.

Food Intake During Races Lasting Between 7 and 24 Hours. Prolonged exercise lasting more than 5 hours, because it is performed at less than 75% $\dot{V}O_2$max, does not affect the rate of gastric emptying. Furthermore, such exercise has no effect on digestion (Cammack et al., 1982; Feldman & Nixon, 1982). Thus, during prolonged exercise you can ingest essentially whatever you choose, although such food should have a relatively high-carbohydrate content. Table 15.4 provides some guidelines for food intake during very prolonged exercise.

Table 15.4   Guidelines for Food Intake for Endurance Exercise Lasting 7 to 24 Hours

1. It is impossible to match caloric intake to energy expenditure during such races.
2. Only foods for which you actually have an appetite and which you can tolerate without side effects should be eaten. Thus, you must experiment in training runs with foods you plan to eat during competition.
3. The foods that you eat should be easily digestible. Examples of such foods include noodles, pasta, and potatoes; fruits such as oranges and bananas; thick soups; and glucose polymer or soluble starch drinks (see chapter 3).
4. Some athletes report a craving for fat-containing foods during prolonged exercise. There appears to be no physiological reason why such foods should be avoided.

Protein

There are few dietary myths greater than those surrounding the protein needs of people who exercise vigorously. Most people are aware that strength-trained athletes, in particular power lifters and weight lifters, have an ability to eat protein in the form of eggs and meat that defies description.

Less well known is that in the 1860s, the Oxford University rowing crew, training on underdone beef and mutton without vegetables, completed a string of nine consecutive victories over Cambridge rowers, who trained only on vegetables, fruit, and bread. The natural, but incorrect, conclusion was that the Oxford rowers' success was due to their diets; thus, the importance of protein in the athlete's diet received unwarranted public credibility. One wonders how the Oxford team might have performed with a little carbohydrate loading! The early pedestrians also ate a great deal of protein, as described in chapter 8.

Protein is a relatively minor fuel during exercise (see Figure 4.5); only during prolonged exercise in the carbohydrate-depleted state do proteins become more important. Even then, protein supplies only about 10% of the total energy requirement and is used as a substrate both for new glucose production in the liver and for oxidation in the Krebs cycle (Evans et al., 1983). Nevertheless, the increased use of proteins during exercise may be sufficient to increase the daily dietary protein requirements of runners and cyclists to about twice (2 g/kg/day) those of sedentary persons (Brouns, 1988; Butterfield, 1987; Lemon, 1987; Meredith et al., 1989a; Tarnopolsky et al., 1988).

The main function of the body protein stores is to provide the basic structure of most body tissues, in particular the muscle proteins actin and myosin (see Figure 1.1), as well as other essential components such as hormones, cellular enzymes, and genes. In all these structures, proteins exist in a dynamic state, that is, they are continually being broken down and replaced by new proteins absorbed from the intestines. This continual protein replacement is known as the *protein turnover rate* and equals about 25 g of protein per day for a 70-kg person.

Stresses such as physical training, severe illness, or major surgery all lead to an increased protein turnover rate. In athletes, this increased rate of protein turnover acts mainly as a noncarbohydrate source of new glucose, especially when the rate of carbohydrate utilization during exercise exceeds the rate of dietary carbohydrate ingestion so that body carbohydrate stores fall (Brouns, 1988). In addition, it seems likely that during the recovery phase after marathon and ultramarathon races, the rate of protein turnover is increased, in part to repair the muscle damage that such events cause (see chapter 10).

It is apparent that these demands for more protein arise from within the body. It is not possible to increase the body's protein metabolism artificially and thereby stimulate muscle growth simply by eating larger amounts of protein in the diet.

The question that we need to ask is this: By how much does exercise, particularly the "muscle sports," increase the protein turnover rate? This is where each expert has a different opinion.

One review (Haymes, 1983) referred to a number of studies that showed that although the protein requirements of athletes involved in intensive training do indeed increase, these requirements exceed 1.7 g per kilogram of body weight, a value that will be met by the increased energy intake of the athlete in training. Thus Haymes (1983) calculated that a 70-kg athlete who eats a diet containing 12% protein and who begins exercising and increases his or her energy intake from 3,000 kcal (12,600 kJ) to 4,000 kcal (16,800 kJ) per day will increase protein intake relative to body weight from 1.3 to 1.7 g per kilogram of body weight.

Support for this conclusion comes from a study by Laritcheva and his colleagues (1978) from the Moscow Institute of Nutrition. They studied a group of top Soviet weight lifters and found that during periods of very intensive training, the protein requirements of some of these athletes went as high as 2.3 g per kilogram of body weight. But even this value was met by a well-balanced diet adjusted to the higher caloric requirements of the athletes' increased daily energy outputs. The authors concluded that excessively high-protein diets were useless, because as the protein content of the diet increased, proportionately less protein was absorbed from the intestine. The study of Tarnopolsky et al. (1988) showed that protein requirements of body builders were, in contrast to those of distance runners, only marginally greater than those of sedentary individuals.

This conclusion brings us to a statement made by an American weight lifter who religiously followed a high-protein diet until a scientific colleague showed him where his money was actually going. "My experience has convinced me that many protein, vitamin and mineral supplements and health foods on the market are not being promoted to meet the unique nutritional requirements of athletes, but rather to make a few people very rich." Enough said.

Fats

The fat in the diet provides a convenient, palatable, and highly concentrated source of energy. Triglyceride is the form in which fat occurs both in foods and in the body's fat stores.

The principal foods contributing fat to the diet are vegetable oil, salad dressing (in particular mayonnaise), meat, the visible fat of meat, the skin of chicken, egg yolk, nuts, olives, avocados, and dairy produce such as milk, cream, cheese, and butter.

These fats may be either saturated or unsaturated. *Saturated* means that most of the chemical bonds in the free-fatty-acid component of the triglyceride molecule are occupied by hydrogen; unsaturated fats have fewer of these bonds occupied by hydrogen.

Animal fats, particularly those found in red meat and dairy produce, are predominantly saturated, whereas vegetable fats are predominantly unsaturated. Unsaturated fats are mostly liquid at room temperature (such as oils); in order to increase the solidity of these fats (so that they can be used to spread, for example, on bread), some of the unsaturated bonds in the free-fatty-acid molecules have hydrogen added in a chemical process known as *hydrogenation*. Polyunsaturated margarines are therefore partially hydrogenated vegetable oils, which contain free fatty acids that are nevertheless more unsaturated than those found in dairy produce, butter in particular.

Dietary fats pose at least three problems:

1. *The fat in the diet is largely "hidden."* In addition, fat is a highly concentrated energy source providing more than twice as much energy per gram than does carbohydrate (see Table 3.2). Thus, a few smears of butter or margarine or a few glasses of whole milk constitute many calories of energy. This high-energy source may be of value to those living on a subsistence diet, but in the developed countries of the world, many of whose citizens are already overfed, the high energy content of fat makes it an undesirable food.

2. *There is a relationship between the fat content of the diet, the blood cholesterol levels of persons living on that diet, and their risks of developing coronary artery disease (see chapter 18).* The risk of colon cancer in both sexes and breast cancer in women is also increased in those who eat a high-fat diet. Thus, the persons and nations with high dietary intakes of saturated fats have an increased incidence of coronary artery disease and cancer; those with a lower intake have reduced incidences of these diseases. On the other hand, the intake of the fats of fish, especially eicosapentantaenoic acid, is associated with a reduced incidence of coronary heart disease (Kromhout et al., 1985; Mehta et al., 1987).

3. *The thermic effect of fat is very little.* Thus, weight gain is far greater from a fat-rich diet than from an equicaloric, carbohydrate-rich diet (Danforth, 1985).

Thus, the practical problems posed by the fat found in the diet are that fat is a high-energy source, it is appetizing and readily satisfies hunger, and its storage in the body is more efficient than is the storage of carbohydrate. The result is that too much fat in your diet may suppress your appetite before you have ingested sufficient carbohydrate to restock your body carbohydrate stores (see Figure 3.6). This is especially important during carbohydrate loading. In addition, it seems that a high-fat diet increases the risk of gaining weight and of developing coronary artery disease and certain cancers.

Vitamins

The vitamins make up a group of unrelated organic compounds that are needed only in minute quantities in the diet but are essential for specific metabolic reactions within the body and for normal growth and development. Thus, vitamins regulate metabolism; they are essential for the metabolic processes that convert fat and carbohydrate into energy; and they assist in the formation of bones and other tissues. Clearly, they are an essential dietary component.

Vitamins fall into two main groups: those that are fat soluble and those that are water soluble. Fat-soluble vitamins are absorbed with dietary fats; they can be stored to some extent in the body and are not normally excreted in the urine. In contrast, water-soluble vitamins are not normally stored within the body, and any excess intake over daily bodily needs is excreted in the urine.

The difference in solubility of the vitamins is therefore important, because solubility determines the extent to which vitamins can be stored in the body.

Because fat-soluble vitamins are readily stored in the body, deficiencies of this group are far less likely than are deficiencies of the water-soluble vitamins, which must be replaced daily. For similar reasons, overdose or intoxication is far more likely to occur with fat-soluble vitamins but may still occur with water-soluble vitamins (Rudman & Williams, 1983). Table 15.5 details information about the fat- and water-soluble vitamins that may have relevance to exercise performance. (The fat-soluble vitamin K, which is involved in blood clotting, has no known role specific to exercise and is therefore excluded from the table.)

Practical Considerations. One of the most frequently asked questions about nutrition is whether athletes require increased intakes of vitamins.

Very little evidence supports the practice of supplementing a nutritionally balanced and adequate diet with additional vitamins (Belko, 1987), even though exercise may increase the requirements of certain vitamins, in particular riboflavin (Belko, 1987; Belko et al., 1983) and also probably vitamin C. Interestingly, the evidence that vitamin C requirements are almost certainly increased by exercise comes from the polar expeditions of Amundsen, Scott, and Shackleton. Although members of all three expeditions ate rations that were totally vitamin C deficient, members of only the latter two expeditions, both of which hauled their own sleds, developed symptoms of scurvy (Huntford, 1985). Thus, despite eating essentially identical diets, none of the members of Amundsen's group developed symptoms of scurvy, almost certainly because their sleds were pulled by dogs and the members consequently exercised considerably less than did members of Scott and Shackleton's expeditions (Norris, 1983).

With the possible exception of folate deficiency, vitamin deficiencies are extremely uncommon in athletes, and the only vitamin deficiencies that have been shown to impair performance are those of thiamine and vitamin C. In addition, no study, including those undertaken by Lindsay Weight at the University of Cape Town (Weight et al., 1988a, 1988b), has yet shown that supplementation with any particular vitamin increases athletic performance in persons eating a normal diet (van der Beek, 1985). The studies of Weight et al. (1988a, 1988b) found that blood vitamin and mineral levels were high in a group of marathon runners and did not rise greatly during 3 months of treatment with a powerful vitamin/mineral supplement.

However, a possibility that cannot be ignored is that at the high doses taken by some athletes, vitamins no longer work in their vitamin roles defined in Table 15.5 but act as drugs in other currently undefined ways. It is possible that those actions could improve athletic performance, but this has not been scientifically proven.

Although, in theory, vegetarians are prone to vitamin deficiencies, in practice, few develop clinical evidence of such deficiencies. Those that do almost always follow the more extreme forms of vegetarian diets.

Table 15.5 The Recommended Dietary Allowance (RDA), Food Sources, Special Functions During Exercise, and Effects of Deficiency and Supplementation of the Vitamins

Vitamin	Recommended dietary allowance (RDA)	Food sources	Special functions during exercise	Effects of dietary deficiency on exercise performance	Effects of dietary supplementation on exercise performance[a]
Fat-soluble vitamins					
Vitamin A	Male 1,000 RE Female 800 RE	Liver, butter, cream, egg yolk, dark green leafy vegetables, yellow fruit and vegetables	Glycogen synthesis; muscle protein synthesis	No effect (Wald et al., 1942)	No effect (Wald et al., 1942)
Vitamin D		Fish-liver oils	Regulation of calcium and phosphate metabolism; bone calcification	No known (Williams, 1984)	No effect (Berven, 1963)
VitaminE	Male 15 IU Female 12 IU	Vegetable oil, wheat germ, nuts, legumes, green leafy vegetables	Antioxidant of polyunsaturated fatty acids	No known (Williams, 1984)	No effect (Sharman, 1971)

566

Water-soluble vitamins

	RDA	Major function	Effect of deficiency	Effect of supplementation
Vitamin B$_1$ (Thiamine)	Male 1.4 mg Female 1.0 mg	Entry of pyruvate into the Krebs cycle; hemoglobin formation	Impairs performance (Archdeacon & Murlin, 1944) Decreases VO$_2$max and lactate turnpoint (van der Beek et al., 1984, 1985)	No effect (Archdeacon & Murlin, 1944) Possible effect (Early & Carlson, 1969)
Vitamin B$_2$ (Riboflavin)	Male 1.6 mg Female 1.2 mg	Energy production in the electron transfer chain	Not known (Williams, 1984) No effect (Belko et al., 1987)	Not known (Williams, 1984) No effect (Belko et al., 1987)
Niacin (Nicotinic acid)	Male 18 mg Female 13 mg	Energy production in glycolysis; fat synthesis; prevents free fatty acid mobilization during exercise	Not known (Williams, 1984)	No effect (Hilsendager & Karpovich, 1964) Impairs performance when taken immediately prior to exercise (Bergström et al., 1969)

Food sources: Nuts, peas, beans, yeast, organ meats, pork, the germ of cereals; Milk, organ meats, eggs, green leafy vegetables; Meat, poultry, fish, whole grain, flours, cereals, nuts, and legumes

[a]The study of Weight et al. (1988a, 1988b) found no effect on running performance of multivitamin supplementation.

(Cont.)

Table 15.5 (Continued)

Vitamin	Recommended dietary allowance (RDA)	Food sources	Special functions during exercise	Effects of dietary deficiency on exercise performance	Effects of dietary supplementation on exercise performance[a]
Vitamin B_6 (Pyridoxine)	Adults 2.0 mg	Liver, whole grain cereals, peanuts, bananas	Formation of hemoglobin, myoglobin, and cytochrome enzymes in the electron transfer chain; synthesis of protein, and of glycogen from noncarbohydrate sources (gluconeogenesis) in the liver; breakdown of glycogen	No effect (Hatcher et al., 1982)	No effect (De Vos et al., 1982)
Biotin	RDA has not been established	Liver, kidney, yeast extracts, nuts, chocolate	Production of glucose from noncarbohydrate sources (gluconeogenesis)	Not known because dietary deficiency almost unknown	Not known (Williams, 1984)

Nutrient	Amount	Food sources	Function		Effect on performance
Pantothenic acid	Not known; probably 5-10 mg	Meat, poultry, fish, whole grain cereals, legumes	Mitochondrial oxidation of pyruvate and free fatty acids	Not known because dietary deficiency almost unknown	No effect (Nice et al., 1984) Possible effect (Early & Carlson, 1969)
Folic acid	Adults 400 µg	Organ meats, deep green leafy vegetables, eggs, whole grain cereals	Red blood cell formation	Not known (Williams, 1984)	Not known (Williams, 1984)
Vitamin B$_{12}$ (Cyanocobalamin)	Adults 3 µg	In animal foods only; organ meats, eggs, milk, muscle meats, fish, poultry	Red blood cell development; carbohydrate and fat metabolism	Not known (Williams, 1984)	No effect (Tin-May-Than et al., 1978)
Vitamin C	Male 45 mg Female 45 mg	Citrus fruits, tomatoes, guavas, cabbage, broccoli, strawberries, potatoes	Synthesis of connective tissue, adrenaline, and cortisol; antioxidant; absorption of iron	Not known (Williams, 1984) Impaired (Suvoticanec-Buzina et al., 1984)	No effect in 10 valid studies reviewed by Williams (1984)

Minerals

The most important minerals in the diet include sodium, potassium, magnesium, calcium, iron, zinc, and copper (see Table 15.6).

Sodium. Sodium is stored mainly in the body fluids with much smaller amounts inside cells. Sodium plays a number of important physiological roles: It maintains the normal water balance and distribution within the body; it determines the blood pressure; and it maintains osmotic equilibrium, acid-base balance, and normal muscular irritability. The total body sodium content is about 80 g.

Two important myths that have developed concerning sodium chloride (salt) are that athletes need to increase their salt intakes when they start training hard and that salt is an important cure for cramps. Let us consider these two questions.

The daily food intake of persons living on the typical Westernized diet has a sodium chloride content of 5 to 20 g (Shephard, 1981). Of this, 3 g occur naturally in the food, 3 to 5 g are added to the food during processing, and the rest is added by the consumer (i.e., from the salt shaker) either in cooking or at the table. Salt is added to the diet largely because it improves the taste of food but also because it acts as a preservative.

Current evidence shows that the body's daily salt requirement is about 0.2 to 0.5 g (Shephard, 1981), about one tenth of what we actually consume. The excess that is ingested is lost in the urine. Even vigorous and prolonged daily exercise increases salt requirements only very slightly, because sweat has a low-salt content that decreases as one becomes more fit and heat acclimatized. Thus, the sweat of heat-acclimatized runners has a very low salt content, so that its composition approaches that of distilled water.

The salt content of sweat in an untrained subject is about 3.5 g of salt per liter of sweat, whereas the sweat of a trained, heat-acclimatized subject contains about 1.8 g of salt per liter of sweat (see Table 4.1). This means that untrained subjects would have to sweat a minimum of 3 L/day and trained, heat-acclimatized athlete up to 6 L/day just to rid themselves of the excess salt in their diets. To induce salt deficits, they would need to exercise even more. But even then, the body has conservation mechanisms that are activated if there is a risk of salt deficiency developing.

I found no published evidence of salt deficiency ever occurring in athletes, even when they exercise hard in a hot environment, providing they are eating normal diets. For example, H.L. Taylor et al. (1943) exercised subjects for a total of 4 hours a day at dry bulb temperatures of either 26.6 °C (80 °F) or 48.9 °C (120 °F). Despite total sweat losses of 5 to 8 L/day, the salt requirements of these subjects were not greater than the 13 to 17 g they ate each day in their normal diets. Similarly, Sohar and Adar (1964) were unable to find evidence of salt deficiencies in any of four groups of Israelis who either exercised or worked vigorously in extreme heat each day.

Table 15.6 Minerals of the Adult Body

Classification	Mineral	RDA	Food sources
Macronutrients (essential at intakes of 100 mg or more per day)	Sodium	500 mg	Table salt, milk, meat, fish, poultry
	Potassium	2-4 g	Cereals, fruit and vegetables
	Magnesium	M 350 mg F 300 mg	Cereals, legumes, nuts, meat, milk
	Calcium	800-1200 mg	Milk, cheese, ice cream, broccoli, oysters
	Chlorine		Table salt
	Sulphur		Eggs, meat, milk, cheese, nuts, legumes
	Phosphorus	800 mg	Milk, cheese, eggs, legumes, nuts, whole grain, cereals
Micronutrients (essential at intakes no higher than a few mg per day)	Iron	M 10 mg F 18 mg	Liver, organ meats, egg yolk, dark green vegetables, legumes, molasses, apricots, prunes, raisins
	Zinc	15 mg	Meats, oysters, legumes, whole grains
	Copper	2 mg	Liver, shellfish, meats, nuts, legumes, whole grain cereals
	Fluorine		Drinking water
	Iodine	M 130 µg F 100 µg	Sea food
	Chromium		
	Cobalt		
Micronutrients (essential, but amounts needed for humans cannot be estimated)	Silicon		
	Vanadium		
	Tim		
	Selenium		
	Manganese		
	Nickel		
	Molybdenum		
Minerals present in humans but whose function is not known	Strontium		
	Bromine		
	Gold		
	Silver		
	Aluminium		
	Bismuth		
	Arsenic		
	Boron		

Note. RDA = recommended daily allowance; M = male; F = female.

On the other hand, there is at least some evidence that a high-salt intake may increase the risk of high blood pressure (hypertension), especially in some subjects who are genetically prone to this condition. For this reason most nutritional authorities advise that daily salt intake in the general population, especially in those with high blood pressure, should be reduced with the ultimate goal of a daily salt intake of 3 g. Their argument is that the taste for salt is an acquired taste and is reversible if the amount of salt added to food is reduced, especially during processing. Adding salt via the salt shaker is, of course, quite taboo. Some authorities even feel that 3 g per day is probably still too high.

Where does this leave the runner? Obviously, we are fortunate that our daily exercise rids us of some of the excess salt in our diets and may therefore protect us against the subsequent development of high blood pressure. The evidence that regular exercise reduces the risk of developing hypertension is presented in chapter 18.

Interestingly, most of the scientific literature on muscle cramps during exercise in the heat (heat cramps) was written in the 1930s and early 1940s (Dill et al., 1936; Talbott, 1935; H.L. Taylor et al., 1943); little work has been done subsequently.

The overriding conclusion (Dill et al., 1936; H.L. Taylor et al., 1943) was that when salt deficiency was induced by very prolonged exercise in the heat in subjects eating severely salt-restricted diets, the predominant symptoms the subjects developed were heat exhaustion with cardiovascular collapse. Muscle cramps were a minor and uncommon feature. Thus, both Dill et al. (1936) and H.L. Taylor et al. (1943) concluded that salt deficiency is only one of the many factors explaining heat cramps, whereas Sohar and Adar (1964) concluded that the evidence linking salt deficiency to muscle cramps is tenuous at best. In fact, it seems that most cases of "heat cramps" described in these reports occurred in persons who also drank copious amounts of fluids while exercising in the heat (Brookbank, 1929). The cramps may really have been caused by hyponatremia resulting from fluid overload rather than from salt deficiency.

Thus, I conclude that muscle cramps that develop during a single bout of prolonged exercise like an ultramarathon are almost certainly not due to salt depletion and therefore do not respond dramatically to salt ingestion.

Chapter 4 discussed the somewhat paradoxical finding that when liberal amounts of both water and salt are ingested during exercise, the amount of salt ingested determines the degree to which dehydration will develop.

Potassium. Potassium is stored in the body mainly inside cells and is found in the diet in citrus fruits, bananas, and tomatoes. The daily potassium requirement is about 2 to 4 g, which is about 4 to 8 times more than the daily salt requirement. The total body potassium store is also about 90 g.

During exercise, potassium is lost in urine and sweat, but these losses are trivial. Thus, the sweat potassium content is only 0.1 to 0.2 g/L (see Table 4.1);

even when eating a low-potassium diet (2 g/day), subjects exercising at 50% $\dot{V}O_2$max for 2 hours a day in the heat (dry bulb temperature 47 °C) showed no evidence of developing potassium deficiency (Costill et al., 1982).

The major factor for runners is that potassium is stored with glycogen in the body; hence, potassium requirements are increased during carbohydrate loading. The ingestion of fruit during carbohydrate loading will adequately cover the additional potassium needs.

The potassium stored with glycogen is released into the bloodstream as exercise progresses and as the intramuscular glycogen stores are utilized. The extra potassium is then lost in sweat and urine in place of sodium chloride; thus, potassium excretion during exercise helps to conserve sodium.

Magnesium. In some countries, magnesium levels in the soil and therefore also in the drinking and irrigation water are low. Persons living in these areas may well have mild magnesium deficiencies, symptoms of which may include impaired exercise tolerance (McDonald & Keen, 1988).

We at the University of Cape Town have found that blood magnesium levels in our local runners are usually in the low-normal range. These findings are suggestive, but not diagnostic, of magnesium deficiency. Whether increased magnesium intakes in these runners would improve their performances is not yet established. Interestingly, magnesium levels are inversely related to $\dot{V}O_2$max and are lowest in individuals with the highest $\dot{V}O_2$max values (Lukaski et al., 1983). The reason for this is unclear, but it does suggest that low blood magnesium levels may not be altogether bad.

Although this is not proven, I feel that low muscle magnesium stores may be a factor explaining muscle cramps in some individuals living in magnesium-deficient geographical regions, and for this reason I normally suggest that persons who are prone to muscle cramps should consider taking magnesium supplements.

Magnesium losses in urine and sweat are, like those of potassium, trivial (see Table 4.1). Thus, the cause of any magnesium deficiency in athletes is almost certainly inadequate dietary intake, not excessive sweat or urine losses.

Calcium. Most of the body's calcium stores exist in bone, and the major complication of calcium deficiency is reduced bone strength due to inadequate bone calcification.

The only athletes likely to be at risk of calcium deficiencies are those females whose diets are abnormal, in particular those whose eating patterns preclude them from eating an adequate amount of dairy products, the major source of dietary calcium. The role of amenorrhea and a low-calcium diet in osteoporosis found in athletic women is discussed in detail in chapters 14 and 16. The important practical point is that a woman who does not menstruate should increase her calcium intake by eating high-calcium foods, in particular dairy produce, and should seek the opinion of a gynecologist regarding the need for estrogen, progesterone, and calcium supplementation.

Iron. Evidence shows that exercise, running particular, causes increased iron losses from the body. Because the daily intake of iron, especially in females, is only marginally above the levels needed to balance normal daily iron losses, the additional iron losses caused by running may cause iron deficiency.

I think that the distance runners most likely to become iron deficient are those who run high weekly mileages, women runners who lose large amounts of blood when they menstruate each month, and those (of either sex) who eat iron-poor diets. Foods that have a high-iron content include liver, red meat, egg yolk, legumes, dark green leafy vegetables, molasses, and whole grains. Vegetarians who eat no meat or eggs are particularly prone to iron deficiency. All at-risk runners could benefit by eating more red meat, liver, or the dark meat of fowls, and some should take iron tablets if their blood hemoglobin levels are found to be sufficiently low to indicate iron deficiency anemia (see chapter 18).

Daily iron requirements of heavily training runners might be as much as 2 mg, but because only 10% of ingested iron is actually absorbed, one should aim to ingest about 20 mg of iron per day. The diet normally provides about 6 mg of iron per 1,000 kcal of energy. Thus, a normal dietary intake of 3,000 kcal will provide 18 mg of iron, which should be sufficient to balance daily iron losses. Problems arise when the daily calorie intake is restricted or the daily iron losses exceed 2 mg. Evidence shows that many elite women runners restrict themselves to as little as 6,300 kJ per day, which provides only 9 mg of iron per day.

Only if the athlete is found to have an iron-deficiency anemia should iron therapy be considered. Total body iron stores are between 3 and 5 g, so an iron-deficient runner taking 200 mg of elemental iron per day would, assuming 10% absorption, require 150 to 250 days (5 to 8 months) to replete his or her iron stores.

A drawback to iron therapy is that iron tablets tend to cause indigestion and constipation. Of the commercially available iron tablets, those least likely to cause these problems are the "slow release" forms and the iron chelates.

Iron is best absorbed when taken with foods high in vitamin C. Tea and coffee greatly diminish iron absorption, as do the oxalates, phytates, and phosphates found in whole-grain foods. By simply drinking orange juice and not tea or coffee with meals, one can increase the iron absorbed from a meal fivefold (Rossander et al., 1979). Similarly, animal protein increases iron absorption from beans and peas.

Zinc. The possibility that distance runners may be zinc deficient was raised by a study in which blood zinc levels were found to be low in a group of runners and lowest in those who trained the hardest (Dressendorfer & Sockolov, 1980).

The symptoms of zinc deficiency are fairly nonspecific (loss of taste and smell, loss of appetite, loss of hair, and skin lesions). We do not know whether zinc deficiency adversely affects running performance, although one study showed increased muscle strength and endurance after zinc supplementation (Krotkiewski et al., 1982). Nor do we know whether the low blood zinc levels measured in long-distance runners necessarily indicated that the runners were truly zinc deficient. Zinc is found mainly in protein foods, and its content is low in high-carbohydrate foods such as fruit, vegetables, grains, and pasta; thus, vegetarian runners are more likely to be zinc deficient. Freeland-Graves et al. (1980) showed that zinc deficiency may indeed occur in vegetarians.

Copper, Chromium, and Other Trace Elements. I found no published evidence of copper, chromium, or trace element deficiencies in runners, even though exercise alters the metabolism of these elements and increases their losses in sweat, urine, and feces (Campbell & Anderson, 1987).

Water

Water requirements during exercise were discussed in chapter 4.

Other Nutritional Additives

I began this chapter with a consideration of the imposter "vitamin B_{15}," and I explained how my own empirical testing in a standard marathon proved to me that this vitamin did not work. Studies confirm this observation and show that the findings of Pipes (1980), which claimed a miraculous 28% increase in $\dot{V}O_2$max in runners taking this substance, were in error and that this vitamin, also known as pangamic acid, has no effect on metabolism or performance during running (M.E. Gray & Titlow, 1982a, 1982b).

In a report in *New Scientist*, Dr. Stephen Fulder (1980) introduced the Western world to the newest wonder drug, the extract of the thorny creeping plant related to the ginseng root and known botanically as *Eleutherococcus senticocus*. The extract of the plant, we are told, has been extensively tested in Russia—thus the popular name "Siberian ginseng"—and has become an official medicine in the Soviet Union. The evidence that this drug improves performance apparently comes from studies conducted on 1,500 athletes at the Lesgraft Institute of Physical Culture and Sports in Moscow.

Somehow, I remain skeptical. I prefer to believe what Frank Shorter once said:

> You get writers who think that there's some kind of magic formula, and they want to be the first to tell the world how to do it. What's the secret? I don't know. But I'll tell you one thing. You don't run 26 miles at 5 minutes a mile on good looks and a secret recipe.

Until proven otherwise, I choose to believe that Siberian ginseng, like vitamin B_{15} and vitamin megadoses (Weight et al., 1988a, 1988b), is relatively useless.

Genetics and proper training will never be beaten by some obscure dietary concoction.

Alcohol

Ethyl alcohol (ethanol-C_2H_5OH) is formed in nature by the fermentation of sugar and is used for several purposes. As a source of fuel for the body, ethanol differs from carbohydrate and fat in three respects.

First, ethanol is essentially foreign to the body and unlike fat and carbohydrate cannot be stored in the body. Second, the metabolic products of ethanol are utilized by muscle only to a limited extent and are almost entirely metabolized in the liver. Third, ethanol is metabolized in the liver at a fixed rate that is unaffected by the ethanol concentration in the blood. The rate of metabolism varies widely in individuals and ranges from 60 to 200 mg per kilogram of body weight per hour (mg/kg/hr). The average rate is usually about 100 mg/kg/hr. This means that a 65-kg person drinking a 30-g dose of ethanol (equivalent to about 70 ml spirits, 180 ml sherry, 250 ml wine, or 850 ml beer) will require 4 hours to metabolize the ethanol. In addition, alcohol provides 7.0 kcal of energy per gram and therefore falls between carbohydrate (4.0 kcal/g) and fat (9.0 kcal/g) in its energy content.

Many runners have the mistaken impression that alcohol can provide a rapid source of energy during exercise. This is clearly incorrect. Ingested ethanol must first be metabolized in the liver to acetaldehyde and then to acetate before it can be used by either the liver or muscles to produce mitochondrial ATP. But a muscle's capacity for acetate metabolism is extremely low and not of the same order as its ability to burn glucose. Thus, alcohol ingestion during exercise will not have any special benefits, and it is certainly not as beneficial as is the intake of glucose polymers or other carbohydrates.

Alcohol has important negative metabolic effects. The metabolism of ethanol to acetaldehyde in the liver causes the accumulation of hydrogen (protons) in the liver. For various reasons, the accumulated hydrogen impairs the liver's ability to produce new glucose (gluconeogenesis) from lactate and other substances.

Also, ethanol in a moderate dose reduces both the amount of glucose released by the liver during exercise and the amount of (blood) glucose used by the active muscles (Juhlin-Dannfelt et al., 1977). Thus, the rate of muscle glycogen utilization during exercise after ethanol ingestion is probably accelerated, and this could compromise endurance during prolonged exercise.

I have a very low tolerance for alcohol; one beer is usually enough to cause clouding of my consciousness and an inability to think clearly. Yet after an ultramarathon I have drunk up to four beers without any noticeable effect on my ability to think clearly. No doubt someone will come up with an explanation for this in due course. It does seem that training increases the rate of alcohol clearance by the liver, at least in rats (Ardies et al., 1989).

But alcohol is not all bad and is probably of value after competition, because it is a pleasant change from the cola drinks drunk during the race. In addition, alcohol will stimulate urine formation after exercise, which may be important in the prevention of kidney stones.

In addition, some evidence shows that a moderate daily alcohol intake may play a beneficial role in the prevention of coronary artery disease (Scragg et al., 1987). One study found that persons who drink no alcohol had the highest mortality rate from coronary artery disease, whereas heavy drinkers, ingesting more than 31 ml of alcohol per day, had the lowest heart disease mortality rate (Backwelder et al., 1980). Unfortunately, the beneficial effects of alcohol ingestion on heart disease mortality were largely negated at alcohol intakes greater than 10 ml/day because of a steep rise in mortality from strokes and cancers in persons ingesting more than 10 ml of alcohol per day. The result was that *total* mortality was lowest in persons ingesting 1 to 10 ml of alcohol per day. However, the risk of breast cancer is increased in women who drink even this relatively small amount of alcohol (Schatzkin et al., 1987b).

DIETARY PRACTICES OF ATHLETES

We have now completed a theoretical consideration of the athlete's diet. But what do athletes actually eat in practice, and are they guilty of any common dietary malpractices that could affect their performances?

Surprisingly, few scientific studies have examined the dietary practices of athletes. Before we consider the studies that have been completed, let us begin by considering the dietary ideas of Alec Nelson (1924) and Arthur Newton.

Nelson emphasized that "all food must be of the freshest and best—English meat, fresh fish and eggs, vegetables straight from the garden and cooked the same day, new milk and butter—and everything only when it is season" (p. 21). He also advised that the menu should be varied as much as possible.

Arthur Newton said this:

The only definite dietary rule that can be laid down for all and sundry would be "eat what you like." . . . Nature generally knows what is needed, and what is needed is right. . . . The mere fact that you like a thing is proof that it is good for you, so long as you don't indulge to excess. . . . But if you perform unorthodox orgies you can never be sure that they won't turn around and bite you. . . . exercise, eat and drink like a healthy man and that's what you will be. (Newton, 1935, p. 53; 1949, p. 71)

Newton came to two main conclusions about diet: Vegetarianism is not appropriate for runners, and with heavy training, a craving for sweet, carbohydrate-containing foods becomes apparent. He observed that the initial tendency at the onset of training hard is to eat more, but that as one becomes fitter, this tendency disappears. I have also observed this but can offer no proven explanation for it. Possibly, increased fitness improves metabolic efficiency and reduces energy losses through the various forms of thermogenesis.

The only other dietary comments made by Newton concern vitamins, which were finally isolated only sometime after Newton began running in 1922.

No doubt such things exist and spend their lives in the foods scientists have allotted them. . . . for the life of me I can't see why athletes should get entangled with them. That their presence has recently been discovered doesn't mean that they've just started: they must have been in various foods as long as mankind has inhabited bodies. Men like Hackenschmidt and Sandow at their prime had no knowledge of them yet they certainly didn't seem to suffer for lack of it. . . . while you are healthy you might just as well disregard them entirely and rely on instinct to decide what is wanted in the way of nourishment. Instinct has been right for thousands of centuries: it is not likely to go wrong in a decade. (Newton, 1947, p. 63)

Scientific Studies

One of the first scientific studies of what athletes actually eat was reported by Barry et al. (1981), who studied 108 Irish Olympic hopefuls and identified a number of dietary malpractices.

The diets contained too much fat (40%), too much protein (15%), and too little carbohydrate (45%). The optimum athletic diet, especially for endurance athletes, should contain up to 70% carbohydrate with about 15% fat and 15% protein. Also, the intakes of the vitamins thiamine and nicotinic acid were suboptimal, and the female athletes' iron and folate intakes were well below their requirements. The authors offered a number of explanations for these malpractices.

• The high intake of dietary protein probably indicated that the athletes still believed that a high-protein intake is essential for strength development.

• The high intake of dietary fat was a result of eating energy-rich foods, in particular animal and dairy produce, fried foods, cakes, and other confectioneries, all of which contain large amounts of hidden fat.

• The suboptimal intakes of thiamine and nicotinic acid were caused by a tendency to eat concentrated energy sources like refined carbohydrates (sugar and white flour and its products) and fat (fried foods, butter or margarine, and confectioneries), all of which have very low contents of thiamine and nicotinic acid.

• The low-iron intakes of the female athletes occurred because they ate less meat (especially kidney and liver) than men. They also ate fewer green leafy vegetables such as broccoli, brussels sprouts, and spinach, which together with kidney and liver are the main dietary folate sources. The authors found a direct relationship between the body folate stores and blood hemoglobin levels in the women athletes; those with the lowest body folate stores also had the lowest hemoglobin levels. The authors suggested that inadequate dietary folate intakes might be one explanation for the low hemoglobin levels in these female athletes.

Other similar studies have shown essentially the same, albeit less severe, dietary errors. The outstanding observations from these studies (Blair et al., 1981; Clement & Asmundson, 1982; Dale & Goldberg, 1982; Short & Short, 1983; P.D. Thompson et al., 1983; van Erp-Baart et al., 1989a, 1989b) point out that although athletes have higher caloric intakes, the percentage contributions of carbohydrate, fat, and protein to athletes' diets are generally not greatly different from those of nonathletes. Certainly there is no evidence that athletes have carbohydrate intakes as high as those recommended by David Costill and his colleagues (see chapter 3).

These studies indicate that the female runner requires a daily energy intake of 8,500 to 10,000 kJ (2,000 to 2,500 cal), whereas the male requires an intake of 12,000 to 14,500 kJ (2,850 to 3,500 cal). However, as we will discuss in chapter 16, many elite female distance runners eat severely calorie-restricted diets that place them at risk of developing menstrual dysfunction and osteoporosis. How they can continue to run when eating so little is a mystery that no one has yet explained.

The optimum athletic diet should include 55% of energy from carbohydrate, 30% from fat, and 15% from protein. Ideally, 350 to 500 g of carbohydrate should be eaten daily (see Figure 3.7). Such a diet corresponds to the healthy or prudent diet advocated by the U.S. Select (McGovern) Committee on Nutrition and Human Needs and to the American Cancer Society diet to reduce diet-related cancers (see Table 15.7).

Relatively few studies have looked specifically at vitamin and mineral intake of runners. The only important mineral and vitamin deficiencies that have been reported commonly among athletes are of iron and folate (Clement & Asmundson, 1982; Dale & Goldberg, 1982). These can be corrected by taking appropriate vitamin and mineral tablets and by eating iron- and folate-rich foods.

Kirsch and Von Ameln (1981) studied the feeding patterns of athletes and found that endurance athletes ingesting 14,000 to 26,000 kJ (3,300 to 6,200 cal) per day followed "nibbling" patterns characterized by frequent (8 to 10 times per day) eating and drinking. Of particular interest was the finding that 45% of the total fluid intake occurred after 8 p.m., suggesting that fluid intake follows a circadian rhythm. This study showed that athletes should always have ready access to food. Fluids, in particular, must be available in the evening.

Tables 15.2, 15.3, and 15.4 provide appropriate eating patterns for normal training, for carbohydrate loading, and for racing in events that last for more than 7 hours.

Table 15.7 Two Recommended Diets

The Healthy or Prudent Diet[a]

Choose a diet from a variety of foods.

Increase carbohydrate consumption to at least 55% of total energy intake.

Reduce sucrose (table sugar) to 25% of total carbohydrate intake.

Reduce fat consumption to 30% of total energy intake.

Reduce saturated fat consumption to 33% of total fat intake by partial substitution with polyunsaturated fat.

Reduce cholesterol consumption to less than 300 mg/day.

Reduce salt intake to about 5 g/day.

Increase consumption of cereals, fruits, and vegetables.

The American Cancer Society Diet to Reduce Diet-Related Cancer

Avoid obesity.

Reduce fat intake.

Eat more high-fiber foods.

Eat foods rich in vitamins A and C.

Eat cruciferous vegetables (cabbage, broccoli, and cauliflower).

Moderate alcohol intake.

Moderate consumption of salt-cured, smoked, and nitrite-cured foods.

[a]From "Nutrition and Sports Performance" by J.R. Brotherhood, 1984, *Sports Medicine*, **1**, p. 352. Copyright 1984 by Adis International Limited. Adapted by permission.

DIET-RELATED IDIOSYNCRASIES

Not everyone can eat all foods. Milk intolerance may cause specific problems, in particular diarrhea and irritable bowel syndrome, in susceptible persons. Sheehan (1975) described essentially the same findings in persons unable to absorb gluten, a protein found in all grain foods except corn and rice. This condition, known as colic disease or gluten enteropathy, is completely cured by avoiding all gluten-containing foods.

So the paradox is that the staple foods of life—bread and milk—may be just the foods that some runners should avoid.

There are other foods to which certain individuals may be allergic and that can cause bizarre symptoms. I received a letter from a runner who thought that chocolate was the bugbear. On giving up chocolate, he found that he could train harder, and he improved his 8-km racing time.

That chocolate caused this runner's problems would only be proved conclusively if his symptoms were completely absent as long as he stayed off chocolate and if the reintroduction of chocolate into his diet, without him knowing it, caused the identical symptoms, whereas the introduction of an inactive substance (placebo) did not. This type of testing is known scientifically as a *crossover reintroduction trial* and is the best basic scientific technique used to determine if a food allergy explains the symptoms present in a particular individual.

Food allergies do indeed exist and should be considered by any athletes with persistent problems, especially exercise-related diarrhea and effort migraine (see chapter 18), that are not helped by conventional medical or other advice.

EXERCISE AND WEIGHT CONTROL

My interest in exercise and weight control began some years ago when a leading runner told me that I was too fat and advised me to set my treadmill on manual and spend my days running, not testing other runners. I suspect that many elite runners share this view and picture me as a potential sumo wrestler.

My medical colleagues, on the other hand, have usually considered me too thin and have enquired for what political cause I am currently on hunger strike. Others ask which diet I am experimenting with. Still others gratuitously offer me their valued medical services; they are intrigued to discover the nature of my terminal illness.

There was, of course, a time when I too thought I could do something about my weight. During those periods of my life when I have been able to run for 2 hours a day, I have lost as much as 5 flabby kilograms in 2 months. But this loss is never permanent. Within 6 weeks of returning to a less arduous training program, my weight slips back to a constant 85 to 87 kg, at least 18% of which constitutes lard.

Why is it, then, that I am apparently unable to lose sufficient weight to become as thin as my elite running friends?

The traditional answer is that I eat far too much for the amount of exercise I take. But we now know that this conventional wisdom is too simplistic.

Human weight control is a very complex problem, far more complex than the conventional idea that being overweight is simply due to an imbalance between daily food intake and energy expenditure. Consider for example, the following studies:

• In 1902, R.O. Neumann (1902) performed a 725-day study on himself. During that time he varied his energy intake over a wide range. His weight refused to change.

• In 1961, G.A. Rose and Williams (1961) studied groups of people who eat a lot and people who eat very little. From each group they were able to select pairs of individuals who did the same amount of exercise and who were of the same mass but whose daily intakes of food differed by a factor of 2.

• Sims and his colleagues (Sims, 1976; Sims et al., 1973) invited a group of Vermont state prisoners to eat as much as they could for 6 months. The prisoners gratefully responded, increasing their daily food intakes by an average of 75%, with some gluttons eating as much as 9,500 kcal daily, or almost 4 times the average daily intake of 2,500 kcal and nearly twice the daily intake of competitors in the Tour de France (Brouns, 1988).

Sims reported the following. First, the prisoners' weights increased for the first few weeks of the experiments and then stabilized.

Second, the equilibrium weights achieved by the prisoners were independent of how much extra food energy each ate; some prisoners were relatively resistant to gaining weight, whereas others who overate to the same degree put on considerably more weight. Miller and Mumford (1967) reported in a similar study that some subjects *lost* weight when eating an extra 10,000 kcal per week.

Third, even those most gluttonous prisoners who ate 4 times their normal daily requirements increased their weights by only between 20 and 25%.

• Sims et al. (1973) also investigated two heavy subjects who had voluntarily dieted so that they were equally as overweight as the prisoners. To equalize their weights with those of the prisoners who ate the most, the two subjects could eat only 1,200 calories (5,000 kJ) of food energy per day. This study showed that individuals whose daily energy intakes differed by a factor of 8 could have the same body weight.

• Sims et al. (1973) also showed that when nonobese subjects are made to become obese by overeating, they require more energy in relation to body surface area for maintenance of the obese state than they require at their natural weight, and they also require more than spontaneously obese subjects. Other studies suggest that this may be because the obese have blunted thermogenic responses to feeding: They heat up less and therefore waste less of the energy contained in the food they eat (Segal et al., 1985, 1987). These people are said to be more "fuel efficient" or "thrifty." Not all studies show this, however (D'Alessio et al., 1988).

• Miller and Parsonage (1975) incarcerated 29 volunteers, all of whom claimed to be unable to lose weight on rigorous slimming diets, in an isolated country house for 3 weeks. On arrival, the subjects' luggage was searched for hidden food, and their car keys were confiscated. All the volunteers were placed on the same 1,500-kcal diet, and their weight losses were determined after 3 weeks. Nineteen of the subjects did actually lose weight on this diet, but nine maintained their weights, and two actually gained weight on what for many people would have been a starvation diet. Those subjects resistant to losing weight were found to have low basal metabolic rates.

• Studies in identical (monozygous) twins showed that genetic, not environmental, factors play the predominant role explaining their body weights (Mayer, 1953) and their body fat contents (Brooke et al., 1975). Similarly, Mayer (1965) found that in the absence of parental obesity, the incidence of obesity in children was 14%; if one parent was obese, this incidence rose to 40%, and if both were obese, the incidence was 80%. An adoption study (Stunkard et al., 1986) showed that the body compositions of adopted children resembled those of their biological parents, not their foster parents, suggesting that hereditary factors are more important than environmental factors in determining body composition.

• Contrary to popular belief, there is absolutely no valid scientific evidence that the obese eat more than lean individuals (Rothwell & Stock, 1981). In fact, some evidence shows that obese females may actually eat less than lean females (Baecke et al., 1983). Rothwell and Stock (1981) concluded that "it is difficult to support the contention that food intake is the primary determinant of body weight in man or experimental animals" (p. 242).

• A growing body of evidence suggests that the body "defends" its weight (Brownell et al., 1987), in part by maintaining a certain size of fat cells—large in obese subjects, small in thin people (Tremblay et al., 1985). Diet and exercise can reduce fat-cell size only up to a point. Once a certain fat-cell size is reached, further weight loss becomes impossible. Reversion to a normal diet and sedentary state causes the fat cells to return to their previous sizes. Interestingly, those fat cells that remain in the body after surgical removal of other fat cells do not enlarge to compensate for the reduced body fat content. Thus, surgical removal of fat may be the only effective method by which a sustained loss of body fat can be achieved.

One mechanism by which the body defends its weight may be that in the face of a reduced energy intake, the body becomes more "fuel efficient," as did Sim's prisoners. That is, the amount of food energy required to maintain a certain body mass is reduced. Brownell et al. (1987) noted the remarkable fuel efficiency of female athletes with amenorrhea and reduced bone density (see chapter 16) and questioned whether exercise training may enhance food efficiency.

The logical explanation for these anomalies is that either of two mechanisms must be operative. Humans must differ either in the amounts of energy that they can actually store from the food they eat or in the amounts of energy they need to maintain a constant body weight (i.e., their basal metabolic rates). In addition, body weight—in particular the size of the body fat stores—must be carefully controlled within certain genetically determined limits by a regulator, sometimes referred to as the *adipostat*.

Most current obesity research centers on the possibility that certain metabolic processes, so-called futile cycles, exist that effectively waste energy by turning the excess energy ingested in food into heat in a process known as *dietary-induced thermogenesis* or the thermic effect of feeding. The theory is that the adipostat regulates the activity of these futile cycles, which are less well developed in the obese than in lean subjects.

Most of the evidence to support this thermogenic control of body weight comes from rat studies. Two British researchers, Nancy Rothwell and Michael Stock (1981), made use of the discovery (previously only known to keepers of rats and not to scientists who lack such practical experience) that rats can be enticed into gross obesity by a "cafeteria diet" that includes such delicacies as pasta, pizza, cake, chocolate, liver pâté, ham, bacon, and hamburgers.

As they become fatter, such rats develop increased masses of specialized fat cells, so-called brown adipose tissue, which is specifically adapted to lose heat. In response to a meal, the brown adipose tissues of these obese rats heat up under the influence of certain hormones released in response to the meal, thereby losing some of the excess energy ingested in the food. This maintains the body weights of the rats at new, albeit elevated, levels. In addition, if the fat rats exercise, their capacities for dietary-induced thermogenesis are increased (J.O. Hill et al., 1983), so that their weight gains on the cafeteria diet are less than those of sedentary rats fed the same diet. Once the cafeteria diet is removed, the fat rats rapidly lose the extra weight they have gained, their brown adipose tissues shrink, and their increased capacities for dietary-induced thermogenesis return to normal.

Unfortunately, although this mechanism is clearly established in rats (Rothwell & Stock, 1981), its role in humans who probably lack sufficient brown adipose tissue is unclear. Furthermore, exercise training may reduce, rather than increase, the capacity for dietary-induced thermogenesis in humans (LeBlanc et al., 1984), at least in the highly trained athlete (Poehlman, 1989). The thermogenic response to caffeine ingestion is also lower in trained than untrained subjects (Poehlman, 1989).

Other factors that are known to be thermogenic and therefore aid weight loss include caffeine, alcohol, nicotine, and certain drugs and hormones, in particular thyroxine. The action of thyroxine is to "uncouple" respiration so that when substrate is oxidized in the mitochondria, greater amounts of heat are released and less ATP is produced, hence a thermogenic effect. Obviously a safe thermogenic drug would have enormous potential for aiding those who wish to be thinner.

The thermogenic effect of nicotine probably explains why persons who stop smoking tend to put on weight and why smokers are generally thinner than nonsmokers despite their eating more (Stamford et al., 1984b). The thermogenic effects of cigarette smoking and caffeine intake probably also explain the tendency of some people wishing to lose weight to live on diets of coffee and cigarettes.

Practical Relevance

I think society in general is excessively concerned about weight, and this concern is particularly evident among endurance athletes like runners who must carry their unsupported weight with them. It is quite true that, up to a point, the less fat we carry, the faster we will run. But I think that each of us has a certain safe body weight that we can reasonably achieve, and even with a superhuman effort we can only reach a shade lower than this weight.

As I see it, the only way to reduce genetically determined optimum body weight is to exercise as much as possible and to diet within reason. Weight loss is increased if breakfast rather than dinner is the main meal of the day and if the food eaten at breakfast is fixed (and disliked) rather than freely chosen (and liked).

Unsubstantiated observations of myself, confirmed in discussions with other runners, suggest that 2 hours of running a day causes body weight to level off, presumably at or near the genetic limit, which may be anything between 3 and 25% body fat for males, with higher values for female athletes (see Figure 3.3). Koplan et al. (1982) found that total weight loss in runners equaled about 1.2 kg for each 10 km run in the week. Thus, an athlete who ran 50 km/week could expect his or her body weight to stabilize at a weight 5 times 1.2 kg, that is, 6 kg lower than prior to exercise. The athlete who ran 100 km/week could expect a total weight loss of 11.2 kg.

The particular benefits of exercise in weight control are as follows (Pavlou et al., 1985):

• The exercise session, particularly if it is intense and prolonged, may cause the metabolic rate to be elevated for some time after exercise (Bahr et al., 1987; Editorial, 1988; Maehlum et al., 1986; Poehlman, 1989). Furthermore, prior exercise may increase the thermogenic effect of food eaten for some hours thereafter (J.C. Young et al., 1986). Thus, additional energy is burned up free of effort.

• Unlike dietary restriction, which causes a loss of water, muscle, and fat, the weight loss caused by exercise training comprises a loss only of body fat, with increases in lean body mass and body water content (J.O. Hill et al., 1987).

• The increased lean body (muscle) mass that results from exercise training should increase the basal metabolic rate, at least in men (Cunningham, 1980); no such effect has been reported in women (Poehlman, 1989). Thus, a higher food intake will be needed to maintain a lower body weight in trained men. In contrast, weight loss by dieting alone causes a loss of lean body mass. Therefore, the basal metabolic rate falls, and progressively less food must be eaten to maintain the reduced body weight. In contrast, exercise may even prevent the fall in resting metabolic rate that accompanies severe caloric restriction (Molé et al., 1989). Unfortunately, there is no scientific evidence that exercise of the legs, for example, can cause a specific (spot) reduction of the fat overlying the leg muscles (Krotkiewski et al., 1979).

• The resting metabolic rate may be chronically elevated in those who train 12 to 16 hours a week (Tremblay et al., 1985).

• Appetite and therefore food intake may fail to adapt immediately to increased physical activity. Thus, there is a period in the beginning of an exercise program when extra weight is lost as food intake fails to meet requirements (Tremblay et al., 1985).

In contrast to a widely held belief, exercise does not appear to stimulate appetite (Thompson et al., 1988) even in the obese (Pi-Sunyer & Woo, 1985). And, not all activities are equally effective in inducing a weight loss. Walking, cycling, and running appear to be the most effective, whereas swimming may be without effect (Gwinup, 1987). The reason for this is unclear.

Growing evidence suggests that genetic factors control the extent to which many of these variables alter with training. Research shows that 40% of the differences in resting metabolic rate between individuals are genetically determined, whereas 81% of the variation in the response of this variable to training is genetically determined (Poehlman, 1989).

Thus, just as there are high and low adaptors to exercise training (chapter 3), so there are those in whom exercise training has no effect on resting metabolic rate (low adaptors) and others in whom a marked effect is found (high adaptors).

The same has been found for the effects of exercise training on the thermic effects of feeding; 72% of the variation in the response of this variable to training is genetically determined (Poehlman, 1989).

Women are at a disadvantage in terms of weight loss; even the leanest, most highly trained female distance runners have about 12 to 15% body fat. Regrettably, one consequence of this modern obsession with weight control and being thin (especially among female gymnasts, ballet dancers, and models) may be the increasing incidence of anorexia nervosa and bulimia among adolescent females in Western society.

ANOREXIA NERVOSA

Anorexia nervosa is a condition in which a person basically stops eating and starts starving to death. The term is misleading, however, because it literally means "loss of hunger on a psychological basis." In fact, there is no loss of hunger in this condition; the person with anorexia nervosa suffers from intense hunger and food preoccupation but will not eat (Blumenthal et al., 1985).

The typical person likely to suffer from anorexia nervosa is an adolescent female from a higher socioeconomic class. Probably she is industrious, introverted, and self-denying; of above average intelligence; a perfectionist; and highly active in sport.

The reason such an intelligent and talented individual would choose to flirt with death is obviously extremely complex, and probably no single theory can explain all aspects of the disease. Some of the most interesting insights into the disease have been provided by medical historian Janet Brumberg (1989).

In her search for the original medical description of the condition, Brumberg discovered that anorexia nervosa was first described simultaneously in 1873 by a

British physician, Sir William Gull, and a French psychiatrist, Charles Lasegue. Whereas Gull concentrated on the medical features of the condition, Lasegue sought a psychological explanation for its development. Lasegue linked the onset of anorexia to a broad set of frustrations arising in the daughters of the 19th century European middle class as they approached adulthood. These frustrations included parental pressures that their daughters should marry "appropriately" and blocked educational or social opportunities.

Brumberg (1989) suggests that 19th century middle-class parents were the first to use love rather than authoritarianism to cement family relationships. The danger was that this expression of love could become suffocating or manipulative and prevent the growth of the individual self-esteem necessary for separation from the family.

Victorians often expressed their love in the form of gifts, the most basic of which was food. At the same time, the culinary standards were improving rapidly, and food and eating habits were increasingly taking on special social significance. Women were not to be seen eating, as food and eating were connected to gluttony, sexuality, aggression, and bodily "indelicacies" such as urination and defecation. Brumberg (1989) notes that for these reasons, constipation was incorporated into the ideal of Victorian femininity.

In addition, the adolescent Victorian girl was not allowed the freedom to express her emotions. Thus refusing food was a silent but potent form of expression:

> Refusing to eat was not as confrontational as yelling, having a tantrum, or throwing things; refusing to eat expressed emotional hostility without being flamboyant. . . . Food refusal, while an emotionally charged behavior, was also discrete, quiet, and ladylike in keeping with the Victorian notion that women were expected to carry reserve further than the male. (Brumberg, 1989, p. 140)

By the turn of the century, slimness had become a sign of social status: "A thin frail woman was a symbol of class and an object of beauty precisely because she was unfit for productive (or reproductive) work. . . . A thin woman signified the idle idyll of the leisured classes" (Brumberg, 1989, p. 189). The result was the appetite had become less of a biological drive and more of a social and emotional instrument.

At about this time, psychoanalyst Sigmund Freud turned his attention to this condition and proposed that anorexia nervosa developed in adolescent girls who wished to keep their bodies small, thin, and childlike, thereby retarding normal sexual development and forestalling adult sexuality. The legend of Wilgefortis (Lacey, 1982) incorporates this interpretation.

Wilgefortis, who lived sometime between A.D. 700 and A.D. 1000 was the seventh daughter of the King of Portugal, a tyrannical man known for his cruelty and grossness. Wilgefortis was horrified to hear that her father had arranged for her to marry the King of Sicily. She had already made a vow of virginity and had planned to give her life to God, not man.

She prayed to God for help. She became ascetic, and, overcoming her appetite, she begged the Lord to deprive her of all her beauty. God granted her prayer by causing her to develop a hairy body (the lanugo hair of the anorectic) and to grow a beard. Her father was so angry that he had Wilgefortis crucified. While on the cross, Wilgefortis prayed for all to remember the passions that encumber all women, and she prayed that any woman who used her as a medium of prayer would be blessed as she had been.

Brumberg (1989) suggests that factors that have influenced the incidence of anorexia nervosa since the end of the World War I include the evolution of the basic institutions of the American beauty culture, including the fashion and cosmetics industries, beauty contests, the modeling profession, and movies, all of which promote the ideal of the slender woman. Thus women increasingly desired slim bodies:

> The body of the new women was a sign of modernity that marked her for more than traditional motherhood and domesticity. With the introduction of birth control, sexuality and reproduction could be separated so that a slender body and willingness to wear more revealing clothes were taken as signs of increased sexual confidence, freedom and enjoyment. A svelte female figure became, for the first time, the ultimate sign and symbol of heterosexual interest and success. (Brumberg, 1989, p. 245)

Additional factors that have come into play since the end of the World War II include medical concerns with the dangers of childhood and adult obesity; the growth of the diet industry to multibillion-dollar status; and the added emphasis of physical fitness and athleticism as criteria for perfection so that "compulsive exercising and chronic dieting have been joined as twin obsessions" (Brumberg, 1989, p. 255). One result has been that the female role models—beauty queens, fashion models, and Playboy centerfolds—are getting thinner (Garner & Garfinkel, 1979, 1980), whereas women are tending to get fatter. The weight of anorexic girls has also become progressively less in recent years.

But Brumberg (1989) concludes that the evolving overemphasis on diet and athleticism cannot adequately explain the recent rise in the incidence of anorexia nervosa. Rather she suggests that modern attitudes toward food and the expectations between the sexes must have played a role.

She suggests that food has become increasingly more available and desirable at the very time when our "obeseophobic" society demands that we eat with restraint. Food has become associated with sociability, status, and sexuality and has been identified as an analogue of the self; Brumberg (1989) cites the example of the hippies of the late 1960s who stopped eating the foods associated with their "bourgeois" upbringing and turned rather to grains, unprocessed foods, and the avoidance of meat. Brumberg (1989) identifies a conflict between the cultural imperative to control appetite and the all-pervasive stimulus to eat.

The second factor that may contribute to increased incidence of anorexia nervosa relates to the stress imposed by the breakdown of family structure. Brumberg (1989) suggests that the young woman of today must view heterosexual relationships with ambivalence as so few such relationships have happy endings. In addition, AIDS poses sexual uncertainties. The young woman of today is therefore forced to develop a professional career to ensure her future security in the event of divorce without forsaking the ideas of marriage and a family.

The result is that young women must fulfill an impossible role, and the demands are extreme and unrelenting. Just as these young women are being challenged and their expectations raised, so there is no coherent support system or philosophy to guide them. The cult of diet and exercise comes closest to a "coherent philosophy of the self . . . of all the messages they hear, the imperative to be beautiful and good by being thin, is still the strongest and most familiar" (Brumberg, 1989, p. 270).

Brumberg (1989) concludes her book with the following:

Anorexia nervosa ultimately expresses the predicament of a very distinctive group, one that suffers from the painful ambiguities of being young and female in an affluent society set adrift by social change. . . . Intelligent, anxious for personal achievement, and determined to maintain control in a world where things as basic as food and sex are increasingly out of control, the contemporary anorectic unrelentingly pursues thinness as a secular form of perfection. In a society where consumption and identity are pervasively linked, she makes nonconsumption the perverse center piece of her identity. In a sad and desperate way, today's fasting girls epitomize the curious psychic burdens of the youthful daughters of a people of plenty. (p. 271)

Anorexia and Running

One of the main reasons I have included a discussion of anorexia in this book is an interesting article that appeared in the world's leading medical journal, the *New England Journal of Medicine*, in February 1983.

The article, written by three running doctors, Alayne Yates, Kevin Leehey, and Catherine Shisslak, from the department of psychiatry at the University of Arizona, carried this dramatic title: "Running—An Analogue of Anorexia?" (Yates et al., 1983).

The article began by noting that the 1970s were characterized by two major social events: (a) increased incidence of anorexia nervosa among adolescent females to the extent that this illness is now regarded as a major public health problem in Western countries and (b) an almost simultaneous increase in the number of joggers and runners in the same countries. The possibility that the two conditions might be related first occurred to the authors during a research project in which they interviewed 60 runners who regularly ran more than 50 miles a week. During these interviews, the authors noted similarities between the characters, lifestyles, and backgrounds of some runners whom they labeled *obligatory runners* and of the anorectic women they were accustomed to treating in their psychiatric practices. The similarities they noted were the following.

Singular Dedication

Although the anorectic person's goal is physical attractiveness and the obligatory runner's goal is physical performance, the authors contend that both subjects pursue their different goals with degrees of dedication that are alarming and potentially dangerous.

Personality Characteristics

As we have already noted, anorectic females are usually model children reared in middle- to upper-class homes, often in families that are overtly concerned with achievement, diet, and exercise. These children tend to be introverted, intensely active, and liable to depression. Some 24% of anorectic women are said to be "very athletic." Typically, anorectic women had a hazy sense of self as children, and they depend on others for opinions of their own self-worth. Successful dieting reduces the anorectic patient's anxiety and introversion and may produce a "high" similar to that experienced by runners.

In their survey, the authors found that their obligatory runners had similar characteristics to these anorectic women. The runners were self-effacing, hardworking, high achievers from affluent families; they were uncomfortable with anger, were reluctant to express emotions, and tended toward introversion. Their heightened commitments to running usually occurred at times of identity crisis, heightened anxiety, or depression. Running improved their senses of self-worth, and the ritualization of shoes, clothing, books, food, training, and racing helped to strengthen these self-images. These obligatory runners were totally obsessed with weight and felt unwell, bloated, anxious, and depressed when they were unable to run.

To explain this, the authors suggested that running may be an effective way for persons who do not like to express anger openly to channel and release that anger. If unexpressed, the accumulated anger would then contribute to the runner's depression or "withdrawal symptoms." Thus, if running is indeed an effective and acceptable release of this pent-up anger for persons who dislike expressing their anger, this would explain the runners' withdrawal symptoms when they stopped running.

Finally, the authors noted that both groups are characterized by asceticism, a tendency to social isolationism, and an aversion to passive receptive pleasures (such as eating, socializing, and visual entertainment).

Cultural Reinforcement

The authors noted that society commends the runner for performance and praises the dieter for slimness. However, the authors also observed that when these pursuits are taken to extremes, a cultural bias becomes apparent, because although we praise overcommitted, elite runners for their dedication and courage (if they compete well despite injuries), anorectic women, the elite of the dieters, are classified as ill and are stigmatized by society.

Age as a Factor of Obsession

Women become anorectic in late adolescence, whereas obligatory runners become obsessed only in their 30s and 40s. The authors suggested that this occurs because a girl's attractiveness really only becomes an issue of self-worth when she enters the dating arena in early or midadolescence. In contrast, the test of male physical powers first occurs in adulthood when the male has achieved a stable career and when, for the first time, he notices that his physical and sexual prowesses begin to decline. So the adult male with an identity crisis runs to overcome the crisis; the heightened physical and sexual prowesses that result from running give him the increased feeling of security and self-worth that he desires.

Conclusions Given in the Article

Yates et al. (1983) concluded that in modern society, most individuals experience some anxieties about appearance or strength and may decide to start diets or exercise programs. In most cases, these lifestyle changes are beneficial. However, a small number of runners and dieters will go overboard in their diet or exercise programs. These people become analogous to religious fanatics or workaholics and are identifiable by extreme inflexibility, adherence to rituals, repetitive thoughts, and intense needs to control themselves and their environments. Something else must be present to push the normal exerciser or dieter into the obligatory or anorectic phase. This, the authors suggest, probably relates to the instability of the self-concept and must therefore place obligatory runners at high risk for depression, anorexia, and other disorders should these runners have to stop running and thereby lose their psychological crutches.

My Comments

I found this article to be one of the most interesting I have ever read in the running literature. In fact, for the authors' profiles of the obligatory runners, they need not have spoken to 60 runners; they could just have questioned me. For I can identify with many of the characteristics described in the article; according to their description I might have been a prime candidate for anorexia had I been a female.

But there are major flaws in some of the authors' arguments and conclusions, or at least there are flaws in the interpretations of this article that have been made by those journalists eager to criticize running.

First, Yates et al. (1983) missed the fundamental issue: Why was there a sudden rise (beginning in the 1970s) in the number of psychologically disturbed people who needed to turn to running or anorexia to find themselves? How did our kind cope before the 1970s?

My point is that neither the running nor the dieting is at fault. Rather, those factors in the family and society psychodynamics (which were identified earlier), and probably inherited psychological characteristics, produce the particular personality type likely to become an anorectic or an obligatory runner; these factors should be identified and treated. Stopping the obligatory runner from running or the anorectic patient from dieting is treating the effect, not the cause of the condition. And the high failure rates in the treatment of both conditions indicate just how ineffectual that approach is.

Second, the authors provided little evidence that obligatory runners actually damage their physical or psychological health to the same degree that anorectic women may damage their health. In fact, I was struck by the remarkable normality of the "abnormal" runners the authors described. The only example they quote of an athlete exhibiting self-destructive behavior comparable to that of an anorectic female was marathon runner Alberto Salazar, who reportedly trained more than 160 km a week on a stress fracture (a physical impossibility even for Salazar) and who has twice run himself into heatstroke or heat exhaustion during road races. In the latter case, of course, the fault lay not with Salazar but with the race organizers who scheduled their races to be run during the heat of the day, thus predisposing one of the world's toughest competitors to injury.

To the best of my knowledge, the only major danger inherent in obligatory running is divorce (and presumably family neglect); a high incidence of divorce has been reported in married couples of which only one partner runs. Yet those same studies showed that the running did not cause the divorce; running acted as a catalyst bringing hidden conflicts into the open.

Third, Yates et al. (1983) did not actually determine the exact number of obligatory runners who are running today. Instead, all the evidence provided was anecdotal and unsubstantiated.

To study further this issue, James Blumenthal and his colleagues (1984) from Duke University compared the psychological profiles of 43 obligatory runners with profiles of 24 patients who had diagnosed anorexia nervosa. The authors found that the psychological profiles of the obligatory runners were quite normal, whereas the profiles of the anorectic patients were clearly abnormal. The authors concluded that "obligatory runners do not suffer from the same degree of psychopathology as do patients with anorexia nervosa" (p. 520).

Weight and Noakes (1987) found that the incidence of abnormal eating patterns of the type present in persons with anorexia nervosa was no greater in groups of female marathon and track runners than it was in the nonrunning population. Abnormal eating patterns were, however, more prevalent in the more competitive women runners, suggesting that some women runners who are at risk for developing anorexia nervosa may use competitive running to control their anorectic tendencies. Clearly, this interpretation cannot explain the attraction running has for the vast majority of women runners.

Fourth, Yates et al. (1983) failed to distinguish between a healthy and a pathological pursuit of perfection. As McCutcheon and Ayres (1983) wrote:

> We have reached a sad state of affairs where perfectionism is a dirty word. . . . it is indeed sad that those who try to reach beyond their limits to pursue excellence are subjected to ridicule. . . . Accusing the dedicated athlete of neuroticism is to libel the pursuit of excellence. (p. 17)

I hope that my own obsessive writing and running also signify perfectionism, not neuroticism!

The truth is that any human activity, be it academics, politics, religion, business, or sport, that provides a solid measure of ego satisfaction, is potentially addictive, particularly for those with hazy self-esteem. So just as there are obligatory runners and dieters, there are obligatory academics, obligatory professionals, obligatory politicians, obligatory priests, and obligatory executives, all of whom probably have similar personalities.

So there it is. Running is no more or no less an analogue of anorexia than is any human activity that improves self-esteem and satisfies the ego. The danger, then, is the personality, not the activity. Running, like all these human activities, is beneficial when it improves feelings of self-esteem and self-worth, because these feelings improve the ways ''obligatory-type'' people cope with life and enhance not only their own lives but also the lives of the people with whom they interact. In fact, if not for the efforts of those self-effacing, hard-working, unaggressive, obligatory high-achievers in all walks of life, the world wouldn't be much of a place in which to live. The dangers arise when the need for ego satisfaction generated by these activities becomes all consuming and introduces the problems described by Yates et al. (1983).

Obligatory runners and dieters, like obligatory people active in any of these activities, need to be aware of the limits to which any single activity can satisfy their ego conflicts without introducing those additional strains that can ultimately be devastating.

FAD DIETS

Another consequence of the relative stability of body weight has been the profusion of fad diets, each claiming to hold the elusive secret that will eventually allow anyone to lose all the weight he or she desires. Of course, all such diets will inevitably fail if, as we have proposed, body weight is controlled on a hereditary basis and can really only be altered markedly and permanently by very radical procedures (like starvation) that are incompatible with a healthy and productive life.

In a review of fad diets, Porcello (1984) divided the 14 most popular fad diets into the following four categories.

- The altered-proportion diets, in which the relative contributions of protein, fat, and carbohydrate to the dietary energy are altered.
- The specific-substance diets, which have been developed around the incorrect premise that specific substances accelerate the breakdown of fats.
- The specific-food-combination diets, which provide two or more special foods, the interaction of which is held to cause weight loss.
- The starvation diets.

The features of these diets are listed in Table 15.8. The most important point is that all fad diets are nutritionally deficient and will lead to impaired health and physical performance if followed rigorously for prolonged periods. The criteria that determine a diet's appropriateness are the following (Porcello, 1984):

- The diet must be medically safe.
- The diet must provide an energy deficit that elicits no more than a 2-lb weight loss per week. Weight loss rates in excess of 2 lb/week can compromise performance and, in young persons, can retard growth.
- The diet must be suited to the individual's lifestyle and food preferences.
- The diet must be convenient to follow and must encourage lifelong eating patterns for the maintenance of weight loss.

VEGETARIANISM

Many athletes choose vegetarian diets. Vegetarian diets may be classified as *lacto-ovo-vegetarian*, in which plant foods are eaten with dairy produce and eggs; lacto-vegetarian, in which dairy produce and plant foods are eaten; and *pure vegetarian*, in which plant foods alone are eaten. Semivegetarians eat some meat (e.g., poultry, seafood, or both).

Most vegetarian adults follow additional dietary practices besides vegetarianism, and the term *vegan* refers to those vegetarians who combine their nutritional practices with a specific philosophy and lifestyle. The most extreme form of vegetarianism is the Zen macrobiotic diet, which falls under the group of specific-substance diets shown in Table 15.8. Table 15.9 lists the nutritional features of the different vegetarian diets.

The Zen macrobiotic diet progresses through 10 stages of dietary restriction (-3 to $+7$), with gradual elimination of animal products, fruits, and vegetables.

Table 15.8 A Descriptive Summary of 14 Fad Diets

Diet	Protein	Carbohydrate	Fat	Vitamins, minerals	Specific comments
Altered-proportion diets					
Dr. Atkins's Revolutionary Diet	High	Low	High	Low in vitamins A and C	High saturated fat and cholesterol; unrestricted calories; ketogenic diet
Calories Don't Count	Normal	Low	Normal	Low in vitamin B_2 and in calcium	Margarine and safflower capsules recommended; ketogenic diet
The Cambridge Diet	Low	Low	Low	Adequate	1,380 kJ a day; ketogenic diet; powdered product
The Complete Scarsdale Medical Diet	High	Low	Low	Low in vitamins A, B_1, and B_2, and in calcium and iron	Less than 4,200 kJ a day
Drinking Man's Diet	High	Low	High	Low in most vitamins	High in saturated fat and cholesterol; alcohol allowed
Macrobiotics	Low	High	Low	Generally inadequate	Progression of very restricted diets
Dr. Stillman's Quick Inches-Off Diet	Low	High	Low	Low in vitamin B_2, calcium, and iron	Claims of spot reducing
Specific-substance diets					
The Grapefruit Diet	High	Low	High	Low in vitamin B_1	High in saturated fat and cholesterol; ketogenic diet
Lecithin, B_6, Apple Cider, Vinegar and Kelp Diet	—	—	Low	Varies with food selection	Low-calorie diet with added substance, which is intended to increase metabolism and fat mobilization
Human Chorionic (HCG) Gonado-tropin Diet	Low	Low	Low	Generally inadequate	2,100 kJ a day
Specific-food-combination diets					
Banana-Milk Diet	Low	Normal	Low	Generally inadequate	4,200 kJ a day supplied by 6 bananas and 3 glasses of milk
The Beverly Hills Diet	Low	High	Low	Generally inadequate	Fruit is staple food for first 3 weeks
Starvation diets					
Starvation Diet	Low	Low	Low	Inadequate	Only water or fruit juice permitted

Note. From "A Practical Guide to Fad Diets" by L.A.P. Porcello, 1984, *Clinics in Sports Medicine*, **3**(3), p. 728. Copyright 1984 by W.B. Saunders Co. Adapted by permission.

Table 15.9 Nutritional Features of Various Vegetarian Diets

Diet	Protein	Carbohydrate	Fat	Vitamins and minerals	Specific comments
Zen macrobiotic diet	Very low (Notes: 1, 2)	High; diet consists mainly of brown rice.	Low	Low in calcium, iron, and vitamins C and B_{12} (Notes: 2-4)	The most restricted diets (grade +7) cause protein calorie malnutrition and growth retardation in children.
Pure vegetarian (vegan)	Will be low in essential amino acids if cereals and legumes are not combined (Notes: 1, 2)	Adequate	Low	Low in high-quality protein, iron, calcium, zinc, magnesium, iodine, and vitamins A, riboflavin, B_{12}, and D (Notes: 2-4)	Because of the high-bulk intake, the diet may not cover energy requirements. Special care must be taken to insure adequate sources of vitamin B_{12}.
Lacto-vegetarian (dairy products only)	Adequate	—Variable—		(Notes: 3, 4)	Milk provides high-quality protein, calcium, and vitamins B_2 and B_{12}.
Lacto-ovo-vegetarian (eggs and dairy products)	Adequate	—Variable—		(Notes: 3, 4)	Eggs provide high-quality protein and vitamin B_{12}.

Notes:
1. Essential amino acid complementation must be practiced (i.e., select foods so that the limited amino acids in one food are supplied in higher concentration in other foods).
2. Pure vegetable and fruit diets without legumes, nuts, and grains are nutritionally inadequate in protein, iron, calcium, riboflavin, B_{12}, and possibly vitamin D.
3. Vitamin B_{12} is found only in animal products.
4. Low-iron content of vegetarian diets is further compounded by their high-fiber content, which impairs iron absorption.

Although the lower level diets can meet nutritional needs, the highest level diet, because it is composed only of cereals, is nutritionally inadequate and will cause growth retardation in children and even death in adults.

A pure vegetarian diet can cover nutritional needs if the following rules are followed:

- To prevent protein deficiency, improve the quality of vegetable protein by combining different protein sources in each meal. Thus, the cereal grains wheat and rice, which are low in the essential amino acid lysine but adequate in methionine, are complemented by legumes such as dry beans, soybeans, and peas, which have adequate lysine but too little methionine.
- Ensure adequate calcium and riboflavin (vitamin B_2) intakes by eating dark green leafy vegetables, legumes, fortified soybean milk, peanuts, almonds, and sesame seeds. As milk provides these two nutrients, lacto-vegetarians do not run the same risk.
- Provide iron, minerals, and vitamins B_1 and B_2 by eating legumes (B vitamins and iron), whole grains (vitamin B_1, iron, and trace elements), and nuts and seeds (B vitamins and iron).
- Avoid vitamin B_{12} deficiency (a potential but uncommon deficiency) by taking vitamin B_{12} supplementation in tablet form or in fortified plant food such as vitamin B_{12}-fortified soybean milk or fermented soybean foods.
- Be aware that deficiencies in vitamins D and B_2 (riboflavin) and in zinc are uncommon despite the low dietary intakes provided by vegetarian diets.
- Remember that pregnancy and growth increase the dietary requirements of protein and certain vitamins and minerals, which may require supplementation.

The benefits of vegetarianism include lower risks of obesity, high blood pressure, diabetes, colon and breast cancer, and coronary atherosclerosis (Fraser et al., 1987), all of which are linked to high dietary intakes of saturated fats (see Table 15.9). In addition, replacing foods of animal source with high-carbohydrate foods will maximize the athlete's ability to replenish carbohydrate stores during heavy training (Nieman, 1988).

16

Special Concerns for Women

"One girl has been credited with the ability to run over the Marathon course of 26 1/4 miles in 3 hrs. 40 mins. 50 secs., a feat which I am disposed to doubt."

Sir Adolphe Abrahams (1930)

"Psychologically, men are more explosive, inconsistent, not enduring, and in pain and exertion—especially among high performance athletes—somewhat snivelling. A woman is the opposite: tough, constant, enduring, level and calm under the pain to which her biology exposes her (during childbirth). On the average she is more patient than a man. Armed with these advantages, women are in a position to do endurance feats previously considered by men to be impossible."

Ernst van Aaken (Carroll, 1981)

"Men and women are not now and may never be physiologically equal."

Christine Wells and Sharon Plowman (1983)

"As long as women are women, I don't think they will surpass men."

Grete Waitz (Waitz & Averbuch, 1986).

Looking back from the security of the 1990s, it is difficult to comprehend the restrictions that women athletes have had to overcome in their quest for athletic equality. New York nursing sister Nina Kuscsik, one of the first women officially to complete a marathon, reviewed the history of women's participation in long-distance running at the 1976 New York Academy of Sciences Conference on the Marathon (Kuscsik, 1977).

Kuscsik suggests that the first female marathoner may have been Melpomene, who allegedly completed the first Olympic Games Marathon in 1896 in about 4-1/2 hours "accompanied by a bicycle escort" (p. 863). Not unexpectedly, her entry had apparently been refused by the Olympic Committee, an action that would have been in accord with the beliefs of Baron Pierre de Coubertin, founder of the Modern Olympic Games. In 1928 de Coubertin stated, "As to the admission of women to the Games, I remain strongly against it. It was against my will that they were admitted to a growing number of competitions" (Kuscsik, 1977, p. 864).

Melpomene was clearly way ahead of her time; in Britain, women runners were ridiculed and labeled "brazen doxies" (p. 863).

In 1921 an international governing body for women's athletics, the Feminine Sportive Federation Internationale (FSFI), was formed. The FSFI successfully lobbied for the introduction of five athletic events for women at the 1928 Olympic Games, including the 800 m as the longest race. Unfortunately, some competitors in the 800-m final collapsed, thereby providing the Olympic Committee with sufficient ammunition to have the event removed from future Games—a move that Kuscsik believes put women's distance running back 50 years.

The idea that women should not tax themselves in competition was supported by physical educators in the United States at that time. The general belief was that women

> are not physically fit for the excitement and strain that this competition affords [and should] play for enjoyment, not to specialize and win. . . . The aim of athletics among women has been the establishment and maintenance of a high standard of health and vigor, rather than some brilliant achievement. (Kuscsik, 1977, p. 865)

The reintroduction of the 800-m event at the 1960 Olympic Games rekindled female interest in long-distance running; the following decade was characterized by the increasingly assertive actions of individuals wishing to participate in long-distance competitions, including marathon races. At that time, the body governing athletics in the United States, the Amateur Athletics Union (AAU), did not allow women to race more than 800 m. In response to growing pressure, this limit was increased tenfold to 5 miles by 1968. But for some, this concession was too little.

In 1963, Californian Merry Lepper completed the Western Hemisphere Marathon in Culver City, California, in 3:37:05 despite having to punch an irate official who tried to remove her from the race.

In 1966 Roberta Gibb Bingay completed the Boston Marathon unofficially in 3:21:00. Will Cloney, the race organizer, insisted that Bingay had not run in *the* Boston Marathon; "she merely covered the same route as the official race while it was in progress" (Kuscsik, 1977, p. 867).

The following year Bingay again completed the race (in 3:27:00), but the attention that year was focused on Kathrine Switzer. Switzer entered the race officially by not disclosing her first name; she started the race in disguise, with a hood covering her head. When it became apparent that a woman was running with the men, race organizers Will Cloney and Jock Semple tried to intercede physically. But a body block administered on Semple by Switzer's football-playing boyfriend dissuaded his further efforts. Switzer finished in 4:30:00; within days her membership in the AAU was terminated on the grounds that (1) she had exceeded the allowable distance for women; (2) she had run with men; (3) she had fraudulently entered an AAU race; and (4) she had run without a chaperone!

But the male bastion was crumbling, and women were finding it easier to run marathons; in addition, their times were improving rapidly. In the New York City Marathon run on September 19, 1971, Beth Bonner and Nina Kuscsik became the first women to break the 3-hour barrier. As a result, the AAU increased the legal limit for women to 10 miles and agreed that "selected" women would in the future be allowed to run marathons. In 1972, women were allowed to enter the Boston Marathon officially for the first time; yet their fight was not over.

The New York City Marathon of that year was allowed to include women only if the women raced in a separate race by starting 10 minutes before the men. But the women competitors had a different idea; when the gun starting their race went off, they sat down and waited the 10 minutes for the men's race to begin.

Faced by this open rebellion and a pending human rights lawsuit for practicing discrimination in a public place (Kuscsik, 1977), the AAU finally capitulated. In 1972, the legal running limit for women was raised to 26 miles, and the AAU declared that men and women could compete in the same races and start from the same starting line at the same time.

Admission of women to ultradistance races followed shortly thereafter. In 1975, women were allowed to compete officially in the Comrades Marathon for the first time. Prior to that time, a handful of women had run the race unofficially, but the numbers were small and their performances were unremarkable.

Recently, the progress of women's distance running has been relentless. The late '70s and early '80s were characterized by the performances of Grete Waitz who, on the global stage provided by the New York City and London marathons, personally lowered the world female marathon record by more than 7 minutes between 1979 and 1983 and proved that the best women distance runners could outrun all but the very best men.

In 1984 another milestone was passed when the women's marathon was finally included in the Olympic Games. American Joan Benoit overcame potentially crippling injury, knee surgery, and illness to win a dramatic race after leading for more than three-fourths of the race.

Norwegian Ingrid Kristiansen, fourth in the inaugural Olympic Marathon, lowered the women's world marathon record to 2:21:06 in 1985; set world records at 5,000 m, 10,000 m, and 15 km; and followed Grete Waitz to become, with Portugal's Rosa Mota, the dominant female marathon runner of the mid-to-late 1980s.

But when historians of the future choose those singular achievements that finally proved women's rightful place with men in the toughest endurance events, they may well include the performances of Paula Newby-Fraser in the 1988 and 1989 Hawaiian Ironman Triathlon and Frith van der Merwe in the 1989 Comrades Marathon.

The Hawaiian Ironman Triathlon, comprising a 2.4-mile sea swim, a 111-mile cycle ride, and a 26-mile run, is considered by many to be the toughest single-day sporting event in the world. Before 1988, the narrowest margin between the winning male and female competitors had been 1:01:12. But in 1988, Paula Newby-Fraser, a Zimbabwean who now lives in San Diego, California, completed the 139-mile course in 11th position overall, in a time of 9:01:01, just 30:01 or 6% slower than that of the male winner; her time in the final 26-mile run (3:07:09) was only 4:27 (2.4%) slower than that of the male winner. In 1989, Newby-Fraser improved her course record to 9:00:56.

Despite having raced excessively in the preceding months, South African Frith van der Merwe finished the 1989 Comrades Marathon in 15th position overall in a field of 11,000 in a time of 5:54:43, a time good enough to have won all the Comrades Marathons prior to 1963 and a time only 2 minutes slower than the best time of the legendary Wally Hayward (chapter 8). When corrected for the expected 10% difference in performance between men and women (chapter 11), her time is the fastest ever run in the race.

The performances of Newby-Fraser and van der Merwe raise the possibility that men and women are indeed not equal and that relative to their respective performances in shorter distance races, women perform better than do men in very prolonged exercise. This is in line with the anthropological evidence that in traditional societies the women performed the chores requiring endurance.

WILL WOMEN EVER RUN AS FAST AS MEN?

Despite the exceptional distance running performances of female athletes like Grete Waitz, Frith van der Merwe, and Eleanor Adams, women's performances remain considerably behind those of the elite men. This raises the question of why there are such differences in running performances between most men and women at all distances.

Chapter 11 referred to the work of Professor Archibald Hill, and Figure 11.1 showed his graph, drawn in 1925, of the differences in running performances between men and women. In Figure 16.1, I have used the same approach as Hill but have plotted the male and female world records current to the end of 1983. A major difference between these new data and those of Hill is that by 1983, women had established world records up to distances of 217 km, a very real change from 1925, when the longest race for which a female record was kept was only 1 km.

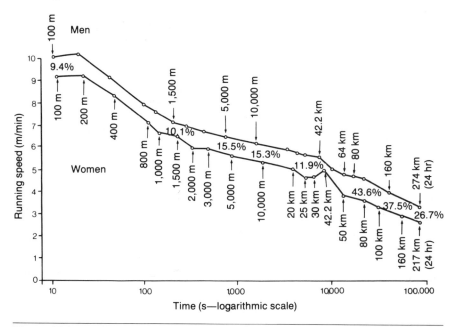

Figure 16.1 World-record performance in males and females at distances from 100 m to 217 km, current to 1983.

Three interesting points arise from the graph. First, the women's performances in 1983 compare quite closely with those of the men of 1925 (compare Figures 11.1 and 16.1).

For example, those who watched the film *Chariots of Fire* will be interested to learn that women today run the 100 and 400 m as fast if not faster than did Harold Abrahams (10.49 vs. Abrahams's 10.6 seconds) and Eric Liddell (47.6 vs. Liddell's 47.6 seconds) in the 1924 Paris Olympic Games.

Second, the women's performances are all at least 9.4% slower than those of the men. This difference, in 1983, was smallest at 100 m (9.4%) and increased to 15.3% at 10 km before suddenly shrinking again to 11.9% at the standard marathon distance. In longer distances, the performance differences between men and women increased further to 44% at 80 km and 27% at 24 hours. Thus, the performance difference between men and women is about 3 times greater for the 24-hour race than it is for the 100 m.

Third, and this is not directly relevant to the comparison between men and women, neither the men's nor the women's performance curve in Figure 16.1 shows the same dramatic fall in performance in races longer than 80 km as the men's performances in 1925 (Figure 11.1, Line A). This can be explained quite simply. As Hill suggested, the best runners of the early 1900s, such as Alf Shrubb and Paavo Nurmi, did not compete in or specifically train for races longer than 16 to 42 km, leaving those races to the poorer runners. But since Arthur Newton's day, progressively faster and more talented runners like Don Ritchie, Bruce Fordyce, and Yiannis Kouros (see chapter 8) have become interested in the marathon and ultramarathon and have improved human performance in those races dramatically.

The same argument can be used to explain the rather poorer performances of women in races longer than 42 km. It seems that for women the glamour event is the standard marathon, and this distance attracts the best athletes. As was the case with the men in 1925, the ultramarathons have not yet attracted the elite female marathon runners (Frith van der Merwe is an exception). For example, the best standard marathon time of Eleanor Adams is more than 25 minutes slower than the world marathon record. Thus, female records in the long ultra-marathon races will continue to be inferior to those of the men until the fastest female marathon runners are attracted to those distances. Indeed the remarkable performances of Frith van der Merwe show what will result when this occurs.

Similarly, the explanation for the relatively poor performances by women in the 5,000 m and 10,000 m is almost certainly that these two events have only recently become popular with women runners. We can expect major improvements in both these records in the near future, as Zola Budd and Ingrid Kristensen demonstrated with their successive large improvements on the world 5,000- and 10,000-m records.

In the next decade or two we can expect women's performances in ultramarathon events to improve remarkably and to approach this apparently uniform 9 to 11% performance difference between men and women. In fact, the performance of Frith van der Merwe in the 1989 Comrades Marathon was exactly 9.9% slower than the best-ever performance of a male in that race.

What these records do not explain are the biological factors responsible for these differences. The interesting scientific question that they do raise is this: Why is the magnitude of the performance difference between men and women really quite similar in both the sprints and in the endurance events (11%)? Is it possible that the same biological factors that cause women to run slower in the sprints also explain why women are slower by a similar margin in the endurance events like the standard marathon? Clearly this contradicts the classic teaching that holds that speed and endurance are determined by different factors. Or does it confirm Arthur Lydiard's belief (Lydiard & Gilmour, 1978) and Gordon Pirie's (1961) observation that potential is determined by 100-m speed?

Although the answers to these questions may never be solved, there are some possible reasons for these differences, which we will now consider.

Body Composition, Maximum Whole-Body Oxygen Consumption ($\dot{V}O_2$Max), and Running Efficiency

The main difference in body composition between men and women is that the average man is considerably heavier and taller than the average woman, and even when men and women are the same height, men are heavier than women. These height differences are the result of the female hormone estrogen, which causes young girls to stop growing approximately 2 years before boys (Wells & Plowman, 1983).

Furthermore, women have twice as much body fat as do equally active men. For example, the percentages of body fat for average men and women are 14% and 24%, respectively (Wells & Plowman, 1983); values for elite male and female runners are 3 to 5% and 8 to 10%, respectively. The implications of these differences in percent body fat are shown in Table 16.1, which demonstrates that at the same body weight as a man, an elite female athlete will have 2.6 kg more fat and therefore 2.5 kg less lean body mass (muscle, bone, skin, and internal organs) than the man. If this 2.6-kg difference is purely due to differences in muscle mass, the 52-kg athletic female will have only 15.4 kg muscle compared to the expected 18-kg of muscle in a 52-kg man, a difference of 14%.

Let us now make two further assumptions. Let us first assume that our male athlete has a $\dot{V}O_2$max of 75 ml/kg/min. If he weighs 52 kg, he will have an

Table 16.1 Comparison of Body Composition of Elite Male and Female Distance Runners of the Same Body Mass

Characteristic	Male	Female
Body mass (kg)	52.0	52.0
% body fat (%)	5.0	10.0
Mass of body fat (kg)	2.6	5.2
Lean body mass (kg)	49.4	46.8
Muscle mass (kg)	18.0	15.4
Peak O_2 uptake per kg muscle mass (L/kg/min)	0.22	0.22
$\dot{V}O_2$max (L/min)	3.9	3.3
$\dot{V}O_2$max (L/kg/min)	75.0	64.0

absolute $\dot{V}O_2$max of 75 ml/kg/min × 52 kg, which equals 3.9 L/min. From this we can calculate that the peak rate of oxygen uptake per kilogram of skeletal muscle in the male is 3.9 L/min/18 kg, which equals 0.22 L/kg/min.

If we next assume that the muscle tissues of men and women have equal abilities to consume oxygen, as seems likely (Washburn & Seals, 1984), then the $\dot{V}O_2$max of our 52 kg female will be 15.4 kg × 0.22 L/min, which equals 3.39 L/min or 64 ml/kg/min.

The implications of this small difference of 2.6 kg body fat carried by the elite female athlete now become obvious. When competing against a male athlete of the same body weight, she will have less muscle and a lower $\dot{V}O_2$max to transport the same absolute body weight.

The first researchers to undertake a scientific study to determine the effects of this excess body fat on the performance difference between men and women were Kirk Cureton and Phillip Sparling (1980) of the University of Georgia at Athens. By adding weight belts to a group of male runners, the researchers artificially increased the masses of the males until the added masses they carried exactly equaled the extra masses of fat carried by a group of female runners, whose body fat contents were 7.5% greater than those of the males. The running performances of these males with and without the added mass were then compared with the performances of the females. Figure 16.2 details some of the differences found by these authors.

These authors found that the distances the men could run in 12 minutes (the 12-minute run test) or the times they could run on the treadmill during a maximum treadmill test (maximum treadmill run time) without added weights were 20% and 34% greater than females; these values were 14% to 23% greater after the men's respective "fat" masses had been equalized. The added weights therefore reduced the male-female difference in running performance by only 30%. Interestingly, the added weights obliterated the 11% difference in $\dot{V}O_2$max but reduced the subjects' 20% difference in running economy to 16%, only a 20% reduction.

The conclusion that I draw from this study, which is somewhat at variance with that of the authors, is that the difference in the running performances between the males and females in this study were due more to inherent differences in muscle power (see chapter 2) and running economy, which were influenced little by the females' extra body fat. Thus, when the males' and females' extra weights had been equalized and their $\dot{V}O_2$max values were the same, the men were still able to run faster and longer because they reached the same $\dot{V}O_2$max values at much higher running speeds (see Figure 16.2). This suggests that even in men and women who have the same $\dot{V}O_2$max values, the men's muscles are superior.

Nevertheless, we cannot dispute Cureton and Sparling's (1980) conclusion that varying amounts of body fat were an important factor explaining as much as 30% of the difference in running performances in this group of men and women; the remaining 70% was likely due to differences in muscle power.

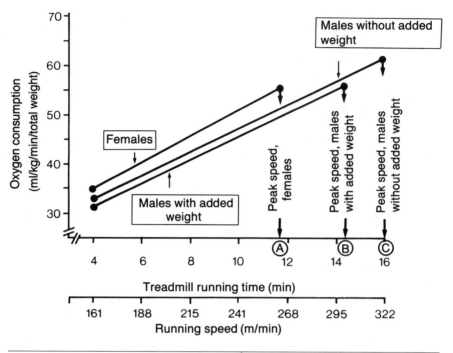

Figure 16.2 Effects of adding weight on the $\dot{V}O_2$max values, running economies, and treadmill running times of males. Comparison to females of equivalent body fat content. *Note.* From K.J. Cureton and P.B. Sparling, "Distance Running Performance and Metabolic Responses to Running in Men and Women With Excess Weight Experimentally Equated," *Medicine and Science in Sports and Exercise,* **12**, p. 291, 1980, © by the American College of Sports Medicine. Adapted by permission.

Another study by Cureton and his colleagues (1986) added further substance to this argument. The authors equilibrated blood hemoglobin levels in a group of matched males and females by withdrawing blood from the males.

This procedure reduced the differences in $\dot{V}O_2$max between males and females from 32 to 24%. More importantly, the difference in maximal running performances between males and females was even less influenced, being reduced from 40% to 32%.

Clearly the intergender difference in blood hemoglobin content is only a minor determinant of different running abilities.

Pate and his colleagues (Pate et al., 1987) reported the most comprehensive study of elite American female middle-distance and marathon runners. The mean $\dot{V}O_2$max values of the best runners were 67 ml/kg/min, equivalent to those of the better American distance runners of the early 1970s whose best performances were also quite similar. Their running economies were similar to those reported in previous studies (J. Daniels et al., 1977).

Percentage $\dot{V}O_2$Max Sustainable During Races

One explanation for the male's superior running ability might be that he can sustain a higher percentage $\dot{V}O_2$max during competition.

However, a number of studies have shown that this is clearly not the case (Conley et al., 1981a; C.T.M. Davies & Thompson, 1979; Wells et al., 1981). At all distances from 5 to 85 km, women can run at equivalent percentage $\dot{V}O_2$max values to the best male runners.

Blood Lactate Turnpoint During Progressive Exercise

The concept of the blood lactate "turnpoint" was discussed in chapter 3, which showed that this parameter is a strong predictor of marathon running performance (see Figure 3.13).

Remarkably, no study has yet reported the lactate "turnpoints" of elite female athletes. However, I suspect that their lactate turnpoints will be the same as those of males of equivalent running abilities.

Capacity for Fat Metabolism

Dr. Joan Ullyot, author of a collection of books on women's running and herself an excellent marathoner, was one of the first to popularize the idea that a woman's relatively greater fatness was an advantage rather than a disadvantage during marathon running (Ullyot, 1976). This idea arose when, in conversation with Dr. Ernst van Aaken, Ullyot mentioned how fresh many elite women runners looked at the finish of the marathon and ultramarathon races. Van Aaken theorized that this must be due to the women's superior capacities to metabolize their more abundant fat stores near the end of marathon and ultramarathon races, when glycogen stores are depleted. "It's simple," van Aaken concluded, "they are running off their fat" (Ullyot, 1976, p. 86).

Next Ullyot spoke to a group of elite female marathoners and asked whether they ever "hit the wall" during marathon races. No, they informed her; the wall was purely a phenomenon that struck the weaker sex.

With these two pieces of information, Ullyot proposed that females will ultimately outperform males, particularly in the longer distance races in which the females' (proposed) greater capacities for fat metabolism will allow them to outperform males when both are equally glycogen depleted. Unfortunately, this attractive theory has not survived the harsh scientific scrutiny of possibly chauvinistic exercise physiologists.

In 1979, David Costill and his colleagues (Costill et al., 1979) showed that men and women, equally trained and with equivalent $\dot{V}O_2$max values, burned equal amounts of fat (45%) during a 60-minute treadmill run. There were also no differences in blood free-fatty-acid or glycerol levels during the run. If the women had greater fat-burning capacities, one would expect their blood free-fatty-acid and glycerol levels to have been higher during the treadmill run.

Not content that they had excluded all possibilities, Costill and his colleagues next took muscle biopsies from all the runners and measured the abilities of these isolated muscle samples to metabolize fat when studied in the test tube (in vitro). The tests showed that this capacity, far from being greater in the women, was actually less, possibly because the women's muscles may have fewer mitochondria.

But other observations indicate that van Aaken's hypothesis is fatally flawed. The evidence in Figure 16.1 clearly shows that relative to men, women perform progressively worse, not better, as the running distance increases.

Liver and Muscle Glycogen Storage Capacity

Differences in endurance between men and women might be explained on the basis of differences in glycogen storage capacity in either muscle, liver, or both. At present, no studies have compared liver glycogen levels in men and women, but muscle glycogen levels and rates of resynthesis after exercise are similar between the genders (Kuipers et al., 1989b).

Muscle Fiber Composition

There are no significant differences in the percentages of slow and fast twitch fibers in the muscles of comparable groups of athletic men and women (Costill et al., 1987; Wells & Plowman, 1983). However, men have larger slow twitch and fast twitch fibers than do women, with the greatest difference being in the size of the fast twitch fibers.

Do these differences in muscle fiber size mean anything? The average man is 30 to 40% stronger than the average female. But this difference is not consistent across all muscle groups, and the intergender differences are greater in the arms than in the legs, possibly because women are less likely than men to lift heavy weights with their arms. In contrast, the intergender difference in leg strength is less, possibly because women use their legs as frequently as do men.

Furthermore, as in the case of $\dot{V}O_2$max, when strength is expressed relative to (fat-free) lean body mass, the intergender differences become less. It seems likely that if strength were ever expressed relative to the muscle cross-sectional area (muscle width), the intergender difference would disappear entirely. Were this the case, it would suggest that the actual muscle tissues of males and females were of the same quality but that men were stronger only because they have more muscle tissue. This question has still to be resolved.

Differences in Heat Tolerance During Exercise

There is no difference between men and women in heat tolerance during exercise. If anything, women may be better able to tolerate exercise in hot, humid conditions because of their large ratios of body surface area to body weight (Haymes, 1984). Women also have a greater skin sweat gland density, but the capacity for sweat production by each gland is somewhat less than in men (Buono & Sjoholm, 1988).

Summary

Having considered the evidence, my feelings are the following.

Women are at a disadvantage because, on average, they are fatter with less total muscle mass than men of equal body mass. Thus, at the same body mass as a man, a woman will have less muscle and therefore a lower $\dot{V}O_2max$ to transport the same body weight. This is a disadvantage particularly in running, in which the body weight must be carried.

The differences in performance between men and women in explosive events such as sprinting or power lifting may be due to the smaller muscle mass of women, or alternatively the muscle tissue per se may be inferior in women. In other words, female muscle may be less able to produce speed or force during contraction than is male muscle.

I suspect that if we were able to compare muscle tissue of the very best male and female athletes in somewhat more detail than is presently possible, we would find that female muscle is simply less good than is male muscle. I say this because there are too many small men, like Sebastian Coe, who can outrun the very best women who are of the same size or even larger and who probably have just as much muscle as do these small men. Furthermore, if muscle mass were the sole factor determining running performance, then all fast runners would be large. Clearly, this is not the case.

Finally, the finding that the female world records, from the sprints to the marathons, are consistently 9 to 11% slower than those of men suggests that the speed and endurance of most women's muscles are less good by about that percentage. I postulate that the biochemical explanation for this can be found not in any differences in the percentage distribution of ST and FT fibers in the muscles of men and women but in differences in muscle myosin ATPase activity, intracellular calcium transport, or both. However, the performances of Newly-Fraser and van der Merwe point to the possibility that the muscles of some women may have greater endurance and superior resistance to fatigue than the muscles of even the best male athletes.

UNIQUE CONSIDERATIONS FOR WOMEN ATHLETES

Professor Christine Wells of the Sport Research Institute of Arizona State University wrote a most complete book for women athletes (Wells, 1991). The reader who requires additional information would be well advised to refer to that book.

The Choice of an Appropriate Sports Bra

Most authorities advise active women to wear specially designed sports bras to minimize breast injury and soreness during strenuous activity. Yet there are few scientific studies of which sports bras are best for use during exercise.

Lorentzen and Lawson (1987) compared the abilities of eight different sports bras to control breast motion during running. Not unexpectedly, they showed that large-breasted women require more rigidly constructed bras than do small-breasted women. The authors suggested that the runner should wear a bra with firm, nonslip, nonstretch straps connected directly or almost directly to nonelastic cups; that the bra should be of firm, durable construction and should have no irritating seams or fasteners next to the skin; and that the silhouette should hold the breasts in a rounded shape close to the body. The bras that best fulfilled these requirements were the Exercise Sports Top (Creative Sports Systems, Irvine, CA), the Lady Duke (Royal Textile Mills, Yancyeville, NC) and the Freedom Frontrunner (Olga, Van Nuys, CA).

Additional criteria proposed by Wells (1991) are that the material used should be absorptive, nonallergic, and nonabrasive; the straps should be wide, nonelastic, and designed so that they do not slip off the shoulders during movement; and the base of the bra should be made of a wide cloth band or similar material to prevent ''riding up'' of the bra over the breasts during running.

Cancer

The risks of benign and malignant cancers of the breast, ovary, uterus, cervix, and vagina; malignant cancers of the digestive system, thyroid, bladder, lung, and other sites; and cancers of the blood-forming tissues (lymphoma, leukemia, myeloma, and Hodgkin's disease) were found to be lower in former college athletes than in nonathletes (Frisch et al., 1985, 1989; Wyshak et al., 1986). The incidence of cancers of the skin including melanomas was not different between the former athletes and nonathletes (Frisch et al., 1989).

The authors concluded that the regular physical activity of the former college athletes reduced their risks of developing these cancers. The risk of osteoporotic fractures developing in later life was not different between former athletes and nonathletes (Wyshak et al., 1987).

These conclusions should be seen as tentative. The lifelong physical activity patterns of these women were not determined; thus, there is no proof that the former athletes were more physically active after leaving college than their peers, although this is likely. The possibility that hereditary factors explained this difference is unlikely, because the family histories of cancer in the athletic and nonathletic groups were the same. The incidence of diabetes was also lower in the group of former college athletes (Frisch et al., 1986).

One avoidable risk factor for breast cancer is alcohol. Two recent studies show that even very moderate amounts of alcohol (two drinks per week) are associated with an increased risk of breast cancer in women (Schatzkin et al., 1987b; Willett et al., 1987).

Premenstrual Symptoms and Endometriosis

Moderate exercise training significantly decreases the severity of premenstrual symptoms (Prior et al., 1986) and reduces the risk for developing endometriosis (Cramer et al., 1986). It is likely that the effects are due to the exercise.

The Effects of Exercise on Menstruation

Three special questions concerning menstruation and exercise require attention.

1. Can strenuous exercise at a young age affect the age of onset of menstruation (menarche), which normally occurs at about 13 years of age?
2. Can strenuous exercise training undertaken after the menarche cause a subsequent cessation of menstruation (secondary amenorrhea), and if so, are any long-term dangers associated with prolonged secondary amenorrhea?
3. Does menstruation influence competitive performance, and if so, can menstruation be controlled before competition? A related question is whether vigorous exercise can influence female fertility independent of any changes exercise might cause in menstrual patterns.

Menarche

Menarche occurs at older ages in athletes than in nonathletes, and menarche is latest in those who compete at the highest levels of their sports. The delay in menarche is about 5 months for each year of training before the menarche. In general, swimmers tend to be the least affected, whereas gymnasts, figure skaters, and ballet dancers have the latest menarches (Malina, 1983). Possible explanations for this follow.

Doctors Rose Frisch and Janet McArthur (1974) postulated that a certain percentage of body fat must be present before menstruation can begin. Hence, poor nutrition may delay menarche.

There is no evidence that athletic girls come from different (lower) social classes than do nonathletes or that they come from larger families. Both these variables are associated with a delayed menarche (Malina, 1983).

The next possibility is that late-maturing girls with late menarches are more likely to succeed in sport. The chief proponent of this hypothesis is Dr. Bob Malina (1983) of the University of Texas at Austin.

The first part of this thesis holds that the physique of the late-maturing girl is different from that of the early maturer and is better suited for athletic success. Late maturers characteristically have long legs for their statures, narrow hips, and generally linear physiques; they have less weight for height and less body fat; and they tend to perform well in motor tasks such as dashes, jumps, and throws. Zola Budd (see Figure 16.3) is an excellent example of the physique of the late maturer.

Early maturers have relatively broad hips, short legs, and excessive fatness, all of which are detrimental to performance, particularly in events in which the body must be projected.

Figure 16.3 Zola Budd.
Note. From The Bettmann Archive.

Malina quotes evidence to show that at least in boys, heavy training does not influence the rate of physical maturation. In other words, training in boys cannot override or indeed influence the normal maturation processes, which are under hormonal control. If the normal maturation processes in girls are also under hormonal control, this suggests that Malina is indeed correct and that exercise selects rather than produces late maturers.

The second part of the Malina hypothesis is that early maturers move away from sport, whereas late maturers are selected toward sport. He points out that early maturers are at a social disadvantage because they are out of phase with the emotional and physiological development of girls their age and particularly boys their age, who in any case mature 2 years later than do girls. The result is that these girls will tend to be socialized away from sport and into activities that, until recently, society has considered to conform more closely with femininity.

Clearly, if the social standing of girls is determined by their abilities to attract the attention of older boys rather than by their athletic achievements, then they will naturally choose to capitalize on their strengths. Incidentally, the only sport for which this argument probably does not apply is swimming, in which early maturers may be at an advantage due to their greater sizes and levels of absolute strength.

In contrast, the late maturer is likely to be socialized into sport because that is where her advantage lies, and her late maturation will keep her less interested in her "feminine" role. Furthermore, her greater success in competitive sport is likely to motivate her to maintain an active interest in sport. As a result, the late maturers comprise the athletic populations of the teens and early 20s.

A third possibility explaining the superior athletic abilities of late maturers may be some factor other than body build. For example, late maturers may have higher $\dot{V}O_2$max values, greater glycogen storage capacities, or more powerful muscle fibers with higher myosin ATPase activity than do early maturers; any or all of these factors might explain the late maturers' superior performances. To date, we have no scientific information to support or dispute this point.

Finally, serious training before menarche could indeed delay it, possibly by slowing accumulation of body fat either by a direct effect of exercise on body mass or through attempts by the athlete to maintain a low body weight by dieting. This could explain why the age at menarche of swimmers is the least affected. Swimmers can afford to be less concerned about diet than are runners, because the swimmer's body weight is supported by the water rather than by the legs. Conversely, ballet dancers particularly (Druss & Silverman, 1979) but also gymnasts, who diet rigorously in order to maintain their sylphlike appearances, would be especially prone to delayed menarche.

There is now growing evidence (Stager et al., 1984b) that competitive sports select the late maturers, whose potentials in most sports are superior to those of early maturers; evidence also shows that menarche is relatively unaffected by vigorous exercise in adolescence. Rigorous dieting with a consequent slowing of the rate of body fat accumulation could further delay menarche in late maturers who participate in activities that traditionally demand slimness for aesthetic appeal.

Menstrual Irregularity

The incidence of menstrual irregularity is higher in most groups of athletes, in particular long-distance runners and ballet dancers, than in nonathletes (Noakes & van Gend, 1988). The question that arises is whether exercise causes this higher incidence of menstrual irregularity or whether females who are prone to menstrual irregularity are more likely to be attracted to vigorous exercise or ballet dancing. Before we consider these two possibilities, let us define what is meant by menstrual irregularity, which can be categorized as follows:

A. Long-term menstrual irregularity

amenorrhea—The absence of any previous menstrual cycles, or menstrual cycles lasting longer than 90 days in a female who has previously menstruated

oligomenorrhea—Menstrual cycles lasting between 35 and 90 days

short luteal phase—Menstrual cycles lasting less than 23 days

B. Short-term menstrual irregularity

This comprises any short-term departure from the normal menstrual pattern experienced by the individual. This might take the form of an early or delayed onset of menstruation or an increased or reduced number of flow days.

At present, the following parameters have been related to menstrual irregularity in female athletes:

- Low percent body fat
- Late onset of menarche
- Heavy training load
- Young age
- Previous menstrual irregularity
- Low parity
- Poor nutrition

Percent Body Fat. Frisch and MacArthur (1974) proposed that a critical percent body fat (17%) is required before a young girl will start menstruating and that a slightly greater percentage (22%) is required for the maintenance of menstruation. With improved nutrition and increased body fat at an early age in North America, there has been a parallel decrease in the age at which menstruation begins, providing indirect support for this hypothesis. In subsequent studies on ballet dancers, Frisch and her colleagues (1980) reported a high incidence of amenorrhea among those dancers with percent body fat levels lower than 22%, thereby further supporting this theory.

Studies of female distance runners have found essentially the same relationship. Young women weighing less than 53 kg who lost more than 4.5 kg after they began running were more likely to develop menstrual irregularities (Speroff & Redwine, 1980).

Another study of 168 women who were classified as inactive controls, "joggers" (who ran 8 to 48 km/week), and "runners" (who ran more than 48 km/week) found that although members of each group had almost identical average heights, the subjects differed greatly with respect to percent body fat and body weight (Dale et al., 1979). The runners were approximately 6 kg below average body weight for height, and their higher incidence of menstrual irregularity correlated with their lower values of percent body fat. Numerous other studies have shown that amenorrheic runners are lighter than normally menstruating runners or controls (Carlberg et al., 1983; Schwartz et al., 1981; Shangold & Levine, 1982; Webb & Proctor, 1983). Amenorrheic runners also tend to be the better performers (Shangold, 1980; van Gend & Noakes, 1987; Webb & Proctor, 1983), and the possible reasons for this have been discussed.

However, the percent body fat theory is not the complete answer (Caldwell, 1982; Malina, 1983; Noakes & van Gend, 1988; Reeves, 1979). For example, some ballet dancers and swimmers who develop irregular menstrual cycles during training become more regular in the off-season even without significant changes in body weight (S.F. Abrahams et al., 1982; J.L. Cohen et al., 1982; Russell et al., 1984). Furthermore, some amenorrheic runners are of normal body weight, and other studies have found no difference in height, weight, or percent body fat between amenorrheic and menstrually regular runners or controls (Dale et al., 1979; Fishman, 1980; Malina et al., 1978; Sanborn et al., 1987; Wakat et al., 1982).

In summary, there is no conclusive evidence that percent body fat plays an exclusive role in determining menstrual patterns in athletes. Rather, percent body fat is likely to be a contributing factor that acts with other variables. One possibility is that loss of fat from specific depots may induce the amenorrhea. Brownell et al. (1987) suggested that depletion of the fat stores distributed below the waist in the hips, thighs, and buttock—the lactation fat stores—may be associated with menstrual dysfunction.

Alternatively, a low percent body fat may be associated with superior athletic potential and the desire to train sufficiently hard to become a top competitor. The stresses of heavy training and intense competition might then induce the menstrual irregularity.

Indeed, one study reported that amenorrheic runners associated more stress with their running than did normally menstruating runners (Schwartz et al., 1981), whereas another study found that amenorrheic runners tend to be more emotionally distressed than normally menstruating runners (Galle et al., 1983).

Another possibility is that the rapidity of weight loss may play a more important role than the amount lost per se, because evidence suggests that a rapid loss of 15% of body weight influences menstruation (McArthur, 1982; Wentz, 1980). Alternatively, the low percent body fat may indicate the presence of an eating disorder.

Age at Menarche. Generally, it has been found that the later the menarche, the higher the incidence of subsequent menstrual irregularity. For example, one study (Feicht et al., 1978) found that amenorrheic middle-distance runners had later ages of menarche than did menstrually regular middle-distance runners (14.1 vs. 13.3 years).

However, the likely explanation for the relationship between a late menarche and subsequent menstrual irregularity is probably that late-maturing girls, who (as we have discussed) are of a different body build than are early maturers, may be more prone to menstrual irregularity than are early maturers. This idea will be elaborated further.

Training Load (Distance Run Per Week). A number of studies show a direct relationship between the degree and frequency of menstrual irregularity and the training load, measured in runners as the distance run per week. One study (Feicht et al., 1978) found that 43% of athletes running more than 128 km/week had menstrual irregularities, and there was a linear relationship between the incidence of amenorrhea and the distance run per week. By comparison, the incidence of amenorrhea among college-age women was found to be only 6%.

However, an exact mileage threshold above which menstrual irregularity occurs has not been established. This implies that there is a wide variation in the individual tolerance to training loads (i.e., each runner possesses a different threshold level above which menstruation is affected).

The mechanism by which high mileage may induce menstrual irregularity is probably a combination of many factors including weight loss and stress-induced hypothalamic dysfunction. Again, training load cannot be considered a primary factor, because other studies have found that training load is unrelated to menstrual status in runners (McArthur, 1982; Schwartz et al., 1981; Shangold, 1980; Shangold & Levine, 1982; Speroff & Redwine, 1980; Wakat et al., 1982). Studies also show that swimmers and cyclists show no increases in the prevalence of amenorrhea with increasing training load (Sanborn et al., 1982), possibly because they maintain body weight and therefore presumably adequate nutritional status with increasing training load.

Age. Younger athletes appear to be more prone to menstrual irregularity. In two large surveys of 900 runners (Speroff & Redwine, 1980) and 550 runners (Lutter & Cushmann, 1982), proportionally more young women developed menstrual irregularities. However, most of these young women also had histories of menstrual irregularity before they even started running, which implies that the running was not the primary cause of the menstrual irregularity. Rather, young girls with menstrual irregularity may be particularly attracted to vigorous exercise like long-distance running.

Previous Menstrual Irregularity. In a survey of women completing the 1979 New York City Marathon, researchers found that the incidence of menstrual irregularity in the respondents was 19% even before they began training (Shangold & Levine, 1982). This is much higher than in the "normal" population (about 6%). The same higher-than-expected incidence of menstrual irregularity before initiation of exercise was found in ballet dancers (S.F. Abrahams et al., 1982) and in a study of competitors in the 1983 Two Oceans Marathon (van Gend & Noakes, 1987).

There can really be only one interpretation of these findings: Some factor that promotes menstrual irregularity may inspire women to take up running, just as women who have late menarche may also be selected toward running. This propensity for menstrual irregularity then continues unchanged while the athlete trains. For this reason, the best predictor of a female's menstrual status after she begins to run is her menstrual status before she begins running (van Gend & Noakes, 1987). If she had regular menstrual periods before she started running, she will likely remain regular after she begins running.

Parity (Number of Children Borne). The evidence suggests that women who have not borne children are more likely to develop running-related menstrual irregularities than are those who have borne children (Baker et al., 1981; Dale et al., 1979).

Nutrition. No published evidence shows that a single nutritional deficiency is uniquely related to menstrual dysfunction in exercising women. One interesting observation came from a study showing that amenorrheic runners ate one fifth the amount of meat eaten by normally menstruating runners (S.M. Brooks et al., 1984). The study found that 82% of amenorrheic runners ate less than 200 g/week of meat (poultry or red meat) and were classified as vegetarians, whereas only 13% of normally menstruating runners ate as little meat. The total animal protein intake was, however, not different between the groups, because the amenorrheic runners ate more dairy produce. Fat intake was lower in the amenorrheic runners, as also reported by Deuster et al. (1986). Thus, a low intake of either red meat or fat may be one factor in menstrual irregularity in athletes.

Another possibility not previously recognized is that there may be a higher than normal incidence of eating disorders among amenorrheic runners. A number of reports (N. Clark et al., 1988; Henry, 1982) found a high incidence of abnormal (anorectic-type) eating patterns in elite North American female runners, and this group of elite runners is particularly prone to menstrual irregularity.

More recently, Weight and Noakes (1987) confirmed that abnormal eating patterns are most prevalent among the most competitive runners. Rosen et al.

(1986) found that 47% of a group of female American collegiate runners practiced one or more pathogenic weight-control behaviors such as self-induced vomiting, binge eating more than twice weekly, or the use of laxatives, diet pills, or diuretics. The prevalence of these abnormal behaviors was even higher among gymnasts (74%). Swimmers, too, were found to use these practices to reduce or control their weights (Dummer et al., 1987). Other studies have noted the low energy intakes of amenorrheic female runners (N. Clark et al., 1988; Drinkwater et al., 1984; Kaiserauer et al., 1989; Marcus et al., 1985; M.E. Nelson et al., 1986; Schweiger et al., 1988; Zierath et al., 1986).

Finally, a relationship between abnormal eating patterns and menstrual dysfunction has been established (Brooks-Gunn et al., 1987a, 1987b; Rippon et al., 1988). In the study of Brooks-Gunn et al. (1987a), 50% of a group of amenorrheic ballet dancers also had past histories of anorexia nervosa; Hamilton et al. (1986) also reported a high incidence of eating disorders in ballet dancers.

Gadpaille et al. (1987) reported that 11 of 13 amenorrheic runners reported major psychiatric disorders, especially depression, in themselves or in first- or second-degree relatives; 62% also had eating disorders. All these findings were significantly different from experiences of normally menstruating runners.

Together, these findings suggest two possibilities (Rippon et al., 1988). One is that women who are prone to menstrual dysfunction are attracted to long-distance running. Socially induced pressures for thinness then induce abnormal eating attitudes and the adoption of the psychological characteristics found in women with anorexia nervosa.

The second possibility is that women who have the psychological characteristics of anorexia nervosa eat calorie-restricted diets from a young age and develop menstrual dysfunction as a result. They then choose professions like modeling, gymnastics, or ballet dancing, for which leanness is an attribute, or physically demanding activities like long-distance running, which will assist in maintaining their leanness. Their menstrual patterns will remain disturbed for as long as they continue to restrict their caloric intakes.

The evidence to date suggests that the menstrual dysfunction seen in women runners may well indicate a disturbed psyche, probably on a hereditary basis. The abnormal eating pattern displayed by such a runner may be a marker and not the primary cause of the abnormality.

Hypothalamic Dysfunction. The hypothalamus is a very specialized area at the base of the brain that is responsible for control of menstruation, among many other things. Current theories hold that the hypothalamus becomes dormant in runners with amenorrhea; thus, it fails to produce those hormones that are necessary to induce the cyclical uterine changes that lead to menstruation (see Figure 16.4).

This is analogous to the situation found in overtrained male runners who also show disturbed hypothalamic function (Barron et al., 1985). The question that remains is, What causes this hypothalamic dysfunction?

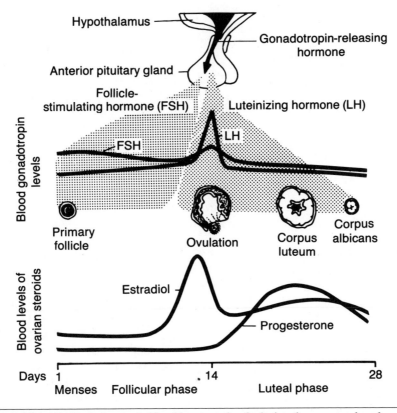

Figure 16.4 Cyclical changes in blood hormone levels during the menstrual cycle.
Note. From "Athletic Menstrual Cycle Irregularity: Endocrine Response to Exercise and Training" by A. Bonen and H.A. Keizer, 1984, *Physician and Sportsmedicine*, **12**(8), p. 79. Copyright 1984 by Jane Hurd.

The current theory is that two groups of brain chemicals, the endorphins and dopamine, are involved. As described in chapters 7 and 18, the endorphins are morphinelike substances that are believed to explain the runner's high. However, the endorphins also stimulate the release of dopamine, which inhibits hypothalamic release of the hormones necessary for inducing the menstrual cycle. Thus, it is suggested that runners with amenorrhea have chronically elevated brain levels of endorphin (Laatikainen et al., 1986) and dopamine, which may "switch off" the hypothalamus.

My feeling is that exercise is not sufficiently stressful to cause this. Rather, I believe that the hypothalamus quits only when several ingredients are present: severe dietary restriction, very strenuous exercise, intensive competition, and a "sensitive" hypothalamus (possibly due to hereditary factors).

Studies Conducted by Me and My Colleagues. In view of the discrepancies in the scientific literature, in 1983 another researcher and I studied the menstrual histories of 108 of the 118 entrants in the 1983 56-km Two Oceans Marathon (van Gend & Noakes, 1987). As a group, these women were in their mid-30s, had been running for about 3-1/2 years, and had, on average, run about six standard marathons and three ultramarathons. On average they trained 80 km/ week, although three trained 180 to 190 km/week. Of these runners, 75% felt that exercise reduced premenstrual tension and menstrual pain.

The first interesting finding was that 40% of these runners had experienced menstrual irregularities before they started running. This was considerably higher than the incidence in a matched-control group, and it confirms that women runners are not "normal," because they have a higher-than-expected incidence of short-term menstrual irregularity even before they start running. We are left to conclude that ultramarathon running attracts women who are prone to menstrual irregularity.

The second finding was that only 9% of the runners had long-term menstrual irregularities, either oligomenorrhea or amenorrhea, and this figure was not different than that of a matched-control group. Furthermore, the overall incidence of long-term menstrual irregularity in the total group of runners was not different from what it had been before they started running. Thus, although the long-term menstrual patterns of some runners did change quite remarkably, equal numbers became either more or less regular once they took up running. Precisely the same finding was made in the study of the New York City Marathon runners (Shangold & Levine, 1982), and together these findings show that running is as likely to produce a normalization as a deterioration in menstrual function.

Glass et al. (1987) also showed that the incidence of menstrual dysfunction in the women competing in the United States Olympic Marathon trial was less than expected and was not greater than that found in less competitive runners reported in other studies. The authors concluded that training load could not be a major factor leading to menstrual dysfunction.

It is of interest to study the variables that were associated with long-term menstrual irregularity in the study of van Gend and Noakes (1987). Typically, the woman with long-term menstrual irregularity was young, had a low body weight, had started running at a young age, and had experienced menstrual irregularity before she started running. She was also a heavy trainer and usually a better-than-average performer. But heavy training and competition did not further influence menstrual status in these athletes. In other words, these women were likely to continue having menstrual irregularities even when they were not competing intensively and training hard.

In contrast to the findings concerning long-term menstrual patterns, van Gend and Noakes (1987) found that 41% of runners reported that they had experienced periods of short-term menstrual irregularity since they started running. These menstrual aberrations appeared to be stress induced, because they typically occurred during periods of heavy training and intensive competition with associated weight loss and rapidly reverted to normal once the athlete had run the race for which she had been training. Unlike long-term irregularity, short-term irregularity bore no relationship to the athlete's weight, the age when she started running, or the distance run in training, showing that short-term and long-term menstrual irregularities are two different conditions affecting different types of athletes.

Thus, the results of our study (van Gend and Noakes, 1987), combined with information reviewed, suggest that running is associated with two different types of menstrual irregularities. The first is a short-term irregularity to which all women runners are prone especially during periods of heavy training, intensive competition, and associated weight loss. The second type is a long-term irregularity that affects a very specific group of runners who may be predisposed because they have particular personality types or body builds and are attracted to lifestyles that include regular vigorous exercise. Thus, the athlete with long-term menstrual irregularity is likely to be a young female who has not had children, who had a late menarche, and who experienced previous menstrual irregularity before she began running. She is likely to be a vegetarian of low body weight, and she may be on a calorie-restricted diet. There may be a past history of anorexia nervosa. She is likely to train heavily and to be a better-than-average performer. Such a woman typically selects a stressful lifestyle, and this sustained level of stress, to which the running in part contributes, may be responsible for the irregular menstrual patterns even before the running commences or after the running is discontinued. All these stresses act to suppress the hypothalamus, which then fails to release the hormones necessary for cyclical menstruation.

Practical Implications. The practical implications of this information are fourfold. First, the athlete who develops short-term menstrual irregularity during periods of heavy training and competition can be reassured that the added stress of competition is the cause and that normal menstruation will resume once the competition is past. In a study of 70 North American distance runners, 83% of whom had some (short-term) menstrual irregularities, it was found that normal menstrual patterns returned within an average of 1.7 months after discontinuation of the exercise, and none of the subjects required more than 6 months to become regular (Stager et al., 1984a).

Second, those runners who are prone to menstrual irregularities will probably be able to recognize themselves from the description I have given. Their normal menstrual patterns are likely to return only if they are able to increase their food intakes and to reduce all the stresses in their lives. For vegetarians, increased meat intakes might assist in the return of menstruation.

Third, runners who develop menstrual irregularities under circumstances that do not fit either of these two descriptions should consult their doctors to ensure that medical conditions unrelated to running (e.g., pregnancy) are not the cause of amenorrhea.

Finally, the vast majority of women, because they do not fit the picture of the highly competitive, heavily dieting runner, need not fear that they will develop amenorrhea with its attendant risks when they start running.

Risks of Prolonged Menstrual Irregularity. Are any risks associated with persistent amenorrhea? The main concern is that women who have persistent amenorrhea and who therefore fail to produce adequate amounts of estrogen may develop "weak," osteoporotic bones, as detailed in chapter 14. Once the bones have lost more than about 10% of their calcium content, they become increasingly liable to fracture. It follows that women with prolonged and persistent amenorrhea will develop decalcified bones, which are at risk of fractures not only in later life but also during the subjects' athletic careers. Other potential risks include the development of uterine and breast cancer (Shangold, 1986).

Persistent amenorrhea, therefore, is not beneficial in the long term, and runners with amenorrhea should seek treatment for the condition. If all that is needed is an increased calorie intake, then that is a small price. Alternatively, drugs that block the action of dopamine or endorphins on the hypothalamus may be effective, but such drugs are not yet commercially available.

To reduce the risk of bone decalcification, amenorrheic runners should increase their intakes of low-calorie, high-calcium foods such as skim milk, low-fat yogurt, and cottage cheese and should ensure that they have daily calcium intakes of 1.2 to 1.5 g. Vitamin D aids in the absorption of calcium; thus, supplementation of this vitamin is of value. Finally, the runner should discuss with a gynecologist knowledgeable of the dangers of prolonged menstrual dysfunction in athletes the need for estrogen therapy, because estrogen therapy will reduce the rate of bone loss and therefore the long-term risks of shinsplints, stress fractures, and ultimately osteoporosis (see chapter 14). Women who are amenorrheic but whose serum estrogen levels are normal require progesterone therapy to reduce the risks that breast or uterine cancer will develop.

Osteoporosis

The likelihood that amenorrheic runners will develop osteoporosis and associated problems was detailed in chapter 14. However, those women who are not amenorrheic and who are physically active have increased bone mass in the femoral neck and the lumbar spine (Pocock et al., 1986), the two sites most commonly involved in osteoporotic fractures in elderly women, and a lower risk of femoral neck fracture (Boyce & Vessey, 1988).

Infertility

Besides being associated with a complete cessation of menstruation, exercise can influence fertility in two other ways.

Exercise can reduce the duration of the luteal phase of the menstrual cycle (Prior et al., 1982; Shangold et al., 1979). This will effectively prevent pregnancy because it will cause sloughing of the uterine lining before any fertilized egg has the chance of becoming established in the womb lining.

In addition, exercise may prevent ovulation. O'Herlichy (1982) reported two amenorrheic Irish runners who failed to ovulate in response to the "fertility pill," clomiphene citrate, even when it was taken in high doses. However, when both stopped running, ovulation was soon induced by normal or low doses of the drug.

That exercise may indeed be a factor in infertility is suggested by the study of B.B. Green et al. (1986). The authors interviewed 346 infertile women attending an infertility clinic and found that infertile women were more likely to participate in vigorous exercise for more than 1 hour a day than were fertile women. Vigorous exercise for less than 1 hour a day was not associated with infertility.

Any woman runner who is having difficulty becoming pregnant should consider that running may be a factor and that discontinuing running may be all that she need do to ensure conception. But occasionally the opposite can occur. A colleague's wife who had struggled for more than a decade to conceive started running and gave birth to her first child 9 months to the day after finishing her first 56-km ultramarathon.

Exercise Performance, the Menstrual Cycle, and the Risk of Injury

The evidence suggests that physical and mental performance does alter during the menstrual cycle, but there is some uncertainty concerning exactly when in the menstrual cycle performance is most affected. In a study in which athletic performance was carefully measured during the entire menstrual cycle, Brooks-Gunn et al. (1986) found that performance in high-intensity, short-duration exercise was best during the menstrual phase of the cycle and worst immediately prior to menstruation, in the premenstrual phase. Whether these findings applied also to more prolonged exercise is not known. The data of Stephenson et al. (1982b) and Nicklas et al. (1989) showed that women performed rather better during maximal exercise testing in the laboratory in the first 8 days than in the last 8 days of the cycle. Body temperatures were also higher during exercise performed in the premenstrual period (Stephenson et al., 1982a). In contrast, Bale and Nelson (1985) found that 50-m swimming performance was best from the 8th to the 15th day of the menstrual cycle but was worst on the 1st day of menstruation. However, because 16 of the 20 swimmers believed that their performances were affected by menstruation, a psychological effect cannot be excluded. For example, impaired performance may result from inattention due to premenstrual discomfort (Pierson & Lockhart, 1963).

How, then, do top women athletes compete effectively at all phases of the menstrual cycle? Either the top athletes may be those who are the least affected by the premenstrual drop in athletic performance or else they use hormone replacement therapy to control their menstrual cycles. Or, they may be amenorrheic and may therefore avoid the premenses—an unstudied benefit of amenorrhea!

Interestingly, women who participate in contact sport are at increased risk of traumatic injury during the premenstrual and menstrual periods, and pill users have a lower incidence of traumatic injuries than non-pill-users (Moller-Nielsen & Hammar, 1989).

Oral Contraceptives and Exercise

Birth Control

Sexually active runners are less likely to use oral contraceptives than are nonrunners. Two independent studies conducted in the United States (Jarrett & Spellacy, 1983a; Shangold & Levine, 1982) showed that runners make far greater use of diaphragms for birth control than do nonrunners (37 to 44% vs. the national average of about 3%) and far less use of oral contraceptives (6 to 13% vs. the national average of 44%). It seems that runners, who are concerned about their health, are particularly concerned about the potential risks of oral contraceptive use.

I will not discuss the relative risks of the use of oral contraceptive pills (Prior & Vigna, 1985); clearly, this is a matter for each woman and her gynecologist. Those experts I have consulted generally agree that the risks of oral contraceptive use are minimal; thus, it is possible that those woman runners who for perceived health reasons choose not to use oral contraceptives may be oversensitive to the potential dangers of those drugs. Alternatively, oral contraceptives may impair running performance (Prior & Vigna, 1985), and this effect may make them less acceptable.

However, one rather disturbing effect of some oral contraceptives is that they decrease blood HDL-cholesterol levels. Because high HDL-cholesterol levels are associated with a reduced incidence of coronary heart disease, anything that reduces blood HDL-cholesterol levels is clearly undesirable. However, regular exercise raises HDL-cholesterol levels in women who use oral contraceptives (D.P. Gray et al., 1983; Merians et al., 1985). All users of oral contraceptives should, in fact, run!

Control of Menstruation

Control of menstruation is necessary if the athlete knows that her performance is affected during the menstrual cycle or if a major race is likely to occur while she is menstruating. To determine this she must establish her menstrual cycle length and must monitor her training and racing performances during the different phases of the menstrual cycle by the careful use of a running logbook.

To ensure that she competes at the most favorable period in her menstrual cycle, the athlete may take either estrogen or progesterone in high doses for varying periods of time. When she stops taking the medication a ''withdrawal bleed'' is induced, similar to the way that menstruation occurs naturally at the end of the menstrual cycle when estrogen and progesterone levels suddenly fall (see Figure 16.4).

Taking this medication shortens one or more of the previous cycles, so that when the athlete is no longer on medication, the competition will fall in her midcycle. If the menstrual cycle needs to be shortened by only a few days, the athlete should take either of these drugs for only 2 to 3 days near the end of the luteal phase. If the cycle needs to be reduced by up to 12 days, these drugs must be taken from Day 5 until Day 14 of the menstrual cycle. Withdrawal bleeding then occurs on Day 16 (Dalton & Williams, 1976).

The athlete who fails to take these precautions and realizes at the last moment that her competition will occur during menstruation can delay menstruation by taking high doses of progesterone in the form of a suppository. This does not, however, prevent the normal deterioration of performance occurring during the premenstrual period.

Potential Hazards of Exercising Vigorously During Pregnancy

Women who choose to exercise during pregnancy must consider four areas of concern (Dale et al., 1982; Gorski, 1985). Not all of these four statements are factual, however.

1. *Exercise compromises the blood flow to the developing fetus.* Until recently, what evidence we had suggested that the blood flow to the fetus may decrease during maternal exercise in both humans (N. Morris et al., 1956) and animals (Lotgering et al., 1983). Different studies suggested that these changes in blood flow are associated with either a decreased (Dale et al., 1982; Jovanovic et al., 1985), an unchanged (Carpenter et al., 1988; Sorensen & Borlum, 1986), or an increased fetal heart rate (Collings & Curet, 1985; Collings et al., 1983; Dressendorfer & Goodlin, 1980) and increased fetal breathing movements (Marsal et al., 1979). More modern studies, however, suggest that fetal blood flow is not impaired by maternal exercise (D.H. Moore et al., 1988; Rauramo & Forss, 1988; Shangold, 1988).

It is difficult to interpret this information (Sady & Carpenter, 1989; Snyder & Carruth, 1984). Most studies of fetal blood flow have been limited to studies of pregnant animals, especially ewes (Lotgering et al., 1983), and these studies indicate that at least during exercise of moderate intensity, compensation for the reduced blood flow occurs so that the fetus continues to receive an adequate oxygen supply despite a reduced total blood flow.

Supportive evidence for this is the finding that babies born to women who have exercised during pregnancy have not shown an increased incidence of abnormalities at birth and have been of normal weight (Collings & Curet, 1985; Collings et al., 1983; Dale et al., 1982; Hall & Kaufmann, 1987; Jarrett & Spellacy, 1983b; Kulpa et al., 1987; Pomerance et al., 1974; Zaharieva, 1972). Only one study (Clapp & Dickstein, 1984) showed that women who continue to exercise vigorously for the duration of pregnancy deliver earlier and have babies of lower birth weights; it seems that these subjects exercised more vigorously than did the mothers in the other studies. However, had the fetuses been exposed to repetitive bouts of hypoxia (inadequate oxygen supply) while their mothers exercised, one would have expected an increased incidence of fetal abnormalities, which was not found. More recently, S.P. Sady et al. (1989) have found that cardiac output is higher both at rest and during exercise in pregnant women. They suggest that the extra blood flow may be perfusing the uterus, thereby maintaining fetal blood flow during exercise.

Despite this, in the absence of more definitive information, it seems that the prudent athlete should avoid very vigorous exercise during her pregnancy.

2. *Blood pH and lactate changes induced by high-intensity exercise may affect the fetus.* Alterations in blood pH levels induced by vigorous exercise could reduce fetal blood flow further, providing another reason the pregnant woman should not exercise vigorously.

3. *Maternal hyperthermia during exercise may affect the fetus.* An elevated maternal temperature (hyperthermia) may be detrimental as it may cause fetal damage (D.W. Smith et al., 1978). Although no studies have measured maternal temperature responses to exercise, the information contained in chapter 4 indicates that a woman exercising moderately in a cool environment for up to 30 minutes will not show a marked rise in body temperature; thus, moderate exercise of this duration is probably quite safe (R.L. Jones et al., 1985).

However, were the pregnant woman to exercise vigorously in hot environmental conditions (wet bulb globe temperature index more than 22 °C) for more than 30 minutes, then her body temperature could possibly reach levels that could cause fetal damage.

4. *Maternal exercise increases the risk of premature labor.* This, fortunately, is one topic on which we have good scientific information. Dr. Gertrud Berkowitz and her colleagues (Berkowitz et al., 1983) from the department of obstetrics and gynecology at the Mount Sinai Medical Center, New York, compared social and health-related data about women who had delivered their babies either prematurely (before 37 weeks of gestation) or after normal gestational periods (over 37 weeks). The authors found that significantly fewer of the women who participated in leisure-time physical activity delivered prematurely and suggested that

exercise might in fact protect against premature labor.

My own interpretation is that some other feature of women who choose to exercise during pregnancy makes them less likely to deliver their babies prematurely. For example, the women least likely to deliver prematurely typically have those social characteristics that are common in the running population: white, upper socioeconomic class, low use of alcohol, good nutrition, and a positive attitude about pregnancy.

Although the authors were able to control for many of these factors in their study, I remain dubious that exercise can in fact reduce the risk of premature delivery. Nevertheless, it is clear that regular moderate exercise during pregnancy certainly does not increase the risk of premature labor, nor does it increase uterine activity (Veille et al., 1985).

Potential Benefits of Exercise During Pregnancy

The benefits of exercise for the pregnant female are said to include the following, but firm scientific evidence on most of these points is lacking (Edwards et al., 1983). What evidence there is indicates that exercise training during pregnancy increases physical fitness without detrimental effects (Erkkola, 1976). These benefits can be grouped into three phases:

1. *Short term.* The mother feels better, has more energy, and suffers less of the common complaints that are associated with pregnancy, in particular constipation, back pain, and reduced energy. Her weight gain is better controlled.

2. *During labor.* The fit mother is better able to cope with whatever happens during delivery, in particular the possibility of complications. Strong abdominal muscles aid the expulsion of the baby, and well-toned pelvic floor muscles stretch better during delivery and recover more quickly afterward.

However, these differences may be more psychological than physical. The studies reported to date found contrasting results of the effects of training during pregnancy on the outcome of labor. In four studies, the labor and delivery experiences of women who had exercised during pregnancy were no different from the experiences of women who had not (Collings et al., 1983; Dale et al., 1982; Kulpa et al., 1987; Pomerance et al., 1974).

In contrast, Erdelyi (1962), who studied the pregnancy outcomes of 172 Hungarian athletes, 66% of whom continued their sporting competition during the first 3 to 4 months of pregnancy, found that these athletes had fewer complications than normal during pregnancy and that there was no increased risk of miscarriage. Labor and delivery were normal, except the rate of Caesarean sections for the athletes was half that of the control group, and the duration of the second stage of labor for the athletes was also half that of the control group.

Hall and Kaufmann (1987) also found a lower incidence of Caesarean section in mothers who had trained during pregnancy; trained mothers also returned home more quickly from the hospital and bore children who recovered more rapidly at birth (Hall & Kaufmann, 1987). Zaharieva (1972) reported that the second stage of labor was only half as long in Olympic athletes as in nonathletes, whereas Wong and McKenzie (1987) found that the third stage of labor was shorter in trained women. Another study (Varrassi et al., 1989) found that trained mothers experienced less pain during labor and had higher serum endorphin concentrations. The blood concentrations of the stress hormones, including cortisol, were lower in trained mothers, suggesting that these women experienced less stress during labor than did the untrained.

3. *Long term.* The woman who has been active during pregnancy will find it easier to lose weight and to recover from the effects of the delivery and pregnancy.

Practical Implications for Pregnant Women

Based on this rather inadequate scientific information, various authors have proposed the following recommendations concerning exercise during pregnancy (Jopke, 1983; Lotgering et al., 1985; Sady & Carpenter, 1989; Snyder & Carruth, 1984).

• The main determinant of the optimum exercise level for the pregnant woman is her prepregnancy fitness and activity levels. Thus, as one writer has said, "Pregnancy is not the time to train for a marathon or a competitive event" (Edwards et al., 1983, p. 89). On the other hand, the average woman (marathon runners and other competitive athletes excluded) can generally continue her regular activity at least for the first 6 to 8 months of pregnancy. It follows, then, that the time to start training is before, rather than after, conception.

• Women who have preexisting chronic medical conditions such as diabetes, heart disease, or high blood pressure (hypertension; Snyder & Carruth, 1984) or who have histories of previous medical problems during pregnancy should probably be discouraged from exercising during pregnancy. Small or underweight women, who statistically have an increased risk of delivering premature and underweight babies, should also be discouraged from exercising, as should overweight adolescents, who frequently begin crash exercise-diet programs once they become pregnant. Weight loss during pregnancy is associated with certain brain abnormalities in the infant; thus, any form of maternal weight loss due to rigorous dieting alone or in combination with exercise must be condemned (Snyder & Carruth, 1984).

• Much of the added physiological stress on the mother during exercise is caused by the added weight of the fetus. Thus, exercises in which the body weight must be carried (e.g., walking, jogging, tennis, and aerobic dance) are more stressful than are those in which the body weight is supported (e.g., cycling and swimming). For this reason, cycling and swimming are the preferred forms of exercise during pregnancy.

- Women who participate in vigorous competitive exercise should decrease their exercise intensities and durations not only after they are pregnant but even when they are likely to conceive. This is necessary because the competitive athlete is more likely to exercise for a prolonged period, thereby increasing her body temperature. Also, hyperthermic damage to the fetus is more likely to occur early after conception. Thus, the competitive athlete should reduce her exercise intensity as soon as she considers it likely that she may be pregnant. Exercise in the heat must be avoided.

It is thought that a rise in body temperature of less than 2 °F is probably safe.

- Dressendorfer (Jopke, 1983) suggested that 20 to 40 minutes of exercise at up to 85% of maximum heart rate is safe and effective. The exercise should be moderate and of short duration so that the risk of hyperthermic damage to the fetus is reduced.

Snyder and Carruth (1984) suggested that the pregnant woman should stretch gently and warm up for about 5 to 10 minutes before she begins her exercise routine. She should then exercise for 15 minutes three to five times a week at a heart rate not exceeding 140 to 150 beats/min. After exercise, she should undertake a 10- to 15-minute cool-down period, during which she walks around and stretches gently until her heart rate is below 100 beats/min. If it takes longer than 5 minutes for the heart rate to fall below 100 beats/min, then the exercise session has been too vigorous. Similarly, if the mother needs to sleep after exercise, she has probably exercised too vigorously.

- Exercise performance becomes gradually impaired during pregnancy, especially during the last 3 months. Therefore, exercise should be more gentle during the last trimester of pregnancy.

- Sports in which there is a risk of injury due to collision are unacceptable. Water skiing and scuba diving are to be avoided, the first because of the danger of forceful entry of water into the uterus causing miscarriage, the latter because of the risk of decompression sickness and the risks associated with exposing the fetus to elevated blood oxygen content.

Sports requiring good balance and coordination need to be avoided or modified during pregnancy because of changes in the center of gravity that make a fall more likely.

There are two "gold" standards against which the effects of exercise during pregnancy must be measured. Does exercise jeopardize or enhance the health of the baby at birth and during its developmental years? Does exercise increase the risk of complications either before or during labor?

The scientific evidence that is available does not show that sensible levels of exercise maintained during pregnancy have any detrimental effects on either of these factors; the evidence does show that such exercise may have certain beneficial effects.

17

Special Concerns for Children

"The less serious running of any description which an athlete indulges in before eighteen, the better for his future prospects."

Alfred Shrubb (1909)

"More champions are marred than made in the days of adolescence through the enthusiasm of parents, the ignorance of games masters or the eagerness of the young athlete himself, who trains and trains, striving always after maximum results, if he is left to his own devices, until he is tired out, both mentally and physically, and becomes utterly stale."

F.A.M. Webster (1948)

"I always remember the words of Gundar Haegg's coach: If you can get a boy in his teens and encourage him to train and not race until he has matured, then you have laid the foundations of an Olympic Champion. I believe that sums up the whole thing. Encourage young athletes, but don't force them. Let them play at athletics and with athletes. If you encourage training from that perspective, their capacity for exercise, and the benefits they draw from it, will astound you."

Arthur Lydiard and Garth Gilmour (1978)

One of the phenomena of modern sport has been the rise of child superstars, particularly in gymnastics and tennis. The sudden success of Zola Budd, in particular, focused attention on the desirability of allowing young children to participate in very intensive training and competition.

The arguments that the performances of child superstars like Zola Budd have evoked are essentially the following:

- The majority of children are too fragile to cope with the physical and psychological rigors of competitive sport.
- When forced to train heavily and to compete intensively, these children must become athletic "burnouts."
- Intensive sporting specialization at a young age robs children of the vital experiences of normal childhood, experiences that can never be relived.

The contrary argument is that none of these points are true and that without intensive training and competitive exposure, these children would never reach such heights of athletic excellence.

In researching the relative merits of these arguments, I discovered that there are really no major studies to give us any firm guidelines on this subject.

SHOULD CHILDREN TRAIN HEAVILY OR COMPETE SERIOUSLY?

Point 1:
Most of the world's outstanding adult endurance athletes of the 1980s did not train heavily, and were not outstandingly successful, as children.

In this discussion I specifically exclude any reference to athletes from Eastern European countries, all of whom, I believe, start quite rigorous and regimented training at a young age. That these countries also produce many great Olympic champions and world-record holders in sports other than distance running is not relevant to the argument. The possibility remains that these outstanding sports stars might have been equally good had they started intensive training in late adolescence. Alternatively, the failure of these countries to produce exceptional distance runners as regularly as they produce exceptional gymnasts, swimmers, sprinters, and rowers might prove that this intensive training approach from a young age is not optimum for future success in distance running.

Certainly the history of athletics in the Western world clearly shows that running and other similar endurance sports are different from gymnastics, ballet, and swimming in which children may need to start intensive training at early ages if they are ever to become world-class contenders. The overwhelming evidence shows that the majority of adult athletes of world standing, including such achievers as Sebastian Coe, were not particularly outstanding and did not train fanatically in their youth.

This was considered to be one of the most important factors determining the successes of the great athletes studied by Hemery (1986). He found that almost without exception, none of these great athletes had specialized in their major sports before the ages of 16 to 18. In almost all cases, the desires to specialize came from the athletes themselves and did not originate from their parents or coaches. Studies of elite Swedish tennis players confirm all these findings. Compared to those tennis players who failed to reach elite status, the most successful players specialized at later ages, came from families that were less likely to contain other tennis players, and were therefore less likely to have been "pushed" into the sport by overenthusiastic parents.

The negative effects of early specialization are probably most notable in the United States, where success as a schoolchild seems to be an almost certain indication that the athlete will never succeed at advanced levels. Two of the most notable American exceptions to this rule have been Jim Ryun and Craig Virgin. On the other hand, neither Frank Shorter nor Bill Rodgers showed outstanding talent at school level, and the same can be said of many world-class athletes (see chapter 8), especially the world-class African marathon runners. For example, neither Zithulele Sinqe nor Willie Motolo, who ran marathons in 2:08:04 and 2:08:15, respectively, both at age 22, trained as youngsters, and they were never coached before age 18. This confirms the overriding importance of genetic ability, not training or coaching, in determining running ability.

Of course these individual examples do not exclude the possibility that late starters might have been better runners if they had started running sooner. But these examples do show that athletes who are not outstanding as children can still make it to the top and may even be more likely to do so in some cases.

My explanation for this is that outstanding athletes seem to have "life expectancies" of about 10 years in top competitive sport. Thus, if they start training hard at the age of 12 years, they will be unlikely to be running at top competitive level much beyond 22 years of age. It follows that the later the athletes start intensive training the better, because their greater physical maturity will allow them to train harder throughout their careers and they will be able to make the most of their peak physical and mental years, which appear to be between the ages of 25 and 35.

Many great athletes and coaches have advocated starting intensive training only when children have matured both physically and mentally. I have already quoted Alf Shrubb and Arthur Lydiard, both of whom felt that it is detrimental for children below the age of 18 to train intensively. A. Nelson (1924) wrote, "Never overwork a young boy. The older he grows the greater is the amount of strain he can bear; then is the time to specialize" (p. 14). Herb Elliott (Lenton, 1981) said the following:

Certainly one of the messages I give kids these days is: "For God's sake do what you enjoy doing and don't get too serious about it." You can have that attitude and approach to athletics until you're about eighteen years of age and still go on to be a world-class performer. You can't in swimming which I think is a disadvantage of that sport. (pp. 25-26)

Jumbo Elliott (Elliott & Berry, 1982) expressed himself similarly when asked how he would advise the parent of a gifted child athlete:

I tell him to let the kid go out and play and have some fun. Forget about hurrying kids into competitive athletics before their bodies are more mature and able to tolerate that kind of work and abuse. It's a bad idea to start children on serious athletic programmes until they are in their teens. Even at that age, too often, some eager parttime amateur coach (who probably teaches history during school hours) pushes far too hard on these young kids, with only one thought in mind—to win. My advice is this—let the kids have fun and grow up a little first. (p. 140)

Grete Waitz's advice (see chapter 16; Waitz & Averbuch, 1986) is that before puberty young children should be encouraged to engage in a range of different sports for enjoyment and to develop overall fitness. If they run, they should race only over the shorter distances and should be involved only in low-key training. This was the way in which both she and Joan Benoit Samuelson, 1984 Olympic Marathon gold medalist, started.

Grete also wrote that the European coaches promote the following guidelines for children's running:

- Children should not specialize in middle distances (800 m to the mile) before 13 to 14 years of age or in long distances (up to 10 km) before 15 to 16 years of age.
- Young runners should first participate in a balanced training program before they specialize.
- Aerobic or endurance training is important for young runners but should only be done at low intensity.
- Young runners should be careful with anaerobic, quality training. Anaerobic training should be avoided before puberty and once begun should be increased only in small amounts from year to year.
- Young runners should practice strength and sprint training.
- Young runners should follow long-term planning, which is crucial to prevent early peaking and burnout.

One of the most regrettable running experiments of which I am aware was undertaken by the medical editor (not George Sheehan) of a now-defunct running magazine. Convinced that hard training by his children was essential if they were to become world champions, he "guided" them to world age-group running records by the time they were 10 years old. After being "world champions" for a few years, they retired from the sport, in which they were no longer interested. I am sure that followers of school athletics in many countries can relate similar examples.

So that is the background. The cards seem to be stacked against the child world champion ever succeeding as an adult world champion; regrettably, this now seems to be the case with Zola Budd. But this rule is far from absolute; Mary Decker-Slaney, the runner whose name will be linked to Zola Budd's forever after the 1984 Olympics, was herself a child prodigy who survived to become an adult world champion!

Point 2:

Children who mature late are more likely to be the better adult athletes.

This may be corollary to Point 1. Possibly, the heavy training and early specialization in youth are not detrimental to adult performance, but rather children who show early promise in any sport, particularly running, are early maturers. The belief that early maturing girls do not make good runners as adults was described in chapter 16. Possibly, the same applies to boys.

Hemery (1986) noted that the majority of the high achievers in the wide variety of sports that he studied were late maturers.

These possibilities deserve further study.

Point 3:

Intensive endurance-type training during early childhood does not seem to have any particular benefits that could not be achieved by the same training after the age of 18 years.

This point inevitably raises a great deal of disbelief (and anger on the part of coaches!). We are naturally inclined to believe that heavy training in childhood and early adulthood, at the very time when the adult body is taking shape, should have the greatest effect. In fact, studies suggest that heavy training in childhood does not have any dramatic effect on those physiological parameters that are believed to improve running performance (Borms, 1986).

For example, J. Daniels and Oldridge (1971) and J. Daniels et al. (1978c) followed different groups of young athletes (initially aged between 10 and 13 years) for up to 6 years and measured their $\dot{V}O_2max$ values and "running economies" approximately every 6 months. The authors found that although absolute $\dot{V}O_2max$ values (in L/min) increased, the $\dot{V}O_2max$ values relative to body mass (ml/kg/min) did not change.

The major change that did occur was a striking decrease in the oxygen cost of running at submaximal speeds due to both growth and training. However, the change in running economy was achieved equally by all athletes regardless of whether they started training at 10, 12, or 13 years of age. Thus, in that study (J. Daniels et al., 1978c) the major benefit of training was an increased running economy, which could probably have been equally well achieved if the athlete had started training at an older age.

Somewhat different results were reported in a group of Japanese runners who were studied annually for 7 years (from age 14 to 21) and who ran 2 hours a day, 5 or 6 days a week (Murase et al., 1981). Relative $\dot{V}O_2$max values increased from 65.4 to 75.5 ml/kg/min during this 6-year period, and there was no further increase in $\dot{V}O_2$max with training after 18 years of age. However, this 15% increase in $\dot{V}O_2$max is no greater than would be achieved by training at an older age. For example, Jim Ryun's $\dot{V}O_2$max value of 81.0 ml/kg/min (see Table 2.1) fell to 65 ml/kg/min when he stopped training and returned to its former value when he again trained hard (J.T. Daniels, 1974a). Other studies focusing on the effect of training on $\dot{V}O_2$max during childhood showed that these changes are of the order of 10 to 20% (Andrew et al., 1972; C.H. Brown et al., 1972; Ekblom, 1969; Eriksson, 1972; Lussier & Buskirk, 1977) and are therefore equal to changes that would be expected in adults undergoing equivalent training.

The degree of muscle mitochondrial enzyme changes with training is no different from that reported in adults (Eriksson, 1972; Eriksson et al., 1973). On the other hand, even when trained, adolescents have lower levels of muscle enzymes than do untrained adults (Fournier et al., 1982), a further indication that even adolescents do not have the physiological requirements necessary for heavy training.

Other predictors of running performance, such as the lactate turnpoint, have yet to be reported in detail in children. Krahenbuhl and Pangrazi (1983) showed that the best 10-year-old runners have higher $\dot{V}O_2$max values, run at higher percentages of $\dot{V}O_2$max, are better sprinters, achieve higher postrace blood lactate levels, and probably have more fast twitch muscle fibers than do 10-year-olds who run poorly.

My interpretation is that these studies simply confirm the fact that hereditary factors are more important determinants of the athlete's ultimate performance than is intensive training at a young age. Furthermore, it seems that after age 16, those runners without the physiological characteristics necessary for athletic success discontinue training (Sundberg & Elovainio, 1982), so that the adolescent athletic population comprises athletes with the physiological characteristics necessary for success.

Point 4:
Children do not drop out of competitive sport because of fatigue.

The concept that children drop out of intensively competitive sport because they physically burn out is false. There is no evidence that either children or adults can train themselves to the point where they suffer lasting physical impairment. Certainly, they can overtrain acutely but the fatigue from overtraining lasts 6 weeks at most (see chapter 10). However, we should not be blind to the relatively common practice, especially in swimming and track athletics, of exposing young children to excessively strenuous and monotonous training for which, because of their age, neither their minds nor bodies are prepared. Although one or two athletes will always survive the abuse inherent to this system and so, regrettably, provide some justification for its retention, the majority fall by the wayside, victims not so much of physical burnout but of mental stagnation.

On the other hand, we tend to forget that many adults drop out of competitive sport when they reach the goals for which they have for so long striven and for which they have sacrificed so much. For example, Roger Bannister stopped competing shortly after he broke the 4-minute mile at a time when he felt that his career and family had become more important (Bannister, 1955). Britain's next mile world-record holder after Bannister, Derek Ibbotson, captured the feeling when he wrote, "In the moment of victory I did not realize that the inner force, which had been driving me to my ultimate goal, died when I became the world's fastest miler. My failure to realize this meant that within a year I was yesterday's hero" (Ibbotson, 1960, p. 13). Herb Elliott, possibly the most talented miler of all time, retired as an unbeaten Olympic champion and world-record holder at the tender age of 22 so that he could study Latin at Cambridge University, where with typical obsessionalism, he chose to cram 4 academic years into 1 (see chapter 8).

So it is, I suspect, with children. I suggest that the majority of successful child athletes quit competitive sport for the same reasons as do adults. Either these children reach the goals they set themselves or they prefer to devote their time developing their other interests or facets of their personalities.

However, another important reason some may stop, which is specific only to children, relates to the pressures to which children are exposed by parents, coaches, and the press during their competitive years. When children approach the age of about 17, they may start questioning whether they really are running for themselves or for their parents, coaches, or country.

Point 5:
Abnormal parental and coaching pressures may be the critical factors determining whether a child enjoys sport and continues to compete after adolescence.

Billie Jean King, surely one of the world's most remarkable athletes, has a brother who is also a professional athlete, a baseball pitcher. When asked whether she thought that she and her brother might have been fortunate in inheriting sporting abilities from their parents, she replied that she and her brother had indeed been very fortunate in their choice of parents, but not for that reason. "My parents were very supportive," stated King, "but they never asked if we won. They asked how we did, whether we gave 100%, and if we were happy with ourselves. You don't have to ask children if they won; you can tell by body language—just look at their shoulders" (Caldwell, 1983, p. 23). It was this supportive, nonmanipulative attitude that she considered to be the most important gift her parents had given her.

Billie Jean's parents understood the basic psychological premise that children's self-esteem is based on what they think their parents think of them. In sport, the parental message can be very subtle or it can be unsubtle, as in the case of the father who allocates pocket money according to the number of points his child scores in a particular sport. Parents who stress the importance of winning risk raising children who, when they doubt whether they can win, may choose not to compete rather than risk losing, a variation of the "fear of success" syndrome discussed in chapter 7. Rather, children must be taught what Billie Jean was taught—that giving 100% is all that matters. In addition, they need to learn how to lose. After all, at least 50% of people involved in competitive sport have to lose.

One of the most endearing stories of learning how to lose properly is related by Roger Kahn (1972). Kahn relates that Joe Black, a former pitcher with the Brooklyn Dodgers baseball team who became a high school coach, took his high school team to watch the Dodgers and meet his old coach, the legendary Casey Stengel. Black introduced his team to Stengel with the following words: "This is my team, Case. They're having troubles. They've lost sixteen out of eighteen games and I wondered what the Old Master thought I ought to teach 'em."

"Lost sixteen out of eighteen, you say?" Stengel scratched his chin. "Well, first you better teach 'em to lose in the right spirit. Children can cope with losing if their parents can."

In contrast to the exemplary and mature attitude of King's parents, some manipulative parents use their children's abilities to serve their own ends. Often parents say that their children "want to" excel in sports, but, one might ask, why would young children "want to" train really hard to run marathons unless they got the message from their parents?

An important point that adults overlook is that children under the age of about 14 do not think abstractly; they do not see rewards beyond the present for the efforts they put in, and so, unlike adults, they do not have long-term goals. So the parents who say that their young children are training to be future world champions are, in fact, expressing parental wishes for these children and, at the same time, very forcefully conveying the parental message. That parental expectations increase the anxiety experienced by children in competition has been shown (Lewthwaite & Scanlan, 1989).

And then there is the final joker in the pack—the coach or possibly the school principal who may suffer from the same problem and whose ego may be so insecure that it depends on the success of student athletes. (Of course, if the athlete also lives in a country that has an ego-identity crisis, then these problems will be expressed on a national scale.)

Clearly, child athletes need egoless parents, egoless coaching, and a mature nation. When these elements are present, the chances are improved that the child athlete will mature to become a confident adult competitor. In addition, the children should always be allowed to determine their own levels of commitment to any particular sport.

Bruce Ogilvie (1983a, 1983b), the sport psychologist discussed in chapter 7, stated that the most important attribute of the coach and indeed the parent is "the quest to become egoless," and he stressed that this must remain a lifelong goal. The goal for coaches and teachers is always to subordinate personal needs to those of the people they are trying to help. Ten very helpful guidelines for parents of sporting children are listed in Table 17.1.

Table 17.1   Guidelines for Parents of Children in Sports

Make sure your children know that win or lose, you love them and are not disappointed with their performances.

Be realistic about your child's physical ability.

Help your child set realistic goals.

Emphasize improved performance, not winning—positively reinforce improved skills.

Don't relive your own athletic past through your child.

Provide a safe environment for training and competition—this includes proper training methods and use of equipment.

Control your own emotions at games and events—don't yell at other players, coaches, or officials.

Be a cheerleader for your child and the other children on the team.

Respect your child's coaches—communicate openly with them. If you disagree with their approach, discuss it with them.

Be a positive role model—enjoy sports yourself, set your own goals, and live a healthy lifestyle.

Note. From "Kids, Parents, and Sports: Some Questions and Answers" by J.C. Hellstedt, 1988, *The Physician and Sportsmedicine*, **16**(4), p. 71. Copyright 1988 by McGraw-Hill. Adapted by permission.

Point 6:

Is it really so bad to be a great athlete only at school?

In other words, why should we be so distraught if our childhood stars suddenly retire? Do we make the same noises when older athletes retire? For example, few adult elite distance runners continue to compete for more than a handful of years, yet no one seems to make a great fuss about that.

So there it is. The problems faced by the child athlete are no different from those faced by the adult. Success, it seems, depends on intense self-motivation, the acceptance of sacrifice, a supportive environment comprising egoless coaching and egoless parents, and gradual progress toward carefully delineated goals.

My personal feeling is that intensive training for young athletes should be delayed for as long as possible; I believe the older the child is when hard training begins, the better. The ultimate performance levels of gifted athletes may be determined ultimately by psychological factors; thus, it is best to start training so that peak physical performance occurs when the mind is strongest.

GUIDELINES FOR SPORTS PARTICIPATION OF YOUNG CHILDREN

Children are not miniature adults; they should be treated as children first and as athletes second. It is important to respect their limitations and to appreciate that children have more intelligence than do adults about their own limitations. Unlike adults, children who are left to their own devices will not drive themselves to the point of injury.

For 6- to 10-year-olds, the emphasis should be on awakening an interest in sports, having fun, and learning basic skills. Children at that age lack the hormones necessary to produce major physiological adaptations to training.

Children between 11 and 14 years should be taught sporting versatility and proper techniques; these children can begin to develop tolerances for increased training loads. A rough guide is that a child of this age can undertake about one third of the training load of an adult. This means that between the ages of 11 and 14, a child can train intensively for no more than 10 to 20 minutes before requiring a rest. At this age, children are motivated by the need to gain the acceptance of peers and are unable to separate judgments about their physical abilities from those about their worth as people (Ogilvie, 1983a). When judged a "failure" on the athletics field, the child will conclude that his or her total being is a failure.

By 15 to 18 years, the child is ready for an increased training load (between half and two thirds of that undertaken by an adult) and for specialized training, including the use of weights. At that age, children are also ready for more intensive competition. However, once again, children are not adults, and they cannot be expected to hold competitive "peaks" for as long as can adults. A.G.K. Brown (1964) suggested that no child should be trained hard for more than 6 or 7 weeks at a time or should be expected to maintain a competitive peak for more than a month. He suggested that the child athlete should peak three times a year, once each summer, spring, and winter or once each term in a three-term school. "If he spends the interim eating and sleeping, good luck to him!" (A.G.K. Brown, 1964, p. 65).

Most of the problems that exist in youth sport result from the inappropriate application of the win-oriented model of professional or elite sport to the child's sport setting (R.E. Smith, 1984). When excessive pressures are placed on winning, children can be deprived of important opportunities to grow personally, to develop their skills, and to enjoy participation. Smith stressed that coaches must understand that success is not synonymous with winning but should be equated with effort and improvement. Because all athletes have the resources for effort, all can be winners if this attitude is promoted.

It is also important to recognize the wide range of maturity differences that can exist among children of the same age. Thus at age 6, maturity levels can vary as much as 4 years; at age 12 by as much as 6 years.

Ogilvie (1983a) suggested that correctly approached, childhood sport should afford children the opportunity to develop strong positive feelings about their bodies. Sport should increase their abilities to interact with others more sensitively through the sharing of physical and emotional experiences and should reinforce positive attitudes toward health maintenance for life.

The Coach's Role: How Not to Do It

In a sadly humorous article entitled *How to Ruin an Athlete*, Richardson (1976) described the most effective way for the coach to break every possible training rule for adolescent athletes. He gave this advice to the "dyed-in-the-wool, true-blue, totally conscientious coach who wants to ensure that his athletes never run again when they finish school" (p.76).

Workouts

Richardson suggested that workouts should have as little variety as possible—each day's training should be the same and should be run on the same course or track. To ensure that the athletes are thoroughly overtrained, they must run sufficiently hard in training so that their performances in races show an impressive deterioration.

Athletes whose racing performances continue to improve are not training sufficiently hard and must undertake more rigorous training schedules, for example, daily sessions of thirty 400-m intervals. All training must hurt, and a point system should be established to identify the most fragile individuals. The following such system has been proposed by Richardson:

Event	Points score
Athlete unable to finish workout	10
Athlete throws up during workout	10
Athlete has to be carried from the field	25
Athlete needs hospital treatment	50
Athlete needs to be hospitalized (per day in hospital)	100
Athlete is crippled for life	500

Athlete dies	750
Athlete dies on field	1,000

Finally, the coach must pay no individual attention to any athlete; the coach should simply materialize at the track, read times off a stopwatch, bark and snarl at the runners, and disappear immediately at the end of each training session. At all times, the coach should keep pressure on the runners by stressing the life-or-death nature of the sport.

Competition

Richardson stressed that all these points apply equally for competition. In addition, he suggested that the coach must set impossible goals for the overtrained runners and should then denigrate their performances individually at the end of each race.

Social and Academic Life

Training athletes a minimum of 4 hours a day will usually ensure that their social and academic lives are nonexistent. But additional predawn workouts must be scheduled for any squad member who can still find time for these unimportant activities.

To stress the unimportance of academics and social life, runners must be punished appropriately if they are found in possession of writing materials or textbooks or are caught doing homework, visiting the library, or dating the opposite sex. Richardson (1976) advised the following:

> Above all, make sure your runners know the price of success. Emphasize that the road to the Olympics is paved with blood, sweat and broken bones. To destroy an athlete, particularly a highly motivated one, requires patience, perseverance and a total lack of understanding. (p. 77)

The Parent's Role

Ogilvie (1983a) listed the following types of parents with negative attitudes:

- The parent who seems unable or unwilling to allow the activity to remain child oriented and who is compelled to judge it by adult standards.
- The parent who is unable to maintain the appropriate emotional distance from the child's activity and makes the child's involvement in sport an extension of his or her own ego.
- The parent who is a "guilt motivator" and who stresses the financial and other sacrifices he or she is supposedly making for the child's sporting success.

- The parent who fantasizes the financial and other rewards that "my child the champion" will bring to the family.

Ogilvie stressed that these adult pressures negate almost all of the fundamental psychological values that sport should provide, such as fun, emotional release, and learning to relate effectively to peers. Furthermore, these adult pressures may stunt the emotional and social growth of the child and can lead to a restricted personality and very shaky ego. The child who senses self-worth purely in terms of a single attribute, in this case athletic ability, runs a very real risk of future emotional trauma should his or her genetic abilities be less than the parents' expressed desires.

Ogilvie (Adler et al., 1982) suggested that the parents of children in competitive sport should answer the following three questions:

- Do you regard the sport as a direct or an indirect measure of the child's worth as a person?
- Have you made athletics a proving ground for the child or vicariously for yourself?
- Do you and your child realize that no matter how remarkable the physical gift, it should not be used to prove one's value as a human being?

Answers to these questions will indicate whether the sport is being approached in the correct or incorrect manner.

Health Considerations

Risk of Injury to the Epiphyseal Growth Plate

The growth of the bones during childhood occurs in a cartilaginous growth plate that separates the bone shaft (metaphysis) from its end (the epiphysis; see Figure 17.1). The cartilaginous growth plate is gradually replaced by bone as the child grows but solidifies into true bone only when the child has matured, usually between the ages of 15 and 19 years.

The main risk posed by the growth plate is that because it comprises cartilage, which is much weaker than bone, it is more likely to be damaged if an external force is applied to the bone (e.g., during a football tackle). Thus, considerable concern has been expressed that vigorous exercise increases the risk of displacement or even death of the growth plate with potentially catastrophic effects. For example, were the growth plate to be displaced in such a way that the epiphysis and the metaphysis were no longer in the appropriate alignment, subsequent growth in that bone would be "skew." If the growth plate were severely damaged, this could result in its death and therefore failure of further growth in the length of that bone. The child who suffered a growth plate injury in one long

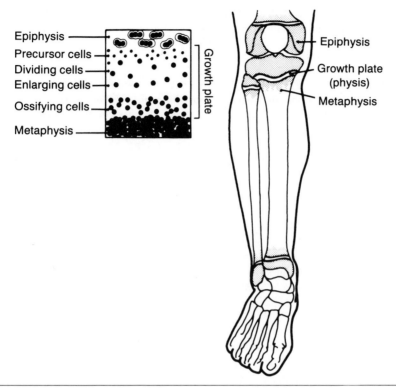

Epiphysis
Precursor cells
Dividing cells
Enlarging cells
Ossifying cells
Metaphysis

Growth plate

Epiphysis
Growth plate (physis)
Metaphysis

Figure 17.1 The epiphyseal growth plate.

bone, such as the tibia or femur, would be left with unequal growth on the two sides of the body.

In 1956 the Committee on School Health of the American Academy of Pediatrics strongly condemned contact sports for schoolchildren (for preadolescents in particular) on the basis that such sports would lead to a high incidence of growth plate injuries (Committee on School Health, 1956). However, subsequent research has clearly established that the risks have been greatly overstated. In a study of 12,338 sporting injuries in children under 15 years of age, R.L. Larson and McMahan (1966) found an incidence of growth plate injuries of only 6%. It appears that the risk of growth plate injuries even in children involved in body contact sports is relatively low and is certainly not a cause of undue concern.

It has also been suggested that children who participate in long-distance running risk damaging their growth plates (Caine & Lindner, 1984). But again it appears that the risks have been overstated, and no one has yet reported a high incidence of these injuries in child runners. Because I have yet to see such an injury in a young runner, I am currently unimpressed with the argument that long-distance running will increase the risk of growth plate injury in children.

Risk of Heat Injury

Several factors are believed to reduce the young athlete's ability to lose heat during exercise in a warm environment. Children produce more metabolic heat per unit mass than do adults during exercise at the same work load. Children also have lower sweating capacities than do adults, reduced abilities to transfer heat from the body core to the body surface (skin), and greater surface-area:-weight ratios, which facilitate heat gain from the environment during exercise in the heat or conversely heat loss to the environment during exercise in the cold. In addition, children acclimatize more slowly to heat than do adults (American Academy of Pediatrics, 1983).

Although these differences do not interfere with the child's ability to exercise in a cool environment, they may limit the child's ability to exercise safely in a warm or hot environment, although not all studies agree on this point (Docherty et al., 1986). Nevertheless, the following recommendations have been made by the American Academy of Pediatrics (1983):

• In hot environmental conditions, children should either reduce the intensities of their activities or avoid exercising for longer than 30 minutes at a time.

• When moving to a hot climate, or at the start of the summer sporting season, children should allow 10 to 15 days for heat acclimatization to occur. During this time, they should gradually increase the intensity and duration of their exercise sessions.

• Children should wear lightweight, porous clothing and should drink fluids regularly during exercise—300 ml per hour for a child weighing 40 kg. Rubberized sweat suits must never be used to produce a loss of weight.

18

Medical Benefits and Hazards of Running

"When death occurs during the performance of physical exertion, two features are as a rule conspicuous: the triviality of the effort, or the discovery of some long pre-existing lesion which had never been suspected. . . . In the majority of deaths that occur during exercise, necropsy reveals disease of such magnitude as to make it almost unbelievable that the sufferer could have survived at all with moderate activity, still less the capacity for outstanding athleticism."

Sir Adolphe Abrahams (1951)

"Health is something the runner goes through on his way to fitness. A way station he hardly notices in his pursuit of the twenty or thirty per cent of his capacity that lies untouched. And health, therefore, is what he risks in training to do his best. Because just beyond fitness and a personal record lies staleness, and with it fatigue and exhaustion and depression and despair."

Dr. George Sheehan (1978b)

"Runners are much like ordinary mortals. They can, sad to say, get sick. They can even die."

James Fixx (1980)

"Recognition of the role of exercise in health is changing as robots and automation now perform most of the laborious tasks that used to be done by

> *muscle power. A cartoon in an American newspaper recently quipped, 'Time was when most men who finished a day's work needed rest. Now they need exercise!' It is encouraging to see this new wisdom grow in popular acceptance.''*
>
> Ralph Paffenbarger (1984)

George Sheehan was one of the first to dare suggest that the majority of runners do not actually run to be healthy. He proposed that runners can be classified into one of three groups—joggers, racers, and runners—according to their motivations for running (Sheehan, 1978b).

Joggers, Sheehan contended, are the physically reborn who preach the gospel of jogging for health and longevity. Narrating evangelical details of how jogging saved their lives, they will bore anyone incautious enough to ask about their running. And as they begin to discuss the evidence that exercise increases longevity and protects against coronary heart disease (with names like Morris and Paffenbarger tripping from their tongues as if these experts were the joggers' nearest and dearest friends), these joggers will be inspecting you carefully, looking for those telltale signs indicating your need for physical reform.

Fortunately for all of us, most joggers grow up. As joggers mature they begin to realize that the passions that motivate people to become healthy are the same as those that transform joggers first into racers and then finally into runners. The boring jogger may sooner or later find that jogging has become boring. The exercise prescription that made the jogger physically healthy has failed to do anything for the mind. The mental challenge to start exercising and get healthy has gone. It is time to move on—to enter a race.

As soon as joggers mail their first race entry forms, they become racers and enter a new world. Racers, you see, no longer have any concern for health. Their sole concerns are performance and the desire to run faster. Every training session, every waking moment, is concerned with what will make these racers run farther in less time. And, because the racers' expectations can never be satisfied, they can never train sufficiently or race enough. The result is that if there indeed are any medical dangers associated with this sport, they occur almost exclusively to the racers.

Sheehan suggested that running competitively (racing) does for the mind what jogging does for the body. The race provides the fear, the excitement, and the physical challenge from which our modern, repetitive, unchallenging nine-to-five lives have sheltered us.

Ultimately, the jogger/racer may evolve into a runner, who is unconcerned about the health aspects of running and whose psyche no longer needs the challenge of the race. This runner runs to meditate, to create, and to become whole. Sheehan (1978b) wrote, "Running is finally seeing everything in perspective. Running is discovering the wholeness, the unity that everyone seeks. Running is the fusion of body, mind and soul in that beautiful relaxation that joggers and racers find so difficult to achieve" (p. 287).

With this introduction, let us discuss the real and perceived medical problems associated with running in general, racing in particular.

ENVIRONMENTAL HAZARDS OF RUNNING

Environmental problems include those posed by sharing our training environment with automobiles and their emissions, a sometimes-unfriendly public, and either hot or cold weather conditions.

Automobiles, Dogs, and an Unfriendly Public

Automobiles pose a serious health threat to runners. If you do not remember the practical tips outlined in chapter 6, you would do well to review them now. It could be worth your life!

In 1979, cardiologist George Burch (1979), former editor of *American Heart Journal*, reported that 8,300 American joggers were killed by automobiles in 1977 and a further 100,000 had been injured. He regarded this as a good enough reason not to jog.

Dr. Paul Milvy (1979), convener of the hugely successful New York Academy of Sciences Marathon Conference (Milvy, 1977, 1978), replied that the data quoted by Burch applied to total pedestrian, not jogging, deaths. He queried whether Burch was faulting the victims rather than the perpetrators of the accidents.

The true extent of this problem is not known. In the study of Koplan et al. (1982), 4% of men and women had been bitten by dogs when running; 0.03% of men and 0.1% of women had been hit by bicycles; and 0.7% of men and 0.5% of women had been hit by motor vehicles. Also, 7% of both males and females had been hit by thrown objects while running. The thrown objects included cans, bottles, ice, liquids, and a rock-filled bag.

A more serious and real problem for female runners is the risk of rape. The avoidance of rape during running hinges on the careful application of the following commonsense rules:

- Run during the daylight hours in the most populated areas.
- Run with a friend, especially when running in less populated areas such as forests and cross-country trails.

- Consider carrying a defensive weapon such as a noxious spray with you.
- If you feel that you are being followed by a potential rapist, take immediate action; *don't* delay. Do not assume that the footsteps you hear behind you are necessarily those of another runner.
- Don't always run the same route at the same time of day on the same day of the week.
- If attacked, act firmly and bravely and try to talk your way out of it. Try, of course, to run away. Should that fail, scream and decide whether to fight or submit.
- Should you decide to fight, fight foul. It helps to have a good knowledge of those parts of the male anatomy that are most vulnerable to kicks and punches!

Automobile Emissions

Two important pollutants in car emissions are lead and carbon monoxide. A South African physician suggested that jogging in a polluted environment causes inhalation of dangerous poisons, leading ultimately to heart failure and brain damage (Grant-Whyte, 1981). This, he felt, could adequately explain the madness of running.

Lead.   Studies show that the content of lead in the blood, at least of runners in countries still using lead gasoline, may indeed be elevated, in some runners to rather high levels (Grobler et al., 1984, 1986; Van Rensburg et al., 1982). The position of runners in other countries has not been established.

High blood lead levels are found particularly in runners in urban areas (Grobler et al., 1986); blood lead levels in rural runners are about 60% lower and are closer to levels found in nonrunners. The source of the lead is almost certainly automobile exhaust fumes, which contain lead due to an "antiknock" factor in gasoline.

How dangerous are these elevated blood lead levels? Current thinking is that even low levels of lead are indeed toxic and that values above 30 μg per 100 ml are unacceptable. Of interest is that only 1.9% of Americans have blood lead levels in excess of 30 μg per 100 ml (Editorial, 1982a), yet the majority of urban runners in countries using leaded gasoline probably have higher values.

What can be done? Obviously, runners in countries in which cars burn leaded gasoline should avoid running next to freeways if possible. Lead levels in air fall as you travel farther away from the road, so run as far from the road as possible. The ultimate answer may be to remove lead from gasoline, but the economic implications may be prohibitive for some countries (Editorial, 1982a).

Carbon Monoxide.   The detailed studies of Honigman et al. (1982) show that carbon monoxide begins to accumulate in the blood during submaximal exercise only when its concentration in the inspired air is more than 6.5 parts per million (ppm). The carbon monoxide has a high affinity for hemoglobin and displaces oxygen, forming carboxyhemoglobin. The formation of carboxyhemoglobin reduces the oxygen-carrying capacity of blood, and this effect may last for up to 4 hours after the cessation of exercise.

Low levels of carboxyhemoglobin do not reduce performance (Horvath et al., 1975), but at carboxyhemoglobin levels of 4%, $\dot{V}O_2$max is reduced. Interestingly, maximal exercise performance is reduced at even lower blood carboxyhemoglobin levels of 3%. There is a linear relationship between the elevated blood carboxyhemoglobin levels and reduced $\dot{V}O_2$max (Folinsbee & Raven, 1984).

Breathing air containing 50 ppm carbon monoxide can cause 5% carboxyhemoglobin levels within 1 hour of jogging. The average level of carbon monoxide in urban traffic is 37 ppm, and this rises to 54 ppm in heavy traffic and even up to 120 ppm at stop signals (Hage, 1982). Carbon monoxide levels peak during rush hour traffic (Hage, 1982) and are elevated for up to 20 m from the side of the road (Aronow, 1972).

Thus, running alongside freeways will cause elevated carboxyhemoglobin levels that may reach 5% within 30 minutes. Similar levels are achieved by running in heavy traffic for 90 minutes. These levels do not affect performance during mild to moderate exercise but have some effect during near-maximal exercise, when $\dot{V}O_2$max will be reduced. Blood carboxyhemoglobin levels will remain elevated for 3 to 4 hours after such exercise. A persistently elevated blood carbon monoxide level is considered by some to be the factor that explains why a cigarette smoker has an increased risk of developing atherosclerosis. Blood carboxyhemoglobin levels of 5% equal those found in persons smoking 10 to 20 cigarettes a day (Nicholson & Case, 1983). Jogging in clean air reduces blood carboxyhemoglobin levels in smokers (Kam, 1980).

Clearly, the avoidance of extreme exposure to high environmental carbon monoxide levels is important. This means that you should avoid running along roads during rush hour and should run at least 20 m away from the cars.

Sulphur Dioxide. Sulphur dioxide is a highly soluble gas that is almost totally absorbed through the nasal passages. However, mouth breathing, particularly at high ventilatory rates during exercise, will cause the sulphur dioxide to travel farther down the air passages, where its effects may become apparent.

Sulphur dioxide is a respiratory irritant that affects normal people only at air concentrations of 1 to 2 ppm. As air levels of sulphur dioxide in all but the most polluted cities very rarely exceed 0.1 ppm, this is not an important pollutant for most runners in many countries. However, asthmatics may be affected at air sulphur dioxide levels as low as 0.5 ppm. The drug cromolyn sodium offers the asthmatic some protection against this effect (Folinsbee & Raven, 1984).

Ozone. Of all the pollutants, ozone is considered to be the most toxic and to have the greatest effect on athletic performance.

Ozone is formed by the effect of ultraviolet radiation on motor car emissions. Ozone levels peak at midday, when the emissions are exposed to peak ultraviolet radiation.

Ozone is a potent airway irritant that can cause respiratory symptoms; at a concentration as low as 0.3 ppm, ozone can interfere with performances of persons exercising heavily. Data indicate that endurance performance is almost certainly affected quite severely by air ozone levels in the range of 0.2 to 0.35 ppm (W.C. Adams & Schelegle, 1983; Gong et al., 1986; Schelegle & Adams, 1986) and that the higher the exercise intensity, the lower the ozone concentration necessary to cause respiratory symptoms and impaired performance (Folinsbee et al., 1984).

Some evidence shows exposure to ozone may reduce the sensitivity of the human airways to its effects, but whether this is truly an adaptive response or represents a diminished response due to ozone-induced airway damage is not known (Folinsbee & Raven, 1984; Foxcroft & Adams, 1986; Hage, 1982).

Temperature

The history of the marathon, more than any other sport, has been etched with the tragedy of heat-related deaths. The marathon race itself commemorates the immortal run of an unknown soldier, fully armored and "hot from battle," to Athens to inform the Greek capital that the invading Persians had been defeated on the plains of Marathon. Within seconds of delivering his news, "Rejoice, rejoice. Victory is ours!", the messenger reportedly died.

Although this particular event is probably mythical (D.E. Martin et al., 1977), genuine tragedies have since been documented in real marathon races. The hero of the 1908 Olympics in London, the diminutive Italian Dorando Pietri, lay in a semicoma desperately close to death for the 2 days following his collapse in the final meters of the marathon. In the 1912 Olympic Games in Stockholm, the Portuguese runner Lazaro collapsed from heatstroke after running 19 miles and died the next day. Jim Peters, the first marathon runner to break the 2:20 barrier, entered the Vancouver Stadium 15 minutes ahead of his nearest rival in the 1954 Empire Games Marathon, only to collapse before reaching the finishing line (see Figure 18.1). The words of the stunned broadcaster, "God! He's running backwards," captured the horror of the moment.

Jackie Mekler, who finished second in the Vancouver Marathon, recalled that environmental conditions were so severe that he chose to run very conservatively, finishing more than 14 minutes slower than his best time. Worse, in accordance with the rules of the day, there were few refreshment stations. Those available were not staffed, because the officials had chosen to return to the stadium to watch the Landy-Bannister mile of the century that was run 20 minutes before Peters arrived in the stadium. Thus, there was no one to tell Peters that he had a huge lead and could win comfortably even if he walked the last 3 km. Fortunately,

Figure 18.1 Jim Peters collapses near the finish of the 1954 Vancouver Empire Games Marathon. Chris Brasher (jacketless in a white shirt), organizer of the London Marathon, is pictured immediately behind Peters.
Note. Photo courtesy of *Sunday Tribune*.

since these disasters, three major changes have reduced the risk of heatstroke occurring during races.

First, races are no longer held in the heat of the day, as was the case in the 1954 Empire Games Marathon. Rather, these races are usually scheduled (with the notable exception of the men's 1984 Olympic Marathon) in the early morning or late evening. Second, facilities for providing athletes with fluid replacement during races have greatly improved. When I ran my first marathon, drinking was allowed only after the first 10 km, and then only every 5 km. Today, refreshment stations are provided every 2 to 3 km and often more frequently at the most popular races. Third, athletes have become aware of the need to acclimatize by training in the heat if they are to run hot-weather marathons and the need to run conservatively in the heat.

But despite these measures, a small number of athletes continue to suffer from heat injury during racing, so it is important to recognize the condition and to know how to treat and prevent it.

The Symptoms and Diagnosis of Heatstroke

The diagnosis is heatstroke when during exercise, the previously healthy athlete shows evidence of marked changes in mental functioning, for example collapse with unconsciousness or a reduced level of consciousness (stupor, coma) or mental stimulation (irritability, aggression, or convulsions), and when these symptoms are associated with a rectal temperature over 107 °F (Peters's was reportedly 109 °F). During the first 48 hours after collapse, a rise in blood levels of certain enzymes that leak from muscle into the blood as a result of heat damage confirms the diagnosis.

The only conditions with which the heatstroke may initially be confused are heart attack (cardiac arrest) or a severe fall in blood glucose levels (hypoglycemia). In patients with cardiac arrest, the heart stops beating and the patient does not breathe; thus, a pulse cannot be felt and the chest wall does not move. In heatstroke, the pulse rate is rapid, usually more than 100 beats per minute, and breathing is more rapid and obvious. Thus, simply feeling the pulse will differentiate between heatstroke and cardiac arrest.

Identifying hypoglycemia is far more difficult. As Sir Adolphe Abrahams, British Olympic team doctor for many years, brother of Harold Abrahams the sprinter, and one of the fathers of modern sports medicine, wrote: "When exhausting exercise is undertaken in circumstances conducive to heatstroke it is impossible to separate the symptoms caused by an accompanying hypoglycaemia" (A. Abrahams, 1951, p. 1188).

The distinction can only be made on the basis of the rectal temperature, which is usually less than 105 °F in hypoglycemic patients, and by measurement of the blood glucose levels.

A simple but practical approach is to first correct any hypoglycemia in a collapsed runner by providing adequate amounts of glucose intravenously. The athlete affected only by hypoglycemia will recover rapidly with this treatment; the condition of the runner with heatstroke will be unaffected.

Causes of Heatstroke

The physiology of body temperature regulation was discussed in chapter 4. In summary, factors that predispose one to heatstroke are those that disturb the equilibrium between the rate of heat production and the rate of heat loss. The rate of heat loss is controlled by the air temperature, air humidity, and the rate of wind movement across the athlete's body. The rate of heat production is determined by the athlete's mass and running speed. Thus, the rate of heat production and the risk of heatstroke are greatest in short-distance races (Noakes et al., 1988a), not in the marathon, as is commonly believed.

The highest incidence of heatstroke in an Olympic running event occurred not in a marathon race but in the 10,000-m cross-country race at the 1924 Olympic Games in Paris. Competing at 3:30 p.m. on a day that was "unbelievably hot"

(Lovesey, 1968), only 15 of the 39 entrants completed the race; four runners collapsed on the track. Lovesey (1968) wrote that the runners arrived looking like "victims from an action on the Front. . . . The state of the pathetic figures who tottered into the stadium in the wake of the leaders so shocked those present that cross-country running was banned from future Olympic track and field programmes" (Lovesey, 1968, p. 112).

Other factors that determine the rate at which the athlete loses heat are (a) clothing, because the more clothing worn, the less heat lost by convection and sweating; (b) the state of heat acclimatization, because heat acclimatization increases both one's ability to lose heat by sweating and one's resistance to an elevated body temperature; and (c) the state of hydration, because dehydration impairs the ability to lose heat by sweating.

For reasons that are presently unknown, only certain individuals are prone to heatstroke. It seems likely that they have hereditary abnormalities of muscle cell metabolism (Noakes, 1987a).

Treatment of Heatstroke

The first priority is to lower the body temperature to below 100 °F as quickly as possible, because the amount of tissue damage caused by the high body temperature is related to the time during which body temperature exceeds that value.

The most effective cooling methods are cold water sprays and a strong fan to blow air over the athlete or ice packs placed over as large an area of the body surface as is possible. The athlete should not be placed in a bath of iced water, because the body temperature could drop too far too rapidly, causing problems during rewarming.

The athlete should be placed in a cool, drafty, shady area, and his or her clothing should be removed. As soon as a cooling procedure has been instituted, correction of dehydration and possible hypoglycemia with intravenous fluids and glucose is essential. Once the body temperature has been reduced to below 100 °F, the athlete should be transported to a hospital for further cooling and observation in case any of the serious complications of heatstroke, in particular kidney failure and organ damage, should occur. It is important that the body temperature be monitored continuously during transport to the hospital and after hospital admission, because the temperature tends to rise once the active cooling procedures cease.

Prevention of Heat Injury

The following proposals for the prevention of heat injury during running are based on the proposals of the American College of Sports Medicine (1975, 1985). Unfortunately, they are not entirely foolproof; some athletes will suffer heatstroke during exercise regardless of the precautions they take. Nevertheless, the overall risk to all athletes will be reduced by close attention to these proposals.

The most important points are that the risk of heatstroke is *inversely* related to the distance of the race (i.e., the risk is least in the longest races), and the risk is *directly* related to the environmental temperature. Here are some tips to keep in mind:

1. Distance races greater than 5 km should not be conducted when the wet bulb globe temperature index exceeds 84 °F (see Table 9.4) or when the dry bulb temperature is greater than 81 °F in summer, less in winter (see Table 9.5). Criteria incorporating CET values (see chapter 9) have yet to be formulated.

2. During periods of the year when daylight dry bulb temperature often exceeds 78 °F, distance races should be conducted before 9:00 a.m. and after 4:30 p.m.

3. The race sponsor and organizer must provide drinking/sponging stations at least every 3 to 4 km for all races longer than 4 km.

4. Runners should be encouraged to drink approximately 100 to 125 ml of fluid every 10 to 15 minutes during competition and to consume approximately 400 to 500 ml of cold water before competition. However, even regular and adequate drinking will not necessarily prevent heat injury, at least in races of up to 10 km (England et al., 1982).

5. Runners should sponge frequently. Water applied to the skin acts as artificial sweat and aids the body's cooling system. In one study, runners who suffered heat injury in a 10-km race had used sponging facilities much less frequently than those who had completed the race safely (England et al., 1982).

6. The runners most likely to develop heat injury are those who

   - are overweight;
   - are inadequately trained;
   - are not acclimatized to the heat;
   - overestimate their running abilities and therefore attempt to run too fast during the race, especially near the end;
   - have suffered heat injury before;
   - are taller than 1.79 m (England et al., 1982);
   - ignore warning symptoms of impending heatstroke such as weakness, clumsiness, stumbling, headache, nausea, dizziness, apathy, aggression, and any gradual impairment of consciousness (J.R. Sutton & Bar-Or, 1980); unfortunately, the majority of runners who develop heat injury have either none or only one of these warning symptoms (England et al., 1982);
   - have recently recovered from febrile illnesses or are harboring illnesses such as influenza, gastroenteritis, or upper respiratory tract infection;
   - become severely dehydrated during exercise; or
   - have genetic predispositions (Jardon, 1982), possibly on the basis of inherited abnormalities of skeletal muscle metabolism (Jardon, 1982; Noakes, 1987a).

However, it should be noted that even elite, highly trained athletes can suffer heat injury if forced to race in inappropriate environmental conditions (Noakes, 1981).

7. All competitors must be educated to train properly and acclimatize for hot weather running; to avoid competition if they have recently been ill or have fevers; to drink adequately during competition; and to stop running if they develop symptoms of impending heatstroke.

8. Responsible and informed personnel should supervise drinking stations. These personnel should have the right to remove from the race any runners who exhibit clear signs of heat exhaustion or impending heatstroke.

9. Suitably qualified medical personnel should be present at all races in which there is a substantial risk of occurrence of heat injury. Such personnel must have free access to a basic medical kit for the immediate treatment of heat injury. The kit should contain at least the following: rectal thermometers, fluids for intravenous administration, "instant" ice packs, and one or two large electric fans.

10. Any previously healthy athlete who collapses and shows a marked alteration in mental functioning during exercise in the heat but who has a measurable pulse should be diagnosed and treated immediately for heatstroke. The rectal temperature should be measured, and a temperature of 107 °F (42 °C)or more will confirm the diagnosis of heatstroke. Immediate priorities are to cool the athlete as rapidly as possible and to call for medical assistance.

Remove the athlete's excess clothing and place him or her in a shady and preferably drafty area. Place ice packs all over the body but especially around the neck, under the armpits, and in the groin. Fan the athlete with an electric fan or towel. If a fan is not available, spray the athlete with a garden hose or place him or her in a cold shower. An athlete who is convulsing requires appropriate drugs administered by a doctor. Monitor the rectal temperature until it falls to 100 °F (38 °C), at which point active cooling can be stopped; thereafter continue to monitor the rectal temperature every 10 minutes. If the temperature begins to rise again, reinstitute active cooling with ice packs.

Ideally, the patient is at this point sent to a hospital for observation and further treatment.

11. Suitable vehicles should be on standby to transport seriously ill athletes to the nearest hospital.

12. All races should end in open, well-exposed areas so that athletes who collapse near the finish of the race can be easily spotted. Deaths from heatstroke have occurred in two North American races because the athletes became disoriented and collapsed in dense vegetation close to the finish, to be discovered too late.

Hypothermia During Running

So much attention has been paid to the dangers of heatstroke during marathon running that we have been slow to appreciate that the opposite condition, hypothermia, can also develop in runners. Hypothermia has long been recognized as a serious condition that often has fatal consequences for mountain hikers (Pugh, 1967), fell runners, and English Channel swimmers (Noakes, 1985; Pugh & Edholm, 1955). The growth in popularity of mass-participation marathons in the northern hemisphere, especially Britain, has focused our attention on the risk of hypothermia developing during marathon and longer races.

Australian Dr. John Sutton was probably the first to consider hypothermia as the cause of death in two runners competing in a "Go-As-You-Please" race to the summit of Mount Wellington in Tasmania in 1903 (Sutton, 1972). The race was held in a snowstorm with a strong wind blowing, and the runners were dressed only in "singlets and light knickers." Soon the competitors in the race were "lying over logs, on the ground, and under trees, too exhausted to continue" (p. 951). Almost certainly, the deceased runners froze to death before they could be rescued.

The first documented case of hypothermia in a marathon runner was reported by Ledingham and his colleagues (1982), who observed a rectal temperature of 95 °F in a runner who collapsed in the Glasgow Marathon, which was run under dry but cold conditions (dry bulb temperature 55 °F) with a strong wind of 16 to 40 km/hr. Subsequently, Maughan (1985) measured rectal temperatures of 59 runners completing the 1982 Aberdeen Marathon, which was run under more favorable weather conditions (dry bulb temperature 55 °F dry with humidity of 75%, and a wind speed of about 26 km/hr). Despite the relatively mild conditions of the race, including the absence of rain, four runners finished the race with rectal temperatures below the normal temperature of 98 °F measured at rest.

Other studies have shown that conditions even in the southern hemisphere can on occasion cause hypothermia (Sandell et al., 1988). A study of all the runners admitted to the medical tent at the end of the 1985 56-km Two Oceans Marathon, which was run under unusually cold conditions for the southern hemisphere (wet bulb globe temperature 68 °F, rain, and a wind of 30 km/hr), showed that eight runners (28% of all collapsed runners) had rectal temperatures below 98 °F. Despite maintaining a running speed in excess of 17 km/hr, one very thin, elite runner collapsed on the course and was brought to the medical tent, where his rectal temperature was found to be 95 °F.

As detailed in chapter 4, three factors predispose an athlete to the development of hypothermia during distance running: the environmental conditions, the athlete's clothing and body build, and the speed at which he or she runs.

Figure 4.2, a and b, allows us to calculate that the effective air temperatures prevailing in the three marathon races previously described, in which runners became hypothermic, would have been between 29 and 33 °F. Were those conditions to prevail for the duration of the race, runners running at 16 km/hr would need to wear clothing providing about 1.1 CLO units, whereas those who were reduced to a walk (5 km/hr) during the race would require approximately 2 CLO units of insulation. It is probable that most runners are unaware of the dangers of marathon running in the cold and so fail to wear clothing that provides sufficient insulation, especially under conditions of precipitation, cold, and, in particular, wind.

Experience with the English Channel swimmers (Pugh & Edholm, 1955) has shown that body build, especially the body muscle content but also the body fat content, is a critical factor determining the rate at which a swimmer will cool down during a long-distance swim. I suspect that the same applies to runners; those who have little body fat and are not muscular will probably be the most affected by the cold and the most likely to become hypothermic. Frank Shorter is one such thin runner who found that he ran poorly in the cold (see chapter 8) and conversely rather well in the heat. Possibly, this indicated that Shorter had difficulty maintaining a normally elevated body temperature when running in the cold.

The role of running speed in protecting against hypothermia has been discussed and is highlighted in Figure 4.2, a and b. The important point to remember is that the change from running to walking has a marked effect on the clothing required to maintain body temperature even at relatively mild effective temperatures. Thus, clothing with at least 4 times as much insulation is required to maintain body temperature at rest at an effective air temperature of 32 °F as when running at 16 km/hr. For this reason, hypothermia is likely to occur in those marathon runners who are lean, lightly muscled, and lightly clothed and who become fatigued and are forced to walk for prolonged periods during marathon races run in effective air temperatures of less than 41 °F. To prevent the condition, simply ensure that extra clothing is available in the event you are forced to walk when running races in cold conditions.

Frostbite

Tissues exposed to very cold temperatures, such as effective air temperatures of −28 °F or lower, will freeze rapidly; if rewarming does not occur within a short time, the frozen tissue dies, requiring amputation.

Toes and fingers are the classic sites of frostbite in mountaineers; in runners, the exposed parts of the face and the hands (if mittens are not worn) are most at risk. However, other, more vital organs may also be in danger.

Dr. Melvin Hershkowitz, a New Jersey physician, reported in *The New England Journal of Medicine* (Hershkowitz, 1977) that after 25 minutes of running at −18 °F in shorts, two T-shirts, a sweater, and a rain jacket that extended just below the belt line, he developed severe pain at the tip of his penis. This forced him to curtail his run 5 minutes later, at which time the physical examination of the sensitive area indicated the presence of early frostbite. Manual rewarming rapidly returned the circulation to the affected area, thereby sparing Dr. Hershkowitz the trauma of amputation. Prevention of recurrence has been achieved by the wearing of an athletic supporter and cotton warm-up pants. Others have suggested that a spare pair of socks placed in the front of the underpants is highly effective.

Sunburn, Skin Cancer, and Cataracts

There is a growing realization that excessive exposure of the skin to the UV-A and UV-B bands of the ultraviolet light from the sun increases the rate at which the skin ages and increases the likelihood that skin cancer will develop. For this reason I advise runners, especially those with skin that burns easily and tans poorly, to protect their skin from sun damage by using sunscreen lotions whenever they run. The face, shoulders, and arms especially need to be protected. In addition, recent evidence indicates that UV-B exposure increases the risk of developing cataracts (H.R. Taylor et al., 1988).

The ease with which the skin burns gives a grading classification of the skin type and determines the sun protection factor (SPF) that is required to prevent sun damage. Skin that always burns easily and never tans is graded as Type 1 skin; skin that burns moderately and tans gradually is Type III skin; skin that rarely burns and tans profusely is Type V skin; whereas skin that never burns and is deeply pigmented is Type VI. Lotions with the following SPFs should be worn by persons with different skin types: Type I skin, SPF 10 or more; Type III skin, SPF 8 to 10; Type V skin, SPF 4; Type VI skin, protection not required. When you are sweating heavily, sunscreen lotions should be applied hourly.

Lifelong care of skin and prevention of sunburn are worthwhile goals, because they will reduce both the rate of skin aging and the risk of developing skin cancer and malignant melanoma.

To prevent cataracts, runners should wear appropriate sunglasses that prevent UV-B transmission.

Altitude

The effects of altitude on exercise performance have been discussed in detail in chapter 11. These are the points to remember:

- Performance decreases proportional to altitude.
- Sea-level athletes are always at a disadvantage.
- Runners should arrive for competition either on the day of competition or 3 weeks beforehand.
- Sea-level runners should expect inadequate performances.

RUNNING AND THE PREVENTION OF CORONARY HEART DISEASE

Although the exact cause of coronary heart disease (coronary atherosclerosis) is unknown, certain risk factors are associated with the disease; the risk of developing the disease increases with the number of risk factors present.

The most important risk factors are

- cigarette smoking;
- elevated blood pressure (hypertension);
- elevated blood cholesterol levels (hypercholesterolemia), in particular a low HDL:total cholesterol ratio;
- physical inactivity;
- low social class;
- of European descent;
- male gender;
- family history of heart disease;
- certain disease states such as diabetes;
- short stature; and
- hostile personality type.

Cigarettes

Smoking, one of the most powerful coronary risk factors, acts to increase the rate of development of coronary atherosclerosis by mechanisms as yet unknown. One important effect is to attenuate the beneficial effects of regular exercise or alcohol consumption or both, which increase serum HDL-cholesterol levels (Stamford et al., 1984a, 1984b).

Heart disease risk rises appreciably with decreasing social status (Lapidus & Bengtsson, 1986; Wing et al., 1987), and males are more prone to heart disease than are females. Risk of heart attack rises when blood pressure is increased above 140/90 mm Hg or when the blood cholesterol level rises above 4.65 mmol/L (Stamler et al., 1986). The contention that very low blood cholesterol levels may be undesirable because of an increased risk of cancer (Schatzkin et al., 1987a) is not supported by other studies (K.M. Anderson et al., 1987; Sherwin et al., 1987).

Race and Family History

There are also racial differences in the incidence of heart disease, which is highest in Europeans and North Americans and lowest in Africans and those living in Third World countries. While this difference may be due to important environmental factors, in particular major differences in dietary fat consumption between these groups, evidence suggests that even when exposed to equivalent risk factors, not all races suffer equivalent rates of coronary heart disease.

Persons who have a family history of heart disease, with the disease occurring in grandparents, parents, uncles, aunts, sisters, or brothers, are at increased risk of heart disease. When such relatives have died from heart disease before the age of 45, the family may carry the genes for very high blood cholesterol levels, so-called familial hypercholesterolemia. Members of families with a history of early deaths from heart attack should consult their doctors and have their blood cholesterol levels and blood pressures monitored.

The reason persons of short stature should be at increased risk of heart disease is unknown.

Personality

Type A personality describes persons with three characteristics: They are highly competitive and ambitious; they have a chronic sense of urgency and speak rapidly and interrupt others frequently; and they are seized by anger and hostility with uncommon frequency. In short, they are unable to sit back and relax. Traditionally, the medical community has believed that such persons have greater risks of developing coronary heart disease than do persons without these characteristics, called *Type B personalities*. It is suggested that of the three personality characteristics, it is the hostility and anger of the Type A personality that explains his or her increased risk of heart disease (R.B. Williams, 1987).

But even "hostility" is not the best description of this personality characteristic. Rather, it appears that a mistrust of others, or cynicism, is the toxic element in the Type A personality that explains this person's apparently increased susceptibility to coronary artery disease. Tutko (Cimons, 1988) suggested that there are two subsets of the Type A person: The Type A-hostile and the Type A-controlled. Tutko argued that the Type A-hostile is the classic Type A person whose actions are motivated by hostility and anger. In contrast, the Type A-controlled is motivated "by excitement and reward—by the challenge of what he is doing. He's like a kid in a candy store. When he wants more, it's because he loves what he is doing" (Cimons, 1988, p. 46).

A study (Ragland & Brand, 1988) suggested that at least after an initial heart attack, the risk of sudden death or heart attack is lower in Type A than in Type B persons. Thus, the degree to which the Type A personality characteristics contribute to an increased risk of coronary heart disease remains uncertain.

Activity Level

Three researchers have contributed significantly to our knowledge of the relationship between activity level and coronary heart disease. Jeremy Morris, Ralph

Paffenbarger, Davis Siskovick, and their colleagues concluded separately that people who actively exercise are probably less likely to suffer from heart attacks.

Morris's Studies

What was probably the first important study suggesting that physical inactivity may be an important risk factor for coronary artery disease was reported in 1953 by Professor Jeremy Morris and his associates at the London School of Tropical Medicine (J.N. Morris et al., 1953). They found that conductors on the London Transport System had a 30% lower incidence of heart disease than did the sedentary bus drivers. A similarly favorable result was found for postal carriers compared to less active postal clerks, who performed sedentary work.

Critical analysis revealed that physical inactivity was not the only difference between the groups. The bus drivers were more overweight, had higher blood pressures and higher blood cholesterol levels, and smoked more than the conductors. These differences were already present even before the subjects were employed, suggesting that fat, heavy smokers with high blood cholesterol levels (who were thus likely to develop heart disease) chose sedentary occupations, whereas thin nonsmokers with low blood cholesterol levels chose active occupations (J.N. Morris et al., 1956; Oliver, 1967). In addition, the job demands of the bus drivers, who had to contend with the crowded London streets, were more stressful than those of the conductors.

These studies showed that important physical and psychological factors determine what occupations people will choose as well as the extent to which they will be physically active either at work or in their leisure time. Some of these physical and psychological variables also influence a person's risk of suffering a heart attack, and this influence is independent of the person's level of activity. Those who choose to exercise either at work or in leisure time are usually those who are at low risk of heart disease, because they tend not to smoke, they come from healthy, long-lived families, and are of high socioeconomic class. Thus, any or all of these factors could explain such people's low incidence of heart disease, whether or not they exercise.

In an attempt to exclude the possibility that persons likely to be at increased risk of heart attack might choose sedentary occupations, Morris's group next studied 16,882 British civil servants, all of whom were involved in sedentary occupations and who were quite similar in respect to their coronary risk factors. These subjects were then subdivided on the basis of whether they performed vigorous exercise in their leisure time or were less active. Vigorous exercise was classified as swimming, tennis, hill climbing, running, jogging, mountain walking, or fast cycling, but these authors did not quantify exactly how often or for how long it was necessary to be vigorously active in order to be placed in this group.

In 1973, these authors published their first findings; the heart attack rate in the vigorously active group was one third that of the less active group (J.N.

Morris et al., 1973). A subsequent study (Chave et al., 1978) showed that vigorous exercise in leisure time even offered a measure of protection for smokers and those with high blood pressure, but (for obvious reasons) these subgroups had higher heart attack rates than did nonsmoking, vigorously active civil servants whose blood pressures were normal.

Morris's group (J.N. Morris et al., 1980) reported that after 13 years of study, they had concluded that the heart attack rate in the vigorously active civil servants was less than one half that of their inactive colleagues. Furthermore, a degree of protection was even present for fat civil servants of small stature who smoked or who had high blood pressure, diabetes, or even chest pains. Of considerable interest was the finding that whereas the heart attack rate in the active group stayed the same between the ages of 40 and 60 years, the rate in the inactive group more than doubled during those years.

J.N. Morris and colleagues (1980) concluded that "vigorous exercise is a natural defence of the body, with a protective effect on the ageing heart against ischaemia and its consequences" (p. 1207). (*Ischemia* means a reduced blood flow and is usually caused by progressive atherosclerotic narrowing of the coronary arteries.)

Paffenbarger's Studies

The next outstanding studies in this field were those by Professor Ralph Paffenbarger and his colleagues (Paffenbarger & Hale, 1975; Paffenbarger et al., 1977, 1978, 1983, 1984). Ralph Paffenbarger (see Figure 18.2) is an experienced ultramarathon runner who has completed the grueling Western States 100 miler, a mountain race through the Sierra Nevadas of northern California, on five occasions. He is currently professor of epidemiology at Stanford University. An excellent review of Ralph Paffenbarger and his work is found in James Fixx's *Second Book of Running* (Fixx, 1980) in a chapter entitled "Is Running Really Good for Us?"

Indeed, it is a sad paradox that James Fixx was one of the few journalists to grasp the complexities involved in scientific studies attempting to measure the cardiovascular benefits of running. His sudden death during exercise was, regrettably, seen by many as proof that exercise could not be good for anyone; Fixx's own meticulous reporting of Ralph Paffenbarger's research (Fixx, 1980) was forgotten in the rush to incriminate jogging as the cause of Fixx's death.

But James Fixx was never under any illusion that running could prevent heart disease absolutely (see his quote at the beginning of this chapter).

In the early 1950s, Paffenbarger decided to study two populations: people who were vigorously active in their occupations (the San Francisco longshoremen study; Paffenbarger & Hale, 1975; Paffenbarger et al., 1977, 1984) and those who were active in their leisure time (the Harvard graduate study; Paffenbarger et al., 1978, 1983, 1984).

Figure 18.2   Professor Ralph Paffenbarger.

The reasons for studying these groups were the following. Excellent medical data had been collected years earlier on both groups, making it possible for Paffenbarger to begin a study on subjects whose medical histories were known for up to 40 years previously. He was therefore able to start a project that covered the life spans of his experimental subjects but that would be completed in his own lifetime. In the Harvard graduate study, for example, Paffenbarger was able to study subjects who had initially enrolled at Harvard as early as 1916.

In addition, the San Francisco longshoremen did not select the nature of work undertaken on the basis of whether they preferred manual or sedentary work, because all longshoremen had to perform hard manual labor at work for a minimum initial 5-year period. In fact, on average, most longshoremen continued heavy work for much longer, an average of 13 years (Paffenbarger et al., 1984). It is fair to conclude that because they could not choose initially whether they were physically active or inactive at work, all must have had similar attitudes toward exercise. Hence, the reasons some subsequently changed to sedentary work were not because they were initially too weak or too unwilling to do manual labor.

In this study, Paffenbarger and his colleagues found that those longshoremen who performed heavy manual labor had a far lower risk of fatal heart attack than did less active longshoremen. As in the studies of Morris and his colleagues, this risk was reduced even in longshoremen who had other coronary risk factors. Protection increased with increasing levels of workday energy expenditure (see Figure 18.3), so that the risk of fatal heart attack was reduced by 50% for a weekly energy expenditure of 39,900 kJ (9,500 kcal).

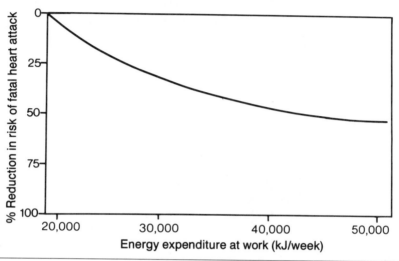

Figure 18.3 The risk of fatal heart attack falls with increasing energy expenditure at work.

Note. From "Epidemiology of Exercise and Coronary Heart Disease" by R.S. Paffenbarger, R.T. Hyde, D.L. Jung, and A.L. Wing, 1984, *Clinics in Sports Medicine*, **3**(2), p. 301. Copyright 1984 by W.B. Saunders Co. Adapted by permission.

In the Harvard graduate study, Paffenbarger et al. (1978) graded leisure-time activity according to the following classification: 10 stairs climbed every working day each week equaled 118 kJ/week (28 kcal/week); one city block walked every working day each week equaled 235 kJ/week (56 kcal/week); participation in light sports equaled 21 kJ/min (5 kcal/min); participation in vigorous exercise equaled 42 kJ/min (10 kcal/min).

Using this classification, Paffenbarger et al. (1984) found that men who reported climbing 50 or more steps each working day had a 20% lower risk of first heart attack than men who climbed less; those who walked five or more blocks daily were at 21% lower risk than those who walked less; and those who reported vigorous sporting activity in leisure time had a 27% lower risk than those who did not exercise vigorously. Interestingly, participation in light sporting activity did not influence cardiac risk.

When total leisure-time physical activity was calculated, researchers found that risk of first heart attack fell with increasing leisure-time physical activity and was 39% lower in those expending more than 8,400 kJ of energy in leisure-time exercise each week (see Figure 18.4). Runners interested in calculating their weekly kilojoule energy expenditure can do so by referring to Figure 2.2.

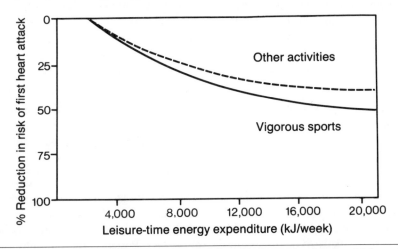

Figure 18.4 The risk of first heart attack falls with increasing levels of leisure-time physical activity.
Note. From "Epidemiology of Exercise and Coronary Heart Disease" by R.S. Paffenbarger, R.T. Hyde, D.L. Jung, and A.L. Wing, 1984, *Clinics in Sports Medicine*, 3(2), p. 306. Copyright 1984 by W.B. Saunders Co. Adapted by permission.

Figure 2.2 shows that the kilojoule energy expenditure per kilogram of body weight (Y axis on the right) increases linearly with increasing running speed. To calculate total energy expenditure during a particular exercise session, all one needs to know is body weight, duration of exercise, and average running speed.

Thus, an 80-kg runner whose average running speed is 10 km/hr (6:00/km) expends approximately 0.83 kJ/kg/min or 58 kJ/min during exercise. To expend more than 8,400 kJ (2,000 kcal) of energy per week, the value shown by Paffenbarger et al. (1984) to be associated with a 39% reduction in heart attack risk, the runner would need to run at that speed for 8,400 ÷ 58 minutes, that is, 144 minutes per week. A 50-kg runner whose average training speed is 16 km/hr (3:45/km) expends approximately 1.14 kJ/kg/min (57 kJ/min) and would need to run 147 minutes per week at that speed to achieve the same total energy expenditure.

There were seven other important findings in this study. First, a leisure-time energy expenditure of less than 8,400 kJ per week was as strong a risk factor for first heart attack as were those other well-established heart attack risk factors—smoking, high blood pressure, and high blood cholesterol. Thus, on the basis of this study, it seems that physical inactivity should be considered as important a risk factor for heart disease as those three factors, a view now supported by researchers from the prestigious Centers for Disease Control in Atlanta, Georgia (Powell et al., 1987).

Second, only Harvard graduates who remained active after graduation were protected from heart attack. The genetically gifted athletes who won fame and glory on the Harvard sports fields in their college days had reduced heart attack rates only if they continued to exercise vigorously in the years following graduation. This suggests strongly that exercise continued for life, not genetic ability, is associated with a subsequent reduction in heart attack risk. In the words of Paffenbarger and his colleagues (1978):

> If it is postulated that varsity sports participation reflects, at least in part, a selective attribute of personal health (cardiovascular fitness), the present findings show that such a selection alone is insufficient to explain lower heart attack risk in later adult years. (p. 173)

More recent findings suggest that if anything, the health of the former university athletes tends to deteriorate rather more rapidly with age than does the health of those who were not athletic during their college years. This is possibly because the body type of the university athlete proficient in sports like football and baseball is more likely to be mesomorphic (muscular). Possibly, mesomorphy is not associated with longevity or good health in later life (Sheehan, 1973).

Third, as other studies show, exercise offered protection even in the face of other coronary risk factors. Thus, Harvard graduates who were short in stature, who had parental histories of heart attack or hypertension, who smoked, who were overweight, or who had high blood pressure levels and histories of diabetes or stroke were still at a 50% lower risk of heart attack if they expended more than 8,400 kJ in leisure-time activities than were graduates with the same risk factors who did not exercise.

Fourth, alumni who reported vigorous leisure-time exercise had a lower risk of fatal heart attack at all levels of total weekly energy expenditure (see Figure 18.4). Thus, additional benefit seemed to be gained by including vigorous exercise in the exercise sessions.

Fifth, those graduates who had suffered heart attacks but who reported 8,400 or more kJ/week of leisure-time energy expenditure had a 29% lower heart attack fatality rate than did those graduates who had also suffered heart attacks but who did not exercise as vigorously.

Sixth, vigorously active graduates had a 27% lower risk of high blood pressure than did less active alumni (Paffenbarger et al., 1983). The heavier the graduate, the greater was the degree to which exercise reduced the risk of developing hypertension.

Seventh, Paffenbarger et al. (1984) calculated that if five risk factors for heart attack (physical inactivity, cigarette smoking, obesity, high blood pressure, and a family history of heart attack) were removed from all longshoremen and Harvard alumni, the risk of heart attack would have been reduced by 88% and 67% in each group, respectively.

Paffenbarger and his colleagues (1986) later showed that the longevity of Harvard alumni who exercised vigorously for life was increased.

Siskovick's Studies

The third researcher who made a significant contribution to this field is David Siskovick, a research cardiologist currently working at the University of North Carolina.

Siskovick and his colleagues (1982, 1984a, 1984b) collected detailed information on all persons dying suddenly from coronary heart disease during a 1-year period in Seattle, Washington. The researchers then excluded from their analysis all those persons who were ill, who had taken time off work, or who had experienced any symptoms before their sudden deaths. The researchers were left with a total of 145 persons who were absolutely healthy right up to the moment that they suddenly died.

Analysis of these data showed that those persons who exercised vigorously on a regular basis had an overall risk of sudden death approximately two thirds lower than that of the nonexercisers (see Figure 18.5). Interestingly, the risk that the sudden deaths in the exercising group would occur while these persons were exercising was increased acutely (vertical line in Figure 18.5), for the duration of the exercise bout, above the overall risk of the nonexercisers. Thus, although the total group of exercisers had a reduced risk of sudden death, that subset of exercisers with advanced heart disease who would ultimately die suddenly were more likely to die while they were exercising rather than when they were at rest.

This finding explains why the sudden deaths of athletes usually occur during exercise and why such events must not be construed to indicate that exercise is dangerous and should therefore be avoided. In fact, if the exercisers were to stop exercising, their risk of sudden death would increase threefold, as shown in Figure 18.5.

To put this in perspective, let us consider the following. Noakes et al. (1984a) and Noakes (1987b) showed that in the population of about 10,000 Comrades Marathon runners, there are approximately three sudden deaths per year, most of which occur as predicted by the data of Siskovick and his colleagues—during or shortly after exercise. If, on the basis of these three deaths per year, marathon running was judged too dangerous and was summarily and effectively banned, the annual risk of sudden death in the group of ultramarathon runners would triple to become equal to that of the nonexercisers in Figure 18.5. Thus, each year after the banning of marathon running, there would be nine, not three, sudden deaths, clearly an undesirable result. Therefore, by allowing our cohort of 10,000 marathon runners to continue running, approximately six lives per year are saved.

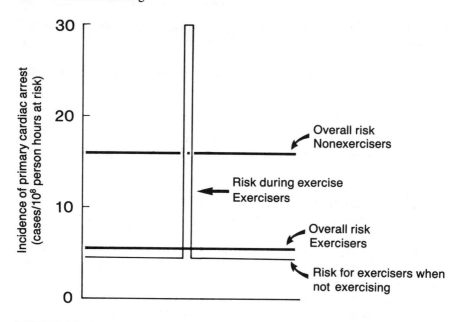

Figure 18.5 Habitual exercise reduces the overall risk of primary cardiac arrest. Note that the risk of cardiac arrest is steeply elevated during exercise in those regular exercisers who are at risk of sudden death.

Note. Based on data from "The Incidence of Primary Cardiac Arrest During Vigorous Exercise" by D.S. Siskovich, N.S. Weiss, R.H. Fletcher, and T.Lasky, 1984, *New England Journal of Medicine,* **311**, p. 876.

The studies of Siskovick and his colleagues confirm the finding that the risk of sudden death is reduced in persons who exercise regularly and suggest that this is almost certainly not due to the presence of confounding variables. However, the authors also indicate a likelihood that those persons who have heart disease in spite of their regular exercise will die during their short period of exercise. Were such persons to avoid all exercise, however, their overall risk of sudden death would be increased, not decreased. Interestingly, the degree of benefit is actually greatest the higher the level of coronary risk; persons who are at low risk of dying suddenly from coronary heart disease benefit less from vigorous physical exercise than do those who are at high risk either because of a family history of heart disease or because they are smokers who have other risk factors already described.

As Siskovick et al. (1984b) stated, "Efforts to discourage clinically healthy persons at risk of primary cardiac arrest from continuing to engage in vigorous exercise may be inappropriate" (p. 625).

In summary, it seems to me that there is now some fairly convincing evidence that those who do sufficient amounts of vigorous exercise probably do have a reduced heart attack risk. This should, however, never be construed as a reason why anyone should exercise. The only reason why people should exercise is because they enjoy it. To exercise solely to prevent having a heart attack is to miss the joy.

EXERCISE AND SUDDEN DEATH IN ATHLETES

If exercise does indeed have a role in preventing heart disease, why do athletes continue to die suddenly during exercise? This is a question that the press in particular seems quite unable to resist. It is interesting to see this phenomenon in its historical perspective.

The Greek physician Galen was one of the first to express an opinion on the risk of exercise to the heart. He wrote:

Athletes live a life quite contrary to the precepts of hygiene, and I regard their mode of living as a regime far more favourable to illness than to health. . . . while athletes are exercising their professions, their body remains in a dangerous condition but, when they give up their professions, they fall into a condition more parlous still; as a fact, some die shortly afterwards; others live for some little time but do not arrive at old age. (cited in Hartley & Llewellyn, 1939, p. 657)

The first modern sport to attract a similar concern was rowing. The seventh Oxford and Cambridge Boat Race, held in 1845, was the first to be rowed on the current course on the Thames between Putney and Mortlake. No sooner had the race moved to this longer course through the British capital than an irate letter written by one Frederick C. Skey, past president and Fellow of the Royal College of Surgeons, appeared in the *Times* of London, charging that "the University Boat Race as at present established was a national folly" (Hartley & Llewellyn, 1939, p. 657). Skey claimed that rowing was bringing young men to early graves.

A scientific study published shortly thereafter by John Morgan (1873), a Birmingham physician, proved that Skey was in error. Morgan showed that the life expectancies of university oarsmen were not reduced. If anything, life expectancies were slightly longer than that of the average Englishman of the period.

Almost a century later, in 1968, this issue was revived by a letter that appeared in the *Journal of the American Medical Association* (Moorstein, 1968) stating that all members of the 1948 Harvard rowing crew had since died "of various cardiac disease," an assertion that was enthusiastically denied by these oarsmen who reported that they were all "alive and well" (T.B. Quigley, 1968).

Surprisingly, cycling was the next sport to attract similar attention. It seems that in the 1890s North Americans suddenly discovered the bicycle, and medicine had another sport about which to express its alarm (M.M. Sherman, 1983). Prospective cyclists were warned that prolonged bending over the handlebars could cause "kyphosis bicyclistarum" or in lay terms "cyclist's stoop," "cyclist's figure," or even "cyclist's spine." Then too there was "cyclist's throat," caused by the inhalation of cold, dusty air, and "cyclist's face," the determined grimace that indicated the excessive tension caused by riding a bicycle. The incidences of hernias and appendicitis were also said to be more common in cyclists, and these too were blamed on the cycling position. Manufacturers were urged to develop a cycle that could be pedaled in the supine position.

As women turned to cycling, special concern was expressed about the particular hazards they faced. Cycling females, it was said, were especially prone to uterine prolapse, distortion of the pelvic bones, and hardening of the muscles of the pelvic floor, all of which would cause difficult labor should these women ever stop cycling long enough to become pregnant.

Finally, there was "cyclist's heart." The working life of the heart was limited to only a certain number of heartbeats, these physicians asserted, and the faster heart rate during cycling would only waste these precious beats and so lead to premature heart failure.

One of the first references to the dangers to the heart caused by running was made in 1909 by five eminent British physicians who started a correspondence in the *Times* of London by stating that "school and cross-country races exceeding one mile in distance were wholly unsuitable for boys under the age of nineteen, as the continued strain involved is apt to cause permanent injury to the heart and other organs" (Editorial, 1938, p. 1258).

Again, this view was easily refuted. In an analysis of 16,000 schoolboys covering a period of 20 years, Lempriere (1930) could find only two cases of sudden death during exercise that were not due to accidents. He concluded that "heart strain through exercise is practically unknown" (p. 269), a conclusion echoed by Sir Adolphe Abrahams (1930, 1951), who denounced the concept of the strained athletic heart.

Running again became a medical cause celèbre in the 1970s as the popularity of the sport mushroomed. One of the first articles to question the safety of such activity reported that half of 59 sudden deaths occurred during or immediately after severe or moderate physical activity, especially jogging. The authors questioned "whether it is worth risking an instantaneous coronary death by indulging in an activity, the possible benefit of which to the human coronary vasculature has yet to be proved" (p. 1327). They also considered "the possible lethal peril of violent exercise to coronary artery disease patients" (Friedman et al., 1973, p. 1327).

The first aspect of this issue that we need to consider is whether running is the real culprit in these deaths during running and is therefore a dangerous activity.

It seems to me that the general public has difficulty understanding this concept, because people tend to assume that there is always a cause-and-effect relationship between any two apparently related phenomena. To explain what I mean, let us consider the following examples.

Imagine that a rugby player is tackled around the neck and thrown to the ground during a match. During this illegal maneuver, the player's neck is broken, resulting in paralyzation. Clearly, in this case there is a direct relationship between the illegal tackle and the subsequent paralysis. Had the player not been playing rugby at that moment and had not been tackled around the neck, that player would not have been paralyzed.

For our second example, let us consider the runner who dies suddenly while running. Can we be certain that had the runner not been running at that particular moment, he or she would still be alive? If that question were put to a physician in a court of law, the physician would not honestly be able to answer that running had been solely responsible for the runner's death. The reason is this: Whereas in the normal course of events people do not suddenly break their necks, a large number of people with heart disease do die each day from heart attacks without ever running. Thus, in running, the condition of sudden death is, unlike the rugby player's broken neck, not specific to sport. The question that then arises is whether running triggered the fatal event.

It is crucial to understand that virtually every person who dies suddenly during exercise has a serious disease, usually of the heart, that adequately explains the cause of death (Noakes et al., 1984a); James Fixx had been a heavy smoker, and his father died at the age of 43 from a heart attack (Noakes, 1987b).

Athletes below the age of 40 who die suddenly during exercise are more likely to have a condition known as hypertrophic cardiomyopathy, in which the heart is abnormally enlarged. An example of such a case was the 25-year-old former international swimming captain and record holder who collapsed after a 5-km jog (Noakes et al., 1984b). However, some young athletes who die suddenly during exercise have genetically elevated blood cholesterol levels (familial hypercholesterolemia), which cause them to develop severe atherosclerosis at very young ages, leading to sudden death in their teens or early 20s.

Another crucial point is that neither coronary atherosclerosis nor hypertrophic cardiomyopathy is caused by exercise, however vigorous. As discussed in the previous section, the cause of coronary atherosclerosis is unknown but is related to certain factors including cigarette smoking, high blood pressure, high blood cholesterol levels, and physical inactivity. If anything, regular exercise acts against the development of coronary atherosclerosis. There is also no evidence that hypertrophic cardiomyopathy is either improved or aggravated by exercise.

Because these athletes have severe or advanced diseases, they are at high risk of dying suddenly, whether they exercise or not. A number of studies have tried to determine whether exercise increases the risk that persons with advanced heart disease will die suddenly during exercise. Some studies have found that moderate exercise does not increase the risk of sudden death (Lynch, 1980; Vuori et al., 1978), whereas others have found that more vigorous forms of exercise, such as cross-country skiing or running, are associated with a fivefold to sevenfold greater risk of sudden death (P.D. Thompson, 1982; P.D. Thompson et al., 1982; Vuori et al., 1978).

The most detailed study of this problem was reported by Paul Thompson and his colleagues (P.D. Thompson et al., 1982). They found that in the state of Rhode Island between 1975 and 1980, 12 men died while jogging, 11 from heart attacks. Five of these men were known to have heart disease before their deaths. These authors calculated that the incidence of death during jogging was 1 death per 396,000 hours of jogging, which is about 7 times the estimated heart attack rate during more sedentary activities. Thus, in that study the evidence clearly showed that jogging increased the risk that the jogger with severe heart disease would die while exercising. The same conclusion can be drawn from the data of Siskovick et al. (1982, 1984a, 1984b).

But this finding should not be used to overestimate the risk of exercise. For example, in the Rhode Island study, there was 1 death per 7,620 joggers per year—clearly an infinitesimal risk for each individual jogger. Furthermore, it would be totally impractical to screen 7,620 joggers in Rhode Island in an attempt to identify the one jogger at risk of sudden death each year. Dr. Peter Wood from the Stanford University calculated on the basis of these data that a middle-aged jogger with no known cardiac disease who decides to continue running for 1 more year is at considerably lower risk of sudden death than is a middle-aged nonrunner who remains inactive during that year (Wood, 1987).

The next important question that needs to be answered is this: If exercise did increase the risk of sudden death, by how much did exercise actually shorten the life expectancy of the runner who was in any case at high risk of dying suddenly and unexpectedly? Indirect evidence that exercise probably does not greatly decrease life expectancy under such circumstances comes from a study of the 1978 Rhode Island blizzard (Faich & Rose, 1979).

In February 1978 a severe blizzard struck Rhode Island, causing the daily death rate from heart attack to increase from the usual February average of 27 deaths per day to 48 deaths per day. This rate remained high for 3 of the first 5 days after the storm but subsequently decreased below the normal daily average, so that the total heart attack deaths for February that year were the same as for previous years. P.D. Thompson (1982) concluded, "These results suggest that the added physical and emotional stress arising from the storm eliminated those who would have succumbed to ischaemic heart disease in the near future" (p. 227). In the same way, jogging deaths may occur in those whose time is up and who are due to die within the next few days or weeks even if they avoided all forms of exercise, including walking.

It is important to remember that severe heart disease may be present even in persons who are extremely physically fit (Noakes et al., 1984b). For example, cases have been reported of marathon runners who completed the 90-km Comrades ultramarathon only weeks before their subsequent deaths from severe advanced heart disease (Noakes et al., 1984a). One 42-year-old runner completed a standard marathon in 3:06 just 3 weeks before autopsy showed he had complete occlusion of one major coronary artery and 75% narrowing, with atherosclerosis, of the other two. In addition, there was evidence of hypertrophic cardiomyopathy (Noakes & Rose, 1984).

It is quite wrong to assume that someone who is fit enough to complete marathon races and even ultramarathon races in quite respectable times cannot have very serious heart disease (Noakes, 1987b).

People who die suddenly during exercise almost always have symptoms of heart disease that they ignored, choosing to continue exercising rather than to seek medical advice. Thus, a study of heart attacks and sudden deaths in marathon runners found that fully 81% of these cases had had warning symptoms (Noakes, 1987b; Noakes et al., 1984a). Six athletes completed marathon races and three had completed the Comrades ultramarathon despite symptoms of chest or abdominal pain sufficiently severe to force them to stop running and to walk and run intermittently. Despite severe chest pain, one athlete continued to run a 16-km race and collapsed at the finish. Another runner continued training for 3 weeks, including a 64-km training run, with chest pain severe enough to force him to walk on numerous occasions.

A large number of people die each day from heart attacks, a point that is usually conveniently ignored by the press. The vast majority of these persons are sedentary, heavy smokers with uncontrolled high blood pressure and elevated blood cholesterol levels. If only those sudden deaths that occur in athletes are reported in the press, the public will naturally get a distorted impression of the relationship between exercise and heart disease.

Finally, as argued in the previous section, the data of Siskovick et al. (1982, 1984a, 1984b) clearly show that persons who have undetected heart disease and who are therefore at risk of sudden death can reduce their overall risk of sudden death if they exercise regularly. During exercise, their risk of death is increased acutely, however (see Figure 18.5).

All these points were rather tragically illustrated by James Fixx's death while running. Fixx was at high risk of heart disease because his father had died from a heart attack at a very young age (43 years). In addition, James had smoked heavily in his earlier years and had a markedly elevated blood cholesterol concentration (Noakes, 1987b).

Fixx unquestionably had warning symptoms that he chose to ignore. His fiancée has said that Fixx complained of chest tightness during exercise and said he was going to Vermont to see whether the fresh Vermont air would not alleviate the symptoms, which he considered to be due to allergy (Higdon, 1984; *Medical World News*, 1984). He promised to see a physician if the symptoms did not improve.

The air did not help, and Fixx died while running on his first day in Vermont. Interestingly, some months before his death, Fixx had visited Dr. Ken Cooper's Aerobic Center in Dallas and had politely refused to undergo an exercise stress test to check the state of his heart. Possibly even then he had an inkling of what was in store.

Autopsy showed that Fixx had severe coronary artery disease with near-total occlusion by atherosclerosis of one coronary artery and 80% occlusion of another coronary artery. There was also evidence of a recent heart attack. In addition, the heart was somewhat large, suggesting the possibility of concurrent hypertrophic cardiomyopathy.

On the day James Fixx died, 1,000 Americans would also have died of heart attacks (Zipes et al., 1981). Had the press bothered to review the features of those heart attack victims, it would have concluded that, at least with regard to his regular exercise, Fixx's death was the exception. The press would have found that heart attacks occur most commonly in males who have high blood pressure, who smoke heavily, who have high blood cholesterol levels, and who take no exercise, a conclusion that is obviously different from that drawn from reports that sensationalize only the exceptions to the rule.

Thus, James Fixx's death followed a familiar pattern and helps emphasize the points already made. One interesting possibility not considered by many is that regular exercise actually allowed James Fixx to outlive his father by 9 years.

Mechanisms Whereby Exercise May Protect Against Heart Disease and Sudden Death

Animal studies show that exercise reduces the rate of development of coronary atherosclerosis in monkeys fed a high-fat atherogenic diet (Kramsch et al., 1981) and increases the resistance of the trained heart to the lethal abnormal heart rhythm, ventricular fibrillation (Billman et al., 1984; Noakes et al., 1983b; Posel et al., 1989), which is the most common mechanism that causes persons with heart disease to die suddenly. Exercise can also discourage habits that are coronary risk factors. For example, in one survey, 81% of men and 75% of women who were smokers stopped smoking when they started running (Koplan et al., 1982).

Another recent study showed that the intensive training for a marathon significantly reduced two other important coronary risk factors, the serum cholesterol levels and the blood pressures of a group of previously sedentary and unfit middle-aged men (Findlay et al., 1987). Body mass and percent body fat were also reduced, and the number who smoked was reduced from 13 to 3. By the end of the study the participants were running about 6 hours a week, equivalent to a weekly energy expenditure of up to 22,000 kJ/week, sufficient to reduce the heart attack risk by about 50%, according to Figure 18.4.

Exercise training may also normalize the increased clotting tendency of the blood of patients with heart disease (Ernst & Matrai, 1987).

Prevention of Sudden Death During Exercise

Is it possible to predict who is likely to die suddenly during exercise and to therefore prevent this tragedy?

It seems entirely logical to assume that it should be possible to identify a person who has heart disease and is at risk of dying suddenly during exercise. But what are the facts?

Two procedures are used to determine if a person has heart disease and may die suddenly during exercise: exercise electrocardiography and coronary angiography. The value of a third method that uses radionuclear techniques to show the functioning of the heart and to delineate areas of heart damage is still being evaluated.

Exercise electrocardiography identifies those who show electrocardiographic changes during exercise that strongly suggest they have heart disease; the test does not conclusively diagnose heart disease. To separate those with from those without the disease, coronary angiography (or radionuclear techniques) must be performed. Coronary angiography clearly identifies those persons who do indeed have coronary heart disease, but the test is not without risk. When a large group is studied, a number of deaths and heart attacks will occur during the procedure (Grayboys, 1979).

In order to test all the joggers in any community, an enormous amount of repetitive and unstimulating work would be involved, from which we would be able to identify a large number who had heart disease sufficiently severe to raise the justifiable concern that they are at risk of dying suddenly during exercise. Does this mean that we must automatically restrict the activities of this entire group in the hope of preventing one sudden death? Worse, must we allow the press to propagate the falsehood that if one such person dies during exercise, anyone wishing to participate in that activity should be discouraged?

Even if we were to stop that single person at risk during exercise, we have no guarantee that his or her life expectancy would be increased by any more than a few hours, days, or weeks. In fact, we might even expedite that person's death, because by preventing him or her from exercising, we may remove that measure of protection that heart patients who exercise seem to enjoy!

In the words of P.D. Thompson et al. (1982), "Physicians can recommend exercise to asymptomatic adults without great concern for possible cardiovascular complications. . . . The risk of exercise is small and suggests that the routine exercise testing of healthy subjects before exercise training is not justified" (pp. 2535, 2537).

The recommendations that other researchers and I have made on the basis of our findings of sudden death in marathon runners are the following (Noakes, 1987b; Noakes et al., 1984a):

- Runners should not assume that completing a marathon will ensure total immunity from coronary heart disease or that reattainment of the ability to run that distance after a heart attack will prevent progression of that disease.
- Runners should seek medical advice and should not force themselves when exertional symptoms develop.
- When consulted by symptomatic runners, doctors should not exclude the possibility of coronary or other life-threatening heart diseases such as hypertrophic cardiomyopathy simply because the athlete is physically fit.

In brief, these researchers and I agree with the conclusion of P.D. Thompson et al. (1982) that only runners who are symptomatic should be exhaustively tested and discouraged from running should a life-threatening cardiac abnormality be discovered.

Because the majority of runners who die suddenly during exercise have, like James Fixx, had warning symptoms, following this simple procedure would reduce the incidence of sudden death during exercise by as much as 80%. Unfortunately, the condition will never be completely prevented because in about 20% of runners, sudden death is the first symptom of heart disease that they experience.

Of course, other forms of physical activity are associated with sudden death but have not attracted quite so much attention in the lay press or even the medical press.

A report in the *Journal of Forensic Science* (Malik, 1979) pointed out that the majority of cases of sudden death during sexual activity occur in early- or late-middle-aged males participating in sexual activity outside wedlock. The condition has yet to be described in a female!

Persons who are especially prone to this form of demise are, obviously, those with heart disease. The following verse, "On Coronary Coupling," was prompted by the findings of Dr. Lenore Zohman, head of cardiac rehabilitation at the Montefiore Hospital in New York, that sexual activity with a new partner is more demanding on the heart and therefore more dangerous for the cardiac patient than is activity with an established partner.

> *Coronary, have a care,*
> *Think before that new affair;*
> *Dr. Zohman studied swingers*
> *And her facts are really zingers.*
>
> *Sex domestic, also straight,*
> *Hardly makes you palpitate;*
> *Heart beats stay at normal rate*
> *When one beds with legal mate,*
> *And the danger that it bears*
> *Looms like—well, two sets of stairs.*
>
> *But roosting in another's nest*
> *Flirts with cardiac arrest;*
> *End result of evening's sport is*
> *Very often rigor mortis.*
> *So seduction's needs are three—*
> *Soft lights, music, ECG.*

(Anonymous)

EXERCISE AND LONGEVITY

If coronary heart disease is the most common cause of death in a typical Western population and if the risk of this disease is reduced in persons who exercise vigorously, then it follows that exercise should enhance longevity. The clearest indication that this is indeed so was reported by Paffenbarger and his colleagues (1986). In an extension of their Harvard graduate study, they showed that those graduates who continued to expend more than 8,400 kJ (2,000 kcal) per week in leisure-time physical activity from age 35 years onward enjoyed a 2-1/2-year gain in life expectancy. Those who began vigorous exercise only after 50 years of age had a 1- to 2-year extension in longevity.

A number of other studies support this conclusion that physical activity probably increases longevity by 1 to 2 years (Heyden & Fodor, 1988; Pekkanen et al., 1987).

Athlete's Heart

The term *athlete's heart* was coined in the late 19th century by those who mistakenly believed that exercise caused heart damage that led to an enlarged, weakened heart and led to death at a young age from heart failure.

In fact, as discussed in an earlier section of this chapter, we now know that persons involved in dynamic, endurance-type activities certainly do not have reduced life expectancies and probably live longer. We also know that a normal heart cannot be damaged by very severe exercise, even at medium altitude, because performance in such activities is limited by proton accumulation in the exercising skeletal muscles, which are forced to stop exercising well before the demands on the heart become excessive. During exercise, the heart simply comes along for the ride, while the skeletal muscles are left to do the work.

Today we use the term *athlete's heart* to describe cardiac characteristics found in trained athletes (see Table 18.1). The heart of the trained athlete has a slow resting heart rate that may be as low as 28 beats per minute in some world-class marathon runners. The maximum heart rate is also slightly reduced in these athletes. The volume of the heart is up to 60% greater in world-class athletes than in untrained subjects, and this enlarged heart pumps more blood with each stroke, both at rest (resting stroke volume) and at maximum exercise (maximum stroke volume). The result is that the maximum cardiac output, the amount of blood pumped each minute by the heart during maximum exercise, and the $\dot{V}O_2max$ are much greater in world-class athletes than in untrained subjects.

In the words of Sir Adolphe Abrahams (1951), "This term [athlete's heart], if legitimately employed, would apply to a heart of superior contractility particularly efficient for the circulatory demands of athletic feats and of violent exercise generally" (p. 1190).

Heart Murmurs

Time was when any heart murmur automatically disqualified anyone from doing any exercise, as happened with Clarence DeMar in the 1910s and Wally Hayward

Table 18.1   Cardiovascular Values in Untrained, Trained, and World-Class
Athletes

Cardiovascular quality	Untrained	Trained	World-class
Resting heart rate (beats/min)	75	60	28-36
Maximum heart rate (beats/min)	185	183	174
Heart volume (ml)	750	820	1,200
Resting stroke volume (ml)	61	80	125
Maximum stroke volume (ml)	120	140	200
Resting cardiac output (L/min)	4.6	4.7	4.5
Maximum cardiac output (L/min)	22.2	25.6	34.8
$\dot{V}O_2$max (ml/kg/min)	41	50	80

Note. Compiled from various sources.

in the 1930s. However, increased medical sophistication has shown that a vast majority of heart murmurs, particularly in athletes, are entirely "innocent" and do not indicate the presence of disease. The interpretation of the meaning of a murmur will depend upon the presence or absence of other findings, which together will then suggest whether the murmur likely is a normal finding or likely signifies heart disease. We now know that up to 80% of runners will be found to have heart murmurs and added (third and fourth) heart sounds when evaluated by experienced cardiologists (Parker et al., 1978; Singh et al., 1975).

Thus, the majority of runners will indeed have heart murmurs that are a feature of their fitness and do not indicate disease. The athlete who is concerned that heart murmurs may indeed be due to disease should consult a heart specialist who, with the aid of sophisticated modern equipment, will be able to establish beyond doubt whether the murmur is or is not due to significant heart disease.

Inflammation of the Heart Muscle (Myocarditis)

In most of the more severe viral infections, in particular influenza, the virus attacks muscle cells throughout the body, causing marked changes in the ultrastructure of these cells and reducing the activities of the important oxidative and glycolytic enzymes essential for cellular energy production (Astrom, 1977; Astrom et al., 1976). This explains why muscle pains and stiffness, much like those felt after a marathon, are common features of many of these infections and why strength and endurance are reduced especially during, but also for some period after, a viral infection (W.L. Daniels et al., 1985).

The heart cells are also frequently involved in such infections, and if strenuous exercise is performed when the heart cells are infected by virus, serious consequences, including sudden death, can result (Neuspiel, 1986).

For this reason, no one should exercise at all during the febrile stage of any viral infection, and one should exercise only very lightly for at least 7 to 10 days after the body temperature has returned to normal. This means that anyone who has influenza within 7 to 10 days of a race must not enter that race; if the infection occurs 10 to 21 days before the race, the athlete may run that event but only at a gentle pace. Only if the infection occurs more than 3 weeks before a race can the athlete run hard in the race, but the chances are that the results will be less than spectacular.

Abnormal Heart Rhythms

When studied during exercise, well-trained runners have a high incidence of abnormal heart rhythms, some of which would normally be considered to indicate serious heart disease (Pantano & Oriel, 1982). Pantano and Oriel concluded that in absence of other symptoms, these variations in heart rhythms are normal and do not indicate heart disease.

High Blood Pressure (Hypertension) in Athletes

Although the evidence shows that vigorous lifelong exercise reduces the likelihood that high blood pressure will develop (Paffenbarger et al., 1983) and that regular exercise is an essential component in the treatment of persons with hypertension (Jennings et al., 1987), some athletes will have or will develop this condition nevertheless and will require treatment.

High blood pressure is considered to be present when the blood pressure readings exceed 140/90 mm Hg. The convention 140/90 means that the average systolic blood pressure, the pressure present in the large arm arteries when the heart is actively contracting, is 140 mm Hg and that the average diastolic pressure, the pressure present when the heart is relaxing, is 90 mm Hg. Blood pressure readings in excess of 140/90 mm Hg are associated with an increased risk for the development of stroke or heart attack; thus persons whose blood pressures exceed these values require treatment.

Currently, there is complete consensus that persons whose blood pressures exceed 140/90 mm Hg should be treated, but there is a lack of agreement about the exact blood pressure reading above which drug therapy becomes essential. My feeling is that blood pressures that are consistently raised above 165/95 mm Hg definitely require drug therapy and that athletes whose blood pressures are raised to these levels should not exercise vigorously until control of their elevated blood pressures is achieved.

Conventional treatment of persons with hypertension follows a "step-care" approach, and the following such approach has been suggested for the management of the hypertensive athlete (Walther & Tifft, 1985).

Step 1: Prescription of one of the following drugs: Prazosin, Clonidine, Methyldopa, or Guanethidine monosulphate. (The status of two newer groups of drugs, the calcium antagonists Verapamil and Diltiazem, and of the ACE inhibitors is currently under investigation. It seems likely that these may yet become the drugs of choice in the treatment of hypertension in athletic persons.)

Step 2: Addition of a low-dose diuretic agent with potassium chloride supplementation of a potassium-sparing agent if the Step 1 medication fails to lower the blood pressure to below 160/90 mm Hg.

If these steps fail, an antagonist of the sympathetic nervous system, so-called beta-receptor antagonists of beta-blockers, may be required. Unfortunately, these drugs produce a number of trying side effects for the athlete; in particular, the drugs very seriously interfere with exercise performance probably through combined effects on the heart, skeletal muscle, and metabolism and should therefore be used only as a last resort.

The nonpharmacological approach entails mild sodium restriction, mild caloric restriction for weight reduction when indicated, and behavior modification, in particular application of relaxation techniques.

THE RESPIRATORY SYSTEM

Exercise-Induced Asthma

Most persons who develop asthma attacks during exercise are aware that they suffer from asthma and will be under medical treatment for this condition. For this reason I will not discuss this topic in any great detail.

In essence, the respiratory airways of asthmatics are especially sensitive to a number of stimuli such as cold air, infections, cigarette smoke, and various allergic stimuli such as house dust, animal dander, and certain foods.

When exposed to these stimuli, the muscles lining the respiratory airways go into spasm, causing severe narrowing of the small air passages. This narrowing acts like a ball valve, allowing air to enter the lung but preventing its escape during normal exhalation. Thus, during an attack, the asthmatic has great trouble exhaling, and his or her lungs become progressively more distended by trapped air, causing progressive respiratory distress.

There are three important points about asthma. First, the condition must be handled by a medical practitioner. Second, the vast majority of asthmatic symptoms can be adequately controlled, if not completely eliminated, by the use of appropriate medication.

Third, running is not the exercise of choice for asthmatics. For reasons that are not entirely clear, running is more likely to produce asthmatic attack than is, for example, swimming. However, if the asthma is well controlled, the patient can run.

Furthermore, far from avoiding sport, asthmatics (especially children) should be as active as possible in sport, because the exercise will frequently reduce the amount of medication needed to control symptoms; a child will benefit from the psychological boost of participating as a normal child in a normal activity.

Respiratory Infections

The high incidence of respiratory infections in competitive runners in the week following major competitions was discussed in chapter 9. The reason for this high incidence is unknown but may be related to (a) trauma to the membranes of the respiratory passages caused by sustained levels of ventilation (such damage will be exacerbated if the environmental temperatures are low) and (b) exercise- and diet-induced (Kono et al., 1988) impairment of the body's resistance to infection due to alterations in the immune system (Lewicki et al., 1987; Nieman et al., 1989). Interestingly, during the time that polio epidemics were common, it was well recognized that vigorous exercise lowered resistance to poliomyelitis virus and increased the risk of more severe paralysis.

Regardless of the mechanism, athletes need to remember that they are at high risk of infection when they race competitively, especially in cold conditions. After such races, athletes should be extremely wary of starting training too soon. At all times runners should remember that an infection inevitably means that they have done too much and are in need of rest, not more training.

When should an athlete with a respiratory or other infection compete again? The most comprehensive advice I could find is that followed by the Swedish cross-country skiers, who are particularly prone to respiratory infections because they train and compete in very cold temperatures.

The advice they receive is the following (Bergh, 1982).

1. Never train hard and never race when you have an infection or are otherwise in poor health. If possible, seek the advice of a physician. Do not train or compete if you

   - have a fever,
   - have a sore throat,
   - have a bad cold, or
   - have just been vaccinated.

2. You can train easily but should not train hard or compete if you
   - have recently been ill or
   - have a light (head) cold—slightly blocked or runny nose with no fever or sore throat.
3. If you have been ill, do not resume training until you are completely well; consult your physician. If you have a cold or other contagious condition, do not train, race, or go to training camps with other athletes.
4. To race when you are not completely well is misguided loyalty to your teammates, club, organization, or leaders. Racing when you are ill can have serious consequences; in so doing you may risk your health or your life.

The Effects of Antibiotic Treatment on Exercise Performance

I am frequently approached by runners who are unwilling to take antibiotics to treat their infections because they fear that antibiotics will jeopardize their performances. The infection jeopardizes their running and indicates that they have overtrained. Antibiotics have not been shown to affect performance adversely (Kuipers et al., 1980).

Fatigue of the Ventilatory Muscles During Exercise

There is now good evidence that the diaphragm and other respiratory muscles become fatigued during both short-duration, high-intensity exercise (Bye et al., 1984) and during more prolonged exercise like standard marathon running (Loke et al., 1982).

Although the implications of this finding are not yet clear, it may indicate that training of the ventilatory muscles by methods other than just running may be necessary.

The Second Wind

The second wind is one of the more interesting and least understood phenomena in exercise physiology. It is defined as the subjective sensation of reduced breathlessness (dyspnea) that comes on after a few minutes of hard exercise.

The first reference to an explanation for this phenomenon that I could find comes from Webster (1948). He suggested, without any experimental justification, the following:

When the second wind, that feeling of renewed energy that the runner experiences, comes on, a certain alkaline substance, created or multiplied in the blood by the process of training, begins to neutralize the acidity which has been produced by exercise activity running on into the beginning of fatigue. (p. 119)

The only scientific studies of the second wind are those of Scharf et al. (1984a, 1984b), who showed that at the onset of the second wind, there is a change in the function of the muscles of inspiration. Specifically, the authors found a reduction in the number of muscle fibers recruited, indicating that the contractility of the inspiratory muscles, particularly the diaphragm, had increased. They suggested that a redistribution of blood flow to the diaphragm and stimulation of the contractility of the inspiratory muscles by adrenaline and other hormones could explain this change.

Further, the authors suggested that the progressive breathlessness that develops during prolonged exercise may represent a reversal of the second wind, that is, a progressive failure of the contractility of the inspiratory muscles, requiring the recruitment of more muscle fiber and causing the subjective sensation of increasing breathlessness.

THE GASTROINTESTINAL SYSTEM

The most common gastrointestinal problems that affect runners, especially during competition, are increased bowel activity causing mild but irritating diarrhea (called "runner's trots") as well as progressive nausea and a disinclination to either eat or drink especially during the last third of marathon and ultramarathon races.

Runner's Trots

Twenty to forty percent of runners are troubled by abdominal cramps, diarrhea, or the urge to defecate during or after competitive running (Keeffe et al., 1984; D.C. Larson & Fisher, 1987; Rehrer et al., 1989b; Riddoch & Trinick, 1988; Sullivan, 1981). These symptoms occur more frequently in men than in women (Keeffe et al., 1984; Riddoch & Trinick, 1988).

The physiological mechanisms that explain why the gastrointestinal symptoms develop during running are not known. My feeling is that exercise per se is not the cause; these symptoms are specific to running and occur with much lower frequency during other activities like cycling or swimming. Thus, it is likely that the increased mechanical mixing and bouncing caused by running (D.C. Larson & Fisher, 1987), possibly aided by increased blood levels of hormones that increase bowel motility (Sullivan et al., 1984), are the principal causes of these symptoms. Symptoms are also more common in runners who become dehydrated by more than 4% during competition (Rehrer et al., 1989c). However, not everyone develops these symptoms when running; thus, other predisposing factors may need to be present.

In chapter 15 I introduced the theory that part of the reason for runner's trots might be mild milk or other food intolerance. One runner told me (Noakes, 1982) that for years he had suffered from intense intestinal cramping that came on a few hours after he had completed a hard training session or a race of more than 5 km. Once the discomfort began, he would have to retire to bed. The spasms of colicky abdominal pain eventually abated about 5 hours later. After much unsuccessful trial and error, that runner finally decided to cut out all dairy produce from his normal diet, which had dramatic results; he was again able to train and race hard without the development of intense abdominal cramping after exercise. He has subsequently had minor recurrences only when he has inadvertently eaten dairy produce that has been disguised in various foods, such as sauces.

Although that runner did not strictly suffer from runner's trots, his story was important to me because after hearing it, I decided to reduce the amount of dairy produce in my own diet. The first result was that I cured myself of an irritable bowel syndrome—a condition of episodic left-sided bowel cramping that is said to be due to psychological factors—and was suddenly able to run any distance race without the need for a pit stop.

When I subsequently discussed this with a gastroenterologist, Dr. Mervyn Danilewitz, he told me that my complaint was not unusual. His own studies (Danilewitz et al., 1984) showed that milk (lactose) intolerance is present in a high percentage (66%) of persons with the irritable bowel syndrome, and he has cured a number of runners with the "trots" by telling them to avoid dairy produce for at least 24 hours before competition.

It is likely that persons who are milk intolerant have reduced amounts of the enzyme lactase in the walls of their small intestines; these people are said to have lactase deficiency or to be lactose intolerant. Lactase is required for the normal breakdown of the milk sugar lactose into its two component simple sugars, glucose and galactose.

The bowel content of lactase is low in all humans at birth but then rises steeply within a few days as the infant starts to drink milk. However, after 2 or 3 years the bowel lactase content falls and, especially in certain races like African Americans, black Africans, Chinese, and Askenazi Jews, can reach very low levels. Only in northern Europeans and their descendants and in certain nomadic African cattle-herding communities is the incidence of lactose intolerance low (Kretchmer, 1972).

The result is that in many communities, there is a wide range in the amounts of bowel lactase present in different individuals. Those who have high contents of lactase will be able to ingest large amounts of dairy produce without developing the symptoms of milk intolerance; those with no lactase at all will be quite unable to metabolize any dairy produce and will have severe milk intolerance. In between are persons like myself who have some bowel lactase and are therefore able to cope with a certain, critical amount of dairy produce. I have found, for example, that I can only manage the milk that I drink in tea and coffee and an occasional piece of cheese or chocolate. Eating my early morning cereal with

100 ml or more of cow's milk precipitates a very severe attack of bowel spasms 4 to 8 hours later.

The reasons why lactase deficiency causes these symptoms are as follows. The lactose that escapes small intestine digestion is greedily attacked by the bacteria present in the large bowel, which rapidly ferment the lactose into organic acids and carbon dioxide. The gases cause the bowel wall to become distended and therefore painful, and the organic acids probably stimulate the muscles in the bowel wall to contract. In addition, water is drawn into the bowel by the osmotic action of the organic acids. The result is that when persons with lactase deficiencies ingest dairy produce, they develop bloating, flatulence, belching, cramps, and watery, explosive diarrhea.

Why lactase deficiency also seems to cause the loose stools during competitive running is not as easy to explain. Possibly, the fermentation by-products of lactose stimulate the bowel to become more active during running.

The practical point is, of course, that anyone who regularly develops diarrhea during running should initially stop taking dairy products for 24 to 48 hours before competition. If this prevents the diarrhea, the runner has discovered the cure. If not, the possibility that the runner may be sensitive to another substance, even fructose (D.E.H. Anderson & Nygren, 1978), must be considered. Another tip is to eat a low-residue diet for 24 to 48 hours before competition (Keeffe et al., 1984; D.C. Larson & Fisher, 1987).

Bloody Diarrhea After Exercise

As many as 20 to 30% of runners may have bloody stools after competitive running (Eichner, 1989; R.L. Fisher et al., 1986; McCabe et al., 1986; L.F. McMahon et al., 1984; Porter, 1983; J.G. Stewart et al., 1984), and in some the condition may mimic serious disease (Cantwell, 1981). At present, the cause of the bleeding is unknown, and even detailed investigations in some runners have failed to find anything that would explain the bleeding (Cantwell, 1981; R.L. Fisher et al., 1986). Other studies found evidence for bleeding from the stomach (Eichner, 1989) or from hemorrhagic colitis (Moses et al., 1988). Bloody diarrhea, which is more common in younger, faster runners (L.F. McMahon et al., 1984) particularly when they have suddenly increased their training or competitive running (J.G. Stewart et al., 1984), resolves within 3 days. The condition has been found in triathletes and cyclists (Eichner, 1989) but does not occur in walkers and is more frequent in runners who ingest analgesic drugs before or after competition (J.D. Robertson et al., 1987). The volume of blood lost is usually inconsequential, amounting to less than 0.5 ml of whole blood a day. Thus, it is unlikely to be an important source of blood loss and could not explain the development of anemia in runners.

If the condition persists beyond 3 days, medical advice should be sought. Causes of bloody diarrhea that will require medical or possibly surgical intervention include bowel infections and bowel tumors. If no cause is found, the athlete should be encouraged to avoid anti-inflammatory drugs for 12 to 24 hours and aspirin for 2 to 3 days before heavy training or competition (Eichner, 1989).

Postexercise Nausea

Heavy or prolonged exercise frequently causes mild nausea and decreased appetite during and for a few hours after exercise. In some runners, vomiting may occur, particularly during or after hard exercise (Keeffe et al., 1984).

Sullivan (1981) found that 6% of runners complained of nausea or retching after competitive running and 50% had reduced appetites for 1/2 to 2-1/2 hours after hard competition. The percentage of runners who reported increases, decreases, or no changes in appetite after an easy run was about equal. These effects should be due to gastroesophageal reflux induced by exercise (C.S. Clark et al., 1989).

Exercise and Cancer of the Colon

A host of studies have shown an inverse relationship between high levels of physical activity at work and a reduced risk of colon cancer (Albanes et al., 1989; Frederiksson et al., 1989; Garabrant et al., 1984; Gerhardsson et al., 1986, 1988; Severson et al., 1989; Slattery et al., 1988; Vena et al., 1985; Wu et al., 1987). This is a novel and currently unexplained finding that might possibly relate to the stimulatory effect of exercise on gastrointestinal motility (Kohl et al., 1988). It is currently believed that cancer of the colon occurs when toxic cancer-forming (carcinogenic) dietary substances remain in contact with the linings of the colon for prolonged periods because of poor bowel motility. However, a general effect may also be present; rats that exercise are more resistant to the development of chemically induced cancers of both the colon (Andrianopoulos et al., 1987) and breast (L.A. Cohen et al., 1988).

Exercise is thought to increase bowel motility, thereby shortening the time it takes for food (and the carcinogenic substances contained in that food) to pass through the bowel—the bowel transit time (Cordain et al., 1986; Keeling & Martin, 1987). Thus, the carcinogenic agents have less time to damage the colon linings and thereby induce cancer; this, it is speculated, reduces the overall risk of colon cancer. However, not all studies find that exercise reduces bowel transit time (Bingham & Cummings, 1989; Meshkinpour et al., 1989).

The transit time of food in the small bowel, where the absorption of most food occurs, is not influenced by exercise (Ollerenshaw et al., 1987). Thus, food absorption should not be influenced by exercise.

THE GENITOURINARY SYSTEM

Bloody Urine (Hematuria) After Exercise

Blood Loss Due to Bladder Trauma

Like most marathoners, I am an obsessional urine watcher—an avid follower of the effects of running, climate, and a host of other minutiae on the production of this critical human end product. And in common with most runners, my concern is never greater than when this process has been most threatened—by those 3 hours of critical renal insult imposed by the marathon race.

Only after that first, ceremonial postrace voiding can we marathoners again feel secure. Imagine what should happen if at this critical first voiding, athletes should see what appears to be their very life blood disappearing before their eyes. The emotional impact is catastrophic. It is enough to suggest complete internal dissolution. A case, one runner said, of total body failure.

This sense of destruction is only compounded by a visit to the doctor. For 10 days later, having survived a series of most exhaustive tests, the athlete is confronted with the assurance that nothing is wrong. The athlete is asked to forget the unforgettable—to dismiss that vision as a figment of postrace dementia.

Fortunately, there is no longer a need for this limited understanding of runner's hematuria. Thanks to the British Royal Navy, we have at least one valid explanation for this diagnostic failure.

With orders to get to the root of the problem, Surgeon Captain Blacklock (1977) of the Royal Navy Hospital in Gosport, Hampshire, investigated a group of naval athletes who developed bloody urine after exercise. He used an operative procedure in which a small fiberoptic tube, a cystoscope, is passed into the bladder allowing its inner walls to be observed. Through his cystoscope, Blacklock saw what he suspected—angry bleeding bruises in the membrane lining the bladder walls. Blacklock repeated the procedure 7 days later and found that the bruises had cleared.

Blacklock proposed that these bruises are caused by the impact of the two walls of the empty bladder against each other during running. Although each impact may by itself be very minor, when they are repeated with each running stride over a long period the trauma can become quite marked. This postulated mechanism would also explain the inconsistency with which any single athlete develops hematuria after exercise: When running with a urine-filled bladder, the athlete would be protected from injury. This proposed mechanism also leads to a simple technique to prevent bladder bruising: Always run with a half-filled bladder, and never urinate immediately before running.

Blood Loss Due to Red Cell Leakage Through the Kidney Glomeruli

The glomeruli of the kidney are networks of blood vessels enclosed in a special membrane through which the blood is filtered as the first stage in the production of urine.

Under normal circumstances, the glomeruli do not allow red blood cells to be filtered into the urine, because these cells are too large to pass through the filtering membrane. However, quite good evidence now shows that a high percentage, if not most, of the red blood cells found in urine after exercise have escaped through the glomeruli (Fassett et al., 1982; Kincaid-Smith, 1982).

This suggests that glomerular permeability is transiently increased during exercise, allowing the passage of some large substances that are normally unable to pass through the glomeruli. Once the exercise stops, these changes reverse themselves within 24 to 48 hours, and the glomerular membrane again becomes impermeable to red blood cells.

Blood Loss Due to Factors Unrelated to Exercise

Hematuria may also be caused by something that has nothing to do with running. Runners are not immune to conventional medical conditions like kidney stones, growths, or infections, all of which may first expose themselves by the passage of bloody urine after exercise.

Hemoglobinuria

Hemoglobinuria is the passage of the red blood cell pigment hemoglobin—the pigment that gives blood its color—in the urine. Hemoglobinuria occurs when the red blood cells traversing the blood vessels in the feet become damaged by the constant impact of the feet against the hard road surface during running. Some cells are destroyed, releasing their contained hemoglobin into the bloodstream; the hemoglobin passes into the kidneys, from whence it is excreted in the urine (Buckle, 1965).

The precipitating factors for hemoglobinuria are hard running surfaces and poorly designed running shoes, in particular shoes that do not absorb sufficient impact shock. Prevention of the condition is usually quite simple and involves the prescription of running shoes with soft midsoles (see Figure 6.2), especially under the forefoot.

However, some athletes are especially prone to hemoglobinuria. Godal and Refsum (1979) and Banga and his colleagues (1979) investigated athletes whose performances dropped inexplicably whenever they commenced hard training. All were found to have genetically fragile red blood cells, which presumably started to break down in large numbers when the athletes exposed their more fragile red blood cells to the trauma of foot-to-road contact.

This caused the runners to become anemic and their performances to fall precipitously. It is entirely possible that other similar types of idiosyncracies predispose some athletes to high rates of red blood cell destruction during exercise, rates that eventually lead to iron-deficiency anemia.

Myoglobinuria

Myoglobinuria is the presence of the muscle protein myoglobin in the urine. It occurs when, for reasons not well understood (Knochel, 1972), myoglobin escapes from the exercising skeletal muscles and appears in the urine.

Unlike hemoglobin, myoglobin is highly toxic to the kidneys and in high concentrations may be an important factor explaining the acute kidney failure that occurs not uncommonly in events like the Comrades ultramarathon (MacSearraigh et al., 1979). A group of researchers from Addington Hospital in Durban (Schiff et al., 1978) found that 57% of a group of Comrades Marathoners had elevated blood myoglobin levels (myoglobinemia) after the race, and 14% had myoglobin in the urine (myoglobinuria).

It seems that runners prone to severe myoglobinuria may have subtle, as yet undefined muscle cell abnormalities that predispose them to acute renal failure and also possibly to heatstroke (Noakes, 1987a).

An Approach to the Management of Bloody Urine

The athlete who passes bloody urine must first decide whether to consult a doctor or not. In general, I advise that the first time the runner passes the bloody urine, he or she should consult a doctor. Depending on the findings of initial testing, the runner would either be able to ignore all subsequent episodes, or would require additional medical evaluation.

The runner should seek medical attention without delay if there is any associated low back (loin) pain or fever; if the bloody urine also occurs when no exercise has been performed; if the condition fails to clear up within 24 to 48 hours after exercise; or if the condition fails to respond to appropriate treatment (soft shoes or running with a half-filled bladder).

Loin pain indicates that the site of bleeding is likely to be the kidney; this is a strong indication that an abnormality like kidney stones is the cause. In this case, an intravenous pyelogram is performed in which a radio-opaque dye similar to that used in coronary angiography is injected into the bloodstream. X rays taken as the dye is excreted by the kidneys allow the outline of the kidneys to be seen so that any abnormalities become immediately apparent.

In contrast, if there is associated lower abdominal (suprapubic) or groin pain or discomfort, or discomfort in the penis, the bleeding is probably of bladder origin.

Similarly, the passage of blood clots suggests that the bleeding comes from the bladder (Editorial, 1982b).

Exercise-related hematuria always resolves within 72 hours (Blacklock, 1977; Editorial, 1982b; Fletcher, 1977; Siegel et al., 1979), so that its persistence beyond 3 days is abnormal and must initially be considered to be due to a disease process like bladder cancer (Mueller & Thompson, 1988) unrelated to running.

Athletic Pseudonephritis

After exercise the urine may contain protein and white and red blood cells; this fact has been known for more than 70 years and led K.D. Gardner (1971) to coin the term "athletic pseudonephritis," because these changes are identical to those found in a very serious kidney disease, glomerulonephritis. Because most forms of glomerulonephritis are ultimately lethal, it is understandable that finding these substances in the athlete's urine would cause considerable concern to those unaware that in athletes such changes are almost always due to exercise, not disease.

Fortunately, there is no reason to believe that these findings are anything but a transient response to exercise that clears completely within 3 days of rest (Fletcher, 1977). It seems likely that the same changes that cause the kidney to leak red blood cells during exercise also cause the kidney to leak large protein molecules and other cells.

Acute Kidney Failure

Exercise-induced acute kidney failure has been described most commonly in Comrades Marathon runners (MacSearraigh et al., 1979), although sporadic cases among standard marathoners have also been described (Lonka & Pedersen, 1987). Although acute kidney failure is not an uncommon complication of heatstroke, in these marathon runners kidney failure developed even though they did not develop heatstroke. The mechanism is unknown and is not simply a result of either severe dehydration or prolonged exercise. In contrast to the widely held belief, kidney function remains essentially unchanged even during prolonged exercise (Irving et al., 1986a).

I suspect that there may be an individual susceptibility to this condition on the basis of a specific musculoskeletal defect that predisposes the muscle to break down during severe exercise and leak myoglobin (Noakes, 1987a). When the myoglobin is filtered through the kidney, the myoglobin acts as a toxin causing the kidney failure. Some researchers believe that the intake of certain analgesic drugs such as aspirin (acetyl salicylic acid), indocid (indomethacin), brufen (Ibuprofen), and naproxen may increase the risk of kidney failure during exercise (Goldszer & Siegel, 1984; Vitting et al., 1986).

The first indication of kidney failure is passing little or no urine for the first 24 hours after a long race. The wise athlete will recognize the seriousness of this sign and will immediately report to the nearest hospital that has a specialized unit for the treatment of kidney failure, in particular a unit able to perform renal dialysis, which the athlete may well require. A runner who fails to recognize this early symptom of kidney failure is likely to start feeling rather ill 36 to 48 hours after the race and will likely develop a severe headache due both to the sudden steep rise in blood pressure and to retained metabolic end products caused by the kidney failure. By this stage, the kidney failure will be well established and the patient will likely have to undergo repeated renal dialysis until the kidneys recover, usually within 10 to 21 days.

Although the condition is seldom acutely fatal, the long-term prognosis of a person who develops acute renal failure during exercise is unknown, nor is it known how the condition might be prevented in those susceptible to it. Probably the most important factor is for runners not to ingest nonsteroidal anti-inflammatory agents during prolonged exercise. These agents are, in any case, probably ineffective during exercise and only increase the likelihood that kidney failure will develop.

Kidney Stones

A survey of entrants in the 1977 New York City Marathon showed an abnormally high incidence, about 5 times normal, of kidney stones among male runners (Milvy et al., 1981). Runners most likely to develop kidney stones were those who had been running for the longest time, who ran the higher mileages in training, and who were the fastest runners. They were also more likely to develop discolored urine after training or racing.

There seems to be a similar high incidence of kidney stones in the population of local runners, and this spurred me and other researchers to study the effects of marathon running on the composition of calcium and other crystals normally present in the urine (Irving et al., 1986b; A.L. Rodgers et al., 1988). These studies found that the urine of marathon runners had the same distribution of calcium crystals as that found in persons at risk of developing kidney stones. Sakhaee et al. (1987) also found that exercise increases the urinary concentration of stone-forming constituents.

These findings are compatible with the well-established observations that kidney stones are more common in persons living in hot environments. Thus, it has been presumed that the repetitive bouts of dehydration caused by running predispose the athlete to the formation of kidney stones, but other factors may also be operative.

For runners the message is clear: Avoid dehydration by drinking as much as possible, especially during but also immediately after exercise, and especially in hot weather.

THE HEMATOLOGICAL (BLOOD-FORMING) SYSTEM

Long-distance runners, females in particular, appear to be especially prone to the development of iron deficiency, which may become apparent as iron-deficiency anemia.

Iron Deficiency in Runners

Iron is needed for three major body processes: the formation of hemoglobin, which binds with oxygen, thereby carrying the oxygen from the lungs to the muscles; the formation of myoglobin, which stores and transports oxygen in the muscle cells; and the formation of a group of enzymes known as the ferrochromes, which exist in the mitochondria (see chapter 2) and whose function is essential for the production of ATP.

Total body iron stores are about 4.0 g, of which 2.7 g are present in hemoglobin, 1.0 g is present as ferritin or hemosiderin in the liver and bone marrow, and 0.3 g are found in myoglobin and the mitochondrial enzymes (P. Jacobs, 1984).

The evidence that we have at present shows that when anyone, an athlete or otherwise, becomes iron deficient, the first stores to be depleted are the liver and bone marrow iron stores. Only when those two stores are depleted does the iron content of the mitochondrial ferrochromes start to fall, and only then do blood hemoglobin levels fall.

Thus, anemia, diagnosed as a fall in the blood hemoglobin content, is probably the final not the first indication of body iron deficiency.

Studies Showing Possible Iron Deficiency in Runners

Body iron stores can be assessed either directly by performing a biopsy of the bone and measuring its iron content or more easily by measurement of the levels of ferritin in the bloodstream. Ferritin levels in the blood bear a direct relationship to the size of the body iron stores; the levels are high when body iron stores are replete and low when body iron stores are depleted.

Low blood ferritin concentrations—below 30 to 50 ng/ml (Clement & Asmundson, 1982; Clement & Sawchuk, 1984; D.N. Dickson et al., 1982; Dufaux et al., 1981)—have been reported in as many as 20% of male competitive long-distance runners. The incidence of low blood ferritin levels among competitive female runners may be even higher. Two studies (Clement & Asmundson, 1982; Nickerson & Tripp, 1983) found that 60 to 80% of female runners had subnormal blood ferritin levels.

Other studies confirmed these findings by directly measuring the bone marrow iron stores. Using a thick needle (not unlike the needle used to perform muscle biopsies) to take bone from the exposed area of the hip bone, Scandinavian (Ehn et al., 1980) and Israeli (Wishnitzer et al., 1983) researchers found the virtual total absence of bone marrow iron stores in different groups of long-distance runners, all of whom had normal blood hemoglobin levels.

Originally, researchers considered that the low serum ferritin levels and the absence of bone marrow iron in these runners must indicate that they were seriously iron deficient even though they were not anemic.

However, Hallberg and Magnusson (1984) offered an alternate and quite plausible explanation. They compared a group of runners with very low serum ferritin levels and absent bone marrow iron stores with runners with high levels of both these parameters. The authors found that the rates of production of red blood cells and their quality were not different between the two groups, suggesting that the low serum ferritin levels and absent bone marrow iron stores did not indicate a true iron deficiency. They suggested that as a result of red cell destruction in the runners' feet while they run, the runners store their iron in the liver rather than in the bone marrow. Thus, the conventional methods used to diagnose iron deficiency in nonrunners are not applicable to runners.

The findings of Matter et al. (1987), Celsing et al. (1986), and Newhouse et al. (1989) are compatible with this interpretation. Matter et al. (1987) found that iron therapy did not improve either the exercise performances, the $\dot{V}O_2$max values, or the running speeds at the blood lactate turnpoint of a group of female runners who had low serum ferritin levels but whose blood hemoglobin levels were normal; similar findings were reported by Newhouse et al. (1989). Celsing et al. (1986) showed that 4 weeks of severely depleted or absent tissue iron stores induced by blood withdrawal did not affect the activities of a variety of iron-dependent mitochondrial enzymes. Maximum exercise tolerance after blood reinfusion was not different from that measured prior to blood withdrawal; thus, the 4 weeks of anemia did not have any long-term effects on performance once blood hemoglobin levels were restored.

All studies concluded that iron therapy should be reserved only for runners whose blood hemoglobin levels are subnormal. In the absence of established anemia, shown by low blood hemoglobin levels, low serum ferritin levels in runners can probably be ignored.

Iron Deficiency With Anemia

Once true iron deficiency develops, the hemoglobin content of the red blood cells falls and the cells become smaller, less able to carry oxygen, and more fragile and have reduced life expectancies. Persons with iron-deficiency anemia suffer from reduced blood oxygen-carrying capacities, which will cause reduced $\dot{V}O_2$max values. With appropriate iron therapy, $\dot{V}O_2$max and running performance improve.

The Possible Causes of Anemia in Long-Distance Runners

The causes of iron-deficiency anemia in runners have not been established. The condition may be due to excessive iron losses in sweat (Lamanca et al., 1988; Paulev et al., 1983; Vellar, 1968) or excessive blood losses in the gastrointestinal tract or in urine due to hematuria, hemoglobinuria, or both due to accelerated intravascular hemolysis (Selby & Eichner, 1986). In some female runners, excessive menstrual blood losses may contribute to iron deficiency. Another cause may be impaired gastrointestinal absorption of ingested iron, which has been reported in some iron-deficient runners (Ehn et al., 1980). A deficient dietary intake must also be considered, because intensively trained runners tend to eat high-carbohydrate, vegetarian-type diets, which usually have low iron contents (see chapter 15). In addition, some elite runners, women in particular, may severely restrict their caloric intakes (see chapter 16).

Low Hemoglobin Levels in Athletes Without Proven Iron Deficiency ("Sports Anemia")

An interesting hematological finding in endurance athletes is that they may have subnormal blood hemoglobin levels without necessarily being iron deficient.

Berry et al. (1949) noted that among competitors at the 1948 Olympic Games, the athletes competing in sports requiring "great endurance" had the lowest hemoglobin levels. The endurance athletes on the 1968 Dutch (De Wijn et al., 1971) and Australian Olympic teams (G.A. Stewart et al., 1972) in particular were found to have blood hemoglobin levels that were lower than those of their team coaches and managers! Interestingly, the Australian athletes with the lowest hemoglobin levels subsequently performed the worst in the Games. Clement and his colleagues (1977) reported essentially the same findings in the 1976 Canadian Olympic team.

The cause of these low hemoglobin levels, called "sports anemia," is currently unknown. Because none of these earlier studies measured blood ferritin levels or performed bone marrow biopsies to measure body iron stores, we do not know whether this sports anemia is due to iron deficiency. Interestingly, Selby and Eichner (1986) found that male and female competitive swimmers showed decreases in hemoglobin levels over a 5-month competitive season; yet their hemoglobin levels did not fall into the anemic range, and the serum ferritin levels were low in 57% of the women and in only 10% of the men. Similar findings have been reported in professional cyclists during the competitive season (Guglielmini et al., 1989). The authors suggest that impaired red cell production and increased breakdown might explain this phenomenon.

I feel that a low hemoglobin level in an endurance athlete is abnormal and requires treatment. An increase in blood hemoglobin levels in response to iron therapy would indicate that iron deficiency was the cause of the low hemoglobin level.

The Anemia of Early Season Training

Since 1966 (Yoshimura, 1966), we have known that a person who starts exercising for the first time or who undergoes a period of very intensive training develops an anemia that can be quite severe, causing blood hemoglobin levels to fall by up to 18% (Londemann, 1978) possibly due to an increased rate of red blood cell destruction. This anemia has been described in rugby players (Yoshimura, 1966); in tennis players and in persons exercising on bicycle ergometers (Shiraki et al., 1977); in Norwegian army recruits participating in a period of intensive training (Londemann, 1978); and in young women participating in an exercise/ fitness class (Hegenauer et al., 1983).

It appears that this anemia corrects itself within about 3 to 8 weeks (Hegenaeur et al., 1983; Shiraki et al., 1977) and can be prevented by eating a high-protein diet (2 g protein per kilogram of body weight per day; Shiraki et al., 1977). The anemia appears to be caused by the release into the bloodstream of a chemical substance (possibly lysolecithin from the spleen) that causes the rapid destruction of a large number of circulating red blood cells. Iron ingestion does not prevent the development of this anemia (Hegenaeur et al., 1983).

To prevent the condition, beginning joggers should increase their dietary protein intakes for the first month or so of their training.

Runners and Blood Donations

Runners frequently ask whether they should donate blood.

In donating blood, the runner loses three ingredients: 500 ml of fluid, approximately 70 g of hemoglobin (equivalent to 220 mg of iron), and many millions of red blood cells. The fluid loss is rapidly replaced within a matter of hours, but the restoration of red blood cells takes considerably longer, at least 3 weeks and possibly much longer in athletes who are iron deficient (see Figure 18.6). Thus, runners who do choose to donate blood should probably not exercise on the day of blood donation because of their reduced blood volumes and should avoid hard competition over any distance until their hemoglobin levels have returned to normal, usually 3 to 6 weeks after donation.

During the time that the athlete has a reduced hemoglobin level, the capacity for severe maximal exercise is reduced, because the anemia causes the $\dot{V}O_2$max to fall 10 to 15% (T. Christensen & Christensen, 1978).

For this reason I suggest that runners who wish to donate blood must first have their blood ferritin and hemoglobin levels measured. If the hemoglobin levels are normal and the ferritin levels are high (greater than 60 ng/ml in a sample collected when the athletes have not run hard for at least 5 days), they may safely donate blood. They should be more careful if their blood ferritin levels are low, and they should take iron supplements and definitely not donate blood if their hemoglobin levels are low (less than 14.5 g/100 ml).

Blood Doping

When Lasse Viren came back from 4 years in the athletic wilderness to win his third and fourth gold medals at the 1976 Montreal Olympic Games, there were those who viewed his success with indignant skepticism.

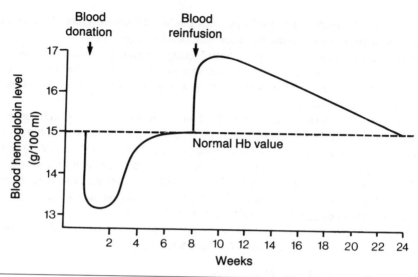

Figure 18.6 The time course of changes in blood hemoglobin levels following blood donation and subsequent reinfusion (blood doping).

Note. From N. Gledhill, "Blood Doping and Related Issues: A Brief Review," *Medicine and Science in Sports and Exercise,* **14**(3), p. 185, 1982, © by American College of Sports Medicine. Adapted by permission.

Some charged that Viren had "blood doped," a technique in which the athlete's circulating red blood cell count is artificially increased by the reinfusion of red blood cells previously drawn from that athlete and stored under special conditions for a minimum of 4 to 6 weeks.

Blood doping or "blood boosting," as it has also been called, violates the Olympic ruling that makes it illegal for any physiological substance to be taken by an abnormal route or in an abnormal quantity for the "sole object of increasing, artificially and in an unfair manner, the performance of that individual while participating in a competition" (Raynes, 1969, p. 145).

In 1976 the central doping issue at the Olympic Games was anabolic steroids. There was no firm evidence that blood boosting worked, so apart from the unsubstantiated charges against Viren, this never became a major issue.

But by the 1980 Olympic Games that had all changed. After those Games, the Finnish runner Kaarlo Maaininka, who won silver and bronze medals in the 10,000- and 5,000-m events, freely admitted to receiving 2 units of blood shortly before these races. Some members of the 1984 United States Olympic Cycling Team also blood doped before those games (Klein, 1985), and Italian Francesco Moser apparently traveled to Mexico City, where he twice lowered the outdoor 1-hour cycling record with "an entourage of two cardiologists and eight men 18 to 20 years of age who were chosen several months before because of their blood type compatibility with Moser'' (Brien & Simon, 1987, p. 2761).

Scientific studies suggest that blood boosting does indeed improve performance, although the mechanism is not known. In 1980, Fred Buick and his colleagues (Buick et al., 1980) performed a study in which each of an elite group of long-distance runners was subjected to a maximal treadmill test, during which $\dot{V}O_2$max and maximal treadmill running time (a measure of endurance performance) were measured. After the test, 900 ml of blood were withdrawn from each athlete and stored. After 5 weeks, blood tests showed that the athletes had recovered from the inevitable anemia that this blood loss caused. The treadmill tests were repeated to insure that the period of anemia had not affected either the athletes' $\dot{V}O_2$max values or their maximum treadmill running times.

After the second treadmill test, half the athletes were reinfused with their own stored blood and the other half received infusions of small amounts of an intravenous salt solution that would not be expected to have any effect on performance. Twenty-four hours later, all athletes were again retested on the treadmill by technicians who had no idea who had received the blood or sham infusions. By doing this Buick ensured that neither athlete nor technician was motivated to extract greater efforts in the knowledge that the runner had been ''boosted.''

After the test, and again under the same rigorous experimental conditions, the athletes received second infusions. Those who had previously received sham infusions now received their blood quotas; those who had already received their blood quotas were given sham infusions. The treadmill tests were repeated 24 hours later, 1 week later, and 4 months later.

Blood reinfusion had a dramatic effect. There was a 6% increase in $\dot{V}O_2$max and a massive 39% increase in treadmill endurance running time. Furthermore, these increases were maintained for 7 days. Since that original study, at least three others have shown essentially similar results (for review see Gledhill, 1982). The most recent study showed that 10-km run time was reduced by 1:09 after infusion of 400 ml of red blood cells (Brien & Simon, 1987). This benefit was still present 13 days after reinfusion, as was also found in a study of cross-country skiers (Berglund & Hemmingson, 1987).

What do these studies mean? Essentially, they confirm observations made in 1972 that showed that blood boosting does improve endurance performance and $\dot{V}O_2$max. Although physiologists originally interpreted these studies as confirmatory evidence that the $\dot{V}O_2$max is limited by the capacity of the heart rather than by the capacity of the skeletal muscle to utilize oxygen (see chapter 2), the case is far from proven (Noakes, 1988b). As discussed in chapter 2, it is now clear that blood doping reduces blood lactate levels during exercise (Spriet et al., 1986) and brings about the lactate turnpoint at a higher running speed (Celsing et al., 1987). These effects are likely to be the more important factors in the increased running performance measured after blood doping (see chapter 2). Blood doping may also enhance heat tolerance during exercise (Sawka et al., 1987).

The possibility that blood doping can be detected is raised by the work of Berglund et al. (1987). They showed that the measurement of serum levels of erythropoietin, iron, and bilirubin can identify 50% of boosted athletes within 7 days of blood doping.

An alternate technique may be to measure the distribution of red blood cell sizes, as the reinfused cells are likely to be larger than the athlete's remaining red blood cells. Thus the size distribution of the athlete's red cells will probably show an abnormal distribution of large cells (Berglund, 1988).

However, even this technique will be unable to detect what is likely to become the new form of blood doping in the 1990s—the use of erythropoietin to stimulate naturally the overproduction of the athlete's own red blood cells.

Erythropoietin is a hormone that is released by the kidney and that stimulates the production of red blood cells by the bone marrow. Advances in biotechnology now make it possible for human erythropoietin to be produced in large quantities. Originally the erythropoietin was developed to treat the anemia that develops in persons with chronic diseases, especially kidney failure. However, it is only a matter of time before athletes begin to use this drug to increase chronically their blood hemoglobin content. A possible advantage of this technique may be that it allows the athlete to perform better not only in competition, but also in training—an advantage not provided by blood doping.

The risks of this technique are not known but could include an increased tendency for blood clotting leading especially to stroke but also possibly to heart attacks. These risks can only be reduced if the use of erythropoietin is medically controlled, a possibility that introduces difficult ethical problems.

Changes in the Blood With Exercise

Changes in Cellular Components

Immediately after very prolonged exercise (marathon or ultramarathon racing), the numbers of white blood cells in the bloodstream increase markedly, a change that reverts to normal within 48 hours (D.N. Dickson et al., 1982). Between 24 and 48 hours after prolonged races, blood hemoglobin levels tend to fall (D.N. Dickson et al., 1982), probably due to excess water retention by the kidneys for the first 3 days after prolonged exercise.

Changes in Chemical Constituents

There are no major changes in the levels of any other blood components, in particular blood urea, uric acid, creatinine, and bilirubin levels after any exercise, regardless of its duration (Noakes & Carter, 1976, 1982).

Marked changes do, however, occur in the activities of certain enzymes in the bloodstream, in particular the enzyme creatine kinase, which normally exists inside the cells and which transfers phosphate from phosphocreatine to form ATP. This enzyme is released into the bloodstream during exercise, probably as a result of muscle cell damage (Noakes, 1987a).

In general, postexercise blood creatine kinase activity varies with the duration of the activity and is higher the longer the race, presumably because the longer the race, the more muscle damage occurs (Noakes, 1987a). Training reduces the extent to which the blood creatine kinase activity rises during and after exercise (Noakes & Carter, 1982), also presumably because training reduces the amount of muscle damage that occurs with exercise (Schwane & Armstrong, 1983).

Finally, elevated creatine kinase activity in the blood is used in the diagnosis of heart attack. Thus, the runner who is admitted to a hospital within 24 hours of a long run may be wrongly diagnosed as having had a heart attack if the doctors are unaware that running causes blood creatine kinase activity to be increased to levels normally found in heart attack patients (Noakes, 1987b; Noakes et al., 1983a).

THE IMMUNE SYSTEM

Exercise and Resistance to Infection

We have already discussed those studies showing that the risk of infection is increased immediately after competitive racing (see chapter 9) and the fact that infection is an important feature of the overtraining syndrome (see Table 10.1). The reasons for these phenomena are unknown, but they probably indicate that the body's immune system and the athlete's resistance to infection are impaired by heavy training and intense competition (Lewicki et al., 1987) and by weight loss (Kono et al., 1988).

Mild exercise releases a protein, endogenous pyrogen (Cannon & Kluger, 1983), which causes the body temperature to rise. It is believed that this elevation of body temperature, similar to the fever stage of infection, is beneficial because it creates an internal environment that is less favorable for the growth and multiplication of invading bacteria and viruses. In addition, blood levels of the antiviral protein interferon increase as does the activity of "killer" white cells (Hanson & Flaherty, 1981; Viti et al., 1985). Thus, mild exercise should reduce acutely the risk that an athlete develops an infection. But the evidence of E. Peters and Bateman (1983) clearly shows that very strenuous, prolonged exercise activates other factors that override this protective mechanism, thereby increasing, not reducing, the risk of infection.

Chronic training appears not to influence immune function even in runners who claim to have had fewer infections since they started running (R.L. Green et al., 1981). However, much is still to be learned of the influence of exercise and overtraining on the immune system (Keast et al., 1988).

Exercise-Induced Anaphylaxis

Anaphylaxis occurs, for example, when persons allergic to bee stings are stung by bees. Sheffer and Austen (1980) and Siegel (1980) described a group of runners (and other athletes) who develop a life-threatening exercise-associated syndrome similar to this. Interestingly, the condition was recognized although not described in detail by A. Abrahams (1951) and may have a familial basis (Longley & Panush, 1987).

The syndrome is characterized by the onset during exercise of severe redness, blistering (urticaria), and itchiness of the skin, face, palms, and soles, associated with (in decreasing order of frequency) cardiovascular collapse; upper respiratory tract airway obstruction due to marked swelling of the throat, causing choking and wheezing; and gastrointestinal symptoms including colic, nausea, or diarrhea. There may also be headaches and vertigo, which can persist for up to 3 days after the attack. The attacks, which can last from 1 to 4 hours, are totally unpredictable. They do not occur with every exercise session and have been reported as frequently as once a month and as infrequently as once every decade. It seems likely that the syndrome occurs in allergic persons only when exercise follows the exposure of those persons to specific proteins (antigens) to which they are allergic. Sources of antigens that have been identified include shellfish, caffeine, and aspirin (Sheffer & Austen, 1980); wheat (Kushimoto & Aoki, 1985); celery (Silverstein et al., 1986); and, believe it or not, running shoes (Noakes, 1983).

Treatment, which must be given immediately if there is shock or serious respiratory obstruction, must include the subcutaneous injection of adrenaline and intravenous injection of antihistamine drugs. The long-term prevention of the condition requires the identification and avoidance of the specific antigens that provoke the attacks for 4 or preferably 6 hours before exercise (Sheffer, 1988).

THE CENTRAL NERVOUS SYSTEM

Effort Headache

This is a poorly understood phenomenon in which a severe headache starts usually after exercise and becomes progressively worse over the next 3 to 6 hours (Massey, 1982).

As one who suffers from this condition, I have observed that my effort headache occurs only when I run more than 24 km and is most likely to occur after the first 2 or 3 long runs I do at the beginning of a new running year. I have found that I will inevitably develop a severe headache after the first marathon I run after a few months of break. When well trained, I seldom have the headaches.

The important point about effort headaches is to know that such a condition exists. If the headaches follow the patterns I have mentioned, you can probably safely assume that they are not due to a serious disease. If the headaches do not follow this pattern or if they become progressively more severe and frequent or are not always related to exercise, then they must be investigated fully by a doctor. Cases in which effort headaches were due to serious disease have been reported (Rooke, 1968).

The effort headache may indicate the presence of a food allergy, in which case an attempt should be made to identify the responsible food (see chapter 15). The drug indomethacin (Indocin) may be useful in this condition (Diamond, 1982).

Endorphins and the Runner's High

The potent pain-relieving (analgesic) actions of the drug morphine have been known for more than 150 years, but it was only in the mid 1950s that the mechanism of action of morphine in the body became clear. The critical finding was that morphine acts on specific morphine receptors lining the outer membranes of many cells throughout the body.

The fact that human cells have receptors for a drug prepared from the poppy plant suggests that the body produces its own morphinelike substances and therefore requires such receptors for the action of these substances. This realization prompted an international search to isolate and identify these endogenous (internally produced) morphine derivatives, which became known as the enkephalins and endorphins. In the decade since their initial isolation, the enkephalins and endorphins have been found to play roles in drug and alcohol dependence, in the pain relief produced by acupuncture, in disorders involving menstruation, in gastrointestinal disorders including stomach ulcers, and in other physiological control mechanisms including the control of blood pressure, respiration, food intake, and drinking behavior (Copolov & Helme, 1983).

When it was found that endorphin levels increase during exercise (for review see Harber & Sutton, 1984), special interest arose in the possibility that elevated endorphin levels might explain the mood changes that occur during running, in particular the euphoria of the runner's high, and the increased resistance to pain that occurs during exercise (Black et al., 1979) and with training (Scott & Gijsbers, 1981).

Currently, the view seems to be that endorphins form part of the natural stress response of the body. When the body is under stress, whether jogging gently or running away from a lion, brain endorphin levels will rise. And because not all stressful events are associated with a high, it follows that elevated endorphin levels will not always produce positive mood changes. However, Allen and Coen

(1987) did show that high doses of naloxone, a drug that blocks the actions of endorphins in the brain, prevents the normal positive mood changes that develop during and after running. The authors suggest that the increased endorphin activity induced by exercise contributes to the postexercise "calmness" experienced by runners.

Thus, the current feeling is that endorphins may play a role in the runner's high and in altering pain perception during exercise. Dr. William Morgan (1985), the psychologist who originally described compulsive running behavior in terms of a chemically based addiction (see chapter 7), seems now less sure about the chemical nature of this addiction. This is in line with the suggestion that the personality, not the activity, determines susceptibility to running addiction.

Exercise and Sleep

Despite the fact the we spend one third of our lives sleeping, the reasons why we need sleep remain ill defined.

There are currently two popular theories about sleep. The first holds that sleep is a dormant period that serves to conserve energy; the second maintains that sleep is needed to restore certain bodily changes that occur during the awake period. Exercise offers an interesting test of these two hypotheses; if sleep has restorative properties, then it would be influenced by the amount of exercise taken during the awake period. And indeed the evidence seems to support the possibility that sleep patterns are influenced by prior exercise (A.F. Morris, 1982).

But of particular interest, especially to athletes involved in exercise lasting more than 24 hours, are the effects of sleep deprivation on exercise performance. For evidence now shows that marked sleep deprivation impairs athletic performance and causes behavioral and minor personality changes (A.F. Morris, 1982). These changes are apparent within 24 hours without sleep and are most marked between 2:00 a.m. and 6:00 a.m. Visual hallucinations and disorders of balance become apparent in almost everyone who exercises without sleep for more than 4 days. Sleep of 3 to 5 hours per night and frequent rest periods reduce the severity of these changes.

Insomnia

A.F. Morris (1982) observed that certain food components such as salt and refined sugars and certain drinks including coffee, some teas, colas, and alcohol may produce insomnia. Similarly, stress and tension generated by the day's activity, in particular travel, and anxiety over approaching competition may make it difficult to sleep. Most sleep medications reduce the quality of sleep, and some produce insomnia. Thus, these medications should never be taken for more than 1 or 2 nights in a row, should not be taken the night before competition, and should not be mixed with other drugs or alcohol. Cigarette smoking also appears to adversely affect the quality of sleep (Bale & White, 1982). Morris recommends that sleep should be induced naturally by the following.

- Unwind slowly from the day's activity (by reading light material, going for a walk, or participating in light conversation), and stick to a regular sleeping pattern (i.e., go to bed at a set time).
- Sleep in a darkened, noiseless room that is warm (15.6 to 17.7 °C; 60 to 64 °F) and well ventilated.
- Sleep in a comfortable bed with your own pillow, bed clothes, and pajamas.
- Take a relaxing bath before going to bed.
- Eat or drink sleep-promoting foods, and avoid sugar, salt, and caffeine. Warm milk and herbal teas are particularly effective.
- Only attempt to sleep when you are feeling sleepy.
- Utilize the progressive relaxation technique described in chapter 7.

Epilepsy

The study of Denio et al. (1989) suggests that persons with epilepsy who exercise have fewer epileptic seizures than those who do not exercise.

THE ENDOCRINE SYSTEM

Diabetes

The major disease of the endocrine system that has relevance to exercise is insulin-dependent diabetes.

This is caused by an absolute lack of the hormone insulin, which is secreted by the pancreas and is essential for the normal regulation of metabolism, both at rest and during exercise. Insulin-dependent diabetes usually has its onset in childhood for reasons that are unclear, although one possibility is that a viral infection causes selective destruction of those pancreatic cells that produce insulin.

Insulin is required for the normal entry of glucose into the muscle cells and therefore for the storage of glucose as glycogen in both muscle and liver. Thus, in the absence of insulin, the untreated diabetic has difficulty dealing with any ingested carbohydrate. The lack of insulin prevents the increased amounts of glucose released from the liver during exercise from entering the muscle cells to act as an important fuel (see Figure 3.2). Thus, blood glucose levels will rise, leading ultimately to coma. Exercise can be rapidly fatal for the untreated or poorly treated diabetic.

The diabetic who is receiving insulin and who wishes to take up exercise should be encouraged to do so, because the training will reduce insulin requirements, improve the quality of diabetic control, and probably reduce the risk of developing the long-term complications of diabetes. Regular exercise also encourages the diabetic to take charge of the disease and will provide the same, if not greater, psychological benefits that are enjoyed by all athletes. With care, selected diabetics can do virtually any exercise, including running the ultramarathons or completing the Ironman triathlon.

The exercising diabetic should follow these guidelines.

- Only consider starting an exercise program if the necessary medical support is available.
- Use an automated blood glucose analyzer to monitor blood glucose levels regularly (every 20 minutes) during exercise.
- Always exercise at exactly the same time of day so that the amount of (injected) insulin in the bloodstream and in body storage sites is always the same. This is essential because the amount of insulin in these sites will determine the body's metabolic response to that exercise.
- Reduce daily insulin injections as exercise levels increase.
- Always carry a supply of rapidly absorbable carbohydrate during exercise, preferably a 20% glucose polymer solution, and drink enough of this solution to maintain a blood glucose level above 3.5 mmol/L at all times during exercise.
- Increase carbohydrate intake after exercise to restock reduced muscle glycogen stores and thus prevent a steep fall in blood glucose levels (hypoglycemia) some hours after exercise.

These guidelines are not meant to be comprehensive. They are offered here simply to remind diabetics that they can and should exercise as much as they wish but that they must approach exercise with diligence and intelligence, with thorough knowledge of exercise physiology (see chapter 2) and metabolism (see chapter 3), and with the backup of suitably qualified and interested medical personnel.

More information can be obtained from two excellent books on the topic (Betteridge, 1987; Cantu, 1982).

Changes in Hypothalamic-Pituitary-Gonadal Hormones and in Fertility and Libido With Training

As I discussed in detail in chapter 16, evidence shows that exercise training in combination with other factors, in particular inadequate nutrition and high levels of competitive and other stresses, can induce cessation of menstruation in female athletes by inhibiting the normal cyclical release of hormones from the hypothalamus and pituitary glands. In females, any failure of the hypothalamus or pituitary glands is immediately apparent, because menstruation ceases. But in men, the condition might not be recognized, because the only likely signs would be a loss of libido and infertility, symptoms to which most male runners would admit only reluctantly. Thus, the question has been posed whether males who train hard also show changes in the function of these glands.

Early evidence for this possibility was the finding (discussed in chapter 10) of hypothalamic-pituitary failure in overtrained male athletes (Barron et al., 1985). This abnormality was not present even in runners who were training in excess of 160 km/week and racing frequently but who were not overtrained.

Three studies (Ayers et al., 1985; Hackney et al., 1988; Wheeler et al., 1984) found reduced blood levels of the male hormone testosterone in trained male distance runners, possibly caused by hypothalamic dysfunction (MacConnie et al., 1986). The study of Ayers and his colleagues showed, however, that these changes were mild and were not associated with changes in libido, sexual performance, or fertility as judged by the quality of the semen produced by these runners. Thus the conclusion is that these low serum testosterone concentrations are not associated with reproductive dysfunction (Cumming et al., 1989; Hackney, 1989).

Interestingly, Ayers et al. (1985) noted that 2 of the 20 runners who they studied were clearly abnormal and were infertile. However, these two runners were thinner, had lost more weight, and had experienced more stress in their lives than had the other runners. The authors felt that these two runners were more typical of the "anorexic-type runners" of the Yates hypothesis, which equates obligatory running in males with anorexia in females (see chapter 15). The authors concluded that heavy training alone was not associated with detrimental effects on libido or sperm production in male runners. However, another study (Baker et al., 1988) found that the pregnancy rates achieved with semen donated from athletic males was less than that from nonathletic males. Semen from athletic males also had decreased volume and decreased motility. Probably the important practical point from these findings is that male runners should consider stopping running if their wives are having difficulty becoming pregnant.

Another possible complication of reduced blood testosterone concentrations in male runners may be a reduced vertebral bone density (Bilanin et al., 1989) similar to that found in amenorrheic females. This finding requires confirmation and explanation, especially because it conflicts with the more accepted belief that physical activity increases bone density (see chapter 14).

Postscript

"We are indeed Masters, I told them. We are professors. We are professionals. We have come into maturity. And we have matured doing what appears to be childish things. Nevertheless, our ability to live with questions and without solutions began when we took to the roads. Our belief in ourselves and in living our own lives developed through our running. It was running that released the treasures in our subconscious and gave us the creativity to put these treasures in substantial form.

Keep running, I told the forties and fifties and sixties looking up at me, the best is yet to come."

Dr. George Sheehan (1983)

My running, which began in search of a sporting challenge, ultimately determined my choice of career. This book then became the natural extension of that mission which, although altered in intent, is now in its twenty-second year. Running provided the material for this book but, more importantly, also the desire and the training in mental doggedness to complete its writing—a task which ultimately became more demanding than any of the sporting challenges I had ever tackled.

In reflection, my greatest pleasure has been to live through and be part of that period during which running underwent the most profound changes in its history, a time when running matured from the deviant pastime of an eccentric few to a mainstream activity enjoyed and understood by millions around the world. In its wake, running has stimulated the mass popularization of many other sports, most notably aerobics, cycling, and the triathlon. And in that process, running has altered so radically that it seems appropriate to reflect on the changes that have occurred in the sport and the implications these might have for its future.

The first great change has been in equipment, particularly running shoes and other apparel; this change is due, in no small part, to a significant scientific input. The discovery and development of EVA (ethylene vinyl acetate) allowed shoes which could better absorb shock to be made. This immediately made the sport more comfortable for, and therefore more accessible, to those bodies like mine which do not conform to the rigid design demands of the elite distance runners.

The introduction of the "Air" and "Gel" midsoles in the past 5 years has really been only an extension and refinement of that original discovery.

The second change has been the intense scientific interest that the running revolution has evoked. Indeed, running has led directly to a major renaissance in research in human physiology. It was Professor A.V. Hill (chapter 9) who wrote that all textbooks of human physiology available in the early decades of this century were based exclusively on studies of frogs! Running stimulated a new generation of exercise physiologists who, like Hill in England and Dill in the United States in the early 1920s, combined their scientific interest with their personal sporting drives and enticed thousands of eager runners, themselves included, to serve as subjects for their scientific studies. And so it has been running and these scientists that have put the human animal back into the physiology research laboratories around the world.

The greatest immediate value of this research has been to establish the cause of running injuries and to develop methods to cure these injuries. As described in chapter 12, most of us as recently as 1975 had absolutely no idea how these injuries should be managed. Today there are few runners, medically trained or otherwise, who cannot sustain a sophisticated discussion on the causes and cures of running injuries. Indeed, the knowledge of most runners on health-related matters is nothing short of remarkable; there must be few groups of sports participants who are as interested or as knowledgeable.

So I suspect that the '70s will be remembered as a decade when the cause of running injuries was first identified and we became able to treat the majority of injured runners successfully.

The '80s on the other hand, saw the dramatic growth in research of the physiological, medical, and health-related aspects of running. During this period our knowledge advanced beyond recognition as exercise scientists applied advanced research techniques from their fields and others' to achieve levels of sophistication previously undreamt.

The result has been that the quality of sports science research experienced a quantum leap in the '80s and began to attract interest, funding, and the quality of scientists that will ensure the continued expansion and progression of the field well into the next century. Indeed, the '80s will be remembered as the dawn of a golden era in exercise physiology research. From it will emerge names which, like Dill and Hill, will echo down the centuries.

The reward for these exercise scientists has been to challenge and disprove many of the antiquated dogmas that have been handed down to us. In addition, the scientists have advanced our knowledge, especially of exercise physiology, more in a single decade than was achieved in the previous eighty years. Our greatest challenge remains the practical application of this sophisticated knowledge to help athletes train in the most appropriate and effective ways.

Probably the most important studies in this era were those of Professors Ralph Paffenbarger and Jerry Morris reported in chapter 18. These studies convincingly showed for the first time that a lack of exercise is a significant risk factor for the development of heart disease, and that regular exercise increases life expectancy. Were a Nobel Prize to be given in the Exercise Sciences, the first recipients, by the proverbial marathon distance, would be Jerry Morris and Ralph Paffenbarger. No longer will future medical students have to suffer, as did I, the tedium of being told by uninspired and uninspiring physicians that exercise is of no value to anyone. In reality, the evidence now indicates that all medical practitioners have the responsibility to actively ensure that all their patients are aware of the health benefits of regular exercise.

Of equal magnitude to the achievements of Morris and Paffenbarger, but in a different discipline, is the work of George Sheehan who single-handedly explained to us why we run and gave us the confidence to believe that this childlike activity has intrinsic value. Like all prophets, Sheehan is a decade or two before his time. Already there is a real danger that his exquisite writings lie forgotten, unknown now to a generation of runners. But their time will surely come.

For already the '90s promises to be the decade when we begin to look more closely at the ways in which our minds influence not only our sporting choices and achievements, but also all aspects of our lives.

For however ignorant we may still be about our physiology, such ignorance is as nothing compared to the dearth of knowledge we have of our mental, spiritual, and philosophical makeup. It was George Sheehan who first taught us to appreciate the importance of this knowledge.

So my sincere hope is that future generations of runners will rediscover the beauty and depth of George Sheehan's writings. My firm belief is that a hundred years hence, when the understanding we currently profess about exercise physiology has passed into antiquity, the timeless value of Sheehan's writing will be appreciated. Like the works of his beloved Thoreau and Emerson, Sheehan's writings will become classics—the most enduring reminder of the running revolution of the 1970s and 1980s.

The third significant change has been the democratization of running, a process that continues to gain momentum. In the '60s and early '70s, running was exclusively an activity for white males usually from the higher intellectual and social strata. Chapter 16 describes just how recently women were accepted into the running family (and just how bitterly some men fought to prevent their admission!). Fortunately, running is no longer the hobby only of the intellectuals, the males, and the well-to-do. It remains only a matter of time before 50% of all runners are women and all strata of society are equally represented.

The 1968 Olympics provided the first glimpse of the exceptional athletic talents of the East African distance runners, especially those from Kenya and Ethiopia. The years since then have confirmed that it is from East and South Africa that the great distance runners of the future will come, further confirming the egalitarian nature of this sport. For the success of these runners proves that neither a gargantuan gross national product nor a major financial investment is necessary for a nation's sons and daughters to succeed in this sport. Money cannot compensate for natural ability, individual desire, and a love of running. Professionalism in running has its limits.

Paradoxically, the fourth major change in this sport has indeed been its move to increasing professionalization. Beginning with the 1976 New York City Marathon, the introduction of the "big city" marathons suddenly gave the world's elite distance runners commercial value, thereby launching the professionalization of distance running.

The commercial value of runners stemmed largely from the widespread media coverage of running events. This coverage brought the excitement of distance running into many millions of homes, thereby helping to promote the sport and leading in no small measure to its rapid growth during the late '70s and early '80s. As more people took to the sport, they stimulated greater interest in the development and marketing of the products they could buy, thereby further stimulating commercial interest in the sport and encouraging the financial investment in sports-related research that led to the exponential growth in our scientific and medical knowledge of ourselves and our sport.

But this popularization of running has not been without a price. In particular, it has brought the specter of depersonalization to a sport which had always been characterized by the affability and friendliness of its participants. For in the days before the revolution, most distance runners in any particular area knew each other, and our races were as much a chance to catch up with each other's news and ideas as they were to compete together. Today this is obviously no longer possible.

In addition, the large amounts of money that can now be earned by the best athletes increases the likelihood that cheating will be attempted. The most obvious cheating techniques are the use of blood doping and banned drugs, especially anabolic steroids, and more recently, erythropoietin, as described in chapter 18.

If those are the changes of the immediate past, what is the future likely to hold?

It is clear that the exponential growth of running that occurred in the '70s will not again be seen.

Growth in the sport has slowed, and there is even the risk that the current popularity of the sport could possibly diminish in the future. Indeed there is some evidence that the running population in Europe is aging (Marti & Vader, 1987), suggesting that fewer young people are taking to distance running, at least in Europe. Concerns have also been expressed about a possible decline in the number of competitive runners in the United States (Blair et al., 1987; Stephens, 1987).

Thus, the question indeed becomes whether the next generation, our children who come to adulthood in the '90s will take to running as we did in the '60s and '70s. Will they respond to those same deep psychological urges that drove us onto the roads? I suspect that, the evidence from Europe and North America notwithstanding, running will continue to be as popular for future generations as it was for us and that the current level of interest in the sport will be maintained and may even increase in the future. As future generations become increasingly conscious of the need to preserve the health of the earth and its environment, it would be incongruous if they were suddenly to ignore their personal health needs. So I foresee that the use of regular exercise for maintaining personal health will increase and will be stimulated by the promotion of employee health by industry.

But unquestionably there will be some important changes in the sport. For example, future runners will likely run fewer marathons and ultramarathons and more shorter distance races. They will likely also participate in more than one sport. Thus, there will be an increased tendency for cross-training, particularly by supplementing running with cycling, swimming, aerobics, and weight training, and especially in the older age groups. So my prediction is that the twenty-year-old runners of the '60s will become the sixty-year-old cyclists of the first decade of the 21st century. But don't exclude the possibility that there will also be a large market for health studios that cater specifically to the special exercising needs of the over-sixties.

With regard to scientific studies, there will be increased emphasis on studies not restricted solely to running. Greater emphasis will also be placed on studies to determine the value of exercise in the aging and diseased populations. Indeed, a major shift in the research interests of the aging exercise physiologists will be to study those aspects of aging that relate specifically to their own sporting interests.

Psychological research will also become increasingly important, reflecting, in part, the shift in emphasis from the body to the mind that is a natural consequence of the aging process.

The '90s will also be the period when we receive the first indications of whether there are dangers with continued heavy running for many years. We will also see whether the fifty-year-olds of the '90s can still run with the same vigor that they did as twenty-year-olds in the '60s, and if not, why not.

So this book or at least this edition (as hopefully there will be more), is at its end. It has, I trust, faithfully recorded the contributions that many from diverse fields have made to the development and growth of this great sport over the past century. Their legacy will be that they nurtured from the most unlikely and ignominious beginnings imaginable (see chapter 8), an activity that has become not only one of the world's most popular competitive sports, but also a recreational pastime enjoyed by millions around the world. And as a by-product, they have provided a major new stimulus for research into human physiology and the role of exercise in health.

For the athlete of the '90s, the most important result is that there never was a better time to be a runner!

References

Abraham, M.W. (1979). Exercise-induced muscle soreness. *The Physician and Sportsmedicine 7* (October), 57-60.

Abraham's, A. (1930). The human machine: its efficiency and limitations. *Lancet 1*, 174-177.

Abrahams, A. (1951). Physical exercise: its clinical associations. *Lancet 1*, 1187-1192.

Abrahams, A. (1961). *The Disabilities and Injuries of Sport.* Elek Books, London.

Abrahams, S.F., P.J.V. Beaumont, I.S. Fraser, D. Llewellyn-Jones (1982). Body weight, exercise and menstrual status among ballet dancers in training. *British Journal of Obstetrics and Gynaecology 89*, 507-510.

Acevedo, E.O., A.H. Goldfarb (1989). Increased training intensity effects on plasma lactate, ventilatory threshold, and endurance. *Medicine and Science in Sports and Exercise 21*, 563-568.

Adams, E. (1987). Ultrarunning for women. In *Training for Ultras*, Andy Milroy (ed.). British Road Runners Club, London, pp. 19-22.

Adams, I.D. (1976). Osteoarthrosis and sport. *Clinics in Rheumatic Diseases 2*, 523-542.

Adams, W.C., E.S. Schelegle (1983). Ozone toxicity effects consequent to prolonged high intensity exercise in trained endurance athletes. *Journal of Applied Physiology 55*, 805-812.

Adler, R., B. Bongar, E.R. Katz (1982). Psychogenic abdominal pain and parental pressure in childhood athletics. *Psychosomatics 23*, 1185-1186.

Ahlborg, B., J. Bergström, J. Brohult, L.G. Ekelund, E. Hultman, G. Maschio (1967a). Human muscle glycogen content and capacity for prolonged exercise after different diets. *Förvarsmedicin 3*, 85-99.

Ahlborg, B., J. Bergström, L.G. Ekelund, E. Hultman (1967b). Muscle glycogen and muscle electrolytes during prolonged physical exercise. *Acta Physiologica Scandinavica 70*, 129-142.

Ahlborg, G., O. Bjorkman (1987). Carbohydrate utilization by exercising muscle following pre-exercise glucose ingestion. *Clinical Physiology 7*, 181-195.

Ahlborg, G., P. Felig (1982). Lactate and glucose exchange across the forearm, legs and splanchnic bed during and after prolonged exercise. *Journal of Clinical Investigation 69*, 45-54.

Ahlborg, G., P. Felig, L. Hagenfeldt, R. Hendler, J. Wahren (1974). Substrate turnover during prolonged exercise in man. Splanchnic and leg metabolism of glucose, free fatty acids, and amino acids. *Journal of Clinical Investigation 53*, 1080-1090.

Ahlborg, G., J. Wahren, P. Felig (1986). Splanchic and peripheral glucose and lactate metabolism during and after prolonged arm exercise. *Journal of Clinical Investigations 77*, 690-699.

Aitken, A. (1983). The supreme ultra road racer. *Athletics Weekly 37* (November 12), 4-9.

Aitken, A. (1984). Bedford. *Marathon and Distance Runner 3* (June), 25-30.

Albanes, D., A. Blair, P.R. Taylor (1989). Physical activity and risk of cancer in the NHANES I Population. *American Journal of Public Health 79*, 744-750.

Aldridge, R., E.B. Cady, D.A. Jones, G. Obletter (1986). Muscle pain after exercise is linked with an inorganic phosphate increase as shown by ^{31}P NMR. *Bioscience Reports 6*, 663-667.

Alexander, M. (1985). *The Comrades Marathon Story*, Third Edition. Juta, Cape Town, South Africa.

Alexander, R.M. (1987). The spring in your step. *New Scientist* (April 30), 42-44.

Alexander, R.M., M. Bennett (1989). How elastic is a running shoe? *New Scientist* (July 15), 45-46.

Allen, M., C.A. Webster, M. Stortz, J. Bruno, L. Cove (1986). Fitness class injuries: Floor surface, malalignments and a new "squat test." *Annals of Sports Medicine 3*, 14-18.

Allen, M.E., D. Coen (1987). Naloxone blocking of running-induced mood changes. *Annals of Sports Medicine 3*, 190-195.

Allen, M.J., M.R. Barnes (1986). Exercise pain in the lower leg. Chronic compartment syndrome and the medial tibial syndrome. *Journal of Bone and Joint Surgery 68-B*, 818-823.

Altshul, V.A. (1981a). Head injuries. *Running 7* (January-February), 12.

Altshul, V.A. (1981b). Should we advise our depressed patients to run? In *The Psychology of Running*, M.H. Sacks, M.L. Sachs (eds.). Human Kinetics, Champaign, Illinois.

Amberson, W.R. (1943). Physiologic adjustments to the standing posture. *Bulletin of the Maryland University School of Medicine 27*, 127-145.

American Academy of Pediatrics (1983). Climatic heat stress and the exercising child. *The Physician and Sportsmedicine 11* (August), 155-159.

American College of Sports Medicine (1975). Position statement on the prevention of heat injury during distance running. *Medicine and Science in Sports 7*, vii-ix.

American College of Sports Medicine (1976). *Guidelines for Graded Exercise Testing and Exercise Prescription*. Lea and Febiger, Philadelphia.

American College of Sports Medicine (1978). Position statement on the recommended quantity and quality of exercise for developing and maintaining fitness in healthy adults. *Medicine and Science in Sports and Exercise 10*, vii-x.

American College of Sports Medicine (1985). Position statement on the prevention of thermal injuries during distance running. *Medicine and Science in Sports and Exercise 17*, ix-xiv.

American College of Sports Medicine (1987). Position stand on prevention of thermal injuries during distance running. *Medicine and Science in Sports and Exercise 19*, 529-533.

Andersen, P., G. Sjogaard (1976). Selective glycogen depletion in the subgroups of Type II muscle fibres during submaximal exercise in man. *Acta Physiologica Scandinavica 96*, 26A-27A.

Andersen, P., J. Henriksson (1977). Capillary supply of the quadriceps femoris muscle of man: Adaptive response to exercise. *Journal of Physiology 270*, 677-690.

Anderson, B. (1975). *Stretching*. World Publications, Mountain View, California.

Anderson, D.E.H., A. Nygren (1978). Four cases of long-standing diarrhoea and colic pains cured by fructose-free diet—A pathogenetic discussion. *Acta Medica Scandinavica 203*, 87-92.

Anderson, K.M., W.P. Castelli, D. Levy (1987). Cholesterol and mortality. 30 years of follow-up from the Framingham Study. *Journal of the American Medical Association 257*, 2176-2180.

Andrew, G.M., M.R. Becklake, J.S. Guleria, D.V. Bates (1972). Heart and lung function in swimmers and non-athletes during growth. *Journal of Applied Physiology 32*, 245-251.

Andrews, H. (1903). *Training for Athletics and General Health*. C. Arthur Pearson, London.

Andrews, H. (1910). The finding of Alfred Shrubb. *The Athletic Field and Swimming World* (February 5), 2.

Andrianopoulos, G., R.L. Nelson, C.T. Bombeck, G. Souza (1987). The influence of physical activity in 1,2 dimethylhydrazine induced colon carcinogenesis in the rat. *Anticancer Research 7*, 849-852.

Apley, J. (1978). So we'll go no more a-jogging . . . *British Medical Journal 1*, 1548.

Archdeacon, J.W., J.R. Murlin (1944). The effect of thiamin depletion and restoration on muscular endurance and efficiency. *Journal of Nutrition 28*, 241-254.

Ardies, C.M., G.S. Morris, C.K. Erickson, R.P. Farrar (1989). Both acute and chronic exercise enhance in vivo ethanol clearance in rats. *Journal of Applied Physiology 66*, 555-560.

Arieli, A., Y. Epstein, S. Brill, M. Winer, Y. Shapiro (1985). Effect of food intake on exercise fatigue in trained and untrained subjects. *European Journal of Applied Physiology 54*, 297-300.

Armstrong, R.B. (1984). Mechanisms of delayed muscular soreness: A brief review. *Medicine and Science in Sports and Exercise 16*, 529-538.

Aronow, W.S. (1972). Effect of freeway travel on angina pectoris. *Annals of Internal Medicine 77*, 669-676.

Asher, R. (1951). Munchausen's syndrome. *Lancet 1*, 339-341.

Åstrand, P.O. (1955). New records in human power. *Nature 176*, 922-923.

Åstrand, P.O., K. Rodahl (1977). *Textbook of Work Physiology*. McGraw Hill, New York.

Astrom, E. (1977). Human skeletal muscle in bacterial infection: Enzyme activities and their relationship to age. *Scandinavian Journal of Infectious Diseases 9*, 193-195.

Astrom, E., G. Friman, L. Pilstrom (1976). Effect of viral and mycoplasma infections on ultrastructure and enzyme activities in human skeletal muscle. *Acta Pathologica Microbologica Scandinavica 84*, 113-122.

Ayers, J.W.T., Y. Komesu, T. Romani, R. Ansbacher (1985). Anthropomorphic, hormonal and psychologic correlates of semen quality in endurance-trained male athletes. *Fertility and Sterility 4*, 917-921.

Backwelder, et al. (Alcohol and mortality)

Baecke, J.A., W.A. Van Staveren, J. Burema (1983). Food consumption, habitual physical activity, and body fatness in young Dutch adults. *American Journal of Clinical Nutrition 37*, 278-286.

Baekeland, F. (1970). Exercise deprivation: sleep and psychological reactions. *Archives of General Psychiatry 22*, 365-369.

Bahr, R., I. Ingnes, O. Vaage, O.M. Sejersted, E.A. Newsholme (1987). Effect of duration of exercise on excess postexercise O_2 consumption. *Journal of Applied Physiology 62*, 485-490.

Bahrke, M.S., W.P. Morgan (1981). Anxiety reduction following exercise and meditation. In *The Psychology of Running*, M.H. Sacks, M.L. Sachs (eds.). Human Kinetics, Champaign, Illinois.

Baker, E.R., R.S. Mathur, R.F. Kirk, H.O. Williamson (1981). Female runners and secondary amenorrhoea. Correlation with age, parity, mileage and plasma hormonal and sex-hormone-binding globulin concentrations. *Fertility and Sterility 36*, 183-187.

Baker, E.R., C. Stevens, R. Lenker (1988). Relationship of exercise to semen parameters and fertility success of artificial insemination donors. *Journal of the South Carolina Medical Association 84*, 580-582.

Bale, P., G. Nelson (1985). The effects of menstruation on performance of swimmers. *Australian Journal of Science and Medicine in Sport 17*, 19-22.

Bale, P., M. White (1982). The effects of smoking on the health and sleep of sportswomen. *British Journal of Sports Medicine 16*, 149-153.

Banga, J.P., J.C. Pinder, W.B. Gratzer, D.C. Linch, E. R. Huehns (1979). An erythrocyte membrane protein anomaly in march haemoglobinuria. *Lancet 2*, 1049.

Bank, W.J. (1977). Myoglobinuria in marathon runners: Possible relationship to carbohydrate and lipid metabolism. *Annals of the New York Academy of Sciences 301*, 942-948.

Banks, P., W. Bartley, L.M. Birt (1976). *The Biochemistry of the Tissues*. John Wiley & Sons, London.

Bannister, R.G. (1955). *The First Four Minutes*. Putnam, London.

Bannister, R.G. (1956). Muscular effort. *British Medical Bulletin 12*, 222-225.

Bannister, R.G. (1981). *The Four-Minute Mile*. Dodd, Mead and Co., New York.

Bannister, R.G., D.J.C. Cunningham (1954b). The effects on the respiration and performance during exercise of adding oxygen to the inspired air. *Journal of Physiology 125*, 118-137.

Bannister, R.G., D.J.C. Cunningham, C.G. Douglas (1954a). The carbon dioxide stimulus to breathing in severe exercise. *Journal of Physiology 125*, 90-117.

Barclay, G.R., L.A. Turnberg (1988). Effect of moderate exercise on salt and water transport in the human jejunum. *Gut 29*, 816-820.

Barron, J.L., T.D. Noakes, W. Levy, C. Smith, R.P. Millar (1985). Hypothalamic dysfunction in overtrained athletes. *Journal of Endocrinology and Metabolism 60*, 803-806.

Barrow, G.W., S. Saha (1988). Menstrual irregularity and stress fractures in collegiate female distance runners. *American Journal of Sports Medicine 16*, 209-215.

Barry, A., T. Cantwell, F. Doherty, J.C. Folan, M. Ingoldsby, J.P. Kevany, J.D. O'Broin, H. O'Connor, B. O'Shea, B.A. Ryan, J. Vaughan (1981). A nutritional study of Irish athletes. *British Journal of Sports Medicine 15*, 99-109.

Bassett, D.R., F.J. Nagle, S. Mookerjee, K.C. Darr, A.V. Ng, S.G. Voss, J.P. Napp (1987). Thermoregulatory responses to skin wetting during prolonged treadmill running. *Medicine and Science in Sports and Exercise 19*, 28-32.

Bassler, T.J. (1977). Marathon running and immunity to atherosclerosis. *Annals of the New York Academy of Sciences 301*, 579-592.

Bates, B.T., L.R. Osternig, B. Mason, S.L. James (1979). Foot orthotic devices to modify selected aspects of lower extremity mechanics. *American Journal of Sports Medicine 7*, 338-342.

Beaulieu, J.E. (1981). Developing a stretching programme. *The Physician and Sports Medicine 9* (November), 59-69.

Bebb, J., J. Brewer, A. Patton, C. Williams (1984). Endurance running and the influence of diet on fluid intake. *Journal of Sport Sciences 2*, 198-199.

Beinart, H. (1986). Olympic Marathon: Experience not required. *Track and Field News* (May), p. 45.

Belko, A.Z. (1987). Vitamins and exercise—An update. *Medicine and Science in Sports and Exercise 19* (suppl.), S191-S196.

Belko, A.Z., E. Obarzanek, H.J. Kalkwarf, M.A. Rotter, S. Bogusz, D. Miller, J.D. Haas, D.A. Roe (1983). Effects of exercise on riboflavin requirements of young women. *American Journal of Clinical Nutrition 37*, 509-517.

Bellet, S., A. Kershbaum, E.M. Finch (1968). Response of free fatty acids to coffee and caffeine. *Metabolism 17*, 702-707.

Belloc, N.B. (1973). Relationship of health practices and mortality. *Preventive Medicine 2*, 67-81.

Benson, H., T. Dryer, L.H. Hartley (1978). Decreased V̇O₂ consumption during exercise with elicitation of the relaxation response. *Journal of Human Stress* (June), 38-42.

Benyo, R. (1983). *The Masters of the Marathon*. Atheneum, New York.

Berg, K., S. Sady (1985). Oxygen cost of running at submaximal speeds while wearing shoe inserts. *Research Quarterly 56*, 86-89.

Berger, B.G. (1984). Running away from anxiety and depression: A female as well as a male race. In *Running as Therapy. An Integrated Approach*, M.L. Sachs, G.W. Buffore (eds.). University of Nebraska Press, Lincoln, pp. 138-171.

Bergh, U. (1982). *Physiology of Cross-Country Ski-Racing*. Human Kinetics, Champaign, Illinois.

Berglund, B. (1988). Development of techniques for the detection of blood doping in sport. *Sports Medicine 5*, 127-135.

Berglund, B., P. Hemmingson (1982). Effects of caffeine ingestion on exercise performance at low and high altitudes in cross-country skiers. *International Journal of Sports Medicine 3*, 234-236.

Berglund, B., P. Hemmingson (1987). Effect of reinfusion of autologous blood on exercise performance in cross-country skiers. *International Journal of Sports Medicine 8*, 231-233.

Berglund, B., P. Hemmingson, G. Birgegard (1987). Detection of autologous blood transfusion in cross-country skiers. *International Journal of Sports Medicine 8*, 66-70.

Bergström, J., L. Hermansen, E. Hultman, B. Saltin (1967). Diet, muscle glycogen and physical performance. *Acta Physiologica Scandinavica 71*, 140-150.

Bergström, J., E. Hultman (1967a). A study of the glycogen metabolism during exercise in man. *Scandinavian Journal of Clinical and Laboratory Investigation 19*, 218-228.

Bergström, J., E. Hultman (1967b). Synthesis of muscle glycogen in man after glucose and fructose infusion. *Acta Medica Scandinavica 182*, 93-107.

Bergström, J., E. Hultman, L. Jorfeldt, B. Pernow, J. Wahren (1969). Effect of nicotine acid on physical working capacity and on metabolism of muscle glycogen in man. *Journal of Applied Physiology 26*, 170-176.

Berkovec, T.D., D.C. Fowles (1973). Controlled investigation of the effects of progressive and hypnotic relaxation on insomnia. *Journal of Abnormal Psychology 82*, 153-158.

Berkowitz, G.S., J.L. Kelsey, T.R. Holford, R.L. Berkowitz (1983). Physical activity and the risk of spontaneous preterm delivery. *Journal of Reproductive Medicine 28*, 581-588.

Berry, W.T.C., J.B. Beveridge, E.R. Bransby, A.K. Chalmers, B.M. Needham, H.E. Magee, H.S. Townsend, C.G. Daubney (1949). The diet, haemoglobin values and blood pressures of Olympic athletes. *British Medical Journal 1*, 300-304.

Berven, H. (1963). The physical working capacity of healthy children. Seasonal variation and effect of ultraviolet radiation and Vitamin D supply. *Acta Paediatrica 148* (suppl.), 1- 22.

Betteridge, J. (1987). *Sport for Diabetics*. A & C Black, London.

Bichovsky-Little, H. (1987). Look after yourself. *New Statesman* (November 27), 22-23.

Bilanin, J.E., M.S. Blanchard, E. Russek-Cohen (1989). Lower vertebral bone density in male long distance runners. *Medicine and Science in Sports and Exercise 21*, 66-70.

Billman, G.E., P.J. Schwartz, H.L. Stone (1984). The effects of daily exercise on susceptibility to sudden cardiac death. *Circulation 69*, 1182-1189.

Bingham, S.A., J.H. Cummings (1989). Effect of exercise and physical fitness on large intestinal function? *Gastroenterology 97*, 1389-1399.

Bird, H.A., A. Hudson, C.J. Eastmond, V. Wright (1980). Joint laxity and osteo-arthrosis: A radiological survey of female physical education specialists. *British Journal of Sports Medicine 14*, 179-188.

Black, J., G.B. Chesher, G.A. Starmer (1979). The painlessness of the long-distance runner. *Medical Journal of Australia 1*, 522-523.

Blacklock, N.J. (1977). Bladder trauma in the long-distance runner: '10,000 metres haematuria.' *British Journal of Urology 49*, 129-132.

Blackwelder, W.C., K. Yano, G.G. Rhoads, A. Kagan, T. Gordon, Y. Palesch (1980). Alcohol and mortality: The Honolulu heart study. *American Journal of Medicine 68*, 164-169.

Blair, S.N., R. Sargent, D. Davidson, R. Krejci (1980). Blood lipid and ECG responses to carbohydrate-loading. *The Physician and Sportsmedicine 8* (July), 69-75.

Blair, S.N., N.M. Ellsworth, W.L. Haskell, M.P. Stern, J.W. Farquhar, P.D. Wood (1981). Comparison of nutrient intake in middle-aged men and women runners and controls. *Medicine and Science in Sports and Exercise 13*, 310-315.

Blair, S.N., H.W. Kohl, N.N. Goodyear (1987a). Rates and risks for running and exercise injuries: Studies in three populations. *Research Quarterly for Exercise and Sport 58*, 221-228.

Blair, S.N., R.T. Mulder, H.W. Kohl (1987b). Reaction to "Secular traits in adult physical activity: Exercise boom or bust?" *Research Quarterly for Exercise and Sport 58*, 106-110.

Blanchard, E.M., B.S. Pan, R.J. Solaro (1984). The effect of acidic pH on the ATPase activity and troponin Ca^{2+} binding of rabbit skeletal myofilaments. *Journal of Biological Chemistry 259*, 3181-3186.

Blickenstaff, L.D., J.M. Morris (1966). Fatigue fracture of the femoral neck. *Journal of Bone and Joint Surgery 48-A*, 1031-1047.

Blom, P.C.S., D.L. Costill, N.K. Vollestad (1987a). Exhaustive running: Inappropriate as a stimulus of muscle glycogen supercompensation. *Medicine and Science in Sports and Exercise 19*, 398-403.

Blom, P.C.S., A.T. Hostmark, O. Vaage, K.R. Kardel, S. Maehlum (1987b). Effect of different post-exercise sugar diets on the rate of muscle glycogen synthesis. *Medicine and Science in Sports and Exercise 19*, 491-496.

Bloom, M. (1981). *The Marathon. What It Takes to Go The Distance*. Holt, Rinehart and Winston, New York.

Blumenthal, J.A., L.C. O'Toole, J.L. Chang (1984). Is running an analogue of anorexia nervosa? An empirical study of obligatory running and anorexia nervosa. *Journal of the American Medical Association 252*, 520-523.

Blumenthal, J.A., S. Rose, J.L. Chang (1985). Anorexia nervosa and exercise. Implications from recent findings. *Sports Medicine 2*, 237-247.

Blumenthal, J.A., R.S. Williams, T.L. Needles, A.G. Wallace (1982b). Psychological changes accompany aerobic exercise in healthy middle-aged adults. *Psychosomatic Medicine 44*, 529-536.

Blumenthal, J A., R.S. Williams, A.G. Wallace, R.B. Williams, T.L. Needles (1982a). Physiological and psychological variables predict compliance to prescribed exercise therapy in patients recovering from myocardial infarction. *Psychosomatic Medicine 44*, 519-527.

Bobbert, M.F., A.P. Hollander, P.A. Huijing (1986). Factors in delayed muscle soreness. *Medicine and Science in Sports and Exercise 18*, 75-81.

Bock, A.V. (1963). The circulation of a marathoner. *Journal of Sports Medicine and Physical Fitness 3* 80-86.

Bock, A.V., C. Van Caulaert, D.B. Dill, A. Folling, L.M. Hurthal (1928). Studies in muscular activity. III: Dynamical changes occurring in man at work. IV: The steady state and the respiratory quotient during work. *Journal of Physiology 66*, 137-174.

Boileau, R.A., J.L. Mayhew, W.F. Riner, L. Lussier (1982). Physiological characteristics of élite middle and long-distance runners. *Canadian Journal of Applied Sport Science 7*, 167-172.

Boje, O. (1936). Der Blutzucker während und nach körperlicher Arbeit [The blood sugar before and after physical work]. *Skandinavisches Archiv für Physiologie 74* (suppl. 10), 1-48.

Bonen, A., H.A. Keizer (1984). Athletic menstrual cycle irregularity: Endocrine response to exercise and training. *Physician and Sportsmedicine 12*, 78-94.

Boobis, L.H. (1987). Metabolic aspects of fatigue during sprinting. In *Exercise Benefits, Limits and Adaptations*, D. Macleod, R. Maughan, M. Nimmo, T. Reilly, C. Williams (eds.). E. & F. N. Spon, London, pp. 116-143.

Borg, G. (1973). Perceived exertion: A note on history and methods. *Medicine and Science in Sports and Exercise 5*, 90-93.

Borg, G. (1978). Subjective aspects of physical and mental load. *Ergonomics 21*, 215-220.

Borms, J. (1986). The child and exercise: An overview. *Journal of Sports Science 4*, 3-20.

Borms, J., P. Van Roy, J.P. Santens, A. Haentjens (1987). Optimal duration of static stretching exercises for improvement of coxo-femoral flexibility. *Journal of Sport Sciences 5*, 39-47.

Böttiger, L.E. (1971). Physical working capacity and age. *Acta Medica Scandinavica 190*, 359-362.

Böttiger, L.E. (1973). Regular decline in physical working capacity with age. *British Medical Journal 3*, 270-271.

Bouchard, C., M. Chagnon, M-C. Thibault, M.R. Boulay, M. Marcotte, C. Cote, J.-A. Simoneau (1989). Muscle genetic variants and relationship with performance and trainability. *Medicine and Science in Sports and Exercise 21*, 71-77.

Bouchard, C., R. Lesage, G. Lortie, J.-A. Simoneau, P. Hamel, M.R. Boulay, L. P'erusse, G. Th'eriault, C. Leblanc (1986). Aerobic performance in brothers, dizygotic and monozygotic twins. *Medicine and Science in Sports and Exercise 18*, 639-646.

Bouchard, C., G. Lortie (1984). Heredity and endurance performance. *Sports Medicine 1*, 38-64.

Boyce, W.J., M.P. Vessey (1988). Habitual physical inertia and other factors in relation to risk of fracture of the proximal femur. *Age and Ageing 17*, 319-327.

Bramble, D.M., D.R. Carrier (1983). Running and breathing in mammals. *Science 219*, 251-256.

Brearly, M.N. (1977). The long jump miracle of Mexico City. In *Studies in Management Science and Systems 5: Optimal Strategies in Sports*, S.P. Ladany, R.H. Machol (eds.). North Holland, Amsterdam, pp. 162-167.

Breihaupt, M.D. (1855). Zur Pathologie des Menschlichen Fusses [The pathology of the human foot]. *Medizin Zeitung 24*, 169-175.

Breslow, L. (1979). A positive strategy for the nation's health. *Journal of the American Medical Association 242*, 2093- 2095.

Bresnahan, G.T., W..W. Tuttle (1950). *Track and Field Athletics*. Henry Kimpton, London.

Brien, A.J., T.L. Simon (1987). The effects of red blood cell infusion on 10-km race time. *Journal of the American Medical Association 257*, 2761-2765.

Brockbank, E.M. (1929). Miners' cramp. *British Medical Journal 1*, 65-66.

Brooke, C.G.D., R.M.C. Huntley, J. Slack (1975). Influence of heredity and environment in determination of the skinfold thickness of children. *British Medical Journal 2*, 719-721.

Brooks, G.A. (1986a). Lactate production under fully aerobic conditions: The lactate shuttle during rest and exercise. *Federation Proceedings 45*, 2924-2929.

Brooks, G.A. (1986b). The lactate shuffle during exercise and recovery. *Medicine and Science in Sports and Exercise 18*, 360-368.

Brooks, S.M., C.F. Sanborn, B.H. Albrecht, W.W. Wagner (1984). Diet in athletic amenorrhea. *Lancet 1*, 559-560.

Brooks-Gunn, J., J.M. Gargiulo, M.P. Warren (1986). The effect of cycle phase on the performance of adolescent swimmers. *Physician and Sports Medicine 14* (March), 182-192.

Brooks-Gunn, J., M.P. Warren, L. Hamilton (1987b). Response. *Medicine and Science in Sports and Exercise 19*, 526-527.

Brooks-Gunn, J., M.P. Warren, L.H. Hamilton (1987a). The relation of eating problems and amenorrhea in ballet dancers. *Medicine and Science in Sports and Exercise 19*, 41-44.

Brotherhood, J.R. (1984). Nutrition and sports performance. *Sports Medicine 1*, 350-389.

Brouns, F. (1988). *Food and Fluid Related Aspects in Highly Trained Cyclists*. Uitgeverij De Vrieseborch, Harleem.

Brouns, F., W.H.M. Saris, J. Stroecken, E. Beckers, R. Thijssen, N.J. Rehrer, F. ten Hoor (1989a). Eating, drinking, and cycling. A controlled Tour de France simulation study, Part I. *International Journal of Sports Medicine 10*, S32-S40.

Brouns, F., W.H.M. Saris, J. Stroecken, E. Beckers, R. Thijssen, N.J. Rehrer, F. ten Hoor (1989b). Eating, drinking, and cycling. A controlled Tour de France simulation study, Part II. Effect of diet manipulation. *International Journal of Sports Medicine 10*, S41-S48.

Brown, A.G.K. (1964). Athletics in schools. In *Modern Athletics by the Achilles Club*, H.A. Meyer (ed.). Oxford University Press, London, pp. 59-71.

Brown, C.H., J.R. Harrower, M.F. Deeter (1972). The effects of cross-country running on pre-adolescent girls. *Medicine and Science in Sports 4*, 1-5.

Brown, J.D., M. Lawton (1986). Stress and well-being in adolescence: The moderating role of physical exercise. *Journal of Human Stress 12*, 125-131.

Brown, J.D., J.M. Siegel (1988). Exercise as a buffer of life stress: A prospective study of adolescent health. *Health Psychology 7*, 341-353.

Brown, R.L. (1983). Overtraining in athletes. A round table discussion. *The Physician and Sportsmedicine 11* (June), 99.

Browne, S. (1986). *A Complete Guide to Running in the Heat*. Travel Publishing Asia Limited, Hong Kong.

Brownell, K.D., S.N. Steen, J.H. Wilmore (1987). Weight regulation practices in athletes: Analysis of metabolic and health effects. *Medicine and Science in Sports and Exercise 19*, 546-556.

Brownlie, L., I. Mekjavic, E. Banister (1987a). Thermoregulation in athletic racing apparel. *Annals of Physiology and Anthropology 6*, 145-155.

Brownlie, L., I. Mekjavic, I. Gartshore, B. Mutch, E. Banister (1987b). The influence of apparel on aerodynamic drag in running. *Annals of Physiology and Anthropology 6*, 133-143.

Brudvig, T.J.S., T.D. Grudger, L. Obermeyer (1983). Stress fractures in 295 trainees: A one-year study of incidence as related to age, sex, and race. *Military Medicine 148*, 666-667.

Brumberg, J.J. (1989). *Fasting girls: The emergence of anorexia nervosa as a modern disears*. Harvard University Press, Cambridge, MA.

Buccola, V.A., W.J. Stone (1975). Effects of jogging and cycling programmes on physiological and personality variables in aged man. *Research Quarterly 46*, 134-139.

Buckle, R.M. (1965). Exertional (march) haemoglobinuria. *Lancet 1*, 1136-1138.

Buffone, G.W. (1984). Running and depression. In *Running as Therapy. An Integrated Approach*, M.L. Sachs, G.W. Buffone (eds.). University of Nebraska Press, Lincoln, pp. 6-22.

Buick, E.J., N. Gledhill, A.B. Froese, L. Spriet, E.C. Meyers (1980). Effect of induced erythrocythemia on aerobic work capacity. *Journal of Applied Physiology 48*, 636-642.

Bunc, V., J. Heller, P. Moravec, S. Sprynarov'a (1989). Ventilatory threshold and mechanical efficiency in endurance runners. *European Journal of Applied Physiology 58*, 693-698.

Buono, M.J., N.T. Sjoholm (1988). Effect of physical training on peripheral sweat production. *Journal of Applied Physiology 65*, 811-814.

Burch, G.E. (1979). Of jogging. *American Heart Journal 97*, 407.

Burfoot, A. (1981a). Evolution of training systems. Parts I-III. *Runner's World 16* (September), 34-73; (October), 81-86; (December), 60-66.

Burfoot, A. (1981b). Training the hard/easy way. *Runner's World 16* (December), 57-105.

Burfoot, A., B. Billing (1985). The perfect pace. *Runner's World 20* (November), 39-83.

Burkett, L.N. (1970). Causative factors in hamstring strains. *Medicine and Science in Sports 2*, 39-42.

Burkett, L.N., W.M. Kohrt, R. Buchbinder (1985). Effects of shoes and foot orthotics on VO_2 and selected frontal plane knee kinematics. *Medicine and Science in Sports and Exercise 17*, 158-163.

Butterfield, G.E. (1987). Whole-body protein utilization in humans. *Medicine and Science in Sports and Exercise 19* (suppl.), S157-S165.

Bye, P.T.P., S.A. Esau, K.R. Walley, P.T. Macklem, R.L. Pardy (1984). Ventilatory muscles during exercise in air and oxygen in normal men. *Journal of Applied Physiology 56*, 464-471.

Byrd, S.K., A.K. Bode, G.A. Klug (1989). Effects of exercise of varying duration on sarcoplasmic reticulum function. *Journal of Applied Physiology 66*, 1383-1389.

Byrnes, W.C., P.M. Clarkson, J.S. White, S.S. Hseich, P.N. Frykman, R.J. Maughan (1985). Delayed onset muscle soreness following repeated bouts of downhill running. *Journal of Applied Physiology 59*, 710-715.

Caine, D.J., K.J. Lindner (1984). Growth plate injury: A threat to young distance runners? *The Physician and Sportsmedicine 12* (April), 118-124.

Caldwell, F. (1982). Menstrual irregularity in athletes: The unanswered question. *The Physician and Sportsmedicine 10* (May), 142.

Caldwell, F. (1983). Parent's role critical says Billy-Jean King. *The Physician and Sportsmedicine 11* (January), 23-24.

Callen, K.E. (1983). Mental and emotional aspects of long-distance running. *Psychosomatics 24*, 133-151.

Cammack, J., N.W. Read, P.A. Cann, B. Greenwood, A.M. Holgate (1982). Effect of prolonged exercise on the passage of a solid meal through the stomach and small intestine. *Gut 23*, 957-961.

Campbell, M.E., R.L. Hughson, H.J. Green (1989). Continuous increase in blood lactate concentration during different ramp exercise protocols. *Journal of Applied Physiology 66*, 1104-1107.

Campbell, W.W., R.A. Anderson (1987). Effects of aerobic exercise and training on the trace minerals chromium, zinc and copper. *Sports Medicine 4*, 9-18.

Cann, C.E., M.L. Martin, H.K. Gerrants, R.B. Jaffe (1984). Decreased spinal mineral content in amenorrheic women. *Journal of the American Medical Association 251*, 626-629.

Cannon, J.G., M.J. Kluger (1983). Endogenous pyrogen activity in human plasma after exercise. *Science 220*, 617-619.

Cantu, R.C. (1982). *Diabetics and Exercise*. E.P. Dutton, New York.

Cantwell, J.D. (1981). Gastro-intestinal disorders in runners. *Journal of the American Medical Association 246*, 1404-1405.

Carlberg, K.A., M.T. Buckman, G.T. Peake, M.L. Riedesel (1983). Body composition of oligo/amenorrheic athletes. *Medicine and Science in Sports and Exercise 15*, 215-217.

Carlile, F. (1963). *Forbes Carlile on Swimming*. Pelham Books, London.

Carlile, F. (1964). Athletes and adaptation to stress. In *Run Run Run*, F. Wilt (ed.). Track and Field News, Los Altos, California.

Carlson, L., R. Havel, L-G. Ekelund, A. Holmgren (1963). Effect of nicotinic acid on the turnover rate and oxidation of the free fatty acids of plasma in man during exercise. *Metabolism 12*, 837-845.

Carmack, M.A., R. Martens (1979). Measuring commitment to running: A survey of runners' attitudes and mental states. *Journal of Sport Psychology 1*, 25-42.

Carpenter, M.W., S.P. Sady, B. Hoegsberg, M.A. Sady, B. Haydon, E.M. Cullinane, D.R. Coustan, P.D. Thompson (1988). Fetal heart rate response to maternal exertion. *Journal of the American Medical Association 259*, 3006-3009.

Carroll, N. (c. 1981). *The Runner's Book*. Canavaun Books, Dublin.

Carter, J.E., C.V. Gisolfi (1989). Fluid replacement during and after exercise in the heat. *Medicine and Science in Sports and Exercise 21*, 532-539.

Carter, J.E.L., F.W. Kasch, J.L. Boyer, W.H. Phillips, W.D. Ross, A. Sucec (1967). Structural and functional assessments of a champion runner—Peter Snell. *Research Quarterly 38*, 355-365.

Carter, R. (1977). Exercise and happiness. *Journal of Sports Medicine 17*, 307-313.

Casal, D.C., A.S. Leon (1985). Failure of caffeine to affect substrate utilization during prolonged running. *Medicine and Science in Sports and Exercise 17*, 174-179.

Catlin, M.E., R.H. Dressendorfer (1979). Effect of shoe weight on the energy cost of running. *Medicine and Science in Sports 11* (Abstract), 80.

Cavanagh, P.R. 1980). *The Running Shoe Book*. Anderson World, Mountain View, California.

Cavanagh, P.R., K.R. Williams (1982). The effect of stride length variation on oxygen uptake during distance running. *Medicine and Science in Sports and Exercise 14*, 30-35.

Celsing, F., E. Blomstrand, B. Werner, P. Pihlstedt, B. Ekblom (1986). Effects of iron deficiency on endurance and muscle enzyme activity in man. *Medicine and Science in Sports and Exercise 18*, 156-161.

Celsing, F., J. Svedenhag, P. Pihlstedt, B. Ekblom (1987). Effects of anaemia and stepwise-induced polycythaemia on maximal aerobic power in individuals with high and low haemoglobin concentrations. *Acta Physiologica Scandinavica 129*, 47-54.

Cerrutty, P.W. (1964). *Middle-Distance Running*. Pelham Books, London.

Chave, S.P.W., J.N. Morris, S. Moss, A.M. Semmence (1978). Vigorous exercise in leisure time and the death rate: a study of male civil servants. *Journal of Epidemiology and Community Health 32*, 239-243.

Chi, M.M., C.S. Hintz, E.F. Coyle, W.H. Martin, J.L. Ivy, P.M. Nemeth (1983). Effects of detraining on enzymes of energy metabolism in individual human muscle fibres. *American Journal of Physiology 244*, C267-C287.

Chow, R., J.E. Harrison, C. Notarius (1987). Effect of two randomised exercise programmes on bone mass of healthy postmenopausal women. *British Medical Journal 295*, 1441-1444.

Christensen, E.H., O. Hansen (1939). Hypoglykämie, arbeitsfähigkeit und ermüdung [Hypoglycemia, the ability to work and the onset of fatigue]. *Skandinavische Archiv für Physiologie 81*, 172-179.

Christensen, T., G. Christensen (1978). The effects of blood loss on the performance of physical exercise. *European Journal of Applied Physiology 39*, 17-25.

Cimons, M. (1988). Futile attraction. *Runner's World* (July), 39-46.

Clancy, W.G. (1980). Runners' injuries. Part Two: Evaluation and treatment of specific injuries. *American Journal of Sports Medicine 8*, 287-289.

Clapp, J.F., S. Dickstein (1984). Endurance exercise and pregnancy outcome. *Medicine and Science in Sports and Exercise 16*, 556-562.

Clark, C.S., B.B. Kraus, J. Sinclair, D.O. Castell (1989). Gastroesophageal reflux induced by exercise in healthy volunteers. *Journal of the American Medical Association 261*, 3599-3601.

Clark, N., M. Nelson, W. Evans (1988). Nutrition education for elite female runners. *The Physician and Sportsmedicine 16* (February), 124-136.

Clarke, R. (1966). *The Unforgiving Minute*. Pelham Books, London.

Clarke, R., N. Harris (1967). *The Lonely Breed*. Pelham Books, London.

Clarke, T.E., E.C. Frederick, L.B. Cooper (1983b). Effects of shoe cushioning upon ground reaction forces in running. *International Journal of Sports Medicine 4*, 247-251.

Clarke, T.E., E.C. Frederick, C.L. Hamill (1983a). The effects of shoe design parameters on rearfoot control in running. *Medicine and Science in Sports and Exercise 15*, 376-381.

Clausen, J.P. (1977). Effects of physical training on cardiovascular adjustments to exercise in man. *Physiological Reviews 57*, 779-815.

Clayton, D. (1980). *Running to the Top*. Anderson World, Mountain View, California.

Clement, D.B. (1974). Tibial stress syndrome in athletes. *Journal of Sports Medicine 2*, 81-85.

Clement, D.B., R.C. Asmundson (1982). Nutritional intake and hematological parameters in endurance runners. *The Physician and Sportsmedicine 10* (March), 37-43.

Clement, D.B., R. Asmundson, C.W. Medhurst (1977). Haemoglobin values: Comparative survey of the 1976 Canadian Olympic Team. *Canadian Medical Association Journal 117*, 614-616.

Clement, D.B., L.L. Sawchuk (1984). Iron status and sports performance. *Sports Medicine 1*, 65-74.

Clement, D.B., J.E. Taunton, G.W. Smart (1984). Achilles tendinitis and peritendinitis: Etiology and treatment. *American Journal of Sports Medicine 12*, 179-184.

Clement, D.B., J.E. Taunton, G.W. Smart, K.L. McNicol (1981). A survey of overuse running injuries. *The Physician and Sportsmedicine 9* (May), 47-58.

Coggan, A.R., E.F. Coyle (1987). Reversal of fatigue during prolonged exercise by carbohydrate infusion or ingestion. *Journal of Applied Physiology 63*, 2388-2395.

Coggan, A.R., E.F. Coyle (1988). Effect of carbohydrate feedings during high-intensity exercise. *Journal of Applied Physiology 65*, 1703-1709.

Coggan, A.R., E.F. Coyle (1989). Metabolism and performance following carbohydrate ingestion late in exercise. *Medicine and Science in Sports and Exercise 21*, 59-65.

Cohen, J.L., C.S. Kim, P.B. May., N.H. Ertel (1982). Exercise, body weight and professional ballet dancers. *The Physician and Sportsmedicine 10* (April), 92-101.

Cohen, L.A., K.W. Choi, C.X. Wang (1988). Influence of dietary fat, caloric restriction, and voluntary exercise on N-nitrosomethylurea-induced mammary tumorigenesis in rats. *Cancer Research 48*, 4276-4283.

Collegian Harriers (1981). *The Distance Runner's Log: To the Lonely Breed*, Ninth Edition. Collegian Harriers: Pietermaritzburg.

Collings, C., L.B. Curet (1985). Fetal heart rate response to maternal exercise. *American Journal of Obstetrics and Gynecology 151*, 498-501.

Collings, C.A., L.B. Curet, J.P. Mullin (1983). Maternal and fetal responses to a maternal aerobic exercise programme. *American Journal of Obstetrics and Gynecology 145*, 702- 707.

Colt, E.W.D., D.L. Dunner, K. Hall, R.R. Fieve (1981). A high prevalence of affective disorder in runners. in *The Psychology of Running*, M.H. Sacks, M.L. Sachs (eds.). Human Kinetics, Champaign, Illinois.

Committee on School Health (1956). Competitive athletics: A statement of policy. *Pediatrics 18*, 672-676.

Conconi, F., M. Ferrare, P.G. Ziglio, P. Droghetti, L. Codeca (1982). Determination of the anaerobic threshold by a non-invasive field test in runners. *Journal of Applied Physiology 52*(4), 869-873.

Conlee, R.K., R.M. Lawler, P.E. Ross (1987). Effect of glucose or fructose feeding on glycogen repletion in muscle and liver after exercise or fasting. *Annals of Nutrition and Metabolism 31*, 126-132.

Conley, D.L., G.S. Krahenbuhl (1980). Running economy and distance running performance of highly trained athletes. *Medicine and Science in Sports and Exercise 12*, 357-360.

Conley, D.L., G.S. Krahenbuhl, L.N. Burkett (1981b). Training for aerobic capacity and running economy. *The Physician and Sportsmedicine 9* (April), 107-115.

Conley, D.L., G.S. Krahenbuhl, L.N. Burkett, A.L. Millar (1981a). Physiological correlates of female road racing performance. *Research Quarterly 52*, 441-448.

Conley, D.L., G.S. Krahenbuhl, L.N. Burkett, A.L. Millar (1984). Following Steve Scott: Physiological changes accompanying training. *The Physician and Sportsmedicine 12* (January), 103-106.

Connett, R.J., T.E.J. Gayeski, C.R. Honig (1984). Lactate accumulation in fully aerobic, working, dog gracilis muscle. *American Journal of Physiology 246*, H120-H128.

Connett, R.J., T.E.J. Gayeski, C.R. Honig (1985). Energy sources in fully aerobic rest-work transitions: A new role for glycolysis. *American Journal of Physiology 248*, H922-H929.

Connett, R.J., T.E.J. Gayeski, C.R. Honig (1986). Lactate efflux is unrelated to intracellular PO_2 in a working red muscle in situ. *Journal of Applied Physiology 61*, 402-408.

Cook, S.D., A.F. Harding, K.A. Thomas, E.L. Morgan, K.M. Schnurpfeil, R.J. Haddad (1987). Trabecular bone density and menstrual function in women runners. *American Journal of Sports Medicine 15*, 503-507.

Cook, S.D., M.A. Kester, M.E. Brunet (1985b). Shock absorption characteristics of running shoes. *American Journal of Sports Medicine 13*, 248-253.

Cook, S.D., M.A. Kester, M.E. Brunet, R.J. Haddad (1985a). Biomechanics of running shoe performance. *Clinics in Sports Medicine 4*, 619-626.

Cooke, R., E. Pate (1985). The effects of ADP and phosphate on the contraction of muscle fibres. *Biophysical Journal 48*, 789-798.

Coon, G.P. (1957). Echoes of the marathon. *New England Journal of Medicine 257*, 1168-1169.

Cooper, A.M. (1981). Masochism and long-distance running. In *The Psychology of Running*, M.H. Sacks, M.L. Sachs (eds.). Human Kinetics, Champaign, Illinois.

Cooper, D. (1986). The megamarathon—24 hours beyond. In *Training for Ultras*, A. Milroy (ed.). Road Runners Publication, London.

Cooper, K.H. (1968). *Aerobics*, Evans and Co., New York.

Copolov, D.L., R.D. Helme (1983). Enkephalins and endorphins. Clinical, pharmacological and therapeutic implications. *Drugs 26*, 503-519.

Cordain, L., R.W. Latin, J.J. Behnke (1986). The effects of an aerobic running program on bowel transit time. *Journal of Sports Medicine and Physical Fitness 26*, 101-104.

Costill, D.L. (1967). The relationship between selected physiological variables and distance running performance. *Journal of Sports Medicine and Physical Fitness 7*, 61-66.

Costill, D.L. (1970). Metabolic responses during distance running. *Journal of Applied Physiology 28*, 251-255.

Costill, D.L. (1977). Sweating: Its composition and effects on body fluids. *Annals of the New York Academy of Sciences 301*, 160-174.

Costill, D.L. (1979). *A scientific approach to distance running*. Track and Field News, Los Altos, California.

Costill, D.L. (1982). Salazar and Clayton. A phyisological comparison of the marathon record holders. *The Runner 4* (March), 20.

Costill, D.L. (1985). The 1985 C.H. McCloy Research Lecture. *Research Quarterly for Exercise and Sport 56*, 378-384.

Costill, D.L. (1986). *Inside Running: Basics of Sports Physiology*. Benchmark Press, Canmet, Indiana.

Costill, D.L., R. Bowers, G. Branam, K. Sparks (1971a). Muscle glycogen utilization during prolonged exercise on consecutive days. *Journal of Applied Physiology 31*, 834-838.

Costill, D.L., R. Bowers, W.F. Kammer (1970). Skinfold estimates of body fat among marathon runners. *Medicine and Science in Sports 2*, 93-95.

Costill, D.L., G. Branam, D. Eddy, K. Sparks (1971b). Determinants of marathon running success. *Internationale Zeitschrift für Angewandte Physiologie 29*, 249-254.

Costill, D.L., R. Cote, W.J. Fink (1982). Dietary potassium and heavy exercise: effects on muscle water and electrolytes. *American Journal of Clinical Nutrition 36*, 266-275.

Costill, D.L., E. Coyle, G. Dalsky, W. Evans, W. Fink, D. Hoopes (1977). Effect of elevated plasma FFA and insulin on muscle glycogen usage during exercise. *Journal of Applied Physiology 43*, 695-699.

Costill, D.L., G.P. Dalsky, W.J. Fink (1978). Effects of caffeine ingestion on metabolism and exercise performance. *Medicine and Science in Sports 10*, 155-158.

Costill, D.L., W.J. Fink, M. Flynn, J. Kirwan (1987). Muscle fibre composition and enzyme activities in elite female distance runners. *International Journal of Sports Medicine 8* (suppl. 3), 103-106.

Costill, D.L., W.J. Fink, L.H. Getchell, J.L. Ivy, F.A. Witzmann (1979). Lipid metabolism in skeletal muscle of endurance-trained males and females. *Journal of Applied Physiology 47*, 787-791.

Costill, D.L., E.L. Fox (1969). Energetics of marathon running. *Medicine and Science in Sports and Exercise 1*, 81-86.

Costill, D.L., H. Higdon (1981). A season in Norway: What makes Grete run? *The Runner* (April), 50-83.

Costill, D.L., E. Jansson, P.D. Gollnick, B. Saltin (1974). Glycogen utilization in leg muscle of men during level and uphill running. *Acta Physiologica Scandinavica 91*, 475-481.

Costill, D.L., D.S. King, R. Thomas, M. Hargreaves (1985). Effects of reduced training on muscular power in swimmers. *The Physician and Sportsmedicine 13* (February), 94-101.

Costill, D.L., J.M. Miller (1980). Nutrition for endurance sport: Carbohydrate and fluid balance. *International Journal of Sports Medicine 1* 2-14.

Costill, D.L., B. Saltin (1974). Factors limiting gastric emptying during rest and exercise. *Journal of Applied Physiology 37*, 679-683.

Costill, D.L., W.M. Sherman, W.J. Fink, C. Maresh, M. Witten, J.M. Miller (1981). The role of dietary carbohydrate in muscle glycogen resynthesis after strenuous exercise. *American Journal of Clinical Nutrition 34*, 1831-1836.

Costill, D.L., H. Thomason, E. Roberts (1973). Fractional utilization of the aerobic capacity during distance running. *Medicine and Science in Sports 5*, 248-252.

Costill, D.L., E. Winrow (1970a). Maximal oxygen intake among marathon runners. *Archives of Physical and Medical Rehabilitation 51*, 317-320.

Costill, D.L., E. Winrow (1970b). A comparison of two middle-aged ultramarathon runners. *Research Quarterly 41*, 135-139.

Counsilman, J.E. (1968). *The Science of Swimming*. Pelham Books, London.

Counsilman, J.E. (1986). The role of the coach in training for swimming. *Clinics in Sports Medicine 5*, 3-7.

Coyle, E.F., A.R. Coggan, M.K. Hemmert, J.L. Ivy (1986a). Muscle glycogen utilization during prolonged strenuous exercise when fed carbohydrate. *Journal of Applied Physiology 61*, 165-172.

Coyle, E.F., A.R. Coggan, M.K. Hemmert, R.C. Lowe, T.J. Walters (1985a). Substrate usage during prolonged exercise following a preexercise meal. *Journal of Applied Physiology 59*, 429-433.

Coyle, E.F., D.L. Costill, W.J. Fink, D.G. Hoopes (1978). Gastric emptying rates for selected athletic drinks. *Research Quarterly 49*, 119-124.

Coyle, E.F., J.M. Hagberg, B.F. Hurley, W.H. Martin, A.A. Ehsani, J.O. Holloszy (1983). Carbohydrate feeding during prolonged strenuous exercise can delay fatigue. *Journal of Applied Physiology 55*, 230-235.

Coyle, E.F., M.K. Hemmert, A.R. Coggan (1986b). Effects of detraining on cardiovascular responses to exercise: Role of blood volume. *Journal of Applied Physiology 60*, 95-99.

Coyle, E.F., W.H. Martin, S.A. Blomfield, O.H. Lowry, J.O. Holloszy (1985b). Effects of detraining on responses to submaximal exercise. *Journal of Applied Physiology 59*, 853-859.

Coyle, E.F., W.H. Martin, D.R. Sinacore, M.J. Joyner, J.M. Hagberg, J.O. Holloszy (1984). Time course of loss of adaptations after stopping prolonged intense endurance training. *Journal of Applied Physiology 57*, 1857-1864.

Cramer, D.W., E. Wilson, R.J. Stillman, M.J. Berger, S. Belisle, I. Schiff, B. Albrecht, M. Gibson, B.V. Stadel, S.C. Schoenbaum (1986). The relation of endometriosis to menstrual characteristics, smoking, and exercise. *Journal of the American Medical Association 255*, 1904-1908.

Cratty, B.J. (1983). *Psychology in Contemporary Sport: Guidelines for Coaches and Athletes*. Prentice-Hall, Englewood Cliffs, New Jersey.

Crews, D.J., D.M. Landers (1987). A meta-analytic review of aerobic fitness and reactivity to psychosocial stressors. *Medicine and Science in Sports and Exercise 19*, S114-S120.

Cumming, D.C., G.D. Wheeler, E.M. McColl (1989). The effects of exercise on reproductive function in men. *Sports Medicine 7*, 1-17.

Cunningham, J.J. (1980). A re-analysis of the factors influencing basal metabolic rate in normal adults. *American Journal of Clinical Nutrition 33*, 2372-2374.

Cureton, K., P. Bishop, P. Hutchinson, H. Newland, S. Vickery, L. Zwiren (1986). Sex difference in maximal oxygen uptake. Effect of equating haemoglobin concentration. *European Journal of Applied Physiology 54*, 656-660.

Cureton, K.J., R.A. Boileau, W.F. Riner (1975). Structural and physiological evaluation of Craig Virgin, 1975 NCAA Cross-country champion. Unpublished Study, *Physical Fitness Research Laboratory*, University of Illinois, Champaign.

Cureton, K.J., P.B. Sparling (1980). Distance running performance and metabolic responses to running in men and women with excess weight experimentally equated. *Medicine and Science in Sports and Exercise 12*, 288-294.

Cureton, K.J., P.B. Sparling, B.W. Evans, S.M. Johnson, U.D. Kong, J.W. Purvis (1978). Effect of experimental alterations in excess weight on aerobic capacity and distance running performance. *Medicine and Science in Sports 10*, 194-199.

Currens, J.H., P.D. White (1961). Half a century of running: Clinical, physiological and autopsy findings in the case of Clarence de Mar (Mr. Marathon). *New England Journal of Medicine 265*, 988-993.

Cyriax, J. (1978). *Textbook of Orthopaedic Medicine*, 10th Edition. Bailliére Tindall, London, 2:10-36.

Czajkowski, W. (1982). A simple method to control fatigue in endurance training. In *Exercise and Sport Biology*, International Series on Sport Sciences, P.V. Komi (ed.). Human Kinetics, Champaign, Illinois, 10:207-212.

Dale, E., D.M. Gerlach, A.L. Wilhite (1979). Menstrual dysfunction in distance runners. *Obstetrics and Gynecology 54*, 47-53.

Dale, E., D.L. Goldberg (1982). Implications of nutrition in athletes' menstrual cycle irregularities. *Canadian Journal of Applied Sports Science 7*, 74-78.

Dale, E., K.M. Mullinax, D.H. Byran (1982). Exercise during pregnancy: Effects on the fetus. *Canadian Journal of Applied Sports Science 7*, 98-103.

D'Alessio, D.A., E.C. Kavie, M.A. Mozzoll, K.J. Smalley, M. Polansky, Z.V. Kendrick, L.R. Owen, M.C. Bushman, G. Boden, O.E. Owen (1988). Thermix effect of food in lean and obese men. *Journal of Clinical Investigation 81*, 1781-1789.

Dalsky, G.P., K.S. Stocke, A.A. Ehsani, E. Slatopolsky, W.C. Lee, S.J. Birge (1988). Weight-bearing exercise training and lumbar bone mineral content in postmenopausal women. *Annals of Internal Medicine 108*, 824-828.

Dalton, K., J.G.P. Williams (1976). Women in sport. In *Sports Medicine*, J.G.P. Williams, P.N. Sperryn (eds.). Edward Arnold, London.

Danforth, E. (1985). Diet and obesity. *American Journal of Clinical Nutrition 41*, 1132-1145.

Daniels, J. (1974b). Physiological characteristics of champion male athletes. *Research Quarterly 45*, 342-348.

Daniels, J., R. Fitts, G. Sheehan (1978b). *Conditioning for Distance Running—The Scientific Aspects*. John Wiley and Sons, New York.

Daniels, J., J. Gilbert (1979). *Oxygen Power. Performance Tables for Distance Runners*. Oxygen Power, Tempe, Arizona.

Daniels, J., G. Krahenbuhl, C. Foster, J. Gilbert, S. Daniels (1977). Aerobic responses of female distance runners to submaximal and maximal exercise. *Annals of the New York Academy of Sciences 301*, 726-733.

Daniels, J., N. Oldridge (1970). The effects of alternate exposure to altitude and sea level on world-class middle-distance runners. *Medicine and Science in Sports 2*, 107-112.

Daniels, J., N. Oldridge (1971). Changes in oxygen consumption of young boys during growth and running training. *Medicine and Science in Sports 3*, 161-165.

Daniels, J., N. Oldridge, F. Nagle, B. White (1978c). Differences and changes in $\dot{V}O_2$max. among young runners 10 to 18 years of age. *Medicine and Science in Sports 10*, 200-203.

Daniels, J.T. (1974a). Running with Jim Ryun: A five-year study. *The Physician and Sportsmedicine 2* (September), 62-67.

Daniels, J.T., N.J. Scardina, P. Foley (1985). $\dot{V}O_2$ submax. during five modes of exercise. In *Proceedings of the World Congress on Sports Medicine, Vienna, 1982*, N. Bachl, L. Prokop, R. Suckert (eds.). Vienna: Urban and Schwartsenberg, pp. 604-615.

Daniels, J.T., R.A. Yarbough, C. Foster (1978a). Changes in $\dot{V}O_2$max. and running performance with training. *European Journal of Applied Physiology 39*, 249-254.

Daniels, W.L., J.A. Vogel, D.S. Sharp, G. Friman, J.E. Wright, W.R. Beisel, J.J. Knapik (1985). Effects of virus infections on physical performance in man. *Military Medicine 150*, 8-14.

Danilewitz, M.D., H. Mohamed, C. Jeppe, J.F. Botha (1984). Incidence of lactose intolerance in Whites with irritable bowel syndrome and symptomatic response to diet. *South African Medical Journal 65*, 1019.

Davey, J.R., C.H. Rorabeck, P.J. Fowler (1984). The tibialis posterior muscle compartment. An unrecognized cause of exertional compartment syndrome. *American Journal of Sports Medicine 12*, 391-397.

Davidson, J., H.G. Gemmell, J.B. Leiper, R.J. Maughan, F.W. Smith (1988). Gastric emptying of moderate volumes of glucose drinks in humans. *Journal of Physiology 387*, 95P.

Davies, C.T.M. (1980a). Metabolic cost of exercise and physical performance in children with some observations on external loading. *European Journal of Applied Physiology 45*, 95-102.

Davies, C.T.M. (1980b). Effects of air resistance on the metabolic cost and performance of cycling. *European Journal of Applied Physiology 45*, 245-254.

Davies, C.T.M. (1980c). Effects of wind assistance and resistance on the forward motion of a runner. *Journal of Applied Physiology 48*, 702-709.

Davies, C.T.M. (1981). Wind resistance and assistance in running. In *Medicine in Sport*, P.E. di Pampero, J.R. Poortmans (ed.). Karger, Basel. 13:199-212.

Davies, C.T.M., M.W. Thompson (1979). Aerobic performance of female marathon and male ultramarathon athletes. *European Journal of Applied Physiology 41*, 233-245.

Davies, C.T.M., M.W. Thompson (1986). Physiological responses to prolonged exercise in ultramarathon athletes. *Journal of Applied Physiology 61*, 611-617.

Davies, K.J.A., L. Packer, G.A. Brooks (1981). Biochemical adaptation of mitochondria, muscle, and whole-animal respiration to endurance training. *Archives of Biochemistry and Biophysics 209*, 539-554.

Davies, K.J.A., L. Packer, G.A. Brooks (1982a). Exercise bio-energetics following sprint training. *Archives of Biochemistry and Biophysics 215*, 260-265.

Davies, K.J.A., A.T. Quintanilha, G.A. Brooks, L. Packer (1982b). Free radicals and tissue damage produced by diet and exercise. *Biochemical and Biophysical Research Communications 107*, 1198-1205.

Davis, J.M., D.R. Lamb, W.A. Burgess, W.P. Bartoli (1987). Accumulation of deuterium oxide in body fluids after ingestion of D_2O-labelled beverages. *Journal of Applied Physiology 63*, 2060-2066.

Daws, R. (1977). *The Self-Made Olympian*. World Publications, Mountain View, California.

Daws, R. (1978). Training to peak. In *The Complete Marathoner*, J. Henderson (ed.). World Publications, Mountain View, California.

de Castella, R., M. Jenkinson (1984). *Deek—The Making of Australia's World Marathon Champion*. William Collins, Australia.

de Coverley Veale, D.M.W. (1987). Exercise dependence. *British Journal of Addiction 82*, 735-740.

Dellinger, B., B. Freeman (1984). *The Competitive Runner's Training Book*. Macmillan, New York.

DeMar, C. (1937). *Marathon*. Stephen Daye Press, Brattleboro, Vermont. Republished in 1981 by New England Press, Shelburne, Vermont.

Dempsey, J.A., P.G. Hanson, K.S. Henderson (1984). Exercise-induced arterial hypoxaemia in healthy human subjects at sea level. *Journal of Physiology 355*, 161-175.

Dempsey, J., P. Hanson, D. Pegelow, A. Claremont, J. Rankin (1982). Limitations to exercise capacity and endurance: Pulmonary system. *Canadian Journal of Applied Sport Science 7*, 4-13.

Denio, L.S., M.E. Drake, A. Pakalnis (1989). The effect of exercise on seizure frequency. *Journal of Medicine 20*, 171-176.

Dennis, S.C., T.D. Noakes, A.N. Bosch (1991). Neither ventilation nor blood lactate show threshold phenomena during progressive incremental exercise tests on trained cyclists. *Journal of Physiology* (Submitted).

Despr'es, J.P., S. Moorjani, A. Tremblay, E.T. Poehlman, P.J. Lupien, A. Nadeau, C. Bouchard (1988). Heredity and changes in plasma lipids and lipoproteins after short-term exercise training in men. *Arteriosclerosis 8*, 402-409.

Detmer, D.E. (1986). Chronic shin splints. Classification and management of medial tibial stress syndrome. *Sports Medicine 3*, 436-446.

Detmer, D.E., K. Sharpe, R.L. Sufit, F.M. Girdley (1985). Chronic compartment syndrome: Diagnosis, management and outcomes. *American Journal of Sports Medicine 13*, 162-169.

Deuster, P.A., S.B. Kyle, P.B. Moser, R.A. Vigersky, A. Singh, E.B. Schoomaker (1986). Nutritional intakes and status of highly trained amenorrheic and eumenorrheic women runners. *Fertility and Sterility 46*, 636-643.

Devas, M.B. (1958). Stress fractures of the tibia in athletes or "shin soreness." *Journal of Bone and Joint Surgery 40B*, 227-239.

Devereaux, M.D., G.R. Parr, S.M. Lachmann, D.P. Page Thomas, B.L. Hazelman (1986). Thermographic diagnosis in athletes with patellofemoral arthralgia. *Journal of Bone and Joint Surgery 68-B*, 42-44.

Devlin, J.T., J. Calles-Escandon, E.S. Horton (1986). Effects of preexercise snack feeding on endurance cycle exercise. *Journal of Applied Physiology 60*, 980-985.

De Vos, A., J. Leklem, D. Campbell (1982). Carbohydrate-loading, vitamin B_6 supplementation and fuel metabolism during exercise in man. *Medicien and Science in Sports and Exercise 14*, 137.

De Vries, H.A. (1981). Tranquillizer effect of exercise: A critical review. *The Physician and Sportsmedicine 9* (November), 47-55.

De Wijn, J.F., J.L. De Jongste, W. Mosterd, D. Willebrand (1971). Haemoglobin, packed cell volume, serum iron and iron binding capacity of selected athletes during training. *Journal of Sports Medicine and Physical Fitness 11*, 42-51.

Diamond, S. (1982). Prolonged benign exertional headache: Its clinical characteristics and response to indomethacin. *Headache 22*, 96-98.

Dickson, D.N., R.L. Wilkinson, T.D. Noakes (1982). Effects of ultra-marathon training and racing on haematological parameters and serum ferritin levels in well-trained athletes. *International Journal of Sports Medicine 2*, 111-117.

Dickson, T.D., P.D. Kichline (1987). Functional management of stress fractures in female athletes using a pneumatic leg brace. *American Journal of Sports Medicine 15*, 86-89.

Dienstbier, R.A. (1984). The effect of exercise on personality. In *Running as Therapy. An Integrated Approach*, M.L. Sachs, G.W. Buffore (eds.). University of Nebraska Press, Lincoln, pp. 253-272.

Dienstbier, R.A., J. Crabbe, G.O. Johnson, W. Thorland, J.A. Jorgensen, M.M. Sadar, D.C. Lavelle (1981). Exercise and stress tolerance. In *The Psychology of Running*, M.H. Sacks, M.L. Sachs (eds.). Human Kinetics, Champaign, Illinois.

Dill, D.B. (1965). Marathoner DeMar: Physiological studies. *Journal of the National Cancer Institute 35*, 185-191.

Dill, D.B. (1968). Physiological adjustments to altitude changes. *Journal of the American Medical Association 205*, 747-753.

Dill, D.B., A.V. Bock, H.T. Edwards, P.H. Kennedy (1936). Industrial fatigue. *Journal of Industrial Hygiene and Toxicology 18*, 417-431.

Dill, D.B., S. Robinson, J.C. Ross (1967). A longitudinal study of 16 champion runners. *Journal of Sports Medicine and Physical Fitness 7*, 4-27.

Dill, D.B., J.H. Talbot, H.T. Edwards (1930). Studies in muscular activity. VI: Response of several individuals to a fixed task. *Journal of Physiology 69*, 267-305.

Dillon, M., A. Milroy (1984). Those were the days. *Marathon and Distance Runner 3* (March), 45-48.

Docherty, D., J.D. Eckerson, J.S. Hayward (1986). Physique and thermoregulation in prepubertal males during exercise in a warm, humid environment. *American Journal of Physical Anthropology 70*, 19-23.

Doherty, J.K. (1964). *Modern Training for Running*. Prentice-Hall, Englewood Cliffs, New Jersey.

Donaldson, S., P. Best, W. Kerrick (1978). Characterisation of the effects of Mg^{2+} on $Ca^{2+}=$ and $Sr^{2+}=$activated tension generation of skinned rat cardiac fibres. *Journal of General Physiology 71*, 645-655.

Donaldson, S.K. (1986). Mammalian muscle fiber types: Comparison of excitation-contraction coupling mechanisms. *Acta Physiologica Scandinavica 128*, 157-166.

Donaldson, S.K.B. (1983). Effect of acidosis on maximum force generation of peeled mammalian skeletal muscle fibres. In *Biochemistry of Exercise*, H.G. Knuttgen, J.A. Vogel, J. Poortmans (eds.). Human Kinetics, Champaign, Illinois, pp. 126-133.

Donaldson, S.K.B., L. Hermansen (1978). Differential, direct effects of H^+ on $Ca^{++}=$activated force of skinned fibres from the soleus, cardiac and adductor magnus muscles of rabbits. *Pflugers Archives 376*, 55-65.

Donnelly, A.E., M. Gleeson, R.J. Maughan, K.A. Walker, P.H. Whiting (1987). Delayed-onset rise in serum lipid peroxide concentration following eccentric exercise in man. *Journal of Physiology 392*, 51P.

Donnelly, A.E., K. McCormick, R.J. Maughan, P.H. Whiting, P.M. Clarkson (1988). Effects of a non-steroidal anti-inflammatory drug on delayed onset muscle soreness and indices of damage. *British Journal of Sports Medicine 22*, 35-38.

Donovan, C.M., G.A. Brooks (1983). Endurance training affects lactate clearance, not lactate production. *American Journal of Physiology 244*, E83-E92.

Downer, A.R. (1900). *Running Recollections and How to Train*. Gale and Polden, London. Facsimile reproduction by Balgownie Books, Aberdeen (1982).

Dressendorfer, R.H., R.C. Goodlin (1980). Fetal heart rate response to maternal exercise testing. *The Physician and Sportsmedicine 8* (November), 90-96.

Dressendorfer, R.H., R. Sockolov (1980). Hypozincemia in runners. *The Physician and Sportsmedicine 8* (April), 97-100.

Dressendorfer, R.H., C.E. Wade, J.H. Scaff (1985). Increased morning heart rate in runners: A valid sign of overtraining? *The Physician and Sportsmedicine 13* (August), 77-86.

Drinkwater, B.L., K. Nilson, C.H. Chestnut, W.J. Bremner, S. Shainholtz, M.B. Southworth (1984). Bone mineral content of amenorrheic and eumenorrheic athletes. *New England Journal of Medicine 311*, 277-281.

Drinkwater, B.L., K. Nilson, S. Ott, C.H. Chesnut (1986). Bone mineral density after resumption of menses in amenorrheic athletes. *Journal of the American Medical Association 256*, 380-382.

Droghetti, P., C. Borsetto, I. Casoni, M. Cellini, M. Ferrari, A.R. Paolini, P.G. Ziglio, F. Conconi (1985). Noninvasive determination of the anaerobic threshold in canoeing, cross-country skiing, cycling, roller, and iceskating, rowing, and walking. *European Journal of Applied Physiology 53*, 299-303.

Druss, R.G., J.A. Silverman (1979). Body image and perfectionism of ballerinas. Comparison and contrast with anorexia nervosa. *General Hospital Psychiatry 10*, 115-121.

Dubowitz, V., A.G.E. Pearse (1960). A comparative histochemical study of oxidative enzyme and phosphorylase activity in skeletal muscle. *Histochemie 2*, 105-117.

Dudley, G.A., W.M. Abraham, R.L. Terjung (1982). Influence of exercise intensity and duration on biochemical adaptation in skeletal muscle. *Journal of Applied Physiology 53*, 844-850.

Dudley, G.A., R. Djamil (1985). Incompatibility of endurance- and strength-training modes of exercise. *Journal of Applied Physiology 59*, 1446-1451.

Dudley, G.A., P.C. Tullson, R.L. Terjung (1987). Influence of mitochondrial content on the sensitivity of respiratory control. *Journal of Biological Chemistry 262*, 9109-9114.

Dufaux, B., A. Hoederath, I. Streitberger, W. Hollman, G. Assman (1981). Serum ferritin, transferrin, haptoglobin and iron in middle and long-distance runners, élite rowers and professional racing cyclists. *International Journal of Sports Medicine 2*, 43-46.

Duffy, E. (1976). The psychological significance of the concept of 'arousal' or 'activation.' In *Psychology in Sport*, A.C. Fisher (ed.). Mayfield Publishing, Palo Alto, California, pp. 90-111.

Dummer, G.M., L.W. Rosen, W.W. Heusner, P.J. Roberts, J.E. Counsilman (1987). Pathogenic weight-control behaviours of young competitive swimmers. *The Physician and Sportsmedicine 15* (May), 75-84.

Early, R., B. Carlson (1969). Water soluble vitamin therapy on the delay of fatigue from physical activity in hot climatic conditions. *Internationale Zeitschrift für Angewandte Physiologie 27*, 43-50.

Eastmond, C.J., A. Hudson, V. Wright (1980). Osteoarthrosis of the hip and knee in female specialist physical education teachers. *Scandinavian Journal of Rheumatology 8*, 264-268.

Edelen, L.G. (1964). Marathon running. In *Run Run Run*, F. Wilt (ed.). Track and Field News, Los Altos, California.

Editorial (1938). After dinner rest awhile? *Lancet 1*, 1258.

Editorial (1982a). The lead controversy. *South African Medical Journal 22*, 793-794.

Editorial (1982b). Haematuria and exercise-related haematuria. *British Medical Journal 285*, 1595-1597.

Editorial (1987). Aching muscles after exercise. *Lancet 2*, 1123-1124.

Editorial (1988). Exercise and energy balance. *Lancet 1*, 392-394.

Edwards, P., P. Beresford, C. Nadon, C. Steeves (1983). Fitness and pregnancy: A round table discussion. *Canadian Journal of Public Health 74*, 86-90.

Ehn, L., B. Carlmark, S. Höglund (1980). Iron status in athletes involved in intense physical activity. *Medicine and Science in Sports and Exercise 12*, 61-64.

Eichner, E.R. (1989). Gastrointestinal bleeding in athletes. *Physician and Sportsmedicine 17* (May), 128-140.

Eide, R. (1982). The relationship between body image, self-image and physical activity. *Scandinavian Journal of Social Medicine 29* (suppl.), 109-112.

Ekblom, B. (1969). Effect of physical training in adolescent boys. *Journal of Applied Physiology 27*, 350-355.

Ekblom, B., G. Wilson, P-O. Astrand (1976). Central circulation during exercise after venesection and reinfusion of red blood cells. *Journal of Applied Physiology 40*, 379-383.

Elliott, H.J. (1961). *The Golden Mile*. Cassell and Co., London.

Elliott, H.J. (1964). The road to Rome. In *Modern Athletics by the Achilles Club*, H.A. Mayer (ed.). Oxford University Press, London.

Elliott, J.F., T.J. Berry (1982). *Jumbo Elliott: Maker of Milers, Maker of Men*. St. Martin's Press, New York.

Emerson, R.W. (1901). Essays, *First and Second Series*, The World Classics, Oxford University Press, London.

England, A.C., D.W. Fraser, A.W. Hightower, R. Tirinnanzi, D.J. Greenberg, K.E. Powell, C.M. Slovis, R.A. Varsha (1982). Preventing severe heat injury in runners: Suggestions from the 1979 Peachtree Road Race experience. *Annals of Internal Medicine 97*, 196-201.

Erdelyi, L.G.J. (1962). Gynecological survey of female athletes. *Journal of Sports Medicine and Physical Fitness 2*, 174-179.

Erickson, M.A., R.J. Schwarzkopf, R.D. McKenzie (1987). Effects of caffeine, fructose, and glucose ingestion on muscle glycogen utilization during exercise. *Medicine and Science in Sports and Exercise 19*, 579-583.

Eriksson, B., P.D. Gollnick, B. Saltin (1973). Muscle metabolism and enzyme activities after training in boys 11-13 years old. *Acta Physiologica Scandinavica 87*, 485-497.

Eriksson, B.O. (1972). Physical training, oxygen supply and muscle metabolism in 11-13 year old boys. *Acta Physiologica Scandinavica* (suppl. 384), 1-48.

Erkkola, R. (1976). The influence of physical training during pregnancy on physical work capacity and circulatory parameters. *Scandinavian Journal of Clinical and Laboratory Investigation 36*, 747-754.

Ernst, E.E., A. Matrai (1987). Intermittent claudication, exercise, and blood rheology. *Circulation 76*, 1110-1114.

Essén, B. (1978). Glycogen depletion of different fibre types in human skeletal muscle during intermittent and continuous exercise. *Acta Physiologica Scandinavica 103*, 446-455.

Essig, D., D.L. Costill, P.J. Van Handel (1980). Effects of caffeine ingestion on utilization of muscle glycogen and lipid during leg ergometer cycling. *International Journal of Sports Medicine 1*, 86-90.

Etnyre, B.R., L.D. Abraham (1986). Gains in range of ankle dorsiflexion using three popular stretching techniques. *American Journal of Physical Medicine 65*, 189-196.

Evans, W.J., E.C. Fisher, R.A. Hoerr, V.R. Young (1983). Protein metabolism and endurance exercise. *The Physician and Sportsmedicine 11* (July), 63-72.

Fabiato, A., F. Fabiato (1978). Effect of pH on the myofilaments and sarcoplasmic reticulum of skinned cells from cardiac and skeletal muscle. *Journal of Physiology 276*, 233-255.

Faich, G., R. Rose (1979). Blizzard morbidity and mortality: Rhode Island 1978. *American Journal of Public Health 69*, 1050-1052.

Farmer, M.E., B.Z. Locke, E.K. Mo'scicki, A.L. Dannenberg, D.B. Larson, L.S. Radloff (1988). Physical activity and depressive symptoms: The NHANES I epidemiologic follow-up study. *American Journal of Epidemiology 128*, 1340-1351.

Farrell, P.A., J.H. Wilmore, E.F. Coyle, J.E. Billing, D.L. Costill (1979). Plasma lactate accumulation and distance running performance. *Medicine and Science in Sports 11*, 338-344.

Fassett, R.G., J.E. Owen, J. Fairley, D.F. Birch, K.F. Fairley (1982). Urinary red-cell morphology during exercise. *British Medical Journal 285*, 1455-1457.

Feicht, C.B., T.S. Johnson, B.J. Martin, K.E. Sparkes, W.W. Wagner (1978). Secondary amenorrhoea in athletes. *Lancet 2*, 1145-1146.

Feldman, M., J.V. Nixon (1982). Effect of exercise on postprandial gastric secretion and emptying in humans. *Journal of Applied Physiology 53*, 851-854.

Felig, P., A. Cherif, A. Minagawa, J. Wahren (1982). Hypoglycaemia during prolonged exercise in normal men. *New England Journal of Medicine 306*, 895-900.

Felson, D.T., J.J. Anderson, A. Naimark, A.M. Walker, R.F. Meenan (1988). Obesity and knee osteoarthritis. The Framingham study. *Annals of Internal Medicine 109*, 18-24.

Findlay, I.N., R.S. Taylor, H.J. Dargie, S. Grant, A.R. Pettigrew, J.T. Wilson, T. Aitchison, J.G.F. Cleland, A.T. Elliott, B.M. Fisher, G. Gillen, A. Manzie, A.R. Rumley, J.V.G.A. Durnin (1987). Cardiovascular effects of training for a marathon run in unfit middle aged men. *British Medical Journal 295*, 521-525.

Fink, W.J., D.L. Costill, M.L. Pollock (1977). Submaximal and maximal working capacity of élite distance runners. Part II: Muscle fibre composition and enzyme activities. *Annals of the New York Academy of Sciences 301*, 323-327.

Fink, W.J., D.L. Costill, P.J. Van Handel (1975). Leg muscle metabolism during exercise in the heat and cold. *European Journal of Applied Physiology 34*, 183-190.

Firer, P. (1989). Etiology and results of treatment of iliotibial band friction syndrome (ITBFS). *American Journal of Sports Medicine 17*, 704.

Fisher, E.C., M.E. Nelson, W.R. Frontera, E.N. Turksoy, W.J. Evans (1986). Bone mineral content and levels of gonadotropins and estrogens in amenorrheic running women. *Journal of Clinical Endocrinology and Metabolism 62*, 1232-1236.

Fisher, R.L., L.F. McMahon, M.J. Ryan, D. Larson, M. Brand (1986). Gastrointestinal bleeding in competitive runners. *Digestive Diseases and Sciences 31*, 1226-1228.

Fishman, J. (1980). Fatness, puberty and ovulation. *New England Journal of Medicine 303*, 42-43.

Fixx, J.F. (1977). *The Complete Book of Running*. Random House, New York.

Fixx, J.F. (1980). *James Fixx's Second Book of Running*. Random House, New York.

Fleg, J.L., E.G. LaKatla (1988). Role of muscle loss in the age-associated reduction in VO_2max. *Journal of Applied Physiology 65*, 1147-1151.

Fletcher, D.J. (1977). Athletic pseudonephritis. *Lancet 1*, 910-911.

Fogelholm, M., H. Tikkanen, H. Naveri, M. Harkonen (1989). High-carbohydrate diet for long distance runners—a practical view-point. *British Journal of Sports Medicine 23*, 94-96.

Folinsbee, L.J., J.F. Bedi, S.M. Horvath (1984). Pulmonary function changes after 1 h continuous heavy exercise in 0.21 ppm ozone. *Journal of Applied Physiology 57*, 984-988.

Folinsbee, L.J., P.B. Raven (1984). Exercise and air pollution. *Journal of Sports Sciences 2*, 57-75.

Fordyce, B. (1981). Bruce Fordyce's Comrades training. In *The Distance Runners Log*. Collegian Harriers, Pietermaritzburg.

Fordyce, B. (1983). Bruce Fordyce: Hotfoot. *Fairlady* (June 1), 99-104.

Fordyce, B. (1985). *Comrades*. Flower Press, Johannesburg.

Fordyce, B. (1989). In A. Milroy *International Ultra Running*. Road Runners Club, London, pp. 31-33.

Forgac, M.T. (1979). Carbohydrate-loading—a review. *Journal of the American Dietetic Association 75*, 42-45.

Foster, C. (1983). $\dot{V}O_2$max. and training indices as determinants of competitive running performance. *Journal of Sports Sciences 1*, 13-22.

Foster, C., D.L. Costill, J.T. Daniels, W.J. Fink (1978). Skeletal muscle enzyme activity, fiber composition and $\dot{V}O_2$max. in relation to distance running performance. *European Journal of Applied Physiology 39*, 73-80.

Foster, C., J. Daniels (1975). Running by the numbers. *Runners' World 10*, 14-17.

Foster, D.W. (1984). Banting Lecture 1984. From glycogen to ketones—and back. *Diabetes 33*, 1188-1199.

Fournier, M., J. Ricci, A.W. Taylor, R.J. Ferguson, R. R. Montpetit, B.R. Chaitman (1982). Skeletal muscle adaptation in adolescent boys: Sprint and endurance training and detraining. *Medicine and Science in Sports and Exercise 14*, 453-456.

Foxcroft, W.J., W.C. Adams (1986). Effects of ozone exposure on four consecutive days on work performance and $\dot{V}O_2$max. *Journal of Applied Physiology 61*, 960-966.

Francis, K.T. (1983). The role of endorphins in exercise: A review of current knowledge. *Journal of Orthopaedic and Sports Physical Therapy 4*, 169-173.

Franklin, B.A., M.T. Forgac, H.K. Hellerstein (1978). Accuracy of predicting marathon time: Relationship of training mileage to performance. *Research Quarterly 49*, 450-459.

Fraser, G.E., W. Dysinger, C. Best, R. Chan (1987). Ischemic heart disease risk factors in middle-aged seventh-day adventist men and their neighbors. *American Journal of Epidemiology 126*, 638-646.

Frederick, E.C. (1983a). Hot times. *Running 9*, 51-53.

Frederick, E.C. (1983b). Overtraining of athletes. Round table discussion. *The Physician and Sportsmedicine 11* (June), 98.

Frederick, E.C. (1986). Kinematically mediated effects of sport shoe design: A review. *Journal of Sports Sciences 4*, 169-184.

Frederick, E.C., T.E. Clarke, J.L. Larsen, L.B. Cooper (1983). The effect of shoe cushioning on the oxygen demands of running. In *Biomechanical Aspects of Sports Shoes and Playing Surfaces*, B. Biggs, B. Kerr (eds.). University of Calgary Printing Press, Calgary, Alberta, pp. 107-114.

Frederick, E.C., J. Daniels, J. Hayes (1984). The effect of shoe weight on the aerobic demands of running. In *Proceedings of the World Congress of Sports Medicine, Vienna, 1982*, N. Bachl, L. Prokop, R. Suckert (eds.). Urban and Schwartzenberg, Vienna, pp. 616-625.

Fredriksson, M., N.O. Bengtsson, L. Hardell, O. Axelson (1989). Colon cancer, physical activity, and occupational exposures. A case-control study. *Cancer 63*, 1838-1842.

Freeland-Graves, J.H., M.L. Ebangit, P.J. Hendrikson (1980). Alterations in zinc absorption and salivary sediment zinc after a lacto-ovo-vegetarian diet. *American Journal of Clinical Nutrition 33*, 1757-1766.

Friberg, O. (1982). Leg length asymmetry in stress fractures. A clinical and radiological study. *Journal of Sports Medicine and Physical Fitness 22*, 485-488.

Friden, J. (1984). Muscle soreness after exercise: Implications of morphological changes. *International Journal of Sports Medicine 5*, 57-66.

Friden, J., V. Kjorell, L-E. Thornell (1984). Delayed muscle soreness and cytoskeletal alterations: An immunocytological study in man. *International Journal of Sports Medicine 5*, 15-18.

Friden, J., J. Seger, B. Ekblom (1988a). Sublethal muscle fibre injuries after high-tension anaerobic exercise. *European Journal of Applied Physiology 57*, 360-368.

Friden, J., J. Seger, M. Sjostrom, B. Ekblom (1983a). Adaptive response in human skeletal muscle subjected to prolonged eccentric training. *International Journal of Sports Medicine 4*, 177-183.

Friden, J., P.N. Sfakianos, A.R. Hargens (1986). Muscle soreness and intramuscular fluid pressure: Comparison between eccentric and concentric load. *Journal of Applied Physiology 61*, 2175-2179.

Friden, J., P.N. Sfakianos, A.R. Hargens, W.H. Akeson (1988b). Residual muscular swelling after repetitive eccentric contractions. *Journal of Orthopaedic Research 6*, 493-498.

Friden, J., M. Sjostrom, B. Ekblom (1983b). Myofibrillar damage following intense eccentric exercise in man. *International Journal of Sports Medicine 4*, 170-176.

Friedman, M., J.H. Manwaring, R.H. Rosenman, G. Donlon, P. Ortega, S.M. Grube (1973). Instantaneous and sudden deaths. Clinical and pathological differentiation in coronary artery disease. *Journal of the American Medical Association 225*, 1319-1328.

Friend, G.E. (1935). Exercise and heart strain. *Practitioner 135*, 265-271.

Frisch, R.E., J.W. McArthur (1974). Menstrual cycles: Fatness as a determinant of minimum weight for height necessary for their maintenance or onset. *Science 185*, 949-951.

Frisch, R.E., G. Wyshak, N.L. Albright, T.E. Albright, I. Schiff (1989). Lower prevalence of non-reproductive system cancers among female forme college athletes. *Medicine and Science in Sports and Exercise 21*, 250-253.

Frisch, R.E., G. Wyshak, N.L. Albright, T.E. Albright, I. Schiff, K.P. Jones, J. Witschi, E. Shiang, E. Koff, M. Marguglio (1985). Lower prevalence of breast cancer and cancers of the reproductive system among former college athletes compared to non-athletes. *British Journal of Cancer 52*, 885-891.

Frisch, R.E., G. Wyshak, T.E. Albright, N.L. Albright, I. Schiff (1986). Lower prevalence of diabetes in female former college athletes compared with nonathletes. *Diabetes 35*, 1101-1105.

Frisch, R.E., G. Wyshak, L. Vincent (1980). Delayed menarche and amenorrhea in ballet dancers. *New England Journal of Medicine 303*, 17-19.

Frizzell, R.T., G.H. Lang, R.S. Lathan (1986). Hyponatremia and ultramarathon running. *Journal of the American Medical Association 255*, 772-774.

Frymoyer, J.W., M.H. Pope, J.H. Clements, D.G. Wilder, B. MacPherson, T. Ashikaga (1983). Risk factors in low back pain. *Journal of Bone and Joint Surgery 65*, 213-218.

Fulder, S. (1980). The drug that builds Russians. *New Scientist 21*, 576-579.

Fullerton, L.R., H.A. Snowdy (1988). Femoral neck stress fractures. *American Journal of Sports Medicine 16*, 365-377.

Gadpaille, W.J., C.F. Sanborn, W.W. Wagner (1987). Athletic amenorrhea, major affective disorders, and eating disorders. *American Journal of Psychiatry 144*, 939-942.

Gaesser, G.A., G.A. Brooks (1980). Glycogen repletion following continuous and intermittent exercise to exhaustion. *Journal of Applied Physiology 49*, 722-728.

Gaesser, G.A., D.C. Poole (1986). Lactate and ventilatory thresholds: Disparity in time course of adaptations to training. *Journal of Applied Physiology 61*, 999-1004.

Gaesser, G.A., D.C. Poole (1988). Blood lactate during exercise: Time course of training adaptation in humans. *International Journal of Sports Medicine 9*, 284-288.

Gaisl, G., G. Wiesspeiner (1988). A noninvasive method of determining the anaerobic threshold in children. *International Journal of Sports Medicine 8*, 41-44.

Galle, P.C., E.W. Freeman, M.G. Galle, G.R. Huggins, S.J. Sandheimer (1983). Physiologic and psychologic profiles in a survey of women runners. *Fertility and Sterility 39*, 633-639.

Galloway, J. (1983). *Galloway's Book of Running*. J.F. Galloway, Armour Circle, Atlanta.

Galloway, J. (1984). *Galloway's Book of Running*. Shelter Publications, Bolinas, California.

Garabrant, D.H., J.M. Peters, T.M. Mack, L. Bernstein (1984). Job activity and colon cancer risk. *American Journal of Epidemiology 119*, 1005-1014.

Gardner, J.B., J.G. Purdy (1970). *Computerized running training programmes*. Tafnews Press, Los Altos, California.

Gardner, K.D. (1971). Athletic nephritis: Pseudo and real. *Annals of Internal Medicine 75*, 966-967.

Garfield, C.A., H.Z. Bennett (1984). *Peak Performance*. Jeremy P. Tarcher, Los Angeles.

Garner, D.M., P.E. Garfinkel (1979). The Eating Attitudes Test: An index of the symptoms of anorexia nervosa. *Psychological Medicine 9*, 273-279.

Garner, D.M., P.E. Garfinkel (1980). Socio-cultural factors in the development of anorexia nervosa. *Psychological medicine 10*, 647-656.

Garrett, W.E., F.R. Rich, P.K. Nikolaou, J.B. Vogler (1989). Computed tomography of hamstring muscle strains. *Medicine and Science in Sports and Exercise 21*, 506-514.

Gayeski, T.E.J., R.J. Connett, C.R. Honig (1985). Oxygen transport in rest-work transition illustrates new functions for myoglobin. *American Journal of Physiology 248*, H914-H921.

Geissler, C.A., M.S. Aldouri (1985). Racial differences in the energy cost of standardized activities. *Annals of Nutrition and Metabolism 29*, 40-47.

Gendel, E.S. (1978). Lack of fitness a source of chronic ills in women. *The Physician and Sportsmedicine 6* (February), 85-95.

George, W.C. (1902). *Training*. Southwood Smith, London.

George, W.C. (1908). *The Hundred-Up Exercise*. Ewart Seymour, London.

Gerhardsson, M., B. Floderus, S.E. Norell (1988). Physical activity and colon cancer risk. *International Journal of Epidemiology 17*, 743-746.

Gerhardsson, M., S.E. Norell, H. Kiviranta, N.L. Pedersen, A. Ahlbom (1986). Sedentary jobs and colon cancers. *American Journal of Epidemiology 123*, 775-780.

Gillespie, A.C., E.L. Fox, A.J. Merola (1982). Enzyme adaptations in rat skeletal muscle after two intensities of treadmill running. *Medicine and Science in Sports and Exercise 14*, 461-466.

Gisolfi, C.V., J.R. Topping (1974). Thermal effects of prolonged treadmill exercise in the heat. *Medicine and Science in Sports and Exercise 6*, 108-113.

Glass, A.R., J.A. Yahiro, P.A. Deutser, R.A. Vigersky, S.B. Kyle, E.B. Schoomaker (1987). Amenorrhea in Olympic marathon runners. *Fertility and Sterility 48*, 740-745.

Gledhill, N. (1982). Blood doping and related issues: A brief review. *Medicine and Science in Sports and Exercise 14*(3), 183-189.

Gledhill, N. (1984). Bicarbonate ingestion and anaerobic performance. *Sports Medicine 1*, 177-180.

Gleeson, M., P.L. Greenhaff, R.J. Maughan (1987). Fasting and high-intensity exercise performance in man. *Journal of Physiology 392*, 52P.

Gleeson, M., R.J. Maughan, P.L. Greenhaff (1986). Comparison of the effects of pre-exercise feeding of glucose, glycerol and placebo on endurance and fuel homeostasis in man. *European Journal of Applied Physiology 55*, 645-653.

Glover, B., P. Schuder (1983). *The Competitive Runner's Handbook*. Penguin Books, New York.

Godal, H.C., H.E. Refsum (1979). Haemolysis in athletes due to hereditary spherocytosis. *Scandinavian Journal of Haematology 22*, 83-86.

Goldszer, R.C., A.J. Siegel (1984). Renal abnormalities during exercise. In *Sports Medicine*, 2nd Edition, R.H. Strauss (ed.). W.B. Saunders, London, pp. 130-139.

Gollnick, P.D., P.B. Armstrong, C.W. Saubert, W.L. Sembrowich, R.E. Shephard, B. Saltin (1973). Glycogen depletion patterns in human skeletal muscle fibres during prolonged work. *Pflugers Archives 344*, 1-12.

Gollnick, P.D., K. Piehl, B. Saltin (1974). Selective glycogen depletion pattern in human muscle fibres after exercise of varying intensity and at varying pedalling rates. *Journal of Physiology 241*, 45-57.

Gollnick, P.D., B. Saltin (1982). Hypothesis: Significance of skeletal muscle oxidative enzyme enhancement with endurance training. *Clinical Physiologist 2*, 1-12.

Gong, H., P.W. Bradley, M.S. Simmons, D.P. Tashkin (1986). Impaired exercise performance and pulmonary function in elite cyclists during low-level ozone exposure in a hot environment. *American Review of Respiratory Diseases 134*, 726-733.

Gonzàlez, E.R. (1982). Premature bone loss found in some non-menstruating sportswomen. *Journal of the American Medical Association 248*, 513-514.

Gordon, B., L.A. Kohn, S.A. Levine, M. Matton, W. De M. Scriver, W.B. Whiting (1925). Sugar content of the blood in runners following a marathon race. *Journal of the American Medical Association 185*, 508-509.

Gorski, J. (1985). Exercise during pregnancy: Maternal and fetal responses. A brief review. *Medicine and Science in Sports and Exercise 17*, 407-416.

Graham, T.E., B. Saltin (1989). Estimation of the mitochondrial redox state in human skeletal muscle during exercise. *Journal of Applied Physiology 66*, 561-566.

Graham, W.F. (1981). The anxiety of the runner: Terminal helplessness. In *The Psychology of Running*, M.H. Sacks, M.L. Sachs (eds.). Human Kinetics, Champaign, Illinois.

Grant, S.J.Y., R.H. Sharp, T.C. Aitchison (1984). First time marathoners and distance training. *British Journal of Sports Medicine 18*, 241-243.

Grant-Whyte, H. (1981). 'Joggitis,' 'marathonitis' and marathon mania. *South African Medical Journal 59*, 849-850.

Graves, J.E., M.L. Pollock, P.B. Sparling (1987). Body composition of elite female distance runners. *International Journal of Sports Medicine 8* (suppl.), 96-102.

Gray, D.P., E. Harding, E. Dale (1983). Effects of oral contraceptives on serum lipid profiles of women runnes. *Fertility and Sterility 39*, 510-514.

Gray, M.E., L.W. Titlow (1982a). B_{15}: Myth or miracle? *The Physician and Sportsmedicine 10* (January), 107-112.

Gray, M.E., L.W. Titlow (1982b). The effect of pangamic acid on maximal treadmill performance. *Medicine and Science in Sports and Exercise 14*, 424-427.

Grayboys, T.B. (1979). The economics of screening joggers. *New England Journal of Medicine 301*, 1067.

Green, B.B., J.R. Darling, N.S. Weiss, J.M. Liff, T. Koepsell (1986). Exercise as a risk factor for infertility with ovulatory dysfunction. *American Journal of Public Health 76*, 1432-1436.

Green, H.J., L.L. Jones, M.E. Houston, M.E. Ball-Burnett, B.W. Farrance (1989). Muscle energetics during prolonged cycling after exercise hypervolemia. *Journal of Applied Physiology 66*, 622-631.

Green, R.L., S.S. Kaplan, B.S. Rabin, C.L. Stranitski, U. Zdziarski (1981). Immune function in marathon runners. *Annals of Allergy 47*, 73-75.

Greenhaff, P.L., M. Gleeson, R.J. Maughan (1987a). The effects of dietary manipulation on blood acid-base status and the performance of high intensity exercise. *European Journal of Applied Physiology 56*, 331-337.

Greenhaff, P.L., M. Gleeson, R.J. Maughan (1988a). The effects of diet on muscle pH and metabolism during high intensity exercise. *European Journal of Applied Physiology* (in press).

Greenhaff, P.L., M. Gleeson, R.J. Maughan (1988b). The effects of a glycogen loading regimen on acid-base status and blood lactate concentration before and after a fixed period of high intensity exercise in man. *European Journal of Applied Physiology 57*, 254-259.

Greenhaff, P.L., M. Gleeson, P.H. Whiting, R.J. Maughan (1987b). Dietary composition and acid-base status: Limiting factors in the performance of maximal exercise in man? *European Journal of Applied Physiology 56*, 444-450.

Gregor, R.J. (1970). *A comparison of the Energy Expenditure During Positive and Negative Grade Running*. M.A. thesis. Ball State University, Muncie, Indiana.

Gregor, R.J., V.R. Edgerton, R. Rozenek, K.R. Castleman (1981). Skeletal muscle properties and performance in élite female track athletes. *European Journal of Applied Physiology 47*, 335-364.

Griest, J.H., M.H. Klein, R.R. Eischens, J. Faris, A.S. Gurman, W.P. Morgan (1981). Running through your mind. In *The Psychology of Running*, M.H. Sacks, M.L. Sachs (eds.). Human Kinetics, Champaign, Illinois.

Grobler, S.R., L.S. Maresky, R.J. Rossouw (1984). Blood lead levels in marathon runners. *South African Medical Journal 65*, 872-873.

Grobler, S.R., L.S. Maresky, R.J. Rossouw (1986). Blood lead levels of South African long-distance road-runners. *Archives of Environmental Health 41*, 155-158.

Guezennec, C.Y., P. Satabin, F. Duforez, D. Merino, F. Peronnet, J. Koziet (1989). Oxidation of corn starch, glucose, and fructose ingested before exercise. *Medicine and Science in Sports and Exercise 21*, 45-50.

Guglielmini, C., I. Casoni, M. Patracchini, F. Manfredini, G Grazzi, M. Ferrari, F. Conconi (1989). Reduction of Hb levels during the racing season in nonsideropenic professional cyclists. *International Journal of Sports Medicine 10*, 352-356.

Guild, W.R. (1957). Echoes of the marathon. *New England Journal of Medicine 257*, 1165-1170.

Guten, G. (1981). Herniated lumbar disk associated with running. A review of 10 cases. *American Journal of Sports Medicine 9*, 155-159.

Guyot, G.W., L. Fairchild, J. Nickens (1984). Death concerns of runners and nonrunners. *Journal of Sports Medicine and Physical Fitness 24*, 139-143.

Gwinup, G. (1987). Weight loss without dietary restriction: Efficacy of different forms of aerobic exercise. *American Journal of Sports Medicine 15*, 275-279.

Hackney, A.C. (1989). Endurance training and testosterone levels. *Sports Medicine 8*, 117-127.

Hackney, A.C., W.E. Sinning, B.C. Bruot (1988). Reproductive hormonal profiles of endurance-trained and untrained males. *Medicine and Science in Sports and Exercise 20*, 60-65.

Hagberg, J.M., E.F. Coyle (1983). Physiological determinants of endurance performance as studied in competitive racewalkers. *Medicine and Science in Sports and Exercise 15*, 287-289.

Hagberg, J.M., J.E. Graves, M. Limacher, D.R. Woods, S.H. Leggett, C. Cononie, J.J. Gruber, M.L. Pollock (1989). Cardiovascular responses of 70- to 79-yr-old men and women to exercise training. *Journal of Applied Physiology 66*, 2589-2594.

Hage, P. (1982). Air pollution: Adverse effects on athletic performance. *The Physician and Sportsmedicine 10* (March), 126-132.

Hall, D.C., D.A. Kaufmann (1987). Effects of aerobic and strength conditioning on pregnancy outcomes. *American Journal of Obstetrics and Gynecology 157*, 1199-1203.

Hallberg, L., B. Magnusson (1984). The etiology of "sports anemia." A physiological adaptation of the oxygen-dissociation curve of hemoglobin to an unphysiological exercise load. *Acta Medica Scandinavica 216*, 145-148.

Hamel, P., J.A. Simoneau, G. Lortie, M.R. Boulay, C. Bouchard (1986). Heredity and muscle adaptation to endurance training. *Medicine and Science in Sports and Exercise 18*, 690-696.

Hamilton, L.H., J. Brooks-Gunn, M.P. Warren (1986). Nutritional intake of female dancers: A reflection of eating disorders. *International Journal of Eating Disorders 5*, 925-934.

Hanson, P.G., D.K. Flaherty (1981). Immunological responses to training in conditioned runners. *Clinical Sciences 60*, 225-228.

Harber, V.J., J.R. Sutton (1984). Endorphins and exercise. *Sports Medicine 1*, 154-171.

Hardwick, J.H. (1912). *Distance and Cross-Country Running*. British Sports, London.

Hartley, P.H-S., G.F. Llewellyn (1939). The longevity of oarsmen. *British Medical Journal 1*, 657-662.

Hartung, G.H., E.J. Farge (1977). Personality and physiological traits in middle-aged runners and joggers. *Journal of Gerontology 32*, 541-548.

Hatcher, L., J. Leklem, D. Campbell (1982). Altered vitamin B_6 metabolism during exercise in man: Effect of carbohydrate modified diets and B_6 supplements. *Medicine and Science in Sports and Exercise 14*, 112.

Hatsell, C.P. (1974). A note on jogging on a windy day. *Institute of Electrical and Electronic Engineers Transactions of Biomedical Engineering 22*, 428-429.

Hauman, R. (1979). Daar's geen keer aan Wally nie [There is no stopping Wally]. *Topsport* (March), 20-42.

Hawley, J.A., S.C. Dennis, B.J. Laidlaw, A.N. Bosch, T.D. Noakes, F. Brouns (1991). Starch provides the highest rates of exogenous carbohydrate oxidation during prolonged exercise. Unpublished manuscript.

Haymes, E.M. (1983). Proteins, vitamins and iron. In *Ergogenic Aids in Sport*, M.H. Williams (ed.). Human Kinetics, Champaign, Illinois, pp. 27-55.

Haymes, E.M. (1984). Physiological responses of female athletes to heat stress: A review. *The Physician and Sports Medicine 12* (March), 45-59.

Heath, G.W., J.M. Hagberg, A.A. Eshani, J.O. Holloszy (1981). A physiological comparison of young and older endurance athletes. *Journal of Applied Physiology 51*, 634-640.

Hegenauer, J., J. Strauss, P. Saltman, D. Dann, J. White, R. Green (1983). Transitory hematologic effects of moderate exercise are not influenced by iron supplementation. *European Journal of Applied Physiology 52*, 57-61.

Heinzelmann, F., R. Bagley (1970). Response to physical activity programs and their effect on health behaviour. *Public Health Reports 85*, 905-911.

Heiser, T.M., J. Weber, G. Sullivan, P. Clare, R.R. Jacobs (1984). Prophylaxis and management of hamstring injuries in intercollegiate football players. *American Journal of Sports Medicine 12*, 368-370.

Heiss, F. (1971). *Unfallverhütung Beim Sports* [Prevention of accidents in sport]. Karl Hoffmann, Schorndorff.

Hellstedt, J.C. (1988). Kids, parents, and sports: Some questions and answers. *The Physician and Sportsmedicine 16* (April), 59-71.

Hemery, D. (1986). *The pursuit of sporting excellence. A study of sport's highest achievers*. Willow Books, London.

Henderson, J. (1969). *Long Slow Distance—The Humane Way to Train*. World Publications, Mountain View, California.

Henderson, J. (1974). *Run Gently, Run Long*. World Publications, Mountain View, California.

Henderson, J. (1976). *The Long Run Solution*. World Publications, Mountain View, California.

Henderson, J. (1977). *Jog, Run, Race*. World Publications, Mountain View, California.

Henderson, J., B. Maxwell (1978). Training to run and race. In *The Complete Marathoner*, J. Henderson (ed.). World Publications, Mountain View, California.

Henricson, A.S., N.E. Westlin (1984). Chronic calcaneal pain in athletes: Entrapment of the calcaneal nerve. *American Journal of Sports Medicine 12*, 152-154.

Henriksson, J. (1977). Training induced adaptation of skeletal muscle and metabolism during submaximal exercise. *Journal of Physiology 270*, 661-675.

Henry, S. (1982). The price of perfection. *The Runner 4* (March), 34-39.

Hershkowitz, M. (1977). Penile frostbite, an unforeseen hazard of jogging. *New England Journal of Medicine 296*, 178.

Hertzog, M. (1952). *Annapurna (8000 m)*. Jonathan Cape, London.

Heyden, S., G.J. Fodor (1988). Does regular exercise prolong life expectancy? *Sports Medicine 6*, 63-71.

Hickson, R.C. (1980). Interference of strength development by simultaneously training for strength and endurance. *European Journal of Applied Physiology 45*, 255-263.

Hickson, R.C., H.A. Bomze, J.O. Holloszy (1977). Linear increase in aerobic power induced by a strenuous programme of endurance exercise. *Journal of Applied Physiology 42*, 372-376.

Hickson, R.C., C. Foster, M.L. Pollock, T.M. Galassi, S. Rich (1985). Reduced training intensities and loss of aerobic power, endurance and cardiac growth. *Journal of Applied Physiology 58*, 492-499.

Hickson, R.C., J.M. Hagberg, A.A. Eshani, J.O. Holloszy (1981). Time course of the adaptive responses of aerobic power and heart rate to training. *Medicine and Science in Sports and Exercise 13*, 17-20.

Hickson, R.C., C. Kanakis, J.R. Davis, A.M. Moore, S. Rich (1982). Reduced training duration effects on aerobic power, endurance, and cardiac growth. *Journal of Applied Physiology 53*, 225-229.

Hickson, R.C., M. Rosenkoetter (1981). Reduced training frequencies and maintenance of increased aerobic power. *Medicine and Science in Sports and Exercise 13*, 13-16.

Hickson, R.C., M.A. Rosenkoetter, M.M. Brown (1980). Strength training effects on aerobic power and short-term endurance. *Medicine and Science in Sports and Exercise 12*, 336-339.

Higdon, H. (1981). Shadows on the wall. *The Runner 4* (November), 46-80.

Higdon, H. (1982). 'Buddy' the fogotten champion. *The Runner 5* (August), 76-85.

Higdon, H. (1984). Jim Fixx: How he lived, why he died. *The Runner 7* (November), 32-38.

Higdon, H. (1985). To everything a season. *The Runner 7* (March), 73-95.

Hikida, R.S., R.S. Staron, F.C. Hagerman, W.M. Sherman, D.L. Costill (1983). Muscle fibre necrosis associated with human marathon runners. *Journal of the Neurological Sciences 59*, 185-203.

Hill, A.V. (1925). The physiological basis of athletic records. *Lancet 2*, 481-486.

Hill, A.V. (1927a). *Living Machinery*. G. Bell and Sons, London.

Hill, A.V. (1927b). *Muscular Movement in Man: The Factors Governing Speed and Recovery From Speed*. McGraw-Hill, New York.

Hill, A.V. (1965). *Trails and Trials in Physiology*. Edward Arnold, London.

Hill, A.V., H. Lupton (1923). Muscular exercise, lactic acid and the supply and utilization of oxygen. *Quarterly Medical Journal 16*, 135-171.

Hill, J.O., J.R. Davis, A.R. Tagliaferro (1983). Effects of diet and exercise training on thermogenesis in adult female rats. *Physiology of Behaviour 31*, 133-135.

Hill, J.O., P.B. Sparling, T.W. Shields, P.A. Heller (1987). Effects of exercise and food restriction on body composition and metabolic rate in obese women. *American Journal of Clinical Nutrition 46*, 622-630.

Hill, R. (1981). *The Long Hard Road. Part One. Nearly to the Top.* Ron Hill Sports, Cheshire, England.

Hill, R. (1982). *The Long Hard Road. Part Two: To the Peak and Beyond.* Ron Hill Sports, Cheshire, England.

Hilsendager, D., P. Karpovich (1964). Ergogenic effect of glycine and niacin separately and in combination. *Research Quarterly 35*, 389-392.

Himann, J.E., D.A. Cunningham, P.A. Rechnitzer, D.H. Paterson (1988). Age-related changes in speed of walking. *Medicine and Science in Sports and Exercise 20*, 161-166.

Holloszy, J.O., E.F. Coyle (1984). Adaptations of skeletal muscle to endurance exercise and their metabolic consequences. *Journal of Applied Physiology 56*, 831-838.

Holmes, B. (1986). Steve Jones finds his wings. *South African Runner* (January), 28-29.

Honigman, B., R. Cromer, T.L. Kurt (1982). Carbon monoxide levels in athletes during exercise in an urban environment. *Journal of the Air Pollution Control Association 32*, 77-79.

Hopkins, P., S.K. Powers (1982). Oxygen uptake during submaximal running in highly trained men and women. *American Corrective Therapy Journal 36*, 130-132.

Hornbein, T.F. (1980). *Everest—The West Ridge.* The Mountaineers, San Francisco.

Horvath, S.M., P.B. Raven, T.E. Dahms, D.J. Gray (1975). Maximal aerobic capacity at different levels of carboxyhemoglobin. *Journal of Applied Physiology 38*, 300-303.

Houmard, J.A., J.P. Kirwan, M.G. Flynn, J.B. Mitchell (1989). Effects of reduced training on submaximal and maximal running responses. *International Journal of Sports Medicine 10*, 30-33.

Howard, J.H., D.A. Cunningham, P.A. Rechnitzer (1984). Physical activity as a moderator of life events and somatic complaints: A longitudinal study. *Canadian Journal of Applied Sport Science 9*, 194-200.

Hughson, R.L. (1980). Primary prevention of heat stroke in Canadian long-distance runs. *Canadian Medical Association Journal 122*, 1115-1119.

Hughson, R.L., L.A. Staudt, J.M. Mackie (1983). Monitoring road racing in the heat. it*The Physician and Sportsmedicine 11* (May), 94-105.

Hughson, R.L., K.H. Weisiger, G.D. Swanson (1987). Blood lactate concentration increases as a continuous function in progressive exercise. *Journal of Applied Physiology 62*, 1975-1981.

Hulkko, A., S. Orava (1987). Stress fractures in athletes. *International Journal of Sports Medicine 8*, 221-226.

Hultman, E. (1967). Studies on muscle metabolism of glycogen and active phosphate in man with special reference to exercise and diet. *Scandinavian Journal of Clinical and Laboratory Investigation Supplement 94*, 1-63.

Hultman, E. (1971). Muscle glycogen stores and prolonged exercise. In *Frontiers of Fitness*, R.J. Shepherd (ed.). Charles C Thomas, Springfield, Illinois, pp. 37-60.

Hultman, E., S. Del Canale, H. Sjoholm (1985). Effect of induced metabolic acidosis on intracellular pH, buffer capacity and contraction force of human skeletal muscle. *Clinical Science 69*, 505-510.

Hultman, E., L.H. Nilsson (1971). Liver glycogen in man. Effects of different diets and muscular exercise. In *Muscle Metabolism During Exercise*, B. Pernow, B. Saltin (eds.). Plenum Press, New York, pp. 69-85.

Hultman, E., L.L. Spriet, K. Sodelund (1987). Energy metabolism and fatigue in working muscle. In *Exercise Benefits, Limits and Adaptations*, D. Macleod, R. Maughan, M. Nimmo, T. Reilly, C. Williams (eds.). E. & F. N. Spon Limited, London, pp. 63-84.

Huntford, R. (1985). *The Last Place on Earth*. Pan Books, London.

Hurley, B.F., P.M. Nemeth, W.H. Martin, J.M. Hagberg, G.P. Dalsky, J.O. Holloszy (1986). Muscle triglyceride utilization during exercise: Effect of training. *Journal of Applied Physiology 60*, 562-567.

Ibbotson, D. (1960). *The 4-Minute Smiler. The Derek Ibbotson Story*. Stanley Paul, London.

Insall, J., K.A. Falvo, D.W. Wise (1976). Chondromalacia patellae. A prospective study. *Journal of Bone and Joint Surgery (Am) 58*, 1-8.

Irving, R.A., R.H. Buck, J. Godlonton, T.D. Noakes (1991). Evaluation of renal function and fluid balance during recovery from exercise induced hyponatremia. *Journal of Applied Physiology* (in press).

Irving, R.A., T.D. Noakes, G.A. Irving, R. van Zyl Smit (1986a). The immediate and delayed effects of marathon running on renal function. *Journal of Urology 136*, 1176-1180.

Irving, R.A., T.D. Noakes, A.L. Rodgers, L. Swartz (1986b). Crystalluria in marathon runners. I: Standard marathon—males. *Urological Research 14*, 289-294.

Ismail, A.H., A.M. El-Naggar (1981). Effect of exercise on cognitive processing in adult men. *Journal of Human Ergology 10*, 83-91.

Ismail, A.H., L.E. Trachtman (1973). Jogging the imagination. *Psychology Today 6*, 79-82.

Ivy, J.L., M.M. Chi, C.S. Hintz, W.M. Sherman, R.P. Hellendall, O.H. Lowry (1987). Progressive metabolite changes in individual human muscle fibers with increasing work rates. *American Journal of Physiology 252*, C630-C639.

Ivy, J.L., D.L. Costill, W.J. Fink, E. Maglischo (1980). Contribution of medium and long chain triglyceride intake to energy metabolism during prolonged exercise. *International Journal of Sports Medicine 1*, 15-20.

Ivy, J.L., A.L. Katz, C.L. Cutler, W.M. Sherman, E.F. Coyle (1988). Muscle glycogen synthesis after exercise: Effect of time of carbohydrate ingestion. *Journal of Applied Physiology 64*, 1480-1485.

Ivy, J.L., W. Miller, V. Dover, L.G. Goodyear, W.M. Sherman, S. Farrell, H. Williams (1983). Endurance improved by ingestion of a glucose polymer supplement. *Medicine and Science in Sports and Exercise 15*, 466-471.

Jackson, M.J. (1987). Muscle damage during exercise: Possible role of free radicals and protective effect of vitamin E. *Proceedings of the Nutrition Society 46*, 77-80.

Jacobs, I. (1987). Influence of carbohydrate stores on maximal human power output. In *Exercise Benefits, Limits and Adaptations*, D. Macleod, R. Maughan, M. Nimmo, T. Reilly, C. Williams (eds.). E. & F. N. Spon Limited, London, pp. 104-115.

Jacobs, P. (1984). The physiology of iron metabolism. *South African Journal of Continuing Medical Education 2* (July), 123-129.

Jacobs, S.J., B.L. Berson (1986). Injuries to runners: A study of entrants to a 10,000 meter race. *American Journal of Sports Medicine 14*, 151-155.

Jacobson, E. (1929). *Progressive Relaxation*. University of Chicago Press, Chicago.

Jain, P.C. (1980). On a discrepancy in track races. *Research Quarterly for Exercise and Sport 51*, 432-436.

James, S.L., B.T. Bates, L.R. Osternig (1978). Injuries to runners. *American Journal of Sports Medicine 6*, 40-50.

James, W. (1958). *Talks to Teachers*. W.W. Norton, New York.

Janal, M.N., E.W.D. Colt, W.C. Clark, M. Glusman (1984). Pain sensitivity, mood and plasma endocrine levels in man following long-distance running: Effects of naloxone. *Pain 19*, 13-25.

Jandrain, B., G. Krzentowski, F. Pirnay, F. Mosora, M. Lacroix, A. Luyckx, P. Lefebvre (1984). Metabolic availability of glucose ingested 3 hours before prolonged exercise in humans. *Journal of Applied Physiology 56*, 1314-1319.

Jansson, E., L. Kaijser (1977). Muscle adaptation to extreme endurance training in man. *Acta Physiologica Scandinavica 100*, 315-324.

Jardine, M.A., T.M. Wiggins, K.H. Myburgh, T.D. Noakes (1988). Physiological characteristics of rugby players including muscle glycogen content and muscle fibre composition. *South African Medical Journal 73*, 529-532.

Jardon, O.M. (1982). Physiological stress, heat stroke, malignant hyperthermia—a perspective. *Military Medicine 147*, 8-14.

Jarrett, J.C., W.N. Spellacy (1983a). Contraceptive practices of female runners. *Fertility and Sterility 39*, 374-375.

Jarrett, J.C., W.N. Spellacy (1983b). Jogging during pregnancy: An improved outcome? *Obstetrics and Gynecology 61*, 705-709.

Jennings, G., L. Nelson, P. Korner, M. Esler (1987). The place of exercise in the long-term treatment of hypertension. *Nephron 47* (Suppl 1), 30-33.

Jetté, M., O. Pelletier, L. Parker, J. Thoden (1978). The nutritional and metabolic effects of a crabohydrate-rich diet in a glycogen supercompensation training regimen. *American Journal of Clinical Nutrition 31*, 2140-2148.

Johnson, L.C. (1964). Morphologic analysis in pathology. In *Bone Biodynamics*, H.M. Frost (ed.). Little Brown and Co., Boston, pp. 587-595.

Johnson, L.C., H.T. Stradford, R.W. Geis, J.R. Dineen, E. Kerley (1963). Histogenesis of stress fractures. *Journal of Bone and Joint Surgery 45-A*, 1542.

Johnston, C.C., C. Slemenda (1987). Osteoporosis: An overview. *The Physician and Sports Medicine 15* (November), 65-68.

Jokl, E., R.L. Anand, H. Stobody (1976). Advances in exercise physiology. *Medicine and Sport 9*, x-xx.

Jones, B.H., J.J. Knapik, W.L. Daniels, M.M. Toner (1986). The energy cost of walking and running in shoes and boots. *Ergonomics 29*, 439-443.

Jones, B.H., M.M. Toner, W.L. Daniels, J.J. Knapik (1984). The energy cost and heart rate response of trained and untrained subjects walking and running in shoes and boots. *Ergonomics 27*, 895-902.

Jones, B.J.M., B.E. Brown, J.S. Loran, D. Edgerton, J.F. Kennedy, J.A. Stead, D.B.A. Silk (1983). Glucose absorption from starch hydrolysates in the human jejunum. *Gut 24*, 1152-1160.

Jones, B.J.M., B.E. Higgins, D.B.A. Silk (1987). Glucose absorption from maltotriose and glucose oligomers in the human jejunum. *Clinical Science 72*, 409-414.

Jones, D.A., D.J. Newham, P.M. Clarkson (1987). Skeletal muscle stiffness and pain following eccentric exercise of the elbow flexors. *Pain 30*, 233-242.

Jones, D.A., D.J. Newham, J.M. Round, S.E.J. Tolfree (1986). Experimental human muscle damage: Morphological changes in relation to other indices of damage. *Journal of Physiology 375*, 435-448.

Jones, K.P., V.A. Ravnikar, D. Tulchinsky, I. Schiff (1985). Comparison of bone density in amenorrheic women due to athletics, weight loss, and premature menopause. *Obstetrics and Gynecology 66*, 5-8.

Jones, R.L., J.J. Botti, W.M. Anderson, N.L. Bennett (1985). Thermoregulation during aerobic exercise in pregnancy. *Obstetrics and Gynecology 65*, 340-345.

Jooste, P.L., A. Van der Linde, N.B. Strydom (1980). Prediction of Comrades Marathon performance. *South African Journal for Research in Sport, Physical Education and Recreation 3*, 47-54.

Jopke, T. (1983). Pregnancy: A time to exercise judgement. *The Physician and Sportsmedicine 11* (July), 139-145.

Jorgensen, U. (1985). Achillodynia and loss of heel pad shock absorbency. *American Journal of Sports Medicine 13*, 128-132.

Jorgensen, U., J. Ekstrand (1988). Significance of heel pad confinement for the shock absorption at heel strike. *International Journal of Sports Medicine 9*, 468-473.

Jorring, K. (1980). Osteoarthritis of the hip: Epidemiology and clinical role. *Acta Orthopaedica Scandinavica 51*, 523-530.

Joseph, P., J.M. Robbins (1981). Worker or runner? The impact of commitment to running and work on self-identification. In *The Psychology of Running*, M.H. Sacks, M.L. Sachs (eds.). Human Kinetics, Champaign, Illinois.

Jovanovic, L., A. Kessler, C.M. Peterson (1985). Human maternal and fetal response to graded exercise. *Journal of Applied Physiology 58*, 1719-1722.

Juhlin-Dannfelt, A., G. Ahlborg, L. Hagenfeldt, L. Jorfeldt, P. Felig (1977). Influence of ethanol on splanchnic and skeletal muscle substrate turnover during prolonged exercise in man. *American Journal of Physiology 233*, E195-E202.

Kahn, R. (1972). *The Boys of Summer*. Harper and Row, New York.

Kaiserauer, S., A.C. Snyder, M. Sleeper, J. Zierath (1989). Nutritional, physiological, and menstrual status of distance runners. *Medicine and Science in Sports and Exercise 21*, 120-125.

Kaltsas, D-S. (1981). Stress fractures of the femoral neck in young adults. *Journal of Bone and Joint Surgery 63-B*, 33-37.

Kam, J.K.-K. (1980). Carboxyhaemoglobin levels between jogging and non-jogging smokers. *Experientia 36*, 1397-1398.

Kannus, P., S. Nittymaki, M. Jarvinene (1987). Sports injuries in women: A one-year prospective follow-up study at an outpatient sports clinic. *British Journal of Sports Medicine 21*, 37-39.

Karlsson, J., B. Saltin (1971). Diet, muscle glycogen and endurance performance. *Journal of Applied Physiology 31*, 203-206.

Karpovich, P., W. Sinning (1971). *Physiology of Muscular Activity*. W.B. Saunders, Philadelphia.

Katz, J., J.D. McGarry (1984). The glucose paradox. Is glucose a substrate for liver metabolism? *Journal of Clinical Investigation 74*, 1901-1909.

Kauss, D.R. (1980). *Peak Performance*. Prentice-Hall, Englewood Cliffs, New Jersey.

Keast, D., K. Cameron, A.R. Morton (1988). Exercise and the immune response. *Sports Medicine 5*, 248-267.

Keating, L. (1982). Pain running through a clot. The saga of a clot running through pain. *South African Runner* (october), 18.

Keeffe, E.B., D.K. Lowe, J.R. Goss, R. Wayne (1984). Gastrointestinal symptoms of marathon runners. *Western Journal of Medicine 141*, 481-484.

Keeling, W.F., B.J. Martin (1987). Gastrointestinal transit during mild exercise. *Journal of Applied Physiology 63*, 978-981.

Keizer, H.A., H. Kuipers, G. van Kranenburg, P. Geurten (1987). Influence of liquid and solid meals on muscle glycogen resynthesis, plasma fuel hormone response, and maximal physical working capacity. *International Journal of Sports Medicine 8*, 99-104.

Kelsey, J.L., P.B. Githens, T. O'Connor, U. Weil, J.A. Calogero, T.R. Holford, A.A. White, S.D. Walter, A.M. Ostfeld, W.O. Southwick (1984). Acute prolapsed lumbar intervertebral disc. An epidemiologic study with special reference to driving automobiles and cigarette smoking. *Spine 9*, 608-613.

Keretzty, A. (1971). Overtraining. In *Encyclopaedia of Sports Science and Medicine*, L.A. Larson, D.E. Hermann (eds.). Macmillan, New York, pp. 218-222.

Kincaid-Smith, P. (1982). Haematuria and exercise-related haematuria. *British Medical Journal 285*, 1595-1597.

King, D.S., D.L. Costill, W.J. Fink, M. Hargreaves, R.A. Fielding (1985). Muscle metabolism during exercise in the heat in unacclimatized and acclimatized humans. *Journal of Applied Physiology 59*, 1350-1354.

Kirkwood, S.P., L. Packer, G.A. Brooks (1987). Effects of endurance training on a mitochondrial reticulum in limb skeletal muscle. *Archives of Biochemistry and Biophysics 255*, 80-88.

Kirsch, K.A., H. Von Ameln (1981). Feeding patterns of endurance athletes. *European Journal of Applied Physiology 47*, 197-208.

Kirwan, J.P., D.L. Costill, H. Kuipers, M.J. Burrell, W.J. Fink, J.E. Kovaleski, R.A. Fielding (1987). Substrate utilization in leg muscle of men after heat acclimation. *Journal of Applied Physiology 63*, 31-35.

Kirwan, J.P., D.L. Costill, J.B. Mitchell, J.A. Houmard, M.G. Flynn, W.J. Fink, J.D. Beltz (1988). Carbohydrate balance in competitive runners during successive days of intense training. *Journal of Applied Physiology 65*, 2601-2606.

Klein, H.G. (1985). Blood transfusion and athletics. Games people play. *New England Journal of Medicine 312*, 854-856.

Knochel, J.P. (1972). Exertional rhabdomyolysis. *New England Journal of Medicine 287*, 927-929.

Kobasa, S.C., S.R. Maddi, M.C. Puccetti (1982). Personality and exercise as buffers in the stress-illness relationship. *Journal of Behavioural Medicine 5*, 391-404.

Koeslag, J.H. (1980). Obesity. In *Basic Medical Sciences*, Third Series. University of Cape Town Postgraduate Medical Centre, Cape Town, South Africa.

Kohl, H.W., R.E. LaPorte, S.N. Blair (1988). Physical activity and cancer. An epidemiological perspective. *Sports Medicine 6*, 222-237.

Kollias, J., D.L. Moody, E.R. Buskirk (1967). Cross-country running: Treadmill simulation and suggested effectiveness of supplemental treadmill training. *Journal of Sports Medicine and Physical Fitness 7*, 148-154.

Komi, P.V., A. Gollhofer, D. Schmidtbleicher, U. Frick (1987). Interaction between man and shoe in running: Considerations for a more comprehensive measurement approach. *International Journal of Sports Medicine 8*, 196-202.

Komi, P.V., J. Karlsson (1979). Physical performance, skeletal muscle enzyme activities and fibre types in monozygous and dizygous twins of both sexes. *Acta Physiologica Scandinavica Supplement 462*, 1-28.

Komi, P.V., J.H.T. Viitasalo, M. Havu, A. Thorstensson, B. Sjödin, J. Karlsson (1977). Skeletal muscle fibres and muscle enzyme activities in monozygous and dizygous twins of both sexes. *Acta Physiologica Scandinavica 100*, 385-392.

Kono, I., H. Kitao, M. Matsuda, S. Haga, H. Fukushima, H. Kashiwagi (1988). Weight reduction in athletes may adversely affect the phagocytic function. *The Physician and Sportsmedicine 16* (July), 56-65.

Koplan, J.P., K.E. Powell, R.K. Sikes, R.W. Shirley, C.C. Campbell (1982). An epidemiological study of the benefits and risks of running. *Journal of the American Medical Association 248*, 3118-3121.

Kostrubala, T. (1984). Running and therapy. In *Running as Therapy. An Integrated Approach*, M.L. Sachs, G.E. Buffore (eds.). University of Nebraska, Lincoln, pp. 112-124.

Kozlowski, S., Z. Brzezinska, B. Kruk, H. Kaciuba-Uscilko, J.E. Greenleaf, K. Nazar (1985). Exercise hyperthermia as a factor limiting physical performance: Temperature effect on muscle metabolism in dogs. *Journal of Applied Physiology 59*, 766-773.

Krahenbuhl, G.S., D.W. Morgan, R.P. Pangrazi (1989). Longitudinal changes in distance-running performance of young males. *International Journal of Sports Medicine 10*, 92-96.

Krahenbuhl, G.S., R.P. Pangrazi (1983). Characteristics associated with running performance in young boys. *Medicine and Science in Sports and Exercise 15*, 486-490.

Kramsch, D.M., A.J. Aspen, B.M. Abramowitz, T. Kreimendahl, W.B. Hood (1981). Reduction of coronary atherosclerosis by moderate conditioning exercise in monkeys on an atherogenic diet. *New England Journal of Medicine 305*, 1483-1489.

Krejci, V., P. Koch (1979). *Muscle and tendon injuries in athletes*. Georg Thieme, Stuttgart, p. 37.

Kretchmer, N. (1972). Lactose and lactase. *Scientific American 227* (October), 70-78.

Krise, R., B. Squires (1982). *Fast Tracks. The History of Distance Running Since 884 B.C.* The Stephen Greene Press, Brattleboro, Vermont.

Kromhout, D., E.B. Bosschieter, C de L. Coulander (1985). The inverse relation between fish consumption and 20-year mortality from coronary heart disease. *New England Journal of Medicine 312*, 1205-1209.

Krotkiewski, M., A. Aniansson, G. Grimby, P. Björntorp, L. Sjöström (1979). The effect of unilateral isokinetic strength training on local adipose and muscle cell morphology, thickness and enzymes. *European Journal of Applied Physiology 42*, 271-281.

Krotkiewski, M., M. Gudmundsson, P. Backström, K. Mandroukas (1982). Zinc and muscle strength and endurance. *Acta Physiologica Scandinavica 116*, 309-311.

Kruk, B., H. Kaciuba-U'Schilko, K. Nazar, J.E. Greenleaf, S. Kozlowski (1985). Hypothalamic, rectal, and muscle temperatures in exercising dogs: Effect of cooling. *Journal of Applied Physiology 58*, 1444-1448.

Kruss, J., J. Gordon, K.H. Myburgh, T.D. Noakes (1989). The influence of inborn athletic potential on choice of profession and exercise habits of paramedical students. *South African Medical Journal 76*, 538-541.

Krzentowski, G., B. Jandrain, F. Pirnay, F. Mosora, M. Lacroix, A.S. Luyckx, P.J. Lefebvre (1984). Availability of glucose given orally during exercise. *Journal of Applied Physiology 56*, 315-320.

Kuipers, H., G.M.E. Janssen, F. Bosman, P.M. Frederik, P. Geurten (1989a). Structural and ultrastructural changes in skeletal muscle associated with long-distance training and running. *International Journal of Sports Medicine 10*, S156-S159.

Kuipers, H., H.A. Keizer, T. de Vries, P. van Rijthoven, M. Wijts (1988). Comparison of heart rate as a non-invasive determinant of anaerobic threshold with the lactate threshold when cycling. *European Journal of Applied Physiology 58*, 303-306.

Kuipers, H., W.H. Saris, F. Brouns, H.A. Keizer, C. ten Bosch (1989b). Glycogen synthesis during exercise and rest with carbohydrate feeding in males and females. *International Journal of Sports Medicine 10* (Suppl 1), S63-S67.

Kuipers, H., F.T.J. Verstappen, R.S. Reneman (1980). Influence of therapeutic doses of amoxicillin on aerobic work capacity and some strength characteristics. *American Journal of Sports Medicine 8*, 274-279.

Kulpa, P., B.M. White, R. Visscher (1987). Aerobic exercise in pregnancy. *American Journal of Obstetrics and Gynecology 156*, 1395-1403.

Kumagai, S., K. Tanaka, Y. Matsuura, A. Matsuzaka, K. Hirakoba, K. Asano (1982). Relationships of the anaerobic threshold with the 5 km, 10 km and 10 mile races. *European Journal of Applied Physiology 49*, 13-23.

Kuscsik, N. (1977). The history of women's participation in the marathon. *Annals of the New York Academy of Sciences 301*, 862-876.

Kushimoto, H., T. Aoki (1985). Masked type I wheat allergy. Relation to exercise-induced anaphylaxis. *Archives of Dermatology 121*, 355-360.

Kuusela, T., J. Kurri, P. Virtama (1984). Stress response of the tibial cortex: A longitudinal radiographic study. *Annals of Clinical Research 16* (suppl. 40), 14-16.

Kyle, C.R. (1979). Reduction of wind resistance and power output of racing cyclists and runners travelling in groups. *Ergonomics 22*, 387-397.

Kyle, C.R. (1986). Athletic clothing. *Scientific American 254* (March), 92-98.

Kyle, C.R., V.J. Caiozzo (1986). The effect of athletic clothing aerodynamics upon running speed. *Medicine and Science in Sports and Exercise 18*, 509-515.

Laatikainen, T., T. Virtanen, D. Apter (1986). Plasma immunoreactive beta-endorphin in exercise-associated amenorrhea. *American Journal of Obstetrics and Gynecology 154*, 94-97.

Lacey, J.H. (1982). Anorexia nervosa and a bearded female saint. *British Medical Journal 285*, 1816-1817.

LaFontaine, T.P., B.R. Londeree, W.K. Spath (1981). The maximal steady state versus selected running events. *Medicine and Science in Sports and Exercise 13*, 190-192.

Lamanca, J.J., E.M. Haymes, J.A. Daly, R.J. Moffatt, M.F. Waller (1988). Sweat iron loss of male and female runners during exercise. *International Journal of Sports Medicine 9*, 52-55.

Lambert, M., T.D. Noakes (1989). Dissociation of changes in $\dot{V}O_2$ max, muscle QO_2 and performance with training in rats. *Journal of Applied Physiology 66*, 1620-1625.

Lane, N.E., D.A. Bloch, H.H. Jones, W.H. Marshall, P.D. Wood, J.F. Fries (1986). Long-distance running, bone density and osteoarthritis. *Journal of the American Medical Association 255*, 1147-1151.

Lane, N.E., D.A. Bloch, P.D. Wood, J.F. Fries (1987). Aging, long distance running, and the development of musculoskeletal disability: A controlled study. *American Journal of Medicine 82*, 772-780.

Lapidus, L., C. Bengtsson (1986). Socioeconomic factors and physical activity in relation to cardiovascular disease and death. A 12 year follow up of participants in a population study of women in Gothenburg, Sweden. *British Heart Journal 55*, 295-301.

Laritcheva, K.A., N.I. Yalovaya, V.I. Shubin, P.V. Smirnov (1978). Study of energy expenditure and protein needs of top weight lifters. In *Nutrition, Physical Fitness and Health*, J. Parizkova, V.A. Rogozkin (eds.). University Park Press, Baltimore, pp. 155-163.

Larson, D.C., R. Fisher (1987). Management of exercise-induced gastrointestinal problems. *The Physician and Sportsmedicine 15* (September), 112-126.

Larson, R.L., R.O. McMahan (1966). The epiphyses and the childhood athlete. *Journal of the American Medical Association 196*, 607-612.

Lau, E., S. Donnan, D.J. Barker, C. Cooper (1988). Physical activity and calcium intake in fracture of the proximal femur in Hong Kong. *British Medical Journal 297*, 1441-1443.

Lavender, G., S.R. Bird (1989). Effect of sodium bicarbonate ingestion upon repeated sprints. *British Journal of Sports Medicine 23*, 41-45.

Le Blanc, J., P. Diamond, J. Cote, A. Labrie (1984). Hormonal factors in reduced postprandial heat production of exercise-trained subjects. *Journal of Applied Physiology 56*, 772-776.

Leach, R.E., M.B. Purnell, A. Saito (1989). Peroneal nerve entrapment in runners. *American Journal of Sports Medicine 17*, 287-291.

Ledingham, I.M., S. MacVicar, I. Watt, G.A. Weston (1982). Early resuscitation after marathon collapse. *Lancet ii*, 1096-1097.

Leger, L., D. Mercier, L. Gauvin (1984). The relationship between %$\dot{V}O_2$max and running performance time. In *Sport and Elite Performers (The 1984 Olympic Scientific Congress Proceedings 3*, 113-119). D.M. Landers (ed.). Human Kinetics, Champaign, Illinois.

Lehman, M., A. Berg, R. Kapp, T. Wessinghage, J. Keul (1983). Correlations between laboratory testing and distance running performance in marathoners of similar performance ability. *International Journal of Sports Medicine 4*, 226-320.

Leiper, J.B., R.J. Maughan (1986). The effect of luminal tonicity on water absorption from a segment of the intact human jejunum. *Journal of Physiology 378*, 95P.

Leiper, J.B., R.J. Maughan (1988). Experimental models for the investigation of water and solute transport in man. Implications for oral rehydration solutions. *Drugs 36* (suppl. 4), 65-79.

Lemon, P.W.R., J.P. Mullin (1980). Effect of initial muscle glycogen levels on protein catabolism during exercise. *Journal of Applied Physiology 48*, 624-629.

Lemon, P.W.R. (1987). Protein and exercise: Update 1987. *Medicine and Science in Sports and Exercise 19* (suppl.), S179-S190.

Lempriere, L.R. (1930). Athletics in schools. *Lancet 1*, 679-681.

Lenton, B. (1981). *Off the Record*. Brian Lenton Publications, Duffy, Australia.

Lenton, B. (1982). Interview: Deek! *Marathon and Distance Runner 1* (September), 14-18.

Lenton, B. (1983a). Franz Stampfl. *Marathon and Distance Runner 2* (November), 27-32; 2 (December), 48-51.

Lenton, B. (1983b). *Through the Tape*. Brian Lenton Publishers, Duffy, Australia.

Levine, S.A., B. Gordon, C.L. Derick (1924). Some changes in the chemical constituents of the blood following a marathon race. *Journal of the American Medical Association 82*, 1778-1779.

Lewicki, R., H. Tch'orzewski, A. Denys, M. Kowalska, A. Goli'nska (1987). Effect of physical exercise on some parameters of immunity in conditioned sportsmen. *International Journal of Sports Medicine 8*, 309-314.

Lewthwaite, R., T.K. Scanlan (1989). Predictors of competitive trait anxiety in male youth sport participants. *Medicine and Science in Sports and Exercise 21*, 221-229.

Li, G., S. Zhang, G. Chen, H. Chen, A. Wang (1985). Radiographic and histologic analyses of stress fracture in rabbit tibias. *American Journal of Sports Medicine 13*, 285-294.

Lichtman, S., E.G. Poser (1983). The effects of exercise on mood and cognitive functioning. *Journal of Psychosomatic Research 27*, 43-52.

Liebetrau, C. (1982). *Psychological Training for Competitive Sport*. Haum, Pretoria, South Africa.

Lindberg, J.S., W.B. Fears, M.M. Hunt, M.R. Powell, D. Boll, C.E. Wade (1984). Exercise-induced amenorrhea and bone density. *Annals of Internal Medicine 101*, 647-648.

Lindenberg, G., R. Pinshaw, T.D. Noakes (1984). Iliotibial band friction syndrome in runners *The Physician and Sportsmedicine 12* (May), 118-130.

Lindinger, M.I., G.J.F. Heigenhauser (1988). Ion fluxes during tetanic stimulation in isolated perfused rat hindlimb. *American Journal of Physiology 254*, R117-R126.

Linnell, S.I., J.M. Stager, P.W. Blue, N. Oyster, D. Robertshaw (1984). Bone mineral content and menstrual regularity in female runners. *Medicine and Science in Sports and Exercise 16*, 343-348.

Liquori, M., J.L. Parker (1980). *Marti Liquori's Guide for the Elite Runner.* Playboy Press, Chicago.

Little, J.C. (1969). The athlete's neurosis: A deprivation crisis. *Acta Psychiatrica Scandinavica 45*, 187-197.

Little, J.C. (1981). The athlete's neurosis: A deprivation crisis. In *The Psychology of Running*, M.H. Sacks, M.L. Sachs (eds.). Human Kinetics, Champaign, Illinois.

Ljungqvist, R. (1968). Subcutaneous partial rupture of the Achilles tendon. *Acta Orthopaedica Scandinavica* (suppl. 118).

Lloyd, T., S.J. Triantafyllou, E.R. Baker, P.S. Houts, J.A. Whiteside, A. Kalenak, P.G. Stumpf (1986). Women athletes with menstrual irregularity have increased musculoskeletal injuries. *Medicine and Science in Sports and Exercise 18*, 374-379.

Loader, W.R. (1960). *Testament of a Runner.* William Heinemann, London.

Lobstein, D.D., B.J. Mosbacher, A.H. Ismail (1983). Depression as a powerful discriminator between physically active and sedentary middle-aged men. *Journal of Psychosomatic Research 27*, 69-76.

Lodwick, G.S., D.I. Rosenthal, S.V. Kathapuram, T.M. Hudson (1987). Fatigue and insufficiency fractures. *Journal of Medical Imaging 1*, 1-9.

Loftin, M., R.A. Boileau, B.H. Massey, T.G. Lohman (1988). Effect of arm training on central and peripheral circulatory function. *Medicine and Science in Sports and Exercise 20*, 136-141.

Loke, J., D.A. Mahler, J.A. Virgulto (1982). Respiratory muscle fatigue after marathon running. *Journal of Applied Physiology 52*, 821-824.

Londemann, R. (1978). Low haematocrits during basic training: Athlete's anaemia? *New England Journal of Medicine 299*, 1191-1192.

Longley, S., R.S. Panush (1987). Familial exercise-induced anaphylaxis. *Annals of Allergy 58*, 257-259.

Lonka, L., R.S. Pedersen (1987). Fatal rhabdomyolysis in marathon runner. *Lancet 1*, 857-858.

Lopes, J.M., M. Aubier, J. Jardim, J.V. Aranda, P.T. MacKlem (1983). Effect of caffeine on skeletal muscle function before and after fatigue. *Journal of Applied Physiology 54*, 1303-1305.

Lorentzen, D., L. Lawson (1987). Selected sports bras: A biomechanical analysis of breast motion during running. *The Physician and Sportsmedicine 15* (May), 128-139.

Lortie, G., J.A. Simoneau, P. Hamel, M.R. Boulay, F. Landry, C. Bouchard (1984). Responses of maximal aerobic power and capacity to aerobic training. *International Journal of Sports Medicine 5*, 232-236.

Lotgering, F.K., R.D. Gilbert, L.D. Longo (1983). Exercise responses in pregnant sheep: Oxygen consumption, uterine blood flow and blood volume. *Journal of Applied Physiology 55*, 834-841.

Lotgering, F.K., R.D. Gilbert, L.D. Longo (1985). Maternal and fetal responses to exercise during pregnancy. *Physiological Reviews 65*, 1-36.

Louw, J. (1989). Predicting your Comrades performance. *Comrades Marathon Update* (January), 12-13.

Lovesey, P. (1968). *The Kings of Distance*. Eyre and Spottiswoode Ltd, Fakenham, Norfolk, England.

Loy, S.F., R.K. Conlee, W.W. Winder, A.G. Nelson, D.A. Arnall, A.G. Fisher (1986). Effects of 24-hour fast on cycling endurance time at two different intensities. *Journal of Applied Physiology 61*, 654-659.

Luger, A., P.A. Deuster, P.W. Gold, D.D. Loriaux, G.P. Chrousos (1988). Hormonal responses to the stress of exercise. *Advances in Experimental Medicine and Biology 245*, 273-280.

Lukaski, H.C., W.W. Bolonchuk, L.M. Klevay, D.B. Milne, H.H. Sandstead (1983). Maximal oxygen consumption as related to magnesium, copper and zinc nutriture. *American Journal of Clinical Nutrition 37*, 407-415.

Lussier, L., E.R. Buskirk (1977). Effects of an endurance training regimen on assessment of work capacity in prepubertal children. *Annals of the New York Academy of Sciences 301*, 734-747.

Lutter, J.M. (1983). Mixed messages about osteoporosis in female athletes. *The Physician and Sportsmedicine 11* (September), 154-165.

Lutter, J.M., S. Cushman (1982). Menstrual patterns in female runners. *The Physician and Sportsmedicine 10* (September), 60-72.

Lydiard, A., G. Gilmou (1962). *Run to the Top*. A.H. and A. Reed, Wellington.

Lydiard, A.G. Gilmour (1978). *Running the Lydiard Way*. World Publications, Mountain View, California.

Lynch, P. (1980). Soldiers, sport and sudden death. *Lancet 1*, 1235-1237.

McArthur, J.W. (1982). Influence of body mass, body composition and exercise. In *The Gonadotropins: Basic Science and Clinical Aspects in Females*, Serona Symposium No. 42, C. Flamigni, J.R. Givens (eds.). Academic Press, New York, pp. 203-215.

McCabe, M.E., D.A. Peura, S.C. Kadakia, Z. Bocek, L.F. Johnson (1986). Gastrointestinal blood loss associated with running a marathon. *Digestive Diseases and Sciences 31*, 1229-1232.

McCann, I.L., D.S. Holmes (1984). Influence of aerobic exercise on depression. *Journal of Personal and Social Psychology 46*, 1142-1147.

MacConnie, S.E., A. Barkan, R.M. Lampman, M.A. Schork, I.Z. Beitins (1986). Decreased hypothalamic gonadotropin-releasing hormone secretion in male marathon runners. *New England Journal of Medicine 315*, 411-417.

McCutcheon, L., A. Ayres (1983). Are runners really like anorectics? *Running Times* (June), 14-18.

McDonald, R., C.L. Keen (1988). Iron, zinc and magnesium nutrition and athletic performance. *Sports Medicine 5*, 171-184.

MacDougall, J.D., P.D. Roche, O. Bar-Or, J.R. Moroz (1983). Maximal aerobic capacity of Canadian schoolchildren: Prediction based on age-related oxygen cost of running. *International Journal of Sports Medicine 4*, 194-198.

McKenzie, D.C., D.B. Clement, J.E. Taunton (1985). Running shoes, orthotics, and injuries. *Sports Medicine 2*, 334-347.

McKenzie, D.C., K.D. Coutts, D.R. Stirling, H.H. Hoeben, G. Kuzara (1986). Maximal work production following two levels of artificially induced metabolic alkalosis. *Journal of Sports Science 4*, 35-38.

McKenzie, R.T. (1923). *Exercise in Education and Medicine*. W.B. Saunders, London.

Mackinnon, L.T., T.W. Chick, A. van As, T.B. Tomasi (1987). The effect of exercise on secretory and natural immunity. *Advances in Experimental Medicine and Biology 216A*, 869-876.

MacMahon, J.R., R.T. Gross (1988). Physical and psychological effects of aerobic exercise in delinquent adolescent males. *American Journal of Diseases in Childhood 142*, 1361-1366.

McMahon, L.F., M.J. Ryan, D. Larson, R.L. Fisher (1984). Occult gastrointestinal blood loss in marathon runners. *Annals of Internal Medicine 101*, 846-847.

McMahon, T.A., P.R. Greene (1978). Fast running tracks. *Scientific American 243* (December), 112-121.

McMahon, T.A., P.R. Greene (1979). The influence of track compliance on running. *Journal of Biomechanics 12*, 893-904.

McNab, T. (1982). *Flanagan's Run*. Hodder and Stoughton, London.

McNaughton, L., D. Preece (1986). Alcohol and its effects on sprint and middle distance running. *British Journal of Sports Medicine 20*, 56-59.

McPherson, B.D., A. Paivio, M.S. Yuhasz, P.A. Rechnitzer, H.A. Pickard, N.M. Lefcoe (1967). Psychological effects of an exercise program for post-infarct and normal adult men. *Journal of Sports Medicine and Physical Fitness 7*, 95-102.

MacRae, H.S-H., S.C. Dennis, T.D. Noakes, A. Bosch (1990). Effects of a 9 week training program on lactate production and removal during progressive exercise in man. *American Journal of Physiology*, (submitted).

MacSearraigh, E.T.M., J.C. Kallmeyer, H.B. Schiff (1979). Acute renal failure in marathon runners. *Nephron 24*, 236-240.

Maehlum, S., M. Grandmontagne, E.A. Newsholme, O.M. Sejersted (1986). Magnitude and duration of excess postexercise oxygen consumption in healthy young subjects. *Metabolism 35*, 425-429.

Malik, M.O.A. (1979). Sudden coronary deaths associated with sexual activity. *Journal of Forensic Science 24*, 216-220.

Malina, R.M. (1983). Menarche in athletes: A synthesis and hypothesis. *Annals of Human Biology 10*, 1-24.

Malina, R.M., W.W. Spirduso, C. Tate, A.M. Baylor (1978). Age at menarche and selected menstrual characteristics in athletes at different competitive levels and in different sports. *Medicine and Science in Sports 10*, 218-222.

Marcus, R., C. Cann, P. Madrig, J. Minkoff, M. Goddard, M. Bayer, M. Martin, L. Gaudiani, W. Haskell, H. Genant (1985). Menstrual function and bone mass in élite women distance runners. Endocrine and metabolic features. *Annals of Internal Medicine 102*, 158-163.

Margulies, J.Y., A. Simkin, I. Leichter, A. Bivas, R. Steinberg, M. Giladi, M. Stein, H. Kashtan, C. Milgrom (1986). Effect of intense physical activity on the bone-mineral content in the lower limbs of young adults. *Journal of Bone and Joint Surgery 68-A*, 1090-1093.

Marsal, K., O. Lofgren, G. Gennser (1979). Fetal breathing movements and maternal exercise. *Acta Obstetrica Gynecologica Scandinavica 58*, 197-201.

Martens, M.A., P. Libbrecht, A. Burssens (1989). Surgical treatment of the iliotibial band friction syndrome. *American Journal of Sports Medicine 17*, 651-654.

Martens, M.A., M. Backaert, G. Vermaut, J.C. Mulier (1984). Chronic leg pain in athletes due to a recurrent compartment syndrome. *American Journal of Sports Medicine 12*, 148-151.

Marti, B. (1988). Benefits and risks of running among women: An epidemiologic study. *International Journal of Sports Medicine 9*, 92-98.

Marti, B., M. Knobloch, A. Tschopp, A. Jucker, H. Howald (1989). Is excessive running predictive for degenerative hip disease? A controlled study of former elite athletes. *British Medical Journal 299*, 91-93.

Marti, B., J.P. Vader (1987). Joggers grow old. *Lancet 1*, 1207.

Martin, B.J. (1981). Effect on sleep deprivation on tolerance of prolonged exercise. *European Journal of Applied Physiology 47*, 345-354.

Martin, D.E., H.W. Benario, R.W.H. Glynn (1977). Development of the marathon from Pheidippides to the present, with statistics of significant races. *Annals of the New York Academy of Sciences 301*, 820-852.

Martin, D.E., R.W.H. Gynn (1979). The marathon footrace. In *Performers and Performances*. Charlces C Thomas, Springfield, Illinois.

Martin, J.E., P.M. Dubbert (1984). Behavioral management strategies for improving health and fitness. *Journal of Cardiac Rehabilitation 4*, 200-208.

Martin, P.E. (1985). Mechanical and physiological responses to lower extremity loading during running. *Medicine and Science in Sports and Exercise 17*, 427-433.

Martinsen, E.W., A. Medhus, L. Sandvik (1985). Effects of aerobic exercise on depression: A controlled study. *British Medical Journal 291*, 109.

Marymont, J.V., M.A. Lynch, C.E. Henning (1986). Exercise-related stress reaction of the sacroiliac joint. An unusual cause of low back pain in athletes. *American Journal of Sports Medicine 14*, 320-323.

Massey, E.W. (1982). Effort headache in runners. *Headache 22*, 99-100.

Massicotte, D., F. Peronnet, C. Allah, C. Hillaire-Marcel, M. Ledoux, G. Brisson (1986). Metabolic response to [^{13}C] glucose and [^{13}C] fructose ingestion during exercise. *Journal of Applied Physiology 61*, 1180-1184.

Massicotte, D., F. P'eronnet, G. Brisson, K. Bakkouch, C. Hillaire-Marcel (1989). Oxidation of a glucose polymer during exercise: Comparison with glucose and fructose. *Journal of Applied Physiology 66*, 179-183.

Matheson, G.O., D.B. Clement, D.C. McKenzie, J.E. Taunton, D.R. Lloyd-Smith, J.G. Macintyre (1987). Scintigraphic uptake of ^{99m}Tc at non-painful sites in athletes with stress fractures. The concept of bone strain. *Sports Medicine 4*, 65-75.

Matin, P., G. Lang, R. Carretta, G. Simon (1983). Scintigraphic evaluation of muscle damage following extreme exercise: Concise communication. *Journal of Nuclear Medicine 24*, 308-311.

Matsui, H., M. Miyashita, M. Kiura, K. Kabayshi, T. Hoshikawa, S. Kamei (1972). Maximum oxygen intake and its relationship to body weight of Japanese adolescents. *Medicine and Science in Sports 3*, 170-175.

Matter, M., T. Stittfall, J. Graves, K. Myburgh, B. Adams, P. Jacobs, T.D. Noakes (1987). The effects of iron and folate therapy on maximal exercise performance in iron and folate deficient marathon runners. *Clinical Science 72*, 415-422.

Maud, P.J., M.L. Pollock, C. Foster, J.D. Anholm, G. Guten, M. Al-Nouri, C. Hellman, D.H. Schmidt (1981). Fifty years of training and competition in the marathon: Wally Hayward, age 70—a physiological profile. *South African Medical Journal 59*, 153-157.

Maughan, R.J. (1985). Thermoregulation in marathon competition at low ambient temperature. *International Journal of Sports Medicine 6*, 15-19.

Maughan, R.J. (1986). Exercise-induced muscle cramp: A prospective biochemical study in marathon runners. *Journal of Sports Science 4*, 31-34.

Maughan, R.J. (1990). Marathon Running. In *Physiology of sports*, T. Reilly, N. Secher, P. Snell, C. Williams (eds.). E. and F.N. Spon, London, pp. 121-152.

Maughan, R.J., J.B. Leiper (1983). Aerobic capacity and fractional utilization of aerobic capacity in élite and non-élite male and female marathon runners. *European Journal of Applied Physiology 52*, 80-87.

Maughan, R.J., D.C. Poole (1981). The effects of a glycogen-loading regimen on the capacity to perform anaerobic exercise. *European Journal of Applied Physiology 46*, 211-219.

Mayer, J. (1953). Genetic, traumatic and enviornmental factors in obesity. *Physiological Reviews 33*, 472-508.

Mayer, J. (1965). Genetic factors in human obesity. *Annals of the New York Academy of Sciences 131*, 412-421.

Medical World News (1984). Jogger Jim Fixx ran a risky race against his family history and CAD warnings. *Medical World News*, August 27.

Mehaffey, J. (1986). De Castella sporting new philosophy. *Asahi Evening News*, August 21.

Mehta, J., L.M. Lopez, T. Wargovich (1987). Eicosapentaenoic acid: Its relevance in atherosclerosis and coronary artery disease. *American Journal of Cardiology 59*, 155-159.

Mellerowicz, H., D.K. Barron (1971). Overtraining. In *Encyclopaedia of Sports Science and Medicine, L.A. Larson, D.E. Hermann (eds.). Macmillan, New York, pp. 1310-1312.*

Mercier, D., L. Leger, M. Desjardins (1986). Nomogram to predict performance equivalence for distance runners. Track Technique 94, 3004-3009.

Meredith, C.N., W.R. Frontera, E.C. Fisher, V.A. Hughes, J.C. Herland, J. Edwards, W.J. Evans (1989b). Peripheral effects of endurance training in young and old subjects. *Journal of Applied Physiology 66*, 2844-2849.

Meredith, C.N., M.J. Zackin, W.R. Frontera, W.J. Evans (1989a). Dietary protein requirements and body protein metabolism in endurance-trained men. *Journal of Applied Physiology 66*, 2850-2856.

Merians, D.R., W.L. Haskell, K.M. Vranizan, J. Phelps, P.D. Wood, R. Superko (1985). Relationship of exercise, oral contraceptive use, and body fat to concentration of plasma lipids and lipoprotein cholesterol in young women. *American Journal of Medicine 78*, 913-919.

Merkel, K.H.H., H. Hess, M. Kunz (1982). Insertion tendopathy in athletes. A light microscopic, histochemical and electron microscopic examination. *Pathology in Research and Practice 173*, 303-309.

Meshkinpour, H., C. Kemp, R. Fairshter (1989). Effect of aerobic exercise on mouth-to-cecum transit time. *Gastroenterology 96*, 938-941.

Messier, S.P., K.A. Pittala (1988). Etiologic factors associated with selected running injuries. *Medicine and Science in Sports and Exercise 20*, 501-505.

Michael, R.H., L.E. Holder (1985). The soleus syndrome. A cause of medial tibial stress (shin splints). *American Journal of Sports Medicine 13*, 87-94.

Mikesell, A., G.A. Dudley (1984). Influence of intensive endurance training on aerobic power of competitive distance runners. *Medicine and Science in Sports and Exercise 16*, 371-375.

Mikkola, J.J. (1929). *Rata-ja Kentta-Urheilun Kasikirja [Track and Field Athletics Handbook]*. Helsinki.

Millar, A.P. (1975). An early stretching routine in hamstring strains. *Australian Journal of Sports Medicine 8*, 107-109.

Millar, A.P. (1976). An early stretching routine for calf muscle strains. *Medicine and Science in Sports 8*, 39-42.

Miller, D.S., P.M. Mumford (1967). Gluttony. Parts I and II. *American Journal of Clinical Nutrition 20*, 1212-1223.

Miller, D.S., S. Parsonage (1975). Resistance to slimming. Adaptation or illusion? *Lancet 1*, 773-775.

Miller, J.M., E.F. Coyle, W.M. Sherman, J.M. Hagberg, D.L. Costill, W.J. Fink, S.E. Terblanche, J.O. Holloszy (1983). Effect of glycerol feeding on endurance and metabolism during prolonged exercise in man. *Medicine and Science in Sports and Exercise 15*, 237-242.

Milroy, A. (1981). *The Long Distance Record Book*. Road Runners Club, London.

Milroy, A. (1983). The remarkable record of the nineteenth century pedestrians. *Ultrarunning* (July-August), 24-26.

Milroy, A. (1987). Personal communication to the author.

Milvy, P. (ed.) (1977). The marathon: Physiological, medical, epidemiological and psychological studies. *Annals of the New York Academy of Sciences 301*, 1-1090.

Milvy, P. (ed.) (1978). *The Long Distance Runner. A Definitive Study*. Urizen Books, New York.

Milvy, P. (1979). On: 'Of Jogging.' *American Heart Journal 98*, 136.

Milvy, P., E. Colt, J. Thornton (1981). A high incidence of urolithiasis in male marathon runners. *Journal of Sports Medicine and Physical Fitness 21*, 295-298.

Mirkin, G., M. Hoffman (1978). *The Sportsmedicine Book*. Little, Brown and Company, Boston.

Mitchell, J.B., D.L. Costill, J.A. Houmard, W.J. Fink, R.A. Robergs, J.A. Davis (1989). Gastric emptying: Influence of prolonged exercise and carbohydrate concentration. *Medicine and Science in Sports and Exercise 21*, 269-274.

Mitchell, J.B., D.L. Costill, J.A. Houmard, M.G. Flynn, W.J. Fink, J.D. Beltz (1988). Effects of carbohydrate ingestion on gastric emptying and exercise performance. *Medicine and Science in Sports and Exercise 20*, 110-115.

Mitchell, J.H., W.C. Reardon, D.I. McCloskey (1977). Reflex effects on circulation and respiration from contracting skeletal muscle. *American Journal of Physiology 233*, H374-H378.

Mitchell, J.B., K.W. Voss (1991). The influence of volume of fluid ingested on gastric emptying and body fluid balance. *Medicine and Science in Sports and Exercise* (in press).

Mitchell, J.H., K. Wildenthal (1974). Static (isometric) exercise and the heart: Physiological and clinical considerations. *Annual Review of Medicine 25*, 369-381.

Miyashita, M., M. Miura, Y. Murase, K. Yamaji (1978). Running performance from the viewpoint of aerobic power. In *Environmental Stress. Individual Human Adaptations*, L.J. Folinsbee, J.A. Wagner, J.F. Borgia, B.L. Drinkwater, J.A. Gliner, J.F. Bedi (eds.). Academic Press, New York, pp. 183-194.

Molé, P.A., J.S. Stern, C.L. Schultz, E.M. Bernauer, B.J. Holcomb (1989). Exercise reverses depressed metabolic rate produced by severe caloric restriction. *Medicine and Science in Sports and Exercise 21*, 29-33.

Moller-Nielsen, J., M. Hammar (1989). Women's soccer injuries in relation to the menstrual cycle and oral contraceptive use. *Medicine and Science in Sports and Exercise 21*, 126-129.

Moodley, D., T.D. Noakes, A.N. Bosch, S.E. Dennis, R. Schall (1991). Exogenous carbohydrate oxidation during prolonged exercise: The effect of carbohydrate type and solution concentration. Unpublished manuscript.

Moore, D.H. (1975). A study of age group track and field records to relate age and running speed. *Nature 153*, 264-265.

Moore, D.H., J.C. Jarrett, P.J. Bendick (1988). Exercise-induced changes in uterine artery blood flow, as measured by Doppler ultrasound, in pregnant subjects. *American Journal of Perinatology 5*, 94-97.

Moore, K. (1982). *Best Efforts: World Class Runners and Races*. Doubleday, Garden City, New York.

Moore, R.L., E.M. Thacker, G.A. Kelley, T.I. Musch, L.I. Sinoway, V.L. Foster, A.L. Dickinson (1987). Effect of training/detraining on submaximal exercise responses in humans. *Journal of Applied Physiology 63*, 1719-1724.

Moorstein, B. (1968). Life expectancy of Ivy League rowing crews. *Journal of the American Medical Association 205*, 106.

Moran, Lord. (1945). *The Anatomy of Courage*. Constable, London.

Morgan, D.W., F.D. Baldini, P.E. Martin, W.M. Kohrt (1989). Ten kilometer performance and predicted velocity at VO_2max among well-trained male runners. *Medicine and Science in Sports and Exercise 21*, 78-83.

Morgan, J.E. (1873). *University Oars*. Macmillan, London.

Morgan, W.P. (1978). The mind of the marathoner. *Psychology Today 11* (April), 38-47.

Morgan, W.P. (1979). Negative addiction in runners. *The Physician and Sportsmedicine 7* (February), 57-70.

Morgan, W.P. (1985). Affective beneficience of vigorous physical activity. *Medicine and Science in Sports and Exercise 17*, 94-100.

Morgan, W.P., D.R. Brown, J.S. Raglin, P.J. O'Connor, K.A. Ellickson (1987). Psychological monitoring of overtraining and staleness. *British Journal of Sports Medicine 21*, 107-114.

Morgan, W.P., D.L. Costill (1972). Psychological characteristics of the marathon runner. *Journal of Sports Medicine and Physical Fitness 12*, 42-46.

Morgan, W.P., D.L. Costill, M.G. Flynn, J.S. Raglin, P.J. O'Connor (1988). Mood disturbance following increased training in swimmers. *Medicine and Science in Sports and Exercise 20*, 408-414.

Morgan, W.P., M.L. Pollock (1977). Psychologic characterization of the élite distance runner. *Annals of the New York Academy of Sciences 301*, 382-403.

Morris, A.E., B.F. Husman (1978). Life quality changes following an endurance conditioning program. *American Corrective Therapy Journal 32*, 3-6.

Morris, A.F. (1982). Sleep disturbances in athletes. *The Physician and Sports-medicine 10* (September), 75-85.

Morris, A.F., L. Lussier, P. Vaccaro, D.H. Clarke (1982). Life quality characteristics of national class women masters long distance runners. *Annals of Sports Medicine 1*, 23-26.

Morris, J.N., S.P.W. Chave, C. Adam, C. Sirey, L. Epstein, D.J. Sheehan (1973). Vigorous exercise in leisure-time and the incidence of coronary heart disease. *Lancet 1*, 333-339.

Morris, J.N., M.G. Everitt, R. Pollard, S.P.W. Chave, A.M. Semmence (1980). Vigorous exercise in leisure-time: Protection against coronary heart disease. *Lancet 2*, 1207-1210.

Morris, J.N., J.A. Heady, P.A.B. Raffle, C.G. Roberts, J.W. Parks (1953). Coronary heart disease and physical activity of work. *Lancet 2*, 1053-1057, 1111-1120.

Morris, J.N., J.A. Heady, P.A.B. Raffle (1956). Physique of London busmen. Epidemiology of uniforms. *Lancet 2*, 569-570.

Morris, N., S.B. Osborn, H.P. Wright, A. Hart (1956). Effective uterine blood flow during exercise in normal and pre-eclamptic pregnancies. *Lancet 2*, 481-484.

Morton, R.H. (1983). The supreme runner: What evidence now? *Australian Journal of Sports Sciences 3*, 7-10.

Morton, R.H. (1984). You can't catch me: I'm the gingerbread man. In *The Fascination of Statistics*. R.J. Brook, G.C. Arnold, T.H. Hassard, R.M. Pringle (eds.), Marcel Dekker, New York.

Moses, F.M., T.G. Brewer, D.A. Peura (1988). Running-associated proximal hemorrhagic colitis. *Annals of Internal Medicine 108*, 385-386.

Mubarak, S.J., R.N. Gould, Y.F. Lee, D.A. Schmidt, A.R. Hargens (1982). The medial tibial stress syndrome. A cause of shinsplints. *American Journal of Sports Medicine 10*, 201-205.

Mueller, E.J., I.M. Thompson (1988). Bladder carcinoma presenting as exercise-induced hematuria. *Postgraduate Medicine 84*, 173-176.

Murase, Y., K. Kobayashi, S. Mamei, H. Matsui (1981). Longitudinal study of aerobic power in superior junior athletes. *Medicine and Science in Sports and Exercise 13*, 180-184.

Murphy, P.C., D.E. Baxter (1985). Nerve entrapment of the foot and ankle in runners. *Clinics in Sports Medicine 4*, 753-763.

Murray, R., G.L. Paul, J.G. Seifert, D.E. Eddy, G.A. Halaby (1989). The effects of glucose, fructose, and sucrose ingestion during exercise. *Medicine and Science in Sports and Exercise 21*, 275-282.

Murray-Leslie, C.F., D.J. Lintott, V. Wright (1977). The knees and ankles in sport and veteran military parachutists. *Annals of Rheumatic Diseases 36*, 327-331.

Mussabini, A., C. Ransom (1913). *The Complete Athletic Trainer*. Methuen, London.

Myburgh, K.H. (1989). The effects of exercise on bone fragility and bone strength in osteoporosis and in health. Ph.D. thesis, University of Cape Town, Cape Town.

Myburgh, K.H., J. Hutchins, A.B. Fataar, S.F. Hough, T.D. Noakes (1990). Low bone density is an etiologic factor for stress fractures in athletes. *Annals of Internal Medicine 113*, 754-759.

Myburgh, K.H., N. Grobler, T.D. Noakes (1988). Factors associated with shin soreness in athletes. *The Physician and Sportsmedicine 16* (April), 129-134.

Nadel, E.R., S.M. Fortney, C.B. Wenger (1980). Effect of hydration state on circulatory and thermal regulations. *Journal of Applied Physiology 49*, 715-721.

Nakamura, Y., A. Schwartz (1972). The influence of hydrogen ion concentration on calcium binding and release by skeletal muscle sarcoplasmic reticulum. *Journal of General Physiology 59*, 22-32.

National Heart, Lung and Blood Institute (1981). *Exercise and Your Heart*. Bethesda, Maryland.

Nelson, A. (1924). *Practical Athletics and How to Train*. Mayflower Press, Plymouth, England.

Nelson, M.E., E.C. Fisher, P.D. Catsos, C.N. Meredith, R.N. Turksoy, W.J. Evans (1986). Diet and bone status in amenorrheic runners. *American Journal of Clinical Nutrition 43*, 910-916.

Nelson, R.C., R.J. Gregor (1976). Biomechanics of distance running: A longitudinal study. *Research Quarterly 47*, 417-428.

Neufer, P.D., D.L. Costill, W.J. Fink, J.P. Kirwan, R.A. Fielding, M.G. Flynn (1986). Effects of exercise and carbohydrate composition on gastric emptying. *Medicine and Science in Sports and Exercise 18*, 658-662.

Neufer, P.D., A.J. Young, M.N. Sawka (1989a). Gastric emptying during exercise: Effects of heat stress and hypohydration. *European Journal of Applied Physiology 58*, 433-439.

Neufer, P.D., A.J. Young, M.N. Sawka (1989b). Gastric emptying during walking and running: Effects of varied exercise intensity. *European Journal of Applied Physiology 58*, 440-445.

Neumann, R.O. (1902). Experimentelle Beitrage Zur Lehre von dem taglichen Nahrungsbedarf des Menschen unter besonderer Berucksichtigung der not wendigen Eiweissmenge [Experimental studies of the daily food requirements with special reference to egg white requirements]. *Archiv Hugiene 45*, 1-87.

Neuspiel, D.R. (1986). Sudden death from myocarditis in young athletes. *Mayo Clinic Proceedings 61*, 226-227.

Newham, D.J., D.A. Jones, S.E.J. Tolfree, R.H.T. Edwards (1986). Skeletal muscle damage: A study of isotope uptake, enzyme efflux and pain after stepping. *European Journal of Applied Physiology 55*, 106-112.

Newhouse, I.J., D.B. Clement, J.E. Taunton, D.C. McKenzie (1989). The effects of prelatent/latent iron deficiency on physical work capacity. *Medicine and Science in Sports and Exercise 21*, 263-268.

Newsholme, E., T. Leech (1983). *The Runner: Energy and Endurance*. Fitness Books. Walter L. Meagher, Oxford.

Newton, A.F.H. (1935). *Running*. H.F. & G. Witherby, London.

Newton, A.F.H. (1940). *Running in Three Continents*. H.F. & G. Witherby, London.

Newton, A.F.H. (1947). *Commonsense Athletics*. G. Berridge, London.

Newton, A.F.H. (1949). *Races and Training*. G. Berridge, London.

Nice, C., A.G. Reeves, T. Brinck-Johnsen, W. Noll (1984). The effects of pantothenic acid on human exercise capacity. *Journal of Sports Medicine and Physical Fitness 24*, 26-29.

Nicholson, J.P., D.B. Case (1983). Carboxyhemoglobin levels in New York City runners. *The Physician and Sportsmedicine 11* (March), 135-138.

Nickerson, H.J., A.D. Tripp (1983). Iron deficiency in adolescent cross-country runners. *The Physician and Sportsmedicine 11* (June), 60-66.

Nicklas, B.J., A.C. Hackney, R.L. Sharp (1989). The menstrual cycle and exercise: Performance, muscle glycogen, and substrate responses. *International Journal of Sports Medicine 10*, 264-269.

Nideffer, R.M. (1976). *The Inner Athlete*. Crowell, New York.

Nideffer, R.M. (1983). The injured athlete: Psychological factors in treatment. *Orthopaedic Clinics of North America 14*, 373-385.

Nideffer, R.M. (1985). *Athletes' Guide to Mental Training*. Human Kinetics, Champaign, Illinois.

Nieman, D.C. (1988). Vegetarian dietary practices and endurance performance. *American Journal of Clinical Nutrition 48* (3 suppl.), 754-761.

Nieman, D.N., L.S. Berk, M. Simpson-Westerberg, K. Arabatzis, S. Youngberg, S.A. Tan, J.W. Lee, W.C. Eby (1989). Effects of long-endurance running on immune system parameters and lymphocyte function in experienced marathoners. *International Journal of Sports Medicine 10*, 317-323.

Nigg, B.M. (1985). Biomechanics, load analysis and sports injuries in the lower extremities. *Sports Medicine 2*, 367-379.

Nigg, B.M., H.A. Bahlsen (1988). Influence of heel flare and midsole construction on pronation, supination, and impact forces for heel-toe running. *International Journal of Sports Biomechanics 4*, 205-219.

Nigg, B.M., H.A. Bahlsen, S.M. Luethi, S. Stokes (1987). The influence of running velocity and midsole hardness on external impact forces in heel-toe running. *Journal of Biomechanics 20*, 951-959.

Nigg, B.M., W. Herzog, J.L. Read (1988). Effects of viscoelastic shoe insoles on vertical impact forces in heel-toe running. *American Journal of Sports Medicine 16*, 70-76.

Nigg, B.M., M. Morlock (1987). The influence of lateral heel flare of running shoes on pronation and impact forces. *Medicine and Science in Sports and Exercise 19*, 294-302.

Nikolaou, P.K., B.L. MacDonald, R.R. Glisson, A.V. Seaber, W.E. Garrett (1987). Biomechanical and histological evaluation of muscle after controlled strain injury. *American Journal of Sports Medicine 15*, 9-14.

Nilsson, L.H., E. Hultman (1973). Liver glycogen in man—the effect of total starvation or a carbohydrate-poor diet followed by carbohydrate refeeding. *Scandinavian Journal of Clinical and Laboratory Investigation 32*, 325-330.

Nilsson, L.H., E. Hultman (1974). Liver and muscle glycogen in man after glucose and fructose infusion. *Scandinavian Journal of Clinical and Laboratory Investigation 33*, 5-10.

Noakes, T.D. (1981). Heatstroke during the 1981 national cross-country championships. *South African Medical Journal 61*, 145.

Noakes, T.D. (1982). Food allergy in runners. *Journal of the American Medical Association 247*, 1406.

Noakes, T.D. (1983). Running shoe anaphylaxis—a case report. *British Journal of Sports Medicine 17*, 213.

Noakes, T.D. (1985). A novel, rapidly fatal approach to the management of hypothermia in long-distance swimmers. *South African Medical Journal 67*, 532.

Noakes, T.D. (1987a). The effects of exercise on serum enzyme activities in humans. *Sports Medicine 4*, 245-267.

Noakes, T.D. (1987b). Heart disease in marathon runners. A review. *Medicine and Science in Sports and Exercise 19*, 187-194.

Noakes, T.D. (1988a). Editorial: Why marathon runners collapse. *South African Medical Journal 73*, 569-571.

Noakes, T.D. (1988b). Implications of exercise testing for prediction of athletic performance: A contemporary perspective. *Medicine and Science in Sports and Exercise 20*, 319-330.

Noakes, T.D. (1990a). Fluid and mineral needs of athletes. In J.S. Torg, R.P. Welsh, R.J. Shephard (eds.) *Current Therapy in Sports Medicine*. B.C. Decker, Toronto.

Noakes, T.D. (1990b). The dehydration myth and carbohydrate replacement during prolonged exercise. *Cycling Science 1*, 23-29.

Noakes, T.D., B.A. Adams, C. Greeff, T. Lotz, M. Nathan (1988a). The danger of an inadequate water intake during prolonged exercise. A novel concept revisited. *European Journal of Applied Physiology 57*, 210-219.

Noakes, T.D., N. Berlinski, E. Solomon, L. Weight (1991c). Serum biochemical changes following intravenous fluid therapy in collapsed ultramarathon runners. *Physican and Sportsmedicine* (in press).

Noakes, T.D., J.W. Carter (1976). Biochemical parameters in athletes before and after having run 160 kilometres. *South African Medical Journal 50*, 1562-1566.

Noakes, T.D., J.W. Carter (1982). The responses of plasma biochemical parameters to a 56 km race in novice and experienced ultra-marathon runners. *European Journal of Applied Physiology 49*, 179-186.

Noakes, T.D., N. Goodwin, B.L. Rayner, T. Brankin, R.K.N. Taylor (1985a). Water intoxication: A possible complication of endurance exercise. *Medicine and Science in Sports and Exercise 17*, 370-375.

Noakes, T.D., L. Higginson, L.H. Opie (1983b). Physical training increases ventricular fibrillation thresholds of isolated rat hearts during normoxia, hypoxia and regional ischemia. *Circulation 67*, 24-30.

Noakes, T.D., G. Kotzenberg, P.S. McArthur, J. Dykman (1983a). Elevated serum creatine kinase MB and creatine kinase BB-isoenzyme fractions after ultra-marathon running. *European Journal of Applied Physiology 52*, 75-79.

Noakes, T.D., V.E. Lambert, M.I. Lambert, P. McArthur, K. Myburgh, A.J.S. Benade (1988b). Carbohydrate ingestion and muscle glycogen depletion during marathon and ultramarathon racing. *European Journal of Applied Physiology 57*, 482-489.

Noakes, T.D., K.H. Myburgh, J.H. Du Plessis, L. Lang, M. Lambert (1990a). Metabolic rate not % dehydration predicts rectal temperature after marathon running. *Medicine and Science in Sports and Exercise* (in press).

Noakes, T.D., K.H. Myburgh, R. Schall (1989a). Peak treadmill running velocity during the $\dot{V}O_2$max test predicts running performance. *Journal of Sports Science* (in press).

Noakes, T.D., K.H. Myburgh, T. Wiggins, C. van der Riet (1990b). Physiological characteristics of elite distance runners (unpublished manuscript).

Noakes, T.D., R.J. Norman, R.H. Buck, J. Godlonton, K. Stevenson, D. Pittaway (1989c). The incidence of hyponatremia during prolonged ultra-endurance exercise. *Med. Sci. Sports Exer.*

Noakes, T.D., R.J. Norman, R.H. Buck, J. Godlonton, K. Stevenson, D. Pittaway (1990c). The incidence of hyponatremia during prolonged ultra-endurance exercise. *Medicine and Science in Sports and Exercise* (in press).

Noakes, T.D., N.J. Rehrer, R.J. Maughan (1991b). The importance of volume in regulating gastric emptying. *Medicine and Science in Sports and Exercise 23*.

Noakes, T.D., A.G. Rose (1984). Exercise-related deaths in subjects with co-existent hypertrophic cardiomyopathy and coronary artery disease. Case reports. *South African Medical Journal 66*, 183-187.

Noakes, T.D., A.G. Rose, J. Benjamin (1984b). Sudden death in a champion athlete. Autopsy findings. *South African Medical Journal 66*, 458-459.

Noakes, T.D., A.G. Rose, L.H. Opie (1984a). Marathon running and immunity to coronary heart disease: Fact vs. fiction. *Clinics in Sports Medicine 3*, 527-543.

Noakes, T.D., M.A. van Gend (1988). Menstrual dysfunction in female athletes. A review for clinicians. *South African Medical Journal 73*, 350-355.

Noakes, T.D., J.A. Smith, G. Lindenberg, C.E. Wills (1985b). Pelvic stress fractures in long-distance runners. *American Journal of Sports Medicine 13*, 120-123.

Noble, B.J., G.A.V. Borg, I. Jacobs, R. Ceci, P. Kaiser (1983). A category-ratio perceived exertion scale: Relationship to blood and muscle lactates and heart rates. *Medicine and Science in Sports and Exercise 15*, 523-528.

Noble, C.A. (1979). The treatment of iliotibial band friction syndrome. *British Journal of Sports Medicine 13*, 51-54.

Noble, C.A. (1980). Iliotibial band friction syndrome in runners. *American Journal of Sports Medicine 8*, 232-234.

Nordemar, R., B. Ekblom, L. Zachrisson, K. Lundqvist (1981). Physical training in rheumatoid arthritis: A controlled long-term study. *Scandinavian Journal of Rheumatology 10*, 17-23.

Norris, J. (1983). The 'scurvy disposition': Heavy exertion as an exacerbating influence on scurvy in modern times. *Bulletin of the History of Medicine 53*, 325-388.

Nose, H., G.W. Mack, X. Shi, E.R. Nadel (1988a). Role of osmolality and plasma volume during rehydration in humans. *Journal of Applied Physiology 65*, 325-331.

Nose, H., G.W. Mack, X. Shi, E.R. Nadel (1988b). Involvement of sodium retention hormones during rehydration in humans. *Journal of Applied Physiology 65*, 332-336.

Nouri, S., J. Beer (1989). Relations of moderate physical exercise to scores on hostility, aggression, and trait-anxiety. *Perceptive and Motor Skills 68*, 1191-1194.

Noyce, W. (1958). *The Springs of Adventure*. John Murray, London.

O'Brien, J. (1982). The road goes on and on. . . . *Marathon and Distance Runner 1* (Sept/Oct), 9-13.

O'Connor, P.J., W.P. Morgan, J.S. Raglin, C.M. Barksdale, N.H. Kalin (1989). Mood state and salivary cortisol levels following overtraining in female swimmers. *Psychoneuroendocrinology 14*, 303-310.

O'Connor, T. (1960). *The 4-Minute Smiler. The Derek Ibbotson Story*. Stanley Paul, London.

Oelz, O., H. Howard, P.E. di Pampero, H. Hoppeler, H. Claassen, R. Jenni, A. Buhlmann, G. Ferretti, J-C. Bruckner, A. Veicsteinas, M. Gussoni, P. Cerretelli (1986). Physiological profile of world-class high-altitude climbers. *Journal of Applied Physiology 60*, 1734-1742.

Ogilvie, B., T.A. Tutko (1971). *Problem Athletes and How to Handle Them*. Pelham Books, London.

Ogilvie, B.C. (1980). The unconscious fear of success. In *Psychology in Sports, Methods and Applications*, R.M. Suinn (ed.). Burgess, Minneapolis.

Ogilvie, B.C. (1981). Quoted by E. Olsen. Speed, strength, guts. *The Runner 3* (February), 46-53.

Ogilvie, B.C. (1983a). The orthopedist's role in children's sports. *Orthopedic Clinics of North America 14*, 361-372.

Ogilvie, B.C. (1983b). Psychology and the élite young athlete. *The Physician and Sportsmedicine 11* (April), 195-202.

O'Herlichy, C. (1982). Jogging and suppression of ovulation. *New England Journal of Medicine 306*, 50-51.

Oliver, R.M. (1967). Physique and serum lipids of young London busmen in relation to ischaemic heart disease. *British Journal of Industrial Medicine 24*, 181-186.

Ollerenshaw, K.J., S. Norman, C.G. Wilson, J.G. Hardy (1987). Exercise and small intestinal transit. *Nuclear Medicine Communications 8*, 105-110.

Olschewski, H., Brück, K. (1988). Thermoregulatory, cardiovascular, and muscular factors related to exercise after precooling. *Journal of Applied Physiology 64*, 803-811.

Orava, S., J. Puranen, L. Ala-Ketola (1978). Stress fractures caused by physical exercise. *Acta Orthopaedica Scandinavica 49*, 19-27.

O'Reilly, K.P., M.J. Warhol, R.A. Fiedling, W.R. Frontera, C.N. Meredith, W.J. Evans (1987). Eccentric exercise-induced muscle damage impairs muscle glycogen repletion. *Journal of Applied Physiology 63*, 252-256.

Orlick, T. (1980). *In Pursuit of Excellence*. Human Kinetics, Champaign, Illinois.

Osler, T. (1967). *The Conditioning of Distance Runners*. World Publications, Mountain View, California.

Osler, T. (1978). *Serious Runner's Handbook*. World Publications, Mountain View, California.

Osler, T., E. Dodd (1979). *Ultra-Marathoning. The Next Challenge*. World Publications, Mountain View, California.

Osler, T.J., E.L. Dodd (1977). Six-day pedestrian races. *Annals of the New York Academy of Sciences 301*, 820-852.

Osterback, L., Y. Qvarnberg (1987). A prospective study of respiratory infections in 12-year-old children actively engaged in sports. *Acta Paediatrica Scandinavica 76*, 944-949.

Owen, M.D., K.C. Kregel, P.T. Wall, C.V. Gisolfi (1986). Effects of ingesting carbohydrate beverages during exercise in the heat. *Medicine and Science in Sports and Exercise 18*, 568-575.

Paffenbarger, R.S., W.E. Hale (1975). Work activity and coronary heart mortality. *New England Journal of Medicine 292*, 545-550.

Paffenbarger, R.S., W.E. Hale, R.J. Brand, R.T. Hyde (1977). Work-energy level, personal characteristics, and fatal heart attacks: A birth-cohort effect. *American Journal of Epidemiology 105*, 200-213.

Paffenbarger, R.S., R.T. Hyde, D.L. Jung, A.L. Wing (1984). Epidemiology of exercise and coronary heart disease. *Clinics in Sports Medicine 3*(2), 297-318.

Paffenbarger, R.S., R.T. Hyde, A.L. Wing, C.C. Hsich (1986). Physical activity, all-cause mortality, and longevity of college alumni. *New England Journal of Medicine 314*, 605-613.

Paffenbarger, R.S., A.L. Wing, R.T. Hyde (1978). Physical activity as an index of heart attack risk in college alumni. *American Journal of Epidemiology 108*, 161-175.

Paffenbarger, R.S., A.L. Wing, R.T. Hyde, D.L. Jung (1983). Physical activity and incidence of hypertension in college alumni. *American Journal of Epidemiology 117*, 245-257.

Pallikarakis, N., B. Jandain, F. Pirnay, F. Mosora, M. Lacroix, A.S. Luyckx, P.J. Lefebvre (1986). Remarkable metabolic availability of oral glucose during long-duration exercise in humans. *Journal of Applied Physiology 60*, 1035-1042.

Palmoski, M.J., R.A. Colyer, K.D. Brandt (1980). Joint motion in the absence of normal loading does not maintain normal articular cartilage. *Arthritis and Rheumatism 23*, 325-334.

Pantano, J.A., R.J. Oriel (1982). Prevalence and nature of cardiac arrhythmias in apparently normal well-trained runners. *American Heart Journal 104*, 762-768.

Panush, R.S., C. Schmidt, J.R. Caldwell, N.L. Edwards, S. Longley, R. Yonker, E. Webster, J. Nauman, J. Stork, H. Pettersson (1986). Is running associated with degenerative joint disease? *Journal of the American Medical Association 255*, 1152-1154.

Pargman, D. (1980). The way of the runner. An examination of motives for running. In *Psychology in Sports. Methods and Applications*, R.M. Suinn (ed.). Burgess, Minneapolis.

Park, J.H., R.L. Brown, C.R. Park, M. Cohn, B. Chance (1988). Energy metabolism of the untrained muscle of elite runners as observed by ^{31}P magnetic resonance spectroscopy: Evidence suggesting a genetic endowment for endurance exercise. *Proceedings of the National Academy of Sciences USA 85*, 8780-8784.

Parker, B.M., B.R. Londeree, G.V. Cupp, J.P. Dubiel (1978). The non-invasive cardiac evaluation of long-distance runners. *Chest 73*, 376-381.

Parkhouse, W.S., D.C. McKenzie (1984). Possible contribution of skeletal muscle buffers to enhanced anaerobic performance: A brief review. *Medicine and Science in Sports and Exercise 16*, 328-338.

Passmore, R., J.V.G.A. Durnin (1955). Human energy expenditure. *Physiological Reviews 35*, 801-836.

Pate, R.R., P.B. Sparling, G.E. Wilson, K.J. Cureton, B.J. Miller (1987). Cardiorespiratory and metabolic responses to submaximal and maximal exercise in elite women distance runners. *International Journal of Sports Medicine* *8* (suppl. 3), 91-95.

Paulev, P-E., R. Jordal, N.S. Pedersen (1983). Dermal excretion of iron in intensely training athletes. *Clinica Chimica Acta 127*, 19-27.

Pavlou, K.N., W.P. Steffee, R.H. Lerman, B.A. Burrows (1985). Effects of diet and exercise on lean body mass, oxygen uptake, and strength. *Medicine and Science in Sports and Exercise 17*, 466-471.

Pavlov, H., J.S. Torg, R.H. Freiberger (1983). Tarsal navicular stress fractures: Radiographic evaluation. *Radiology 148*, 641-645.

Pedersen, B.K., N. Tvede, L.D. Christensen, K. Klarlund, S. Kragbak, J. Halk-jr-Kristensen (1989). Natural killer cell activity in peripheral blood of highly trained and untrained persons. *International Journal of Sports Medicine 10*, 129-131.

Pekkanen, J., B. Marti, A. Nissinen, J. Tuomilehto, S. Punsar, M.J. Karvonen (1987). Reduction of premature mortality by high physical activity: A 20-year follow-up of middle-aged Finnish men. *Lancet i*, 1473-1477.

Perry, S.W., M.H. Sacks (1981). Psychodynamics of running. In *Psychology of Running*, M.H. Sacks, M.L. Sachs (eds.). Human Kinetics, Champaign, Illinois.

Peters, E., E. Bateman (1983). Ultra-marathon running and upper respiratory tract infections. An epidemiological survey. *South African Medical Journal 64*, 582-584.

Peters, J. (1955). *In the Long Run*. Cassell, London.

Peters, J.H., J. Johnston, J. Edmunson (1957). *Modern Middle and Long Distance Running*. Nicholas Kaye, London.

Peters, K. (1981). Conversation with . . . Steve Scott and Herb Elliott. *Running 6* (June), 16-18.

Peters-Futre, E., T.D. Noakes, R.I. Raine, S.E. Terblanche (1987). Muscle glycogen repletion during active post-exercise recovery. *American Journal of Physiology 253*, E305-E311.

Petray, C.K., G.S. Krahenbuhl (1985). Running training instruction on running technique, and running economy in 10-year-old males. *Research Quarterly for Exercise and Sport 56*, 251-255.

Pierson, W.R., A. Lockhart (1963). Effect of menstruation on simple movement and reaction time. *British Medical Journal 1*, 796-797.

Pinshaw, R., V. Atlas, T.D. Noakes (1983). The nature and response to therapy of 196 consecutive injuries seen at a runner's clinic. *South African Medical Journal 65*, 291-298.

Pipes, T.V. (1980). The effects of pangamic acid on performance in trained athletes. *Medicine and Science in Sports and Exercise 12*, 98.

Pirie, G. (1961). *Running Wild*. W.H. Allen, London.

Pirnay, F., J.M. Crielaard, N. Pallikarakis, M. Lacroix, F. Mosora, G. Krzentowski, A.S. Luyckx, P.J. Lefebvre (1982). Fate of exogenous glucose during exercise of different intensities in humans. *Journal of Applied Physiology 53*, 1620-1624.

Pirnay, F., M. Lacroix, F. Mosora, A. Luyckx, P. Lefebvre (1977). Effect of glucose ingestion on energy substrate utilization during prolonged muscular exercise. *European Journal of Applied Physiology 36*, 247-254.

Pi-Sunyer, F.X., R. Woo (1985). Effect of exercise on food intake in human subjects. *American Journal of Clinical Nutrition 42* (suppl. 5), 983-990.

Plaatjies, M. (1986). Marathoner's injury trends all the same. *The Star*, September 3.

Pocock, N.A., J.A. Eisman, M.G. Yeates, P.N. Sambrook, S. Eberl (1986). Physical fitness is a major determinant of femoral neck and lumbar spine bone mineral density. *Journal of Clinical Investigation 78*, 618-621.

Podolsky, R.C., Schoenberg, M. (1983). Force generation and shortening in skeletal muscle. In *Handbook of Physiology. Volume 10: Skeletal Muscle*, L.D. Peachey, R.H. Adrian, S.R. Geiger (eds.). American Physiological Society, Bethesda, Maryland, pp. 172-187.

Poehlman, E.T. (1989). A review: Exercise and its influence on resting energy metabolism in man. *Medicine and Science in Sports and Exercise 21*, 515-525.

Pollock, M.L. (1977). Submaximal and maximal working capacity of élite distance runners. Part 1: Cardiorespiratory aspects. *Annals of the New York Academy of Sciences 301*, 310-321.

Pollock, M.L., C. Foster, D. Knapp, J.L. Rod, D.H. Schmidt (1987). Effect of age and training on aerobic capacity and body composition of master athletes. *Journal of Applied Physiology 62*, 725-731.

Pollock, M.L., L.R. Gettman, A. Jackson, J. Ayres, A. Ward, A.C. Linnerud (1977). Body composition of elite class distance runners. *Annals of the New York Academy of Sciences 301*, 361-370.

Pomerance, J.J., L. Gluck, V.A. Lynch (1974). Physical fitness in pregnancy: Its effect on pregnancy outcome. *American Journal of Obstetrics and Gynecology 119*, 867-876.

Porcello, L.A.P. (1984). A practical guide to fad diets. *Clinics in Sports Medicine 3*, 723-729.

Porter, A.M.W. (1982). Marathon running and the caecal slap syndrome. *British Journal of Sports Medicine 16*, 178.

Porter, A.M.W. (1983). Do some marathon runners bleed into the gut? *British Medical Journal 287*, 1427.

Porter, K., J. Foster (1986). *The Mental Athlete*. Ballantine Books, New York.

Posel, D., T.D. Noakes, P. Kantor, M. Lambert, L.H. Opie (1989). Exercise training after experimental myocardial infarction increases the ventricular fibrillation threshold before and after the onset of reinfarction in the isolated rat heart. *Circulation 80*, 138-145.

Powell, K.E., H.W. Kohl, C.J. Caspersen, S.N. Blair (1986). An epidemiological perspective on the causes of running injuries. *The Physician and Sportsmedicine 14*, 100-114.

Powell, K.E., P.D. Thompson, C.J. Caspersen, J.S. Kendrick (1987). Physical activity and the incidence of coronary heart disease. *Annual Review of Public Health 8*, 253-287.

Powers, S.K., S. Dodd, J. Lawler, G. Landry, M. Kirtley, T. McKnight, S. Grinton (1988). Incidence of exercise induced hypoxemia in elite endurance athletes at sea level. *European Journal of Applied Physiology 58*, 298-302.

Powers, S.K., S. Dodd, R. Deason, R. Byrd, T. McKnight (1983). Ventilatory threshold, running economy and distance running performance of trained athletes. *Research Quarterly for Exercise and Sport 54*, 179-182.

Pretorius, D.M., T.D. Noakes, G.A. Irving, K.E. Allerton (1986). Runner's knee: What is it and how effective is conservative treatment. *The Physician and Sportsmedicine 14*, 71-81.

Prior, J.C., B. Ho Yuen, P. Clement, L. Bowie, J. Thomas (1982). Reversible luteal phase changes and infertility associated with marathon training. *Lancet 2*, 269-270.

Prior, J.C., Y. Vigna (1985). Gonadal steroids in athletic women: Contraception, complications and performance. *Sports Medicine 2*, 287-295.

Prior, J.C., Y. Vigna, N. Alojada (1986). Conditioning exercise decreases menstrual symptoms. A prospective controlled three month trial. *European Journal of Applied Physiology 55*, 349-355.

Prokop, L. (1963-64). Adrenals and sport. *Journal of Sports Medicine and Physical Fitness 3-4*, 115-121.

Protzman, R.R. (1979). Physiologic performance of women compared to men: Observations of cadets at the United States Military Academy. *American Journal of Sports Medicine 7*, 191-194.

Prud'homme, D., C. Bouchard, C. Leblanc, F. Landry, E. Fontaine (1984). Sensitivity of maximal aerobic power to training is genotype-dependent. *Medicine and Science in Sports and Exercise 16*, 489-493.

Pugh, L.G.C.E. (1958). Muscular exercise on Mount Everest. *Journal of Physiology 141*, 233-261.

Pugh, L.G.C.E. (1966). Accidental hypothermia in walkers, climbers, and campers: Report to the Medical Commission on Accident Prevention. *British Medical Journal 1*, 123-129.

Pugh, L.G.C.E. (1967a). Athletes at altitude. *Journal of Physiology 19*, 619-646.

Pugh, L.G.C.E. (1967b). Cold stress and muscular exercise, with special reference to accidental hypothermia. *British Medical Journal 2*, 333-337.

Pugh, L.G.C.E. (1970a). Oxygen uptake in track and treadmill running with observations on the effect of air resistance. *Journal of Physiology 207*, 823-835.

Pugh, L.G.C.E. (1970b). The influence of wind resistance in running and walking and the mechanical efficiency of work against horizontal or vertical forces. *Journal of Physiology 213*, 255-276.

Pugh, L.G.C.E. (1972). The gooseflesh syndrome (acute anhidrotic heat exhaustion) in long-distance runners. *British Journal of Physical Education 3* (March), IX-XII.

Pugh, L.G.C.E., J.L. Corbett, R.H. Johnson (1967). Rectal temperatures, weight losses and sweat rates in marathon running. *Journal of Applied Physiology 23*, 347-352.

Pugh, L.G.C.E., O.G. Edholm (1955). The physiology of Channel swimmers. *Lancet 2*, 761-768.

Puranen, L., L. Ala-Ketola, P. Peltokallio, J. Saarela (1975). Running and primary osteoarthritis of the hip. *British Medical Journal 2*, 424-425.

Quigley, B.M. (1982). 'Biorhythms' and men's track and field world records. *Medicine and Science in Sports and Exercise 14*, 303-307.

Quigley, T.B. (1968). Life expectancy of Ivy League rowing crews. *Journal of the American Medical Association 205*, 106.

Radford, P.F. (1985). The art and science of training and coaching athletes in late 18th and early 19th century Britain. *Proceedings of the HISPA International Congress*, J.A. Glasgow.Mangan (ed.). 1-5 July.

Ragland, D.R., R.J. Brand (1988). Type A behavior and mortality from coronary heart disease. *New England Journal of Medicine 318*, 65-69.

Raglin, J.S., W.P. Morgan (1987). Influence of exercise and quiet rest on state anxiety and blood pressure. *Medicine and Science in Sports and Exercise 19*, 456-463.

Rauramo, I., M. Forss (1988). Effect of exercise on maternal hemodynamics and placental blood flow in healthy women. *Acta Obstetrica Gynecologica Scandinavica 67*, 21-25.

Ravussin, E., C. Bogardus, K. Scheidegger, B. LaGrange, E.D. Horton, E.S. Horton (1986). Effect of elevated FFA on carbohydrate and lipid oxidation during prolonged exercise in humans. *Journal of Applied Physiology 60*, 893-900.

Raynes, R.H. (1969). The doping of athletes. *British Journal of Sports Medicine 4*, 145-162.

Reed, M.J., J.T. Brozinick, M.C. Lee, J.L. Ivy (1989). Muscle glycogen storage postexercise: Effect of mode of carbohydrate administration. *Journal of Applied Physiology 66*, 720-726.

Reeves, J. (1979). Estimating fatness. *Science 204*, 881.

Rehrer, N.J., E. Beckers, F. Brouns, F. ten Hoor, W.H.M. Saris (1989a). Exercise and training effects on gastric emptying of carbohydrate beverages. *Medicine and Science in Sports and Exercise 21*, 540-549.

Rehrer, N.J., F. Brouns, E. Beckers, F. ten Hoor, W.H.M. Saris (1990). Gastric emptying with repeated drinking during running and bicycling. *International Journal of Sports Medicine* (in press).

Rehrer, N.J., G.M.E. Janssen, F. Brouns, W.H.M. Saris (1989b). Fluid intake and gastrointestinal problems in runners competing in a 25-km race and a marathon. *International Journal of Sports Medicine 10* (Suppl 1), S22-S25.

Reidman, S. (1950). *The Physiology of Work and Play*. The Dryden Press, New York.

Ribeiro, J.P., R.A. Fielding, V. Hughes, A. Black, M.A. Bochese, H.G. Knuttgen (1985). Heart rate break point may coincide with the anaerobic and not the aerobic threshold. *International Journal of Sports Medicine 6*, 220-224.

Richards, R., D. Richards, R. Whittaker (1984). Method of predicting the number of casualties in the Sydney City-to-Surf fun runs. *Medical Journal of Australia 141*, 805-808.

Richardson, B. (1976). How to ruin an athlete. *Runner's World 11* (February), 76-77.

Richie, D.H., S.F. Kelso, P.A. Bellucci (1985). Aerobic dance injuries: A retrospective study of instructors and participants. *The Physician and Sportsmedicine 13* (February), 130-140.

Riddoch, C., T. Trinick (1988). Gastrointestinal disturbances in marathon runners. *British Journal of Sports Medicine 22*, 71-74.

Rippon, C., J. Nash, K.H. Myburgh, T.D. Noakes (1988). Abnormal eating attitude test scores predict menstrual dysfunction in lean females. *Internal Journal of Eating Disorders* (in press).

Roberts, A.D., R. Billeter, H. Howald (1982). Anaerobic muscle enzyme changes after interval training. *International Journal of Sports Medicine 3*, 18-21.

Roberts, K.M., E.G. Noble, D.B. Hayden, A.W. Taylor (1988). Simple and complex carbohydrate-rich diets and muscle glycogen content of marathon runners. *European Journal of Applied Physiology 57*, 70-74.

Robertson, J.D., R.J. Maughan, R.J.L. Davidson (1987). Faecel blood loss in response to exercise. *British Medical Journal 295*, 303-305.

Robertson, R.J., J.E. Falkel, A.L. Drash, A.M. Swank, K.F. Metz, S.A. Spungen, J.R. LeBoeuf (1987). Effect of induced alkalosis on physical work capacity during arm and leg exercise. *Ergonomics 30*, 19-31.

Robertson, R.J., R. Gilcher, K.F. Metz, C.J. Caspersen, T.G. Allison, R.A. Abbott, G.S. Skrinar, J.R. Krause, P.A. Nixon (1984). Hemoglobin concentration and aerobic work capacity in women following induced erythrocythemia. *Journal of Applied Physiology 57*, 568-575.

Robinson, S., H.T. Edwards, D.B. Dill (1937). New records in human power. *Science 85*, 409-410.

Robinson, S., P.M. Harman (1941). The effects of training and of gelatin upon certain factors which limit muscular work. *American Journal of Physiology 133*, 161-169.

Rodgers, A.L., K.G. Greyling, R.A. Irving, T.D. Noakes (1988). Crystalluria in marathon runners. II: Ultra-marathon—males and females. *Urological Research 16*, 89-93.

Rodgers, B., J. Concannon (1982). *Marathoning*. Simon and Schuster, New York.

Rogers, M.A., C. Yamamoto, J.M. Hagberg, W.H. Martin, A.A. Ehsani, J.O. Holloszy (1988). Effect of 6 d of exercise training on responses to maximal and sub-maximal exercise in middle-aged men. *Medicine and Science in Sports and Exercise 20*, 260-264.

Rontoyannis, G.P., T. Skoulis, K.N. Pavlou (1989). Energy balance in ultramarathon running. *American Journal of Clinical Nutrition 49*, 976-979.

Rooke, E.D. (1968). Benign exertional headache. *Medical Clinics of North America 52*, 801-808.

Rorabeck, C.H. (1986). Exertional tibialis posterior compartment syndrome. *Clinical Orthopaedics 208*, 61-64.

Rorabeck, C.H., P.J. Fowler, L. Nott (1988). The results of fasciotomy in the management of chronic exertional compartment syndrome. *American Journal of Sports Medicine 16*, 224-227.

Rorabeck, C.H., R.B. Bourne, P.J. Fowler (1983). The surgical treatment of exertional compartment syndromes in athletes. *Journal of Bone and Joint Surgery 65-A*, 1245-1251.

Rose, G.A., T.R. Williams (1961). Metabolic studies on large and small eaters. *British Journal of Nutrition 15*, 1-9.

Rosen, L.W., D.B. McKeag, D.O. Hough, V. Curley (1986). Pathogenic weight control behaviour in female athletes. *The Physician and Sportsmedicine 14* (January), 79-86.

Ross, C.E., D. Hayes (1988). Exercise and psychologic well-being in the community. *American Journal of Epidemiology 127*, 762-771.

Rossander, L., L. Hallberg, E. Björn-Rasmussen (1979). Absorption of iron from breakfast meals. *American Journal of Clinical Nutrition 32*, 2484-2489.

Rost, F. (1986). Stitch, the side pain of athletes. *New Zealand Journal of Medicine 99*, 469.

Roth, D.L., D.S. Holmes (1987). Influence of aerobic exercise training and relaxation training on physical and psychologic health following stressful life events. *Psychosomatic Medicine 49*, 355-365.

Rothwell, N.J., M.J. Stock (1981). Regulation of energy balance. *Annual Review of Nutrition 1*, 235-256.

Round, J.M., D.A. Jones, G. Cambridge (1987). Cellular infiltrates in human skeletal muscle: Exercise induced damage as a model for inflammatory muscle disease? *Journal of Neurological Science 82*, 1-11.

Rovere, G.D. (1987). Low back pain in athletes. *The Physician and Sportsmedicine 15*, 105-117.

Rudman, D., P.J. Williams (1983). Megadose vitamins. Use and misuse. *The New England Journal of Medicine 309*, 488-489.

Rushall, B.S. (1979). *Psyching in Sport. The Psychological Preparation for Serious Competition in Sport.* Pelham Books, London.

Russell, J.B., D. Mitchell, P.I. Musey, D.C. Collins (1984). The relationship of exercise to anovulatory cycles in female athletes: Hormonal and physical characteristics. *Obstetrics and Gynecology 63*, 452-456.

Ryan, A.J. (1978). Injections for tendon injuries: Cure or cause. *The Physician and Sportsmedicine 6* (September), 39.

Ryan, A.J. (1983). Overtraining of athletes. Round table discussion. *The Physician and Sportsmedicine 11* (June), 93-110.

Ryan, A.J., T.L. Bleiler, J.E. Carter, C.V. Gisolfi (1989). Gastric emptying during prolonged cycling exercise in the heat. *Medicine and Science in Sports and Exercise 21*, 51-58.

Ryder, H.W., H.J. Carr, P. Herget (1976). Future performance in footracing. *Scientific American 234* (June), 108-119.

Sachs, M.L. (1984a). The mind of the runner: Cognitive strategies used during running. In *Running as Therapy: An Integrated Approach*, M.L. Sachs, G.W. Buffone (eds.). University of Nebraska Press, Lincoln, Nebraska, pp. 288-303.

Sachs, M.L. (1984b). The runner's high. In *Running as Therapy: An Integrated Approach*, M.L. Sachs, G.W. Buffone (eds.). University of Nebraska Press, Lincoln, Nebraska, pp. 273-287.

Sachs, M.L., D. Pargman (1984). Running addiction. In *Running as Therapy: An Integrated Approach*, M.L. Sachs, G.W. Buffone (eds.). University of Nebraska Press, Lincoln, Nebraska, pp. 231-252.

Sachs, M.L., G.W. Buffone (1984). *Running as Therapy: An Integrated Approach*. University of Nebraska Press, Lincoln, Nebraska.

Sacks, M.H. (1979). A psychodynamic overview of sport. *Psychiatric Annals 9*, 127-133.

Sacks, M.H. (1981). Running addiction: A clinical report. In *The Psychology of Running*, M.H. Sacks, M.L. Sachs (eds.). Human Kinetics, Champaign, Illinois.

Sady, S.P., M.W. Carpenter (1989). Aerobic exercise during pregnancy. Special considerations. *Sports Medicine 7*, 357-375.

Sady, S.P., M.W. Carpenter, P.D. Thompson, M.A. Sady, B. Haydon, D.R. Coustan (1989). Cardiovascular response to cycle exercise during and after pregnancy. *Journal of Applied Physiology 66*, 336-341.

Sahlin, K., J. Henriksson (1984). Buffer capacity and lactate accumulation in skeletal muscle of trained and untrained men. *Acta Physiologica Scandinavica 122*, 331-339.

Sakhaee, K., S. Nigam, P. Snell, M.C. Hsu, C.Y. Pak (1987). Assessment of the pathogenetic role of physical exercise in renal stone formation. *Journal of Clinical Endocrinology and Metabolism 65*, 974-979.

Salazar, A. (1981). Quoted by Olsen E. Alberto Salazar: Body and soul. *The Runner 3* (February), 24-31.

Salminen, A., K. Hongisto, V. Vihko (1985). Lysosomal changes related to exercise injuries and training-induced protection in mouse skeletal muscle. *Acta Physiologica Scandinavica 120*, 15-19.

Saltin, B. (1973). Metabolic fundamentals in exercise. *Medicine and Science in Sports 5*, 137-146.

Saltin, B. (1981). Muscle fibre recruitment and metabolism in prolonged exhaustive dynamic exercise. *Ciba Foundation Symposium 82*, 41-58, Pitman Medical, London.

Saltin, B., J. Henriksson, E. Hygaard, P. Andersen (1977). Fibre types and metabolic potentials of skeletal muscles in sedentary man and endurance runners. *Annals of the New York Academy of Sciences 301*, 3-29.

Saltin, B., J. Karlsson (1971). Muscle glycogen utilization during work of different intensities. In *Advances in Experimental Medicine and Biology*, B. Pernow, B. Saltin (eds.). Plenum Press, New York, 11, pp. 289-299.

Saltin, B., P-O. Astrand (1967). Maximal oxygen uptake in athletes. *Journal of Applied Physiology 23*, 353-358.

Saltin, B., P.D. Gollnick (1983). Skeletal muscle adaptability: Significance for metabolism and performance. In *Handbook of Physiology, Section 10, Skeletal Muscle*, L.D. Peachey, R.H. Adrian, S.R. Geiger (eds.). American Physiological Society, Bethesda, Maryland.

Samet, J.M., T.W. Chick, C.A. Howard (1982). Running-related morbidity: A community survey. *Annals of Sports Medicine 1*, 30-34.

Samorajski, T., C. Delaney, L. Durham, J.M. Ordy, J.A. Johnson, W.P. Dunlop (1985). Effect of exercise on longevity, body weight, locomotor performance, and passive avoidance memory of C57BL/6J mice. *Neurobiology of Aging 6*, 17-24.

Sanborn, C.F., B.H. Albrecht, W.W. Wagner (1987). Athletic amenorrhea: Lack of association with body fat. *Medicine and Science in Sports and Exercise 19*, 207-212.

Sanborn, C.F., B.J. Martin, W.W. Wagner (1982). Is athletic amenorrhoea specific to runners? *American Journal of Obstetrics and Gynecology 143*, 859-861.

Sandell, R.C., M.D. Pascoe, T.D. Noakes (1988). Factors associated with collapse following ultramarathon foot races. A preliminary study. *The Physician and Sportsmedicine 16* (September), 86-94.

Saris, W.H.M., M.A. van Erp-Baart, F. Brouns, K.R. Westerterp, F. ten Hoor (1989). Study on food intake and energy expenditure during extreme sustained exercise: The Tour de France. *International Journal of Sports Medicine 10*, S26-S31.

Satabin, P., P. Portero, G. Defer, J. Bricout, C-Y. Guezennec (1987). Metabolic and hormonal responses to lipid and carbohydrate diets during exercise in man. *Medicine and Science in Sports and Exercise 19*, 218-223.

Sawka, M.N., R.C. Dennis, R.R. Gonzalez, A.J. Young, S.R. Muza, J.W. Martin, C.B. Wenger, R.P. Francesconi, K.B. Pandolf, C.R. Valeri (1987). Influence of polycythemia on blood volume and thermoregulation during exercise-heat stress. *Journal of Applied Physiology 62*, 912-918.

Scharf, S.M., H. Bark, D. Heimer, A. Cohen, P.T. Macklem (1984a). "Second wind" during inspiratory loading. *Medicine and Science in Sports and Exercise 16*, 87-91.

Scharf, S.M., P. Bye, R. Pardy, P.T. Macklem (1984b). Dyspnea, fatigue and second wind. *American Review of Respiratory Diseases 129* (Suppl.), S88-S89.

Schatzkin, A., R.N. Hoover, P.P. Taylor, R.G. Ziegler, C.L. Carter, D.B. Larson, L.M. Licitra (1987a). Serum cholesterol and cancer in the Nhanes 1 epidemiologic followup study. *Lancet 2*, 298-301.

Schatzkin, A., D.Y. Jones, R.N. Hoover, P.R. Taylor, L.A. Brinton, R.G. Ziegler, E.B. Harvey, C.L. Carter, L.M. Licitra, M.C. Dufour, D.B. Larson (1987b). Alcohol consumption and breast cancer in the epidemiologic follow-up study of the First National Health and Nutrition Examination Survey. *New England Journal of Medicine 316*, 1169-1173.

Schedl, H.P., J.A. Clifton (1963). Solute and water absorption by the human small intestine. *Nature 199*, 1264-1267.

Scheffer, A.L., K.F. Austen (1980). Exercise-induced anaphylaxis. *Journal of Allergy and Clinical Immunology 66*, 106-111.

Schelegle, E.S., W.C. Adams (1986). Reduced exercise time in competitive simulations consequent to low level ozone exposure. *Medicine and Science in Sports and Exercise 18*, 408-414.

Schiff, H.B., E.T.M. MacSearraigh, J.C. Kallmeyer (1978). Myoglobinuria, rhabdomyolysis and marathon running. *Quarterly Journal of Medicine 47*, 463-472.

Schmidt, V., K. Bruck (1981). Effect of precooling maneuver on body temperature and exercise performance. *Journal of Applied Physiology 50*, 772-778.

Schoene, R.B., S. Lahiri, P.H. Hackett, R.M. Peters, J.S. Milledge, C.J. Pizzo, F.H. Sarnquist, S.K. Boyer, D.J. Graber, K.H. Maret, J.B. West (1984). Relationship of hypoxic ventilatory response to exercise performance on Mount Everest. *Journal of Applied Physiology 56*, 1478-1483.

Schomer, H.H. (1984). *Mental Strategies and the Perception of Effort: Implications for the Psychological Preparation of Marathon Runners*. PhD thesis. University of Cape Town, South Africa.

Schomer, H.H. (1986). Mental strategies and the perception of effort of marathon runners. *International Journal of Sports Psychology 17*, 41-59.

Schomer, H.H. (1987). Mental strategy training programme for marathon runners. *International Journal of Sports Psychology 18*, 133-151.

Schulz, R., C. Curnow (1988). Peak performance and age among superathletes: Track and field, swimming, baseball, tennis, and golf. *Journal of Gerontology 43*, P113-P120.

Schwane, J.A., R.B. Armstrong (1983). Effect of training on skeletal muscle injury from downhill running in rats. *Journal of Applied Physiology 55*, 969-975.

Schwane, J.A., S.R. Johnson, C.B. Vandenakker, R.B. Armstrong (1983). Delayed-onset muscular soreness and plasma CPK and LDH activities after down-hill running. *Medicine and Science in Sports and Exercise 15*, 51-56.

Schwane, J.A., J.S. Williams, J.H. Sloan (1987). Effects of training on delayed muscle soreness and serum creatine kinase activity after running. *Medicine and Science in Sports and Exercise 19*, 584-590.

Schwartz, B., D.C. Cumming, E. Riordan, M. Selye, S.S.C. Yen, R.W. Rebar (1981). Exercise-induced amenorrhea: A distinct entity? *American Journal of Obstetrics and Gynecology 141*, 662-670.

Schweiger, U., F. Herrmann, R. Laessle, W. Riedel, M. Schweiger, K-M. Pirke (1988). Caloric intake, stress, and menstrual function in athletes. *Fertility and Sterility 49*, 447-450.

Scott, V., K. Gijsbers (1981). Pain perception in competitive swimmers. *British Medical Journal 283*, 91-93.

Scragg, R., A. Stewart, R. Jackson, R. Beaglehole (1987). Alcohol and exercise in myocardial infarction and sudden coronary death in men and women. *American Journal of Epidemiology 126*, 77-85.

Scrimgeour, A.G., T.D. Noakes, B. Adams, K. Myburgh (1986). The influence of weekly training distance on fractional utilization of maximum aerobic capacity in marathon and ultramarathon runners. *European Journal of Applied Physiology 55*, 202-209.

Scully, T.J., G. Besterman (1982). Stress fracture—a preventable training injury. *Military Medicine 147*, 285-287.

Segal, K.R., B. Gutin, J. Albu, F.X. Pi-Sunyer (1987). Thermic effects of food and exercise in lean and obese men of similar lean body mass. *American Journal of Physiology 252*, E110-E117.

Segal, K.R., B. Gutin, A.M. Nyman, F.X. Pi-Sunyer (1985). Thermic effect of food at rest, during exercise, and after exercise in lean and obese men of similar body weight. *Journal of Clinical Investigations 76*, 1107-1112.

Selby, G.R., E.R. Eichner (1986). Endurance swimming, intravascular hemolysis, anemia and iron depletion. New perspective on athlete's anemia. *American Journal of Medicine 81*, 791-794.

Selye, H. (1950). *The physiology and pathology of exposure to systematic stress*. Acta Inc., Montreal.

Selye, H. (1957). *The Stress of Life*. Longmans, Green and Co., London.

Severson, R.K., A.M. Nomura, J.S. Grove, G.N. Stemmermann (1989). A propsective analysis of physical activity and cancer. *American Journal of Epidemiology 130*, 522-529.

Shangold, M., R. Freeman, B. Thysen, M. Gatz (1979). The relationship between long-distance running, plasma progesterone and luteal phase length. *Fertility and Sterility 31*, 130-133.

Shangold, M.M. (1980). Sports and menstrual function. *The Physician and Sportsmedicine 8* (August), 66-71.

Shangold, M.M. (1986). How I manage exercise-related menstrual disturbances. *Physician and Sports Medicine 14* (March), 113-120.

Shangold, M.M. (1988). Exercise-induced changes in uterine artery blood flow, as measured by Doppler ultrasound, in pregnant subjects. *American Journal of Perinatology 5*, 187-188.

Shangold, M.M., H.S. Levine (1982). The effect of marathon training upon menstrual function. *American Journal of Obstetrics and Gynecology 143*, 862-869.

Sharman, I. (1971). The effects of vitamin E and training on physiological function and athletic performance in adolescent swimmers. *British Journal of Nutrition 26*, 265-276.

Sharp, M.W., R.R. Reilley (1975). The relationship of aerobic physical fitness to selected personality traits. *Journal of Clinical Psychology 31*, 428-430.

Sharp, R.L., D.L. Costill, W.J. Fink, D.S. King (1986). Effects of eight weeks of bicycle ergometer sprint training on human muscle buffer capacity. *International Journal of Sports Medicine 7*, 13-17.

Sheehan, G.A. (1972). *Encyclopedia of Athletic Medicine*. Runner's World Publications, Mountain View, California.

Sheehan, G.A. (1973). Longevity of athletes. *American Heart Journal 86*, 425-426.

Sheehan, G.A. (1975). *Dr. Sheehan on Running*. World Publications, Mountain View, California.

Sheehan, G.A. (1978a). *Dr. George Sheehan's Medical Advice for Runners*. World Publications, Mountain View, California.

Sheehan, G.A. (1978b). *Running and Being. The Total Experience*. Simon and Schuster, New York.

Sheehan, G.A. (1980). *This Running Life*. Simon and Schuster, New York.

Sheehan, G.A. (1983). *How to Feel Great 24 Hours a Day*. Simon and Schuster, New York.

Sheffer, A.L. (1988). Anaphylaxis. *Journal of Allergy and Clinical Immunology 81*, 1048-1050.

Sheldon, W., C.W. Dupertuis, E. McDermott (1954). *Atlas of Men*. Harper, New York.

Sheldon, W.H., S.A. Stevens (1945). *The Varieties of Human Temperament*, 3rd Edition. Harper, New York.

Shellock, F.G., W.E. Prentice (1985). Warming-up and stretching for improved physical performance and prevention of sports-related injuries. *Sports Medicine 2*, 267-278.

Shephard, R.J. (1981). *Physiology and Biochemistry of Exercise*. Praeger Publishers, New York.

Shephard, R.J., T. Kavanagh (1978). Fluid and mineral needs of middle-aged and postcoronary distance runners. *The Physician and Sportsmedicine 6* (May), 90-102.

Sherman, M.M. (1983). Are exercise ailments cyclical? *New England Journal of Medicine 309*, 858-859.

Sherman, W.M., G. Brodowicz, D.A. Wright, W.K. Allen, J. Simonsen, A. Dernbach (1989). Effects of 4 h preexercise carbohydrate feedings on cycling performance. *Medicine and Science in Sports and Exercise 21*, 598-604.

Sherman, W.M., D.L. Costill, W.J. Fink, F.C. Hagerman, L.E. Armstrong, T.F. Murray (1983). Effect of a 42.2 km footrace and subsequent rest or exercise on muscle glycogen and enzymes. *Journal of Applied Physiology 55*, 1219-1224.

Sherman, W.M., D.L. Costill, W.J. Fink, J.M. Miller (1981). Effect of exercise-diet manipulation on muscle glycogen and its subsequent utilization during performance. *International Journal of Sports Medicine 2*, 114-118.

Sherwin, R.W., D.N. Wentworth, J.A. Cutler, S.B. Hulley, L.H. Kuller, J. Stamler (1987). Serum cholesterol levels and cancer mortality in 361 662 men screened for the multiple risk factor intervention trial. *Journal of the American Medical Association 257*, 943-948.

Shiff, H.B., E.T.M. MacSearraigh, J.C. Kallmeyer (1978). Myoglobinuria, rhabdomyolysis and marathon running. *Quarterly Journal of Medicine 47*, 463-472.

Shiraki, K., T. Yamada, H. Yoshimura (1977). Relation of protein nutrition to the reduction of red blood cells induced by physical training. *Japanese Journal of Physiology 27*, 413-421.

Short, S.H., W.R. Short (1983). Four-year study of university athletes' dietary intake. *Journal of the American Dietitic Association 82*, 632-645.

Shorter, F., M. Bloom (1984). *Olymic Gold. A Runner's Life and Times*. Houghton Mifflin, Boston.

Shorter, F., M. Bloom (1984). *Olympic Gold. A Runner's Life and Times*. Houghton Mifflin, Boston.

Shrubb, A. (1909). *Long Distance Running and Training*. Imperial News, Toronto.

Shrubb, A. (1910). *Running and Cross-Country Running*. Health and Strength, London.

Siegel, A.J. (1980). Exercise-induced anaphylaxis. *The Physician and Sportsmedicine 8* (January), 95-98.

Siegel, A.J., C.H. Hennekens, H.S. Solomon, B. Van Boeckel (1979). Exercise-related hematuria. *Journal of the American Medical Association 241*, 391-392.

Silverstein, S.R., D.A. Frommer, B. Dobozin, P. Rosen (1986). Celery-dependent exercise-induced anaphylaxis. *Journal of Emergency Medicine 4*, 195-199.

Simoneau, J.A., G. Lortie, M.R. Boulay, M. Marcotte, M.C. Thibault, C. Bouchard (1986). Inheritance of human skeletal muscle and anaerobic capacity adaptation to high-intensity intermittent training. *International Journal of Sports Medicine 7*, 167-171.

Sims, E.A.H. (1976). Experimental obesity, dietary-induced thermogenesis, and their clinical implications. *Clinics in Endocrinology and Metabolism 5*, 377-395.

Sims, E.A.H., E. Danforth, E.S. Horton, G.A. Bray, J.A. Glennon, L.B. Sallans (1973). Endocrine and metabolic effects of experimental obesity in man. *Recent Progress in Hormonal Research 29*, 457-496.

Sinclair, J.D. (1951). Stitch: The side pain of athletes. *New Zealand Medical Journal 50*, 607-612.

Singh, R., R.S. Crampton, J.A. Horgan (1975). Physical, electocardiographic, echocardiographic and hemodynamic features of the athletic heart syndrome. *Clinical Research 23*, 8A.

Siskovich, D.S., N.S. Weiss, R.H. Fletcher, T. Lasky (1984a). The incidence of primary cardiac arrest during vigorous exercise. *New England Journal of Medicine 311*, 874-877.

Siskovich, D.S., N.S. Weiss, R.H. Fletcher, V.J. Schoenbach, E.H. Wagner (1984b). Habitual vigorous exercise and primary cardiac arrest: Effect of other risk factors on the relationship. *Journal of Chronic Diseases 37*, 625-631.

Siskovich, D.S., N.S. Weiss, A.P. Hallstrom, T.S. Inui, D.R. Peterson (1982). Physical activity and primary cardiac arrest. *Journal of the American Medical Association 248*, 3113-3117.

Sjödin, B., I. Jacobs (1981). Onset of blood lactate accumulation and marathon running performance. *International Journal of Sports Medicine 2*, 23-26.

Sjödin, B., I. Jacobs, J. Karlsson (1981). Onset of blood lactate accumulation and enzyme activities in M. vastus lateralis in man. *International Journal of Sports Medicine 2*, 166-170.

Sjödin, B., R. Schele (1982). Oxygen cost of treadmill running in long distance runners. In *Exercise and Sport Biology* P.V. Komi (ed.). Human Kinetics, Champaign, Illinois, pp. 61-67.

Sjoüdin, B., J. Svedenhag (1985). Applied physiology of marathon running. *Sports Medicine 2*, 83-99.

Sjogaard, G., R.P. Adams, B. Saltin (1985). Water and ion shifts in skeletal muscle of humans with intense dynamic knee extension. *American Journal of Physiology 248*, R190-F196.

Sjostrom, M., J. Friden, B. Ekblom (1987). Endurance, what is it? Muscle morphology after an extremely long distance run. *Acta Physiologica Scandinavica 130*, 513-520.

Sjostrom, M., C. Johansson, R. Lorentzon (1988). Muscle pathomorphology in m. quadriceps of marathon runners. Early signs of strain disease or functional adaptation? *Acta Physiologica Scandinavica 132*, 537-542.

Slattery, M.L., M.C. Schumacher, K.R. Smith, D.W. West, N. Abd-Elghany (1988). Physical activity, diet, and risk of colon cancer in Utah. *American Journal of Epidemiology 128*, 989-999.

Slovic, P. (1977). Empirical study of training and performance in the marathon. *Research Quarterly 48*, 769-777.

Smart, G.W., J.E. Taunton, D.B. Clement (1980). Achilles tendon disorders in runners—a review. *Medicine and Science in Sports and Exercise 12*, 231-243.

Smith, D.A., T.V. O'Donnell (1984). The time course during 36 weeks' endurance training of changes in V̇O₂max and anaerobic threshold as determined with a new computerized method. *Clinical Sciences 67*, 229-236.

Smith, D.W., S.K. Claren, M.A.S. Harvey (1978). Hyperthermia as a possible teratogenic agent. *Journal of Pediatrics 92*, 878-883.

Smith, E.L., C. Gilligan, M. McAdam, C.P. Ensign, P.E. Smith (1989). Deterring bone loss by exercise intervention in premenopausal and postmenopausal women. *Calcified Tissues International 44*, 312-321.

Smith, E.L., D.M. Raab (1986). Osteoporosis and physical activity. *Acta Medica Scandinavica 711* (suppl.), 149-156.

Smith, E.L., P.E. Smith, C.J. Ensign, M.M Shea (1984). Bone involution decrease in exercising middle-aged women. *Calcified Tissues International 36* (suppl. 1), S129-S138.

Smith, L.S., T.E. Clarke, C.L. Hamill, F. Santopietro (1986). The effects of soft and semi-rigid orthoses upon rearfoot movement in running. *Journal of the American Podiatric Medical Association 76*, 227-233.

Smith, R.E. (1984). The dynamics and prevention of stress-induced burnout in athletics. *Primary Care 11*, 115-127.

Smuts, J.C. (1951). *The Thoughts of General Smuts*. Juta, Cape Town, South Africa.

Snider, M.P., W.G. Clancy, A.A. McBeatt (1983). Plantar fascia release for chronic plantar fasciitis in runners. *American Journal of Sports Medicine 11*, 215-219.

Snyder, A.C., D.R. Lamb, C.P. Salm, M.D. Judge, E.D. Aberle, E.W. Mills (1984). Myofibrillar protein degradation after eccentric exercise. *Experientia 40*, 69-70.

Snyder, D.K., B.R. Carruth (1984). Current controversies: Exercising during pregnancy. *Journal of Adolescent Health Care 5*, 34-36.

Sohar, E., R. Adar (1964). Sodium requirements in Israel under conditions of work in hot climate. *Unesco Arid Zone Research 24*, 55-62.

Sohn, R.S., L.J. Micheli (1984). The effect of running on the pathogenesis of osteoarthritis of the hips and knees. *Medicine and Science in Sports and Exercise 16*, 150.

Sole, C.C., T.D. Noakes (1989). Faster gastric emptying for glucose-polymer and fructose solutions than for glucose in humans. *European Journal of Applied Physiology 58*, 605-612.

Sonstegard, D.A., L.S. Matthews, H. Kaufer (1978). The surgical replacement of the knee joint. *Scientific American 238* (January), 44-51.

Sorensen, K.E., K.G. Borlum (1986). Fetal heart function in response to short-term maternal exercise. *British Journal of Obstetrics and Gynaecology 93*, 310-313.

Sorock, G.S., T.L. Bush, A.L. Golden, L.P. Fried, B. Breuer, W.E. Hale (1988). Physical activity and fracture risk in a free-living elderly cohort. *Journal of Gerontology 43*, M134-M139.

South African Runner (1987a). Fast and furious for Matthews. *South African Runner* (September), 33.

South African Runner (1987b). Xolile Yawa. *South African Runner* (June), 45.

Speroff, L., D.B. Redwine (1980). Exercise and menstrual function. *The Physican and Sportsmedicine 8* (May), 42-52.

Spriet, L.L. (1987). Muscle pH, glycolytic ATP turnover and the onset of fatigue. In *Exercise benefits, Limits and Adaptations*, D. Macleod, R. Maughan, M. Nimmo, T. Reilly, C. Williams (eds.). E. & F. N. Spon Limited, London, pp. 85-102.

Spriet, L.L., N. Gledhill, A.B. Froese, D.L. Wilkes (1986). Effect of graded erythrocythemia on cardiovascular and metabolic responses to exercise. *Journal of Applied Physiology 61*, 1942-1948.

Squires, R.W., E.R. Buskirk (1982). Aerobic capacity during acute exposure to simulated altitude, 914 to 2,286 metres. *Medicine and Science in Sports and Exercise 14*, 36-40.

Squires, R.W. (1982). *Improving Your Running*. Stephen Greene Press, Lexington, Kentucky.

Stacoff, A., J. Denoth, X. Kaelin, E. Stuessi (1988). Running injuries and shoe construction: Some possible relationships. *International Journal of Sports Biomechanics 4*, 342-357.

Stager, J.M., B. Ritchie-Flanagan, D. Robertshaw (1984a). Reversibility of amenorrhea in athletes. *New England Journal of Medicine 310*, 51-52.

Stager, J.M., D. Robertshaw, E. Miescher (1984b). Delayed menarche in swimmers in relation to age at onset of training and athletic performance. *Medicine and Science in Sports and Exercise 16*, 550-555.

Stamford, B.A., S. Matter, R.D. Fell, S. Sady, P. Papanek, M.K. Cresanta (1984a). Cigarette smoking, physical activity, and alcohol consumption: Relationship to blood lipids and lipoproteins in premenopausal females. *Metabolism 33*, 585-590.

Stamford, B.A., S. Matter, R.D. Fell, S. Sady, P. Papanek, M.K. Cresanta (1984b). Cigarette smoking, exercise and high density lipoprotein cholesterol. *Atherosclerosis 52*, 73-83.

Stamler, J., D. Wentworth, J.D. Neaton (1986). Is relationship between serum cholesterol and risk of premature death from coronary heart disease continuous and graded? *Journal of the American Medical Association 256*, 2823-2828.

Stampfl, F. (1955). *Franz Stampfl on Running*. Herbert Jenkins, London.

Stanish, W.D., S. Curwin, M. Rubinovich (1985). Tendinitis: The analysis and treatment for running. *Clinics in Sports Medicine 4*, 593-609.

Stanish, W.D., R.M. Rubinovich, S. Curwin (1986). Eccentric exercise in chronic tendinitis. *Clinical Orthopedics 208*, 65-68.

Starek, P.J.K. (1982). Athletic performance in children with cardiovascular problems. *The Physician and Sportsmedicine 10* (February), 78-89.

Staron, R.S., R.S. Hikida, F.C. Hagerman, G.A. Dudley, T.F. Murray (1984). Human skeletal muscle fibre type adaptability to various workloads. *Journal of Histochemistry and Cytochemistry 32*, 146-152.

Stephens, T. (1987). Secular trends in adult physical activity: Exercise boom or bust? *Research Quarterly for Exercise and Sport 58*, 94-105.

Stephens, T. (1988). Physical activity and mental health in the United States and Canada: Evidence from four population surveys. *Preventive Medicine 17*, 35-47.

Stephenson, L.A., M.A. Kolka, J.E. Wilkerson (1982a). Metabolic and thermoregulatory responses to exercise during the human menstrual cycle. *Medicine and Science in Sports and Exercise 14*, 270-275.

Stephenson, L.A., M.A. Kolka, J.E. Wilkerson (1982b). Perceived exertion and anaerobic threshold during the menstrual cycle. *Medicine and Science in Sports and Exercise 14*, 218-222.

Stevens, E.D. (1983). Effect of the weight of athletic clothing in distance running by amateur athletes. *Journal of Sports Medicine and Physical Fitness 23*, 185-190.

Stewart, G.A., J.E. Steel, A.H. Toyne, M.J. Stewart (1972). Observations on the haematology and iron and protein intake of Australian Olympic athletes. *Medical Journal of Australia 2*, 1339-1343.

Stewart, J.G., D.A. Ahlquist, D.B. McGill, D.M. Ilstrup, S. Schwartz, R.A. Owen (1984). Gastro-intestinal blood loss and anemia in runners. *Annals of Internal Medicine 101*, 843-845.

Stones, M.J., A. Kozma (1986). Age by distance effects in running and swimming records: A note on methodology. *Experiments in Aging Research 12*, 203-206.

Strachan, A.F., T.D. Noakes, G. Kotzenberg, A.E. Nel, F.C. De Beer (1984). Creactive protein levels during long-distance running. *British Medical Journal 289*, 1249-1251.

Stripe, P. (1982a). Running economy on air-soles. *Nike Research Newsletter 1* (1), 1-2.

Stripe, P. (1982b). The effect of shoe weight on the aerobic demands of running. *Nike Research Newsletter 1* (4), 1-2.

Stripe, P. (1983). Rearfoot control, cushioning and shoe design. *Nike Research Newsletter 2* (1), 1-3.

Stuart, M.K., E.T. Howley, L.B. Gladden, R.H. Cox (1981). Efficiency of trained subjects differing in maximal oxygen uptake and type of training. *Journal of Applied Physiology 50*, 444-449.

Stunkard, A.J., T.I.A. Sorensen, C. Hanis, T.W. Teasdale, R. Chakraborty, W.J. Schull, F. Schulsinger (1986). An adoption study of human obesity. *New England Journal of Medicine 314*, 193-198.

Styf, J., L. Korner, M. Suurkula (1987). Intramuscular pressure and muscle blood flow during exercise in chronic compartment syndrome. *Journal of Bone and Joint Surgery 69-B*, 301-305.

Suboticanec-Buzina, K., R. Buzina, G. Brubacher, J. Sapunar, S. Christeller, N. Milanovic (1984). Vitamin C status and physical working capacity in adolescents. *International Journal of Vitamin and Nutrition Research 54*, 55-60.

Subotnick, S.I. (1979). *Cures for Common Running Injuries*. Macmillan, New York.

Sullivan, S.N. (1981). The gastro-intestinal symptoms of running. *New England Journal of Medicine 304*, 915.

Sullivan, S.N., M.C. Champion, N.D. Christofides, T.E. Adrian, S.R. Bloom (1984). Gastrointestinal regulatory peptide responses in long-distance runners. *The Physician and Sportsmedicine 12* (July), 77-82.

Sundberg, S., R. Elovainio (1982). Cardiorespiratory function in competitive endurance runners aged 12-16 years compared with ordinary boys. *Acta Paediatrica Scandinavica 71*, 987-992.

Surbey, G.D., G.M. Andrew, F.W. Cervenko, P.P. Hamilton (1984). Effects of naloxone on exercise performance. *Journal of Applied Physiology 57*, 674-679.

Sutker, A.N., D.W. Jackson, J.W. Pagliano (1981). Iliotibial band syndrome in distance runners. *Physician and Sportsmedicine 9* (October), 69-73.

Sutton, G. (1984). Hamstrung by hamstring strains: A review of the literature. *Journal of Orthopaedic and Sports Physical Therapy 5*, 184-195.

Sutton, J.R. (1972). Community jogging vs. arduous racing. *New England Journal of Medicine 286*, 951.

Sutton, J.R., O. Bar-Or (1980). Thermal illness in fun running. *American Heart Journal 100*, 778-781.

Sutton, J.R., N.L. Jones, L.G.C.E. Pugh (1983). Exercise at altitude. *Annual Review of Physiology 45*, 427-437.

Svedenhag, J., B. Sjödin (1985). Physiological characteristics of elite male runners in and off-season. *Canadian Journal of Applied Sport Sciences 10*, 127-133.

Talbott, J.H. (1935). Heat cramps. *Medicine 14*, 323-376.

Tanaka, K., Y. Matsuura (1984). Marathon performance, anaerobic threshold, and onset of blood lactate accumulation. *Journal of Applied Physiology 57*, 640-643.

Tanaka, K., Y. Matsuura, S. Kumagai, A. Matsuzaka, K. Hirakoba, K. Asano (1983). Relationship of anaerobic threshold and onset of blood lactate accumulation with endurance performance. *European Journal of Applied Physiology 52*, 51-56.

Tanaka, K., Y. Matsuura, A. Matsuzaka, K. Hirakoba, S. Kumagai, S.O. Sun, K. Asano (1984). A longitudinal assessment of anaerobic threshold and distance running performance. *Medicine and Science in Sports and Exercise 16*, 278-282.

Tarnopolsky, M.A., J.D. MacDougall, S.A. Atkinson (1988). Influence of protein intake and training status on nitrogen balance and lean body mass. *Journal of Applied Physiology 64*, 187-193.

Tarrant, J. (1979). *The Ghost Runner*. Athletics Weekly, Rochester, England.

Taunton, J.E., D.B. Clement, G.W. Smart, J.P. Wiley, K.L. McNicol (1985). A triplanar electrogoniometer investigation of running mechanics in runners with compensatory overpronation. *Canadian Journal of Applied Sports Science 10*, 104-115.

Taylor, H.L., A. Henschel, O. Mickelsen, A. Keys (1943). The effect of the sodium chloride intake on the work performance of man during exposure to dry heat and experimental heat exhaustion. *American Journal of Physiology 140*, 439-451.

Taylor, H.R., S.K. West, F.S. Rosenthal, B. Munoz, H.S. Newland, H. Abbey, E.A. Emmett (1988). Effect of ultraviolet radiation on cataract formation. *New England Journal of Medicine 319*, 1429-1433.

Temple, C. (1980). *Cross Country and Road Running*. Stanley Paul, London.

Temple, C. (1981). *Challenge of the Marathon*. Stanley Paul, London.

Terrados, N., J. Melichna, C. Sylven, E. Jansson, L. Kaijser (1988). Effects of training at simulated altitude on performance and muscle metabolic capacity in competitive road cyclists. *European Journal of Applied Physiology 57*, 203-209.

Terray, L. (1975). *Conquistadors of the useless. From the Alps to Annapurna*. Victor Gollancz Ltd., London.

Thaxton, L. (1982). Physiological and psychological effects of short-term exercise addiction on habitual runners. *Journal of Sports Psychology 4*, 73-80.

Thom, W. (1813). *Pedestrianism, or an Account of the Performance of Celebrated Pedestrians During the Last Century: With a Full Narrative of Captain Barclay's Public and Private Matches and an Essay on Training*. Brown and Frost, Aberdeen, Scotland.

Thompson, D.A., L.A. Wolfe, R. Eikelboom (1988). Acute effects of exercise intensity on appetite in young men. *Medicine and Science in Sports and Exercise 20*, 222-227.

Thompson, P.D. (1982). Cardiovascular hazards of physical activity. *Exercise and Sports Science Reviews*. Terjung R.L. (ed.). Franklin Institute Publishers, Philadelphia. 10, pp. 208-235.

Thompson, P.D., E.J. Funk, R.A. Carleton, W.Q. Sturner (1982). Incidence of death during jogging in Rhode Island from 1975 to 1980. *Journal of the American Medical Association 247*, 2535-2538.

Thompson, P.D., B. Lazarus, E. Cullinane, L.O. Henderson, T. Musliner, R. Eshleman, P.N. Herbert (1983). Exercise, diet, or physical characteristics as determinants of HDL-levels in endurance athletes. *Atherosclerosis 46*, 333-339.

Thomson, J.A., H.J. Green, M.E. Houston (1979). Muscle glycogen depletion patterns in fast twitch fibre subgroups of man during submaximal and supramaximal exercise. *Pflügers Archives 379*, 105-108.

Thoreau, H.D. (1862). In *The Portable Thoreau (1977)*. Penguin Books, New York.

Thorstensson, A. (1986). Effects of moderate external loading on the aerobic demand of submaximal running in men and 10 year-old boys. *European Journal of Applied Physiology 55*, 569-574.

Tin-May-Than, Ma-Win-May, Khin-Sann-Aung, M. Mya-Tu (1978). The effect of vitamin B_{12} on physical performance capacity. *British Journal of Nutrition 40*, 269-273.

Tobin, C. (1984). *New Zealand's Olympic Gold Miler*. John McIndoe Limited, Dunedin, New Zealand.

Topp, R. (1989). Effect of relaxation or exercise on undergraduates' test anxiety. *Perceptive and Motor Skills 69*, 35-41.

Tremblay, A., J.P. Despres, C. Bouchard (1985). The effects of exercise-training on energy balance and adipose tissue morphology and metabolism. *Sports Medicine 2*, 223-233.

Tucker, A., J.M. Stager, L. Cordain (1984). Arterial O_2 saturation and maximum O_2 consumption in moderate-altitude runners exposed to sea level and 3,050 m. *Journal of the American Medical Association 252*, 2867-2871.

Turnbull, A. (1989). The race for a better running shoe. *New Scientist 15* July, 42-44.

Turnbull, R. (1985). Turnbull and Temane—The team triumphant. *South African Runner* (November), 26-27.

Ullyot, J. (1976). Women's secret weapon. In *Van Aaken Method*, E. Van Aaken (ed.). World Publications, Mountain View, California.

Uram, P. (1980). *The Complete Stretching Book*. Anderson World, Mountain View, California.

Urhausen, A., T. Kullmer, W. Kindermann (1987). A 7-week follow-up study of the behaviour of testosterone and cortisol during the competition period in rowers. *European Journal of Applied Physiology 56*, 528-533.

Van Aaken, E. (1976). *Van Aaken Method*. World Publications, Mountain View, California.

Van der Beek, E.J. (1985). Vitamins and endurance training. Food for running or faddish claims? *Sports Medicine 2*, 175-197.

Van der Beek, E.J., W. van Dokkum, J. Schrijver, J.A. Wesstra, H. van Weerd, R.J.J. Hermus (1984). Effect of marginal vitamin intake on physical performance of man. *International Journal of Sports Medicine 5* (suppl.), 28-31.

van der Merwe, F. (1990). Frith's winning ways. *Femina* (January), 38-40.

van der Merwe, F.J.G. (1987). Britse invloed op atletiek in die Wes-Kaap tot 1932. Ongepubliseerde, M.A. (Geskiedenis) - verhandeling, Universiteit van Stellenbosch [British influence.on athletics in the Western Cape until 1932. Unpublished, M.A. (History) dissertation, University of Stellenbosch].

van Erp-Baart, A.M.J., W.H.M. Saris, R.A. Binkhorst, J.A. Vos, J.W.H. Elvers (1989a). Nationwide survey on nutritional habits in elite athletes. Part I. Energy, carbohydrate, protein, and fat intake. *International Journal of Sports Medicine 10* (suppl. 1), S3-S10.

van Erp-Baart, A.M.J., W.H.M. Saris, R.A. Binkhorst, J.A. Vos, J.W.H. Elvers (1989b). Nationwide survey on nutritional habits in elite athletes. Part II. Mineral and vitamin intake. *International Journal of Sports Medicine 10* (suppl. 1), S11-S16.

van Gend, M.A., T.D. Noakes (1987). Menstrual patterns of ultramarathon runners. *South African Medical Journal 72*, 788-793.

Van Rensburg, J.P., W.H. Van der Walt, A. Van der Linde, A.J. Kielblock, N.B. Strydom (1982). Lead absorption in distance runners exposed to motor vehicle exhaust fumes. *South African Journal for Research in Sport, Physical Education and Recreation 5*, 21-44.

Varrassi, G., C. Bazzano, W.T. Edwards (1989). Effects of physical activity on material plasma beta-endorphin levels and perception of labor pain. *American Journal of Obstetrics and Gynecology 160*, 707-712.

Veille, J-C., A.R. Hohimer, K. Burry, L. Speroff (1985). The effect of exercise on uterine activity in the last eight weeks of pregnancy. *American Journal of Obstetrics and Gynaecology 151*, 727-730.

Vellar, O.D. (1968). Studies of sweat losses of nutrients. *Scandinavian Journal of Clinical and Laboratory Investigation 21*, 157-167.

Vena, J.E., S. Graham, M. Zielezny, M.K. Swanson, R.E. Barnes, J. Nolan (1985). Life time occupational exercise and colon cancer. *American Journal of Epidemiology 122*, 357-365.

Verde, T., R.J. Shephard, P. Corey, R. Moore (1982). Sweat composition in exercise and in heat. *Journal of Applied Physiology 53*, 1540-1545.

Videman, T. (1982). The effect of running on the osteoarthritic joint: An experimental matched-pair study with rabbits. *Rheumatology and Rehabilitation 21*, 1-8.

Viitasalo, J.T., M. Kvist (1983). Some biomechanical aspects of the foot and ankle in athletes with and without shinsplints. *American Journal of Sports Medicine 11*, 125-130.

Viti, A., M. Muscetolla, L. Paulesu, V. Bocci, A. Almi (1985). Effect of exercise on plasma inferon levels. *Journal of Applied Physiology 59*, 426-428.

Vitting, K.E., N.J. Nichols, G.R. Seligson (1986). Naproxen and acute renal failure in a runner. *Annals of Internal Medicine 105*, 144.

Vollestad, N.K., P.C.S. Blom (1985). Effect of varying exercise intensity on glycogen depletion in human muscle fibres. *Acta Physiologica Scandinavica 125*, 395-405.

Voloshin, A., J. Wosk (1982). An in vivo study of low back pain and shock absorption in the human locomotor system. *Journal of Biomechanics 15*, 21-27.

Volpin, G., C. Milgrom, D. Goldsher, H. Stein (1989). Stress fractures of the sacrum following strenuous activity. *Clinical Orthopaedics 243*, 184-188.

Vuori, I., M. Makäräinen, A. Jääskeläinen (1978). Sudden death and physical activity. *Cardiology 63*, 287-304.

Wahrenberg, H., P. Engfeldt, J. Bolinder, P. Arner (1987). Acute adaptation in adrenergic control of lipolysis during physical exercise in humans. *American Journal of Physiology 253*, E383-E390.

Waitz, G., G. Averbuch (1986). *Grete Waitz—World Class*. Warner Books, New York.

Wakat, D.K., K.A. Sweeney, A.D. Rogol (1982). Reproductive system function in women cross-country runners. *Medicine and Science in Sports and Exercise 14*, 263-269.

Wald, G., L. Brouha, R. Johnson (1942). Experimental human vitamin A deficiency and ability to perform muscular exercise. *American Journal of Physiology 137*, 551-556.

Walker, J. (1988). In: Mile Mannered. *Runner's World 23* (February), 29.

Wallensten, R. (1983). Results of fasciotomy in patients with medial tibial syndrome or chronic anterior-compartment syndrome. *Journal of Bone and Joint Surgery 65-A*, 1252-1255.

Wallensten, R., E. Eriksson (1984). Intramuscular pressures in exercise-induced lower leg pain. *International Journal of Sports Medicine 5*, 31-35.

Wallin, D., B. Ekblom, R. Grahn, T. Nordenborg (1985). Improvement of muscle flexibility. A comparison of two techniques. *American Journal of Sports Medicine 13*, 263-268.

Walther, R.J., C.P. Tifft (1985). High blood pressure in the competitive athlete: Guidelines and recommendations. *The Physician and Sportsmedicine 13* (May), 92-114.

Ward, A. (1964). *Modern Distance Training*. Stanley Paul, London.

Ward-Smith, A.J. (1986). Altitude and wind effects on long jump performance with particular reference to the world record established by Bob Beamon. *Journal of Sports Sciences 4*, 89-99.

Warhol, M.J., A.J. Siegel, W.J. Evans, L.M. Silverman (1985). Skeletal muscle injury and repair in marathon runners after competition. *American Journal of Pathology 118*, 331-339.

Warren, B.L. (1984). Anatomical factors associated with predicting plantar fasciitis in long-distance runners. *Medicine and Science in Sports and Exercise 16*, 60-63.

Warren, B.L., C.J. Jones (1987). Predicting plantar fasciitis in runners. *Medicine and Science in Sports and Exercise 19*, 71-73.

Warren, M.P., J. Brooks-Gunn, L.H. Hamilton, L.F. Warren, W.G. Hamilton (1986). Scoliosis and fractures in young ballet dancers. Relation to delayed menarche and secondary amenorrhea. *New England Journal of Medicine 314*, 1348-1353.

Washburn, R.A., D.R. Seals (1984). Peak oxygen uptake during arm cranking for men and women. *Journal of Applied Physiology 56*, 954-957.

Webb, J.L., A.J. Proctor (1983). Anthropometric, training and menstrual differences in three groups of American collegiate female runners. *Journal of Sports Medicine and Physical Fitness 23*, 201-209.

Webster, F.A.M. (1948). *Why? The Science of Athletics*. Nicholas Kaye, London.

Weight, L., T.D. Noakes (1987). Is running an analogue of anorexia? A survey of eating disorders in female distance runners. *Medicine and Science in Sports and Exercise 19*, 213-217.

Weight, L.M., K.H. Myburgh, T.D. Noakes (1988a). Vitamin and mineral supplementation: Effect on the running performance of trained athletes. *American Journal of Clinical Nutrition 47*, 192-195.

Weight, L.M., T.D. Noakes, D. Labadarios, J. Graves, P. Jacobs, P.A. Berman (1988b). Vitamin and mineral status of trained athletes including the effects of supplementation. *American Journal of Clinical Nutrition 47*, 186-191.

Weir, J., T.D. Noakes, K. Myburgh, B. Adams (1987). A high carbohydrate diet negates the metabolic effects of caffeine. *Medicine and Science in Sports and Exercise 19*, 100-105.

Wells, C.L. (1991). *Women, Sport, and Performance: A Physiological Perspective* (2nd ed.). Human Kinetics, Champaign, Illinois.

Wells, C.L., L.H. Hecht, G.S. Krahenbuhl (1981). Physical characteristics and oxygen utilization of male and female marathon runners. *Research Quarterly 52*, 281-285.

Wells, C.L., S.A. Plowman (1983). Sexual differences in athletic performance: Biological or behavioral. *The Physician and Sportsmedicine 11* (August), 52-63.

Wentz, A.C. (1980). Body weight and amenorrhea. *Obstetrics and Gynecology 56*, 482-487.

West, J.B., J.J. Boyer, D.J. Graber, P.H. Hackett, K.H. Maret, J.S. Milledge, R.M. Peters, C.J. Pizzo, M. Samaja, F.H. Sarnquist, R.B. Schoene, R.M. Winslow (1983a). Maximal exercise at extreme altitudes on Mount Everest. *Journal of Applied Physiology 55*, 688-698.

West, J.B., P.H. Hackett, K.H. Maret, J.S. Milledge, R.M. Peters, C.T. Pizzo, R.M. Winslow (1983b). Pulmonary gas exchange on the summit of Mount Everest. *Journal of Applied Physiology 55*, 678-687.

Wheeler, G.D., S.R. Wall, A.H. Belcastro, D.C. Cumming (1984). Reduced serum testosterone and prolactin levels in male marathon runners. *Journal of the American Medical Association 252*, 514-516.

Wildmann, J., A. Kruger, M. Schmole, J. Niemann, H. Matthaei (1986). Increase of circulating beta-endorphin-like immunoreactivity correlates with the change in feeling of pleasantness after running. *Life Sciences 38*, 997-1003.

Wiley, J.P., D.B. Clement, D.L. Doyle, J.E. Taunton (1987). A primary care perspective of chronic compartment syndrome of the leg. *The Physician and Sportsmedicine 15* (March), 111-120.

Wilkes, D., N. Gledhill, R. Smyth (1983). Effect of acute induced metabolic alkalosis on 800 m racing time. *Medicine and Science in Sports and Exercise 15*, 277-280.

Willett, W.C., M.J. Stampfer, G.A. Colditz, B.A. Rosner, C.H. Hennekens, F.E. Speizer (1987). Moderate alcohol consumption and the risk of breast cancer. *New England Journal of Medicine 316*, 1174-1179.

Williams, A.F. (1981). When motor vehicles hit joggers: An analysis of 60 cases. *Public Health Reports 96*, 448-451.

Williams, C., M.L.G. Nute (1983). Some physiological demands of a half-marathon race on recreational runners. *British Journal of Sports Medicine 17*, 152-161.

Williams, K.R. (1985). The relationship between mechanical and physiological energy estimates. *Medicine and Science in Sports and Exercise 17*, 317-325.

Williams, M.H. (1984). Vitamin and mineral supplements to athletes: Do they help? *Clinics in Sports Medicine 3*, 623-637.

Williams, R.B. (1987). Refining the Type A hypothesis: Emergence of the hostility complex. *American Journal of Cardiology 60*, 27J-32J.

Williford, H.N., J.B. East, F.H. Smith, L.A. Burry (1986). Evaluation of warm-up for improvement in flexibility. *American Journal of Sports Medicine 14*, 316-319.

Willoughby, A. (1977). Jogging about. *Runner's World 18*, 17.

Wilmore, J.H., C.H. Brown, J.A. Davis (1977). Body physique and composition of female distance runners. *Annals of the New York Academy of Sciences 301*, 764-776.

Wilson, V.E., N.C. Morley, E.I. Bird (1980). Mood profiles of marathon runners, joggers and non-exercisers. *Perceptual and Motor Skills 50*, 117-118.

Wilt, F. (1972). Conditioning of runners for championship competition. *Journal of the American Medical Association 221*, 1017-1021.

Wilt, F. (1973). *How They Train. Volume 2: Long Distances* (2nd ed.). Track and Field News, Los Altos, California.

Wing, S., P. Dargent-Molina, M. Casper, W. Riggan, C.G. Hayes, H.A Tyroler (1987). Changing association between community occupational structure and ischaemic heart disease mortality in the United States. *Lancet 2*, 1067-1070.

Winget, C.M., C.W. DeRoshia, D.C. Holley (1985). Circadian rhythms and athletic performance. *Medicine and Science in Sports and Exercise 17*, 498-516.

Wishnitzer, R., E. Vorst, A. Berrebi (1983). Bone marrow iron depression in competitive distance runners. *International Journal of Sports Medicine 4*, 27-30.

Wolf, J.G. (1971). Staleness. In *Encyclopedia of Sports Science and Medicine*, L.A. Larson, D.E. Herrmann (eds.). Macmillan, New York, pp. 1048-1051.

Wolffe, J.B. (1962). The heart of the athlete. *Journal of Sports Medicine and Physical Fitness 2*, 20-23.

Wong, S.C., D.C. McKenzie (1987). Cardiorespiratory fitness during pregnancy and its effect on outcome. *International Journal of Sports Medicine 8*, 79-83.

Wood, P.D. (1987). In: The health benefits of exercise: A round table. *The Physician and Sportsmedicine 15* (November), 124.

Wu, A.H., A. Paganini-Hill, R.K. Ross, B.E. Henderson (1987). Alcohol, physical activity and other risk factors for colorectal cancer: A prospective study. *British Journal of Cancer 55*, 687-694.

Wyndham, C.H., N.B. Strydom (1969). The danger of an inadequate water intake during marathon running. *South African Medical Journal 43*, 893-896.

Wyndham, C.H., N.B. Strydom, W.P. Leary (1966). Studies of the maximum capacity of men for physical effort. Part II: The maximum oxygen intakes of young, active Caucasians. *Internationale Zeitschrift für Angewandte Physiologie 22*, 296-303.

Wyndham, C.H., N.B. Strydom, A.J. Van Rensburg, A.J.S. Benade (1969). Physiological requirements for world-class performances in endurance running. *South African Medical Journal 43*, 996-1002.

Wyngand, J.W., R.M. Otto, T.K. Smith, H.R. Perez (1985). The metabolic cost of running in sand and on concrete. *Medicine and Science in Sports and Exercise 17*, 237.

Wyshak, G., R.E. Frisch, N. Albright, T. Albright, I. Schiff (1986). Lower prevalence of benign diseases of the breast and benign tumors of the reproductive system among former college athletes compared to non-athletes. *British Journal of Cancer 54*, 841-845.

Wyshak, G., R.E. Frisch, T.E. Albright, N.L. Albright, I. Schiff (1987). Bone fractures among former college athletes compared with nonathletes in the menopausal and postmenopausal years. *Obstetrics and Gynecology 69*, 121-126.

Yamaji, K., R.J. Shephard (1987). Grouping of runners during marathon competition. *British Journal of Sports Medicine 21*, 166-167.

Yates, A., K. Leehey, C.M. Shisslak (1983). Running—An analogue of anorexia? *New England Journal of Medicine 308*, 251-255.

Yoshimura, H. (1966). Sports anemia. In *Physical Activity in Health and Disease*, K. Evand, K.L. Andersen (eds.). Universiteitsforlaget, Oslo, pp. 74-78.

Young, A.J., M.N. Sawka, L. Levine, B.S. Cadarette, K.B. Pandolf (1985). Skeletal muscle metabolism during exercise is influenced by heat acclimation. *Journal of Applied Physiology 59*, 1929-1935.

Young, J.C., J.L. Treadway, T.W. Balon, H.P. Gavras, N.B. Ruderman (1986). Prior exercise potentiates the thermic effect of a carbohydrate load. *Metabolism 35*, 1048-1053.

Young, K. (1978). Going over the wall. In *The Complete Marathoner*, J. Henderson (ed.). World Publications, Mountain View, California, pp. 123-126.

Young, M., F. Sciurbam, J. Rinaldo (1987). Delirium and pulmonary edema after completing a marathon. *American Review of Respiratory Diseases 136*, 737-739.

Young, R.J., A.H. Ismail (1976a). Relationship between anthropometric, physiological, biochemical and personality variables before and after a four month conditioning program for middle-aged men. *Journal of Sports Medicine and Physical Fitness 16*, 267-276.

Young, R.J., A.H. Ismail (1976b). Personality differences of adult men before and after a physical fitness program. *Research Quarterly 47*, 513-519.

Young, R.J., A.H. Ismail (1977). Comparison of selected physiological and personality variables in regular and non-regular adult male exercisers. *Research Quarterly 48*, 617-622.

Zaharieva, E. (1972). Olympic participation by women. Effects on pregnancy and childbirth. *Journal of the American Medical Association 221*, 992-995.

Ziegler, S. (1978). An overview of anxiety management strategies in sport. In *Sport Psychology: An Analysis of Athlete Behavior*, W.F. Straub (ed.). Mouvement, New York, pp. 257-264.

Zierath, J., S. Kaiserauer, A.C. Snyder (1986). Dietary patterns of amenorrheic and regularly menstruating runners. *Medicine and Science and Sports and Exercise 18*, S55-S56.

Zipes, D.P., J.J. Heger, E.N. Prystowsky (1981). Sudden cardiac death. *American Journal of Medicine 70*, 1151-1154.

Zucker, P. (1985). In: Eating disorders in young athletes: A round table. *The Physician and Sportsmedicine 13* (November), 89-106.

Zylstra, S., A. Hopkins, M. Erk, M.M. Hreshchyshyn, M. Anbar (1989). Effect of physical activity on lumbar spine and femoral neck bone densities. *International Journal of Sports Medicine 10*, 181-186.

Index

Absorption, intestinal, 58-63
Acclimatization, 110-114
Acetylcholine, 8
Achilles tendon, 179, 500, 510, 530-535
Actin, 7
Acute muscle tears, 526-528
Adams, Eleanor, 353-356, 601, 603
Addiction, running, 248-259
Addison's disease, 423-424
Adenosine triphosphate, 5-6, 8, 18, 85. *See also* (ATP)/ (ADP)(Pi) ratio; Oxygen-independent ATP production
Adipose tissue, 59-60
Adipostat, 583
Adrenaline, 62
Affleck-Graves, J., 41-42
African runners, 292-293
Aging, 22, 185, 186, 214-215, 438-442
Air resistance, 33-35
Air temperature, 80, 107-108, 117, 382-386
Alcohol, 131, 404-405, 576-577, 611
Allen, Mark, 103
Altitude, 22-23, 33-34, 367-369, 398, 442, 658
Alveoli, 17-18, 20
Amateur Athletics Union, 599, 600
Amenorrhea, 424, 516, 517-518, 583
American College of Sports Medicine, 169
Anaerobic glycolysis. *See* Oxygen-independent glycolysis
Anaerobic threshold. *See* Lactate turnpoint
Anaphylaxis, 700
Anatomical distribution of injuries, 540-541
Andrews, Harry, 268
Anemia, 574, 693-695
Animal fats, 563
Ankle injuries, 548
Ankle pronation, 173, 174, 176, 177, 178, 180, 454-455
Anorexia nervosa, 253, 586-593, 618
Antiinflammatory drugs, 533
Anxieties, 236-237, 243-244, 258-259
Appetite, 395
Arch supports. *See* Orthotic devices
Arms, 66, 93, 102-103
Army conscripts, Scandinavian, 70-71
Arousal, 236-238
Asics shoes, 176
Associative strategies, 168, 241, 242, 388-389, 401-402
Asthma, 680-681
Astley Belt races, 346-348
Athletes, 10, 160
Athletes, elite, 23-25, 27-29, 215-216, 220, 221, 225-226. *See also* Elite runners
Athlete's heart, 677
Athletic events, 427-437. *See also* Racing
Athletic neurosis, 251
Athletic pseudonephritis, 690
ATP, 5-6, 8, 18, 85
(ATP)/(ADP)(Pi) ratio, 97-98
Autogenic phase training, 238
Automobile emissions, 648-650
Automobile traffic, 196-197

Back pain, 542-543
Ballistic stretching, 468
Banana-lasted shoes, 178
Bannister, Roger, 148, 219-230, 433, 636
Barclay, Captain, 343-345
Base training, 157-159, 190
Bathing, 110-111, 388, 407
Beamon, Bob, 430
Bedford, Dave, 152, 312-313
Beginning runners. *See* Novice runners
Belief systems, 231-232
Belly breathing, 193-194
Benoit, Joan, 501, 600-601
Bicycling, 22, 40, 41, 103, 670
Binks, Joe, 267
Biomechanical factors in injury, 504
Biorhythms, 442-444
Birth control, 623-624
Bladder trauma, 687
Blood, 607, 698-699
Blood capillaries, 97
Blood circulation, 536-539
Blood donations, 695
Blood doping, 20-21, 695-698
Blood loss, 688-690
Blood pressure, 572, 679-680
Board lasted shoes, 176
Body fuels, 60-80
Body organs, 64
Body temperature, 104-131, 650-658. *See also* Thermogenesis
Body weight, 64, 116-117, 399. *See also* Weight control
Bones, 202, 511-524
Borg, Gunnar, 184-185
Boston Marathon, 81, 270
Bowel movements, 377, 392. *See also* Diarrhea
Bowerman, Bill, 154
Brain, 66
Breakdown point, 457
Breakfast, 380-381, 400
Breast cancer, 577, 611
Breathing, 193-195
Brooks, George, 92
Brumberg, Jane, 586-587, 588-589
Budd, Zola, 612, 630-631, 634
Bulimia, 586
Bursa injuries, 546
Buttock pain, 543

Caffeine, 78-79, 380-381
Calcium, 8, 86, 516, 517-518, 523, 573
Calf muscles, 510, 517, 544
Cambered roads, 391-392
Canadian athletes, 220
Cancer, 577, 610-611, 686
Capillaries, 197
Carbohydrates
    absorption of, 121-124
    body storage of, 65-67
    dietary, 60-62, 76, 92, 123, 556-561. *See also* High-carbohydrate diet

digestion of, 58-59
gastric emptying and, 124-127
in prolonged exercise, 128-129, 130
in ultramarathons, 393
Cardiac disease, 169-171, 659-680
Cardiac output, 21. *See also* Heart rate
Carlile, Forbes, 155-156
Carmack/Martens Committment to Running
Scale, 256-257
Carroll, Noel, 215, 259
Castella, Robert de, 313-315
Cataracts, eye, 658
Cecal slap, 391
Cellulite, 6
Children, 28, 29, 31, 252-253, 630-644
Chondromalacia patella, 501
Chromium deficiency, 575
Chronic muscle tears, 528-530, 543
Cigarette smoking, 659
Citric acid cycle, 61-62
Clarke, Ron, 287-290
Clayton, Derek, 29, 51-52, 152, 293-294, 433
Clothing
in body temperature control, 109-110
choice of, 182
for cold-weather exercise, 112, 114
environmental conditions and, 113
for marathons, 379-380
running efficiency and, 31-32, 35-36
for ultramarathons, 393
CLO units, 109-110, 112
Clunk foot type, 494
Clustering tactic, 388
Coaching, 136, 162-163, 190, 208-209, 640-641
Coe, Sebastian, 609, 631
Cold acclimatization, 112-114
Colic disease, 580
"Collapse-point theory", 203
Colt, Edward, 250-251
Compartment syndromes, 536-538
Competition, 222-223, 241-243, 402-403
Comrades Marathon
acute kidney failure and, 690
age records for, 438-440
course of, 138
Fordyce and, 529
hypoglycemia and, 82
hyponatremia and, 116
muscle cell damage and, 422
Newton and, 136-137, 139-140
running times for, 55, 431
sudden death and, 667
women and, 600, 601
Concentric muscular contractions, 12
Contraceptives, 624-625
Contractions, muscle, 6-9, 12-15, 86-87, 99, 100
Contract-relax stretching, 468
Cooper, A. M., 253
Cooper, Dave, 356
Cooper points, 243
Coping thoughts, 169
Copper deficiency, 575
Coronary angiography, 169-170
Coronary atherosclerosis, 169-170, 671
Coronary heart disease, 169-171, 659-680

"Corpse reviver", 403
Corrected effective temperature, 382-383
Cortisone injections, 533, 544
Costill, David, 71-72, 212
Counsilman, James E., 412-414
Courses, 376-377,399. *See also* Cambered roads; Flat
courses; Gradients; Road running; Surfaces, running
Cramps, 8-9, 530, 572, 609, 644
Creatine phosphate, 85
Creativity, mental, 207, 246
Cross-bridge cycle, 7, 86
Cross frictions, 529
Crossover reintroduction trial, 581
Cross-training, 102-103
Cummings, William, 264-266
Curved-lasted shoes, 178
Cycling, 22, 40, 41, 103, 670

Daniels, J., 44-45, 46
Davies, C. T. M., 39-44, 83
Davies, Mervyn, 34
Death, sudden, 669-676
De Castella, Robert (Deek), 313-315
Decker-Slaney, Mary, 634
Deerfoot of Cattaraugus, 263-264
Defensive running, 196-197
Dehydration, 108-109
Dellinger, Bill, 154-155
DeMar, Clarence, 270-271, 677
Dengis, Pat, 152
Depression, mental, 244
Detraining, 99-101
Diabetes, 703-704
Diagnosis and treatment, medical, 169-171, 487-554.
See also Medical considerations
Diarrhea, 414, 415, 418, 419, 421, 683-686
Diet. *See also* Breakfast; Nutrition
of athletes, 577-580
Barclay on, 345
for beginners, 197-198
body carbohydrate stores and, 66
fad, 593-594, 596
high-carbohydrate, 69-75, 80-81, 84, 371-373
in marathons, 377, 405-406
of pedestrians, 349-350
preexercise, 77-83
in ultramarathons, 393
zen macrobiotic, 594-595
Diet-induced thermogenesis, 583-584
Digestion, 58-63
Digital neuritis, 547
Digital neuroma, 548
Discipline, personal, 167-169
Dissociative strategies, 168, 241-242
Distance training, 145-146, 185-187
Divorce, 592
Downhill running, 12, 340, 391, 420, 507, 536. *See
also* Gradients
Drafting tactic, 33, 34, 388
Dress. *See* Clothing
Drinking, 108-109, 115-131, 388, 393. *See also* Thirst
Drinks
alcoholic, 131, 404-405, 576-577, 611
contents of, 117-121
high-carbohydrate, 82, 388, 403-404
salt-containing, 404

Drinks (continued)
water, 126
Drugs, antiinflammatory, 533
Dry bulb temperature, 384, 387
Dynamic muscle contractions, 12-15

Eccentric muscular contractions, 12
Economy, running, 25-36
Edelen, Leonard "Buddy", 290-292
Efficiency, running, 25-36
Effort. See Exertion
Electrolytes, 117, 119
Eleutherococcus senticosus, 575
Elite athletes, 23-25, 27-29, 215-216, 220, 221, 225-226
Elite runners, 64, 82-83, 116, 241, 261-361
Elliott, Herb, 191, 285-287, 433
Elliott, Jumbo, 163
Emotional control, 232
Endorphins, 250, 254-255, 701-702
Endurance training, 92, 96-103
Energy metabolism, 57-103
Enjoyment rating, 192
Environmental conditions, 107-108, 113, 198-199, 385-386, 397-398
Environmental temperature, 80, 107-108, 117, 382-386
Enzymes, 100
Epilepsy, 703
Epiphyseal growth plate, 642-644
Estrogen, 516, 517, 604
Ethylene vinyl acetate, 174
Euphoria, 250, 701-702
Exercise
benefits of, 243-247
body fuels for, 75-80, 131
body temperature control in, 104-131
carbohydrate ingestion during, 128-129, 130
duration of, 40-41
energy metabolism in, 57-103
fluid intake during, 115-131
glycogen use and, 67-75, 81
infection resistance and, 699-700
lactate turnpoint and, 90-91
liver glycogen and, 81-83
sleep and, 702-703
stretching, 197, 381, 466-484
sudden death and, 669-676
supramaximal, 84-96
weight control and, 581-586
Exercise dependence. See Addiction, running
Exercise testing, maximal, 169
Exertion, 184-185, 186, 192, 242. See also Work capacity; Work load
Expert runners. See Elite runners
Extrinsic injuries, 452, 456
Extroversion, 550

Fad diets, 593-594, 596
Failure, 235-236
Fartlek. See Speed work
Fasting, 79
Fatigue, 93
Fats. See also Adipose tissue
animal, 563
body storage of, 63-65
dietary, 62, 76, 99, 563-564
digestion of, 59-60
metabolism of, 607-608
soluble vitamins in, 564-565, 566
Fatty acids, free, 62, 78, 79, 81, 98

"Fear-of-success/competitive-inhibition" syndrome, 235-236
Femoral stress fractures, 545
Fibers, muscle, 9-15, 69, 608-609
Fibula, 546
Finnish runners, 273-274, 275, 277
Fitness, 76-77, 101, 243, 244, 339-340. See also Detraining; Training
Fixx, James, 662, 673-674, 676
Flat courses, 196
Fluid intake, 108-109, 115-131, 388, 393. See also Drinks
Food allergies, 581
Food intake. See Diet; Nutrition
Footfall, 195
Foot injuries, 547-549
Fordyce, Bruce
hypoglycemia and, 82
logbooks of, 164
on marathon preparation, 529
on muscle fatigue, 422
on overtraining, 414, 418
performance of, 603
tapering of, 365
training of, 331-340
Framing (psychology). See Segmenting (psychology)
Free fatty acids, 62, 78, 79, 81, 98
Freud, Sigmund, 587
Front thigh injuries, 544
Frostbite, 657-658
Fructose, 72-73, 75, 122-123
Fuels, body, 60-80

Gait, 454, 517. See also Stride
Galloway, Jeff, 214-215
Gardner, James, 47, 49-50
Gastric emptying rate, 60, 119-121, 124-127, 128, 129
Gavuzzi, Peter, 141
Gear, marathon, 377
Gender factor, 22, 31, 45, 47, 65. See also Women
Genetic factors
in endurance training, 102
in muscle fiber types, 10
running injuries and, 503-504, 508, 516, 523, 532
in ultramarathon performance, 357
George, Walter, 264-266
Gilbert, J. R., 44-45, 46
Ginseng, 575
Gluconeogenesis, 6
Glucose, 59, 61, 122-123, 124
Glucose polymer solutions, 126, 129
Gluten enteropathy, 580
Glycogen
body storage of, 65-67
environmental temperature and, 80
exercise and, 67-75, 76, 79, 81
interval training and, 88-90
levels of, 608
resynthesis of, 69-75, 84
Glycolysis, anaerobic, 6, 61, 85-90
Goal setting, 168, 240-241
Gradients, 35, 406. See also Downhill running; Uphill running
Graham, Fred, 258-259
Groin pain, 543-544

Habeler, Peter, 23
Halberstadt, Johnny, 82
Hamstring injuries, 527-528
Hard-day/easy-day training program, 154-155, 188

Hard training program, 206-212
Hardy personality, 245
Hayward, Wally, 181-182, 322-325, 434, 438, 440, 601, 677
Hazards of running, 645-705
Headache, 700-701
Health awareness, 246-247
Health considerations, 447-464
Heart disease, 169-171, 659-680
Heart rate, 94-95, 185, 186, 417, 418. *See also* Cardiac output; Pulse rate
Heart rhythms, abnormal, 679
Heat acclimatization, 110-111, 366
Heat, body, 104-131, 650-658
Heat cramps. *See* Cramps
Heat stress, 383, 384, 386
Heatstroke, 652-656
Heel bruises, 539-540
Heels, shoe, 173, 176-179
Helms Trophy, 137
Hematuria, 687, 688
Hemoglobinuria, 688-689
Heparin, 79
Heritability. *See* Genetic factors
High-carbohydrate diet, 69-75, 80-81, 84, 371-373
High-carbohydrate drinks, 82, 388, 403-404
High-intensity training. *See* Peaking training
Hill, A. V., 18-19, 427-428, 435, 602, 603
Hill, Ron, 294-303
Hills. *See* Gradients
Holistic training, 164-165, 193
Hormone-sensitive lipase, 62
Hurst, Len, 266-267
Huxley, A. F., 6-7
Hydrogenation, 563
Hydrogen-ion concentration, muscle, 85-86
Hypermobile foot type, 494-495, 502, 503
Hypertension, 572, 679-680
Hypertrophic cardiomyopathy, 171, 671
Hypoglycemia, 79, 81-83, 424, 652
Hypomania, 251
Hyponatremia, 115-116, 572
Hypothalamic dysfunction, 618-619, 704-705
Hypothermia, 112, 114, 656-657
Hypotonic solutions, 129

Iatrogenic injury syndrome, 552
Iliotibial band friction syndrome, 506-509
Infection, 396, 397, 681-682, 699-700
Infertility, 622-623
Inflammation of heart muscle, 678-679
Injuries, 235, 449-554
Insomnia, 702-703
Insulation. *See* Clothing
Insulin, 62, 79, 703-704
Insulin-induced hypoglycemia, 424
Intermediate foot type, 495
Interval training, 88, 274-275
Intestinal absorption, 58-63
Intrinsic injuries, 453, 456, 488
Introversion, 550
Inverse stretch reflex, 467
Iron deficiency, 574, 692-695
Isometric muscle contractions, 12-15

Jokl, Ernst, 429-430
Jones, Steve, 315-316
Joseph, Paul, 256-257

Keating, Len, 538-539

Keino, Hezekia Kipchoage (Kip), 292-293
Kidneys, 688-691
King, Billie Jean, 636-637
Knee injuries, 500-509
Kolehmainen, Hannes, 154, 268-269
Kouros, Yiannis, 350-353, 434, 603
Krebs cycle, 61-62
Kyle, Chester R., 33

Lacing, shoe, 179
Lactase deficiency, 684-685
Lactate metabolism, 21, 88-96, 99
Lactate "shuttle", 92-93
Lactate turnpoint, 90, 607
Landy, John, 222-223
Lane choice, 445
Lead runners, 402-403
Leg injuries, 546
Lemonade, 403
Lewis, Carl, 430
Lipase, hormone-sensitive, 62
Liquori, Marti, 163, 191
Little, Crawford, 251
Liver glycogen, 66, 68, 69, 76, 79, 81-83, 608
Loedolff, Willie, 439
Logbooks, 163-164, 192-193
Long slow distance training, 144-145, 157
"Long-swing" athletes, 160
Lopes, Carlos, 316-317
Louw, Jan, 52-53, 55
Lupton, Hartley, 18-19
Lydiard, Arthur, 155, 157, 189, 209

Macrobiotic diet, 594-595
Magnesium, 573
Marathon runners. *See also* Ultramarathon runners
    hypoglycemia in, 81-82
    mental strategies of, 241-242
    Mikkola on, 274
    muscle cell damage in, 420
    in Olympic Games, 360-361
    overtraining of, 418, 419
    post-race physiology of, 118
    sudden death of, 171
    training of, 203, 263-321
Marathons, 362-407. *See also* Ultramarathons
March fractures, 519
Martens, Rainer, 256
Masochism, 252-253
Maximal exercise testing, 169
Maximum achieved work load, 21
Maximum alveolar oxygen-diffusing capacity, 20
Maximum heart rate, 185, 186
Maximum oxygen consumption
    age and, 22, 438, 440
    altitude and, 367-369
    detraining and, 99-101
    lactate turnpoint and, 92
    maintenance of, 40-41
    oxygen-independent ATP production and, 53, 56
    as performance predictor, 38-47, 50-53
    running efficiency and, 25-30, 604-607
    static exercise and, 14
    theory of, 18-25
    training and, 36-37, 211
Maximum ventilation rate, 20
Maximum work capacity. *See* Speed, running
Medical considerations, 246, 390, 447-464, 645-705
Medical diagnosis and treatment, 169-171, 487-554
Mekler, Jackie, 325-328

Menopause, 516, 518
Menstruation, 193, 424, 516, 517-518, 574, 583, 611-624
Mental creativity, 207, 246
Mental imagery, 239-240, 388-389
Mental training, 150, 167-169, 191, 217-260, 373-376
Mercier/Leger/Desjardins nomogram, 50, 51
Merrick, Dave, 451
Merwe, Frith van der, 340-343, 601, 603, 609
Messner, Reinhold, 23
Metabolism, 84-103, 116
Metatarsals, 547-549
Midsoles, shoe, 173-176
Mikkola, J.J., 273-274
Milk intolerance, 580, 684-685
Minerals, dietary, 570-575
Mitochondria, 4-5, 98-101
Morgan, William P., 241-242, 249, 254
Morris, Jeremy, 661-662
Morton, Hugh, 434-436
Motivation, 25-26, 167-169
Motor-nerve end plates, 8
Munchausen syndrome, 551-552
Muscles
  carbohydrate uptake of, 121-124
  contractions of, 6-9, 12-15, 86-87, 99, 100
  cramped, 8-9, 530, 572, 609, 644
  in endurance training, 96-103
  glycogen and, 65-66, 68
  injured, 524-530
  overtrained, 419, 422
  progressive relaxation of, 239
  stiff, 93
  structure and function of, 2-15, 69, 608-609
Myocarditis, 678-679
Myofibrils, 3
Myofilaments, 3
Myoglobin, 9
Myoglobinuria, 689
Myosin, 7
Myosin adenosine triphosphatase, 9, 86

Narcissism, 252-253
National Heart, Lung and Blood Institute (U.S.), 170, 171
Nausea, 686
Nelson, Alec, 144
Nerve injuries, 539
Neuritis, digital, 547
Neuroma, digital, 548
Neurosis, athletic, 251
Newton, Arthur, 135-165
  on diet, 578
  on hypoglycemia, 83
  on marathons, 397-407
  on mental effort, 207
  performance of, 434
  on sleep, 198
  on stride, 30, 31
Nicotinic acid, 79
Nike Tailwind shoes, 175-176
Noakes Running Shoe Pronation-Testing Technique, 177
Nocturnal cramps, 530
Novice runners
  shinsplints and, 515
  shoes for, 172
  stress fractures and, 522, 546
  training of, 199-200, 203-204, 309, 421
  women as, 458

Nurmi, Paavo, 269, 271-276
Nutrition, 555-597. See also Diet

Obsessive-compulsive behavior, 251-252
Ogilvie, Bruce, 245
O'Leary Belt races, 346-347
O'Leary, Daniel, 345-348
Olympic Games, 228, 360-361
Oral contraceptives, 624-625
Organs, body, 64
Orthotic devices, 32, 498, 505, 510, 533-534
Osgood-Schlatter syndrome, 511
Osler, Tom, 45, 47, 48, 158-159, 410, 435, 437
Osteitis pubis, 543-544
Osteoarthritis, 462-464
Osteoclasts and osteoblasts, 514
Osteoporosis, 518, 622
Overtraining, 149-150, 190, 199, 408-425
Owens, Jesse, 429
Oxygen consumption, maximum. See Maximum oxygen consumption
Oxygen cost of running, 25-36
Oxygen-independent ATP production, 53, 56
Oxygen-independent glycolysis, 6, 61, 85-90
Oxygen transport, 16-56

Pacing, 33, 372, 387-388, 392-393, 400-401, 406
Paffenbarger, Ralph, 662-667
Pangamic acid, 555
Parents of child athletes, 641-642
Passing tactic, 402-403
Passive stretching, 468
Peaking training, 95-96, 155, 159-162, 190, 208-215
Pedestrianism, 262, 348-350
Pelvic stress fractures, 543
Perception of exertion, 184-185, 186, 192, 242
Performance, running
  altitude and, 658
  heat-impaired, 111
  menstruation and, 623-624
  prediction of, 38-56, 93-94, 370-371, 397, 434-436, 437
  preexercise diet and, 80-83
  world records of, 426-446
Peroneus tendinitis, 548
Personality, 244-245, 660
Peter Bent Brigham Hospital, 81
Peters, Jim, 109, 278-282, 435, 650-651
pH, muscle, 85-86
Phosphofructokinase, 86
Physiotherapy, 534, 544
Pirie, Gordon, 282-285
Plantar fasciitis, 509-511
Play, 259
Plods, 414, 421
Popliteal artery entrapment syndrome, 538
Popliteus tendonitis, 536
Potassium, 560, 572-573
Prediction of performance, 38-56, 93-94, 370-371, 397, 434-436, 437
Pregnancy, 625-629
Primary affective disorder, 250-251
Progesterone, 573
Progressive relaxation technique, 239
Pronation, ankle, 173, 174, 176, 177, 178, 180, 454-455
Proteins, 60, 62-63, 561-563
Pseudonephritis, 690

Psychology
  of injury, 549-554
  of overtraining, 422
  in training, 150, 167-169, 191, 217-260, 373-376
Pubic symphysitis, 543-544
Pugh, Griffiths, 33
Pulse rate, 185, 192. See also Heart rate
Purdy, Jerry, 47, 49-50
Pyruvate, 61

Quadriceps, 12, 340, 544-545
Quality of life, 244
Quigley, Brian, 443-444

Racial groups, 31
Racing, 189-190. See also Marathons; Time-trials;
  Ultramarathons
Radiant heat, 107-108
Rape, 647
Reinforcement control, 168
Relaxation techniques, 237-239
Respiratory infections, 681-682
Rest
  Fordyce on, 337
  injury and, 460-461, 534
  after marathons, 396-397, 407
  before marathons, 377-378
  Newton on, 150-152, 407
  thirteenth training law on, 191
Rigor complex, 8
Ritchie, Don, 328-331
Road running, 196-197
Robbins, James, 256-257
Rowell, Charles, 346-348, 434
Runners. See Elite runners; Marathon runners; Novice
  runners; Ultramarathon runners
Runner's high, 250, 701-702
Runner's knee, 500-505
Runner's trots, 683-685
Runner's World Shoe Survey, 498
Rushall, Brent S., 220, 221, 225-226
Ryder, H. W., 430-433, 434
Ryun, Jim, 632, 635

Salazar, Alberto, 10-11, 29, 592
Salt-containing drinks, 404
Salt, dietary, 117-119, 122, 393, 404, 570-572
Sarcomeres, 3
Scandinavian army conscripts, 70-71
Scenic areas, 196
Schedules, training, 187-188
Scott, Dave, 103
Second wind, 682-683
Segmenting (psychology), 241, 374-375, 401-402
Self-concept, 233-235
Self-discipline, 167-169
Selfish Runner's Syndrome, 215-216
Self-talk, 169
Sex factor, 22, 31, 45, 47, 65. See also Women
Sexual activity, 378
Shaping (psychology), 167-168
Sharpening. See Peaking training
Sheehan, George, 450-452, 501, 580, 646-647
Shinsplints, 511-518, 537-538, 546
Shoes, 32, 171-182, 379-380, 458, 489-498
Shorter, Frank, 303-307, 575, 632, 657
"Short-swing athletes", 160
Shrubb, Alfred, 267-268, 269
Siberian ginseng, 575

Siskovick, David, 667-669
Skeletal muscles. See Muscles
Sleep, 198, 377-379, 399-400, 702-703
Sliding filament theory of muscle contraction, 6-7
Slip lasted shoes, 176
Smoking, cigarette, 659
Snell, Peter, 157, 160
"Soda loading", 96
Sodium bicarbonate, 96
Sodium chloride, 117-119, 122, 393, 404, 570-572
Soles, shoe, 172-173
Soleus syndrome, 513
Specialized training, 147-149, 190
Speed, running, 18-20, 116, 117, 427-437, 445-446.
  See also Time-trials
Speed work, 153-154, 187, 208-212, 336-337, 359
Splanchnic shunt, 18
Sponging, 110-111, 388
Sporting events, 427-437. See also Racing
Sports anemia, 694
Sprinting, 56, 85, 97
Stampfl, Franz, 224-225
Starches, 6, 123-124
Start of marathons, 386-387, 400-401
Static contractions, 12-15
Static stretching, 468
Stengal, Casey, 637
Stiffness, muscle, 93
Stimulus-belief system-behavior pattern, 230-232
Stimulus control, 168
Stitches (physiology), 194-195, 391
Stopwatches, 386-387
Straight-lasted shoes, 178
Stress, 199, 235-236
Stress fractures, 518-524, 546
Stress, heat, 383, 384, 386
Stress resistance, 245-246
Stress testing, 169
Stretching exercises, 197, 381, 466-484
Striated muscles. See Muscles
Stride, 30, 31, 454, 455. See also Gait
Submaximal training, 92, 96-103
Substrate oxidation, 98
Subtalar pronation syndrome, 548
Sudden death, 669-676
Sugar-containing drinks, 82, 388, 403-404
Sunburn, 658
Sunshine, 107-108
"Supercompensation effect", 74
Superplods, 415, 418, 419, 421
Supramaximal exercise, 84-96
Supramaximal training. See Sprinting
Surfaces, running, 32-33, 445-446, 457-458, 499
Surgery, 462, 534-535
Sweat, 107, 109
Sweat rate, 111, 116-117
Swedish runners, 31
Swimming, 151-152, 155-156, 412, 413, 422, 429, 442

Tactics, racing, 402-403. See also Clustering tactic;
  Drafting tactic; Passing tactic
Tapering, 151-152, 191, 338, 365, 369, 399
Temane, Matthews Selepe, 317-321
Temperature
  bodily, 104-131, 650-658
  environmental, 80, 107-108, 117, 382-386
Tendon injuries, 530-536
Tension, 243-244
Thermogenesis, diet-induced, 583-584

Thighs, 12, 340, 544-545
Thirst, 149-150. *See also* Drinking
Thirty-six week training program, 200-203
Thompson, M. W., 39-44, 83
Thought control, 232-233, 238
Thrombosis, 538-539
Tibial stress syndrome, 511-518
Times, racing, 43, 55, 370-371
Time-trials, 146-147, 189-190
Trace element deficiencies, 575
Training, 166-216. *See also* Coaching; Detraining; Fitness; Overtraining; Peaking training; Speed work
   base, 157-159, 190
   carbohydrate storage and, 65
   endurance, 92, 96-103
   Fordyce's rules of, 335-340
   frequency of, 142-144
   hard, 206-208
   hard/easy, 154-155, 188
   holistic, 164-165
   injury and, 458, 498-499
   interval, 88, 274-275
   laws of, 182-193
   long slow distance, 144-145, 157
   maximum oxygen consumption and, 36-37
   mental, 150, 167-169, 191, 217-260, 373-376
   minimal, 164
   muscle glycogen levels and, 72
   Newton's rules of, 142-154
   practical implications of, 101-102
   psychological aspects of, 243-259
   schedules for, 187-188
   specialized, 147-149, 190
   for ultramarathons, 366
   Waitz's rules of, 310
   weekend, 210-211
Transcontinental Race, 140-141
Treadmills, 22, 34
Triathlons, 103
Triglycerides, 6, 59
Trochanteric bursitis, 546
Tropomyosin, 7
Troponin-C, 8
Twenty-week hard-training program, 206-212

Ultramarathon runners, 321-361
Ultramarathons, 203-204, 212-215, 356-361, 392-393
Ultraviolet bands, 658
Uphill running, 420, 510. *See also* Gradients
Upper thigh muscles, 12, 340, 544-545
Urination, 392, 395
U.S. National Heart, Lung and Blood Institute, 170, 171

Van der Merwe, Frith, 340-343, 601, 603, 609
Vegetarianism, 574, 577, 594-595, 597
Ventilation rate, maximum, 20
Viren, Lasse, 157, 417, 418, 695-696
Virgin, Craig, 51-52
Viscoelastic shoe insoles, 498
Vitamin B_{15}, 555-556
Vitamin-B-complex tablets, 560
Vitamins, 564-569
$\dot{V}O_2$max. *See* Maximum oxygen consumption

Waitz, Grete, 307-312, 414, 415, 418, 601, 633
Waking procedures, 378-379
Walking, 148-149, 200, 381, 387-388, 390-391
Warm-up, 381
Water ingestion, 126
Water intoxication, 115-116, 572
Water-soluble vitamins, 564-565, 567
Weather, 107-108, 113, 198-199, 385-386, 397-398
Weekend training, 210-211
Weight control, 109, 555-597. *See also* Body weight
Weight lifters, 11
Weights, training, 32
Weston, Edward Payson, 345-346
Wet bulb globe temperature index, 108, 382-383
Whole-body damage, 423-425
Wilgefortis, 587-588
Wind, 33-35, 107, 113
Wind chill factor, 114
Withdrawal symptoms, 249-250, 254
Women, 598-629. *See also* Gender factor
   calcium deficiency in, 516, 517-518, 523
   foot injuries of, 547
   as marathoners, 429
   medical complaints of, 246
   performance by, 428
   stress fractures in, 522
Work. *See* Exertion
Work capacity, maximum. *See* Speed, running
Work (livelihood), 257-258
Work load, maximum achieved, 21
World records, 427-437, 442-444

X-ray diagnosis, 459-460, 520, 529

Yawa, Xolile, 321, 322

Zapotek, Emil, 152, 228, 276-277
Zen macrobiotic diet, 594-595
Zinc deficiency, 574-575